Contents

Encyclopedia of
Major League Baseball Teams

Encyclopedia of
Major League
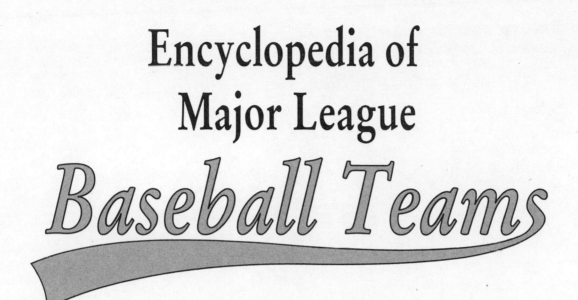

Donald Dewey &
Nicholas Acocella

HarperCollins*Publishers*

HarperCollins books may be purchased for educational, business, or sales promotional use. For information, please write to: Special Markets Department, HarperCollins Publishers, Inc., 10 East 53rd Street, New York, N.Y. 10022.

FIRST EDITION

Designed by George J. McKeon

Library of Congress Cataloging-in-Publication Data

Dewey, Donald.
    Encyclopedia of major league baseball teams / by Donald Dewey &
Nicholas Acocella. — 1st ed.
      p.   cm.
    ISBN 0-06-270049-9
    1. Baseball—United States—Clubs—History.   2. Major League
Baseball (Organization)—History.   I. Acocella, Nicholas, 1943–   .
II. Title.
GV875.A1A36   1994
796.357'64'0973—dc20   92-43303

93 94 95 96 97 AC/RRD 10 9 8 7 6 5 4 3 2 1

For Francesca and the SAPs (Sid Gribetz,
Alan Willinger, and Paul Sternheim)

Acknowledgments

This book would not have been possible without the generous assistance of many people both inside and outside organized baseball.

The authors would like to thank the media relations staffs of the major league teams. Thanks are also owed to Lori Alfieri and Marilyn I. Bellemore of The Rhode Island Historical Society, James C. Anderson of The Filson Club, Philip Bergen of The Bostonian Society, Terry Carlson of The Minnesota Historical Society, Emily Clark of The Chicago Historical Society, Barbara Dawson of The Cincinnati Historical Society, Denny J. Day of The Franklin County Historical Society, Kevin Kennard of The Historical Society of Delaware, James Marshall of The Toledo–Lucas County Public Library, Dale Ogden of The Indiana State Museum, Beverly Osborne of The Worcester Historical Museum, and Judith Simonson of The Milwaukee County Historical Society.

In addition, the staffs of The National Baseball Library in Cooperstown—especially Patricia Kelly and the rest of the people in the photo collection—and The New York Public Library were patient and cooperative.

A special word of appreciation goes to Joseph Overfield, the guru of baseball in Buffalo; Chuck Patterson, who provided background on the Boston and Milwaukee Braves; and Professor Jerry Jay Wright of Pennsylvania State University at Altoona, who generously shared his research with us.

And, finally, our gratitude to Bart Acocella and Jean and Lisa Casko, whose patience and diligence in helping prepare the manuscript knew no bounds.

Introduction

The most significant innovation of the National League charter drafted on February 2, 1876 was its declaration that it represented a pact among signatory clubs rather than among players, as had been the case with earlier professional efforts. With this corporate distinction, organized baseball took on the structure that it has maintained to this day; from that New York meeting at the Grand Central Hotel, and notwithstanding all the publicity given in recent years to multimillion-dollar player signings, the prerogative to write a contract has had precedence over the individual who has agreed to put his name to it. Asked once how he would have fared in the era of free agency, Joe DiMaggio didn't fantasize about a money figure, but alluded to the deeper foundations of the baseball business by cracking that New York Yankees' owner George Steinbrenner would have had to make him a partner.

The concept of the team as the game's fundamental organizational unit has spawned a double history of major league baseball—one part of it incorporating the feats and failures of the field, the other part embracing the success and bankruptcies of those who have underwritten the passions and statistics attending actual play. While parallel in the broadest sense of chronology, the two histories taken together have also attested to the autonomies and antagonisms between diamond events and executive calculations, starting with the denial of the shibboleth that, where professional sports are concerned, winning is everything. On the contrary, as the dual histories of major league clubs make clear, even winning on the field is important only to the extent that it bolsters a franchise's multiple functions—as a commercial aggregate of players, managers, coaches, owners, and front office personnel, as well as stadium seats, concession-stand merchandise, and parking areas; as a community emblem; as a league plank; and, assuming particular importance in recent decades, as a mass media program. Only by evaluating all of these factors can we begin to understand such apparent anomalies as winning teams (the Oakland Athletics of the 1970s) that created more organizational friction than harmony, losing teams (the New York Mets of the 1960s) that profited from being losers, and profitable teams (the Brooklyn Dodgers of the 1950s) that seized the first opportunity to move elsewhere.

For most of the twentieth century, the difference between a major and a minor league team has been clear: the National and American leagues have said which was which. In the nineteenth century, before farm systems were established, the distinction was often not so evident. In taking most of its players from the previously existing National Association in 1876, for example, the National League could claim with justification that it employed the most developed talents in the game, at least among those interested in pursuing it as an occupation. With the participation of New York, Boston, Philadelphia, Chicago, Cincinnati, and St. Louis, the NL founders could also say that they had representation in the largest metropolitan markets in the country at the time. And, in the financial commitments of their owners, the eight original NL franchises (the above-mentioned plus Hartford and Louisville) sought to certify not only their own longevity, but that of the league as a whole as an interstate enterprise that extended from Massachusetts to Missouri. In short, even before they became major through their power to mandate what was minor, the teams of the National League were *big*. From that starting point, the story of professional baseball has amounted to a chronicle of the league's maneuvers to maintain its dominance of the sport—at first alone, for some years in alliance with the American Association, and ultimately in association with the American League.

In terms of comparable playing talent, financial investment, and organization, there have been six conspicuous challenges to the primacy of the NL: the American Association in 1882 and 1891, the Union Association in 1884, the Players League in 1890, the American League in 1901, and the Federal League in 1914. In addition, there have been a number of other, murkier attempts to rival the NL's monopoly, ranging from the stillborn (the Second American Association in 1894 and the New American Association in 1900) to the largely tactical (the Continental League in 1959). Yet another source of alternative play, but parallel rather than competitive because of the social proscriptions of the day, were the black circuits that flourished for about thirty years after the establishment of the Negro National League in 1920.

The clubs belonging to the NL's most serious challengers usually set up quarters in heavily populated cities and promoted highly skilled players, a good number of whom were lured away from the NL itself by the prospect of more money, greater playing time, or some private consideration such as being able to perform in a native city. Except for the American League, their Achilles heel was organization, in terms of both the failing commitment and resources of individual teams and the inability of the rebel leagues as a whole to stave off NL pressures aimed at destroying them. In some cases (the 1882 American Association), the NL reached its objective with the carrot of persuading the upstart to adopt its regulations as the price for recognition and survival; in other instances (the Players League), it used a stick to compel unconditional surrender; and in still other conflicts (the Federal League), it employed both the carrot and the stick to buy off some and crush others.

The American League's ability to withstand the NL's pressures and to appropriate part of the definition of major league baseball stemmed precisely from the far more meticulous preparations of organizers Ban Johnson, Charles Comiskey, and Clark Griffith; in the parlance of the game, they not only had the tools, they went into the struggle with "an idea." Long before Griffith had called upon his prominence in NL playing circles to attract stars to the new league and even before Johnson had succeeded in his coy stratagem of invading big city markets in the guise of a minor league operation, the foundations for a cohesive network of teams had been laid with the functioning of the Western League. Although many Western League franchises were dropped or transferred before evolving into the major league AL in 1901, they represented the pattern from which Johnson and his associates learned to make corrections and which impressed bankrollers like Charles Somers enough to keep financing the venture at critical junctures. The NL then made its contributions to the undertaking by alienating a substantial number of its star players with laughable salaries and by being both gullible and arrogant enough to give credence to Johnson's avowals that he wanted to play only at a minor league level in such cities as Boston, Philadelphia, and Chicago. It

didn't help, either, that by the time the NL woke up to the presence of a full-fledged rival on many of its doorsteps and endeavored to apply the same strong-arm tactics that it had resorted to against earlier competitors, the burgeoning yellow journalism of the day sprang to the discovery of a new gang of bullies. Where the AL was concerned, the NL not only had to extend a carrot, but also an invitation to the garden where it had grown.

With the AL franchises added to the NL's associative monopoly, the room for further competition was narrowed even more, making it somewhat remarkable that a pretender like the Federal League lasted twice as long as the Union Association and the Players League. For all practical purposes, in fact, the mutual coexistence agreement reached between the NL and AL at the beginning of the century left only the relatively untapped areas of the West, the South, and Canada as potential arenas for new challenges. This possibility was precluded, however, as long as most of the game's celebrated stars had eastern or midwestern backgrounds, the cities of the three areas grew at only modest rates, travel was both physically difficult and economically prohibitive, and public media interest was restricted. As it developed, it was the west, the south, and Canada that ended up hosting an appreciable number of the farm clubs that the major leagues got used to calling their own. And, by the time player backgrounds, market populations, travel times, and media attitudes had ceased to be impediments for the regions, it was the existing big leagues that were there first to exploit their new commercial viability by the transfer (Los Angeles and Atlanta) and addition (Seattle and Toronto) of franchises.

Since the dissolving of the Federal League following the 1915 season, challenges to the presumptive place of the two major leagues have been mostly intramural; i.e., involving an internal rearrangement of player–management, team–league, or league–league relations, but glancing off the right of the two circuits united as Major League Baseball to exercise their monopoly. This has hardly been a coincidence because it was a suit brought by a Federal League club, the Baltimore Terrapins, that prompted the 1922 finding of the U.S. Supreme Court that the interstate reach of the two leagues still did not subject them to antitrust laws because they did not engage in "trade or commerce in the commonly accepted use of those words."

In the wake of the Supreme Court's decision, and despite periodic blustering by congressmen to take another look at the game's exemption from the antitrust statutes, Major League Baseball has not had to fight wars so much as gear up for police actions. Some of these it has won (the right to maintain a farm system), some it has lost (the reserve clause), and some it has drawn (the hurried expansion accords worked out to calm litigious citizens in Kansas City in 1967 and Seattle in 1969), but none of the conflicts posed a real threat to the dominance of Major League Baseball itself. In this sense, even such notable advances by the players as Jackie Robinson's breaking of the color barrier in 1947 and Dave McNally and Andy Messersmith's breakthrough to free agency in 1975 were matters of reform rather than revolution.

As epitomized by the 1975 free agency ruling and the companion verdict establishing salary arbitration, the contract rights of players have triggered many of Major League Baseball's internal conflicts. There have also been several cases of individual franchises creating problems because of insufficient finances or reckless (or, sometimes, merely unorthodox) management; but, in contrast to the less solidified leagues that were dragged into an abyss by such difficulties, the NL and AL have been able to respond to their organizational crises by making loans, forcing changes in ownership, smoothing the way for a transfer to another city, or a combination of all three. In more than seventy years, there have been only two instances when internal feuding or the exercising of authority seemed on the verge of calling into question the compactness of the leagues themselves: a 1920 dispute among AL clubs over the nomination of Judge Kenesaw Landis as the first commissioner that stirred plans for dissolving the junior circuit and expanding the NL to twelve teams, and Commissioner Happy Chandler's decision in 1947 to suspend the Chicago White Sox for its refusal to pay a fine. The agitation for abandoning the AL lasted three days, the suspension of the White Sox two weeks, and that during the offseason.

On occasion, clubs have suffered as much from too much cooperation as from conflict. At the turn of the century, for instance, there were so many other NL teams represented in the financing of the Giants that New York president Andrew Freedman and his Cincinnati counterpart John T. Brush found it logical to propose that the league as a whole take over player contracts and assign players to various franchises on an annual basis. In a milder variation on this syndicate notion of competition, it was the Giants who had the upper hand a couple of decades later in practically dictating successive ownerships to the Boston Braves. In the 1950s and 1960s, the Kansas City Athletics functioned as little more than a major league farm team for the Yankees, and had the record to prove it (the worst in big league history for a club of any longevity). Another umbilical relationship was that of the Cubs with Branch Rickey, who while with both the Cardinals and Dodgers had little trouble talking Chicago out of its star players. One of the more telling consequences of free agency has been the elimination of much of this coziness between particular franchises.

Free agency has come in for a great deal of criticism for discouraging the loyalty of a player toward the team that developed him or with which he became a star. Such assertions totally ignore the history of major league teams, where the one-franchise player such as Ted Williams, Brooks Robinson, or George Brett has always been the exception rather than the rule, and often even an exception only because the organization holding his contract has not been satisfied with a trade offer for his services. Questions about Darryl Strawberry's loyalty to the Mets or Barry Bonds's to the Pirates don't address the issue of Boston's loyalty to Tris Speaker, Detroit's to Hank Greenberg, Pittsburgh's to Ralph Kiner, and New York's to Tom Seaver, to mention only four of the scores of Hall of Famers who were dealt away as soon as their teams considered it to their benefit. The lore of the game even celebrates such front office executives as Rickey, Bill Veeck, Frank Lane, and Whitey Herzog for their readiness to sever a player's ties to a specific club (the most frenetic trader of them all was probably Bing Devine when he was with the Cardinals in the 1960s and 1970s).

On the question of loyalty, as in other matters, major league teams benefit from a fuzziness in public perception that is normally not there in the case of an individual player. The relatively more benign view of team activities is the product of a number of things: broadcasters and public relations people promoting a franchise line successfully; sportswriters and media pundits adopting the easy cynicism of nobody-ever-said-life-was-fair; a defensiveness that, for better or worse, the team is the only game in town; and the belief, reinforced with every passing year and additional generation of survival, that the club transcends any of its single seasons, specific front office policies, or, even, individual owners. Major League Baseball refers to the process as tradition.

The big league clubs also benefit from the clouds that enwrap their financial status. Rare is the month that some Major League Baseball spokesman doesn't decry the imminent bankruptcy of some franchise or the deficits allegedly afflicting almost every team outside New York, Chicago, and Los Angeles not owned by a brewer. And still, despite all the proclaimed losses, new owners continue to pay spiraling millions for franchises, incumbent owners continue to give millions to players, and the only owners getting out of the game are those who have lost millions in their other enterprises or who have decided to pass their twilight years without the aggravation of league meetings. Moreover, when there has been an ownership change in recent years, the buyers have almost always included front office executives from the outgoing-regime (for example, Montreal in 1990) or prominent local businessmen (for instance, Seattle in 1992)—hardly prime candidates for buying a pig in a poke. Even short of estimating revenues from ticket sales, certain financial contours become discernible through this fog, such as community subsidies (Dodger Stadium is the last ballpark built with private capital), tax relief (especially in the depreciation of players as organizational assets, as pioneered by Arnold Johnson of the Kansas City Athletics), and merchandising (the ability to get customers to pay for the jackets, caps, and other paraphernalia that serve as advertising vehicles for the business).

Then there is the misperception regarding the role of television. In everything from imposing lights on Wrigley Field to furnishing owners with more money for raising the stakes in free agent poker, the medium's effect on baseball has been considerable. But this is not the same thing as contending, as many have, that income from national television contracts has become so central to its profitability that Major League Baseball has slipped to the status of a minority partner in the relationship between the medium and the sport. If that is in fact the situation, then the NL and AL have lost sight of their own monopoly in having the best players, the best markets, and the best organization in what is called the national pastime. They would also have had to overlook the fact that commercial and cable networks—the former in disarray and the latter poised in the early 1990s for an explosive expansion—have greater need than ever for the kind of stable scheduling they can provide.

Major League Baseball has not, however, become so absent-minded after generations of striving to its present position. Underneath all the rhetoric and propaganda emanating from league offices, it still regards the networks as just one more strand (albeit a thick one) in its organizational web. The NL and AL have, in fact, netted substantially more than large contract payments from dealings over the years with NBC, CBS, ABC, and ESPN, and they are hardly

likely to have forgotten it. For starters, they have been able to blame the medium for all the violations of tradition (the lights in Chicago, World Series games on frigid nights, commercialization of almost every aspect of the game—including calls to the bullpen and the announcing of lineups) that they themselves ostensibly hold dear. Second, they have tightened their grip on the sport still further through all the recognition (star players, team logos, ballpark contours) and merchandising elements that television has fused into an industry. Most recently, at the beginning of the 1990s, the leagues have even been able to exploit forecasts of the end of their golden agreements with the networks by enlisting that eventuality as sufficient reason for raising ticket prices, seeking caps on player salaries and the elimination of arbitration, and exploring pay-per-view prospects.

Another advantage arising from Major League Baseball's agreements with the national networks has been the relative containment of disputes between small-market and big-market franchises. If the Game of the Week in its various manifestations has always gone out of its way to schedule a New York, Chicago, or California club, it has also been obliged to accommodate as an opposing team, or in a backup game, small-market clubs like Pittsburgh and Milwaukee. The result at a public relations level has been the generally positive impression of a full menu of Major League Baseball's offerings for the viewing public (with regrets that this or that entree isn't available on a given day). More to the point for the teams, the network money has been shared out equally among the clubs in the two leagues, making big-market (New York, Los Angeles) and small-market (Cincinnati, Seattle) franchises equal beneficiaries.

On the other hand, there has been anything but democracy in the accords reached by individual teams with local cable stations, such as MSG in New York, and with locally headquartered superstations, such as WWOR in New York, WGN in Chicago, and TBS in Atlanta. Unlike the network revenues, the money from these deals has been spread around scarcely at all, prompting increasing agitation from the smaller franchises for some kind of sharing arrangement—a demand first voiced by Bill Veeck for metropolitan telecasts back in the 1950s. But if the question of revenue sharing has challenged Major League Baseball to reappraise its internal structure, it is not because television has defined that structure or obtained carte blanche to make the sport subject to its own interests, but because the medium has merely underlined the long-standing disparities that the two leagues have always tolerated in the relations between small-market and big-market franchises.

It is true, for instance, that WGN has become so important for the profit volume (not survival) of the Cubs that, in 1992, the club went to court to block proposals to shift it to the Western Division as of 1993 because that would have meant additional later games at Mountain and Pacific starting times for the superstation's audience in eastern zones of the country. But those who denounced the league's surrender to such a broadcasting calculation overlooked the fact that the only reason the Cubs were—aberrantly—in the Eastern Division to begin with was another NL concession in 1968 to the even-bigger-market Mets, who were ready to torpedo the whole concept of divisional play if they didn't get Chicago and St. Louis to visit Shea Stadium nine times a year each, geographic logic be damned. It was not television, but franchise self-interest, that declared that Atlanta and Cincinnati were west of Wrigley Field and Busch Stadium.

When all the smoke has been cleared away from the sport's posturing, and as long as it enjoys its privileged exemption from antitrust regulations, the only force equal to even its most richly endowed franchise is Major League Baseball itself; i.e., the entirety of economic, social, and political factors adding up to the self-interests of the associated teams. Every decision made, whether pertaining to a lockout of players, a bargaining stance on television contracts, or a relentless teasing of an eager candidate member such as Tampa-St. Petersburg, requires no more justification than the argument of having been "in the best interests of baseball"—a claim second only to "in the interests of national security" for concealing the manipulative and the embarrassing behind the purportedly protective and self-explanatory. Nor, especially after the events around Fay Vincent's pressured resignation in September 1992, can there be any doubt about who has the last word on what the "best interests" happen to be.

Like the Boston fans who didn't show up to watch Braves' games and Brooklyn's economic downturn in the 1950s, Vincent gave the owners plenty of immediate alibis for the move they agreed to make. He got involved too visibly in player-management negotiations, he brokered the arrangement that gave AL clubs only 22 percent of the entry fees to be paid by Colorado and Florida for joining the NL, he tried to impose realignment on the NL, he was hasty in approving the sale of the Giants to Tampa Bay interests, and he issued threats against front office executives of the Yankees for having tes-tified before the Players Association in the Steve Howe drug case. But none of these episodes was as important as the attitude of the owners that Vincent had begun to lose sight of his function as their spokesman, that he forgot that he was only a well-paid employee and not an independent party with superentity powers.

However Vincent developed such a vision of his task, it wasn't with an historical appreciation of the work of his predecessors in the commissioner's office. For all his erratic pronouncements, not even Kenesaw Landis quite confused himself with Major League Baseball; he knew full well that even his disciplining of single franchises in such matters as the chattel status of farmhands had the endorsement of the majority of owners who couldn't boast of a vast minor league organization. Conversely, when the owners had an ideal public relations pitchman for their interests, they discovered to their regret that accepting his advice in questions other than that role could be disastrous; it was in October 1985, for example, that Peter Ueberroth planted the seed of the collusion against free agents that would end up costing the teams tens of millions of dollars, as well as numerous star players for some of them. Past commissioners also knew how to save their noblest rhetoric until they could no longer be hurt by it; thus, it was not until he had already been shown the door in 1952 that Happy Chandler could assert that he "always regarded baseball as our National Game that belongs to 150 million men, women, and children, not to sixteen special people who happen to own big league teams."

Whatever his timing, Chandler was wrong—at least insofar as the owners define Major League Baseball. No more striking evidence of this came than in the aftermath of Vincent's resignation, when Chicago White Sox owner Jerry Reinsdorf told reporters that it was now possible to "run the business for the owners, not the players or the umpires or the fans." As long as the owners accept this definition of Major League Baseball, it will not be the fault of the players, television, city councils, or even power-driven commissioners if the game someday runs into a brick wall. While it remains exempt from antitrust laws and while its dominance makes the emergence of a serious revival unlikely, the only way Major League Baseball will be beaten is for the clubs grouped within it to beat themselves—not precisely what has been meant by baseball as a team game.

Donald Dewey
Nicholas Acocella

A Note on Leagues

A total of six separate major leagues have been officially acknowledged by the Office of the Baseball Commissioner, based on findings of the Special Baseball Records Committee:

The National League (NL)	1876–Present
The American Association (AA)	1882–1891
The Union Association (UA)	1884
The Players League (PL)	1890
The American League (AL)	1901–Present
The Federal League (FL)	1914–1915

For the best descriptions of the founding and demise of each of the six major leagues, see the following entries:

National League founding	Chicago Cubs, page 120
American Association founding	Pittsburgh Alleghenys, page 444
American Association demise	Chicago, page 146
Union Association founding and demise	St. Louis Maroons, page 481
Players League founding	Brooklyn Wonders, page 75
Players League demise	Chicago Pirates, page 145
American League founding	Cleveland Indians, page 207
Federal League founding	Chicago Whales, page 168
Federal League demise	Newark Peppers, page 331

The following table chronicles the evolution of the six leagues and the transient nature of the various franchises:

Year	League	Teams
1876	NL	Boston, Chicago, Cincinnati, Hartford, Louisville, New York, Philadelphia, St. Louis
1877	NL	New York and Philadelphia dropped Brooklyn replaces Hartford
1878	NL	Indianapolis, Milwaukee, and Providence replace Brooklyn, Louisville, and St. Louis
1879	NL	Buffalo and Cleveland replace Indianapolis and Milwaukee Syracuse and Troy added
1880	NL	Worcester replaces Syracuse
1881	NL	Detroit replaces Cincinnati
1882	AA	Baltimore, Cincinnati, Louisville, Philadelphia, Pittsburgh, St. Louis
1883	NL	New York and Philadelphia replace Troy and Worcester
	AA	Columbus and New York added
1884	AA	Brooklyn, Indianapolis, Toledo, and Washington added Richmond replaces Washington during the season
	UA	Altoona, Baltimore, Boston, Chicago, Cincinnati, Philadelphia, St. Louis, Washington

		During the season, Kansas City replaces Altoona, Pittsburgh replaces Chicago, St. Paul replaces Pittsburgh, Wilmington replaces Philadelphia, and Milwaukee replaces Wilmington
1885	NL	St. Louis replaces Cleveland
	AA	Columbus, Indianapolis, Richmond, and Toledo dropped
1886	NL	Kansas City and Washington replace Buffalo and Providence
1887	NL	Indianapolis and Pittsburgh replace Kansas City and St. Louis
	AA	Cleveland replaces Pittsburgh
1888	AA	Kansas City replaces New York
1889	NL	Cleveland replaces Detroit
	AA	Columbus replaces Cleveland
1890	NL	Brooklyn and Cincinnati replace Indianapolis and Washington
	AA	Rochester, Syracuse, and Toledo replace Baltimore, Cincinnati, and Kansas City New Brooklyn franchise replaces old one Baltimore replaces Brooklyn during the season
	PL	Boston, Brooklyn, Buffalo, Chicago, Cleveland, New York, Philadelphia, Pittsburgh Cincinnati added after the season but never plays
1891	AA	Boston, Cincinnati, and Washington replace Rochester, Syracuse, and Toledo Milwaukee replaces Cincinnati during the season Chicago added after the season but never plays
1892	NL	Baltimore, Louisville, St. Louis, and Washington added
1899	NL	Baltimore, Cleveland, Louisville, and Washington dropped
1901	AL	Baltimore, Boston, Chicago, Cleveland, Detroit, Milwaukee, Philadelphia, and Washington
1902	AL	St. Louis replaces Milwaukee
1903	AL	New York replaces Baltimore
1914	FL	Baltimore, Brooklyn, Buffalo, Chicago, Indianapolis, Kansas City, Pittsburgh, St. Louis
1915	FL	Newark replaces Indianapolis
1953	NL	Milwaukee replaces Boston
1954	AL	Baltimore replaces St. Louis
1955	AL	Kansas City replaces Philadelphia
1958	NL	Los Angeles and San Francisco replace Brooklyn and New York
1961	AL	Minnesota replaces Washington California and new Washington franchise added
1962	NL	Houston and New York added
1966	NL	Atlanta replaces Milwaukee
1968	AL	Oakland replaces Kansas City
1969	NL	Montreal and San Diego added
	AL	Kansas City and Seattle added
1970	AL	Milwaukee replaces Seattle
1972	AL	Texas replaces Washington
1977	AL	Seattle and Toronto added
1993	NL	Colorado and Florida added

About This Book

The clubs covered in the *Encyclopedia of Major League Baseball Teams* are those that have been represented in the six officially acknowledged major leagues (*see* A Note on Leagues). Teams are arranged alphabetically by name of club. In cases of more than one team from the same city (e.g. New York Giants, New York Mets), the franchises are listed in the chronological order of their formation.

There are separate entries for teams that have been shifted from one city (Milwaukee Braves) to another (Atlanta Braves). Anyone who contends that the Brooklyn Dodgers–Los Angeles Dodgers or Seattle Pilots–Milwaukee Brewers constitute the same franchise has not talked to a native of Brooklyn or Seattle.

Many ballparks have had different names, depending on an owner of the moment (Robison Field in St. Louis, for example). The authors have indi-cated the most famous name at the heading to each entry and explained changes in the text.

To avoid cluttering the text, the authors have avoided cross-references. Historical episodes affecting more than one team have usually been covered in all pertinent entries from the point of view of the particular club.

The list of managers at the end of each entry covers pilots who have been contracted for their jobs and coaches who were asked to fill in for an extended period.

It should also be noted that, as reflected in the standings at the end of the relevant entries, the National League played a split season in 1892 as a means of providing more incentive for a postseason showdown in its enlarged (twelve-team) circuit. Both the National and American leagues played a split season in 1981 because of a players' strike.

Altoona Mountain Citys

Union Association, 1884	**BALLPARK:** COLUMBIA PARK
RECORD: 6–19 (.240)	**OTHER NAMES:** PRIDE, OTTOWAS

Playing in the smallest city in major league history, in a league hastily assembled and woefully ill-organized, Altoona was a franchise doomed from its inception.

Despite having only 25,000 inhabitants in the mid-1880s, Altoona had a prominent history of local amateur baseball when, in March 1883, a group of local businessmen, headed by lawyer Arthur V. Dively and clothier William W. Ritz, formed a semi-professional baseball club that competed against other Pennsylvania teams. The team drew an average of 1,600 fans in 1883, and flushed with their initial success, the directors sought to place their club in an organized league for the 1884 season. Their first choice was the Inter-State Association, which had teams in Pennsylvania, New Jersey, and Delaware. But Altoona's membership in the Inter-State Association was short-lived: In February, half of the Association's clubs jumped to the Eastern League. Too late to go along with the defectors to the minor league, Dively and Ritz suddenly found themselves wooed by Henry Lucas, founder and backer of the Union Association, a prospective major league. Lucas was interested in the city mainly because it was a convenient stopover for other projected UA teams traveling east and west.

Lucas, whose accuracy often got lost in his enthusiasm, was at least publicly overwhelmed by Altoona's credentials. He claimed alternately that the Pennsylvania Railroad and Philadelphia executives in that company were behind the Altoona franchise. This must have surprised the 16 local businessmen who were the actual investors in the club and who were busily engaged in selling public shares at $1

each to raise money. Lucas visited Altoona on March 8, six days after the club's acceptance into the UA, and donated $2,500 to the treasury, fully half of the necessary start-up capital.

The Mountain Citys opened the 1884 UA season in Cincinnati, where they were billed as the "Famous Altoonas." (Local partisans called the team the Pride or the Ottowas.) The club's initial billing was a prime example of Lucas's hyperbolic boosterism, because of the nineteen players who appeared in an Altoona uniform, only outfielder Jack Leary had any prior major league experience—and he batted .091 for Altoona.

By even the mediocre standards of the UA, the Mountain Citys were demonstrably overmatched. They lost their first eleven games. The defense and pitching were abominable, making 53 errors and giving up 92 runs in the eight games against Lucas's St. Louis Maroons. By late May, the Mountain Citys were a financial disaster. Attendance slipped to as low as 200 and, despite a weekly promotion that offered free admission to women, the average number of spectators for seventeen games was only slightly more than 1,000. State blue laws prohibited Sunday games, a prohibition the city of Altoona took seriously.

Profiteering by at least two shareholders contributed to the financial distress. James Goetz, a tailor, contracted to make not only two sets of uniforms—at $18 per uniform—but also matching brown traveling suits for every player—at $35 each. Hatter Malcolm Westfall provided uniform hats ($10 each) and brown derbys to match the traveling suits ($8 each). This sartorial extravagance cost over $1,000, a fifth of the club's initial capital.

Eventually, the club fell into arrears in salary payments, and players either scrambled off to other teams or withheld their services until they received their money. On May 29, Lucas met with the Altoona directors and, with the mythical Pennsylvania Railroad angels long forgotten, refused to subsidize the club's losses. The directors paid the players what they were owed and Altoona became the first of the UA clubs to disband. Having also forgotten the reason he had found Altoona so useful, Lucas moved the franchise to Kansas City, 1,000 miles to the west.

ALTOONA MOUNTAIN CITYS

Annual Standings and Manager

Year	Position	W	L	Pct.	GB	Manager
1884	Partial Season	6	19	.240	—	Ed Curtis

Atlanta Braves

National League
1966–Present

BALLPARK: ATLANTA–FULTON COUNTY STADIUM

RECORD: 2030–2269 (.472)

The arrival of the Braves in Atlanta in 1966 was one of major league baseball's noisier events. For one thing, the franchise moved into Georgia a year later than had been planned because of a lawsuit that had kept it in Milwaukee for a lame duck 1965 season. For another, the National League's approval of the transfer caused a tidal wave in the American League, where Kansas City Athletics operator Charles Finley threatened to sue his fellow owners for not fulfilling a pledge to give him first shot at the Atlanta market. This in turn led the AL to endorse Finley's move of the Athletics to Oakland and set in motion the maneuvers that would end in the expansion of both leagues in 1969. Amid all these financial and legal rumblings, Atlanta's enthusiasm for the first twentieth-century franchise in the Deep South was almost drowned out.

As portable franchises went, the Braves were one of the better ones. In fact, except for the Dodgers, it was the only team since 1900 to shift its quarters after having played at least .500 ball the season before moving, and absolutely the only one to maintain that level for the first year in its new city. Reflecting the power tradition it had established during its thirteen-year tenure in Milwaukee, the club's principal assets were home-run king Hank Aaron, All Star catcher Joe Torre, and future batting champion Rico Carty. The 1966 roster was also dotted with past and future luminaries like Eddie Mathews, Felix Millan, Felipe Alou, and knuckleball specialist Phil Niekro. For further entertainment there was Bobby Bragan, the manager who liked putting together unorthodox lineups (power hitters leading off, for example) as much as he liked baiting umpires. What all this added up to was an Atlanta team that led the league in home runs and runs scored, but that still finished fifth because of bad pitching and weak defense.

Through their first couple of years in Atlanta, the Braves as a franchise seemed distracted by the pot of gold they had been handed in their new fan territory and virginal television market. This encouraged something less than sensitivity toward individual players and the organization's long-term needs. In one particularly notorious episode, on New Year's Eve in 1966, Mathews, who had been with the Braves franchise since its days in Boston and who had amassed numbers that would eventually get him to Cooperstown, had to find out through a reporter that he had been traded to the Astros. When the Atlanta press chided management for such shabby behavior, the team sent a letter of apology to "Edward" Mathews (his name is Edwin). The Braves also mishandled a number of complaints from black and Latin players about some of the realities of living in

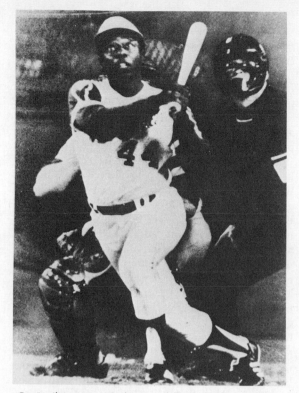

On April 8, 1974, Hank Aaron follows the flight of the drive off Al Downing of the Dodgers that became his record-setting 715th home run. *National Baseball Library, Cooperstown, NY*

the New South, eventually concluding that the main problem was manager Bragan and replacing him with dugout warhorse Billy Hitchcock for the end of the inaugural season and most of 1967. By the time Ken Silvestri was rushed in for the final weekend of 1967, the team was in seventh place with the franchise's worst record (77–85) since its final year in Boston, in 1952.

Although 1969 will always be associated with the Miracle Mets of the NL Eastern Division, not too many people invested their savings predicting that the Braves would win the Western Division that sea-

Although most record books record the venerable Satchel Paige as having ended his career with Kansas City in 1965, he was signed by the Braves in 1968 in order to qualify him for a major league pension. He was released without appearing in a game as soon as he qualified.

son, either. With one major exception, the club broke spring training with the same general look it had had in 1968, when new manager Lum Harris had brought it back to mediocrity with a .500 mark. The one significant change was the addition of first baseman Orlando Cepeda, obtained in a preseason trade with the Cardinals for the popular Torre. At first, the front office's justification for the deal—that Cepeda was a proven winner and that Torre had begun to decline offensively because of too many years crouched behind the plate—cut little ice with Atlanta fans. But then Cepeda started to contribute the 22 homers and 88 RBIs that would back Aaron's 44 round-trippers, Niekro's 23 wins, and Millan and Clete Boyer's steady defensive work in the infield as the keys to the division flag. Merely being the Surprise Braves, however, the team went down to defeat in three consecutive games against the Mets in the League Championship Series, in spite of a home run from Aaron in each of the contests.

Aaron's relationship with Atlanta was not unlike that of Willie Mays with San Francisco: While acknowledged as a superstar, he was also viewed by fans as an immigrant from Milwaukee, as not being quite local enough a hero. Just as San Francisco fans had displayed more enthusiasm for Cepeda and Willie McCovey, Atlanta fans showed greater attachment to players who came into their own in Fulton County Stadium; for instance, Niekro and, later, Dale Murphy. Also as in the case of Mays, there was a perceptible warming toward Aaron near the end of his career, especially in 1973–74 when he was chasing, and then eclipsing Babe Ruth's all-time home run record. But there were also differences in the relationships between the two stars and their fans. Unlike the often spectacular Mays, Aaron personified quiet efficiency on the field, rolling up his magnificent offensive numbers (for example, twenty straight years of at least 20 homers) with relentless consistency rather than dramatic flair, hauling down fly balls, throwing out runners, and stealing bases with maximum economy. On the relatively few occasions that he deliberately drew attention to himself, it was to criticize a situation that Mays seldom spoke about—baseball's treatment of blacks. More often than not, Aaron's criticisms elicited little more than condescending reassurances from the major league establishment. But even the commissioner and the two league offices had to pay attention when, during the pursuit of Ruth's mark and despite general enthusiasm for the feat, Aaron received so much hate mail from lunatics around the country dedicated to preserving "a white man's record" that he had to be given police protection. It was an experience that years later he would recall as vividly as his 715th home run and that helped his decision on one occasion to stand up Commissioner Bowie Kuhn at a ceremony in the outfielder's honor to protest baseball's lethargy in naming blacks to managerial and significant administrative posts.

If Atlanta's division win in 1969 had come as a sweet surprise, its plummet back down to fifth place in 1970 caused an equally bitter shock. What made the tumble even more bewildering was the actual *improvement* from the previous year in many of the key hitting categories. Among those shining were Cepeda (34 homers, 111 RBIs), Aaron (38 homers, 118 RBIs), and Carty (25 homers, 101 RBIs, and a league-leading .366 average). Where the trouble lay was a pitching staff on which three of the five starters had an ERA of more than four runs a game and a leaky defense. For the next four years, the Braves were the most erratic team in the league, twice playing better than even and twice barely escaping a finish in the cellar of the Western Division. Almost all of Atlanta's accomplishments for the first half of the 1970s stemmed from an offense that established Fulton County Stadium as a launching pad that made even Wrigley Field seem like a pitcher's park by comparison. The signal offensive feats over the period included catcher Earl Williams belting 33 homers and being named NL Rookie of the Year in 1971; Aaron, Darrell Evans, and Davey Johnson making Atlanta the only club in history to have three hitters with at least 40 homers in one season (1973); and Ralph Garr winning the battling title in 1974. About the only positive notes in the pitching were Niekro's no-hitter over the Padres in 1973, the knuckleballer's 20 wins the following year, and Buzz Capra's NL–leading 2.28 ERA, also in 1974.

As might be expected from a team showing little consistency, attendance stayed below the one million mark in the early 1970s. Equally predictable, Harris was fired. Where the novelty came in was in the appointment of Mathews, the player who had been dispatched so curtly by the franchise, as Harris's successor in the final weeks of the 1972 season. The novelty wore off fast enough. Mathews lasted only to the midway point in 1974 before he too was told that his services were no longer required. The firing stunned not only Mathews, but also his friend and one-time companion slugger Aaron, who immediately made it clear that the only good to come out of the ouster would be if General Manager Eddie Robinson appointed a black like himself as the new skipper. Robinson not only ignored that suggestion in

favor of his special assistant Clyde King, but seemed to go out of his way to offend both Mathews and Aaron by giving King the first multiyear deal for an Atlanta manager.

The climax of Aaron's pursuit of Babe Ruth's record also occurred in 1974. Aaron had ended the previous season one homer short of the mark, so the outfielder spent the winter answering questions about whether he thought he could break the record on Opening Day in Cincinnati in 1974. Braves owner William Bartholomay, the insurance man who had been operating the team since its final years in Milwaukee, had his own answer to the question. Disgruntled by the falling attendance in Atlanta, Bartholomay was adamant that he wasn't going to hand Cincinnati the gate attraction of Aaron's 714th and 715th home runs and made it clear that he wanted the slugger to sit out the opening series against the Reds and perform his heroics at home. This business maneuver drew a storm of criticism from traditionalists in the sports press and prompted Commissioner Kuhn to intervene with an order to have Aaron in the starting lineup for the opener against the Reds. Aaron responded by tying Ruth's mark with the first swing of his bat in the first inning. But that was it. Bartholomay got his wish when 53,775 poured into Fulton County Stadium on the cold and miserable night of April 8, 1974 and saw Aaron tag Al Downing of Los Angeles for his 715th. It was to be the final great moment in a Braves uniform for Aaron who, after some earlier indications that he was going to retire altogether, agreed to a trade to the Milwaukee Brewers following the end of the season.

The Braves entered 1975 lacking more than Aaron. They were also without Dick Allen, the slugger who had rejected an offseason trade to the team and so had to be reswapped to the Phillies. For their part, third baseman Evans and shortstop Larvell Blanks showed that the team lacked defense by combining for 61 errors in the infield. Rookie Rowland Office proved that the team had even misplaced its traditional offense by leading the club with a soft .290 average (3 homers and 30 RBIs). Manager King demonstrated that multiyear contracts lacked something when he was kicked back upstairs to assist Robinson in a switch with Connie Ryan. And most conspicuous of all by their absence were Atlanta's fans, only 534,000 of whom (representing a single-season drop of 446,000) bothered to buy a ticket to see a fifth-place club.

Then came Ted Turner. Declaring that he was an owner who "cared," Turner, a cable television millionaire, purchased the franchise from Bartholomay and his partners in January 1976 for an estimated $12 million. His first surprise move was to keep Bartholomay as the team's chairman of the board. Then, with the baseball establishment still smarting over the successful challenge to the reserve rule mounted that winter by pitchers Andy Messersmith and Dave McNally, the new Braves owner went out and signed Messersmith to a long-term deal, part of which called for the pitcher to wear uniform number 17 as a living billboard advertising Turner's cable superstation. While none of the other owners were about to admit in public that Turner had undermined a move to blackball Messersmith, some of them had plenty to say when he (and White Sox president Bill Veeck) skirted that season's lockout of spring training camps by inviting minor leaguers down to Florida on schedule. Although technically not a break with the ownership lockout because no big leaguers were involved, Turner's action was interpreted as a disturbing sign of his tendency to do things his own way and would be remembered down the road. On the other hand, he went along with the other owners on a contractual prerogative that allowed teams to cut by 20 percent the salary of any player who announced that he intended playing out his option year. In the case of the Braves for 1976, this amounted to twenty-four players.

The 1976 season was little more than an interlude between Turner's spring and fall clashes with other owners and the league office. In what was to be the second of four straight cellar finishes, Atlanta led the league in nothing but injuries (at one point seven players, including Messersmith, were hobbling around on crutches). On the other hand, Turner personally jacked up the gate appeal of the team by such stunts as jumping out onto the field to welcome a Braves' home run hitter at home plate and joining the grounds crew in sweeping the field. Antics of the kind added almost 300,000 more customers for the year.

Some of the laughter died after the season. No sooner had Turner announced that he had signed outfielder Gary Matthews as a free agent for 1977 than Kuhn smacked him with a tampering charge, levied a fine of $10,000, and stripped the Braves of their first-round amateur draft pick in January. The Giants, the team that had lost Matthews, were not satisfied and went to Kuhn with further tampering accusations. Following a review of the new evidence, the commissioner increased his penalties to a one-year suspension of Turner and Atlanta's loss of its June draft selection as well. Turner's response was threefold: the firing of general manager John Alevizos for having illegally approached Matthews before the end of the 1976 season, the raising of a giant billboard advertisement welcoming the outfielder to Atlanta, and the suing of Kuhn over the suspension.

Turner's case wasn't heard until April 28–29, 1977, by which time he had rattled the NL again by telling Braves skipper Dave Bristol to take a few days off while he himself stepped in as "acting manager." Once again the stunt was primarily aimed at getting the Atlanta faithful to forget about the wretched play of the Braves; in fact, on the day that Turner decided to take over for Bristol, the team lost its 16th straight game. With coach Vern Benson actually calling the shots in the dugout, the owner presided over a seventeenth consecutive loss but expressed himself as thrilled by the experience. NL President Chub Feeney was less so. Drawing upon an old regulation that prohibited players and managers from owning stock in the club that employed them, Feeney prevented Turner from doing a repeat performance, and Bristol was reinstated to guide the team to the most losses (101) it has ever suffered.

In court, Turner fared only slightly better. After hearing the evidence about the alleged tampering and reviewing Kuhn's right to impose the penalties that he had, a judge upheld the fine and the year's suspension but returned the draft picks to the Braves. Turner, who at one point during the proceedings threatened to give the commissioner's attorney "a knuckle sandwich" for his cross-examination tactics, accepted the verdict and, to help himself forget the Braves for a year, went off to win the America's Cup.

The next phase of the team's development was largely carried out under Bobby Cox, brought in to replace Bristol as manager for the 1978 season. Although the team was to remain mired in the cellar for another couple of years, Cox had slightly more to build on than his immediate predecessors. One of the most important new pieces was Bob Horner, a third baseman signed out of Arizona State University as the nation's number one draft pick. Horner, who was to win NL Rookie of the Year honors in 1978, went directly from college ball to hitting a home run in his third major league at bat. Also during 1978, Larry McWilliams and Gene Garber teamed up to end the season's biggest story—Pete Rose's 44-game hitting streak.

Aside from Horner, the franchise's major hope lay in Dale Murphy, a quiet-spoken Mormon as lanky as Horner was chunky but with equal power. For more than two years, Murphy's progress was stymied by the team's inability to decide if he was a catcher, a first baseman, or an outfielder. Constantly switched among the positions, he failed to develop any consistency at the plate until he was placed in the outfield for good in 1980. Murphy supporters claimed that he was too much of a nice guy during all the indecision. The same charge of passivity could never be leveled against Horner. Prior to beginning only his second year of professional ball, the third baseman and his agent held out for free agency because of a discrepancy in his contract. The dispute ended in a three-year pact worth $1.2 million—the highest amount ever doled out to a Braves player. When Horner hit 33 homers, drove in 98 runs, and batted .314 in his sophomore season, it seemed like an equitable deal for both sides. But when the slugger started slowly in 1980 and showed a few more pounds than could be justified as muscle, Turner made clear his feeling about the contract by snapping that he wanted his "money's worth" and ordering Horner to the minor leagues to play himself back into shape. This provoked tensions with general manager John Mullin, who insisted that even an overweight Horner was one of the best hitters in the league, and with the Major League Players Association, which filed a grievance against Atlanta for "improper disciplinary action." The third baseman sat for a couple of days, and then went on to finish second in homers in the league.

Turner's impatience with Horner struck many as ironic given the huge amounts of money he was throwing out for free agents in those same years. In 1979, he agreed to pay reliever Al Hrabosky $170,000 annually over 30 years, the gimmick being the owner's assurances that the pitcher would have a place on one of the cable network's stations upon retirement. Even more galling to other owners than a pact that ran through the year 2009 was Turner's 1980 signing of outfielder Claudell Washington for five years for a sum barely falling short of $5 million. Up to that point in his career, Washington had never hit more than 13 homers in a season and had batted .300 only once; in his five and a half seasons with the Braves, the outfielder would prove to be solid but hardly spectacular. As for Hrabosky, whose antics on the mound had earned him the sobriquet of The Mad Hungarian, he managed no more than seven saves in three seasons before quitting. Eventually, he settled his contract with the Braves before going on to his desired broadcasting career—with the Cardinals.

Despite overseeing the team's transition back to respectability, Cox was not around when the Braves finally cashed in their potential in 1982. With Torre coming back as manager and Bob Gibson as the team's pitching coach, Atlanta started the season by winning its first thirteen games. From that point on, it was mainly a question of whether any of the other Western Division teams—particularly, the Dodgers or Giants—would be able to surpass a less than imposing division leader. The Dodgers did—and didn't. In a two-week period at the end of July and beginning of August, Los Angeles charged from its third-place standing 10 games behind the Braves to first place, along the way sweeping Atlanta in consecutive weekend series. Then the Braves righted themselves from a streak of 19 losses in 21 games and went back on top. The battle went on right down to the final weekend of the season, when Atlanta found itself a mere game ahead of both the Dodgers and the Giants and needed the two California teams to knock each other off to back into the division title.

Although the Braves had barely crawled into the League Championship Series and were quickly run off the field in three straight games by the Cardinals, the winners of the Eastern Division, 1982 seemed to restore the franchise. And, indeed, for the next two seasons with Torre still in command, the Braves had a few things to boast about: two second-place finishes, back-to-back Most Valuable Player awards for Murphy (1982–83), and an all-time attendance record of 2,119,935 in 1983. But it wouldn't be too long before the team was back to battling to stay out of the cellar (and generally failing) and before an Atlanta merchandiser was making a lot of money from bumper stickers that told the Braves to "get out of town—and take the Falcons with you."

The first big setback came with a series of wrist and hand injuries to Horner that made him miss almost 60 games in 1983 and just about all of 1984.

He would never be the same player again, despite one moment of glory on July 6, 1986 when he hit four balls out of the park in a game against Montreal (a contest the Braves still managed to lose). The always-questionable pitching fell into a steady decline, especially after the team's burgeoning ace, Pascual Perez, was suspended in 1984 for drug use. Torre's relations with the front office also began to sour, prompting periodic reports that Niekro was being groomed to replace him, that Niekro was about to take on the extra job of pitching coach, or, simply, that Niekro had a private line to Turner for issuing all his criticisms of the way the club was being handled. In a move later described by some as a Pyrrhic victory for Torre, the Braves backed off from a contract offer to the knuckleballer following the 1983 season and let him sign with the Yankees as a free agent. Torre was under no illusions that he did not have to deliver big in 1984. When all he could manage was a second-place tie with Houston and a record two games under .500, he was discharged in favor of Eddie Haas, a long-time manager in Atlanta's farm system.

Whether it was Haas who was out of his depth (the impression of many in Atlanta) or a team that once again needed a total overhaul, the Braves of 1985 were a drab reminder of the very bad old days. But for a brief moment at the start of the 1986 season, when the club woke up on the morning of July 4th only a game-and-a-half out of first place, the general dreariness continued for the rest of the decade under Bobby Wine, Chuck Tanner, and Russ Nixon. For his part, Turner, who had once zealously promoted the Braves as America's Team and who had pursued free agents like Pete Rose with the argument that his cable operations made every Atlanta player a national household name, appeared rarely at Fulton County Stadium, devoting more time to his International Goodwill Games and to soccer's World Cup, both of which he insisted preempt television coverage of baseball.

The single constant through the team's deterioration was Murphy. While would-be phenoms came and went, the outfielder continued to be among the league's most prodigious power hitters. But by 1990, with even Atlanta's own broadcasters lamenting that the most popular player in the history of the franchise might never again play in a postseason game and suggesting that this prospect was beginning to tell on his abilities, the writing was on the wall for a deal. It came on August 4th, when Murphy and pitcher Tommy Greene were shipped to the Phillies for a trio of players who brought little to Atlanta by

way of return. Not even his Philadelphia uniform prevented Braves fans from giving Murphy a special day in Atlanta in 1991.

In their search to get somebody to lead the franchise out of the doldrums in 1986, the Braves went back to Cox, this time bringing him in as general manager. While the team foundered on the field, Cox concentrated on the Braves' farm system, and especially on a group of pitchers who had either been drafted from Atlanta's advantageous winter selection position (Tom Glavine, Steve Avery, Kent Mercker) or sent down for further development after being obtained in trades (John Smoltz). By 1990, all these prospects would be in Georgia. Along with them came outfielders Dave Justice (1990 NL Rookie of the Year) and Ron Gant (the third player in Braves history to clout 30 homers and steal at least 30 bases). As it turned out, the manager by then was Cox himself, who took over from Nixon in June 1990.

After another cellar finish, the Braves embarked on their busiest winter since moving to Atlanta. To begin with, John Schuerholz was brought in from Kansas City to replace Cox as general manager. Over the next few months, Schuerholz signed free agents Terry Pendleton, Sid Bream, Rafael Belliard, and Juan Berenguer, insisting that the club's biggest needs were infielders who could catch the ball and relievers who could bail out the young starters. A few weeks into the 1991 season, Schuerholz obtained fleet-footed outfielder Otis Nixon from Montreal in exchange for a minor league catcher. What nobody, not even the team's own general manager or manager, anticipated was that these would be the final ingredients for the first team in NL history to go from last place one year to the pennant the next.

The Atlanta season built slowly, with the team still nine games behind the Dodgers in July. Although Pendleton, Bream, and Belliard all came through to close up infield leaks and Gant was launched on another 30–30 year, the team was hobbled significantly by a back injury to Justice. Even when the lefty slugger came back to the lineup, there were injuries to Berenguer and middle-reliever Marvin Freeman and, most devastatingly, a drug test on Nixon that disqualified him from play just when he was hitting near .300 and leading the league in steals. The Braves persevered. Glavine won 20, Avery 18, and Smoltz went 11–2 over the second half of the year. To replace Berenguer, Schuerholz acquired Alejandro Peña in a late August trade with the Mets; Peña earned a save in every one of his 11 save situations. Offensively, Pendleton closed in on the batting title, Gant saved most of his homers to put the team ahead or in a tie, and Justice ended up with numbers that seemed to ridicule his two-month absence.

In the LCS against Pittsburgh, Atlanta fans sparked some resentment among Native Americans by painting their faces and resorting to their "grandstand chop" to show their support for the team. The protests revived debate about the racial insensitivity involved in team names like Braves, Indians, and Redskins. On the field, meanwhile, the Braves and Pirates battled through two extra-inning games and two 1–0 contests before Smoltz finally claimed the league title with a shutout in the seventh game. In the event, the LCS was only a warmup for the World Series against Minnesota, like Atlanta a pennant winner after having spent the previous year in the basement of its division. With their handkerchief-waving fans cheering them on in the Metrodome, the Twins beat the Braves in the first two games; with their chopping fans cheering them on in Fulton County Stadium, the Braves took the next three contests. Back in Minnesota, a dramatic eleventh-inning home run by Kirby Puckett off Charlie Leibrandt settled the sixth game. Then in Game Seven, veteran Jack Morris matched zeroes with Smoltz for nine innings. Atlanta blew an easy chance to score the game's first run with a base-running lapse by Lonnie Smith in the eighth inning, and finally succumbed in the tenth to a bases-loaded pinch-single by Gene Larkin off reliever Mike Stanton. The classic game capped what had become a "feel-good" series, with the two un-derdog clubs inspired by such unlikely heroes as Atlanta second baseman Mark Lemke (three triples, nine hits, fine defense). Despite the loss to Minnesota, more than 600,000 fans showed up at an Atlanta parade for the franchise's most successful team up to that point.

The point was surpassed in 1992, when the Braves won four more games than in the previous year and took another division championship. Pendleton was again the primary offensive force, and proved to be all the more vital with both Gant and Justice having mediocre seasons. On the mound, Glavine reached the 20-victory mark for the second straight year. The playoffs against the Pirates went to a tingling seventh game, when, with Pittsburgh just one out away from the pennant, Francisco Cabrera, a seldom-used twenty-seventh player who had been commuting between Atlanta and Richmond for several years, came off the bench to single home the tying and flag-clinching runs; Cabrera's two RBIs marked the only time a post-season game ended with the home team coming from behind in its final at bat. Once again, however, the World Series proved to be one rung too many, with the Braves losing to the Blue Jays in six games.

In the expansion draft held in November, the Braves had the tainted honor of seeing prime pitching prospect David Nied go as the very first selection by Colorado. But they more than compensated for the loss by signing Greg Maddux, the 1992 Cy Young winner, as a free agent.

ATLANTA BRAVES

Annual Standings and Managers

Year	Position	W	L	Pct.	GB	Managers
1966	Fifth	85	77	.525	10	Bobby Bragan, Billy Hitchcock
1967	Seventh	77	85	.475	24½	Billy Hitchcock, Ken Silvestri
1968	Fifth	81	81	.500	16	Lum Harris
1969	First	93	69	.574	+3	Lum Harris
1970	Fifth	76	86	.469	26	Lum Harris
1971	Third	82	80	.506	8	Lum Harris
1972	Fourth	70	84	.455	25	Lum Harris, Eddie Mathews
1973	Fifth	76	85	.472	22½	Eddie Mathews
1974	Third	88	74	.543	14	Eddie Mathews, Clyde King
1975	Fifth	67	94	.416	40½	Clyde King, Connie Ryan
1976	Sixth	70	92	.432	32	Dave Bristol
1977	Sixth	61	101	.377	37	Dave Bristol, Ted Turner
1978	Sixth	69	93	.426	26	Bobby Cox
1979	Sixth	66	94	.413	23½	Bobby Cox
1980	Fourth	81	80	.503	11	Bobby Cox
1981	Fourth	29	25	.463	9½	Bobby Cox
	Fifth	25	27	.481	7½	Bobby Cox
1982	First	89	73	.549	+1	Joe Torre

1983	Second	88	74	.543	3	Joe Torre
1984	Second	80	82	.494	12	Joe Torre
1985	Fifth	66	96	.407	29	Eddie Haas, Bobby Wine
1986	Sixth	72	89	.447	23½	Chuck Tanner
1987	Fifth	69	92	.429	20½	Chuck Tanner
1988	Sixth	54	106	.338	39½	Chuck Tanner, Russ Nixon
1989	Sixth	63	97	.394	28	Russ Nixon
1990	Sixth	65	97	.401	26	Russ Nixon, Bobby Cox
1991	First	94	68	.580	+1	Bobby Cox
1992	First	98	64	.605	+9	Bobby Cox

Postseason Play

LCS	0–3 versus New York	1969	WS	3–4 versus Minnesota	1991
	0–3 versus St Louis	1982		2–4 versus Toronto	1992
	4–3 versus Pittsburgh	1991			
	4–3 versus Pittsburgh	1992			

Baltimore Orioles

American Association, *1882–1889*	**BALLPARKS:** NEWINGTON PARK (1882) UNION PARK (1882–1889)

RECORD: 403–519 (.437)

For a club that was to evolve into one of the National League's most successful franchises, the Baltimore Orioles' American Association beginnings were inauspicious. As a last-minute replacement for a Brooklyn team, the Orioles were a hastily assembled collection of rookies and has-beens whose owners were more interested in the sale of beer than baseball.

Twenty-four-year-old backer-manager-shortstop Henry Myers had played one game with Providence in 1881; no one else on the opening day roster had been in the major leagues in 1881. All in all, it was a dismal crew that finished last in every offensive and pitching category and made 490 errors, also an association worst, in 73 games. The .207 team batting average was the second worst for a full season in baseball history. (The worst was the same Orioles' .204 mark in 1886). The only bright spot in the first year was the opening of Union Park on May 17th, a week into the season. A double-decked facility that could hold 6,000 fans, Union Park was part of an entertainment complex—including a restaurant, a dance hall, and grounds for concerts—where Henry

R. Von der Horst and his brother Herman H. sold the beer they brewed at the Von der Horst Brewing Company. The accent on beer made the fans so rowdy that barbed wire had to be installed to separate them from the field and umpires.

In 1883, the Von der Horsts took over ownership of the franchise, and sold minority interests to A. J. Houck and Billy Barnie. Stepping in as manager, Barnie brought the Orioles home last again in 1883, this time in an expanded eight-team association; the Von der Horsts did rather better, realizing a profit reported variously at $10,000 and $30,000.

Although Barnie never put together a consistent contender, he was aggressive in player recruitment. One of his catches was first baseman Tommy Tucker, who led all association batters with a .372 average in 1889. His most significant pick, however, was Matt Kilroy, whose 46 wins in 1887 are the most ever by a lefthander in baseball history. Kilroy's 513 strikeouts in his rookie season of 1886 is also among the least approachable baseball records. No one since 1893, when the distance between home plate and the pitcher's rubber was established at 60' 6'', has reached 400 strikeouts, and even in Kilroy's era only four pitchers reached that figure.

Harry Von der Horst always had a professional rivalry with fellow German immigrant and team owner–beer merchant Chris Von der Ahe of St. Louis. By the end of the decade, the success of Von der Ahe's team and his imperious attempts to dominate the association so irked Von der Horst that, despite his team's third .500-plus season, he needed only the shove provided by Von der Ahe's unilateral selection of a new AA president to resign from the AA and place the Orioles in the minor Atlantic Association for the 1890 season. This switch enabled Von der Horst to continue selling his beer to the fans, to avoid the catastrophic financial consequences of the AA's struggle with Players League, and to husband his resources for another day.

BALTIMORE ORIOLES

Annual Standings and Managers

Year	Position	W	L	Pct.	GB	Managers
1882	Sixth	19	54	.260	32½	Henry Myers
1883	Eighth	28	68	.292	37	Billy Barnie
1884	Sixth	63	43	.594	11½	Billy Barnie
1885	Eighth	41	68	.376	36½	Billy Barnie
1886	Eighth	48	83	.366	41	Billy Barnie
1887	Third	77	58	.570	18	Billy Barnie
1888	Fifth	57	80	.416	36	Billy Barnie
1889	Fifth	70	65	.519	22	Billy Barnie

Baltimore Monumentals

Union Association, 1884   **BALLPARKS:** BELAIR LOT
                                 MADISON AVENUE GROUNDS

RECORD: 58–47 (.552)

Despite their winning record and third-place finish, the Monumentals never managed to accomplish their purpose of competing directly with the American Association Baltimore Orioles. The club's main attractions were left fielder Emmett Seerey, who led the team in batting with a .311 average; third baseman Yank Robinson, who went on to a 10-year major league career; and Bill Sweeney, who led the UA with 40 wins.

Aside from some decent players, the Monumentals had adequate backing. A. H. Henderson, a local mattress manufacturer, was a major investor; I. W. Lowe served as club president. The team helped drive the Eastern League Baltimore club out of existence, and took over that minor league team's home field on Madison Avenue for some home games late in the summer. With all this, though, the franchise was no match for the sixth-place Orioles, who had already become the darlings of Baltimore fans.

A financial disaster, the Monumentals didn't even bother to attend a league meeting in December, and were dropped from the circuit. A month later, the Union Association folded.

Footnote Player: Harry Wheeler is the only player in major league history to play for five different teams in a season. The outfielder's 1884 odyssey started with the American Association St. Louis Browns. After 5 games, he jumped to the Kansas City Unions, for whom he appeared in 14 games, one of them as a pitcher. Then he switched to the UA Chicago Pirates (20 games), moved with the franchise to Pittsburgh (17 games), and ended his peregrinations—and his career—with 17 games for the Monumentals. He hit .244 for the year.

BALTIMORE MONUMENTALS

Annual Standings and Managers

Year	Position	W	L	Pct.	GB	Managers
1884	Third	58	47	.552	32	Charlie Levis, Bill Henderson

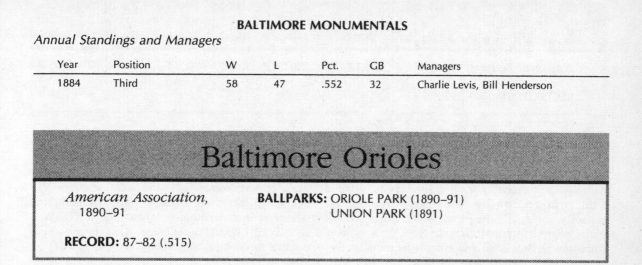

Baltimore Orioles

American Association, 1890–91	**BALLPARKS:** ORIOLE PARK (1890–91) UNION PARK (1891)

RECORD: 87–82 (.515)

When the Brooklyn Gladiators of the American Association folded in late August 1890, Harry Von der Horst, then operating his Baltimore Orioles in the minor league Atlantic Association, answered a request to rejoin the higher league. Only manager Billy Barnie and four players from the Orioles' previous AA stay were part of the team that finished the 1891 season with a 15–19 record.

The Orioles gained respectability the following season, the AA's last, with a third-place finish. Sadie McMahon tied for the league lead with 34 wins. Rookie John McGraw batted .272 in 33 games. Left fielder George Van Haltren batted .318 and took over as manager for the last six games when Barnie moved to Philadelphia.

On May 11, 1891, Von der Horst transferred the Orioles to a new 8,000-seat ballpark, across the street from Oriole Park, where the Orioles had been playing. Very quickly, the grandiose official designation of the Baltimore Baseball and Exhibition Grounds gave way to the less formal Union Park. Right field at Union Park sloped toward a 16-foot wooden fence and into an undrainable mud puddle caused by seepage from Brady's Run, a stream that constantly invaded the park.

After an opening day attendance of 10,500, the Orioles played to middling crowds and lost money. The NL ended up absorbing the organization and three other AA franchises for the 1892 season.

BALTIMORE ORIOLES

Annual Standings and Managers

Year	Position	W	L	Pct.	GB	Managers
1890	Partial Season	15	19	.441	—	Billy Barnie
1891	Third	72	63	.533	21	Billy Barnie, George Van Haltren

Baltimore Orioles

National League, 1892–1899   **BALLPARK:** UNION PARK

RECORD: 644–447 (.590)

Perceived as the exemplar of scrappy baseball and as the inventors of every tactic from the bunt to the hit-and-run, the Orioles in their National League incarnation are probably the 19th century team most familiar to modern fans. Their image and their familiarity are largely the products of the long managerial reigns of John McGraw in New York, Wilbert Robinson in Brooklyn, and Hughie Jennings in Detroit, three skilled raconteurs ready to hold forth whenever the opportunity arose.

The Oriole myth has always centered on the abrasive McGraw. Bill Clarke, Robinson's back-up catcher and for many years the baseball coach at Princeton University, said of him: "Even when the ball beat him to second by twenty feet, his mind would be sorting over arguments to give the umpire—while his feet aimed for the ball in the baseman's hand." More than by McGraw, however, the Orioles were molded and led by Ned Hanlon, one of the master strategists of baseball who came to Baltimore from Pittsburgh early in 1892. Hanlon's first major move was to trade right fielder George Van Haltren, a proven .330 hitter, to Pittsburgh for 20-year-old future Hall of Famer Joe Kelley. Other elements of Baltimore's future success were already present. Robinson, who went 7-for-7 in the first game of a double-header on June 12, was already the regular catcher. McGraw was a brash, light-hitting 19-year-old utility player. But the combination could not pull the Orioles out of dismal twelfth- and tenth-place finishes—for the worst combined record for the year—in the split season.

Resuming his quest for a winner in 1893, Hanlon traded shortstop Tim O'Rourke, who was hitting .363 at the time, to Louisville for 25-year-old Hughie Jennings, who was batting .136. Late in the season, he bought Steve Brodie for $1,000; a malcontent in St. Louis, Brodie became a .300 hitter in Baltimore. Finally, the manager traded his third baseman Billy Shindle and right fielder George Treadway to Brooklyn for aging slugger Dan Brouthers and Willie Keeler, a diminutive 22-year-old left-handed third

baseman. In addition to all his activity in the player market, Hanlon purchased 25 percent of the club's stock from Van der Horst and became organization president with complete control over operations. Van der Horst never questioned Hanlon's authority; whenever anyone inquired about one of Hanlon's seemingly bizarre deals, Van der Horst simply pointed to the lapel button he wore that said, "Ask Hanlon."

A few pieces needed rearranging. Keeler's days as an infielder ended, and he was installed in right field. The quiet man among the rowdy Orioles, Keeler batted an astounding .389, racking up 1,099

WILLIE KEELER
"HIT 'EM WHERE THEY AINT!"
BASEBALL'S GREATEST PLACE-HITTER;
BEST BUNTER. BIG LEAGUE CAREER
1892 TO 1910 WITH N.Y. GIANTS,
BALTIMORE ORIOLES, BROOKLYN SUPERBAS,
N.Y. HIGHLANDERS. NATIONAL LEAGUE
BATTING CHAMPION '97-'98.

National Baseball Library, Cooperstown, NY

hits in his five seasons in Baltimore. Asked once to put his thoughts on hitting down on paper, he issued his famous dictum: "I have already written a treatise and it reads like this: 'Keep your eye clear and hit 'em where they ain't; that's all.' " To make room for Brodie, Kelley moved from center to left, where he hit better than .300 six straight years with a high of .393 in 1894. McGraw went from short to third to make room for Jennings.

Hanlon matched his keen eye for talent with a belief in drilling his team in such fundamentals as hitting the cutoff man and having the pitcher cover first on ground balls to the first baseman's right. To take advantage of the greater pitching distance introduced in 1893, he devised the Baltimore chop and reemphasized the discredited bunt, especially the squeeze. The extra split-second it took for a pitch to reach the batter gave baserunners an edge that helped six Orioles steal more than 30 bases in 1894. Defensively, the new pitching distance allowed the Orioles to prevent double steals by having the pitcher cut off the catcher's throw to second.

Taking an extra base became the norm. The aggressive, almost suicidal, McGraw and the place-hitting wizard Keeler perfected the hit-and-run. Testing outfielders' arms at every opportunity, all eight starters had 20 or more doubles, and the team's 150 triples (in 128 games) is still a record. With all eight starters batting over .300 and driving in more than 90 runs, Baltimore swept past the favored Giants by winning 27 out of their last 30 games to take the pennant by 3 games.

Constantly seeking an edge, the Orioles conspired with head groundskeeper Tom Murphy to tailor the field to their style of play. The baselines were sloped sufficiently toward fair territory to keep bunts from rolling foul. The dirt in front of home plate was packed hard to give Baltimore chops a higher bounce; equally hard was the dirt in the basepaths in order to give runners a better footing.

Groundskeeping tricks soon led to less legitimate ploys. Allowed to grow conveniently long, the outfield grass became a hiding place for extra balls strategically placed to be substituted for ones hit in the gaps by opponents. Orioles' runners saved considerable time going from first to third on the inside edge of the basepath: While the umpire was looking somewhere else, the runner often skirted second base by ten feet. Robinson would throw his catcher's mask into the basepath to trip runners. McGraw would hook a finger in the belt of a tagging runner. With a runner on third, the team's third base coach would

bolt for home to confuse both pitcher and catcher. So notorious did the Orioles become that everyone outside Baltimore rooted against them, and the baseball world hailed Boston's pennant victory on the last weekend of the 1897 season as the triumph of good, clean baseball over the scurrilous brand played in Maryland.

Not content with clever plays and whatever else they could get away with, the Orioles were also masters of invective and intimidation. They would sit on the bench and file their spikes to a sharp edge in full view. Umpires as well as opponents were victims of intentional spikings. Baltimore's brawls became legendary. McGraw's with Tommy Tucker on May 16, 1894 so preoccupied fans that a fire in the right field bleachers went unnoticed even though it eventually destroyed Boston's South End Grounds. The vituperation aimed at fans, opponents, umpires, and even each other became so offensive that the NL mandated $100 fines for vulgarity in 1895. This hardly deterred Jennings from the sarcasm that made him despised by all opponents and some teammates or McGraw from the loud profanity that won him the hated nickname of Muggsy.

John Heydler, an umpire in the 1890s and subsequently NL president, charged years later that the Orioles were "mean, vicious, ready to maim a rival player or umpire." In fact, they were no worse than some other teams, most notably the Cleveland Spiders. The general level of decorum around the league was so bad in the 1890s that umpires won the right to remove players from games, and in 1898 Cincinnati's president, John T. Brush, persuaded other owners to pass his "measure for the suppression of obscene, indecent, and vulgar language upon the ballfield" that established a system of negative points and disciplinary hearings for various offenses. What made the Orioles different was that their rowdiness was tactical; what made Brush's plan ineffectual was that the fans loved the rowdiness. Hanlon happily paid whatever fines were imposed on his players, and the Orioles realized a phenomenal $40,000 profit in 1894 alone.

The Orioles' weak spot was always pitching. Realizing that pitchers would need more rest to throw effectively from the new distance, Hanlon instituted a three-man rotation that kept changing because of injuries (to Sadie McMahon, Duke Esper, and George Hemming), ineffectiveness (by Tony Mullane), a holdout (by Bill Hawke), and a suspension (to Bert Inks). In 1894, Hanlon shuttled ten players onto and off the mound and the roster; McMahon (25–8) anchored the staff until a sore shoulder drove him to the sidelines in late August when Kid Gleason (15–5), purchased from St. Louis in June, succeeded him.

The Temple Cup, an ornate two-and-a-half-foot trophy on a 12-inch onyx pedestal, was donated in 1894 by Pittsburgh sportsman William C. Temple for the winner of a best-four-out-of-seven postseason series between the first- and second-place teams in the National League. The pennant-winning Orioles did not take the 1894 series seriously: They regarded themselves as the NL champions, and no exhibition series against the second-place Giants was going to change that. The Giants swept the series, to the jubilation of everyone outside Baltimore.

The Orioles won the pennant again in 1895. McMahon returned in August to reel off 10 consecutive wins, but he was never again so effective. Hoffer won 30, but the hitters carried the day, with Jennings, McGraw, Keeler, and Kelley all hitting .365 or better. After the regular season, the ninth-place Giants claimed that they, as holders of the Temple Cup, should compete against the first-place Orioles. That notion brushed off, Baltimore promptly lost the series for a second successive time, to the second-place Cleveland Spiders. Baltimore's one victory came at home amidst a shower of eggs and rocks directed at the visitors.

Another Baltimore pennant in 1896 produced a Temple cup rematch with the Spiders. The Orioles finally came out on top, sweeping the Spiders, but they earned only $200 each. The grumbling over proceeds left the public sour, especially after the players refused to attend a benefit in their honor unless they received a share of the take. A second-place finish in 1897 led to a second consecutive Temple Cup Victory, this time four games to one over pennant-winning Boston. The winners' shares were $310 each. Four consecutive lopsided victories, lack of interest by both fans and players, and a sense that the pennant winners had nothing to win and everything to lose, destroyed the ill-conceived postseason championship. Even Temple recognized that his grand plan had not been taken seriously when the Baltimore and Boston players held a joint banquet at which they used the Cup as a communal wine goblet.

In addition to juggling his pitching staff in the mid-1890's, Hanlon had to compensate for injuries to key players. Bill Clarke caught more games than the continually injured Robinson in 1896, 1897, and 1898. McGraw played in only 96 games in 1895 because of a malaria attack and only 23 the following year when he came down with typhoid fever. McGraw's, and

especially Robinson's, retrospective laments about the toughness of the old Orioles and the softness of twentieth-century players were half-truths at best.

Besides plugging holes left by injuries and illness, Hanlon made a second series of startlingly successful trades. In 1895, rookie George Carey replaced Brouthers. In 1896, Hanlon traded Gleason to the Giants for first baseman Jack Doyle. Doyle stayed two years, hitting .339 and .354, then went to Washington along with second baseman Heinie Reitz for his first baseman Dan McGann, who had his only 100 RBI year in Baltimore; second baseman Gene DeMontreville, who hit .328 in 1898; and pitcher Doc McJames, whose 27 wins led the staff. When Brodie's average dropped below .300 in 1896, Hanlon dealt him to Pittsburgh for Jake Stenzel (.353 in 1897).

In 1897, Keeler had his best season, one of the best ever. In 128 games, he had 239 hits (192 of them singles) for a .424 average. (In the contemporary 162-game season, it would take 293 hits to match his pace.) Keeler's 44-game hitting streak that year remained the standard until Joe DiMaggio's 56-game streak in 1941.

Hanlon and Von der Horst profited greatly from all the feistiness, hitting, and winning. In the final three-game series of 1897 alone, 56,000 people showed up to watch the Orioles lose two out of three—and the pennant—to Boston. Boston won the last game before 30,000, the largest crowd of the nineteenth century.

The 1898 season was less profitable, despite the NL's reversion to a 154-game season after several years of a 132-game schedule. The players, understanding that more games meant more money for the owners, threatened to strike until their demand for commensurate pay raises was met. The entire Baltimore payroll was a mere $39,000, and Hanlon received $10,000 of that. Four stars received the legal, though often violated, $2400 maximum for players.

A Brooklyn-Baltimore syndicate ownership was born in 1899 out of slipping patronage for Baltimore's second consecutive second-place finish. Claiming losses of $400 a day, the club announced an effective merger with the Dodgers under which Von der Horst owned 40 percent of each club and Hanlon 10 percent, with the other 50 percent in the hands of Brooklyn's Ferdinand Abel and Charlie Ebbets. Hanlon came out as both president of Baltimore and manager of Brooklyn; in the former capacity, he sent Keeler, Kelley, Jennings, McGann, McJames, Hughes, and Maul to the Dodgers to work for him in the latter role.

McGraw took over the remnants of the Orioles and managed to outfox Hanlon several times. First, he insisted that his boss–rival select the players he wanted for Brooklyn by April 15, then he hid Joe McGinnity from him by convincing the rookie right-hander to take something off his curveball until after that date; McGinnity won 28 games for the Orioles. Next, without telling Hanlon, McGraw traded De-Montreville. When an irritated Hanlon demanded DeMontreville and pitcher Jerry Nops for his Brooklyn squad, McGraw retaliated by going to the press and gaining Von der Horst's support; DeMontreville and Nops remained in Baltimore. In the end, Brooklyn won the pennant, with the Orioles in fourth place 15 games out. But, incredibly, Baltimore out-drew Brooklyn on the road, causing considerable embarrassment to the syndicate owners. The Orioles might even have come closer had McGraw's wife not died

on August 31, sending the manager into an 11-day seclusion and the team into a tailspin during his absence.

By the end of the 1899 season, the NL owners had decided to cut back to eight teams. Baltimore was the only one of the four cities to be dropped that had both a winning record and a history of profitability. It was, nevertheless, a natural for pruning because syndicate baseball had been soundly criticized in the press and resented by the fans; getting rid of Baltimore would, the owners hoped, restore some of their credibility. Besides, the league voted the Baltimore (read Brooklyn) owners a buyout fee of $30,000 and the right to dispose of the team's players, which meant that the best of them, especially McGinnity, ended up in Brooklyn.

BALTIMORE ORIOLES

Annual Standings and Managers

Year	Position	W	L	Pct.	GB	Managers
1892	Twelfth	20	55	.267	34½	George Van Haltren, John Waltz, Ned Hanlon
1892	Tenth	26	48	.361	25	Ned Hanlon
1893	Eighth	60	70	.462	26½	Ned Hanlon
1894	First	89	39	.695	+3	Ned Hanlon
1895	First	87	43	.669	+3	Ned Hanlon
1896	First	90	39	.698	+9½	Ned Hanlon
1897	Second	90	40	.692	2	Ned Hanlon
1898	Second	96	53	.644	6	Ned Hanlon
1899	Fourth	86	62	.581	15	John McGraw

Baltimore Orioles

American League,
1901–1902

BALLPARK: AMERICAN LEAGUE PARK

RECORD: 118–153 (.435)

From the sudden appearance of Baltimore in the American League to the club's equally abrupt disintegration and transfer to New York two years later, team and league were locked in a rancorous struggle. From the beginning, there was no possibility that the Orioles, rooted in the more permissive National League and epitomized by truculent John McGraw, could fit comfortably in the AL, which had been organized by Ban Johnson as an orderly, decorous rival to the senior circuit. Although the marriage didn't

last long, it was the delight of the tabloids while it did.

Slated to be part of a resuscitated American Association in 1900, the Orioles had to wait a year to rejoin the major leagues when the new AA died aborning. Then, in October of that year, Johnson announced his intention of challenging the NL directly by rechristening his Western League and moving into several eastern cities, including Baltimore. McGraw, with the faithful Wilbert Robinson in tow, was the obvious choice to head the Baltimore franchise. The bulk of the $40,000 initial capital came from 29-year-old stockbroker Sydney S. Frank, with McGraw and Robinson among the minority investors.

The franchise's first problem was finding a ballpark. McGraw had secured a lease on Baltimore's Union Park, but Harry Von der Horst and Ned Hanlon, the Baltimore half of the Baltimore–Brooklyn syndicate, contended that his lease was for the land but not the park. Hanlon sent armed guards to the site, where they set up headquarters in the clubhouse and occupied first base. McGraw partisans invaded, overcame the defense of the groundskeepers, and took possession of third base. City marshals established a peacekeeping mission in the neutral left field bleachers. When the courts finally settled the issue, McGraw was evicted, forcing him to begin construction on an 8,500-seat steel-and-concrete grandstand on the site of the old American Association park. At the same time, McGraw assembled his team by raiding NL teams for such players as outfielder Cy Seymour, catcher Roger Bresnahan, and pitcher Joe McGinnity.

The Orioles were in third place a third of the way into the season, but by then McGraw had undermined Johnson's vision of the AL by complaining repeatedly about the incompetence of umpires, especially John Haskell. He was thrown out of a game for the first time—by Haskell—less than two weeks into the season and shortly thereafter suspended for five days for his tantrums during a series against the Athletics. He earned a forfeit by sending Harry Howell back to the mound after the pitcher had been ejected. (Mike Donlin was tossed out of the same game for throwing the ball at the umpire.) Orioles rookie first baseman Burt Hart was suspended for what turned out to be forever for slugging Haskell.

The climax came on August 21st when, with McGraw absent with one of several serious knee injuries he suffered that year, McGinnity protested a close call at first base, stomped on umpire Tom Connally's foot, and squirted tobacco juice in his face. Donlin punched Detroit shortstop Kid Elberfield for attempting to come to Connally's rescue before the Baltimore police intervened by arresting Elberfield! McGinnity and shortstop Bill Keister, annoyed at the interference by the police, tried to rescue Elberfield, so they too were dragged off to court along with a fan named Allen who had become involved in the fracas. The sitting judge, who happened to be a minority stockholder and secretary of the Orioles, dismissed the charges against the three ballplayers and fined Mr. Allen $20. Meanwhile, Connally had for-

feited the game to Detroit and escaped with the help of mounted policemen. McGinnity had to travel to Chicago, accompanied by McGraw, to plead forgiveness from Johnson, who limited the pitcher's punishment to a twelve-day suspension. The season ended with Baltimore in fifth place and some semblance of peace between McGraw and Johnson.

The Orioles had begun the 1901 season with overflow crowds on the first two days of play. But despite a league-leading .294 team batting average, they finished sixth in attendance, drawing only 142,000 fans, and barely broke even. McGraw and his associates, who by the end of 1901 included a new president and major stockholder, John K. Sonny Mahon, knew that Baltimore's days in the AL were numbered. Johnson's grand design, going head to head with the NL in as many cities as possible, required a franchise in New York. McGraw even made several off-season trips to New York to interview potential investors and investigate possible locations for a ballpark.

The 1902 season was a disaster from the very start, when McGraw was thrown out on opening day in Boston. Several days later, he punched an official from the Dodgers who had come to lure outfielder Jimmy Sheckard to Brooklyn. On April 31, he launched into prolonged arguments with umpire Jack Sheridan, first for calling interference when McGraw bumped a runner, then for refusing to allow McGraw a base when he was hit by a pitch. The next day, McGraw was hit five times, but each time Sheridan refused to give him first base; the fifth time McGraw sat down in the batter's box and refused to get up until Sheridan ran him. The truce between them violated, Johnson suspended the Orioles' manager for five days. Then, on May 24th, McGraw's

In 1901, John McGraw came as close as anyone before Branch Rickey to breaking baseball's color line. Recognizing the major league caliber of the skills of Charlie Grant when he saw him playing for the Eastland Hotel team in Little Rock, Arkansas, for the amusement of patrons, McGraw planned to pass the second baseman off as a half-Cherokee with the unlikely name of Chief Tokahoma. But Charles Comiskey, the White Sox owner, blew the whistle on the deal with the threat that "if Muggsy really keeps this Indian, I will get a Chinaman of my acquaintance and put him on third."

career as an everyday player came to an abrupt end when Dick Harley of the Tigers was caught off third on an attempted double steal, came back into the base with his spikes high, and slashed McGraw's knee.

On June 18th, McGraw met secretly with Andrew Freedman, the Giants owner. A year and a half earlier, Freedman had compared the possibility of his hiring McGraw to New York's annexing the moon; now the two concocted a scheme to embarrass the American League. The first part of the plan was for McGraw to get suspended again, hardly a chore. The Baltimore manager picked his spot, a call by Tom Connally, on June 28th, that Seymour had missed the bag rounding third. With Kelley in a supporting role, McGraw put on a wild performance that earned his team a forfeit from Connally and an indefinite suspension for himself from Johnson.

Next he had to get out of his contract with Baltimore. This he accomplished by reminding the board of directors that he had $7,000 coming as reimbursement for club expenses and by offering to cancel the debt if he were let go. Free of his obligations to the Orioles, McGraw secretly signed a four-year contract to manage the Giants. The contract was not made public until July 9th, and by then McGraw had completely severed his relationship with the Orioles by selling his stock in the club for $6,500.

Not content with his escape, McGraw set out to destroy the Baltimore franchise. On July 16th, Joseph C. France, acting for Freedman, who had financial support from Cincinnati owner John T. Brush, bought 201 of the 400 shares in the Baltimore franchise. The mastermind of the deal, McGraw even traded his half-interest in the Diamond Cafe, a combination saloon-bowling alley-billiard parlor he owned with Wilbert Robinson, for his partner's share in the Orioles, then included those shares in the sale. For one uncomfortable day for the AL, the owner of the NL New York Giants held a majority of the stock in the Baltimore Orioles. He used the twenty-four hours to release McGinnity, McGraw, Bresnahan, first baseman Dan McGann, and pitcher Jack Cronin, and sign them for New York. Cincinnati's share of the spoils was Kelley, who became player–manager, and Seymour. As part of the deal, Brush also sold the Reds to the Fleischman brothers, who were friends of Freedman.

The next day, when only five players showed up at the ballpark, the Orioles lost by forfeit. Johnson negated Freedman's purchase of the Orioles, assumed control of the franchise in the name of safeguarding the interests of the other stockholders, appointed Robinson manager, and had the other AL clubs provide castoffs to play out Baltimore's schedule. The Orioles, playing over .500 ball and in fifth place on July 16th, dropped precipitously to last place and stayed there.

For the 1903 season, Johnson found a New York backer, Frank Farrell, who bought out the remaining Baltimore stockholders and transferred the franchise to New York.

BALTIMORE ORIOLES

Annual Standings and Managers

Year	Position	W	L	Pct.	GB	Managers
1901	Fifth	68	65	.511	13½	John McGraw
1902	Eighth	50	88	.362	34	John McGraw, Wilbert Robinson

Baltimore Terrapins

Federal League, 1914–1915	**BALLPARK:** TERRAPIN PARK
RECORD: 131–177 (.425)	**OTHER NAMES:** BALTFEDS

The Baltimore Terrapins had an influence on baseball out of all proportion to either their success or their longevity. Their importance stemmed from a Supreme Court decision that came at the end of a tortuous seven-year odyssey through the American judicial system and that established unequivocally the iron supremacy of organized baseball and its exclusive right to be regulated by no authority but its own.

The team's beginning held considerable promise. On Opening Day, 1914, 28,000 fans crowded into the new 15,000-seat Terrapin Park directly across the street from the home field of the International League Orioles to watch the Terrapins beat Buffalo 3–2. The club was a community venture: Six hundred stockholders put up more than $164,000, about half of which was spent on the ballpark. The largest share of stock belonged to Baltimore legend Ned Hanlon, who had managed the National League Orioles to three pennants in the 1890s.

The strength of the Terrapins in 1914 was their pitching: Both Jack Quinn (26–14) and George Suggs (24–14) finished in the top five in victories to lead the Baltfeds to a third-place finish, only 4½ games out of first place. But a year later, the pitching staff fell apart, Quinn fell to 9 wins and a league-leading total of 22 losses; Suggs was 13–17, with a 4.14 ERA; and newcomer and future Hall of Famer Chief Bender, recruited from the Philadelphia Athletics, turned in an abysmal 4–16 performance. Last in the FL in batting average as well as in ERA, the Terrapins dropped to eighth place, 40 games out of first and 24 games behind seventh-place Brooklyn.

With the FL collapsing, Terrapins' president Carroll W. Rasin sought to make a deal with the American and National leagues. The Baltimore directors considered a proffered $50,000 buyout inadequate because the club had lost $75,000 in 1915 after a modest profit of $9,000 in 1914. When club attorney Stuart Jawrey proposed that the Baltimore directors be allowed to purchase a major league franchise for $250,000, he was ridiculed. Charlie Ebbets of the Brooklyn Dodgers spoke for the majority in calling Baltimore "one of the worst minor league towns in this country," adding: "You have too many colored population, to start with. They are a cheap population when it gets down to paying their money at the gate." With that, Jawrey gave up.

In the following weeks, Rasin attempted to resolve the situation by combining the Terrapins with Jack Dunn's Orioles. Dunn, however, refused either to surrender his IL franchise and become manager of the new franchise or to purchase the Terrapins for the asking price of $100,000; he agreed only to purchase Terrapin Park for $25,000. When Rasin refused FL president James Gilmore's final offer of $75,000, the settlement left Baltimore out. Early in January, the U. S. Justice Department, in response to a complaint by Baltimore, refused to investigate, claiming

it saw no violation of antitrust laws. Left with no alternative other than abandoning their investment, the stockholders voted $50,000 to pursue the issue in court. The first suit, filed in U. S. District Court in Philadelphia on May 19, 1916, accused organized baseball of trying to destroy the FL and establish a monopoly, and asked for $900,000 in damages. Inexplicably, Jawrey withdrew the suit on June 11, 1917, the first day of hearings, only to refile it in another federal district court, in Washington, D.C. on September 20. This time, the suit included the FL engineers of the settlement: Gilmore, Chicago Whales president Charles A. Weeghman, and Newark Peppers president Harry F. Sinclair.

Eighteen months later, Judge Wendell Philips Stafford ended the nineteen-day trial of *Federal Baseball Club of Baltimore vs. National League* with instructions to the jury that there had been violations of federal antitrust legislation. The jury awarded Baltimore treble damages and legal fees, for a total of $254,000. Organized baseball immediately appealed to the U.S. Court of Appeals for the District of Columbia. On December 6, 1920, Chief Justice Constantine J. Smyth reversed the trial court on the grounds that baseball was not commerce at all and was, therefore, not subject to laws proscribing restraint of trade in interstate commerce.

Now it was Baltimore's turn to appeal, to the U. S. Supreme Court. On May 29, 1922, Chief Justice Oliver Wendell Holmes wrote the unanimous opinion upholding the appellate court. Holmes ruled that, while baseball was certainly played for money, it was not "trade or commerce in the commonly accepted use of those words," because "personal effort, not related to production, is not a subject of commerce," and incidental movement across state lines does not make interstate commerce out of an activity that is not commerce to start with. Holmes, almost parenthetically, endorsed the reserve clause as necessary "to retain the services of sufficient players," even though organized baseball's lawyers had downplayed the controversial clause that had resulted in numerous legal defeats for the owners.

Contrary to some modern understanding, no court ever claimed that baseball was not a business. Justice Smyth did rule that baseball was a sport, but the contrast he drew was with trade, which involves the manufacture or sale of tangible goods, not with business. This distinction exempted from the antitrust laws not only baseball, but all entertainers, doctors, lawyers, and everyone else involved in a service industry. In this sense, Holmes's ruling was hardly surprising. What was surprising was that, one year later, Holmes ruled that vaudeville *was* interstate commerce even though the opinion forced him into minuscule distinctions in the degrees of interstate activity. What is even more surprising is that baseball's exemption has survived for seventy years—longer than the reserve clause.

BALTIMORE TERRAPINS

Annual Standings and Managers

Year	Position	W	L	Pct.	GB	Managers
1914	Third	84	70	.545	4½	Otto Knabe
1915	Eighth	47	107	.304	40	Otto Knabe

Baltimore Orioles

American League,
1954–Present

BALLPARKS: MEMORIAL STADIUM (1954–1991)
ORIOLE PARK AT CAMDEN YARDS (1992–Present)

RECORD: 3291–2885 (.533)

The successors to the St. Louis Browns, the Orioles have shucked that team's tradition of haplessness and ineptitude to become the most successful club on the field since the inception of divisional play. At the same time, inadequate patronage has often deprived the franchise of the operating expenses necessary to sustain the success of the organization.

The Orioles were born on September 29, 1953, when the AL, after several false starts, finally approved the transfer of the Browns and the sale of the club to a Maryland syndicate headed by attorney Clarence Miles for $2.475 million. The new owner raided the Philadelphia Athletics for its management team, Art Ehlers in the front office and Jimmy Dykes on the field, and fielded a team consisting largely of the young players assembled by St. Louis owner Bill

Brooks Robinson's fielding acrobatics typified the aggressive defense of the Baltimore teams of the 1970s. *National Baseball Library, Cooperstown, NY*

Veeck. The club lost its first game, played in Detroit on April 13, 1954, by a score of 3–0, with Steve Gromek outdueling Don Larsen. The O's added 99 more losses before their first season ended (Larsen lost 21 to lead the AL), with an offense so inadequate that Vern Stephens' 8 home runs and 46 RBIs led the team. The novelty of major league baseball produced a profit of $900,000, but, even before the season had ended, Miles took the drastic step of hiring White Sox manager Paul Richards to replace both Ehlers and Dykes in 1955.

Given a $250,000 fund for player procurement, Richards spent $700,000 within two years—a spree that later prompted Baltimore front office executive Jack Dunn to observe: "Paul was the only man in baseball who had an unlimited budget and exceeded it." Most of the money went for signing young players, including five bonus babies who, under existing rules, had to be carried by the team. When the roster became clogged with unproductive, untested youngsters, Richards began to bend the rules; among other violations, he placed bonus baby Jim Pyburn on the disabled list without cause and tried to hide the signing of pitcher Tom Borland by having him play an exhibition game under the alias Jack Moreland. The results were, in the first instance, a ruling by Commissioner Ford Frick that, in the future, a doctor's note would be required to place a player on the DL and, in the second, a $2,000 fine for the Orioles and an additional $2,500 penalty for Richards personally. Internally, these difficulties led to a shift in strategic direction toward trading to achieve immediate results.

Richards took to the new policy as enthusiastically as he had to the old one. On November 18 and December 1, 1954, he completed the largest trade in baseball history in two stages. The key elements in what turned out to be an eighteen-player swap were Larsen, pitcher Bob Turley, and shortstop Billy Hunter, who went to the Yankees for, among others, catcher Gus Triandos, outfielder Gene Woodling, and shortstop Willie Miranda. Richards's hectic quest for a radical turnaround in the team's fortunes almost produced an even bigger deal: In 1956, he offered Kansas City general manager Parke Carroll a 25-for-25 swap of complete rosters, a deal that fell through mainly because Carroll could not reach Athletics' owner Arnold Johnson before the expiration of the June 15th trading deadline.

Richards's razzle-dazzle with players had its parallel in the boardroom. Upset by his difficulties with the commissioner's office and angered by the signing of Bruce Swango, a bonus player who had

difficulty pitching in front of crowds and had to be released without ever appearing in a game, the team directors demanded an accounting. The scapegoat turned out to be Miles, who was replaced by a triumvirate in November, 1955. Investment banker Joseph Inglehardt, who owned the largest piece of club stock, supported Richards, while new club president James Keelty supported efforts to build slowly through the farm system; in the middle was attorney Zanvyl Krieger, who tried to keep peace between the other two. Keelty's strategy lay in the hands of farm director Jim McLaughlin, the only front office holdover from the Browns, who methodically built the superior minor league network that would become the source of the franchise's later success.

Richards's one-man show was curtailed in November 1958, when the triumvirate told him to choose between his two titles. With Richards electing to remain in the dugout, Lee MacPhail was brought in as general manager. A year later, Inglehardt, who had accumulated 30 percent of the organization's stock, had enough power to force out Keelty and replace him as president with MacPhail.

Meanwhile, Richards had picked up knuckleballer Hoyt Wilhelm on waivers in 1958, and the first

In 1958, Jack Harshman became the only pitcher to hit two home runs in two games in the same season.

fruits of McLaughlin's farm system had begun to show. An eventual Hall of Famer, Wilhelm led the AL in ERA (2.19) in 1959, then moved to the bullpen until 1962 to support the Kiddie Corps pitching of Milt Pappas, Chuck Estrada, Jack Fisher, and Steve Barber. While the organization's primary emphasis

The most anticipated pitching prospect in baseball history was probably Baltimore farm hand Steve Dalkowski, who averaged almost two strikeouts an inning while toiling for Kingsport in 1957 and who was clocked regularly at more than 100 miles an hour. Dalkowski's problem, which prevented him from ever appearing in a major league game, was his control: Although he fanned 121 in 62 innings, he also walked 129, leading to a record of 1–8 and an ERA of 8.13.

in the late 1950s was on pitching, it also produced shortstop Ron Hansen, Rookie of the Year in 1960, and Brooks Robinson, who took over third base as a

Footnote Player: On May 3, 1963, pitcher Buster Narum walloped a home run in his only plate appearance for Baltimore. Six days later, he was farmed out, and never played for the team again.

Because of the presence of knuckleballer Hoyt Wilhelm on the staff, Paul Richards designed an enlarged glove for his catchers in 1960. The mitt measured 50 inches in circumference and 15.5 inches in diameter. Subsequent rule changes restricted the so-called "pancake mitt" to 38 inches in circumference.

regular in 1958. Hall of Famer Robinson went on to a 23-year career, all of it with the Orioles, during which he hit .267 with 268 home runs and revolutionized the playing of third base. His career year, which won him an MVP Award, came in 1964, when he hit .317 with 28 homers and an AL-leading 118 RBIs. Another addition, first baseman Jim Gentile,

On May 9, 1961, Jim Gentile clouted grand slams in consecutive at bats against Minnesota's Pedro Ramos and Paul Giel. He is the only player to have accomplished this.

hit 21 homers in 1960 and followed that up with a .302 average, 46 homers, and 141 RBIs. Gentile, the first Oriole to drive in more than 100 runs in a season, was not Richards's favorite player; the manager even pinch hit for him in one game after he had stroked two home runs.

The Oriole organization supported the creation of an expansion franchise for Washington, D.C. after the transfer of the original Senators to Minnesota simply because no one in the front office had thought that wooing D.C. fans would be productive. Richards, more interested in protecting players, suggested to Earl Weaver, manager of Baltimore's top farm club in Syracuse, that outfielder Chuck Hinton fake an injury to deflect interest in him in the expansion draft; when Weaver refused to cooperate, the Orioles lost Hinton, as well as pitcher Dean Chance and the veteran Woodling. Having finished second in 1960 and with the team on its way to another runnerup showing in 1961, Richards, who had always resented having to give up total control of the club, departed on September 1st to assume the dual role of manager-GM in Houston. His successor,

coach Lum Harris, finished out the season, then followed his erstwhile boss to Texas.

MacPhail's choice as the next manager, Billy Hitchcock, presided over a slide to seventh place; worse, he lacked the respect of the players. Pappas attacked him openly in the press, Gentile ignored all the rules and taunted him in the clubhouse. MacPhail's contribution was to cut the salaries not only of Pappas and Gentile, but of Barber and Hansen as well. The result was a fourth-place finish and increased resentment among the players. In 1964, Hank Bauer, an ex-Marine and ex-Yankee, was brought in to restore order. Under Bauer, the first great Oriole team began to come together; Boog Powell took over at first in 1965, Davey Johnson at second in 1966. Together with Robinson and future Hall of Famer Luis Aparicio, obtained from the White Sox early in 1963, they formed the best infield in the AL. Paul Blair was the best defensive center fielder in baseball. The only missing element was a power hitter with the impact to put the team over the top. Then, on December 9, 1965 the Orioles acquired outfielder Frank Robinson from Cincinnati for Pappas, pitcher Jack Baldschun, and outfielder Dick Simpson. The final decision on the deal, all but completed by MacPhail before his departure on December 7th to become top assistant to Commissioner William Eckert, was left to new GM Harry Dalton; MacPhail's parting advice was to try to get the Reds to throw in another player.

The Orioles ran away with the pennant in the first half of 1966, then spent the last half "limping away with it," as Dalton put it. Frank Robinson had a Triple Crown, MVP season (.316 BA, 49 HR, and 122 RBI, as well as AL-leading totals in slugging and runs scored); he added a World Series MVP when the Orioles swept the Dodgers. The righthand-hitting slugger went on to play six seasons in Baltimore, building up what would eventually be a career total 586 homers (fourth place on the all-time list) and a place in Cooperstown in 1982. Robinson, described at the time of the trade as a "Grade A Negro" by *The Sporting News,* had displayed no strong sense of racial identity until he moved to Baltimore. At first, he refused even to join the local NAACP unless its leaders would guarantee that he would not have to make public appearances as long as he was in baseball. A change resulted from his difficulties in finding acceptable housing in segregated Baltimore and from the Oriole organization's initial indifference to his situation. Eventually, he became an outspoken critic of a racism that he felt was so endemic to baseball that it allowed pitchers, specifically California's Jim Coates, to throw at black hitters with impunity. He later became baseball's first black manager, with Cleveland.

Among those who enjoyed the 1966 World Series victory was a new owner, Jerold Hoffberger, whose National Brewing Company had sponsored Baltimore televised games since 1963. In late 1964, Inglehardt, with 32 percent of the club's stock, had tried to buy out Krieger's 17 percent. Unwilling to sell his shares or to buy Inglehardt's, Krieger acted as intermediary for Hoffberger, a contentious and humorless corporate type who bought out the majority partner and several smaller investors for $1.5 million on May 26, 1965 and who would spend the next thirteen years fighting with everyone in baseball outside the Oriole organization. Hoffberger's first move was to bring Frank Cashen in from his brewery to be executive vice-president. A year later, when MacPhail, his authority compromised by Cashen's presence, left, Hoffberger elevated Dalton from farm system director to head of player personnel.

Hoffberger's contribution to the Orioles was the full flowering of the farm system. On June 8, 1965, major league baseball held the first draft of amateur players; other teams selected twenty to thirty players, the Orioles selected seventy. That talent pool made it possible to replace aging players such as Aparicio and Johnson with Mark Belanger and Bobby Grich, rookies trained in Oriole fundamentals. Although the owner's paternalistic approach worked in the front office, it was out of step with player attitudes in the era of Marvin Miller and the Players Association. Between 1960 and 1968, every Oriole player representative was released, traded, or left unprotected in expansion drafts. Only when Brooks Robinson assumed the post of player representative did the harassment end. In the events leading up to the spring training strike of 1972, Hoffberger clashed repeatedly with Miller, who accused the Baltimore owner of trying to force players to desert the union.

Whatever the truth of that specific allegation, Hoffberger was something less than the "hardline reactionary" that Miller charged; in fact, he supported an increase in pension benefits, the issue in the 1972 stoppage, and disapproved strenuously of the tactics of Ray Grebey, head of the owners' Player Relations Committee. After the 1972 strike, the Oriole owner boycotted owners' meetings until 1976, when he abandoned his disdainful aloofness only to join forces with George Steinbrenner of the Yankees and Charlie Finley of the A's in an effort to oust Commissioner Bowie Kuhn.

Hoffberger was big on delegating authority, and rarely interfered in personnel decisions. In 1967, when Bauer allowed the team to lapse into complacency, it was Cashen who fired the team coaches and replaced them with Earl Weaver, George Bamberger, and Vern Hoscheit from the Rochester farm club. Meant as a warning, the move made Bauer surly and resentful and resulted in his firing as well, during the 1968 All Star Game break. Bauer's successor was Weaver, who had written the organization's instructional book and who had been Dalton's protégé for some time. In his first three full seasons, Weaver finished first in the AL East, winning more than 100 games each year, including a franchise high 109 in 1969; swept the LCS all three years, against Minnesota twice and the A's once; and won a World Series (against the Reds in 1970), while losing two (to the Mets in 1969 and the Pirates in 1971).

Weaver was a firm believer in the odds and employed an elaborate set of index cards detailing every player's performance against every opponent. He abhorred bunting and used platooning in inspired ways. His trademark, the backwards-turned-cap, facilitated face-to-face confrontation at close quarters without violating the rule prohibiting contact with an umpire. The tactic did not prevent his being ejected a record ninety-one times, including both ends of one doubleheader, and suspended six times in his final seven seasons. Many of his dirt-kicking tantrums were, however, well-staged events to lift the team. In the fourteen full seasons of his first tour of duty with the club, Weaver won six division titles (including four pennants) and finished second five times relying almost unwaveringly on a formula of superior pitching, excellent fielding, and the three-run homer.

In his nineteen-year big league career, reliever Dick Hall uncorked only one wild pitch.

In 1970, Dave McNally became the first pitcher to hit a grand slam in a World Series game.

Brooks Robinson, Blair, and Belanger maintained Baltimore's standing as the best defensive team in the AL. First baseman Boog Powell won the MVP Award in 1970 and averaged more than 30 homers and 100 RBIs from 1969 to 1971. Dalton got Mike Cuellar in December 1968, and the lefty reeled off 20 or more wins in each of the next three pennant-winning seasons and tied for the Cy Young Award in 1969. Southpaw Dave McNally also won at least 20 in each of the same three seasons, tying Cuellar for the league lead with 24 in 1970, while Jim Palmer won 20 in 1970 and 1971. After Dalton traded pitcher Tom Phoebus and several spare parts to get Pat Dobson from San Diego in December 1970, the new addition won 20 to complete the first pitching staff since the 1920 White Sox to include four 20-game winners. The consistency with which the Orioles produced 20-game winners owed much to the pitching coaches on Weaver's staff: Bamberger from 1968 to 1977, then Ray Miller.

Palmer, a rookie in 1965, had hurt his arm in the 1966 World Series and missed most of the 1967 and all of the 1968 seasons. He then came back to win 20 or more games eight times, leading the AL in that category three times, in ERA twice, and in shutouts once. His three Cy Young Awards and lifetime record, 286–152 over nineteen seasons, all with Baltimore, won him a Cooperstown plaque in 1990. The stormy relationship between Palmer and Weaver centered around the pitcher's nagging ailments and the manager's insistence that Palmer pitch his way through imagined pain. Weaver claimed to keep a calendar based on the Year of the Back and the Year of the Ulnar Nerve; asked whether he had any incapacities of his own, the manager replied, "One big one: Jim Palmer."

The Orioles won AL East Championships in 1973 and 1974, only to lose both pennant playoffs to Oakland. The team had never drawn well, and would in fact not reach the two-million mark until 1983. But when it failed even to sell out its home games in the 1974 LCS, Hoffberger contemplated selling out. Fixated on the threat of Congressional wrath over the lack of a major league team in Washington, Kuhn pushed the overtures of a group headed by former General Motors president Edward Cole that would either have moved the club to the

capital or made it a regional team by putting a stadium between the two cities. Hoffberger, who had opposed the transfer of the second AL Washington Senators to Texas in 1972, was committed to keeping the Orioles in Baltimore and to building regional support without embracing the idea of a mutually convenient location. To Kuhn's chagrin, he threw his support behind a Maryland referendum to authorize construction of a new stadium. But in November 1974, while he was negotiating the possible sale of the franchise to local developer Ralph DeChiaro, the referendum was defeated. When DeChiaro discovered that Hoffberger was also discussing a deal with former Browns' owner Veeck, the developer pulled out of further discussions. Veeck, despite the legislative defeat of a $4 million state loan to assist his bid, was on his way to buying the club when, in May 1975, Cashen took the organization off the market.

The Washington problem would not go away, however. At the December 1976 major league meetings, Kuhn got the AL and NL to approve a resolution calling on the Orioles to play "a suitable number of games" in Washington to preclude another club's moving there. Hoffberger ignored the implied threat, but the strongarm tactic encouraged further thoughts of selling out.

Meanwhile, with Cashen moving back to the beer business, Hank Peters became the Oriole general manager and the effective head of the organization. Peters was ill-equipped to face the impending free agent revolution. On April 2, 1976, he traded outfielder Don Baylor and 1975 20-game winner Mike Torrez, both of whom were threatening to play out their options, to Oakland for outfielder Reggie Jackson and pitcher Ken Holtzman. Jackson, whose three-year $675,000 demand was outside Baltimore's realm, signed for one year at $200,000, sending the team into turmoil; Grich and Holtzman, having signed for considerably less than Jackson, were particularly irate. The rancor between players and front office continued all year (Peters at one point called Holtzman "a cancer on our team") until the first free agency reentry draft in which the Orioles lost Jackson, Holtzman, Grich, 20-game winner Wayne Garland (who refused to play for Weaver), and reserve outfielder Royale Stillman. Only Charlie Finley's

Oakland A's lost more players. What's more, the Orioles were able to sign only one free agent, infielder Billy Smith, to whom no other club had made an offer.

The decision to go with younger players had been a conscious one. Doug DeCinces had already supplanted Brooks Robinson at third base. Ken Singleton, acquired with Torrez from Montreal for McNally and outfielder Rich Coggins in December 1974, hit 24 homers in 1977. First baseman Lee May, picked up from Houston the same month, hit 27; so did Rookie of the Year DH Eddie Murray. Mike Flanagan and Dennis Martinez were the new arms out of the farm system to supplant Palmer. In addition, Peters conned the Yankees into trading their best prospect, lefthander Scott McGregor, along with pitchers Rudy May, Tippy Martinez, and Dave Pagan, and catcher Rick Dempsey in exchange for pitchers Holtzman, Doyle Alexander, Grant Jackson, and Jimmy Freeman and catcher Ellie Hendricks. The No Name Orioles finished in a tie for second.

A year later, after the Orioles had lost almost a quarter of a million dollars, stockholding members of Hoffberger's family wanted out. Cashen wanted to buy, but couldn't get the backing. Kuhn served as intermediary for a bid by former Secretary of the Treasury William Simon, but Hoffberger smelled the recurring Washington odor in the offer and turned it down. In August 1979, the owner finally announced the sale of the club to Washington attorney Edward Bennett Williams, who was also president of the Washington Redskins football team. Despite Williams's pronounced D.C. connections, he pledged to keep the team in Baltimore. The deal was not completed until after the season, which saw Flanagan win the Cy Young Award, Singleton lead the offense with 35 homers and 111 RBIs, and the Orioles take the AL East and knock off California in the LCS. Despite another seven-game World Series loss to the Pirates, the season resulted in a $1.5 million profit. The team's success almost doubled the selling price to $12 million.

In 1980, Steve Stone, signed as a free agent in November 1978, won 25 games, the most ever by an Oriole pitcher, and the switch-hitting Murray matured into a .300 hitter with 32 homers and 116 RBIs

In his major league debut on September 1, 1978, Sammy Stewart established a big league mark by striking out seven batters in a row.

as the team finished second. In the strike season of 1981, Murray led the AL in RBIs and tied for the lead in homers; Dennis Martinez tied for the lead in wins; Sammy Stewart lost the ERA title only because his number of innings pitched was rounded to the next whole number; and the Orioles finished the split schedule with the second best overall record in the AL East. In 1982, Murray again hit .316 with 32 homers and 110 RBIs, and Rookie of the Year shortstop Cal Ripken, Jr. had 28 homers and 93 RBIs. Finishing second in his final year, Weaver became so adept at platooning left fielders Gary Roenicke and John Lowenstein that they became known as Lowenicke, while combining for a .288 average with 45 homers and 140 RBIs.

Williams and Peters clashed over a successor to Weaver, with the inexperienced owner finally yielding on his choice of Frank Robinson to the experienced general manager's selection of Joe Altobelli. Ripken (.318, 27, 102, MVP) and Murray (.306, 33, 111) led the attack during the season, with the pitching taking over in the postseason (a 0.49 ERA in the four-game LCS against Chicago and 1.60 in the five-game World Series triumph over the Phillies).

After that, mediocrity set in. One source of the trouble was the steady departure of key front-office and scouting personnel following the exits of Dalton and then Cashen. McLaughlin, who had survived as head of scouting until the late 1970s, had become old and difficult and alienated the rest of the scouting staff. To the chagrin of Peters, Williams's main front office move was the appointment of Doug Melvin as the chairman's personal talent evaluator.

The 1985 season began with some hope after Williams had laid out $12 million to sign outfielders Fred Lynn and Lee Lacy and reliever Don Aase; he also insisted, over Peters's objections, on trading for second baseman Alan Wiggins, a speedy leadoff batter with drug problems. The three free agents lived up to expectations, but Wiggins created clubhouse strife and ended up banished to the minor leagues by Weaver, who had come out of retirement to guide a decidedly forlorn club before calling it quits for good. Weaver was replaced by coach Cal Ripken, Sr., who, on September 14, 1987, ended his son's streak of having played in every inning (a total of 8,243) of all 904 Oriole games since June 5, 1982; remaining intact was Ripken, Jr.'s consecutive game streak that reached 1,708 games by the end of the 1992 season. (In 1987, when his younger son Billy joined the team, Ripken, Sr. became the first to manage two sons.) At the end of 1987, Peters left, accepting some of the blame for the team deterioration, but laying most of it on what he called "the non-professionals;" no one had any doubt whom he meant. The departure of Peters gave Williams the opportunity to bring in an entirely new management team. Sensitized by the furor over Dodger executive Al Campanis's claims that blacks lacked the skills to hold front office positions and acutely aware that there were no blacks serving in the Baltimore front office in any capacity, Williams appointed Frank Robinson a special assistant to the president and Calvin Hill vice-president for administrative personnel. The new general manager was Rollie Hemond, the new farm director, talent evaluator Melvin. As it turned out, the front office overhaul was Williams's last major act with the Orioles. Suffering from terminal cancer, he turned over control of the club to Larry Lucchino, an associate in his law firm. At the time, the team, headed for the worst season in its history, had just finished losing its first 21 games, a major league record for futility at the beginning of a season. Williams died in August 1988; in December, his widow, Agnes Neil Williams, sold the club, for $70 million, to a group headed by Eli Jacobs, a computer equipment millionaire; R. Sargent Shriver, a brother-in-law of the Kennedy family; and Lucchino, who continued as president.

In 1989, with Frank Robinson as manager, the Baby Birds, built around Cal Ripken, Jr., took advantage of a greatly weakened AL East to finish second. Robinson elected to return to the front office in the middle of the 1991 season and surrendered the man-agerial reins to former catcher Johnny Oates. In 1992 the team moved amid much fanfare into Camden Yards, a new downtown stadium built along traditional asymmetrical lines. Favorite public relations features of the new arena are the B & O warehouse 460 feet away from home plate behind the right-field wall, and the fact that the saloon run by Babe Ruth's father once stood in the middle of the new center field. Free agent pickup Rick Sutcliffe inaugurated the facility on April 6 by blanking Cleveland on five hits. It was an auspicious beginning to a comeback season that saw the team climb to third place, finishing 7 games behind division-winning Toronto. Standouts included righthander Mike Mussina (18–5) and center fielder Mike Devereaux (24 homers and 107 RBIs). The appeal of Oates's young team and the attraction of the new ballpark combined to draw more than 3.5 million fans, a club record.

Following the 1992 season, debt-plagued owner Jacobs went looking for a buyer before his holdings were taken over by creditors. In the meantime, the club adopted in a very big way baseball management's new tactic of letting go of veteran players rather than offer arbitration. One casualty was Billy Ripken, made dispensable following the signing of free agent second baseman Harold Reynolds. Cal Ripken, Sr. also announced his retirement as a coach, but neither that decision nor Billy's departure prevented Cal, Jr. from signing a contract that made him one of the highest paid players in the league.

Camden Yards. *Courtesy of the Baltimore Orioles / Jerry Wachter*

BALTIMORE ORIOLES

Annual Standings and Managers

Year	Position	W	L	Pct.	GB	Managers
1954	Seventh	54	100	.351	57	Jimmy Dykes
1955	Seventh	57	97	.370	39	Paul Richards
1956	Sixth	69	85	.448	28	Paul Richards
1957	Fifth	76	76	.500	21	Paul Richards
1958	Sixth	74	79	.484	17½	Paul Richards
1959	Sixth	74	80	.481	20	Paul Richards
1960	Second	89	65	.578	8	Paul Richards
1961	Third	95	67	.586	14	Paul Richards, Lum Harris
1962	Seventh	77	85	.475	19	Billy Hitchcock
1963	Fourth	86	76	.531	18½	Billy Hitchcock
1964	Third	97	65	.599	2	Hank Bauer
1965	Third	94	68	.580	8	Hank Bauer
1966	First	97	63	.606	+9	Hank Bauer
1967	Sixth*	76	85	.472	15½	Hank Bauer
1968	Second	91	71	.562	12	Hank Bauer, Earl Weaver
1969	First	109	53	.673	+19	Earl Weaver
1970	First	108	54	.667	+15	Earl Weaver
1971	First	101	57	.639	+12	Earl Weaver
1972	Third	80	74	.519	5	Earl Weaver
1973	First	97	65	.599	+8	Earl Weaver
1974	First	91	71	.562	+2	Earl Weaver
1975	Second	90	69	.566	4½	Earl Weaver
1976	Second	88	74	.543	10½	Earl Weaver
1977	Second*	97	64	.602	2½	Earl Weaver
1978	Fourth	90	71	.559	9	Earl Weaver
1979	First	102	57	.642	+8	Earl Weaver
1980	Second	100	62	.617	3	Earl Weaver
1981	Second	31	23	.574	2	Earl Weaver
	Fourth	28	23	.549	2	Earl Weaver
1982	Second	94	68	.580	1	Earl Weaver
1983	First	98	64	.605	+6	Joe Altobelli
1984	Fifth	85	77	.525	19	Joe Altobelli
1985	Fourth	83	78	.516	16	Joe Altobelli, Earl Weaver
1986	Seventh	73	89	.451	22½	Earl Weaver
1987	Sixth	67	95	.414	31	Cal Ripken
1988	Seventh	54	107	.335	34½	Cal Ripken, Frank Robinson
1989	Second	87	75	.537	2	Frank Robinson
1990	Fifth	76	85	.472	11½	Frank Robinson
1991	Seventh	67	95	.414	24	Frank Robinson, Johnny Oates
1992	Third	89	73	.549	7	Johnny Oates

*Tie

Postseason Play:

LCS				WS		
	3–0 versus Minnesota	1969			4–0 versus Los Angeles	1966
	3–0 versus Minnesota	1970			1–4 versus New York	1969
	3–0 versus Oakland	1971			4–1 versus Cincinnati	1970
	2–3 versus Oakland	1973			3–4 versus Pittsburgh	1971
	1–3 versus Oakland	1974			3–4 versus Pittsburgh	1979
	3-1 versus California	1979			4–1 versus Philadelphia	1983
	3-1 versus Chicago	1983				

Boston Braves

National League,
1876–1952

RECORD: 5118–5598 (.478)

BALLPARKS: SOUTH END GROUNDS (1876–1914)
FENWAY PARK (1914–15; 1946)
BRAVES FIELD (1915–1952)

OTHER NAMES: RED STOCKINGS, RED CAPS, BEANEATERS,
NATIONALS, DOVES, RUSTLERS, AND BEES

For better and worse, the Braves were a team of firsts. They played in the first National League game, executed the first player transaction between major league clubs, and were the first to realize that a manager had to be more than a player who filled in a lineup card. It was Braves' owners who awoke baseball to the advantages of the reserve clause, to the benefits of tailoring parks around teams instead of vice versa, and to the long-range implications of air travel for franchise shifts and expansion. On the diamond, the club was one of the league's strongest powers in the nineteenth century—and almost as much of a doormat in the twentieth century. Even its two twentieth century pennants, in 1914 and 1948, are usually viewed as having had a lot of the astonishing and a little of the miraculous.

Boston entered the National League with as fearsome a reputation as any club could have. Between 1872 and 1875, the city's Red Stockings franchise in the National Association had not only taken four consecutive championships, but had done so with the startling record of 205 wins and only 50 losses over that span. This prompted no less a baseball eminence than Albert Spalding to declare on one occasion that "just as Boston was the cradle of liberty for the nation, so also was it the cradle in which the infant game was helped to a healthy maturity." Nobody had more of a hand than Boston hurler Spalding in dumping the infant out of its cradle and onto its feet. Approached by William Hulbert after the 1875 National Association season, the pitcher and teammates Ross Barnes, Deacon Jim White, and Cal

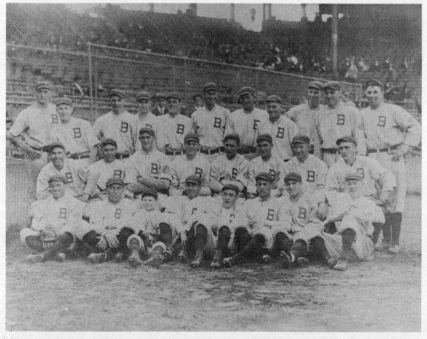

The 1914 Miracle Braves. *National Baseball Library, Cooperstown, NY*

McVey agreed to jump to the Chicago White Stockings, thereby devastating the Red Stockings and creating a crisis for the NA in general. Boston president Nathaniel Apollonio first sought to have the four players banned from organized baseball, but when Hulbert and Spalding outmaneuvered him by finding enough backing to start their own National League, Apollonio had little choice but to give assent to the dissolution of the NA and join the fledgling circuit.

As visitors against Philadelphia on April 22, 1876, Boston won the first NL game, 6–5. An estimated 3,000 spectators saw the winners score twice in the ninth inning to end an atrocious defensive contest in which 20 errors were committed. The win went to Joe Borden, sardonically referred to as "Josephus the Phenomenal" because his name wasn't Josephus and because, despite a no-hitter in his rookie NA year for Philadelphia in 1875, he was anything but phenomenal. The very first NL batter was Boston shortstop George Wright, who grounded out. Firsts by teammates included: first hit by center fielder Jim O'Rourke, first run batted in by right fielder John Manning, first run scored by catcher Tim McGinley, and first steal by first baseman Tim Murnane. The game proved to be a good start to a bad season; Boston ended up in fourth place, 15 games behind Spalding's White Stockings. The organization's major source of pride in 1876 was that the Red Stockings were the only NL club to fulfill a seventy-game schedule.

Although he would be eclipsed by his successors in the art of the contract, Apollonio left his own mark on management-player relations in his sole NL year. After the much-touted Borden made it clear that he was never going to vindicate the three-year contract he had been given (at $2000 per year), Apollonio demanded that he work off the money as a groundskeeper. If the organization president had counted on the pitcher seeking a buyout to spare him humiliation, he had miscalculated because Borden immediately set about mending fences and cutting the grass at the South End Grounds. In the end, it was the team that had to offer the buyout, and at some three-quarters of the originally stipulated sum.

Prior to the start of the 1877 season, the team's board of directors announced a series of executive changes that left Apollonio out as president, Arthur H. Soden in as his replacement, James B. Billings in as treasurer, and William Conant in as secretary. For the better part of the next thirty years, Soden, Billings, and Conant (known as the Triumvirs) ruled not only Boston baseball, but were a dominant management voice (second only to Chicago's Spalding) for the sport as a whole. The first among equals was Soden, a manically frugal man who came to the organization from a background that included everything from pharmaceutical supplies and roofing to banks and railways. It was he who fathered the reserve clause that kept players bound to their clubs through an indefinite option year at the lapse of a specified contract; who became interim president of the NL when Hulbert died in 1882; and who kept other franchises afloat when he deemed them necessary for the league's survival. Advancing money to other teams did not come easily for Soden: He and his two associates were in fact so miserly that they often did their own ticket collecting at the ballpark so as not to have to pay others to do it, openly encouraged players to go into the stands and wrestle with fans if necessary to recover foul balls, and abolished all complimentary tickets except for passes for themselves (good for two admissions each). When outfielder Charlie Jones complained during a road trip that he hadn't been paid in weeks and asked what he was owed, Soden replied that he would look into the matter when the team returned to Boston, then proceeded to strand the player in Cleveland and accuse him of jumping the team. Soden's lies kept Jones blackballed from the game for the 1881 and 1882 seasons. The amount of money owed to him? $378.

After their drab debut season, the Red Stockings rebounded to win two straight pennants. The key to both wins was Tommy Bond, a righthander who rolled up 40 victories in both 1877 and 1878. One of the earliest practitioners of the curveball, Bond was

Although he failed to live up to his promise with Boston, Joe Borden does deserve credit for pitching the first no-hitter in National League history, against Cincinnati on May 23, 1876. The trouble is, the official scorer for the game was O. P. Caylor of the Cincinnati *Enquirer*, who had a personal rule that walks constituted hits (it was not until 1887 that the NL experimented with the same idea). Because Borden surrendered two bases on balls in his effort, credit for the first big league no-hitter is usually given to St. Louis's George Washington Bradley, who accomplished the feat in a contest against Hartford on July 15, 1876.

even credited for awhile with having developed the pitch, although he himself always admitted having picked it up from Candy Cummings. Another important contributor to the 1877 flag was Deacon White, who returned to Boston from the White Stockings to lead the league in hitting. It was a short-lived reunion, however, with White taking off once again after the season, this time for Cincinnati, because he objected to Soden's policy of requiring players to pay for their own uniforms.

The Red Stockings took another big personnel hit after the 1878 season, when shortstop George Wright and outfielder Jim O'Rourke defected to Boston's regional rival, Providence. It was the departure of Wright and O'Rourke that inspired Soden's proposal for a reserve clause to take effect for the 1880 season. At first, other NL owners, especially those more concerned about getting players rather than losing them, agreed only to exercising "ownership" rights over five players per team, with the others free to continue making their own freelance deals at the expiration of contracts. It required eight years, and a graduated rise in the number of players affected, for the clause to be applied to every player bound contractually to an organization.

The loss of players like Wright and O'Rourke, together with arm miseries suffered by Bond, doomed Boston for several years. With the attendance also dipping sharply, the Triumvirs resorted to the classic baseball solution of firing the manager. Harry Wright was let go on the eve of the 1882 season and was replaced by John Morrill, a nimble defensive infielder for the club since its first season. Morrill had the team back on top within two years, mainly because of the surprising hitting of second baseman and assistant manager Jack Burdock (.330 in 1883) and the pitching of Jim Whitney and Charlie Buffinton. The 1883 pennant was useful in more than one way to Soden, then engaged in a campaign to buy out seventeen minority stockbrokers. For years, the investors had tolerated Soden's refusal to pay out dividends on the grounds that profits had to be put back into improving the team; when the same line was taken after the pennant season, most of the stockholders announced that they were fed up and sold out.

Although the team slipped back to second place in 1884, it was a season that could have been a lot worse. The rise of the Union Association that year was helped no little by Soden's reserve clause, and organizers of the new league took particular aim at the Boston franchise. But despite a club in the city that boasted the services of such former Red Stockings as George Wright, Murnane, and Bond, and a twenty-five-cent admission price that undercut the NL's fifty-cent tariff, Boston held its own.

Morrill stayed at the helm for another four years of mediocrity, during which the team had a barely visible offense and a pitching staff that practically had to come up with shutouts to win. The same Whitney–Buffinton combination that had posted 61 victories in 1883 dropped 59 games only two years later. Bill Stemmeyer contributed 22 wins in 1886, but he also threw a record 64 wild pitches in a mere 41 games. In the same year, Stemmeyer's batterymate Pat Dealey committed an NL-record 10 passed balls in a single contest. Performances like Dealey's paved the way for Boston's most startling move of the decade, the purchase of catcher King Kelly from Chicago before the 1887 season.

By any standard, Kelly was the most popular player in the history of the Boston franchise; he was also its most innovative and (to the ownership) most exasperating. It was Billings, the treasurer third of the Triumvirs, who first had the idea that there was nothing in NL rules preventing one club from dealing a player to a second club for cash and who proposed the Boston purchase of Kelly to Chicago president Spalding. When Spalding relayed the Boston proposal to him, Kelly initially refused, saying that ballplayers were not horses or dogs to be shuffled around at will. He changed his mind after Spalding began dropping big hints that he would receive a much bigger salary in Boston than he would in Chicago. Finally, under the impression that the Triumvirs would pay him $5,000, Kelly gave his consent, and was peddled to Boston for $10,000. While Spalding was counting his profits from the first major league inter-club transaction of players, Kelly arrived in Boston, where he was informed by Billings that his salary would actually be $2,000, in line with the league ceiling. Kelly was about to explode when Billings added that the Triumvirs would be happy to pay him $3,000 more if he would consent to having his picture taken with his new employers. Kelly consented. (The team carried out a similar ploy a year later in purchasing pitcher John Clarkson, also from Chicago for $10,000. Local papers referred to Clarkson and Kelly as "the $20,000 Battery.")

Kelly's extravagant personality (he frequently rode to games in a carriage pulled by two white horses or his fans) was the oil on Morrill's water. No matter how well he performed between the lines (his first season in Boston included 84 stolen bases, 102

MIKE J. (KING) KELLY

COLORFUL PLAYER AND AUDACIOUS

BASE-RUNNER. IN 1887 FOR BOSTON

HE HIT .394 AND STOLE 84 BASES.

HIS SALE FOR $10,000 WAS ONE OF

THE BIGGEST DEALS OF BASEBALL'S

EARLY HISTORY.

National Baseball Library, Cooperstown, NY

runs scored, and a .322 average), the future Hall of Famer remained mostly newsworthy for predictions that he would soon take over from the self-effacing Morrill as manager. It wasn't long before players were choosing sides between the extrovert catcher and the introvert manager, Kelly himself was blowing hard that the King didn't need anybody's job, and Morrill was telling friends that he was annoyed that so much attention was being devoted to a single player. The break finally came in the spring of 1889, when the Triumvirs asked Morrill to captain the scrubs in a preseason game against the regulars, captained by Kelly. The outraged Morrill refused, and was sold to Washington twenty-four hours later. But instead of Kelly taking over, the manager's job went to Jim Hart. This saved Kelly some bad press, but did nothing to staunch editorial attacks on Soden, Billings, and Conant for their shabby treatment of Morrill. The consensus was that the exhibition game had merely been a pretext by the owners to get rid of Morrill after he had asked for a salary increase.

Hart took over a club that included four players picked up by Soden from the NL franchise in Detroit that had been forced to retire from the league after the 1888 season; the players, obtained for a total of $26,000, were first baseman Dan Brouthers, catchers Charlie Bennett and Charlie Ganzel, and second baseman Hardy Richardson. Brouthers led the league in hitting and Clarkson topped NL pitchers in both wins (49) and ERA (2.73), as Hart's Beaneaters (a name in general use by the end of the decade) rose back up to only a game behind pennant-winning New York. The race was not settled until the final hours of the season, when Boston lost a clutch game to Cleveland, in part because Kelly was too hung over to play. Kelly made the defeat all the more awkward when he jumped off the bench in the middle of the contest to protest an umpire's decision and had to be escorted from the park by police. The incident precipitated both charges of police brutality and reports that some NL owners were pressuring Boston to suspend its raucous catcher.

The 1890s were the most successful decade in the Boston organization's history. After a disillusioning fifth-place finish in 1890, the club went on to win five pennants before the dawning of the new century; the 1897–1898 teams in particular have generally been regarded as the best ever to play NL baseball in New England. The managerial brain behind the club's success was Frank Selee, the first NL pilot without playing experience. Selee's fortes were the hit-and-run and the steal. He was also considered one of the league's best scouts; among his finds were Jimmy Collins, Fred Tenney, and Chick Stahl. Even on a team that generally gave its managers a long leash (seven had a tenure of at least six straight years), Selee's thirteen years in a row were far and away the record for longevity.

But not even Selee could overcome the effects of the Brotherhood War in 1890. Among the Beaneaters who defected to the Boston entry in the Players League were Kelly, Brouthers, Charlie Radbourne, Richardson, Billy Nash, and Joe Quinn. The reverse side of the coin was that, with so many roster spots open, the Triumvirs stepped up their scouting and came up with first baseman Tommy Tucker, second baseman Bobby Lowe, shortstop Herman Long, and Hall of Fame righthand pitcher Kid Nichols—all mainstays of the winning teams later in the decade. While Lowe later became famous for being the first major leaguer to hit four home runs in one game (on May 30, 1894 against Cincinnati), Nichols wasted little time in establishing himself as perhaps the best of all nineteenth-century pitchers by winning 27 games in his rookie year. Among his most conspicuous feats were winning 30 or more games in seven straight years and winning at least 20 in ten straight seasons. His career record of 360–203 included 533 complete games.

Even more than the Union Association, the Players League owed its revolt to Soden's reserve clause; also like the UA, the PL was bent on waging an attendance battle on the Boston owner's home preserve. But despite the fact that the PL team managed by Kelly won the pennant and the Beaneaters finished a mediocre fifth, the competition was a mutually lethal tie where fans were concerned. With other Brotherhood franchises faring even worse, the PL died after one season, and players like Nash and Quinn returned to the Triumvirs. But Soden had little time to celebrate because he created still a third rival when he signed outfielder Harry Stovey to a contract. Along with infielder Lou Bierbauer, Stovey had jumped to the Brotherhood from the Philadelphia club in the American Association; following the dissolution of the PL, the two players found their names missing from the lists of protected big leaguers obligated to return to their teams of origin, and so declared themselves free agents. Stovey wound up on Boston and Bierbauer landed on Pittsburgh. When organized baseball's National Board upheld both players, the AA declared war on Soden by establishing a Boston club under manager Art Irwin that included former Beaneaters Richardson, Brouthers, and Buffinton. Both teams ended up winning their league flags, but the season proved to be the swan song for the AA; it folded some of its clubs into an enlarged NL for 1892 and disbanded the others.

With no city rivals to worry about for the rest of the decade, the Beaneaters concentrated on winning pennants. With Nichols and Jack Stivetts both winning 35 games, the team compiled 102 victories in the split season of 1892 and came out with the best overall record. The split season was an attempt to replace the inter-league championship series by having the winners of the two halves of the schedule meet in a fall showdown. The winners were Boston and the Cleveland Spiders. Sensitive to accusations that Boston might have deliberately let the Spiders win the second half so he could pocket the receipts accruing from the playoffs, Soden initially refused Cleveland's challenge for the postseason series, but then relented before pressures from the other NL franchises. Boston ended up sweeping the series in five games. The split season idea was, however, dropped after its one-year trial because of the lack of fan interest.

In 1893, Nichols turned in another 33 wins, while the outfield duo of Hugh Duffy and Tommy McCarthy batted .363 and .346, respectively. Although both players performed for other clubs during their careers, they were particularly productive for Boston. In nine seasons with the Beaneaters, Duffy not only hit over .300 eight times, but managed a soaring .438 (with 18 homers, 145 RBIs, and 160 runs) in 1894, the second year in which moving the mound to 60'6" had caused an onslaught of slugging. While not attaining Duffy's statistical heights, McCarthy bolstered his .300 years with the best outfield glove in the league. The players were christened The Heavenly Twins for their joint efforts on the diamond, their friendship off the field, and their common contractual holdout prior to the start of the 1894 season.

The contributions of Duffy and McCarthy notwithstanding, the club slowed down again in the middle of the decade. Aside from Nichols, the pitching was spotty, with Stivetts in particular having on and off years. The team also had its share of tragedies and disasters. In January 1894, catcher Bennett lost both legs when he slipped trying to reboard a train in Kansas City. In May, South End Grounds lost a good part of its grandstand to a fire that reportedly began when a lighted cigarette set off discarded peanut shells; the blaze went unnoticed for vital minutes because fans were distracted by a field brawl between Tommy Tucker and Baltimore's John McGraw. Because of the fire, the Beaneaters had to reschedule many home games for the road while the park was being repaired.

Boston was the first major league team to win 100 or more games in a season, a feat disguised by the fact that they accomplished it in 1892, the year of the split-season schedule. The club put together half-season records of 52–22 and 50–26 for an overall 102–48 record.

It was because of Tommy McCarthy's practice in the 1890s of tapping fly balls back and forth between his bare and gloved hands while advancing on the infield, that the National League adopted the rule allowing runners to move up as soon as a fly touches a fielder, not only when a clean catch or error is made.

After three years in the middle of the pack, the club regained league dominance in 1897 and 1898. Aside from veterans Nichols, Duffy, Lowe, and Long, the team featured Ted Lewis and Fred Klobedanz in the rotation, Tenney at first, Collins at third, and Stahl and Billy Hamilton in the outfield. To go with Nichols's 59 wins over the two seasons, Lewis turned in 47 victories and Klobedanz 45; a lifetime .295 hitter, the defensive specialist Tenney also tightened up the infield by pioneering the 3–6–3 double play; Hall of Famer Collins hit .346 and .328, drove in more than 100 runs each season, and led the NL in home runs in 1898; Stahl contributed averages of .358 and .311; and Hamilton, a steal in a trade with Philadelphia for Nash, batted .358 and .369. The club's efforts did not bring unalloyed joy to Soden, however, because of declining attendance both years, in part because of a distracted public concern about the Spanish–American War and in part because of a widespread feeling that the Beaneaters had no real competition.

Soden had a lot more to complain about in 1899. To begin with, Boston lost its dominance to a Brooklyn club suddenly filled with Baltimore all-stars following a deal between Harry Von der Horst and Charlie Ebbets that was typical of the era of syndicate baseball. Along with injuries or off years by Hamilton, Duffy, Collins, and Nichols, the Baltimore–Brooklyn transaction dropped the Beaneaters to second place, eight games off the lead. Second, despite the powerful competition provided by Brooklyn, Boston fans were still conspicuous by their absence, with the war still raging and amid growing criticism that South End Grounds was not only uncomfortable but also, as evidenced by the 1894 fire, dangerous. If anything, the team's success on the field the previous two years only magnified the emptiness of Soden's periodic promises to give the ballpark an overhaul. Third, many of the players began accusing the Triumvirs of giving more money to threatened league franchises than to their own personnel. Lastly, the resentment against the owners began to color relations between the players and Selee, especially where catcher Marty Bergen was concerned.

From 1896 to 1899, Bergen, a defensive specialist with little offensive clout, had done most of the team's catching. He had also done most of the team's brooding, announcing at various intervals that he needed a few days off and then ignoring threats of suspensions and fines to return to his farm in nearby North Brookfield, Massachusetts. Although some players warned Selee and the owners that Bergen

had to be treated with kid gloves, most of them were angered that he seemed able to come and go as he wished. A truce of sorts reigned during the 1898 season, after Bergen had lost a son, but then the catcher himself turned the tension back on by saying that he couldn't play with the Beaneaters because they reminded him of his lost boy. With the press generally on Bergen's side during his crisis, Soden confined himself to lecturing the player to "rise above (his) spells," until after the 1899 season, when a delegation of Beaneaters warned that they would not return to the club if Bergen was still on it. The threat became academic on January 19, 1900, when Bergen used a razor and an axe to kill his wife, three-year-old son, infant daughter, and himself.

Another Beaneater who ran afoul of his teammates was pitcher Klobedanz, who supplemented his income after the 1898 season by scabbing as a scene-shifter during a strike by a theatrical union. Union-minded Boston players hounded the southpaw off the team, and he soon disappeared into the minors.

After an uneventful 1900 season, things went from bad to worse. Soden was confronted with still another challenge to his monopoly on the Boston market when Ban Johnson announced that his new American League would field a team in the city in 1901. The news climaxed months of attempts by Johnson to get NL approval for his venture in return for which he promised not to enter into direct competition with franchises from the older league. As a chief spokesman for the NL, Soden not only rejected Johnson's offer, but warned that he and other league owners were ready to finance a revived American Association to beat off the AL; to back up his threat, he contacted Art Irwin with a plan to set up an AA franchise in Boston at Charles River Park. Stung by such a reaction, Johnson stepped up his own plans to settle a franchise in Boston, and it wasn't long before he had leased land for the new club. His bluff called, Soden quickly backed off his promises to Irwin and had to watch the birth of the Boston Red Sox. As if this were not bad enough, Heavenly Twin Duffy announced that he had played out his option for the Beaneaters and, reserve clause or not, was jumping to take over the new AL franchise in Milwaukee as manager. Despite the significance of this contractual challenge, Soden did nothing but shrug that Duffy was through as a player anyway. This proved to be still another miscalculation when Duffy, now installed as one of Johnson's most active recruiters, talked Collins into taking over as player–manager of the Red Sox. In his turn, Collins persuaded pitcher Lewis and outfielders Stahl and Buck Freeman to join him on the AL's Boston team.

For the most part, the Nationals (as they were now called almost as regularly as the Beaneaters) went through the motions in 1901. Not only did they wind up as a literally .500 club in fifth place, but they lost both local publicity and attendance battles to the exciting, second-place Red Sox. The season was barely over when Selee was replaced by Al Buckenberger. For one more year, the steady play of Tenney at first and the pitching of Vic Willis and Togie Pittinger kept Boston respectable in third place. But then the roof fell in: Between 1903 and 1913, the club managed to rise as high as fifth only once, and finished in the cellar five times, including four straight years (1909–1912).

Although Buckenberger would never have been confused with a genius in any case, his tenure as manager was not aided by a particularly friendly relationship between Tenney and Soden. On more than one occasion, Buckenberger expressed himself as baffled by Tenney's reluctance to accept big contract offers from AL clubs at the height of the new league's raiding, making it obvious to listeners that his own life would have been easier if the first baseman had accepted one of the bids. When Soden rewarded Tenney's loyalty with a multiyear contract and even stepped in to pay fines for the player incurred from on-the-field fights, Buckenberger had little doubt that his replacement was already wearing a Boston uniform. Soden waited only long enough to team up with Conant to buy out Billings's stock and reduce the front office trio to a duo. When Tenney was finally given Buckenberger's post for the 1905 season, it became clear that his friendship with Soden was at least partly based on a mutual appreciation for the dollar. With marching orders that it was more important that he save the franchise money than win a pennant and that he would receive a bonus if he accomplished that goal, Tenney went about earning his incentive by ordering players to, among other things, use splintered bats and run into the stands during games to retrieve foul balls. The new manager's mania reached its crest during a game in which he accused umpire Bill Klem of keeping balls that belonged to the club and attempted to search the arbiter.

Together with the general decline of the club and the popularity of the Red Sox, the buy-out of Billings and the penny-pinching of Tenney fueled reports that Soden and Conant were about to unload the franchise. Although the two remaining Triumvirs issued perfunctory denials of their desire to sell, it was the loyal Tenney who effectively undercut their public stance by admitting that he had tried to put together a purchasing consortium prior to the 1906 season but had been unable to raise a nickel. This only worsened the negotiating position of Soden and Conant with prospective buyers, forcing them to sit still through the 1906 season, when Boston finished last for the first time in its thirty-year history. The farcical club, which at one point lost nineteen straight games, had four 20-game losers and the essence of a light-hitting outfielder by the name of Gene Good, whose .151 average was 25 points higher than his weight.

With the nightmare of the 1906 campaign over, Tenney had better luck when he asked Pittsburgh owner Barney Dreyfuss to meet with Soden and Conant to discuss the sale of the team. Under the impression that he was going to be partnered with Dreyfuss in another syndication deal, Tenney attended an October meeting in New York, where he was surprised to find a former coal miner by the name of George B. Dovey sitting with the Pittsburgh owner. Under the terms of the deal worked out at the session, Dovey and his brother John put up $75,000 for the franchise, players, and grounds, and also relieved Soden and Conant of past obligations on the ballpark lease. Tenney bought enough stock to make him the second largest stockholder in the franchise, but it wasn't until the new board of directors convened a short time later that he realized that the Dovey brothers hadn't been fronting for Dreyfuss as the chief stockholder, but rather for their most recent employer, a Pittsburgh theatrical entrepreneur named John Harris. For all practical purposes, however, the Doveys operated the team—a fact so evident to Boston newsmen that they began referring to the club as the Doves.

Aware of the organization's image problem with the Boston public, the Doveys set about scoring some immediate public relations points. They made a show of consulting with former Triumvir Billings, by far the most popular member of the previous ownership, all the more so after having been squeezed out by Soden and Conant. The Doveys then turned their attention to the ballpark, where they installed an electric scoreboard and padded bleacher seats. Not in the least embarrassed by their ties to Dreyfuss, they went to the Pirates for their first deal, obtaining outfielder Ginger Beaumont and second baseman Claude Ritchey for utility infielder Ed Abbaticchio. Unfortunately, once the 1907 season began, all of the Doveys' efforts only added up to a modest rise to seventh place. The Doveys responded by doing the traditional thing in untraditional circumstances—firing the manager, who also happened to be the organization's second largest shareholder. Knowing that the Doveys also wanted to get rid of him as a player, Tenney thought that he had them over a barrel in demanding a 25 percent profit for his stock. The brothers laughed and then traded him to the Giants in an eight-player deal. This not only astonished Tenney, but rankled NL President Harry Pulliam, who declared himself opposed to somebody playing for one team while having a financial interest in a second. But despite Pulliam's order to get rid of his Boston stock, Tenney held onto his investment, arguing that the league had no right to force him to sell out for what he considered an unfair price. Pulliam pulled back, not least because of the fears of some league owners (notably Dreyfuss) that the issue could only spark closer looks at their own involvements with more than one franchise.

To replace Tenney as manager, the Doveys brought in Joe Kelley, a future Hall of Famer who was then winding down his career as an outfielder-first baseman. It turned out to be a short-lived love affair, especially after one of the players obtained in the trade with the Giants, catcher Frank Bowerman, spent most of the drab 1908 season second-guessing every one of the new pilot's decisions. When Kelley demanded that the Doveys get rid of Bowerman, he was met only with additional criticism that he himself wasn't playing enough and leading the team from the field. The inevitable announcement of Kelley's "resignation" and Bowerman's succession came as soon as the season was over.

If the 1908 season had been a disaster, 1909 turned into pure catastrophe. On the field, the club set a new franchise record of 108 losses. In the dugout, Bowerman spent the first three months of the season bemoaning his inability to get the club going, then going off to the nearest telephone to persuade John McGraw to get him back to the Giants. By July,

Bowerman was back on his Michigan farm with an apparent nervous breakdown, and Harry Smith was running the team. But even this development was overshadowed by George Dovey's sudden death in June at the age of 48; an autopsy blamed a lung hemorrhage. Brother John took over the reins and hired Fred Lake to manage the club for the 1910 season. The choice of Lake was considered something of a public relations coup in Boston because he took the job after a salary raise demand had left him out in the cold with the Red Sox. Once again, however, the publicity plus became a performance minus, when Lake failed to get the Doves out of last place.

In December 1910, New York lawyer William Hepburn Russell approached Harris and Dovey with an offer to buy the franchise. Harris said he wasn't interested, but countered with an offer to purchase the Tenney shares for which Russell held power of attorney. When Russell reported back to Tenney that he could finally unload his stock at a good price, the former manager gave his approval to the purchase, only to learn that Harris had in the meantime changed his mind about selling and was ready to listen to a reasonable offer. Over the next couple of weeks, Harris changed his mind a couple of more times, but finally agreed to yield the team for $100,000 to a syndicate that included Russell, Boston publishers Louis and George Page, and Boston insuranceman Frederick Murphy. As his manager, Russell turned immediately to client Tenney, but the latter declined the job unless the new owners bought up all his stock and gave him a free hand to tear up what he described as "a rotten club." Russell acceded to both conditions, and Lake was gone almost as fast as he had arrived.

Tenney's free hand to remold the club produced a record of 44–107, the second lowest winning percentage in franchise history. The most notable new face was the legendary Cy Young, obtained in July to boost ticket sales; Young was the first of many Hall of Famers a breath short of retirement (among the others were Rube Marquard, Ed Walsh, George Sisler, Johnny Evers, Babe Ruth, and Al Simmons) that the team added over the years for box office reasons. Tenney wasn't much more successful in the clubhouse than on the field, in part because of the managerial ambitions of veterans like Johnny Kling and Buck Herzog. The situation was about the same in the front office, where Russell and the Pages were at loggerheads over practically every organization move. The strain began to tell on Russell, and the final two months of the season were filled with rumors of another imminent sale. Besieged by his partners, the ineffective play of his team, and demands that he commit himself to never selling out to non-local interests, Russell finally cracked, dying of a heart attack at the end of November 1911.

Despite the heightened sensitivity in Boston about the dangers of selling the club again to outsiders, it was in fact another three New Yorkers who stepped forward to lay down $187,000 to take over from the Russell group. The biggest baseball name in the trio was John Montgomery Ward, the Hall of Famer who had led the Players League revolt and who had devoted himself to his New York legal practice since retiring as a player–manager after the 1894 season. It was Ward who, determined to get back into baseball, talked millionaire contractor James Gaffney into putting up the money for the purchase. Gaffney, a former policeman who had built up his personal fortune through diligent use of his Tammany Hall contacts, brought along John Carroll, another Tammany influence peddler. Like the Doveys, the new owners immediately set about to win back fans by refurbishing South End Grounds, while disclosing that they were also looking for a site to erect a more modern stadium. As team president, Ward didn't lose any points, either, when he replaced Tenney with Kling. Gaffney's first significant decision for the franchise was to rebaptize the team the Boston Braves, a reference to his Tammany Hall association, and to redesign club uniforms so that they bore the profile of a Native American warrior. After years of being called Beaneaters, Nationals, Doves, and even Rustlers (during Russell's brief reign), the franchise finally had the nickname that would even outlast its presence in Boston.

It didn't take long for Ward to lose his enthusiasm about reentering the game. His first cold shower came when he claimed several players off the waiver list, only to have their names removed immediately; this prompted suspicions that the NL's old guard was still resentful of Ward's anti-management background, not only in having organized the Brotherhood, but also in having defended a number of players in individual suits brought against clubs. The president also made clear his disappointment at not being able to persuade the 45-year-old Young to return to anchor the otherwise nameless pitching staff. Once the season got underway and the Braves showed that their new owners and new uniforms had not affected their on-field performance, Ward came under increasing fire from Gaffney, who wasn't accustomed to backing also-rans. Finally, in July, Gaffney announced Ward's resignation and his own succession to the presidency. Ward told one news-

man that he was glad to be out of what he termed "a bughouse."

The 1912 team had several players worthy of mention. One was Walter Dickson, who was rushed into the breech to assume Young's anchoring role and ended up with a record of 3–19. At shortstop the club had Frank O'Rourke, whose .122 batting average was a testament to his defensive abilities. But the most conspicuous member of the team was shortstop Rabbit Maranville, who began a twenty-three-year Hall of Fame career that would become as famous for his on-field and off-field clowning as for his vest-pocket catches and clutch hitting. Any list of Maranville's antics on the diamond would have to include: going up to bat by crawling through the legs of the home plate umpire, sticking eyeglasses on umpires, and, on the pretext of administering first aid to a cut-up arbiter, "discovering" one facial nick after another until he had completely painted his victim in iodine. His off-field exploits ran the gamut from walking on the window ledges of high-rise buildings to pursuing a modest stage career of singing, telling jokes, and demonstrating his belt-buckle catches. Gaffney was only the first of several owners who would complain that Maranville was driving him mad—and also only the first of several who would acknowledge that he had the best infield glove in the league and that he was box office.

For the 1913 season, Gaffney replaced Kling with George Stallings. Courteous to the point of courtliness before and after a game, Stallings was as abusive and belligerent a manager as baseball has ever seen during play. Although he became known as the Miracle Man after piloting Boston to a pennant in 1914, he was also known to his contemporaries as Bonehead—not because of his own mental deficiencies, but because that was a common term of his own in summoning or discussing his players. His managerial career, in Boston as elsewhere, was marked by difficulties with stars, sometimes to the point of blows in the clubhouse; on the other hand, he had a reputation for building up the self-confidence of players less than gifted and getting surprising performances out of them. Stallings's superstitiousness about paper was an Achilles heel that rivals were quick to exploit; the Pirates and Cubs, in particular, frequently assigned a bench player to a seat close to the Boston dugout for the sole purpose of shredding apart a newspaper to distract Stallings.

Under Stallings, the Braves quit the cellar for the first time in five years in 1913. With nothing to lose and with Gaffney's approval, he spent most of that season and the offseason overhauling the roster, to the point that only four players who had served under Kling (Maranville, catcher Hank Gowdy, and pitchers Otto Hess and Lefty Tyler) were still in Boston uniforms in 1914. Key transactions included the trading of Sweeney to the Cubs for veteran Johnny Evers; the acquisition of outfielder Possum Whitted from the Cardinals for pitcher Hub Perdue; and the purchase of pitchers Dick Rudolph and Bill James from the minor leagues. Few of the moves seemed worth the effort, however, when the club started the season by losing 18 of its first 22 games. Admitting that the team's outfield was especially weak, Stallings platooned lefty–righty, offensive–defensive, speed–slugging in so many combinations that, by the end of the year, eleven different outfielders had seen service. The low point came at the beginning of July, when the team not only found itself in last place 15 games behind the Giants, but even lost an exhibition game to a team made up of employees of a soap company.

The second half of the season was a different story. Staging one of the greatest comebacks in baseball history, the Braves won 52 of their last 66 games, passing all seven other teams between July 19th and September 8th. Among the position players, the most pivotal factor was Evers, who teamed with Maranville to give the club the tightest infield defense up the middle in the league and whose relentless badgering of teammates not to let down made him a stereophonic set with Stallings. The starting pitching was almost invulnerable over the second half, with James finishing at 26–7 with a 1.90 ERA and Rudolph 27–10 and 2.35. Enthusiasm for the team reached such proportions in Boston that even Red Sox owner Joseph Lannin offered Gaffney the use of the more modern Fenway Park for games in August and September. It was at Fenway, for a crucial morning–afternoon doubleheader against the Giants on Labor Day, that the Braves set the all-time Boston record for baseball attendance in a single day by selling 36,000 tickets to the first game and another 40,000 to the second contest. It was also in the American League ballpark that the club capped its startling season by sweeping the heavily favored Athletics of Connie Mack in the World Series.

For most of the season, 1915 appeared to be a replay of 1914. Once again, the team found itself last

Cuban Dolf Luque became the first Latin American pitcher in the major leagues when he debuted for Boston in 1914.

in July and, once again, it ripped through the rest of the league in August and the first half of September. But with James going down with a bad arm, Rudolph blowing hot and cold, and the club hitting only .240 (the lowest in the NL), the drive ended in a second-place finish, seven games behind the Phillies. In the middle of the aborted pennant run, on August 18, the club finally moved out of South End Grounds to the newly constructed Braves Field. Most of the money for the facility had been raised by Boston stockbroker Arthur Wise, who had played a similar role in the financing of Fenway Park. Regarding the design of the new stadium, Gaffney had insisted that it be spacious enough to allow inside-the-park homers in all outfield directions, it being his contention that fans preferred seeing players running around the bases rather than trotting around them. The result was a field that measured 402 feet down each foul line and 550 feet to dead center. It would not be until 1925 that a Boston player, outfielder Bernie Neis, managed to hit a ball over the left field fence even in batting practice; later that same season, New York catcher Frank Snyder walloped the first official home run into the left field seats.

Gaffney didn't stay around very long to admire his new facility. In January 1916, he announced that he was selling the team to a consortium of Boston bankers and politicians for a price that was said only to be "considerably higher" than the $187,000 he had put up in 1912. Although there were reports at the time that Gaffney's move was dictated by his intention of buying the Giants in his native New York, it turned out that he merely saw a chance to make a big profit and took it. The new owners—who included the bankers behind the financing of Braves Field—named Wise as the treasurer to look after their interests and brought in ex-Harvard football coach Percy Haughton to assume the presidency and head up baseball operations. Haughton immediately gave a new three-year contract to Stallings, who also bought some stock in the new organization.

Relations between Stallings and Haughton got off to a dreary start when the team president addressed the players before an exhibition game in spring training and urged them to curb their use of foul language on the field, substituting words like "good" and "nice" for other four-letter words whenever they made an error or missed hitting a ball. When first baseman Sherry Magee followed this advice by shouting "good, good, good!" after a ball bounced over his head, the vitriolic Stallings had to be restrained from jumping on his player. Haughton also made the mistake of going along with a scheme by business manager B. M. Hapgood to schedule a series of twenty exhibition games up and down the east coast, even if that meant keeping the players confined to the train every night. After a week of this oppressive routine, Maranville organized the players in a passive resistance strike, with everyone refusing to shave and donning only blue work shirts and loud ties. When some of the locals in the towns they visited confused Boston players with bums and even (in one case) escaped jailbirds, Haughton ordered Hapgood to modify the schedule.

Although they finished a spot lower in the standings in 1916 than they had the year before, the Braves actually made a tougher run at the pennant in a four-way race with Brooklyn, Philadelphia, and New York. The biggest disappointment of the year was Evers, who went from jockeying his teammates to snarling at them, and who could bat no higher than .216. When Evers showed up the following season in the same mood, he was packed off to the Phillies. None of the organization's other problems were dispatched so easily. Between 1917 and 1932, the club rose only once as high as fourth and then, after attaining that modest plateau a couple of more times in the mid-1930s, flopped back down into the league's nether regions until after World War II.

For the consortium fronted by Haughton, World War I meant daily threats of losing players to the draft and diminishing attendance. After rejecting what it considered an insufficient bid from Stallings and Hapgood for buying the franchise, the group announced after the 1918 season that it was selling to George Washington Grant, a one-time motion picture distributor in England then busy with various speculative ventures in New York. The trouble with a number of Grant's ventures was that they somehow involved the New York Giants, raising suspicions in Boston that he was little more than a stalking horse for John McGraw and that the Braves were on the verge of being turned into a New York farm club. It was McGraw, for instance, who had brought Grant together with Haughton. Grant was not only partnered with McGraw in an attempt to buy a Havana race track, but had both a Wall Street office and a box at the Polo Grounds adjoining those of New York owner Charles Stoneham. In rebutting the charges that he was being maneuvered by the Giants, Grant insisted that his interest in the Braves went back as far as 1911, when he had sought to buy the team from Russell but had been outbid by Gaffney and Ward. He also promised that he would move to Boston, and not be another outside owner.

As it turned out, Grant never left New York.

One of the most famous games in baseball history was played in Boston on May 1, 1920, when Joe Oeschger dueled Brooklyn's Leon Cadore to a 1–1, 26-inning tie. The contest was halted because of darkness. Only three balls were used in the entire game, which didn't even last four hours. Among the many records established was Oeschger's feat of hurling 16 consecutive scoreless innings in one game.

Moreover, the Braves suddenly had active trade partners in the Giants, with three deals being pulled off within months of the sale of the club. Safely ensconced in Manhattan, Grant didn't pay too much attention to the hostility of the Boston press, or to the growing cynicism of the fans toward the franchise. When Stallings urged him to spend money on decent players, he pleaded poverty, and dared the manager to quit. Stallings finally agreed to go in November 1920, and was replaced by his long-time aide Fred Mitchell.

Mitchell surprised everyone by steering the team to a fourth-place standing and its first .500 record since 1916. The principal reason for the surge was the .300 hitting of outfielders Billy Southworth, Walton Cruise, and Ray Powell. Southworth's effort amounted to something of a vindication because he had come to the club in an unpopular exchange with Pittsburgh for local hero Maranville, and at the start of the season Boston fans made sure he knew that he was not wanted at such a price. Grant also had reason to be satisfied with Mitchell's managing for a readiness to dole out fines that covered an appreciable part of the team's road expenses. Only when some dailies began to question whether the fines were more motivated by the owner's financial priorities than by the manager's disciplinary intentions, did Mitchell ease up.

One year later, with the team's plummet back into the NL basement, Grant had enough. Once again availing himself of McGraw as a middleman, he sold the franchise to Emil Fuchs, a former judge and deputy attorney general of New York State who had subsequently compiled a small fortune through his private legal practice. Although no sale figures were announced, both sides conceded that Grant had more than recouped his original $400,000 investment. McGraw was also instrumental in satisfying Fuchs's one condition for the sale—talking former Giants' ace Christy Mathewson into coming in as Boston president. If anyone in New England had still doubted the dependence of the Braves' franchise on Manhattan moneymen and their cronies at the Polo Grounds, the February 11, 1923 announcement of Grant's deal with Fuchs was something of a clinching argument. But unlike Grant, Fuchs set up quarters in Boston and set about cultivating the local writers. Within a few months, he was calling the local sports reporters his "board of directors," treating them to one banquet after another, and actually going to them for advice on player trades. He also voiced confidence that Mitchell was the ideal manager for leading the team back to the first division.

Mitchell wasn't; no sooner had the Braves dropped exactly 100 games for a second straight year in 1923 than Mathewson got rid of him. Then, in November, the club announced still another swap with the Giants in which they surrendered Southworth and hurler Joe Oeschger for outfielders Casey Stengel and Bill Cunningham and shortstop Dave Bancroft; Bancroft was also appointed Mitchell's successor. According to McGraw, the Giants had given up "the best shortstop in the game" only because "we want to help Matty over in Boston."

Bancroft had a tough start in demonstrating that he might also be a competent manager. Two months before the start of the 1924 season, Boston third baseman Tony Boeckel, who had batted .313, .289, and .298 the previous three seasons, was killed on a highway near San Diego after he had survived a car crash with a truck, but had then been struck by a second vehicle while awaiting the arrival of police. In May, the veteran Rube Marquard, whom Bancroft had counted on for steadying his pitching staff, was operated on for appendicitis, ending up with only six mound appearances for the year. In July, it was Bancroft's own turn to submit to an appendectomy. It added up to another last-place finish and a third consecutive season with 100 defeats on the nose.

On his feet for the entire 1925 season, Bancroft did slightly better, batting .319 as a shortstop and piloting the club to fifth place. His secret weapon was Dick Burrus, a lefthand-hitting first baseman who batted .340 and had 87 RBIs; Burrus had not worn a big league uniform since 1920 and would have only one more season as a regular. Among the missing was Stengel, who, realizing that his playing days were winding down, had asked Fuchs for the managership of Boston's farm team in Worcester; he proved to be so impressive at the job that, a few weeks into the 1925 season, he was also made president of the club. But then, with a chance to take over the more talented Toledo minor league club in 1926, Stengel asked Fuchs for his release. When the judge

said no, Worcester manager Stengel directed his request to Worcester president Stengel, who immediately granted his pilot's wish and passed on copies of the release to Fuchs and to Commissioner Landis. Landis threatened to declare the paper game null and void, but Fuchs told him not to bother.

During the 1925 World Series, Mathewson succumbed to the lung ailment that had been wearing him down since he had been gassed in World War I. Fuchs himself took over as president, with Connecticut real estate developer Albert Powell being elected vice-president. A few months later, Powell attempted a board of directors coup, but fell short of the necessary shares and sold out his interest. Charles Adams eventually succeeded to the vice-presidency and to effective number two command.

Bancroft labored through two more seasons with miserable clubs, then was given permission to make a deal for himself. He eventually signed with the Dodgers for $30,000, with $10,000 of the amount going back to Fuchs. Named as the new manager was journeyman catcher Jack Slattery. Slattery never had a chance. Even in announcing his new pilot, Fuchs made it clear that he knew little about him, that he had been the choice of several Boston writers who suggested the Braves needed a local man to take over the club. Then, only hours after naming Slattery as manager, Fuchs made the far more startling announcement that the team had obtained Rogers Hornsby from the Giants in exchange for outfielder Jimmy Welsh and catcher Shanty Hogan. It took about six weeks into the season for Slattery to step aside for Hornsby.

Hornsby proved again that he was the premier second baseman in baseball by leading the league with a .387 batting average. As the manager between at bats, however, he did little but alienate his players, on occasion even accusing them of depriving him of RBI opportunities in their greater concern about the game. This attitude added up to another finish near the bottom of the league. Nevertheless Fuchs rewarded Hornsby at the end of August with a six-year contract at $40,000 a year. But even as the franchise was coming under attack for the deal, especially from writers close to players resentful of Hornsby's selfishness, the Rajah himself approached Fuchs with the idea of trading him to the Cubs in exchange for some young players who would be more useful to Boston over the long run. With even the recipient of his largesse suggesting that he had made a serious error with his multiyear contract, Fuchs turned the negotiations with the Cubs over to Adams. Adams ended up with a boatload of players who did little for the Braves, but he also came away with the gratitude of his team and a whopping $200,000 in the exchange. Riding the crest of sudden popularity in Boston, Adams also pressed Fuchs to save the organization more money by taking over himself as manager for the 1929 season. Over the protests of other owners in the league, Fuchs agreed to go down to the dugout. To assist him during games, the Judge reacquired the veteran shortstop Maranville from the Cardinals.

The positive side of the 1929 season was that the club won more games than it had under Slattery and Hornsby. The negative side was just about everything else. Fuchs no sooner managed the team through a decent April than he was called away to New York to a trial. When he offered the managership to Maranville, the shortstop refused the post unless he was given a five-year contract. Not about to repeat his mistake with Hornsby, Fuchs retained his title for the rest of the year, with Maranville and coach Johnny Evers actually calling the shots, often at cross-purposes. When the Judge himself found the time to return to the bench, his strategies scandalized his two veteran aides and provoked laughter from the rest of the team. On more than one occasion, for instance, Fuchs defied the book by pinch-hitting righties for lefties when the opposing pitcher was righthanded; more often than not, his explanation for the unorthodox move was that he hadn't noticed with what arm the pitcher was throwing. He didn't think much of the squeeze play, either, telling the bench one day that it wasn't "the honorable way" to score a run. Fuchs also brought to the bench his proclivity for long-winded stories, which he related to the players even in the middle of crucial game situations and often to the irritation of umpires, who had to remind the manager that he was preventing one of his hitters from getting up to the plate.

It hardly came as news that Fuchs's managerial career came to an end with the close of the 1929 season; his replacement was Bill McKechnie, a dour disciplinarian who played everything by the book and who had a reputation for being as good with pitchers as he was out of his depth with hitters. McKechnie ended up piloting Boston for eight seasons,

as many as Stallings had and second only to Selee. To his credit, he steered four of those clubs to better than .500 records; on the down side, his 1935 team's basement finish at 38–115 represented the nadir of the franchise.

One of the pleasant surprises awaiting McKechnie in 1930 was outfielder Wally Berger. Obtained from the Los Angeles minor league team for some of the cash pocketed in the Hornsby deal, Berger was that rarest of all Braves' species—a rookie who could hit. In his debut season, the righthand-hitting outfielder slugged a then-rookie record 38 homers, drove in 119 runs, and batted .310. Over six succeeding seasons, he never batted below .288 or clouted fewer than seventeen homers, twice again topping the thirty mark in circuits and going over the one hundred RBI mark three more times.

Despite the club's return to respectability in the first part of the 1930s, Fuchs started to sink under the debts that he had accumulated with Adams and other creditors. By the end of the 1934 season, he was barely able to keep a good face on what had deteriorated to a desperate situation. Then he made two moves that finished him. On the eve of the 1934 winter meetings, he announced his ambition of turning Braves Field over to dog racing and moving the Braves into Fenway Park. Red Sox President Tom Yawkey said nothing doing, NL President Ford Frick called the idea "absolutely preposterous," and Commissioner Landis said that he would resign rather than allow it. Fuchs immediately backed down, but the origins of his scheme became apparent when the Gaffney estate, which still owned the ballpark, countered with its own threat to throw the Braves out and lease the stadium to the Boston Kennel Club. With Fuchs red in the face over his aborted deal with Gaffney trustees and Yawkey refusing to budge on his refusal to let the Braves use Fenway, the NL held a meeting that was ostensibly about the dog racing issue but that was actually about Fuchs's solvency.

Between September 4th and September 15th in 1929, the Braves played nine straight double-headers. At one point in the skein, they set a record for futility by losing ten games in five days.

Footnote Player: Al Spohrer was a backup catcher who did his most famous receiving when he got into a ring at Boston Garden on January 10, 1930 to fight Art Shires, another big leaguer who thought of himself as a prize fighter. Some 17,000 customers watched Shires batter Spohrer to a TKO finish in the fourth round. Commissioner Landis stepped in soon afterward to ban any further such bouts. Spohrer and Shires ended up as teammates on the 1932 Braves.

By the end of the session, the league had agreed to guarantee the Gaffney estate a reduced leasing fee on Braves Field and to contribute to Boston's spring training expenses. As for Fuchs, he was permitted to remain as Braves' president, but on condition of either resolving his debts, selling his equity, or turning it over to Adams and his other creditors by August 1st.

With his reprieve, Fuchs made even more headlines by signing Babe Ruth to a Boston contract. Well past his prime as the game's greatest slugger, Ruth agreed to a $25,000 deal for becoming a part-time player, a vaguely defined "second vice-president," and a trouble-provoking "assistant manager." No sooner had the ink dried on the pact than the Bambino told reporters that he expected to take over as manager eventually. After an initial phase of assuring everyone that he didn't feel threatened by Ruth, McKechnie began to show his displeasure with the signing, first by exploding against lesser players and then by sinking into a funk that gradually overtook the entire team. Ruth wasn't much happier. It took him only a couple of weeks into the season to realize that he was second vice-president of nothing, that nobody in the organization took his managerial aspirations seriously, and that he was only a drawing card for a last-place team that had little else to attract fans. The breaking point came when Fuchs demanded that he play an exhibition game with a bad knee. On May 25th in a game against Pittsburgh, Ruth summoned up what was left of his hitting prowess and clouted three homers and a single, and drove in six runs. After a subsequent hitless contest against Cincinnati and a final at bat against Philadelphia, he called a press conference on June 2nd to announce his retirement. Fuchs acted more relieved than McKechnie, conceding that he would have released the home run king if he hadn't quit.

The Ruth fiasco was Fuchs's last hurrah. Unable to meet the August 1st deadline, he resigned as president. Adams, who was left holding the bag for a club that managed to win only 2 of 30 games between mid-August and mid-September, appointed McKechnie as temporary president and declared his willingness to sell the team to anyone who offered a reasonable price. When no such offer was put on the table, Adams undertook a financial reorganization of the franchise with the blessings of the league. The key

man in the restructuring was Bob Quinn, who was elected president. Adams had become a heavy investor in a Massachusetts race track, so he was barred by Landis from either holding stock or being an officer, but he continued to control the team through the estimated $325,000 that was still owed to him.

Quinn, who already had associations with losing teams with the Red Sox and Dodgers, got off to a typically bad start by deciding that one of the franchise's problems was that it was called the Braves. To eliminate this hardship, he held a contest soliciting a new name. After sorting through such proposals as the Bankrupts and the Basements, the newspaper writers called in to judge the submissions decided on the Bees, if for no other reason than it would make their own headline-composing colleagues happy. With the club no longer called the Braves, Braves Field was also renamed National League Park. On the more substantive issue of the club roster, it took Quinn less than two seasons to reduce to two (pitcher Danny MacFayden and first baseman Elbie Fletcher) the players who had also served under Fuchs. McKechnie, who was widely viewed as getting more out of his players than any other manager would have and who also remained close to Adams, beat Quinn to the punch by signing on with the Reds after the 1937 season. At first, Quinn played down the significance of McKechnie's departure, contending that he had a more than able successor in Donie Bush. But when negotiations with Bush fell through at the last minute, the team announced that Casey Stengel would be taking over. Although familiar to Boston fans for the fast one that he had pulled on Fuchs in managing to get out from under his Worcester contract, Stengel had also become known for the clown act he had put on as the pilot of Quinn's wretched Brooklyn clubs; for the most part, it was this aptitude that characterized his tenure in Boston as well. In his six years as manager, Stengel turned out clubs that finished fifth once, sixth once, and seventh four times.

Even when Boston had a good player in the late 1930s and early 1940s, he didn't last long. In 1940 alone, the organization's continuing need for cash prompted such essentially money deals as sending pitcher Jim Turner to the Reds; pitchers MacFayden and Johnny Lanning to the Pirates; second baseman Tony Cuccinello to the Giants; catcher Al Lopez to the Pirates; pitcher Lou Fette to the Dodgers; and outfielder (and future batting champ) Debs Garms to the Pirates. If nothing else, the transactions persuaded a covey of Boston businessmen that Quinn knew the value of a dollar, for shortly after the opening of the 1941 season, they agreed to back him in a

In 1935, Ben Cantwell, the supposed ace of the Boston pitching staff, won 4 games and lost 25. He is the last 25-game loser in the major leagues.

syndicate to buy out the debt to Adams that amounted to 73 percent of the value of the franchise. Among the shareholders in the group were Stengel and construction magnate Lou Perini. Quinn also took the occasion to restore the name Braves to both the team and the ballpark.

The 1942 team featured Ernie Lombardi, the first Boston player to win the batting title since Hornsby in 1928. Lombardi, obtained in a cash transaction before the season, was one of several familiar National Leaguers to wear a Braves uniform during World War II. Another was Hall of Famer Paul Waner, who was a member of the club when he recorded his 3,000th hit on June 19, 1942. Among the other veterans who came and went in the early 1940s were Frenchy Bordagaray, Connie Ryan, Johnny Hopp, Joe Medwick, Bill Lee, and Mort Cooper. The best of the newcomers during the war years was lefty-hitting outfielder Tommy Holmes, who ended up with a .302 average over an eleven-year career that included ten seasons with Boston. Holmes had his greatest season in 1945, when he batted .352, led the league in doubles, homers, and slugging percentage, drove in 117 runs, and scored 125. Indicative of the generally lackluster offensive history of Boston, Holmes's 1945 production accounts for a majority of the seasonal records held by Boston Braves players.

Midway between sixth-place finishes in the off-season of 1943–1944, Perini and fellow-construction industry millionaires Guido Rugo and Joseph Maney announced that they were tired of their role in the ownership syndicate and offered either to sell out their stock at the original purchase price or buy out the other shareholders at the same rate. Within two months, the Three Little Steam Shovels, as the trio was called in the press, had total control over the franchise. Quinn remained as president, but Stengel, who had never managed to entertain Perini on or off the field, was out in favor of coach Bob Coleman. Coleman, whose background had mainly been in the minor leagues, lasted little more than a year before resigning and turning the team over to Del Bissonette to finish out the 1945 season. Whether the low-key, almost invisible Coleman would have lasted any longer in any case was debatable, because Perini, like most other big league owners, mainly marked time during the war years, hiring bodies rather than talents. Even the one significant change in the organization in the period—John Quinn's succession to the presidency in place of his father, who was demoted to the post of minor league director—seemed like corporate doodling.

It was another story in 1946. With the war over,

Perini began implementing promises that he had been making for two years about infusing the franchise with new blood. To begin with, he announced boldly that the Braves were going to sign the best manager in baseball, and then went out and reached agreement with Billy Southworth, who arguably fit such a description after having won three pennants in six years for the Cardinals. Next, he installed lights for night games and launched a whole series of promotions aimed at attracting Boston fans back to Braves Field. Only too aware of the success the Cardinals, Yankees, and Dodgers had enjoyed since they had built up their farm systems, he enlarged his scouting department and established an important farm club in Milwaukee in the American Association. Finally, he went on a buying and trading tear. Between February and July 1946, Perini instigated or gave his approval to twelve deals, only three of which actually cost Boston players.

The payoff for all the movement was Boston's first .500 record since 1938 and first first-division finish since 1934. Moreover, the team set a new attendance mark of 969,673—nearly double the previous record established in 1933; the twenty-four night games played at home drew more than 568,000 fans. On the field, the most productive players were Holmes and Hopp, who both batted over .300, and righthander Johnny Sain, who came back from the war to post the first of three straight 20-win seasons. If there was a negative side to the season, it came on Opening day when an estimated 5,000 fans had their clothes ruined by freshly painted seats that had not dried. For the rest of the year, accountants and lawyers had to pore over some 13,000 damage claims; after separating the hustlers from the genuinely aggrieved, the club ended up paying out the relatively small sum of $6,000 in cleaning bills. To avoid having the suits a daily occurrence, Perini asked Red Sox owner Yawkey to allow the Braves to play in Fenway Park until all the paint at Braves Field had dried; Perini not being Fuchs and wet paint not being dog races, Yawkey agreed.

The 1947 team inched a little further up the ladder to third place. Third baseman Bob Elliott hit .317 with 22 homers and 113 RBIs, Holmes batted above

Baseball's first team yearbook was the *Braves' Sketch Book*, devised by promotions director Bill Sullivan in 1946. It sold an estimated 22,000 copies.

Second baseman Bama Rowell inspired Bernard Malamud's climactic scene in the novel *The Natural*, when he smashed the Bulova clock atop the right field scoreboard in Ebbets Field on Memorial Day in 1946. The blow shattered the clock and showered Brooklyn outfielder Dixie Walker in glass. In the work by the Brooklyn-born Malamud, the home run by fictional hero Roy Hobbs won a pennant for the New York Knights. The reality was somewhat different, with Rowell having to wait forty-one years even to collect the watch that Bulova had promised to anyone who hit the clock.

.300 again, and Sain went 21–12. But moving to center stage in May and remaining there for the rest of the season (and the rest of the Braves' stay in Boston) was southpaw Warren Spahn, who posted a 21–10 record and led the league in ERA. Already twenty-five years old when he won his first major league game after coming out of the service in 1946, Spahn ended up winning more games (363) than any lefthander in the history of the game. His feats over a twenty-one year career included thirteen 20-game seasons (tying him with Mathewson for the most), most career shutouts (63) by a lefty, and league leader in victories eight times, strikeouts four times, and ERA twice. It was not until he reached the age of thirty-nine that he pitched his first no-hitter, but he hurled a second one a year later at the age of forty. Spahn was elected to the Hall of Fame in 1973.

For the first time in more than thirty years, the Braves entered the 1948 season in full expectation that they could win the pennant. With the nucleus of the team already in place, the front office used the offseason to supply the finishing touches—buying slugging outfielder Jeff Heath from the Browns and acquiring veteran second baseman Eddie Stanky from the Dodgers to team up with young shortstop Alvin Dark. Buoyed by a new five-year contract, Southworth pushed his collection of journeymen and rookies into first place in early June, saw them hold the lead for most of the summer, topple back to second in late August, and then return to the top for good after sweeping a September 6 doubleheader from Brooklyn. Among the position players, the standouts were Dark (.322 and Rookie of the Year), his double-play partner Stanky (.320) , Heath (.319, 20 homers, 76 RBIs), and Elliott (23 homers and 100 RBIs). Although the season's starting rotation be-

came associated with the despairing cry of "Spahn, Sain, and pray for rain," it was in fact largely a one-man show, with Sain leading the league with 24 wins. On the other hand, Spahn actually had one of his few so-so years, notching only 15 victories and seeing his ERA balloon to 3.71 a season after leading the NL in that category. After Spahn came Bill Voiselle with 13 wins and Vern Bickford with 11.

The World Series was anticlimactic for more than one reason. Throughout September, Boston fans had entertained visions of the city's first local post-season duel, all the more so when Braves and Red Sox players began sniping at one another in the press. But then the Red Sox collapsed in a tie-breaking play-off, and the Braves were left to face Cleveland. The final disappointment occurred when the Indians rode considerably stronger pitching to a championship in six games. In three contests Boston was held to a single run, and in a fourth it was shut out altogether. The team's major consolation was a 1–0 defeat of Bob Feller in the opening game, largely because umpire Bill Stewart missed a crucial pickoff of Boston pinch-runner Phil Masi at second base; Masi eventually scored the game's only run. For Perini, the solace was a profit of $210,000 from the World Series, which topped off the take from still another single-season attendance record (1,455,438).

After the season, storm clouds formed over the team. The first sign of trouble came a couple of days after the World Series, when Freddie Fitzsimmons quit as a coach, leaving heavy hints strewn all over his path that he could no longer tolerate Southworth's authoritarian airs. That Southworth had always been something of a martinet was no secret to anyone in Boston, St. Louis, or anywhere else he had managed, but as long as he had kept winning, his players generally put up with it and his employers promoted it as a virtue. When Quinn began emphasizing Southworth's role in the 1948 pennant during player contract negotiations that winter, however, he raised a flame under a cauldron, and several Braves spent the winter on the phone with one another wondering how their manager had won the NL flag by himself. None of this boded well for spring training, and Southworth immediately made it worse by devising new rules directed at keeping the players on the field or in their rooms as much as possible. Even before the team arrived in Boston for its home opener, there was speculation that Stanky, Southworth's sharpest critic on the team, would take over as pilot.

Then a series of injuries plagued the team. Heath, who had broken his ankle prior to the 1948

World Series, was not able to play until August. Sain hurt his arm and lost 17 games before he bothered to tell anyone. First baseman Earl Torgeson separated his shoulder during a game, then broke his thumb in a clubhouse fight with outfielder Jimmy Russell. Along with other minor but nagging aches, these setbacks drove the Braves out of first place in early June and dumped them all the way to fourth. By the middle of August, Southworth could stand no more, and asked to be relieved for the remainder of the season. He was replaced not by Stanky, but by coach Johnny Cooney. If reports of their manager's breakdown were meant to soften the hostility of the players, they failed in their objective. When the team met to divvy up the fourth-place money, Southworth was voted merely a half-share.

Faced with getting rid of the manager or some of the rebellious players for the 1950 season, Perini let the three years still on Southworth's contract settle the issue for him, and traded the middle infield combination of Stanky and Dark to the Giants for sluggers Sid Gordon and Willard Marshall, shortstop Buddy Kerr, and pitcher Sam Webb. Although Gordon gave the team a couple of good seasons, the deal proved far more profitable to the Giants, when Stanky and Dark provided the heart for New York's legendary comeback against Brooklyn in 1951.

After another fourth-place finish in 1950, Perini decided to give Southworth one more year to restore the euphoria of 1948. It was a decision that he and Meany took alone, however, after squeezing out Rugo, the third Little Shovel, from the team's vice-presidency. If Southworth doubted that he was running out of time, he merely had to hear another off-season announcement that Holmes was being sent to Hartford for managerial experience. In the event, Holmes loitered in Connecticut only until June 1951, when Southworth told Perini that his health was more important to him than the opportunity for watching still another fourth-place showing. What became clear immediately upon Holmes's return to Boston was that he had not picked up any significant managerial experience and still sought to address his charges as teammates. Just as bad, he insisted on coaching at third base, another job for which he was not suited, and soon had Braves' runners being thrown out at a frenzied rate. For the rest of the 1951 season, Perini pretended not to hear the criticism leveled against the manager from both the press and grandstands. If Holmes qualified as a manager on no other level, he did so as a financial bargain, and the two remaining Little Shovels made little attempt to hide their new priority of saving money. In August,

the franchise's shortage of cash became evident to everyone when Boston sold Sain to the Yankees for minor league righthander Lew Burdette and $50,000. Before the start of the 1952 season, Elliott was also gone, traded to the Giants for relief pitcher Sheldon Jones and $40,000.

Even though the organization's attitude toward money and the departure of Sain and Elliott did not offer much hope of a first-division club in 1952, there was at least widespread anticipation that the club would benefit from the arrival of rookie third baseman Eddie Mathews and shortstop Johnny Logan. In what proved to be his final mistake, however, Holmes started the season with the light-hitting Johnny Cusick at short, precipitating gripes from the bench that finally persuaded Perini and Quinn that Holmes was not the best manager available in the organization. After thirty-five games, he was replaced by Charlie Grimm, the pilot of the organization's minor league club in Milwaukee. The team finished 16 games under .500 for Grimm and 25 games under overall for a seventh-place showing. The main sources of solace were indeed Logan and Mathews. Taking over from Cusick with the arrival of Grimm, Logan batted .283 and displayed a Maranville-like fire in assuming command of the infield. Mathews hit only .242, but launched his Hall of Fame career with 25 homers. Before his retirement in 1968, he would clout 512 roundtrippers and top the forty mark four times.

Although they didn't know it at the time, the 8,822 fans who showed up at Braves Field on September 21 to see Boston lose to Brooklyn 8–2 were the last ones to see an NL game in the city. The final crowd itself was indicative of the team's main problem: The highest attendance for a game all year was 13,405 in early July. The total 1952 count was a mere 282,000, comparable to the worst years of World War II. But even as he was lamenting more than one million dollars in losses between 1950 and 1952, Perini and his brothers Joseph and Charles were busy buying up the stock of Maney, Rugo, and a few minor shareholders. Amid much speculation that the buying spree was a prelude to shifting the franchise to Milwaukee, Perini and his brothers noted only that the Wisconsin city had been promised a major league team for years. Then, on March 18, 1953, with spring training already underway and groundskeepers already preparing Braves Field for the new season, the official announcement came that the Perinis were indeed moving the club to Milwaukee. A vote by the other NL owners was a formality. For his part, Giants' owner Horace Stoneham, apparently forgetting the ties established by his father and John McGraw with a long line of Boston owners, shed few tears for the transfer, claiming that "we never took a nickel out of Boston." Dodgers owner Walter O'Malley said little for the public record, but he would later admit that Perini had opened his eyes to the real consequences of air travel for big league baseball. In fact, before the decade was out, two more NL franchises and two in the AL would also pull up stakes and move to other cities.

BOSTON BRAVES

Annual Standings and Managers

Year	Position	W	L	Pct.	GB	Managers
1876	Fourth	39	31	.557	15	Harry Wright
1877	First	42	18	.700	+7	Harry Wright
1878	First	41	19	.683	+4	Harry Wright
1879	Second	54	30	.643	5	Harry Wright
1880	Sixth	40	44	.476	27	Harry Wright
1881	Sixth	38	45	.458	17½	Harry Wright
1882	Third	45	39	.536	10	John Morrill
1883	First	63	35	.643	+4	Jack Burdock, John Morrill
1884	Second	73	38	.658	10½	John Morrill
1885	Fifth	46	66	.411	41	John Morrill
1886	Fifth	56	61	.479	30½	John Morrill
1887	Fifth	61	60	.504	16½	John Morrill
1888	Fourth	70	64	.522	15½	John Morrill
1889	Second	83	45	.648	1	Jim Hart
1890	Fifth	76	51	.571	12	Frank Selee
1891	First	87	57	.630	+3½	Frank Selee
1892	First	52	22	.702	+2½	Frank Selee
	Second	50	26	.658	3	Frank Selee
1893	First	86	43	.667	+5	Frank Selee
1894	Third	83	49	.629	8	Frank Selee
1895	Fifth*	71	60	.542	16½	Frank Selee
1896	Fourth	74	57	.565	17	Frank Selee
1897	First	93	39	.705	+2	Frank Selee
1898	First	102	47	.685	+6	Frank Selee
1899	Second	95	57	.625	8	Frank Selee
1900	Fourth	66	72	.478	17	Frank Selee
1901	Fifth	69	69	.500	20½	Frank Selee
1902	Third	73	64	.533	29	Al Buckenberger
1903	Sixth	58	80	.420	32	Al Buckenberger
1904	Seventh	55	98	.359	51	Al Buckenberger
1905	Seventh	51	103	.331	54½	Fred Tenney
1906	Eighth	49	102	.325	66½	Fred Tenney
1907	Seventh	58	90	.392	47	Fred Tenney
1908	Sixth	63	91	.409	36	Joe Kelley
1909	Eighth	45	108	.294	65½	Frank Bowerman, Harry Smith
1910	Eighth	53	100	.346	50½	Fred Lake
1911	Eighth	44	107	.291	54	Fred Tenney
1912	Eighth	52	101	.340	52	Johnny Kling
1913	Fifth	69	82	.457	31½	George Stallings
1914	First	94	59	.614	+10½	George Stallings
1915	Second	83	69	.546	7	George Stallings
1916	Third	89	63	.586	4	George Stallings
1917	Sixth	72	81	.471	25½	George Stallings
1918	Seventh	53	71	.427	28½	George Stallings
1919	Sixth	57	82	.410	38½	George Stallings
1920	Seventh	62	90	.408	30	George Stallings

1921	Fourth	79	74	.516	15	Fred Mitchell
1922	Eighth	53	100	.346	39½	Fred Mitchell
1923	Seventh	54	100	.351	41½	Fred Mitchell
1924	Eighth	53	100	.346	40	Dave Bancroft
1925	Fifth	70	83	.458	25	Dave Bancroft
1926	Seventh	66	86	.434	22	Dave Bancroft
1927	Seventh	60	94	.390	34	Dave Bancroft
1928	Seventh	50	103	.327	44½	Jack Slattery, Rogers Hornsby
1929	Eighth	56	98	.364	43	Emil Fuchs, Rabbit Maranville, Johnny Evers
1930	Sixth	70	84	.455	22	Bill McKechnie
1931	Seventh	64	90	.416	37	Bill McKechnie
1932	Fifth	77	77	.500	13	Bill McKechnie
1933	Fourth	83	71	.539	9	Bill McKechnie
1934	Fourth	78	73	.517	16	Bill McKechnie
1935	Eighth	38	115	.248	61½	Bill McKechnie
1936	Sixth	71	83	.461	21	Bill McKechnie
1937	Fifth	79	73	.520	16	Bill McKechnie
1938	Fifth	77	75	.507	12	Casey Stengel
1939	Seventh	63	88	.417	32½	Casey Stengel
1940	Seventh	65	87	.428	34½	Casey Stengel
1941	Seventh	62	92	.403	38	Casey Stengel
1942	Seventh	59	89	.399	44	Casey Stengel
1943	Sixth	68	85	.444	36½	Casey Stengel
1944	Sixth	65	89	.422	40	Bob Coleman
1945	Sixth	67	85	.441	30	Bob Coleman, Del Bissonette
1946	Fourth	81	72	.529	15½	Billy Southworth
1947	Third	86	68	.558	8	Billy Southworth
1948	First	91	62	.595	+6½	Billy Southworth
1949	Fourth	75	79	.487	22	Billy Southworth
1950	Fourth	83	71	.539	8	Billy Southworth
1951	Fourth	76	78	.494	20½	Billy Southworth, Tommy Holmes
1952	Seventh	64	89	.418	32	Tommy Holmes, Charlie Grimm

*Tie

Postseason Play

WS	4–0 versus Philadelphia	1914
	2–4 versus Cleveland	1948

Boston Reds

Union Association, 1884	**BALLPARK:** UNION PARK
RECORD: 58–51 (.532)	**OTHER NAME:** RED STOCKINGS

Despite being the last Union Association club to be admitted to the league, the Reds were hardly an afterthought. Henry V. Lucas, the UA's founder and president, spent the months before the opening of the 1884 season crisscrossing the eastern half of the country seeking financial backing for a franchise he knew was necessary if the UA was to take on the National League in the latter's stronghold. Lucas finally found Boston backers in Frank E. Winslow, who became club president, and George Wright, the star shortstop of the Cincinnati Red Stockings of 1869–1870. Wright agreed to come aboard only after Lucas consented to use baseballs manufactured by Wright and Ditson, a sporting goods firm in which the former player was a partner.

With only about a month to recruit players before opening day, Winslow and Wright had to be content with a team that included primarily youngsters, only some of whom showed promise. One who did was Tim Murnane, who had been with Boston in the NL and was the opening day manager as well as the first baseman. Rookie Cannonball Crane, who later became a pitcher of some note, played right field and hit 12 homers. Another rookie, Tommy McCarthy, batted .215 as a part-time outfielder; he was the only future Hall of Famer to play in the UA. Other recruits came from various sources, including independent teams in New Hampshire and even Bates College in Maine.

The strength of the team was its pitching. Dupee Shaw jumped from the NL Detroit Wolverines in midseason and led the staff with a 21–15 record. Behind him were Walter Burke, 19–15 in his only major league season, and the aging Tommy Bond, 13–9 before he jumped to the American Association Indianapolis Blues.

The Reds ended up with a winning record and finished fourth, but they were 34 games behind the pennant-winning St. Louis Maroons. Fan interest was minimal, and the club had no effect on its NL Boston rivals, whose attendance increased from 138,000 in 1883 to 146,000 in 1884. The UA expelled the Reds for

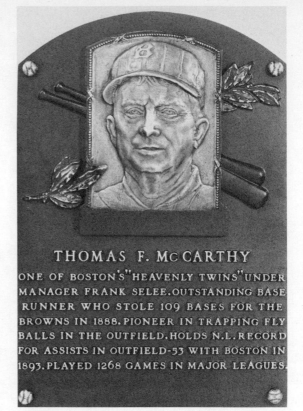

THOMAS F. McCARTHY
ONE OF BOSTON'S "HEAVENLY TWINS" UNDER MANAGER FRANK SELEE. OUTSTANDING BASE RUNNER WHO STOLE 109 BASES FOR THE BROWNS IN 1888. PIONEER IN TRAPPING FLY BALLS IN THE OUTFIELD. HOLDS N.L. RECORD FOR ASSISTS IN OUTFIELD-53 WITH BOSTON IN 1893. PLAYED 1268 GAMES IN MAJOR LEAGUES.

National Baseball Library, Cooperstown, NY

failure to attend a league meeting on December 18, but the expulsion was a mere gesture because the UA itself survived only until mid-January.

BOSTON REDS

Annual Standings and Managers:

Year	Position	W	L	Pct.	GB	Managers
1884	Fourth	58	51	.532	34	Tim Murnane, Tom Furniss, Jake Morse

Boston Reds

Players League, 1890	**BALLPARK:** CONGRESS STREET GROUNDS
RECORD: 81–48 (.628)	**OTHER NAME:** RED STOCKINGS

King Kelly, Boston's most popular player in the nineteenth century, was the heart and soul of the Players League Reds. He managed the team to the league's only pennant, hit .326, and played shortstop, catcher, and the outfield. More generally, Kelly's initial willingness to join the PL gave the new league credibility, and his subsequent unwillingness to accept an unprecedented $10,000 advance to return to the National League bolstered the circuit's sagging spirits.

The backers of the Reds, Charles A. Prince and Julian B. Hart, adopted the crosstown NL club's former name. They also adopted a good part of the NL team's roster. Aside from Kelly, the biggest catch was first baseman Dan Brouthers, who batted .330 and was an outspoken supporter of the Brotherhood and the PL. Left fielder Hardy Richardson (.326), second baseman Joe Quinn (.301), center fielder Tommy Brown (.276), third baseman Billy Nash (.266), and pitchers Charlie Radbourne (27–12) and Bill Daley (18–8) also made the move from the NL's South End Grounds to the PL's Congress Street field.

The offer to Kelly to return to the NL was made by Albert C. Spalding, president of the NL Chicago club and the mastermind of the NL's retaliation against the PL. Authorized by the other owners to lure one star player into breaking ranks, Spalding

chose Kelly for his $10,000 offer. Kelly asked for ninety minutes to think it over, took a long walk, then rejected the bid.

"I want the $10,000 bad enough," Kelly told Spalding, "but I've thought the matter over, and I can't go back on the boys. And neither would you." Spalding claimed later that he then shook Kelly's hand, congratulated him on his loyalty, and loaned him $500.

Neither Kelly's loyalty to the cause nor the winning of the only PL pennant proved very important once the PL backers sat down with the NL to hammer out a peace. In November, while the other PL backers were accepting buyouts, Prince asserted the league's strength and predicted that "the organization will remain essentially whole." His public stance was a ploy to achieve a private goal—shifting his team to the AA. NL Boston owner Arthur Soden initially resisted giving approval to an invasion of his territory, but, in the interests of ending the war with the PL, finally relented.

BOSTON REDS

Annual Standings and Manager

Year	Position	W	L	Pct.	GB	Manager
1890	First	81	48	.630	+ 3½	King Kelly

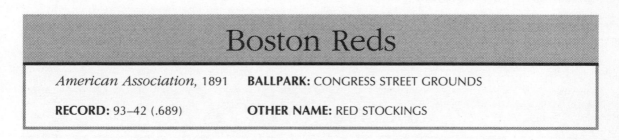

Boston Reds

American Association, 1891	**BALLPARK:** CONGRESS STREET GROUNDS
RECORD: 93–42 (.689)	**OTHER NAME:** RED STOCKINGS

The transfer of the Reds from the Players League to the American Association in January 1891 was a triumph both for Charles A. Prince, the franchise owner who gained the respectability of being part of an established league, and for the AA, which had long sought to place a club in Boston. At the same time, however, the humiliating membership conditions imposed by Arthur Soden, president of the Boston NL club—prohibition of the use of the name Boston in the club title and a fifty-cent admission fee—were bound to create trouble.

The trouble came even before the start of the season. Harry Stovey, who had played right field for the PL Reds, officially belonged to the AA Philadelphia Athletics, the team for which he had played in

1889. But the Athletics of 1891, under entirely different ownership, neglected to include Stovey (and second baseman Lou Bierbauer) on their reserve list on the understanding that the outfielder was to be reassigned to Prince's Reds. But when Stovey, dissatisfied with Prince's offer, accepted a better one from Soden, the war was on.

In terms of personnel, Prince was well equipped for the battle. He had been allowed to keep first baseman Dan Brouthers (whose .350 average led the AA in 1891) and center fielder Tommy Brown (.321) from his PL roster; and he added right fielder Hugh Duffy (.336) and third baseman Duke Farrell (.302) to his roster. The team scored more than a thousand runs, and, with George Haddock (34–11) and Charlie

Buffinton (29–9) on the mound, coasted to the AA pennant by 8½ games.

Soden's NL team also won its pennant, and the two Boston clubs were about evenly matched in a ferocious competition for patronage until August, when Prince pulled off a coup that promised to tip the balance in his favor. In that month, the AA Cincinnati Porkers folded, and King Kelly, their manager, was allowed to choose his next team. His selection of the Reds brought the fans out to Congress Street Grounds to see their idol.

Kelly's signing coincided with the formation of NL and AA committees to negotiate a peace. By the time the two groups met in Washington on August 25th, Kelly, after only four games with the Reds, had succumbed to an offer by Soden that included a huge contract and a trip to Europe. The fans, loyal only to Kelly, shifted their allegiance once again. Then, when the Reds' board of directors abandoned the fifty-cent admission price in retaliation, Prince resigned and was succeeded by Julian B. Hart. Cutting the price of tickets in half proved fruitless: Prince's team kept winning, but so did Soden's, and it had the King.

The AA conferees in Washington demanded Kelly's return and withdrew from the talks when the NL delegation stalled, asserting that it lacked the authority to send Kelly back. The AA's reaction was to fire its president, Louis Kramer, on the grounds that he had known about the pirating of Kelly before it happened—this despite a wire from Hart to the conference that the loss of Kelly should not influence the peace talks, because the player's skills had eroded too far for him to remain in the Reds' plans.

At the end of the season, Hart challenged Soden to a championship series, but NL President Nick Young refused to allow the two teams to meet, and the AA declared the Reds world champions. It turned out to be a hollow declaration: The Reds were a financial failure, and the AA magnates realized that, if the circuit's best team could not show a profit, the rest of the league was living on borrowed time. The result was the amalgamation of the two leagues. Prince, who still had considerable money invested in the AA club, negotiated a $30,000 buyout from Soden. Prince later demanded $50,000, but compromised at $37,000 when he realized that he might end up with nothing because there were enough AA votes without his to dissolve the association and permit four of its franchises to join the NL.

BOSTON REDS

Annual Standings and Manager

Year	Position	W	L	Pct.	GB	Manager
1891	First	93	42	.689	+ 8½	Art Irwin

Boston Red Sox

American League, 1901–Present	**BALLPARKS:** HUNTINGTON AVENUE BASEBALL GROUNDS (1910–1911) FENWAY PARK (1912–Present) BRAVES FIELD (1915–1916 WORLD SERIES; 1929–1932)
RECORD: 7241–6961 (.510)	
	OTHER NAMES: AMERICANS, PURITANS, PILGRIMS, SOMERSETS

The Red Sox have worked hard at their image as a major league Sisyphus forever pushing their burden up the steep incline, only to near the crest and topple back down again. They have had to work hard at it because much of the record contradicts such an image. At the beginning of the century, for instance, Boston was the most successful team in baseball, winning six flags and emerging victorious in every one of its World Series. In the middle of the century, the Brooklyn Dodgers suffered more late-season and postseason agonies than the Red Sox have yet to experience. In recent decades, the club has not only lost season-making games that it appeared to have won, but also won eleventh-hour showdowns that it appeared to have lost. The only undeniable fact through all the gilded Red Sox pathos is that the franchise has not nailed down a world championship since 1918. But then again, it is the organization that peddled away Tris Speaker and Babe Ruth, came ever so near to neglecting Ted Williams, spurned opportunities to sign Jackie Robinson and Willie Mays, and allowed Carlton Fisk to walk away in the prime of his career. Even Sisyphus used two hands.

Boston was a late addition to Ban Johnson's American League in 1901. Originally, Johnson had planned on staying out of the city in the hope of minimizing National League hostility toward his rival circuit; only when the NL rejected any notion of cooperation between the leagues and floated the idea of a new, obeisant American Association to hamper the AL, did he substitute Boston for Buffalo on his roster of clubs. Financing for the team came from coal magnate Charles Somers, who also owned the Cleveland franchise and who supplied emergency funds for several other clubs in the fledgling league. While the NL had a number of owners who epitomized syndicate ownership by holding interests in more than one team, Somers was something of a

On September 28, 1960, Ted Williams connects during his final plate appearance in the major leagues for the last of his 521 home runs. The blow, off Baltimore's Jack Fisher, was later commemorated in a noted essay by John Updike. *AP/Wide World Photos*

syndicate unto himself, and was arguably more responsible than anyone for keeping the AL in business during its formative years.

Until 1907, the new team was known by a variety of nicknames, starting with the Americans to distinguish it from the Beaneaters in the NL. Johnson's incessant speeches about the moral high road that he demanded his teams take encouraged the use of Puritans for awhile, but that soon became interchangeable with Pilgrims. Together with various local landmarks of the same name, Somers's own monicker inspired the briefly used Somersets. Finally, in 1907, after the Beaneaters had dropped the last dab of red from their uniform socks, the AL franchise moved in to grab the name Red Sox.

The establishment of the AL squad in Boston proved to be disastrous for the Beaneaters, who had been the toast of baseball only a couple of years before. To begin with, Jimmy Collins, the Beaneater third baseman and future Hall of Famer, defected to the Americans as player–manager and took along three teammates—pitcher Ted Lewis and outfielders Buck Freeman and Chick Stahl. The jumps helped gut the Beaneaters overnight, offering the instant promise that the new team would be the best game in town. The promise became even more of a reality when Collins talked righthander Cy Young, the most successful hurler in baseball history, and his battery-mate, Lou Criger, into leaving the Cardinals.

The club debuted in Baltimore on April 26th, going down to the Orioles, 10–6. The second game was even worse, with Baltimore bashing Young by a count of 17–6. After several more beatings in Philadelphia, Washington, and (again) Baltimore, the club finally took up residence at the hastily constructed Huntington Avenue Baseball Grounds on May 8, defeating the Athletics by a 12–4 score. As gratifying as the victory was, the franchise was cheered even more by an overflow crowd of some 11,000—9,000 more than attended a Beaneaters' home contest against defending NL champion Brooklyn the same day. It was the start of a year-long story, with Collins's squad outdrawing the NLers by almost two to one; indeed, twenty years would have to pass before the eventually named Braves attracted more fans than the AL club. Making the choice easier for Bostonians was the insurgents' second-place finish (the Beaneaters came in fifth), only four games behind the White Sox. The stars of the campaign were Young, who led the league in both victories (33) and ERA (1.62), and Freeman, who averaged .345 with 114 RBIs. The same duo excelled the following season, when Young

again led AL moundsmen with 32 wins and Freeman produced a league-high 121 RBIs.

After the 1902 season, the AL and NL opened the negotiations that ended with a January 1903 peace agreement. As part of the settlement, righthander Vic Willis, who had been set to follow Collins and the others from one Boston franchise to the other, had to stay put in the NL. The truce also persuaded Somers that he was no longer needed on the scene; after looking around futilely for a local buyer, he sold his controlling interest in the club to Henry Killilea, a Milwaukee attorney. Killilea delegated much of his authority to business manager Joe Smart. Being an outsider without the novelty that had made Somers acceptable, the new owner was not particularly popular in Boston, and even less so when his aide Smart showed himself to be the kind of corner-cutting operator that had helped sour fans on Arthur Soden as the Braves' owner. The atmosphere around the team was chilled further by a series of player feuds, usually triggered by the division of the clubhouse into Irish Catholic and non-Irish Catholic cliques. When Smart criticized Collins for not controlling the players, he became the first of several front office people whom the pilot barred from the locker room.

Despite the tensions, in 1903 the Pilgrims rolled to their first pennant by the comfortable margin of 14½ games over the Athletics. Young paced the league for the third time in a row with 28 wins, while Bill Dinneen and Long Tom Hughes also reached the magic circle of 20 wins. Although his average slipped below .300, lefty-swinging Freeman repeated as the best offensive performer, hitting more homers (13) and knocking in more runs (104) than anyone else in the AL. In mid-September, when it was clear that Boston and Pittsburgh were not going to be detoured from championships, Killilea and Pirates' owner Barney Dreyfuss agreed to meeting in a best-of-nine postseason competition. The accord for the first World Series was, however, easier said than done. While Johnson and other AL officials generally acknowledged the initiative as a final legitimization of the league, there was some disturbance among NL owners for precisely the same reason. Killilea also had problems with his own players, whose contracts officially ran out on September 30th and who initially balked at facing the Pirates unless they were given the entire proceeds from the games. While Dreyfuss (who had the Pirates under contract until mid-October) watched and considered dropping the idea, Killilea entered into tense talks with the players, eventually winning their consent to a further two weeks' salary plus a bonus.

The first World Series got off to an inauspicious start when Young revealed that he had been approached by gamblers to drop his starts in return for $20,000. In a climate laden with the first on-field rivalry between the leagues, Johnson sought to capitalize on the disclosure by praising Young's honesty and suggesting that an NL pitcher might not have been so quick to reject the bribe. Between the lines, Boston had little to be smug about at first, losing three of the first four games to Pittsburgh ace Deacon Phillippe. But then the club rallied behind an equal effort by Dinneen, ending up as the first World Series champions by winning five out of eight. Dinneen's three wins included two shutouts. The triumph was almost overshadowed, however, by revelations that Smart had made some pocket money by scalping tickets.

With the prospect of the league's most important triumph going sour, Johnson insisted that Killilea get rid of Smart. When that didn't stem the unfavorable publicity, the AL president then brokered the sale of the franchise to General Charles Henry Taylor, publisher and editor of the Boston *Globe*. From the beginning, Taylor made no bones about the fact that he was interested in the team only as an outlet for his son John I. Taylor, a wastrel who had failed at the newspaper business and at everything else he had considered amusing himself with.

Johnson continued to pull the strings behind the scenes, with the league's interests rather than Boston's his first priority. Shortly after engineering the sale of the club, be pressured Taylor into shipping Hughes to the Highlanders in exchange for Jesse Tannehill. Although the deal worked out to the enormous benefit of the Pilgrims, it had been inspired by Johnson's determination to strengthen the New York franchise. The same thinking was behind the AL president's pressure on Taylor to send the New Yorkers outfielder Patsy Dougherty in exchange for infielder Bob Unglaub in June 1904. The loss of Dougherty, who had batted .342 and .331 in his two seasons, infuriated Boston fans; it turned out to be only the first in a long series of atrocious swaps with New York.

Even without Dougherty, the Pilgrims captured the flag again in 1904. The race was a struggle against the Highlanders that went right down to the final day of the season before it was decided on a wild pitch by New York ace Jack Chesbro. Young, Dinneen, and Tannehill all won more than twenty games, and Norwood Gibson contributed another

seventeen victories. In a generally punchless year, Freeman's 84 RBIs not only paced the club, but was the second highest total in the league. Equally important, the team stayed healthy all year; the roster was in fact so stable that only eighteen players wore Boston uniforms during the season, establishing a major league record. The Pilgrims didn't get the opportunity to repeat their World Series success: Mainly because he feared having to face his city rivals the Highlanders, Giants' owner John T. Brush had ruled out any appearance by his club in postseason competition. When even the Giants' players protested the decision, the issue was settled once and for all by their manager John McGraw, who sought to defend Brush by blasting all AL teams as unworthy of meeting his NL pennant winners. If nothing else, the resultant controversy gave Boston a moral victory.

Over the next seven years, the team needed every victory that it could get, ending up in the second division four times and dropping to the cellar altogether in 1906. The team owner was the cause of most of the problems the team had. Taylor had poor relationships with the players, with Collins, with subsequent managers, and he was unable to deal effectively with other clubs. After Collins had discovered the newspaper heir in the clubhouse in the middle of the 1905 season chastising some members of the team, he banned him from the premises; Taylor's response was to sit near a passageway that led from the field to the dressing room and to offer his comments as the players passed by. By the beginning of the 1906 season, with the Pilgrims launched on a twenty-game losing streak, Collins lashed out at the owner for undermining his efforts and announced that he was giving up his managerial title to concentrate on playing. Johnson restored peace for a few weeks, but then Collins quit a second time, and for good. Outfielder Stahl was named to take over the club for the final three weeks.

Boston righthander Joe Harris shares the AL record for most innings pitched in a game—24. On September 1, 1906, both Harris and Jack Coombs of Philadelphia went all the way in an overtime contest that was finally won by the Athletics, 4–1. Harris didn't have too much luck the rest of the year, either, going 2–21 on the season and concluding his three-year career with a mark of 3–30.

The crisis only deepened. After being signed to manage in 1907, Stahl had a change of mind during spring training; negotiations over his salary followed, and he returned to the job. Soon after the agreement, however, he committed suicide by drinking carbolic acid. Players who discovered him near death reported that Stahl's last words were "Boys, I couldn't help it; it drove me to it," but there was little consensus on what the *it* was. Taylor next went to pitcher Young, but he begged off after seven games, saying that he couldn't both pitch and manage. Drafted after Young was University of Illinois Athletic Director George Huff, who lasted for little more than a week before deciding that the campus was better for his health than ostensible charges who referred to him sarcastically as "The Professor." Unglaub, the infielder who had cost Dougherty, took over for twenty-eight games, losing twenty of them, before he in turn was replaced by Deacon McGuire. By the time the revolving door had stopped at the end of the season, the five managers had produced a seventh-place finish that was remarkable at least insofar as it represented a distinct improvement over the previous year.

When he wasn't busy criticizing his players or trying to convince his managers to stay, Taylor was concluding one unpopular player exchange after another. Even the Dougherty–Unglaub transaction faded into insignificance after future batting champion George Stone was swapped to the Browns for the aging Jesse Burkett, Collins was peddled to the Athletics for .239-hitting third baseman Jack Knight, Dinneen was exported to the Browns for winless Beany Jacobsen, and future NL home-run leader Gavvy Cravath was sold to the White Sox. Causing the biggest storm of all was the February 1909 trading of Young to the Indians for pitchers Jack Ryan and Charlie Chech and an estimated $12,500. Although never confirmed, reports at the time asserted that Taylor surrendered Young in the midst of an all-night drinking session with Cleveland owner Somers.

There were compensations. With the veterans being traded and sold away, McGuire and successors Fred Lake and Patsy Donovan were forced to go with younger players such as outfielders Tris Speaker and Harry Hooper, both eventual Hall of Famers. Lake was at the helm in 1909 when the club put an uncharacteristic stress on base-stealing and finished a surprising third. Eight players had at least fifteen steals, and four of them more than twenty-five. Leading the pack was center fielder Speaker who in his first year as a regular batted .309 to go along with his thirty-five thefts. The lefty swinger would have six more seasons batting better than .300 for the Red Sox before being traded to the Indians in 1916. The lefty-hitting Hooper, Speaker's equal as a defensive wizard, probably has the least impressive numbers of any outfielder in Cooperstown (only five seasons of hitting .300, never more than eleven homers or forty steals), but his contemporaries viewed him as one of the game's best all-around players.

The club's unexpected showing in 1909 raised some expectation that there would be another World Series in Boston in 1910, but it didn't come until 1912 because of continuing turmoil in the executive suite, in the dugout, and on the field. Even the emergence of Speaker as a franchise star had as much to do with the obtuseness of teams like the Giants and Pirates as it did with Taylor's perspicacity; in fact, the outfielder had offered his free agent services to both NL teams after Taylor had hesitated over a new contract for 1908 and had wound up playing for a minor league squad in Arkansas before being repurchased by Boston. Despite his managerial success in 1909, Lake was fired after the season because of salary demands and criticism of Taylor's interference with the club. When Donovan began grousing about the same problem, Johnson tried to persuade General Taylor that his son was in need of another hobby. Largely because Taylor had invested heavily in the construction of Fenway Park and wanted to see the project through to its completion, nothing happened until December 1911, when Johnson announced that Taylor had sold a half-interest in the club to Jimmy McAleer, a veteran manager and important recruiter for the AL in its infant years, and Bob McRoy, the AL president's own chief assistant for many years. Although the younger Taylor stayed around as a vice-president and his father maintained fifty percent control of the franchise and total control of the Fenway Park property, McAleer and McRoy assumed effective command.

The new regime's first order of business was replacing Donovan with Jake Stahl, brother of the tragic Chick Stahl. He ended up presiding over the single greatest year in franchise history as the Red Sox cruised to the pennant with 105 victories. The performances of the year were turned in by Speaker and righthander Joe Wood: While the outfielder batted .383 with 98 RBIs and an AL-leading 10 homers, the hurler swept to a record of 34–5 (1.91 ERA) that included sixteen consecutive victories at one point. Hugh Bedient and Buck O'Brien also won 20 each.

The World Series against the Giants was billed as Boston's revenge for McGraw's 1904 snub, and through the first five games, the Red Sox appeared well on their way to vindicating most betting odds by taking a 3–1 lead (the second game ended as an eleven-inning tie). But then McAleer insisted that Stahl give the ball to O'Brien for the clincher, and the rookie was routed in the first inning of Game Six. Back in Fenway for the seventh game, McRoy instigated a public relations mess when he sold seats that had been occupied in previous home games by a local booster group calling itself the Royal Rooters. Enraged that their cheering section had been taken away from them, the Royal Rooters marched around the field to protest the eviction, refusing to let the contest start until police were called in. Wood, who had been Stahl's original choice for the clincher, then went out to the mound and got battered like O'Brien in the first inning. Between the denunciations of the franchise by the Royal Rooters and a sinking feeling that the team was about to blow the Series, little more than 17,000 Bostonians showed up for the finale, which pitted Bedient against New York great Christy Mathewson. At the end of seven innings, the clubs were locked in a 1–1 tie. Stahl then called on Wood, who retired the Giants in the eighth and ninth innings but surrendered what seemed to be a fatal run in the top of the 10th. In the bottom of the frame, however, New York outfielder Fred Snodgrass muffed an easy fly ball, first baseman Fred Merkle and catcher Chief Meyers let an even easier foul ball by Speaker drop untouched, and Speaker and third baseman Larry Gardner cashed in on the woeful fielding by driving in the two runs that gave Boston the world championship. Despite the scare he had given everyone with his performance in the seventh game, Wood ended up with three of the Red Sox wins.

Injuries, especially a broken hand suffered by Wood, sent the club reeling back to fourth the following season, but that was only one of its problems. The Boston clubhouse was riven by another feud with religious overtones (referred to by writers of the day as pitting Masons against members of the Knights of Columbus); the primary antagonists were Speaker and Wood, on one side, and second baseman Heinie Wagner and catcher Bill Carrigan, on the other. For Johnson, however, Wagner and Carrigan were being abetted by McAleer, and the AL president inspired some press reports that Stahl was about to replace the team boss. The infuriated McAleer retaliated by bouncing Stahl in favor of Carrigan—a

move that only reinforced Johnson's belief that the club president was the main source of all the trouble and that led Speaker and Wood to move gingerly around the clubhouse. Johnson waited until the end of the 1913 season, then, with McAleer off on a world tour with Charles Comiskey and McGraw, once again exercised his authority in franchise matters to complete the sale of the McAleer–McRoy holdings to Boston and New York real estate man Joseph Lannin for some $200,000. Although the Taylor family continued to hold on to its share of the franchise and Fenway Park, Lannin assumed operational control.

With McAleer out of the picture and a modus vivendi established with Speaker, Carrigan remained on the job in 1914, returning the club to second place. The story of the year was southpaw Dutch Leonard, who set the all-time ERA record for pitchers with at least 200 innings by posting a mark of 1.01. For Lannin, Leonard's performance and the club's resurgence were offset by the rise of the Federal League and the new owner's need to offer hefty raises to Speaker and other regulars to prevent them from defecting to the rival circuit. The real estate tycoon also took the battle to the Federals by bankrolling three teams in the minor International League, which found some of its markets invaded by the FL. In purchasing the IL franchise in Providence outright, Lannin gave impetus to a long association with the Rhode Island club as an incubator for Red Sox talent. Equally important, his financial assistance to the Baltimore organization of Jack Dunn put him in a position to acquire two of the minor league's chief pitching talents, Babe Ruth and Ernie Shore. Even at that, however, Boston was third on line for the two hurlers. Cincinnati, which had the first shot, was not impressed and turned them down. The Athletics, whom Dunn had sought out for a deal, said no only because Connie Mack didn't have enough cash on hand. Along with catcher Ben Egan, Ruth and Shore were shipped to Boston for $8,000. Although his power feats would later overwhelm his pitching, lefty Ruth turned in three straight seasons of 18, 23, and 24 victories, and in 1916 led the AL in both ERA (1.75) and shutouts (9). Righty Shore had his best year in 1915, when he won 19 and had an ERA of 1.64. The pitchers cemented their association in baseball lore on June 23, 1917, when Ruth walked the lead-off batter in a game with Washington, got ejected for protesting, and was replaced by Shore, who, after the Senators' baserunner was thrown out trying to steal second, retired the next twenty-six hitters for what was credited as a perfect game.

With Ruth and Shore combining for 37 wins, Rube Foster racking up another 19, and Wood pacing the league in ERA (1.49), Boston finished ahead of Detroit by 2½ games in 1915 to take the flag. The pitching strength was needed, because only Speaker broke .300 with a .322 mark and Lewis's 76 RBIs were the club high. The World Series was more of the same, with Foster, Shore, and Leonard holding the Phillies to a combined batting average of .182 and taking the championship in five games. In return for having lent the Braves Fenway Park for the 1914 World Series, Boston played its home games at the recently opened Braves Field, where record crowds of 40,000 showed up for the third and fourth games.

The World Series had barely ended when the Federal League's two-year operation also shut down, prompting Lannin to cut back on the salaries that he had raised in 1914. While all of the affected players grumbled, Speaker made it clear that he would not wear a Boston uniform again until he received at least what he had been making during the FL's existence. The tug-of-war between the owner and the outfielder continued throughout spring training and right up to opening day, when Lannin suddenly announced that he had traded Speaker to Cleveland for pitcher Sam Jones, infielder Fred Thomas, and $55,000. Although the swap was portrayed as strictly the outcome of Speaker's holdout against Lannin, Johnson lurked once again in the background as an influential figure, talking the Boston owner into dealing only with the Indians, where a long-time crony, James Dunn, had just taken over as owner and needed a gate attraction. The fact that Speaker had never been offered to other teams angered the Yankees, who were in the market for an outfielder and who had begun to view Johnson as a franchise enemy.

Despite the absence of Speaker and an offense that was even frailer than it had been the year before, the club rode its superior pitching to another pennant in 1916. Ruth took over as the ace of the staff with 23 wins, while Leonard and Carl Mays each chipped in with 18. Only third baseman Gardner hit over .300, and his 62 RBIs was also a team high. In the World Series against Brooklyn, the Red Sox again emerged on top in five games, with Shore producing two wins and Gardner belting two home runs and driving in six runs. The postseason meeting was most noteworthy for the Game Two duel between Ruth and the Dodgers' Sherry Smith, which went 14 innings before a pinch-hit single by Del Gainor settled matters in favor of Boston.

Earlier in the 1916 season, Lannin had bought out the Taylor interests in the club, including Fenway Park. No sooner had the Series against the Dodgers ended, however, than he disclosed that he was looking to sell the team, having decided that he had made about as much money as he was ever going to make from it. In December, New York theatrical producers Harry Frazee and Hugh Ward bought the Red Sox from Lannin for an estimated $1 million. For reasons never fully clarified, Johnson approved the deal, even though Frazee and Ward paid for the purchase mostly with promissory notes, the owners gambling that they would be able to meet their commitments through 1917 profits. Suspicions that Johnson might have shared the small amount of real cash transferred to Lannin were never confirmed.

The first move by the new owners was to try to persuade Carrigan to give up his plans to retire from baseball for the banking business and return as the manager; when that didn't work, they tapped second baseman Jack Barry for the post. In what would become typical of his bamboozling of the local press, Frazee spent much of his first off-season as a baseball executive hinting coyly that he was about to spend a lot of money for a big name player; although speculation pointed to either Ty Cobb or Walter Johnson as the target of the purchase, the only name of any weight involved in a Boston deal prior to the 1917 season was Wood, who was shipped off to Cleveland to rejoin Speaker. Frazee's assurances that Barry would deliver another pennant didn't materialize after the club went into a September nosedive following a five-month battle with the White Sox. Still worse, the outbreak of World War I cast a pall over attendance and over the team president's confidence that he could make good on his outstanding paper to Lannin. By the end of the season, Frazee had to hide behind no-comment replies to reports that he had once again put the club on the market for $1.5 million to be able to pay off Lannin.

Although Barry was criticized for running a

The scoring rules in 1918 deprived Babe Ruth of a 715th home run. In the bottom of the ninth inning in a tied game with Cleveland on July 8th, Ruth clouted a drive into the right field seats. Because a runner who had been on first scored the winning run, the Bambino was credited only with the bases necessary (a triple) to push the tie-breaker across the plate.

first-place team into second place, the second base-man was on his way back to the helm for a second season when he was drafted by the Navy. In quick order, Lewis, Shore, Gainor, pitcher Herb Pennock, and several others were also drafted, giving the Red Sox a decidedly skeletal look on the eve of the 1918 season. But mainly because of the pitching of Mays (21 wins) and both the hurling (13 wins) and hitting (a league-leading 11 home runs with 66 RBIs and a team-leading .300) of Ruth, Boston surprised even its most ardent fans by taking the flag in the war-shortened year under manager Ed Barrow. In the World Series against the Cubs, Ruth threw a 1–0 shutout in the opening game, then went 7⅓ more scoreless frames in the fourth game; the two efforts extended the lefthander's scoreless innings in World Series play to 29⅔, a big league mark that wasn't surpassed until 1961 and that he would always claim gave him more satisfaction than his subsequent slug-ging feats. In addition to Ruth's two masterful per-formances, Mays contributed a pair of 2–1 victories to give Boston its fifth world championship in as many tries. The Series was almost suspended prior to the fifth game when players from both teams ganged up to demand more money. The threatened strike was averted only when an inebriated Johnson talked Red Sox player representative Hooper into taking the field in the name of patriotism because of the ongoing war. The meeting with Chicago was the last World Series in which neither club hit a home run (Boston hit only .186 as a team) and the last to be won by a club from Massachusetts.

After World War I, the Red Sox found them-selves with serious roster problems because of the return of conscripts; like other clubs, Boston decided that the best solution to the overcrowding was to deal away its higher-salaried veterans, providing more playing time for the prospects who had slipped into the lineup in 1917 and 1918. In the particular case of Frazee, the fire sales were also a remedy for the money that he was losing steadily in his New York theatrical ventures. The first to go were Shore and Lewis, in a December 1918 swap with the Yan-kees that netted pitchers Slim Caldwell and Slim Love, catcher Roxy Walters, outfielder Frank Gilhooley, and $15,000. A month later, Frazee put the Yankees on hold while he whipped through five more deals with other clubs, mainly getting cash in return; the biggest name to go was Leonard, who brought $7,500 from the Tigers. Though he didn't need any incentive for further transactions, the Bos-ton owner got it in midseason, when Mays stormed off the mound during a game, accusing his team-

mates of deliberately sabotaging him and declaring that he would never play for the Red Sox again. After a series of futile efforts to talk the righthander back to the club, Frazee sold him to the Yankees for $40,000, with two minor league pitchers thrown in to dress up the exchange. And then the brouhaha started.

Furious that Frazee had not suspended Mays for his one-man strike and that the Yankees had also turned a blind eye to what he viewed as primarily a disciplinary problem, Johnson nullified the deal and ordered league umpires not to allow Mays to appear on the field in a New York uniform. The Yankees retaliated by getting an injunction against Johnson's order, enabling Mays to take the mound but also dividing the league into two acrimonious factions. Supporting the New York position were Frazee and Chicago owner Charles Comiskey, who had his own agenda of bitterness against Johnson; among other things, the three clubs recalled the AL president's maneuvers in whisking Speaker off to Cleveland in 1916, charging that he had been planning a similar transaction of Mays to the Indians. While the two sides (Johnson was backed by the other five teams) traded lawsuits throughout the 1919 season, the AL office published two sets of statistics, one of them excluding the games in which Mays appeared. Be-cause the pitcher's performance (a record of 9–3) rep-resented the difference between a third- and fourth-place finish for New York, Johnson also froze the World Series shares paid out to runner-up teams. The turning point of the dispute proved to be an alliance forged by the Red Sox, Yankees, and White Sox with the eight NL teams to prevent the re-election of Garry Herrmann, a Johnson crony, as chairman of the ruling National Commission. With his authority on the body threatened, the AL chief agreed to recognize the Boston–New York deal and to award the Yankees a third-place share of the World Series proceeds; in return, the Yankees with-drew their lawsuits and there was no further block-ing of Herrmann's re-election. (Only a year later, the same 11 AL and NL teams would take on Johnson again, making moves to set up an enlarged National League if Johnson didn't agree to the election of Kenesaw Mountain Landis as the first baseball com-missioner.)

Back in Fenway Park, meanwhile, Ruth spent the 1919 season rewriting the game's offensive his-tory, leading the league with an unprecedented 29 home runs and also setting the pace with 114 RBIs. Thus it came as all the more of a shock when Frazee, in December, sold the outfielder–pitcher to New

York for $100,000 plus a $350,000 loan. Frazee's immediate defense of the deal was that not even Ruth's hitting had prevented Boston from finishing sixth and that he could use the money to rebuild the team. What he didn't say was that the cash went largely for keeping the musical *No! No! Nanette* on the boards; the only part of the funds that stayed within the franchise went for the purchase of outfielder Tim Hendryx, who had one good year, and benchwarmer Gene Bailey, who had none.

With Ruth gone, the Red Sox had lost their last brake before the abyss. After two fifth-place finishes in 1920 and 1921, Boston finished last eight out the following nine years, went fifteen consecutive seasons without reaching .500, and did not even sneak back to fourth place until 1934. The absolute nadir was reached in 1932, when the club compiled a record of 43–111 (.279), ending the season 64 games behind the Yankees. If there was a key supporting player to the New York pillaging of the franchise, it was Barrow, who resigned as manager after the 1920 campaign and then joined the Yankees to go on the receiving end of all the deals that he had hated while in Fenway Park. Only a few weeks after his defection, he exploited Frazee's shortage of cash to help engineer a trade that sent future Hall of Famer Waite Hoyt and All Star catcher Wally Schang to New York. Other exchanges in the early part of the decade in which Barrow figured prominently stripped the Red Sox of pitchers Jones and Joe Bush and shortstop Everett Scott in December 1920, of third baseman Joe Dugan and outfielder Elmer Smith in July 1922, and of outfielder Harvey Hendrick and pitchers George Pipgras and Pennock in January 1923. The Dugan trade caused an uproar when the Browns, then battling the Yankees for the pennant, accused the Red Sox of being New York's silent partners in the race. In good part because of the St. Louis protest, the two leagues introduced the June 15th trading deadline that remained in effect for more than sixty years.

As disastrous as Frazee's dealings with New York were, there was as much of a rank odor in the owner's acknowledgement that, in the wake of the Ruth deal and the accompanying loan, he "consulted" regularly with Yankees' officials on all important matters affecting the Boston franchise. This became obvious in October 1922, when Ruppert hit the roof because he hadn't been "consulted" about a Frazee swap with Detroit that had brought the Red Sox outfielder Babe Herman, infielder Danny Clark, and pitchers Carl Holling and Howard Ehmke along with $25,000 in return for second baseman Del Pratt

and hurler Rip Collins. Informed that the Yankees had also been interested in Ehmke, Frazee's abject response was that he had already cashed the $25,000 check, so he couldn't do the Yankees' bidding by canceling the trade.

Appalled spectators to the New York–Boston relationship included Johnson, who had lost much of his authority to Landis, but who never ceased working behind the scenes to get rid of Frazee. He received some help from the Boston owner himself in 1922, when, again anxious to cash a check, Frazee sold outfielder Frank O'Rourke to Toronto of the International League without first securing waivers from the Phillies. Philadelphia's protest not only forced Frazee to erase the sale to Toronto, but also cost him the friendly sentiments of the NL clubs in general. With Comiskey still reeling from the Black Sox scandal and the Yankees too compromised in their affairs with Boston, Johnson tightened the screws on the friendless Frazee in the summer of 1923, finally succeeding in brokering a sale of the franchise to a group headed by Bob Quinn, then the business manager of the Browns and regarded as close to the AL president. Quinn's chief source of the $1.5 million for paying off Frazee was Palmer Winslow, an Indiana millionaire in the glassworks business.

Although there were no tears in Boston for Frazee's disappearance from the scene, Quinn's arrival hardly signalled any dramatic improvement on the field; on the contrary, the team slipped only more deeply into the second-division coma that would enfold it for another decade. The main difference was that, whereas Frazee had become a symbol for pompous failure and self-interest, Quinn embodied little but haplessness. Quinn didn't have a Babe Ruth to trade away, so he had to be content with giving away future batting champion Buddy Myer to the Senators for two pitchers who never saw a .500 record and three other warm bodies. It didn't help Quinn's reign, either, that his chief backer Winslow died not long after financing the purchase of the club and that he himself took a bath in the 1929 stock market crash, making him even more dependent on player-for-cash transactions in the Frazee tradition.

One of the other consequences of Barrow's resignation after the 1920 season was a march of managers through the decade that included future Hall of Famers Hugh Duffy and Frank Chance, Quinn's St. Louis skipper Lee Fohl, and, for a second time, Carrigan. None of them did anything with clubs that ranked at the bottom of the standings not only in the pennant race, but also in most pitching and offensive categories. The Wall Street crash that cost Quinn heavily in 1929 also took its toll on Carrigan's bank in Maine, and he returned home for good at the end of the decade to see what could be saved. His replacement was Wagner, the former second baseman who had been at the center of the clubhouse troubles with Speaker and Wood in the early teens. The best performances of the 1920s came from second baseman Pratt in 1921 (.324 with 100 RBIs), righty Jones in the same year (23 wins), and Ehmke in 1923 (20 victories). On the other hand, six Boston pitchers chalked up the most losses in the league in one season or another of the decade.

The 1930s did not start off any better. In one of the more excusable transactions completed with the Yankees, Quinn peddled hurler Red Ruffing to the Bronx in exchange for outfielder Cedric Durst and $50,000. The deal was made after the righthander had led the AL in losses two years in a row (and with very high ERAs), had gotten off to an 0–3 start in 1930, and had put together an overall record of 39–96 in a Boston uniform. Unfortunately for Red Sox fans, the Yankees were proven right once again in their estimation of Boston talent because Ruffing went 234–129 over the rest of his career and wound up being elected to the Hall of Fame in 1967. In 1931, Danny MacFayden made the mistake of winning 16 games for the team, so it was hardly news that the Yankees came calling for him with another $50,000 check early in the 1932 season. The managerial musical chairs also continued in the early 1930s. Wagner lasted only a single season, and was replaced by Shano Collins. Collins steered the team to ten more wins in 1931, but it went to his head: After making predictions about a first-division finish the following season, he began ticking away on the bench through an 11–46 start, then finally exploded about everything from the team's woeful performance to the sale of MacFayden, and resigned. His successor was Marty McManus, who liked telling people that Quinn had offered him the job while he was in church and that he instantly had another reason to feel humbled.

There were a couple of bright spots at the beginning of the 1930s. In 1931, outfielder Earl Webb set the all-time record for doubles in a season, clouting 67 two-baggers; the extra-base hits crowned an all-around impressive offensive year in which the lefty swinger also batted .333, drove home 103 runs, and scored another 96. A year later, the same Webb was traded to the Tigers for first baseman Dale Al-

In 1933, Boston trainer Doc Woods left Dale Alexander under a heat lamp in the clubhouse, then went out to watch the game for a few minutes. He got so caught up in a Red Sox rally that he forgot about Alexander until the first baseman suffered third degree burns and, later, gangrene poisoning. The trainer's forgetfulness effectively ended the first baseman's career.

exander and outfielder Roy Johnson. Although neither of the acquisitions was a defensive wizard, Alexander ended up as the first player to win a batting championship after being traded in the middle of a season, and Johnson turned in several solid hitting years. Another acquisition of the period was catcher Rick Ferrell, who, though he played for several clubs in an eighteen-year Hall of Fame career, put up his best offensive numbers as a member of the Red Sox.

Ferrell came to Boston in May 1933 in the first trade completed by Tom Yawkey, who had taken over the franchise from the wilting Quinn. The beneficiary of a large family trust and a nephew of a former owner of the Detroit Tigers, the 30-year-old Yawkey got the team for little more than the $350,000 that Quinn had run up in debts. (At the end, the outgoing owner even had to borrow off his insurance policy to meet the payroll.) Three days after obtaining Ferrell, he sent the Yankees $100,000 in exchange for former Red Sox hurler Pipgras and third baseman Billy Werber. Though Pipgras was near the end of the line, nobody in New England missed the significance of Boston paying New York for players rather than the other way around; better yet, the deal produced more than symbolism when Werber led the AL in steals two years in a row and gave the club some solid infield defense and clutch hitting.

Over the next four years, Yawkey worked zealously at removing the stench that had hung over the franchise since Frazee's administration. One early project was overhauling Fenway Park; with a nudge from a grandstand fire during the 1933 season, he spent about $750,000 replacing the facility's wooden structure with a steel and concrete frame. To take over daily baseball operations, he hired Hall of Fame second baseman Eddie Collins as general manager. It was Collins who recommended the Ferrell and Werber transactions and who waved Yawkey's bankroll

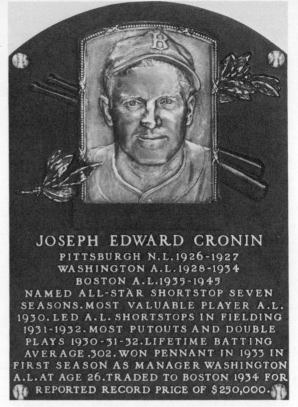

JOSEPH EDWARD CRONIN
PITTSBURGH N.L. 1926-1927
WASHINGTON A.L. 1928-1934
BOSTON A.L. 1935-1945
NAMED ALL-STAR SHORTSTOP SEVEN
SEASONS. MOST VALUABLE PLAYER A.L.
1930. LED A.L. SHORTSTOPS IN FIELDING
1931-1932. MOST PUTOUTS AND DOUBLE
PLAYS 1930-31-32. LIFETIME BATTING
AVERAGE .302. WON PENNANT IN 1933 IN
FIRST SEASON AS MANAGER WASHINGTON
A.L. AT AGE 26. TRADED TO BOSTON 1934 FOR
REPORTED RECORD PRICE OF $250,000.

National Baseball Library, Cooperstown, NY

at other clubs incessantly during the mid-1930s as a clinching argument for a deal. Among the noted names made available to the Red Sox by Yawkey's cash were pitchers Lefty Grove, Rube Walberg, Wes Ferrell (Rick's brother), and Flint Rhem; outfielders Bing Miller, Heinie Manush, and Doc Cramer; shortstop Lyn Lary; and second baseman Max Bishop. Two deals stood out. After allowing McManus to finish the 1933 season and then bringing in Bucky Harris as manager the following year, Yawkey stunned the AL by paying Clark Griffith $225,000 (plus Lary) for Washington shortstop-pilot Joe Cronin. The Hall of Famer would continue to play the same dual role for Boston until after World War II. Following the 1935 season, Yawkey and Collins made one of their periodic raids on Mack's Athletics, coming away with slugger Jimmie Foxx in return for $150,000 and two minor leaguers. In Foxx's first four years with Boston, he hit between 35 and 50 home runs and drove in between 105 and 175 runs; in 1938, the righthanded slugger won his third MVP award for leading the AL in batting (.349), RBIs (175), and walks (119), while also bashing 50 homers, 33 doubles, and scoring 139 runs.

The good news about all of the Yawkey–Collins moves was the return of fans to Fenway Park after many years of alienation reinforced by the Depression. By the middle of the decade, the Red Sox were back to outdrawing the Braves on a regular basis. The bad news was that not even sparkling years such as that enjoyed by Foxx in 1938 brought the club a pennant. The closest Boston came in the 1930s were two second-place finishes in 1938 and 1939, both of them at some distance from the Yankees. Foxx aside, the best individual efforts in the period came from the southpaw Grove, who won four ERA titles, and Ferrell, who turned in 25 victories one year and 20 in another. Ferrell was also the most volatile member of the club, given to storming off the mound in the middle of a game if he didn't like an umpiring call or

the defense of one of his teammates; when Collins traded both Ferrells and outfielder Mel Almada to Washington in June 1937 for pitcher Bobo Newsom and outfielder Ben Chapman, the local press dubbed it the Harmony Deal because of its anticipated impact on the Boston clubhouse.

Although there were no championship flags raised over Fenway in the late 1930s, fans got their first look at two of the most important players in franchise history. In 1938, Bobby Doerr took over second base, a position he would hold until back problems forced his retirement after the 1951 season. One of the best offensive middle infielders to play the game, Doerr had six seasons of more than 100

RBIs and twelve straight years of double figures in homers. In 1944, the Hall of Famer won the MVP trophy for a career-high batting average of .325. Even Doerr was eclipsed, however, by the arrival in 1939 of Ted Williams, considered by many as the equal of Ruth as baseball's greatest power hitter. Yawkey and Collins preferred spending money on proven big leaguers rather than developing a farm system, so Williams came to the attention of Boston only after both the Cardinals and Yankees had approached him in his senior year in high school with contract offers. The outfielder's mother had insisted on a $1,000 signing bonus, however, so St. Louis and New York backed off. Even when Williams began putting up impressive numbers for San Diego, Yawkey refused to give in to the bonus demand until persuaded otherwise by Collins's top aide, former AL umpire Billy Evans.

Williams's statistics in nineteen years for the Red Sox approached the uncanny. A lifetime .344 hitter and .634 slugger, he took six batting titles, including one in 1941, when his .406 marked the last time that a major leaguer reached the .400 level. He led the AL in home runs four times, in RBIs four times, in runs scored six times, in doubles twice, in walks eight times, and in annual slugging average nine times. With all his long-ball hitting, the lefty swinger topped the fifty mark in strikeouts only twice—in his first two years in the league; with all his imposing numbers, he still missed almost six full seasons at the peak of his career to World War II, the Korean conflict, and injuries. In 1941, while Joe DiMaggio was batting .406 during his 56-game hitting streak, Williams batted .412 over the same span. In 1957, he established the record for most consecutive times on base by putting together four homers, two singles, nine walks, and one hit by pitch in sixteen successive plate appearances. In 1958, he became the oldest player to win a batting title (forty years and twenty-eight days). With the numbers went the drama. With his average standing at .3995 and eligible to be rounded off to .400 on the final day of the 1941 season, Williams insisted on playing both games of a doubleheader, collecting six hits and gaining six points. In the 1941 All Star Game, he hit a home run with two out in the ninth inning to provide the winning margin. In the 1946 All Star contest, he ran up on Rip Sewell's eephus pitch and deposited it over the wall. In his final at bat in 1960, he tagged his 29th home run of the season, providing a fitting climax to John Updike's noted essay on the farewell performance.

The frequently truculent Williams also provided

critics with constant ammunition. After being sent down to the minors after an initial trial in the 1930s, he announced boldly to some veterans standing around that he would be back soon enough and make more money than all of them combined. When writers got on his case for some fielding lapses, he completed a tour of the bases on a home run by spitting up at the Fenway Park pressbox. Struck out in a key situation in one game, he fired his bat at the screen behind home plate; following another failure in a clutch appearance, he went back out on the field and punted his glove against the wall.

With Williams keying the offense, the Red Sox returned to regular contending status in the 1940s (except for a couple of World War II years when the club had Doerr and little else). Moving into center field at the beginning of the decade was DiMaggio's brother Dom, who, though he lacked his sibling's power, was perhaps his equal defensively and one of the best leadoff hitters (.298) in the league for most of his eleven-year career. Cronin began reducing his playing time, but not soon enough to head off one of the team's worst deals—the 1940 sale of Peewee Reese to the Dodgers. The manager's eventual infield replacement was Johnny Pesky, a lefty swinger who batted over .300 in six of his first seven seasons and who teamed ably with Doerr on double plays. Boston's best pitcher over the first half of the 1940s was Tex Hughson, who led the league with 22 wins in 1942 and in winning percentage with an 18–5 record two years later. In 1945, Boo Ferriss also arrived on the scene, making his major league debut with consecutive shutouts and going on to 21 wins.

With the end of the war, the Red Sox returned in full force, winning 105 games for the second best season in franchise history and making a farce of the 1946 pennant race. Williams led the offense with a .342 average, 38 homers, and 123 RBIs, and got plenty of help from Doerr (116 RBIs) and first baseman Rudy York (119 RBIs), who had been acquired from the Tigers in an offseason deal. On the mound, Ferriss showed that he was no flash in the pan by going 25–6, Hughson won 20, and Mickey Harris contributed another 17. Making it even sweeter for Yawkey, a record 1.4 million fans watched the romp—almost double the 1945 attendance and without the benefit of night ball (not introduced to Fenway Park until 1947).

The World Series against St. Louis, widely forecast as another walk in the park, turned out to be anything but. Through the first six games, the teams went back and forth, with lefty Harry Brecheen winning twice for the Cardinals and Ferriss turning in a shutout in Game Three. In the finale, St. Louis took a 3–1 edge on Ferriss in the fifth inning, only to see Boston come back in the visiting eighth to tie the score. Then, in the bottom of the frame, Harry Walker drove a double into the left-center alley to send Enos Slaughter on a tear around the bases from first; taking the relay from center fielder Leon Culberson, Pesky hesitated a vital second or two, and by the time he got the ball home, Slaughter had scored what turned out to be the world championship run. Local historians have usually pointed to Pesky's hesitation as the first note of the Boston Postseason Blues.

Despite a Triple Crown for Williams in 1947, the team didn't get close to another postseason appointment because of arm injuries suffered by all three of its 1946 mound stars—Ferriss, Hughson, and Harris. Following the season, the club monopolized the headlines of sports pages for much of November, first with the announcement that Cronin was moving upstairs to replace Collins as general manager, then with the startling selection of long-time Yankees' manager Joe McCarthy as the new skipper, and, finally, with two significant trades with the Browns. In the first deal, the Red Sox shipped off six second-stringers and the considerable sum of $310,000 to obtain slugging shortstop Vern Stephens and southpaw Jack Kramer. A few hours later, Yawkey wrote another check for $65,000 and sent it along with shortstop Sam Dente and a couple of minor leaguers to St. Louis for righthander Ellis Kinder and infielder Billy Hitchcock. While Stephens added 29 home runs and 137 RBIs to the club's offense in 1948, Kramer and Kinder combined for 28 wins. On top of big years from Williams (.369 for another batting title and 127 RBIs) and Doerr (27 homers and 111 RBIs) and a successful debut by southpaw Mel Parnell (15 victories), the contributions of the newcomers kept Boston in a tingling duel with Cleveland, New York, and Philadelphia for most of the season, until the campaign ended with the Red Sox and Indians tied for the lead. Facing a winner-take-all playoff game, McCarthy elected to give the ball to journeyman Denny Galehouse instead of to either Kinder or Parnell, both of them well rested, and watched the veteran get blown away by Lou Boudreau's pennant winners, 8–3. The question of Why Galehouse? was added to that of What Was Pesky Thinking? in the Doomsday Book of Boston baseball.

The next year proved to be equally excruciating. In a year-long struggle with the Yankees, the Red Sox overcame a slow start to win 28 of 35 between late July and late August, then ran off an eleven-game winning streak in September. What it all came down to were the season's final two games at Yankee Stadium, with Boston holding a one-game lead and needing to win only once for the flag. In the opener, New York evened things up with a 5–4 victory over Parnell. Then, with everything once again on the line, Kinder and Yankees' righthander Vic Raschi went through seven innings with New York leading on the strength of a first-inning run. McCarthy opted to pinch-hit for his starter in the top of the eighth, prompting a weary Parnell and an all-but-finished Hughson to come in for the bottom of the frame during a four-run New York outburst. When Boston staged a three-run rally in the ninth and even got the tying run to the plate before finally going down, the question of Why a Pinch-Hitter for Kinder? was added to the litany of remorse.

The new decade brought none of the anguish of the 1946 World Series, the 1948 playoff, or the final weekend of the 1949 season for the simple reason that the team didn't get as close to winning again; in fact, it would not be until 1967 that Boston would get a new taste of postseason competition. The reasons for the franchise's decline were many. One was Williams, who broke his elbow during the 1950 All Star Game, then got drafted into military service for the Korean hostilities, then just got old. A second was the failure to protect the slugger in the lineup with enough bats that would make it risky to keep walking him. A third was the perennial lack of pitching behind one or two good starters and an almost equally frequent need to find a stopper around whom it would be possible to anchor the rest of the staff. But most of all, the Red Sox of the 1950s were conspicuous for their resistance to signing black players.

Although the local press usually went out of its way to exonerate Yawkey of racism, the fact remained that he at least tolerated the whites-only policies of Collins, Cronin, and organization men like Specs Torporcer, and showed none of the energy on the race question that he displayed on most other matters. By and large, he left it up to Collins to do the dirty work, such as in 1945, when the Boston city council was pressuring the club to offer tryouts to blacks. For the general manager, it was "beyond (his) understanding how anyone can insinuate or believe that all ballplayers, regardless of race, color, or creed, have not been treated in the American way as far as having an equal opportunity to play for the Red Sox." Shortly after that pronouncement, Collins supervised a tryout for three black players, among whom was Jackie Robinson; the for-show-only trial produced the verdict that none of the players had big league potential. In 1949, it was Cronin's turn to ignore the enthusiastic recommendation of scout George Digby that the club sign Birmingham outfielder Willie Mays, available at the time on a first-come-first-serve basis for only $5,000. Later on, a couple of blacks were given minor league pacts, where organization reports about their progress were replete with such descriptions as "Earl Wilson—a nice colored boy." It was not until 1959, a mere three years before Robinson's induction into the Hall of Fame, that Boston became the last team to integrate by including infielder Pumpsie Green on the roster. Over the years that followed, the race question would continue to hang over the franchise to the point that numerous black free agent stars refused even to consider putting on a Boston uniform.

McCarthy, who had come in for more fan and press criticism in his short stay with the Red Sox than he had put up with in sixteen years with the Yankees, walked away from the team near the middle of the 1950 season. His successors for the rest of the decade—Steve O'Neill, old Cleveland nemesis Boudreau, Pinky Higgins, and Billy Jurges—generally kept the team above .500, but also ensconced in the middle of the standings. The least popular of all the pilots was probably Boudreau, who, in addition to having the capital crime of the 1948 playoff on his record, committed another felony as soon as he took over in 1952 in announcing that no one on the club, including Williams, was an untouchable if the right deal came along.

The decade had its share of tragedies and shining moments. In 1952, outfielder Jimmy Piersall, who had animated the stands with his aggressiveness on the basepaths and brilliant defense, suffered a nervous breakdown from the ills that he subsequently described in the best-selling *Fear Strikes Out.* In 1954, Parnell broke his pitching arm, just about ending his career except for one moment on July 14, 1956, when he rediscovered his abilities to throw a no-hitter against the White Sox. In 1956, the club was sent reeling by the death of 25-year-old first baseman Harry Agganis; considered one of the organization's hottest prospects and a box-office draw for the city's substantial Greek community, Agganis was felled by a pulmonary embolism while recovering from an attack of pneumonia. Among the brighter notes was Billy Goodman's batting title in 1950; the only twentieth-century player to capture the hitting crown while serving in a utility role, the lefty-swinging Goodman played one game at shortstop, five at second base, twenty-one at first, twenty-seven at third,

and forty-five in the outfield. The best trade pickup of the period was right fielder Jackie Jensen, who was swiped from Washington in December 1953 in exchange for pitcher Mickey McDermott and outfielder Tom Umphlett. With the Red Sox, the righty slugger led the AL in RBIs three times, had at least 100 RBIs five times, and hit between 20 and 35 homers six times. Jensen's power numbers and great arm netted him the MVP award in 1958. He retired after the 1959 campaign because of fear of flying, attempted a comeback a couple of years later, then walked away for good.

If the 1950s were uninspired, the next decade started out as a reminder of the woeful Frazee–Quinn seasons, with the club enduring another eight-year stretch of less than .500 ball. Following the retirement of Jensen in 1959 and Williams in 1960, there was even an uncharacteristic lack of power in the regular lineup until Higgins, promoted from manager to general manager for the 1963 season, decided to forget about Dick Stuart's atrocious defense and acquired the first baseman known as Doctor Strangeglove in a trade with the Pirates. Stuart did what he was good at in two seasons, hitting a total of 75 homers and driving in 232 runs; he also did what he was bad at, leading the league in errors for his position both years. Another light early in the 1960s was lefthand-hitting Pete Runnels, who won the batting crown in both 1960 and 1962. The most accomplished pitcher was righthander Bill Monbouquette, who won 20 in 1963 for a seventh-place club.

The most important development for the franchise in the period was the maturing of two sluggers who would become synonymous with Boston fortunes and misfortunes for many years to come. In 1961, lefty-swinging Carl Yastrzemski took over Williams's left field post to initiate a twenty-three-year Hall of Fame career spent exclusively at Fenway. A rare case of one Cooperstown resident directly succeeding another at a defensive position, Yastrzemski led the league in every significant offensive category except triples and steals in one year or another. His single greatest season was 1967, when he won the Triple Crown (and the MVP award) with 44 homers, 121 RBIs, and a .326 mark. That year he also paced the league with 112 runs scored and cracked 31 doubles. The batting title was one of three that he collected on his way to 3,419 hits overall, while his lifetime 646 doubles, 1,844 RBIs, and 1,845 bases on balls all ranked him within the top ten when he retired. While more of a free swinger than Yastrzemski, Tony Conigliaro raised equal Hall of Fame expectations when he joined the team in 1964 and clouted 24 home runs. The following season, the 20-year-old outfielder became the youngest player ever to lead the AL in homers when he belted 32 round-trippers. After a similarly productive campaign in 1966, Conigliaro seemed well on his way to bettering all his numbers in 1967, when he was beaned by Jack Hamilton of the Angels in an August contest. The tragic accident caused the righthand-hitting slugger to remain on the sidelines until 1969. After seeming to overcome serious vision and balance problems, he returned to wallop 20 homers in 1969, then muscled up for his biggest year of all in 1970 by belting 36 homers and driving in 116 runs. But the power display was deceptive, and nobody knew it better than the Boston front office, which, convinced that Conigliaro's eye problems were only going to get worse, traded him off to the unsuspecting Angels for reliever Ken Tatum after the campaign. In California, the outfielder's physical ills and an ensuing psychological crisis caused him to announce his retirement in the middle of the season.

The promise of Yastrzemski and Conigliaro was not enough for Yawkey after a ninth-place finish in 1965, so he ousted Higgins as general manager, replacing him with business manager Dick O'Connell. For the next ten years, O'Connell would be the chief architect of Boston's return to the front ranks of the league. It didn't happen overnight; in fact, O'Connell did little more in 1966 than to swap second-line players while the team again finished next to last. No sooner had the season ended, however, than he announced the signing of Dick Williams as manager. The announcement did not exactly stop people in their tracks on Boston Common since Williams's only managerial experience of note had been with Toronto of the International League and the Red Sox had already passed through Jurges, Higgins, Pesky, Billy Herman, and Runnels in the decade; in the words of one local wit, the only difference between Williams and his immediate predecessors was that "they at least were all good players, while he wasn't." But in 1967, in what became known as the year of the Impossible Dream, Williams negotiated the club through as torrid a pennant race as the league had ever seen to wind up a mere game ahead of both Detroit and Minnesota and only three ahead of Chicago. The victory marked the only time in the twentieth century that a team took a flag by picking up nine places in the standings from one year to the next.

The ingredients for the pennant win started with the manager, whose taskmaster personality startled players who had grown accustomed to the casual approach of Pesky, Herman, and Runnels. When he wasn't putting players in their place, Williams was persuading them that they were the best talents in the league, otherwise he wouldn't have taken the job to begin with. The most conspicuous believers on the squad were Yastrzemski, who tore through AL pitching with his Triple Crown, and Jim Lonborg, whose 22 wins were a league high. In their first World Series since Pesky had watched Slaughter careen around the bases, the Red Sox once again found themselves up against the Cardinals—and once again went down in seven games as St. Louis righthander Bob Gibson won three times.

The biggest carryover from the pennant winning year to 1968 was the Fenway Park attendance, which had led the AL in 1967 for the first time in fifty-two years with 1.7 million and rose still further to just short of the two-million level. Yastrzemski also repeated to some degree with another batting title, although his .301 mark in the Year of the Pitcher was a record low for a hitting champion and his power numbers fell off considerably. But Yaz's relative decline was nothing compared to that of other members of the team, especially Lonborg, who fell to six victories because of a knee injury. The collapse brought out Williams's penchant for criticizing individuals in acidic terms that made for good reading, but unnerved the team. At that, the manager might have gotten away with his tactic if, early the following season, he hadn't included Yastrzemski on his hit list after fining the star for not running out a grounder. Yawkey, who had come to consider himself a second father to Yaz, got involved, and it wasn't long before the club was divided between factions favoring the owner and the outfielder and those behind Williams. The tensions came to a predictable end two weeks before the conclusion of the 1969 season, when Williams was fired. Despite his previous popularity, Yastrzemski heard it from Fenway fans for some time afterward because of the widespread perception that he had been responsible for ousting the field brains behind the Impossible Dream.

In general, the 1970s were the club's best decade since the teens. But while never finishing below third in the Eastern Division, the team could claim only one title, encouraging the image of a squad of selfish underachievers who couldn't wait to grab their salaries and leave the ballpark in twenty-five separate cabs. In 1972, the team was riven by the players' strike that delayed the opening of the season. Among those skeptical of the walkout were Yastrzemski, outfielder Reggie Smith, and shortstop Rico Petrocelli,

Fenway Park. *National Baseball Library, Cooperstown, NY*

who dwelt on Yawkey's personal generosity toward them and who came under accusations of elitism from teammates. Yawkey himself conceded that he had been outflanked by the new militancy of players, and, especially after the failed impact of the 1973 owners' lockout during spring training, began talking about getting rid of the franchise. Although he backed down whenever he was approached by an interested buyer, he projected an uncertainty that was soon felt throughout the organization.

The owner had another reason to hate the thirteen-day strike that cancelled the beginning of the 1972 season: Because of an ensuing unbalanced schedule, the Red Sox played one game less than the Tigers, and ended up 1/2 game behind Detroit when the final curtain fell on the season. For consolation, there was the emergence during the year of two of the club's most important players for the rest of the decade—pitcher Luis Tiant and catcher Carlton Fisk. Picked up for practically nothing after being released by Minnesota, Tiant led the league in 1972 with his 1.91 ERA, then went on to win 20 games in three seasons and 18 in a fourth. The righty's vast assortment of pitches and pre-delivery swivel, which left him almost facing second base in his release motion, made him one of the team's most popular gate attractions. Fisk, the best receiver in the history of the franchise, took over the regular job with a .293 average, 22 homers, and a league-leading 9 triples. Through the rest of the 1970s, he would vie with

Thurman Munson of New York for the title of premier catcher in the league, not only delivering with power at the plate and showing uncommon defensive agility, but assuming a dictatorial command of the pitching staff.

O'Connell kept other bodies coming and going. After Eddie Kasko had brought the club to within a half-game of the division title in 1972, he stumbled over a series of clubhouse feuds and key injuries the following season, and was replaced as manager by ex-catcher Darrell Johnson. On the trade front, the club made more good deals than bad ones, but this fact was obscured by another exchange with the Yankees—reliever Sparky Lyle for outfielder-infielder Danny Cater—that awoke memories of the transactions completed by Frazee and Quinn with New York. The best O'Connell move of the period was an October 1973 swap of Smith and Tatum to the Cardinals for righthander Rick Wise and outfielder Bernie Carbo. For one thing, the trade removed Smith, whose increasing petulance had provoked a number of clubhouse scenes, most notably with free-spirited and union-minded lefthander Bill Lee. More than that, Wise slipped into a regular spot in the rotation, while Carbo became the league's best fourth outfielder. Unfortunately for the dour Johnson and his successor Don Zimmer, Carbo also joined with Lee, the veteran Ferguson Jenkins, and a couple of other players in a cutup clique that called itself the Loyal Order of the Buffalo Heads—a name proposed by Jenkins because of his view that Zimmer was a buffalo and the buffalo was the dumbest animal on earth. For a couple of years, the mockeries of the Buffalo Heads, aimed at the manager's office, the front office, and baseball in general, were a lightning rod for trouble. Buffalo though he might have been in Jenkins's eyes, Zimmer found it even harder to live down Lee's description of him as a gerbil. The pilot exacted his revenge by insisting that O'Connell get rid of every one of his taunters.

Although Zimmer ultimately emerged as the bad-guy manager of the decade, he was not rated any worse by the players than his predecessor Johnson. A strict by-the-book strategist who barely covered his distaste for having to deal with the media, Johnson became an early target of anonymous criticisms that some local sportswriters seemed only too eager to record. At one point in the 1975 season, both Lee and Fisk were sources of charges that the manager was "incoherent" in his dealings with the team. In the heat of the pennant race that year, second baseman Doug Griffin told newsmen that Boston would win the division title despite having Johnson around. Yastrzemski's opinion of the manager emerged at the end of the season, when, with the division already wrapped up, he asked for permission to fly to Florida for a one-day business trip, was told no, then went anyway. During the clubhouse celebrations after the clinching of the pennant, Johnson avoided the team altogether, sitting in his private office and drinking beer with Oakland outfielder Joe Rudi, a hunting partner.

That the Red Sox had anything to celebrate in 1975 was largely due to the splashy arrival in the AL of outfielders Fred Lynn and Jim Rice. The lefty-swinging Lynn became the only major leaguer to win both Rookie of the Year and MVP awards in the same year for his .331 average, 21 home runs, and 105 RBIs. For his part, the righty-hitting Rice contributed a .309 mark with 22 home runs and 102 RBIs. In the LCS, Boston made quick work of Oakland in a three-game sweep, with Tiant pitching a three-hitter in one contest and Yastrzemski sparkling in the field as well as at bat. The one sour note of the series, which became even more pronounced in the World Series, was the absence of Rice, who had broken his arm in a late season game against the Tigers.

The World Series against Cincinnati's Big Red Machine offered some of the most memorable moments of the postseason competition between the leagues. The duel opened with Tiant tossing a five-hit shutout, then Cincinnati coming back on two ninth-inning runs against Lee and reliever Dick Drago to

win the second contest by a 3–2 count. A festival of home runs (six) in Game Three kept the clubs knotted until Joe Morgan singled in the winner for the Reds in the 11th inning. Tiant starred again in Game Four with another complete-game victory, but Tony Perez erased that in Game Five with a pair of home runs. In a riotous sixth meeting at Fenway, the Reds held a 6–3 lead into the eighth inning, when Carbo came off the bench to even matters with a three-run pinch-homer. For the next three frames, the bullpens exchanged blanks (with the help of a game-saving catch in the 11th inning by Boston right fielder Dwight Evans), setting the stage for Fisk and a shot over the Green Monster in the 12th inning that was assisted into baseball lore by the catcher's frantic waving for the ball to remain fair as it twisted out toward the foul line. Boston fans barely had time to digest what many called the most thrilling Series game ever played, when the teams took the field for the finale. For five innings, Lee held a 3–0 lead, then surrendered two runs in the sixth and another in the seventh. Still, Boston had the homefield edge and its ace reliever Jim Willoughby on the mound, when Johnson suddenly added to the Doomsday Book. With two out and nobody on in the home eighth, the manager chose to hit for Willoughby, leaving the ninth inning in the hands of the inexperienced Jim Burton. Morgan promptly singled in the run that gave Cincinnati the world championship and contributed the question Why a Pinch-Hitter for Willoughby? to Boston's rueful litany.

Nineteen seventy-six was a mess. To start off with, Fisk, Lynn, and shortstop Rick Burleson all dithered on the field after O'Connell refused to give in to their contract demands. With free agent winds blowing around the sport as a result of the Messersmith–McNally ruling, the tension between the players and the front office made Boston a center of the coming storm. Then, even as he was refusing to accede to his own players, O'Connell announced in June that he had bought outfielder Rudi and reliever Rollie Fingers from Charlie Finley's A's for $1 million each. The deal, which was soon nullified by Commissioner Bowie Kuhn "in the best interests of baseball," had the immediate effect of turning Boston players against the front office with the predictable criticism that, if the franchise had money to pay for Rudi and Fingers, why didn't it have it to pay the three local heroes? More than that, however, disclosure of the Boston–Oakland agreement enraged other AL owners because it suggested a monetary worth players eligible for free agency could put on their own services. As a representative of the old guard,

Minnesota's Calvin Griffith even singled out the Red Sox, rather than the Braves of Ted Turner or the Yankees of George Steinbrenner, as the franchise most responsible for abetting salary inflation.

In the event, O'Connell did sign Fisk, Lynn, and Burleson, but only after exhausting months during which scouting director Haywood Sullivan undercut some of his authority by leaking particulars of the negotiations to a local radio show and in an organizational confusion brought on by the death of Yawkey in July. Never as close to Jean Yawkey as he had been to her late husband, O'Connell spent most of his free time away from the contract negotiations trying to put together a syndicate to buy the team. In November 1976, he fulfilled all of the worst nightmares of owners like Griffith by signing reliever Bill Campbell as the first reentry draft free agent; Campbell, who had made $23,000 for the Twins in 1976, signed a four-year pact valued at $1 million. Another beneficiary of the agreement was Sullivan, who used the money paid to Campbell and that agreed to in the contracts with Fisk, Lynn, and Burleson as convincing arguments to Jean Yawkey that the general manager should be allowed to spend only what she personally approved. Yawkey's order to that effect made it clear that Sullivan had replaced O'Connell as the hierarchy's top star—a fact borne out during the rival bidding for the team.

There were several suitors for the franchise, but the finalists turned out to be A-T-O, the parent company of Rawlings Sporting Goods, and a syndicate that was fronted by Sullivan and Buddy LeRoux, a former trainer for the Red Sox who had in the meantime hustled his way through various profitable real estate deals. Despite the fact that the Sullivan–LeRoux offer was for some $15.5 million, almost all of it in paper, while A-T-O's tender was $18.5 million in cash and hard securities, Yawkey threw some of her own money into the lower bid and then, in September 1977, announced that this was the one she was accepting. A-T-O immediately went to court to challenge the propriety of an executor who doubled as a purchaser, but was defeated by the vague language in Yawkey's will, which instructed his wife only to sell the franchise "to the best advantage." No sooner did that ruling come down than Yawkey took over as president, LeRoux as vice-president, and Sullivan as general manager in place of O'Connell.

The AL was much harder to convince than the courts. Noting the serious undercapitalization of the new ownership, league owners warned Sullivan not even to attempt to seek endorsement for the sale until he had obtained more solid financing. For its part, the Players Association went on the offensive when it discovered that the State Street Bank and Trust had financed the Sullivan–LeRoux purchase on condition of severe restrictions on free agent offers, player salaries, and farm system investments. Despite all these storm signals, Sullivan and LeRoux submitted their bid for league approval at the end of the year, and were voted down decisively. It required another six months before the pair raised enough capital by selling limited partnerships and getting Yawkey to increase her commitment to $5.5 million, to win the backing of the other owners.

Prior to being forced out, O'Connell replaced Johnson as manager with Zimmer. Whatever his relations with Lee, Jenkins, and the other members of the Loyal Order of the Buffalo Heads, Zimmer steered the club to its most successful back-to-back years since the Carrigan era. In 1976, his major force was Tiant, who won 21 games. In 1977, free agent Campbell silenced a lot of the criticism about his contract by winning 13 games and saving 31 others. But even Campbell was eclipsed by a power explosion that featured a league-leading 39 homers from Rice, 33 from first baseman George Scott, 30 from third baseman Butch Hobson, 28 from Yastrzemski, and 26 from Fisk; Rice, Hobson, Yaz, and Fisk also all had 100 or more RBIs. Unfortunately, the 1977 season also revealed Zimmer's limitations as a handler of pitchers, with Jenkins, Wise, and Lee all jerked in and out of the rotation because of their outspokenness and Campbell worn to a frazzle through overuse. As would be the case for the next couple of years, Zimmer also found himself talking to a wall whenever he pressed Sullivan for more pitching help; overwhelmed by his multiple duties in the new era of free agency, the general manager offered little response other than to promote untested rookies from Pawtucket.

With the ownership question finally settled a few weeks into the 1978 season, the club gave some indications that it would be able to concentrate on baseball by getting out of the starting gate fast and, by mid-July, running up a lead as big as 14½ games over the Yankees. Contributing to the fast break were off-season acquisitions Dennis Eckersley (who would lead the rotation with 20 wins), Mike Torrez (who would win 16), and second baseman Jerry Remy (who gave the team speed at the top of the order). For his part, Rice was embarked on another banner year that would add up to the AL high in home runs (46) and RBIs (139). Even through the winning, however, Zimmer continued having trouble with Lee and other pitchers, who not only questioned his mound smarts, but warned that he and Sullivan had cut off their noses to spite their faces in preseason deals that had relieved the club of Jenkins, Carbo, and Willoughby. When the team went into a tailspin in the second half of the season, at one point losing 14 of 17 games to allow New York back into the race, the clubhouse atmosphere went from tense to overtly hostile. The last ingredient for what loomed as one of the worst collapses in baseball history was added when Hobson, who had been playing for most of the year with floating chips in his elbow, asked Zimmer to bench him for the good of the team; the third baseman, often cited by the manager as the essence of the team player, had become so pathetic defensively that he was rarely able to throw the ball to first on the fly, in the process ringing up a league-leading 43 errors. With Scott also sidelined by injuries, the Red Sox appeared to suffer a coup de grace in a four-game September sweep by the Yankees at Fenway; in the series, dubbed the Boston Massacre by locals, the visitors outscored the home team by a count of 42–9.

But the club wasn't through. Although the Yankees got ahead by 3½ games at one point, Boston forged back to win eight in a row and secure a tie at the end of the regular season. With everything on the line in a one-game playoff, Torrez took a 2–0 lead into the seventh inning, when New York shortstop Bucky Dent lifted a fly ball into the screen above the Green Monster for a three-run home run. Reliever Bob Stanley yielded two more runs, while his Bronx counterpart Goose Gossage choked off Red Sox rallies in the final two frames. As though the defeat had not been excruciating enough, Zimmer heard it from fans all winter that one of the late-inning rallies might have turned out differently if he had not been in such a hurry to unload Carbo, leaving his bench nearly empty when he needed a pinch-hitter against Gossage. Neither Zimmer nor Sullivan needed any reminders of Lee's warnings, and it was hardly news when the southpaw was peddled to Montreal in the offseason. What did shock Boston players, on the other hand, was Sullivan's refusal to re-sign free agent Tiant. Told that the Cuban righthander had gone off to the Yankees, Yastrzemski spoke for most of the team when he accused the front office of "tearing out our heart and soul."

Zimmer himself survived to within a few games of the end of the 1980 season, despite blistering criticism not only from local call-in shows and the grandstand, but even from the team announcer, former outfielder Ken Harrelson. That he lasted as long as he did was partly due to Sullivan's own siege mentality against the growing criticisms of LeRoux, viewed as the main inspiration for Harrelson's attacks on the manager (and, by extension, the general manager). When Sullivan finally pulled the plug on Zimmer in September 1980, replacing him with Ralph Houk, he insisted that the pilot could not be held completely accountable for the team's failure to get back into postseason play. He was right: It had been Sullivan himself who had rejected Zimmer's constant urgings for backup players like shortstop Buddy Harrelson and veteran pitchers like Tommy John and Charlie Hough on the grounds that the franchise had cheaper options in Pawtucket.

On the field, the club closed out the decade with little to show but a couple of individual honors. On September 12, 1979, Yaz cracked his 3,000th hit, becoming the first American Leaguer to attain that plateau and also collect 400 home runs. Lynn and Rice continued their offensive displays, with the former winning the batting title with a .333 mark, both of them clouting 39 homers, and Rice winning an RBI duel with his teammate 130–122.

The 1980–81 offseason brought more big trouble, when the contracts that Burleson, Lynn, and Fisk had signed in 1976 all clicked into a walk year. Deciding that Burleson's asking price for another pact was too steep, Sullivan packaged the shortstop and the fragile Hobson to the Angels in return for third baseman Carney Lansford, outfielder Rick Miller, and reliever Mark Clear. A second deal that would have sent Lynn to the Dodgers for first baseman Mike Marshall and pitchers Steve Howe and Joe Beckwith came undone at the eleventh hour when the outfielder told Los Angeles that he would only sign a one-year contract. For some weeks, Sullivan negotiated with both Lynn and Fisk for a new pact. But then, whether because he simply forgot or received some tactical legal advice that was disastrous, the Red Sox executive was late in mailing out the existing contracts to the two stars, making them free agents. During a hearing before a grievance board, Lynn agreed to go to the Angels in a deal for Rudi and pitchers Frank Tanana and Jim Dorsey. Fisk's free agent status was upheld and, after he rejected a Sullivan offer, he signed with the White Sox. Thanks to their ineptitude in the signing saga, the team's general partners earned the names Dumwood Sullivan and Shoddy LeRoux from one Boston sportswriter.

Although hailed as a pitcher's manager, Houk had only one hurler (bullpen ace Clear in 1982) reach even 14 wins during his four-year tenure. On the other hand, the club continued to produce offensive leaders. In the strike-shortened season of 1981, Lansford peppered balls off the Green Monster in left field to win a batting crown (.336). Also taking advantage of the split-campaign was right fielder Evans, who ended up in a four-way tie for the home run lead with his 22 blasts. In 1983, Wade Boggs won the first of his five batting championships in Boston with a .361 average, while Rice paced AL sluggers with 39 homers and 126 RBIs. The following year, it was the turn of center fielder Tony Armas to lead the way in both round-trippers (43) and runs batted in (123). Notwithstanding such contributions, the team remained mired in the middle of the Eastern Division, finally exhausting Houk, who retired at the end of the 1984 season in favor of John McNamara.

The next chapter of the front office follies was written in June 1983, when LeRoux claimed that he had majority backing from the organization's limited partners and staged a full-dressed coup, bringing his team into Fenway Park and declaring himself in charge; as general manager, the former trainer called on nobody less than former foe O'Connell. For two days, the franchise operated with two independent administrations, meaning that it worked with none. Even after Sullivan and Yawkey obtained a restraining order against their partner, everything remained at a standstill. Finally, long weeks after the takeover attempt, the Massachusetts Superior Court decided that LeRoux's move was illegal; at the same time, however, it rejected another petition by Sullivan and Yawkey that would have forced the insurgents to sell out their interest in the club, estimated as representing forty-two percent of the capital. LeRoux appealed the verdict and almost a year later, not only heard the first ruling upheld, but was also ordered to sell out. In the front office overhaul that followed, Sullivan moved up the ladder with the title of Chief Executive Officer, while Lou Gorman was hired away from the Mets to take over as general manager.

Under McNamara in 1985, the club got another batting championship from Boggs (.368) and had its first 15-game winner (Dennis [Oil Can] Boyd) since 1979, but still couldn't budge beyond the .500 mark in fifth place. Over the winter, Gorman went to his former employers in New York for a deal that landed righthanders Calvin Schiraldi and Wes Gardner in exchange for southpaw Bob Ojeda—a transaction that was to benefit the Mets in more ways than one. Then, only a few days before the opening of the 1986 season, Gorman went back to New York, this time to the Yankees, to acquire designated hitter Don Baylor in a swap for Mike Easler. In the astonishing pennant-winning season that followed, Baylor not only led the team in slugging with his 31 home runs and 94 RBIs, but took over as the clubhouse force that the Red Sox had been missing since Tiant.

Wade Boggs. *Courtesy of the Boston Red Sox*

But 1986 was hardly all Baylor. After a couple of seasons that had raised concern about the health of his arm, righthanded fastballer Roger Clemens exploded against the league, winning his first 14 decisions. In addition to accumulating the numbers (24–4, AL-leading ERA of 2.48) that would make him an easy winner of both the Cy Young and MVP awards, Clemens stepped in repeatedly as the stopper, ending team skids whenever it was his turn in the rotation. On April 19th, The Rocket, as fans called him, established a major league record by striking out 20 batters in a game against Seattle.

In the LCS against the Angels, Clemens failed in two starts in the first four games, and the club went into the ninth inning of the fifth game only three outs away from elimination. But, in one of the most dramatic comebacks in league history, the Red Sox wiped out California's three-run lead on two-run homers by Baylor and late-season acquisition Dave Henderson. Although the Angels came back to tie the contest in the bottom of the frame, Henderson hit a sacrifice fly in the eleventh inning that proved to be the winner. Given a second life, the club bashed California pitching by scores of 10–4 and 8–1 in the last two games to win its first flag since 1975.

The World Series against the Mets turned out to be even more dramatic than the LCS; this time, however, it was Boston that played the role of unlikely victim. The Red Sox took a quick two-game lead on a four-hit shutout by Bruce Hurst and an eighteen-hit outburst at Shea Stadium. When the Series moved to Fenway, Ojeda and Ron Darling rode some timely home run hitting to even the Series, but then Hurst returned for another masterful complete-game victory. The sixth game at Shea, comparable only to the sixth game in the 1975 Series, saw the teams battle evenly through nine innings, then Henderson spark a two-run rally in the tenth with another clutch homer. What followed was the Inning That Would Live in Infamy. With only three outs to go for a world championship, Schiraldi retired the first two batters quickly. But then Gary Carter, pinch-hitter Kevin Mitchell, and Ray Knight singled, Stanley came in to yield the tying run on a wild pitch, and Mookie Wilson hit a grounder through Buckner's legs to plate the winning tally. The aftermath of one of the most agonizing losses in World Series history added another line to the Doomsday Book; to wit, Where Was Dave Stapleton?—a reference to the backup first baseman whom McNamara had usually put in for defense in the late innings. But though the loudest criticism over the loss centered around Buckner's error, McNamara himself was the first to note that it

had been the ex-Met Schiraldi and Stanley who had given up the key hits and the wild pitch. To back up the manager, both relievers returned in Game Seven to help fritter away still another Boston lead and give the Mets the world championship.

In 1987, Boggs won another batting title and Clemens ended up with another 20 wins, but there was little else that was positive about the season. Clemens and Gedman were both at the center of bitter contract disputes during spring training, future Hall of Famer Tom Seaver announced his retirement after another contract conflict, and injuries limited Rice to thirteen home runs and Boyd to a mere seven mound appearances. With the club mired in fifth place, Sullivan cut some of his contract overhead by dealing off Baylor, Henderson, and Buckner; on the other hand, the general manager opened himself to fresh ridicule by having his son Marc (.169) carried as the platoon catcher.

The snickering prompted by the presence of the younger Sullivan was nothing compared to that aroused in 1988, when Boggs was sued for palimony payments by a woman he had been seeing during team trips for some years. After denying the relationship, the married third baseman acknowledged the substance of her assertions, this causing some of the bluer noses in Boston (and within the Red Sox hierarchy) to demand that the batting champion be traded. Bogg's situation became even more ticklish when the litigant, Margo Adams, named other Red Sox players who had been living it up on the road, this leading to several clubhouse fights. Despite all the controversy, Boggs not only won another batting title with a .366 average, but became the first player ever to record six straight seasons of at least 200 hits.

In good part because of the fallout over the Adams suit, the Red Sox slogged through the first half of 1988, barely playing .500. At the All Star break, Sullivan and Gorman replaced McNamara with long-time minor league manager Joe Morgan, who promptly piloted the team to 12 straight victories and 19 out of 20. With that thrust, the club was able to overcome some mediocre performances by Clemens and another bad year by Rice to squeak past Detroit for the division title. The LCS against Oak-

In 1987, Don Baylor set the major league record for being hit by a pitched ball. By the time he retired, he had reached first base the hard way 267 times.

land was a catastrophe, with Hurst losing twice in a four-game sweep.

The decade closed with the franchise drawing more than 2.5 million for the first time. Otherwise, the 1980s went out sourly. After various run-ins with Morgan, both Rice and Stanley were released. The manager himself took to ripping the determination of several of the players, and attracted criticism in turn by leaving the team's spring training camp to serve as the grand marshal of a St. Patrick's Day parade in his hometown. On the field, the biggest performance came from first baseman Nick Esasky, who hit 30 homers and drove in 108 runs. Despite the departure of the free agent Esasky at the end of the season, the team rebounded in 1990 to take another division title. The generally limp offense (even Boggs fell to .302 and centerfielder Ellis Burks led the club with 89 RBIs) was offset by another big year from Clemens (21 wins, 1.93 ERA) and the steady influence of righthander Mike Boddicker (17 victories). The return match against the Athletics in the LCS was even more embarrassing than the 1988 series: Not only did Boston again go down in four straight, but it scored only one run in each of the contests. The closest thing to a Red Sox Moment came in the finale, when Clemens was kicked out in the second inning after surrendering three runs and trying to take out his frustrations on the umpires.

After a second-place finish in 1991, the club fired Morgan on the grounds that he had lost contact with the players; former third baseman Hobson was appointed his successor. One of Hobson's first moves was to bring back his old manager Zimmer as a

On April 12, 1992, the Red Sox went into the record book for limiting the Indians to two hits in a doubleheader. In the opening game, southpaw Matt Young pitched eight hitless innings, but still lost, 2-1, because of several walks. In the nightcap, Roger Clemens yielded only two singles to gain Boston a split on the day. While Young's game did not qualify as a no-hitter because he hurled only eight innings, it marked the first time that a rookie catcher (John Flaherty) made his debut by helping to keep opposition batters hitless.

coach. The announcement caused hardly a ripple.

Under the new field leadership the team collapsed completely, finishing last for the first time since 1932. With only free agent acquisition Frank Viola offering any support to Clemens, the pitching was as chaotic as ever. Even more striking, the usually reliable offense disappeared, with Boggs slipping to .259, slugger Jack Clark hitting only one home run in Fenway Park, and other pivotal players spending more time on the disabled list than on the field. The highlight of the season was June 15, when reliever Jeff Reardon chalked up his 342nd save to break the record held by Rollie Fingers. Before the end of the year, however, Reardon, who had been totally ineffective after surpassing Fingers, was also gone—sold to Atlanta. He was followed in the off-season by Boggs, who signed as a free agent with the Yankees.

BOSTON RED SOX

Annual Standings and Managers

Year	Position	W	L	Pct.	GB	Managers
1901	Second	79	57	.581	4	Jimmy Collins
1902	Third	77	60	.562	6½	Jimmy Collins
1903	First	91	47	.659	+14½	Jimmy Collins
1904	First	95	59	.617	+1½	Jimmy Collins
1905	Fourth	78	74	.513	16	Jimmy Collins
1906	Eighth	49	105	.318	45½	Jimmy Collins, Jake Stahl
1907	Seventh	59	90	.396	32½	George Huff, Bob Unglaub, Deacon McGuire
1908	Fifth	75	79	.487	15½	Deacon McGuire, Fred Lake
1909	Third	88	63	.583	9½	Fred Lake
1910	Fourth	81	72	.529	22½	Patsy Donovan
1911	Fifth	78	75	.510	24	Patsy Donovan
1912	First	105	47	.681	+14	Jake Stahl
1913	Fourth	79	71	.527	15½	Jake Stahl, Bill Carrigan
1914	Second	91	62	.595	8½	Bill Carrigan
1915	First	101	50	.669	+2½	Bill Carrigan

1916	First	91	63	.591	+2	Bill Carrigan
1917	Second	90	62	.592	9	Jack Barry
1918	First	75	51	.595	+2½	Ed Barrow
1919	Sixth	66	71	.482	20½	Ed Barrow
1920	Fifth	72	81	.471	25½	Ed Barrow
1921	Fifth	75	79	.487	23½	Hugh Duffy
1922	Eighth	61	93	.396	33	Hugh Duffy
1923	Eighth	61	91	.401	37	Frank Chance
1924	Seventh	67	87	.435	25	Lee Fohl
1925	Eighth	47	105	.309	49½	Lee Fohl
1926	Eighth	46	107	.301	44½	Lee Fohl
1927	Eighth	51	103	.331	59	Bill Carrigan
1928	Eighth	57	96	.373	43½	Bill Carrigan
1929	Eighth	58	96	.377	48	Bill Carrigan
1930	Eighth	52	102	.338	50	Heinie Wagner
1931	Sixth	62	90	.408	45	Shano Collins
1932	Eighth	43	111	.279	64	Shano Collins, Marty McManus
1933	Seventh	63	86	.423	34½	Marty McManus
1934	Fourth	76	76	.500	24	Bucky Harris
1935	Fourth	78	75	.510	16	Joe Cronin
1936	Sixth	74	80	.481	28½	Joe Cronin
1937	Fifth	80	72	.526	21	Joe Cronin
1938	Second	88	61	.591	9½	Joe Cronin
1939	Second	89	62	.589	17	Joe Cronin
1940	Fourth*	82	72	.532	8	Joe Cronin
1941	Second	84	70	.545	17	Joe Cronin
1942	Second	93	59	.612	9	Joe Cronin
1943	Seventh	68	84	.447	29	Joe Cronin
1944	Fourth	77	77	.500	12	Joe Cronin
1945	Seventh	71	83	.461	17½	Joe Cronin
1946	First	104	50	.675	+12	Joe Cronin
1947	Third	83	71	.539	14	Joe Cronin
1948	Second	96	59	.619	1	Joe McCarthy
1949	Second	96	58	.623	1	Joe McCarthy
1950	Third	94	60	.610	4	Joe McCarthy, Steve O'Neill
1951	Third	87	67	.565	11	Steve O'Neill
1952	Sixth	76	78	.494	19	Lou Boudreau
1953	Fourth	84	69	.549	16	Lou Boudreau
1954	Fourth	69	85	.448	42	Lou Boudreau
1955	Fourth	84	70	.545	12	Pinky Higgins
1956	Fourth	84	70	.545	13	Pinky Higgins
1957	Third	82	72	.532	16	Pinky Higgins
1958	Third	79	75	.513	13	Pinky Higgins
1959	Fifth	75	79	.487	19	Pinky Higgins, Billy Jurges
1960	Seventh	65	89	.422	32	Billy Jurges, Pinky Higgins
1961	Sixth	76	86	.469	33	Pinky Higgins
1962	Eighth	76	84	.475	19	Pinky Higgins
1963	Seventh	76	85	.472	28	Johnny Pesky
1964	Eighth	72	90	.444	27	Johnny Pesky, Billy Herman
1965	Ninth	62	100	.383	40	Billy Herman
1966	Ninth	72	90	.444	26	Billy Herman, Pete Runnels
1967	First	92	70	.568	+1	Dick Williams
1968	Fourth	86	76	.531	17	Dick Williams
1969	Third	87	75	.537	22	Dick Williams, Eddie Popowski
1970	Third	87	75	.537	21	Eddie Kasko
1971	Third	85	77	.525	18	Eddie Kasko
1972	Second	85	70	.548	½	Eddie Kasko

1973	Second	89	73	.549	8	Eddie Kasko
1974	Third	84	78	.519	7	Darrell Johnson
1975	First	95	65	.594	+4½	Darrell Johnson
1976	Third	83	79	.512	15½	Darrell Johnson, Don Zimmer
1977	Second*	97	64	.602	2½	Don Zimmer
1978	Second	99	64	.607	1	Don Zimmer
1979	Third	91	69	.569	11½	Don Zimmer
1980	Fourth	83	77	.519	19	Don Zimmer, Johnny Pesky
1981	Fifth	30	26	.536	4	Ralph Houk
	Second*	29	23	.558	1½	Ralph Houk
1982	Third	89	73	.549	6	Ralph Houk
1983	Sixth	78	84	.481	20	Ralph Houk
1984	Fourth	86	76	.531	18	Ralph Houk
1985	Fifth	81	81	.500	18½	John McNamara
1986	First	95	66	.590	+5½	John McNamara
1987	Fifth	78	84	.481	20	John McNamara
1988	First	89	73	.549	+1	John McNamara, Joe Morgan
1989	Third	83	79	.512	6	Joe Morgan
1990	First	88	74	.543	+2	Joe Morgan
1991	Second*	84	78	.519	7	Joe Morgan
1992	Seventh	73	89	.451	23	Butch Hobson

*Tie

Postseason Play

LCS	3–0 versus Oakland	1975	WS	5–3 versus Pittsburgh	1903
	4–3 versus California	1986		4–3 versus New York	1912
	0–4 versus Oakland	1988		4–1 versus Philadelphia	1915
	0–4 versus Oakland	1990		4–1 versus Brooklyn	1916
				4–2 versus Chicago	1918
				3–4 versus St. Louis	1946
				3–4 versus St. Louis	1967
				3–4 versus Cincinnati	1975
				3–4 versus New York	1986

Brooklyn Hartfords

National League, 1877   **BALLPARKS:** UNION GROUNDS
                                    HARTFORD BALL CLUB GROUNDS
RECORD: 31–27 (.534)

The first franchise ever to be shifted from one city to another without changing ownership, the Brooklyn Hartfords were greeted less than enthusiastically by local fans when they were transferred from Connecticut. Only gamblers found the Hartfords an adequate substitute for the New York Mutuals, who had played at Brooklyn's Union Grounds the year before. However, following New York's prohibition of pool selling, the most popular form of baseball betting, in 1877, the gamblers were forced to ply their trade by telegraph from Hoboken, New Jersey. With the fans disenchanted and the gamblers exiled, almost no one showed up for games.

On the whole, the Hartfords of Brooklyn (as they were officially known) played fairly well with what was for the most part the same team that had performed in New England in 1876. John Cassidy, a utility player in Hartford, became the right fielder and the team leader in batting (.378) in Brooklyn. The club played almost all of its home games at Union Grounds, returning to Hartford for only one contest. But it added little glory to the history of Union Grounds, the first enclosed ballpark, which had opened in 1863 but which was an outdated and rundown facility by 1877.

Club president Morgan Bulkeley, who rarely came to Brooklyn, considered firing manager Bob Ferguson and revamping the lineup for 1878. He resigned Cassidy and several other players, but as losses mounted upwards to $2,500, reconsidered and disbanded the club at the end of the 1877 season, failing even to attend the NL meeting in December.

BROOKLYN HARTFORDS

Annual Standings and Manager

Year	Position	W	L	Pct.	GB	Manager
1877	Third	31	27	.534	10	Bob Ferguson

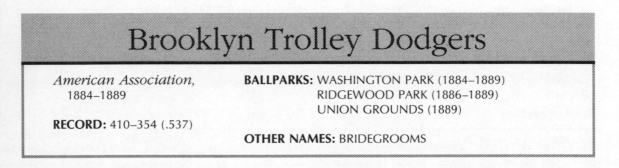

Brooklyn Trolley Dodgers

American Association,
1884–1889

RECORD: 410–354 (.537)

BALLPARKS: WASHINGTON PARK (1884–1889)
RIDGEWOOD PARK (1886–1889)
UNION GROUNDS (1889)

OTHER NAMES: BRIDEGROOMS

The American Association career of the franchise that was eventually to become the Brooklyn Dodgers was, in many ways, a condensed version of its more fabled National League descendant. Both spent a considerable percentage of their time in their respective leagues as mediocrities; both had intense rivalries with St. Louis; both evolved into a winner; and both bolted—the AA Trolley Dodgers to the NL and the Dodgers, decades later, to the West Coast.

The franchise, the brainchild of former New York *Herald* editor George Taylor, actually began in the minor league Interstate Association, where it won the 1883 pennant. There was nothing minor league about Brooklyn, however: With more than 600,000 people, it was the third largest city in the United States. The club owners—casino owners Charles Byrne and Ferdinand Abel—also had sufficient capital to back a major league club, so that when the AA went shopping for four expansion clubs during the Union Association war of 1884, Brooklyn was a natural choice.

The Trolley Dodgers, named for an activity familiar to every resident of the bustling city, finished ninth in their first major league season with former newspaperman Taylor as manager. Club president Byrne, looking forward to a total overhaul for 1885, hired Charlie Hackett, the Cleveland manager, not

only to leave the NL for Brooklyn, but to bring with him some of his better players. When the Cleveland club folded, Hackett sequestered seven players in a Cleveland hotel for the required ten-day waiting period before one club could hire another's released players. *The New York Times* called Hackett's coup "the biggest sensation that was ever made in baseball," a description that proved somewhat inflated when the four players who actually stuck with Brooklyn—first baseman Bill Phillips, third baseman George Pinckney, outfielder Pete Hotaling, and pitcher John Harkins—could raise the team to no higher than fifth.

Hackett wasn't even around at the end to see that. When the ex-Clevelanders and the Brooklyn

> **W**hile some critics considered the gambling hall wealth of Brooklyn co-owner Ferdinand Abel unsavory, he had a similar opinion of fellow baseball owners. "Whenever I go to a baseball meeting," he once said, "I never forget to check my money and my valuables at the hotel before entering the session chamber."

holdovers formed feuding factions and began trying to make each other look bad, Byrne stepped in, fined the culprits $500 each, and took over as manager himself. The owner stayed on the job in 1886, steering the team up to third, sixteen games behind the pennant-winning St. Louis Browns. But the club slipped again to sixth the following year. The bright spot was Henry Porter's 33–21 and 27–19 records in the two years.

At the end of the 1887 campaign, Byrne retired as manager and hired Bill McGunnigle in his stead. Then he bought the entire New York Mets franchise to get first baseman Dave Orr, shortstop Paul Radford (whom McGunnigle moved to center field), and left fielder Darby O'Brien. Not yet content, Byrne worked out a series of deals with St. Louis Browns president Chris Von der Ahe. The blockbuster was the $13,500 purchase of pitchers Bob Caruthers and Dave Foutz; Byrne also wrote another check to Von der Ahe for $5,000 for catcher Doc Bushong. Caruthers won 29 and lost 15 and, with the help of rookie flash Mickey Hughes (25–13), kept the newly rechristened (because several players had recently married) Bridegrooms in first place until August; the rebuilt Browns surged past them, however, to win the pennant by six games.

Despite their deals, the Brooklyn–St. Louis rivalry festered at every level. Byrne's distaste for Von der Ahe was founded on a disagreement over how the AA should compensate visiting clubs. The Browns' owner wanted a percentage of the gate, largely because his powerhouse team was such an attraction around the league; with $50,000 invested in his franchise, Byrne, whose Bridegrooms drew best at home, was happy giving—and receiving—a guaranteed amount to clubs that drew small crowds at home. The feud between the Brooklyn and St. Louis owners was exacerbated by Byrne's opinion of Von der Ahe as an ignoramus and a buffoon. For their part, the players were anxious to avenge their defeat of 1888. Even McGunnigle threatened to jump off the Brooklyn Bridge if he didn't beat the Browns in 1889.

The season began inauspiciously when the Washington Park grandstand burned down in May. Home games were shifted to the road (except for one played at the site of the old Union Grounds) until the completion of a new Washington Park on June 20. In the meantime Sunday games continued at Ridgewood Park.

After trailing St. Louis until the latter part of August, the Bridegrooms surged into first place and prepared for a crucial two-game series on September 7th and 8th. The Brooklyn players were so obsessed with beating St. Louis that they made a pact to practice celibacy. The first game ended in a fiasco, when, with St. Louis leading 4–2 in the eighth inning and darkness approaching, Von der Ahe set up a row of lighted candles in front of the visitors bench. Umpire Fred Goldsmith, failing to take the hint, ordered play to continue even after Brooklyn fans knocked over several candles with beer cups and started a small fire. St. Louis manager Charlie Comiskey refused to let his team take the field in the ninth inning, prompting a barrage of beer bottles and a forfeit win for Brooklyn. When Von der Ahe refused to allow his team to play the next day as well, the Browns forfeited that game, too.

The two games loomed large in the pennant race. AA president Wheeler C. Wikoff and the board of directors debated for weeks, then reversed the umpire's decision in the first game, awarding it to St. Louis on the grounds that Goldsmith should have called the game because of darkness; the second forfeit stood. The compromise managed to displease both sides and had dire repercussions both for Wikoff and for the AA as a whole. Before that, though, the Bridegrooms won the pennant, edging the Browns by two games. Caruthers led the AA with 40 wins against only 11 losses.

Brooklyn lost the first subway series to the New York Giants six games to three. As soon as the series was over, the AA turned to electing a new president. The ineffectual Wikoff, who could resolve neither the issue of how to divide gate receipts nor the St. Louis forfeits to anyone's satisfaction, was no one's candidate for re-election. On November 13, in what amounted to a struggle for control of the AA in the face of the impending Players League war, L. C. Krauthoff of Kansas City and Zack Phelps of Louisville surfaced as rivals. Byrne and three other owners supported the former, Von der Ahe and three allies favored the latter. The impasse was broken the next day when Byrne and Cincinnati president Aaron Stern resigned from the AA and applied for membership in the NL, which was meeting simultaneously in the same hotel.

> **W**ashington Park was named for George Washington, whose headquarters during the Battle of Long Island, the Vechte-Cortelyou House, stood on the site. The 1699 stone structure, the oldest building in New York City, served the ballpark as a ladies room.

BROOKLYN TROLLEY DODGERS

Annual Standings and Managers

Year	Position	W	L	Pct.	GB	Managers
1884	Ninth	40	64	.385	33½	George Taylor
1885	Fifth	53	59	.473	26	Charlie Hackett, Charlie Byrne
1886	Third	76	61	.555	16	Charlie Byrne
1887	Sixth	60	74	.448	34½	Charlie Byrne
1888	Second	88	52	.629	6½	Bill McGunnigle
1889	First	93	44	.679	2	Bill McGunnigle

Brooklyn Gladiators

American Association, 1890   **BALLPARKS:** RIDGEWOOD PARK
　　　　　　　　　　　　　　　　　　　　　LONG ISLAND GROUNDS

RECORD: 26–73 (.263)

To combat the defection of the Bridegrooms to the National League and the formation of the Players League Wonders, the American Association created the Gladiators, a makeshift franchise, to represent the AA in Brooklyn. But the Glads played their weekday games not in Brooklyn, but in Ridgewood on the Queens side of the border between the two counties, and its Sunday games even farther away in Maspeth, Queens.

Formation of the new team fell to William A. Wallace, a printer with the New York *Press*. He and his president–manager, 23-year-old former minor league player Jim Kennedy, assembled a team of castoffs and rookies without futures. Nine different pitchers took the mound for the Gladiators; not one

had a winning record. Only third baseman Jumbo Davis batted over .300, and he played only 38 games for the team after spending the early part of the season with St. Louis.

No one in Brooklyn—or Queens, for that matter—was fooled by this sorry ensemble. Both the Bridegrooms (who were winning the NL pennant) and the Wonders (who finished second in the PL) were easier to reach and easier to watch, so the Gladiators attracted minimal crowds. Stumbling badly toward what would have been a last-place finish had they completed the season, the team disbanded on August 25th and the franchise was turned over to the Baltimore Orioles.

BROOKLYN GLADIATORS

Annual Standings and Manager

Year	Position	W	L	Pct.	GB	Manager
1890	Partial Season	26	73	.263	—	Jim Kennedy

Brooklyn Wonders

Players League, 1890   **BALLPARK:** EASTERN PARK

RECORD: 76–56 (.576)

Because John Montgomery Ward was the manager and part-owner of the Wonders, the Brooklyn franchise became a major focus of the war waged between the National League and the rebellious Players League.

It was Ward, a former star pitcher with Providence and an equally illustrious shortstop with the Giants, who founded the Brotherhood of Professional Baseball Players with eight New York teammates in late 1885, partly as a benevolent society but also partly to combat a prevailing $2,000 salary cap. Within a year, more than 100 players belonged to the Brotherhood; within two, it won recognition from the NL, which agreed to include an explicit reserve clause in every player contract rather than have the pacts generically refer to the rule in baseball's governing instrument, the National Agreement. For fear of revealing that its salary limitation rule was a paper farce, however, the league refused to consider Ward's request for full salary disclosure. The NL also played out a charade, promising the Brotherhood it would lift the cap if the American Association went along, lobbied the AA to refuse, and then, while Ward and other Brotherhood leaders were away on A. G. Spalding's around-the-world tour in 1888, passed a new player classification plan that called for a $2,500 salary limit.

There was strong sentiment among many players for a strike, but Ward counseled them not to break their current contracts, but to refuse to sign a new one for the 1890 season. Ward, a lawyer and no radical, actually considered the reserve clause a necessary evil. He also refused to make the organization part of the American Federation of Labor or the Knights of Labor.

When John Montgomery Ward was belatedly elected to the Hall of Fame in 1964, the baseball establishment proved it had a long memory by omitting any reference to his participation in the Players League from his commemorative plaque.

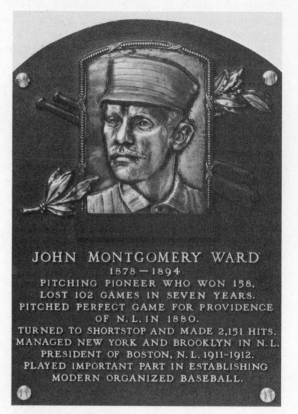

National Baseball Library, Cooperstown, NY

The two sides spent the 1889 season in a delicate mutual avoidance of negotiations over stated grievances. Then, in November, Ward issued a manifesto announcing formation of the PL. More than half the players in the NL bolted to the new league, which offered joint player–backer boards of directors; guaranteed, three-year, no-cut contracts; profit sharing; and purse money for the top seven teams. Relations with the AA were less bitter, and in December, Ward and Chris Von der Ahe of the St. Louis Browns even discussed a merger.

Ward invested in both the New York and Brooklyn clubs, and signed on to manage and play shortstop for the latter. The bulk of the financing for the

Brooklyn franchise came from a group of local businessmen, headed by financier George W. Chauncey, that spent $100,000 to build Eastern Park in the East New York section of the city. Brooklyn was turned into a major battleground where the Wonders—named for a local bread company—had to take on the well-financed NL Bridegrooms.

The first battle was not played on the field, however; it took place in January 1890, in New York State Supreme Court, where Giants owner John B. Day sought an injunction against Ward's appearing for the Wonders. Day's lawyer argued that Ward was in the same position as period opera singer Johanna Wagner, who had been enjoined from breaking a contract with a promoter. Judge Morgan Joseph O'Brien denied the injunction on the grounds that the contract Ward had signed in 1889 did not "expressly provide the terms of a contract to be made in 1890," and because there was no mutuality in a contract that bound one party for ten days and the other indefinitely; the ruling was in effect a body blow to the reserve clause.

Joining Ward, who hit .337 and stole 62 bases, were first baseman Dave Orr, who hit .373 and lost the batting crown by less than one point; second baseman Lou Bierbauer (.306) and pitcher Gus Wey-

hing (30–16). Though not considered a contender at the beginning of the season, Ward's Wonders finished second, only 6½ games behind powerhouse Boston. However, they managed to attract fewer than 80,000 fans. (The Bridegrooms' turnstiles clicked more than 120,000 times.)

The war was too much for the Brooklyn backers. In late 1890, one of them, Wendell Goodwin, joined a secret meeting of committees from all three leagues. While they agreed about little except to meet again, the PL delegation revealed the extent of its league's losses, and the NL moved in for the kill. Separate deals between NL owners and PL backers proliferated. The PL tried vainly to include players in the negotiations before everything was lost, but the NL and AA refused. In a last-ditch effort, Ward formed a committee with two PL backers to seek a consolidation with the NL, but this too failed.

On November 10, the Wonders' major backers—Chauncey, Goodwin, and John Wallace—announced that they had bought sixteen percent of the Bridegrooms for $40,000 and had abandoned the Wonders and the PL. Several smaller shareholders held out for several years, during which they harassed the Bridegrooms, but for all practical purposes Ward's Wonders were no more.

BROOKLYN WONDERS

Annual Standings and Manager

Year	Position	W	L	Pct.	GB	Manager
1892	Second	76	56	.576	6½	John Montgomery Ward

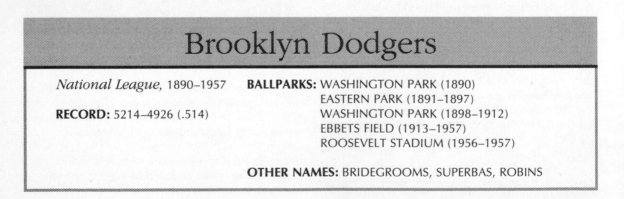

Brooklyn Dodgers

National League, 1890–1957

RECORD: 5214–4926 (.514)

BALLPARKS: WASHINGTON PARK (1890)
EASTERN PARK (1891–1897)
WASHINGTON PARK (1898–1912)
EBBETS FIELD (1913–1957)
ROOSEVELT STADIUM (1956–1957)

OTHER NAMES: BRIDEGROOMS, SUPERBAS, ROBINS

What Babe Ruth was to baseball as an individual player, the Dodgers were as a franchise. In its sixty-seven-year history, the team commingled the excellence of the Yankees and Cardinals, the agonies of the Red Sox and Cubs, and the buffoonery of the

expansion Mets to produce a legend that has only grown since the Dodgers' transfer to Los Angeles following the 1957 season. Aside from feeding off signal personalities like Charlie Ebbets, Wilbert Robinson, Larry MacPhail, Leo Durocher, Branch Rickey,

Aside from breaking down racial barriers, Jackie Robinson rewrote the story of twentieth-century baseball with his psychological terrorizing of opponents. *UPI/Bettmann Newsphotos*

and Jackie Robinson, the club gained its fabled status for its identification with the Brooklyn community—to the point that its departure for California has been viewed almost as much of a cause as an effect of the New York borough's economic and social decline in midcentury. But, their association with blue-collar informality and community ties notwithstanding, it was also the Dodgers who pointed the way to the megabusiness that major league baseball would become through the wooing of the mass media of radio, television, and advertising. This, as much as historical precedents like Jackie Robinson's crashing of racial barriers or legendary tales of cheap owners and vain managers, has been the team's most significant legacy.

Brooklyn left the National League by moving from one coast to the other, but its entrance into the senior circuit was the result of a much more local shift. On November 14, 1889, ten days after rebellious players had announced their intention of setting up a competitive league that would dispense with the reserve clause, owners from the NL and the American Association gathered at simultaneous conferences in Manhattan's Fifth Avenue Hotel to discuss strategy and possible retaliatory measures.

When Charles Byrne, president of the AA Brooklyn Bridegrooms, didn't like what he heard, he left his league's meeting and, with Cincinnati's Aaron Stern in tow, marched down the hall to join the NL session.

Because Byrne had been paying the highest salaries in either the AA or the NL, he was left relatively unaffected by the mass defections set off by the formation of the new Players League; in fact, in the offseason between being a member of the AA and of the NL, the Bridegrooms lost only one player—backup catcher-outfielder Joe Visner. With his 1889 AA pennant winners still intact, therefore, it didn't come as too much of a shock when the NL's youngest member inaugurated its season on April 28, 1890 by thrashing Philadelphia, 11–0. Not too many gray days followed, either, with the club going on to take the pennant by 6½ games.

Through the transition, the Bridegrooms (so named because a number of players on the team were married within a brief period of time in 1888) were managed by Bill McGunnigle, the first of several Brooklyn pilots who had inordinate pride in his own tactical abilities. Among the McGunnigle brainstorms was a plan to install an electric plate in the batter's box that would be connected by wire to the dugout so that hitters would know through an impulse code whether a fastball or curve was coming. This idea came to nothing when an electrician pointed out that the signal might fry the batter in his shoes.

For all their success in their maiden NL season, neither the Bridegrooms nor McGunnigle could do much about the heavy losses suffered by the team at the gate. The problem was the existence of two other Brooklyn teams—the AA Gladiators who had replaced the Bridegrooms in their original league and the club organized by the PL Wonders. As part of the Players League settlement, Byrne and his partner, Ferdinand Abel, agreed to merge their club with the Wonders, whose owner George Chauncey insisted on two conditions: that the NL team move from Washington Park to his own Eastern Park and that his manager, John Montgomery Ward, replace McGunnigle.

The Bridegrooms launched Eastern Park as an NL stadium on April 27, 1891 by blowing a lead in the ninth inning to the Giants and losing 6–5. Just as in 1890, the opening day result was a harbinger of things to come—both for the 1891 season (when the club finished sixth) and for the next seven years in Chauncey's ballpark (never higher than third). While the bloom faded from the Bridegrooms on the field, sportswriters decided that, after a couple of years of marriage, it had also dropped off the name of the team, so they offered alternatives. During Ward's two-year tenure as manager, for example, the club was referred to as Ward's Wonders after the consolidation of the NL and PL Brooklyn franchises. When Ward stood aside for Dave Foutz in 1893, the team became Foutz's Fillies. Then came the period of Ned Hanlon's Superbas, a name derived from a popular vaudeville act of the time. But none of these names gained official status. Nor, for that matter, did another—the Trolley Dodgers—inherited from the days in the AA. The Dodgers as the Dodgers were still some years off.

The first season-long holdout was Brooklyn pitcher Tom Lovett, who declined a $3,000 contract for 1892 because it was for less than he had made the year before. Lovett, who had compiled records of 30–11 in 1890 and 23–19 in 1891, refused to be victimized by the league-wide salary slash imposed after the dissolution of both the Players League and the American Association.

During its Eastern Park years, the club started being noticed for the characters who would always seem drawn to its roster. One of the first conspicuous personages was Brickyard Kennedy, a four-time 20-game winner whose pitching talents were forever being eclipsed by his misadventures in the big city. On one occasion, for instance, he set out from his Brooklyn home for a game against the Giants in the Polo Grounds, got lost, and had to ask a policeman for directions. Somewhere in the middle of the conversation, the cop understood that Kennedy was from Ohio and wanted to get back there. The pitcher was eventually taken off a train heading for the Midwest.

The most important member of the Brooklyn franchise in the 1890s was a former scorecard vendor and ticket taker who had started with the club when it was in the AA and spent most of the decade working his way up the ladder to gain Byrne's confidence. Then, only hours after Brooklyn had agreed to cede its municipal charter and become a borough of the City of New York, 38-year-old Charles Hercules Ebbets announced some new beginnings of his own by revealing that he had bought a minority interest in the club and, with Byrne confined to bed with a fatal illness, would be running the franchise. Three days later, Byrne died, and Ebbets moved up to the club's presidency. He wasted little time in making his presence felt. Within months the team had abandoned Eastern Park and was moved into a newly built Washington Park, erected across the street from the facility that the Bridegrooms had played in for their inaugural 1890 season. After watching the club lose its opening day game to Philadelphia by a 6–4 score before an overflow crowd of 14,000, Ebbets made the first of what he thought were useful suggestions to manager Billy Barnie to improve the team's play. When Barnie showed little inclination to go along with the advice and continued to pilot what was clearly going to be a second-division team, he was shown the door and replaced by outfielder Mike Griffin. The change lasted only four days (and three losses), whereupon Griffin decided that he was a better player than a manager and Ebbets decided that he could be as good a manager as a president. The club finished tenth in a twelve-team league.

Even worse from Ebbets's point of view, the team's flagging efforts on the field, combined with some home front worries about the Spanish-American War, contributed to a 40 percent drop in attendance from the previous year. Realizing that he had been in over his head, the club president summoned newsmen to announce that he had persuaded

Griffin to return as pilot for the 1899 season. But no sooner had Ebbets made his commitment than he and Baltimore Orioles owner Harry von der Horst entered into an arrangement that would change the face of baseball for years to come. In an era in which conflict of interest was a precept foreign to the sport, Von der Horst and Ebbets created an interdependent relationship between the two franchises. When all the shuffling of stock was done, Chauncey and the Byrne estate had been bought out and the two factions—Abel and Ebbets from Brooklyn and Von der Horst and Hanlon from Baltimore—each owned half of both clubs. While Abel and Von der Horst held most of the stock, Ebbets and Hanlon retained operating control.

For the Baltimore half of the syndicate, the advantage of the deal was the satisfaction of a years-long desire to get into the New York market; for the Brooklyn pair, the plusses were Hanlon, first baseman Dan McGann, shortstop Hughie Jennings, outfielders Willie Keeler and Joe Kelley, and pitchers Doc McJames and Jay Hughes—a considerable part of the teams that had kept Baltimore in either first or second place from 1894 to 1898. The transaction was also significant for the players who were left out of it: Orioles John McGraw and Wilbert Robinson, who would end up pursuing different avenues in their career-long relationships with the Dodgers; and should-have-been manager Griffin, who refused to report as a mere player under the newly appointed Hanlon, sued Ebbets for breach of contract, and eventually settled for $2,250. Despite a lifetime .299 average, the 33-year-old Griffin never played in the majors again.

Under the terms of the interlocking arrangement, Hanlon held on to his title as president of Baltimore. There were few questions in Brooklyn about his loyalties, however, when, thanks mainly to his fellow expatriates from Baltimore, he led the team to a first-place finish by eight games over runnerup Boston. While McGann and Jennings showed only flashes of their best, Keeler hit .377 and Kelley .330. Hughes led the staff with 28 wins, and McJames chipped in with 19; Jack Dunn and Brickyard

Kennedy also contributed 20 victory seasons. Another flag followed in 1900 in a streamlined eight-club league that allowed another Oriole, pitcher Joe (Iron Man) McGinnity, to leave his collapsed franchise and hurl 29 victories for Brooklyn.

The champagne was still being poured to celebrate the consecutive pennants when sour grapes appeared on the table. Enthusiastic as he was over Hanlon's on-field handling of the team, Ebbets could not forget the fact that he, as club president, was earning only $4,000 a year while his nominal underling, the highest paid man in a baseball uniform, was taking down almost three times that much. Matters came to a head in February 1901, when Ban Johnson announced his intention of going head-to-head against the NL with his gradually evolving American League. Hanlon, who had never been all that at ease in Brooklyn or with Ebbets, began to pressure Von der Horst to get in on the new venture by transferring Brooklyn back to Baltimore and enlisting in Johnson's circuit. Fortunately for Ebbets, Von der Horst liked Hanlon about as much as the president did and, instead of using his significant minority interest to vote for a shift to Maryland, offered to sell his stock. In 1902, Ebbets bought out Abel and then, after obtaining the necessary $30,000 from Brooklyn furniture dealer Henry Medicus, also bought out Von der Horst. The newly acquired stock, together with his own minority share, allowed Ebbets to assume the owner's chair. His first order of business was to call a board meeting at which his own salary was raised to $10,000 and Hanlon's cut to $7,500.

It was Ebbets's only important triumph for years to come. If he had counted on Hanlon's resigning because of the salary slash, he was disappointed. With his old third baseman McGraw named to the manager's spot in the AL Baltimore franchise and with no other attractive offers on the horizon, Hanlon stayed put in Brooklyn until 1905. On the other hand, the players who had been making both Hanlon and the franchise look good took the offers waved at them by Johnson's new league. Among the notable defectors were outfielder Fielder Jones and second baseman Tom Daly, who jumped to the Chicago White Sox; third baseman Lave Cross, who joined the Philadelphia Athletics; and McGinnity, who only had to hear that Baltimore was back in business under McGraw to leave Brooklyn. Worse was to come with the January 1903 accord between the National and American leagues when, as part of the effort to untangle a cat's cradle of verbal and written commitments and to put an end to league jumping, Keeler was awarded to the New York High-

In 1899, Charlie Ebbets cancelled the franchise's experiment with Ladies Day following complaints from male fans that the women in attendance chatted throughout the game and let their children run around the grandstand.

lander forerunners of the Yankees. What made some of the defections especially hard for Ebbets to swallow was that they ultimately benefited the New York Giants. After McGraw had been suspended for abusing AL umpires, for instance, he leaped at an opportunity to manage the Giants, and took pitching ace McGinnity back over to the NL with him. The same inter-league agreement that cost the Dodgers Keeler also permitted the Giants to reclaim the future Hall of Famer Christy Mathewson from the St. Louis Browns.

The roots of the Dodger–Giant rivalry, the most raucous in the history of baseball, stretched back to the pre-NL games between the Brooklyn Atlantics and New York Knickerbockers. If there were any primordial springs to it, they surely included the relative proximity of the teams and the distinct class perceptions that Brooklyn was the fortress of the blue-collar worker and Manhattan the bulwark of the starched-collar (or, later, white-collar) employee. These differences were only exacerbated by the economic and political conditions that compelled Brooklyn to become part of New York City in 1898 and by the complex civic feelings attending that development. Within strictly baseball terms, the rivalry was intensified by seven decades of players, managers, and owners on both sides who often sounded more dedicated to winning city bragging rights than a league pennant. (Typical of the rivalry was the successful effort by Giants' owner Andrew Freedman to persuade his City Hall friends to vote down a proposed subway station for Washington Park in 1898.) The final element in the explosive mixture was the itinerant ways of many players and managers—one year wearing a Brooklyn uniform and swearing destruction on New York and a year later wearing the other uniform and repeating the oath in the opposite direction. From John Montgomery Ward to Leo Durocher, the convert brought more to the battle than his converters.

When it came to actual games, Ebbets had a great deal more to lament. Although the 1920s and 1930s would bring other low points, the years between 1903 and 1914 were the most abysmal in franchise history, with the team never once rising to the first division. Members of the club during the period included catcher Bill Bergen, statistically the worst hitter ever to pick up a bat; pitcher Henry Schmidt, who won 21 games in his rookie year and then retired because he hated living in the East; first baseman Tim Jordan, whose 12 homers in both 1906 and 1908 were enough to lead the league; and Nap Rucker, a gifted southpaw whose brilliant duels with

the Giants' Mathewson and ten-year 2.42 ERA added up to a mere 134–134 mark because of his lack of hitting support. At the end of the 1905 season, the only one in which the Dodgers came in dead last, Ebbets had his excuse to get rid of Hanlon, and replaced him with Patsy Donovan. Donovan presided over three more years of bad baseball before giving way to Harry Lumley, a Brooklyn outfielder who had already seen his best playing years. Lumley lasted only one season before he too was shown the door, in favor of Bill Dahlen.

With his players unable to attract fans, Ebbets spent a lot of the franchise's Dark Age thinking up other ways to get the turnstiles spinning. One ploy that he would return to repeatedly was to think up "free entertainments" that would skirt the league's ban on paid admissions to Sunday games. On April 17, 1904, for example, he announced no charge for a contest between the Dodgers and Braves; the only requirement was that fans had to buy scorecards—which just happened to be color-coded according to prices that corresponded to those for seating in the boxes, grandstands, and bleachers the rest of the week. When he resorted to the same gambit a week later against the Phillies, however, he ended up bringing down the wrath of the league when the police marched onto the field and arrested not only the starting Brooklyn battery of pitcher Ed Poole and catcher Fred Jackson, but also Philadelphia leadoff batter Frank Roth. An initial hearing acquitted Poole, Jackson, and Roth of violating city Sabbath laws, but that ruling was overturned and fines were levied against the players and their clubs. Philadelphia and other NL teams warned Ebbets that they would not be part of his schemes again.

But the Brooklyn president had more ambitious plans for elevating attendance figures than slipping in the odd Sunday game. If the new Washington Park represented a decided improvement over Eastern Park, the facility still had its drawbacks. One was its relatively modest seating capacity of 18,000. Another was the row of tenements (known locally as Ginney Flats) outside the outfield fences that afforded hundreds of spectators good views of the action without having to buy anything but the beer served by the landlords of the buildings. More generally, the park was a typical nineteenth-century wooden structure; that is, vulnerable to fire, as had already been proven in the Polo Grounds, Washington, and Chicago in the first decade of the twentieth-century. Deciding that nothing would do but a steel-and-concrete structure along the lines of the stadium opened by the Athletics in Philadelphia in 1909,

Ebbets and his attorney Bernard York scouted out an area east of Prospect Park known as Pigtown and began purchasing the property parcel by parcel in the utmost secrecy. It was not until some four and a half acres had been secured that Ebbets invited sportswriters to a dinner on the evening of January 2, 1912 to reveal his intention of building the park that would be known as Ebbets Field.

After several earlier, unrealistic target dates, Ebbets Field was opened on April 5, 1913 for an exhibition game between the Dodgers and the Yankees. (The first NL game, a 1–0 win by Philadelphia, was played four days later.) The stadium, designed by Brooklyn architect Clarence Van Buskirk, had a capacity of 24,000 and dimensions that would make it popular with NL batters for the next forty-odd years. To the belated awareness of both Ebbets and Van Buskirk, however, all 24,000 spectators were expected to enter the park through an elegant but markedly cramped rotunda, prompting immediate warnings that the facility might one day turn out to be a worse firetrap than the wooden structure it had replaced. Ebbets got the message and had other entrances cut into walls on either side of the rotunda.

Ebbets Field cost the team president more than second thoughts about his rotunda. Originally confident that the stadium would cost less than a million dollars, Ebbets bought out Medicus in 1912 so that he would have full claim to the receipts promised by the new park. But as delay followed delay during the year, he realized that he had overextended himself and had to sell 50 percent of his stock back to contractors Edward and Stephen McKeever in order to complete the project. By the time the park opened the following year, Stephen McKeever in particular had become a conspicuous host of the proceedings. Unlike his somewhat diffident brother Edward and the business-first Ebbets, McKeever was a gregarious man who had earned the conversational title of Judge not for any judicial standing, but because of his intimacy with Brooklyn's Democratic Party bosses and his proprietorial air at social conclaves. In the vein of Will Rogers, Stephen McKeever was said never to have met a man he didn't like; in contrast to Rogers, he himself let everyone know a few years later whom he considered an exception to that rule.

Ebbets and McKeever were not the only important people in the organization in the years leading up to World War I. Where the players were concerned, perhaps the most important of all was Larry Sutton, an ex-printer and former minor league umpire from New Jersey hired by Ebbets as a scout. With an eye for talent never surpassed in the history of major league ball, Sutton became directly respon-

Ebbets Field. *National Baseball Library, Cooperstown, NY*

sible for the appearance in Brooklyn uniforms of (among others) outfielders Zack Wheat and Casey Stengel and pitchers Burleigh Grimes and Dazzy Vance—all of whom would eventually have plaques at Cooperstown. The first of Sutton's discoveries was Wheat, who went hitless against Mathewson in his debut at the Polo Grounds on September 11, 1909. The following day, however, he got the first two of the 2,884 hits he would total over an eighteen-year career with the Dodgers and a concluding season with the Athletics.

Through the 1913 season, Wheat, the hapless Rucker, and batting champion Jake Daubert were about all the Dodgers had to boast about. Already concerned that his inadequate team was going to make the outlay for his new stadium a business fiasco, Ebbets was put back on his heels altogether by news of the formation of the rival Federal League and the organization of a Brooklyn team in the circuit. Remembering only too well what had happened to his best players when the AL had come into existence, the president had little alternative but to offer key members of the team multiyear pacts at salaries twice as high as he would have paid under normal circumstances. He also decided that the team needed—quickly—a manager who would not only prove more successful than Dahlen, but equally adept at distracting sportswriters and fans from the FL Tip-Tops. The most obvious candidate, Giants' coach Wilbert Robinson, agreed to a pact to take over the team in 1914.

Robinson, who was probably the most popular baseball figure in New York City at the time, had been charming writers ever since joining former Baltimore teammate McGraw at the Polo Grounds in 1911. No less a sportswriting notable than Damon Runyon had decided that the roly-poly Robinson had perfected his soft-soap character to such a degree that he deserved being referred to only and always as Your Uncle Wilbert. The only reason he was even available for the Brooklyn job was because of a falling out with McGraw over a missed sign in the 1913 World Series—a minor enough incident as far as Robinson and most other people would have been concerned, but an occasion for the steel-tempered McGraw to slash back through years of indignities he had allegedly suffered by associating with his coach. Robinson remained as Brooklyn manager until 1931, by which time the team had added Robins to the list of team names. The bird designation was not always meant in a complimentary fashion.

In 1914, Ebbets almost precipitated the first players strike of the century when he assigned first baseman Clarence Kraft to the minor leagues. Although Ebbets dispatched Kraft to the Newark team in Class AA, the Nashville club of the Class A Southern Association immediately recalled a claim that it had on the player's services should he ever be demoted from the major leagues. The National Commission backed the Nashville claim, but Kraft himself didn't, arguing that he couldn't be shipped out to a Class A team (for less money) unless he were rejected by all the intermediate leagues. The player was backed by Dave Fultz, head of the Players Fraternity who immediately got the support of players around the league to strike on the issue. Despite an onslaught of press criticism that he was "a menace to the game," Fultz prevailed, and Ebbets had to pay an estimated $2,500 to Nashville for compensation, while Kraft was allowed to remain with Newark.

With the only consistent performances coming from Stengel and righthander Jeff Pfeffer over his first two seasons, Robinson steered the club up the standings by a couple of notches, its 1915 record of 80–72 representing its first winning season since 1903. Then, in 1916, Your Uncle Wilbert collected all the chips, riding solid years from Wheat and Daubert and 25 wins from Pfeffer to the pennant. Making it all the sweeter was that the club clinched the flag in a game against the Giants that so infuriated McGraw that the New York manager stalked off the field before it was over. Noting that the Dodgers' victory had been made possible by several New York errors and that many Giant players despised their manager as much as they continued to like Robinson, runnerup Philadelphia demanded that NL President John Tener investigate the possibility that the game had been thrown deliberately. Tener dismissed the accusation, and neither New York team would ever again be charged with trying to help the other.

Charlie Ebbets played a role in the consolidation of the Loews movie theater chain. Skeptical that people would ever sit still for a lengthy motion picture, Marcus Loew arranged with Ebbets in 1914 to use Ebbets Field for the showing of Thomas Ince's six-reel *The Wrath of the Gods*. After more than 21,000 people paid their way into the park to see the film and an accompanying live show, Loew began buying up the theaters that were to bear his name for decades. Ebbets got half the proceeds from the Ebbets Field showing.

The World Series against the Red Sox went to Boston in five games. It featured one of the greatest pitching duels in the history of postseason play—a fourteen-inning thriller in Game 2 in which Babe Ruth prevailed over Sherry Smith by the score of 2–1.

With the FL out of the way and the preventive multiyear contracts expiring, Ebbets celebrated the team's first pennant in sixteen years by slashing salaries across the board. The move elicited threats from several players (including the starting outfield of Wheat, Stengel, and Hi Myers) of a strike, which in turn only prompted Ebbets to farm out some of the lesser lights involved. Fortunately for Ebbets, his allies included Brooklyn *Eagle* sports editor Abe Yager, who made no bones about the fact that a strike would leave blank pages in the newspaper. Yager, until then most noted for recording Willie Keeler's self-description as a batter who "hits 'em where they ain't," took it upon himself to send Wheat a telegram in the name of Ebbets inviting the outfielder to discuss their differences at the team's Hot Springs, Arkansas training camp. The gambit worked, and Wheat ended up leading the parade of protesters back into the Brooklyn fold.

The United States's entry into World War I gave Ebbets another opportunity to get around the laws against Sunday baseball. With the backing of the U.S. Navy, he announced that a July 1, 1917 band concert at Ebbets Field would raise money for the Red Cross and war-related charity organizations—and that, as an extra inducement to music lovers, the Dodgers and Phillies would play immediately after the tubas had been packed away. Not even the presence of 1,500 marching sailors on the field before the concert prevented New York police from arresting both Ebbets and Robinson. But although both were found guilty of violating the blue laws, they gained a moral victory when their fines were suspended. A couple of years later, in 1919, State Senator Jimmy Walker, the future mayor, sponsored a successful bill that allowed local communities to decide whether or not they wanted Sunday baseball. To nobody's surprise, McKeever's friends down at Brooklyn Borough Hall said they saw nothing wrong with it.

Between the military draft and Ebbets's resentment toward the players who had threatened to strike, the 1918 roster lacked several familiar names. Among the absent was Stengel, who had been traded to Pittsburgh for shortstop Chuck Ward and two pitchers of no particular distinction. The swap looked even worse to Brooklyn fans after it was announced that Ward had been drafted and one of the pitchers had a draft-exempt offseason job that he couldn't

leave. But the third player, who had been strongly recommended by Larry Sutton despite a 3–16 record for the Pirates, turned out to be Burleigh Grimes, the spitballer who would top the 20-win mark four times for the Dodgers and end up with 270 victories over his nineteen-year career.

After another fairly dismal season in 1919, the team won its second pennant in five years in 1920, thanks largely to the hitting of Wheat and Myers, the pitching of Grimes, and the solid defensive work of catcher Otto Miller. But just as the Dodgers had entered the 1916 World Series under the cloud of the Philadelphia allegations about collusion with the Giants, they had to deal this time with an ambitious Brooklyn district attorney who discovered political capital in rumors that the same gamblers who had been involved in the 1919 Black Sox scandal had approached Brooklyn players. Only after he had hauled Ebbets and the whole team down to his office amid a carnival of publicity did Harry Lewis solemnly announce that he had found "not. . . . a single suspicion" of a Dodger plot to throw the games with the Cleveland Indians.

The gamblers spared themselves an unnecessary expense: The Indians took the best-of-nine Series, five games to two. Ebbets had some off-field grief, too, when Brooklyn righthander Rube Marquard was arrested for scalping tickets. Although the pitcher was given only a nominal fine, Ebbets quickly bundled him off to Cincinnati.

Another twenty-one years would elapse before Brooklyn returned to the World Series. Through the rest of the 1920s and the 1930s, the team could manage only one second-place and two third-place finishes. In the eyes of his critics, it was Ebbets's miserliness that drove the franchise down a road it would need two decades to get off again. A typical lashing of the period came from a New York *Herald* columnist covering the 1922 season opener who as-

On May 1, 1920, the Dodgers played the longest game in major league history—a twenty-six-inning, 1–1 tie in which Brooklyn's Leon Cadore and Boston's Joe Oeschger both went the distance. The following day, the team lost to Philadelphia 4–3 in a thirteen-inning contest. Then, the day after that, the Braves were once again the winning opponent in a 2–1 nineteen-inning affair. All told, the club played fifty-eight innings in three days without gaining a victory.

serted that "President Ebbets was in the parade but dropped a dime just before the band signaled the start of the procession, and the parade moved on while he was searching for it." When the team owner protested such a caricature, the columnist came back the next day to declare: "I was in error when I wrote that Squire Ebbets held up the Opening Day parade by searching for a dime he had dropped. The president of the Brooklyn club has informed me that the amount involved was fifteen cents."

Even on the rare occasions that the team did find itself in a pennant race in the 1920s, there were headaches. In September of 1924, for example, with the Giants invading Ebbets Field with a slight half-game lead over Brooklyn, all hell broke loose when the descending crowds numbered thousands more than the park's capacity. Despite emergency calls for extra police, the mob not only stormed through the rotunda and leaped over grandstand walls to get in, but uprooted a telephone pole and used it as a battering ram to knock down the centerfield gate. Fearful of making the situation even worse by cancelling the game, Ebbets ordered ropes to be stretched across the field to keep in spectators standing on the grass. In the course of the game (a hectic affair won by the Giants 8–7), the teams combined for eleven ground-rule doubles into the crowd.

The team's return to second-division ignominy in 1925 was not witnessed by Ebbets. After a strenuous offseason of meetings around the country and only slightly more rest at the club's spring training site in Clearwater, Florida, the 65-year-old owner collapsed and died in his Waldorf Astoria suite on the eve of the home opener in Brooklyn. Macabre detail then followed macabre detail. While the Dodgers were playing their home opener against the Giants, the hearse bearing Ebbets's body passed by the ballpark on its way to his home in Flatbush. Two days later, the hearse recovered the body to drive it around both the outfield of Ebbets Field and the one-time team home at Washington Park. After a funeral service at Holy Trinity Episcopal Church attended by more than 2,000 people, the motorcade with Ebbets's remains drove through bone-chilling weather to Greenwood Cemetery. Once there, mourners had to stand in a shivering rain while gravediggers widened the hole for the unexpectedly big coffin. Among those shivering was sixty-six-year-old Edward McKeever, named the day before as Ebbets's successor as club president. But eleven days later, after a bout with influenza that he had picked up at the cemetery, McKeever died, too.

With both his brother and Ebbets dead, Steve McKeever, Dodger treasurer, had every reason to expect that he would move into the presidency. But at a stockholders meeting in May, the Ebbets family put its fifty percent ownership behind manager Robinson and refused to back down. Figuring that Robinson's simultaneous duties in the dugout would make him something of an absentee chief of the franchise and would leave effective control in his own hands, Judge McKeever gave in. It was a mistake. In announcing his readiness to take on the dual tasks of president and manager, Robinson also made it clear from the outset that he wished to get out from under his field responsibilities "gradually." It was to that end that he appointed Wheat his so-called "assistant manager" and often remained in the grandstands during games while the outfielder ran the club. It turned out to be a no-win situation on three different levels. First, Wheat showed little aptitude for the job, and Robinson had to return to the dugout just in time to preside over a seventh-place finish. Second, because the team wasn't quite bad enough to finish below Chicago, it lost first drafting rights to slugging Toledo outfielder Hack Wilson, whom Robinson had been coveting for months. Third, Robinson became the first man McKeever had ever ran across that he didn't like.

Robinson's attempt to wear two hats also cost him the benevolent attention of the New York press. The first rupture appeared when the Brooklyn *Eagle,* noting that the team's stockholders had tried to pass off his election to the presidency as unanimous, said a vote of the kind confirmed that "the common sense of the common people is a common fallacy." Far sharper was a clash between Uncle Wilbert and the New York *Sun* after the paper had run a cartoon in 1926 mocking the high salaries being made by then-unproductive stars like Grimes and contrasting them with the meager earnings of southpaw Jesse Petty, the club's most effective hurler. When Robinson called the paper to protest the publication of players' salaries, *Sun* sports editor Joe Vila doubled the poison by not only reporting the phone call, but by ordering the paper never again to print either Robinson's name or the term Robins for the team. From that point on, the *Sun* (and later other dailies) recognized the Brooklyn franchise as the Dodgers—and as an organization run by what became known as The Daffiness Boys.

As one of the Daffiness Boys, McKeever was enraged that Robinson's undiplomatic phone call had also exposed him and the entire franchise to daily media taunting, and he unleashed a torrent of abuse on the manager–president whenever the latter

made the mistake of dropping by the executive offices. The attacks grew so predictable that Robinson
avoided his office altogether and began operating as
president from a suite at the St. George Hotel in
Brooklyn Heights.

Despite their familiarity with the second division, some Dodgers of the 1920s had genuine ability.
In 1922, Sutton talked Ebbets into acquiring Dazzy
Vance, a 30-year-old righthander who till then had
been known mainly for his wildness and a sore arm.
Ebbets agreed only because he wanted Vance's
catcher Hank DeBerry, and the New Orleans team
that owned both players refused to deal them sepa-
rately. Vance, whose arsenal included a fastball,
curveball, and a tattered piece of uniform shirt that
gave many batters too much pause, ended up with
more victories than any other Brooklyn pitcher. Babe
Herman made his debut in 1926; a first baseman–
outfielder, Herman's lifetime .324 average over thirteen seasons was to become overshadowed by
largely invented stories of his clumsiness on the field.

Aside from Vance and Herman, Robinson's
greatest asset entering the 1927 season was Joe Gilleaudeau, son-in-law of the late Ebbets and the
spokesman for the family's 50-percent share of the
franchise. During the offseason, amid reports that an
illness first reported as the flu was about to kill Mc-
Keever, Gilleaudeau took it upon himself to offer
Robinson a three-year extension on his manager's
contract. McKeever got out of bed in a flash, but too
late to stop the new pact. Over the following two
seasons, the Judge shared his laments about Robinson with any sportswriter handy. Finally, with the
rest of the league complaining that the Brooklyn
front office situation was holding up attendance payments, NL President John Heydler called a conference of the principals in an attempt to restore order.
In February 1930, Heydler announced a compromise
of sorts: a new two-year contract for Robinson as
manager but his resignation as president and member of the board of directors; confirmation of Gilleaudeau and appointment of a new Ebbets family
representative to the board; confirmation of Mc-
Keever and appointment of his ally, attorney Frank
York, to the board; appointment of York to the presidency; appointment of Walter Carter, a brother-in-
law of Chief Justice Charles Evans Hughes, to the
board as a deadlock-breaking fifth vote.

It took only a few months for other NL owners
to realize that the compromise had resolved nothing,
had in fact entrusted the presidency to a lawyer who
admitted that he knew little about baseball and had
stripped the franchise's only baseball man, Robin-

son, of effective authority. Still, the owners mainly
crossed their fingers, hoping that a better team on the
field would alleviate some of Brooklyn's problems.
For a good part of 1930, this turned out to be more
than wishful thinking. The Dodgers came alive behind Herman, first baseman Del Bissonette, and first-
year catcher Al Lopez to throw a scare into the far
more talented Cardinals and Giants. Even after the
team had lapsed back into fourth place, it could brag
about its first one-million-plus year at the gate. Mc-
Keever was so optimistic that the showing was only
a hint of things to come that he pushed the board of
directors for an expansion of Ebbets Field seating
and gave selected players like Lopez unsolicited
raises.

The respite lasted no longer than one year. At
the end of the 1931 season, with the team once again
barely keeping its head above water, a board meeting decided that Robinson had to go. His replacement, on the recommendation of Carter, was Max
Carey, an outfielder Robinson had imported a few
years earlier in the expectation that he would serve
as a Wheat-style "assistant manager." Noting that
Carey's real name was Carnarius, Tommy Holmes of
the *Eagle* suggested that the club be called the Ca-
naries instead of the Robins. Instead, the managerial
switch provided the final excuse for all of the city's
papers to refer to the team as the Dodgers.

Carey, a hard-nosed disciplinarian, made his
presence felt at once. Realizing how much leverage
he had with Carter, McKeever, and York, he successfully pressed for the purchase of slugger Hack Wilson and then, after Herman had threatened to sit out
the season to protest a salary cut, for the dealing of
the Babe to the Reds in exchange for infielders Joe
Stripp and Tony Cuccinello and catcher Clyde Sukeforth. Unfortunately, Carey's foresight was not as
good as his powers of persuasion. The Hack Wilson
who came to the Dodgers was not the fabled slugger
who had once driven in 190 runs in a season, but a
prematurely old thirty-two-year-old who had become reliable only for expanding his waistline and
drinking himself into a stupor. Not only did Herman
go on to more .300 seasons in other uniforms, but a
throw-in in the Cincinnati deal, catcher Ernie Lombardi, ended up with two batting titles.

Carey delayed the inevitable in 1932, managing
to finish third on the strength of a 20-win season
from southpaw Watty Clark, a batting title from outfielder Lefty O'Doul, and the field leadership and
clutch hitting of catcher Lopez. Midway through the
season, York finally had enough of pretending to be
the president of a baseball franchise and resigned,

leaving the way open for McKeever, at the age of seventy-eight, to realize his dream of taking over the presidency. The move was largely cosmetic, however, with Gilleaudeau and the Judge's son-in-law, Jim Mulvey, coming to a private arrangement that no significant decisions would be made for the organization without their approval. If this wasn't sign enough of the continuing chaos in the Brooklyn front office, both Gilleaudeau and Mulvey (an executive for the Metro-Goldwyn-Mayer film company) made it clear that they would confine their sway to periodic board meetings, neither having any interest in getting any closer to actual baseball operations. To handle these chores, they relied on front office aides Dave Driscoll and John Gorman.

Driscoll lasted only until the middle of the 1933 season, when there was a general cry for his head after he had traded O'Doul and Clark, the bulwarks of the 1932 club, to the Giants in exchange for first baseman Sam Leslie. In fact, the trade proved beneficial for Brooklyn; O'Doul was on his last legs and Clark did nothing for New York, while Leslie batted over .300 in his two seasons with the Dodgers. But the uproar gave McKeever the room he needed to usher in former Boston Red Sox owner Bob Quinn as the team's new general manager. Loyalties to Driscoll aside, Gilleaudeau and Mulvey saw Quinn as the authoritative baseball man neither had any desire to become. When the writers covering the team turned on the franchise once again for firing the popular Driscoll, Quinn countered the hostility with repeated assurances that things would get better.

They didn't, not for another seven years, but by then Quinn had contributed a couple of chapters of his own to the legend of the Daffiness Boys. It was Quinn, for example, who was the first to hear of a somewhat humdrum press conference given by New York manager Bill Terry at the 1933–34 winter meetings during which the Giants pilot, in the course of running down the NL teams and their prospects, noted that Brooklyn had not made any deals and sardonically asked if "Brooklyn (was) still in the league?" Incensed that his inertia in the trade market was being criticized, the new general manager turned the quote into a battle cry for the Dodger faithful for the upcoming season. Moreover, riding his own angry momentum, Quinn persuaded the board of directors that Carey was not the manager to lead the team into the fray and that he should be replaced by former Dodger outfielder Stengel. It was Stengel who was in the dugout when, in the waning hours of the season, Brooklyn took the two games from the Giants that cost the New Yorkers the pen-

nant to the Cardinals and that allowed the Brooklyn *Times-Union* to publish the banner headline: YES, INDEED, MR. TERRY, THE DODGERS ARE STILL IN THE LEAGUE.

Stengel's three-year reign as manager didn't bring good baseball, but it did bring the daffiness of the front office down to the field in much more calculated ways than had been the case with Herman's occasional stumbling or Wilson's groggy pursuit of line drives. The ideal man for charming newsmen and keeping their eyes away from the team's second-division finishes, Stengel was given to such antics as protesting inclement weather conditions by coaching at third base with an umbrella over his head and arranging races between his players so he could make a few dollars from reporters. Aiding him in the sideshows were players like Frenchy Bordagaray, an able enough hitter, but a fashion plate in the outfield who couldn't kick a habit of holding onto his hat before chasing down a ball that had been hit over his head.

In 1935, Stengel had another outfielder, Len Koenecke, who initially gave signs only of sharing Bordagaray's talent for self-absorption. In one incident, Stengel ordered a hit-and-run with Koenecke at bat. Koenecke swung and hit a dribbler in front of home, the catcher pounced on the ball to get the runner at second but fired it into center field; the center fielder retrieved the ball to get the runner at third, and all the while Koenecke remained at home plate arguing with the umpire that the ball had been foul. As Stengel jumped up and down on his hat in the coach's box, the outfielder was tagged out at the end of a catcher-center fielder-third baseman-catcher double play. On other occasions, Koenecke was given to wandering off bases on the mistaken assumption that a first out was a third out and to trotting out to the wrong defensive position. Finally, after exhausting Stengel's patience with one too many lapses of the kind during a series in St. Louis, he was sent back to Brooklyn on a train ahead of the rest of the team. He never made it. On a stopover in Detroit, Koenecke left the train, chartered a plane, went berserk aboard the plane, and was killed by a blow to the head from a fire extinguisher that had been meant only to control him. In later years, Stengel would blame himself for not having recognized the symptoms of Koenecke's mental distress.

More direct in his approach was pitcher Van Lingle Mungo, a righthander who had been seen as the key to the team's future when he joined the Dodgers in 1931 but who had become a magnet for bad luck whenever he took the mound. By his fifth season of good but unsuccessful pitching, Mungo had turned into a walking bad mood prone to throwing a punch, especially after a couple of drinks. The apotheosis of Mungo's career was probably reached at the outset of the 1936 season, when, resolved to get over the temper tantrums that had cost him in the past, he started on Opening Day against the Giants at the Polo Grounds, gave up a run in the first inning, got into a fight that led to his ejection from the game in the second inning, came back the next day to go down again 1–0 on an error, and then lost a third game three days later when two of his fielders collided on what should have been the final out of the game. Following the third loss in a week, Mungo left the team with the announcement that he could no longer play with "semi-pros." A sympathetic Stengel talked him back to Brooklyn, and refused front office pressures to levy a fine. Mungo eventually ended up winning eighteen games, but also managed to lose nineteen.

Following the 1935 season, with his promises for better times ahead unfulfilled, Quinn resigned as general manager to take over the presidency of the Braves. His successor was John Gorman, the longtime road secretary who instantly went from being one of the boys around the press pool to a secretive, almost paranoid, general manager. Gorman had plenty to be secretive about, at least in the beginning. No sooner had the certified accountant gained parity with Quinn in NL circles than he surrendered Lopez, infielder Tony Cuccinello, and a couple of other bodies to his former boss in exchange for three players who did nothing for Brooklyn. When, over the next few months, he also practically gave away Bordagary and second baseman Lonny Frey, Gorman earned his niche among the Daffiness Boys. But what was overlooked at the time was that he also pulled off three deals between December 1936 and October 1937 that proved crucial to the franchise's climb back to respectability. The first, with the Pirates, brought the club infielder Cookie Lavagetto; the second, with the Giants, yielded pitcher Freddy Fitzsimmons; and the third and most important of all, with the Cardinals, made Leo Durocher a Dodger. A few days after the Durocher deal, in October 1937, Gorman abruptly announced his "resignation," returned to public accounting in his native Connecticut, and was never again seen around Ebbets Field.

Stengel's charm wore out after the 1936 season. Even though he still had a year left on his contract (so had Carey), the organization decided that, in view of steadily declining attendance, the Brooklyn faithful preferred winning teams to entertaining

managers. The next pilot could not have been more unlike Stengel—Burleigh Grimes, the Attila-tempered spitballer who was called Old Stubblebeard by his legions of detractors. One of Grimes's first moves in taking over the team was to grouse to reporters that he was making much less money to manage the club than Stengel was making to sit in his living room. Some solid play from Lavagetto aside, things went generally downhill from there in 1937.

But Brooklyn fans were not the only ones unamused by the franchise's dead-end management. For years, other league owners had been complaining about the deterioration of the organization, which had last shown a profit in 1930. The final straw was 1937, when the average home attendance was little more than 6,000. Moreover, even the few fans who put in an appearance did so in a facility that was literally rotting away, with thousands of broken seats remaining unrepaired and the outfield walls beginning to crumble. If anybody made the mistake of griping about the conditions, he was likely to be hauled out of the park by roughnecks who had been ostensibly hired as ushers but whose main task was making sure the catcalls to the field were held to a minimum. The situation was no better at the team's Montague Street offices, where the telephone was frequently turned off for nonpayment of bills and where the most common visitors were process servers. It was this organizational tableau that inspired cartoonist Willard Mullin of the New York *World-Telegram* to portray the Dodgers as an Emmett Kelly-like bum.

If the franchise survived at all in the 1930s, it was largely due to the Brooklyn Trust Company, which had a half-million dollars in Dodger IOUs that it did not foreclose on only because the bank also held a mortgage to Ebbets Field and saw nothing to be gained by shutting down the team. Instead, Brooklyn Trust went to NL President Ford Frick with the argument that it was also in the league's interest to come up with a fully qualified baseball man who could rescue the franchise. Frick's first thought was Cardinals' general manager Branch Rickey, then known to be having troubles with the St. Louis owners. But Rickey declined, and instead recommended Larry MacPhail, a one-time protégé who had been having troubles of his own with the Cincinnati franchise he had recently turned around with the help of such innovations as night games and radio coverage. The 48-year-old MacPhail, known as The Great Mouthpiece for his irritating, raspy voice, took the job.

Operating with the title of executive vice-president and assured of a totally free hand in running the franchise, MacPhail got Brooklyn Trust chief George McLaughlin to cough up some $400,000 for new players, a complete overhaul of Ebbets Field, and the installation of lights. The biggest chunk of money for players (an estimated $75,000) went for slugging first baseman Dolf Camilli, then engaged in a contract tug-of-war with the Phillies. More money was spent for Ernie Koy, an outfield prospect for the Yankees. The stadium refurbishments included a new paint job, new seats and concession stands, and the discarding of the franchise's traditional green-and-gold uniforms for its grandstand toughs in favor of new (Dodger) blue colors for young, freshly hired ushers. With the installation of the lights, MacPhail demonstrated that his grand designs for reviving the franchise were matched only by his luck.

Convinced that night baseball would prove to be as beneficial to Brooklyn as it had been to Cincinnati, MacPhail set June 15th for Ebbets Field's first game under the arcs. To give more splash to the event, he organized various pregame festivities, including an elaborate fireworks display and a race between Koy and 1936 Olympic champion Jesse Owens. At the last minute, he had to make time for an additional ceremony when 700 citizens of Midland Park, New Jersey insisted on presenting a watch to fellow townsman Johnny Vander Meer, the Cincinnati southpaw who had pitched a no-hitter against Boston in his previous start. What neither MacPhail nor any of the 38,748 fans in the stands could have dreamed possible was that Vander Meer would then go out and complete the only back-to-back no-hitters in baseball history—and in the process make Brooklyn's inaugural night game more of a conversation piece for the rest of the season than an army of publicists would have managed. Attendance for the year ended up in the neighborhood of 750,000 more than double the 1937 total.

Not all of MacPhail's promotion schemes had happy endings. In what was originally seen as a master stroke, the Dodger boss also announced the hiring of Babe Ruth—ostensibly as a first base coach, but mainly as a pregame sideshow for his batting practice shots over the rightfield wall. Although the batting practice gimmick attracted fans, everything else went haywire. It took only a few games for the Dodger players to realize that Ruth was not much of a coach. It took less than that for the fabled slugger to start arguing with Grimes and shortstop Durocher. When Ruth decided that he couldn't do worse than some of the players in the regular lineup and declared his desire to make a comeback, Grimes ridiculed the suggestion and cemented his mutual animosity with the Babe. The finale came after the World Series, when MacPhail announced that Durocher would be taking over from Grimes as manager for the 1939 season. Ruth, who had been led on by some cryptic remarks by MacPhail that he would be the next Dodger pilot, left the team in bitterness at what he perceived as a betrayal.

MacPhail made more enemies in the Polo Grounds and Yankee Stadium when he announced, in December 1938, that he was breaking his agreement with the other two New York clubs not to broadcast games on the radio. It was a decision that would revolutionize baseball's relationship with the mass media and make the Dodgers a constant presence in living rooms, in bars, and on street corners. The key to the move was Red Barber, a Mississippi-born preacher who had started out with MacPhail in Cincinnati and who now brought his colorful idioms (arguments were "rhubarbs," pitchers with 0–2 counts on batters were sitting in "the catbird seat") to a New York audience that embraced them with wonder, amusement, and finally, enthusiasm. On August 26, 1939, Barber would be in his own catbird seat as the broadcaster for the first televised game, and on August 10, 1951, he would also cover the first game televised in color. Throughout their stay in Brooklyn, the Dodgers were to remain the most potent attraction for advertising revenue in sports.

If any other sign of the franchise's new directions were needed, it came shortly after MacPhail's arrival, with the announcement that McKeever had died of pneumonia at the age of 83. The final tribute to the Judge came when his friends at Borough Hall approved an ordinance renaming the Cedar Place boundary of Ebbets Field McKeever Place. The Daffiness Boys were no more.

At first sight, the Durocher Boys who took the field in 1939 did not look much better than the players who had been boring fans through most of the decade. With only Camilli and Lavagetto as reliable players in the lineup, most predictions were that

Leo Durocher on Larry MacPhail: "There is no question in my mind that Larry was a genius. There is that thin line between genius and insanity, and in Larry's case it was sometimes so thin that you could see him drifting back and forth. . . ."

In addition to Red Barber, the Dodgers had several other radio and television announcers during their Ebbets Field days. They included Barber
protégé Vin Scully, Ernie Harwell, Connie Des-
mond, actor Alan Hale, and Andre Baruch.
Baruch, a spokesman for the Lucky Strike spon-
sors of the team, was very much out of his depth,
as evidenced by one of his more famous calls of
"There's a popup around the mound. . . . it goes
into the upper deck in left field for a home run."

Durocher would argue his way out of a job before
too long. By this time his often public clashes with
MacPhail rivaled his notorious umpire baiting. But
with an eye for talent that his roaring personality
had usually overshadowed, MacPhail spent more of
the Brooklyn Trust Company's money during the
offseason for pitchers Hugh Casey and Whitlow
Wyatt, and then in July 1939 purchased the contract
of outfielder Dixie Walker from Detroit. All three
players had been plagued by injuries and generally
given up as broken prospects, with Casey carrying
around an additional reputation as a hard drinker. In
the event, Walker (soon to become The People's
Cherce) showed a useful stroke and the two pitchers
some effectiveness in the team's first .500 season
since 1932.

Equally important from MacPhail's point of
view, 1939 saw the return of fans (almost a million of
them) as the twenty-sixth player. In one celebrated
instance of the restored enthusiasm in the grandstands, fans took up a collection to pay a $25 fine that
Durocher had incurred for trading punches with Giants first baseman Zeke Bonura. The intention was to
change the money into pennies, then throw the coins
on the field and have NL officials crawl around to
retrieve them. Only when NL President Frick intervened with warnings to MacPhail and Durocher was
the plan called off. To show the franchise's gratitude
for the successful year at the gate, MacPhail gave
away a car at the last home game—then fired Durocher for almost costing the team a third-place finish
by starting a rookie pitcher. One writer estimated
that it was about the twentieth time Durocher had
been fired (and then immediately rehired) during
the season.

Although 1940 did not bring the pennant that
MacPhail, in his beerier moments in the early hours,
had predicted, it brought almost all of the important
pieces that would be needed for the flag that was

won in 1941. In some fast shuffling with his mentor
Rickey after the commissioner's office had released a
number of minor leaguers as free agents, MacPhail
laid claim to Pete Reiser, a shortstop soon to be found
more suited to the outfield and later to become synonymous with reckless charges into outfield walls.
MacPhail also snared Pee Wee Reese from the Red
Sox minor league system. From St. Louis he received
one-time triple crown winner Joe Medwick, who, although beaned in his very first at bat against the
Cardinals and never quite the same player afterward,
produced a couple of .300 seasons and had a beneficial effect on his old Cardinal roommate Durocher.
Before the calendar year was out, MacPhail would
also pick up pitcher Kirby Higbe from the Phillies
and catcher Mickey Owen from the Cardinals.

While the team was finishing second to the club
that MacPhail had put together in Cincinnati, the
Dodger boss remained busy implementing ideas that
he was convinced would galvanize the sport. On
May 7, 1940, for example, the Dodgers traveled from
St. Louis to Chicago on two planes, becoming the
first team to travel by air en masse. After both Medwick and Reese were beaned, MacPhail, with help
from researchers at Baltimore's Johns Hopkins University, came up with the forerunner of present day
batting helmets—bands that could be sewn into the
players' caps.

The last significant addition to the team was second baseman Billy Herman, acquired in a trade with
the Cubs a few weeks into the 1941 season. Beating
off a late-season run by the Cardinals, Brooklyn took
its first pennant in twenty-one years by the margin of
2½ games, in the process compiling the franchise's
best record since 1899. Higbe and Wyatt both won 22
games to lead the league; Casey won 14 and saved 7
others; Camilli belted more homers (34) and knocked
in more runs (120) than anybody else in the league to
capture MVP honors; and Reiser hit .343 to win the
batting championship. Ecstatic when the team
clinched in Boston and alerted to the thousands of
fans awaiting the Dodger train in Grand Central Station, MacPhail cabbed up to the 125th Station so he
could get aboard and be part of the welcome. What
he didn't know was that Durocher had arranged for
the train to bypass the station so none of the players
would wander off to nearby saloons. Convinced that
the train whizzing by him had been another Durocher slap at him, MacPhail once again fired his manager, this time in the middle of the team's celebration
banquet. A few hours later, Durocher was back.

MacPhail's fury reached new heights after the
World Series against the Yankees. The Series went to

New York in five games, with the turning point coming in the fourth game when catcher Owen couldn't hold on to a third strike against Tommy Henrich in the ninth inning for the last out. Instead of evening the Series at two games apiece, the passed ball permitted the Yankees to stage a winning rally and go on to their championship the next day. It was after this setback that the *Eagle* coined the familiar Brooklyn cry of WAIT TILL NEXT YEAR. It was also after this defeat that MacPhail first threatened to ask waivers on the entire team, then, with a few belts to help his negotiating prowess, offered the entire roster of players to the St. Louis Browns in exchange for the Missouri club. St. Louis officials waited a few seconds too long to respond, and the proposal was withdrawn.

One of MacPhail's most popular innovations was the hiring of organist Gladys Gooding in 1942. Gooding—the answer to a hoary local riddle about who was the only person to have played for the Dodgers, basketball Knicks, and hockey Rangers—got into hot water almost immediately when she played "Three Blind Mice" at the appearance of the umpires on the field. The tune was directed particularly at umpire Bill Stewart, who doubled as a hockey referee and who had angered Rangers' fans with some questionable calls the previous winter. Stewart protested the ironic melody, and Gooding had to go back to singing the National Anthem and playing more innocuous tunes.

Grandstand music was also provided at Ebbets Field by a band calling itself the Dodger Sym-Phony. The Sym-Phony's forte was following an opposition batter back to the bench after he had made out with the jeering tune of "Go wash your feet, go wash your feet," then clanging cymbals and booming a bass drum at the moment the player sat down. Some players, notably Walker Cooper, tantalized the musicians by refusing to sit down for long minutes, but always ended up being kaboomed down anyway.

With only Lavagetto lost immediately to the draft at the outbreak of World War II, the Dodgers entered the 1942 season with every expectation of repeating. When even Lavagetto was replaced by future Hall of Famer Arky Vaughan through a trade with Pittsburgh, the team's confidence bordered on arrogance. Early season stories were as often about the poker games organized on the trains by Durocher and his coach Charlie Dressen as they were about developing pitching arms or improved batting eyes. By early August, the team had a lead of 10½ games over the Cardinals and seemed invincible—to everybody but MacPhail. Especially after Reiser was

injured after crashing into an Ebbets Field wall, the Dodger boss kept after Durocher, at one point entering the clubhouse to rave at the manager and the team for underestimating St. Louis. That particular scene came to an end when Walker bet MacPhail that the Dodgers would win the pennant by at least eight games, and the executive had to back away from wagering against his own team. But by the end of the season, with the Cardinals settled in first place by two games, MacPhail's dire warnings had proven accurate. Ironically, the second-place 1942 team finished with four more victories than the 1941 pennant winner, and those 104 wins were the second most ever recorded by a Brooklyn team.

If Durocher and his players were stunned by their second-place standing, they were even more dismayed by the announcement in late September that MacPhail had resigned. The official reason given for the move was that he was anxious to contribute to the war effort and had accepted a commission as a major in the Army's office of Service and Supplies. But while true as far as it went, the man who had saved the Dodger franchise had also been taken aback when the board of directors had made no attempt to talk him out of his decision. MacPhail's problems with the board were twofold. The first was his swaggering and boozy style that offended several stockholders. The second was money. While it was true that he had made enough for the franchise to be able to pay off its loan from the Brooklyn Trust Company, to reduce most of the mortgage on Ebbets Field, and to build up one of the league's best farm systems, he had always been a little elusive when it had come to paying dividends, insisting that the club had to put its profits back into the operation. At the same time, he himself had continued to draw one of the biggest front office salaries in the major leagues.

It didn't take long for the team to come up with a successor. Following what was probably his greatest achievement as the general manager of the Cardinals, Rickey announced at the end of October that he was leaving St. Louis. About a month later, Mulvey, the McKeever son-in-law who had originally wanted Rickey instead of MacPhail, confirmed that the sixty-one-year-old teetotaler, most famous for organizing St. Louis's vast system of minor league affiliates, would be taking over the Dodgers. Many of the sportswriters who had become accustomed to MacPhail's lavish spending on them bemoaned the change. A few went further than that, and in print. For columnist Jimmy Powers of the *Daily News*, for instance, Rickey was simply El Cheapo, a reference to the cost-cutting policies of the St. Louis Cardinals

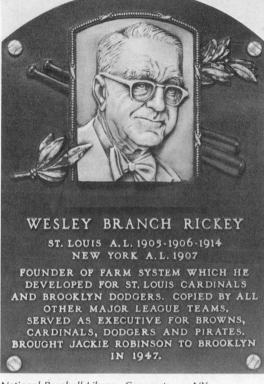

WESLEY BRANCH RICKEY

ST. LOUIS A.L. 1905-1906-1914
NEW YORK A.L. 1907

FOUNDER OF FARM SYSTEM WHICH HE
DEVELOPED FOR ST. LOUIS CARDINALS
AND BROOKLYN DODGERS. COPIED BY ALL
OTHER MAJOR LEAGUE TEAMS.
SERVED AS EXECUTIVE FOR BROWNS,
CARDINALS, DODGERS AND PIRATES.
BROUGHT JACKIE ROBINSON TO BROOKLYN
IN 1947.

National Baseball Library, Cooperstown, NY

(that had actually been forced on Rickey by owner Sam Breadon). For Tom Meany, Rickey would always be The Mahatma because he fulfilled writer John Gunther's description of Gandhi as "a combination of God, your own father, and Tammany Hall." What none of these writers foresaw was that Rickey would bring even more radical changes to the Dodger franchise than MacPhail had.

At first though, like other big league teams, Brooklyn struggled through the war years with over-the-hill stars, teenagers, and medical rejects. Among those parading through Ebbets Field in the early 1940s were Paul Waner, his brother Lloyd, Johnny Cooney, and outfielder Ben Chapman (back as a pitcher). The teenagers included 16-year-old Tommy Brown, 17-year-old Eddie Miksis, and 17-year-old Chris Haughey. The second-time-around Dodgers numbered among them manager Durocher (who came out of retirement twice to plug infield holes), Bordagaray, and Herman (who pleased myth-makers when he singled in his first comeback at bat, then promptly tripped over first base). The draft exemptions ran the gamut from pitchers Jack Franklin and Tom Sunkel (both with one blind eye) through

shortstop Clancy Smyres (only one good kidney) to pitcher Tommy Warren (shell-shocked). With such ingredients, Durocher finished third twice and seventh once.

Rickey, meanwhile, was busy on several fronts. To make sure the farm system started by MacPhail would not dry up, he sent out 20,000 letters to high school coaches around the nation asking for recommendations. To bankroll his plans, he sold off Camilli (who refused to report to the Giants), Medwick, and Wyatt; in fact, of the twenty-two transactions he engineered between February 1943 and October 1946, twelve of them brought the Dodgers not players, but straight cash. The only player obtained in that period from another NL club who would have an impact on the Dodgers after the war was second baseman Eddie Stanky. Among the future luminaries who put in token appearances before going off to war were pitcher Ralph Branca and Gil Hodges, then a shortstop-third baseman.

By the time the war ended, Rickey had also secured his position in the club hierarchy. In 1944, together with John Smith of the Charles Pfizer Chemical Company and a corporation lawyer named Walter O'Malley, he purchased the 25 percent share of the team held by the estate of Ed McKeever. A year later, the same trio spent $750,000 for the 25 percent share held by Gilleaudeau and the Ebbets' heirs. Though Mulvey and his wife Dearie, the daughter of Judge McKeever, refused to sell their 25 percent as well, the two deals meant that, for the first time since 1924, the franchise wasn't being run by estate executors.

Those who had anticipated a personality clash between Durocher and Rickey were disappointed for several years. While the brash manager and sanctimonious general manager could not have been more different on the surface, they shared several important things: the winning years of the Gashouse Gang in St. Louis, respect for one another's talents, and a knack for knowing when to cut their losses. In 1943, one of the losses was Durocher aide Dressen, whose gambling habits made him the perfect fall guy for Rickey's crackdown on the highly publicized poker games during team trips. In typical Rickey fashion, however, Dressen was rehired a few months after being fired at a salary some $1,500 lower than his original one. For his part, Durocher agreed that poker games were not the best image for a baseball team in the middle of the war and imposed his own rule of only "penny ante" games.

The biggest strain on the Rickey–Durocher relationship in the war years came in 1943, after the manager had suspended pitcher Bobo Newsom for allegedly blowing a game to the Pirates by ignoring a sign from catcher Bobby Bragan. The move prompted infielder Vaughan to challenge Durocher to a fight, mutual charges that some of the writers on the Dodger beat had blown the problem out of proportion, and threats by both Vaughan and Walker to leave the team. Matters came to a head when Rickey gathered Durocher, the players, and some of the writers together in the clubhouse before a game and had everyone say his piece. By the time the meeting had ended, the writers had successfully refuted Durocher's double-talk, Newsom was telling everyone that he had been exonerated, and Durocher was telling Dressen to get ready to succeed him because he was about to resign. But Rickey held firm, and instead traded away Newsom and didn't disguise his satisfaction when Vaughan announced his retirement at the end of the season. The most lasting scar from the incident was Durocher's hostility toward Walker for having sided with the protesting players. Although Rickey had no intention of also jettisoning The People's Cherce, and Walker would go on to win the batting championship the following year, the groundwork had been set for one of the general manager's shrewdest player moves a few years later.

In retrospect, Rickey's solidarity with Durocher seemed motivated in good part by the general manager's belief that he had the ideal manager for dealing with what was gong to be the most significant development in twentieth-century baseball—racial integration. This permitted him to set aside incidents that even MacPhail might have been hard pressed to ignore. In the midst of the 1945 season, for example, Durocher and an Ebbets Field guard were charged with felonious assault for beating up a veteran who had been heckling the manager from behind the Dodger dugout. Despite having to pay the victim $6,500 to settle a civil suit and then having to go through a criminal trial (at which Durocher and the guard were acquitted), Rickey stood fast. He also calmed his abstinence instincts when he discovered that Durocher had been feeding liquor to southpaw Tom Seats to help the pitcher overcome his nervousness about appearing on the mound; as with Newsom, it was Seats who was eventually sent packing.

The Rickey plan for integrating baseball began to take shape May 7, 1945, when he announced the formation of the Brown Dodgers as Brooklyn's entry in a new Black United States Baseball League. The announcement elicited little reaction, despite Rickey's cryptic references during a press conference to black players who might some day join the whites-

> The first black manager in organized whites-only baseball was Roy Campanella. Campanella was given the lineup card by manager Walter Alston in June 1946 after Alston had been kicked out of a minor league game between the Nashua farm team of the Dodgers and the Lawrence Millionaires. Campanella steered Nashua to a 7–5 victory.

only version of organized baseball. Five months later, he made his intentions a lot clearer when he disclosed that Jack Roosevelt Robinson, a shortstop for a Negro League team in Kansas City, had signed a contract to play for the Brooklyn farm team in Montreal in 1946. One of the tests Rickey had put Robinson through before signing him was to sit the player in his office and expose him to a couple of hours of racial slurs and epithets, in the interests of preparing him for the abuse of opposing dugouts and winning agreement that the first black player would "have guts enough not to fight back." Although Robinson didn't need the refresher course in hatred, he pledged to turn the other cheek if that was the price for breaking the color line. To assist his orientation in Montreal, Rickey also signed black pitchers John Wright and Roy Partlow for the International League club.

Initial reaction among the Dodger players to the signing of Robinson was summed up by the Alabamian Walker's shrug that as long as he was playing for the Royals in Canada, it was neither here nor there. Through the 1946 season, the team had more immediate problems in dueling the Cardinals for the pennant, finally having to settle for second place after losing two games in a postseason playoff. The indifference evaporated rapidly when Robinson led Montreal to the International League pennant and Rickey announced that the Dodgers and their principal farm club would train together in Cuba prior to the 1947 season. It didn't take Walker long to read the writing on the wall, or to circulate a petition among the players demanding that the team vow not to promote Robinson to Brooklyn. Alerted to the initiative but still not certain how many players agreed with Walker, Durocher fulfilled Rickey's expectations of his behavior by calling a midnight meeting of the club in Havana and advising the protesters that they could "wipe their ass" with the petition. The following evening, Rickey called in Walker, Bragan, and other players suspected of being involved in the protest and, making his intentions definite, gave them the choice of accepting Robinson as a teammate or going elsewhere. But when Walker chose the trade route, Rickey quickly backed down. It would be another year before he would be able to persuade Pittsburgh that it was doing him a favor by accepting an all-star outfielder who couldn't coexist with a black teammate and who was still resented by his manager for the Newsom–Vaughan fracas. By that time, of course, Walker was also decidedly past his prime—a detail as obscured by Rickey as the value he put on the two players he received in exchange from the Pirates, pitcher Preacher Roe and third baseman Billy Cox.

Robinson's Dodger debut on April 15, 1947 marked the beginning of the team's drive to almost a decade of dominance in the league. Until 1957, the club that would be characterized by writer Roger Kahn as the Boys of Summer would finish third once (in 1948) and either first or second every other year. As it turned out, the Boys of Summer would also prove to be the last chapter of baseball in Brooklyn.

In his maiden season, Robinson not only had to put up with the slurs, spikes, and beanballs from his opponents and the iciness on the part of his own teammates, but he also had to learn a new position, first base, under the eyes of tens of thousands of fans who were either hoping or fearing that he would fail. Robinson met all the challenges and by the second month of the season had won over most of the team, especially shortstop Reese and second baseman Stanky. The vicious taunts of adversaries like Phillies manager Ben Chapman and the deliberately brutal slides of players like Enos Slaughter and Joe Garagiola of the Cardinals, only served to bring the Brooklyn players closer together. But in the season that was to culminate in a Dodger pennant and his own honors as Rookie of the Year, Robinson brought more than the first black face. Even his league-leading 29 steals didn't quite convey the daring tactics he brought to his running game—jockeying off bases to distract pitchers and catchers, and luring outfielders into throwing behind him so he could take the extra base. With Robinson and the style of play he had imported from the Negro leagues, opposition errors, wild pitches, and passed balls occurred as often as his own straight steals. It was no coincidence, either, that the hitters following him in the lineup all batted around .300 or that the team as a whole took on an arrogant edge.

Robinson wasn't the only charter member of the Boys of Summer to make his presence felt in 1947. As the anchor of the club, Reese batted .284, with 73

One of Carl Furillo's unofficial jobs in right field was making sure that no opposition batter hit a ball off a sign advertising Abe Stark's clothing store. The reward for the batter would have been a new suit. After years of saving Stark merchandise, Furillo decided that he was entitled to a suit, and asked for one. He received only a pair of slacks. Stark went on to become president of the New York City Council and Brooklyn Borough President.

RBIs and an NL-leading 104 walks. Playing center field was Carl Furillo, soon to move over to right where he would become even more of a People's Choice than Walker; Furillo batted .295 with 88 RBIs and showed the arm that would soon earn him the nickname The Reading Rifle. On the same day that Robinson made his debut, future Hall of Famer Duke Snider began his big league career with a pinch-hit single. Hodges was also back, this time as a backup catcher.

There was also a significant absence during the 1947 season. Six days before Opening Day, Happy Chandler announced that Durocher was being suspended for the year for what was termed an "accumulation of unpleasant incidents in which he has been involved which the commissioner construes as detrimental to baseball." The suspension followed months of tangled charges and recriminations among Durocher, Rickey, and MacPhail, who had bought into the Yankees after World War II. Other principals in the maelstrom were Hearst columnist Westbrook Pegler, actors George Raft and Laraine Day, and Durocher's on-and-off crony Dressen.

The trouble began after the 1946 season, when Pegler issued a call for Rickey to fire Durocher because the manager was all too frequently seen with Raft and a couple of professional gamblers close to the actor. Under Rickey's urging, Chandler summoned Durocher and extracted a promise from him to change his friends. But just as the situation seemed resolved, MacPhail weighed in with the claim that Durocher had come to him to ask for the Yankee managing job. Rickey, already furious that MacPhail had signed away Dressen as a coach, immediately agreed to a new contract with Durocher and stood by while the Dodger pilot called MacPhail a liar and asserted that he had actually turned down an offer instigated by the Yankee official. A couple of weeks later, MacPhail enraged Rickey further by poaching a second Brooklyn coach, Red Corriden. While all this was going on, Pegler increased his attacks, insinuating among other things that the commissioner didn't really care about Durocher's associates because Chandler was from Kentucky and all Kentucky politicians were crooks.

Durocher didn't need Pegler to stay in newsprint. Barely exonerated of the attack on the Ebbets Field heckler, he began dating the rising Hollywood star Day, then still legally married. When the actress's husband started feeding gossip columns the details of the adultery, Day and Durocher flew off to Mexico to get her a quickie divorce and then returned to Texas to get married. Pegler and various church groups couldn't decide which they abhorred more—the association with gamblers, the flagrant adultery, or the instant divorce and remarriage. For its part, the Catholic Youth Organization (CYO) of Brooklyn announced that it was withdrawing from a Dodger Knot Hole promotion for kids because "the present manager . . . is not the kind of leader we want to idealize and imitate."

With Robinson's debut at hand, Rickey played down the grumbles of his partners and continued to support Durocher. But then, during a March 8, 1947 exhibition game against the Yankees in Havana, the Dodger general manager himself added fuel to the fire when he spotted MacPhail sitting in the Yankee box with two of the same gamblers Chandler had warned Durocher away from. First Rickey, then Durocher, demanded an explanation from Chandler about his apparent double standard in policing managers and franchise owners. This in turn set off MacPhail, who not only accused Rickey and Durocher of slandering him, but asked that Chandler investigate a regular Brooklyn *Eagle* column written under Durocher's name that had little pleasant to say about anybody connected to the Yankees. Chandler had no alternative but to call in all the principals for a hearing. After listening to everyone's story, he fined both the Dodgers and Yankees $2,000 for "a public controversy damaging to baseball"; fined Dodger traveling secretary Harold Parrott $500 for ghosting the *Eagle* attacks on the Yankees; suspended Dressen for thirty days for breaking an agreement with Rickey that he would leave the Dodgers only to manage (not coach) another team; and bounced Durocher for twelve months for incidents dating back to the team poker games in the early 1940s. As for MacPhail, he was exonerated of

Leo Durocher sits with George Raft during the 1946 World Series. Six months later, the Brooklyn manager was suspended for a year for, among other things, associating with the actor. To Raft's left are restaurateur Toots Shor and Joe DiMaggio. *UPI/Bettmann Newsphotos*

having invited the gamblers into the Yankee box, but was also reprimanded for having floated the stories of Durocher managing the Yankees to help his old field leader work out a more advantageous contract with Rickey. This latter suggestion did nothing for Durocher's relations with Rickey.

With Durocher gone and Sukeforth showing little interest in managing except as an emergency fill-in, Rickey turned to Burt Shotton, a former aide with the Cardinals who had retired to Florida at the age of sixty-two. Shotton was as colorless as Durocher was bumptious, to a point that he even declined to wear a uniform, preferring to remain confined to the dugout (as stipulated by NL rules) in his street clothes. Nevertheless, it was Shotton who steered the team through the shoals of Robinson's debut year and a hard challenge from St. Louis to win the flag. Once again, however, it was WAIT TILL NEXT YEAR as far as the World Series was concerned, with the Dodgers falling to the Yankees in seven games. As consolation prizes, the club took away two of the most dramatic moments in World Series history: Lavagettos' two-out, pinch-double in the ninth inning of the fourth game that broke up Bill Bevens's no-hitter and gave Brooklyn a 3–2 victory, and left fielder Al Gionfriddo's circus catch against Joe DiMaggio in the sixth game. Neither Lavagetto nor Gionfriddo (nor Bevens, for that matter) would return in 1948.

One who did return the following season was Durocher, but there was little doubt from spring training that he had outstayed his welcome with Rickey. To make matters worse, he took to sniping at Shotton for having won the pennant with "his" players and at Rickey for worrying only about money by dealing Stanky to the Braves after the second baseman had demanded a substantial pay raise. When the Dodgers began floundering beneath both the Braves and Cardinals, Rickey sought to contain the publicity damage as much as possible by dropping hints to Durocher that he should resign. But Durocher refused all the way up to the All Star Game, where as Shotton's replacement he had the right to skipper the NL. The game ended up being the last one ever managed by Durocher as a Dodger. When Horace Stoneham called Rickey to request permission to talk to Shotton as a possible replacement for Mel Ott as manager of the Giants, Rickey said no—but gave permission instead for Stoneham to approach Durocher. Within days, Durocher had moved to the Polo Grounds and Shotton was back in Ebbets Field.

Although the Stanky deal had indeed been prompted by salary considerations and contributed mightily to Boston's pennant win in 1948, it also set in motion a number of lineup changes in Brooklyn that would benefit the team for years to come. To replace Stanky at second, Robinson was moved from first; to replace Robinson, Hodges was moved out from behind the plate; and to take over first-string catching duties, Roy Campanella was promoted from the minors. With Reese solidified at short and Cox coming over from the Pirates to handle third, the Boys of Summer infield was in place by the end of 1948. In 1949, the last big piece was installed with Snider taking over center and Furillo moving to right (a number of players, including Robinson and Hodges, would play left over the next few years). Especially with the other regulars all righthanded, the lefty-swinging Snider wasted little time in becoming one of the NL's most menacing sluggers.

The team rebounded from its somewhat chaotic 1948 season to win the pennant again in 1949. The keys were Robinson, who won the batting title and the league's MVP award; Hodges, Snider, and Furillo, all of whom drove in 100 runs; Campanella's defense; and Rookie of the Year Don Newcombe, who led the staff with seventeen wins. Once again, however, a stronger Yankee team prevailed in the World Series, this time in only five games.

If Dodger fans were heartsore after another postseason failure in 1949, they needed a transplant after excruciating, back-to-back setbacks on the final day of NL play in both 1950 and 1951. In 1950, the foe was Philadelphia's Whiz Kids, who ended decades of Phillies misery by bolting out ahead of the pack early in the year and beating off all comers until September. Then, on September 19th, 9 games behind and in third place, the Dodgers made their long-awaited move. Led by Newcombe and Roe on the mound (both would win 19) and by Hodges, Snider, and Campanella on offense (all three would hit more than thirty homers), the club closed the gap to two games on the final weekend of the season. Needing both games against the Phillies to force a playoff, the Dodgers took the first contest before a roaring Ebbets Field crowd, then sent Newcombe out for the finale against Philadelphia ace Robin Roberts. After five scoreless innings, the Phillies broke through for a run, only to be matched by an inside-the-park homer by Reese. In the bottom of the ninth inning, Snider singled to center for the apparent winning run, but Cal Abrams, starting off from second and being pursued on the basepaths by Reese, was thrown out at home by Richie Ashburn. When neither Furillo nor Hodges could get the winning run across, the Dodgers went into the tenth inning and went down on an opposite-field, three-run homer by Dick Sisler.

The season was barely over when Milt Stock, the third base coach who had sent in Abrams, was fired (this despite the fact that he had little choice in the matter with Reese already steaming into third base behind Abrams). But then, on October 26th, there was an even more significant announcement: Rickey was out.

Ever since he had borrowed the capital he needed to join with Smith and O'Malley in the purchase of 75 percent of the club, Rickey had lamented his personal financial situation. With his five-year contract as president and general manager up, and with O'Malley in particular toting up all the demerits of the Durocher and MacPhail controversies, he was not at all certain that he would be given a new pact, so he sought to beat his partners to the punch by offering to sell his original $350,000 investment. But in typical fashion, he also made sure that O'Malley and the Smith estate would pay heavily for the privilege by arranging (through Pittsburgh owner John Galbreath) for a rival buy out offer from New York real estate developer William Zeckendorf, who put $1.05 million on the table. O'Malley, who was learning fast about boardroom skills, realized that the only alternative to meeting the price was to risk having Zeckendorf team up with the Mulveys to frustrate his designs for the franchise, so he and Smith's widow came up with the money.

A week after succeeding Rickey as club president, O'Malley began bringing in his own team. To take over baseball operations, he promoted Buzzy Bavasi, a MacPhail man, to the post of general manager. Another MacPhail protégé, Fresco Thompson, was given control of the farm system. Then, to make his point even clearer, he substituted MacPhail's favorite coach (and former Cincinnati pilot) Dressen for Rickey confidant Shotton.

Dressen fit the Dodger franchise pattern of managers perfectly. Known as Jolly Cholly for his outgoing manner and constant whistling to gain attention on or off the ballfield, he represented another rising note in the alternating up and down managerial personalities that stretched back through Shotton, Durocher, Grimes, Stengel, Carey, and Robinson (and that would be extended again when he was replaced eventually by stolid Walter Alston). Second, like McGunnigle, Hanlon, Durocher, and so many others, Dressen took a back seat to no one in admiring his own managing abilities. More than one writer would claim that he had never heard Dressen use a sentence without the word "I" in it. Dressen himself would admit to saying to his players once when trailing 9–0 in the middle of the game, "hold them there and I'll think of something." Whatever his faults, he was held in such respect that most of the Boys of Summer, especially Reese and Robinson, said he was the best manager they ever had.

Despite Sisler's traumatic home run, the Dodgers were favored again to go all the way in 1951. With Carl Erskine joining Newcombe, Roe, and Branca in the rotation, the only open question entering the season was left field, and that seemed to be resolved in June when Bavasi engineered an eight-player trade with the Cubs that brought All Star Andy Pafko to Brooklyn. When Pafko showed that he had lost little of his power and complemented Snider and Furillo in the outfield defensively as well as offensively, Dressen was moved to tell reporters that the runner-up Giants "will never bother us again." By August 11, the Dodger lead over New York had grown to 13½ games, with Roe (22–3), Newcombe (20–9), Hodges (40 homers, 103 RBIs), and Campanella (33 homers, 108 RBIs, .325, MVP) on their way to particularly brilliant years. But then on August 12th the Giants had shaved a game off the lead and were launched on the greatest comeback drive in major league history. By the time September had been spent, the teams were heading for a best-of-three playoff, Brooklyn getting even that far only by virtue of an heroic fielding and hitting display by Robinson against Philadelphia on the final day of the regular season.

The most famous of all playoff series began with Branca yielding homers to Bobby Thomson and Monte Irvin and losing 3–1. The following day, Dodger rookie Clem Labine evened the score with a 10–0 shutout that benefited from three Brooklyn homers. Then, on October 3, with Newcombe taking a 4–1 lead into the ninth inning at the Polo Grounds, the implausible happened. After three hits and only one out, Newcombe was lifted for Branca, who grooved a 0–1 pitch that Thomson hit for "'the shot heard 'round the world" and a Giants pennant.

As after the Abrams debacle in 1950, the Thomson homer cost a Dodger coach his job—in this case Sukeforth, for having implied to Dressen that Branca looked better in the bullpen than either Erskine or Labine and stood the best chance of getting the Giants out. (It certainly didn't help that Sukeforth had been another confidant of Rickey's.) What Branca didn't lose psychologically in the playoffs he lost physically the following spring when he fell through a chair in the clubhouse, tilted his pelvis, and injured his arm by attempting a new motion to compensate for his aches. Newcombe was also lost to the team when he was drafted into military service. But despite these two blows to their rotation and other injuries to Cox and Furillo, the Dodgers stormed through the season with only a modest challenge from the Giants. If the team had a most valuable player, it was Rookie of the Year Joe Black, a reliever who led the staff with 15 wins and 15 saves. But still again, it was the Yankees waiting in the World Series and, still again, the club went down to New York, this time after a full seven games.

With Newcombe still in the Army, Bavasi sought to beef up the pitching staff for 1953 by obtaining Russ Meyer from the Phillies in a complex four-team trade. With Pafko gone in a deal with the Braves, Dressen moved Robinson to left field and installed Jim Gilliam, that year's NL Rookie of the Year, at second base. The results were 105 victories, the most in franchise history. Although Erskine won 20 and Meyer came through with 15 more victories, the story was almost completely in the team's offense. For the first of five consecutive seasons, Snider hit at least 40 home runs. He was matched by Campanella, who became the only catcher in history to reach the same mark and whose 142 RBIs and .312 average netted him his second MVP award. Then there were Hodges and Furillo.

Next to Reese, Hodges was the most popular member of the Boys of Summer. Neither quick-tempered like Snider, intense like Robinson, nor moody like Furillo, he built his constituency from an image of a strong, silent man who had become the best defensive first baseman in baseball and whose power feats included clouting four homers in one game (against Boston, on August 31, 1950). In addition, Hodges was a year-round Brooklyn resident, as often to be encountered in the groceries and laundromats of Flatbush as on the diamond at Ebbets Field. It thus became a mini-crisis for the entire borough when he went hitless in 21 at bats in the 1952 World Series and began the following season by going 14 for 75. The player became inundated with rosary beads, rabbits' feet, and four-leaf clovers.

Footnote Player: Bill Sharman, the future basketball great for the Boston Celtics, was called up late one September in the early 1950s. Although he never appeared in a big league game, he was thrown out of one when umpires decided that he was doing too much heckling from the bench.

Then, in June, a priest named Herbert Redmond placed Hodges forever within Brooklyn lore by telling his parishioners: "It's too warm this morning for a sermon. Go home, keep the commandments, and say a prayer for Gil Hodges." A couple of days later, the first baseman erupted for a season that would add up to 31 homers, 122 RBIs, and a .302 batting average.

Furillo earned special admiration from Brooklyn fans for his uncanny mastery of the rightfield wall in Ebbets Field and his particularly ferocious play against the Giants. Few were the drives that banged off the home team's rightfield scoreboard (and dozens of jutting edges), its adjoining billboards, or crowning screen that didn't end up directly in the outfielder's glove. Along with Robinson, Furillo was at his best when he faced former manager Durocher, and there were few series between the clubs that didn't have both players hitting the ground to avoid beanballs. But in a game at the Polo Grounds on September 6, 1953, the rivalry between the teams reached new levels of bitterness after New York rookie Ruben Gomez hit Furillo on the wrist. At first, the outfielder was successfully blocked from going out to the mound after Gomez. But then, as he stood on first base and heard Durocher's catcalls from the dugout, he sprang toward the New York bench after the manager. With umpire Babe Pinelli shouting "Get him, Carl, get him!," Furillo started swinging into the pile of bodies that had accumulated around him and Durocher. When everyone was finally separated, Furillo realized that one of the Giants had stepped on his hand in the melee, fracturing the palm and breaking a finger. Although the injury caused him to miss the rest of the regular season, it also allowed him to sit on a .344 batting average that gave him the hitting title.

Despite what was probably the most formidable team in the history of the franchise, the Dodgers fell to the Yankees for the fifth straight time in the World Series, four games to two. As deflating as this was, O'Malley was even more concerned by the fact that the second-place Braves had drawn 650,000 more fans than the Dodgers in their new Milwaukee home. He was also quick to note the three main reasons for the edge: a bigger stadium, more parking space, and a blackout on local television coverage of games.

Ever since Carey and Stengel had collected money for not managing, the franchise had become wary of offering more than one-year pacts to its pilots. When the same offer was made to Dressen after the 1953 season, however, his wife Ruth wrote to O'Malley pointing out the virtues of her husband

and demanding a three-year contract. O'Malley didn't agree, Dressen procrastinated, and then O'Malley said no when the manager had a change of heart. The new pilot for 1954 was Walter Alston, a veteran of the Dodger farm system.

Alston's reception in Brooklyn was decidedly cool. First, there were the newspaper headlines asking WALTER WHO? and WHO HE? Then there were the insistent reports that he had gotten the job only after Reese and farm system director Thompson had turned it down and that both of them were ready to jump in at any time if the freshman skipper proved inadequate. Perhaps worst of all, Alston walked into a clubhouse that reeked with sympathy for Dressen and regret that Reese hadn't succeeded him.

The promise of a bad year was fulfilled. Newcombe was finally back from the Army, but developed shoulder problems that limited him to nine wins. Robinson sustained a leg injury that did nothing to assist him in a battle of the bulge, Campanella sat out a good part of the season after bone chip surgery on his wrist, and Cox had slowed down to a bench player.

The 1955 season began with some significant absences. The most conspicuous of these was the *Eagle*, the daily paper that had practically grown up with the team and the demise of which was viewed as symptomatic of the borough's general economic and social decline. Also gone were Roe and Cox, both dealt to the Orioles in the offseason. Their absences were made up for by a recovered Newcombe, who won 20, and by a combination of Don Zimmer, Don Hoak, and Sandy Amoros that moved in and out of the lineup with Robinson to give the team even more clout. Although Snider was a worthy candidate with his 42 homers and 136 RBIs, the MVP award went for the third time to Campanella, not only for his 32 homers and 107 RBIs, but for his handling of a pitching staff that was decidedly unexceptional after Newcombe. The club clinched the pennant on September 8th, the earliest in NL history.

The 1955 World Series against the Yankees was NEXT YEAR. After splitting the first six games, the teams matched up in a thriller at Yankee Stadium between southpaws Johnny Podres and Tommy Byrne, finally won by Brooklyn 2–0. The only runs in the game were driven in by Hodges, the goat of the 1952 series. But even the efforts of Podres and Hodges were overshadowed by the turning point of the game in the sixth inning, when left fielder Amoros, inserted that inning for defense, made a spectacular catch on a drive by Yogi Berra down the

left field foul line, then relayed the ball to Reese, who fired a strike over to Hodges at first to complete a double play that effectively ended the chances of the Yankees. The Dodger victory prompted explosive celebrations in Brooklyn, with schools and many businesses shut down for a triumphal parade the next day. The phone company estimated that more people picked up receivers in the hours immediately after the game than had after the announcement of the end of World War II.

Through all the euphoria, O'Malley remained the center of business reality. Noting that the team had reached its attendance peak of 1.8 million all the way back in Robinson's debut year of 1947, he announced that the Dodgers would play a handful of games in 1956 and 1957 in Jersey City's Roosevelt Stadium. He made little attempt to mask the one and only true reason for the move—to persuade city officials that he was serious about wanting a facility larger and more modern than Ebbets Field, even if that meant leaving Brooklyn altogether. Despite the threat, the city continued to say no to his specific proposal for building a new park in downtown Brooklyn, offering instead the Queens site that would one day become the location of Shea Stadium.

Despite all the distractions of O'Malley's gradually embittered negotiations with the city and of the odd games played in Jersey City (usually to no more than ten or twelve thousand fans), 1956 turned out to be one of the team's most exciting seasons, with the pennant not decided until the final day. Partly because of this greater tension and partly because of the stirrings of some civic groups worried that the club might indeed go elsewhere, attendance rose by more than 166,000 over the championship year. After lagging behind Milwaukee most of the year, the Dodgers went into the final weekend a game behind, whereupon they swept the Pirates three straight while St. Louis was taking two out of three from the Braves. The team had arrived that far on Newcombe's greatest season, when his 27–7 record netted him both the Cy Young and MVP awards and made him the only one ever to snare both those honors plus a Rookie of the Year recognition; Labine's 10 wins and league-leading 19 saves; Snider's 43 homers and 101 RBIs; and Furillo's relentless clutch hitting in September. Then there was Sal Maglie.

The ace of the Giants for years, Maglie had embodied everything Brooklyn fans had come to hate about Durocher's New Yorkers. His nickname, The Barber, was the result of his penchant for "shaving" the chins of batters he thought had too much of the plate. When the Giants waived the righthander to the Indians in the middle of the 1955 season, Brooklyn fans were relieved that he had apparently come to the end of the road. When Bavasi announced in May 1956 that his contract had been purchased from the Indians, the reaction was astonishment. But, after some obligatory photographs with Furillo and Robinson to show that bygones were bygones, Maglie earned Ebbets Field cheers by compiling a 13–5 mark with the lowest ERA on the staff. In the final week of the season, he raised his performance level a notch further by first pitching a no-hitter against the Phillies and then by beating the Pirates in the game that would give the team first place for good.

It was also Maglie who shared the mound for the single greatest pitching performance in World Series history, when his five-hitter against the Yankees in the fifth game came up short of Don Larsen's perfect game, 2–0. In a return to pre-1955, the Dodgers went down to New York in seven games.

Two weeks after the World Series, O'Malley disclosed that the team had sold Ebbets Field to real estate developer Melvin Kratter for $3 million, then taken a lease on the park for three years with an option to rent it for two additional years. While optimists noted that this commitment could keep the club in the stadium until 1961, their ranks were not particularly heavy, especially after the city showed marked reluctance even to investigate the feasibility of the downtown site desired by O'Malley for a new facility. The single break from the off-season speculation about the future of the franchise came in December when Bavasi announced that he had traded Robinson to the Giants for journeyman pitcher Dick Littlefield and an estimated $30,000. Robinson's playing for the Giants was even more unthinkable than Maglie's playing for the Dodgers, but at first the future Hall of Famer said only that he was "'considering'' retirement. It emerged a month later that he had already sold the exclusive story of his retirement to a magazine and was bound contractually not to tip his hand until the periodical hit the newsstands. Despite strong pressures from Giants' owner Stoneham to come back for one more year, Robinson said no.

Robinson's last couple of years in Brooklyn were not especially happy ones. Physically, he was plagued by a number of leg injuries and a ballooning waistline that just about killed his running game. Never at ease with O'Malley, he found himself at odds even more frequently with Alston, especially after an incident in which the manager remained in the dugout while he carried on a long argument with an umpire over a play at second base. Robinson's relations with the press had also undergone a change in the seasons following his debut. The more he asserted his rights on the diamond as just another player and forgot about Rickey's stricture to turn the other cheek, the more even the sportswriters who had originally supported his arrival (for example, Dick Young of the *Daily News*) fell back on suggestions that he was arrogant and compared him unfavorably to other black players, most frequently the genial Campanella. Robinson's swan song turned out to be the sixth game of the 1956 World Series, when his 11th-inning drive over the head of old nemesis Enos Slaughter gave the Dodgers a 1–0 victory and kept them alive for a seventh game against the Yankees.

Just as Robinson's arrival had coincided with the suspension of Durocher, his departure coincided with the suspension of baseball in Brooklyn altogether. Through the early months of 1957, O'Malley moved quickly. First he arranged a swap of minor league franchises with Chicago's Phil Wrigley that gave him title to Los Angeles's Wrigley Field and territorial prerogatives over the city. Then he traded the park to the city of Los Angeles for the Chavez Ravine site where he intended building a new stadium. The last obstacle fell away in August, when Stoneham of the Giants announced that he would be moving his club to San Francisco for the following year, thus fulfilling an NL condition that more than one team would have to move west for the transfer to be viable from the point of view of the league's travel schedule. The official announcement came a week after the conclusion of the season, on October 8, when a terse communiqué said only that "the stockholders and directors of the Brooklyn Baseball Club have today met and unanimously agreed that necessary steps be taken to draft the Los Angeles territory.''

In their final Brooklyn season, the Dodgers slipped back to the record (84 wins) and the standing (third) they had last occupied in 1948, before the full assemblage of the Boys of Summer. The final Ebbets Field game took place on September 24, 1957, with rookie southpaw Danny McDevitt besting the Pirates 2–0 before a scant crowd of 6,702—about the average turnout back in the worst days of the Daffiness Boys. It was an appropriate reminder of the fact that, as imaginative as MacPhail and Rickey might have been, it had fallen to O'Malley to devise the greatest innovation of all for Brooklyn baseball—no baseball.

BROOKLYN DODGERS

Annual Standings and Managers

Year	Position	W	L	Pct.	GB	Managers
1890	First	86	43	.667	+6	Bill McGunnigle
1891	Sixth	61	76	.445	25½	John Montgomery Ward
1892	Second	51	26	.662	2½	John Montgomery Ward
	Third	44	33	.571	9½	John Montgomery Ward
1893	Sixth*	65	63	.508	20½	Dave Foutz
1894	Fifth	70	61	.534	20½	Dave Foutz
1895	Fifth*	71	60	.542	16½	Dave Foutz
1896	Ninth*	58	73	.443	33	Dave Foutz
1897	Sixth*	61	71	.462	32	Billy Barnie
1898	Tenth	54	91	.372	46	Billy Barnie, Mike Griffin, Charlie Ebbets
1899	First	101	47	.682	+8	Ned Hanlon
1900	First	82	54	.603	+4½	Ned Hanlon
1901	Third	79	57	.581	9½	Ned Hanlon
1902	Second	75	63	.543	27½	Ned Hanlon
1903	Fifth	70	66	.515	19	Ned Hanlon
1904	Sixth	56	97	.366	50	Ned Hanlon
1905	Eighth	48	104	.316	56½	Ned Hanlon
1906	Fifth	66	86	.434	50	Patsy Donovan
1907	Fifth	65	83	.439	40	Patsy Donovan
1908	Seventh	53	101	.344	46	Patsy Donovan
1909	Sixth	55	98	.359	55½	Harry Lumley
1910	Sixth	64	90	.416	40	Bill Dahlen
1911	Seventh	64	86	.427	33½	Bill Dahlen
1912	Seventh	58	95	.379	46	Bill Dahlen
1913	Sixth	65	84	.436	34½	Bill Dahlen
1914	Fifth	75	79	.487	19½	Wilbert Robinson
1915	Third	80	72	.526	10	Wilbert Robinson
1916	First	94	60	.610	+2½	Wilbert Robinson
1917	Seventh	70	81	.464	26½	Wilbert Robinson
1918	Fifth	57	69	.452	25½	Wilbert Robinson
1919	Fifth	69	71	.493	27	Wilbert Robinson
1920	First	93	61	.604	+7	Wilbert Robinson
1921	Fifth	77	75	.507	16½	Wilbert Robinson
1922	Sixth	76	78	.494	17	Wilbert Robinson
1923	Sixth	76	78	.494	19½	Wilbert Robinson
1924	Second	92	62	.597	1½	Wilbert Robinson
1925	Sixth*	68	85	.444	27	Wilbert Robinson
1926	Sixth	71	82	.464	17½	Wilbert Robinson
1927	Sixth	65	88	.425	28½	Wilbert Robinson
1928	Sixth	77	76	.503	17½	Wilbert Robinson
1929	Sixth	70	83	.458	28½	Wilbert Robinson
1930	Fourth	86	68	.558	6	Wilbert Robinson
1931	Fourth	79	73	.520	21	Wilbert Robinson
1932	Third	81	73	.526	9	Max Carey
1933	Sixth	65	88	.425	26½	Max Carey
1934	Sixth	71	81	.467	23½	Casey Stengel
1935	Fifth	70	83	.458	29½	Casey Stengel
1936	Seventh	67	87	.435	25	Casey Stengel
1937	Sixth	62	91	.405	33½	Burleigh Grimes
1938	Seventh	69	80	.463	18½	Burleigh Grimes
1939	Third	84	69	.549	12½	Leo Durocher
1940	Second	88	65	.575	12	Leo Durocher

1941	First	100	54	.649	+2½	Leo Durocher
1942	Second	104	50	.675	2	Leo Durocher
1943	Third	81	72	.529	23½	Leo Durocher
1944	Seventh	63	91	.409	42	Lco Durocher
1945	Third	87	67	.565	11	Leo Durocher
1946	Second	96	60	.615	2	Leo Durocher
1947	First	94	60	.610	+5	Clyde Sukeforth, Burt Shotton
1948	Third	84	70	.545	7½	Leo Durocher, Burt Shotton
1949	First	97	57	.630	+1	Burt Shotton
1950	Second	89	65	.578	2	Burt Shotton
1951	Second	97	60	.618	1	Charlie Dressen
1952	First	96	57	.627	+4½	Charlie Dressen
1953	First	105	49	.682	+13	Charlie Dressen
1954	Second	92	62	.597	5	Walter Alston
1955	Fist	98	55	.641	+13½	Walter Alston
1956	First	93	61	.604	+1	Walter Alston
1957	Third	84	70	.545	11	Walter Alston

*Tie

Postseason Play

WS	1–4 versus Boston	1916
	2–5 versus Cleveland	1920
	1–4 versus New York	1941
	3–4 versus New York	1947
	1–4 versus New York	1949
	3–4 versus New York	1952
	2–4 versus New York	1953
	4–3 versus New York	1955
	3–4 versus New York	1956

Brooklyn Tip-Tops

Federal League, 1914–1915   **BALLPARK:** WASHINGTON PARK

RECORD: 147–159 (.480)   **OTHER NAMES:** BROOKFEDS

The Brooklyn Federal League club was one of the upstart league's most influential franchises because of the wealth and involvement of its owner, Robert B. Ward, whose thirteen Tip-Top bakeries produced almost two hundred and fifty million loaves of bread in 1913. At first, Ward declined to call his club the Tip-Tops, denying an attempt to use baseball as an advertising vehicle for his bakeries; he wanted to call the team the Brookfeds. By 1915, however, the club's official scorecard referred to the team as the Tip-Tops, and all qualms about advertising the bread were forgotten.

The Tip-Tops' front office was all Wards: Robert

The Ward brothers built five eighty-foot light towers at Washington Park in preparation for introducing night baseball in 1916. A postseason exhibition involving Federal League players and local semipros was to have been the trial for regularly scheduled games under the lights every Monday, Tuesday, Thursday, and Friday.

as president; brothers George and Walter as vice-president and secretary-treasurer, respectively; and the illustrious John Montgomery Ward, who was not related, as business manager (in 1914 only). The team played in a new cement and steel stadium on the site of the old wooden Washington Park. Opening day there was not scheduled until May 11th because the Wards anticipated difficulties with construction unions protesting the Tip-Top bakeries' non-union hiring policies. It wasn't until April 17th, four days after the season began, that the concrete for the grandstand was poured. Amid much fanfare, the Tip-Tops lost the home opener to Pittsburgh, as Howie Camnitz five-hit the home team to defeat Tom Seaton 2–0. Only 15,000 fans showed up, leaving about 4,000 empty seats in the new facility.

Manager Bill Bradley had former Brooklyn great Willie Keeler as a coach; right fielder Steve Evans, whose .348 average was second best in the FL and included 12 home runs; and Seaton, 25–13 with a 3.03 ERA. The one that got away was Giants ace Rube Marquard, who signed a two-year, $20,000 contract with the Brookfeds after the Giants turned down his request for a $1,500 advance. Marquard signed a false affidavit swearing he was not under contract to the Giants and accepted a $1,500 advance from Ward. When the truth came out, the hurler had to return to New York, and John McGraw had to reimburse Ward to prevent the owner's suing the pitcher for fraud.

The Tip-Tops stayed in contention a good part of the season and finished a respectable fifth, but the club was compelled to lower ticket prices because of faltering attendance. Although it was already clear after the first season that the FL was in trouble, the Tip-Tops fortified themselves for the 1915 season by the addition of Benny Kauff, whose transfer to Brooklyn was part of the deal that saw the pennant-winning Indianapolis Hoosiers transplanted to Newark. Kauff hit a game-winning three-run homer

on opening day but felt cheated when John Montgomery Ward's successor as business manager, Dick Carroll, withheld the $500 he had been advanced by the Hoosiers. When the outfielder defected to the NL Giants, FL president James Gilmore suspended him for ten days and fined him $100. The flamboyant Kauff, who had once declared "I'll make Cobb look like a bush leaguer if I can play for the Giants," was prevented from appearing for the New Yorkers when the Boston Braves complained that McGraw was hiring a contract jumper. Kauff first sought reinstatement from organized baseball's National Commission, then, rebuffed, conveniently forgot his promise to retire if he couldn't play for the Giants and went back to the Feds. By then, Robert Ward had soured on him and entertained the possibility of letting him go to the Whales. Kauff, however, hired John Montgomery Ward as his attorney and was reinstated on the Tip-Tops when he threatened to sue.

Kauff went on to lead the FL in batting for a second consecutive year with a .342 average. Lee Magee, who jumped from the St. Louis Cardinals to play second base and manage the Tip-Tops, hit .323. But the defense was the worst in the league, and the team dropped to seventh place. Magee was fired as manager toward the end of the season and replaced by John Ganzel.

On October 19th, Robert Ward suffered a fatal heart attack. Ban Johnson suggested that "the Federal League put him under the sod as he could not stand the strain of worries and losses." On the contrary, Ward had offered another million dollars to the cause if Gilmore thought the Feds could win the war. But even with Ward's backing, Gilmore had concluded that they might be able to bluff organized ball into a decent settlement, but there was no way they could win. Ward had lost more than $800,000, and his brothers, lacking the stomach to continue the fight, joined the consensus that defeat was inevitable. The Ward family received $400,000 (in twenty annual installments) of the total settlement package of $600,000 and turned over ownership of Washington Park to the Brooklyn Dodgers.

The right field wall at Washington Park carried an admonition to the fans: "Baseball players are all human, and therefore love applause. If you want a winning team, root for them, speak well of them to your friends, and while we are here let us all be clean of speech—so that ladies may find it pleasant to come often."

Footnote Player: Ed Lafitte, a descendant of New Orleans pirate Jean Lafitte, is the only pitcher to throw a no-hitter but never a shutout. Lafitte's no-hitter was a 6–2 victory over Kansas City on September 19, 1914.

BROOKLYN TIP-TOPS

Annual Standings and Managers

Year	Position	W	L	Pct.	GB	Managers
1914	Fifth	77	77	.500	11½	Bill Bradley
1915	Seventh	70	82	.461	16	Lee Magee, John Ganzel

Buffalo Bisons

National League, 1879–1885 **BALLPARKS:** RIVERSIDE PARK (1879–1883)
OLYMPIC PARK (1884–1885)

RECORD: 314–333 (.485)

In 1879, when the Bisons joined the National League from the loosely constituted International Association, there was no certainty that the league would be able to survive, let alone achieve its goal of dominating baseball. Support for joining the NL was not universal. Management was particularly apprehensive that the NL's mandatory 50¢ admission fee would drive away fans. Further, team captain Davy Force, who had played in the NL in its first two seasons before joining the Bisons, had seen firsthand the league's financial instability and expressed his misgivings in a letter to Buffalo management.

Nevertheless, Buffalo entered the NL for the 1879 season with essentially the same team that had done so well in the International Association the year before. The single addition was catcher-manager John Clapp, who led the club to a surprisingly strong third place finish in 1879, due primarily to the pitching of rookie Pud Galvin (37–27). One of the greatest pitchers of the nineteenth century, Galvin, tied for sixth place on the all-time win list with 361 victories (219 of them with the Bisons), was elected to the Hall of Fame in 1965.

In 1880, Clapp moved on to Cincinnati and was replaced by Bill McGunnigle, who was in turn replaced by Sam Crane after only seventeen games. Galvin dropped to 20–37 after an early season holdout. The Bisons finished seventh.

Josiah Jewett, son of the founder of the Jewett Stove Company, became president of the Bisons in 1881 and brought in Orator Jim O'Rourke as player-manager. He also added heavy-hitting Hall of Fame first baseman Dan Brouthers and former NL batting

National Baseball Library, Cooperstown, NY

champion Deacon Jim White to the club. Brouthers and White, along with Hardy Richardson and Jack Rowe, who had been a big part of the Bisons since 1879, became the Big Four who were supposed to lead the Bisons to glory.

Jewett ran the team very much according to the rules. At an NL meeting on October 4, 1880, Buffalo had opposed continuing the year-old reserve rule on the grounds that it had not served its primary purpose of suppressing salaries. Jewett reversed the team's original policy and enforced the reserve rule with particular severity against outfielder Curry Foley. In 1882, Foley batted over .300 and on May 25 against Cleveland became the first player in the NL to hit for the cycle, including a grand slam home run. Early the next season, however, the outfielder became severely ill. Under the suspension rule, the Bisons were under no obligation to pay him as long as he was too sick to play; at the same time, the club could continue to claim his services for as long as it chose. This Jewett did not only for the 1883 season but also for 1884; in fact, Foley never played again despite the efforts of several minor league teams to sign him.

The Bisons finally made a ($5,000) profit in 1883 while finishing fifth. Jewett used the money to cover part of the $6,000 cost of building Olympic Park, which had a partially covered grandstand and a louvered ventilation system, both of which were innovations. But when, for the fourth time in six seasons, the Bisons could finish no higher than third in 1884, Jewett and the other shareholders changed their attitude. With no prospect for a pennant in the near future, the owners decided to unload their high-priced players. The first to go was ace pitcher Galvin, who had always presented problems to management. His 1880 holdout had forced the club to woo him back from an outlaw league in California. Three years later, he had complained loudly that the team's new blue uniforms made him look fat. But as long as he was one of the league's best pitchers (46 victories in both 1883 and 1884), the club had tolerated his idiosyncrasies. In mid-July, 1885, however, with his effectiveness diminished, Galvin was sold to the American Association Pittsburgh Alleghenys for $1,500. This simul-

taneously put $1,500 in the club's coffers and relieved it of Galvin's $2,500 salary—even though there was no rule permitting one team to sell a player contract to another. Galvin blasted the greed, charging the club with unwillingness to pay his salary.

Footnote Player: Before joining the Bisons, George Derby spent two years with the Detroit Wolverines, winning forty-six and losing the same number. But as Pud Galvin's "change" pitcher in 1883 he won only two and lost ten. The climax came on July 3rd when Derby lost to Chicago 31–7, going the distance against sixty-seven batters and giving up sixteen extra-base hits—both still records. The good news was that he walked only one batter in what turned out to be his last major league game.

On September 17th, the Bisons sold the entire team to the Detroit Wolverines for $7,000. With the club's finances approaching the disastrous, the sale was a ruse that allowed Buffalo to retain its NL franchise—at least until the end of the season—while recouping its losses. The resultant furor almost undid the deal. NL President Nick Young ruled that the players still belonged to the Bisons, but Brouthers, Richardson, Rowe, and White refused to return to Buffalo, claiming that they had been released and could sign anywhere they chose. Unable to play either for Detroit, because that would violate Young's ruling, or for Buffalo, because that would compromise their position, the four sat out the rest of the 1885 season. Although officially unsanctioned, the deal became a *fait accompli* in 1886 when, with Buffalo out of the league, the Big Four joined Detroit without protest.

The Bisons played out the 1885 season with inexperienced recruits and players no one else wanted. They suffered through repeated trouncings and minimal crowds, closing the season—and their existence—at home against Providence on October 7th. The gate receipts for that day amounted to $3.

BUFFALO BISONS

Annual Standings and Managers

Year	Position	W	L	Pct.	GB	Managers
1879	Third	46	32	.590	10	John Clapp
1880	Seventh	24	58	.293	42	Bill McGunnigle, Sam Crane
1881	Third	45	38	.542	10½	Jim O'Rourke

1882	Third*	45	39	.536	10	Jim O'Rourke
1883	Fifth	52	45	.536	10½	Jim O'Rourke
1884	Fifth	64	47	.577	19½	Jim O'Rourke
1885	Seventh*	38	74	.339	49	Jack Chapman, Pud Galvin, George Hughson

*Tie

Buffalo Bisons

Players League, 1890   **BALLPARK:** OLYMPIC PARK

RECORD: 36–96 (.273)

The inclusion of the Bisons in the ranks of the Players League was, to a great extent, the result of the insistence by Detroit Wolverines' third baseman Deacon White and shortstop Jack Rowe that they play in Buffalo regardless of the dictates of the reserve rule.

In 1889, White and Rowe owned stock in the Buffalo franchise in the International League. White was forty-one years old and, although Rowe was a decade younger, both were planning to retire and wanted to play their last season in Buffalo; White had even been named president of the club. When Detroit sold both infielders to Pittsburgh, they refused to report, prompting Detroit president Frederick Stearns to threaten: "White may have been elected president of the Buffalo club or president of the United States, but that won't enable him to play ball in Buffalo. He'll play ball in Pittsburgh or get off the earth."

As late as June 1889, White and Rowe were still not in uniform. They agreed to go to Pittsburgh only when John Montgomery Ward, the president of the players' Brotherhood, persuaded them to honor the reserve rule but not sign a contract. White arrived in Pittsburgh in the middle of June still angry. "No man can sell my carcass unless I get at least half," he grumbled to the press. Pittsburgh president William A. Nimick responded by giving White a $5,000 salary prorated for the rest of the year and a $1,250 bonus for having been sold.

The following winter, after the formation of the PL had been announced, a chain reaction of franchise shifts brought White and Rowe back to Buffalo. The PL had intended to challenge the NL in all eight of its cities, but then the NL dropped its Washington and Indianapolis franchises to admit the AA defectors Cincinnati and Brooklyn; the PL abandoned plans to enter the cities that the NL had rejected and included Brooklyn and Buffalo instead. White and Rowe were joined by catcher Connie Mack and center fielder Dummy Hoy as player–investors; the roster included eleven former members of the dropped Washington club. The Cincinnati *Enquirer* called the Bisons a "home for respectable old men," obviously a jibe at White because the rest of the squad was relatively young.

With Rowe as manger, the Bisons got off to a blistering start, defeating Cleveland in their first four games by scores of 28–2, 15–8, 19–7, and 18–5. By May 15th, however, the club had sunk to last place and never got out. The collapse was a collaborative effort. The Bisons scored the fewest runs and had the lowest batting average in the league, while the pitching, with a staff ERA of 6.11, gave up the most runs in the league.

Finishing last, 20 games out of seventh place, the Bisons drew only about 61,000 customers despite a refurbished Olympic Park. Unlike the rest of the PL, Buffalo couldn't even claim that the competition had done it in, because the city's International League team had fled to Montreal on June 3rd. When the peace settlement between the PL and NL came, the Bisons were simply ignored. All the other PL franchises had an NL rival with which it could negotiate either a buyout or consolidation; alone in its market, Buffalo had no alternative but to go out of business.

BUFFALO BISONS

Annual Standings and Manager

Year	Position	W	L	Pct.	GB	Manager
1890	Eighth	36	96	.273	46½	Jack Rowe

Buffalo Blues

Federal League, 1914–1915   **BALLPARK:** INTERNATIONAL FAIR ASSOCIATION GROUNDS

RECORD: 154–149 (.508)   **OTHER NAMES:** BUFFEDS

The Buffalo Federal League Club was a prime example of the reasons a third major league was doomed from the beginning. The franchise backers, who included founder Walter F. Mullen and club president William E. Robertson, took on one of the more formidable minor league clubs, the International League Bisons, and it soon became clear that there wasn't enough room in the small Buffalo market for a strong minor league club and one with major league pretensions. Along the way to disaster, however, the Buffeds pulled off one of the FL's great coups—the snaring of first baseman Hal Chase from the Chicago White Sox.

In less than two months, the Buffeds built a new wooden park, the International Fair Association Grounds (better known as Federal Park), that seated 20,000. Typically bad weather kept the opening day crowd to only about 14,000, and a bases-loaded walk by Gene Krapp that provided Baltimore with the winning run sent the crowd home unhappy as well as cold. The Buffeds' one established player was Russ Ford, an emery ball specialist from the American League Highlanders; Ford (20–6, 1.82) anchored a pitching staff that included five other hurlers with more than ten wins. Shortstop Baldy Louden, recruited from the Tigers, hit .313, and center fielder Charlie Hanford, the only member of the Bisons to jump to the rival Feds, chipped in with a .291 average, 10 home runs, and 90 RBIs. But what enabled the team to get into the first division and even remain a contender for a part of the season was the dramatic arrival of Chase in late June.

Chase had signed a contract with the Chicago White Sox for $6,000, one-fourth of which was spe-cifically to recompense him for giving the club the right to reserve him for the following season. This ploy to legitimize the reserve clause, though common at the time, sent the first baseman into high dudgeon over his right to play where he chose. Grabbing a trick from the owners' bag, he gave the White Sox ten days' notice, the standard advance notice a club had to give a player before releasing him, then took off for Buffalo. Charles Comiskey, the White Sox owner, secured an injunction to prevent Chase from playing for Buffalo, but Robertson hid the player in a hotel room until his debut on June 25th. After only two innings, the Erie County sheriff served Chase with the papers, putting him out of the lineup for several weeks until a judge refused to make the injunction permanent. The ruling, on July 21st, was a resounding condemnation of the "despotism of the monopoly established by the National Agreement" and the "species of quasi-peonage" to which it reduced ballplayers by taking away their property rights to their labor and to enter into a contract. Returning to the Buffeds, Chase hit .347 in seventy-three games to help lift them to fourth place.

The ultimate losers were the IL Bisons, who drew just over 100,000 to the Buffeds' 185,000. By August, the minor league club was floundering to the point that AL president Ban Johnson sent it $3,200 to help make its payroll. At the beginning of the 1915 season, Bisons' manager Patsy Donovan challenged the Buffeds to a one-game, winner-take-all showdown, with the loser vacating the territory. The Buffeds refused the challenge, but both organizations might have been better off had they accepted. The Bisons sank even deeper into the hole the Feds had created for them, requiring additional subsidies and eventually a friendly takeover by Boston Red Sox owner Joseph L. Lannin.

The Buffeds, renamed the Blues for 1915, added outfielder Jack Dalton (.293) from the Dodgers and pitcher Hugh Bedient (15–18) from the Red Sox. Although Ford slipped to 5–9, Schulz (21–14) and Anderson (19–13) more than made up the difference. As for Chase, he led the league in home runs with 17 and played his usually flashy first base.

None of this was sufficient to overcome the franchise's small market or Buffalo's weather, which conspired to reduce attendance to an even lower level than it had been in 1914. By the end of the season, despite lowered ticket prices and subsidies provided

by Harry Sinclair of the Newark club, cumulative losses had reached $170,000, with a total debt of more than $50,000. The FL settlement after the season excluded Buffalo, whose debts had forced it to forfeit its franchise. On July 21, 1916, the franchise declared bankruptcy, claiming almost $90,000 in debts. The bankruptcy court sold the ballpark for $55,000, with the land to be used for residential development. In September, Mullen, the real estate developer who had first advanced the idea of Buffalo's entry into the FL, announced his willingness to accept Buffed stock (which had been sold to the general public) as a down payment on one of the plots of land where the ballpark had stood.

BUFFALO BLUES

Annual Standings and Managers

Year	Position	W	L	Pct.	GB	Managers
1914	Fourth	80	71	.530	7	Harry Schlafly
1915	Sixth	74	78	.487	12	Harry Schlafly, Walter Blair, Harry Lord

California Angels

American League, 1961–Present

RECORD: 2482–2637 (.485)

BALLPARKS: WRIGLEY FIELD (1961)
DODGER STADIUM (1962–1965)
ANAHEIM STADIUM (1966–Present)

OTHER NAMES: LOS ANGELES ANGELS

Although only the Royals and Mets among expansion teams have appeared in more postseason series, the Angels have created an image of more wastrel than winner. In fact, throughout its three decades of existence, the club has been saddled with organizational indecisiveness, tragic luck, and a seeming mania for tossing good millions after bad millions. Sitting in the saddle has been former cowboy screen star Gene Autry, whose failure to qualify for the World Series had become almost as much of a rallying cry for the franchise by the 1990s as winning one for the Gipper had once been for Notre Dame. But Autry, as much as any of the dubious general managers working under him for thirty years, was also a primary source of the organizational confusion and incoherent spending policies frustrating the team's pennant ambitions. Much less explicable have been

the persistent tragedies that have cost many Angels their lives.

The expansion Angels were created on October 26, 1960 at an American League owners' meeting in New York that also sanctioned the transfer of Calvin Griffith's Washington Senators to Minneapolis–St. Paul and brought into existence a new big league team in the nation's capital. Hank Greenberg, the Hall of Fame slugger who was then a part-owner of the Chicago White Sox, went to work immediately putting together a syndicate that included fellow Hall of Famer Ralph Kiner, White Sox partner Bill Veeck, and San Diego banker C. Arnholt Smith. But no sooner had the Greenberg group been formed than Dodgers' owner Walter O'Malley, supported by Commissioner Ford Frick, stepped forward to claim Los Angeles as his exclusive territory. O'Malley's

Gene Autry found it much easier to ride his horse Champion through Hollywood westerns than to mount a championship team in the American League. *AP/Wide World Photos*

than the originally bruited compensation, O'Malley won for himself—and the rest of the NL—the senior circuit's right to reenter the New York market with the Mets in 1962.

So hastily was the deal with the Autry group hammered out that the new AL owners chose their first general manager—Fred Haney—while literally on their way to the press conference announcing the agreement. In accord with Autry and Reynolds, Haney went after Casey Stengel as the team's first manager, but Stengel declined on the grounds that he was committed to making no further career moves until *The Saturday Evening Post* had completed serializing his autobiography. With the expansion draft only days away, Haney then balanced the candidacies of Leo Durocher and Bill Rigney, decided that Durocher wouldn't have the patience to cope with a team that was starting from scratch, and came down in favor of Rigney. Because of Haney's long friendship with Los Angeles general manager Buzzy Bavasi and Rigney's with San Francisco general manager Chub Feeney, the Angels went into the draft armed with the detailed scouting reports compiled by the Dodgers and Giants. There was little question that this added intelligence gave them the edge on the new Washington Senators in the selection derby, enabling them to pick up the still-unknown minor leaguers Dean Chance from Baltimore, Buck Rodgers from Detroit, and Jim Fregosi and Fred Newman from Boston. As the Dodgers had in 1958, the Angels made sure that their inaugural season roster had room for bulky Steve Bilko, a first baseman whose slugging feats (and gargantuan whiffs) had made him a box-office magnet for minor league fans in the Los Angeles area for years.

The Angels played their first game in Baltimore on April 11, 1961, with the veteran Ted Kluszewski hitting two homers and righthander Eli Grba (the team's first selection in the draft) defeating a strong Orioles team 7–2. The club then dropped its next seven games and had as its chief consolation for the season the fact that its 70 wins (the most by an expansion team in an inaugural year) left it a mere half-game behind the Twins and comfortably in front of the Athletics and Senators. The other principal story of the year was Wrigley Field, a bandbox in which the power alleys were only five feet more distant than the 340-foot left field foul pole. Not too surprisingly, the facility set the all-time major league record for most home runs in a season—248. Five Angels—Bilko, catcher Earl Averill, and outfielders Ken Hunt, Leon Wagner, and Lee Thomas—each hit at least 20 round-trippers. Despite the fireworks

move was no belated awakening to competition in the Los Angeles market, because the AL expansion had been in the offing a year or more and the Dodgers had already suggested a $450,000 indemnification fee for giving up their exclusivity rights. What O'Malley had not counted on, however, was having to compete for southern California fans against the flamboyant showman Veeck. When AL owners could not persuade Greenberg to yield on the issue of his partner, the deal became unstuck.

Autry entered the scene through his Golden West broadcast operation, which had been quick to sign a tentative agreement with the Greenberg syndicate for airing Angels' games on KMPC. With Greenberg out of the picture, Autry and his partner Bob Reynolds paid $2.1 million for twenty-eight players made available through the expansion draft, gave O'Malley another $350,000 as indemnification, and agreed to lease Dodgers-owned facilities for at least five years—an initial season in Wrigley Field and the next four at Dodger Stadium, then still under construction. In exchange for taking $100,000 less promised by the long-ball hitting, Wrigley's small capacity of little more than 20,000 kept attendance down to a bare 600,000, about one-third of what the Dodgers drew that season at the Coliseum.

Mainly because of the lowest overhead in the league, the Angels declared a small profit for 1961, and immediately made the first in a long series of organizational miscalculations by paying out dividends instead of using the money to build up a farm system. The chronic lack of long-range planning was translated most immediately into forty-one deals involving fifty-four players over the first two seasons of the franchise's existence—most of the swaps for second-line position players and journeymen relievers needed because of a previous peddling off of another second-line position player and journeyman reliever.

If the franchise's modest success in 1961 nudged it down ill-advised paths, its stunning rise to third place in 1962 accelerated the misdirection for years to come. The good news was that the team stayed in the pennant race well into September, throwing a scare into the much better endowed Yankees and Twins. Offensively, the key men were Wagner (37 homers, 107 RBIs), Thomas (26 homers, 104 RBIs), and second baseman Billy Moran (17 homers, 74 RBIs). The lineup and infield defense were also bolstered near the end of the season by Rigney's decision to turn shortstop over to Fregosi; the righthand hitter would be as much of a franchise player as the early Angels had for the next decade. The pitchers were led by righthander Chance, who won 14, saved 8 others, and finished up with an ERA of under 3. But on and off the field, the most noted hurler of all on the 1962 Angels was southpaw Bo Belinsky.

Probably no major leaguer has received more publicity for doing less than the screwballer Belinsky. By the time he had finished an eight-year career that included lengthy stays in the minors and on the disabled list, he had won a mere 28 games, arriving at double figures only in his rookie year and even then losing more than winning. Just once, in 1964 when he was 9–8, did he stack up more victories than losses. In 1962, however, Belinsky burst on a stodgy baseball scene with a reputation as a womanizer, pool hustler, and all-around bon vivant, and promptly added value to all these pastimes by racking up his first five decisions; one of the wins was a May 5 no-hitter against Baltimore, the organization from which the Angels had drafted the lefty and that had rejected a bid from California to take him back after an unimpressive showing in spring training. Thanks in part to his media-intense surroundings in

Los Angeles and in part to aging Hearst columnist Walter Winchell's doting on him as a perfect partner for doubledating actresses the newsman wanted to impress, Belinsky was soon as much of a regular feature in gossip columns as he was on sports pages. With no attempt to disguise his footloose habits, he was linked at one time or another with Iran's Queen Soraya and actresses Ann-Margret, Connie Stevens, and Tina Louise. The lengthiest relationship of all was with actress Mamie Van Doren, whose regular presence at Dodger Stadium in low-cut outfits out-Hollywooded the Hollywood atmosphere surrounding the Dodgers and did nothing to hurt the Angel gate. For awhile, the team also tolerated increasing coverage being given to Belinsky's rowdy influence on other Angels, particularly pitching ace Chance, who by his own admission rarely skipped the all-night parties, night club shows, and pool games that attracted his roommate.

The party started to peter out when, after going 6–1 in his first seven decisions, Belinsky hit a wild streak (he led the AL in walks in 1962) and went 4–10 for the rest of the year. Rigney, who had disliked the pitcher's style from the beginning and who had sought in vain to persuade Haney to send him back to Baltimore during spring training, appeared to have more success when he urged the general manager to use Belinsky as bait in ongoing trade talks with Kansas City for reliever Dan Osinski; A's president Charlie Finley agreed to accept Belinsky as "a player to be named later" after the season in exchange for Osinski. But then A's manager Hank Bauer, who was either very careless or very nimble about evading a problem he didn't want, let Belinsky know that he was the player-to-be-named-later. The pitcher, who had no desire to leave Los Angeles for Kansas City, waited until the team arrived in New York for a game against the Yankees and, assured of maximum media coverage, announced that he knew all about the deal between Haney and Finley and that he wasn't going anywhere; moreover, he challenged both the commissioner's office and the AL to look into a situation where a player who was already traded might have been representing the league in the World Series. The ploy worked. Commissioner Frick threw the hot potato to the American League, and AL President Joe Cronin passed it on to Finley and Haney behind a warning that everyone's interests might best be served by replacing Belinsky in the deal. An infuriated Haney persuaded the A's to accept lefty Ted Bowsfield as a substitute.

About the only members of the organization who were not ambivalent about Belinsky were

Rigney, who didn't want him around, and Chance, who very much did. Haney and Autry, in particular, changed their minds whenever Rigney announced a new fine against the hurler for missing a curfew, then changed them back again whenever his appearance on the mound or in a newspaper photograph boosted gate receipts. The conflicting signals from the top were very much in evidence in the spring of 1963, when Belinsky was still with the club, still rooming with Chance, and still drawing fines with regularity. Then in late May, Rigney again appeared to have prevailed when Belinsky's 1–7 record (with an ERA approaching 6) argued convincingly for a stay back in the minors. Because the Angels' chief farm club was in Hawaii, however, Belinsky had no problem accepting the demotion, to the point that he resisted a recall to Los Angeles in August. With tales of his Hawaiian adventures added to those in California, the southpaw actually received a $2,000 raise for the 1964 season despite an overall performance of 2–9, with a 5.75 ERA. To some degree, the incentive paid off, because Belinsky responded with his only winning season. But the 1964 campaign also featured a punchup with Los Angeles *Times* sportswriter Braven Dyer, after which there was a perceptible change in the media coverage of Belinsky's antics. He was dealt to the Phillies over the winter for Rudy May and, under increasing drinking and arm problems, started wandering around the National League from Philadelphia to Houston to Pittsburgh to Cincinnati. After failing in an attempt to catch on with St. Louis in 1971, he called it quits.

If the Belinsky saga reflected the special box office priorities of a franchise under the Hollywood stars, the disasters that began afflicting the club in 1962 lent an air of movie spookiness to organization operations. In April of that year, outfielder Hunt, who had walloped 25 homers in his rookie season the year before, stood flexing his back on the on-deck circle, snapped his collarbone, and never played a full schedule again. In August, veteran reliever Art Fowler was struck in the face by a line drive during batting practice and lost his vision in one eye. In 1964, a car accident put paid to the promise shown by lefty Ken McBride. That same season, the club paid out $300,000 signing bonuses to college stars Rick Reichardt and Tom Egan, only to have Reichardt's potential thwarted by the loss of a kidney and Egan's by a beanball that broke his jaw and cost him vision in an eye. In 1965, rookie Dick Wantz pitched himself into the rotation in spring training, but was dead of a brain tumor four months later. In 1968, bullpen ace Minnie Rojas lost his wife and two

children, and was himself permanently paralyzed in an auto accident. Other road accidents killed infielder Chico Ruiz in 1972, reliever Bruce Heinbechner in 1974, and shortstop Mike Miley in 1977. In 1978, Lyman Bostock, one of the league's premier hitters, was shot to death as an innocent bystander. After surrendering a game-tying gopher pitch to Boston's Dave Henderson that eventually turned the tide in favor of the Red Sox in the 1986 LCS, relief specialist Donnie Moore suffered bouts of depression that ended in his suicide.

While the majority of these tragedies were still in the offing after the club's unexpectedly strong showing in 1962, Autry and Haney abetted the organization's professional fall by deciding that the team needed no significant overhaul to remain an AL contender. It was in this context that club president Reynolds conceded some years later that the third-place finish was "harmful'" in its overall impact. "From top to bottom, we overestimated what we had and underestimated what we had to do," Reynolds declared. "We were lulled into a false sense of security." But in addition to the overconfidence fostered by the 1962 showing, Haney in particular came in for criticism on other fronts, as well. One repeated charge during his tenure was that the no-longer-young cronies who made up most of his scouting staff refused to go into black neighborhoods to look at high school and sandlot prospects and so, in effect, instituted racial criteria for developing players; although the franchise continually denied such allegations, the fact was that the only black player signed over the first five years of the team's existence was Dick Simpson. A disciple of Branch Rickey, Haney also was frequently accused of adopting the Mahatma's scatter-gun strategy of signing prospects in quantity rather than by selective commitment in the hope that two or three of the players would turn out to be of major league caliber.

What it all added up to was another seven years before California got back up as high as third and another ten years after that before it could claim its first division title. Not that the franchise didn't have a few consolations along the way.

On April 19, 1966, the team got out from under its tenancy at Dodger Stadium to move into its own Anaheim Stadium, in the process formally changing its name from the Los Angeles Angels to the California Angels. The opening game, played before 31,660, went to the visiting White Sox, 3–1. The best performance of the decade came from Chance in 1964, when he took the AL Cy Young Award with a record of 20–9 (including 11 shutouts) and a league-leading

1.65 ERA. Also noteworthy was the ill-starred Rojas's 1967 mark of 12 wins and 27 saves. Among the familiar names who came and went were Jimmy Piersall, Joe Adcock, Vic Power, Curt Simmons, Bill Skowron, and future Hall of Famer Hoyt Wilhelm. The two worst diamond moments of the 1960s came on July 31, 1963, when Paul Foytack surrendered a record four consecutive homers to Cleveland's Woodie Held, Pedro Ramos, Tito Francona, and Larry Brown, and August 18, 1967, when Jack Hamilton beaned 22-year-old Boston slugger Tony Conigliaro, sending him along a path of visual and general physical deterioration to death before the age of forty-five. (Hamilton himself never fully got over the accident, and was out of baseball within two years.)

As muddle-headed as the front office often seemed during Haney's reign, matters did not get much better after he stepped down following the 1968 season. In the space of eight years, Autry hired three baseball operations chiefs, each of whom had some critical things to say about his predecessor and each of whom brought in a brand new team of administrative and scouting personnel. Complicating the situation even further was Autry's aggressive pursuit of free agents in the late 1970s, a priority that made the team's farm system even more of an afterthought—at least until ownership decided that free agents weren't the solution and demanded to know why no instant stars were coming up from the Pacific Coast League. Although the Angels weren't the only franchise that shifted gears every few years, they were the only one sitting in southern California's baseball vineyard and watching hundreds of prospects walk out from under its nose to other organizations.

Haney's immediate successor was Dick Walsh, a former official for the Dodgers who had been O'Malley's spokesman for problems having to do with the Angels' occupancy of Dodger Stadium. Despite the fact that even Reynolds had once described him as "the vice-president in charge of saying no" for O'Malley and nobody connected with the Angels could think of any particularly positive experiences with him, Walsh was brought in amid descriptions that he was the ideal man to work with Rigney in returning the club to the status of a contender. It wasn't too long before the "no-nonsense" tag applied initially to the new general manager gave way to such unflattering descriptions as dictatorial, paranoid, and untruthful. Working with an extraordinary seven-year contract, Walsh involved himself in every aspect of the team, to the point that several key administrators quit because of his refusal to delegate authority. One of the earliest enemies he made was the city of Anaheim, which charged him with nickel-and-diming municipal employees assigned to the stadium and constantly breaking hiring commitments. His mania for cutting costs extended to a written memo to the equipment manager that the players were using too many towels. In a more notorious incident, he sent a letter to the home of a pitcher advising him that he could expect no salary increase because he had contracted a venereal disease; the pitcher's wife opened the letter and was soon suing for divorce. In 1971, when star shortstop Fregosi announced that he needed an operation for a foot tumor, Walsh told him the team couldn't afford his absence and refused authorization for the surgery; it was only a couple of months later that Fregosi, in increasing pain, checked himself into a hospital. Episodes of the kind earned Walsh the nickname of the Smiling Python in the clubhouse, and more than one player tried to go over his head to Autry and Reynolds to ask for a trade or a new general manager. The intensity of the players' dislike for him got to the point in 1971 that they tried to hit him with line drives during batting practice, and he had to be hustled off the field by members of the coaching staff.

Walsh's relations with Rigney were not much better. While Rigney was always careful not to attack the general manager for the record, he let his newspaper friends know over and over that he had turned down offers from Detroit and other AL teams only because of his friendship with Autry and the owner's request that he assure some franchise continuity after the departure of Haney. The continuity lasted only until the end of May 1969, when Walsh declared that the team didn't appear to be trying enough and appointed Lefty Phillips as the new pilot. After taking over a club that was 17 games under the break-even mark, Phillips steered the Angels to within 3 games of .500. A year later, he had California back up to the winning percentage of its surprise 1962 season. But the resurgence came amid an organizational deterioration that extended from Autry to the clubhouse and that ultimately left the manager out to dry. Almost as fabled as Casey Stengel for his original syntax, Phillips himself only worsened the situation by being unable to communicate with any coherence to his players or explain his moves to the media.

At the center of much of the club's turmoil with the dawning of the 1970s was outfielder Alex Johnson, obtained in a deal with Cincinnati after the 1969 season. Hailed by Walsh as the heart of the team's revived offense, Johnson appeared to vindicate the general manager's prophecy by becoming only the fourth player to take a batting title in the year immediately after crossing over to the AL from the NL. But even in the midst of his big year, Johnson got into regular tangles with teammates, the front office, the league office, and the press, usually ascribing the troubles to racism and his own admitted bitterness that "baseball is anti-black." He became so abusive to sportswriters covering the team, including one incident when he poured coffee into the typewriter of Dick Miller of the Los Angeles *Herald Examiner*, that they refused to enter the clubhouse when he was around. Another frequent sparring partner was infielder Chico Ruiz, who had come to the Angels in the same trade with the Reds and who went at Johnson, fists flailing, at the batting cage, in the dugout, and in the locker room. Although Phillips issued a couple of fines during the season, he complained to anyone who listened that he had received orders from Walsh to play down disciplinary incidents, both because of Johnson's performance between the lines and fears that the organization would

again be the target of charges that it was indeed anti-black.

In 1970, the trouble started in spring training, when Johnson insisted on standing in the shade of a light tower on defense on a hot Palm Springs day, and was benched. It was merely the first of an unprecedented series of disciplinary fines, suspensions, and benchings levied against the outfielder by Phillips; through the first seventy-one games on the California schedule, Johnson was hit with an astounding twenty-nine fines. Repeatedly, Phillips demanded that Walsh get rid of the slugger, or at least come out publicly to support his own disciplinary stand. But even after the manager declared flatly in the wake of one early-season episode that Johnson would never play for the Angels again, the general manager confined his reactions to assurances that everybody would eventually cool down. With Phillips's authority shattered, some of the players took it upon themselves to go after Johnson for his regular disinclination to run out ground balls or chase after long drives. Center fielder Ken Berry had to be pulled off the much larger Johnson in the shower room. Pitcher Clyde Wright threatened to whack him with a stool after Johnson had fired a soda bottle at him. The climactic incident came in late June, when Ruiz, one of several Angels known to carry guns, pulled a pistol on his tormentor. A couple of days later, the club finally announced that it was suspending Johnson indefinitely for "failure to hustle and improper mental attitude."

Johnson retaliated by filing a grievance with the Players Association. Association director Marvin Miller argued successfully before an arbitration panel that the player was suffering from mental stress and should have been put on the disabled list with his salary restored; it was the first time in baseball history that a player was disabled for emotional rather than physical problems. The 1971 LCS was barely underway when California unloaded its problem by trading Johnson and catcher Gerry Moses to Cleveland in return for outfielder Vada Pinson, hurler Alan Foster, and infielder Frank Baker.

Another problem involving Phillips during the 1971 campaign was former Red Sox slugger Conigliaro, who, in a deal with Boston the previous winter, had ended up on the club that had put such a dent in his career. Although he had amazed everyone with a comeback fifty-six homers over two seasons after being out of baseball for an entire year, Conigliaro had also kept Red Sox officials awake at night with periodic distress calls about lingering eye problems, and they did not hesitate too long when

Asked in 1971 why some highly touted rookies were not fulfilling their promise, manager Lefty Phillips replied: "Our phenoms ain't phenominating."

Walsh offered them a package for his services. Conigliaro's fears proved more than justified when he got off to a bad start with the Angels and specialists confirmed that his vision was deteriorating. But in an atmosphere dictated by the bad feeling against Johnson and a sense that Walsh didn't know what he was doing, the outfielder's teammates as well as Phillips saw Conigliaro as just another malingerer and began taunting him about his frequent requests to sit out games. Conigliaro finally had enough and, after being unable to sleep after an extra-inning night game, called a bizarre press conference shortly before dawn to say that he feared "ending up in a straitjacket with the other nuts" on the team and was thinking about retiring. Phillips's reaction was to say that the outfielder belonged in a mental hospital, while Walsh announced that Conigliaro was being placed on the voluntary retirement list and was being docked his pay for the remainder of the season. Like Johnson, Conigliaro sued the club through the Players Association, contending that the Angels should have been aware of his eye problem and placed him on the disabled list before worries about vision destabilized him to the point of his threatening to retire. Once again, association director Miller prevailed before an arbitration board, and California was forced to turn over the rest of Conigliaro's salary. The Angels never sought compensation from the Red Sox, despite Walsh's accusations that Boston had known about the outfielder's condition before dealing him.

Walsh's second-thinking about the Conigliaro trade was unsolicited because both the general manager and Phillips had been fired prior to the verdict. The breaking point for Autry apparently came when Walsh testified during the Johnson grievance hearing that Ruiz had indeed threatened the outfielder with a pistol, and this after the owner had been assured that no weapon had been involved. Walsh subsequently tried to doubletalk his way out of the contradiction by blaming Reynolds for not relaying one of his messages to Autry, but the incident only revived charges in other quarters that the official was not above lying when he deemed it in his immediate interests. Named to succeed Walsh was Harry Dalton, then Baltimore's director for player personnel.

Like Walsh, Dalton moved into his office with warnings that the club needed a total overhaul before it could be regarded as a serious force. After the Yankees turned down his request to interview Ralph Houk for the managerial opening, the new general manager gave the job to Del Rice, a veteran catcher who had been the first player to sign a contract with the Angels and who had subsequently coached and managed throughout the organization. But even Rice raised his eyebrows two days after his appointment when Dalton announced that the coaching staff would include Bobby Winkles, a guru of collegiate ball at Arizona State University who had declared his intention of eventually managing in the major leagues.

Less than a week after hiring Rice and the coaches, Dalton completed the most significant trade in franchise history to that point by sending Fregosi to the Mets in exchange for righthanders Nolan Ryan and Don Rose, catcher Francisco Estrada, and outfielder Leroy Stanton. Fregosi, whom Autry had often described as being as close to him as a son, was stunned by the deal and blamed it on an attempt by Dalton to clean house of any player associated with the Haney and Walsh regimes. Dalton had three justifications for the swap: the foot injury that had slowed down the club's captain and shortstop, the power potential of Stanton, and, most of all, Ryan. Prior to the arrival of the southpaw staff of Chuck Finley, Mark Langston, and Jim Abbott in the early 1990s, in fact, California pitching had largely been broken down into periods of Before Ryan, Ryan, and After Ryan. Before leaving the team again as a free agent at the end of the 1979 season, the fireballer led the AL in strikeouts seven times, topping the 300 mark five times on his way to the all-time record for whiffs. His 1973 total of 383 strikeouts also set a new high for a single season. Moreover, it was as an Angel that he hurled the first four of his seven no-hitters. Although often criticized for his wildness and for won-lost records that hovered near the .500 level, Ryan's prime years (with the Angels and then with the Astros) were spent with teams that did not remind anybody of the 1927 Yankees; his 22–14 finish in 1974, for example, was his second consecutive 20-win season for a club below the breakeven line and represented the first time that a last-place finisher in the AL had sported a 20-game winner since the 1951 Browns had come alive for Ned Garver. Ryan also proved invaluable to the Angels as a gate attraction, with thousands more fans descending on his starts at Anaheim Stadium in the hope of seeing a new strikeout record or another no-hitter.

With Ryan added to a staff that already had Rudy May and previous twenty-game winners Wright and Andy Messersmith, Rice and Dalton went into the 1972 season confident that they had enough pitching for a run at the division title. They did—but that was all that they had. While all four starters averaged fewer than three runs a game and combined for a 1.80 ERA over the last two months of the campaign, the bullpen was incendiary and the hitting bordered on the pathetic, with only first baseman Bob Oliver knocking in as many as 70 runs. Dalton didn't wait too many days following the season (and a fifth-place finish) to oust Rice. There was a cursory attempt to pry Dick Williams away from Oakland, and then Winkles got the job that he had been expected to get for some time.

With the completion of another big trade at the end of November, Winkles also got a rival manager on the bench. Setting a situation similar to that endured by Rice, Dalton announced that the team had acquired outfielders Frank Robinson and Bobby Valentine, pitchers Bill Singer and Mike Strahler, and infielder Billy Grabarkewitz from the Dodgers in exchange for Messersmith and third baseman Ken McMullen. Robinson, then winding down his Hall of Fame career, had not made any secret of his managerial ambitions, or of wanting to be the first black pilot in the big leagues. Initially, however, the swap appeared to pay only big dividends when Robinson led the team in homers (30) and RBIs (97) and Singer joined Ryan as a twenty-game winner; the only bad part of the deal seemed to be the broken leg suffered by Valentine in May just when he appeared to be on the verge of fulfilling predictions of an All Star career. It was another story in 1974, however, with Robinson and a couple of the other veterans criticizing Winkles's moves in the press, Winkles accusing Robinson of seeking his job, and Dalton emulating Walsh in trying to pretend that nothing was happening. In mid-June, in what he had apparently counted on as an air-clearing move, Winkles told a meeting of players that he had asked Dalton to trade Robinson for the good of the club; the tactic backfired immediately when Dalton replied that he was considering no such move. A couple of weeks later, Winkles was gone amid a consensus from those close to the team that he had been as bad dealing with the older players as he had been successful bringing along the younger ones.

If Robinson had figured on becoming the first black manager on a team located in conservative Orange County, he was immediately disabused of the notion when the Angels paid the A's $50,000 to approach Williams once again. Then working for a real estate mogul in Florida but still under formal contract to the Oakland organization, Williams signed a pact with California that covered him through the 1977 season. In an attempt to head off trouble before it began, he named Robinson team captain. The change had no instant effect on the diamond, where the club played out the string to its first cellar finish, but it calmed the mood in the clubhouse. Before the year was out, Robinson was traded to Cleveland, where he would realize his ambition to be the first black manager in the major leagues.

Williams took the team into the 1975 season with a vow that he would never manage a last-place club again; he was wrong. There was something of a consolation, however, in the club's entertaining aggressiveness on the basepaths, with outfielder Mickey Rivers (70) and second baseman Jerry Remy (34) leading the way to 220 stolen bases, the most by a major league team since the 1916 Browns had swiped 234. In his determination to recast the club with an accent on youth, Williams also got 16 wins and an AL-leading 269 strikeouts from twenty-one-year-old southpaw Frank Tanana, plus another 16 victories from Ed Figueroa in his first full season. But the results were decidedly more mixed for a so-called Incubator Infield of Bruce Bochte at first, Remy at second, Mike Miley at short, and Dave Chalk at third, prompting another disastrous change of direction by Dalton at the end of the season. Resolved to get some punch for the lineup, the general manager acquired Bobby Bonds from the Yankees in exchange for Figueroa and Rivers, then picked up Bill Melton from the White Sox for Jim Spencer. Bonds and Melton combined for only 16 homers and 96 runs batted in, and the team's rise from sixth to fourth was mainly due to repeat starring performances from Tanana and Remy and the collapse of both the Rangers and White Sox.

Another major factor was the relief in the clubhouse when Williams was fired near the end of July 1976. Entering that season, Williams had tried to act like a good soldier in the wake of the deals with the Yankees and White Sox that had not only cost him Figueroa and Rivers, but that had also signalled more front office confusion. As the season wore on, however, with injuries and still-missing offense taking turns as an excuse for another dismal showing, the manager began to reveal some of the martinet demeanor he had been infamous for in Oakland and Boston. He started shouting at the players on the field and in the dugout, became unresponsive to player requests, and, in an interview that all but guaranteed his departure, declared that the only major leaguers on the club were Ryan, Tanana, and Remy. In June, the manager and California broadcaster Don Drysdale visited Autry and tried to persuade him to dump Dalton; the plan of the one-time Brooklyn Dodger farmhands was that Drysdale would take over as general manager. Incensed by what he saw as an attempted palace coup, Autry dismissed both men with only a vague promise to confer with Dalton about the state of the team. A couple of weeks later, after a clash between Williams and Melton that almost ended in punches, the club announced that coach Norm Sherry was taking over as manager. After going 39–57 with Williams, the team played the rest of the season at a 37–29 clip.

In spite of the fact that they had played .500 in only three of their first sixteen seasons, the Angels went into 1977 as favorites in the Western Division. The reason was Autry's decision the previous winter not only to enter the newly opened free agent market, but to sweep it clean of as many star players as possible. Within nine days of negotiations, the club had laid out $5.2 million to obtain the services of outfielder Joe Rudi, shortstop Bobby Grich, and designated hitter Don Baylor. Once again, however, there proved to be relatively little substance behind the glare, with all three of the free agents either going down with serious injuries or falling far short of expectations. Baylor, the one least affected by ailments, had such an unproductive second half of the fifth-place season that he had to ask the club to provide security for his family at Anaheim Stadium against threatening and abusive fans.

With the writing on the wall as early as July, Dalton announced still another managerial change, firing Sherry in favor of Dave Garcia. Like his predecessors, Sherry packed his bags with parting shots at the front office, claiming that he had been made a scapegoat for injuries and Dalton's inability to find bench players who could make up for some of the personnel losses. In another twist in the franchise's ongoing melodrama, Dalton also rehired Robinson as a batting instructor. Once again, the rumors started that the outfielder-designated hitter had been brought in as an eventual managerial replacement.

Another one of Garcia's problems was the ongoing tension between his two ace pitchers. Tanana blamed a sore arm on Dalton's inability to strengthen the relief corps and the indulgence of Ryan's preference for a four-man rotation, even after the introduction of the designated hitter; Ryan's rebuttal was to accuse Tanana of living it up between starts.

Garcia lasted at the helm of the team only until June of the following year, by which time there had been an even more significant change in the front office. Concluding after his investment in the three free agents that the organization needed somebody to control finances more scrupulously, Autry brought in as president former Dodgers' general manager and Padres' chief executive Buzzie Bavasi, then in retire-

ment. The move scalded Dalton, who saw Bavasi as a general-manager-in-waiting, and Red Patterson, who had been appointed president a couple of years before in succession to the retiring Reynolds. But while Patterson decided that he was too old (sixty-eight) to go after another job and accepted a demotion to a vaguely defined role as a special assistant to Autry, Dalton found himself at loggerheads immediately with Bavasi at the latter's insistence that $400,000 be cut from the player development budget. Fortunately for Dalton, even before he could submit his resignation, he received an offer to take over as general manager of the Brewers. Within a few weeks of becoming guardian of the treasury, Bavasi had full charge of California's baseball operations.

Bavasi's first personnel move—signing free agent Minnesota outfielder Bostock to a four-year pact—marked still another reversal to a barely stated policy priority. The team itself justified the agreement with Bostock's unquestioned abilities and a trade of Bonds to the White Sox before he reached free agent eligibility. But over the next couple of off-seasons, saving clearly became secondary again to spending when inflated contracts were tendered to second-line free agents such as Rick Miller and Jim Barr and in a headline-making swap with the Twins that reeled in future Hall of Famer Rod Carew for some $4 million.

Garcia went into the 1978 season knowing that he wasn't going to last long, and not because of Robinson. Already at the end of the previous season, Autry had drawn a $5,000 tampering fine from Commissioner Bowie Kuhn for declaring that he would like to have Kansas City manager Whitey Herzog (a former Angels' coach) as his pilot. Then, during the winter, the owner made no secret of contacts with the Twins in an attempt to pry away Gene Mauch. Garcia ended up hanging on until June 1st when, with the Angels only 1½ games out of first, he was replaced by Fregosi. Autry's "son" kept the club playing at Garcia's level for the rest of the year for California's first second-place finish. The season ended on a tragic note, however, with the death in September of Bostock.

Fregosi was at the helm when the team won its first division title in 1979. Even before the season started, the franchise was ahead of the game when the signing of Carew sparked a run on ticket booths at Anaheim Stadium. When the final numbers were in, home attendance had eclipsed the 1978 record of 1,755,386 by a margin of some 768,000 for a total of 2,523,575. The key to the Angels' success was offense. Baylor became the first (and only) designated hitter to take MVP honors for a performance that included 36 homers and top league totals in both RBIs (139) and runs scored (120). Other major contributors were Grich (30 homers, 101 RBIs), Dan Ford (21 homers, 101 RBIs), and third base find Carney Lansford (19 homers, 79 RBIs). Among the pitchers, Ryan and David Frost both won 16, but, even more important, the bullpen finally showed some tenacity, with John Montague proving especially valuable over the final weeks. Montague came to the club from Seattle in late August only after Bavasi had gotten into a wrestling match with reporter Jim Ruffalo, who had suggested that the team was more interested in saving a few dollars than in purchasing the relief pitching it needed to stay on top in the final weeks.

The LCS was more notable for what happened off the field than on it. With only Carew and Ford showing any consistent punch, California went down rather tamely to Baltimore in four games. During a team flight, however, the Angels regained the sports headlines when broadcaster Drysdale accused free agent hurler Barr of not showing effort, and a brawl was avoided only when Fregosi ordered Drysdale to stick to his play-by-play.

The 1980s brought the Angels appreciably better records, considerably more spending, but still no pennant. The club played at .500 or better five times, making the most of it in a somewhat weak division by finishing first twice, second twice, and third once. The big names of the decade—some of them much more successful than others—included Reggie Jackson, Fred Lynn, Doug DeCinces, Bob Boone, Lance Parrish, Tommy John, and Don Sutton. The parade of managers also continued, with Mauch, John McNamara, Mauch again, Cookie Rojas, and Doug Rader succeeding Fregosi. In the front office, there was superficially more stability with Bavasi lasting through 1984 and Mike Port running the club for the remainder of the decade—but also more stagnation, with Port showing little sense of long-range planning.

The results of the 1980 season were the absolute reverse of the previous year, with the Angels plunging all the way back down to sixth, from three games ahead in the standings to thirty-one behind. Not only did every one of the team's regular position players (except Carew) decline, but relief specialist Mark

In 1983, as a representative of the Angels, Fred Lynn hit the only grand-slam homer in the history of the All Star Game.

On September 16, 1987, Bob Boone caught his 1,919th game, eclipsing the major league record held by Al Lopez. Boone ended his career with 2,225 games behind the plate.

Clear's 11–11 record was the best on the staff. Hopes for a decent starting rotation went out the window when Ryan jumped to the Astros as a free agent, his projected replacement Bruce Kison joined Frost on the disabled list, and the Mets reneged on a completed deal that would have sent righthander Craig Swan to California. To make matters worse, Autry began criticizing his "son" Fregosi in public, declaring at one point that California's Salt Lake City farm team offered better baseball entertainment. Autry, whose behavior was attributed by some to the loss of his wife during the season, also brought back Rigney as a special assistant and said nothing to contradict the former manager's loud second-guessing of Fregosi. The temperature was raised still further after the season, when Mauch was announced as the new Director of Player Personnel. The inevitable occurred the following May, when the personnel director replaced Fregosi in the dugout. Like so many before him, Fregosi went out blasting the organization's inability to adopt a coherent development policy and its financial waste in buying up any player with some marquee quality for the short-term, local goal of outdrawing the Dodgers.

The only baseball man with more of a reputation than Autry for falling down inches from the finish line was Mauch, and he consolidated it with stunning defeats in the 1982 LCS against Milwaukee and again in the 1986 championship series against Boston. With a Murderer's Row lineup that counted six players (Jackson, Baylor, DeCinces, Lynn, Grich, and Brian Downing) with at least 19 homers, the 1982 Angels still had to overcome spotty pitching from all but lefthander Geoff Zahn to get into the playoffs against the Brewers. There, they seemed to have left the worst of the season behind them when John and Kison hurled complete-game victories in the first two contests. But then the Brewers came roaring back for three straight victories in Milwaukee, and the team returned to the West Coast still without a pennant.

Following the LCS, Mauch asked to be allowed out of his contract so that he could stay at home with his fatally ill wife, and John McNamara was brought in as a replacement. McNamara stayed on the job for two years—time enough for him to understand the talk about the franchise hex when a plague of injuries in 1983 prevented him from fielding even once the lineup that he had projected for the season during spring training. With Port replacing Bavasi, Mauch returned for the 1985 season, falling a single game short of Kansas City for another division title. It was no mean feat, considering that five of the regular position players were at least 34 years old (one of them, Carew, collected his 3,000th hit against Minnesota's Frank Viola on August 4th). A season later, with all of the same players except Carew back and still another year older, Mauch confounded all preseason expectations by guiding his Last Hurrah Gang (as the press called it) to the title. The principal new addition was first baseman Wally Joyner, who batted .290 with 22 homers and 100 RBIs; DeCinces and Downing also hit more than 20 homers and drove in more than 90 runs. The starting rotation featured Mike Witt (18 wins), Kirk McCaskill (17), and the veteran Sutton (15), with the ill-fated Donnie Moore saving 21 and winning 4 as the bullpen ace.

As in 1982, the Angels came out of the gate fast in the LCS against the Red Sox, winning three of the first four games. Then in the fifth game, with the team leading in the ninth inning by the score of 5–2 and needing only three outs for its first flag, disaster struck in the form of two-run homers from former Angel Baylor and Dave Henderson. Although California came back to tie in the bottom of the ninth, it then had to enter an overtime from which it never returned: After Boston won the fifth game in the 11th inning, it regained the home field advantage of Fenway Park to demolish the Angels' staff in games six and seven and take the pennant. Within a couple of months of the devastating defeat, Autry and Bavasi had severed their ties with Last Hurrah Gang members DeCinces, Grich, Jackson, Rick Burleson, Ruppert Jones, Terry Forster, and Vern Ruhle; most of the others were released or traded away before the end of the following year. In classic franchise style, DeCinces bowed out accusing Port of being "gutless" about adopting a development policy and sticking to it.

The rest of the decade saw Autry's second wife Jackie playing a more active role in organization affairs, but the team on the field still alternating from prospects to old-timers, depending on the losing streak of the moment. The radical shifts in front office temperament put everyone on the defensive, including Mauch's successor Cookie Rojas, who became a joke around the league for managing in fear of becoming still another scapegoat. Rojas could have saved himself the bother because he was eventually singled out anyway, and replaced by Doug Rader.

Jim Abbott. *The California Angels*

The brightest side of the franchise entering the 1990s was, uncharacteristically, its pitching staff, with farm products Jim Abbott and Chuck Finley joining with free agent acquisition Mark Langston to give the Angels the best three starting southpaws on a team since the Dodgers in the 1960s. Abbott also brought national attention for the fact that he made the majors despite having been born without a right hand. Langston made his debut in a California uniform a memorable one when, on April 11, 1990, he teamed with Witt to toss a no-hitter. Another key arm at the beginning of the decade was that of reliever Bryan Harvey, who led the AL in saves in 1991 with 46.

In 1991, with the club headed for last place despite a .500 mark, there were more traumatic changes, with former Angels' receiver Buck Rodgers

In 1988, coach Moose Stubing managed the last eight games of the year in place of the fired Cookie Rojas, and lost them all to tie the record for the most managerial losses without a win established by George Creamer of the American Association Pittsburgh Alleghenys in 1884.

coming in to replace Rader as manager and Whitey Herzog taking over the front office baseball operations from Port. Only a few weeks on the job, Herzog admitted that he had been stymied in his attempts to re-sign free agent Joyner by some abiding hostility between the first baseman (who ended up going to the Royals) and Autry's second wife. "Well, at least this experience taught me something about the organization," Herzog declared.

Herzog's education did little for the team in 1992, with the Angels losing nine more games than they had in the previous year. Most of the blame was laid at the doorstep of such aging sluggers as Von Hayes, Hubie Brooks, Lance Parrish, and Gary Gaetti and of the injured Harvey. The organization also showed that it had lost none of its bent for the tragic and near-tragic, when a May 21 crash of the team bus on the New Jersey Turnpike incapacitated Rodgers for three months, left 11 others injured, and narrowly missed being a catastrophe. Following the season, the Autrys showed little inclination to reopen their checkbooks, setting in motion the loss of Harvey to the Marlins in the expansion draft and the trading of Abbott to the Yankees for three prospects. Newcomers for 1993 included the long-in-the-tooth Chili Davis (for a return engagement via free agency) and Kelly Gruber (in a trade with Toronto).

CALIFORNIA ANGELS

Annual Standings and Managers

Year	Position	W	L	Pct.	GB	Managers
1961	Eighth	70	91	.435	38½	Bill Rigney
1962	Third	86	76	.531	10	Bill Rigney
1963	Ninth	70	91	.435	34	Bill Rigney
1964	Fifth	82	80	.506	17	Bill Rigney
1965	Seventh	75	87	.463	27	Bill Rigney
1966	Sixth	80	82	.494	18	Bill Rigney
1967	Fifth	84	87	.522	7½	Bill Rigney
1968	Eighth	67	95	.414	36	Bill Rigney
1969	Third	71	91	.438	26	Bill Rigney, Lefty Phillips
1970	Third	86	76	.531	12	Lefty Phillips
1971	Fourth	76	86	.469	25½	Lefty Phillips
1972	Fifth	75	80	.484	18	Del Rice
1973	Fourth	79	83	.488	15	Bobby Winkles
1974	Sixth	68	94	.420	22	Bobby Winkles, Dick Williams
1975	Sixth	72	89	.447	25½	Dick Williams
1976	Fourth*	76	86	.469	14	Dick Williams, Norm Sherry
1977	Fifth	74	88	.457	28	Norm Sherry, Dave Garcia
1978	Second*	87	75	.537	5	Dave Garcia, Jim Fregosi
1979	First	88	74	.543	+3	Jim Fregosi
1980	Sixth	65	95	.406	31	Jim Fregosi
1981	Fourth	31	29	.517	6	Jim Fregosi, Gene Mauch
	Seventh	20	30	.400	8½	Gene Mauch
1982	First	93	69	.574	+3	Gene Mauch

1983	Fifth*	70	92	.432	29	John McNamara
1984	Second*	81	81	.500	3	John McNamara
1985	Second	90	72	.556	1	Gene Mauch
1986	First	92	70	.568	+5	Gene Mauch
1987	Sixth*	75	87	.463	10	Gene Mauch
1988	Fourth	75	87	.463	29	Cookie Rojas
1989	Third	91	71	.562	8	Doug Rader
1990	Fourth	80	82	.494	23	Doug Rader
1991	Seventh	81	81	.500	14	Doug Rader, Buck Rodgers
1992	Fifth*	72	90	.444	24	Buck Rodgers

* Tie

Postseason Play

LCS	1–3 versus Baltimore	1979
	2–3 versus Milwaukee	1982
	3–4 versus Boston	1986

Chicago Cubs

National League,
1876–Present

RECORD: 8852–8229 (.518)

BALLPARKS: 23RD STREET GROUNDS (1876–1877)
LAKEFRONT PARK (1878–84)
WEST SIDE PARK (1885–1892)
SOUTH SIDE PARK (1891–1893)
WEST SIDE PARK (1893–1915)
WRIGLEY FIELD (1916–Present)
COMISKEY PARK (1918)

OTHER NAMES: WHITE STOCKINGS, COLTS, ORPHANS

As the oldest continuous franchise in major league baseball, the Cubs have seen it all, done it all—and seen it all done to them. Once synonymous with the on-field and off-field power of the National League, the team has over more recent generations come to suggest a futility both more endearing and more classical than that of the Boston Red Sox. But, all its modern fabulists notwithstanding, there has never been anything particularly fateful about the club's generally weak showings since the mid-1940s: Aside from a couple of good years in the 1980s, the team has simply not been up to its NL rivals, let alone to its own successes in the 1880s and in the first and fourth decades of this century.

February 2, 1876 saw the birth of triplets—of the National League, of the major leagues as they are commonly defined today, and of the Chicago franchise, initially known as the White Stockings, but that would come to be called the Cubs. The triple delivery was primarily the work of William Hulbert, owner of the Chicago franchise in the proto-major league National Association. Galled by the dominance of the NA's Boston Red Stockings, Hulbert made a secret offer in June 1875 to pitcher Al Spalding, the ace of the New England team, to jump to his club for the 1876 season. Not only did Spalding agree, but he in turn persuaded three star teammates—first baseman Cal McVey, second baseman Ross Barnes, and catcher Deacon White—to make the switch with him. By the end of June, with the NA season in full swing, The Big Four, as they were called in Boston, had all inked pacts with Chicago for the following year. Not satisfied with that coup, Hulbert then pried first baseman Cap Anson away from the NA's Philadelphia franchise.

Mainly because of the star quality of the Boston defectors, the NA did not move against them immediately, even though the agreements became public

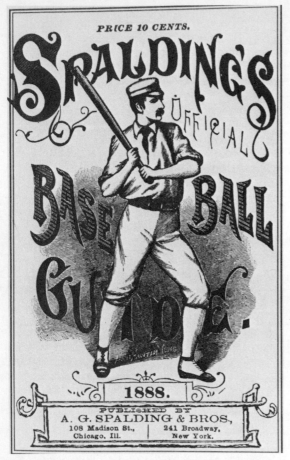

PRICE 10 CENTS.

SPALDING'S OFFICIAL BASE BALL GUIDE.

1888.

PUBLISHED BY
A. G. SPALDING & BROS.,
108 Madison St.,   241 Broadway,
Chicago, Ill.   New York.

Albert Spalding's power in the early days of major league baseball extended to his claims of furnishing the only official information on the game. *National Baseball Library, Cooperstown, NY*

The charter agreement for the establishment of the National League stipulated among its main points:

—an entry fee for every franchise of $100.

—a minimum population of 75,000 for franchise members.

—no more than one club from each member city.

—exclusion of any franchise opposed by two members from the original eight.

—a commitment by all members to play out the schedule; a failure to do so would mean expulsion.

—a pledge by members not to "employ any player who has been dismissed by the league or any member club."

—the banning of drinking and gambling on playing grounds.

—a $5 payment per game of umpires.

Noting that the NL was an agreement among clubs rather than players, as had been the case with the National Association, Al Spalding justified the structure by declaring: "Like every other form of business enterprise, Base Ball depends for results on two interdependent divisions, the one to have absolute control and direction of the system, and the other to engage—always under the executive branch—the actual work of production."

Bob Addy, a Chicago outfielder in 1876, is generally credited with being the first player to slide into a base. Addy is said to have pioneered the technique while playing for the Rockford (Illinois) club in 1866.

knowledge soon enough and even though association rules proposed expulsion for anyone involved in signing a future contract during the playing season. Emboldened by the league's timidity toward the four Red Stockings, Hulbert decided not to wait and see whether he would be singled out for expulsion, instead moving swiftly to supersede the entire association with a new league. After picking up the support of the NA's westernmost franchise in St. Louis and independent teams in Cincinnati and Louisville, he bearded the owners of the circuit's four eastern clubs (New York, Philadelphia, Boston, and Hartford) at Manhattan's Grand Central Hotel on February 2, 1876. At the meeting, Hulbert outlined his plan for a reorganization that would "wipe away.... inflated salaries, players jumping from one team to another during the season, gambling scan-

dals, team imbalances, and incomplete schedules." The owners bought the plan and charted a constitution for the National League of Professional Base Ball Clubs. Also at Hulbert's suggestion, they threw their names into a hat, with the first one extracted (Hartford's Morgan G. Bulkeley) appointed league presi-

On May 2, 1876, second baseman Ross Barnes hit the first NL home run. It was the only one that he hit that season.

dent and the first five the circuit's board of directors. A month later, the remnants of the National Association dissolved what had been baseball's first professional league.

With Spalding cut in for 25 percent of the team's profits and also serving as manager, the White Stockings (the name was carried over from the NA club) played their first NL game on April 25, 1876, blanking Louisville 4–0. The manager himself applied the whitewash, and it was the first of his league-leading 47 wins. In fact, there weren't too many categories in which a Chicago player didn't lead the league, as the White Stockings rolled up a .788 won-lost percentage in taking the first pennant. Among the position players, Barnes led in hits, doubles, triples, walks, and batting average (.429), center fielder Paul Hines tied for the most doubles, and White led in RBIs.

Having won the league's first pennant, the White Stockings then proceeded to become the circuit's first bust by plunging to fifth place in a six-team league in their sophomore season. The main reason for the drastic falloff was the reduction of The Big Four to The Big One, as only McVey lived up to his billing by batting .368. Spalding had to leave the mound for first base because of an arm injury, and would soon retire altogether. Not yet restricted by the reserve clause, White defected back to Boston. As for Barnes, he was victimized by a rule change that wiped out the "fair-foul" hit in which a ball was tapped into fair territory and then angled off over a foul line before nearing the pitcher or an infielder; because this had been the second baseman's specialty, its elimination brought a drop in his batting average of 157 points.

Their feet wet, the principals of the franchise spent the remainder of the decade consolidating the roles that would make them the league's primary force in nineteenth-century baseball. Spalding moved to the front office as a prelude to being elected club president in 1882 after Hulbert's death. From there, he would not only run the White Stockings, but would emerge as the sport's chief propagandist, being responsible for, among other things, the legend that identified Abner Doubleday as the originator of the "pure American game" of baseball. One of the main vehicles of his sway over the league was the annual *Spalding Baseball Guide,* which first appeared in 1877 and which purported to contain all relevant news and statistics on a given season. When he wasn't running the Cubs, making his voice heard at NL councils, and publishing his version of diamond and front office events, Spalding was building up the sports goods business that bore his name and became a monopolistic supplier for years of balls, bats, and other equipment. In fact, there was little about the nineteenth-century game that didn't have the Spalding imprint. He also had his radical moments. In 1882, suspicious that some of the statistics submitted to his *Guide* might have been doctored under home pressure, he decreed that Chicago's official scorer would remain anonymous—even from the team and the league; it emerged only many years later that the scorer was a woman, Elisa Green Williams, and that she had not even told her family what she did for a living. As early as 1883, Spalding also pressed the league to allow the installation of light towers at Lakefront Park; although spurned in his initiative for night ball, the Chicago owner had the lights put up anyway for something of a mini-fantasy promotion for fans eager to slide into bases or view the batter's box from the pitcher's mound. Spalding was elected to the Hall of Fame in 1939.

Second only to Spalding in nineteenth-century Chicago baseball was Anson, who became Cap instead of Adrian as soon as he was made captain-manager of the club in 1879. As a player, Anson was one of the greatest hitters in baseball history, forging a lifetime average of .334 over a twenty-two-year career in which he slipped below .300 only twice. Among his accomplishments were leading the league in hitting three times, in RBIs four times, and in doubles twice. The righthand-hitting first baseman was the first major leaguer to compile 3,000 hits, and in relatively short seasons. As a manager, Anson called the shots for five pennant-winning clubs between 1880 and 1886; he pioneered such stratagems as the hit-and-run, platoons, and a pitching rotation, and was one of the first to insist on the usefulness of spring training. Anson also knew the value of showmanship, anticipating John McGraw's custom of parading his champion players from their hotel to a visiting ballpark in open barouches—the better to provoke resentment from local fans and get them to buy a ticket. At one time or another, he also dressed up the team in Navajo robes, blue bloomers, form-fitting pants, and even dress suits. The manager's personality was something else: When he wasn't ordering around his players like an obsessed drill sergeant, he was attacking opponents and umpires with

The 1877 White Stockings are the only NL team to go through an entire season without hitting a home run.

his fists; on several occasions, he closed the club-house to Spalding for interfering. Most notoriously, he was an unapologetic racist who was given to referring to blacks as "chocolate-covered coons" or "no-account niggers" and who refused to play an 1884 exhibition game against Toledo because the team's catcher, Fleet Walker, was black. It was Anson's refusal to play Toledo (a decision backed completely by Spalding) that caused team owners to ban blacks from major league baseball until the arrival of Jackie Robinson after World War II. Like Spalding, Anson was elected into the Hall of Fame in 1939.

When Anson took over as manager in 1879, he found some welcome additions to the roster thanks to the offseason dissolution of franchises in Milwaukee and Indianapolis; in fact, the team was so sanguine about the arrival of outfielder Abner Dalrymple, catcher Silver Flint, and third baseman Ned Williamson that it predicted a pennant for itself. Instead, it could do no better than fourth, largely because of a kidney infection that sidelined Anson and a line drive off the head of ace pitcher Terry Larkin that not only finished his career, but eventually drove him to insanity and suicide. One year later, however, Chicago not only won the pennant, but did so with a winning percentage (.798) never matched in the National or American league. The main contributors were center fielder George Gore (winner of the batting title at .360), left fielder Dalrymple (NL highs in hits and runs scored), and pitchers Larry Corcoran (43 wins and a 1.95 ERA) and Fred Goldsmith (the league's best winning percentage at 21–3).

Under pressure from William Hulbert, the NL agreed to color-coordinate players by position in 1882, thereby making Hulbert's partner, Al Spalding, an even richer sporting goods entrepreneur. Under the system, every player on every team wore white pants, white belts, and white ties, with only different-colored socks distinguishing the teams. Beyond that, caps and shirts were determined by position: baby blue for pitchers, scarlet for catchers, scarlet and white for first basemen, orange and black for second basemen, maroon for shortstops, blue and white for third basemen, white for left fielders, red and black for center fielders, and gray for right fielders. The system was dropped after a year because of the protests of team owners over the expense involved.

Although the White Stockings never again came so close to an .800 pace, their 1880 performance set the pattern for most of the first part of the decade. In 1881, the pennant drive was fueled by Anson's league-leading numbers in batting, hits, and RBIs, and by Corcoran's pace-setting 31 wins. In 1882, Anson and Gore were again the big sticks, while Corcoran took ERA honors at 1.95 and totaled 55 victories in tandem with Goldsmith. The same pair combined for 59 wins in 1883, but Chicago fell short of New York and had to settle for second place. An otherwise disastrous 1884 season was brightened by a batting championship for King Kelly and an asterisk-worthy show of power. Prior to the campaign, Spalding had talked the league into changing the Lakefront Park ground rule that had defined as a double any ball hit over the right field fence, which was 250 feet from home plate. With such drives ruled home runs for one brief year, Chicago belted 142 round-trippers—the most in baseball until the Murderers' Row Yankees of 1927. Oddly, the biggest beneficiaries of the change were, for the most part, righthanded hitters—Anson who hit 21 (including 5 in two days), second baseman Fred Pfeffer with 25, and, especially, third baseman Williamson, who not only led the NL with 27, but who, on May 30th, became the first big leaguer to belt three in one game.

With their move to the first version of West Side Park in 1885, the White Stockings went back to the more varied game that had been so successful for them at the beginning of the decade; still, after a year-long battle with the Giants, it was a home run in the final hours of the season by Pfeffer against New York that provided the room for another pennant. Although Anson enjoyed another banner year at the plate and four different players scored at least 100 runs, the big story was pitcher John Clarkson's 53 wins (second highest to Charlie Radbourne's 60 for Providence a year earlier). For the righthander, it was the first of eight straight seasons with at least 25 victories; he also struck out 318 batters to lead the league in that category for the first of four seasons. Clarkson, who ended up with 326 wins in a relatively short twelve-year career, was elected to the Hall of Fame in 1963.

With the schedule expanded by a dozen games to 124 for 1886, Anson brought in Jocko Flynn to bolster Clarkson and Jim McCormick as a three-man staff; the result was a 24–6 record by the rookie that may have left him third best on the staff (Clarkson won 35 and McCormick 31), but that proved to be the difference in another pennant struggle, this time with Detroit. Offensively, the biggest production came from Anson and Kelly. While the manager batted .371 with 117 runs scored and a league-leading 147 driven home, the colorful Kelly played all over the field (nine games at first base, six at second, five at short, eight at third, fifty-six in the outfield, and fifty-three behind the plate) while winning his second batting crown and leading the NL in runs scored for the third straight time. If people had the tendency to keep their eyes on the light fixtures when Spalding entered a room and to reach for their coats when Anson did, they were just as likely to smile when Kelly showed up. Major league baseball's first matinee idol, the flamboyant, mustachioed jack-of-all-trades never did anything quietly when he could attract attention with a little more effort. Anson's habit of having the whole team arrive at out-of-town ballparks in open carriages had nothing on Kelly's custom of having his private carriage pulled by two white horses (when not by fans themselves) to both home and away games. An inveterate gambler, he wasted little time even pretending to hear the moralistic advice tendered at regular intervals by both Spalding and Anson. With all that, the righthand hitter never left his dash outside the turnstiles, producing a .307 average over sixteen years and becoming a byword for both hit-and-run plays and sliding into bases. He was elected to the Hall of Fame in 1945.

After both the 1885 and 1886 pennant wins, the White Stockings met the American Association St. Louis Browns in a championship series, and wished they hadn't. The loss in 1886 so baffled Spalding that he insisted that it could have only occurred because key players like Kelly and Gore had been drunk before taking the field. This was no idle speculation from an owner who, earlier in the year, had been so fired up by his temperance outlook that he had lobbied all NL teams to hire private detectives to tail players both during and after the season for the purpose of enforcing total abstinence. None of the other teams was enthusiastic about adding private eyes to their payrolls, but that didn't prevent Spalding and the fanatically dry Anson (he drank only water) from forcing the White Stockings to take the pledge at a bizarre ceremony at the owner's Chicago sporting goods store. Spalding then had his players put under surveillance anyway, and managed to collect enough fines to pay off his detectives without dipping into the club treasury. But with the second consecutive loss to St. Louis in the postseason competition, Spalding became more than sympathetic to Anson's regular laments that some White Stockings had gotten so out of hand that fines were not enough of a response. Only a few weeks after the end of the season,

he sold or released Kelly, Gore, and McCormick. All three had coincidentally been demanding substantial raises for 1887.

The sale of Kelly to Boston for $10,000 caused the greatest sensation—both because of the player's enormous popularity and for the unprecedented sum involved. Spalding rejected all the criticism, claiming that he had made the deal at Kelly's request; the catcher had in fact agreed to go after being told that he would receive a substantial raise in Boston that he stood no chance of getting in Chicago. The most lasting significance of the deal was that it opened Spalding's eyes to the money to be made in peddling his players; a year later, he sold Clarkson to Boston for another $10,000. At the very least, the two deals were above the table, which, according to some NL owners, could not have been said about Spalding's involvement in the Union Association, the short-lived league that rose and fell within the single season of 1884. Suspicions that the Chicago president had more than a rival interest in the UA were spurred by the fact that one of the league's major recruiters worked as a sales clerk in Spalding's sporting goods store.

With the departure of stars like Kelly, Gore, and McCormick after the 1886 season, the club took on such an unfamiliar, young look that the press began calling it the Colts. (The name became even more common after Anson appeared in the vaudeville show, *The Runaway Colt*.) Aside from Anson himself, the team's best player in the second half of the decade was outfielder Jimmy Ryan, who put together three .300-plus seasons and a home run title on his way to an eighteen-year career that saw him bat .309 overall. Although the club continued to play first-division ball, it could not recapture the glory days at the beginning of the decade, and would in fact not win the pennant again until 1906. Spalding's biggest splurge during the period was organizing baseball's first world tour during the offseason of 1888–89.

As owner and propagandist, Spalding was never more visible than he was during the 1890 war with the Players League, the circuit set up by the Players' Brotherhood to combat the most flagrant abuses of the reserve clause. As an owner, he had plenty of reason to be visible because every one of his key players except Anson, third baseman Tom Burns, and pitcher Bill Hutchison defected to the rebel league. With the assistance of *Spalding Guide* editor Henry Chadwick, he played point man for other NL and AA owners in issuing continuous denunciations of John Montgomery Ward, the other prominent Brotherhood player representatives, and their backers. When that wasn't enough, he had cronies like

O. P. Caylor and Harry Palmer put on the staff of the New York *Sporting Times,* where they described the Players League supporters as "drunken knaves" and "men without principle, who knew not how to keep their words and had no sense of shame." It was also Spalding who, behind the guise of exploring peace possibilities with PL representatives after the 1890 season, inveigled them into admitting how bad their financial situation was, then told his fellow NL owners to accept nothing but unconditional surrender. He got what he asked for, although he ended up spending $18,000 to buy out the PL franchise in Chicago.

With the return of star players like Pfeffer and Ryan from the PL in 1891, Chicago seemed headed for another NL pennant until it was overtaken by Boston in a late September rally. Anson didn't take the defeat lightly, even accusing New York of deliberately losing a crucial four-game series to Boston because the Giants wanted an eastern club to win the flag. The manager had more reason for bitterness before the 1892 season with the announcement that Spalding, while still the major stockholder, was stepping down as organization president in favor of James Hart. Anson had disliked Hart since the world tour in 1888, when the executive had served as the group's business manager; Hart had disliked Anson ever since finding out that the manager had been the only member of the traveling group to refuse to contribute to the purchase of a pair of diamond cufflinks that Spalding had wanted to give the business manager for his services.

While the rest of the NL tended to view Hart only as Spalding's mouthpiece, Anson viewed Spalding's gradual absorption with other matters as a sign that Hart's power was only going to grow, and not to his (Anson's) benefit. With the passing of the years, he inveighed against the former president for encouraging him to buy more stock in the club, then

working with Hart behind the scenes to make sure that he couldn't actually buy any. When the club announced before the 1898 season that Anson's contract wasn't being renewed and Spalding sought to sugarcoat the pill by offering to stage a benefit game for the manager, Anson declared that he didn't need any charity.

Anson went out swinging on the field. In his goodbye in a Chicago uniform, he not only became the first player to collect 3,000 hits (on July 18th), but, at the age of forty-six, established himself as the oldest player to post a .300 average for a full season. Indeed, offense was the name of the game for the Colts for most of the decade, especially after the pitching mound had been pushed back to 60'6" for the 1893 season. The club's most dazzling performer in the period was center fielder Bill Lange, whose feats at bat, on the bases, and in the field drew the same sort of raves that Willie Mays would excite more than a half-century later. After debuting in 1893 with a .281 mark, Lange averaged over .337 for the next six seasons. The righthand-hitting outfielder retired after the 1899 season, so that he could concentrate on raising his children.

With Anson out of the picture after more than two decades, the team went from being known as the Colts to the Orphans. But though fans generally resented the departure of the long-time manager, they were intrigued enough by the team to set a franchise attendance record of 400,000 in 1898. What they got for their money were clubs that forecast the pattern of the Cubs in the mid-twentieth-century—fast breaks out of the gate that were followed by a slow descent to the lower regions of the standings. Tom Burns and Tom Loftus each had two-year stints as manager, without any noticeable difference in the team's success.

With one important exception, the Chicago pitchers of the 1890s took a long time to adjust to the mound's increased distance from home plate. The

---

Chicago holds the record for both the most runs scored by a team in one game and the most runs scored by a club in one inning. On June 29, 1897, the team clobbered Louisville by the never-equalled count of 36–7. Fourteen years earlier, on September 6, 1883, Chicago had erupted for an unmatched 18 runs in the seventh inning of a contest against Detroit. In the latter explosion, shortstop Tommy Burns belted two doubles and a home run.

Footnote Player: Many players hold an obscure record, but Walt Wilmot, an outfielder for Chicago in the 1890s, holds three of them. On September 30, 1890, Wilmot was called out twice in the same game for being hit by a batted ball; on August 22, 1891, he was the first player to be walked six times in one game; and on August 6–7, 1894, he had eight stolen bases in two consecutive games.

exception was Clark Griffith, who had six twenty-win seasons in the decade and who would get into Cooperstown in 1946 on the basis of his 240 career wins. Unfortunately for the club, Griffith was also one of the first Chicago players lured across town to the new American League franchise that set up major league operations in 1901. With Griffith as player-manager, numerous teammates followed him, to the point that sportswriters decided that still another name change—to the Remnants—was in order for the franchise. Although this sarcasm never attained the popularity of Orphans or Colts, it accurately described the state of the club that took the field at the second version of West Side Park. Moreover, it acted like a thumbscrew on Spalding, who not only had to see his players defect to the new league, but who was also powerless to do anything about Charles Comiskey's decision to call his AL organization the White Stockings (later shortened to White Sox by the headline writers of local papers), because that name had fallen into disuse since the Players League war. In an attempt to salvage something at least on the level of nicknames, Spalding insisted that the club be called the Colts, thereby eliminating the Anson implications in Orphans as much as the connotations of Remnants. The most lasting solution came, however, from the Chicago *Daily News* on March 27, 1902 with the suggestion that the rebuilding team be called the Cubs. After a few more years of the Colts, the *Daily News* proposal won acceptance from fans.

Frank Selee took over the helm in 1902. With Johnny Kling showing the ability to be a full-time catcher, Selee shifted second-string receiver Frank Chance out from behind the plate to first base. Chance, who fought the move because he didn't think he could play the position, became an institution at first base, winding up with a career that spanned seventeen seasons and entitling him to election to the Hall of Fame in 1946. At shortstop, the manager installed rookie Joe Tinker, whose fancy glove and clutch bat got him into Cooperstown in the same year as Chance. In the middle of September, another rookie, Johnny Evers, replaced veteran Bobby Lowe at second base and began his march toward the same 1946 appointment with the Hall of Fame. It was on September 15, 1902, that the three infielders pulled off the first Tinker-to-Evers-to-Chance double play.

The pitching staff began showing more promise in 1903, when lefty Jake Weimer won 21 in his rookie season. But the biggest break came after the season when, during the first City Series between the two Chicago teams, Cubs' ace Jack Taylor was accused

Joe Tinker and Johnny Evers turning a double play.
National Baseball Library, Cooperstown, NY

by Hart of having thrown three games to the White Sox. Although Taylor adamantly denied the charge, Hart packed him off to the Cardinals for Mordecai (Three Finger) Brown. Slapped with his nickname because of a childhood accident on his Indiana farm, Brown proved so valuable to the Cubs that even the shredder that had cost him complete use of two of his fingers was turned into a tourist attraction. What attracted Selee was a knuckleball that gave the right-hander six straight twenty-win seasons, a career total of 239 victories, and an overall ERA of 2.06. Brown, who had several years when his ERA was closer to one than to two, was elected to the Hall of Fame in 1949.

With Frank (Wildfire) Schulte inserted as the regular left fielder and Ed Reulbach brought up to bolster the rotation headed by Brown and Weimer, the Cubs of 1905 seemed poised to better their second-place finish of the year before. But then Selee's violent coughing fits were diagnosed as tuberculosis. Ignoring the urgings of friends and family members to retire, the manager lasted through the first half of the season, but in a weakening condition that cast a pall over the team. Another distraction came with the announcement that Hart had sold his interest in the franchise to Charles Taft of Cincinnati and that the Ohio magnate was installing Charles Murphy as president. Despite local resentment that he was nothing more than a front for the outsiders from Cincinnati, Murphy made his first move a significant one—insisting that Selee retire. The ailing manager selected Chance as his replacement.

Chance made his influence felt in a series of off-season exchanges that were to push Chicago over the top. The most important deals saw outfielder Jimmy Sheckard come over from the Dodgers and third baseman Harry Steinfeldt arrive from the Reds. Steinfeldt had cost Chicago the starter Weimer, so Chance later completed a second swap with Cincinnati to obtain pitcher Orval Overall. The staff was strengthened additionally through the acquisition of southpaw Jack Pfeister from the minor leagues.

The first of three consecutive flags came in 1906. That year also saw the modern NL record for winning percentage set when Chance's machine won 116 games and finished twenty lengths ahead of runner-up New York. Oddly, although the club boasted three .300 hitters (Chance, Steinfeldt, and Kling), nobody had the kind of monstrous offensive year that might have been expected from such a dominant won-lost percentage as .763. Steinfeldt's 83 RBIs were the team's (and league's) high, and only Chance scored 100 runs. The pitching was another story. In one of his finest seasons, Brown hurled ten shutouts among his twenty-six wins and posted a league-low ERA of 1.04. Replacing Weimer in the rotation, the lefty Pfeister went 20–8, with a 1.56 ERA. Reulbach's 19–4 was good enough to lead the NL in winning percentage; he surrendered a modest 1.65 runs a game. Other big years came from Carl Lundgren (17 wins, 2.21), Overall (12 wins, 1.88), and even the returning Jack Taylor (12 wins, 1.83).

In what was expected to be the cherry on their cake for the year, the heavily favored Cubs then met the crosstown White Sox in the World Series. Known to one and all as the Hitless Wonders, the AL club lived up to its reputation by batting a mere .198 in six games, but stifled the Cubs at .196 and came away with a stunning world championship.

The 1907 season was largely a replay of 1906, with the pitching again making a mockery of the pennant race. While only Chance batted as high as .293, Overall and Brown notched 20 wins each, and Overall (1.70), Brown (1.39), Lundgren (1.17), Pfeister (NL-leading 1.15), and Reulbach (1.69) all overwhelmed opposition hitters. In the first of two consecutive World Series encounters with the Tigers, the Cubs played the ALers to a 3–3 twelve-inning tie in the opener, then swept the next four games.

The third straight pennant came after a season-long struggle with both New York and Pittsburgh. The turning point of the race occurred on September 23rd at the Polo Grounds when, with two out and two on in a 1–1 game, Giants' shortstop Al Bridwell singled in what appeared to be the winning run to put the home team a game up in the standings. But when Evers noticed that Fred Merkle, the New York runner on first, had failed to touch second before running to the clubhouse, he called for the ball to record a forceout. What followed was torn from the pages of the Keystone Kops. Chicago outfielder Solly Hofman heaved the ball over Evers's head; New York pitcher Joe McGinnity, seeing what Evers was up to, grabbed for the ball before Tinker could get to it and fired it toward the left field stands; another ball suddenly appeared on the field, and Evers tagged second with it; umpire Hank O'Day took a long look at the thousands of rejoicing New York fans on the field around him, mumbled an Out call, and then hastened off to the clubhouse. Only later that night did NL president Henry Pulliam confirm the putout and restore the game to a tie, but then, inexplicably, he allowed the two teams to proceed the following day with a regularly slated game without ordering them to resume the deadlocked contest first. Merkle's Boner, as the play was to be called, led to a makeup game on October 8th that Chicago won for the pennant. That the club was still alive at that point was largely due to Brown and Reulbach, who combined for 53 wins. Brown and Overall had shutouts in another World Series rout of Detroit. The games were marred by charges that owner Murphy was pocketing extra ticket money for himself; the matter was dropped after Murphy added $800 to the players' pool.

Impressed by his win in a state pool tournament, Kling announced after the season that he was going to retire from baseball and concentrate on green tables. According to Murphy, it was the catcher's "desertion" of the club that cost a fourth straight pennant in 1909. In fact, even without Kling, the Cubs won 104 games and romped over everybody except the Pirates, who won 110. Brown again led the staff with 27 wins and an ERA of 1.31. After scratching out as a pool professional, Kling returned in 1910, only to find himself having to share time behind the plate with Jimmy Archer and having to put up with a lot of resentment for his year's hiatus. But with Brown and rookie King Cole winning 20 and Holman and Schulte leading the offense, the Cubs won their fourth pennant in five years. The bad news started toward the end of the campaign, when Evers

One of the most famous verses ever inspired by baseball was penned by Franklin P. Adams of the New York *Evening Mail* in 1910. Entitled *Baseball's Sad Lexicon*, it said in part:
These are the saddest of possible words—
Tinker to Evers to Chance
Trio of bear cubs and fleeter than birds
Tinker to Evers to Chance
Thoughtlessly pricking our gonfalon bubble,
Making a Giant hit into a double,
Words that are weighty with nothing but trouble—
Tinker to Evers to Chance.
The popularity of the New York writer's lament is credited with having played an important role in the election of the Chicago players to the Hall of Fame, because the number of twin killings they were actually involved in was not that high; in fact, Pittsburgh infielders playing in the same period topped them regularly.

broke his leg and had to sit out the World Series against Connie Mack's Athletics. What he missed was a Philadelphia championship in five games.

The Philadelphia victory, helped along by twelve Chicago errors, underlined the aging of the team, starting with Chance himself. Before the 1911 season had progressed too far, both Kling and Steinfeldt were dealt off. The team also had to get along without Evers, who suffered a nervous breakdown, and Overall, who retired at the age of twenty-nine. Mainly because of a big offensive year from Schulte (the league leader in homers and RBIs, with 21 and 121, respectively) and another dominating performance on the mound by Brown (21 wins and 13 saves), the club still managed to come in second. After the season, the team suffered a couple of more blows when Jim Doyle, who had replaced Steinfeldt at third base, died of an appendicitis attack and Chance was revealed to have developed a blood clot in his head from having been hit by too many pitched balls. It was while Chance was in the hospital that Murphy just about ended an era for the franchise when he accused several players of being drunkards and warned that they were on their way out. An infuriated Chance, who had been having contract problems with Murphy for years, rose from his hospital bed to deny the charges, calling them a pretext for not yielding to the salary demands of several key members of the club. The outburst was one of the

main reasons why Chance was shown the door at the end of the 1912 season.

Although Murphy promised some franchise continuity by making Evers Chance's replacement, it wasn't quite the kind the owner had expected. As soon as the appointment was announced, Tinker, who hadn't spoken to his double-play partner off the field in years because of an imagined slight over who had once hailed a cab first, demanded to be traded; he was accommodated in an eight-player swap with the Reds that was of little benefit to Chicago. Brown, Sheckard, and Reulbach followed Tinker to other cities. Once the 1913 season got underway, Evers showed why he had been nicknamed The Crab by getting into a series of rows with his players, some of them on the diamond during games. In one incident, Bridwell, whose single had set into motion Merkle's Boner in 1908 and who had been purchased to succeed Tinker at shortstop, took a swing at his manager in the midst of an argument about where he should be playing the opposition hitters. In another episode, outfielder Tommy Leach ran in from his position to the mound to take on Evers for what he concluded had been ridicule of his defensive play.

Given all the dissension on the team, it did not come as a surprise when Murphy fired Evers at the end of the year in favor of former umpire O'Day. But when the owner also let it be known that he was working on a deal to send the second baseman to the Braves and Evers responded by threatening to jump to the newly-organized Federal League, NL president John Tener summoned Murphy to a meeting in Cincinnati. With Murphy's angel Taft and a couple of other Chicago stockholders in attendance, Tener ripped into the Cubs' president for causing the potential loss of a star like Evers to the Feds, recalled some of his other administrative imbroglios, and suggested that he withdraw from the scene. Under an agreement worked out shortly afterward, Taft bought the stock Murphy had in the club. As for Evers, he ended up being traded to Boston anyway.

Managers came and went for the next few years, with Roger Bresnahan succeeding O'Day, Tinker Bresnahan, and Fred Mitchell Tinker. None of them was able to lift the team above fourth. The club's best player in the period was southpaw Hippo Vaughn, who posted twenty wins or more five times between 1914 and 1919, took an ERA title, and led the league twice in strikeouts. It was Vaughn who, on May 2, 1917, hooked up with Fred Toney of Cincinnati in a double no-hitter for nine innings, before finally surrendering two safeties to the Reds in the tenth inning and losing, 1–0.

In 1916, after two years of long-distance ownership, Taft sold the franchise to a group headed by Charles Weegham, a cafeteria and dairy magnate who had been the chief stockholder in the Chicago entry in the Federal League. Among Weegham's partners were fish wholesaler William Walker and chewing gum tycoon William Wrigley. As part of the deal, Weegham pulled the Cubs out of West Side Park and moved them to the facility that had been used by his FL franchise; known initially as Weegham Park and then as Cubs Park, the stadium was redubbed Wrigley Field in 1926. The first NL game to be played on the premises took place on April 20, 1916, and saw the Cubs down the Reds in eleven innings, 7–6. The three name changes in less than a decade reflected Weegham's fast exit from the franchise and Wrigley's equally rapid consolidation of power. By the beginning of 1918, the chewing gum king had taken so much stock in exchange for loans to the financially strapped Weegham that he was the organization's single biggest shareholder; by the end of the year, he had pressured Weegham's ouster as president, replacing him with manager Mitchell and bringing in former newspaperman Bill Veeck as vice-president. Wrigley gained an absolute majority of the stock in 1921.

Prior to the 1918 season, the Cubs acquired future Hall of Famer Grover Cleveland Alexander from the Phillies in an exchange that they were confident would restore them to the front ranks of the league. They were half-right: While indeed storming back to win the pennant by a comfortable 10½ games over New York, the pivotal deal turned out to be not the one for Alexander, who was drafted into the army shortly after reporting, but for Lefty Tyler, obtained from the Braves. Together with Vaughn (who led NL hurlers in wins and ERA) and righthander Claude Hendrix (19 wins), Tyler's 19 victories and 2.00 ERA were more than enough to compensate for another generally weak hitting attack.

Because of travel restrictions imposed by the War Department, the league offices agreed that only one switch of venue would be permitted during the World Series against the Red Sox. When Chicago drew the first three games at home, it concluded a deal with the AL White Sox to use the larger Comiskey Park for the contests. Not only were the attendance results mediocre, but the tepid turnout further diluted a prospective players' share of the proceeds that had already been watered down by a new regulation assigning monies to third- and fourth-place teams and by a public relations-inspired donation to war relief. On the trip to Boston after the third game,

players on both teams agreed to demand a meeting with the league presidents before taking the field again. With the threat of a strike in the air before Game Four at Fenway Park, Cubs' representative Les Mann and his Red Sox counterpart Harry Hooper made their case to NL officials without getting anywhere. But then AL president Ban Johnson showed up three sheets to the wind, and so wore down the players with a rambling plea to their patriotism that the World Series was resumed. The Cubs went down in six games. The offense was so anemic for both clubs that a mere nineteen runs were scored in the six contests.

One of Weegham's contractual ploys came back to haunt the franchise in 1919, when it was discovered that Mitchell was managing on a player's pact. League rules forbade a player from holding down an executive position at the same time, so Wrigley replaced him as president with Veeck. Mitchell, who hadn't actually appeared in a game as a player for some years, initially voiced bafflement at why he wasn't just given a regulation manager's contract, then later on expressed suspicion that it had been Veeck himself who had engineered the move. Over the next two years, however, the team had other problems that dwarfed the presidency dispute. In July 1919, Mitchell gave Veeck an ultimatum to get rid of pitcher Phil Douglas or find another pilot; Douglas, who had become notorious for his drinking sprees, and who would later be outlawed for offering to throw games, was shipped off to the Giants. The following year, pitcher Hendrix was yanked from a starting assignment at the last minute amid rumors that he had accepted money to throw a game to the Phillies. Alexander, back from the army, was rushed in as a substitute and lost, precipitating a league investigation. The inquiry's first casualty was Hendrix, who was kicked out of baseball along with fellow pitcher Paul Carter; far more important, the probe into the Chicago–Philadelphia game ultimately led to the unraveling of the infamous Black Sox scandal in the 1919 World Series.

The Cubs were no mere spectators to the investigation of the 1919 World Series. It was a franchise stockholder, advertising executive A. D. Lasker, who responded to the reports of the gambling manipulations by proposing that the major leagues establish a panel of Three Just Men to oversee the sport. Wrigley was less than enthusiastic about the politicians and other luminaries suggested by Lasker, so he came forward with an alternative proposal to appoint one man as overall governor. His candidate, federal judge Kenesaw Mountain Landis, signed a seven-year contract on November 12, 1920, becoming the first commissioner of baseball.

After the 1918 World Series, the club again hit the skids for close to a decade, being little more than a .500 outfit. The best pitching efforts of the period were turned in by Alexander in 1920 (an NL-leading 27 wins and 1.91 ERA) and righty Charlie Root in 1927 (an NL-leading 26 victories). Until stomach problems caught up to him, Charlie Hollocher continued to belie the image of no-hit shortstops, turning in season marks of .340 in 1922 and .342 in 1923 to wind up his abbreviated seven-year career with a .304 average. The 1920s also saw the arrival of catcher Gabby Hartnett, who would dominate the league at his position well into the following decade. In twenty years of major league service (nineteen of them with Chicago), the righthand-hitting Hartnett averaged .297, with 236 homers. Oddly, though he had some very big years (especially 1930, when he hit .339 with 37 homers and 122 RBIs), the catcher never once led the league in any offensive category. It was his steadiness at the bat and defensive brilliance that got him elected to the Hall of Fame in 1955.

Mitchell lasted as pilot through the 1920 campaign, when Veeck and Wrigley made the same mistake that Murphy had made in 1913 by bringing in Evers. Once again, the former infielder got into an endless series of tangles with his players, with Vaughn quitting the club in July after a particularly bitter argument and never returning. Evers was fired in August and succeeded by backup catcher Bill Killefer. Although he stayed on the job until the beginning of the 1925 season, Killefer had little to show for it except a reputation as a physical fitness advocate whose spring training program included having the players run up and down hills for hours on Wrigley's private preserve on Catalina Island. Things got even worse in 1925, when Veeck finally decided to make a change halfway through the season. Certain that Rabbit Maranville, unexcelled as a cutup, would train his energies toward becoming a shrewd manager, Veeck was stunned when the shortstop only stepped up his antics, especially after victories that he (and other members of the team) celebrated as though they had been pennant-clinching games. During a fifty-game stint as pilot, Maranville (among other things) engaged in a headline-making fight with a Brooklyn cab driver, ambushed club traveling secretary John Seys in various ways, including dropping water balloons on him from a hotel window, and emptied a spittoon over fellow passengers on a train. It was after the spittoon incident that Veeck entrusted the club to George Gibson for the final

weeks of the campaign. Together, Killefer, Maranville, and Gibson guided the club to its first cellar finish.

Breaking with the club tradition of hiring managers off the bench, Veeck found his next pilot, Joe McCarthy, in Louisville of the American Association. The choice aroused some grumbling among the players, and especially from Alexander. When the team got off to a slow start, not least because Alexander was hitting the bottle more regularly than the catcher's mitt, McCarthy stemmed further criticism of his tentativeness and inexperience by asking Veeck to get rid of the one-time ace as a negative influence; the front office complied, Alexander was sold to the Cardinals, and McCarthy began asserting his authority with fewer questions.

Using his experience with the American Association to the maximum, McCarthy talked Veeck into acquiring outfielders Riggs Stephenson and Hack Wilson from the minor league. In his first eight seasons with the Cubs, the righthand-hitting Stephenson never batted below .319; in fact only in the final year of his fourteen-season career did he hit below .297. With a mark of .336, Stephenson has the highest lifetime average next to the outlawed Shoeless Joe Jackson for players not in the Hall of Fame. Wilson, who did get elected to Cooperstown, in 1979, turned into one of the great power hitters of the era. In his first three years with Chicago, he led the league in homers, but even this was only a prelude to 1930, when he established the NL record for home runs with 56 and the major league mark for RBIs with 190. A portly righthand hitter, Wilson was eventually undone by the bottle, which just about washed him up by his early thirties.

Drawn mainly by Wilson's bashing and the club's return to offense, 1,163,347 fans paid their way into the newly-doubledecked Wrigley Field in 1927; it was the first time that an NL franchise had drawn a million. The attendance record also disproved the shibboleth, maintained by many teams into the 1940s, that radio coverage of games hurt ticket sales. In fact, a decade before Larry MacPhail of Cincinnati received credit for exploding this myth, the Cubs drew 7,845,700 spectators for the seven-year period between 1925 and 1931 while the games were being broadcast on as many as five stations in the Chicago metropolitan area. This turnout, for a club that averaged fourth in the standings in the years in question, represented a growth of 119 percent over the previous seven-year period when none of the games had been broadcast and the club had played at a similar pace.

With the addition of outfielder Kiki Cuyler from the Pirates, the team stayed in the pennant race through the entire 1928 season, ultimately having to settle for third place, four games behind pennant-winning St. Louis and two behind runnerup New York. The final touch was added in November 1928, when Veeck obtained NL hitting great Rogers Hornsby from the Braves in exchange for pitchers Socks Seibold, Percy Jones, and Bruce Cunningham, infielder Fred McGuire, catcher Lou Leggett, and $125,000. The second baseman promptly proved his worth by batting .380, with 47 doubles, 39 homers, 149 RBIs, and league-leading totals in both runs scored with 156 and slugging average with .679. In addition to Hornsby, the offense featured Wilson's .345 with 39 homers and an NL-high 159 RBIs, Cuyler's pace-setting 43 steals, and a .362 mark from Stephenson. Pat Malone led league pitchers with 22 wins, and Root contributed the highest winning percentage with his 19–6 ledger. The team still wasn't good enough to overcome the Athletics, who took the World Series in five games. To add insult to injury, Philadelphia defied an 8–0 deficit in the seventh inning of the fourth game, clobbering Cubs' hurlers for ten runs and holding on for a 10–8 victory.

Like other major league teams, the Cubs bashed the liveliest of all lively balls around in 1930. The season that saw Wilson set the NL mark for home runs and the big league record for RBIs also saw the center fielder's .356 average come up short before Stephenson's .367 and barely edge Cuyler's .355. Shortstop Woody English and Hartnett also hit better than .330. Despite so much slugging, it was a season of more pain than gain, with the club winding up two games behind St. Louis. Throughout the year, there were recurrent reports that McCarthy was on his way out, primarily because of a testy reply to Wrigley during the offseason after the owner had criticized Chicago's performance in the World Series against the Athletics. Most of the reports had the manager going to the Braves as part of a secret codicil to the Hornsby trade that allegedly gave Boston first rights on his services if he were to leave the Cubs; in the event, after resigning four days prior to the end of the season, McCarthy ended up with the Yankees. Hornsby was named as his successor.

Although he lasted slightly longer, Hornsby was the second coming of Evers, and it was a rare week during his tenure that he wasn't berating a player or a player wasn't attacking him. A particular target in 1931 was Wilson, who shared the manager's general philosophy that a dollar not spent was a dollar wasted, but who preferred spending his in saloons

Hack Wilson. *National Baseball Library, Cooperstown, NY*

After Chicago catcher Gabby Hartnett had himself photographed with gangster Al Capone during a game in 1931, Commissioner Kenesaw Landis issued an edict forbidding players, managers, and coaches from going near spectators while a game was in progress.

instead of at the race tracks that Hornsby favored. A combination of too many late nights and unrelieved tensions with the field boss brought about the outfielder's total offensive collapse and got him packed off to the Cardinals after the season in exchange for righthander Burleigh Grimes.

Wilson wasn't Hornsby's only problem, either. Despite the return of the heavy ball, almost every member of the pitching staff declined from 1929, reviving charges that had been heard during the Rajah's managing days in St. Louis that the only thing he knew about pitching was that he could hit it. Only Wrigley's fondness for Hornsby, along with the money that the second baseman had borrowed from the franchise to cover his track losses, prevented another change of managers.

Hornsby lost Wrigley as a shield in January 1932,

when the chewing gum manufacturer died at the age of 70. In replacing his father, Phil Wrigley confirmed Veeck at his post, and even gave him additional organizational power. With future Hall of Famer Billy Herman replacing Hornsby as the full-time second baseman and righthander Lon Warneke charging toward a league-leading 22 victories, the Cubs got off to a good enough start to keep Veeck from bringing in a new pilot. But then, in August, with the club only nine games above .500, the president finally acted, naming first baseman Charlie Grimm as the new skipper. Relieved to be free of Hornsby, the team went 37–20 for the rest of the season, a pace good enough to outdistance the Pirates by four games. In dividing up the prospective World Series pool, the players made two controversial decisions: voting nothing to Hornsby and approving a half-share for shortstop Mark Koenig. Hornsby filed a protest with Landis about being cut out, but the commissioner ruled that the money belonged to the players and could be shared out as they deemed fit. As for Koenig, while it was true that he appeared in only 33 games, it was equally true that the former Yankee's .353 average and his nimbleness at completing the double play for that stretch was one of the primary factors in the pennant win. His one-time teammates from New York thought so, because the Yankees began taunting the Cubs for their stinginess as soon as the Series began. It was within the context of increasingly abusive exchanges between the clubs that, in the third game, Babe Ruth walloped a home run off Root that, according to legend, he had predicted beforehand by pointing to center field and that, according to the Cubs, he had not called at all. The blast turned out to be the main talking point of a Series that was otherwise a travesty, with the Yankees belting eight homers and sweeping four games.

Little more than a year after Wrigley's death, Veeck also passed away, leaving the presidency to Walker, Weeghman's original partner. As a baseball executive, Walker belonged to the category of ravers—getting into regular screaming matches with Grimm, firing the manager for answering him back, then rehiring him as soon as he had calmed down again. A couple of decent finishes notwithstanding, the president had some things to scream about, starting with an attendance dip in the Great Depression year of 1933 of more than 400,000 from the previous season. It was also a period of disillusioning deals, with both Babe Herman and Chuck Klein coming to the club in apparent steals and then failing to produce at anticipated levels. Walker could hardly complain about either of the Grimm-inspired trades

because he completed an even worse one without consulting the manager—sending slugger Dolf Camilli to Philadelphia for weak-hitting first baseman Don Hurst. It was decisions like the Hurst swap that prompted Phil Wrigley to buy out Walker and replace him as president with Charles (Boots) Weber, an executive in another branch of the Wrigley family's enterprises.

By 1935, a completely recast team (except for catcher Hartnett and second baseman Herman among the regulars) had left the 1932 flag winners a distant memory. But then, in good part because of twenty-one consecutive victories down the home stretch, the Cubs beat out St. Louis and New York for another pennant. Grimm's biggest gamble was replacing himself at first base with nineteen-year-old Phil Cavarretta; the lefty-swinging Cavarretta paid off with 82 RBIs and a solid .275 average. Other big years came from Hartnett (an MVP award for a .344 average and 91 RBIs), Herman (.341 and a league-leading 227 hits and 57 doubles), and left fielder Augie Galan (league-leading numbers in steals and runs scored). Both Warneke and righthander Bill Lee won 20. The World Series was another disappointment, however: Despite two wins from Warneke and an arm injury that kept Detroit slugger Hank Greenberg in the dugout for most of the action, the Tigers emerged as the world champions in six games.

In what was taking shape as a pattern of one-season-forward-and-two-seasons-back, Chicago sat out the next two postseason competitions with the AL, although the team held on to first place for chunks of both 1936 and 1937. Off the field, the biggest news was the increasing involvement of Wrigley in baseball affairs, encouraged no little by the yes-men who had come to surround him. While most of the coterie was from the chewing gum company, neither Weber nor chief scout Pants Rowland was particularly distinguished as an independent voice, either. It was mainly because of their timidity before Wrigley's passing doubts, for instance, that the club turned down an opportunity in 1936 to purchase Joe DiMaggio from the same San Francisco team that had sent Galan to Chicago. On the other hand, Wrigley's enthusiasm for the perpetually distracted Tuck Stainback kept the backup outfielder on the roster for four years. In that time, Stainback became most noted for remaining at his outfield position until his opposition counterpart came out to inform that three outs had been recorded, for charging out to his position from the dugout after his teammates had made merely two outs, and for catching fly balls and then tossing them to his fellow outfielders thinking the inning was over while adversaries circled the bases.

One area in which Wrigley did excel was in product research. Using some of the same techniques that had made his gum company so prosperous and that anticipated the mania for minuscule statistics in the 1970s and 1980s, the owner brought in a battery of statisticians to break down every conceivable game situation involving pitchers and hitters, all in the interests of getting a better picture of team productivity. Other specialists began filming Chicago's players for a closer look at their mechanics. It was also in the mid-1930s that Wrigley ordered his field announcers and broadcasters never to refer to the home park without qualifying it as "Beautiful Wrigley Field," and then set about to make the claim true. In a remodeling that would be carried out over a couple of phases, he approved Bill Veeck, Jr.'s proposal to pad the walls with ivy and engineer Otis Shepard's suggestion to erect a hand-operated scoreboard above the center field bleachers.

In spite of a much-trumpeted preseason deal that had brought Dizzy Dean to the club in exchange for three players and $185,000, the Cubs got off to a lethargic start in 1938, sparking rumors of a managerial change. On July 20, Grimm submitted his resignation, lobbied for Hartnett as his successor, and got a job in the radio booth as a reward for not forcing Wrigley to fire him. Under Hartnett, the team gained new life, charging after the Pirates through August and September. The turning point of the season came on September 28th at Wrigley Field, when, with the two contenders tied in the bottom of the ninth inning and darkening skies making suspension of play imminent, Pittsburgh reliever Mace Adams got two quick outs, but then, instead of rolling, underhanding, or just holding on to the ball, grooved a curve for what became fabled as Hartnett's Homer in the Gloamin'. The blast put the Cubs ahead of the Pirates to stay, and three days later Chicago had another flag. Once again, however, the World Series was a sweep by the Yankees.

Between 1939 and 1944, the team put together five losing seasons in a row for the first time in its history. One reason was former sportswriter Jim Gallagher, who struck Wrigley as the second coming of Bill Veeck, Sr. and who was named the franchise's first general manager in 1941. Unfortunately for the Cubs, Gallagher's on-the-job training included a lot of disastrous trades with the Dodgers that became an organization habit well into the 1950s. The Cubs' executive got the ball rolling in May 1941 when he dispatched Herman to Brooklyn in exchange for infielder Johnny Hudson, outfielder Charlie Gilbert,

and $65,000. In August, he sold southpaw Larry French to Ebbets Field for the waiver price. About a week later he let Galan go to the Pacific Coast League, and was probably not very surprised when Brooklyn hauled the outfielder back from California within a few days. Then, on June 6, 1944, in what some writers mused was Gallagher's attempt to define D-Day as Dodgers-Day, he swapped second baseman Eddie Stanky to Brooklyn for lefty Bob Chipman.

When Gallagher moved into the front office, he found catcher Jimmie Wilson newly installed as Hartnett's successor as manager. It turned out to be a strained partnership, with the pilot doubting Gallagher's baseball expertise and the general manager continually expressing doubts that Wilson had any strategic plan other than to play hot hitters and bench cold ones. That Wilson remained the manager until 1944 was largely due to World War II and the reluctance of all baseball front offices to make big changes on teams that were, organizationally, content to run out the ground ball until the conflict was over. On one subject, however, Gallagher and Wilson found agreement—never explaining their moves, or even announcing them, to the press. Stung by criticism for one thing or another, both club officials created even more of a public relations mess for the franchise by having trades acknowledged by the team doing business with the Cubs and by having lineup changes revealed through the public address announcer or by the batter getting into the box. It was because of the chill that descended over the media's relations with Gallagher and Wilson in the early 1940's that Wrigley felt compelled to get over his own indifference to the press and to become more public relations-minded after the war.

One of the biggest problems that Gallagher found waiting for him was Chicago's farm sys-

In 1943, Phil Wrigley organized the All-American Girls Professional Baseball League as a financial hedge against the major leagues' being shut down by World War II. The league, which remained in operation until 1954, had teams in Illinois, Indiana, Wisconsin, and Michigan, with such names as the Rockford Peaches, the Chicago Colleens, the Fort Wayne Daisies, and the Kalamazoo Lassies. Among the managers were Hall of Famers Jimmie Foxx and Max Carey.

tem—or lack of one. Because of a belief that minor league clubs should be allowed to develop on their own terms, Wrigley had always eschewed the farm chain system that had made the Cardinals and Yankees so successful. The club's major provider of talent over the years, the Los Angeles Angels of the Pacific Coast League, was owned by Wrigley personally, not by the Cubs, and often dealt players to other major league teams if they made better offers than Chicago. Another high minor league club, the American Association Milwaukee Brewers, survived on Wrigley's subsidies, but also went its own way when there was an advantage in doing so. Before Gallagher's insistence that the organization could only thrive with stricter agreements with the minor leagues, however, Wrigley gave the green light to an expansion that brought the franchise a twenty-team network of working agreements or outright ownership by 1947.

The war years brought the usual collection of unripe rookies, over-the-hill veterans, and career minor leaguers. The most conspicuous of all the team's follies was outfielder Lou Novikoff, whose minor league slugging had promised another Babe Ruth but whose aversion to the ivy on the Wrigley Field walls had all the team's specialists and even outsiders laboring in vain for four years to demonstrate that there was no danger of poison ivy or hay fever if he would go back after a ball. Novikoff never accepted the demonstrations (at one point, teammates even chewed some of the ivy to prove that it had no harmful effects), and continued running back toward the infield in pursuit of balls that had caromed above his head; moreover, his power output during his four-year stay added up to fifteen homers. On the other hand, the club came up with a genuine power hitter in outfielder Bill (Swish) Nicholson, who led the NL in both home runs and RBIs in 1943 and 1944; the lefty-swinging Nicholson and Philadelphia's Mike Schmidt (in 1980 and strike-shortened 1981) are the only NLers to have accomplished this feat.

When the Cubs lost thirteen straight at the beginning of the 1944 season, Gallagher had a ready excuse for removing Wilson as manager and bringing back Grimm. Although he achieved little in his reunion year, Grimm was at the helm when the team dismayed preseason prognosticators and surged to a pennant in 1945. Two of the most important contributors to the drive were Stan Musial, the St. Louis star whose induction into the Navy unquestionably accounted for a three-game difference between the teams at the end of the year, and the Cincinnati Reds, who lost twenty-one of twenty-two encounters with

Chicago during the campaign. On the club itself, the offense was galvanized by Cavarretta, who took MVP honors by winning the batting title (.355), driving in 97 runs, and scoring 94. Right behind Cavarretta in the MVP polling was center fielder Andy Pafko, who led the team with 110 RBIs. The pitching staff was anchored by righthanders Hank Wyse (22 wins) and Claude Passeau (17), but the turning point for the season came on July 27, when Gallagher paid the Yankees $97,000 for the services of southpaw Hank Borowy. Borowy ended up going 11–2 with a NL-leading 2.13 ERA.

Against widespread cracks that neither team was good enough to win, the Cubs and Tigers slogged through a seven-game World Series before Detroit emerged as the champion. The defeat was Chicago's seventh straight in a World Series; worse, it was to be the team's last appearance in an interleague championship series. Even second place in the NL stayed out of reach until the introduction of divisional play in 1969.

If nothing else, the Cubs were highly quotable for the rest of the 1940s. In his new zeal to communicate with the public, owner Wrigley periodically took out ads to apologize for the showing of the club and to promise better days ahead. A standby of Chicago press releases for years was a so-called "Cubs' Platform" that stated the organization's goals as:

1. A world championship.
2. Continued comfort for fans.
3. Making Wrigley Field America's finest recreation center.
4. Baseball's premier farm system.

The fourth item proved to be as elusive as the first; only a couple of years after Gallagher had talked Wrigley into entering agreements with twenty minor league teams, the number had been halved. The clubs that remained seemed incapable of developing a big league hitter, prompting one of baseball's more noted tales. To a wire in which a scout informed him that he had "Spotted a pitcher who stopped a good team cold for nine innings; only one foul fly hit out of the infield," Grimm was purported to have responded: "Forget the pitcher. Send the guy who hit the foul." Even more popular was the barb provoked by years of watching shortstop Roy Smalley fire throws into the first base seats: Instead of "Tinker to Evers to Chance," it was "Miksis to Smalley to Addison Street." Another cherished franchise moment—Hartnett's Homer in the Gloamin'—had its ludicrous sequel on April 30, 1949, when Pafko made what appeared to be a diving catch on a drive by St. Louis's Rocky Nelson to end a 3–2 game, only to have umpire Al Barlick call it a trap. While Pafko raged at Barlick, Nelson chased a pinch runner around the bases for a Cardinal win on his Homer in the Glove.

On June 14, 1949, Wrigley concluded that part of the club's problem was that both Grimm and Gallagher were holding down the wrong jobs, so he kicked the manager upstairs to a vice-presidency that effectively reduced the general manager's powers; named to succeed Grimm in the dugout was Frankie Frisch. Although hired principally for his Gashouse Gang style on the field and in the clubhouse, Frisch wasted little time in exploiting his friendship with the perennially bemused Grimm to have a big say in team transactions. Their first joint effort in October 1949 left them in a room alone with Brooklyn's Branch Rickey, and when they came out again, they had surrendered $100,000 of Wrigley's money for pitcher Paul Minner and first baseman Preston Ward. A few weeks later, Grimm and Frisch cornered Boston's Lou Perini during the winter meetings with the declared intention of coming away with either ace Warren Spahn or top prospect Johnny Antonelli; they ended up with over-the-hill Bill Voiselle. Buoyed by these fiascos, Gallagher ridiculed the notion of Grimm and Frisch attempting to deal with Rickey. Not only wasn't the Brooklyn president flattered, he advised newsmen not to pay attention to Gallagher, whom he described as "a glorified office boy."

However reduced his own power, Gallagher made it sufficiently uncomfortable in the executive offices for Grimm to tire of all the infighting and leave the club only six months after being given his vice-presidency. Frisch didn't wait for Wrigley to fill the void by increasing Gallagher's powers again; instead, he persuaded the owner to hire Wid Matthews away from the Dodgers and to demote Gallagher to business manager. That wasn't good news for Gallagher, but it wasn't so good for the Cubs, either, because Matthews proved even more vulnerable to his mentor Rickey's wiles. The worst of several deals with Brooklyn occurred on June 15, 1951, when Chicago unloaded Pafko, catcher Rube Walker, second baseman Wayne Terwilliger, and pitcher Johnny Schmitz in exchange for outfielder Gene Hermanski, catcher Bruce Edwards, infielder Eddie Miksis, and pitcher Joe Hatten. The sports pages of the Chicago press let out a scream, terming the deal "the great daylight robbery" and "Wrigley insanity." So disbelieving were some local sportswriters that Matthews would give away Pafko for so little return that they printed ludicrous rumors for the rest of the year that there would be a second part of the swap after the

season in which Chicago would pay Brooklyn a couple of hundred thousand dollars for either Duke Snider or Carl Furillo.

Among those who couldn't accept the Pafko trade was manager Frisch, and his officially off-the-record comments soon got back to Matthews. A month after the deal with Brooklyn, Frisch was out in favor of Cavarretta. Two of the rare positive developments in the period were both brought about by a Gallagher-worked deal in June 1949 with the Reds in which Chicago obtained outfielders Frankie Baumholtz and Hank Sauer. While Baumholtz provided several years of solid service as a center fielder and leadoff man, Sauer's home-run hitting made him one of the most popular players in franchise history. In his first four seasons with the team, the right-handed hitter took advantage of Wrigley Field's friendly confines to crack at least 31 round-trippers, then, after an injury-plagued campaign, came back to total 41 in a fifth season. In 1952, Sauer's 37 homers and 121 RBIs (both NL highs) netted him an MVP crown for a last-place club.

Convinced that Sauer's kind of slugging was the way out of the morass for the team, Matthews spent the offseasons of both 1951 and 1952 trying to come up with another power hitter. His first attempt, which even Wrigley later on admitted having snickered at, was to go back once again to the Dodgers and offer the righthanded starter Bob Rush for no less than Furillo, first baseman Gil Hodges, and second baseman Bobby Morgan; for once, the Dodgers said they weren't interested. In June of 1953, however, Matthews found the next best thing to the Dodgers when he went to Rickey, by then with Pittsburgh, and discovered that he was still eager for any deal that involved Wrigley's money. The key items in what amounted to a ten-man trade were the Cubs' acquisition of NL home run champion Ralph Kiner (like Sauer, a slow-footed righthand hitter) and Rickey's pocketing of $150,000. For the next couple of seasons, Kiner and Sauer alternated between going down with injuries and bashing home runs, while Baumholtz ran himself ragged trying to cover the alleys for both of them and the team remained mired in the second division.

After the Cubs had lost fifteen of their first twenty spring training games in 1954, Cavarretta made the mistake of going to Wrigley and warning him that the team was going to be as bad as the one that had finished seventh the year before. For his pains, Cavarretta was summarily fired as a "defeatist" and replaced by former third baseman Stan Hack, who then guided the squad to another

ERNEST BANKS
"MR. CUB"
CHICAGO N. L., 1953-1971
HIT 512 CAREER HOMERS WITH MORE THAN
40 IN A SEASON FIVE TIMES. HAD RECORD
FIVE GRAND-SLAMS IN 1955. FIRST TO BE
ELECTED N.L. MOST VALUABLE PLAYER TWO
SUCCESSIVE YEARS, 1958-59. LED LEAGUE
IN HOME RUNS AND RUNS BATTED IN TWICE
AND SLUGGING PCT. ONCE. ESTABLISHED
RECORDS FOR MOST HOMERS IN SEASON BY
SHORTSTOP (47 IN 1958) AND FOR FEWEST
ERRORS (12) AND BEST FIELDING AVERAGE
(.985) BY A SHORTSTOP IN 1959.

National Baseball Library, Cooperstown, NY

seventh-place standing. Most of the attention during the year was concentrated around the middle of the infield, where second baseman Gene Baker and shortstop Ernie Banks were the first black players to wear Chicago uniforms. Originally, Baker had been touted as the more gifted of the pair, but his star faded rapidly next to the accomplishments of the righthand-hitting slugger who eventually became known as Mister Cub. In nineteen years with the team, Banks clouted 512 home runs and drove home 1,636 runs. Five times he hit more than 40 homers in a season, and eight times he drove in more than 100 runs. In 1958 and 1959, he won back-to-back MVP awards for teams that finished fifth. Banks, who ended up playing more games at first base than at shortstop, entered the Hall of Fame in 1977.

Aside from Banks, Cubs' fans had little to entertain them in the 1950s. Even when there were spurts toward respectability, they were usually exhausted by July 4th, leaving pundits to debate whether the need to play under the summer sun at lightless Wrigley was as much responsible for the club's inertia as bad players. A good part of the decade was spent

counting down on trumpeted five-year development plans that first Matthews and then his successors indicated as the means for fielding a contender. On October 11, 1956, Wrigley announced the biggest one-whack sweep in franchise history when he told reporters that Hack, Matthews, and Gallagher had all resigned. The new manager was ex-catcher Bob Scheffing, Los Angeles Angels' President John Holland took over Matthews's portfolio, and, to a roar of laughter along Lake Michigan, Grimm returned still again, this time as vice-president with vaguely defined duties. Thanks to a league-leading 182 homers in 1958 and to Banks and tireless relievers Don Elston and Bill Henry in 1959, the Scheffing-Holland-Grimm triumvirate boosted the team as high as fifth at the end of the decade. But Wrigley was still dissatisfied, and fired Scheffing for the ever-flexible Grimm.

On his third go-round, Grimm lasted little more than a month of the regular season in 1960. Claiming that the change was being made for health reasons, Wrigley next went to Lou Boudreau, one of the team's radio-television broadcasters. Grimm had been given a broadcasting job after his first ouster and a vice-presidency after his second one, so Wrigley showed a weakness for symmetry by appointing him to *both* the broadcasting booth and another vice-presidency after his third exit. It wasn't long before Boudreau rejoined Grimm behind a microphone, either: As soon as the Hall of Famer met with Wrigley and Holland at the end of the season and insisted on a two-year contract to continue, he was fired as pilot.

In getting rid of Scheffing for Grimm at the end of the 1959 season, Wrigley had held forth on the expendability of field bosses, declaring in part: "I believe there should be relief managers just like relief pitchers, so you can keep rotating them." To the astonishment of the baseball world, the Chicago owner translated his theories into practice in December 1960, when he announced that, instead of a single successor to Boudreau, he had decided to institute a college of coaches—a nucleus of eight veteran baseball men who would rotate throughout the season as managers, coaches, and instructors, not only on the

On November 21, 1959, the Cubs were part of the first modern interleague trade not requiring waivers, when they sent first baseman Jim Marshall and pitcher Dave Hillman to the Red Sox for first baseman Dick Gernert.

Cubs, but also on the organization's other teams. To drive home the point that "a player in the organization is a Cub no matter where he plays," Wrigley said there would be no further reference in franchise literature to *minor* league teams. Named as members of the first college were Grimm, Rip Collins, Rube Walker, Harry Craft, Bobby Adams, Goldie Holt, El Tappe, and Vedie Himsl.

Inevitably, the rotation system came in for a lot of criticism, both from traditionalists who objected to it on principle and some of the Cubs' own players, who were soon complaining about receiving contradictory instructions from different coaches. With regard to the team's statistical performance, the difference wasn't so discernible, although there was one exception: Whereas the Cubs of the 1950s had lingered near the bottom of the standings because of poor players, the teams of the early 1960s remained buried despite a number of burgeoning stars. Among those winning regular jobs at the start of the decade were third baseman Ron Santo, second baseman Ken Hubbs, shortstop Don Kessinger, and outfielders Billy Williams and Lou Brock. For Chicago, the most accomplished was Williams, who launched a Hall of Fame career in 1961 by taking NL Rookie of the Year honors. In an eighteen-year career (sixteen of them with Chicago), the lefty swinger compiled a .290 mark that included a batting title and thirteen straight seasons of at least 21 homers (for an overall total of 426). The most starcrossed was Hubbs, who gained a second straight Rookie of the Year award for the team in 1962, but who was killed in a plane crash prior to the 1964 season. Future Hall of Famer Brock became most noteworthy as the central player in the worst trade in franchise history, when he was swapped to St. Louis on June 15, 1964 for outfielder Doug Clemens and pitchers Bobby Shantz and Ernie Broglio.

After two years of the rotating coaches and no visible progress on the field, Wrigley decided that the core problem was not bad players or the instabilities built into his system, but what he termed a "lack of centralized objectives." To fix this, he named Air Force Colonel Robert Whitlow as the organization's "athletic director," emphasizing that even Holland was to report to the career military man.

In 1962, Buck O'Neill became the first black to be named as a major league coach.

Whitlow's first move was to whittle at the rotation system itself by naming Bob Kennedy as "head coach" for an indeterminate period. For a few months, Whitlow and Kennedy practiced peaceful coexistence, but when the colonel tried to give Kennedy some advice on the club's pitching rotation in August 1963, the head coach exploded, ordering him to stay away from pitching tutor Fred Martin and the players. Wrigley's silence before the clash only encouraged Kennedy to assert a more traditional managerial authority over the team. Although there was still a changing of the guard to Lou Klein in the latter half of 1965, other members of the rotation system began drifting away to other jobs. The breakup of the college of coaches coincided with the resignation of Whitlow as athletic director and Wrigley's lament that the colonel's ideas had been "too far ahead of their time." Aside from installing an auxiliary fence in the center field bleachers, nobody could quite pinpoint what ideas Wrigley had in mind.

With Whitlow out of the picture, the Chicago owner abandoned his experiment completely, and named Leo Durocher as the manager for 1966. At his first press conference, Durocher, who hadn't been in charge of a team for almost ten years, set the bumptious tone that was to characterize his stay with the club until 1972. His first point was that he was "the manager and only the manager—don't ever use the word coach around me." His second was that he was going to see to it that the team stopped its practice of bringing up good players (such as Lou Brock) and then trading them away before they had blossomed. And, in reference to the club's 1965 finish, he insisted that the "Cubs are not an eighth-place team." The latter assertion came back to haunt him for years when, in 1966, Chicago proved his argument by finishing tenth.

The 1966 cellar finish notwithstanding, Durocher did restore the team to respectability. It was at his urging that Holland completed two of the organization's best deals before the 1966 season: getting catcher Randy Hundley and pitcher Bill Hands from the Giants and outfielder Adolfo Phillips and pitcher Ferguson Jenkins from the Phillies. While Hundley became one of the premier defensive receivers of his era, Jenkins, a righthander, turned into the bulwark of a pitching staff that for years had relied almost exclusively on aging veterans. Put into the rotation in 1967, Jenkins ripped off twenty wins for the first of six consecutive seasons—a feat all the more remarkable in hitter-friendly Wrigley Field. By the end of his nineteen-year career, the Canadian native would rack up 284 victories, earning him election to Cooperstown in 1991.

Even with Jenkins, Hundley, Williams, and what was regarded as the best infield in the major leagues, the Cubs were unable to rise above contending status, mainly because of a lack of depth behind Jenkins and Hands and of a dependable third outfielder to go with Williams and veteran slugger Jim Hickman. But with the dawning of the 1969 campaign, even these problems seemed relatively minor compared to the deficiencies faced by the other clubs in the newly created Eastern Division. What followed was the worst debacle in Chicago history, with the team holding first place for 155 days, but still winding up eight games behind the Miracle Mets.

The first problem was Durocher, whose emphasis on winning at all costs followed his traditional path of progressing from confidence building to relentless pressuring. Among the consequences of this approach was an insistence on playing his regulars without pause: Banks, Kessinger, Santo, Williams, and Hundley all played in 151 games or more, Jenkins led the league in starts, and lefty Ken Holtzman and Hands were right behind him.

The exhausted players began bickering among themselves. In one notorious incident, Santo, till then the clubhouse leader, lashed into rookie center fielder Don Young for losing two balls that cost the team a critical game to the Mets. Although Santo apologized the following day for his outburst, and later called it the worst mistake of his career, he was booed by Wrigley Field fans down the stretch and lost a good deal of credibility with his teammates. It didn't help either that Young, the center of the controversy, *was* in over his head and that Durocher had insisted on trading his best alternative, the popular Phillips, midway through the season. The manager was also criticized for leaving the team at two separate junctures during the season to attend to private business and for keeping umpires in a state of agitation against the team with his incessant baiting. What it all added up to was the blowing of an 8½ game lead in mid-August before New York's momentous drive over the final weeks of the season.

The Cubs came close again in 1970, but the beginning of the new decade was mainly marked by increasing tension between Durocher and his players. The worst blowup came on August 23, 1971, when, after asking the players to air their grievances, Durocher charged Santo with being so egotistical that the third baseman had demanded that the club or-

ganize a Ron Santo Day at Wrigley Field. When Santo not only denied the allegation but went at Durocher with his fists, the latter pulled off his uniform and announced that he was retiring. Although some of the players applauded the decision, a majority warned that a Durocher exit under such circumstances could only rebound against Santo, and called in Holland to mediate the crisis. Durocher came back, but in an atmosphere that Jenkins described as "an armed truce," with neither side talking to the other except in game situations. Expectations that Wrigley would make a managerial change at the end of the year were disappointed when the owner issued a statement that read in part: ". . . . . Leo is the team manager and the 'Dump Durocher Clique' might as well give up. He is running the team, and if some of the players do not like it and lie down on the job, during the offseason we will see what we can do to find them happier homes."

Wrigley backed up his words by unloading some anti-Durocher players, but it didn't help. On July 25, 1972, a carefully worded statement asserted that Durocher was "stepping aside" in favor of Whitey Lockman. Durocher maintained that he had not been fired, and while not exactly contradicting him, Wrigley and Holland didn't confirm the claim, either. Under the much milder Lockman, the Cubs completed the season at a .600 pace, but still finished eleven games behind the Pirates.

Lockman turned out to be the first of four managers who saw the club through the rest of the decade with little distinction other than reaching .500 (achieved once). Aside from the fact that none of them (Jim Marshall, Herman Franks, and Joey Amalfitano being the others) provoked the controversies sparked by the college of coaches and Durocher, their principal common denominator was a background in the Giants' system. The club wrote a small footnote to managerial history on May 8, 1973, when Banks took over as pilot after Lockman had been kicked out of a game; it was the first recorded instance of a black managing even temporarily in the major leagues. Wholesale roster changes took place after the 1973 and 1974 seasons, with Santo, Jenkins, Hundley, Williams, Kessinger, and second baseman Glenn Beckert all dispatched elsewhere. In trying to get rid of Santo, Holland had management's first unhappy experience with the recently approved five-and-ten rule that empowered a player who had been with the same team for five years and who had a total of ten years' service in the majors, to say no to a proposed trade. When Santo insisted on that right in refusing to go to the Angels in a deal for southpaw Andy Hassler, Holland threatened to cut the slugger's salary by twenty percent. This only toughened Santo's stance, and he dared the club to release him altogether. After several attacks by Wrigley on the so-called Woolworth Rule, the Cubs obtained Santo's permission for a trade to the White Sox.

Although the Cubs continued drawing well even during the losing years of the early 1970s, the franchise claimed deficits because of higher salaries and overhead. Wrigley first insisted that the problem could be resolved by exciting winning teams, and to this end he quickly forgot the torments of only a few years previously by going back to Durocher in 1975 and asking him to return as manager. Durocher agreed to come back only as general manager, and suggested Maury Wills as a manager, but Wrigley rejected the notion.

The owner then changed his strategy to saving money instead of trying to make it at a greater rate: after the 1975 season, he slid Holland off into semiretirement as an advisor and installed the fiscalminded Salty Saltwell, Wrigley Field operations chief, as the new general manager. Saltwell neither helped nor hurt in 1976, but that wasn't enough for Wrigley, who at one point during the season blasted the players as "clowns." In November 1976, he announced another series of changes that left Holland out altogether, returned Saltwell to park operations, and brought Kennedy back as vice-president in charge of baseball affairs. Wrigley didn't get the opportunity to see how the latest facelift would affect the team: On April 12, 1977, he died at the age of 82.

Wrigley's son William took over the organization and made it his first order of business to stress that the family had no intention of selling the team and no intention of installing light towers atop Wrigley Field. The assurances were deemed necessary because of enormous inheritance taxes that the heir had to pay on his parents' estate (his mother passed away around the same time as his father) and increasing league pressures to bring night ball to Chicago. The main attractions under the sun at the end of the decade were relief specialist Bruce Sutter's herculean efforts to save what games the rocky starting rotation kept close until the late innings and slugger Dave Kingman's titanic blasts over the left field wall. Sutter's emergence as the NL's premier closer made him the club's most marketable player, and he ended up being sent to the Cardinals after the 1980 season. As for Kingman, the righthand-hitting outfielder-first baseman continued his career habit of mixing his long-ball prowess with league-leading numbers in

strikeouts and crass off-the-field incidents; typical of the latter was the dumping of ice water on a reporter in spring training in 1980. Kingman was traded to the Mets prior to the 1981 season.

Kennedy did not endear himself to Cubs' fans with either trade. The general manager also disappointed local expectations when he chose the uninspiring Preston Gomez as Amalfitano's successor as manager in 1980, after the names of former Wrigley Field favorites like Santo and Hundley had been mentioned prominently; worse, he fired Gomez in July and went right back to Amalfitano. When the team got off to another slow start in 1981, Wrigley bounced Kennedy and brought back former manager Franks as the general manager. For Franks, the appointment turned out to be a lame duck position twice over: Almost as soon as he entered his office, major league players began a six-week strike and, a couple of days after that, Wrigley announced that he was selling his eighty-one percent of the franchise to the Chicago *Tribune* for $20.5 million. The deal, which went into effect officially after the season, ended the Wrigley family's sixty-five-year association with team.

The key member of the new front office under the *Tribune* was former Philadelphia manager Dallas Green, who took on the title of executive vicepresident. The abrasive Green also took on the city of Chicago when he indicated from the start that he considered the installation of lights at Wrigley necessary if the franchise hoped to survive. While fans were digesting this declaration of things to come, the new Cubs' boss moved to make over the organization in his own (Philadelphia) image, importing cronies like Lee Elia to manage and Gordon Goldsberry to direct scouting operations. In a deal that would rank with the greatest ever made by Chicago, Green also went to the Phillies to unload shortstop Ivan DeJesus in exchange for veteran shortstop Larry Bowa and Philadelphia's prize farm hand, infielder Ryne Sandberg. Over the next couple of seasons, he would also pry away from his former employers catcher Keith Moreland, pitcher Dick Ruthven, and outfielders Gary Matthews and Bob Dernier.

For all its pledges of bringing a "new tradition" to Wrigley Field, the Green regime had a rocky first couple of years, winding up in fifth place, 19 games off the pace, both seasons. The primary problem was a pitching staff that depended too much on exhausted veterans like Jenkins (re-signed as a free agent) and whose best arm belonged to a closer, Lee Smith, who didn't have all that many games to close. None of this sat well with Cubs' fans, who had to read almost every day about Green's desire for lights or his plan to demolish the center field scoreboard (he ended up having to settle for an electronic auxiliary scoreboard under the existing one). The result was an atypically hostile crowd for Wrigley Field as the club continued to flounder near the bottom of the Eastern Division. Finally, in August 1983, Elia exploded, calling Chicago fans "garbage" and getting off such gems as "eighty-five percent of the people in this country work. The other fifteen percent come out to Wrigley to boo my players." Whatever Green might have felt about Elia's remarks, he received prompt orders from the circulation-dependent *Tribune* to get himself a new manager, and Elia was replaced within days by administrative assistant Charlie Fox. When the season ended, Fox returned upstairs to make room for Jim Frey as the pilot.

Entering the 1984 season, Green knew that he was running out of time to make good on his promise to bring a pennant to Chicago. The biggest sign of his tightened leash was the hiring of Jim Finks, general manager of the NFL Chicago Bears, as president and head of the franchise. Green was also getting as good as he was giving on the lights issue: First, a group calling itself Citizens United for Baseball Sunshine (CUBS) took to rallying the city to its banner; second, an increasingly hostile press ridiculed worries about the Cubs losing LCS or World Series home dates because of television demands for night games, pointing out that the Chicago team was far from qualifying for postseason competition; third, the Illinois state legislature approved a bill prohibiting night games at Wrigley Field. What ended up saving Green was a series of trades early in 1984 that added pitchers Rick Sutcliffe, Scott Sanderson, and Dennis Eckersley to the staff. The club then went on to its first taste of postseason battle since 1945.

With the righthander Sutcliffe contributing an astonishing 16–1 record and sailing to Cy Young honors, the Cubs outdistanced the Mets by 6½ lengths to win their first divisional title. As crucial to the team as the rotation of Sutcliffe, Eckersley, Sanderson, Ruthven, and lefty Steve Trout was the bullpen of Smith and Tim Stoddard: Between them, the two righthanders won 19 and saved 40. Among the position players, the standout was second baseman Sandberg, who won the NL MVP award for a .314 average that included 19 homers, 36 doubles, a league-leading 19 triples, 32 steals, 84 RBIs, and 114 runs. Sandberg also provided the turning point to the season on June 23rd when, in a slugfest with the Cardinals, he hit game-tying homers in both the ninth and tenth innings, giving the team room to

prevail in the eleventh inning by the rowdy score of 11–10.

With the club set to meet the Padres in the LCS, Commissioner Bowie Kuhn confirmed Green's years-old warnings by announcing that, if Chicago advanced to the World Series, it would lose the NL's scheduled advantage in playing the first two and last two games at home so that NBC could be accommodated for evening telecasts. The issue became academic when Chicago lost three straight to San Diego after winning the first two games, but there was not much doubt that Wrigley Field was close to ending its daylight-only policy. With at least the divisional title in his pocket and the tide turning in his favor on the lights issue, Green received his reward from the ownership with the December announcement that Finks was resigning as president and would be replaced by the executive vice-president.

For Green, that was as happy as the ending got. The following year, the team made medical history of sorts by losing every one of its five starters to injuries for extended periods. With only Smith pitching with any consistency, the club fell off to fourth, the first of four consecutive seasons that it would again finish shy of the .500 mark. Frey lasted until June 12, 1986, when he was replaced by Gene Michael. The colorless Michael did nothing to dis-

Ryne Sandberg. *Stephen Green*

tract attention from Green's regular rages over the team's performance or his continued sniping at community leaders for refusing to budge on the lights issue, even after the NL had given him further ammunition by declaring that the Cubs would have to play future LCS games at Busch Stadium in St. Louis. Management's most decisive act during the year was firing a ballgirl because she had appeared in *Playboy*.

Prior to the 1987 season, Green made his biggest offensive pickup since Sandberg when he signed free agent Andre Dawson. In the face of the multimillion-dollar pacts being offered players of his caliber, the slugging outfielder signed a blank contract, challenged Green to fill in the amount, then went on to an MVP season that made him the cheapest $500,000 slugger in baseball. But aside from Dawson's NL-leading 49 homers and 137 RBIs and a comeback year by Sutcliffe (18 victories), there was little to celebrate in the campaign. In September, Michael told reporters that he had no desire to return the following year, and was fired then and there. While Frank Lucchesi took the reins for what remained of the schedule, Green hinted that he himself would return to the dugout in 1988 as a prelude to turning the team over to coach John Vukovich. But that plan went out the window when Green was asked to resign in October. Ex-manager Frey was welcomed back as general manager, and he immediately named long-time friend Don Zimmer as pilot.

The lights issue finally came to a head in 1988. Although it had dominated local sports controversies only since the Wrigley family had sold out to the *Tribune*, the question had in fact dogged the franchise ever since Spalding had sought to install towers around Lakefront Park. In the 1930s, Bill Veeck, Jr. had kept at Phil Wrigley to make lights part of the remodeling of Wrigley Field, but the owner rejected the idea. Only a couple of years later, however, Wrigley himself prepared for night games, to the point of having light towers shipped to the ballpark. But with the Japanese bombing of Pearl Harbor, he changed his mind again, mainly in apprehension that the government was going to curtail baseball altogether for the duration of the war; the light towers ended up being donated to the Great Lakes Naval Base for the war effort. It was this history that was on the table at a February 25th meeting of all interested parties, with the *Tribune*'s representatives threatening to move the team to a new facility in the suburbs, the NL making it clear that no postseason games could ever be played on Addison Street, and some local politicians coming to a conclusion that, thanks to the lobbying efforts of CUBS, they had overestimated the opposition of their constituencies to NL night games in the city. Under the terms of an agreement hammered out that day, the city council repealed ordinances banning lights, the Cubs agreed to play only a "minimal number" of night contests to placate the neighborhood around the ballpark, the *Tribune* committed itself to staying at Wrigley through the 2002 season ("if feasible"), and the NL threw in the bone of an All Star Game for the stadium. The first night game took place against the Phillies on August 8th, but was postponed by rain after three innings; the following evening, the Cubs got their first home contest under the lights into the books, defeating the Mets, 6–4.

As for the team in 1988, its main selling point was the maturation of four top prospects—first baseman Mark Grace, shortstop Shawon Dunston, outfielder Rafael Palmiero, and righthanded starter Greg Maddux. The performances of the quartet did a great deal to obscure the club's less than mediocre finish and a disastrous deal by Frey in which bullpen stopper Smith was sent to the Red Sox for pitchers Calvin Schiraldi and Al Nipper. The general manager had a lot more luck with his next big deal in the offseason of 1988–89, making Palmiero the key concession in a swap with the Rangers that netted southpaw reliever Mitch Williams. While driving Zimmer frantic with his habit of walking the bases loaded before he got down to cases, Wild Thing, as Williams became known, buttressed a starting staff of Maddux (19 wins), Mike Bielecki (18), and Sutcliffe (16) with 36 saves for another division title. The principal offense came from Sandberg (30 homers and .290), Grace (.314 and 79 RBIs), and Rookie of the Year outfielder Jerome Walton (.293). Even more to the delight of the franchise, the team's winning ways drew a record 2,491,942 fans to the turnstiles. In addition to the club's appeal as winners, Zimmer himself became something of an attraction for his pudgy, pop-eyed appearance, volcanic explosions against umpires, and tactics that ranged from the highly imaginative to the bizarre (e.g., hit-and-run plays on full counts with the bases loaded and less than two outs). The LCS against the Giants turned into a hitting duel between first basemen Grace and Will Clark: While Grace had 11 hits in 17 at bats for a .647 mark and drove home 8 runs, his California counterpart topped him by going 13-for-20 for a .650 average and 8 RBIs. With that kind of offense dominating, San Francisco took the series in five games.

The 1990s brought continued slugging from Sandberg and Dawson and the confirmation of Maddux as one of the league's premier righthanders, but little else. In 1990, Sandberg belted 40 homers to become the first second baseman to lead the NL in that category since Hornsby in 1925. Prior to the 1991 season, the team spent lavishly in the free agent market, coming up with slugger George Bell and pitchers Danny Jackson and Dave Smith; only Bell produced to any degree, and even he was traded to the White Sox following the season. Early in the 1991 campaign, Zimmer was discharged by team president Donald Gresenko in favor of Jim Essian. After a few weeks of silence on the reasons for the move, the commissioner's office announced that it had been probing the manager's long-known race track betting habits. Zimmer was said to have been absolved of any wrongdoing for "insufficient evidence."

After the season, Gresenko himself was removed, with Stanton Cook coming in as president. Other moves saw Frey being shown the door for veteran AL front office executive Larry Himes and Jim Lefebvre succeeding Essian. But the biggest move of all was one that didn't happen. Early in 1992, Commissioner Fay Vincent announced that the addition of Florida and Colorado in 1993 was the perfect time to realign the league with more geographic logic, moving the Cubs and Cardinals to the Western Division and transferring the Braves and Reds to the East. Although the plan was initially welcomed by many clubs, especially by Atlanta with its interest in building a divisional rivalry with the Marlins, everything began to go sour when Chicago declared its opposition. The team's main bone of contention was that shifting to the West would have inconvenienced eastern viewers of its WGN superstation, forcing them to watch more games at later Mountain and Pacific starting times and thereby threatening lower ratings and less advertising. Cook also objected to Vincent's strongarm tactics in imposing the realignment in the avowed "best interests of baseball." When the commissioner refused to back down, the Cubs went to court and secured a restraining order against the move. Vincent's actions were ultimately viewed by the owners as another instance of his attempts to gain independent power and helped to increase pressures for his removal.

Under Lefebvre, the club got only one game better in 1992. The highlight of the season was Maddux's mound performance, where his record of 20–11 and a 2.18 ERA earned him the Cy Young nod. After year-long bickering over a new contract, however, the free agent hurler walked off to the Braves in November. Refusal to grant Dawson more than a one-year pact also led to the outfielder's decision to go to the Red Sox. For 1993, the club scrambled to fill the holes left by Maddux and Dawson by signing free agents Jose Guzman and Candy Maldonado, respectively. Other new arrivals included southpaw relievers Randy Myers and Dan Plesac.

CHICAGO CUBS

Annual Standings and Managers

Year	Position	W	L	Pct.	GB	Managers
1876	First	52	14	.788	+6	Al Spalding
1877	Fifth	26	33	.441	15½	Al Spalding
1878	Fourth	30	30	.500	11	Bob Ferguson
1879	Fourth	46	33	.582	10½	Cap Anson
1880	First	67	17	.798	+15	Cap Anson
1881	First	56	28	.667	+9	Cap Anson
1882	First	55	29	.665	+3	Cap Anson
1883	Second	59	39	.602	4	Cap Anson
1884	Fourth*	62	50	.554	22	Cap Anson
1885	First	87	25	.777	+2	Cap Anson
1886	First	90	34	.726	+2½	Cap Anson
1887	Third	71	50	.587	6½	Cap Anson
1888	Second	77	58	.570	9	Cap Anson
1889	Third	67	65	.508	19	Cap Anson
1890	Second	84	53	.613	6	Cap Anson
1891	Second	82	53	.607	3½	Cap Anson
1892	Eighth	31	39	.443	21	Cap Anson
	Seventh	39	37	.513	14	Cap Anson
1893	Ninth	56	71	.441	29	Cap Anson
1894	Eighth	57	75	.432	34	Cap Anson
1895	Fourth	72	58	.554	15	Cap Anson

1896	Fifth	71	57	.555	18½	Cap Anson
1897	Ninth	59	73	.447	34	Cap Anson
1898	Fourth	85	65	.567	17½	Tom Burns
1899	Eighth	75	73	.507	26	Tom Burns
1900	Fifth*	65	75	.464	19	Tom Loftus
1901	Sixth	53	86	.381	37	Tom Loftus
1902	Fifth	68	69	.496	34	Frank Selee
1903	Third	82	56	.594	8	Frank Selee
1904	Second	93	60	.608	13	Frank Selee
1905	Third	92	61	.601	13	Frank Selee, Frank Chance
1906	First	116	36	.763	+20	Frank Chance
1907	First	107	45	.704	+17	Frank Chance
1908	First	99	55	.643	+1	Frank Chance
1909	Second	104	49	.680	6½	Frank Chance
1910	First	104	50	.675	+13	Frank Chance
1911	Second	92	62	.597	7½	Frank Chance
1912	Third	91	59	.607	11½	Frank Chance
1913	Third	88	65	.575	13½	Johnny Evers
1914	Fourth	78	76	.506	16½	Hank O'Day
1915	Fourth	73	80	.477	17½	Roger Bresnahan
1916	Fifth	67	86	.438	26½	Joe Tinker
1917	Fifth	74	80	.481	24	Fred Mitchell
1918	First	84	45	.651	+10½	Fred Mitchell
1919	Third	75	65	.536	21	Fred Mitchell
1920	Fifth*	75	79	.487	18	Fred Mitchell
1921	Seventh	64	89	.418	30	Johnny Evers, Bill Killefer
1922	Fifth	80	74	.519	13	Bill Killefer
1923	Fourth	83	71	.539	12½	Bill Killefer
1924	Fifth	81	72	.529	12	Bill Killefer
1925	Eighth	68	86	.442	27½	Bill Killefer, Rabbit Maranville, George Gibson
1926	Fourth	82	72	.532	7	Joe McCarthy
1927	Fourth	85	68	.556	8½	Joe McCarthy
1928	Third	91	63	.591	4	Joe McCarthy
1929	First	98	54	.645	+10½	Joe McCarthy
1930	Second	90	64	.584	2	Joe McCarthy, Rogers Hornsby
1931	Third	84	70	.545	17	Rogers Hornsby
1932	First	90	64	.584	+4	Rogers Hornsby, Charlie Grimm
1933	Third	86	68	.558	6	Charlie Grimm
1934	Third	86	65	.570	8	Charlie Grimm
1935	First	100	54	.649	+4	Charlie Grimm
1936	Second*	87	67	.565	5	Charlie Grimm
1937	Second	93	61	.604	3	Charlie Grimm
1938	First	89	63	.586	+2	Charlie Grimm, Gabby Hartnett
1939	Fourth	84	70	.545	13	Gabby Hartnett
1940	Fifth	75	79	.487	25½	Gabby Hartnett
1941	Sixth	70	84	.455	30	Jimmie Wilson
1942	Sixth	68	86	.442	38	Jimmie Wilson
1943	Fifth	74	79	.484	30½	Jimmie Wilson
1944	Fourth	75	79	.487	30	Jimmie Wilson, Charlie Grimm
1945	First	98	56	.636	+3	Charlie Grimm
1946	Third	82	71	.536	14½	Charlie Grimm
1947	Sixth	69	85	.448	25	Charlie Grimm
1948	Eighth	64	90	.416	27½	Charlie Grimm
1949	Eighth	61	93	.396	36	Charlie Grimm, Frankie Frisch
1950	Seventh	64	89	.418	26½	Frankie Frisch
1951	Eighth	62	92	.403	34½	Frankie Frisch, Phil Cavarretta

1952	Fifth	77	77	.500	19½	Phil Cararretta
1953	Seventh	65	89	.422	40	Phil Cavarretta
1954	Seventh	64	90	.416	33	Stan Hack
1955	Sixth	72	81	.471	26	Stan Hack
1956	Eighth	60	94	.390	33	Stan Hack
1957	Seventh*	62	92	.403	33	Bob Scheffing
1958	Fifth*	72	82	.468	20	Bob Scheffing
1959	Fifth*	74	80	.481	13	Bob Scheffing
1960	Seventh	60	94	.390	35	Charlie Grimm, Lou Boudreau
1961	Seventh	64	90	.416	29	Harry Craft, Vedie Himsl, Lou Klein, El Tappe
1962	Ninth	59	103	.364	42½	El Tappe, Lou Klein, Charlie Metro
1963	Seventh	82	80	.506	17	Bob Kennedy
1964	Eighth	76	86	.469	17	Bob Kennedy
1965	Eighth	72	90	.444	25	Bob Kennedy, Lou Klein
1966	Tenth	59	103	.364	36	Leo Durocher
1967	Third	87	74	.540	14	Leo Durocher
1968	Third	84	78	.519	13	Leo Durocher
1969	Second	92	70	.568	8	Leo Durocher
1970	Second	84	78	.519	5	Leo Durocher
1971	Third*	83	79	.512	14	Leo Durocher
1972	Second	85	70	.548	11	Leo Durocher, Whitey Lockman
1973	Fifth	77	84	.478	5	Whitey Lockman
1974	Sixth	66	96	.407	22	Whitey Lockman Jim Marshall
1975	Fifth*	75	87	.463	17½	Jim Marshall
1976	Fourth	75	87	.463	26	Jim Marshall
1977	Fourth	81	81	.500	20	Herman Franks
1978	Third	79	83	.488	11	Herman Franks
1979	Fifth	80	82	.494	18	Herman Franks, Joey Amalfitano
1980	Sixth	64	98	.395	27	Preston Gomez, Joey Amalfitano
1981	Sixth	15	37	.288	17½	Joey Amalfitano
	Fifth	23	28	.451	6	Joey Amalfitano
1982	Fifth	73	89	.451	19	Lee Elia
1983	Fifth	71	91	.438	19	Lee Elia, Charlie Fox
1984	First	96	65	.596	+6½	Jim Frey
1985	Fourth	77	84	.478	23½	Jim Frey
1986	Fifth	70	90	.438	37	Jim Frey, Gene Michael
1987	Sixth	76	85	.472	18½	Gene Michael, Frank Lucchesi
1988	Fourth	77	85	.475	24	Don Zimmer
1989	First	93	69	.574	+6	Don Zimmer
1990	Fourth*	77	85	.475	18	Don Zimmer
1991	Fourth	77	83	.481	20	Don Zimmer, Jim Essian
1992	Fourth	78	84	.481	18	Jim Lefebvre

* Tie

Postseason Play

LCS	2–3 versus San Diego	1984	WS	2–4 versus Chicago	1906
	1–4 versus San Francisco	1989		4–0 versus Detroit	1907
				4–1 versus Detroit	1908
				1–4 versus Philadelphia	1910
				2–4 versus Boston	1918
				1–4 versus Philadelphia	1929
				0–4 versus New York	1932
				2–4 versus Detroit	1935
				0–4 versus New York	1938
				3–4 versus Detroit	1945

Chicago Browns

Union Association, 1884   **BALLPARKS:** SOUTH SIDE PARK
LAKEFRONT PARK

RECORD: 33–35 (.459)

Pitted against the White Stockings of Albert Spalding and Cap Anson, the National League's most powerful and most influential franchise, the Union Association Browns never had the faintest chance of success. Franchise backing came from A. H. Henderson, a mattress manufacturer from Baltimore who also owned a portion of the UA club in that city.

With a decidedly unimpressive roster, Henderson and UA President Henry Lucas made a determined effort to entice Larry Corcoran to desert the White Stockings for the Browns. One of the premier pitchers of the 1880s, Corcoran had won 135 games in four years, upon which he demanded the astronomical salary of $4,000 from Spalding, if only to irritate the White Stockings owner sufficiently to gain his release. Corcoran subsequently lowered his asking price to $2,500, but, when Spalding countered with an offer of $2,100, the pitcher signed with the Browns. Corcoran had made a fatal error, however: Eight days earlier he had sent Spalding a telegram requesting a new contract and a $400 advance. Spalding and NL President A. G. Mills interpreted the request as a legally binding agreement and threatened Corcoran with expulsion if he did not sign formally with the White Stockings. When Spalding sent Anson to the pitcher's Camden home, Corcoran capitulated, signed for $2,100, and even borrowed $600 from the NL to buy back his advance from the Browns.

The NL contemplated a long war with the Unions. As early as February 1884, Mills had suggested that Spalding secure a lease on South Side Park for 1885 to deprive the Browns of a future home; that facility, Mills offered, could be used either by a Chicago minor league club in the Northwestern League or by the Chicago reserve team, a scheme devised by Spalding to tie up as many players as possible. For the first few weeks of the 1884 season, the Chicago Reserves played at Lakefront Park when the White Stockings were out of town, but crowds were sparse and losses high, and they were soon disbanded.

The Chicago reserve team played a central part in one of the more curious episodes of the UA war. Samuel G. Morton was the secretary of the minor Northwestern League, but he was also an employee of Spalding's sporting goods business in Chicago *and* the operator of a baseball employment agency that funneled players to the UA. Morton used Spalding's store as a headquarters for his agency, which, through his Northwestern League connection, gained access to information about players all across the country. Morton's questionable activities, which Spalding later admitted were carried on with his complicity, were exposed when Morton attempted to hire Browns' right fielder Joe Ellick to manage the Chicago Reserves. A furious Mills put a stop to the mercenary dealings with the enemy and chastised both Morton and Spalding.

The relationship between the Browns and the White Stockings was a complicated one. Spalding, never adverse to extra income, allowed his UA rivals to play a few games in Lakefront Park. But he probably did so knowing that nothing could save the Browns. In August, having lost $15,000, Henderson and Lucas abandoned Chicago and moved the franchise to Pittsburgh.

CHICAGO BROWNS

Annual Standings and Manager

Year	Position	W	L	Pct.	GB	Manager
1884	Partial Season	33	35	.459	—	Ed Hengle

Chicago Pirates

Players League, 1890   **BALLPARK:** SOUTH SIDE PARK
                                                                  WEST SIDE PARK
RECORD: 75–62 (.547)

For the Players League to succeed, it was imperative that it field a team that could compete with the formidable National League White Stockings. This it managed to do through the simple expedient of recruiting most of its NL rival's players. More important, the club won the attention of Chicago's fans, and drew nearly 149,000, close to fifty percent more than the attendance at the White Stockings games.

Owner John Addison, a wealthy contractor, teamed up with White Stockings' second baseman Fred Pfeffer to recruit third baseman Ned Williamson, shortstop Charlie Bastian, center fielder Jimmy Ryan, right fielder Hugh Duffy, and catcher Duke Farrell. To fill out the lineup, they raided the American Association St. Louis Browns for first baseman-manager Charlie Comiskey, third baseman Arlie Latham, left fielder Tip O'Neill, and pitcher Silver King. A second pitcher, Mark Baldwin, came from the AA Columbus Solons.

The Pirates set up shop in a new facility, South Side Park, across the street from the future site of the old Comiskey Park; they also played several games in the White Stockings' West Side Park. Baldwin and King tied for the league lead in wins (32 each), while the entire outfield of O'Neill, Duffy, and Ryan batted over .300. Despite these performances, the Pirates, considered a major contender at the beginning of the season, finished fourth.

As soon as the season ended, backers of various PL clubs, devastated by losses, sought to make separate deals with the NL. On October 9, three-man committees from each of the three leagues held a preliminary meeting, raising suspicions in the Brotherhood that the owners were about to sell out the players. It was then that Addison offered a hotly debated resolution to include three players—John Montgomery Ward of Brooklyn, Ned Hanlon of Pittsburgh, and Art Irwin of Boston—in the committee deliberations. Although the resolution went to the heart of the PL's concept of backer–player parity, it ultimately helped to destroy the league when the NL and the AA refused to meet with the players, who in turn insisted that all negotiations end if they could not play a part. The conflict between backers and players was precisely what Spalding had hoped for: It wasn't long before PL backers were scurrying to make individual settlements with their NL counterparts.

The battle for Chicago ended when Ryan and Williamson broke ranks with the players and asked to return to the White Stockings' fold. Addison, his business sense overwhelming his sentiment for the spirit of the Brotherhood and the PL, announced his intention of selling the Pirates to Spalding for $25,000—$10,000 in cash and $15,000 in White Stockings stock. Threats of lawsuits by the players put off the final sale until December 29th. The final deal included $18,000 in cash, which Addison, loyal to the spirit of the PL in the end, distributed among backers, player–investors, and just plain players (as back salary). Addison himself received $15,000 worth of stock in the newly syndicated New York Giants and a season pass to White Stockings' games.

CHICAGO PIRATES

Annual Standings and Manager

Year	Position	W	L	Pct.	GB	Manager
1890	Fourth	75	62	.547	10	Charlie Comiskey

Chicago

American Association, 1891	**BALLPARK:** NONE
RECORD: NONE	

Nameless and gameless, the Chicago American Association franchise was created amid the turmoil that followed the collapse of the Players League in late 1891. The franchise played a major role in the settling of that strife and in the eventual emergence of the consolidated twelve-team National League.

In the first two years of its existence, the AA had contemplated invading Chicago, but had satisfied itself with its strongholds in New York and Philadelphia the first year and with consolidating its gains in its second season. From 1884 to 1890, the two leagues were at peace, and the gentlemen's agreement that guaranteed every owner a monopoly within his market precluded any incursion into Chicago. In 1891, however, the era of friendly rivalry came to an abrupt end, and a new struggle for supremacy in the baseball world broke out between the two leagues. The weaker AA, spurred to action by the NL's pirating of association players, fought for its very existence during the 1891 season. At the close of that season, on October 22, 1891, the AA announced the retaliatory formation of a Chicago franchise, financed by restaurateur George H. Williams, who had raised $50,000 in capital.

While the invasion directly threatened the interests of the NL's strongest club, it also created a some-

what awkward nine-team association. No one knew whether the AA would expand further or drop one of its weaker clubs. Williams didn't wait to find out the size or shape the association would assume in 1892. First, he signed Sam Morton as his manager. Then he launched a direct attack on his intended adversary, hiring second baseman Fred Pfeffer (for the impressive sum of $7,000), outfielder Walt Wilmot, and catcher Malachi Kittredge away from the White Stockings. He also raided the Giants, coming away with star pitcher Amos Rusie (for $6,800).

With an interloper doling out such extravagant salaries, the NL owners set about to destroy the AA altogether by offering four clubs—St. Louis, Louisville, Baltimore, and Washington—membership in a twelve-club NL, provided they could convince two other clubs to accept a buyout and become part of the two-thirds majority necessary to disband the AA.

When the two leagues met jointly in Indianapolis on December 15th, the NL was still shy of the votes it needed to effect its coup. Williams was among the hardliners against consolidation. But when Columbus, Boston, and Philadelphia came to terms and accepted the other owners' offers, he accepted the inevitable and settled for a buyout of $14,000.

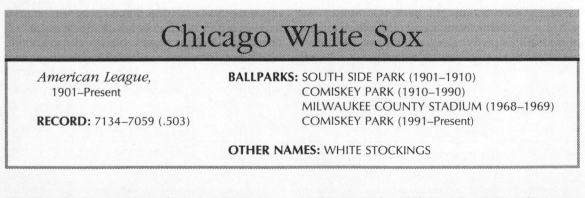

Chicago White Sox

American League, 1901–Present	**BALLPARKS:** SOUTH SIDE PARK (1901–1910)
	COMISKEY PARK (1910–1990)
	MILWAUKEE COUNTY STADIUM (1968–1969)
RECORD: 7134–7059 (.503)	COMISKEY PARK (1991–Present)
	OTHER NAMES: WHITE STOCKINGS

The White Sox haven't always been the Hitless Wonders, but they have come close. Mainly because of a cavernous ballpark that encouraged an emphasis on

pitching, speed, and defense for some eighty years, the club has produced more slugging within its executive suites than on the diamond. While the formula has worked often enough to keep Chicago's head above water in terms of overall won–lost percentage, it has also sparked extended periods of athletic ennui and front office frenzies that have both bored and bewildered fans. The franchise has also been bedeviled by what its sympathizers have variously called the Comiskey Curse, the Black Sox Curse, and the Cissell Curse. But more to the point of the organization's preoccupations has been the Cubs Curse and the persisting apprehension that the White Sox are doomed to remain the Second City's second team.

The rivalry between the two Chicago teams began even before the American League gained major league status. In 1900, Western League President Ban Johnson won approval from the National League to shift the St. Paul franchise of his minor circuit to Chicago. The fly in the ointment was James Hart, owner of the NL club in the city, who went along with the majority only on three conditions: that the new club set up quarters south of 35th Street, that it not use the name Chicago, and that it give the NL franchise the right to draft two of its players every year. Johnson and Charles Comiskey, owner of the Western League team, went along with the first stipulation in renovating a vacant cricket field at 39th and Wentworth. But though Comiskey also vowed not to identify his franchise explicitly with the city of Chicago, he got back at Hart by nicknaming the club the White Stockings, the original name of the NL team. The draft stipulation went by the boards a year later when the NL refused to consider incorporating some of Johnson's teams into an expanded loop and the insurgents declared the Western League (renamed the American League) a rival major circuit.

The White Stockings played their first AL major league contest on April 24, 1901, defeating Cleveland by the score of 8–2. It was the beginning of a pennant-winning charge that not only won instant respectability for the team, but that allowed it to outdraw Hart's NL entry by some 150,000. Heading the team on the field was playing manager Clark Griffith, who led his own pitching staff with 24 wins. The club's success overshadowed an incident that was to cause an ever-widening rift between Comiskey and

For headline writing purposes, the Chicago *Tribune* shortened the club's name from White Stockings to White Sox soon after the team began playing.

Johnson and repercussions for years to come. On August 21st, Johnson banned shortstop Frank Shugart and pitcher Jack Katoll for firing baseballs at umpire John Haskell. When Griffith defended his players and demanded that Haskell be kicked out of the league as an incompetent, Johnson interpreted it as an assault on his league staff and countered that Griffith was the real culprit for not knowing how to control his players. Although he did not challenge the ousters of Shugart and Katoll, Comiskey fumed that there had been other attacks on umpires without similar penalties. All of this served as grist for the mill of other AL owners who had grown wary of the league president's close ties to Comiskey and who started to play on Johnson's noted vanity to the point that he went out of his way to demonstrate his "objectivity" by censuring the Chicago owner whenever the opportunity arose. (Shugart never played another major league game, while the reinstated Katoll failed in a comeback attempt the following season).

Almost a year to the day later, in 1902, Johnson got over his reservations about Griffith, and asked him to leave Chicago to head up the AL franchise that was due to start playing in New York the following season. Comiskey was hardly enthusiastic about losing his manager, but bowed to Johnson's argument that the New York team was too vital to the future of the league as a whole to be entrusted to anyone with less visibility than Griffith. Pitcher Nixey Callahan took over the club in 1903, and managed to last until June of the following year despite a mediocre effort from the team and a number of incidents provoked by the pilot's reliance on the bottle and his fists for resolving problems. Callahan's successor was outfielder Fielder Jones.

It was under Jones that the squad known as the Hitless Wonders captured Chicago's second pennant in 1906. Hitless they were indeed: The team batting average was .230, its slugging average .286, and its homer total 6, with only Jones himself hitting more than 1. On the other hand, the club was merciless in its deployment of the hit-and-run, the use of the stolen base (eight players ended up in double figures), and the gobbling up of any ball hit on the ground or in the air. Also crucial, Jones received stellar efforts from righthander Frank Owen, who won 22, lefty Nick Altrock, who took 20, and southpaw Doc White, who notched 18. The season also saw righthander Ed Walsh take the Hall of Fame trail with 17 victories, 10 of them shutouts. Using a spitball that he had picked up from journeyman Elmer Stricklett in 1904, Walsh racked up 195 wins in his fourteen-year career; more impressive, he retired with an ERA of 1.82, the low-

Commissioner Kenesaw Mountain Landis (rear left) questions Swede Risberg and Chick Gandil (to his immediate left) during the probe into the 1919 World Series. *UPI/Bettmann Newsphotos*

est in baseball history. Walsh was elected to Cooperstown in 1946.

As enthralling as the pennant run had been, especially during a nineteen-game winning streak in August, it could not compare with the excitement around the only World Series played between the two Chicago teams. With its all-time record of 116 wins, the Cubs' squad represented an ideal Goliath for the David of the Hitless Wonders. Inner-city fever for the games was so rampant that those unable to buy tickets at the ballpark were accommodated at a theater and an armory, where they could receive direct telegraph reports of the play-by-play; in the most general use of the term, these relays amounted to the first "broadcast" of major league baseball. Expectations were not disappointed. Thanks partly to the last minute insertion of backup infielder George Rohe into the lineup and the pitching of Walsh, the White Sox defeated the heavily favored NL team in six games. Rohe, who was drafted into service after shortstop George Davis had been injured, cracked crucial triples in the first and third games. Walsh won twice, including a two-hit shutout in the third game. In living up to their reputations, the ALers as a club batted only .198, but the Cubs batted two points lower than even that.

In the middle of clubhouse celebrations after the

sixth and deciding game, Comiskey wrote out a check for $15,000 and told Jones to spread it around among the players. It was an unlikely gesture from an owner who had already built a reputation as one of the most tight-fisted in baseball. As the players discovered a few months later, however, it wasn't so strange, after all, because Comiskey informed them that the "bonus" for their World Series performance was also their raise for 1907. This announcement was followed by weeks of turmoil, with numerous players refusing to report to spring training; their ranks included Jones, who told newsmen he would rather retire than bow to such an underhanded ploy. Comiskey's response was to offer Jones a substantial raise as player–manager, with the hope that he would act as something of a Pied Piper in bringing the other players into line. It worked; although the grumbling continued all season, the revolt died, and the players focused on the pennant race, which was not settled (in Detroit's favor) until the final week of the season. On the other hand, the episode contributed mightily to Comiskey's image as an owner who cried poverty whenever his players asked for better contracts, but who threw away thousands of dollars regularly in entertaining his well-heeled associates in city restaurants and rustic retreats.

There was more of the same in 1908, when

Ed Walsh, the major leagues' last 40-game winner. *National Baseball Library, Cooperstown, NY*

Walsh put together one of the greatest performances in AL pitching history (40–15, 1.42 ERA, 11 shutouts, 269 league-leading strikeouts), only to be denied his request for a salary of $7,500 after the campaign. Comiskey's refusal to grant Walsh the contract was all the more astonishing insofar as the righthander earned his numbers for a team that was even more hitless than the 1906 Wonders—batting only .224, slugging a nearly invisible .271, and hitting a pathetic 3 home runs. Walsh wasn't alone in going unappreciated. Instead of winning plaudits for keeping his inoffensive lineup in the race until the very last day of the season, Jones was lambasted by the press for entrusting the decisive contest against the Tigers to the southpaw White instead of righthander Frank Smith. When White was shelled and the second guessing ensued, Jones again announced his retirement, and this time stuck to it. It took another seven years and four more managers (including a second tenure by the relatively more sober Callahan) before the club returned to being more than an also-ran.

On July 1, 1910, the White Sox moved from their one-time cricket grounds to newly constructed Comiskey Park. The facility's reputation as an overly symmetrical, open-air warehouse stemmed from Comiskey's refusal to finance a cantilevered structure that would have eliminated the large number of support girders and allowed for a greater sense of intimacy; its fame as a pitcher's paradise was rooted to a considerable degree in the owner's decision to have Walsh accompany design engineers during grandstand-laying phases of construction so that he might offer an insider's insights. The pitcher's most significant insight was that the foul lines should be 363' in both left and right field and that the center field wall ought to be 420' away from home plate. Symptomatic of the kind of ball that would be played on the premises for the next eight decades, St. Louis won the opening game, 2–0; the losing pitcher was Walsh. It was not until July 31st that the White Sox hit their first home run at home, and even that drive off the bat of Lee Tannehill hit the left field corner and then rolled through the fence. At that, the fact that Tannehill even reached the corner was a rarity for a team that set the modern record for a lack of offense—a .212 average and a .261 slugging mark.

Outfielder Patsy Dougherty led the club in batting with a .248 average and in RBIs with 43.

Among those donning a Chicago uniform in the doldrums years before World War I was Hal Chase, the first baseman whose defensive talents were second only to his willingness to throw games if the money made it worthwhile. With the White Sox, however, Chase eschewed pocket money from fixes in favor of challenging the contract that prevented him from accepting a much higher offer to play for the insurgent Federal League. The first baseman's weapon was a clause in existing player contracts that allowed a team to release a player with a letter declaring its intention ten days in advance; according to Chase, such a stipulation should have been equally valid for a player, so he wrote a letter to the club, announcing his free agency. Comiskey's appeal against the ploy was unsuccessful. Third baseman Harry Lord also defected to the FL after invoking the ten-day clause.

Comiskey invited contract trouble of another kind in December 1914, when he made the franchise's most important purchase to that date by acquiring second baseman Eddie Collins from the Athletics. The price for the future Hall of Famer was stiff: $50,000 to Philadelphia and a five-year $75,000 guaranteed contract to Collins on top of a $15,000 signing bonus. In the years to come, the infielder's elevated salary would trigger a number of club jealousies and help create the factionalism that made it easier for gamblers to approach players on the eve of the 1919 World Series. At the time, however, the Collins contract was viewed as nothing but a positive sign that the organization was bent on returning to the top of the standings. There was a similar reaction to the trade the following August that brought Chicago outfielder Joe Jackson from Cleveland in exchange for outfielders Braggo Roth and Larry Chappell, pitcher Ed Klepfer, and $31,500. Considered by his contemporaries as the AL's most accomplished hitter, the lefty-swinging outfielder hit .356 over a thirteen-year career that ended ignominiously with his involvement in the 1919 World Series fix.

In the face of raids by the FL and then by the U.S. Selective Service, the White Sox used the World War I years to cobble together the best all-around team in the league. In addition to Collins and Jackson, the key position players were outfielders Hap Felsch and Nemo Leibold, third baseman Buck Weaver, and catcher Ray Schalk (elected to the Hall of Fame in 1955); a second wave brought shortstop Swede Risberg and veteran first baseman Chick Gandil. The mound staff was headed by Ed Cicotte, Lefty

Williams, and Red Faber. The righthanded Faber remained a franchise favorite long after he had seen his best years, ending up with 254 wins in 20 seasons of service and a ticket to the Hall of Fame in 1964.

By 1916, the club was back as a contender, winding up only two games behind Boston. The reins were in the hands of Pants Rowland, who avoided the mistakes of his predecessors in turning a deaf ear to Comiskey's advice by even soliciting the owner's counsel on strategic field matters.

In 1917, the team went over the top with what turned out to be the most successful season in franchise history. Leading the way to 100 wins were Felsch (.308, 102 RBIs), Cicotte (28 wins), and southpaw reliever Dave Danforth (11 wins and 11 saves). There was something of a stain on the flag, however, in the persistent reports that the Tigers were paid off by the White Sox to lose a pair of crucial doubleheaders in early September. Lending credence to the reports was the gaggle of gamblers that seemed drawn to the White Sox all season. In one notorious June incident at Fenway Park, dozens of them stormed the field in the fifth inning of a game in an attempt to force a forfeit in favor of Chicago that would insure their bets. The invasion was turned back, but not before Weaver and backup infielder Fred McMullin, both to be implicated in the 1919 scandal, slugged it out with the trespassers.

In the World Series against the Giants, the White Sox again found themselves as underdogs, and again upset expectations by emerging as champions in six games. The turning point of the Series came in the final game, when New York third baseman Heinie Zimmerman found himself in a one-sided rundown play and chased Collins futilely across home plate with the winning run. The most significant performance was turned in by Faber, who notched three of Chicago's four victories. The righthander also added to baseball's legendary boners in the second game, when he completed what might have been a successful steal of third base, except for the fact that teammate Weaver was already standing on the bag.

The following year was a franchise nightmare. With Jackson, Collins, Felsch, Risberg, Faber, and Williams all drafted by the army or in war-related jobs, the club flopped into sixth place. Worse, the steadily building tensions between Comiskey and Johnson finally exploded in a bitter wrangle over minor league pitcher Jack Quinn. The trouble started when Comiskey received permission from the ruling three-man National Commission to negotiate directly for the services of the hurler, till then under contract to the Pacific Coast League's Vernon team;

the authorization was granted after the PCL, like other professional leagues, had announced an abbreviated season because of wartime restrictions. But while Comiskey was securing Quinn's name on a Chicago contract, the Yankees were busy concluding a deal for his services with the Vernon club. When the dispute was brought before the board of Johnson, NL president John Heydler, and Cincinnati president Garry Herrmann, the National Commission acknowledged that its ignorance of the New York negotiations had misled Comiskey, but ruled that the Vernon franchise had a priority in disposing of the player and awarded Quinn to New York. Johnson had always been the commission's strongest voice, so an infuriated Comiskey blamed the decision on the AL president and sought to remove him from his post. In the end, however, only the Yankees and Red Sox got behind the drive. Quinn went on to 247 victories in an unprecedented twenty-three-year pitching career.

The ill-fated 1919 season began with the disclosure that Rowland was leaving the team to become part-owner of a minor league franchise in Milwaukee. His successor as manager was Kid Gleason, a one-time pitcher and second baseman whose chief character trait was belligerence. It didn't take Gleason long to see that he had inherited not only one of baseball's most gifted teams, but also one of its most troubled. With the principal exception of Collins, most of the stars bitterly resented Comiskey's tightwad ways. They also resented the financial security that made Collins indifferent to their situation, and went out of their way to express it. During fielding practice, for example, even the second baseman's keystone partner Risberg confined his tossing to Gandil and Weaver. Risberg and Gandil didn't think too much of Schalk, either, for sticking up for Collins, and the catcher had his problems with Felsch for much the same reason. As for Jackson, he wondered aloud more than once why his batting prowess hadn't entitled him to the same kind of contract given to Collins. What all this came down to during pregame exercises was a lot of throwing between Collins and Schalk, while the rest of the first-stringers ignored both of them. Once the game began, however, it was another story, and though threatened by Cleveland and New York for awhile, the 1919 Chisox held on to first place for most of the season on their way to a relatively neat pennant. The pitching stars were Cicotte and Williams, who combined for 52 wins, but the team also boasted an offense that led the league in batting (.287). Particularly striking for the franchise of the Hitless Wonders, every regular

except the defense-oriented Risberg batted a minimum of .275. The biggest bat of all belonged to Jackson, who swatted opposition pitchers for .351, with 96 RBIs.

In sheer box-score terms, the club lost the World Series to the Reds, five games to three (it was the first of three straight best-of-nine postseason competitions). For the White Sox, the best performances, statistically, came from Jackson (12 hits and 6 RBIs), Weaver (11 hits), and southpaw Dickie Kerr (2 wins). Williams, on the other hand, was tagged with three defeats, including a first-inning routing in the final game.

Suspicions that something was amiss arose immediately with the first game, when the Reds pounded Cicotte for a 9–1 win. When Comiskey voiced his doubts to NL president Heydler, however, he was viewed only as a sore loser; the deeply hostile Johnson had an identical response when Heydler relayed Comiskey's suspicions to him later on in the Series. It was not, in fact, until almost a year afterward that Comiskey succeeded in persuading a Cook County grand jury to look into the games. The owner's move came on the heels of charges in a Philadelphia newspaper that not only had several White Sox players thrown the World Series in 1919, but they had also taken money to lose some crucial games during a late-season eastern swing in 1920, allowing the Indians to take over the lead in the AL. The allegations were made by Billy Maharg, a gambler and one of several former marginal major leaguers who would be implicated in the fix as participants, accessories before the fact, or accessories after the fact. By the end of September, both Cicotte and Jackson were in front of a grand jury and pulling in Williams, Risberg, Weaver, Gandil, Felsch, and McMullin as co-conspirators. It was after this testimony that, according to baseball legend, a boy approached Jackson and pleaded, "say it ain't so, Joe." With the exception of Gandil, who had retired immediately after the 1919 World Series, all the players named were suspended by Comiskey pending the outcome of their trial.

Although the Chicago Eight were the center of attention, they were hardly alone on the stage. The gambling ranks were represented by codefendants Carl Zork and David Zelser, by New York kingpin Arnold Rothstein (who might or might not have organized the fix), and by former prize fighter Abe Attell (who might have been working for Rothstein or might have just used his name to impress cohorts). The baseball community was spoken for not only by Maharg and players (Chase and Rube Benton among them) said to have had knowledge of the fix, but also by former White Sox pitcher Bill Burns, who testified that he personally delivered $10,000 to Cicotte's hotel room after Cincinnati's opening-game victory. Comiskey could hardly escape the headlines, either, especially when otherwise censorious editorials allowed as how the players might never have been tempted to go along with the gamblers if they had been paid decently in the first place. As for AL president Johnson, he might have enjoyed Comiskey's predicament a lot more if he hadn't been reminded of his own skepticism about a fix when first approached on the subject by Heydler, and if he hadn't had to cope with widespread denunciations of the National Commission as ineffective for dealing with the gambling problem. It was within this atmosphere that several major league franchises called for an overhaul of the ruling council and proposals were put forward for the establishment of a supervisory office of governors from outside the sport. Cubs' owner Bill Wrigley lobbied successfully, instead, for the appointment of Judge Kenesaw Mountain Landis as the first baseball commissioner. If Comiskey had a consolation in seeing the crosstown Cubs provide the solution to the administrative mess, it was that Johnson lost a lot of his power and that the grand jury also heard a lot of testimony about a fix involving one of Wrigley's own pitchers, Claude Hendrix.

There was no specific law covering fixing games in Illinois, so the eight players, Zork, and Zelser were indicted on a somewhat ambiguous charge of conspiring to defraud the White Sox, the people of Chicago, and the members of the team not party to the bribes. The narrowness of this count became immediately obvious when Michael Ahearn and Thomas Nash, lawyers who had made their reputations defending such gangland figures as Al Capone, pointed out that the Chicago team had made almost twice as much money in 1920 as it had in 1919, notwithstanding the constant press rumors of some hanky-panky during the World Series against the Reds. It didn't hurt, either, that Jackson had batted .375 in the games, Weaver .324, and McMullin .500. Even arguments that the White Sox had deliberately committed twelve errors were offset by the defense's observation that the Reds had made an equal number. But mainly because the jury had to reach a decision on the basis of the non-existent injury caused to the club's financial situation, a verdict of not guilty was handed down on August 2, 1921, after some two weeks of testimony. It was just one of the oddities of the proceedings that, though he had been cited as an aggrieved party in the indictment, Comiskey footed the legal bills of Ahearn and Nash.

For Landis, the important thing was not the jury's decision, but the impracticality of the original indictment and the statements by most of the players acknowledging their collusion with Burns and other middlemen from gambling circles. Twenty-four hours after the jury issued its finding, he banned the eight White Sox with the pronouncement that "no player who throws a ballgame, no player that undertakes or promises to throw a ballgame, no player that sits in conference with a bunch of crooked players and gamblers where the ways and means of throwing a game are discussed and does not promptly tell his club about it will ever play baseball." In subsequent years, most of the outlawed players sought reinstatement through one legal avenue or another, but were unsuccessful. Especially embittered was Weaver, who was not accused in any testimony of being an active member of the conspiracy. Landis's hard line against the third baseman and his teammates aroused a great deal of criticism among those who were not content to view his treatment of the eight players as the salvation of the major leagues. For one thing, he disregarded much stronger evidence a few years later in another betting case involving superstars Ty Cobb and Tris Speaker, declaring the outfielders innocent of any wrongdoing. More generally, the commissioner's icy response to the appeals of Weaver was in sharp contrast to his frequent championing of individual player rights. The most often-heard explanation for his attitude was that he was determined to use the 1919 scandal to establish his credentials as a no-nonsense baseball czar.

The fallout from the scandal on the team was considerable. With the nucleus of the club put on the sidelines for good, Chicago tumbled into seventh place in 1921 and didn't rise again even to third until 1936. Physically and psychologically wearied by the betrayal and its legal aftermath, Comiskey devoted

The second-place 1920 White Sox had four 20-game winners—Red Faber (23), Lefty Williams (22), Dickie Kerr (21), and Ed Cicotte (21). The feat would go unmatched for more than a half-century, until the 1971 Baltimore Orioles got 21 wins from Dave McNally and 20 victories each from Pat Dobson, Mike Cuellar, and Jim Palmer.

Buck Weaver, the eighth man out in the Black Sox scandal.
National Baseball Library, Cooperstown, NY

The odd man out when the major leagues banned the spitball in February 1920 was Frank Shellenback. The White Sox had assigned the righthander temporarily to Vernon in the Pacific Coast League and inadvertently neglected to include him among the practicing spitballers to be grandfathered into an exemption. Shellenback, who never returned to the majors, went on to compile a record of 315 wins and 192 losses in the high minor leagues over more than twenty years.

Most of the interest generated by the team until the middle of the 1930s came from off-the-field events—scandalous, comic, and tragic. In 1923, the southpaw Kerr, who had won two games in the 1919 Series, was placed on the ineligible list by Landis because he pitched against some of the ostracized Black Sox in a semipro game. In 1926, the team signed Moe Berg, a catcher who was far more formidable as a scholar of Sanskrit, spokesman for freeing Sacco and Vanzetti, multilinguist, and, later, spy for the O.S.S. than as a ballplayer. One of the team's better talents of the decade, outfielder Johnny Mostil, tried to kill himself with a razor before the 1927 season in apparent despair over an affair with teammate Faber's wife. Bill Cissell, a shortstop-second baseman, gained grim preternatural status among fans as the Cissell Curse when he disappointed expectations of an all-star career, took to the bottle, wandered around Comiskey Park for some years as a part-time laborer, then ended up dying of malnutrition. On another note altogether, first baseman Art Shires, who liked to refer to himself as Art the Great, spent his off-hours promoting a second career as a boxer until a challenge to Cubs' outfielder Hack Wilson prompted Landis to step in and curtail all such moonlighting.

On the field, the team's best offensive performers of the 1920s were outfielders Mostil and Bibb Falk, along with first baseman Earl Sheely; all three of them compiled lifetime .300 averages. In 1931, the team installed Luke Appling at shortstop—a position he would hold on to until 1950. In his twenty major league seasons, the righthand-hitting Appling batted .310, with two hitting titles; an expert at fouling off pitches to wear down the pitcher, he was elected to the Hall of Fame in 1964. The doldrums years also saw the coming and going of outfielder Smead Jolley and first baseman Zeke Bonura, both of whom defined the one-dimensional player. A .305 batsman in his brief four-year career, Jolley's problem was any ball hit in the air, on the ground, or off the wall. Bonura, whose power was such that he put together back-to-back years with 20 home runs despite playing in Comiskey Park, was more noted for his *olé* plays at first base. The chief moundsman of the period was Ted Lyons, who won 20 games three times and compiled a record of 260–230 over a dragged out twenty-one-season career; the righthander was elected to Cooperstown in 1955.

most of his remaining energy to buying and trading players in an increasingly frantic attempt to rebuild the team. He also hired and fired managers with regularity; among those taking turns at the helm were Collins, Schalk, and former Cubs' heroes Frank Chance and Johnny Evers. In one way or another, all of them echoed the sentiments of Donie Bush, who resigned under pressure after the 1931 season with the observation that "there's no future for anybody managing this club."

The end for Comiskey came on October 26, 1931, after a number of years of living as a virtual recluse. Disenchantment with the organization had settled in so deeply that a proposal to rebaptize one of the streets around the stadium as Comiskey Road met with sarcastic suggestions that it be renamed Seventh Place instead. Taking over the franchise was Comiskey's son Lou, an overweight forty-six-year-old who was seldom seen without Turkish cigarettes or macaroons in his hand. But belying his image, the younger Comiskey made his first deal one of the franchise's most notable—paying Connie Mack $100,000 for outfielders Al Simmons and Mule Haas and second baseman Jimmy Dykes. Dykes emerged as the most important of the acquisitions when he took over the club as manager in May 1934 and remained at the helm until after World War II.

Under Dykes, the White Sox reached the .500 level in 1936 for the first time in ten years. Aside from the club's improved play on the field, the manager reawakened interest in the franchise by his regular baitings of AL rivals; his most widely quoted cut was a description of New York pilot Joe McCarthy as "a push-button manager" for the latter's ability to sit back and watch players like Lou Gehrig and Joe DiMaggio win games for him with a minimum of strategic effort. Among the players who contributed to the club's revival in the late 1930s was righthander Monty Stratton, who won 15 games two years in a row with a darting fastball that was dubbed the "gander." But just as Stratton was being tipped as the next Faber, what local writers called the Comiskey Curse or the Cissell Curse returned in the form of a November 1938 shooting accident that eventually cost the hurler a leg. Stratton's struggle to make a comeback (he managed to appear in some low minor league games) was later the subject of a Hollywood movie with Jimmy Stewart.

By the late 1930s, Comiskey had been won over to the argument that the club could never hope to go all the way against other powerhouses in the league unless it played in a ballpark more conducive to long-ball hitting. But the owner's plan to move out of the stadium that had been erected as a monument to his father was bogged down by a series of financial calculations that made it clear that some outside money would be required to build a new facility in a Chicago suburb. Comiskey was still procrastinating when his always frail physical condition deteriorated sharply; on July 18, 1940, he died of a heart attack complicated by pneumonia. What followed were years of wrangles that made the club's efforts to stay above water in the standings of almost secondary importance. Under the terms of the Comiskey will, the franchise was left in trust to Lou's son Charles Comiskey II until he reached the age of 35; at the time of his father's death, the youngest Comiskey was a college student in his teens. An ambiguous stipulation of the will, however, also empowered its executor, the First National Bank of Chicago, to sell the franchise if it was deemed to be in financial straits. No sooner had First National Bank vice-president John Gleason taken a seat on the franchise's board of directors than he stormed through the loophole with the claim that a baseball team was a bad risk for a bank and announced his intention of seeking a buyer. This prompted Comiskey's widow and two daughters to haul the bank into a probate court, where a judge backed their argument that the executor of a will was bound to protect an estate, not liquidate it. In 1941, Lou Comiskey's widow Grace regained control of the team and declared herself president; her elder daughter Dorothy, recently married to White Sox pitcher Johnny Rigney, took over as treasurer.

Throughout Lou Comiskey's run as owner, he had depended almost exclusively on Harry Grabiner to oversee every front office detail in trading, financial, and ballpark maintenance matters. As a reward for his services, Grabiner, who had started with the franchise as a peanut vendor at the beginning of the century, was singled out in the will for a guaranteed ten-year contract at $25,000 a year. While Grace Comiskey had never warmed to the executive, she emulated her husband in depending on Grabiner to keep the baseball operation going. Grabiner ended up remaining with the organization until 1945, but chiefly because neither side wanted to admit to executive suite tensions during World War II.

With Appling and even the aging Lyons, among others, in military service, the wartime White Sox were a typical gathering of fifth wheels and retreads. The best offensive player of the period was the no-longer-young outfielder Wally Moses, who led the league in doubles and triples in different campaigns and who swiped 56 bases in 1943. The most pitching wins in a season came from Bill Dietrich with 16 in 1944, but, reflecting the club's seventh-place finish, he also lost 17. Past and future familiar names who

The White Sox are the answer to the often-asked question of what team's players all had exactly the same batting averages after a game as they had entering it. On April 16, 1940, Cleveland's Bob Feller pitched a no-hitter against Chicago on Opening Day.

called Comiskey home included Ed Lopat, Hal Trosky, and Tony Cuccinello. Cuccinello was the victim of a bizarrely-timed release when, with only two games to go in 1945, he was informed that he would not be signed for the following season because of the scheduled return of so many young players from the armed services; when he got the word, the third baseman was locked in a duel with New York second baseman Snuffy Stirnweiss for the AL batting title. Stirnweiss ended up winning a silver bat by .00009 points, the smallest margin in baseball history.

In 1945, Grabiner tried unsuccessfully to persuade Grace Comiskey to sell the team to him and Bill Veeck. Comiskey didn't trust the offer, not least because Grabiner had been the one to advise against another offer from Veeck four years earlier. The vice-president left the team to be replaced by Lester O'Connor, a long-time associate of Landis who preferred to leave the commissioner's office after the judge had died and after he had been passed over as a successor. As a general manager, O'Connor was a disaster, and not only because of an ill-advised 1948 trade sending Lopat to the Yankees for catcher Aaron Robinson and pitchers Fred Bradley and Bill Wight. The executive's most glaring gaffe was the signing of Chicago prep school pitcher George Zoeterman in 1947 in the face of regulations (that he himself helped draft) prohibiting such raids on high schoolers. When O'Connor argued that the regulation covered only teenagers playing within the National Federation of State Athletic Associations and not those playing for the kind of private school attended by Zoeterman, Chandler exploded at the legal hairsplitting, nullified the contract, and fined the White Sox $500. O'Connor countered with a refusal to pay the fine, causing Chandler to announce that he was suspending Chicago from the AL, the first and only time that such a measure was to be invoked. The suspension lasted from October 24 to November 4, 1947, at which point AL president Will Harridge intervened at the request of the schedule makers who

did not know whether or not to arrange the 1948 season with a Chicago team. Harridge had barely called a meeting in Cleveland to order when the proceedings were interrupted by a message from Minneapolis that the college student Comiskey had announced his intention of paying the fine in order to put an end to the embarrassment. The young owner's move signalled the beginning of the end for O'Connor, who acknowledged that he had entered the Cleveland meeting resolved to maintain his position as a point of legal principle.

Dykes lasted until May 1946, when one of his habitual demands for a contract extension was rejected by Grace Comiskey. Despite an agreement by both sides not to announce the pilot's decision to resign until a replacement was found, the news surfaced in a newspaper gossip column, forcing O'Connor to go to Lyons hurriedly as the new manager. The ex-pitcher was at the helm through the 1948 season, one of the worst in franchise history. In addition to suffering 101 losses and finishing in the basement, the club became an object of ridicule around the league for not even being able to arrange travel schedules without missing trains, losing luggage, or showing up at the wrong hotel; the travel secretary was Frank McMahon, a brother-in-law of the team president. About the only bright note of the campaign was sounded on July 18, when outfielder Pat Seery added his name to the short list of major leaguers who have hit four home runs in one game; Seery did it in an 11-inning affair against the Athletics. As soon as the season ended, the team underwent its biggest overhaul in decades. O'Connor, who had been marking time since the Zoeterman affair, resigned before he could be fired, and was replaced by Frank Lane. Lyons, who had muttered more than once in his two-and-a-half-year stint that he had never asked to be manager, was replaced by Jack Onslow. And, following a two-year apprenticeship with one of the club's minor league affiliates, Chuck Comiskey moved to Chicago to play a more assertive role in the organization.

The new general manager Lane did not gain his sobriquet of Trader from his dabblings on Wall Street. In his very first move, he placed the entire club on waivers to gauge what other general managers thought of his players. What followed over his reign of slightly less than seven years was an orgy of exchanges involving close to one hundred separate deals at the major league level. To get the ball rolling only a couple of weeks after replacing O'Connor, Lane sent catcher Robinson to the Tigers for southpaw Billy Pierce and $100,000; Pierce developed into the franchise pitcher for the 1950s, winning 20 games twice and capturing the ERA title in 1955. Another steal was the October 1949 acquisition of second baseman Nellie Fox from the Athletics in return for backup receiver Joe Tipton; the embodiment of the grit of the Go-Go Sox of the 1950s, Fox teamed with shortstop Luis Aparicio to furnish Chicago with one of baseball's best double-play combinations for years, and also took MVP honors for leading the team into another World Series in 1959. A third vital swap was completed in April 1951, when Lane and the general managers of the Athletics and the Indians engaged in a three-way transaction that netted the White Sox Minnie Minoso; the fleet, righthand-hitting outfielder represented the club's main offensive threat for most of the decade. Lane also earned himself a footnote in baseball lore by being one of the few executives to outwit Branch Rickey of the Dodgers. After getting Rickey to speculate on what he *might* ask for Brooklyn farm prospect Chico Carrasquel if he were ever interested in swapping the shortstop, Lane waited a few days, then called the Dodgers' president and said he accepted the asking price. Rickey's disclaimers that he had never actually offered Carrasquel got lost in a lot of doubletalk about honoring one's word, with the upshot being that the Brooklyn executive surrendered Carrasquel for a couple of minor leaguers.

With most of Lane's big trades still to come, Onslow's managerial tenure was marked by only marginal progress on the field and a great deal of strife in the clubhouse. Most of the tensions grew out of the pilot's military bearing and the refusal of part-timers like Tipton and Steve Souchock to knuckle under. Lane was ready to find a new dugout leader at the end of the 1949 season, but was stymied by Grace Comiskey's refusal to pay off the second year of Onslow's contract while the latter vacationed under the sun somewhere. When the club lost 22 of 30 games at the start of the 1950 campaign, however, Lane gained an ally in Chuck Comiskey, who threatened to resign as vice-president if his mother did not agree to a change. Coach Red Corriden took over the team for the remainder of the 1950 season, but only as an interim solution. The following offseason the club announced that Paul Richards would be the new manager. Despite initial scorn in Chicago that the Comiskeys had once again gone for the cheapest instead of the best, the arrival of Richards marked the beginning of the franchise's most successful era. Although the club won only one pennant in the period because of superior New York squads, it embarked on a streak of seventeen straight seasons of playing

better than .500 ball. Moreover, the White Sox resurgence coincided with the deterioration of the Cubs into a regular inhabitant of the NL's lower depths, making the AL team all the more attractive at the box office.

The main selling point of the White Sox during the 1950s was a club speed that showed up not in relatively modest stolen base totals, but in the ability of just about every regular except catcher Sherm Lollar to take the extra base and force the defense into errant throws. Leading the Go-Go Sox, as they were dubbed, were speedster outfielders Minoso, Jim Rivera, and Jim Busby, and, later, shortstop Aparicio. As the craftiest bat wielder of them all, the otherwise slower Fox kept his teammates spinning around the bases by punching hits to all fields. The small ball tactics were epitomized by the 1959 pennant-winning club's ability to fashion a run out of little more than a walk by Aparicio, a stolen base, a grounder to the right side by Fox, and a sacrifice fly by Jim Landis or Lollar. The corollary of such a minimalist offense was a pitching staff able to hold one- and two-run leads, and the club found the necessary ingredients, especially in the latter part of the decade, in Pierce, Dick Donovan, Early Wynn, and relievers Turk Lown and Gerry Staley.

Not even the team's revival, however, checked the ongoing front office soap opera of squabbles and resentments. One brushfire erupted in January 1952, when Chuck Comiskey, smarting over the credit being given to Lane and Richards for restoring the club to the first division in 1951, demanded a hefty pay raise for being the one to bring in the general manager and the manager in the first place. He was particularly irked by an attendance bonus clause that had been given to Lane. When his mother and other members of the board refused, Comiskey resigned, charging that family attorney Thomas Eagan was manipulating his mother and sisters. Lane was not much happier than Comiskey after the latter had furnished local papers with the details of his salary. When Comiskey got over his pique six months later

Jack Harshman, a southpaw who won 48 games for the White Sox in four seasons in the 1950s, had 21 home runs among his 76 major league hits—the highest ratio of round-trippers to safeties in baseball history. Harshman also played some first base and the outfield during his career.

and reassumed his role as vice-president, he found the general manager as reluctant to forgive as Comiskey himself was to forget that a nominal subordinate was making more money than he was. Lane's relations with Grace Comiskey began crumbling after the 1952 season, when the general manager endorsed a Bill Veeck proposal entitling visiting teams to a share in the profits accruing from local television coverage. The team president ordered Lane to disassociate himself from Veeck and vote against all revenue-sharing proposals.

With the team on its way to a fourth successive first-division finish in September 1954, Richards went to Comiskey seeking a long-term contract that would also raise his annual earnings to the level already attained by a couple of other AL managers. When he received nothing more than a promise for a small increase in his bonus clause, he jumped to the Orioles in the twin role of general manager and manager. The flustered Lane tapped coach Marty Marion as Richards's replacement. Although Marion kept the club in contention through September of the following season, he found Richards a hard act to follow, and was constantly criticized for his strategic limitations. The criticisms also spilled over to include Lane, who became more frequently depicted as the lesser partner in the former collaboration with Richards.

The next explosion occurred near the end of the 1955 season, when Lane, infuriated by an umpiring decision that went against Chicago, confronted AL president Harridge at Comiskey Park and shouted obscenities about the caliber of the league's arbiters. The next day Harridge fined Lane $500 for the outburst, prompting Chuck Comiskey to enter the fray by denouncing his general manager for embarrassing the franchise. When Grace Comiskey declined to back Lane, he resigned. Soon after the end of the season, a front office shakeup saw Chuck Comiskey and his brother-in-law, the former pitcher Rigney, given dual control over baseball operations. The moves confirmed Rigney's wife Dorothy as the organization's new power, with Chuck, now over 30, still considered too immature to run the franchise.

When Marion could do no better than a fifth consecutive third-place finish in 1956, he was removed for Al Lopez. Lopez turned out to be not merely the most successful manager in the history of the franchise, but also the only AL pilot who, first with the 1954 Indians and then with the 1959 White Sox, interrupted what would have been an otherwise staggering sixteen straight pennants by the Yankees. At first, however, even Lopez had to take a back seat to still further turmoil in the boardroom, this time

The most quotable of the Chicago players at mid-century was brash outfielder Jim Rivera. Told in 1956 that Al Lopez had been signed to manage the club, Rivera told reporters: "It isn't everybody who can inherit a player like me when they get the job." After catching an Opening Day toss in Washington from President John F. Kennedy in 1961, the outfielder brought the ball back to the chief executive for an autograph, looked it over, then said: "You'll have to do better than that, John. This is a scribble I can hardly read."

occasioned by the death of Grace Comiskey in December 1956. As had been the case with her husband Lou's will, Grace's last testament caused a lot of confusion, and little of it to son Chuck's benefit. Ignoring her male heir's expectations of succeeding her as president, Grace awarded elder daughter Dorothy enough stock to give her control of the franchise, with Chuck getting the rest. Another block of shares was to be held in trust for Chuck until, at the age of 35, he could claim it and finally assume majority control, as originally decreed by Lou. Chuck, however, was not content to wait that long, and over the next eighteen months he and his sister dragged one another from courtroom to courtroom over everything from the validity of the will to the numerical makeup of the board of directors to arguments that Dorothy had taken silverware from Grace's house that should have been given to Chuck. The battle eventually wore down Dorothy, but not in ways foreseen by her brother: Instead of surrendering, she went looking for an outside buyer for her fifty-four percent of the club's stock.

Act II began with Dorothy offering Chuck her stock at the going market price, and her brother, enraged that he wasn't receiving preferential treatment, turning her down. Dorothy next went to perennial White Sox hawk Veeck, who immediately purchased a sixty-day option on the stock and got busy trying to round up the $2.7 million that he needed for the

On September 30, 1956, 16-year-old Jim Derrington became the youngest starting pitcher in major league history. He lost the game to Kansas City, and would be washed up as a major leaguer by the age of 18.

shares. Once Veeck got into the picture, the youngest Comiskey changed his mind about having been cold-shouldered by Dorothy and offered her a deal as heavy on tax benefits as in actual cash. Insurance company executive Charlie Finley then topped the offers of both Veeck and Chuck Comiskey. When Dorothy tried to buy back the option that she had given Veeck in order to consider one of the other two offers, the veteran baseball man declined. This led to an unlikely alliance of the two Comiskeys in a courtroom to challenge the right of Dorothy to cede an option to anyone outside the family. While Chicago papers cavorted over the doings of the Battling Comiskeys, Judge Robert Dunne plowed through the mounds of paper that attorneys from every side had dropped on his desk and finally ruled, on March 5, 1959, that Dorothy had been within her rights to grant the option to Veeck and that, whatever her second thoughts on the matter, he was entitled to the majority stock holding if he paid for it as contracted. Dunne also lashed into both Comiskeys for turning the Chicago courts into their private rumpus room.

A couple of days after the court decision, Veeck took over as majority partner with a consortium that included Hall of Famer Hank Greenberg and banker Arthur Allyn. Greenberg became a vice-president, but Chuck Comiskey maintained a parallel title. In his typical promotional style, Veeck sought to make light of his tribulations with the family by throwing out the first ball on Opening Day to Chuck; the ball bounced five feet in front of home plate, and so did the attempt to make people believe that the tensions between the would-be scion and the new owners were a thing of the past.

In the meantime, however, there were the distractions of Veeck's endless enticements to fans who wanted laughs with their double plays and the team's first flag since the benighted 1919 meeting with the Cincinnati Reds. In the first category, the owner staged a "Martian invasion" by midgets led by Eddie Gaedel of St. Louis Browns fame and sought to rejuvenate his slumping left fielder Al

BILL VEECK

OWNER OF INDIANS, BROWNS AND WHITE SOX. CREATED HEIGHTENED FAN INTEREST AT EVERY STOP WITH INGENIOUS PROMOTIONAL SCHEMES, FAN PARTICIPATION, EXPLODING SCOREBOARD, OUTRAGEOUS DOOR PRIZES, NAMES ON UNIFORMS. SET M.L. ATTENDANCE RECORD WITH PENNANT-WINNER AT CLEVELAND IN 1948; WON AGAIN WITH 'GO-GO' SOX IN 1959. SIGNED A.L.'S FIRST BLACK PLAYER, LARRY DOBY IN 1947 AND OLDEST ROOKIE, 42 YEAR OLD SATCHEL PAIGE IN 1948.
A CHAMPION OF THE LITTLE GUY.

National Baseball Library, Cooperstown, NY

Smith by inviting anyone with that last name to a game for free; what the fans who attended Al Smith Night saw was the outfielder drop a fly ball that cost Chicago the game. In the second category, the White Sox took advantage of the injury-wracked Yankees to go into first place in mid-July and stay there until the clinching on September 22nd. Aside from Fox, who won his MVP for a .306 average that barely expressed his overall leadership value to the club, other notable offensive contributions came from Aparicio with a league-leading 56 steals and from Lollar with 22 homers and 84 RBIs. The pitchers were led by future Hall of Famer Wynn, who had endured a rough season in 1958 after coming to Chicago in a trade for the popular Minoso; in 1959, the 39-year-old righthander took major league Cy Young honors for his 22 wins.

In a World Series dominated by relief pitching (neither side recorded a complete game), the White Sox went down in six games to the Dodgers. The biggest bat in the Chicago lineup belonged to veteran first baseman Ted Kluszewski, who had been

The most bizarre rally in baseball annals took place April 22, 1959, when the White Sox scored 11 runs in the seventh inning of a game against Kansas City. The offensive display consisted of 10 walks, a hit batsman, three Athletics' errors, and a lone single by Chicago outfielder Johnny Callison. The White Sox won the game, 20–6.

acquired from Pittsburgh toward the end of the regular season and who weighed in with 3 homers, 10 RBIs, and a .391 average.

For most of the 1960s, the team was more respectable than thrilling. The slide away from the status of a feverish contender began in the 1959–1960 offseason, when Veeck pulled off as bad a series of trades as ever managed by a baseball executive in such a period; even worse, they involved the sacrificing of prospects and left the organization's farm system in wretched condition. In the first of the big swaps, Veeck sent first baseman Norm Cash, catcher John Romano, and third baseman Bubba Phillips to the Indians for the graying Minoso, catcher Dick Brown, and pitchers Don Ferrarese and Jake Striker. In the second one, he parted with outfielder Johnny Callison, getting third baseman Gene Freese back from the Phillies. Finally, he obtained outfielder Roy Sievers from the Twins in return for catcher Earl Battey, first baseman Don Mincher, and $150,000. The least that could be said for the players surrendered in the three deals was that, with the exception of Phillips, they all played in subsequent All Star games. The biggest contributions from the players obtained came from Sievers, who provided some punch in the middle of the lineup for two seasons, and from the returning local hero Minoso, whose two home runs on Opening Day in 1960 allowed Veeck to set off a spray of rockets and other fireworks from the Comiskey Park scoreboard that he had refurbished at a cost of $350,000.

For most of the 1960 season, Veeck had more on his mind than the team that was settling into third place for keeps. In June, he underwent an amputation of what remained of his left leg (originally damaged in a war accident) and intimated to friends that doctors had found other problems that persuaded him it was time to put his affairs in order. After many months of tests, the ailment was disclosed as a stretching of blood vessels in the head, for which the only effective remedy was resting and withdrawing from baseball. Even before he had received advice to leave the White Sox to others, Veeck had been spending a lot of energy in trying to get his partner Greenberg into the driver's seat for the new Los Angeles franchise that was due to come into the league as a part of the 1961 expansion. When the franchise ended

In 1960, the White Sox became the first team to put players' names on uniforms.

In 1960, reliever Alan Worthington announced his retirement on religious principles because he couldn't tolerate Bill Veeck's use of the scoreboard to steal signs.

up being awarded to Gene Autry, Veeck and an equally disappointed Greenberg let it be known that they would consider selling out. In June 1961, comedian Danny Thomas and attorney Bernard Epton announced that they had acquired a seven-day option with a $4.8 million offer for the franchise—a tactical mistake because Veeck had conceded no such option and decided that there was less than met the eye in the tender. The Veeck-Greenberg majority interest was ultimately sold to Arthur Allyn, Jr., son of one of the outgoing owners; with the transaction, the White Sox became a subsidiary of the Artnell conglomerate of oil and clothing companies.

As for Comiskey, he ended up in the middle of another complicated fiasco in an attempt to gain the control that had been promised him for more than twenty years. First, he sold his forty-six percent interest in the franchise to a group headed by Chicago insurance company executive William Bartholomay for $3.5 million. The idea was that, with that forty-six percent in its pocket, the Bartholomay syndicate would attract enough investors to overwhelm Allyn with an offer for total control, after which Comiskey would be given the opportunity to buy a majority interest right back, making a profit for one and all. Unfortunately for the heir, however, Allyn rejected the Bartholomay offer, leaving the Comiskey name cut off from the franchise for the very first time. Moreover, when Bartholomay and his associates saw that they were going to have little leverage with their forty-six percent, they sold it to Allyn, giving the latter the absolute control that Chuck Comiskey had been dreaming about since his college days.

In 1963, Lopez and the club revived somewhat with the first of three straight second-place finishes. In none of the three seasons did any member of the team drive in 100 runs, while the only .300 batter in that span was outfielder Floyd Robinson, who barely made it in 1964 with his .301. On the other hand, the team got some solid starting pitching from southpaws Gary Peters and Juan Pizarro and exceptional relief from knuckleballers Hoyt Wilhelm and Eddie Fisher. But then, just as the postwar dynasty of the Yankees finally ended and the league was thrown wide open again, Chicago began to have trouble playing at a .500 level. Lopez was not around for the start of the slide: Following ulcer problems and other ailments, he announced his resignation on November 4, 1965. His own choice for a successor was his chief lieutenant Cuccinello, but the team hired Eddie Stanky instead.

Under Stanky, the White Sox didn't return to first place, but they did return to the headlines. Stanky's insistence on strict curfews, a dress code, and a regular calisthenics program had the players falling over one another to complain anonymously to reporters. His attacks on rival players and managers sharpened grandstand expectations of on-field brawling. His prolonged arguments with umpires contributed regular photographs to the sports pages. Both the benefits and limitations of these tactics became evident in 1967. On the one hand, the pilot's firebrand style kept the team in the middle of a year-long struggle with Boston, Detroit, and Minnesota; on the other hand, all the shouting and contentiousness papered over the fact that the team was decidedly short on talent, as evidenced by outfielder Ken Berry's .241 being the highest batting average on the squad. The pudding provided the proof the following year, when most of the same players tumbled into eighth place, thirty-six games off the pace. Long before that point was reached, Stanky had alienated himself from just about everybody in Chicago by blaming the media for the club's failure, imposing countless fines on the players for perceived on-field and off-field rule infractions, compromising his coaches by making them look like his private spies on the players, and criticizing the front office for trades made and not made. In early July, the team announced that the manager had resigned "for the good of the club" and that Lopez had consented to fill in while the search for a permanent replacement went on. The search didn't end until the closing of the 1970 season, when Chuck Tanner was hired after two half-years each by Lopez and Don Gutteridge.

The best thing that happened to the White Sox toward the end of the 1960s was the 1969 collapse of the Cubs against the Miracle Mets. Allyn spent much of the period agitating for a new downtown stadium, spurred on by incidents of racial violence around Comiskey Park that he claimed were chiefly responsible for diminishing attendance (only 7,756 showed up for Opening Day in 1968, in the immediate wake of the assassination of Martin Luther King). In an effort to make his case more urgent to the city fathers, he agreed to play ten home games in Milwaukee's County Stadium—ostensibly in order to give the league an incentive for including Milwaukee in

its planned 1969 expansion, but mainly to find ammunition if he sought to sell the team to a Wisconsin lobbying group headed by Bud Selig. The results were mixed: The ten games in Milwaukee in 1968 accounted for one-third of Chicago's home attendance for the year, but the following season, with the expansion franchises already consigned to Seattle and Kansas City and the Milwaukee group publicizing efforts at an outright purchase, even the major league-starved fans to the north stayed away from the lackluster White Sox. Selig, for one, wasn't discouraged, and he offered Allyn $13 million for the franchise—a proposal that was matched in short order by Texas millionaire Lamar Hunt, who wanted to move the club to Dallas. By this juncture, however, Allyn had received clear word from the league that it would never approve a sale that called for abandoning the Chicago market; on September 24, 1969, he took the only way out left to him by selling fifty percent of his Artnell stock to his younger brother John and retiring to Florida.

The start of a new decade under a new owner brought the worst team in franchise history, with the White Sox ringing up 106 losses and burying themselves so deeply in the cellar of the Western Division that they finished nine games behind even the fifth-place Brewers. The pitching was so bad that middle reliever Lee Stange's 1–0 record was the only one on the entire staff that was over .500. Offensively, the most conspicuous contribution came from third baseman Bill Melton, whose 33 home runs marked the first time that a Chicago player had hit 30 or more. A sign of the times, however, was that Melton belted his 30th in a Comiskey Park game attended by only 672 fans. John Allyn didn't even wait until the end of the season before he got rid of Ed Short as general manager and brought in former Northwestern athletic director Stuart Holcomb to head baseball operations. It was Holcomb who filled in the rest of the new regime by picking Tanner as manager, Johnny Sain as pitching coach, and Roland Hemond as director of player personnel. Holcomb spent the off-season reducing the team's actuarial table and picking up role players like outfielders Jay Johnstone and Pat Kelly; but his most important exchange, mirroring Allyn's pledge to bring some animation back to the South Side, was in dispatching the somnolent voices of Bob Elson and Red Rush to Oakland for the rasping, sarcastic Harry Caray, who revived the team's broadcast appeal.

The 1971 club achieved a twenty-three-game turnaround from the previous season. Melton hit another 33 homers, and led the league doing so, but the most unexpected development was Sain's conversion of Wilbur Wood from a so-so reliever into the ace of the rotation. For the first of four straight years, the knuckleballer turned in 20 wins, and also threw at least 320 innings. For Sain, it was another demonstration that the only thing he did more consistently than irritate higherups with his independent attitude was develop twenty-game winners. After the season, the club pulled off a deal with the Dodgers that landed the most emblematic player of Chicago in the early 1970s, slugger Dick Allen. Over the next three years, for both better and worse, the White Sox became the Chicago Allens, with Holcomb, Hemond, and Tanner taking every occasion to point out that the first baseman-outfielder was the franchise meal ticket. Allen got the relationship off to a rocky start when he dropped out of sight after lamenting to friends that he was growing weary of being dealt from team to team. When he showed up for spring training after long weeks of remaining incommunicado, he was signed to the biggest contract in the history of Chicago sports, then went out to bat .308 and lead the AL in home runs (37), RBIs (113), walks (99), and slugging average (.603)—all of which added up to an MVP trophy. His big offensive year also brought White Sox rooters back to Comiskey Park; for the first time in seven years, the franchise topped one million.

Asserting that Allen had saved the franchise, Holcomb and Hemond announced during the offseason that the slugger had been signed to a brand new contract that established him as baseball's highest-paid player. This rankled several players, especially righthander Stan Bahnsen, who had been offered only a modest raise for winning 21 games, and second baseman Mike Andrews and outfielder Rick Reichardt, who had been advised that they would be cut if they had bad years. When Bahnsen, Andrews, and Reichardt threatened to play through the 1973 campaign without signing a contract, Holcomb invoked the automatic renewal clause. Other members of the team voiced dismay during spring training at the herculean efforts being made by Tanner and Hemond for saving a roster spot for Hank Allen, Dick's brother, who was at the end of an undistinguished major league career. The climate didn't get any healthier when Dick Allen fractured his fibula in a play at first base in late June and was sidelined for the remainder of the year. When he was injured, Allen was batting .313 with 16 homers; without him, and because of some other injuries to regulars, the club fell from second to fifth.

On the same day that Allen was hurt, Holcomb announced that the club was releasing Reichardt, as it had previously gotten rid of one of the other contract rebels, Andrews. The remaining holdout, pitcher Bahnsen, quickly agreed to terms, but it proved to be a Pyrrhic victory for Holcomb. Already incensed that the general manager had released Johnstone at the beginning of the season over another contract protest, Tanner went to the newspapers with a complaint that the front office was stripping him of veteran backups over pocket-money differences and forcing him to press inexperienced rookies into late-inning situations. Although Tanner was right, suspicions about his motives in going public with his complaint arose as soon as Hemond jumped in on the manager's side, in the process laying out his resume for running the club's baseball affairs. By the end of July, tensions among the three had gotten to a point that Allyn intervened—on the side of the pilot and the director of player personnel. Without saying anything to Holcomb, the owner flew to Boston to meet the team and assure Tanner that the general manager was on his way out; without saying anything to Allyn, Holcomb told Chicago newspapers that he was resigning. After the owner and the departing general manager had finished accusing each other of professional discourtesy, Hemond took over as vice-president and new general manager.

Allen's third and final year with the team was the most eventful of all. Although he came back in 1974 in perfect health and got a quick start on another league-leading power performance, the first baseman showed a gradually decreasing interest in the club's .500 fortunes as the season wore on. When his hitting put the team ahead in a game, however marginally, he persuaded the cooperative Tanner to yank him for the last couple of innings so he could avoid having to meet with sportswriters after the contest. Finally, on September 14, he called a gathering of his teammates and announced his decision to quit baseball that very day. Tanner bade his star farewell with the praise that "he was the greatest player I ever saw." Allyn and Hemond were more reserved. After the season was over, the pair realized that the money they had saved by not having to pay Allen for the last three weeks had been more than offset by the reduced crowds at Comiskey over that period. It didn't end there. That fall, Allen announced a change of heart, saying he intended to return to Chicago. When Hemond responded by trading him to Atlanta for $5,000 and second-string catcher Jim Essian, Allen said he would never play on a southern team. Hemond said that was Atlanta's problem, and washed his hands of the whole affair. As it turned out, the Braves did indeed swap the slugger back to his original team, the Phillies; obscured amid all the goodbyes was the fact that, even having missed a good three weeks of the 1974 season, Allen ended up winning the AL homer title.

The White Sox had a couple of other luminaries besides Allen on their roster in the early 1970s. One was Ron Santo, the veteran Cubs' third baseman who had come to the team in 1974 after exercising his 5-and-10 rights in rejecting a proposed swap to California. At the end of his career, Santo brought little but box office nostalgia to the club, though Allen also accused him of trying to turn his teammates against him (it was after Santo's own retirement in the fall of 1974 that Allen had his second thoughts about returning to Chicago). Another presence was southpaw Jim Kaat, picked up from Minnesota when his career seemed to be at an end; in his only two full seasons with the White Sox, Kaat racked up forty-one victories, mainly because of a quick pitch that sometimes caught umpires napping as much as batters. The first part of the decade also saw the arrival from the minors of the fireballing duo of Terry Forster and Goose Gossage. At one point or another, the club tried to make both of them starters, but their biggest numbers with Chicago (as with a host of subsequent teams) were registered from the bullpen. While wearing a White Sox uniform, each led the AL in saves—Forster in 1974, Gossage in 1975. By 1975, Bucky Dent had become the team's regular shortstop.

One of the reasons that Gossage and Dent got so much playing time in 1975 was that they didn't cost the team much, and that criterion had come to guide Allyn's every move. Among the creditors on the attack against the franchise were the Internal Revenue Service and Allyn's brother Arthur, who went to court to claim a half-million dollars he said he still had coming from his sale of the franchise in 1970. The situation had grown so critical that the club had to sell receiver Ed Herrmann to the Yankees in April 1975 because it couldn't pay his salary. In June, Allen was forced to sell outfielder Buddy Bradford to the Cardinals to meet the team payroll. When not even that was enough, he went to the AL for help but found little sympathy; the league had its own ideas for resolving the crisis.

In an elaborate scheme aimed at simultaneously liquidating a series of Seattle lawsuit threats that had been hanging in the air since the Pilots had moved to Milwaukee in 1970 and at putting an end to the constant attempts by Finley to move out of Oakland, the league tried to pressure Allyn into selling the White Sox to a Washington State group that included comedian Danny Kaye, thereby leaving Chicago open to a transfer by the Athletics. In no mood to please the league, Seattle, or Finley, Allyn sent the other owners reeling when, instead, he accepted a bid from a syndicate headed by the physically rehabilitated Veeck. The league's response was to vote down the proposed sale behind the argument that Veeck's debenture stock method of purchase suggested serious undercapitalization; in what amounted to a public relations gesture, however, the other owners also gave the prospective buyers ten days to come up with $1.2 million in hard cash to support their tender, letting it be known in private that they didn't expect Veeck to be able to deliver. They were wrong. While local television boosters ignited a campaign called Save Our Sox, asking for public donations toward the $1.2 million, and Illinois politicians began assailing the league with letters and telephone calls, Veeck scrambled after the money, putting it together from a network of friends and associates in several cities. Their bluff called, the other owners held their noses as they welcomed baseball's Barnum back into their ranks. Under the terms of the sale, Veeck and his partners paid $8 million for seventy-five percent of the team stock; Allyn retained a twenty percent share.

Veeck's successful return made him 2-for-4 in his attempts over the years to buy the White Sox. Three weeks later, however, he admitted to wishing that he had struck out on this particular occasion because of the revolutionary ruling granting free agency. With insufficient capital to afford high-priced free agents, Veeck initiated his "rent-a-player" plan of acquiring stars in the last years of their contracts, knowing that he was going to have to let them walk elsewhere after a single campaign. The most successful use of this tactic (though it did cost the team Gossage and Forster) came in 1977, when the White Sox obtained free-agents-to-be Richie Zisk and Oscar Gamble and rode their combined 61 home runs to 90 victories for the first time since 1965. That same season of a decidedly livelier ball saw the club as a whole belt an unprecedented 192 homers (nine players finished in double figures) and a record-breaking 1,657,135 fans (more than the two previous seasons together) troop through Comiskey Park turnstiles. The Veeck promotions this time around included ethnic nights highlighting just about every culture represented in Chicago, belly dancers, a so-called Anti-Superstition Night when witches were invited to cast spells on the opposition, baseball clown Max Patkin, and the reactivating of the fifty-four-year-old Minoso as a designated hitter for three games (he got one single in eight official at bats). It was also Veeck, and not the usually cited New York Mets of the mid-1980s, who started the practice of having players take curtain calls from the dugout after hitting a home run. And, perhaps most traumatically of all for those who had to wear them, it was another one of the owner's inspirations that led the team to play briefly in shorts.

Managers came and went. As soon as he took over, Veeck bounced Tanner in order to bring back Richards, but after so many years, the one-time Go-Go pilot had become a Growl-Growl one, and he was replaced soon enough by Bob Lemon. The Hall of Fame pitcher took Manager of the Year honors in 1977, but at the beginning of the following season came under fire from some of his players for his extremely laid back style. Veeck held his fire in public while trying to swing a managerial trade with the Yankees of Lemon for Billy Martin, but when that came to nothing, he simply disposed of the pilot in favor of Larry Doby. Doby—the first black player in the AL under Veeck at Cleveland in the late 1940s and the second black manager after Frank Robinson—was little more than another gimmick. Amid criticism that he didn't know how to use his bullpen, he was replaced after a half-season by Don Kessinger, a one-time Chicago favorite for the Cubs. Although a stickler for fundamentals in a way that neither Lemon nor Doby had been, Kessinger did not survive a single season, mainly because of clubhouse tensions prompted by what some players called overbearing beliefs in hypnotism and born-again Christianity. Veeck's reading of the criticism was too much passivity on the team, and he readily accepted the manager's resignation in August 1979. Tony LaRussa was named to succeed Kessinger.

Following the team's power surge in 1977, there was something of a three-year lull in between-the-lines entertainment. Chicago's offense consisted in good part of outfielder Chet Lemon, whose 1979 average of .318 was the club's highest in twenty-five years. With fan interest again on the wane, Veeck began looking into the possibility of moving the club to Denver in either an outright sale or a transfer that would net him and his partners some new community financing. To make ends meet, he rented out Comiskey Park regularly to rock concert organizers and stepped up his own promotions—in both cases ultimately paying a heavy price. The rock concerts not only tore up the field and necessitated several costly resoddings, but also forced the postponement

of games because of bad playing conditions. On July 12, 1979, to the snickers of other league owners, Veeck got his comeuppance as a promoter when a local disc jockey's stunt in blowing up disco records produced a mob scene of thousands of fence jumpers running wild on the field between games of a doubleheader, with policemen trying futilely to restore order and firemen trying to put out the blazes caused by the so-called Disco Demolition. With public opinion turning against him, Veeck announced that the franchise was up for sale again, thereby setting the stage for still another lengthy series of skirmishes with the league.

On August 22, 1980, Veeck revealed that he had reached agreement with Edward DeBartolo to sell the franchise for $20 million. A multimillionaire who had made his fortune in shopping malls, hotels, and banks, DeBartolo was also well known in sports circles for being the chief stockholder in the NHL Pittsburgh Penguins and three race tracks, as well as for being the father of the owner of the NFL San Francisco Forty-Niners. Over the next four months, however, the other AL owners raised one objection after another to the deal, citing DeBartolo's past involvement in efforts to win a major league franchise for New Orleans, his association with the race tracks, and the fact that he would have been an absentee proprietor. Not even DeBartolo's willingness to commit himself to an indemnity payment if he moved the club out of Chicago, his announced intention of selling his interests in the race tracks, or his pledge to spend twenty percent of every year in Chicago, moved the league. The AL attitude became so suspicious that Italian-American groups accused the owners of objecting to DeBartolo just because of his ethnic background; others speculated that the objection was based on the businessman's unsavory underworld connections. With DeBartolo forced out of the picture, Veeck had to conclude an alternative deal for the same $20 million with a partnership headed by real estate magnate Jerry Reinsdorf and former television sports producer Eddie Einhorn.

With new money at the top, the club was able to take advantage of an administrative blunder by the Red Sox and sign catcher Carlton Fisk; because Boston had not sent him his new contract by the prescribed date, the league's premier receiver had become eligible for free agency. Although many would always primarily identify the righthand-hitting slugger with the Red Sox, Fisk would actually spend a lot more time as a member of the White Sox, with whom he eventually set a franchise career home run record and also passed Johnny Bench for most homers by a catcher. A couple of weeks after signing Fisk, Reinsdorf and Einhorn threw another couple of hundred thousand dollars at the Phillies to obtain outfielder Greg Luzinski. Along with the home-grown Harold Baines, the two acquisitions provided most of the punch for the club's third-place show in the first half of the 1981 strike season, and also accounted for most of the pop in another third-place finish in 1982. The latter standing was somewhat mis-leading, however, to the extent that the team had to win 15 of 18 in the final hours of the campaign to wind up that high; in fact, it was a season riven with conflict between the ownership and LaRussa, espe-cially after the manager's top aide, pitching coach Ron Schueler, was fired at the All-Star break. Schueler was ousted despite having had a big hand in the development of LaMarr Hoyt, who led the league with 19 wins.

There was nothing at all tainted about the team's Western Division title in 1983, with the White Sox outdistancing the second-place Royals by a full 20 games, the biggest such edge in AL history. Using a remark by Texas manager Doug Rader ("They win ugly—they get six hits, but they get six runs with them") as a rallying cry, the Win Uglies stayed near the rest of the pack until August, but then went on a 46–15 tear. Once again, Hoyt led the league, this time with 24 victories, including thirteen straight at the end of the season, and was awarded Cy Young hon-ors. Right behind Hoyt was Rich Dotson with 22 triumphs, including ten in a row during the conclu-sive hot streak. Offensively, the club boasted four hitters (Fisk, Baines, Luzinski, and Ron Kittle) who reached the seats at least twenty times, a first for the franchise; the righthand-hitting Kittle also drove across 100 runs, and was named Rookie of the Year. Hoyt got the team off to a good start in the LCS against Baltimore by pitching a five-hitter, but there-after it was all Orioles, with the White Sox scoring merely three runs in four games. The crusher was a tenth-inning home run by Baltimore outfielder Tito Landrum that broke up a scoreless nail-biter in the finale.

Chicago's home run hitting in 1983 came amid some criticism of batting coach Charlie Lau's stress on a contact approach. But as Lau had demonstrated during two earlier stays with Kansas City, his phi-losophy did not at all preclude the long ball for play-ers so gifted, and, again as with the Royals, many of the White Sox defended his methods vigorously in the course of the season. Thus it was all the more of a blow when, shortly before the 1984 season, Lau died of cancer. With a series of nagging injuries also

exacting a toll on just about everyone except Baines, the squad slid to fifth place. Among the pitchers, Hoyt went from leading the league in victories to leading it in losses, and was packed off at the end of the year to San Diego in a swap that brought short-stop prospect Ozzie Guillen, utilityman Luis Salazar, and pitchers Bill Long and Tim Lollar. The only pos-itive development on the pitching staff was the 15 wins of future Hall of Famer Tom Seaver, obtained from the Mets in the compensation draft; the right-hander posted 16 more victories the following year, including his 300th (against the Yankees on August 4th). The uproar raised in New York over the White Sox selection of Seaver played a major role in the elimination of the compensation pool, which had been created with the idea of reimbursing to some degree teams that had lost star players to free agency In 1982, the White Sox had also been the first team to pick up somebody through the compensation route, obtaining catcher Joel Skinner from the Pittsburgh organization.

By the middle of the decade, Reinsdorf and Ein-horn were showing the same antsiness about the team's mediocre play as had many of their predeces-sors. Making them even more impatient was the change in ownership of the Cubs that had brought the Chicago *Tribune* into baseball's executive circles; not only had the media giant injected new money into the NL club, but it used its newsstand and radio–television broadcasting dominance to devote about ten words about the Cubs for every one spent on the White Sox. With even Harry Caray taking his "Take Me Out to the Ballgame" act (originally inspired by Veeck) to Wrigley Field, Chicago's AL franchise started having doubts that it was even the second team in the city. Hemond, who had weathered one storm after another over the years, came under fire from both sides—the owners warning him that third place was not good enough and LaRussa complain-ing that the front office had become too timid to trade. Finally, with the 1985 season in the books, Reinsdorf made his move in making White Sox broadcaster Hawk Harrelson general manager and reducing Hemond to the usual advisory role.

On May 8, 1984, the White Sox and Brewers began the longest night game in major league history—a 25-inning affair lasting eight hours and six minutes. The contest was decided the following day on a home run by Harold Baines, giving Chicago a 7–6 victory.

With the loudly opinionated, stetson-wearing Harrelson, Reinsdorf had hoped to generate enough news interest to win back a couple of lines even on the sports pages of the *Tribune*; that was about all that he got. With LaRussa making efforts to play the good soldier, the new general manager's first decision was to shift the thirty-eight-year-old Fisk to left field, in order to be able to play catching prospects Skinner and Ron Karkovice. Harrelson's second move was to overwhelm LaRussa with specialty coaches, insisting in particular that every team needed different pitching tutors for starters and relievers. The Fisk experiment lasted only a few weeks into the season, when the embarrassed veteran, backed by a pitching staff that had missed his presence behind the plate, returned to catching. The coaching exuberance created a number of incidents at spring training, when one-time stars like Allen, Willie Horton, Don Drysdale, and Moe Drabowsky kept bumping into LaRussa's permanent staff, physically as well as philosophically. When the manager protested that enough was enough, the general manager tried to talk Billy Martin out of one of his retirements with the Yankees. The effort became so widely reported that LaRussa demanded a vote of confidence; he got one on May 9, if only because Martin proved unavailable. Six weeks later, however, after some Harrelson mouthing off about the team's performance and some rejoinders from LaRussa that the general manager wasn't exactly Branch Rickey as a trader, Jim Fregosi was brought in as the pilot.

A couple of weeks after Fregosi arrived to take over for LaRussa, Tom Haller was added to the front office with duties suspiciously like those assigned previously to Harrelson. Between them, Haller and Harrelson made one of the worst trades of the year in shipping outfielder Bobby Bonilla to the Pirates in exchange for pitcher Jose DeLeon; they also sent Seaver to the Red Sox and then immediately replaced him with another aging future Hall of Famer, Steve Carlton. By September, with the team wallowing in the lower depths of the Western Division, Harrelson had become a rare visitor to Comiskey Park; he submitted his resignation a few days before the end of the season. In October, Haller was out, too, replaced as general manager by Larry Himes.

The team's humdrum play in the middle of the decade continued—as did the nervousness about the future of the organization. The next field of battle was the insistence of Reinsdorf and Einhorn that the club needed a new stadium if it hoped to go on operating in Chicago. While city and state legislators got bogged down in one legislative argument after another, Reinsdorf and Einhorn grew less subtle in their threats to move, to the point where they opened negotiations with St. Petersburg officials regarding shifting the franchise to Florida. By the start of 1988, St. Petersburg had begun construction on a dome that would cost $140 million and seat 43,000 and announced plans for enlarging the Cardinals' spring training site of Al Lang Field as a temporary quarters for the Chisox in 1989. On June 27, only three days before the deadline that the Illinois legislature had to approve final details for building a new Chicago stadium, Florida officials disclosed that Reinsdorf and Einhorn had taken a fifteen-year lease on the dome and had hammered out an accord for the fourth-best television package in the majors. With Governor James Thompson finally pulling out all the stops to save the franchise for the state, the Illinois legislature put the finishing touches on the construction bill with literally minutes to spare. Key ingredients of the agreement called for a new Comiskey Park to be built directly across the street from the existing structure by March 1, 1991 and for the White Sox to receive a series of attendance subsidies if the gate dipped below stipulated levels for the first ten years of occupancy. The reaction by Reinsdorf and Einhorn to the pact was muted enough to suggest that they would not have been all that heart-broken if Illinois lawmakers had failed to reach an agreement.

Himes and Fregosi did not exactly represent a meeting of the minds. While the manager pressed the front office for some deals that would add experience, especially in the outfield, the general manager, at the instruction of the ownership, spent a lot of time trimming the financial sails, to the point where the White Sox had the lowest payroll in the major leagues at the end of the decade. None of the players lobbied for a Larry Himes Fan Club, either, especially with the executive's preoccupation with travel rules such as wearing socks with shoes. But while he was forced to forget about expensive free agents, Himes was also able to take advantage of Chicago's high position in the annual amateur draft and come up with arguably better prospects in the late 1980s than any other general manager in the league; among those inked to Chicago contracts in the latter part of the decade were pitchers Jack McDowell and Alex Fernandez, third baseman Robin Ventura, and first baseman-outfielder Frank Thomas.

Neither Fregosi nor Himes himself was around to see the prospects blossom at the beginning of the 1990s. Fregosi was the first to go, fired after the 1988 season for Jeff Torborg. Torborg lasted at the helm through the 1991 campaign, when he was released from his contract to accept a more lucrative offer from the Mets; his successor was Gene Lamont. Himes clashed with Reinsdorf in 1989 over his insistence that the club trade Baines while they could still get appreciable value for the designated hitter, whose leg injuries over the years had reduced him to an offense-only player. Although Reinsdorf eventually agreed to a trade with the Rangers that brought infielder Scott Fletcher, outfielder Sammy Sosa, and pitcher Wilson Alvarez to Chicago, he also made it clear how much he liked Baines by retiring the lefthand-hitting slugger's number before a game against Texas later in the season. Himes lingered another year, when he was replaced by one-time pitching coach Schueler.

The most conspicuous performer for the White Sox in the late 1980s and early 1990s was reliever Bobby Thigpen, whose 57 saves in 1990 established a new major league record. In both 1988 and 1989, the righthander had saved 34, adding another 30 in 1991. Prior to the maturation of Ventura and Thomas in 1991, the club's best offensive prospect since Baines had been first baseman Greg Walker, who had clouted at least 24 homers in three different seasons in the 1980s. On July 30, 1988, however, Walker suf-

fered the first of a series of seizures that were ultimately diagnosed as a viral inflammation of the brain's blood vessels, and his career just about came to an end. For White Sox loyalists, Walker was merely the latest victim of the Cissell Curse.

Moving into the new Comiskey Park in time for the 1991 season, the White Sox rode their young bats to a second straight second-place finish, but also to much more disappointment that they hadn't gone all the way. It was amid this fallout that Schueler seemed only too happy to let the conservatively tactical Torborg go off to the Mets and replace him with Lamont. 1992, however, saw the team struggling through the season even to finish third, despite the presence in the lineup of Tim Raines and George Bell (both acquired in trades) to support Ventura and Thomas. The biggest on-field development was the emergence of McDowell as a 20-game winner; the biggest milestone Fisk's 350th home run, the most by a catcher. For his part, Reinsdorf spent most of the year working baseball's back rooms to force out Fay Vincent as commissioner; many compared his position in the game's business echelons to that once held by Walter O'Malley of the Dodgers.

CHICAGO WHITE SOX

Annual Standings and Managers

Year	Position	W	L	Pct.	GB	Managers
1901	First	83	53	.610	+4	Clark Griffith
1902	Fourth	74	60	.552	8	Clark Griffith
1903	Seventh	60	77	.438	30½	Nixey Callahan
1904	Third	89	65	.578	6	Nixey Callahan, Fielder Jones
1905	Second	92	60	.605	2	Fielder Jones
1906	First	93	58	.616	+3	Fielder Jones
1907	Third	87	64	.576	5½	Fielder Jones
1908	Third	88	64	.579	1½	Fielder Jones
1909	Fourth	78	74	.513	20	Billy Sullivan
1910	Sixth	68	85	.444	35½	Hugh Duffy
1911	Fourth	77	74	.510	24	Hugh Duffy
1912	Fourth	78	76	.506	28	Nixey Callahan
1913	Fifth	78	74	.513	17½	Nixey Callahan
1914	Sixth*	70	84	.455	30	Nixey Callahan
1915	Third	93	61	.604	9½	Pants Rowland
1916	Second	89	65	.578	2	Pants Rowland
1917	First	100	54	.649	+9	Pants Rowland
1918	Sixth	57	67	.460	17	Pants Rowland
1919	First	88	52	.629	+3½	Kid Gleason
1920	Second	96	58	.623	2	Kid Gleason
1921	Seventh	62	92	.403	36½	Kid Gleason
1922	Fifth	77	77	.500	17	Kid Gleason
1923	Seventh	69	85	.448	30	Kid Gleason
1924	Eighth	66	87	.431	25½	Frank Chance, Johnny Evers
1925	Fifth	79	75	.513	18½	Eddie Collins

1926	Fifth	81	72	.529	9½	Eddie Collins
1927	Fifth	70	83	.458	29½	Ray Schalk
1928	Fifth	72	82	.468	29	Ray Schalk, Lena Blackburne
1929	Seventh	59	93	.388	46	Lena Blackburne
1930	Seventh	62	92	.403	40	Donie Bush
1931	Eighth	56	97	.366	51	Donie Bush
1932	Seventh	49	102	.325	56½	Lew Fonseca
1933	Sixth	67	83	.447	31	Lew Fonseca
1934	Eighth	53	99	.349	47	Lew Fonseca, Jimmy Dykes
1935	Fifth	74	78	.487	19½	Jimmy Dykes
1936	Third	81	70	.536	20	Jimmy Dykes
1937	Third	86	68	.558	16	Jimmy Dykes
1938	Sixth	65	83	.439	32	Jimmy Dykes
1939	Fourth	85	69	.552	22½	Jimmy Dykes
1940	Fourth*	82	72	.532	8	Jimmy Dykes
1941	Third	77	77	.500	24	Jimmy Dykes
1942	Sixth	66	82	.446	34	Jimmy Dykes
1943	Fourth	82	72	.532	16	Jimmy Dykes
1944	Seventh	71	83	.461	18	Jimmy Dykes
1945	Sixth	71	78	.477	15	Jimmy Dykes
1946	Fifth	74	80	.481	30	Jimmy Dykes, Ted Lyons
1947	Sixth	70	84	.455	27	Ted Lyons
1948	Eighth	51	101	.336	44½	Ted Lyons
1949	Sixth	63	91	.409	34	Jack Onslow
1950	Sixth	60	94	.390	38	Jack Onslow, Red Corriden
1951	Fourth	81	73	.526	17	Paul Richards
1952	Third	81	73	.526	14	Paul Richards
1953	Third	89	65	.578	11½	Paul Richards
1954	Third	94	60	.610	17	Paul Richards, Marty Marion
1955	Third	91	63	.591	5	Marty Marion
1956	Third	85	69	.552	12	Marty Marion
1957	Second	90	64	.584	8	Al Lopez
1958	Second	82	72	.532	10	Al Lopez
1959	First	94	60	.610	+5	Al Lopez
1960	Third	87	67	.565	10	Al Lopez
1961	Fourth	86	76	.531	23	Al Lopez
1962	Fifth	85	77	.525	11	Al Lopez
1963	Second	94	68	.580	10½	Al Lopez
1964	Second	98	64	.605	1	Al Lopez
1965	Second	95	67	.586	7	Al Lopez
1966	Fourth	83	79	.512	15	Eddie Stanky
1967	Fourth	89	73	.549	3	Eddie Stanky
1968	Eighth*	67	95	.414	36	Eddie Stanky, Al Lopez
1969	Fifth	68	94	.420	29	Al Lopez, Don Gutteridge
1970	Sixth	56	106	.346	42	Don Gutteridge, Chuck Tanner
1971	Third	79	83	.488	22½	Chuck Tanner
1972	Second	87	67	.565	5½	Chuck Tanner
1973	Fifth	77	85	.475	17	Chuck Tanner
1974	Fourth	80	80	.500	9	Chuck Tanner
1975	Fifth	75	86	.466	22½	Chuck Tanner
1976	Sixth	64	97	.398	25½	Paul Richards
1977	Third	90	72	.556	12	Bob Lemon
1978	Fifth	71	90	.441	20½	Bob Lemon, Larry Doby
1979	Fifth	73	87	.456	14	Don Kessinger, Tony LaRussa
1980	Fifth	70	90	.438	26	Tony LaRussa
1981	Third	31	22	.585	2½	Tony LaRussa
	Sixth	23	30	.434	7	Tony LaRussa

1982	Third	87	75	.537	6	Tony LaRussa
1983	First	99	63	.611	+20	Tony LaRussa
1984	Fifth*	74	88	.457	10	Tony LaRussa
1985	Third	85	77	.525	6	Tony LaRussa
1986	Fifth	72	90	.444	20	Tony LaRussa, Jim Fregosi
1987	Fifth	77	85	.475	8	Jim Fregosi
1988	Fifth	71	90	.441	32½	Jim Fregosi
1989	Seventh	69	92	.429	29½	Jeff Torborg
1990	Second	94	68	.580	9	Jeff Torborg
1991	Second	87	75	.537	8	Jeff Torborg
1992	Third	86	76	.531	10	Gene Lamont

*Tie

Postseason Play

LCS	1–3 versus Baltimore	1983	WS	4–2 versus Chicago	1906
				4–2 versus New York	1917
				3–5 versus Cincinnati	1919
				2–4 versus Los Angeles	1959

Chicago Whales

Federal League, 1914–1915   **BALLPARK:** WEEGHMAN PARK, 1914–1915

RECORD: 173–133 (.565)   **OTHER NAMES:** CHIFEDS

When the Federal League rose from a struggling minor league to challenge the American and National leagues in a head-on war for players and patronage, the challenge was largely the work of one man, James A. Gilmore, minority stockholder in the Chicago Whales. Also-rans in the six-team minor circuit of 1913, the Whales emerged as the most successful franchise in the loop's two-year fling as a major league.

The 1913 version of the FL had franchises in Indianapolis, Cleveland, St. Louis, Pittsburgh, Chicago, and Covington, Kentucky (which moved in midseason to Kansas City). Even before the end of the season, FL owners began to make plans to secure new financial backing, invade more major league cities, secure more suitable stadiums, and raid the established leagues for players. The timidity of FL President John T. Powers was unsuited to this more ambitious agenda, so he was cast aside for Gilmore, a millionaire coal dealer who persuaded Otto Stifel and Philip Ball of St. Louis, Robert B. Ward of Brooklyn, and Charles A. Weeghman of Chicago to buy into the idea of a new major circuit.

Gilmore, who had lost $7,000 to $8,000 backing the Whales, convinced 40-year-old Weeghman, who had made a fortune with a chain of lunch counters, to invest $26,000 in the club, promising him that that would be the full extent of the commitment. Realizing that the investment was far more open-ended, Weeghman recruited William Walker, whose Chicago-based wholesale fish business was the largest in the Midwest; between them, they laid out $412,000 before the Whales played their first game of the 1914 season. A considerable percentage of their money went to build Weeghman Park on Chicago's North Side. The park, a showcase for the FL, entered the NL with the Whales at the end of the 1915 season and was eventually renamed Wrigley Field.

Unlike the AL or the NL, the FL was a group venture whose stock was jointly held by all the backers, each of whom had to put up a $25,000 bond and its ballpark lease as a good faith gesture. Even when it came to recruiting players, the teams cooperated: Of the 264 players to appear for the Feds, 172 had played in the AL or NL and 81 of those either broke major league contracts or ignored the reserve clause in their contracts. The lure, of course, was money. On the field, FL rules mirrored those of the other two leagues. Although there had been discussion of allowing a designated hitter to replace the pitcher in the batting order, this and other innovations were rejected on the naive assumption that the FL would eventually be admitted to organized baseball and that a uniformity of rules would hasten that day.

The second player to join the Feds—and the one whose signing made the biggest splash—was the Cincinnati Reds' Joe Tinker. As part of the Tinker to Evers to Chance pennant-winning Chicago Cubs of the first decade of the century, Tinker's December 1913 defection to the Whales, with whom he signed a $12,000 contract to manage and play shortstop, alerted the established leagues to the intensity of the impending war. Tinker's major catches were center fielder Dutch Zwilling, who contributed a .313 batting average and 15 home runs (good enough to tie for the league lead), and Claude Hendrix, whose 29 victories (against only 11 losses) led the FL and whose 1.69 ERA was second to teammate Adam Johnson's 1.58.

Tinker's recruiting misadventures included catcher Bill Killefer, the most celebrated "flip flop" of the FL war. A five-year veteran, Killefer, who had been with the Phillies in 1913, signed a three-year $17,500 contract with the Whales in January, 1914, after having reached a verbal agreement with Philadelphia. Twelve days later, he signed a Phillies contract for $19,500. FL attorney Edward E. Gates sought a federal court injunction to prevent Killefer from playing for the Phillies on the grounds that the catcher had fulfilled his old contract with the team, that he had signed a valid new one with the Whales, and that his skills were unique and would be impossible to replace. Judge Clarence W. Sessions of the Grand Rapids, Michigan, Federal District Court, while excoriating Killefer as "a person upon whose pledged word little or no reliance can be placed," refused to grant the injunction. Neither Sessions nor the Sixth Circuit Court of Appeals, which upheld his decision, defended the reserve clause, however. In fact, the court pronounced that the reserve clause lacked "the necessary qualities of definiteness, certainty, and mutuality" to be binding.

Even without Killefer, the Whales finished a close second in 1914, 1½ games behind Indianapolis, leading the FL in both ERA (2.44) and homers (51). The Whales also led the FL in attendance, outdrawing the Cubs, who finished third in the NL. Encouraged by this showing, Weeghman redoubled his efforts to increase his share of the Chicago market

and build a winner. Toward the first end, he set up a combination giveaway-raffle at his restaurants: Every patron who bought a meal got a free ticket to see the Whales and the opportunity to win another. In addition, he eliminated noisome vendors from Weeghman Park, replacing them with food stands behind the last row of seats. Toward the second end, he raided the Cubs for George McConnell, who led the FL in victories with a 25–10 record. Left fielder Les Mann, a recruit from the world champion Boston Braves, hit .306. With these additions, the Whales led the FL in homers (50) for a second consecutive year and won the closest pennant race in major league history, beating out St. Louis by one percentage point on the last day of the season.

The race might have been a runaway had the Whales been able to retain Walter Johnson, a 28-game winner with the Washington Senators in 1914. Unable to come to terms with the Senators, the pitcher went home to await a better offer. What he got was a letter from the Senators lowering their original offer and threatening automatic renewal of his contract under the reserve clause. Weeghman sent Tinker to Kansas to see the pitcher. The face-to-face meeting lasted about twenty minutes, after which Tinker had Johnson's name on a contract calling for a $6,000 advance on a three-year contract at $17,500 a year. The same day, Johnson got a letter from Washington manager Clark Griffith telling him that the first letter, written by Senators President Harry Minor, had been a mistake. Griffith and Johnson met in Kansas City where the manager preyed on the righthander's loyalty to the club and his teammates. The only explanation Johnson gave for reneging on his deal with Tinker was that he "did not treat the Federal League right. I bungled it, no doubt."

In 1914, Gilmore, who took over as league president in August, had audaciously suggested that the FL pennant-winning Indianapolis Hoosiers play the winners of the World Series for a putative world championship. When the Whales won the 1915 pennant, Gilmore proposed a three-way round robin World Series among the Whales, the Red Sox, and the Phillies. Failing in that, he encouraged a Chicago championship series involving the Whales, Cubs, and White Sox. Weeghman distributed form letters to the fans to be mailed to the mayor of Chicago importuning him to convince the AL and NL clubs to participate. The Whales had again drawn better than the fourth-place Cubs, but not as well as the third-place White Sox. When neither team responded to the challenge, the FL minted medallions declaring the Whales "Champions of the World."

For Gilmore, both proposed championship series were part of a larger scheme to exact a favorable settlement from organized baseball. Gilmore, who had known as early as July that the Feds were faltering, engineered a grand plan that included a threat to move the Newark Peppers into New York City. The stumbling block was a suit Gilmore and Weeghman had filed on January 5, 1915 in the Federal District Court for Northern Illinois, the domain of Judge Kenesaw Mountain Landis, who almost eight years earlier had fined Standard Oil $29 million for violations of federal antitrust statutes. Relying on the trustbusting reputation Landis had earned in the Standard Oil case, Gilmore and the Feds expected a speedy and favorable decision on their nine-count accusation that organized baseball was a monopoly in restraint of interstate trade. The Feds sought nothing less than the elimination of the reserve clause and, effectively, the free agency of every major and minor league player.

What Gilmore had not counted on was that Landis was not above allowing his personal preferences to dictate his official acts. Anticipating a decision by Landis the judge, they neglected to take into account Landis the baseball fan. In the hearings held in January, Landis asked Gates, representing the FL, "Do you realize that a decision in this case may tear down the very foundations of the game so loved by thousands?" To both sides he issued the admonition that "any blows at the thing called baseball would be regarded by this court as a blow to a national institution." Reluctant to render a decision that on the merits would have had to favor the Feds, Landis simply did nothing for months.

In the meantime, the Feds played the 1915 season. In October, Gilmore and several FL owners attended the World Series to talk about the terms for a settlement. Two months later, Gilmore, invited to attend the NL annual meeting in New York to discuss peace, declined on the spurious grounds that the FL's plans to invade New York were too far along; nevertheless, he and FL backer Harry Sinclair met privately on December 13 with NL president John Tener and several owners and outlined a peace. Joined by AL President Ban Johnson, and a league delegation

on December 17, the three leagues and representatives of the minor leagues met to ratify the deal. The major impediment to the accord was the suit pending for eleven months before Landis. Completely misreading the judge's delaying tactics, the AL and NL negotiators feared that they would be subject to charges of contempt if they went ahead with a settlement before the case was decided; the FL participants feared that they could be accused of joining the very antitrust conspiracy they were attacking in court. Both sides agreed to sound out the judge before proceeding. Relieved of the burden of choosing between his judicial duty and his inclination toward the traditions of the baseball establishment, Landis dismissed the case, clearing the way for the final signing of a treaty on December 22.

The settlement cost organized baseball $600,000 in various buyouts. Weeghman was brought into the fold when he purchased the Cubs for $500,000; the down payment was $100,000 with the NL kicking in half of that amount. Weeghman brought Tinker along as manager and moved his new club into Weeghman Park.

Though the Feds lost upwards of $2.5 million, the venture was hardly the dismal failure that the established major leagues wanted the public to perceive. Weeghman and Ball (who had purchased the St. Louis Browns) had been admitted to the fraternity. Other FL owners received cash awards that compensated them for some of their losses; one or two may even have emerged with a profit. Both sides suffered losses, but the NL was probably the hardest hit and was also the first to broach the subject of a settlement.

The losers were the players, whose salaries fell back to levels more acceptable to the owners and who would never again have a third major league defying the reserve clause and bidding for their services. In 1916, Gilmore summed up his conversion from a vantage point outside baseball: "There is no room for three major leagues. The reserve clause, to which I objected, is vitally important to clean promotion of the sport."

CHICAGO WHALES

Annual Standings and Managers

Year	Position	W	L	Pct.	GB	Managers
1914	Second	87	67	.565	1 ½	Joe Tinker
1915	First	86	66	.566	+.001	Joe Tinker

Cincinnati Reds

National League, 1876–1880   **BALLPARKS:** LINCOLN PARK GROUNDS (1876)
                                                          AVENUE GROUNDS (1876–1879)
RECORD: 125–217 (.365)   BANK STREET GROUNDS (1880)

OTHER NAMES: PORKOPOLITANS

The greatest misfit among the charter members of the National League was the first version of the Cincinnati Reds; or, more accurately, the first *three* versions because, officially, the Reds were three successive franchises. The first of these, a charter member of the NL, lasted until June of 1877; the second existed until September 1879; the third played the 1880 season.

The inclusion of a Cincinnati club in the NL's inaugural season was a virtual necessity, because the city was the home of the fabled, undefeated Red Stockings of 1869–1870, the first all-professional team. Attempting to capitalize on this tradition, owner Josiah Keck, whose meatpacking business gave the team its first nickname, the Porkopolitans, secured as his team's home field Lincoln Park Grounds, where the old Red Stockings had played. Keck also had two players—first baseman-manager Charlie Gould and second baseman Charlie Sweasy—who had played for the legendary Red Stockings. But unlike the Red Stockings, the team Keck assembled was dreadful; it won only 9 of its 65 games and finished last, 42½ games behind pennant winning Chicago. Further, the Reds never fit comfortably into the priggish and rigid NL.

The Reds also floundered financially. Even the introduction of Ladies Day could not prevent the club from losing money as fast as it lost games, a trend that continued into the 1877 season. After only 3 victories in the first 17 games, Keck simply pulled the plug on June 18th and released all his players rather than suffer the losses he expected from the team's first scheduled road trip.

Although New York and Philadelphia had been expelled for an almost identical offense at the end of the 1876 season, the NL couldn't tolerate a vacancy in June—or a seven-team schedule for the rest of the season. A group of eight local businessmen led by J. Wayne Neff scrambled to reassemble a team and continue the schedule, but William Hulbert, president of both the NL and its Chicago franchise, informed them that approval would have to be by unanimous

consent because the franchise had not paid its June dues of $100. Securing that approval took three weeks, a hiatus that caused considerable confusion about Cincinnati's status.

Some newspapers carried league standings with the Reds included; others left the Reds out; still others printed both sets of standings side by side. Apparently, the only one who remained unconfused was Hulbert. His emissary, Lewis Meacham, who often used his official capacity as sports editor of the Chicago *Tribune* to act as apologist for Hulbert, went to Cincinnati and signed the team's second baseman-outfielder Jimmy Hallinan (whom he bailed out of jail after a barroom fight) and slugging outfielder Charley Jones to Chicago contracts. This obvious conflict of interest provoked a storm. Meacham maintained that, because Keck had properly released the players and the new owners had imprudently neglected to sign them to contracts during the interregnum, they were fair game. In the end, Hulbert got to keep Hallinan, but he had to return Jones to the Reds after only two games with Chicago. The legal rationalization for the compromise was that Jones's signing with Chicago was contingent upon the disbanding of the Cincinnati franchise, which may or may not have happened; the actual reason was that the new owners in Cincinnati could not possibly reconstitute the team without its most popular player. The second version of the Reds played its first game on July 3. The club went on to a 12–28 record, good for a sixth-place finish when combined with the record of Keck's team.

The matter of Cincinnati's status was put to rest—at least officially—in December, when the new franchise was expelled from the league and its record for the entire season retroactively disallowed because of the old franchise's nonpayment of its June dues. Then, the next day, the replacement franchise that had played out the season was readmitted as a member in good standing. This charade somehow satisfied everyone's sense of justice.

The first edition of the Reds produced a number of firsts: the first southpaw hurler (change pitcher Bobby Mitchell) in 1878, the first player to wear glasses (pitcher Will White), and the first brother battery (Will and Deacon White)—both in 1877.

For a change, the excitement the Reds generated on the field in 1878 eclipsed the boardroom and backroom fireworks. Led by third baseman-manager Cal McVey, they climbed all the way to second place, four games behind Boston, on the strength of the hitting of their outfield—slugger Jones, veteran Lip Pike, and sophomore King Kelly—and the superlative pitching of Will White (30–21).

Deacon White, Will's brother, became the new manager in 1879 but lasted only sixteen games. In that brief span, he alienated O. P. Caylor, a sportswriter who was often at the center of events in Cincinnati baseball and who wanted to be named the team's official scorer; White brought in his brother-in-law instead. The public consensus was that the Reds needed a catcher, since Kelly and everyone else who tried had trouble handling Will White's pitches; instead, Deacon White signed shortstop Ross Barnes, who had won the first NL batting championship but whose superstar days were behind him. He also released southpaw Bobby Mitchell for no apparent reason, leaving the team with only one pitcher.

Caylor had a field day with these moves, and the clubhouse critics followed his lead. White was fired as manager during the first eastern swing, with McVey taking over. Largely on the strength of Will White's 43 victories and the hitting of Kelly and ex-manager Deacon White, the club finished the season over .500 in fifth place. But while the Reds improved on the diamond, clubhouse difficulties actually worsened under McVey. When Mike Burke, who yielded the shortstop spot to Barnes, was released, he started a fight with McVey on the field. Caylor supported Burke, and the fans, disgusted with the dissension, stayed home.

The fundamental problem was that the team had polarized. The three high-priced stars—Deacon White, Barnes, and McVey, each of whom made $2,000—all wanted to run the team. Many of the other players, each of whom made only $800, resented the stars' attitudes and salaries. As attendance dropped, the club sank deeper into the red. When losses reached $10,000, Neff, who held one-third of

the stock, decided to cut his losses. On September 24, he gave all the players notice that their services would not be required after October 1. The consequences of the near-collapse were grave and long lasting. To prevent the spread of Cincinnati's star system, in which three players made as much money as the rest of the players combined, the NL held a special meeting on September 29 at which it passed the first primitive but effective reserve rule to curb salaries. The vote was unanimous, with Hulbert casting Cincinnati's proxy.

At the regular league meeting on December 4, the Cincinnati club quietly resigned from the league and, equally quietly, the third edition of the Reds, led by Justus Thorner, was admitted in its place. The new ownership cleaned house, keeping only the White brothers and outfielder Blondy Purcell from the 1879 team. The result was a last-place finish.

Mindful of Neff's experience, three successive presidents—Thorner, Nathan Menderson, and W. H. Kennett—risked offending the league's notions of respectability by selling beer and abetting Sunday baseball to increase revenues. The prohibitions were grounded less in moral fervor than in the conviction that drinking attracted rowdies and gamblers who drove away the better elements of society, the only clientele that could assure maximum profits. But Cincinnati, with its large German immigrant population's preference for both beer and Sunday entertainment, disproved the theory. The Reds realized about $1,000 from the rental of its park to non-league teams for Sunday games and showed a profit of about $3,000 from its concession stands.

The Reds were pounded publicly for these lapses, most prominently by the Worcester Spy. Cincinnati's defenders responded by reminding the Spy that larger cities like Cincinnati, with their larger crowds, increased the revenues of franchises in smaller cities like Worcester.

At a special league meeting on October 6, the carping escalated into a power struggle. The other seven clubs agreed that, at their regularly scheduled meeting in December, they would pass rules prohibiting both the sale of spirits in league parks and any use of those parks for Sunday games. President Kennett, representing Cincinnati, refused to sign the pledge. Two days later, the seven passed another resolution threatening termination of Cincinnati's franchise unless it promised to vote for the proposed legislation, then without blinking terminated that franchise for its failure to comply with legislation the league would not enact until two months later.

CINCINNATI REDS

Annual Standings and Managers

Year	Position	W	L	Pct.	GB	Managers
1876	Eighth	9	56	.138	42½	Charlie Gould
1877	Sixth	15	42	.263	25½	Lip Pike, Bob Addy
1878	Second	37	23	.617	4	Cal McVey
1879	Fifth	43	37	.538	14	Deacon White, Cal McVey
1880	Eighth	21	59	.263	44	John Clapp

Cincinnati Reds

American Association,
1882–1889

BALLPARKS: BANK STREET GROUNDS (1882–1883)
LEAGUE PARK (1884–1889)

RECORD: 549–396 (.581)

The Reds—and the American Association itself—were born when O. P. Caylor, sports editor of the Cincinnati *Enquirer,* formed an independent club in 1881 and took it to St. Louis for a weekend series. Caylor, who had been incensed over the National League's expulsion of the Reds in 1880, had already tried twice to establish a new league. Thus, when the exhibitions in St. Louis proved successful, he and Justus Thorner, who had been president of the NL Reds, were ready for a call from Horace B. Phillips of Philadelphia to meet in Pittsburgh with the specific intention of forming a rival to the established league. When no one else—not even Phillips—showed up for the meeting, Caylor and Thorner had a chance encounter with Al Pratt, a former National Association pitcher then working as a Pittsburgh bartender. Pratt referred the two Cincinnatians to H. Denny McKnight, a local businessman who had been president of the International Association Pittsburgh Alleghenys. Together, they concocted a preposterous plot: To each of the clubs that had thought so little of the idea of establishing a new league, they sent a telegram implying that each recipient was the only one who had failed to show up, and inviting them to a second meeting. Amazingly, the ruse succeeded and the AA was formed at a subsequent meeting at the Hotel Gibson in Cincinnati.

The Reds were the sartorial hits of the new league, with each player wearing a different color cap and silk shirt. Manager–catcher Pop Snyder (in scarlet) led the team to the AA's first pennant. Third baseman Hick Carpenter (gray and white) led the hitters with a .342 average. Rookie second baseman Bid McPhee (black and yellow) hit only .228, but his flashy defense was an instant crowd-pleaser. Will White (sky blue) led the AA with 40 victories.

Searching for an excuse to wage war on the new AA, the NL settled on the contracts of two young infielders, Dasher Troy and Sam Wise, who had jumped from the NL Detroit Wolverines. Wise, who had signed with the Reds, turned around and defected back to the Boston NL club. At first, Caylor tried alternately to cajole and threaten Wise; then, the Reds sought an injunction from a Massachusetts court to prevent the shortstop from appearing for Boston and to force his return to Cincinnati. This effort, the first time baseball went to the courts to settle its intramural squabbles, ended in failure for the Reds, who had to be content with the hollow act of expelling Wise.

Relations between the two leagues had thawed

Footnote Player: Backup first baseman Henry Luff was fined $5 in 1882 for being about a century ahead of his time. The penalty was levied by manager Pop Snyder for making a one-handed catch. Luff's reaction was to quit the team.

sufficiently by the end of the season for the Reds to schedule a championship series with the NL pennant-winning Chicago club. The AA had banned all intercourse with its rival, so Cincinnati formally released all its players, then allowed them to sign brief contracts with a dummy organization put together for the sole purpose of playing against the White Stockings. The Reds and White Stockings traded 2–0 shutouts on October 6th and 7th before AA president McKnight put a stop to the contests by threatening the Reds with expulsion for violating league rules. The AA board of directors later exonerated the Reds of any wrongdoing when it studied the potential profit in such postseason championships.

The ensuing peace between the leagues brought prosperity in its wake. Although they slipped to third place in 1883, the Reds showed a profit of $25,000. Then came the Union Association war, which was fought with particular ferocity in Cincinnati, where Thorner, who had left the Reds in 1883 to join the Unions, managed to get the lease on the Bank Street Grounds for the UA Outlaw Reds. Replacing Thorner as the central figure in running the Reds was Aaron Stern, who hastily built a new park three blocks away on the site of an abandoned brickyard, so hastily, in fact, that the grandstand collapsed on opening day, injuring several fans. There were even reports of one death, a story the Outlaw Reds spread with private glee and public gravity.

With Caylor, a vituperative bantam as manager in 1885 and 1886, and Gus Schmelz, with his Teutonic red beard in charge on the field for the final three AA seasons, the Stern regime hit its stride after the UA war. The owner showed himself to be a cross between a shrewd and penny-pinching businessman and a downright cheat. In 1887, Stern gleefully accepted $1,000 for the scorecard concession at League Park. He also accepted $100 and free telegraphic service for the sale of baseball scores to Western Union, even though it was clear that the company sold the scores to professional gamblers. A year later, he sold Western Union exclusive wire rights to Reds games for an unspecified amount. For $75 he sold the right to sell cushions in the grandstand. To club treasurer Louis Hauck he wrote in preparation for the 1887 season: "I shall now commence to figure our expenses as low as they can possibly be made and I shall spend as little money as possible in running the Cincinnati club." To accomplish this he cut off all free tickets and put players—in uniform—at the turnstiles to save on ticket takers' salaries.

Stern's greatest scam was directed at other clubs. One game of the 1887 world championship series between the NL Detroit Wolverines and the AA St. Louis Browns was played in Cincinnati, with Stern contracted to get 20 percent of the gate. Injudiciously, he wrote out his instructions to Hauck on how to maximize that profit, telling the treasurer to claim that the turnstiles were broken and simply to tell St. Louis and Detroit how many tickets had been sold. He specified that the tickets sold at Hawley's, a downtown store, were to be excluded from the count; "I want to make all I can," he wrote.

Not content with petty pilfering, Stern attempted to capitalize on his second-place finish after Detroit won the series with the Browns, claiming that as the only AA team to beat the Browns in their season series, the Reds were entitled to a one-game playoff with the champions. Detroit turned him down.

Two years later, the Reds were out of the AA—and in the NL. The immediate cause of Stern's walkout was a deadlock over the election of a new president of the association. With the vote hopelessly tied 4–4, the Reds—along with Brooklyn—dealt the AA a major blow by exercising their right to resign from the league and were immediately accepted into the NL.

Second baseman Bid McPhee played all eight seasons with the Reds in the American Association without using a glove. He did not adopt the new fashion until well into the 1890s, after he had moved with the club to the National League. Amazingly, he made more putouts than any other second baseman in history, and ranks fourth in assists on the all-time list.

CINCINNATI REDS

Annual Standings and Managers

Year	Position	W	L	Pct.	GB	Managers
1882	First	55	25	.688	+11½	Pop Snyder
1883	Third	61	37	.622	5	Pop Snyder
1884	Fifth	68	41	.624	8	Will White, Pop Snyder

1885	Second	63	49	.563	16	O. P. Caylor
1886	Fifth	65	73	.471	27½	O. P. Caylor
1887	Second	81	54	.600	14	Gus Schmelz
1888	Fourth	80	54	.597	11½	Gus Schmelz
1889	Fourth	76	63	.547	18	Gus Schmelz

Cincinnati Outlaw Reds

Union Association, 1884   **BALLPARK:** BANK STREET GROUNDS

RECORD: 69–36 (.657)

When the Union Association changed its policy of respecting existing National League and American Association contracts on July 1, 1884, the door was opened for a midseason round of raids on the existing leagues. The primary beneficiary of the more aggressive stance was the Outlaw Reds, who turned a mediocre club into a contender with one dramatic stroke.

The Outlaw Reds had never been innocents. To open the season, they recruited first baseman Martin Powell and pitcher Dick Burns (from the NL Detroit Wolverines), pitcher George Washington Bradley (from the AA Philadelphia Athletics), center fielder Bill Harbidge and catcher John Kelley (from the NL Philadelphia Phillies), second baseman Sam Crane (from the AA New York Mets), shortstop Jack Jones (from the AA Louisville Eclipse), and shortstop Frank McLaughlin (from the AA Pittsburgh Alleghenys). Not content with pirating players, the team also gained control of the AA Reds park, Bank Street Grounds. The franchise's primary backer was Justus Thorner, a past president of Cincinnati clubs in both the NL and the AA. The AA club ended up playing only three blocks away, so the competition for fans became ferocious. Tickets were sold on street cars to the parks; hawkers for each club filled the streets;

fans on the way to one park were shanghaied to the other.

Not only was the battle for patronage rowdy, the Outlaw Reds themselves raised more than a little hell. Thorner tried to impose discipline: After 35 games, he fired outfielder-manager Dan O'Leary, whose idea of discipline was to take his players out drinking and to bet on his team's games. Thorner also expelled McLaughlin for a drunken tear after a sweep by Boston.

In August, the owner pulled his master stroke. The NL had raided the Unions, so Thorner felt it justifiable to "take what players we can get." The players he could get were pitcher Jim McCormick, shortstop Jack Glasscock, and catcher Fatty Briody of the NL Cleveland Blues. Glasscock said he had "played long enough for glory," and Briody succinctly called the deal "a matter of dollars and cents." Briody hit .337 in 22 games, Glasscock an eyebrow-raising .419 in 38 games; McCormick won 21 and lost only 3, making him, along with Bradley and Burns, one of the Outlaw Reds' three 20-game winners. Nevertheless, the Outlaw Reds fell short of the pennant by 21 games and lost $15,000. Thorner expressed an interest in entering the American Association, but got nowhere. The club neglected even to send a representative to the final UA meeting in January 1885.

CINCINNATI OUTLAW REDS

Annual Standings and Managers

Year	Position	W	L	Pct.	GB	Managers
1884	Second	69	36	.657	21	Dan O'Leary, Sam Crane

Cincinnati Reds

National League, 1890–Present	**BALLPARKS:** CROSLEY FIELD (1890–1970) RIVERFRONT STADIUM (1970–Present)
RECORD: 7970–7768 (.506)	**OTHER NAMES:** RED STOCKINGS, REDLEGS

Nephews of baseball's first professional team, the Reds have contributed a number of their own firsts to the major leagues, especially during the Larry MacPhail era of the 1930s. Prior to the Big Red Machine clubs of the 1970s, however, the franchise was one of the senior league's most lackluster outfits, winning only four pennants in eighty years. The organization has also been associated with an inordinate number of suicides and gambling scandals.

The Reds joined the National League in 1890, when Aaron Stern, owner of Cincinnati's franchise in the American Association, jumped to the league, along with Brooklyn, in protest over an effort by St. Louis president Chris Von der Ahe to install a puppet AA president. Among the players Stern brought with him were pitcher Tony Mullane and second baseman Bid McPhee. Under Tom Loftus, the club finished a decent fourth with a record that in other years might have been sufficient to win a pennant. It

was a fate that was to befall the Reds several other times during the 1890s, with even a couple of .600-plus records boosting them no higher than third. Except for the first half of the split season of 1892, the team never even managed to finish within ten games of first place until the pennant season of 1919.

Stern did not linger for so much frustration. At the end of the club's first season, he sold out for some $40,000 to a group of Players League backers. But the deal turned out to be a pig in a poke for the new owners when the NL simply chartered a totally new Cincinnati franchise and gave it to clothing merchant John T. Brush as a reward for shuttering his small-market Indianapolis team after the 1889 season. Brush immediately declared that he liked what he had seen the previous season, and kept Loftus and practically the entire 1890 squad. This perspective lasted no longer than a few weeks into the new season, when several players became more noted locally

Pete Rose acknowledges the Riverfront Stadium crowd after singling off San Diego's Eric Show on September 11, 1985, for his record-breaking 4,192nd hit. *Courtesy of the Cincinnati Reds*

for their drinking sprees than for their diamond achievements and Loftus began issuing fines and suspensions with dreary regularity. To make a difficult situation worse, Brush purchased the contract of aging star Pete Browning, who joined the all-night tooters. By the end of the year, a totally demoralized club found itself in seventh place and Loftus found himself out of a job. Brush's only consolation for the year was that the Reds had beaten off an attendance challenge from King Kelly's AA Cincinnati Porkers; the Porkers were forced to move to Milwaukee in August.

The club made two key moves prior to the 1892 season—signing Charlie Comiskey as manager and bringing in Frank Bancroft as business manager. At the end of a solid if not brilliant playing career, Comiskey was a cold shower on the cutup Reds and had carte blanche from Brush to get rid of players that he didn't want. During his playing days, the first baseman was also credited with being the first to play off the bag (rather than directly on it) to cut down grounders into right field; by importing this defensive tactic, Comiskey tightened up the Reds' infield considerably, to the point that both he and second baseman McPhee led the NL in double plays. A tireless promoter who helped develop baseball in several foreign countries, Bancroft brought his talents to Cincinnati to keep fans interested even while the team was floundering on the field. Among his most lasting contributions to the organization was persuading the league that opening days should be ballyhooed as semi-holidays and that Cincinnati, as the home of the first professional club, should have the privilege of inaugurating every season.

For all his no-nonsense approach and tactical ingenuity, Comiskey could do little during his tenure but keep the team near the .500 mark most of the time. Ultimately, his reign was more memorable for a couple of games and a couple of individuals than for winning baseball. The first of the noteworthy games took place on May 6, 1892, when a scoreless 14-inning contest against Boston at League Park (Crosley Field in its first incarnation) had to be suspended because of the glare of the sun in batters' eyes. Because of that episode, all ballparks subsequently had to be laid out so that hitters ended up standing in the shadows of the West and right fielders in the glare of the East. (Since this meant that pitchers stood with their left arms to the South, lefthanders soon became known as southpaws.) Another footnote to baseball history was written on October 15, 1892, when, on the last day of the season, one Bumpus Jones walked into the Cincinnati club-

house and told Comiskey that he could outpitch anybody on the staff. Having nothing to lose in the finale, Comiskey sent Jones out to the hill, where the twenty-two-year-old righthander became the only hurler in baseball history to throw a no-hitter in his big league debut. Invited back for spring training in 1893, Jones ended up with only one more major league victory.

Among the players Comiskey had inherited from Loftus was Arlie Latham, a third baseman who grew so progressively lazy at going after grounders that, well into the twentieth century, "doing a Latham" was big league parlance for waving futilely at a passing groundball. Another member of Comiskey's 1894 team was Dummy Hoy, the deaf outfielder widely believed to be the reason umpires began confirming their vocal calls with arm and hand signals. During his stay in Cincinnati, Comiskey also spent a lot of time mediating between Brush and *Commercial-Gazette* sportswriter Ban Johnson, who rarely let a day go by without roasting the Reds' owner for one perceived fault or another. But when Johnson heard of a vacancy in the presidency of the minor Western League, he didn't hesitate to have Comiskey ask Brush to use his influence to get him the job. Although he detested Johnson as much as Johnson detested him, Brush did exactly that, telling associates that it was a good way of stopping the daily *Commercial-Gazette* attacks on him. The Western League soon served as the launching pad for Johnson's rival American League. Suggestions that Comiskey had manipulated Brush into recommending Johnson for some ulterior motive gained credibility after the 1894 season, when the manager resigned from the Reds to buy the St. Paul franchise in the Western League and position himself to march into the AL with his sportswriter friend.

Named to replace Comiskey was Buck Ewing, the catcher who had introduced squatting into his profession in 1880. Regarded by many as the best all-around player of the nineteenth century, Ewing also made something of a mark as a pilot, becoming the only Cincinnati manager with at least five years service never to preside over a losing season. Still, as in the case of Comiskey, this was largely a consolation prize for a club that was never able to mesh its pitching, offense, and defense.

Matters only got worse in 1900, when Brush decided that one of the club's problems was Ewing's uninspired leadership, and replaced him with Bob Allen. With only first baseman Jake Beckley doing any hitting (.341 with 94 RBIs) and nobody doing any memorable pitching, Allen's Reds dipped below

.500 for the first time since Comiskey's departure. To put a cap on the season, the League Park grandstand burned down in late May, making it necessary for fans to accept temporary seating for the rest of the year. Following the 1901 season, another big blaze forced a total overhaul of the park and its fanciful renaissance as the Palace of the Fans. The principal features of the redone facility were grandstand columns and pillars copied from the 1892 Chicago World's Fair and so-called "rooters' rows" along the first and third base lines where beer was served by the glass, twelve for a dollar. With the suds flowing so freely and the fans separated from the field only by a wire screen, both Cincinnati and visiting players came to dread the rooters' rows and wasted few tears when these areas too were destroyed by fire following the 1911 season.

Although it managed to rise as high as third only once in the period, the team paraded several well-known baseball names through the manager's job in the first decade of the twentieth century. Succeeding Allen was the popular McPhee, who played his entire eighteen years in the majors on Cincinnati clubs. Little more than a year after taking the job, McPhee decided that there were too many headaches (and grandstand boos) in being a manager, and so he quit. After an interregnum of Bancroft, future Hall of Famer Joe Kelley jumped to the Reds from the AL franchise in Baltimore, not only giving Cincinnati a new outfielder-manager, but giving Brush some satisfaction in his decade-old enmity toward league president Johnson. In 1906, it was the turn of another old Baltimore Oriole, Ned Hanlon, who stuck around just long enough to lead the club to two sixth-place finishes before concluding that he didn't know how to deal with losers. After a year with John Ganzel at the helm, the decade ended with the Hall of Fame righthander Clark Griffith assuming field command.

Brush was not around for most of the changes, although generations of Cincinnati fans would come to regret that he didn't leave sooner than he did. The problem was righthander Christy Mathewson, the main piece of what was arguably the worst trade in

major league history. In 1900, the Giants purchased Mathewson conditionally from a Norfolk, Virginia minor league team to see if he was worth the $1,500 being solicited for his services. When Mathewson lost three games, he was immediately sent back south and the deal canceled. At the end of the season, Brush put up the then-going draft price of $100 for the pitcher, but then turned right around to deal him to New York for aging Amos Rusie. The most benevolent interpretation of the trade has been that Brush was on the verge of selling out in Cincinnati and taking over the Giants and wanted to have the future Hall of Famer waiting for him in New York. The bottom line, however, was that the Giants saved themselves $1,500, Norfolk lost $1,400, Rusie didn't win any games for the Reds, and Mathewson went on to compile 373 victories (tied with Grover Cleveland Alexander for the most in NL history).

It was in August 1902 that Brush finally did step down, selling the franchise to as motley a crew as has ever sat on the board of directors of a baseball team. The main parties were Cincinnati mayor Julius Fleischmann; Fleischmann's brother Max, who ran the family's yeast company; George Cox, a political boss who had few equals in his reputation as a corrupt thug; and August (Garry) Herrmann, chairman of the municipal waterworks board. The transaction was finalized when Cox threatened to build a new city street through the Palace of the Fans if an agreement wasn't reached.

Herrmann was named president and chief of baseball operations. Even for a business renowned for its outsized personages, the new Cincinnati boss seemed like a character out of *Dick Tracy*. Called a "walking delicatessen" by some, he seldom ventured anywhere without an ample supply of sausages that he would munch on whenever the opportunity presented itself. On more than one occasion, he bolted from a public function because of some mixup that had left sausages unavailable. When he wasn't proclaiming his addiction to meat, Herrmann was boasting of his beer-drinking prowess. In case anybody missed his bluster in bars, taverns, and hotel dining rooms, he could be recognized as the portly gentleman with a taste in checked suits and big diamond rings. Even his name Garry came to him expansively—it stood for Garibaldi, and had been given to him arbitrarily by an employer who wanted to think of all his charges as great European historical figures.

For all his personal extravagance, Herrmann was regarded as a reliable (or pliable) enough baseball executive to be entrusted with the swing vote on the three-man National Commission that presided

Frank Bancroft's 16-game tenure with the Reds in 1902 was his seventh managerial assignment, a major league record; previously he had led Worcester, Detroit, Cleveland, Providence, and Indianapolis in the National League and Philadelphia in the American Association.

over the game until 1920, when Kenesaw Mountain Landis was elected the first commissioner. In this role, Herrmann broke deadlocks between the presidents of the National and American leagues to issue edicts that had a binding effect not only on the major leagues, but on minor league clubs as well. In one incident that went right to the stomach of Herrmann's concerns, he cast a vote compelling the owner of a San Francisco team to pay $2,500 for second baseman Eddie Colligan even though the infielder had been in a hospital with a broken leg at the time of the purchase. When the San Francisco owner, J. Cal Ewing, protested the decision, Herrmann replied that Ewing should have informed himself of Colligan's condition before paying money for him. Shortly afterward, Herrmann received five barrels of sauerkraut COD from Ewing, only to fork some into his mouth and discover it was rancid. When Herrmann protested to Ewing, the San Francisco owner replied that Herrmann should have informed himself of the sauerkraut's condition before paying money for it.

The Reds had some hitting at the beginning of the twentieth century, though not as much as it might have counted on. The most severe blow was the loss of outfielder Sam Crawford to the Tigers in 1903 following a settlement of the war between the National and American leagues. It was in fact Herrmann's decision not to sue over Crawford's announced defection to Detroit that paved the way for the general agreement between the leagues. While in Cincinnati, the outfielder had led the league in homers in 1901, in triples in 1902, and had contributed three .300 averages in four seasons. Before being sold to the Cardinals after the 1903 season, Beckley also remained a consistent .300 hitter. A third offensive threat was outfielder Cy Seymour, who batted .342, .313, and a league-leading .377 before Herrmann decided that his slow start in 1906 was a good occasion to deal him to the Giants for another lump of money. One of the more curious achievements of the period was outfielder Fred Odwell's league-leading total of nine homers in 1905; Odwell hit only one more round-tripper in his four-year career.

Like Comiskey, Clark Griffith came to Cincinnati with a long view that didn't include the Reds. Even before being appointed manager for the 1909 season, he had made it clear to Herrmann that he would have never taken the job if a similar opening had been available with Washington in the AL. Throughout his three-year tenure, he never dropped his eyes from events over in the junior circuit, especially those having to do with the Washington fran-

chise he would eventually take over. Not surprisingly, Griffith's Cincinnati teams were not much better than their predecessors. On the other hand, the 1911 squad provided the manager with a mental note for future use on the potential of Latin players, when Cubans Armando Marsans and Rafael Almeida were purchased on the recommendation of Bancroft. Both players were subject to endless racial taunts around the league, not least in their home park from drunken fans.

Perhaps the most influential game played at the Palace of the Fans during Griffith's three-year term did not involve the Reds at all, but Elks teams from Cincinnati and nearby Newport, Kentucky. On June 19, 1909, Herrmann gave his okay to inventor George Cahill to install five temporary towers of light batteries in the facility for the first experimental night game. Although flies and popups above the range of the lights created problems for the fielders, Herrmann went on record as predicting the inevitability of night baseball.

The 1912 season brought still another overhaul to the ballpark on McLean and Western avenues, again necessitated by a fire the previous fall. Reopened as Redland Field, the steel-and-concrete structure did away with the ornate pillars and rowdy rooters' rows in favor of a simple grandstand that could seat almost 25,000 and provide room for a few thousand more standees. Along with an all-but-new facility came a new manager, former umpire Hank O'Day. O'Day's chief cachet as Cincinnati pilot was his former career as an arbiter: When the team got off to a good start, several rival managers began grousing that umpires were giving Cincinnati the benefit of close calls because of solidarity with their ex-colleague. The charges died out as soon as the Reds fell back to their familiar standing somewhere between the middle and tail end of the pack. Even when he had been winning, however, O'Day did not have much job security; as in the case of Ganzel in 1908 with Griffith hovering in the wings, Herrmann had never disguised his disappointment at not having been able to get Joe Tinker to manage the club in 1912—or his intention to keep pursuing the Cubs shortstop for the job. In December 1912, Herrmann achieved his quest, and ended up wishing he hadn't.

To obtain Tinker, the Reds completed an eight-player exchange with the Cubs that stood as the biggest trade in franchise history until 1971, at least for the number of bodies involved. But no sooner had the infielder taken over as player-manager than he began to echo the laments of Hanlon that he wasn't accustomed to associating with losers. After Herrmann vetoed a couple of trade suggestions, Tinker turned his tongue on the team president, charging that the executive was more interested in saving money for his extravagant parties than in buying players who would make the team a winner. When the feud hit the newspapers, the general reaction among Cincinnati fans who had suffered through years of mediocre play was to support Tinker.

Tinker's sense of vindication lasted only until he discovered that Herrmann and the Fleischmanns had created a new post on the team for somebody whose sole function would be to go on road trips and report on the activities of the pilot and players. When the organization refused Tinker's demand to drop the spy idea, he declined to sign a contract for the new year. A few days later, Herrmann sold his shortstop-manager to the Dodgers and obtained Buck Herzog from the Giants as the new skipper. Tinker ended up jumping to the Federal League rather than report to Brooklyn. The spy, Harry Stevens, undertook his assignment the following year. At one point in the season, Herrmann ordered him to Baltimore to make recommendations on two players that the minor league franchise owed the Reds. Stevens, who had absolutely no scouting credentials, endorsed the purchase of shortstop Claude Derrick, who played exactly two games for Cincinnati, and outfielder George Twombly, who batted .211 in a 150-game career. On the other hand, the special assignment scout recommended against the acquisition of Baltimore pitchers Ernie Shore and Babe Ruth.

Although the Reds lost relatively few players during the Federal League raids, Herrmann bitterly resented the loss of each one. The defections helped make the 1914 version of the Reds the worst to date with its 94 losses; Herzog became so frantic in his search for a winning formula that none of the club's outfielders logged 100 games. But then, with the dissolution of the FL after 1915, Cincinnati joined other NL and AL clubs in picking up the best of the jobless. Among those signing on with the Reds was Hal Chase, probably the best defensive first baseman in the game until the 1980s and a solid hitter; unfortunately, Chase also had credentials as possibly the most corrupt player in major league history. His stay with the Reds, which was to last through the 1918 season, followed significant stints with both the Yankees and White Sox during which he was regularly accused of betting on his team, betting against his team, and throwing games.

In Cincinnati, Chase began still another chapter of scandal by first establishing his bonafides as the best player on the team: In his very first at bat, he inherited a two-strike count from a batter thrown out of the game for protesting an umpire's call, cracked the first pitch he saw in the NL for a double, stole third on the next delivery, and, after a walk, stole home as part of a double steal. He then went on to lead the league in batting and, for a couple of years, encourage indications that he had reformed.

With only Chase doing any conspicuous hitting and the club mired near the bottom of the standings again, it was only a matter of time before Herrmann pulled the plug on Herzog. When he did, in mid-July, it was with the flair of the so-called Hall of Fame Trade—Herzog and outfielder Wade Killefer going to the Giants in return for future Cooperstown residents Christy Mathewson, Edd Roush, and Bill McKechnie.

The trade was not without its snaggles. To begin with, the initial press reports that had Herzog returning to New York also named Chase as the new manager, prompting fans in Cincinnati to cheer the first baseman's every move during a couple of games in which catcher Ivy Wingo was actually calling the shots. Second, Chase himself took to his new People's Choice reception and wasn't too happy when he discovered that the Reds were going to put Mathewson in the manager's chair. Third, Mathewson immediately dashed any hopes that he would also bolster the team's sagging starting rotation by announcing his retirement as a player. (He ended up returning for one game in September—a 10–8 slugfest in which he barely prevailed over Chicago's Mordecai Brown.) As it turned out, the steal of the deal for the Reds was outfielder Roush, who went on to build an eighteen-year Hall of Fame career with a .323 batting average. A lefthanded slap hitter and one of the best defensive center fielders of his era, Roush won two batting titles for Cincinnati (including in his debut year of 1917) and had a remarkable ten-year skein in which he never hit below .321 (the highest minimum for so long by all NL players except Honus Wagner). To the consternation of Herrmann, the only thing that Roush did as consistently as hit was to hold out at the beginning of a season—almost always skipping spring training while he waited for the organization to appreciate his worth. Roush was elected to Cooperstown in 1962.

Mathewson spent most of the remainder of 1916 and all of the following year trying to put together a pitching staff. His efforts appeared to pay off in 1917, when he got the club over .500 for the first time in eight years, largely on the arms of Pete Schneider (20 wins, 1.98 ERA) and Fred Toney (24 wins, 2.20 ERA). Toney was also the protagonist of one of baseball's most memorable games when, on May 2 in Chicago, he locked up with Hippo Vaughn in a double no-hitter through nine innings, emerging as the winner when the Reds scratched out a run with two hits and an error in the top of the 10th.

The Reds had an even better record in 1918 than in 1917, but their success was overshadowed by new travails precipitated by Chase. The trouble began in July when Mathewson became suspicious of the frequency with which the usually sure-handed first baseman was making wild throws on plays in which a pitcher had to cover first. Together with a lot of unusual whispering between Chase and second baseman Lee Magee (NL leader in errors for his position), Mathewson decided that the errant tosses were a sign that his first baseman was back to his old tricks, and had little trouble persuading Herrmann to suspend him for the remainder of the year. The team waited until the season was over, then brought formal charges of throwing games against Chase. NL President John Heydler held a hearing on January 30, 1919, at which he heard testimony from Herrmann, several Cincinnati pitchers, New York manager John McGraw (the Giants were involved in one of the games allegedly thrown), and a couple of sportswriters. On the other hand, Heydler did not hear directly from Mathewson, who had in the meantime accepted an officer's commission in the US Army's Chemical Warfare Division and was in Europe. Without the chief accuser on the scene, and with records indicating that Chase had hit a homer to win one of the contests he had reputedly tried to fix, Heydler ruled against the Reds.

But the story didn't end there. McGraw, who had laced his testimony with praise for Chase's natural abilities, announced in the wake of the hearing that the Giants would be interested in obtaining the first baseman, and Herrmann wasted little time in delivering him to New York in exchange for catcher Bill Rariden. For the first two months of the 1919 season, Chase performed up to expectations; but as the year wore on, McGraw began to have the same suspicions as Mathewson had had, especially with regard to games pitting New York against the surprisingly contending Reds. Finally, in August, Heydler disclosed that he had never completely closed his investigation into the original Cincinnati charges and had come up with evidence (several canceled checks) that confirmed Mathewson's accusations that Chase had been betting against Cincinnati while a member of the team. That alone was sufficient for getting the man known as Prince Hal suspended for life, but it subsequently emerged that both Chase

and Giants' third baseman Heinie Zimmerman had also approached several of their teammates to throw games against the Reds. Zimmerman joined Chase in permanent exile.

Despite the emergence of Roush and the steady play of Heinie Groh at third, the Reds entered the 1919 season in a state close to a shambles. On top of the fallout over the Chase hearings, Herrmann revealed before the start of the year that he had given up trying to reach Mathewson, who was still somewhere in Europe with the army, and had decided to install Pat Moran as manager. Although Moran had directed an unexceptional Philadelphia team to the pennant in 1915, he was no Mathewson where Cincinnati fans were concerned, and his arrival was generally viewed as killing time until Mathewson returned to resume his rebuilding, especially of the pitching staff. The nearest thing to a reliable starter was Hod Eller, a "shine ball" artist whose specialty of smoothing down one side of the ball with a foreign substance was rumored to be on the verge of being outlawed. (It was banned, but not until after the season.) As it turned out, however, it was Moran who drove the Reds to the top even more unexpectedly than he had the Phillies, giving the franchise its first NL flag.

The ingredients for the club's best showing since coming into the league were several, starting with another batting title from Roush and Groh's defensive primacy at third and pesky .310 average. Southpaw Slim Sallee, considered just about washed up at thirty-four when he was obtained from the Giants on waivers before the start of the season, had a career year with a 21–7 record. Another waiver pickup (from the Yankees) Ray Fisher won 14, lefty Dutch Ruether 19, and anchor man Eller 20. If there was a turning point in the season, it came in the middle of August when the Reds traveled to the Polo Grounds for three consecutive doubleheaders against the second-place Giants and came out with four victories. Feelings for the series ran so high that Herrmann, increasingly obsessed by the prospect of a franchise pennant after so many years, ordered the players to pack their own bottled water lest they be poisoned in New York. The final standings showed Cincinnati finishing nine games ahead of McGraw's club.

The prize for the Reds' first NL flag was the notorious World Series identified with the Black Sox of Chicago. Although volumes would be written about the scandal that ended the careers of eight White Sox players for allegedly accepting or knowing about payoffs to throw the postseason games to

Cincinnati, suspicions subsequently emerged that a few of the Reds had also been open to bribes from gamblers. Roush, for one, went on record as saying that he had such misgivings about the effort of some of his teammates in the opening game that he complained to Moran. The manager then called in Eller, who confirmed that he had had to threaten a couple of gamblers who had approached him. No Cincinnati player was named in the criminal investigation conducted a year later into the Series, although the involvement of former Red Chase as a middleman between two gambling factions kept speculation alive about his ex-teammates.

By the accounting of some of the principals, only the opening game of the best-of-nine series was actually given away, with White Sox ace Ed Cicotte taking a deliberate 9–1 bashing. The incriminated players did not receive all the money due them, one story goes, so they then resolved to play seriously. However that might be, the underdog Reds took the Series in eight games, getting back-to-back shutouts in the fourth and fifth games from Jimmy Ring and Eller. Eller was the overall mound star with two complete-game victories and 15 strikeouts in 18 innings. The offense was led by the Cincinnati outfield: Greasy Neale, who had 10 hits and a .357 average; Pat Duncan, who drove in 8 runs; and Roush, who made the most of a mere 6 hits by scoring 6 runs and driving in 7.

The Reds did not return to the World Series for twenty years. In between were periods of respectable contenders (the first half of the 1920s), also-rans (the late 1920s), and abysmal losers (a good part of the 1930s). Barely a year after the team had been celebrating its first world championship, Moran was back at the task of trying to assemble a pitching staff. Most of the onus for the decade fell on Dolf Luque and, especially, Eppa Rixey and Pete Donahue—all of whom won 20 games in 1923. Picked up from the Phillies in a 1920 trade, Rixey managed three 20-win seasons for a club that grew progressively more anemic in hitting. Often picked out as being among the players least deserving of election to the Hall of Fame (he entered in 1963) for his career mark of 266–251, the lefthander helped define hard-luck pitching over his twenty-one-year career. He also held the record for most victories by an NL lefthander before the arrival of Warren Spahn. Between 1922 and 1926, the righthander Donahue won a minimum of 16 games every season, breaking into the 20-win column three times.

Aside from Roush, the team's biggest offensive threat through most of the decade was catcher Bubbles Hargrave, who ended up with a career average of .310 for twelve big league seasons. By 1926, Hargrave became the first full-time receiver to win a batting title.

Well into 1923, the franchise was still being dogged by its association with the Black Sox scandal. Herrmann himself was partly responsible for keeping that specter visible when he challenged an NL ban on pitcher Rube Benton. Benton had stirred a hornet's nest in the summer of 1920 when he accused former Cincinnati manager Buck Herzog of having asked him to throw a game to the Reds in 1919 in the heat of the pennant race against the Giants; the pitcher had been with New York at the time. With the investigation into the Black Sox underway, Herzog gained a few paragraphs of newsprint by countering with the charge that Benton had made $1,500 off the World Series through his knowledge of the payoffs; to back up his allegation, he got NL players Tony Boeckel and Art Wilson to sign affidavits swearing that Benton had boasted to them of his winnings on the Reds. Summoned before the grand jury looking into the World Series, Benton acknowledged that he had made money off the Chicago loss, but that it was only $20 and that it was based on nothing more than general rumors about a fix. Once he was off the stand on that matter, he reiterated his allegations against Herzog, saying that the former Cincinnati skipper had approached him in a Chicago bar and that a bartender would back up his story. Although NL President Heydler made it clear that he just wanted Benton to go away, he was forced to action by the increased public attention to the Black Sox investigation. Heydler ended up going to Chicago with Benton to search out the bartender, but once in the Windy City, the pitcher said he was disoriented by the conversion in the meantime of bars to speakeasies and couldn't remember in which saloon the conversation with Herzog had supposedly taken place. The infuriated Heydler then passed the word that Benton would not be welcomed on any 1922 NL roster.

At the start of the 1923 season, however, Herrmann and Moran agreed that the lefty's performance during a year in exile in the American Association indicated that he could still pitch, and asked Heydler to approve his reinstatement. Heydler insisted that the hurler's well-known penchant for strong drinks and fast race horses were reason enough to brand him as "morally undesirable," arguing that Commissioner Landis agreed with him. With half the league dedicated to strong drinks and race horses, Herrmann deduced that Heydler had lost his objectivity and went over his head to Landis. The commissioner not only reinstated Benton, but took the opportunity to blast the officials, players, and newspapers that had disparaged his character without evidence.

Benton did not receive the warmest reception ever accorded a new Cincinnati player. Not only was he a reminder of the blot that would always be attached to the Reds' World Series victory, but his charges against Herzog raised the even grimmer notion that the team hadn't even won the pennant fairly. Then, in August, there was still another reason for fans to talk about the hold of gamblers on big league baseball, and in particular on games involving the Reds. Following a five-game massacre by the Giants that effectively squelched Cincinnati's pennant chances, a sheet called *Collyer's Eye* charged that outfielder Duncan and second baseman Sammy Bohne had been contacted by gamblers before the series against New York. Duncan and Bohne denied the allegations before Heydler, then filed separate $50,000 suits against the periodical; the two cases were settled out of court for unspecified amounts.

Herrmann had other problems in the 1920s. In 1923, he scheduled an exhibition game in Allentown, Pennsylvania, then was forced to call it off at the last minute when bad weather played havoc with the Reds' traveling plans. Unfortunately, nobody had bothered to announce the cancellation to an estimated 4,000 Allentown residents who converged on the local ballfield, learned that the Reds would not be coming, and staged a riot during which hundreds of dollars were stolen from the stadium box office. Herrmann refused to indemnify the owners of the Allentown team, asserting that the chaos was their fault for not having provided rainchecks. In 1924, Moran showed up for spring training in such a debilitated state after a winter of hard drinking that he was immediately moved to an Orlando hospital where he died several days later; the official cause of death was listed as Bright's disease. After a decent but hardly glorious season under new pilot Jack Hendricks, the club was dealt another blow when Jake Daubert, who had held down the first base job since 1919 and who had been named captain earlier in the year, died after a complex operation for gallstones and appendicitis. Then, following a frustrating 1926 season when the team had come within a breath of overtaking the pennant-winning Cardinals, Herrmann decided that the time had come to unload Roush, and the outfielder was dealt to the Giants for first baseman George Kelly. Although there was some outcry in Cincinnati over the loss of the club's best player, Herrmann had chosen the most propi-

tious moment possible for the move because Roush remained under lingering criticism for making an unlikely error in a late September game against the Braves that put Cincinnati's flag chances in the grave for good.

Mainly because of a growing hearing problem that he admitted had taken much of the joy out of the game for him, Herrmann stepped down as president in October 1927. Named as his successor was C. J. McDiarmid, an attorney who had been serving as organization secretary. During what turned out to be a relatively brief tenure, McDiarmid distinguished himself only for lacking his predecessor's patience with holdout players: Whereas Herrmann had put up with Roush's annual strikes and similar actions by Heinie Groh, Hughie Critz, and others, the new president simply peddled away contract balkers.

By the end of the 1920s, the single biggest shareholder in the team was Kentucky pharmacist Lou Widrig, who fell just short of exercising control over the organization. During the 1929 season, Widrig was approached by millionaire auto dealer and real estate operator Sidney Weil to sell out his interest. The pharmacist quoted a price that he knew would be too steep for Weil, then forgot about the tender. It was a mistake: Within a couple of weeks, the aggressive Weil had taken advantage of Widrig's unpopularity with other shareholders and, with the help of some extravagant buying offers, negotiated himself into control of the club. The new owner accepted McDiarmid's resignation and installed himself as president. To replace Hendricks, who quit after the 1929 season, he appointed Dan Howley.

After a long drought in player transactions on a major league level, the Reds under Weil declared themselves ready to deal. Not having a farm system like the Cardinals or a surplus of big-league talent like the Giants, however, the intentions produced very little for a couple of years but the purchases of aging AL outfielders Harry Heilmann and Bob Meusel and a waiver pickup of shortstop Leo Durocher from the Yankees. It was not until spring training in 1932 that Weil completed a swap that would help remake the franchise—the acquisition of catcher Ernie Lombardi, outfielder Babe Herman, and third baseman Wally Gilbert from the Dodgers in return for infielders Tony Cuccinello and Joe Stripp and catcher Clyde Sukeforth. A year after that, Durocher and two second-line pitchers were sent to St. Louis for hurlers Paul Derringer and Allyn Stout and second baseman Sparky Adams. Lombardi would end up in the Hall of Fame, while Derringer would post four 20-win seasons for the Reds.

Before Lombardi and Derringer helped Cincinnati to its second World Series appearance in 1939, the franchise had to survive the bleakest period in its history, finishing in the basement four straight years and not even sneaking back into the first division until 1938. Not surprisingly, the club's languid play prompted another parade of managers, with Howley generating a line that produced Donie Bush, Bob O'Farrell, Charlie Dressen, Bobby Wallace, and Bill McKechnie. The personalities involved ran a gamut from Howley's mild-mannered philosophical approach to Dressen's obstreperous dedication to creating action, even if that meant putting one player on the roster (third-string catcher Gus Brittain) whose principal task in 1937 was starting brawls on the field.

Brittain wasn't the only player of the decade who would have qualified for an entry in Characters of the Game. In his three-and-a-half seasons with the club, Durocher became so infamous for his debts and his appeals to Weil for hundred-dollar loans that he became known around the organization as C-Note. Two other notables were pitcher Biff Wysong and catcher Bob Asbjornson. Scheduled to make his big-league debut in a 1930 game against the Phillies, Wysong was first given an "appreciation day" by hundreds of fellow Clarkson, Ohio natives; he then went out to the mound and got shellacked by the margin of 18–0. In 1931, Asbjornson was the center of similar pregame festivities in Boston during which he received a hefty check. In the game, the receiver clouted his one and only major league homer. His elation was cut short, however, when he realized after the game that no one had signed the check. When he arrived at a restaurant after the game for a dinner in his honor he was chagrined to discover that no one had showed up. The 1933 pitching staff included Jack Quinn, then officially listed as fifty years old but suspected of being a couple of years older; the righthander, who had started his big-league career with the Yankees in 1909, went 0–1 in fourteen appearances. In 1934, the club suffered through several weeks of a slump by rookie left fielder Link Blakely before the lefthanded hitter put together a couple of good offensive games; urged by a local news vendor to demand more money on the basis of his awakening, Blakely announced that he wouldn't play again unless he was paid more, was shipped off to the minors, and never appeared in a major league game again.

For Weil, there was little that was entertaining about presiding over a cellar club. What he had originally conceived of as a sideline became a full-time

In 1934, Larry MacPhail made the Reds the first team to offer season-long ticket plans to fans. In another MacPhail innovation that season, the Reds were the first club to travel by plane, flying from Cincinnati to Chicago for a series.

business when his brokers added up his losses in the 1929 stock market crash. For all his initial enthusiasm for raising salaries and paying high prices for players if that was the way back to the top of the league, he would be complaining a year later that he had overpaid for the organization and the Redland Field property. To keep going, he borrowed against his stock from the Central Trust Company, whose president, Charles Dupuis, tried a balancing act between the Reds' baseball needs and the bank's money priorities with decreasing success. By the end of the 1933 season, Weil had had his fill of both the club's losing and the bank's intrusions, and resigned as president and board member; Dupuis also quit his board seat in favor of two other Central Trust trustees. Then, amid incessant reports of an imminent sale of the franchise, the club announced in early November that it was hiring Larry MacPhail to take over baseball operations.

One of the most innovative figures in baseball history, MacPhail had already had a picaresque career before arriving on the scene to revolutionize the major leagues. An attorney by education, he gained some fleeting fame during World War I by joining with seven other soldiers in an attempt to kidnap the Kaiser in a heavily guarded castle in Holland; though the group managed to penetrate the fortress, MacPhail came away with only an ashtray for his daring. After the war, he was involved in everything from refereeing football games to running a glass factory and selling automobiles. In the late 1920s, he bought into the American Association's minor league team in Columbus and stayed on as president after selling it to the Cardinals. Within four years, he had built up the club to a pennant winner, impressing St. Louis vice-president Branch Rickey in the process. By then, in what turned out to be a typical turn of events in his lifelong love-hate relationship with the Cardinal executive, he also infuriated Rickey by refusing to part with Columbus second baseman Burgess Whitehead in the middle of the 1933 season unless he received five players as compensation to assure the AA team of its pennant. Rickey ceded the players, Columbus won the pennant, but MacPhail

LELAND STANFORD MacPHAIL
"LARRY"

DYNAMIC, INNOVATIVE EXECUTIVE MADE HIS
MARK AS PROGRESSIVE HEAD OF THREE CLUBS–
CINCINNATI REDS, BROOKLYN DODGERS AND
NEW YORK YANKEES–FROM 1933 TO 1947. WON
CHAMPIONSHIPS IN BOTH LEAGUES–WITH
DODGERS IN 1941 AND YANKEES IN 1947.
PIONEERED NIGHT BALL AT CINCINNATI IN
1935. ALSO INSTALLED LIGHTS AT EBBETS FIELD
AND YANKEE STADIUM. ORIGINATED PLANE
TRAVEL BY PLAYING PERSONNEL AND IDEA
OF STADIUM CLUB. HELPED SET UP EMPLOYEE
AND PLAYER PENSION PLANS.

National Baseball Library, Cooperstown, NY

was fired the day the season ended. About a month later, it was Rickey who recommended MacPhail for the Cincinnati job.

Then 43 years old, MacPhail wasted little time in overhauling the last-place Reds. Before spring training arrived, he worked out seven deals, the most noteworthy of which brought over catcher O'Farrell from the Cardinals as a playing manager. But the trades and the new pilot (O'Farrell wouldn't survive even a single season) were the least of the moves. Aware of how restricted his power was under the eye of the Central Trust Company, the new general manager persuaded Powel Crosley, whose interests included automobiles, radio manufacturing, and

Footnote Player: The Reds were so strapped for money in 1933 that they signed sandlot amateur Eddie Hunter for an honorarium as a backup infielder. Hunter got into one game as a backup third baseman, but never got to bat or had a fielding chance.

broadcasting, to sink $175,000 into the organization's preferred stock, and for an additional sum, to secure options on eighty percent of the common stock; shortly afterward, the industrialist purchased just enough of the common shares to assert complete control. The ownership change was notarized with the redesignation of Redland Field as Crosley Field.

The Central Trust taken care of, MacPhail began building up the kind of farm system that had proven so successful for Rickey in St. Louis. Before the 1934 season arrived, he worked out accords with six minor league clubs, including Toronto in the International League; to supply prospects for the farm teams, he appointed Milt Stock as chief scout and director of tryout camps. Finally, turning his attention to the deteriorating state of Crosley Field, he ordered the park completely repainted and bought bright red uniforms for the ushers and ticket takers.

Despite all his moves, MacPhail warned fans that they couldn't expect a dramatic turnaround in a single season, and he proved to be an accurate prophet when the team again finished in the basement in 1934. Concluding that O'Farrell did not know how to inspire less than brilliant players, the general manager brought in Dressen in late July; over the last two months, the club won almost as many games as it had in the first four and lost seventeen fewer. In September, Cincinnati also got a look at the first impressive player to come through the organization's hastily assembled farm system—first baseman Frank McCormick. In a thirteen-year career that would be mainly spent in Crosley Field, the righty-hitting McCormick topped .300 eight times, winding up a whisper below that level overall at .299. As a Red, he led the league in hits three straight years, in doubles once, and in RBIs once.

In 1935, the team's abandonment of the cellar after four consecutive seasons took second place to the first major league night game, on May 24 at Crosley Field between the Reds and Phillies. MacPhail, who had introduced night ball in Columbus with some success, won over skeptical NL owners to the experiment mainly because they had been making only nickels and dimes with their forays into Cincinnati anyway and had little to lose. MacPhail being MacPhail, he wasn't content just to advertise the game and nod to some groundskeeper at the appointed hour to switch on the lights. To begin with, there were military bands and fireworks displays, the latter culminating in configurations of an American flag and an enormous C with REDS in the middle. Then there was an elaborate presentation of the special guests, who included George Cahill, the tech-

The first major league night game, played in Crosley Field on May 24, 1935, between Cincinnati and Philadelphia. *UPI/Bettmann Newsphotos*

nician who had given Herrmann a demonstration of night baseball back in 1909, and George Wright, the last surviving member of the original Cincinnati Red Stockings. Finally, the signal went not to some Crosley Field groundskeeper, but to Washington, D.C., where President Franklin Delano Roosevelt activated the lighting system with a remote control button from the White House. The Reds put the finishing touches to the evening by defeating Philadelphia 2–1 behind Derringer; the attendance was 20,422.

Next to night games, MacPhail's most lasting influence on the Reds (and on baseball in general) stemmed from his insight that the broadcast media could help rather than hinder stadium attendance. A vital ally in this belief was announcer Red Barber, whose down-home twang and gentle humor introduced baseball to millions of people in the Ohio area, then later in New York. Barber's play-by-play not only delivered a game to a hundred times more fans than could have seen it at the ballpark, but underlined the sport's dramatic values and brought out the variety of its personalities. Thanks to Barber and those who followed him to the microphones, the players took on human dimensions not always apparent in the relatively dry sportswriting of the era.

For all his business foresight and association

with Crosley, MacPhail was not quite a darling of the organization's board of directors. He insisted on running the Reds by reinvesting profits in further promotions and renovations—denying dividends to stockholders while he himself sat on a hefty base salary and an attendance bonus. Whenever this strategy was challenged, MacPhail went into a temper tantrum, daring the board to do without him. In September 1936, one such scene ended with the general manager punching out Crosley. It took only a few days for the club to announce that MacPhail had "resigned" and was being replaced by Warren Giles, then head of Rochester's International League franchise. It was Giles—with the front office help of Frank Lane and Gabe Paul—who was on hand in 1939 and 1940 to reap the benefits of the organizational overhaul instigated by MacPhail.

The Giles administration got off to a bad start with another plunge by the team back to the cellar. One of the new general manager's problems was Dressen, who, during afterhours drinking sessions with sportswriters, loudly proclaimed his opinion that MacPhail had gotten a raw deal. Even when Dressen's popular scrappy image with fans began to fade and some of the Reds' players began complaining about his brusque dugout manner, Giles held his fire until he could find a suitable replacement. But then, in early September, Dressen himself brought the issue to a head by demanding to know whether he would be back the following season and, told that he would not be, resigned in favor of Bobby Wallace for the final thirty games. The roster problems faced by Giles were compounded by nagging reminders that the organization—specifically, MacPhail—had made several administrative mistakes that had cost the team good players. The most conspicuous of these errors was MacPhail's misjudgment in 1935 that future Hall of Famer Johnny Mize, on a look-see loan to the Reds from the Cardinals, would never recover from knee problems and should be returned to St. Louis.

As the 1937 winter meetings demonstrated, Giles himself was not immune to bad front office moves. In a classic instance of the best-trades-are-the-ones-that-aren't-made, the Reds announced in December that they had traded Lombardi to the Cubs, but then had to eat their words when Chicago owner Phil Wrigley vetoed the deal; Lombardi won the first of his two batting titles that year. More consciously, the club made two other important moves during the offseason in hiring Bill McKechnie as the new manager and in shortening the distances to Crosley Field's outfield fences. The latter decision helped Lombardi increase his homer total from 9 to 19 and outfielder Ival Goodman from 12 to 30 in the space of a single year. With the 1938 season already underway, Giles scored the team's biggest swap coup since the 1932 exchange for Lombardi when, at the urging of McKechnie, he sent catcher Spud Davis, pitcher Al Hollingsworth, and $50,000 to the cash-starved Phillies for pitcher Bucky Walters. Walters had broken into the major leagues as a third baseman in 1931, but had subsequently been converted to the mound by Philadelphia. In ten seasons with the Reds, he would rack up the overwhelming majority of his 198 career victories, leading the league three times with 20-win years, taking two ERA titles, and establishing himself as a workhorse with marks in appearances and innings pitched.

But neither Walters's arrival nor the 21 wins registered by Derringer were the pitching story for Cincinnati in 1938. On June 11th and 15th, southpaw Johnny Vander Meer became the only hurler to throw consecutive no-hitters when he blanked the Braves in Boston 3–0 and then repeated the trick in Brooklyn against the Dodgers 6–0. Lending added drama to the performance against the Dodgers was the fact that the game was the first to be played under the lights in Ebbets Field and had been pro-

moted by old friend MacPhail with the same gusto that he had brought to the 1935 contest in Cincinnati. As though the 38,748 screaming fans needed any more tension, Vander Meer walked the most precarious of tightropes in the ninth inning when, after getting Buddy Hassett on a ground ball, he walked three straight batters to fill the bases and bring McKechnie to the mound; after the visit by the manager, the lefthander induced Ernie Koy to hit into a forceout at the plate and Durocher to tap a soft fly to Harry Craft. Although the back-to-back no-hitters prompted enthusiastic predictions about Vander Meer's career, he in fact never won more than 18 games in a season and ended up with a lifetime mark below .500 (119–121).

With two significant additions, McKechnie brought the fourth-place 1938 Reds all the way to the top the following year. The new faces were third baseman Billy Werber, obtained from the Athletics for cash, and reliever Junior Thompson, who won 13 games with a 2.54 ERA in a combined role as long man and closer out of the bullpen. The other major contributors to the franchise's second flag were Derringer and Walters, who won 52 games between them, McCormick, who led the league in RBIs and hit .332, and Goodman, who batted .323 with 84 RBIs. The worst part of the season for the team was the World Series, which the Yankees swept.

Much the same cast was back in 1940, when the club took its second consecutive pennant. The biggest changes saw Joe Beggs (12 wins) and Jim Turner (14) brought in to bolster the mound staff, and rookie Mike McCormick (.300) taking over in left field. Walters, Derringer, and Thompson threw up a combined 58 wins, Frank McCormick drove in 127 runs with a .309 mark, and Lombardi hit over .300.

A cloud descended over the team in early August, however, when reserve catcher Willard Hershberger committed suicide in a Boston hotel room by severing his jugular vein with a razor. Hershberger had been despondent for some days before his fatal act, and had even alluded to his intentions in a dugout conversation with McKechnie. As he admitted later, McKechnie had written off the forewarning as a passing mood, attributable in particular to Hershberger's glumness that he had called a pitch against Harry Danning of the Giants that had been whacked for a grand slam that had defeated the Reds in a midseason game. The Boston tragedy tantalized feature writers for some time, especially because of the lack of a suicide note. It also underlined the unusual number of suicides associated with Cincinnati baseball. In 1896, righthander Cannonball Crane ended his life by drinking chloral acid. In 1911, utilityman

Danny Mahoney chose carbolic acid. Pea Ridge Day, a member of the 1926 staff, shot himself to death. Still another pitcher, Benny Frey, couldn't cope with his demotion to the minors by the Reds in 1937 and killed himself by running the engine of his car in a sealed-off garage.

Hershberger's death and an ankle sprain suffered by Lombardi near the end of the season forced McKechnie to reactivate the forty-year-old Jimmie Wilson from the coaching lines. One of the NL's premier receivers in his prime, Wilson proved more than equal to the task over the final games of the regular season and then in the World Series against Detroit. Showing that he still had some zip in his arm, he gunned down the only Tiger runner who attempted to steal in the seven-game duel that ended with Cincinnati's second world championship; on the other hand, he himself stole a base and banged out 6 hits in 17 plate appearances. In addition to Wilson, the stars in the victory over the Tigers were Walters and Derringer, who each won two games, outfielder Jimmy Ripple, who drove in 6 runs on 7 hits, and Werber, whose 10 hits included 4 doubles.

With the coming of the 1941 season, the Reds entered another long, dry period that would not end until 1961. In general, the problem in the 1940s was lack of hitting, while that of the 1950s was lack of starting pitching. For the eleven-year period between 1945 and 1955, one or the other shortcoming would prevent the team from even reaching .500, though it never quite dropped into the basement. The march of managers over the years included pitcher Walters, Hall of Famer Rogers Hornsby, and veteran catcher Birdie Tebbetts. Along the way, Giles moved from team general manager to president (and ultimately, NL President), leaving his righthand man Paul to head up daily baseball operations.

Like every other big league club, the Reds limped through the World War II years with some makeshift lineups. In 1944, they were reduced to hav-

ing to use fifteen-year-old Joe Nuxhall, the youngest player to appear in the majors in the twentieth century; in two-thirds of an inning, the southpaw yielded two hits and five walks, retiring for the season with an astronomical 67.50 ERA. In 1945, the staff went in the opposite direction, with seven hurlers over thirty-five, the most senior being forty-six-year-old Hod Lisenbee. Still, McKechnie negotiated four first-division finishes, primarily on the strength of consistent clutch hitting by Frank McCormick, solid performances from Walters, and the unexpected success of Elmer Riddle in 1941 (ERA title) and 1943 (most NL wins).

The club's single most dominating performance during the 1940s came from Ewell Blackwell in 1947. Known as the Whip for a treacherous side-armed, buggy-whip delivery, the six-foot, six-inch righthander won sixteen straight games on his way to league-leading totals in victories and strikeouts. Even more startling, Blackwell came within two outs of repeating Vander Meer's feat of consecutive no-hitters (and against the same teams) when, on June 18, he held the Braves hitless, and then, four days later, got one out in the ninth inning before surrendering a single to Eddie Stanky of the Dodgers. Also like Vander Meer, Blackwell would end up with something less than a brilliant career: Despite being singled out by Ralph Kiner and other righthanded sluggers of the period as the toughest pitcher in the league, he closed out an injury-plagued ten seasons with the Reds, Yankees, and Athletics a mere four games above .500, at 82–78.

Shortly after the war, the team began picking up the sluggers that would give the franchise its identity through the 1950s. The most conspicuous of the long-ball hitters was lefty-swinging first baseman Ted Kluszewski, whose bulging biceps eventually inspired the team's sleeveless uniforms. Although he was a relatively slow starter in the major leagues, hitting only 74 homers in his first five seasons as a regular, Kluszewski hit his stride in 1952, reaching the 40-plateau for the first of three straight campaigns. Another long-ball threat on the 1948 team was Hank Sauer, a righthand-hitting outfielder who demolished all previous club power marks with 35 round-trippers. In one of the franchise's worst trades, Sauer and center fielder Frankie Baumholtz were shipped to Chicago during the 1949 season for outfielders Peanuts Lowery and Harry Walker. On the other hand, the Reds pulled off one of their best trades after the 1952 season, when they packaged catcher Joe Rossi and outfielders Cal Abrams and Gail Henley for Pittsburgh in return for center fielder

Rogers Hornsby wound up his managerial days with two clubs paying him for doing nothing. When he moved to Cincinnati from St. Louis in the middle of the 1952 season, Hornsby brought along a guaranteed contract from the Browns that he continued to collect on. After being fired by the Reds before the end of the 1953 season, he also continued collecting on a second guaranteed pact that he had signed with the NL team.

Gus Bell. An outstanding defensive player, Bell contributed to the Crosley Field power displays in the 1950s by hitting at least 27 homers three times and driving in a minimum of 100 runs four times.

The most potent of all the Cincinnati squads of the era was the 1956 team, whose 221 homers tied the 1947 Giants for most long balls by a NL club in one season. The blasters were led by Kluszewski (35), right fielder Wally Post (36), Bell (29), starting catcher Ed Bailey (28), third baseman Ray Jablonski (15), backup catcher Smokey Burgess (12), and reserve first baseman George Crowe (10). But the team's best all-around player was left fielder Frank Robinson, who launched his Hall of Fame career by swatting 38 homers (to tie Wally Berger's record for the most by an NL rookie), batting .290, and scoring a league-leading 122 runs. For the next two decades, the righty-hitting Robinson would pile up one distinction after another, especially as a Red (1956–65) and, after a disastrous trade, as an Oriole (1966–71). Among his accomplishments: 586 career home runs; eleven seasons of at least 30 homers; the only player to win MVP awards in both leagues (with the Reds in 1961 and the Orioles in 1966); Triple Crown winner in 1966; slugging average leader four times; and at least 100 RBIs six times. While winding down as a player, Robinson also became the first black big league manager when he took over the Indians in 1975. For all his impressive statistics, Robinson's most enduring legacy as a player was as the ultimate hustler, as likely to win a game for his team by taking out a second baseman to thwart a double play as by hitting a ball into the stands.

The 1956 power splurge was good box office, with the franchise recording one million customers for the first time. A year later, the same popular enthusiasm for the team produced a campaign to stuff the ballot boxes in the All Star game voting, with every starting player except first baseman Crowe winning election. NL President Ford Frick, under pressure from other teams and howls of protest around the country, intervened to sit down third baseman Don Hoak and shortstop Roy McMillan in favor of more accomplished players. The perception of the organization and its fans as being acutely provincial was also reinforced during the decade by Crosley's decision to rename the club the Redlegs lest somebody get the idea that its traditional nickname imply some association with Communism.

In the late 1950s, with the bloom off the power hitters and many of the power hitters themselves off to other teams, Crosley began seriously entertaining offers to shift the franchise to New York, which had been stripped of its NL teams with the moves of the Dodgers and Giants to California after the 1957 season. What ultimately stymied the deal was a brace of Congressional investigations into the antitrust status of baseball and league fears that any franchise movement at the time would only point up how major league teams gave priority to the market place over sporting loyalties.

After three gray seasons in which the team had wound up a lot closer to the bottom of the league than the top, Cincinnati entered the 1961 campaign with few predictions of a first-division standing. A list of the club's most valuable assets extended little beyond Robinson, center fielder Vada Pinson, the potential of southpaw Jim O'Toole, and the baseball smarts of manager Fred Hutchinson. On the opposite side of the ledger were the resignation of Paul during the offseason, so that he could accept a job with the expansion Astros, and the death of Crosley in spring training, which revived reports of the organization's either being sold or transferred. When the Reds won only 6 of their first 24 games, there was still less reason to suspect that this would be the worst patch of the season and that they would end up with their first flag in twenty-one years.

The first element in the turnaround was offseason dealing that brought pitcher Joey Jay from the Braves and third baseman Gene Freese from the White Sox. Righthander Jay, the first Little League alumnus to break into the majors, led the team with 21 wins, while Freese clouted 26 homers and drove in 87 runs. Three weeks into the season, Bill DeWitt, Paul's successor as president and general manager, settled down the infield defense by acquiring second baseman Don Blasingame from the Giants. Aside from Jay, the pitching staff saw O'Toole fulfill his promise with 19 victories, veteran Bob Purkey chip in with 16 wins, and the bullpen tandem of Jim Brosnan and Bill Henry put together 12 wins and 32 saves. Offensively, Robinson had an MVP season of 37 homers, 124 RBIs, and a .323 average; Pinson just missed out on the batting title by averaging .343; and first baseman Gordy Coleman weighed in with 26 homers and 87 RBIs. The World Series proved to be something of an anticlimax when the greatest longball team in history, the 1961 Yankees of Roger Maris and Mickey Mantle, won relatively easily in five games. Nevertheless, the club's surprise pennant and the return of some 1.1 million fans to Crosley Field ended speculation about a franchise shift.

In terms of wins and losses, most of the rest of the 1960s was a prelude to the arrival of the Big Red Machine. The closest brush with another pennant came in 1964, when the Reds, Phillies, Giants, and Cardinals all battled down to the final hours of the season before St. Louis emerged the victor. If there was a sentimental favorite that year, in and outside Cincinnati, it was the Reds because of the brain tumor that had left Hutchinson with only a few months to live and that made it impossible for him to carry on as the head of the team during the September stretch. Hutchinson died in November at the age of forty-five. Under Dick Sisler, Don Heffner, and Dave Bristol, the club played well enough to stay above .500 for four out of five years, but was generally not up to the level of the Cardinals, the two California teams, or even the Cubs.

Shortly after replacing Paul as president, DeWitt negotiated the purchase of the team from the Crosley estate. He remained as owner until 1966 when, following a dismal year by the Reds and unrelenting criticism from the press and fans for having traded AL MVP Robinson to the Orioles the previous winter for pitchers Milt Pappas and Jack Baldschun, he sold out to a group headed by Cincinnati publisher Francis Dale and brothers William and James Williams. Robinson was not the only public relations problem DeWitt had during his reign. In 1962, reliever Brosnan published his journal of the 1961 pennant race to general praise everywhere except in baseball front offices. Although nowhere near as candid or racy as Jim Bouton's subsequent *Ball Four*, Brosnan's *Pennant Race* bothered DeWitt and his fellow executives for being less than reverential about baseball customs and their guardians; the Reds' president forbade the pitcher from any further writing on the basis of contractual clauses prohibiting players from making statements that could be interpreted as being detrimental to baseball. After the reliever had a so-so year in 1962, DeWitt was only too happy to send him off to the White Sox.

The first of the Big Red Machine players to arrive was Pete Rose, the switch-hitting infielder-outfielder who would be dubbed Charlie Hustle for his belly-flop style of play, who would close out a twenty-four-year career with more hits than anyone else in the history of the game, and who would be denied immediate entry into the Hall of Fame because of his gambling. As a second baseman in 1963, Rose immediately alerted the NL what it was up against when he won Rookie of the Year honors. A lifetime .303 hitter, his subsequent achievements included: three batting titles; averaging .300 or more fifteen times; leading NL batters in hits seven times and in doubles five times; scoring 100 runs ten times.

Rose's most productive year was probably 1973, when he was named MVP for winning the batting title with a .338 average, hitting 36 doubles, driving in 64 runs, and scoring 115 times. His most magnetic season, however, was 1978, when he pursued Joe Dimaggio's 56-game hitting streak before national cameras, finally having to settle for tying Willie Keeler for the NL record of 44 games. While not especially gifted as a fielder, Rose's doggedness and intense working habits permitted managers to move him around over the years from second base to the outfield to third base to first base; he was elected or named to the All Star team seventeen times at five different positions. In addition to retiring with the most hits (4,256) in baseball history, Rose amassed the most games (3,562) and at bats (14,053), finished second on the all-time list for doubles (746) and fourth for runs scored (2,165).

The next Big Red Machine players in place were Tony Perez and Johnny Bench. A first baseman for most of his career, righthand-hitting Perez was shifted to third base for several seasons in the late 1960s and early 1970s in order to accommodate the bat of Lee May. Probably the most consistent clutch hitter on all the pennant-winning teams of the 1970s, Perez had seven consecutive years of 20 or more homers, and nine overall. Between 1967 and 1977, he drove in at least 90 runs every year. Bench, elected to the Hall of Fame in 1989, ended his seventeen-year career in 1983. A defensive giant with a knack for seeing the team's generally humdrum pitching staffs through crises, he totaled 389 homers, including two seasons (1970 and 1972) of 40-plus when he led the league; his six 100-plus RBI years also counted a couple of NL-leading performances. The righthand-hitting slugger captured two MVP trophies—in 1970 (.293, 45 homers, 148 RBIs, 97 runs scored, 35 doubles) and 1972 (.270, 40 homers, 125 RBIs, 100 walks).

Ironically, Cincinnati's most dominating pitcher until at least the arrival of Tom Seaver from the Mets in 1977 (and, arguably, beyond that) had nothing to do with the club's renaissance in the 1970s. In the 1960s, righthander Jim Maloney notched eight straight seasons of double-figure victories, including 20-win seasons in 1963 and 1965. A fastballer once clocked at a whisker below 100 miles an hour, Maloney also tossed two no-hitters during his career, and lost an anguishing third one when the Mets broke through against him in the 11th inning. By the time Sparky Anderson arrived to take over Cincinnati's drive to its first division title and the NL pennant in 1970, however, shoulder and Achilles tendon

Johnny Bench. *National Baseball Library, Cooperstown, NY*

injuries had reduced the thirty-year-old hurler to a disabled-list spectator, and he was out of baseball a year later.

The hiring of Anderson to replace Bristol at the end of the 1969 season came as a surprise to anyone who had associated the former Phillies infielder only with that very small group of players who performed as regulars for one year but otherwise never wore a big league uniform. Anderson was the choice of general manager Bob Howsam, who had come to the Reds from the Cardinals in the late 1960s. A Branch Rickey protégé, Howsam had a marked respect for the way the Dodgers (as organized by his mentor back in the 1940s) did things, and it didn't hurt Anderson in the slightest that he was a product of that system.

To Howsam's manner of thinking, Anderson was also the ideal enforcer of an image of a tradition-bound franchise that was simultaneously open to creative money-making ideas. What this specifically translated to in Cincinnati was, on the one hand,

introducing a prep school dress code that compelled players to remain clean-shaven with short hair and to wear uniform pantlegs at a prescribed height and, on the other hand, moving the team into Riverfront Stadium, with its quintessentially untraditional artificial surface, antiseptic atmosphere—but, most of all, increased seating capacity.

Whatever else this approach did, it worked. In the first ten years of occupying Riverfront, the franchise drew an estimated 21 million fans. What most of the heartlanders came to watch was the best team in the NL—with its six divisional titles, four pennants, and three second-place finishes. In 1970, 1975, and 1976, the club won more than 100 games, with its 1975 record of 108–54 the best in franchise history. On the level of individual honors, four Reds won the MVP award six times in the decade—Bench in 1970 and 1972, Rose in 1973, Joe Morgan in 1975 and 1976, and George Foster in 1977.

The first of the divisional titles came in 1970, when the club rolled over runnerup Los Angeles by

14½ games. The team boasted three players (Bench, Perez, May) with more than 30 homers, an unlikely 20 wins from Jim Merritt, 18 more from Gary Nolan, and a crucial 35 saves and 6 wins from Wayne Granger. While favored to take the Pirates in the LCS, the Reds did it improbably—with strong starting performances from Nolan and Merritt and middle-inning relief from Milt Wilcox, to sweep a pitchers' series. The World Series against the Orioles was something else, with only May's seven hits and eight RBIs worthy of Cincinnati memory from the five-game Baltimore win.

In 1971, the Reds endured their only losing season of the decade, but there were consolations. In May, the club completed one of the most profitable swaps in its history when it acquired outfielder Foster from the Giants in return for backup shortstop Frank Duffy and minor league pitcher Vern Geishert. With Cincinnati, Foster led the league in homers twice, in RBIs three times, and in runs scored once; in his MVP year of 1977, he became one of only five NL players to tag more than 50 homers in a season. In November, Howsam pulled off the franchise's biggest blockbuster ever when he obtained second baseman Morgan, third baseman Dennis Menke, outfielders Cesar Geronimo and Ed Armbrister, and pitcher Jack Billingham from Houston for May, second baseman Tommy Helms, and utility player Jim Stewart. While Menke was at the end of the trail, Geronimo became the regular center fielder for the decade, Billingham the team's most effective righthander, and Armbrister a valuable pinch-hitter. But towering over all of them was the lefty-hitting Morgan, who was elected to the Hall of Fame in 1990. The personification of the winning player, he racked up six straight seasons of averages between .288 and .327, stolen base totals between 49 and 67, homers between 16 and 27, and both walks and runs scored over the 100 mark. His two MVP titles in 1975 and 1976 were also in acknowledgement of a defense that, together with shortstop Dave Concepcion, gave the Reds the tightest middle infield of the period.

With just about all the pieces in place, the team romped to another division title in 1972, and again bested the Pirates in the LCS, though this time by the much tighter margin of three games to two. The pennant turned on the final inning of the fifth game when, trailing 3–2, Bench led off the ninth by hitting a solo home run, Perez and Menke singled, and Pittsburgh righthander Bob Moose uncorked a wild pitch to send in the winning run. The World Series again ended the season on a sour note, with the Reds not able to overcome the four homers and nine RBIs of

Oakland catcher Gene Tenace in a seven-game duel.

Spearheaded by Rose's MVP year, the team overcame a daunting eleven-game lead by Los Angeles in early July to win the division title again in 1973. Billingham's 19 wins and lefty Don Gullett's 18 victories overcame an injury to Nolan, and Dan Driessen offset some of the lineup woes brought on by Concepcion's broken ankle. But the LCS against the Mets turned into a nightmare when the underdog New Yorkers prevailed in five games. The most memorable moment of the playoffs occurred in the fifth inning of the third game when Rose's hard slide into second precipitated punches with Mets' shortstop Bud Harrelson and then mass disorders in the Shea Stadium grandstands. Only when Mets players begged fans to calm down did Cincinnati lose a brief hope of winning the key game through forfeit. The following day, Rose rubbed it in against booing fans when he hit a game-winning homer off Harry Parker in the 12th inning, but it proved to be Cincinnati's final roar.

After a disappointing 1974 in which the Reds almost—but not quite—repeated their overtaking of the Dodgers, the club went all the way in 1975 for its third world championship. Changes for the year included the insertion of lefty-hitting Ken Griffey in right field and Anderson's reliance on the bullpen tandem of righty Rawley Eastwick and southpaw Will McEnaney to the point that he gained a reputation as Captain Hook. In the LCS, quick work was again made of the Pirates (a three-game sweep), setting the stage for a marathon seven-game struggle against the Red Sox. In what might have been the single most exciting World Series contest played up to that time, the two teams went back and forth in Game Six until Boston catcher Carlton Fisk homered in the twelfth inning to give the home team a 7–6 victory. Undeterred, the Reds overcame a 3–0 deficit in the final game to score two runs in the sixth, one in the seventh, and the winner on Morgan's single in the ninth. The pitching hero was Eastwick, with two wins and one save.

The next year, 1976, proved much easier. The club not only outdistanced the Dodgers by 10 games for the division title, but then went on to sweep both the Phillies in the LCS and the Yankees in the World

In the 1975 World Series against Boston, Dan Driessen became the first National League designated hitter.

Series. Aside from Morgan's MVP play, the most noteworthy aspect of the regular season was that the pitching staff was the first in the NL to have seven pitchers with at least 11 victories; among them was righthander Pat Zachry (14–7), who shared Rookie of the Year honors with San Diego's Butch Metzger. Rose again proved to be a postseason star when he led the team with six hits in the sweep over the Phillies, and Foster hit clutch homers in the first and third games. Against the Yankees, Bench was the principal offensive weapon, with eight hits, two homers, and six RBIs.

The Reds didn't get much of an opportunity to turn complacent after their 1976 cakewalk. In November, lefty Gullett announced that he was signing with the Yankees as a free agent; Anderson immediately attacked the hurler as an ingrate. At the December winter meetings, Howsam dropped a bombshell by trading Perez and McEnaney to the Expos for pitchers Woodie Fryman and Dale Murray. The deal was made over the strenuous objections of Rose and Morgan, who warned Howsam about the effect of the first baseman's absence on team chemistry. Rose himself did little for that chemistry when, on the eve of spring training, he expressed his resentment over the five-year, $1-million contract given to Concepcion during the offseason, dropping a large hint that he would follow Gullett's example at the expiration of his own contract if the front office did not reward his long service. When Howsam offered to add $50,000 to his existing $188,000-a-year pact, Rose said no, demanding a two-year agreement at $400,000 annually. Not for the last time, a financial negotiation centering around Charlie Hustle dominated Cincinnati sports pages, and the Rose loyalists were not tardy in dropping an avalanche of letters on Howsam's desk. On the eve of the 1977 season, the two sides agreed on $750,000 for two years.

Howsam's busiest day of the year was June 15th, when he completed five deals within the space of a few hours. The headline-maker was a swap with the

Mets that brought Tom Seaver in exchange for Zachry, reserve infielder Doug Flynn, and minor league outfielders Steve Henderson and Dan Norman. Along with Foster's MVP production, Seaver's 14–3 record the rest of the year was the diamond highlight of the season for the team. Although the Reds didn't win anything in 1977, Commissioner Bowie Kuhn paid them a backhanded compliment in December by scotching a deal with the Athletics on the grounds that it would have made them too strong. The controversy started when Howsam announced that he had acquired southpaw ace Vida Blue from Oakland in return for minor league first baseman Dave Revering and the substantial sum of $1.75 million. Kuhn, who had already vetoed other fire sale deals by Oakland owner Charlie Finley, immediately warned that he would permit the transaction with the Reds only if it were reshaped to include "more players and less money." Howsam responded with a threat to sue Kuhn for interfering in Cincinnati business, but found little sympathy around the rest of the NL, where there was indeed a fear that a rotation headed by Seaver and Blue would make the pennant race a joke. Cincinnati eventually made its peace with Kuhn's pronouncement, and ended up sending Revering to Oakland for reliever Doug Bair.

Although the Reds remained in the 1978 race down to the wire, Rose dominated most of the attention, first by getting his 3,000th hit off Montreal's Steve Rogers on May 5th, then by chasing after the DiMaggio consecutive game hit streak. Seaver also had a moment of glory on June 16th when he threw his one and only career no-hitter against the Cardinals. Otherwise, the news was mainly bad. A stomach muscle pull kept Morgan on the sidelines for an extended period and crimped his hitting (.236) when he did play. A predominantly untested pitching staff (Tom Hume, Paul Moskau, Mike LaCoss) gave Seaver little support. By June, Bench was complaining that Anderson had lost his ability to motivate the club, Rose was making more sounds that he would leave if he didn't receive the going market rate for free agents of his caliber, and Howsam was saying goodbye altogether on the grounds that he wanted to reduce his work load because of his age.

Dick Wagner was named as the new general manager upon Howsam's resignation. After the team had completed a postseason trip to Japan, Wagner sent tempers rising all over Cincinnati by announcing the firing of Anderson and the hiring of John McNamara. The decision came as a shock even to Anderson, whose .596 winning percentage as a manager to that point had been topped only by Joe Mc-

So economical was the Reds' 1976 World Series sweep of the Yankees that only nine Cincinnati players came to bat during the four games. In addition to designated hitter Dan Driessen, the hitters were Tony Perez, Joe Morgan, Dave Concepcion, Johnny Bench, Pete Rose, George Foster, Cesar Geronimo, and Ken Griffey.

Carthy and Frank Selee. Among the many protesting the move was Cincinnati mayor Gerald Spring, who accused the team of "going bananas" and urged that Wagner be fired instead. The general manager justified the switch to McNamara by contending that the club had become complacent under Anderson.

Wagner's popularity didn't rise any higher when he lost out to the Phillies for Rose's free-agent services. It was thus within a decidedly chilly atmosphere that McNamara worked a minor miracle by turning the efforts of declining stars, untested rookies, and journeymen into another division title in 1979. The biggest pluses were a career year from Concepcion (.281, 16 homers, 84 RBIs), Ray Knight's ability to shine (.318 with 79 RBIs) through critical comparisons to his third base predecessor Rose, Foster's 30 homers, and the .318 hitting of speedster outfielder Dave Collins. In the LCS, the Pirates got a measure of revenge for the first portion of the decade by yielding a mere five runs to Cincinnati in a three-game sweep.

If the Reds were the NL's most predictable first-place club in the 1970s, they were almost equally reliable as a second-place finisher in the 1980s. The chief exceptions were the split season of 1981, when the club's overall record was actually the best in the major leagues but useless before a convoluted half-and-half standings formula, and 1982, when the team dropped into the cellar with the worst record in franchise history. The runnerup finishes were largely deceptive, insofar as the team was seldom a serious contender in September. Just as Pittsburgh had dominated the Eastern Division in the 1970s and never reached the LCS in the 1980s, Cincinnati was the only Western Division club in the NL to remain a spectator to the decade's postseason play.

The comings and goings were constant at all levels. At the start of the decade, the Williams brothers tightened their grip on the organization and, despite his unpopularity, gave Wagner a five-year contract. The general manager ended up working out only two-and-a-half years of the pact, getting the axe in July 1983 when the team showed every sign of repeating as last-place finishers. To much surprise (and relief, by some), Wagner's successor turned out to be Howsam, talked out of retirement in what was openly acknowledged as a stopgap measure. The nature of the temporary solution became clearer the following season when the Williamses sold out to auto dealer Marge Schott. By then, however, Howsam had used his relatively brief time with the franchise to make significant changes on both the roster and in the manager's office.

When reliever Jim Kern was traded to the Reds by the Mets in the 1982 deal for George Foster, he refused to shave off his beard. Facial hair was in violation of the team's rigid dress code, so the righthander was shipped immediately to the White Sox.

Wagner's chief cachet for the Williams' ownership was as a spokesman for organization austerity, so that none of the club's stars at the start of the decade entertained any serious thought of being able to negotiate new free-agent contracts. Morgan left for the Astros after the 1980 season, Collins for the Yankees the following year. Also during the 1981–1982 off-season, the team traded away prospective free agent Griffey to the Yankees and prospective free agent Foster to the Mets, getting little in return in either deal except much smaller salary obligations. One who did remain was Bench, but on conditions that proved to be embarrassing to both the club and the player himself. Declaring that he no longer wanted to catch, Bench won over Wagner and McNamara to the idea that he be allowed to close out his career as a third baseman. The result in 1982 was not only a team-leading 19 errors, but a marked lack of range that had pitchers moaning about having the All Star catcher behind them rather than in front of them. Bench finally called it quits after the 1983 season.

With Seaver also sent back to the Mets the previous winter, the only remnants of the winning 1970s teams that Howsam found on his return in 1983 were Concepcion and Driessen. The club had in fact declined so steeply that the biggest RBI man for the season was slap-hitting second baseman Ron Oester, who drove across 58 runs. In his first two player moves to rebuild offensive respectability, Howsam signed free agents Perez and Dave Parker. While the aging Perez had been reduced to little more than a pinch-hitter, Parker ended up leading the team in most offensive categories in 1984. Unfortunately, there was little to lead for most of the season, and Howsam had only made matters worse by hiring as manager Vern Rapp, a drill sergeant who had gained a reputation as the horror of the league during an earlier managing stint with the Cardinals. But then, on August 16th, most Reds' fans were ready to forgive everything with the announcement that a trade with Montreal was bringing back Rose as player-manager.

For better and worse, the second half of the 1980s in Cincinnati was almost all Rose. As a player, he showed that he still had something left when he batted a hustling .365 over the final weeks of the 1984 season. The following year, he conducted another national media event by inserting himself into the lineup for some 400 at bats in pursuit of Ty Cobb's all-time hit record. After some organization scares that he would accomplish the feat on the road in Chicago, he got base hit number 4,192 off San Diego's Eric Show before a capacity crowd at Riverfront Stadium on September 11th. Oddly, for a player as aware of the media as Rose was, he never made a happening of his retirement as a player, merely removing his name from the active roster after the 1986 season with some vague suggestion that he might one day reactivate himself.

As a manager, Rose brought together all his fabled field instincts and encyclopedic knowledge of both players and the rule book to guide the club to four straight second-place finishes. Although most expectations were that he would be an able motivator but something of a disaster where pitching was concerned, there were extended periods when just the opposite seemed to be the case. His most successful year statistically was 1985, but in 1987 he kept the team on course through numerous injuries to key players and had to depend on nimble use of the bullpen of John Franco, Rob Murphy, and Frank Williams to bail out one of the least effective starting rotations in the league. The season also saw him clashing with Parker and other veterans in the clubhouse and Schott becoming more vocal in her criticisms of the club's addiction to second place. Parker was packed off to Oakland at the end of the year; not daring to move against the popular Rose, Schott made the first of what turned out to be a continuing series of front office changes by firing general manager Bill Bergesch and signing Murray Cook as his successor.

The owner had a lot more to complain about in 1988, when Rose engaged in such a protracted argument with umpire Dave Pallone over an early season call that he was held responsible for provoking a near-riot by Riverfront fans and suspended for a month. Reds' broadcasters Joe Nuxhall and Marty

Brennaman were also censured by the league office for attacking Pallone on the air, describing him as (among other things) "incompetent" and "a scab," the latter a reference to the arbiter's arrival in the NL during an umpires' strike some years earlier. The incident took on added resonance when Pallone acknowledged some time later that he was gay, suggesting that he had set off the on-field explosion not only for a professional judgment that he had never been regarded as among the league's best, but also because he was an obvious target for some of the macho notions about baseball held in Cincinnati.

As it turned out, even the Pallone episode was merely a prelude to the chaos that engulfed the team in 1989. In spring training, Commissioner A. Bartlett Giamatti revealed that he was looking into the possibility that Rose had been betting on baseball games, including some involving his own Reds, and that the Cincinnati pilot was in debt to various bookmakers for an estimated $500,000. The months that followed were a circus of accumulating evidence about Rose's addiction to betting on major sports, independent print and television investigations linking him with shadowy figures around the country, countermoves by the manager's attorneys challenging the credentials of Giamatti and his investigator John Dowd, and repeated denials by Rose that there had been any baseball betting. Through it all, Rose rejected any thought of stepping down as manager, declaring that he had nothing to feel guilty about.

Eventually, the media pressure became so great that Rose decided not to lead the team up to Cooperstown for the annual exhibition game played after induction ceremonies lest he distract attention from Bench, one of the year's inductees. Then, finally, with the suit challenging Giamatti's authority still bouncing between different courts, the manager and the commissioner announced an agreement on August 24th by which Rose was banned permanently from baseball.

The accord was hardly the last act of the drama. Although the agreement made no mention of Rose's alleged betting on baseball (an important concession to him in view of possible criminal prosecution), Giamatti couldn't even get through his initial press conference disclosing the arrangement without reiterating his belief in those specific charges. Rose himself continued issuing denials in this regard, and for a long while also spurned notions that his monumental losses to bookmakers over the years (estimated in the millions) indicated an addiction to gambling.

Barely a week after the agreement had been an-

On September 16, 1988, Tom Browning pitched the franchise's only perfect game, blanking Los Angeles, 1–0.

nounced, a heart attack killed Giamatti at the age of fifty-one. The commissioner's death prompted off-the-record claims by some of his intimates that the Rose case had literally exhausted the life out of him. While ignoring Giamatti's lifelong chain-smoking, assertions of the kind were still another blow to the Rose image, and it didn't improve over the next few months when he seemed so desperate for money that he ran to card shows to sell his autograph at inflated prices and to home-shopping networks to peddle the trophies and memorabilia that he had amassed over the years.

In the summer of 1990, a federal court found Rose guilty of tax evasion and sentenced him to several months in prison. On top of that, the committee charged with overseeing Hall of Fame election procedures voted in 1991 that his ban also made him ineligible for consideration as a member of Cooperstown. The decision—based on Hall of Fame regulations about the moral character of candidates—provoked a storm of controversy, especially in view of the presence in the baseball shrine of racists like Cap Anson, assailants like Ty Cobb, drunkards like Grover Cleveland Alexander, and numerous others who should have come up as short of this criterion as Rose.

Rose's resignation in August 1989 opened the way for Cincinnati to have a Yankee look the following year, with former George Steinbrenner employees Bob Quinn installed as general manager and Lou Piniella taking over as manager. The New York connection was solidified further through two important deals—the acquisition of first baseman Hal Morris from the Yankees and the swapping of Franco for Mets' southpaw reliever Randy Myers. With otherwise the same club that Rose and his brief successor Tommy Helms had managed in 1989, Piniella steered the team to the Western Division title, an LCS victory over Pittsburgh, and a startling sweep of the Athletics in the World Series.

The division race was a question of getting ahead early and staying there; in fact, though the Reds occupied first place all but one day of the regular season, they were a less than .500 club in the second half of the campaign and survived because of a torrid first half. Offensive honors were spread widely around the team, with third baseman Chris Sabo and outfielder Eric Davis hitting more than 20 homers, shortstop Barry Larkin (.301) laying claim to being the best all-around player at his position in the NL, the ex-Yankee Morris batting .340, and Mariano Duncan (.306) proving to be an invaluable role player at second base, shortstop, and the outfield. The key

to the pitching was the trio of relievers—Myers, southpaw Norm Charlton, righthander Ron Dibble—who fancied themselves as The Nasty Boys for their redneck truculence and roaring fastballs. Southpaw Tom Browning was the only starter to win even 15 games. Statistically, the club was something of an anomaly, with only three of its starters reaching low double figures in wins and none of its position players scoring 100 runs or driving in 90.

In a revival of their competition in the 1970s, the Pirates and Reds battled through six LCS games before Cincinnati emerged with the pennant. The loudest bat belonged to right fielder Paul O'Neill, who had three doubles and a homer among his eight hits. Considered a clear underdog to the powerhouse Athletics, the team made short work of the World Series. Righthander Jose Rijo was named MVP for allowing only one run in his two victories. Outfielder Billy Hatcher had a monstrous series by collecting seven straight hits and breaking numerous offensive records, ending up with four singles, four doubles, and a triple in twelve official at bats; the righthanded hitter also drew two walks and was hit by a pitch.

If there was a negative aspect to the season, it was attributed to Schott, who alternately aroused snickers of derision for the public pampering of her pet St. Bernard Schottzie and cries of protest over her methodical, cost-cutting dismantling of the organization's farm system. By 1991, her mania for making a few dollars extra had reached the point of evicting Quinn from his Riverfront Stadium box so that she could sell the seat. In another damaging episode, team physician Michael Lawhon quit amid charges that Schott's cost-cutting measures had made it impossible for him to treat the players properly. The 1991 campaign was also marked by several incidents involving The Nasty Boys, who lost their charm by firing baseballs gratuitously at hitters, runners, and even, in one instance, fans in the stands. Dibble was suspended three times before finally announcing that he would seek psychological counseling.

The club's collapse back to fifth place in 1991, together with Schott's obsessive bean counting, sparked speculation that Piniella would be elsewhere in 1992. Instead, he won an agreement to have more of a say in front office dealings, and flashed his power immediately by acquiring lefty Greg Swindell from Cleveland, Tim Belcher from Los Angeles, Bip Roberts from San Diego, and Dave Martinez from Montreal. The chief costs were Myers (to the Padres) and Davis (to the Dodgers), the latter having worn out superstar hopes with annual ailments that kept him sidelined for significant portions of the season.

But despite an estimated swelling of the team's salaries by $35 million, Piniella could get the team back no higher than second—a fate sealed by serious injuries during the season to Rijo, Browning, Morris, and Sabo. The brightest on-field developments were Roberts's 10 straight hits in September, enabling him to tie the NL record, and Dibble and Charlton's becoming the first bullpen tandem to register at least 25 saves each. On the other hand, Piniella and Dibble also engaged in one of the ugliest manager–player fistfights in some years after the pitcher reacted truculently to being removed from a game.

Throughout the season, Schott bristled over the additional $35 million buying only a runnerup team, so there was little shock when Quinn was fired at the end of the year. Named as the new general manager was 31-year-old organization man Jim Bowden. When Piniella accepted an offer to manage the Mariners, Bowden named former Big Red Machine first baseman Perez as his successor. In other moves during the offseason, he signed free agent John Smiley to replace the departing Swindell, obtained slugger Kevin Mitchell from the Mariners for Charlton, landed speedster outfielder Roberto Kelly from the Yankees in return for O'Neill, and inked free agent first baseman Randy Milligan.

Initial enthusiasm that the Latin Perez's appointment marked a decisive gain for minorities was short-lived. In short order, Bowden not only appointed as coaches rival managerial candidates Oester and Dave Miley, but also signed on as hovering advisers such veteran dugout chiefs as Davey Johnson, Bobby Valentine, and Jack McKeon. But even these hirings were overshadowed by disclosures that Schott had made a practice of issuing slurs against blacks, Jews, and Asians in her daily business activities. The charges came to light during a lawsuit filed by Tim Sabo, the team's controller until he was fired in August 1991. Sabo's revelations, which were subsequently backed up by several other people both in and out of the Reds' organization, cited Schott as referring to Parker and Davis as her "million-dollar niggers," as saying that she would "rather have a trained monkey than a nigger" working for her, and as voicing admiration for Hitler's distrust of the Jews ("though he did go too far").

The disclosures caused a furor beyond baseball. While Schott scrambled to hire more blacks and Latins for the organization and insisted that she hadn't "meant anything" by her remarks, national civil rights leaders demanded that she be ousted from the game and that baseball owners finally make good on their vague promises to open up jobs for more minorities. In the middle were the other team owners, who were called on to discipline one of their own while they themselves had organizations almost as lily-white as Cincinnati's. Particularly damaging to the other owners was testimony from a former administrative assistant for the Athletics that Schott had shared her racial remarks with other league executives during a conference call—an incident that none of them seemed to recall.

After months of dragging their feet on the case because of a fear that Schott would go to court to challenge any ouster move, the owners announced in February 1993 that she was being suspended until November and fined $25,000. The decision only solidified the impression that Schott's crassness was merely a stylistic variation of the mentality of many other owners. The recently promoted Bowden was given effective charge of the team for 1993.

CINCINNATI REDS

Annual Standings and Managers

Year	Position	W	L	Pct.	GB	Managers
1890	Fourth	77	55	.583	10½	Tom Loftus
1891	Seventh	56	81	.409	30½	Tom Loftus
1892	Fourth	44	31	.587	8½	Charlie Comiskey
	Eighth	38	37	.507	14½	Charlie Comiskey
1893	Sixth*	65	63	.508	20½	Charlie Comiskey
1894	Tenth	55	75	.423	35	Charlie Comiskey
1895	Eighth	66	64	.508	21	Buck Ewing
1896	Third	77	50	.606	12	Buck Ewing
1897	Fourth	76	56	.576	17	Buck Ewing
1898	Third	92	60	.605	11½	Buck Ewing
1899	Sixth	83	67	.553	19	Buck Ewing
1900	Seventh	62	77	.446	21½	Bob Allen
1901	Eighth	52	87	.374	38	Bid McPhee

1902	Fourth	70	70	.500	33½	Bid McPhee, Frank Bancroft, Joe Kelley
1903	Fourth	74	65	.532	16½	Joe Kelley
1904	Third	88	65	.575	18	Joe Kelley
1905	Fifth	79	74	.516	26	Joe Kelley
1906	Sixth	64	87	.424	51½	Ned Hanlon
1907	Sixth	66	87	.431	41½	Ned Hanlon
1908	Fifth	73	81	.474	26	John Ganzel
1909	Fourth	77	76	.503	33½	Clark Griffith
1910	Fifth	75	79	.487	29	Clark Griffith
1911	Sixth	70	83	.458	29	Clark Griffith
1912	Fourth	75	78	.490	29	Hank O'Day
1913	Seventh	64	89	.418	37½	Joe Tinker
1914	Eighth	60	94	.390	34½	Buck Herzog
1915	Seventh	71	83	.461	20	Buck Herzog
1916	Seventh*	60	93	.392	33½	Buck Herzog, Christy Matthewson
1917	Fourth	78	76	.506	20	Christy Matthewson
1918	Third	68	60	.531	15½	Christy Matthewson, Heinie Groh
1919	First	96	44	.686	+9	Pat Moran
1920	Third	82	71	.536	10½	Pat Moran
1921	Sixth	70	83	.458	24	Pat Moran
1922	Second	86	68	.558	7	Pat Moran
1923	Second	91	63	.591	4½	Pat Moran
1924	Fourth	83	70	.542	10	Jack Hendricks
1925	Third	80	73	.523	15	Jack Hendricks
1926	Second	87	67	.565	2	Jack Hendricks
1927	Fifth	75	78	.490	18½	Jack Hendricks
1928	Fifth	78	74	.513	16	Jack Hendricks
1929	Seventh	66	88	.429	33	Jack Hendricks
1930	Seventh	59	95	.383	33	Dan Howley
1931	Eighth	58	96	.377	43	Dan Howley
1932	Eighth	60	94	.390	30	Dan Howley
1933	Eighth	58	94	.382	33	Donie Bush
1934	Eighth	52	99	.344	42	Rick O'Farrell, Charlie Dressen
1935	Sixth	68	85	.444	31½	Charlie Dressen
1936	Fifth	74	80	.481	18	Charlie Dressen
1937	Eighth	56	98	.364	40	Charlie Dressen, Bobby Wallace
1938	Fourth	82	68	.547	6	Bill McKechnie
1939	First	97	57	.630	+4	Bill McKechnie
1940	First	100	53	.654	+12	Bill McKechnie
1941	Third	88	66	.571	12	Bill McKechnie
1942	Fourth	76	76	.500	29	Bill McKechnie
1943	Second	87	67	.565	18	Bill McKechnie
1944	Third	89	65	.578	16	Bill McKechnie
1945	Seventh	61	93	.396	37	Bill McKechnie
1946	Sixth	67	87	.435	30	Bill McKechnie
1947	Fifth	73	81	.474	21	Johnny Neun
1948	Seventh	64	89	.418	27	Johnny Neun, Bucky Walters
1949	Seventh	62	92	.403	35	Bucky Walters
1950	Sixth	66	87	.431	24½	Luke Sewell
1951	Sixth	68	86	.442	28½	Luke Sewell
1952	Sixth	69	85	.448	27½	Luke Sewell, Rogers Hornsby
1953	Sixth	68	86	.442	37	Rogers Hornsby, Buster Mills
1954	Fifth	74	80	.481	23	Birdie Tebbetts
1955	Fifth	75	79	.487	23½	Birdie Tebbetts
1956	Third	91	63	.591	2	Birdie Tebbetts
1957	Fourth	80	74	.519	15	Birdie Tebbetts
1958	Fourth	76	78	.494	16	Birdie Tebbetts, Jimmy Dykes

1959	Fifth*	74	80	.481	13	Mayo Smith, Fred Hutchinson
1960	Sixth	67	87	.435	28	Fred Hutchinson
1961	First	93	61	.604	+4	Fred Hutchinson
1962	Third	98	64	.605	3½	Fred Hutchinson
1963	Fifth	86	76	.531	13	Fred Hutchinson
1964	Second*	92	70	.568	1	Fred Hutchinson, Dick Sisler
1965	Fourth	89	73	.549	8	Dick Sisler
1966	Seventh	76	84	.475	18	Don Heffner, Dave Bristol
1967	Fourth	87	75	.537	14½	Dave Bristol
1968	Fourth	83	79	.512	14	Dave Bristol
1969	Third	89	73	.549	4	Dave Bristol
1970	First	102	60	.630	+14½	Sparky Anderson
1971	Fourth*	79	83	.488	11	Sparky Anderson
1972	First	95	59	.617	+10½	Sparky Anderson
1973	First	99	63	.611	+3½	Sparky Anderson
1974	Second	98	64	.605	4	Sparky Anderson
1975	First	108	54	.667	+20	Sparky Anderson
1976	First	102	60	.630	+10	Sparky Anderson
1977	Second	88	74	.543	10	Sparky Anderson
1978	Second	92	69	.571	2½	Sparky Anderson
1979	First	90	71	.559	+1½	John McNamara
1980	Third	89	73	.549	3½	John McNamara
1981	Second	35	21	.625	½	John McNamara
	Second	31	21	.596	1½	John McNamara
1982	Sixth	61	101	.377	28	John McNamara, Russ Nixon
1983	Sixth	74	88	.457	17	Russ Nixon
1984	Fifth	70	92	.432	22	Vern Rapp, Pete Rose
1985	Second	89	72	.553	5½	Pete Rose
1986	Second	86	76	.531	10	Pete Rose
1987	Second	84	78	.519	6	Pete Rose
1988	Second	87	74	.540	7	Pete Rose
1989	Fifth	75	87	.463	17	Pete Rose, Tommy Helms
1990	First	91	71	.562	+5	Lou Piniella
1991	Fifth	74	88	.457	20	Lou Piniella
1992	Second	90	72	.556	8	Lou Piniella

*Tie

Postseason Play

LOCS	3–0 versus Pittsburgh	1970		WS	5–3 versus Chicago	1919
	3–2 versus Pittsburgh	1972			0–4 versus New York	1939
	2–3 versus New York	1973			4–3 versus Detroit	1940
	3–0 versus Pittsburgh	1975			1–4 versus New York	1961
	3–0 versus Philadelphia	1976			1–4 versus Baltimore	1970
	0–3 versus Pittsburgh	1979			3–4 versus Oakland	1972
	4–2 versus Pittsburgh	1990			4–3 versus Boston	1975
					4–0 versus New York	1976
					4–0 versus Oakland	1990

Cincinnati Reds

Players League, 1890   **BALLPARK:** NONE

RECORD: NONE

The sale of the National League Cincinnati Reds to a syndicate of Players League backers in October 1890, appeared at first to be a major coup for the PL; it ended as a farce. It also made the Reds the only franchise to belong to three major leagues in less than one year.

As the only NL owner not challenged directly by the PL, Aaron Stern should have been in good shape: He had been able to keep most of his players from the PL raiders, and he had drawn more than 130,000 customers in 1890. Nonetheless, he had lost money, and rumors that he would sell to the Brotherhood persisted. Stern denied the rumors—when he wasn't claiming that he would sell only for cash. He kept neither of these commitments—selling out to PL interests for $40,000 and getting only half the purchase price in cash.

The PL Reds played some exhibition games in October while the syndicate owners, headed by Albert L. Johnson of Cleveland, made sounds about seeking a local buyer. At the same time, however, they were meeting with the NL to settle the terms of the PL's dissolution. The Johnson group eventually found itself with a franchise but without a league.

The NL had anticipated that the syndicate would have reached an accommodation with John T. Brush, who had been awarded the NL Cincinnati franchise after Stern's defection, but Johnson spurned all of Brush's offers. Instead, he negotiated his way into the American Association, then turned around and, using his new league membership as leverage, permitted the NL as a whole to buy him out for $30,000.

Appalled at Johnson's duplicity, the AA hastily tossed together a new Cincinnati club, the makeshift Porkers, to combat Brush's Reds. The AA also secured an injunction against the NL, preventing it either from paying Johnson the $30,000 or from taking over his title to the Cincinnati franchise. Two AA owners who had stock in Cincinnati claimed that Johnson had merely been holding their shares in trust and could not, therefore, sell them; Johnson claimed that they had given him their shares. The ensuing court battles were not settled until Johnson's death in 1901, when the money, which had been held in escrow for a decade, was divided among the surviving participants and the heirs of those who had died. When the last penny had been counted out, the PL Cincinnati Reds still hadn't played an official game.

Cincinnati Porkers

American Association, 1891   **BALLPARK:** PENDLETON PARK

RECORD: 43–57 (.430)

For raucus adventure, wild antics, and just plain fun, the Porkers have never been matched in major league baseball. Created to challenge the Reds, who had jumped from the American Association to the National League, the team did nothing conventionally.

With Chris Von der Ahe of the St. Louis Browns holding three-quarters of the stock, the Porkers were a joint venture by association owners, who felt required to field a team in Cincinnati. The syndicate owning the club placed Edward Renau in nominal charge as president, but Von der Ahe, no shrinking violet, consistently meddled in operations.

The ballpark, which was located in Pendleton (just east of Cincinnati's city limits), was almost impossible to reach except by a one-hour steamboat ride. The manager was aging star and bon vivant King Kelly, whose concept of leadership included allowing players to pick which position they wanted to play on a given day, providing ample supplies of food and alcohol to enliven the lengthy post-game discussions, and being in the vanguard whenever the team marched into court to face charges of violating Pendleton's ordinance against Sunday baseball. Kelly became something of a local hero when he was found not guilty, three times, of contravening the local blue laws—each time immediately after completing a Sunday game. The players, a collection of Players League veterans who could find no other home, were more than willing to follow Kelly's rambunctious lead: On the field the brawls began on opening day against Von der Ahe's Browns and became almost a daily feature thereafter.

What is remarkable is that between all the eating and drinking and brawling the team won as often as it did—and lasted as long as it did. Even for the association, which had always been less prim than the NL, the Porkers were too much. In mid-August, John T. Brush, owner of the NL Reds, paid Von der Ahe $12,000 to vacate the Cincinnati territory. The deal came while the AA was negotiating with the Western Association Milwaukee Brewers to replace the Porkers. Von der Ahe claimed that all he was doing by dumping Cincinnati and wooing Milwaukee was fending off the Western Association's threat to the AA. He promised there would be another AA team in Cincinnati before long; he was wrong.

CINCINNATI PORKERS

Annual Standings and Manager

Year	Position	W	L	Pct.	GB	Manager
1891	Partial season	43	57	.430	—	King Kelly

Cleveland Forest Citys

National League, 1879–1884

RECORD: 242–299 (.447)

BALLPARK: KENNARD STREET PARK

OTHER NAMES: BLUES

The Forest Citys achieved special importance not for their five seasons as a member of the National League, but for the nature of their demise and the disposition of their players. A direct casualty of the Union Association war, the club's death throes forced a reconsideration of how major league teams did business with one another, with results that affected the game for 100 years.

The Forest Citys were a relatively successful (32 wins, 20 losses, 4 ties) independent club in 1878, when NL president William Hulbert decided that Cleveland, with its population of 150,000, was a perfect market for helping him realize his ambition of expanding the league from six to eight teams. Sporting flashy checkered uniforms, the club was anything but an instant success: The star of the team was workhorse pitcher Jim McCormick, who won 20 and lost 40 and, as field manager, led the team to a weak sixth-place finish. The following year, with a much improved lineup that included second baseman Fred Dunlap, shortstop Jack Glasscock, left fielder Ned Hanlon, and right fielder Orator Shaffer, McCormick improved his record to 45–28 and the team's position to third.

The improvement was short-lived. Mike McGeary took over as manager and third baseman in 1881, but after only eleven games, seven of them losses, he requested his release and was replaced by McCormick. Toward the end of the season, the NL blacklisted Ed (The Only) Nolan for "general dissipation and insubordination." Dunlap batted .325, but the rest of the team slipped badly and finished seventh.

The Forest Citys became the Blues when the NL

Outfielder Dave Rowe pitched one game for Cleveland, on July 24, 1882. He gave up 29 hits and 7 walks. The 35 runs charged to him is a major league record for one game.

mandated specific colors for 1882 uniforms. Cleveland was assigned a navy blue that caught the eye more than the white (Chicago), red (Boston), gray (Buffalo), gold (Detroit), light blue (Providence), green (Troy), or brown (Worcester) handed out elsewhere. In addition to the new uniforms and the new name, there was also a new manager, J. Ford Evans, who relinquished the presidency to C. H. Bulkley to take over daily operations; he led the club to a 42–40 record, good for sixth place.

In 1883, under Frank Bancroft, the Blues moved up two notches to fourth and began to look like a team with a future. But the Union Association war of 1884 hit Cleveland harder than any other NL team. Dunlap broke the reserve clause in his contract to sign with the St. Louis Maroons before the season began; Glasscock, McCormick, and catcher Fatty Briody jumped their contracts in August to join the Cincinnati Outlaw Reds. With Glasscock and McCormick gone, attendance plummeted, as Clevelanders declined to watch the minor leaguers brought in as replacements by new manager Charlie Hackett. Bulkley, needing $5,000 just to finish the season, sought assistance from NL president A. G. Mills. Mills persuaded the other seven clubs to split the gate receipts 50/50 when Cleveland visited, but to accept the usual 70/30 split when playing in Cleveland.

Bulkley, his club crippled beyond salvation, sold the franchise for $2,500 to Henry V. Lucas, the owner of the Maroons. Assuming that he had purchased the Blues' player contracts as well as the Cleveland franchise, Lucas prepared to wait the required ten days before signing the players. But the Brooklyn Bridegrooms of the American Association moved first, and hid seven players in hotel rooms where Lucas could not reach them. On the tenth day, the Bridegrooms signed all seven players.

The ensuing uproar almost caused a new war between the leagues. Owners on both sides, realizing that business as usual could not continue, authorized a secret meeting of a joint committee in Saratoga on August 24, 1885, to revise the National Agreement that defined their relationship. The new rules, announced in October, included a provision that allowed only clubs in the same league to negotiate with a player in the first ten days after he was released or his club disbanded; after the tenth day, clubs in the other league would be permitted to make offers. This innovation eventually led to the waiver rule that dictated, until recent years, how each league could approach the other's players.

In 1885, Cleveland, out of the NL for a full season, won its final contest, although in the courts rather than on the field. Lucas, miffed over the loss of the seven players to Brooklyn, had refused to pay the $2,000 he owed the Cleveland franchise; Bulkley sued him for the money and won.

CLEVELAND FOREST CITYS

Annual Standings and Managers

Year	Position	W	L	Pct.	GB	Managers
1879	Sixth	27	55	.329	31	Jim McCormick
1880	Third	47	37	.560	20	Jim McCormick
1881	Seventh	36	48	.429	20	Jim McCormick, Mike McGeary
1882	Sixth	42	40	.512	12	Jim McCormick, Fred Dunlap
1883	Fourth	55	42	.567	7½	Frank Bancroft
1884	Seventh	35	77	.313	49	Charlie Hackett

Cleveland Blues

American Association, 1887–1888	**BALLPARKS:** AMERICAN ASSOCIATION PARK (1887–1888) BEYERLE'S PARK (1888)

RECORD: 89–174 (.338)

When the Pittsburgh Alleghenys left the American Association after the 1886 season, the league chose as a replacement a Cleveland club formed by Frank De Haas Robison, the owner of two local streetcar lines. Robison's initial interest in baseball stemmed almost exclusively from the game's potential effect on patronage of his Payne Avenue line, at the end of which he built American Association Park.

The makeup of the team showed his lack of interest. Only right fielder Fred Mann, who led the club with a .309 average, came from the Alleghenys, and he was dispatched in midseason to the AA Philadelphia Athletics. The rest of the squad was made up of rookies and castoffs who finished a dismal last under manager Jimmy Williams.

In 1887, Williams and team secretary Davis Hawley discovered shortstop Ed McKean with Rochester of the International League and catcher Chief Zimmer with Poughkeepsie of the Hudson River League. The following year, they managed to get

> The first Native American to reach the major leagues was Jim Toy, a first baseman with the Blues in 1887. Toy, who was part Sioux, batted .222 in 109 games.

pitcher Jersey Bakely reinstated after he had been forced to spend three years on the sidelines because of his participation in the Union Association. With McKean beginning to come into his own (a .299 average to lead the team), Zimmer taking over behind the plate, and Bakely winning 25, the Blues rose to sixth place. Williams wasn't around to see the improvement, however, having given way to Tom Loftus in midseason.

When the demise of the Detroit Wolverines created an opening in the National League for the 1889 season, Robison leapt at the opportunity to join the older, better-run, and more lucrative circuit.

CLEVELAND BLUES

Annual Standings and Managers

Year	Position	W	L	Pct.	GB	Managers
1887	Eighth	39	92	.298	54	Jimmy Williams
1888	Sixth	50	82	.379	40½	Jimmy Williams, Tom Loftus

Cleveland Spiders

National League, 1889–1899	**BALLPARKS:** NATIONAL LEAGUE PARK (1889–1890) LEAGUE PARK (1891–1899) WESTERN LEAGUE PARK (1891–1899)

RECORD: 738–764 (.491)

What is best remembered about the Cleveland Spiders is that they compiled the worst full-season record of any team in the history of major league

baseball; except for that one year, however, they actually had a winning record. Further, the Spiders, for the better part of their twelve years in the National

League, rivaled the Baltimore Orioles as the rowdiest, most intimidating team in the game.

The winning habit took several years to develop; in their first three seasons, the Spiders finished in the bottom half of the league and changed managers three times. But the intimidation of umpires and opponents began almost immediately after Frank De Haas Robison brought his American Association Blues to the NL and renamed them the Spiders because so many of the players were tall and spindly. Their slight frames proved no bar to violent brawls. In a typical game against the Giants on August 14, 1889, umpire Jack Powers was jumped on by third baseman Patsy Tebeau, shortstop Ed McKean, and second baseman Cub Stricker when he reversed a decision that had originally gone in the Spiders' favor. Powers required a police escort to get out of the clubhouse.

The 1889 season ended on a sour note when Cleveland lost to the Giants in a game which Boston had offered the Spiders $1,000 if they won. The Players League war of 1890 offered further lows when every player except McKean, pitcher Ed Beatie, and catcher Chief Zimmer jumped to the Brotherhood. Lightning and an ensuing fire destroyed the grandstand at National League Park in June. Then, in less than two years, Hall of Famer Cy Young made his debut; the Players League collapsed; Jimmy McAleer, who was to become a sterling defensive center fielder, returned to the fold; second baseman Cupid Childs, who would hit over .300 in five of the next seven seasons, made his debut; Tebeau was appointed manager; and Jesse Burkett, arguably the best hitter of the nineteenth century and a Hall of Famer since 1946, arrived.

The expansion of the NL to twelve teams in 1891 produced an experiment with a split season. The Spiders finished first in the second half, entitling them to a postseason series with first-half winner Boston. Boston won the league championship handily. The postseason series kept both teams out of a conspiracy among NL owners to drive down player salaries. In order to save two weeks of payroll, the other clubs released every player at the end of the season even though contracts ran until November 1st. The profits for the six games of the series more than compensated Boston and Cleveland for the two weeks extra salary the clubs had to pay.

The Spiders hit their stride mid-decade, finishing second to the Baltimore Orioles in both 1895 and 1896. Burkett, who hit .356 over eight seasons in Cleveland, won back-to-back batting championships in 1895 and 1896 with averages of .409 and .410.

Young racked up 241 wins in nine years, including seasons in which he led the NL in wins (35 in 1895) and strikeouts (140 in 1896). Second-place finishes gave the Spiders the right to meet the Orioles for the Temple Cup, a postseason contrivance to inject excitement into the one-league monopoly. In the first series, in 1895, Young beat the Orioles three times and Burkett hit .500 to spearhead a four-out-of-five triumph; in the second championship series, the Orioles swept.

It wasn't only in the won-lost columns that the Spiders rivaled the Orioles. Tebeau's style of play was as ferocious as that of John McGraw in Baltimore. The Cleveland manager was even jailed for his attack on an umpire who decided it was too dark to continue a game in Louisville in 1896; Tebeau, McAleer, McKean, and Burkett were fined by the NL over the incident, and other NL teams proposed a boycott of Cleveland until the Spiders mended their ways. Robison headed off the threat by securing an injunction against both the collection of the fines and the boycott. In another episode, Tebeau and backup catcher Jack O'Connor pursued Cleveland sports-

National Baseball Library, Cooperstown, NY

writer Elmer Pasco to a saloon and thrashed him in retaliation for what he had written about the Spiders.

Even though they dropped to fifth place in 1897, the Spiders had their best year at bat. Led by Burkett (.383), six starters hit better than .300. The phenom was Native American Indian right fielder Lou Sockalexis, who was hitting .413 until he injured his foot jumping out of a whorehouse window; he finished the season at .338. In the middle of a second consecutive fifth-place finish marked by paltry attendance figures, Robison arranged to have almost every home game in the last two months of 1898 played on the road. Fan apathy, Sunday blue laws (which forced the Spiders to play in more distant Western League Park), and the sixty-day road schedule conspired to keep home attendance down to about 70,000 for the season. When fans threatened a boycott in retaliation for Robison's desertion of the city, he indulged in the then-legal practice of syndicate baseball by purchasing the St. Louis Browns at a bankruptcy auction on March 14, 1899. Within a few weeks, he left Cleveland in the hands of his brother Stanley, took personal charge in St. Louis, and engaged in a wholesale exchange of players between the two clubs. Moving to St. Louis in the most one-sided trade in baseball history were future Hall of Famers Young, Burkett, and Bobby Wallace; manager-first baseman Tebeau; 23-game winner Jack Powell; Childs and McKean; and right fielder Harry Blake. In return, Cleveland received a combination of over-the-hill types and authentic nobodies. Third baseman Lave Cross was named manager, but in June, when it became clear that he could still hit, he was shipped back to St. Louis.

The Cleveland press immediately began calling the team the Misfits, the Leftovers, the Discards, and the Castoffs. The rescheduling of home games to the road began immediately; the Robisons even changed the Opening Day venue from Cleveland to St. Louis, where 15,200 fans showed up to watch the newly renamed Perfectoes win 10–1. The Cleveland *Plain Dealer*, accurately assessing the impending disaster, reported the game under a headline that read, "The Farce Has Begun."

The exploits of Lou Sockalexis, a Penobscot Indian from Maine, in a summer league in the early 1890s inspired Gilbert Patten, who managed in the league, to write the Frank Merriwell stories under the pen name Burt L. Standish.

On the grounds of decorum, two more home games were transplanted to the road when Frank Robison's daughter died. Cleveland finally came home on May 1st with a record of 1–7, to win the home opener in front of 500 fans. The high point of the season came on May 20th and 21st, when the Spiders beat Philadelphia and Louisville for their longest winning streak of the season. Cleveland fans barely paid attention to the team, with crowds sinking to as small as seventy-five. Pittsburgh came away from a three-game series with a $64 share of the gate receipts, less than half of the hotel bill for its stay in Cleveland.

After July 1, the team (soon called the Wanderers and the Exiles) played only six games at home. Its record over that period was 9 wins and 86 losses. From August 26th until the end of the season, it won 1 and lost 40, including a major league record of 24 in a row. When all the pounding was over, the Spiders had a record of 20 wins and 134 losses, a .130 percentage, the lowest in major league history. They finished a mind-numbing 84 games out of first place and 35 games out of eleventh place in the twelve-team NL. After their last game, the players gave club secretary George Muir a diamond locket as a reward for being "the only person in the world who had the misfortune to watch us in all of our games."

For the Robisons, everything turned out exactly as they had planned—or almost. Their grand design of moving all their quality players to St. Louis where they would win a pennant failed when the Perfectoes finished fifth. But the rest of the scheme fell into place nicely. After releasing or selling off any remaining player with talent, the highest salary on the team was a mere $2,500; total operating expenses were a paltry $45,000. Income was even lower, because only 6,088 fans showed up for the twenty-four home games—an average of about 250 people per game.

Having stripped the Cleveland franchise of everything, the Robisons sought to sell. They negotiated with interests in Detroit, a move the NL rejected because Detroit was a smaller market than Cleveland, and Toronto, an idea that no one took seriously. Throughout the year there were rumors that the NL would be streamlined, shucking two teams or even four. The final rumor proved true: In March 1900, the NL paid the Robisons $25,000 for their franchise rights in Cleveland, assumed the last three years of the lease on National League Park for $5,000 a year, and closed down the team. The Robisons got to keep their St. Louis franchise.

CLEVELAND SPIDERS

Annual Standings and Managers

Year	Position	W	L	Pct.	GB	Managers
1889	Sixth	61	72	.459	25½	Tom Loftus
1890	Seventh	44	88	.333	43½	Gus Schmelz, Bob Leadley
1891	Fifth	65	74	.468	22½	Bob Leadley, Patsy Tebeau
1892	Fifth	40	33	.548	11½	Patsy Tebeau
	First	53	23	.697	+3	Patsy Tebeau
1893	Third	73	55	.570	12½	Patsy Tebeau
1894	Sixth	68	61	.527	21½	Patsy Tebeau
1895	Second	84	46	.646	3	Patsy Tebeau
1896	Second	80	48	.625	9½	Patsy Tebeau
1897	Fifth	69	62	.527	23½	Patsy Tebeau
1898	Fifth	81	68	.544	21	Patsy Tebeau
1899	Twelfth	20	134	.130	84	Lave Cross, Joe Quinn

Cleveland Infants

Players League, 1890   **BALLPARK:** BROTHERHOOD PARK

RECORD: 55–75 (.423)

The Brotherhood of Professional Base-Ball players evolved into the Players League on Bastille Day, July 14, 1889, at a meeting when John Montgomery Ward first announced his intention to form a new league. Among those attending the Brotherhood session was Albert L. Johnson, a Cleveland streetcar line operator and the brother of Cleveland Mayor Tom J. Johnson. Johnson was genuinely offended by the reserve clause, which he viewed as an affront to his progressive view of the United States. But he was also a practical businessman who saw the heavy traffic on Frank Robison's streetcar line carrying customers to see Frank Robison's National League Cleveland Spiders. Both motives impelled him to agree to back a PL franchise in Cleveland.

Johnson, described by Ward as an "organizing genius," managed to win over the nucleus of the Spiders team: second baseman Cub Stricker; third baseman Patsy Tebeau; outfielders Paul Radford, Jimmy McAleer, and Larry Twitchell; catcher Sy Sutcliffe; and pitchers Henry Gruber, Ed Bakely, and Darby O'Brien. A young Ed Delahanty jumped from the NL Philadelphia Phillies to play shortstop, and Henry Larkin came from the American Association Philadelphia Athletics to play first base and manage

until he was succeeded by Tebeau in midseason. But the biggest catch was the pride of the AA, Pete Browning, who left Louisville to join the Infants.

Johnson's raids produced very little: Despite Browning's league-leading .373 batting average and the club's league-leading .286, the Infants languished in seventh place. Although the club outdrew the Spiders, the Cleveland market could produce only about 106,000 paying customers between the two teams. Johnson lost approximately $340,000 on his venture, but, unfazed, he struck what he thought would be a decisive blow for the PL by assembling a syndicate to purchase the NL Cincinnati Reds. Buoyed by the coup, Ward suggested a peace conference at which Chicago president Albert Spalding, leading the NL forces, bluffed the PL delegates, including Johnson, into revealing the extent of their losses. In the ensuing scramble to make separate deals, Johnson tried to sell the NL both the Infants and his share in the Cincinnati franchise for $40,000; the NL owners, sensing victory, declined. As the PL dissolved around him, Johnson tried to reach an accommodation with Frank Robison, but the Spiders' owner would have none of it. In the end, Johnson had to swallow both his pride and his Cleveland losses.

CLEVELAND INFANTS

Annual Standings and Managers

Year	Position	W	L	Pct.	GB	Managers
1890	Seventh	55	75	.423	26½	Henry Larkin, Patsy Tebeau

Cleveland Indians

American League,
1901–Present

BALLPARKS: LEAGUE PARK (1901–1932; 1934–1936)
MUNICIPAL STADIUM (1932–Present)

RECORD: 7193–7018 (.506)

OTHER NAMES: BLUES, BRONCOS (OR BRONCHOS), NAPS, AND MOLLY MCGUIRES

The drabbest major league franchise since midpoint in the century, the Indians are actually surprising in not having a worse record than they do. That they remain above .500 despite failing even to attain third place since 1968 largely reflects their solid teams after the world wars and in the 1930s. But that said, the club's mere three pennants in more than nine decades makes it the caboose of the league among non-expansion franchises. The wonder isn't that there have been numerous attempts over the years to move the team away from Cleveland and its justifiably alienated fans, but that none of the initiatives has succeeded.

The Blues, as they were first known for the color of their uniforms, moved into Cleveland in 1900 as a member of the minor Western League of Ban Johnson. Transplanted from Grand Rapids, the club was owned by coal magnate Charles Somers and haberdasher John Kilfoyl, both of whom got into the venture on Johnson's assurances that the Western League (rebaptized the American League) would develop into a major circuit as soon as its teams played a season and attracted local followings. When Johnson proved to be correct, it was in significant part because of Somers's financial assistance. In addition to bankrolling his own Cleveland franchise, the millionaire kept Connie Mack afloat in Philadelphia, advanced substantial loans to the St. Louis Browns, supplied the capital needed to build Comiskey Park in Chicago, and paid all the bills for the Boston club for a couple of years. Somers's open checkbook also made it easier for his manager,

Jimmy McAleer, to lure some key players away from the National League. The best of the pickups was Cubs' third baseman Bill Bradley, who became a hot corner fixture in Cleveland for almost ten years.

The Blues debuted as a major league team on April 24, 1901—an 8–2 loss to the White Sox; because the other three games scheduled to be played that day were rained out, the contest also formally inaugurated the American League. The Opening Day defeat was followed by eighty-one others, and the team managed to finish ahead of only the chaotic Milwaukee Brewers. Southpaw Pete Dowling ignited an organization tradition of less than brilliant lefty pitching by leading the league with 26 losses (4 of them with Milwaukee before being traded). After the season, Johnson prevailed on Somers and Kilfoyle to allow McAleer to take over the Brewers (who were being shifted to St. Louis) for the good of the league; named as the new manager was Bill Armour. Unlike his predecessor, Armour found himself with a club that boasted two future Hall of Famers. The first one was righthander Addie Joss, who made his debut with 17 victories and a 2.77 ERA; for the rest of his career, Joss never again posted such a high ERA. When he was struck down by meningitis at the age of 31 after nine big league seasons, he had compiled four 20-win years and a composite run yield of 1.88, second in baseball history to Ed Walsh. Joss was elected to the Hall of Fame in 1978, after the waiving of the eligibility regulation requiring at least ten years of major league service.

It was also in the second year of the club's ex-

The memory of Louis Sockalexis, the first Native American in the major leagues, inspired a Cleveland fan to suggest Indians as a new team name in a 1915 contest. Sockalexis, who played for the National League Spiders between 1897 and 1899, is shown here in the uniform of a Poland Springs, Maine, amateur club. *National Baseball Library, Cooperstown, NY*

In the opening day game against Chicago on April 24, 1901, Cleveland second baseman Erv Beck doubled for the American League's first extra-base hit. The following day, Beck also clouted the league's first home run.

istence that it acquired one of the greatest position players in its history—Nap Lajoie. A lifetime .339 hitter regarded as without equal for his graceful defense, the second baseman landed in Cleveland along with outfielder Elmer Flick and pitcher Bill Bernhard as the solution to a legal suit aimed at forcing the three players back to the NL Phillies, from whom they had all jumped to the AL Athletics after the 1900 season. In changing leagues without changing cities, the trio had become vulnerable to a Pennsylvania court injunction barring them from playing in the state and making them unavailable to Connie Mack except as road players. With little choice in the matter, Mack went along with a Johnson proposal to deal the three to Cleveland for a small amount of money, catcher Ossee Schreckengost, and second baseman Frank Bonner; the major cost to Somers and Kilfoyle was not being able to use Lajoie, Flick, and Bernhard in Philadelphia games against the Athletics. The righthand-hitting Lajoie more than made up for that with his reign of terror against the rest of the schedule. In his thirteen years of service with the club, he won two batting titles (and arguably a third), batted well over .300 eleven times, led the league in doubles and slugging average twice and in runs batted in once. When he retired after a twenty-one-year career, he had amassed 3,251 hits—reason enough for his 1937 election to Cooperstown.

The other two pickups from the Athletics were no slouches either. Flick also ended up in the Hall of Fame (elected in 1963), for a thirteen-year career that produced a .315 average and a reputation as one of the early century's swiftest flyhawks. He led the league in hitting once, in slugging once, in steals twice, and in triples three times. Somers thought so much of the lefthand-hitting Flick that he turned down a straight one-for-one swap with Detroit for Ty Cobb in 1908. As for Bernhard, he had four big winning seasons for the team, including 23 victories in 1904.

Despite the presence of Joss and the three former Philadelphia players, the team sputtered along for three seasons under Armour as no better than a middle-of-the-pack also-ran. One problem was an unreliable defense, a second was lack of pitching depth, and a third was the club's less than complete respect for Armour's strategic talents. Making the manager's position all the more difficult was Lajoie, whose popularity was so immediate that a Cleveland *Press* poll in 1903 made the Naps an easy winner in a search for a new nickname for the squad. It was anything but a surprise when Armour submitted his resignation after the 1904 season and was immedi-

In 1903, shortstop Johnny Gochnauer established the twentieth-century record for errors when he made 98 miscues. His fielding average for the year was .869.

Cleveland players Nap Lajoie and Harry Bay were the first subjects of a motion picture shot on baseball. Lajoie and Bay went through some motions for a camera during a postseason exhibition series against Cincinnati in 1903.

It was because of Cleveland protests that baseball owners introduced a rule after the 1908 season stipulating that any called-off game having a mathematical bearing on the pennant race had to be made up. In 1908, Cleveland lost the pennant to Detroit by the margin of a half-game because of a Tigers' rainout.

ately replaced by the second baseman. It still wasn't until 1908, however, that the club made a genuine run at the pennant, in part because of a series of debilitating injuries to key players and in part because of growing evidence that Lajoie had bitten off more than he was able to chew in doing double service as the team's pilot and leading hitter. By 1908, in fact, the same Cleveland *Press* that had been conducting the chorus of hosannas for the infielder had taken up the role of chief critic of his managerial smarts, questioning everything from his daily lineup and starting rotation to his increasing outbursts of temper against umpires, rivals, and his own players. With this as the background, the 1908 squad finally jelled and got into a dogfight with the Tigers and White Sox that continued through the month of September and reached its dramatic peak on October 2nd in a duel between Joss and Chicago's Walsh, the two stingiest hurlers in baseball history. Although Walsh allowed a mere four hits and fanned fifteen, he also uncorked a pitch that went off catcher Schreckengost's mitt, was officially ruled a wild pitch, and permitted Cleveland to score the only run of the game. For his part, Joss did nothing more than pitch a perfect game. But though the mound masterpiece was immediately hailed as the turning point in the AL race, the Naps instead lost their concluding games to the Chisox and the Browns, while the Tigers took advantage of a rainout to finish a half-game on top of the standings. The pennant agony so unnerved Kilfoyle that his health deteriorated and he stepped aside as club president. Somers, who had previously only wanted the title of vice-president despite being the franchise's number one man, reluctantly took over the top spot and brought in Ernest Barnard as vice-president and head of baseball operations.

Next to Somers, Barnard, a one-time college coach and the editor of the Columbus *Dispatch,* was the most influential executive in the early days of the organization. No sooner had he taken over as vice-president than, a decade before Branch Rickey turned it into a science, he sold Somers on the idea of establishing regular farm system working agreements with a string of minor league franchises; Somers ended up investing heavily in several teams in the network, which included New Orleans, Toledo, Portland (Oregon), Waterbury (Connecticut), and Ironton (Ohio).

A year after its almost-pennant, Cleveland was back near the bottom of the standings; the fall came despite a successful return to the city by Cy Young, baseball's all-time winner who had started his career with Cleveland's NL team in 1890. By the beginning of September, the frayed Lajoie had run out of gas, and asked Somers to appoint a new manager. Though he insisted initially that the change was being made only for the remainder of the 1909 season, the owner tapped Deacon McGuire for the post; it was only after the conclusion of the campaign that, in the face of Lajoie's adamance against returning, McGuire was given the job on a definitive basis. With the second baseman again only a player, the *Press* went back to its periodic task of finding a new nickname for the club, and acknowledged its own surprise when fans once again voted for Naps.

The next few years brought one big name and several big controversies. The name was outfielder Joe Jackson, whom Somers acquired from the still-helpful Mack in July 1910. Although the lefthanded slugger had been touted for a couple of years as Philadelphia's prime prospect, Jackson himself had asked out of the organization because of what he considered "Eastern" taunts of his rural background; with slightly more western Cleveland, he ripped the league apart for all or parts of five seasons with batting marks of .387, .408, .395, .373, and .338, and was off to a .331 average in 1915 before the swap with Chicago that sent him to his appointment with the Black Sox scandal. The first of the controversies arose on the last day of the 1910 season, when Lajoie, in a neck-and-neck fight with Cobb for the hitting title, found a suspiciously cooperative St. Louis defense during a doubleheader, enabling him to dump six bunt singles during an eight-hit afternoon. Although the Cobb-hating Browns were so transparent in their intention that Johnson banned St. Louis manager Jack O'Connor after the season, the Detroit outfielder was still declared the winner by one point. There the matter rested until 1981, when *Sporting News* researcher Paul MacFarlane rechecked the records, discovered that Cobb had been credited erroneously with one hit, and called for the crown to be reassigned to Lajoie. Commissioner Bowie Kuhn overruled the appeal for fear of opening a Pandora's box of revised statistics.

The second controversy exploded in April 1911, with the team in shock from the sudden death of Joss. Although the pitcher's funeral was scheduled to be held in Toledo on the same day that Cleveland was slated to open the season in Detroit, neither Somers nor the Tigers would countenance the idea of postponing the opener a day, prompting a revolt by the Naps. With first baseman George Stovall as their spokesman, the players handed a petition to manager McGuire for delivery to Somers, then left Detroit for Toledo before the document was ever presented. Both McGuire and the Detroit management had inflammatory stories that the team had pulled an illegal strike, but Somers stepped in to soothe all parties, and the opener was held the following day, as the players had requested all along. The incident only worsened already brittle relations between the tart-tongued McGuire and the team, which almost to a man wanted Stovall as pilot. The players appeared to get their way toward the end of the season, when McGuire stepped aside and the first baseman was named to succeed him for the final seventeen games. But unknown to the club, Somers had completed yet another deal with Mack for aging first baseman Harry Davis, with the specific intention of appointing him the manager for 1912. The official announcement of Davis's selection during the offseason preceded by only a couple of weeks the trading of Stovall to the Browns.

It was a fairly surly bunch of Cleveland players who reported for the 1912 season. Aside from Lajoie, Jackson, and lefthander Vean Gregg, few of them showed a disposition to play for Davis, and the results were not long in coming when the team plopped into fifth place to stay midway through the year. Davis resigned in favor of 28-year-old center fielder Joe Birmingham. The choice went over with everybody except Lajoie, who questioned Birmingham's credentials as a big league pilot at every opportunity. Relations between the manager and the star arrived at a breaking point in June 1913, when Birmingham benched Lajoie for the first time in the future Hall of Famer's career for not hitting; a week

did not go by for the rest of the season without Lajoie lashing into Birmingham either on the bench or in the sports pages. When the manager asked for front office support, he received little beyond double-talk from Somers and Barnard. Birmingham himself also gained some grandstand protection from the unexpected rise of the club to third place, to a large extent because of his handling of youngsters like shortstop Ray Chapman, catcher Steve O'Neill, and pitchers Fred Blanding and Willie Mitchell.

The following year, the bottom fell out. The first blow came with the formation of the rival Federal League and the on-and-off threats of its organizers to move into Cleveland. To head off this move, Somers shifted the minor American Association franchise that he had in Toledo to League Park, the idea being that local fans would have some kind of baseball without the Feds even when Cleveland was on the road. All this succeeded in doing was showing the city that the owner's minor league club was better than his major league one, because Toledo finished fifth in the AA while Birmingham's squad dropped all the way to the cellar; to make the point even clearer, Barnard and Birmingham kept moving players from one team to the other throughout the season. The net result was still 102 defeats, the most suffered by the franchise until 1991. Lack of interest in the club was such that, while the baseball-minded could turn out an estimated 80,000-strong for an amateur game played at the Brookside Park amphitheater in 1914, only 186,000 of them passed through the gates at League Park for the entire year.

For Somers, it was the beginning of the end. Overextended by almost 2 million dollars, he completed six straight transactions between the end of the 1914 season and the following August that were aimed primarily at helping his sagging treasury. The first of the deals was the headline-making sale of Lajoie to the Athletics; at the end of the line, the second baseman had asked to play out his days in the city where he had started his career. On August 21, 1915, Somers also got rid of Jackson in the exchange with the White Sox that brought Cleveland outfielders Braggo Roth and Larry Chappell, pitcher Ed Klepfer, and $31,500. The money from the sales was too little too late, however, and creditor banks ended up taking away all of Somers's baseball properties except the minor league franchise in New Orleans. Acting as agent for the creditors, AL president Johnson eventually found a buyer in Chicago-based James Dunn, head of a railroad construction firm.

The passing of the old guard once again got the *Press* polling its readers for an appropriate name for the team. Even prior to Lajoie's departure, the paper had gotten into the habit of referring to the squad as the Molly McGuires—an extremely loose historical allusion to the fact that the players were restive employees of the coal mining boss Somers (but having nothing to do with ex-pilot McGuire). The name never really caught on with anybody but Somers himself, and became moot altogether after the owner was forced to step down. The *Press*'s newest poll came out in favor of Indians, in honor of former (NL) Cleveland Spiders' outfielder Lou Sockalexis, a Penobscot Indian whose passing was announced while the survey was being conducted. Adoption of the nickname Indians, with associated logos and caricatures, exposed the franchise to numerous charges over the years that it was promoting racial stereotypes, but a succession of Cleveland owners into the 1990s dismissed the accusation and refused to change the name still again.

The new owner Dunn's first move was to name Bob McRoy, a onetime assistant to AL president Johnson, Cleveland general manager. His second move was to stir up a fight with the city's papers by announcing that Barnard was out of the new administration; after a lot of unsubtle pressuring by the dailies, Dunn assigned Barnard to vague duties in the front office. Two years later, with McRoy ailing, Barnard regained his old position as the head of the club's baseball operations. The front office squabbles were completely overshadowed, however, by an April 1916 swap with the Red Sox that brought future Hall of Famer Tris Speaker to the team. Speaker had become available because of a lengthy contract dispute with Boston owner Joseph Lannin that so embittered the outfielder that he refused to report to spring training. Even after the deal had been announced, Speaker refused to budge from the sidelines until he received a $10,000 payment as part of the transaction, and received it personally from Lannin. When the Red Sox owner dragged his feet on the demand, Johnson had to step in to guarantee the $10,000 personally.

Although the lefty-swinging Speaker had surged to major league baseball's front ranks with his first nine seasons in Boston, he ultimately played an even more influential role in his eleven years wearing a Cleveland uniform. In his debut season in Ohio, he led the circuit with a .386 batting average, a .502 slugging mark, and 41 doubles. Subsequently, he topped the .300 level nine more times, with many of the averages closer to .400. It all added up to a .344 lifetime average and election to Cooperstown in 1937. But as valuable as he was as a player, Speaker

Tris Speaker. *National Baseball Library, Cooperstown, NY*

was also in effect the team's manager from the day he arrived. Rarely did nominal pilot Lee Fohl make an important move in the lineup or with the starting rotation without first consulting his center fielder; even more striking, Fohl made pitching changes in the course of a game only after decoding prearranged signals from Speaker in the outfield. Speaker also had a big say in front office transactions, and it was on his advice that the franchise acquired several former Boston teammates. The most important of these was Joe Wood, who went from being a washed-up pitcher in Boston to a valuable platoon outfielder in Cleveland.

With Speaker providing most of the punch, the Indians improved by 20 games in the standings in 1916 and by another 11 the following season. By 1918, the team was back to being regarded as a legitimate pennant contender, especially with the maturation of Stan Coveleski and Jim Bagby in the starting rotation. But then the club ran into a brick wall, when no fewer than nine roster players were drafted for World War I military service and Speaker got into a blistering argument with an umpire that cost him a one-week suspension at the peak of the pennant race; the Indians ended up 2½ games behind Boston. Expectations were even higher the following season, particularly in the wake of a deal with the Athletics that netted third baseman Larry Gardner and outfielder Charlie Jamieson (who never batted below

The 1916 Indians were the first AL team to wear numbers on uniforms, on the sleeves. The practice was not fully adopted until some years later.

.291 in the first thirteen of his fourteen seasons with the organization). The obstacle this time around turned out to be the relationship between Fohl and Speaker. In a big game against the Yankees in August, Fohl either misunderstood the hand signals from his center fielder or ignored them in selecting reliever Fritz Coumbe to come in from the bullpen to face Babe Ruth in a clutch situation. When Ruth clouted a homer, the already agitated Speaker let everyone in the stands know how he felt about the relief choice, prompting Fohl to leave the bench before the end of the game and to submit his resignation shortly afterward. Having to take over the club in name as well as in fact, Speaker lost his concentration as a player for the only time in his career and dropped below the .300 mark, taking the club down with him.

Cleveland finally cashed in its chips in 1920. While the rest of baseball was waking up to the reports that there had been some hanky-panky during the previous year's World Series between Chicago and Cincinnati, Speaker was putting the finishing touches to one of the strongest teams in franchise history. A key element of the fine tuning was a bizarre contract with pitcher Slim Caldwell that ordered the righthander, whose career had been floundering at the bottom of a bottle, to drink himself into a stupor after every starting assignment, but that also called for his immediate release should he touch a drop at any other time. Caldwell responded with the only 20-win season of his twelve-year career. Even better were Bagby, who topped the league with 31 victories, and Coveleski, who contributed 24. Offensively, the team ran away from the league in average (.303), doubles, triples, walks, runs scored, and runs batted in. At the head of the onslaught was playing manager Speaker, who hit .388 and drove home 107 runs.

The flag did not come cheaply. In a Polo Grounds game against the Yankees on August 16th, starting shortstop Ray Chapman took a fastball in the head from submarine specialist Carl Mays and, after twenty-four hours of agony, died of a fractured skull. The diamond's first and only beaning fatality staggered the club, especially Speaker, who was so broken up that he declined to attend the infielder's funeral. In less than a week, the Indians had dropped out of the first-place standing they had held for some time, showing little sign that they would be able to rebound from the gloom cast by Chapman's death. To make matters worse, the team had to keep issuing statements urging anonymous Cleveland fans to stop their lunatic threats to get even with Mays the next

time the Yankees came to town. That the club overcame its gloom was due in large measure to the purchase of minor league shortstop Joe Sewell in early September; in appearing in the final twenty-two games of the season, Sewell rekindled the squad's fire offensively and defensively to make the difference in a two-game edge over Chicago. Even that margin, however, carried a price tag with late August reports that the same White Sox players who had allegedly thrown the 1919 World Series to the Reds, had accepted further bribes to cave in to the Indians. Although there was never definitive evidence proving the charges, various baseball officials, most notably NL president John Heydler, pointed a finger at Cleveland as one of the nerve centers of baseball betting. The most lasting effect of the accusations was to make Dunn and everybody else associated with the franchise defensive about Cleveland's pennant win; as late as 1948, when the club won its second AL flag, the controversy was reflected in cracks that the team had finally arrived in the World Series legitimately.

On the eve of the World Series against Brooklyn, Speaker asked the ruling National Commission to grant special permission for Sewell, who had been acquired after the eligibility deadline of September 1st, to play the postseason games. Johnson and Heydler, already with their plates full with a grand jury investigation of the 1919 World Series and other purported bribery cases, immediately passed the buck to the Dodgers; it turned out to be about the last nondecision of the commission, because Judge Kenesaw Landis was sworn in shortly afterward as the game's first commissioner. As for Brooklyn, it knew it had little choice in the matter: Between behind-the-scenes pressures not to create more bad publicity for the sport and its own reluctance to seem to be taking advantage of Chapman's death, it granted Cleveland permission to carry Sewell on the roster. In the event, the shortstop had a woeful Series, committing six errors and batting only .174, but Cleveland still overcame a slow start of two losses in the first three games to win, 5 games to 2. The pitching star was Coveleski, who allowed only two runs in three complete-game victories. Game Five was one of the most memorable in World Series history because of three firsts for postseason competition achieved by the Indians—a home run by a pitcher (Bagby); a grand slam home run (Elmer Smith); and, especially, an unassisted triple play (by second baseman Billy Wambsganss, who caught a line drive off the bat of Clarence Mitchell, touched second base to double off Pete Kilduff, and then tagged Otto Miller).

Another twenty-eight years passed before the team played before World Series bunting again. The best pitchers of the 1920s were Coveleski, George Uhle, and Wes Ferrell. In 1921, Coveleski won more than 20 for the fourth year in a row; although he never again gained the magic number for the Indians, he also led the league in ERA in 1923. The righthander was elected to the Hall of Fame in 1969 on the basis of 215 wins and an overall ERA of 2.88. Uhle never reached Coveleski on a career level, but he still won 200 games and had a couple of seasons when he was even better; in 1926, for example, he topped AL hurlers with 27 triumphs. Uhle was also useful coming off the bench as a pinch-hitter; his .288 lifetime mark is the highest for a pitcher who did not play another position for an extended time and who had at least 500 at bats. On the other hand, Ferrell's hitting abilities were so well known that they often overshadowed his pitching accomplishments; between 1929 and 1932, for instance, he had four consecutive 20-win seasons. Ferrell's most noted batting accomplishments are the 9 home runs that he hit in 1931 and the 38 in his career, both long-ball marks for a pitcher.

Aside from Speaker and Jamieson, Cleveland's most consistent offensive performer in the 1920s was Sewell, who went on to a .312 Hall of Fame career. The shortstop's particular forte was being able to make contact, and he set most of the important records for strikeout infrequency. His average of only one whiff for every 63 at bats leaves even category rivals like Lloyd Waner and Tommy Holmes distant runners-up. Another Hall of Famer who joined the team in the decade was outfielder Earl Averill, who was in double figures in homers for every one of his ten full seasons with Cleveland and who posted a .318 mark for his career. Averill, who reached Cooperstown in 1975, also had nine years when he batted in a minimum of 90 runs and ten seasons in a row of scoring at least 100.

On the eve of the 1922 season, owner Dunn was felled by a bad heart; for the next five years, the franchise was run by his widow and Barnard. While there were constant attempts to find a new buyer, it was not until November 17, 1927 that a group of

On August 26, 1926, righthander Dutch Levson defeated the Yankees in both ends of a doubleheader by scores of 5–1 and 6–1. He is the last major league pitcher to hurl two complete-game victories on the same day. Levson had no strikeouts in either contest.

Cleveland businessmen headed by John Sherwin and Alva and Chuck Bradley concluded an offer to take over. Alva Bradley, who with his brother owned a large amount of downtown Cleveland real estate and an appreciable part of the banks, hotels, and stores on it, took over as president—a post he would hold until after World War II. To run the team's day-to-day baseball operations, the new owners brought in Billy Evans, a former umpire who was later inducted into the Hall of Fame.

As for Speaker, he remained at the managerial helm until 1926, when, largely thanks to Uhle's 27 wins and a big offensive contribution (.358 and 114 RBIs) from first baseman George Burns, he had the club battle the Yankees right down to the wire before having to accept second place. For Speaker, however, the near-win was forgotten quickly in the heat of a postseason investigation into charges that he, Wood, Cobb, and Detroit pitcher Dutch Leonard had colluded in a fix back in the black year of 1919. The probe was sparked by Leonard himself, who late in the 1926 season sent Commissioner Landis a pair of yellowed letters that appeared to implicate the Indians and Tigers in a plot to assure Detroit a third-place finish behind Chicago and Cleveland; according to Leonard, the four players had shared the proceeds from bets placed on the game (won by Detroit) of September 25, 1919. A disbelieving Landis took a long time to round up testimony in the case, partly because Leonard refused to go east from his California home to offer personal testimony and the commissioner himself was forced to travel to the west coast. But even as the judge was trying to be discrete about his inquiries, the Tigers called a press conference to announce that Cobb had resigned as manager and, a few weeks later, Barnard summoned reporters to a similar announcement that Speaker

Jack Graney, a Cleveland outfielder from 1908 to 1922, was the first player to go from the diamond to the broadcast booth upon his retirement.

On April 16, 1929, Earl Averill became the first AL hitter to clout a home run in his first major league at bat.

was also leaving his post. While Speaker seemed satisfied to note that neither of the Leonard letters mentioned him by name, Cobb charged that the whole controversy had been ignited by Detroit owner Frank Navin, who had been trying to get out from under the playing manager's big contract for years. Before the accusations finished flying, both Cobb and Speaker also dragged AL president Johnson into the fray, noting that he didn't like either outfielder and alleging that he had used $20,000 of AL money to pay Leonard for the letters.

Johnson and Landis didn't like each other any more than the AL president and the two outfielders did, so the use of his name didn't hurt the players' case with the commissioner, who was already vexed by Leonard's refusal to travel to Chicago to confront his purported co-conspirators. Thus it did not come as a total shock when, on January 17, 1927, Landis exonerated Cobb, Speaker, and Wood. Privately he urged Cobb and Speaker (Wood was already out of the big leagues and working as a baseball coach at Yale) to ignore the many offers they had received from the NL since resigning their player-manager posts and to remain in the junior loop; for either of them to leave the AL, Landis said, would amount to a victory for Johnson anyway. After considering their alternatives, including the possibility of suing Leonard and baseball for defamation of character, Cobb decided to go to the Athletics and Speaker to the Senators. Johnson voiced skepticism over the outcome of the investigation, but then so did many others.

Speaker's immediate successor, Jack McCallister, came and went in the final year before Dunn's widow sold the franchise to Sherwin and the Bradleys, and did nothing to impress the new owners with his sixth-place finish. If nothing else, the club's next three managers—former Indians' shortstop Roger Peckinpaugh, Hall of Fame hurler Walter Johnson, and long-time Cleveland catcher Steve O'Neill—were far more familiar to local fans than McCallister. In terms of the annual standings, however, while they all usually kept the team above .500, none of them could get the club closer than ten games to the pennant winner; even when Peckinpaugh's 1932 charges finished 22 games above the break-even point, for instance, they still ended up 19 behind the Yankees. The worst friction of the decade was between Johnson and Evans, with the latter telling anyone who would listen that it had never been his idea to hire the one-time Washington great as field boss. Evans received plenty of ammunition from the players for his dislike of Johnson. Long-simmering tensions in the clubhouse boiled over in May 1935, when Johnson unilaterally

released two veterans, third baseman Willie Kamm and catcher Glenn Myatt, behind assertions that they were the ringleaders of a team plot to get rid of him. Kamm went over the heads of the Cleveland front office to Landis, demanding that the commissioner open an investigation to clear his name. Landis eventually issued a statement vindicating the two players, but also reaffirmed Johnson's contractual right to cut loose any player he didn't want. Evans promptly hired the 35-year-old Kamm as a Cleveland scout and applauded the decision of the Giants to sign the 38-year-old Myatt.

The incident didn't end there. When Averill tried to round up some public support for Johnson, fans generally sympathetic to the outfielder booed him. At one point, management was so apprehensive about the grandstand attitude toward the manager that extra police were assigned to League Park and concession stand beverages had to be dispensed in soft cups rather than bottles. The breaking point for Bradley came on Sunday, July 28th, when a mere 5,000 fans showed up for a game against league-leading Detroit. Although Bradley had weathered the crowd hostility with the philosophy that it was good for business, the ensuing indifference toward a team that was going nowhere, under a manager that nobody but Averill seemed to like, led him to fire Johnson in favor of O'Neill. Evans had little time for crowing, however, for he too was gone after the end of the season when he declined to accept a pay cut from the increasingly strapped ownership. To save a little more money, Bradley eliminated the office of general manager altogether, bringing in long-time chief scout Cy Slapnicka as a special assistant.

One of the biggest events for the franchise during the decade of the 1930s was the opening of massive Cleveland Municipal Stadium on July 31, 1932. Originally built in the hope of attracting that year's Olympics to Cleveland, the facility's circular design imposed tremendous disparities in the outfield distances, suggesting to some a Polo Grounds West and creating further uncertainty for the franchise over the years about what kind of offensive team should be sought. But ever since hosting its inaugural game between Cleveland and Philadelphia (a 1–0 shutout by the Athletics' Lefty Grove), the park has aroused even more debate about its sheer size. On the positive side, its official opening capacity of 78,000 has allowed Cleveland to set the AL records for largest attendance for a single day game (74,420 in 1973), a doubleheader (84,587 in 1954), and a night game (78,382 in 1948). On the other hand, it is the least intimate stadium in the major leagues, with even crowds of 20,000 and 30,000 looking like minor clusters of spectators huddled within the vast arena. Making matters worse are frequent bone-chilling winds blowing off Lake Erie that have earned the facility the sobriquet of The Mistake by the Lake. Bradley took his time committing the franchise to playing all its games in the stadium. After playing all their home dates there in 1933, in fact, the Indians moved back to League Park for the following season and continued to call the older installation their main quarters until after World War II. Until then, the club played at Municipal only when it anticipated particularly big crowds, on Sundays, holidays, and, later, weekday nights.

Averill was not the only player to provide offense for the club in the 1930s. In 1931, outfielder Joe Vosmik worked his way into the regular lineup with 117 RBIs and the first of several .300 years; the right-handed hitter's biggest performance came in 1935, when he led the AL in doubles and triples, drove in 110 runs, and batted .348. An even more potent bat, before a migraine condition forced a premature retirement, belonged to first baseman Hal Trosky, who belted between 19 and 42 homers every year between 1934 and 1940 and who had six straight seasons of at least 100 RBIs (including 142 to lead the league in 1936); the righty slugger retired with a career average of .302. The later part of the decade also saw debuts by third baseman Ken Keltner and shortstop Lou Boudreau, both of whom would become league stars in the 1940s. For a single game, nobody in major league history was more productive than shortstop Johnny Burnett, who, on July 10, 1932, cracked seven singles and a pair of doubles in an 18-inning contest against Philadelphia.

Aside from Ferrell, the team's most reliable starter for the better part of the decade was Mel Harder, who won 20 in 1934, then followed that up with 22 victories the following season. The period's most unreliable starter, on the other hand, was Johnny Allen, whose assorted antics on and off the field ultimately overshadowed his 20 wins in 1936 and his astonishing 15–1 record in 1937. Allen's chief problem was a temper that was easily set off by either alcohol or the taunting of opposition players, who caught on very early that the righthander was a model "rabbit ears." His blotter with the Indians included one incident when he ripped apart a Boston hotel lobby, another when he tried to deck third baseman Odell Hale for making an error that cost him a sixteenth straight win in 1937, and a regular series of fines for one infraction or another. On June 7, 1938, however, Allen entered Cleveland lore for good

when, in a game against the Red Sox, he stalked off the mound rather than obey umpire Bill McGowan's demand that he cut off the sleeve of his tattered undershirt, which was conveniently flapping in the eyes of Boston batters with the release of every pitch. With time called and Fenway Park fans becoming increasingly agitated, Allen sat on the bench rejecting pleas from manager Ossie Vitt and teammates that he allow the trainer to snip off the offending sleeve. Finally out of patience, Vitt announced that he was fining the pitcher $250 for leaving the mound without permission; Allen's departing words were to tell Vitt and McGowan to go to hell and to announce his intention of retiring. A couple of days later, Bradley met the team in New York and restored something like peace when he bought the undershirt from Allen for the same $250 that he had been fined. The owner then had the garment put on display in a Cleveland department store operated by his brother, where it remained until the Hall of Fame requested it for its own exhibition.

Ferrell, Harder, and Allen all turned out to be lesser pitching stories, however, than righthander Bob Feller, who was signed in 1936. Only 17 when he was spotted by Slapnicka, Feller carried the franchise for almost fifteen years, riding a blazing fastball and wicked curve to 266 career victories that included six 20-win seasons and seven years of leading the league in strikeouts. The Iowa native had three no-hitters during his career, the most notable of which was his Opening Day mastery of the White Sox on April 16, 1940. His single most successful season was probably 1946, when he overwhelmed AL hitters with 26 victories, 36 (out of 42) complete games, 10 shutouts, 348 strikeouts, and a 2.18 ERA. Feller entered Cooperstown in 1962.

Feller's career with the Indians was almost still-born due to the haste of Slapnicka in getting him to a major league mound. Although mindful of rules that called for players of Feller's age to be signed only to minor league contracts, the team official sought to protect his flank with a lot of paperwork dodges while throwing in the righthander against major league hitters—first in a midseason exhibition game with the Cardinals, then in regular season AL games. The irregularity was brought to Landis's attention immediately, but the commissioner said nothing until he received a formal complaint from the owner of a minor league club in Des Moines who had been beaten to the hurler by Slapnicka. After hearing testimony from all concerned, there seemed little doubt that Landis had enough grounds to declare Feller a free agent and allow him to accept one of the big money contracts that were already being waved at his family by the Yankees, Red Sox, and Tigers. But in the end, it was the interest of these very teams, especially the perennial contenders from New York and Detroit, that appeared to dictate the judge's decision to leave the pitcher where he was; both Feller and his father had also indicated a preference for Cleveland. As for the Des Moines club that had brought the complaint, Landis decided that it was at least entitled to a $7,500 indemnity from the Indians for the way the major league organization had behaved in the affair.

About six months later, Slapnicka tried a reverse dodge in hiding slugger Tommy Henrich in the Cleveland farm system. When Henrich protested to the commissioner's office that he was being denied a legitimate shot at the majors, Landis upheld the complaint and declared the outfielder a free agent. Henrich then signed with the Yankees for a $25,000 bonus. In response to the Landis ruling, Slapnicka took the bizarre position that the protest to the commissioner had been inspired by ex-general manager Evans and accused him of a "breach of ethics" for telling Henrich his rights.

With the coming of Vitt as manager in 1938, the club entered another tormented phase that made the Johnson days seem like a honeymoon. To the new pilot's credit, his three years at the helm produced 252 victories. With Feller overcoming fears of a sore arm by leading the league with 27 victories and the middle infield combination of shortstop Boudreau and second baseman Ray Mack startling the league with its defensive wizardry, the 1940 club in particular enthralled Cleveland with its season-long battle with the Tigers for the top spot. As it turned out, it was Vitt's overuse of Feller, bringing him in from the bullpen in a critical late-season game against Detroit and watching him surrender a spray of clutch hits, that ultimately kept the Indians out of the World Series by the margin of a single game. But in comparison to what he provoked off the field for practically his entire stay, even Vitt's unwise use of Feller was negligible.

The manager's first problem was his penchant for criticizing a player to reporters, to Bradley and Slapnicka, and even in shouts to the field from the dugout, but rarely to his own face. When the players weren't mumbling to each other over this treatment, they were muttering about the constant changes in the lineup that were often based on little more than a pinch-hitter's single or a regular's 0–for–4. Within the steadily poisoned climate between the manager and the team, the club began venting its frustrations on the field in altercations with umpires and rival players. One exception was outfielder Jeff Heath, who subsequently acknowledged starting fights on his own bench in the hope that Vitt would try to break them up. Along the way, there were also several cases of players asking to be traded to another organization or attempting to sound out Slapnicka on what it would take to force a change in managers. Although Slapnicka never gave the players any particular reason for hope because the team was playing better than at any time in two decades, Vitt himself concluded that the executive was plotting with Heath and a couple of others; this in turn prompted a cold war between the manager and Bradley's righthand man.

The breaking point came in June 1940, during a game in Fenway Park in which the Red Sox were lathering Feller. When Vitt shouted out "There's my star out there, the great Feller. How can I win a pennant with him?", he emboldened Harder and Trosky to organize a delegation of veterans that visited Bradley and demanded that a new pilot be named. The president spurned the protest, but then unwittingly confirmed the substance of the meeting to Cleveland *Plain Dealer* beat writer Gordon Cobbledick. In a matter of hours, the local dailies were practically unanimous in branding the players as Crybabies, implying that Vitt was just too hardnosed for them. The Crybabies tag followed the team from city to city for the rest of the season, with crowds in Detroit particularly ugly about throwing everything from baby bottle nipples to jars of baby food at the Indians. Although the players eschewed any further public protests, they agreed among themselves to act more subtly against Vitt's rule; for example, deciding that the manager was too timid to employ the hit-and-run play, they worked out a second set of signs among themselves to use the tactic when Harder, Allen, or catcher Frankie Pytlak thought it appropriate. The squad still ended up a game behind Detroit.

Although Vitt got through the season, he didn't get much further. Back came Peckinpaugh for 1941, a season that became mostly noteworthy in Cleveland for the July 17th night game (attended by a then-record 67,468) in which southpaw Al Smith and righthander Jim Bagby, Jr. stopped Joe DiMaggio's 56-game hitting streak with the help of a couple of sizzling fielding plays by third baseman Keltner. Following the campaign, Slapnicka stepped aside, citing health reasons in general and conceding that his almost daily tribulations with Vitt had taken more of a long-term toll than he had anticipated; Peckinpaugh was kicked upstairs to run daily baseball operations. In the ensuing speculation about Peckinpaugh's successor in the dugout, almost everybody in both leagues was named except the man who got the job—the 24-year-old Boudreau. The choice was the inspiration of Peckinpaugh, who himself holds the record for being the youngest manager in baseball history, having taken over the 1914 Yankees at the age of 23.

After a couple of rough seasons when he admitted to being intimidated by his older charges and when his defensiveness created a lot of problems with the media, Boudreau was seen as a worthy successor to Lajoie and Speaker as a player-manager. He also flourished as a player during the decade, progressing from a smooth-fielding shortstop to a smooth-fielding shortstop with one of the most lethal bats the AL had seen at his position. A batting champion in 1944 and a regular league leader in doubles, the righthand swinger put everything together for an MVP trophy in 1948, when he hit .355, with 18 homers, 34 doubles, 106 RBIs, and 116 runs scored. Boudreau was elected to the Hall of Fame in 1970.

No sooner had Boudreau been handed the reins for the 1942 campaign than Trosky was forced into retirement by his migraine condition and Feller became one of the first major leaguers to enlist in the military after the bombing of Pearl Harbor. The two developments were a portent for the war years, with the club's best players either enlisting or being drafted and the leftovers capable of only middle-of-the-pack finishes. Aside from Boudreau himself, who failed an army physical because of arthritic ankles, the best players during the period were Keltner, outfielder Heath, and pitchers Bagby, Allie Reynolds, and Steve Gromek. It was also during the war that Bob Lemon tried to break into the Cleveland lineup as a third baseman. With the end of the hostilities, Lemon was shifted to the outfield for a brief period before a final conversion to the mound. In thirteen years of pitching, the righthander racked up 207 victories, including seven 20-win seasons. He entered Cooperstown in 1976.

After another mediocre year in 1945, majority stockholder Sherwin began putting out feelers for a sale of the franchise. Aside from his own tepid interest in baseball other than as an investment, Sherwin had become bogged down in organization affairs more than he had counted on because of the deaths of several of the partners belonging to the original 1927 purchasing group; by the mid-1940s, in fact, five widows sat on the club's board of directors. Ignoring pleas from Bradley, Sherwin and members of his family sold out their majority interest for $1.6 million to promoter-extraordinaire Bill Veeck on June 21, 1946. The Veeck group included long-time White Sox official Harry Grabiner and also counted among its minority partners comedian Bob Hope. The Veeck era was short—but also the most eventful in franchise history.

With Grabiner at his side, Veeck set out immediately to fulfill his declared intention of raising Cleveland baseball from the dead. In a matter of weeks in the middle of the 1946 season, he reached out to the fans in everything from reversing a policy against keeping foul balls to extending an invitation to any radio station in the city to broadcast Indians' games for free. Rarely did the club play back-to-back home games without promotions like ethnic nights or midget racing. For pregame clowning, baseball comedians Max Patkin and Jackie Price were hired with the official title of coach; between innings, an orchestra played the popular songs of the period. By his own admission, the new owner had also planned to add more color to the dugout by hiring Casey Stengel as the manager and demoting Boudreau to player-only status. But at a dinner shortly after the sale of the club, Boudreau persuaded his new bosses that, unless he were traded altogether, he could only create a lot of problems for any successor by merely being around. Veeck remained skeptical, especially about Boudreau's stiffness in handling the media, but had little desire to trade the shortstop.

It didn't take long for the Indians to become the most talked about franchise in the league—and with the record-breaking gate figures to prove it (helped appreciably by the team's move to Municipal Stadium for good in 1947). With the signing of Larry Doby near the end of the 1947 season, the club was also the first in the circuit to break the color barrier, breached earlier in the year in the NL with Jackie Robinson's arrival in Brooklyn. A second baseman for the Negro leagues, Doby did little in his few appearances in his maiden season, his evident nervousness serving to reinforce the commonly-held opinion that he was just another Veeck box-office ploy. That changed in 1948, when the Indians moved Doby to the outfield, where he came through with a .301 mark. Over the next eight years, the lefthand-hitting slugger never hit fewer than 20 home runs, twice leading AL batters in that category. Unlike Robinson and Branch Rickey, Doby had made no pledge to Veeck about turning the other cheek, so that opposing teams got the message early that brushback pitches or deliberate spikings were going to be answered immediately.

The team that Doby joined at the end of 1947 was considerably different from the one that Veeck and Grabiner had inherited from Bradley and Peckinpaugh. The new regime's first deal, in the autumn of 1946, was also one of its biggest—acquiring slugging second baseman Joe Gordon from the Yankees in return for Reynolds. With Mack no longer needed as Boudreau's keystone partner, Veeck then made a second swap with New York in which he sent the second baseman and catcher Sherm Lollar east in exchange for pitchers Gene Bearden and Alan Gettel and outfielder Hal Peck. A third trade of the period saw outfielder Gene Woodling going to Pittsburgh for veteran catcher Al Lopez. Gordon and Bearden, in particular, were among the most prominent contributors to Cleveland's renaissance in the late 1940s, but it was another deal that Veeck didn't make that had the city in an uproar. Mindful of Boudreau's observation that he had managed the club too long ever to be carried only as a player again, Veeck got himself into a public relations quagmire at the end of the 1947 season when he entertained an offer from the Browns to send his shortstop, outfielder George Metkovich, and two minor leaguers to St. Louis in return for shortstop Vern Stephens, outfielder Walt Judnich, and pitchers Jack Kramer and Bob Muncrief. As soon as the newspapers got word of the proposal, Boudreau supporters organized protest demonstrations and petitions demanding that Veeck leave town instead of their hero. When he realized what he had wrought, Veeck ran all over Cleveland, going from bar to restaurant to bar, to admit as personally as he could that he had made a mistake while also denying that a deal had been completed or that it had even been his idea to begin with. Popular opinion continued to run against the owner until early November, when he summoned Boudreau to a peace-making session and, rather than get rid of him, gave him a new two-year contract as the team's player-manager. The only condition that Veeck attached to the pact was that he, not Boudreau, would choose the club's coaches for 1948. By the time the new season rolled around, the manager found himself surrounded by veteran baseball men like Bill McKechnie, Muddy Ruel, and former star pitcher Harder.

The 1948 season was frenetic. It ultimately came down to a pennant-deciding playoff game against the Red Sox, but even one of the most intense races in league history had to battle all year with Veeck for attention. First, there was the owner's decision to take advantage of the club's potential power by adding an auxiliary fence to the outfield walls of Municipal Stadium; the payoff was that both Gordon and Keltner hit more than 30 homers, while Boudreau, Doby, first baseman Eddie Robinson, and catcher Jim Hegan also hit double figures. Then there was his incessant search for the "extra piece," leading to

deals for third baseman-outfielder Bob Kennedy and pitchers Russ Christopher and Sam Zoldak. But even these valuable pickups were overshadowed by Veeck's second dip into the Negro leagues in mid-season and his signing of the venerable Satchel Paige. Estimated as being anywhere from 47 to 57 years old when he took a major league mound for the first time, the righthander went 6–1 with a 2.48 ERA in seven starts and fourteen relief appearances; two of his wins were complete-game shutouts. Not only did the promotions continue, but in one of his more inspired moves, Veeck didn't even allow the fact that the Indians, Red Sox, and Yankees were all deadlocked at the top of the standings with only hours left in the campaign to prevent him from staging Good Old Joe Earley Night on September 28. Earley had drawn the honor for no better reason than having written a letter to Veeck questioning why the team's promotions seemed to ignore the average fan. More than 60,000 fans showed up to see Earley and his wife presented with an automobile and other gifts; they also stuck around for a 11–0 victory over the White Sox. Even that attendance total, however, paled before some of the other crowds drawn to Municipal Stadium in the course of the year. On Opening Day, for instance, the gate reached 73,163; on the final day of the season, with the outcome of the race still in question, the number was 74,181. It did not come as too much of a surprise when the overall total for the year—2,620,627—shattered all previous big league records.

Apart from Boudreau's MVP effort and the offense that was energized by moving in the fences, the story of the year between the lines was southpaw Bearden, who went 20–7 and led the AL in ERA with 2.43. The lefty, who neither before nor after 1948 managed more than eight wins in a season, was so effective that he was chosen ahead of both Lemon (20 wins) and Feller (19) to pitch the decisive playoff duel against Boston; although rocky at the beginning of the game, he rode two homers and two singles by Boudreau to an 8–3 victory and Cleveland's first pennant in twenty-eight years. Bearden appeared only once in the World Series against the Braves—a five-hit shutout in Game Three. Otherwise, the star of the Series—taken by the Indians in six games— was Lemon, who won both his starts.

The 1948 season was a tough act to follow, and the 1949 season came up short. Although the club stayed in the running for most of the summer, it finally collapsed under diminished efforts from everybody except Doby and Lemon. Veeck himself had a hard job getting into the spirit of the campaign because of the death of Grabiner immediately after the World Series; by midseason, however, he had broken in former Detroit slugger Hank Greenberg as a new aide and was again coming up with aggressive promotion ideas. His most discussed show of the year was the ritualistic burying of the world championship flag after it had become obvious that the Indians were not going to be able to overtake the Yankees and the Red Sox. Events of the kind on top of the team's contending status added up to another 2.2 million fans. Unfortunately for Veeck, not even that total saved him from a personal economic crisis when his wife sued him for divorce. With his only finances tied up in the team, he was forced to sell the club to Cleveland insurance executive Ellis Ryan and Greenberg.

For much of the 1950s, the Indians were the AL's Other Club—the one that also beat up mercilessly on weak sisters like the Browns, Senators, and Athletics, but that wasn't quite as good as the dynasty that had arisen in Yankee Stadium. At the beginning of the decade in particular, the club's pitching staff of Lemon, Feller, Early Wynn, and Mike Garcia was second to none, not even the Yankees.

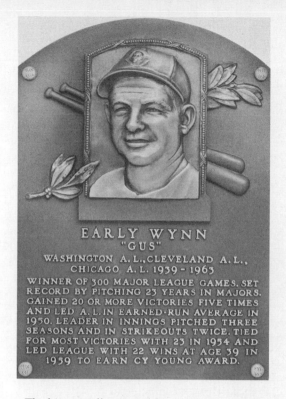

EARLY WYNN
"GUS"
WASHINGTON A.L., CLEVELAND A.L.,
CHICAGO A.L. 1939 - 1963
WINNER OF 300 MAJOR LEAGUE GAMES. SET RECORD BY PITCHING 23 YEARS IN MAJORS. GAINED 20 OR MORE VICTORIES FIVE TIMES AND LED A.L. IN EARNED-RUN AVERAGE IN 1950. LEADER IN INNINGS PITCHED THREE SEASONS AND IN STRIKEOUTS TWICE. TIED FOR MOST VICTORIES WITH 23 IN 1954 AND LED LEAGUE WITH 22 WINS AT AGE 39 IN 1959 TO EARN CY YOUNG AWARD.

The biggest offensive additions at the start of the new decade were third baseman Al Rosen, first baseman Luke Easter, and second baseman Bobby Avila:

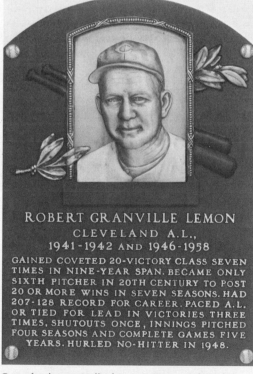

ROBERT GRANVILLE LEMON
CLEVELAND A.L.,
1941-1942 AND 1946-1958
GAINED COVETED 20-VICTORY CLASS SEVEN TIMES IN NINE-YEAR SPAN. BECAME ONLY SIXTH PITCHER IN 20TH CENTURY TO POST 20 OR MORE WINS IN SEVEN SEASONS. HAD 207-128 RECORD FOR CAREER. PACED A.L. OR TIED FOR LEAD IN VICTORIES THREE TIMES, SHUTOUTS ONCE, INNINGS PITCHED FOUR SEASONS AND COMPLETE GAMES FIVE YEARS. HURLED NO-HITTER IN 1948.

One of only two Hall of Fame trios to pitch in the same starting rotation. The other threesome was Chief Bender, Eddie Plank, and Rube Waddell of the Athletics. *National Baseball Library, Cooperstown, NY*

ROBERT WILLIAM ANDREW FELLER
CLEVELAND A.L. 1936 TO 1941
1945 TO 1956
PITCHED 3 NO-HIT GAMES IN A.L., 12 ONE HIT GAMES. SET MODERN STRIKEOUT RECORD WITH 18 IN GAME, 348 FOR SEASON. LED A.L. IN VICTORIES 6 (ONE TIE) SEASONS. LIFE TIME RECORD: WON 266, LOST 162, P.C., 621, E.R. AVERAGE 3.25, STRUCKOUT 2581.

Rosen led the league in homers twice, RBIs twice, and won MVP honors in 1953; Easter clubbed 86 homers between 1950 and 1952; and Avila won the batting championship in 1954. Boudreau survived through the 1950 season, when he took his twin roles as shortstop and manager to the Red Sox; he was replaced by Lopez. It was Lopez who was at the helm in 1954, when the team established the AL record for wins in a season (111) and gave the Yankees (who won 103) a rest from the World Series. The Cleveland juggernaut was led by Rosen and Doby, who combined for 56 homers and 228 RBIs, and by Avila, who won the batting title with a .341 mark. The pitching staff was even more impressive, with its overall ERA of 2.78 the lowest in the AL since 1918. Starring on the mound were Wynn and Lemon with 23 wins apiece, Garcia with the ERA title, and the relief tandem of lefty Don Mossi and righty Ray Narleski. But though figured as overwhelming favorites in the World Series against the Giants, the Indians went down four straight times in games that became most memorable for Dusty Rhodes's pinch hits and Willie Mays's spectacular catch on Vic Wertz's long drive in the eighth inning of the first game. It was the last appearance by the club in postseason competition.

Within two years of its pennant win, the team was plummeting toward the bottom of the standings, and shedding Municipal Stadium customers as extra weight. Between 1956 and 1958, the franchise that had only a few years before set the pace for attendance in baseball was at the bottom of the list with the Washington Senators. The reasons for the sudden reversal were numerous, starting with the failure of the organization's minimal farm system, the predilection of Greenberg for veteran players who were closer to retirement than their peak years, and a local press that never let up on the club's deficiencies, creating even more ill will in the grandstands than the team might have deserved normally. The only domestic-bred player who did everything expected of him was right fielder Rocky Colavito, whose long-ball power and strong throwing arm made him one of the most popular players ever to take the field for the franchise. Colavito's biggest years were 1958 and 1959, during which he belted 83 home runs and drove in 224 runs. Another outfielder developed in the Cleveland system, Roger Maris, was dealt away before he blossomed. The chief pitching prospect of the decade, southpaw Herb Score, was just coming into his own when a line drive off the bat of Gil McDougald in May 1957 struck him in the eye and effectively ended his mound dominance.

Among the players acquired by Greenberg to try to fill the void were ex-Pittsburgh teammate Ralph Kiner, former Boys of Summer third baseman Billy Cox, one-time Giants' ace Sal Maglie, and erstwhile Detroit regular Hoot Evers—none of whom brought much to the table. As for the press, it seemed to have a hard time getting over Veeck, and never warmed up to the administrations that followed. Greenberg, for one, accused the city's leading dailies of turning a still-respectable team into a mockery in the eyes of the fans. Lopez echoed this charge in 1956, when he blamed sportswriters for encouraging fans to boo Rosen, who had been forced to leave a game with a broken nose.

The decline at the turnstiles together with the stumbling on the field served as fertile ground for rumors that the club was going to follow the example of franchises like the Boston Braves, St. Louis Browns, and Philadelphia Athletics and shift operations to another city. Greenberg, in particular, was reported as urging the organization's board of directors to vote for a move to Los Angeles before the Dodgers or another NL team got there. Instead, the majority ownership of insurance executives Ryan and Mike Wilson opted in 1957 to sell their stock to a syndicate headed by William Daley, a Cleveland millionaire with railroad and banking interests. With the franchise tied even more tightly to the city, Greenberg, too, cashed in his stock, bidding goodbye with a blast at the fans and the press for being unable to support a major league team.

Greenberg's successor as general manager was Frank Lane, who demonstrated why he was known as The Trader by completing almost sixty major league deals between December 1957 and December 1960. Players came and went by the score—sometimes because they filled an immediate need, other times because they promised a lot for the future, still other times only because Lane was bent on capturing media attention. Among the most familiar names passing through Cleveland in the period were Mickey Vernon, Billy Martin, Jimmy Piersall, Granny Hamner, and Don Newcombe. Two transactions stood out. In the first, announced on June 15, 1958, Lane sent Maris, pitcher Dick Tomanek, and first baseman Preston Ward to Kansas City in return for first baseman Vic Power and shortstop Woodie Held. The transaction was sharply denounced by several AL teams because it left the slugging prospect Maris with a club—the Athletics—that operated as a major league affiliate of the Yankees. Lane, who had rejected a couple of direct New York offers for Maris and who did not enter into a single trade with the

Yankees during his stay in Cleveland, took the public stance that he was not responsible for Kansas City's future dealings (which did, indeed, include sending Maris on to the Bronx).

The outcry in AL front offices over the swap with the Athletics was nothing, however, compared to the grandstand protests when Lane sent the popular Colavito to the Tigers in the spring of 1960 in exchange for batting champ Harvey Kuenn. The official justification for the swap was that the Indians were in more immediate need of consistency at the plate than the long ball, but that excuse faded before statistics that showed Colavito ahead of Kuenn in just about every important offensive category except doubles and batting average. The real trigger for the deal was the fear in the front office that Colavito's power numbers and appeal to the fans were putting him in a Boudreau-like position to demand a significant salary increase. In any case, the outfielder continued his long-ball hitting with the Tigers, while Kuenn lasted only a single season in Cleveland before being sent on to the Giants.

The traffic in players was paralleled by regular movement in and out of the managerial chair. Following Lopez's departure after the 1956 season, the parade included Kerby Farrell, Bobby Bragan, former star second baseman Gordon, Jimmy Dykes, Mel Mc-Gaha, and Birdie Tebbetts. Dykes was obtained from the Tigers for Gordon in an unprecedented swap of non-playing managers arranged by Lane and his Detroit counterpart Bill DeWitt. But the deepest impression was left by Bragan, whom local lore attributed with casting a hex on the club after he was fired in the middle of the 1958 season. Although Bragan himself insisted that the story arose from the overnight rantings of a Cleveland disc jockey, it was a good enough pretext for the management of the late 1980s to promote a pregame "de-hexing" ceremony by a witch; the promotion was successful, but the team continued to lose. Bragan was also the source of one of the game's more quoted remarks, when he told reporters that Lane had fired him by declaring: "I don't know how we're going to get along without you, Bobby, but starting tomorrow, we're going to try."

Lane wrote his own walking papers in January 1961 after the Daley ownership, tired of ploys like the Dykes-Gordon trade and still taking heat for the Colavito-Kuenn exchange, refused to consider a better contract for him. Lane was succeeded by Gabe Paul, whose association with the franchise over the next couple of decades as general manager, president, and part-owner corresponded with its near-

bankruptcy. The best players on the team in the first half of the 1960s were slugger Leon Wagner and pitcher Sam McDowell; Colavito also returned in 1965 for two more big power years before being sent off again for good. While he managed to win 20 games only once for a team that more often than not lost its struggle to reach .500, McDowell was the talk of the league for years for the velocity that allowed him to top AL pitchers in strikeouts for five seasons. The southpaw was eventually undone by a drinking problem.

By the early 1960s, Daley had come around to Greenberg's way of thinking that the club was never going to succeed in Cleveland, and started putting out feelers for a shift to Seattle. As soon as the approaches were publicized, Paul took advantage of a backlash against the millionaire to form a syndicate and snap up the franchise himself. Paul sat in the owner's chair for about four years before cash shorts forced him to sell out to a group headed by frozen food king Vernon Stouffer. Stouffer promptly began losing money in his other enterprises and, together with the continued bleeding of the team's books, realized that he couldn't afford the Indians. But he ended up holding on for more than four years, rejecting several buyout offers along the way as inadequate; among the suitors was Cleveland shipping company boss George Steinbrenner. Finally, in 1972, Stouffer, too, was gone, with the club coming under the control of sports entrepreneur Nick Mileti. Mileti's reign was very short and very unsweet; in fact, he spent most of his year in the executive boardroom changing the organization from a corporation to a limited partnership in order to save on taxes and lure new investors. The league went along, but at the price of forcing him to relinquish control of the franchise to computer magnate Ted Bonda. One of Bonda's first moves was to bring in Phil Seghi as the general manager.

With the exception of a brief return to third place in 1968, the team had little to brag about between the mid-1960s and mid-1970s except individual pitching performances. In 1968, the story was Luis Tiant, who won 21 and led the league with a franchise-record 1.60 ERA. In 1970, McDowell won his 20. In 1972, spitballer Gaylord Perry, obtained from the Giants for McDowell in one of the organization's better trades, paced AL hurlers with 24 victories. But the downside of the individual efforts was never too far from view. A year after winning 21, Tiant led the league in losses. McDowell's 20 wins represented his last good year. And, offsetting the swap for Perry, the club completed a series of devastating exchanges.

Cleveland's Joe Adcock holds the record for the earliest protest of the year. On opening day in 1967, the manager waited until Indians' leadoff man Vic Davalillo had taken the first delivery of the season from Kansas City's Jim Nash, then called time to protest the new white shoes being worn by Charlie Finley's team. The claim was disallowed the next day by AL president Joe Cronin.

In reacquiring Colavito from the White Sox in 1965, for example, the Indians surrendered future stars Tommy John and Tommie Agee. In a transaction that raised a lot of ethical questions because it was worked out just before Paul left the team to go to New York, Cleveland shipped third baseman Graig

Nettles, who had hit 71 homers in three previous seasons, to the Yankees in exchange for outfielders Charlie Spikes and Rusty Torres, infielder Jerry Kenney, and catcher John Ellis. A couple of years later, Seghi renewed contacts with the Yankees to present the New Yorkers with first baseman Chris Chambliss and pitchers Dick Tidrow and Cecil Upshaw for hurlers Fritz Peterson, Steve Kline, Fred Beene, and Tom Buskey.

The managers during the period—George Strickland, Joe Adcock, Johnny Lipon, and Ken Aspromonte—were mostly distinguishable by the sizes of their uniforms. An exception was Alvin Dark, who was responsible for the club's brief comeback in 1968 but who then, serving as his own general manager, ran the team so far into the ground that there were daily reports that it was on the verge of moving to Denver, New Orleans, or Florida. One catastrophe that would have certainly been avoided under the

Cleveland player–manager Frank Robinson, the first black manager, homered in his first at–bat after taking charge of the Indians. *UPI / Bettmann Newsphotos*

religiously dry Dark was the July 4, 1974 Beer Night that began with fans able to celebrate the holiday with the brew they wanted at ten cents a cup and that ended with a ninth-inning riot on the field and a forfeit win for the visiting Texas Rangers.

It was following the 1974 season that Bonda took a leaf from Veeck's book and appointed Frank Robinson as baseball's first black manager. Robinson added to the drama of the choice in his first at bat in the 1975 season when, serving as Cleveland's designated hitter, he belted a home run. That height was never reached again. Although he got the club back to the .500 level in 1976 after nine straight seasons of more losses than wins, the future Hall of Famer found himself in a regular series of skirmishes with Perry, Ellis, and other players who either didn't like his sharp tongue or his assumption that anybody who wasn't as good as he had been simply wasn't trying hard enough. Robinson lasted until June 19, 1977, when he was replaced by Jeff Torborg.

As bad as the Indians had been through the 1960s and most of the 1970s, they got still worse. From 1977 to 1991, through a march of eight managers extending from Torborg to Mike Hargrove, they endeavored to reach as high as fourth in the Eastern Division once, breaking the .500 wall only in 1979, the split-season of 1981, and 1986. The span also produced three seasons with at least 100 losses, with the 105 defeats suffered in 1991 a franchise mark. With the arrival of the 1990s, in fact, the Indians had consolidated their hold on being the major league team absent from postseason competition the longest; even counting the expansion clubs created in the 1960s and 1970s, only the Mariners had been as zealous about playing nothing more than regular season games.

Bonda's computer company, IBC, sold the franchise in 1977 for $6 million to a syndicate headed by transportation tycoon Steve O'Neill. Under the terms of the agreement, O'Neill put up $4 million, with the rest coming from partners like Bonda himself and Paul, who returned from the Yankees to begin another stint as franchise president. If Bonda had emulated Veeck in choosing Robinson as a manager, Paul seemed most inspired this time around by Lane, as he worked out seventeen deals in the course of his first year. The one that drew the most comment was the dispatch of popular third baseman Buddy Bell to the Rangers for his Texas counterpart Toby Harrah.

What was heard with even more frequency was the reluctance of players to put on a Cleveland uniform and play before a few thousand fans in the cold cavern that was Municipal Stadium. This aversion took on even greater importance in the fledgling age

Footnote Player: Larry Littleton went hitless in 23 at bats for the Indians in 1981, trying the major league record for most at bats without getting a hit in a career. The mark had been set by Mike Potter of the Cardinals, who had stretched his 0–23 over two seasons, in 1976 and 1977.

of free agency; right into the 1990s, the most noted free agents signed by the club were Baltimore 20-game winner Wayne Garland, who agreed to a ten-year pact in 1977 before pacing the league in losses and then going down with a rotator cuff tear, and New York Mets field leader Keith Hernandez, who inked a two-year contract in 1990 and then spent all except forty-three games of it on the disabled list with hamstring problems.

The 1980s saw still more flux in the ownership. In 1982, Edward DeBartolo made a serious bid for the team with the intention of moving it to New Orleans. The tender was considered so attractive to the O'Neill ownership that it influenced parallel attempts by Paul to sign Billy Martin as a manager; when Martin refused to consider anything less than a five-year contract to protect himself against a lame duck bargain, Paul cut off the talks. DeBartolo, who had been thwarted by AL owners in earlier tries to buy the White Sox, ended up withdrawing his bid when he sensed the same opposition lining up against him. He did not bother renewing his offer a year later, when O'Neill died and Paul began interviewing prospective buyers for the dead owner's family. In 1984, E. F. Hutton executive David LeFevre appeared to have clinched a $16 million deal for the O'Neill estate's 60 percent holding, but the agreement came unhinged when the National Football League Browns refused to grant better terms for the use of Municipal Stadium and several minority Indians' shareholders filed suit on charges that they were about to be shortchanged. The LeFevre negotiations marked Paul's swan song for the organization.

With the sale question still hanging in the air, the team announced the appointment of Peter Bavasi as president and the elevation of Seghi to head of all baseball operations. The arrival on the scene of Bavasi, who only a short time before had worked as a lobbyist for bringing baseball to St. Petersburg, revived speculation of a franchise move; so rife was the conjecture that even the new president's decision to take the big C off players' caps and replace it with the Chief Wahoo logo was viewed as a preliminary step to a shift. It was during Bavasi's reign, in December 1986, that the club was indeed sold, but once again to local interests—to real estate developers Richard and David Jacobs. A month after the transaction, Bavasi resigned to take over a computer sports information company. Hank Peters was brought in some months later as the new president.

Managers continued to vie with players for turns at the team's revolving door. Torborg was succeeded by Dave Garcia, who seemed content merely to get a squad on the field for more than three years. Garcia finally gave way to Mike Ferraro, who had to quit after little more than a half-season in 1983 because of kidney cancer. Next up was Pat Corrales, who was given a "perpetual" contract by Bavasi, then learned the meaning of perpetuity by being bounced for Doc Edwards during the 1988 campaign. John Hart, John McNamara, and Mike Hargrove followed along. If nothing else, the team engineered some imaginative trades in the 1980s and early 1990s. In 1983, the Indians sent fading righthander Len Barker to the Braves for outfielder Brett Butler and third baseman Brook Jacoby, both of whom became regulars for some years. That same season, the club pulled off a five-for-one blockbuster, shipping outfielder Von Hayes to the Phillies in return for outfielder George Vukovich, pitcher Jay Baller, catcher Jerry Willard, and infielders Julio Franco and Manny Trillo. The following season, Cleveland helped assure the Cubs of an Eastern Division win in the NL by sending Rick Sutcliffe to Chicago, but solidified its own lineup by acquiring outfielders Mel Hall and Joe Carter in the exchange. After several years of imposing offensive numbers, Carter was dealt to San Diego in 1990 for outfielder Chris James, infielder Carlos Baerga, and catcher Sandy Alomar, Jr.; Alomar was named Rookie of the Year in 1990.

Aside from those contributed by Carter, Hall, and Franco, the team had several other noteworthy performances in the 1980s. The most puzzling was that turned in by the cocky Joe Charboneau in 1980; after winning Rookie of the Year honors and adding a modicum of excitement to team proceedings, the outfielder suffered a couple of injuries and crashed through to a new definition of a one-year wonder. When he wasn't injured (which was often), one of the club's biggest lineup threats was first baseman Andre Thornton, who hit more than 30 home runs three times. Outfielder Cory Snyder also raised great expectations for his power toward the end of the decade, but his murderous strikeout ratio ultimately sent him on the road to several teams in a quest for simply surviving as a major leaguer. The pitching was generally abysmal, with the nadir reached in 1987, when the aged Phil Niekro and Tom Candiotti, both knuckleballers, led the team with seven wins each. The most reliable hurler for a few years was reliever Doug Jones, who between 1988 and 1990 broke most of the team's bullpen records by saving 112 games; in 1988, the righthander also set a league mark by registering saves in fifteen consecutive appearances.

As the franchise entered the 1990s, there was little doubt that hope for significant change lay with the prospects for building a new downtown stadium that would get the club out from under a burdensome lease with the NFL Browns for the Mistake by the Lake. The project, a political football for years in a city with widespread economic difficulties, was finally firmed up in 1992 with a target opening in 1994. Club officials immediately predicted that the new facility would make it less difficult for the team to attract top-flight free agents and would restore winning play.

Even going into their final season in the old park in 1993, the Indians were able to boast some of the best young players in the league. One was outfielder-designated hitter Albert Belle who, recovered from alcohol problems a couple of years earlier, belted 34 homers and drove in 112 runs during the 1992 season. In that same year, outfielder Kenny Lofton set a new AL Rookie record with 66 stolen bases, and righthander Charles Nagy assumed the ace's position on the staff by winning 17 games with an ERA of 2.96. The best player of all, however, was second baseman Baerga, who in 1992 became the first ALer at his position to hit .300 with at least 200 hits, 20 homers, and 100 RBIs.

Tragedy struck the club a couple of weeks into spring training in 1993, when a boating accident took the lives of bullpen ace Steve Olin and setup man Tim Crews and seriously injured veteran southpaw Bob Ojeda, who had been signed as a free agent during the offseason.

CLEVELAND INDIANS

Annual Standings and Managers

Year	Position	W	L	Pct.	GB	Managers
1901	Seventh	54	82	.397	29	Jimmy McAleer
1902	Fifth	69	67	.507	14	Bill Armour

1903	Third	77	63	.550	15	Bill Armour
1904	Fourth	86	65	.570	7½	Bill Armour
1905	Fifth	76	78	.494	19	Nap Lajoie
1906	Third	89	64	.582	5	Nap Lajoie
1907	Fourth	85	67	.559	8	Nap Lajoie
1908	Second	90	64	.584	½	Nap Lajoie
1909	Sixth	71	82	.464	27½	Nap Lajoie, Deacon McGuire
1910	Fifth	71	81	.467	32	Deacon McGuire
1911	Third	80	73	.523	22	Deacon McGuire, George Stovall
1912	Fifth	75	78	.490	30½	Harry Davis, Joe Birmingham
1913	Third	86	66	.566	9½	Joe Birmingham
1914	Eighth	51	102	.333	48½	Joe Birmingham
1915	Seventh	57	95	.375	44½	Joe Birmingham, Lee Fohl
1916	Sixth	77	77	.500	14	Lee Fohl
1917	Third	88	66	.571	12	Lee Fohl
1918	Second	73	54	.575	2½	Lee Fohl
1919	Second	84	55	.604	3½	Lee Fohl, Tris Speaker
1920	First	98	56	.636	+2	Tris Speaker
1921	Second	94	60	.610	4½	Tris Speaker
1922	Fourth	78	76	.507	16	Tris Speaker
1923	Third	82	71	.536	16½	Tris Speaker
1924	Sixth	67	86	.438	24½	Tris Speaker
1925	Sixth	70	84	.455	27½	Tris Speaker
1926	Second	88	66	.571	3	Tris Speaker
1927	Sixth	66	87	.431	43½	Jack McCallister
1928	Seventh	62	92	.403	39	Roger Peckinpaugh
1929	Third	81	71	.533	24	Roger Peckinpaugh
1930	Fourth	81	73	.536	21	Roger Peckinpaugh
1931	Fourth	78	76	.506	30	Roger Peckinpaugh
1932	Fourth	87	65	.572	19	Roger Peckinpaugh
1933	Fourth	75	76	.497	23½	Roger Peckinpaugh, Walter Johnson
1934	Third	85	69	.552	16	Walter Johnson
1935	Third	82	71	.536	12	Walter Johnson, Steve O'Neill
1936	Fifth	80	74	.519	22½	Steve O'Neill
1937	Fourth	83	71	.539	19	Steve O'Neill
1938	Third	86	66	.566	13	Ossie Vitt
1939	Third	87	67	.565	20½	Ossie Vitt
1940	Second	89	65	.578	1	Ossie Vitt
1941	Fourth*	75	79	.487	26	Roger Peckinpaugh
1942	Fourth	75	79	.487	28	Lou Boudreau
1943	Third	82	71	.536	15½	Lou Boudreau
1944	Fifth*	72	82	.468	17	Lou Boudreau
1945	Fifth	73	72	.503	11	Lou Boudreau
1946	Sixth	68	86	.442	36	Lou Boudreau
1947	Fourth	80	74	.519	17	Lou Boudreau
1948	First	97	58	.626	+1	Lou Boudreau
1949	Third	89	65	.578	8	Lou Boudreau
1950	Fourth	92	62	.597	6	Lou Boudreau
1951	Second	93	61	.604	5	Al Lopez
1952	Second	93	61	.604	2	Al Lopez
1953	Second	92	62	.597	8½	Al Lopez
1954	First	111	43	.721	+8	Al Lopez
1955	Second	93	61	.604	3	Al Lopez
1956	Second	88	66	.571	9	Al Lopez
1957	Sixth	76	77	.497	21½	Kerby Farrell
1958	Fourth	77	76	.503	14½	Bobby Bragan, Joe Gordon
1959	Second	89	65	.578	5	Joe Gordon

1960	Fourth	76	78	.494	21	Joe Gordon, Jimmy Dykes
1961	Fifth	78	83	.484	30½	Jimmy Dykes
1962	Sixth	80	82	.494	16	Mel McGaha
1963	Fifth*	79	83	.488	25½	Birdie Tebbetts
1964	Sixth*	79	83	.488	20	Birdie Tebbetts
1965	Fifth	87	75	.537	15	Birdie Tebbetts
1966	Fifth	81	81	.500	17	Birdie Tebbetts, George Strickland
1967	Eighth	75	87	.463	17	Joe Adcock
1968	Third	86	75	.534	16½	Alvin Dark
1969	Sixth	62	99	.385	46½	Alvin Dark
1970	Fifth	76	86	.469	32	Alvin Dark
1971	Sixth	60	102	.370	43	Alvin Dark, Johnny Lipon
1972	Fifth	72	84	.462	14	Ken Aspromonte
1973	Sixth	71	91	.438	26	Ken Aspromonte
1974	Fourth	77	85	.475	14	Ken Aspromonte
1975	Fourth	79	80	.497	15½	Frank Robinson
1976	Fourth	81	78	.509	16	Frank Robinson
1977	Fifth	71	90	.441	28½	Frank Robinson, Jeff Torborg
1978	Sixth	69	90	.434	29	Jeff Torborg
1979	Sixth	81	80	.503	22	Jeff Torborg, Dave Garcia
1980	Sixth	79	81	.494	23	Dave Garcia
1981	Sixth	26	24	.520	5	Dave Garcia
	Fifth	26	27	.491	5	Dave Garcia
1982	Sixth*	78	84	.481	17	Dave Garcia
1983	Seventh	70	92	.432	28	Mike Ferraro, Pat Corrales
1984	Sixth	75	87	.463	29	Pat Corrales
1985	Seventh	60	102	.370	39½	Pat Corrales
1986	Fifth	84	78	.519	11½	Pat Corrales
1987	Seventh	61	101	.377	37	Pat Corrales, Doc Edwards
1988	Sixth	78	84	.481	11	Doc Edwards
1989	Sixth	73	89	.451	16	Doc Edwards, John Hart
1990	Fourth	77	85	.475	11	John McNamara
1991	Seventh	57	105	.352	34	John McNamara, Mike Hargrove
1992	Fourth*	76	86	.469	20	Mike Hargrove

* Tie

Postseason Play

WS	5–2 versus Brooklyn	1920
	4–1 versus Boston	1948
	0–4 versus New York	1954

Colorado Rockies

National League, 1993   **BALLPARK:** MILE HIGH STADIUM

Along with the Florida Marlins, the Rockies were born as a National League franchise in time for the 1993 season. It was an arduous delivery. After seven years of lobbying and formal presentations, the organization remained in executive suite turmoil right up to a few weeks before its inaugural spring training, with major stockholders coming and going. The main constant in all the movement was the consolidation of the Coors Brewing Company as a decisive voice in the new club's affairs.

Denver had been viewed as a prime location for a big league franchise as far back as the 1960s when Charlie Finley had flirted with the idea of moving his Kansas City Athletics to the Colorado capital. For a number of years, oilman Marvin Davis had been particularly active in trying to attract a team to the virgin Rocky Mountain territory. It was not until August 1985, however, that a new basic agreement between management and players authorized the expansion of the NL by two teams and stirred local interests into organizing for a club. Another five years had to pass before still another basic agreement enabled the league to publish a timetable calling for expansion by 1993. In December 1990, the candidates were reduced to six—three from Florida and one each from Denver, Buffalo, and Washington, D.C.

The months that followed reflected worse on the selectors than on the candidates. Although there was little argument over a $95-million entry fee affixed for each of the new franchises, there was a great deal of irritation in the American League for being cut out of the spoils. Even when the NL agreed to include the junior circuit in the deal, there was enough squabbling over how many players each league would have to make available to the new franchises to force Commissioner Fay Vincent to put the entire selection process on hold for several weeks. Finally, with various newspapers reporting that Denver and Miami had been selected, Vincent had little choice but to confirm them as the winners on June 10, 1991. It took still another two weeks for the leagues to come up with a complicated expansion draft formula exposing NL teams to the loss of three players each and eight AL clubs to the same maximum. At that, some AL owners continued to grumble at having to divide only $42 million of the total $190 million due from the Rockies and Marlins.

A prime mover in winning the franchise for Colorado was Francesco Peña, a one-time mayor of Denver who was subsequently appointed Secretary of Transportation in the Clinton administration. The key to Peña's success was in forcing a business alliance among John Antonucci, chief executive officer of the Ohio-based Superior Beverage Group; Peter Coors, head of the brewing company; and Michael Monus, head of another Ohio firm, the Phar-Mor drugstore chain. Together with investments from several Colorado businessmen, they announced their financial capability as topping $140 million. But no sooner had the ink dried on the entry contracts than the FBI accused Monus of embezzling money from Phar-Mor, and he had to withdraw. In January 1993, Antonucci also withdrew amid indications that Coors was using baseball's emphasis on local ownership as an excuse for strengthening his own power within the organization. The brewer also had his name attached to a new stadium set to be completed in time for the 1995 season.

The club's point man for baseball decisions was Bob Gebhard, a veteran of both the Minnesota and Montreal front offices. In what was saluted as an imaginative move, Gebhard tapped Don Baylor as Colorado's first manager. The appointment came after several years of suspicions that Baylor, synonymous with winning teams throughout his playing career, was being denied a managerial post because he was black and outside the old boy network.

In the November 1992 expansion draft, the Rockies won a coin flip with the Marlins and took Atlanta righthander David Nied as their first pick. Among the familiar names they picked up were Charlie Hayes, Jody Reed, Kevin Reimer, and Joe Girardi. Reed was immediately traded to the Dodgers for pitcher Rudy Seanez, while Reimer was sent to the Brewers for Dante Bichette. After months of assurances by other owners that the draft would stock the new teams with far better players than had been the case in earlier expansions, the resultant rosters promised little more than cellar dwellers. To take advantage of the higher altitude at Mile High Stadium, the club also went into the free agent market for potential sluggers such as Andres Galarraga and Darryl Boston. The franchise's immediate payoff was its first-game attendance of 80,227, the largest crowd ever to see a regular season single game.

Columbus Colts

American Association, 1883–1884	**BALLPARK:** RECREATION PARK
	OTHER NAMES: SENATORS, BUCKEYES
RECORD: 101–104 (.493)	

The Colts were born of the euphoria over the American Association's first financially successful season and killed by the financial devastation left by the war with the Union Association. In the course of their short, rollercoaster existence, their main impact was in the fight for Sunday baseball.

When the AA first challenged the National League with a six-team league in 1882, there was room for a second major circuit, and everyone made money. Emboldened by this success, the AA expanded to eight teams in 1883, adding New York and Columbus to its roster. The Colts, assembled mostly from other association teams by president H. T. Crittenden and manager Horace Phillips, finished sixth, but broke even financially. If there was a franchise player, it was pitcher Frank Mountain, who won 26 games but also led the AA in losses with 33.

The Colts of 1884 played in an environment so different that it made them dramatically more competitive than the 1883 squad. The UA had lured several dozen AA players with its promise of abolishing the reserve rule; in addition, the AA itself expanded to twelve clubs, further diluting the talent pool. Under new manager Gus Schmelz, the team leapt to second place, only 6½ games behind the Mets. Mountain (23–17) and Rookie Ed Morris (34–13) were the difference.

Sunday baseball had been a major plank in the AA's platform from the beginning. But the religious establishment used every weapon imaginable to combat the growing tendency toward what it regarded as a violation of the Sabbath; in Columbus, the attack came in the resurrection of an old city ordinance prohibiting any form of work on Sunday. The club turned the tables, however, by getting an injunction against the operation of streetcars under the same ordinance. The retort kept so many people from getting to church that the churchmen quit the battle.

The Colts faced a different—and more formidable—threat at the end of the season. The twelve-team AA had been a financial disaster and, with the collapse of the UA, there was no longer any necessity to lock up so many players, Four clubs had to go, and Columbus, one of the smallest cities in the AA, was a clear choice for elimination. The Pittsburgh Alleghenys, piloted since the end of 1884 by former Colts' skipper Phillips, took over virtually the entire Columbus roster for $6,000, enough for the Columbus directors to vote themselves a 120 percent dividend before closing down the franchise.

The King of Concessions, Harry M. Stevens, got his start in Columbus when he marched into the Colts' offices, announced his dissatisfaction with the scorecards the club was selling, declared his ability to design a better one, and came away with a contract to print and sell his product.

COLUMBUS COLTS

Annual Standings and Managers

Year	Position	W	L	Pct.	GB	Managers
1883	Sixth	32	65	.330	33½	Horace Phillips
1884	Second	69	39	.639	6½	Gus Schmelz

Columbus Solons

American Association, 1889–1891	**BALLPARK:** RECREATION PARK
RECORD: 200–209 (.489)	**OTHER NAMES:** SENATORS, BUCKEYES

When Columbus reentered the American Association in 1889 as a replacement for Cleveland, which had defected to the National League, it was by far the smallest city in the AA. Nonetheless, local businessmen, headed by Conrad Born, welcomed the opportunity to bring major league baseball back to the Ohio city.

With Al Buckenberger as manager, Columbus put together a makeshift team centered around one genuine star, first baseman Dave Orr who hit .327, and one curiosity, lefthanded third baseman Lefty Marr. Mark Baldwin won 27 games, but also led the AA in losses with 34; the Solons came home in sixth place.

With the formation of the Players League in 1890, Orr, Baldwin, and several other Solons jumped the team. Despite these losses, Columbus, under a succession of three managers, rose to second place on career years from left fielder Speed Johnson (.346), catcher Jack O'Connor (.324), and pitcher Hank Gastright (30–14).

The financial disaster and public distress over the PL war compelled the NL and AA to consider remedies. The most talked about possibility came from Allan W. Thurman, a Columbus director and president of the AA who was dubbed The White Winged Angel of Peace for his plan to consolidate all three leagues into two eight-team circuits. Thurman's eloquence propelled him onto the three-man National Board that was established to govern baseball in the aftermath of the PL crisis. Selected board chairman, a position out of all proportion to the power Columbus wielded in the AA, he cast the deciding vote in the panel's condoning of Pittsburgh's pirating of Lou Bierbauer and Boston's signing of Harry Stovey, players to whom the AA had a claim. The outcry against the Columbus official, who was accused of being a traitor and a toady for Albert Spalding of Chicago, led to his ouster as AA president; soon thereafter, he quit the National Board and baseball altogether.

Columbus's reward for Thurman's loyalty to the National Agreement was a raid by the piratical NL Pittsburgh club on third baseman Charlie Reilly. The Solons retaliated with a lawsuit to prevent Reilly's transfer, but lost the suit.

The trade war between the NL and the AA was over almost before it began. Columbus, its finances a shambles, began talking about capitulation in June. At season's end, with the Solons in fifth place, Born and his associates accepted $18,000 as their share of the NL's buyout of AA clubs en route to absorbing four clubs and reshaping itself as a twelve-team league.

COLUMBUS SOLONS

Annual Standings and Managers

Year	Position	W	L	Pct.	GB	Managers
1889	Sixth	60	78	.435	33½	Al Buckenberger
1890	Second	79	55	.590	10	Al Buckenberger, Gus Schmelz, Pat Sullivan
1891	Fifth	61	76	.445	33	Gus Schmelz

Detroit Wolverines

National League, 1881–1888   **BALLPARK:** RECREATION PARK

RECORD: 426–437 (.494)

At their meeting in December 1880, National League owners elected Detroit to replace the expelled Cincinnati franchise. The Wolverines' first season, in which they finished a respectable fourth and showed a more-than-respectable profit of $12,000, was uneventful. Before its second season even began, however, the club found itself a central party in the NL's war with the American Association.

Initially the AA gave the NL little cause for alarm, because its six franchises were selected to avoid a head-on challenge in any of the older circuit's eight markets; teams from the two leagues even played each other in twenty exhibition games before the start of the regular season. But trouble erupted when two Detroit infielders, Dasher Troy and Sam Wise, signed contracts with the AA's Philadelphia and Cincinnati teams, respectively, in the spring of 1882. The Wolverines insisted that the pair were their property even though they had not been among the five players reserved by the club.

NL President William Hulbert backed Detroit, summarily dismissing the association's potential effect on his league and arrogantly refusing even to recognize its existence. Troy, pleading ignorance of the association's intention to play on Sunday, eventually returned to the Wolverines, while Wise signed with the NL Boston team.

The association struck back by stating its intention of reviewing the cases of blacklisted NL players, establishing a network of subordinate teams, and threatening to take legal action to get back players who had jumped to the NL. In August 1882, Detroit catcher Charlie Bennett signed a preliminary agreement with the association's Pittsburgh Alleghenys and accepted a $100 advance on his salary. However, before he signed the actual contract, Detroit beat Pittsburgh's contract offer to the receiver, causing the Alleghenys to seek a federal court injunction to prevent Bennett from playing for the Wolverines in 1883. The court ruled that Bennett and the Alleghenys had no valid contract, only an unenforceable agreement to agree.

Earlier in 1882, the Wolverines had become embroiled in a controversy of a different sort. Detroit President W. G. Thompson, suspicious of the work of umpire Dick Higham, accused the arbiter of colluding with gamblers to fix games. At a special league meeting on June 24th in Detroit, Thompson, who was also the mayor of the city, produced testimony by a handwriting expert that linked Higham to a gambler. Higham, whose associations with gamblers dated back to his playing days in the 1870s, resigned on the spot.

After four seasons in which they never finished higher than fourth, the Wolverines became more aggressive about going after players. In June 1885, John T. Brush, owners of the Indianapolis team in the faltering minor Western League, sent his manager Bill Watkins to Detroit to inquire about purchasing the franchise. Detroit President Joseph H. Marsh, who had succeeded Thompson in 1883, refused to sell and turned around and hired Watkins as *his* manager. Watkins brought with him eight Indianapolis players, most notably outfielder Sam Thompson.

The following season, Detroit purchased the entire Buffalo franchise for $7,000 in order to acquire Dan Brouthers, Hardy Richardson, Jack Rowe, and Deacon Jim White. Acquisition of the Big Four set off a storm of protest that almost led to the team's expulsion from the league. The players themselves remained undecided about what to do until a member of the Wolverines' board of directors took them to his country home and prevailed upon them to sign with Detroit for the 1886 season. With the Big Four under contract, the Wolverines had in place almost all of the elements of their 1887 championship team.

Boston President Arthur Soden posed another obstacle, however, when he led a movement to give visiting teams a flat fee of $100 per game instead of 30 percent of the gate. Soden's proposal included a threat by the eastern teams—New York, Philadelphia, and Washington, as well as Boston—to bolt the NL if they did not have their way. The eastern owners were especially irate that Detroit, in a smaller market than theirs, had burdened itself with a huge payroll that it could only meet with the help of its 30

SAMUEL LUTHER THOMPSON
DETROIT N.L., PHILADELPHIA N.L.
1885 - 1898; DETROIT A.L. 1906
ONE OF THE FOREMOST SLUGGERS OF
HIS DAY. LIFETIME BATTING AVERAGE
.336. BATTED BETTER THAN .400 TWICE.
GREAT CLUTCH HITTER. COLLECTED
200 OR MORE HITS IN A SEASON THREE
TIMES. TOPPED N.L. IN HOME RUNS AND
RUNS BATTED IN TWICE.

National Baseball Library, Cooperstown, NY

percent share of big-city fans' half-dollars. Frederick Kimball Stearns, millionaire owner of a pharmaceuticals business who had followed Marsh to the head of the Detroit franchise, was unmoved by the threat, and he was backed by Chicago president Albert Spalding. The eventual compromise—a flat $125 visitor's share except on holidays, when the home team would get to keep only half the gate—ended up satisfying no one. The disgruntled Stearns then did some threatening of his own, even applying to the American Association for membership. Bluff or not, the other NL owners were not overjoyed by the possibility of losing the Big Four and their fans altogether, so the Wolverines were granted an exemption from the new formula. A year later, the NL adopted a more palatable plan for visiting teams—twenty-five percent of the gate with a $150 guarantee.

In 1886, the Big Four and Lady Baldwin, whose 42 wins were the most ever by a lefthander, led a surge upward from a sixth-place finish the year before. In a new 126-game schedule, the team's record of 87–36 was equivalent to winning 114 or 115 games in a modern 162-game schedule. Unfortunately, the

White Stockings were even better, so Detroit had to settle for the best second-place record in baseball history.

In 1887, the team slipped to 79 wins and 45 losses, but that was good enough to lead the NL by 3½ games over Philadelphia. Stearns immediately challenged the St. Louis Browns, winners of the AA pennant for the third consecutive year, to a fifteen-game series "for the title of world champions." The conditions Stearns laid down were the purchase of a $200 pennant, a 75 percent share of the receipts for the winners, and the unprecedented use of two umpires in a game. With captain-center fielder Ned Hanlon directing the action on the field, the Wolverines won 8 of the first 11 games—and 10 of 15 overall—to take the title.

By opening day of 1888, Detroit had still another president, Charles W. Smith. It also had less of a club. Second baseman Fred Dunlap had been sold to Pittsburgh, and many of the remaining players had spent the entire offseason partying in celebration of their victory over the Browns. A plague of injuries also hit the team. The fans lost interest, the team lost money, and Smith and Stearns lost the desire to compete. Frustrated over paying high salaries while competing in a market of fewer than 200,000 people, the owners unloaded both their players and their franchise. Brouthers, Richardson, Bennett, and catcher Charlie Ganzel were shipped to Boston; White, Rowe, and Hanlon went to Pittsburgh; Thompson was sold to Philadelphia; pitcher Charlie Getzein ended up in Indianapolis. Four lesser lights—and the franchise itself—were bought by Cleveland interests. The Detroit shareholders walked away with about $45,000.

DETROIT WOLVERINES

Annual Standings and Managers

Year	Position	W	L	Pct.	GB	Managers
1881	Fourth	41	43	.488	15	Frank Bancroft
1882	Sixth	42	41	.506	12½	Frank Bancroft
1883	Seventh	40	58	.408	23	Jack Chapman
1884	Eighth	28	84	.250	56	Jack Chapman
1885	Sixth	41	67	.380	44	Charlie Morton, Bill Watkins
1886	Second	87	36	.707	2½	Bill Watkins
1887	First	79	45	.637	+3½	Bill Watkins
1888	Fifth	68	63	.519	16	Bill Watkins, Bob Leadley

Detroit Tigers

American League, 1901–Present

BALLPARKS: BENNETT PARK (1901–1911)
TIGER STADIUM (1912–Present)

RECORD: 7371–6861 (.518)

From their very first game in the American League, the Tigers have had few equals as an offense-minded franchise. While the team has produced four 200-win pitchers over the years, they have been the exception to an attack that has been perennially heavy on slugging outfielders and first basemen and that has been aided markedly by the friendly contours of the club's two home ballparks. Now considered a bulwark of the junior circuit, Detroit had to survive two early-century attempts to eliminate it from existence—the first one plotted by AL founder Ban Johnson and the second one by Johnson's enemies

A charter member of the AL, the Tigers made their debut on April 25, 1901 in a Bennett Park contest against Milwaukee that drew almost double the facility's official capacity of 6,000. Entering the ninth inning nine runs down to the Brewers, the club put together an improbable ten-run rally for a 14–13 triumph. It was the beginning of a generally successful season highlighted by Roscoe Miller's 23 wins and shortstop Kid Elberfeld's .310 average. The manager for the maiden campaign was George Stallings, who had been calling the shots since the mid-1890s when Detroit had been a member of the forerunner to the AL, the minor Western League. Stallings always claimed that he was the first one to dub his players Tigers after having them don black-and-yellow striped socks in 1896. Other sources attribute the nickname to Detroit *Free Press* sports editor Philip Reid, who was said to have used it because of the sock color's similarity to the athletic uniforms of Princeton University.

Aside from being the manager, Stallings was also a partner in the team ownership with Jim Burns—a state of affairs that Johnson had accepted only because it was the fastest way of assuring a league franchise in Detroit. For the AL president, however, Stallings's incessant invective on the field against rival players and umpires was exactly what he didn't need in his efforts to present the junior circuit as a decorous alternative to the brawling National League, and it was a rare week that went by in 1901 that he wasn't issuing warnings or fines to the Detroit pilot. The antagonism between the men boiled over in August, when Johnson received reports that Stallings and Burns had almost come to blows over the manager's attempts to maneuver Detroit into the NL. With Johnson accusing him of trying to wreck the AL and Burns charging him with financial irregularities, Stallings announced his willingness to sell his interest in the club. But that wasn't enough for Johnson, who, using the excuse of countercharges from Stallings about his partner's financial finaglings, also forced out Burns. Taking over the

Ty Cobb steals third against Philadelphia on a fourth ball to teammate Sam Crawford on August 24, 1909. The third baseman is Frank (Home Run) Baker.
National Baseball Library, Cooperstown, NY

franchise was Samuel Angus, a Detroit insurance man and railroad contractor; among those whom Angus brought along with him was his chief bookkeeper Frank Navin. Navin, who wasted little time in climbing up the ladder of the organization, had a big say in the hiring of Frank Dwyer as manager—and just as much of a big say in ousting him after the season for not preventing the club's plunge to seventh place and the worst won-lost percentage that it would have for fifty years.

Less than twelve months after he had ripped Stallings for trying to take the Tigers out of the AL, Johnson was busy trying to take them out of Detroit. Convinced that the franchise's low attendance figures in the first two years were only going to get worse, the league official lined up backers for a new ballpark in Pittsburgh, with every intention of moving the team to Pennsylvania in time for the 1903 campaign. The shift was thwarted only when, as part of the peace agreement reached between the AL and NL in January of 1903, Johnson pledged to stay out

of Pittsburgh in return for the junior loop's being allowed to move into New York. Detroit gained another benefit from the pact when the leagues resolved that outfielder Sam Crawford, who had jumped to the Tigers from the Reds after the 1902 season, could stay where he was. Crawford remained with the club for fifteen years, during which he put together the best part of his .309 career average and all-time primacy in triples. The lefthanded hitter, who was inducted into the Hall of Fame in 1957, led the AL in three-base hits five times (he had also topped the NL once) and finished in double figures in the category in all but two of his nineteen major league seasons.

In the same week that the two leagues were ironing out their differences, Win Mercer, a Detroit pitcher who had been tapped to succeed Dwyer as manager, committed suicide in a San Francisco hotel by connecting a rubber tube to a gas jet. A note left behind warned of the evils of gambling and womanizing—both of which had occupied Mercer as much as pitching had over most of his career. On Johnson's recommendation, Angus next gave the managerial job to Ed Barrow. Barrow, like his own successors Bobby Lowe and Bill Armour, spent a good deal of his time fighting with Navin about everything from player salaries to trades made and not made. Things didn't get any easier for the dugout bosses when William H. Yawkey bought out Angus before the 1904 season and depended on Navin's judgments even more than his predecessor had. It added up to one mediocre finish after another, with the club never getting closer to first place than 15½ games between 1902 and 1906.

There were consolations. By the middle of the decade, George Mullin had settled in as the franchise ace. One of the few pitchers in Tigers' history who didn't owe most of his wins to a thundering offense behind him, Mullin fashioned a career ERA of 2.82 in fourteen years of big league service; a five-time 20-game winner, he ended up with 228 victories.

Another important presence was second baseman Germany Schaefer, who provided AL fans with the kind of entertainment that NL spectators would expect a few years later from Rabbit Maranville. On at least two occasions, the not-greatly gifted Schaefer called home runs in the middle of a game. After delivering one such blow, he slid around the bases while delivering play-by-play on his own antics; on the other occasion, he carried his bat with him, stopping at each base and aiming it at the pitcher as though it were a rifle. Undoubtedly, the most famous of all Schaefer numbers was his stealing of first base in a 1908 contest against Cleveland. The infielder made his return run after an earlier theft of second had not drawn a desired throw from the catcher to allow Detroit outfielder Davy Jones to score from third. No sooner had Schaefer reoccupied first than he took off for second again, this time drawing the throw from the catcher; both he and Jones were called safe. Schaefer's inventiveness did not amuse the dour Johnson, who promptly issued a regulation against baserunners advancing backwards; the NL followed suit a short time later.

Even Schaefer's antics, however, were to be eclipsed quickly by Ty Cobb, who joined the club in August 1905. Regarded by many as the greatest player in the history of baseball, Cobb became a member of the team as the result of a complicated arrangement with the Sally League club in Augusta, Georgia that permitted Detroit to use its facilities for spring training in return for which righthander Ed Cicotte was assigned to the minor league organiza-tion; Augusta also agreed to give the Tigers first drafting rights to its players in August. Chosen in that draft, Cobb served notice at once that he was not going to be easy to get along with when he protested that he wasn't receiving any of the money from the deal that was sending him to the major leagues. The personal troubles that would dog the outfielder's big league career were also immediately put on display; three weeks before the purchase of his contract, Cobb's mother had been arrested for the fatal shooting of his father. Prosecutors linked the episode to the woman's alleged infidelities, but the defense argued successfully after many months of trial delays that the elder Cobb had been mistaken for a burglar and killed accidentally.

Cobb made his big league debut on August 30th, belting a two-run double off New York's Jack Chesbro. It was the first of 4,191 safeties—a record that stood until surpassed by Pete Rose in the 1980s. The lefty-hitting outfielder's .367 average over his twenty-four-year career still stands as the highest in baseball history, as does his 2,245 runs scored. Between 1907 and 1915, Cobb won nine straight batting titles, then added another three later on; not counting his maiden year, when he had only 150 at bats, he never hit below .320, and three times topped .400. He also left a mark on just about every other batting category, leading the league in doubles three times, in triples four times, in runs scored five times, in runs batted in four times, in steals six times, and in slugging average eight times. Although he broke into double figures in home runs only twice, he even managed to lead the league in that category when his nine round-trippers in 1909 were high. In a celebrated incident in 1925, Cobb, who had been fuming for some years about the attention being given to Babe Ruth, told reporters that, even with the odd batting stance that left several inches between his hands on the bat, he could have hit 30 or 40 home runs a year if he had wanted to; he then went out and clouted three in that day's game to prove his point. The Georgia Peach, as writers got used to calling him, was the very first player elected to the Hall of Fame in 1936, getting the nod even before Ruth.

Manager Bill Armour's juggling of the switch-hitting Boss Schmidt, the righthand-hitting Freddie Payne, and the lefthand-hitting Jack Warner behind the plate in 1906, marked the first extensive use of platooning.

If Cobb's double off Chesbro quickly established his playing credentials, his appearance in the on-deck circle arrogantly waving three bats before that debut just as swiftly ignited the tensions with teammates that would vie with the outfielder's diamond accomplishments throughout his career. By his own admission many years later, Cobb, a southern Protestant, expected nothing except trouble from his teammates, mostly northern Irish-Catholics, even before joining the club. In his first years, his chief nemesis was left fielder Marty McIntyre, who showed his feelings about the Georgian by giving opposition catchers clear shots at throwing him out on the basepaths and by feinting after fly balls that would end up dropping and making the center fielder Cobb look bad. After one such maneuver by McIntyre, pitcher Ed Siever became so infuriated with Cobb for costing him a game that he went after him in a hotel lobby; Cobb was kicking the hurler in the head when teammates came along to pull him away. McIntyre's fly ball tactic became so notorious (and popular with teammates) that when Hughie Jennings took over as manager in 1907, his first move was to switch Cobb to right field so he and the left fielder would be separated. Jennings's solution came almost too late because, wearied by the hostility around him, Cobb had begun carrying a gun in 1906 and eating most of his meals alone. By the middle of the season, he was so worn out that he was granted a couple of weeks leave from the team. It emerged subsequently that Cobb had suffered a nervous breakdown and had entered a Detroit sanitarium, where he remained for about a month.

Crawford was another member in good standing of the anti-Cobb faction, and was always good for such quotes as "He's still fighting the Civil War and he sees us as just damn Yankees." Crawford wasn't far off the mark, because a number of the most violent incidents off the field involved Cobb against blacks, whom he as a matter of course referred to as "niggers." In one 1907 episode in Detroit, he got into an argument with a black groundskeeper about the condition of the spring training field in Augusta and ended up choking the man's wife when she sought to intervene. In 1909, he slapped a black elevator operator in Cleveland for being "insolent," precipitating a brawl with knives and a security man's billyclub. Although Navin persuaded the hotel to back off from a civil suit that had been threatened, the Cleveland district attorney pressed an assault charge, making it necessary for Cobb to skirt Ohio in the team's travels for some time. In 1914,

Cobb attacked a Detroit butcher for reputedly insulting his wife, then used the butt of his gun against a black shop assistant.

While the player's racism *per se* hardly kept Navin awake at night, it was another element in the volatile mix that encouraged constant newspaper reports that, batting titles or not, the Tigers were on the verge of trading their star. The only seriously contemplated deal, however, was a swap at the end of the 1907 season that would have sent Cobb to Cleveland in exchange for outfielder Elmer Flick, and the Indians said no to that precisely because of Cobb's reputation for making trouble.

In 1907, with Cobb winning the first of his silver bats, the Tigers captured their first pennant. The turning point of the campaign came during a late September game against contending Philadelphia, when Cobb clouted a 9th-inning homer to knot the contest and an interference call in the 14th inning nullified an extra-base hit that would have left the Athletics with the winning run in easy scoring position. The interference call (made after Crawford slammed into a security guard while pursuing a long drive toward an overflow crowd at Shibe Park) sparked a melee on the field among players of both teams, police, and fans. When order had been restored, the clubs played for another deadlocked three innings before darkness descended; Philadelphia manager Connie Mack always claimed that the interference call cost the Athletics the flag.

Aside from Cobb's league-leading .350 average, 212 hits, 116 RBIs, and 49 steals, Detroit got a big offensive performance from Crawford, who led the AL in runs scored (102) while belting 17 triples and 34 doubles. The mound sensation of the year was Wild Bill Donovan, who set the franchise record for winning percentage with his 25–4. Lefty Ed Killian also won 25, and Mullin had the rare twentieth-century mark of 20 wins and 20 losses. Beyond the players, the most significant change from the club

In addition to his other talents, Ty Cobb took three turns on the mound during his career. In 1918, he made two appearances for a total of four innings, and was slapped around to the tune of a 4.50 ERA. But in 1925, at the age of 38, he took it upon himself to nail down a victory, retiring opposition hitters in order for an inning and earning a save.

that had finished sixth the year before was the arrival of Jennings. In contrast to Armour, who had sat on the bench in street clothes and a boater, Jennings was a raucous field leader who coached at third base with a whistle that kept his team on its toes as much as it unnerved opposing pitchers. The manager's old Oriole style was only too familiar to Johnson, who had sought unsuccessfully to talk Navin out of buying the Hall of Fame shortstop's contract from the Eastern League franchise in Baltimore.

The World Series against the Cubs was an embarrassment for Detroit. The highlight as far as the Tigers were concerned was the opening game, which was declared a 3–3 tie after twelve innings. In the next four games, the team scored the grand total of three runs, presenting Chicago with an asterisked sweep. Detroit's inept performance in the World Series took much of the luster off the pennant win, as did the fact that the franchise still ranked seventh in season attendance for the year. Complaining of money shorts, Yawkey eagerly accepted additional capital offered by Navin, making the one-time bookkeeper a partner and organization president. Navin immediately found himself in bitter contract negotiations with several key players, including Cobb and Mullin. Before finally coming to an agreement near the end of spring training in 1908, Cobb made clear the reasons for his balkiness: "It isn't a question of principle with me. I want the money."

The 1908 and 1909 seasons brought two more pennants and two more hitting crowns for Cobb. The 1908 race was again a squeaker, with matters not decided until Donovan shut out the White Sox on the very last day of the season. Once again, however, Detroit's reward for the flag was a postseason meeting with the Cubs, who this time tarried for five games before bringing the world championship to the NL.

The next year, the club held off a September rush by the Athletics for its third straight pennant. Aside from taking the batting title, Cobb became the only player in franchise history to win the Triple Crown by also leading the AL in homers (9) and RBIs (107). The pitching story was Mullin, with a league-leading 29 victories, and Ed Willett, who notched 21. With the Pirates instead of the Cubs as a World Series rival, the Tigers put up more of a battle, but still came out on the short end of seven games. The star of the Series was Pittsburgh hurler Babe Adams, who pitched three complete-game victories, including a shutout in the last game. Honus Wagner also won a sideline duel with Cobb that had been billed as a showdown between the two best hitters in baseball: While the Detroit outfielder managed only a .231 mark, the Pittsburgh shortstop averaged .333.

The Tigers' third straight World Series loss infuriated Johnson, who knew exactly where to place the blame: "We do all right in the World Series," the AL president told reporters, "except when that damn National Leaguer Jennings gets into it."

Instead of a fourth consecutive pennant, 1910 brought another major controversy involving Cobb. With the club out of the race by midseason, interest in Detroit was focused on the tight batting race between the feisty outfielder and Cleveland second baseman Nap Lajoie. On the final day of the season, St. Louis manager Jack O'Connor, a charter member of the Hate-Cobb Club, ordered his third baseman Red Corridan to play on the rim of the outfield grass, thereby allowing Lajoie to dump six bunt singles in the course of a doubleheader. But then Johnson and his chief statistician stepped in, ruling that Cobb had still emerged with the better average; moreover, the AL president threw O'Connor out of the league and levied fines on other members of the Browns.

There the matter stood until 1981, when *Sporting News* researcher Paul MacFarlane came across a hit erroneously attributed to Cobb and that, when subtracted, returned the title to Lajoie. Despite the evidence at hand, however, Commissioner Bowie Kuhn rejected MacFarlane's arguments and insisted that Cobb was still the batting leader.

Although the Tigers didn't, Cobb had what was arguably the best of all his years in 1911, when he led the league in batting (.420), hits (248), doubles (47), triples (24), runs (147), RBIs (144), and stolen bases (83). (Batting averages throughout the AL soared because of the use of a cushioned cork ball.) His performance convinced even lingering skeptics that he was the dominant force in the game, and he was regarded as box office even off the field: After the season, he made the first of several ventures into show business, touring in the lead role in a vaudeville chestnut called *A College Widow*.

The following season, with the team moving from Bennett Park to the facility that would change names over the years from Navin Field to Briggs Stadium to Tiger Stadium, Cobb got off to another quick start on his way to a .410 mark. But even the outfielder's sixth straight batting title was overshadowed by the events that began to unwind at New York's Hilltop Park on May 15th. After listening for several innings to the heckling of a fan subsequently identified as Claude Luecker, Cobb climbed into the stands and began punching and kicking his antagonist. At a stirring from some nearby fans to attack the outfielder, Crawford and several other players grabbed bats to make sure that the fight stayed private. When stadium police finally intervened, Cobb was sent off the field, where he told reporters that Luecker had been assailing him every time the Tigers played in New York, but that he had reached his limit when the fan had started calling him "a half-nigger." Informed that Luecker had lost four of his fingers in a printing press accident, Cobb shrugged that he didn't care "if he has no feet."

Johnson's response was to suspend Cobb indefinitely for both going into the stands and being the first to use what he described as "vicious language." To the astonishment of everyone who had been following team events, the Detroit players were unanimous in signing a telegram to Johnson that warned that they would boycott a game against the Athletics on May 18th if Cobb were not reinstated immediately. As soon as he heard of the telegram, Navin ordered Jennings and his coaches to find college and semipro players in the Philadelphia area in case the team went through with its threat; Navin's principal concern was a $1,000-a-day fine he would be subject to for not fulfilling the club's schedule.

On May 18th, the Tigers showed up at Shibe Park with Cobb, then promptly left again when umpires Bill Dinneen and Bull Perrine reiterated that Cobb couldn't play. The team that took the field for Detroit was made up of Jennings, coaches Deacon McGuire and Joe Sugden, and twelve area amateurs. Among them were future priest Aloysius Travers, who pitched all nine innings of the 24–2 shellacking administered by the Athletics; Ed Irvin, a catcher whose entire major league career would consist of two triples in three at bats; and Billy Maharg, the only one of the pickups who would play another major league game (for the Phillies in 1916), but who became more noted for being a whistle blower in the 1919 Black Sox scandal.

As soon as he heard about the farcical contest against Philadelphia, Johnson met with the Detroit players to issue a warning that they would all be blacklisted if they didn't play their next scheduled game against Washington. At this point, Cobb stepped in to urge his teammates not to jeopardize their careers because of him. The players took the field against the Senators after being fined $100 each for the strike against the Athletics. Because he had helped to settle the crisis, Cobb himself got off with a ten-day suspension and a $50 fine, with even the suspension made retroactive.

While he seldom found sympathy for his off-field actions in the Detroit press, Cobb was always able to count on the support of public opinion in Georgia in his various entanglements. That backing proved particularly valuable prior to the 1913 season, when the outfielder got into his almost-annual dispute with Navin over a new contract. The club president only stopped dragging his feet over a demanded $2,000 raise when Georgia Senator Hoke Smith announced that Navin's treatment of Cobb was a sign that Congress should consider major league baseball a trust.

Aside from pitcher Willett and backup third baseman Baldy Louden, Detroit's biggest loss during the Federal League wars in 1914 and 1915 was in the higher salaries that Navin had to pay to Cobb, Crawford, and his other stars to make sure that they weren't tempted away by the rebel circuit. World War I was another story, with as many as twelve members of the roster drafted into military service. The closest thing to a tragedy, however, once again involved Cobb, who volunteered for service in the U.S. Army's chemical warfare division after the 1918 season. Only a couple of weeks before the armistice halting the hostilities, Cobb and former New York pitching great Christy Mathewson were co-instructors in a gas mask test in France that went wrong. Cobb stumbled out of the test chamber several precious seconds ahead of Mathewson, who would have lung problems brought on by the gas for the rest of his short life.

The teens years introduced several players who became franchise all-stars. The first was outfielder Bobby Veach, who compiled eight .300 seasons for the Tigers on his way to a lifetime .310 average. An even greater offensive performer was outfielder Harry Heilmann, who spent four better-than-average years with the team before exploding in 1919 with a .320 mark; it was the first of twelve straight .300 seasons during which the righthanded hitter won four batting titles and topped the .400 mark once (in 1923). Heilmann, who was elected to the Hall of Fame in 1952, also had eight years of belting at least 40 doubles and driving in more than 100 runs. Pitching for the period was principally in the hands of southpaw Harry Coveleski, older brother of Hall of Famer Stan Coveleski, and Hooks Dauss. Coveleski, who never won more than six games in any other season, notched three straight 20-win years between 1914 and 1916. Dauss, the all-time leader in victories for the franchise, won 221 games in a fifteen-year career spent exclusively in the Motor City. Aside from his rookie year in 1912, when he made only two appearances, he was in double figures in wins every season of his career, reaching the 20-mark three times.

On the eve of the 1919 season, Yawkey died of a stroke. Some months later, his estate sold his half-interest in the franchise to auto-body builder Walter Briggs and John Kelsey, also in the auto business. The new partners immediately voiced confidence in Navin. For his part, however, Navin had run out of faith in Jennings, especially when the Tigers broke from the gate in 1920 with 13 straight losses and flopped to seventh place. Navin's announcement after the campaign that Jennings was stepping down after fourteen years was hardly a shock; what did catch many unaware was that Cobb, who had had trouble enough getting along with teammates, was named as Jennings's successor.

For a few days in November 1920, Cobb's appointment threatened to be academic because of a boardroom plot that would have eliminated Navin's Tigers from the major leagues. The machinations were set into motion when the Chicago Cubs proposed that the ruling National Commission of Johnson, NL president John Heydler, and Cincinnati's president Garry Herrmann be replaced by a single, outside civilian, ideally Chicago federal judge Kenesaw Mountain Landis. The Cubs' proposal, prompted by various fixing scandals that the National Commission had done nothing to prevent, was backed by the other seven NL teams, and the White Sox, Yankees, and Red Sox as well.

Despite being able to count on only five votes, Johnson rebuffed the plan as an encroachment on his own power, at the same time pleading with the owners not to cause another fracas that would have brought baseball bad headlines. The eleven teams weren't buying: At a November 8th meeting in Chicago, they agreed to form a new National League of twelve clubs, with Heydler serving as president. In addition to the eleven franchises voting for the initiative, the new league also was to include a Detroit team having nothing to do with Johnson loyalist Navin.

The Detroit owner wasn't *that* loyal, however: As soon as he heard of the eleven-team plan, he contacted the secessionists and brokered another conference of all sixteen clubs and the two league presidents on November 12th. At this second meeting, Johnson was forced to read the writing on the wall, Landis was elected baseball's first commis-

sioner, and Navin held on to the major leagues' only team in Detroit.

Cobb piloted the club for six years, gaining the .500 plateau five times but generally emulating Jennings in beefing up the offensive attack at the cost of the pitching. To make the mound situation worse, he endorsed a trade of Howard Ehmke to Boston (where the righthander won 39 games in his first two seasons) and ignored glowing scouting reports on farmhand Carl Hubbell, who was eventually sold to the Giants.

The loudest new bats in the first half of the 1920s belonged to outfielders Heinie Manush and Bob Fothergill. The lefty-swinging Manush broke into the league in 1923 with an average of .334—the first of eleven times that he would reach .300 on his way to a lifetime mark of .330 and membership in the Hall of Fame. Fothergill complemented Manush from the right side of the plate, batting .326 over his twelve-year career. Cobb himself did not enter his twilight years quietly, batting between .338 and .401 during his managerial tenure. He was also at the center of another statistical controversy in 1922, when AP reporter Fred Lieb overrode an error decision by the official scorer at a New York-Detroit game, crediting Cobb with the hit that ended up putting him over .400. Although Lieb had no official standing for making the ruling, the league office accepted the AP decision.

Compared to his earlier years, Cobb's behavior was relatively mild during his reign as manager. The one person he made an exception for was Ruth, who had eclipsed him as the league's glamour boy and who wasn't shy about underlining the fact. Cobb's usual comeback was to taunt the swarthy-skinned Ruth as a "nigger" and to point out as loudly as he could the New York slugger's supposed aversion to personal hygiene. It was cracks of the kind ("Something around here really stinks like a polecat") that led to a riot at Navin Field in June 1924. Using the excuse of a King Cole pitch that drilled the Yankees' Bob Meusel, Ruth and Cobb tackled each other near home plate, with the Bambino swearing that he was going to get even for all of Cobb's riding. Before the stars could be separated, an estimated 1,000 fans had also flooded the field, while hundreds of others smashed up grandstand seats. The game was ultimately forfeited to the Yankees.

In October 1926, Navin dropped a bombshell with the announcement that Cobb was retiring as both a player and manager; a month later, Cleveland player-manager Tris Speaker also stepped down.

Both stars had been forced to resign amid allegations by ex-Detroit pitcher Dutch Leonard that they, the hurler, and former Indians' outfielder Joe Wood had conspired to fix a game on September 25, 1919 in the interests of assuring the Tigers a third-place finish behind the White Sox and Cleveland. As evidence of his charges, Leonard sent two letters to Johnson that had been sent to him by Wood after the reputed fix; the AL president was said to have paid the pitcher $20,000 for the documents.

Despite Johnson's insistence that the affair had been dealt with effectively with the resignations of Cobb and Speaker, Landis stepped in to hold his own investigation. After going to California to interrogate Leonard, the commissioner ignored the extremely suggestive wording of the Wood letters to rule that the fix charges were unfounded. Leonard's behavior was attributed to his resentment over the fact that Cobb had released him in 1925 and that Speaker had declined to give him a tryout with Cleveland.

The matter did not end there. Accusing Johnson and Navin of having whipped up the scandal as a means of tearing up his multi-year contract with the Tigers, Cobb let it be known that he was considering a suit against everybody involved for slander. For his part, Johnson ridiculed Landis's finding, claiming that the commissioner was holding something back. Never one to let others play with his reputation, Landis promptly called for a meeting of AL owners that had only one item on the agenda—a choice between him and Johnson. Before the meeting was held, the owners voiced approval for the commissioner's actions and forced Johnson into a sabbatical that he never truly returned from; Navin was put in charge of the league's day-to-day business. With Johnson off the scene, Cobb and Speaker rejected offers from several NL clubs for their services; the two stars remained in the AL—Cobb with the Athletics and Speaker with the Senators.

The Wood-Leonard letters were not the only storm that Cobb had to weather during the 1926–1927 offseason. Even as Landis was probing the September 1919 game, Swede Risberg, one of the Chicago Eight, came forward with separate accusations that Cobb and the Tigers had thrown two consecutive doubleheaders to the White Sox for cash in the heat of the 1917 pennant race; Risberg was backed up in his allegations by another member of the Black Sox, Chick Gandil. A parade of witnesses to Landis's office refuted the Risberg-Gandil charges by a count of 35-2, noting only that Chicago players had taken up a collection for Detroit pitchers following the sea-

son for some key victories over the contending Red Sox, a fairly common practice in the period.

After acquitting Cobb and the other Tigers of collusion in the case, Landis issued a series of rules covering gambling in baseball. Key provisions established a statute of limitations on charges like those made by Risberg and Leonard, permanent expulsion for any player wagering on a game with which he was involved directly, and one-year suspensions for betting on third teams or for rewarding opposition players for having beaten third teams.

In 1927, without Cobb for the first time in more than two decades, the Tigers embarked on a seven-year stumble around the middle and bottom of the standings in which they attained .500 merely twice. The bad news during the period included a little bit of everything. Managers George Moriarty and Bucky Harris both had personality clashes with the players that made for better reading than the box scores. A suddenly colorless team in the late 1920s drew little, with the nadir reached on September 25, 1928, when only 404 fans were on hand to watch a home game against Boston. Navin took another financial blow in the 1929 stock market crash, sparking rumors of an imminent sale of the franchise.

On the credit side, there was the continued hitting of Heilmann and the arrival of Dale Alexander, a bad-field good-hit first baseman who averaged .343, .326, and .325 in his only full seasons with the team. But most of all, the late 1920s and early 1930s were significant for the debuts of future Hall of Famers Charlie Gehringer and Hank Greenberg.

Gehringer, a second baseman, spent his entire nineteen-year career with the Tigers, ending up with a mark of .320. His achievements included a batting title in 1937, twice leading the league in doubles and once in triples, driving in at least 100 runs seven times, and scoring 100 or more twelve times. Greenberg, a first baseman, was one of the AL's most prodigious power hitters in the 1930s, when he led the circuit in home runs and RBIs four times. His 183 RBIs in 1937 stand as the league record, and his total of 58 home runs the following year has been topped only by Roger Maris since. Greenberg had come close to selecting the Yankees over the Tigers, but changed his mind after being taken to Yankee Stadium by New York scout Paul Krichell and watching Lou Gehrig go through pregame drills.

Throughout his career, Greenberg suffered a lot of overt and covert prejudice for his Jewish background; during his run at Ruth's home run record in 1938, for instance, he received some of the same kind of hate mail that Hank Aaron would receive many years later while chasing Ruth's career home run standard.

A couple of days short of the 1933 season, Harris announced his resignation as manager. As much in need of a box-office personality to draw crowds as a winning strategist, Navin went to none other than Ruth, who had frequently proclaimed his ambition to pilot a big league club. But faced with the most serious offer he was to receive for becoming a manager, Ruth asked Navin to hold off on a meeting until he returned from a series of scheduled personal appearances in Hawaii. By the time the slugger came back from the islands, the Detroit owner had spent $100,000 to purchase catcher Mickey Cochrane from the Athletics and had named him to the post. In his first year at the helm, Cochrane delivered the first Detroit pennant since 1909 with a team that also racked up the organization's best won-lost percentage (.656) for a season.

Offensively, the keys to the Detroit attack in 1934 were what were known as the G Men—Gehringer, Greenberg, and left fielder Goose Goslin, who had been acquired from Washington a week after Cochrane had come over from Philadelphia. While most of the Hall of Famer's career was spent with the Senators, Goslin turned in three impressive seasons

for the Tigers, including his .305 batting average, 100 RBIs, and 100 runs scored in 1934. The other two G Men were even better: Gehringer contributed a .356 average with 50 doubles, 127 RBIs, and an AL-leading 134 runs, while Greenberg produced an average of .339 with 26 homers, a league-leading 63 doubles, 139 RBIs, and 118 runs. The pitching staff was headed by Schoolboy Rowe, who went 24–8, and Tommy Bridges, who finished at 22–11.

The World Series against St. Louis, however, turned out to be a replay of the Tigers' early-century failures against Chicago and Pittsburgh: The Cardinals took the world championship in seven games. The series became most noteworthy for the seventh game, when the Cardinals jumped off to a quick 8–0 lead, Joe Medwick got into a scuffle with Tigers' third baseman Marv Owen, and spectators in the left field grandstand began pelting the NL outfielder with fruit and other objects. Landis, who was on hand for the game, finally had to ask St. Louis manager Frankie Frisch to remove Medwick to avoid an unseemly forfeit, an even more unseemly riot, or both.

The Tigers finally broke their postseason hex in 1935, after the G Men had led the way to another pennant. The world championship secured at the expense of the Cubs was all the more surprising in that

The "G Men": Goose Goslin, Hank Greenberg, Charlie Gehringer. *National Baseball Library, Cooperstown, NY*

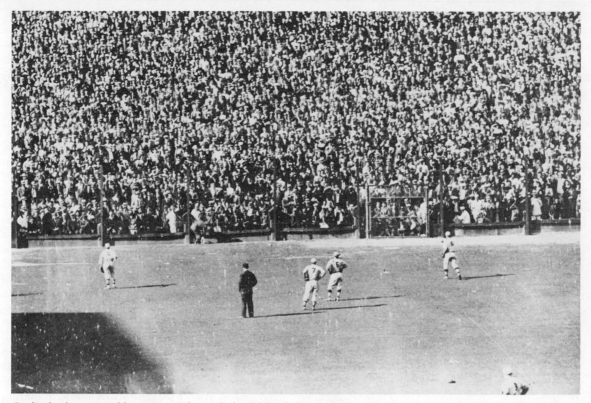

Cardinals players stand by as Detroit fans pelt the field with fruit and debris aimed at Joe Medwick (number 7) in the final game of the 1934 World Series. *National Baseball Library, Cooperstown, NY*

Greenberg, who had won MVP honors for his AL-leading 36 homers and 170 RBIs during the season, was injured in the second game and had only six plate appearances for the entire Series. The chief engineers of the victory in six games were Bridges, who had two complete-game wins, and right fielder Pete Fox, who had three doubles and a triple among his team-leading 10 hits.

No sooner had the celebrating died down in Detroit than the franchise was hit by a series of disasters. A month after the final World Series game, Navin died of a heart attack. Moving in as the team's sole owner, Briggs appointed Cochrane to a vice-presidency and appointed his own son Spike as organization treasurer. Cochrane's first step in his new dual role was to purchase the contract of former Philadelphia teammate Al Simmons from the White Sox. Simmons delivered as hoped with a .327 mark and 112 RBIs, but the deal was a mistake otherwise. The slugger resented Cochrane's authoritarian airs, Cochrane resented Simmons for assuming that he was entitled to special treatment, and many of the other Tigers resented the way Cochrane had just handed

right field to Simmons and benched World Series hero Fox.

If all that wasn't enough to ruin the 1936 season, a wrist injury to Greenberg twelve games into the campaign was; the team's leading power hitter didn't pick up a bat again for the year. It all became too much for Cochrane, and he was sent home by Briggs for a rest in midseason and replaced by coach Del Baker. Cochrane reassumed command of the team in 1937, and probably wished that he hadn't. On May 25th, facing New York pitcher Bump Hadley at Yankee Stadium, he suffered a triple skull fracture when he was hit on the temple. For four days he hovered between life and death, before finally being taken off the critical list. The beaning ended his playing career, though he was able to return as manager later in the season.

By 1938, sportswriters were questioning Cochrane's ability to serve as both manager and general manager, suggesting that he was still suffering from his beaning. On August 6th, Briggs removed Cochrane from both his posts, tapping Baker again as manager and naming Jack Zeller as general manager. Although the team was no better than fourth in the standings, Briggs had his consolations, including the addition of outfield upper decks that raised the capacity of the home park to 56,000; in conjunction with the expansion, the owner also consolidated his identification with the franchise by renaming Navin Field Briggs Stadium. The 1938 season was also the year of Greenberg's pursuit of Ruth's home run record and the settling in of Rudy York as one of the league's premier power hitters. After a debut of 35 home runs and 103 RBIs in 1937, the righthanded slugger came through with 33 round-trippers and 127 RBIs. Initially assigned to third base and then to catching, the defensively limited York eventually ended up at first base, with Greenberg switching to the outfield.

The Tigers' 1940 pennant win followed an off-season that prompted many to wonder whether the team would ever win again. The doubts were raised by a January announcement that Landis was releasing ninety-one Detroit farmhands as free agents and ordering the franchise to pay more than $47,000 to another fifteen who had been victimized by deliberate burial in its minor league system. At the eye of the storm was Zeller, who had been the organization's farm director since 1926, when Navin had brought him in as a Mister Clean after indications that his other scouts had been recommending only players whose purchase had netted them a few dollars on the side. According to Landis, however, Zeller and Cecil Coombs, business manager of a minor league team in Fort Worth, had been conniving even more grandly in a whole series of coverups and fake contracts aimed at allowing the Tigers to maintain control over players for whom they had no immediate need. The release of the prospects led many to predict that the club would suffer for years, but the only noteworthy loss turned out to be outfielder Roy Cullenbine. Zeller saved his job mainly by exonerating Briggs of any collusion in the affair.

The principal ingredients in the 1940 flag were another dominating effort by Greenberg (an MVP trophy for his .340 average and league-leading 41 homers and 150 RBIs), York's 33 homers and 134 RBIs, the field leadership of newly acquired shortstop Dick Bartell, 21 wins from the much-traveled

In August 1937, Rudy York set the major league record for home runs in one month when he clouted 18.

Bobo Newsom, a 16–3 record fashioned by Rowe, and 17 saves by reliever Al Benton. For all that, the Tigers also had the decisive help of their chief rivals, the Indians, who played the season with one eye on the standings and the other on ways of dumping their unpopular manager Ossie Vitt. The Crybaby Indians, as they were called, were still in contention on the final weekend of the season, when Baker, reluctant to use one of his aces against Bob Feller, threw rookie Floyd Giebell into the breach; the righthander, who had only just been called up from the minors, stifled Cleveland for a 2–0 victory that clinched the pennant. Giebell won only two other major league games.

The World Series against the Reds went to seven games before the Tigers once again went down to the NL—its fifth postseason loss in six tries. The world championship was decided with a nail-biting duel between Newsom and Cincinnati's Paul Derringer that saw the Tigers enter the seventh-inning with a 1–0 margin, only to have the Reds rally for two winning runs. A turning point of the inning came when Bartell, in a freeze similar to that of Johnny Pesky in the 1946 World Series between the Cardinals and Red Sox, held a relay throw for precious seconds while the Reds scored the tying run. The winner was then driven in on a sacrifice fly by the weak-hitting Billy Myers.

The next three years quickly obliterated memories of how very close the club had come to a championship. Nineteen days into the 1941 season, Greenberg became the first AL player drafted into military service. Newsom got through the 1941 season, but no further, after leading the AL in losses. Baker himself lasted only through the 1942 season, the first year since the pre-Cobb days of 1906 that none of the regulars reached .300. The new manager was Steve O'Neill, who brought the club home to a second straight fifth-place finish in 1943.

With one exception, the team's brightest prospects in the early 1940s were pitchers. Dizzy Trout won 20 twice, and led the league in victories in 1943 and in ERA in 1944. Although he won 20 only once, Virgil Trucks could be as dominating as any pitcher in the league, as evidenced by his strange 1952 season, when he won 5 and lost 19, but notched two no-hitters, a one-hitter, and a two-hitter. Better than both righthanders was the southpaw Hal Newhouser, the only Detroit pitcher in Cooperstown (elected in 1992). His 207 career victories included three straight 20-win seasons between 1944 and 1946, plus a fourth attainment of the magic circle in 1948; in all four years, his wins were the most in the AL.

Newhouser, who also led the circuit in ERA in 1945 and 1946, is the only pitcher to have won back-to-back MVP awards (1944 and 1945).

The most noteworthy position player picked up by the team in the early part of the decade was outfielder Dick Wakefield, who became baseball's first bonus baby when he signed a contract for $52,000 plus an automobile in 1941. In his first full season in Detroit in 1943, the lefty swinger battled Luke Appling for the batting championship down to the final weeks before falling back to the runnerup spot. A year later, Wakefield was granted an extended leave from the Navy, enabling him to play a key offensive role (.355 in 78 games) in the Tigers' pennant struggle with the Browns. After coming out of the Navy for good in 1946, he challenged Ted Williams to a $1,000 bet that he would win the batting title, bringing Commissioner Happy Chandler on the run with warnings to both outfielders. Neither player won the title, but while Williams averaged .342, Wakefield closed out at a mere .268. He would never again show the form that had made him the focus of attention in Detroit during Greenberg's absence.

With Newhouser and Trout combining for 56 wins, and Wakefield, York, and third baseman Pinky Higgins providing the key offense, Detroit entered the final weekend of the 1944 campaign a game ahead of St. Louis, with the prospect of playing the Senators while the Browns had to take on the Yankees. The improbable happened: The Tigers could only split four contests with Washington, and St. Louis swept its final four with New York to win its one and only pennant.

There was a happier ending to a similar finish in 1945, largely because Greenberg had come back in midseason and the team had reacquired Cullenbine, the outfielder it had lost to the Landis free agent ruling in 1940. This time around, some odd schedule-making prompted by Clark Griffith's desire to make extra money by renting out Griffith Stadium to the National Football League Redskins, saw runnerup Washington finish its season a full week before first-place Detroit. Requiring only three wins in their last eight games to nail down the flag, the Tigers stumbled through the week, not nailing down matters until Greenberg hit a grand slam on the last day of the season.

Once again, Detroit's World Series foe was Chicago—an encounter that most pressbox critics wrote off as a showdown between gnats. Greenberg and Newhouser were the big names in the club's seven-game victory, with the former driving in seven runs and scoring seven and the latter overcoming a first-game shellacking to turn in two complete-game victories.

Immediately after the triumph over the Cubs, Zeller resigned as general manager and was replaced by George Trautman. With the club in need of a shortstop and with Greenberg's back flaring up regularly, Trautman decided to kill two birds with one stone by dealing York to the Red Sox for glove man Eddie Lake and moving Greenberg back to first base from the outfield.

A few weeks after the start of the 1946 season, he completed what turned out to be one of the best trades in franchise history—sending outfielder Barney McCoskey to the Athletics for third baseman George Kell. A .306 hitter in fifteen years of major league service, Kell would win the batting title with a .343 mark in 1949, and also lead the league in doubles in both 1950 and 1951. The righthanded hitter was elected to the Hall of Fame in 1983.

Kell was Trautman's main legacy to the Tigers because after only a year on the job, the executive was selected to head up the National Association of minor league clubs and left Detroit. The move had more than usual consequences when Greenberg, who had been making sounds all year about retiring and going into business with his in-laws (the department store Gimbels), applied for the job as Trautman's successor. Briggs turned him down on the grounds that he wasn't qualified, eventually bringing in ex-umpire and one-time Cleveland general manager Billy Evans. The owner then had Greenberg put on the waiver list, no other AL club claimed him (even with his bad back, he had again led the league in home runs and RBIs in 1946), and he ended up with the Pirates. There seemed little doubt that the old boy network was at work in agreeing to let the slugger out of the league.

If Trautman left a positive impression with his swap for the third sacker Kell, Evans left an equally negative one in November 1948 with one of the organization's worst deals, acquiring catcher Aaron Robinson from the White Sox in exchange for lefty prospect Billy Pierce and $100,000. As always, the franchise proved to be more perceptive in evaluating its young position players than its pitchers, and solid major leaguers such as Hoot Evers, Johnny Groth,

The Tigers were the last AL team to install lights, playing their first home night game on June 15, 1948—a 4–1 victory over Philadelphia.

and Vic Wertz moved into the starting lineup. In another running motif, however, almost all the top players coming through the system were outfielders, precipitating some ill-advised trades for an infielder to go with Kell or a catcher who could hit his weight. While the drought of infielders would finally be abated somewhat with the promotion of shortstop Harvey Kuenn in 1953, it was not until 1964 that the club could also claim, in Bill Freehan, a first-rate receiver.

The doldrums of the late 1940s were lifted temporarily when Detroit charged into second place in 1950, but then they descended again with a vengeance: For the rest of the decade, the team managed only two first-division finishes, and both of them were fourth-place shows. Managers came and went, with the parade taking in Red Rolfe, Fred Hutchinson, Bucky Harris on a second tour, Jack Tighe, Bill Norman, and Jimmy Dykes. There were even more changes in the front office. In January 1952, Briggs died, leaving the running of the club to a board of trustees. The trustees weathered the team's tepid box office performance until 1956, but then opened the bidding; among those making offers for the franchise were Bill Veeck and Charlie Finley. In the end, it was Spike Briggs who was instrumental in the decision to sell to a syndicate headed by broadcast executive John Fetzer for $5.5 million. For services rendered, Briggs was kept around as general manager and vice-president, but that arrangement ended the following year after he made one cutting remark too many about the ownership's baseball smarts. Briggs was replaced by John McHale, the fifth general manager of the decade (former star Gehringer and Muddy Ruel had taken turns after Evans); McHale would be succeeded by Rick Ferrell and Bill DeWitt before the end of the 1950s.

The team was not without its attractive players in the period. The first was Kuenn, who became the first Tiger to win Rookie of the Year honors by breaking in with a .308 average and a league-leading 209 hits in 1953. In his Detroit uniform, the righthanded line-drive hitter would top the loop in safeties three more times, pave the way in doubles three times, and win the batting title in 1959. A year after Kuenn came Al Kaline, who would reach the Hall of Fame on the basis of his twenty-two-year career with the Tigers during which he batted .297, clouted 399 home runs, and won eleven Gold Gloves for his defensive prowess and exceptional right field throwing arm. In 1955, the 20-year-old Kaline, who never spent a day in the minor leagues, became the youngest player ever to win the hitting crown. One of the more entertaining

players of the decade was left fielder Charlie Maxwell, whom Briggs plucked off a waiver list in 1955 when the Orioles tried to sneak him through the AL to complete a trade with the Braves. The lefty power hitter had four seasons of 24 homers or more for the club, but became especially noted for his long-ball feats on Sunday; 40 of Maxwell's 148 career blasts were hit on the seventh day. The best pitchers of the 1950s were righthanders Jim Bunning and Frank Lary. Bunning led the league with 20 wins in 1957, and in strikeouts in both 1959 and 1960. Lary won 21 in 1956 and 23 in 1961, but gained particular distinction for his taming of the slugging Yankees. He defeated New York seven times in 1958, and twenty-eight times overall in a career that would have otherwise been under .500.

The arrival of DeWitt as president and general manager after the 1959 season sparked three notable exchanges with the Indians of general manager Frank Lane. In the first one, the Tigers made what was arguably the best deal in their history in acquiring first baseman Norm Cash from Cleveland for backup infielder Steve Demeter. With the help of some illegal hollowing out of his bat, the lefty-swinging Cash won the hitting title in 1961 with a .361 mark, had eleven seasons of at least 22 home runs (including 41 in 1961), and ended up with 377 round-trippers. Less than a week after obtaining Cash in April 1960, DeWitt and Lane pulled off the most controversial swap of the period in dealing consistency (Kuenn) for power (outfielder Rocky Colavito). While Kuenn lasted only one year in Cleveland, Colavito belted 35, 45, and 37 homers in his three years in a Detroit uniform. The third trade between the executives was more in the nature of the bizarre—an exchange of managers Dykes and Joe Gordon, the first time that non-playing pilots had ever been swapped.

While the front office moves in 1960 revived interest in the Tigers at the gate, they hardly affected the club's position in the standings. Looking for substance rather than the novelty offered by the trade-obtained Gordon, Fetzer was on the verge of appointing Casey Stengel manager for 1961, when doctors advised the veteran pilot against returning to work. Bob Scheffing was Fetzer's second choice, and it was the ex-catcher at the helm when the team rode big power years from Cash and Kaline to its most victories since 1934. Unfortunately, it was also the season that Roger Maris and Mickey Mantle led the homer-hitting Yankees on a romp through the AL, so that Detroit still finished second, eight off the pace. The club then dropped back down to mediocre finishes for the next several years again. DeWitt was replaced in 1962 by Jim Campbell, Scheffing in the middle of 1963 by Charlie Dressen. Dressen's tenure was marked by two heart attacks and a kidney infection, the latter proving fatal in August 1966. Bob Swift, a coach who took over for Dressen after both his heart attacks, also died after the 1966 season, of cancer. Campbell's next choice of a pilot was Mayo Smith.

Although Smith took over the club with some less than sparkling credits as the former field boss of the Phillies and Reds, he proved to be the right man in the right job. He shook up the infield by benching the line-drive-hitting but fielding-weak Jerry Lumpe, moved a stiff-legged Dick McAuliffe from shortstop to second base, and inserted the offensively woeful but slick-moving Ray Oyler at short. That change plus MVP-type seasons from catcher Freehan and righthander Earl Wilson kept the team in contention against the Red Sox until the very last out of the season, when McAuliffe, in a game against the Angels, chose the worst possible moment to crack into a double play that gave Boston the pennant; it was the only double play the infielder hit into all year. The flag drive was also hampered by righthander Denny McLain's baffling foot injury on his way to an apparent 20-win season. McLain's ailment would raise even more questions a couple of years later when he was linked to gamblers.

It was the same McLain, however, who became the sweetheart of baseball in 1968, when he took both MVP and Cy Young honors for a 31-win season that made a joke out of the pennant race. It was the first time that a major leaguer had notched 30 wins since the Cardinals' Dizzy Dean in 1934 and the only time that any Detroit hurler attained the plateau. So dominating was McLain that only two other members of the staff had to win more than 10 to contribute to the team's romp—southpaw Mickey Lolich with 17 and Wilson with 13. Offensively, the club had a little bit of everything. Cash, Freehan, and left fielder Willie Horton all had 25 homers or more, and right fielder Jim Northrup's 21 blasts included 4 grand slams, 3 of them in one week.

Statistically, Ray Oyler is the worst hitter in the history of the AL for players with at least 1,000 at bats. In his 1,265 official appearances, the shortstop had only 221 hits, for an average of .175. Only once, in 1967, did he even reach the .200 level.

If Smith had returned the club to the winner's circle by inserting Oyler at shortstop, he reversed himself in the World Series against St. Louis by sitting down the .135 hitter, moving utilityman Mickey Stanley from the outfield to short, and restoring Kaline, who had been injured, to the picket line with Horton and Northrup. The veteran Kaline turned out to be a big offensive plus with 11 hits and 8 RBIs in a seven-game struggle that finally went to Detroit. Lolich took MVP honors by posting three complete-game victories. The World Series was played against a background of racial tensions around the country following the assassination of Martin Luther King earlier in the year. Fears of a violent eruption in Detroit had also been fueled by the mass vandalizing of Tiger Stadium after the crushing defeat in the final game of 1967. In the event, the biggest outpouring on the streets was for the victory parade for the world champions.

The next couple of seasons brought other kinds of trouble. As the climax to a long-simmering feud with Johnny Sain over the latter's co-manager status with the mound staff, Smith got Campbell to fire the pitching coach during the 1969 campaign. The decision rankled McLain and Wilson, in particular. Although he posted another AL-leading 24 wins, McLain plagued Smith all year with a series of tardy arrivals for games and a lackadaisical approach to his work schedule between starts, this in turn creating a good deal of resentment among the other pitchers. The most heated controversy erupted during the All Star Game, when the righthander, slated to start for Smith's AL squad, showed up late for the pregame hoopla in Washington, then left the capital altogether to return to Detroit for a dental appointment after rains had forced a one-day postponement of the contest. By the time McLain got back to Washington the following day, Smith had given his start to Mel Stottlemyre. Horton, who had become the team's most consistent power hitter, struck a nerve with Tiger fans with his nonchalant pursuit of a few drives into the left field corner and his frequent strikeouts; by May of 1969, he was being booed so constantly that he left the team for a couple of days.

Things got worse in 1970, with the club dropping under .500 for the first time in seven years. McLain was again at the center of the storm, drawing two suspensions from Commissioner Bowie Kuhn and a third from Campbell that limited his season to fourteen games and a 3–5 record. The first Kuhn punishment came in February, when the hurler was implicated in an investigation of a Michigan bookmaker who had profited from the Tigers' loss to the

Red Sox in 1967, the year that McLain had been side-lined with his mysterious foot problem. When sportswriters sought to question him about the investigation during spring training, McLain dumped ice water on them, causing Campbell to act. Kuhn's second suspension was announced near the end of the season, after McLain had been accused of brandishing a gun in a Chicago restaurant. Fetzer and Campbell finally had had enough and, on October 9th, announced the trade of the righthander to the Senators in an eight-player deal that had a great deal to do with Detroit's recovery in the early 1970s. McLain was still officially under suspension when the exchange with Washington was worked out, so Kuhn himself was involved in the talks, and even emceed the press conference disclosing the agreement.

In return for sending pitchers McLain and Norm McRae, third baseman Don Wert, and outfielder Elliott Maddox to the Senators, the Tigers landed shortstop Ed Brinkman, third baseman Aurelio Rodriguez, and pitchers Joe Coleman and Jim Hannan. Although Hannan's contributions were negligible, the righthanded Coleman notched two 20-win seasons and 62 victories in his first three years with Detroit; equally important, Brinkman and Rodriguez gave the club a defense on the left side of the infield that was second to none.

In preparation for the 1971 season, Campbell also made another big move when he fired Smith and brought in Billy Martin as manager. Martin made sounds throughout the 1971 campaign that he would have liked a few younger players instead of aging veterans like Kaline, Cash, and McAuliffe, but he managed to keep the club an interesting runnerup to the Orioles. The star of the year was Lolich, who went from pacing the league in losses in 1970 to leading in victories with 25. The ex-Senator Coleman chipped in with 20, and southpaw Fred Scherman won 11 and saved 20 more.

Against all expectations, Martin's 1972 roster not only didn't include fresh faces in the starting lineup, but was bolstered by the addition of even more graying players, such as Tony Taylor, Frank Howard, and Woodie Fryman. Southpaw Fryman, in particular, turned out to be a steal after his contract was purchased in August. Down the final weeks of the season in a seesaw battle against Boston for first place, the veteran National Leaguer won 10 and lost only 3, providing a necessary third starter behind Lolich's 22 wins and Coleman's 19. Overall, the pitching staff's 2.96 ERA was good enough to offset

Footnote Player: Southpaw Les Cain, who pitched for the Tigers in 1968 and between 1970 and 1972, won the only legal judgment requiring that a baseball team compensate him for the rest of his life. In 1973, the Michigan Bureau of Workmen's Compensation upheld Cain's claim that Billy Martin had ruined his career by forcing him to pitch with a sore arm and ordered Detroit to pay him $111 a week for life. The two sides later agreed upon a single lump sum payment. Cain's lifetime record was 23–19.

a blinking offense and give the Tigers their first half-pennant since the start of divisional play in 1969.

Equally important in the division race was an early-season players' strike that forced the postponement of some games, created an imbalanced schedule, and allowed Detroit to edge into the LCS by the thinnest of margins—a mere half-game. In the playoffs against the heavily favored Athletics, the Tigers overcame two quick victories by Oakland to even the series at four games, only to fall in the fifth and decisive contest.

Having reached postseason play within two years, Martin showed again why he was a short-term success and long-term travail by precipitating incidents that ended with his firing before the end of the 1973 season. During spring training, he quit for a day after he couldn't get his way with Campbell over some roster cuts. A few weeks into the season, he ignored the general manager's warnings about leaving the club to fly off to Kansas City for private business. During a series against the Indians, he was so infuriated by a winning effort by Cleveland spitballer Gaylord Perry that he ordered Coleman and Scherman to throw at hitters, then proudly admitted doing so. AL president Joe Cronin suspended him for three days, and before he could return, he was fired by Campbell in favor of coach Joe Schultz. About the only bright spot of the season was reliever John Hiller, who returned from a 1971 heart attack to win 10 games and save 38 others. Even Coleman, who won 23 games, lost seven in a row during a late-season stretch when the club was still entertaining some hope of getting back into contention.

With Ralph Houk taking over in 1974, Campbell finally agreed to getting rid of some of the older players Martin had been agitating about for a couple of years. McAuliffe was traded to the Red Sox before the start of the season, Cash was released, Northrup was sold to the Expos, and, after the campaign, Kaline announced his retirement. Before applying for his pension, Kaline recorded his 3,000th hit (on September 24th), becoming the first AL player to reach that plateau since Eddie Collins in 1925. There was not too much else to applaud in a last-place season that was billed as a rebuilding year but that saw only outfielder Ron LeFlore among the prospects getting any significant playing time. LeFlore joined the Tigers after coming out of a penitentiary, where he had served a term for robbery. Although he became a top base-stealer for several years, he was eventually undone by his strikeouts, a series of injuries, and a number of run-ins with old-school managers.

In 1976, the Tigers found a bonafide slugging prospect in lefty-swinging first baseman Jason Thompson and reaped big offensive rewards by slipping Rusty Staub into the role of designated hitter, but nobody came close to Mark Fidrych in dominating not only the club, but the entire league. A nonroster player when he arrived for spring training and a full-time occupant of the bullpen bench until five weeks into the season, the righthander went on to

Mark ''The Bird'' Fidrych. *Courtesy of Detroit Tigers*

fascinate the country with his mound skills and idiosyncrasies. Fidrych talked to the ball, got down on his hands and knees to landscape the pitching hill, and ran over to shake the hands of infielders in the middle of innings if they made a particularly sparkling play. Initially resentful that the hurler was trying to show them up, even opposition batters came to realize that there was nothing false or calculated about the enthusiasm of the Tiger who became known as The Bird. There wasn't anything false about his record or drawing power, either. On the mound, Fidrych easily took Rookie of the Year honors with his 19 wins and league-leading ERA of 2.24; he also hurled twenty-four complete games for tops in that category. Financially, he was a godsend for a franchise that was otherwise hard put to persuade fans that climbing out of the cellar was a goal worth watching first-hand. In his twenty-nine starts at home and on the road, he drew 899,969 spectators; at Tiger Stadium, his pitching turns drew 605,677, or some 60 percent of the year's attendance. According to one *Wall Street Journal* analyst, Fidrych was personally responsible for about $1 million of team revenues in 1976. Tragically, the Bird turned out to be a short-lived phenomenon. In spring training in 1977, Fidrych tore the cartilage in his right knee, postponing his debut in his sophomore year until late May. After a couple of shaky starts, he seemed to be coming around (six wins, 2.89 ERA) when tendinitis in his pitching arm decked him for the year. He won only four more games for the Tigers before retiring in 1980.

Without Fidrych, the Tigers limped through the rest of the decade, with Staub and Thompson providing most of the offense and an array of pitchers pointed to as the staff anchor for years to come. The only prediction that wasn't wrong was Jack Morris, who posted his first winning season (17–7) in 1979, then went on to win more games than any other big league pitcher in the 1980s. By the end of the decade, the team had also called up such future stars as shortstop Alan Trammell, second baseman Lou Whitaker, outfielder Kirk Gibson, and catcher Lance Parrish.

Houk lasted through 1978, when he retired and was replaced by Les Moss. But only one-third of the way into the 1979 campaign, Campbell bounced Moss in favor of Sparky Anderson, who had been unceremoniously cut loose by Cincinnati after having been the brains behind the Big Red Machine. Anderson signed one of the biggest pacts ever given to a manager to that time—$125,000 a year through 1984. One of his first moves was to endorse the dealing of Staub to Montreal, charging that the designated hitter's contract holdout during spring training had left him out of shape.

In his first few years, Anderson's impact was hardly noticeable, with the Tigers playing well enough to stay above .500, but not well enough to scare division rivals. Under his tutelage, however, the club gradually built up a franchise-record eleven straight seasons of better-than-even ball, and won everything in the division in both 1984 and 1987. Anderson was the perfect manager for Detroit, because the team's traditional pitching shorts after one or two starters were best served by a strategist who had become known as Captain Hook for his regular use of the bullpen. As far as his roster as a whole was concerned, on the other hand, Anderson showed himself to be the very opposite of impatient—rarely going the trade route in any significant way once he chose twenty-five players in spring training. Not that his spring evaluations were always correct; indeed, few managers proved to be as wrong so loudly as Anderson, in his chronic predictions that untested rookies (Chris Pittaro and Ricky Peters, among them) were only a foot away from the Hall of Fame. He also took a black eye for his evaluation of third baseman Howard Johnson as an essentially defensive player who lacked the fortitude needed to survive in the big leagues; it was with this justification that he dealt the switch-hitting slugger to the Mets after the 1984 season for righthander Walt Terrell.

A foretaste to the team's return to the World Series came in 1983, when Morris posted his first 20-win season and Trammell confirmed that he could hit as well as field. After the season, Fetzer announced the sale of the franchise to Domino's Pizza king Tom Monaghan for $43 million. In the front office shakeup that followed, Campbell went from general manager to president and Bill Lajoie was brought in to take over Campbell's old job. In what turned out to be two pivotal moves before the start of the 1984 season, the team also signed lefty-hitting Darrell Evans as a free agent and completed a deal with the Phillies in which outfielder Glenn Wilson and catcher John Wockenfuss were sent to the NL in exchange for southpaw relief pitcher Willie Hernandez and first baseman Dave Bergman.

For all practical purposes, the Eastern Division race in the AL in 1984 ended on opening day, when the Tigers joined the Murderers Row Yankees of 1927 as the only AL teams to occupy first place every day of the season. The club got out of the gate with nine straight wins, had a record of 35–5 by mid-May, and ended up 15 games ahead of second-place Toronto.

The pitching force of the year was reliever Hernandez, who snatched both the MVP and Cy Young awards for his 9 wins, 32 saves, 1.92 ERA, and AL-leading 80 appearances. Among the position players, Parrish and Gibson contributed 60 homers and 189 RBIs between them, while Trammell and Whitaker gained recognition as the best all-around middle infield duo in years.

Lack of suspense in the pennant race did not prevent a record 2.7 million fans from descending on Tiger Stadium during the year. In the LCS against Kansas City, Detroit continued to exhibit its superiority in a three-game sweep. The World Series against San Diego was another romp, with the club winning in five games. Morris won twice, Hernandez saved two more, and Gibson drove in seven. MVP honors, however, went to Trammell for his nine hits, six runs batted in, and five runs scored. Anderson's triumph made him the first manager to win a World Series in both leagues.

Hopes that the franchise was launched on a dynastic reign were quickly dashed when it slumped to third place the next two seasons. In 1985, a porous defense was added to declines by just about every front-line pitcher and position player. The biggest positive development was designated hitter Evans's 40 home runs, good enough to lead the league; at the age of 38, the lefty swinger was the oldest player ever to pace the circuit in the power category. In 1986, Morris rebounded for 21 wins, and all four infielders (Evans, Whitaker, Trammell, and third baseman Darnell Coles) had at least 20 home runs, but the club was once again derailed by its lack of defense and pitching depth. To make matters worse, Parrish couldn't agree to terms with the club after the season and walked off to the Phillies as a free agent.

Another turnaround in 1987 was largely the result of some last hurrah performances, Anderson's reversal of habit in pressing for a couple of midseason acquisitions, and the blossoming of a couple of young players; it didn't hurt, either, that the Blue Jays went into one of the worst eleventh-hour collapses in the league's history. Among the veterans, Evans again startled those who had dismissed him as washed up by belting 34 homers and driving in 99; he was the first 40-year-old ever to reach the 30-mark in four-baggers. For his part, Trammell put together the finest of all his seasons by hitting .343 with 28 home runs and 105 RBIs. Looking for right-handed offense in the middle of the season, Lajoie picked up former NL batting champion Bill Madlock from the Dodgers; in some 300 at bats, Madlock contributed 14 homers and 50 RBIs as the lineup's designated hitter. In August, the club made an equally important deal in picking up righty Doyle Alexander from the Braves; although the transaction cost top prospect John Smoltz, Alexander was a marvel over the final weeks of the campaign, going 9–0 in 11 starts. Parrish's defection was compensated for to some degree by Matt Nokes, who, while nowhere near his predecessor defensively, belted 32 home runs.

Despite all these individual contributions, the Tigers still found themselves on the verge of elimination in the final week of the season, when Toronto suddenly blew six games in a row. With the division title on the line in the season finale, lefty Frank Tanana took the mound against the Blue Jays' Jimmy Key. Tanana did not make any mistakes, Key made one—a solo home run to outfielder Larry Herndon, and the half-pennant went to Detroit by the score of 1–0. As it turned out, it was the club's last moment of glory for the decade. In the LCS against Minnesota, all the defensive troubles that had been apparent but contained during the season came to the fore, enabling the Twins to win in five games.

Thanks largely to reliever Mike Henneman, the team remained competitive in 1988, and might have won it all except for a circulatory problem that felled key starter Jeff Robinson in August. The second-place finish was somewhat unexpected in that, like Parrish the previous season, Gibson had taken the free agency route before the start of the campaign; the outfielder was one of a handful of players who gained his freedom after an arbitrator ruled that major league owners had been colluding in discouraging free agents from leaving their organizations. The bill for defecting players such as Parrish and Gibson came due in 1989, when the Tigers plummeted to the basement with the second worst record in franchise history. Anderson was so unnerved by what was clearly going to be an arduous season that he collapsed in May and had to be sent home for a three-week rest.

In 1990, Monaghan brought in college football coach Bo Schembechler as president and kicked Campbell upstairs as a figurehead club chairman of the board; Schembechler did little over the next couple of years but mouth whatever Monaghan told him to say. That same year, however, the franchise struck gold by signing Cecil Fielder, who had played the previous season in Japan. A bulging righthanded hitter, the first baseman became the first ALer since 1961 to top the 50-homer mark when he led the loop with 51 round-trippers. In 1991, he came right back to hit 44 more, tying Oakland's Jose Canseco for the lead, and the year after that, walloped another 35. In all three seasons, Fielder led the AL in RBIs—a league feat accomplished previously only by Babe Ruth. The slugger was the centerpiece of a team that tore through the AL in the early 1990s with the long ball, but that was equally torn through for its vulnerability to the strikeout. At the same time, the club's pitching was never less impressive, with the starting rotation consisting of the well-traveled Terrell, the graying Tanana, and another veteran of Japan, Bill Gullickson.

Monaghan, who had adopted a relatively benign posture over his first few years of running the franchise, came under fire for several reasons at the beginning of the new decade. The biggest source of trouble was his campaign to pressure the city into building a new stadium behind the argument that Tiger Stadium had become too much of an eyesore and was structurally unfit for the two-million-plus customers needed every year to keep the franchise afloat. That crusade was opposed not only by traditionalists who viewed Tiger Stadium as third only to Wrigley Field and Fenway Park in representing the spirit of the game, but by voters who, in March 1992, rejected any notion of a municipal tax for paying for a new facility. Monaghan's response to the vote was to announce his interest in selling out.

The owner also came in for a great deal of criticism for not intervening in the firing of popular Detroit broadcaster Ernie Harwell after the 1991 season. Although Monaghan and Schembechler both blamed the decision on the station covering the club's games, it was also obvious that neither executive had been enthusiastic about some of Harwell's on-air observations during the losing seasons of 1989 and 1990.

In August 1992, Monaghan dropped the other shoe by announcing that he had reached an agreement to sell the club to Mike Ilitch, a rival pizza

In 1991, Rob Deer became the first player in big league history to hit at least 25 home runs without batting .200. The outfielder averaged only .179 while clouting his 25 round-trippers.

chain owner of Little Caesar's. Before the shoe, however, came a couple of dirty socks—Monaghan faxing Schembechler that he was out, then informing Campbell of a similar decision by phone while the veteran organization executive was attending induction ceremonies at the Hall of Fame. The biggest beneficiary of the moves when Ilitch took over after the season was Jerry Walker, who at least initially had some clout to go with his general manager's title.

The new owner made it clear at once that he had deeper pockets than his predecessor—giving huge contracts to Fielder, the aging Whitaker, and Gullickson, the latter of whom had won 20 games in 1991 mainly because of his ability to hang on for at least five innings in slugfests. The club's other big hopes for the 1993 season were catcher Mickey Tettleton and shortstop Travis Fryman, who had combined for 52 homers and 179 RBIs the previous year.

DETROIT TIGERS

Annual Standings and Managers

Year	Position	W	L	Pct.	GB	Managers
1901	Third	74	61	.548	8½	George Stallings
1902	Seventh	52	83	.385	30½	Frank Dwyer
1903	Fifth	65	71	.478	25	Ed Barrow
1904	Seventh	62	90	.408	32	Ed Barrow, Bobby Lowe
1905	Third	79	74	.516	15½	Bill Armour
1906	Sixth	71	78	.477	21	Bill Armour
1907	First	92	58	.613	+1½	Hughie Jennings
1908	First	90	63	.588	+½	Hughie Jennings
1909	First	98	54	.645	+3½	Hughie Jennings
1910	Third	86	68	.558	18	Hughie Jennings
1911	Second	89	65	.578	13½	Hughie Jennings
1912	Sixth	69	84	.451	36½	Hughie Jennings
1913	Sixth	66	87	.431	30	Hughie Jennings
1914	Fourth	80	73	.523	19½	Hughie Jennings
1915	Second	100	54	.649	2½	Hughie Jennings
1916	Third	87	67	.565	4	Hughie Jennings
1917	Fourth	78	75	.510	21½	Hughie Jennings
1918	Seventh	55	71	.437	20	Hughie Jennings
1919	Fourth	80	60	.571	8	Hughie Jennings
1920	Seventh	61	93	.396	37	Hughie Jennings
1921	Sixth	71	82	.464	27	Ty Cobb
1922	Third	79	75	.513	15	Ty Cobb
1923	Second	83	71	.539	16	Ty Cobb
1924	Third	86	68	.558	6	Ty Cobb
1925	Fourth	81	73	.526	16½	Ty Cobb
1926	Sixth	79	75	.513	12	Ty Cobb
1927	Fourth	82	71	.536	27½	George Moriarty
1928	Sixth	68	86	.442	33	George Moriarty
1929	Sixth	70	84	.455	36	Bucky Harris
1930	Fifth	75	79	.487	27	Bucky Harris
1931	Seventh	61	93	.396	47	Bucky Harris
1932	Fifth	76	75	.503	29½	Bucky Harris
1933	Fifth	75	79	.487	25	Bucky Harris, Del Baker
1934	First	101	53	.656	+7	Mickey Cochrane
1935	First	93	58	.616	+3	Mickey Cochrane
1936	Second	83	71	.539	19½	Mickey Cochrane
1937	Second	89	65	.578	13	Mickey Cochrane
1938	Fourth	84	70	.545	16	Mickey Cochrane, Del Baker

1939	Fifth	81	73	.526	26½	Del Baker
1940	First	90	64	.584	+1	Del Baker
1941	Fourth*	75	79	.487	26	Del Baker
1942	Fifth	73	81	.474	30	Del Baker
1943	Fifth	78	76	.506	20	Steve O'Neill
1944	Second	88	66	.571	1	Steve O'Neill
1945	First	88	65	.575	+1½	Steve O'Neill
1946	Second	92	62	.597	12	Steve O'Neill
1947	Second	85	69	.552	12	Steve O'Neill
1948	Fifth	78	76	.506	18½	Steve O'Neill
1949	Fourth	87	67	.565	10	Red Rolfe
1950	Second	95	59	.617	3	Red Rolfe
1951	Fifth	73	81	.474	25	Red Rolfe
1952	Eighth	50	104	.325	45	Red Rolfe, Fred Hutchinson
1953	Sixth	60	94	.390	40½	Fred Hutchinson
1954	Fifth	68	86	.442	43	Fred Hutchinson
1955	Fifth	79	75	.513	17	Bucky Harris
1956	Fifth	82	72	.532	15	Bucky Harris
1957	Fourth	78	76	.506	20	Jack Tighe
1958	Fifth	77	77	.500	15	Jack Tighe, Bill Norman
1959	Fourth	76	78	.494	18	Bill Norman, Jimmy Dykes
1960	Sixth	71	83	.461	26	Jimmy Dykes, Joe Gordon
1961	Second	101	61	.623	8	Bob Scheffing
1962	Fourth	85	76	.528	10½	Bob Scheffing
1963	Fifth*	79	83	.488	25½	Bob Scheffing, Charlie Dressen
1964	Fourth	85	77	.525	14	Charlie Dressen
1965	Fourth	89	73	.549	13	Charlie Dressen, Bob Swift
1966	Third	88	74	.543	10	Charlie Dressen, Bob Swift, Frank Skaff
1967	Second*	91	71	.562	1	Mayo Smith
1968	First	103	59	.636	+12	Mayo Smith
1969	Second	90	72	.556	19	Mayo Smith
1970	Fourth	79	83	.488	29	Mayo Smith
1971	Second	91	71	.562	12	Billy Martin
1972	First	86	70	.551	+½	Billy Martin
1973	Third	85	77	.525	12	Billy Martin, Joe Schultz
1974	Sixth	72	90	.444	19	Ralph Houk
1975	Sixth	57	102	.358	37½	Ralph Houk
1976	Fifth	74	87	.460	24	Ralph Houk
1977	Fourth	74	88	.457	26	Ralph Houk
1978	Fifth	86	76	.531	13½	Ralph Houk
1979	Fifth	85	76	.528	18	Les Moss, Sparky Anderson
1980	Fifth	84	78	.519	19	Sparky Anderson
1981	Fourth	31	26	.544	3½	Sparky Anderson
	Second*	29	23	.558	1½	Sparky Anderson
1982	Fourth	83	79	.512	12	Sparky Anderson
1983	Second	92	70	.568	6	Sparky Anderson
1984	First	104	58	.642	+15	Sparky Anderson
1985	Third	84	77	.522	15	Sparky Anderson
1986	Third	87	75	.537	8½	Sparky Anderson
1987	First	98	64	.605	+2	Sparky Anderson
1988	Second	88	74	.543	1	Sparky Anderson
1989	Seventh	59	103	.364	30	Sparky Anderson
1990	Third	79	83	.488	9	Sparky Anderson
1991	Second*	84	78	.519	7	Sparky Anderson
1992	Sixth	75	87	.463	21	Sparky Anderson

* Tie

Postseason Play

WS			LCS		
	0–4 versus Chicago	1907		2–3 versus Oakland	1972
	1–4 versus Chicago	1908		3–0 versus Kansas City	1984
	3–4 versus Pittsburgh	1909		1–4 versus Minnesota	1987
	3–4 versus St. Louis	1934			
	4–2 versus Chicago	1935			
	3–4 versus Cincinnati	1940			
	4–3 versus Chicago	1945			
	4–3 versus St. Louis	1968			
	4–1 versus San Diego	1984			

Florida Marlins

National League, 1993   **BALLPARK:** JOE ROBBIE STADIUM

Even before they took the field for their first game in April 1993, the Marlins showed more of a knack for pressing the right business buttons than other big league clubs had exhibited for decades. The person doing most of the pressing was Wayne Huizenga, the multimillionaire owner of the Blockbuster Video company.

Although a viable candidate for a franchise since the National League first announced in 1985 its intention to expand to 14 teams, the Miami area was widely considered an underdog to Tampa-St. Petersburg as a Florida venue. Reasons included racist attitudes toward Miami's heavily Latin population, the southern city's unstable weather, and the promises both leagues had given to Tampa-St. Petersburg over the years after the aborted transfers of existing franchises to the twin cities. But that picture began to change in March 1990, when Huizenga, a minority investor in the football Dolphins, laid out $30 million to secure half-ownership of Joe Robbie Stadium. It was the start of an intense campaign of White Papers and public relations gimmicks aimed at persuading baseball's expansion committee that Miami was the preferable site. Particularly crucial in the lobbying effort were a pair of exhibition games between the Yankees and Orioles held at Joe Robbie Stadium in March 1991; the contests drew 113,000 fans. It didn't hurt, either, that Blockbuster Video handled video production for Major League Baseball Properties and was the sole retail and rental outlet for the sport's official line of videotapes.

Commissioner Fay Vincent announced the awarding of two new franchises to Huizenga and the Colorado Rockies in June 1991; formal ratification came from the owners about three weeks later. The entry fee was $95 million, which Huizenga declared ready to pay in cash. Contradicting earlier indications, the Marlins' owner then disclosed that the club would be designated by state rather than city for the avowed purpose of increasing its appeal to all Floridians. The move annoyed residents of Miami, but positively infuriated others, not least in Tampa-St. Petersburg. A year later, Tampa-St. Petersburg interests would have even more to complain about when Huizenga, after taking a public stand suggesting that he favored the transfer of the San Francisco Giants to the twin cities, was known to have worked feverishly behind the scenes to keep the California club in the Bay Area.

Insisting that he would stay out of his organization's day-to-day baseball operations, the Florida owner brought in Carl Barger as president and Dave Dombrowski as general manager. Both appointments created some ripples: Barger's because of conflict of interest accusations when he sought to hold on for awhile to his post as president of the Pirates, Dombrowski's because, in leaving a similar position with the Expos, he cleaned out the Montreal front-office and scouting department to accompany him. NL President Bill White finally had to intervene to put a stop to the raids on the Expos.

Rene Lachemann, the epitome of the old boy

network, was tapped as the team's first manager. In the expansion draft held in November 1992, on the other hand, the club generally went for youth instead of familiar names, making Toronto minor league outfielder Nigel Wilson its first selection. Exceptions were veteran reliever Bryan Harvey (California), southpaw starters Danny Jackson (Pittsburgh) and Greg Hibbard (White Sox), and outfielder Junior Felix (California). As soon as the draft was completed, however, the club swapped Jackson to the Phillies and Hibbard to the Cubs for more young prospects. Among the free agents picked up during the offsea-

son were third baseman Dave Magadan, ancient knuckleballer Charlie Hough, and Orestes Destrade, a slugging first baseman who had recorded impressive numbers in Japan.

Only a few hours before the start of the expansion draft, Barger died of a heart attack. While this prompted some speculation that Dombrowski would wield even more power in the organization, there appeared to be little doubt that Huizenga himself would also have more of a say in the baseball operations that he claimed to want to keep at a distance.

Hartford Dark Blues

National League, 1876   **BALLPARK:** HARTFORD BALL CLUB GROUNDS

RECORD: 47–21 (.691)

One of the clubs carried over from the National Association to the fledgling National League, The Dark Blues were a relatively strong team in a relatively weak market. They had finished third in the NA's last season, and managed the same standing in the NL's inaugural campaign.

Morgan Bulkeley, who had made the Aetna Insurance Company the largest insurance firm in the country, was the Hartford president. When the NL's board of directors was chosen, the first club name out of the hat was Hartford's, making Bulkeley president of the league as well. He served only one year, took a relatively minor interest in league affairs, and years later was elected to the Hall of Fame solely on the basis of his luck at having been drawn first.

Neither the hitting of right fielder Dick Higham (.327) nor the pitching of one of the league's best hustlers, Tommy Bond, did much for attendance at the Hartford Baseball Grounds. One of Bulkeley's solutions was to prohibit local newspapers from disseminating the score of a game until it was over. The hope was that the habitués of local saloons and pool halls would pay to go the park instead of having the progress of games delivered to them for the cost of the afternoon paper. Most of them didn't.

As losses mounted, rumors proliferated. One had it that The Dark Blues would play in Brooklyn in 1877. On August 14th, the Hartford management denied the Brooklyn rumor flatly, making Bulkeley the

HON. MORGAN G. BULKELEY

FIRST PRESIDENT OF THE NATIONAL LEAGUE AND A LEADER IN ITS ORGANIZATION IN 1876 WHICH LAID THE FOUNDATION OF THE NATIONAL GAME FOR POSTERITY.

National Baseball Library, Cooperstown, NY

> *Footnote Player:* Arthur Candy Cummings is usually credited with inventing the curveball. After appearing for several professional teams between 1866 and 1875, Cummings went 16–8 with five shutouts for Hartford in 1876. He pitched only one more year in the National League, going 5–14 for Cincinnati in 1877.

first baseball owner to deny that his team would move to another city for financial reasons. At the end of the 1876 season, the club was indeed shifted to Brooklyn.

Bulkeley himself went on to become mayor of Hartford, governor of Connecticut, and a United States senator.

HARTFORD DARK BLUES

Annual Standings and Manager

Year	Position	W	L	Pct.	GB	Manager
1876	Third	47	21	.691	6	Bob Ferguson

Houston Astros

National League,
1962–Present

BALLPARKS: COLT STADIUM (1962–1964)
ASTRODOME (1965–Present)

RECORD: 2388–2571 (.482)

OTHER NAMES: COLT .45s

For all their splashy attire, grandiose playing facilities, and Texas backing, the Astros have been very modest in their accomplishments over three decades of National League baseball. Houston has never reached the World Series, appeared in only two League Championship Series, and attracted two million fans only twice. On the other hand, the team can put in a claim for being the only expansion club in the NL not to finish in the cellar in its maiden season and for being part of the two most exciting LCS playoffs since the start of divisional play in 1969.

Along with the New York Mets, Houston was brought into the NL as a compromise solution to the Continental League's designs on major league baseball. The engine behind the franchise was the Houston Sports Association, a group put together in the late 1950s by public relations man George Kirksey and Texaco heir Craig Cullinan, Jr. to lure big league ball to the city. It was only after thwarted tries at getting the Cardinals, Athletics, and Indians to transfer to Texas that Kirksey and Cullinan threw in with the Continental League. Their behind-the-scenes maneuverings in Washington, especially with fellow

Texan and Senate Majority Leader Lyndon Johnson, were of fundamental importance in getting the National and American leagues to seek some kind of accord with the insurgent circuit fronted by Branch Rickey.

The agreement between the NL and the Houston Sports Association was announced officially on October 17, 1960. By that time, however, it was a somewhat different association. With Cullinan reluctant to assume full financial control and determined to involve as many community leaders as possible in the venture, and with idea man Kirksey in no position to bankroll anything, the door was wide open for Robert E. Smith to step in. Smith, regarded by many as the richest man in the state, brought along a long-time associate, Judge Roy Hofheinz. The arrival on the scene of Hofheinz produced some immediate fallout when Gabe Paul, who had been persuaded to leave the general managership of the Cincinnati Reds to take over the new franchise's day-to-day baseball operations, walked away from a three-year contract only shortly after signing it, suggesting that he would not have lasted long with the judge.

The Houston Astrodome, the first indoor facility for playing baseball in either the National or American League. *National Baseball Library, Cooperstown, NY*

One who did—at least relatively—was Kirksey. Although reduced to being just another employee under Hofheinz, Kirksey had a hand in every significant development leading up to the fielding of the first Houston team. It was he who handled the secret negotiations that got Paul Richards away from the Baltimore Orioles for the position that Gabe Paul had backed out of and the club official who sounded out Harry Craft about becoming the new team's first manager. Never without a promotional scheme, it was also Kirksey who proposed that one way of firming up a pending advertising deal with the Colt Firearms Company would be to call the team the Colt .45s. When Smith and Hofheinz countered that it should be Houston fans to name the team by ballot, good soldier Kirksey organized the vote. Weeks later, after ferreting through what he said was more than 10,000 letters, he announced that the winner was—surprise—the Colt .45s. Smith and Hofheinz were suspicious, but by then Kirksey's cronies in the Houston media had also been using Colt .45s too familiarly for the name to be dismissed. Hofheinz tolerated it for three years, until the move into the Astrodome gave him an excuse for scrapping it in favor of something in keeping with the space age image of the city.

The aged, untested, and mediocre players put in the window by the NL for the October 1961 expansion draft did not enthuse Richards, and he didn't mind saying so. After taking veteran utilityman Ed Bressoud as his first choice, Richards concentrated on younger players, leaving the more familiar names to the Mets and hoping that he would get lucky. The twenty-three players chosen by the end of the draft cost the franchise $1.8 million. As the first selected player to sign a contract, infielder Bob Aspromonte became the first Houston major leaguer.

Aside from the expansion draft, Richards stocked the organization with high school and junior college prospects. Among his first discoveries was Rusty Staub, the outfielder-first baseman who would become one of the franchise's first bonafide stars. To get Staub, however, Kirksey, a last-minute negotiating substitute for Richards, also agreed to sign his brother to a three-year contract for $50,000 and his father to a scouting job. When they heard about the terms of the agreement, Richards and Hofheinz saw to it that Kirksey did no further contract negotiating for the team.

For their first three years, the Colt .45s played in Colt Stadium, a temporary facility that was put under construction at exactly the same time as the adjoining Astrodome; in fact, the park was considered so temporary that nobody even bothered to mark the power alley measurements (an estimated 395 feet) on the outfield walls. On the other hand, what Colt Stadium had in infinite abundance were giant mosquitos that forced the grounds crew to spray insect repellent between half innings and that earned the park the epithet of Mosquito Heaven.

The Colt .45s played their first game on April 10, 1962—an 11–2 bashing of the Cubs that featured two homers by outfielder Roman Mejias. The game was also an omen insofar as Houston would finish the season in eighth place ahead of not only the fellow-expansion Mets, but also Chicago.

If Houston fans were expecting even better results the following year, they were disappointed. What they got—aside from the first of three straight ninth-place finishes—was a better look at the shining pitching amid the murky offense that would be the team's trademark for most of the future. The best example of the team's makeup was righthander Ken Johnson, who in 1964 became the first pitcher in baseball history to lose a nine-inning no-hitter, 1–0 to the Reds.

Hofheinz used the team's first couple of years to build up his power in the boardroom, eventually eclipsing even Smith, his original sponsor, as the franchise's most important voice. When the gradually embittered Smith finally challenged the judge to buy him out, he was stunned to receive an offer that effectively reduced him to a minority stockholder. Only with the passing of some years did it emerge that Hofheinz had found the money by hocking himself up to the eyebrows, his most persuasive collateral being the prospects offered by his pet project, the indoor Astrodome.

On September 27, 1963, the Colt .45s sought to give their fans a glimpse of the future by starting nine rookies in a game against the Mets. The players were: P-Jay Dahl; C-Jerry Grote; 1B-Rusty Staub; 2B-Joe Morgan; 3B-Glenn Vaughan; SS-Sonny Jackson; OF-Brock Davis, Aaron Pointer, and Jimmy Wynn. Dahl lasted only three innings in a 10–3 Mets bashing and never appeared in another major league game. Vaughan played in nine games and then also disappeared. Davis and Pointer had several trials with Houston. The others, including Hall of Famer Morgan, had substantial careers—mainly for other teams.

On September 29, 1963, John Paciorek of Houston went 3-for-3 in a game against the Mets. When a back injury prevented him from ever playing again, he retired with the most hits by any player with a perfect 1.000 batting average.

Things were no smoother on the baseball operations front. Ever since he had become general manager, Richards was less than enthusiastic about Craft as field manager, because that appointment had been made at the instigation of Gabe Paul, Kirksey, and Cullinan. Richards proposed a change to Lum Harris in the middle of the 1964 season, and Hofheinz went along—with the understanding that the new manager had better produce some results when the team moved to the Astrodome in 1965. When Harris's Astros won one game less than the 1964 Colt .45s had, he went out the door, and took Richards with him. Even twenty years later, Richards could remain bitter enough to reject a reporter's suggestion that Hofheinz was his own worst enemy by remarking that "not while I'm alive he isn't."

In place of Harris and Richards, Hofheinz appointed Texan Grady Hatton and Spec Richardson, respectively. The last of the old guard to go was Kirksey, who had been gradually squeezed by the judge into smaller and smaller offices to carry out less and less meaningful tasks. Kirksey had a measure of satisfaction, however, when he received three times the expected price for his two-percent share in the Houston Sports Association after some pointed hints that he might sell his holding to Smith.

Shamelessly trumpeted as the Eighth Wonder of the World, the Astrodome (officially called the Harris County Domed Stadium) was financed by an $18 million general obligation bond. By the time parking lots, site roads, and other accessories had been factored in, the bill for the project came to $31.6 million. The very first game played on the premises was a preseason exhibition against the New York Yankees on April 9, 1965, with the Astros prevailing in 12

Although it had no predecessors in either the National or American league, the Astrodome was not the first indoor stadium. That distinction belongs to the facility built under Manhattan's 59th Street Bridge in 1939 for use by the New York Cubans of the Negro League.

innings by the score of 2–1. The 47,876 who showed up saw New York's Mickey Mantle hit baseball's first indoor home run. Three days later, on April 12th, NL action got underway with Philadelphia's Chris Short throwing a four-hitter and Dick Allen hitting a two-run homer to defeat Houston, 2–0.

It didn't take long for some of the dome's structural flaws to become obvious. Players complained in particular about its 4,500 plastic skylights, which caused fielders to lose fly balls in the roof and prompted them to wear helmets at their positions for day games. When Hofheinz ordered the skylights painted over, thereby reducing the day lighting by as much as 40 percent, the field's natural grass quickly began to wither. It was in response to this latter condition that an artificial surface was introduced (to the Astrodome, to baseball, and to professional sports in general) in time for the 1966 home opener.

The Houston players who took the indoor field in the last half of the 1960s were seldom equal to their forward-looking surroundings. The main exceptions were Staub and fellow-slugging outfielder Jimmy Wynn, second baseman Joe Morgan, and catcher Jerry Grote. The principal pitching prospects were future 20-game winner Larry Dierker, lefty Mike Cuellar, and righthanders Dave Giusti and Don Wilson. Except for Dierker and Wilson, however, every one of them would be traded off by Richardson before fully realizing their potential, which, in Morgan's case, would mean the Hall of Fame. What was especially mystifying about many of Richardson's deals was that they were made with an eye to obtaining long-ball hitters (such as Lee May, Donn Clendenon, and Curt Blefary) who would have been better off in any park *except* the cavernous Astrodome.

Richardson also strove mightily to enforce an All-American Boy image on the team according to which the players were completely devoted to the harmony of the organization and were happy to go along with its strict curfews and other rules. Hofheinz did his best to intensify this "family" atmosphere by declining to pay players by check, insisting instead that they write out their own personal checks to withdraw the salaries that had been deposited in

a local bank in which the judge had a large holding. As he proudly pointed out to anyone who asked about the policy, the maneuver allowed the bank to hold on to the money a little longer and got the players used to thinking about his institution when it came to financial matters.

Hatton's run as manager ended 61 games into 1968, when he turned the team over to Harry Walker. The Hat, as he had been known since his playing days for a nervous habit of constantly readjusting his cap while in the batter's box, was regarded as without equal among hitting coaches and just the cure for one of the league's most anemic offenses. Walker's second and related reputation was for endless monologues on hitting that by and large left his listeners timing his spiels as much as picking up any useful pointers from them. Hardly a week went by without a Houston paper reporting some new clubhouse hilarity prompted by Walker's monologues—a development that Hofheinz found less than delightful. But what the judge (and much of the folklore about Walker) ignored was that The Hat was also a canny strategist who, when he wasn't jabbering about the secrets he had uncovered about hitting, enjoyed the respect of most of his players.

In 1969, Walker solidified his reputation by steering the Astros to their first .500 season. Although the team still sported one of the league's weakest offenses and clearly benefited from the inauguration of divisional play and the presence of the expansion of San Diego Padres in its division, it rode the arms of Dierker (20–13, 2.33 ERA), Wilson (16 wins), and Fred Gladding (28 saves) to its first meeting with respectability. The little-hit, strong-pitching personality of the club could not have been better exemplified than by the back-to-back games of April 30 and May 1: In the first contest, Cincinnati's Jim Maloney no-hit Houston; the next day, Wilson returned the favor by tossing a no-hitter against the Reds.

Over the next couple of seasons, the Astros slipped back to two games under .500, but both times improved on their fifth-place finish in 1969 to land in fourth. More significantly, and reflecting Walker's long hours in the batting cage with the players, the club boasted three .300 hitters in 1970 (Dennis Menke, Cesar Cedeno, and Jesus Alou) who were able to take some of the offensive burden off slugger Wynn. The team also turned over first base to Bob Watson, who became a mainstay in the middle of the lineup for many years.

Despite these positive developments, Hofheinz was growing impatient, not least because the Mets,

The first game to be played on Astroturf took place on April 18, 1966, with Los Angeles rookie Don Sutton picking up the first of his 324 career wins with a 6–3 decision over Houston. The losing pitcher was Hall of Famer Robin Roberts.

which had entered the league with the Astros, had already secured one world championship and had settled in as a regular Eastern Division contender. Persuaded by Richardson that the team was only one power hitter away from the playoffs, the judge gave his approval to a deal that sent the popular Texan Morgan, Menke, pitcher Jack Billingham, and outfielders Cesar Geronimo and Ed Armbrister to Cincinnati in exchange for home-run-hitting first baseman Lee May and infielders Tommy Helms and Jimmy Stewart. May responded in 1972 with a team-leading 29 homers and 98 RBIs, Helms played a steady second base, and the Astros climbed to second in the Western Division with an unprecedented 84 wins. On the other hand, Morgan and the others had a big hand in Cincinnati's finish ahead of Houston.

The second-place finish in 1972 took place under another cloud as well—the removal of Walker. With little more than 30 games left on the schedule, Hofheinz decided that the best way to keep the team from going into a sputter was to bring in a manager accustomed to lashing the horses down the stretch. His choice was Leo Durocher, who was most famous for piloting the Miracle Giants of 1951, but who had also recently become infamous for managing the Foldup Cubs of 1969. The Astros of The Lip barely played .500 for the final month and closed out 10½ lengths behind the Reds.

The following season was even worse. With Houston fans optimistic for the first time that the team could get into postseason action, injuries to Dierker and catcher Johnny Edwards, resentment and even open mockery of Durocher's old-school abrasive style, and the manager's own debilitating intestinal ailment, added up to a fourth-place flop. Durocher quit before the end of the season, begging off for health reasons but leaving the clear impression that he had been devastated by the players' contempt for his constant hectoring and predictable game tactics.

There were fewer expectations in 1974, and the team (now under Preston Gomez) lived up to them with another fourth-place finish and an even .500 winning percentage. Gomez left his strongest imprint when he yanked Wilson out of a game after the right-hander had hurled eight no-hit innings but was trailing 2–1. The move to a pinch hitter recalled an identical decision that the manager had made piloting the Padres a couple of years earlier and caused similar protests that he lacked a sense of drama. What Gomez mainly lacked about a year later was a job.

The 1975 season was a watershed year for the franchise. Even before spring training had begun, the team was felled by the news that Wilson had died of carbon monoxide poisoning in January. With an obtuseness that was to be repeated almost as tragically a few years later with another pitcher, the club insisted for a long time that Wilson's death was an accident; only after some years did it acknowledge that the hurler, an insecure man who had been known to pop pills to overcome his fear of taking the mound, had actually committed suicide. Whatever spanky clean image the club had hoped to maintain with its story about Wilson, everything came apart shortly afterward with the disclosure that Hofheinz could not meet $38 million in debts to franchise creditors. In a hurried move to stave off bankruptcy, the judge agreed to share his power with creditor representatives on a three-man committee. There he found himself instantly in the minority on a vote to oust Richardson and replace him with John Mullen as general manager. But after only a few weeks on the job, Mullen himself had a falling out with the committee and was succeeded by Tal Smith.

When Smith moved into the front office, he found a team playing out the string toward a cellar finish that would represent the lowest point in the first three decades of the team's history. His first order of business was to get rid of Gomez and bring in Bill Virdon as manager. Only too aware that the club's uncertain finances would discourage the pursuit of free agents and wary of repeating the Joe Morgan error with a trade of Watson or Cedeno, Smith became a full-time student of the waiver wire and the scouting reports on players who were spending most of their time on the bench, coming up with pitcher Joaquin Andujar and infielder Art Howe.

With the return of some stability, the Astros bounced back to a third-place finish in 1976, still a couple of games under .500 but 21 games closer to first. The keys to the season were the blossoming of fireballing righthander J. R. Richard into a 20-game winner, the steady relief work of Ken Forsch, the hitting and running of Cedeno, and the clutch RBIs of Watson. Another promising sign for the future

The Astrodome's indoor facilities could not prevent a game from being rained out on June 15, 1976. The contest had to be called off because ten inches of rain and strong winds prevented fans, umpires, and stadium workers from getting to the arena.

was the June announcement that Hofheinz had given up the battle and sold the franchise to his chief creditors—the General Electric Credit Corporation and the Ford Motor Credit Corporation. (In 1978, GE would sell out its interest to Ford.)

Virdon's biggest problem in the first couple of years was injuries—particularly to Cedeno, whose various pulls, breaks, and fractures bedeviled his career and ultimately prevented him from becoming one of the game's superstars. Without the outfielder in the middle of the lineup, the team's fortunes largely depended on Watson and, as ever, pitching. In the latter category, Richard developed from a prospect to a front-line starter to the league's most dominating mound force. While turning in consecutive seasons of 20, 18, 18, and 18 wins, he also became the first righthander in the NL to strike out 300 batters (1978) and came back the following season (1979) to do it again. Only once between 1976 and 1980 did his ERA reach 3.00.

The ticking bomb of free agency and salary arbitration exploded against the Astros in 1978 when several players went to newspapermen to complain that the team would never be competitive without going after top stars on the market, and Watson decided that the atmosphere had degenerated enough to demand a trade. But in 1979, exceeding all expectations, the team went down to the final days of September before winding up a game-and-a-half behind the Reds. The surge was largely the result of the pitching of Richard, Joe Niekro (21 wins), Andujar, and Joe Sambito; the timely hitting of Jose Cruz; and the acquisitions before the season of catcher Alan Ashby, shortstop Craig Reynolds, and outfielder Jeffrey Leonard. On the other hand, the club's 49 homers for the year were only one more than the 48 hit by Chicago's Dave Kingman to lead the league.

There was another change in 1979: still another shuffling of the franchise's ownership papers. This time, the Ford Motor Credit Corporation sold the team to John McMullen, a New Jersey-based shipbuilder and naval architect. Under the terms of the sale, McMullen and his family took over 34 percent of the club, with 10 percent going to New York attorney David Le Fevre and the remaining 56 percent being spread among nineteen investors in the Houston area.

The Astros finally fulfilled the hopes that their fans had for the team in the 1980 season. With Cruz and Cedeno leading the offense, Niekro contributing another 20-game season, and Nolan Ryan, Forsch, and Vern Ruhle combining for another 35 wins, the team eked out a special playoff win against the Dodgers (after blowing a three-game lead on the final weekend of the season at Dodger Stadium) to capture its first division title.

Not even the four sweaty games played against Los Angeles remained vivid in the mind, however, after the LCS against Philadelphia. Following a relatively mild opening game in which the Phillies defeated the Astros 3–1, the teams proceeded to play four consecutive extra-inning contests in which pinch hitters, relief pitchers, and bench players took center stage. But in the end, and despite an especially brilliant 12-for-19 offensive display by outfielder Terry Puhl, Philadelphia, not Houston, went off to meet Kansas City in the World Series.

It fell to the newly installed McMullen regime to distract attention from the team's success on the diamond, and it went about the task with a vengeance. Under the heading of positive events, the new ownership abandoned penurious policies where free agents were concerned, first by signing Ryan to a four-year contract valued at $4.5 million and then by spending more money to bring back the popular Morgan as a sparkplug for the club. On the other hand, the club showed even less class than the Hofheinz regime had about Wilson's suicide when it did nothing to rebut press claims that it considered Richard "too lazy" in his work habits. When the righthander, who had complained of sluggishness for some time, collapsed on the field during practice and was eventually diagnosed as having suffered a stroke, it was too late to salvage his career. The incident bred a nationwide debate that baseball people in general, not just the Astro management, would have been less passive about the pitcher's symptoms if they had not satisfied the stereotype about "lazy blacks."

Then, in still another echo of the franchise's earlier executive suite machinations, McMullen announced that Smith was out as general manager. The principal reason was an attendance clause that had been written into Smith's contract and the owner's conclusion that the franchise could no longer afford the architect of the team's 1980 success. In an uproar over the decision, a group of the organization's limited partners got together and offered to buy McMullen out. When that failed, the dissidents went to court and sued for a constitutional change that would make the club a corporation rather than a partnership. Under the terms of the new charter, McMullen found himself on the kind of three-man administrative committee Hofheinz had once had to accede to—in this instance with certified public accountant Jack Trotter and retired millionaire Herb Nyland. It was this committee that gave approval to the signing of former Yankees executive Al Rosen as the new general manager and to the signing of Don Sutton as another costly free agent.

The 1980 season was one of only two in which the Astros reached the two-million mark in home attendance (the other was the Astrodome's inaugural 1965 season). While the chief reason for the relatively tepid attendance over the years was the team's often uninspired play, there were other factors as well. First, there were the economic hard times that began to descend on Houston as a whole in the 1970s because of the world fuel crisis. In addition, until the franchise undertook a $60-million expansion and renovation project in November 1987, the Astrodome had ranked behind only the Big O in Montreal and Candlestick Park in San Francisco in minimal atmospheric and physical amenities. But for many baseball people, including new general manager Rosen, even these factors would not have weighed so heavily on the attendance if not for the basic dimensions of the dome.

From the day that it opened for baseball in 1965, the Houston Astrodome stood as a pitcher's paradise and a home run hitter's nightmare. Even though Richardson had not allowed the park's great alley distances to deter him from seeking power hitters, and despite individual successes like that of Wynn, there was never much doubt that a club having to play half its games in such surroundings would have to feature strong pitching, solid defense, and line drive hitters with speed who could make the most of the artificial turf. In the minds of baseball people like Rosen, however, idiosyncratic conditions of the kind bred schizophrenic teams that played one way while at home and another way while on the road, usually to their detriment. Moreover, their argument went, line drive hitters and pitchers (excepting a phenomenon like Ryan) were rarely magnets at the ticket booth, offered no long-view promise for prospective season-ticket holders, and were definitely weak selling points for radio-television advertisers. Thus, in what was to become the recurring theme of his five-year stay in the Astros' front office, Rosen told a reporter shortly after being named as Smith's successor: "I really believe we have to look into shortening the dimensions. I'm convinced a lot of players get mentally depressed hitting in the dome over a long period of time. On the other hand, you can develop bonafide heroes by making the park fairer to the hitters, and that wouldn't hurt at the gate."

Rosen did not get his shortened dimensions (a critical ten feet down the two foul lines) until promising sluggers Glenn Davis and Kevin Bass were about to assert their presence in 1985. In the meantime, like Smith, he oversaw a club that went just as far as its pitching took it. In the split season of 1981, that meant riding Ryan, the new free agent acquisition Sutton, and reliever Sambito into the special pre-LCS elimination playoffs on the basis of having the best second half in the Western Division. Against the Dodgers, the club won the first game on a 9th-inning homer by Ashby and the second on an 11th-inning pinch-hit single by Denny Walling, but then went down in three straight games to end its season.

If 1981 was the short season, 1982 lasted far too long. With Sambito out for most of the year and punch-hitter Phil Garner leading the power offensive with 13 homers, not even solid mound performances from Ryan, Niekro, and Sutton could lift the team above fifth place. Cedeno, who had never quite lived up to his oppressive billing as "a second Willie Mays" and whose value as a "family" player plummeted after a manslaughter charge in his native Santo Domingo, was traded to the Reds for Ray Knight. Virdon, who had been given a new contract before the arrival of Rosen, was replaced in midseason by the general manager's man, Bob Lillis, an original Astro. And Sutton, ascribing his relatively inconsistent mound performance to family pressures, offered to give back his $500,000 signing bonus if the club would deal him to some team in his native California. He was accommodated halfway—by being traded at the end of August, but to Milwaukee for outfielder Bass and southpaw Frank DiPino.

With Lillis at the helm for the next three years, the Astros posted records good for second- or third-place finishes. Offensively, Bass, Puhl, Cruz, Reynolds, Ashby, and Bill Doran seemed interchangeable in their left-handed approach to line-drive swinging. From the right side, shortstop Dickie Thon appeared on the verge of becoming baseball's stellar shortstop both offensively and defensively until he was beaned by Mike Torrez of the Mets in April of 1984.

Pitching continued to be the team's trademark. Between 1977 and 1984, Niekro won more games than any righthander in the NL and was second overall only to Steve Carlton of the Phillies. For his part, Ryan stepped up his assault on the record book—in 1983 surpassing Walter Johnson for the all-time strikeout mark, in 1985 becoming the first pitcher to record 4,000 strikeouts. Another important righthander on the 1985 staff was Mike Scott, who had labored through two seasons in a Houston uniform with little distinction after being obtained from the Mets. Prior to spring training in 1985, however, Rosen sent Scott to pitching guru Roger Craig to learn how to throw the split-finger fastball. Scott came back to post an 18–8 record.

Putting Scott together with Craig was one of Rosen's last inspirations for the Astros. Amid rumors that the general manager had an offer on the table from San Francisco's Bob Lurie to take over the Giants, the team announced in September of 1985 that Dick Wagner had been appointed as the new head of baseball operations. The other shoe fell a few weeks later when Lillis was sent packing and replaced by Hal Lanier.

With Lanier stressing fundamentals in a "run and gun" offense, Houston sprang out of the box in 1986 with 15 wins in their first 21 games. It was a pace that seldom slowed for the rest of the season, with the club's 96 victories and 10-game finish ahead of second-place Cincinnati franchise records. The key players were Scott, who won the Cy Young Award for his 18 victories, 306 strikeouts, and 2.22 ERA; first baseman Davis, who might or might not have needed the shortened dimensions of the Astrodome for his 31 homers and 101 RBIs; a then-record 33 saves by Dave Smith; and the running of Doran, Bass, and Billy Hatcher. More generally, Lanier snatched most Manager of the Year citations for his nimble use of platoon players like Garner and Walling and of setup relievers like Charlie Kerfeld, Aurelio Lopez, and Larry Andersen. The strength of the second-line players was evident in the club's 24 wins in its final at bat.

Even the Astros' thrilling 1980 LCS against the Phillies paled next to the playoff games against the Mets in 1986. The series finale—a sixth-game, sixteen-inning dogfight in which New York rallied from a three-run deficit in the ninth inning, Houston came back from elimination on a Hatcher home run in the fourteenth inning, and the Astros finally went down with the tying and winning runs on base in the 16th inning—has been called the greatest postseason game ever played. In the end, Houston's fate was decided by Scott and Smith: the former who had already pitched two complete wins and who would have been on the mound again if there had been a seventh game, the latter who blew two late-inning leads and whose record of effectiveness against the rest of the league was equal only to his history of ineffectiveness against the Mets.

The next two seasons under Lanier marked a return to mediocrity. In 1987, the club finished last in the league in hits and total bases and next to last in batting and runs scored. Aside from Davis's slugging, the offense was so weak that Ryan could convert a league-leading ERA of 2.76 and a league-leading 270 strikeouts into only 8 wins while losing 16 times. It was the same story in 1988.

Given the team's quick relapse after the 1986 division title, change was inevitable again. At the end of the 1987 season, declaring that he and Lanier could no longer work together, Wagner stepped down as general manager and was replaced by his assistant Bill Wood. Wagner's move followed weeks of snipings by Lanier that the front office had done nothing to help the team and amid indications that McMullen agreed with his manager. The following year, with Wood no more active in the trade market than Wagner had been and with the team tumbling into fifth place, Lanier had somebody else to blame when he was fired in favor of former infielder Howe. Howe took on the job on the understanding that he would be overseeing a rebuilding process.

In the event, the rebuilding had two phases. To begin with, the team began getting rid of its aging regulars (Cruz, Reynolds, Ashby, Puhl). For his part, Ryan went off as a free agent to the Rangers. But the gain in the actuarial tables was hardly discernible at first, partly because the team remained surprisingly competitive in 1989 and didn't hesitate to import other veterans like Buddy Bell, Rafael Ramirez, Jim Clancy, and Rick Rhoden.

The halfway measures stopped in 1990, for two principal reasons. The first was that a large number of players—Davis, Smith, Andersen, Danny Darwin, and Juan Agosto among them—were eligible for free agency or were entering the last year of their contracts. The second was that McMullen, in his 70s and disappointed that nobody else in his family had his interest in the team, had decided to sell the franchise and concentrate on potentially more profitable racing enterprises. To make the club more attractive to prospective buyers, he ordered Wood to get rid of as many free agents as possible in exchange for young players due only the major league minimum and to cold-shoulder the free agents who couldn't be traded. Acting on this directive, Wood pulled off deals with the Red Sox and Orioles in 1991, obtaining first baseman Jeff Bagwell, outfielder Steve Finley, and pitcher Pete Harnisch. In 1992, the Astros were especially conspicuous in their adoption of the minor league contract business tactic, i.e., offering bonafide major league free agents minor league pacts to come to spring training as non-roster players, then revaluing

On September 25, 1986, Mike Scott clinched Houston's division win with flair—by hurling a no-hitter against San Francisco.

their contracts if they made the team. Among those who made the club through such a door were out-fielder Pete Incaviglia and pitchers Doug Jones, Rob Murphy, and Joe Boever.

McMullen finally succeeded in selling the club in July 1992, getting a reported $115 million from Drayton McLane, owner of a grocery distribution company and the second largest stockholder in the Wal-Mart Corporation. McLane took over just as the club was rising from the bottom of the second division to respectability. Buoyed by Bagwell, Finley, Harnisch, reliever Jones, and home-grown products Craig Biggio, Luis Gonzales, and Eric Anthony, the Astros surprised the league in 1992 by returning to the .500 mark. The showing was all the more unexpected because of an arduous 26-game, 28-day road trip that the team had to make in August because the Astrodome had been rented out for the Republican national convention. The single best performance came from bullpen ace Jones, who saved 36 games, won 11 others, and recorded an ERA of 1.85. Carrying through on promises to spend as much as was necessary to restore the club to contending status, McLayne laid out big dollars in the off-season to revolutionize his starting rotation with the signing of free agents Doug Drabek and Greg Swindell.

HOUSTON ASTROS

Annual Standings and Managers

Year	Position	W	L	Pct.	GB	Managers
1962	Eighth	64	96	.400	36½	Harry Craft
1963	Ninth	66	96	.407	33	Harry Craft
1964	Ninth	66	96	.407	27	Harry Craft, Lum Harris
1965	Ninth	65	97	.401	32	Lum Harris
1966	Eighth	72	90	.444	23	Grady Hatton
1967	Ninth	69	93	.426	32½	Grady Hatton
1968	Tenth	72	90	.444	25	Grady Hatton, Harry Walker
1969	Fifth	81	81	.500	12	Harry Walker
1970	Fourth	79	83	.488	23	Harry Walker
1971	Fourth*	79	83	.488	11	Harry Walker
1972	Second	84	69	.549	10½	Harry Walker, Leo Durocher
1973	Fourth	82	80	.506	17	Leo Durocher, Preston Gomez
1974	Fourth	81	81	.500	21	Preston Gomez
1975	Sixth	64	97	.398	43½	Preston Gomez, Bill Virdon
1976	Third	80	82	.494	22	Bill Virdon
1977	Third	81	81	.500	17	Bill Virdon
1978	Fifth	74	88	.457	21	Bill Virdon
1979	Second	89	73	.549	1½	Bill Virdon
1980	First	93	70	.571	+1	Bill Virdon
1981	Third	28	29	.491	8	Bill Virdon
	First	33	20	.623	+1½	Bill Virdon
1982	Fifth	77	85	.475	12	Bill Virdon, Bob Lillis
1983	Third	85	77	.525	6	Bob Lillis
1984	Second*	80	82	.494	12	Bob Lillis
1985	Third*	83	79	.512	12	Bob Lillis
1986	First	96	66	.593	+10	Hal Lanier
1987	Third	76	86	.469	14	Hal Lanier
1988	Fifth	82	80	.506	12½	Hal Lanier
1989	Third	86	76	.531	6	Art Howe
1990	Fourth*	75	87	.463	16	Art Howe
1991	Sixth	65	97	.401	29	Art Howe
1992	Fourth	81	81	.500	17	Art Howe
* Tie						

Postseason Play

LCS	2–3 versus Philadelphia	1980
	2–4 versus New York	1986

Indianapolis Blues

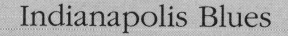

National League, 1878   **BALLPARKS:** SOUTH STREET PARK
EXPOSITION GROUNDS

RECORD: 24–36 (.400)

The inclusion of the Blues in the National League in 1878 was the consequence of an expedient promise by league president William Hulbert to admit the best independent team from each season—provided that club had played its games under NL rules. The Blues were the first and only beneficiary of an experiment that turned sour when Indianapolis proved incapable of supporting a major league franchise.

From its inception, the NL had a difficult relationship with the independent clubs, many of which considered themselves the equal of NL teams. At the conclusion of the NL's first season in 1876, Hulbert spelled out league policy toward the implicitly lesser teams: To ask them to enter, he said, "under equal obligation with ourselves would be to invite them to bear financial burdens that many of them would be unable and unwilling to assume, while to invite them to join us and at the same time deny them equal participation in any of the rights and privileges which we enjoy, would be a proposition unworthy of ourselves and disparaging or disrespectful to them." The sanctimonious tone of the declaration did little to quell the hostility of the independents toward the league. Only slightly more helpful was the formation of a confederation of thirteen previously independent clubs allied with the NL.

In 1877, the Blues won 73, lost 40, and tied 8 games—the best record among the independents. In the fallout from the Louisville Crooks scandal, the NL needed three new clubs merely to retain its 1877 quota of six teams. Hulbert, conveniently forgetting his proclamation of the year before, accepted the Blues into the league for the 1878 season.

From the beginning, dismally small crowds made it clear that Indianapolis could not hold its own. In late August, to bolster attendance, the club played several home games at Exposition Grounds on the site of Three Rivers Stadium in what was then Allegheny, Pennsylvania. Within a month, several players had signed 1879 contracts with other teams, an entirely permissible practice in pre-reserve rule days.

Team morale sank even lower in early June when owner W. T. Pettit suspended his ace pitcher, Ed (The Only) Nolan, on suspicion of throwing games. Nolan, a curious character who would play only for inferior teams, only for a high salary, and only if he were the sole pitcher, had once summarily left a club when he had been required to share the mound duty. While he was cleared of the charges against him in June, the hurler was suspended again on August 17th after Pettit discovered that he had fabricated a telegram from a fictitious brother named Bill requesting a visit. Nolan had spent his day off not with a sick brother, but with what the Indianapolis *Journal* called "a beautiful habitué of an avenue assignation house, who has ruined more men in this city than she can count on the jeweled fingers of both her hands." Suspended for a second time, Nolan took his lover on a trip to New York. The romance cost him dearly when the league honored Pettit's suspension and kept the pitcher out of the NL until 1881.

Between suspensions, Nolan won 13 and lost 22, even though he gave up only 2.57 earned runs per game. His primary support came from right fielder Orator Shaffer (.338) and manager-left fielder John Clapp (.304), but the team could do no better than fifth place in the six-team league.

Facing a deficit of about $2,500, Pettit withdrew his club from the league on December 4th and left Indianapolis owing money to the players.

INDIANAPOLIS BLUES

Annual Standings and Manager

Year	Position	W	L	Pct.	GB	Manager
1878	Fifth	24	36	.400	17	John Clapp

Indianapolis Blues

American Association, 1884   **BALLPARK:** BRUCE GROUNDS

RECORD: 29–78 (.271)

One of the most counterproductive American Association defenses in the Union Association war of 1884 was its decision to add four teams to keep as many players as possible out of the clutches of the Unions. The willing victims included a group of Indianapolis businessmen headed by Joseph Schwabacher, who became president of the AA Blues.

The new Indianapolis directors hired as their manager Jim Gifford, who recruited a sorry collection of rookies and rejects. The hero of the team was rookie pitcher Larry McKeon, who had an ERA of 3.50 but who won just 18 while leading the AA with

41 losses. By season's end, thirty-five players had put on a Blues uniform: nineteen of them had no prior major league experience and seventeen of them had no major league future. By late August, Gifford was gone, replaced by Bill Watkins. The Blues avoided last place only because a Washington club that suspended operations during the season had to be replaced by one from Richmond.

At its December meeting, the UA threat having been thwarted, the AA summarily dropped Indianapolis as part of its reversion to an eight-team league.

INDIANAPOLIS BLUES

Annual Standings and Managers

Year	Position	W	L	Pct.	GB	Managers
1884	Eleventh	29	78	.271	46	Jim Gifford, Bill Watkins

Indianapolis Hoosiers

National League,
1887–1889

BALLPARKS: ATHLETIC PARK (1887–1889)
INDIANAPOLIS PARK (1888–1889)

RECORD: 146–249 (.370)

It was not until March 8, 1887, only twenty-four days before opening day, that the National League awarded Indianapolis the franchise vacated by the St. Louis Maroons. The $12,000 purchase price covered virtually the entire St. Louis roster, including star shortstop Jack Glasscock and slugging third baseman Jerry Denny. Glasscock demanded $3,000 for the season, and Denny received $2,600 plus relocation costs.

From the beginning, the players rebelled against the stern discipline of manager Watch Burnham, whose only qualification for the job was that he had

brought the availability of the Maroons to the attention of Louis Newberger, John T. Brush, and the other Indianapolis businessmen who invested in the club. The animosity between Burnham and the players boiled over less than a month into the season when the players refused to practice in uniforms that had gotten wet because of a leaky roof. Burnham fined each player $5, then, fearing that the directors would not support him, wrote a letter of apology on behalf of the entire team, signed team captain Glasscock's name to it, and sent the letter to the board. Discovering Burnham's clumsy forgery almost immediately, the board replaced him with its secretary, Fred Thomas, while announcing publicly that the pilot had resigned because his father had been injured in an accident.

Two weeks later, the board reinstated Burnham as a reward for having gone to Nashville and recruited Larry Corcoran, once one of the best pitchers in the NL. (Corcoran lost the only two games he pitched for the Hoosiers.) The players greeted Burnham's return with renewed antagonism and, after the facts behind his resignation and the board's coverup of his duplicity became public in June, they became equally hostile to the board. To head off an open rebellion, the directors fired Burnham a second time and reinstalled Thomas for several weeks until Horace Fogel took over.

Unsurprisingly, the Hoosiers finished dead last, 43 games out of first place and 11 games out of seventh place. Equally predictable, there was a major shakeup in the administration: 30-year-old Harry Spence was named manager, and vice-president Brush, owner of the When Department Store, was elevated to the presidency.

While it lacked the high drama of the year before, the 1888 season had its moments. First baseman Dude Esterbrook became an instant fan favorite after he punched Chicago catcher Mark Sullivan, but he was gone before the end of the year. Glasscock came down with malaria and missed 22 games. Rumors abounded that Spence would be fired and Frank Bancroft would be brought in to manage. President Brush accompanied the team on an eastern swing to ascertain for himself the truth of stories about excessive drinking on train trips.

In their second season, the Hoosiers climbed into seventh place, but the marginal improvement could not save Spence's job. Bancroft did indeed take over in 1889, but the Hoosiers lost 31 of their first 50 games under him and 42 of 67 overall. In late July, Glasscock, sufficiently recovered to bat .352, became manager; the only Hoosier pilot to compile a winning record, he led the club to a 34–33 record the rest of the way for a second consecutive seventh-place finish.

As a team, the Hoosiers folded when the NL fortified itself in anticipation of its struggle with the Players League—a struggle hastened by Brush with one of the most mindless schemes ever devised to suppress player salaries. Brush's so-called Classification Plan called for the owners to grade each player not on performance but on deportment and to pay players according to their classifications: $2,500 for A players, $2,250 for B's, $2,000 for C's, $1,750 for D's, and $1,500 for E's. In effect, an abstemious utility infielder could make more money than a .350 hitter who enjoyed good whiskey and good times. The plan went into effect only because John Montgomery Ward, president of the Brotherhood of Professional Baseball Players, was away on Albert Spalding's around-the-world tour, and there was no one else to organize resistance. As might have been expected, the owners began violating the rule almost immediately with bonuses and incentives for star players, whatever their personal habits. The players petitioned several times to have the scheme rescinded, but the owners persisted in paying lip service to it throughout the 1889 season. Their adamance only strengthened the resolve of the players to establish their own league.

The PL became a reality in 1890, with New York as the primary battleground because it was the largest market and because Ward had led a slew of Giants' stars to the rebel circuit. To keep the NL New Yorkers on their feet, Brush sold them Glasscock, Denny, rookie pitcher Amos Rusie, and several other players; other Hoosiers were scattered around the NL and the American Association. In return, Brush

AMOS WILSON RUSIE
"THE HOOSIER THUNDERBOLT"
INDIANAPOLIS N.L., NEW YORK N.L.,
CINCINNATI N.L., 1889-1895
1897-1898 AND 1901
GENERALLY CONSIDERED FIREBALL KING OF
NINETEENTH-CENTURY MOUNDSMEN. NOTCHED
BETTER THAN 240 VICTORIES IN TEN-YEAR
CAREER. ACHIEVED 30-VICTORY MARK FOUR
YEARS IN ROW AND WON 20 OR MORE GAMES
EIGHT SUCCESSIVE TIMES. LED LEAGUE IN
STRIKEOUTS FIVE YEARS AND LED OR TIED
FOR MOST SHUTOUTS FIVE TIMES.

National Baseball Library, Cooperstown, NY

received a $60,000 cash settlement—a substantial profit over his $15,000 investment—and the opportunity to buy the Cincinnati Reds. After some initial excitement over newspaper speculation that the NL Pittsburgh franchise would move there, Indianapolis had to settle for a spot in the Indiana State League.

INDIANAPOLIS HOOSIERS

Annual Standings and Managers

Year	Position	W	L	Pct.	GB	Managers
1887	Eighth	37	89	.294	43	Watch Burnham, Fred Thomas Horace Fogel
1888	Seventh	50	85	.370	36	Harry Spence
1889	Seventh	59	75	.440	28	Frank Bancroft, Jack Glasscock

Indianapolis Hoosiers

Federal League, 1914   **BALLPARK:** GREENLAWN PARK

RECORD: 88–65 (.575)   **OTHER NAMES:** HOOSIERFEDS, HOOFEDS

The only major league franchise to win a pennant in its only year of existence, the Hoosiers were a success by accident. The centrally organized Federal League signed players to league contracts and then distributed them to individual teams. Indianapolis, one of the smaller cities in the FL, was not the league's choice to have a powerhouse team, but a pennant fell into the laps of club president J. Ed Krausse and manager Bill Phillips.

The Hoosier's allotment of players included veterans Frank LaPorte (second base, .311); Vin Campbell (center field, .318); George Mullin (14–10, 2.70 ERA); and Cy Falkenberg (25–16, 2.22 ERA, and a league-leading 236 strikeouts). Joining them were youngsters Bill McKechnie (shortstop, .304); Al Scheer (left field, .306); reserve outfielder Edd Roush (.325); and George Kaiserling (17–10, 3.11 ERA). The franchise player, however, was right fielder Benny Kauff, who led the Federals in batting (.370), hits (211), doubles (44), runs (120), and stolen bases (75).

An opening day 3–0 loss to St. Louis, with 15,000 fans in attendance, proved to be a misleading beginning for Indiananapolis's season. The Hoosiers battled Chicago and Baltimore to the last week of the season, finishing 1½ games ahead of the former and 4½ ahead of the latter. They also battled—and beat—the local minor league team.

None of it was sufficient; no one took the Hoosiers' pennant seriously. Their challenge to the American and National league champions went ignored. At first, when the FL decided to move into the New York metropolitan area for the 1915 season, it toyed with the idea of moving the Kansas City club, owned by oil millionaire Harry Sinclair; legal considerations forced the FL powers to reconsider and uproot the Hoosiers instead. Sinclair abandoned his Kansas City interests, took over the Indianapolis franchise, and moved it to Newark, New Jersey.

INDIANAPOLIS HOOSIERS

Annual Standings and Manager

Year	Position	W	L	Pct.	GB	Manager
1914	First	88	65	.575	+1½	Bill Phillips

Kansas City Unions

Union Association, 1884	**BALLPARK:** ATHLETIC PARK
RECORD: 16–63 (.203)	

When Altoona gave up its franchise in the Union Association in early June, UA president Henry V. Lucas was forced for the first of several times to seek a midseason replacement. He turned to Kansas City, a booming community, where he found an angel in Americus V. McKim, a 44-year-old malt and grain merchant.

McKim, who had sought a franchise in the UA before the season began, was still sufficiently anxious to bring major league baseball to Kansas City that he accepted the most restrictive condition ever imposed on a club: Even though the Unions' games would count in their opponents' championship records, Kansas City could not win the pennant. In effect, the Unions would be in the UA, but would have no official record.

Ignoring his second-class status, McKim rented Athletic Park for $500 and doubled its capacity to 4,000, hired former UA umpire Alexander Crawford to be organization secretary, and began to assemble a team. So hastily was the club put together that many of the players met for the first time when they assembled for their first game; several of them were put at positions they had never played before. The turnover was extraordinary: No fewer than fifty players appeared for the Unions in their brief existence. Two of them—second baseman Charlie Berry and right fielder Frank Shaffer—came from Altoona; most of the others were from reserve teams, minor league clubs, or other UA squads. As a team, this collection hit a mere .199.

Twenty-six-year-old outfielder Harry Wheeler jumped from the AA St. Louis Browns to become the manager. He lasted only four games (all losses) as the manager and only fourteen as the right fielder. A local pharmacist named Matt Porter, who succeeded Wheeler, compiled a 3–13 record and even put himself in the lineup in center field for three games. Next came Ted Sullivan, who had been Lucas's deputy with the St. Louis Maroons until June 13th, when he quit because of the owner's repeated interference in the running of the club. An inveterate promoter and self-promoter who almost twenty years later published a popular book, *Humorous Stories of the Ball Field*, Sullivan also played three games in the outfield for the Unions.

Despite their sorry performance, the Unions were good box office. At the end of the season, McKim announced at a team banquet that the club had made a $7,000 profit. This may have been an exaggeration, but, compared to most other UA clubs, Kansas City must have done fairly well because McKim was one of the league's few backers who pronounced himself eager for a second season. Sullivan made a trip east to sign new players, and McKim, who also had plans to build a new ballpark, attended the UA's annual meeting on December 18th and voted to reelect Lucas president. He even attended the final meeting, held on January 15, 1885, after Lucas had defected to the National League, but by this time only the Milwaukee backers shared his enthusiasm for continuing the obviously failed venture. Only the two clubs showed up, so they voted to dissolve the UA.

KANSAS CITY UNIONS

Annual Standings and Managers

Year	Position	W	L	Pct.	GB	Managers
1884	Partial Season	16	63	.203	—	Harry Wheeler, Matt Porter, Ted Sullivan

Kansas City Cowboys

National League, 1886   **BALLPARK:** LEAGUE PARK

RECORD: 30–91 (.248)

The admission of the Cowboys to the National League was an eleventh-hour solution to the failure of backers in Indianapolis to fund a franchise. Americus V. McKim, who had financed the Union Association Kansas City club in 1884; Joseph J. Heilm, who ran a Kansas City brewery owned by his St. Louis family; and English-born James Whitfield, who was sports editor of the Kansas City *Times*, raised $25,000 and secured the eighth NL berth on February 10, 1886.

Dave Rowe, hired as the center fielder-manager, oversaw a draft of has-beens and were-to-bes to fill out his roster. The club's troubles began almost immediately when a cyclone ripped through the city in May; it was the high point of the season. The most noted players were a pair of righthanded hurlers, Grasshopper Jim Whitney and Stump Weidman, both of whom had seen better days. Each won 12 games, while Weidman's 36 losses led the NL, with Whitney's 32 right behind him. Weidman created a sensation when, during the Cowboys' first trip to Detroit, he was presented with a diamond ring by the local owners and fans for past services. The Detroit *Free Press* objected on the grounds that the gifts had come from professional gamblers, with whom Weidman had been altogether too friendly during his tenure with the Wolverines.

In an era marked by rabid umpire baiting, the Cowboys—especially McKim—were conspicuous enough to provoke criticism from the usually affable NL president Nick Young. At one time or another, every league umpire resigned after a run-in with the unruly Kansas City players and fans. Young spent the summer promising the members of his umpiring staff that, if they would return to the fold, they would not have to work any more Kansas City home games.

The vast distance other teams had to travel to reach Kansas City to play against dismal competition before sparse, unruly crowds was the undoing of the franchise. Heim and McKim had sought to remedy one of their problems by lowering their admission price, but the NL treated their request to deviate from the mandatory 50-cent charge as heresy. With the Cowboys mired in seventh place at the end of the season and the St. Louis Maroons financially strapped, there were persistent rumors that both clubs would be dropped. McKim, reading the situation accurately, sold his share of the Cowboys in October to Charles D. Axman and E. E. Menges, two local businessmen.

Kansas City's status as a major league city then took two severe blows in succession. First, the Pittsburgh Alleghenys resigned from the American Association and were accepted into the NL, which temporarily became a nine-team league. After the AA refused the Cowboys' application to replace Pittsburgh, the Kansas City owners first tried to purchase the Cleveland club that had been given the Alleghenys' spot in the AA, then arranged to purchase the Maroons for $15,000. It was a marriage that would never be consummated.

Rowe publicly maintained to the end that Kansas City would go to court to prevent being expelled. But, at its March 9, 1887 annual meeting, the NL refused to authorize the Cowboys' purchase of the Maroons, bought out the St. Louis club itself for $12,000, admitted Indianapolis to consolidate all eight of its teams east of the Mississippi River, and dumped Kansas City. Heim and his associates were forced to accept the NL's offer of $6,000 for their holdings and players.

KANSAS CITY COWBOYS

Annual Standings and Manager

Year	Position	W	L	Pct.	GB	Manager
1886	Seventh	30	91	.248	58½	Dave Rowe

Kansas City Blues

American Association,
1888–1889

BALLPARKS: ASSOCIATION PARK (1888)
EXPOSITION PARK (1889)

RECORD: 98–171 (.364)

Kansas City got its third opportunity to field a major league team within five years when the Brooklyn Trolley Dodgers purchased the entire New York Mets franchise and created an opening for the American Association's 1888 season. Joseph J. Heim, who had been the primary owner of the National League Cowboys, was back as president of the AA club; so was Dave Rowe as manager.

With a record not much better than the Cowboys' and an eighth-place finish, the Blues were hardly a great success. Third baseman Jumbo Davis led the hitters with a .267 average, and Henry Porter's 37 losses led the AA against only 18 victories. Rowe, who lasted only 50 games, was succeeded by second baseman Sam Barkley, who survived 57 games, and then by Bill Watkins.

In 1889, John W. Speas succeeded Heim as president, and had a somewhat improved team with which to work. Rookie outfielders Jim Burns (.301) and future Hall of Famer Billy Hamilton (.304) added

some punch, and the club crawled up one notch to seventh place.

At the end of the season, the Blues became enmeshed in the struggle to elect a new president of the association. The faction led by Chris Von der Ahe of St. Louis favored Zach Phelps of Louisville; Kansas City's choice was one of its own directors, L. C. Krauthoff, who also had the backing of Cincinnati, Brooklyn, and Baltimore. The highly respected Krauthoff had been the first choice of a majority of clubs, but he had sacrificed his front-runner status by refusing to agree to special considerations for Von der Ahe's Browns. With the vote hopelessly deadlocked, Cincinnati and Brooklyn, wary of Von der Ahe's influence with Phelps, bolted to the NL. The Kansas City directors, stripped of their allies and mindful of the dangers of the impending Players League war, resigned from the AA and joined the minor league Western Association.

KANSAS CITY BLUES

Annual Standings and Managers

Year	Position	W	L	Pct.	GB	Managers
1888	Eighth	43	89	.326	47½	Dave Rowe, Sam Barkley, Bill Watkins
1889	Seventh	55	82	.401	38	Bill Watkins

Kansas City Packers

Federal League, 1914–1915

BALLPARK: GORDON AND KOPPEL FIELD

RECORD: 148–156 (.487)

The one Federal League franchise up against only minor league competition, the Packers still fared

worse than other teams in the circuit sharing markets with the National and American leagues. The main reason was simply that the market was too small to support a big league baseball team, let alone a club bogged down in mediocrity.

The Packers got off on the wrong foot when the minor league American Association Kansas City franchise obtained an injunction to prevent tampering with its players. Even though the injunction expired after a few weeks, it was enough of a warning signal for club president C. C. Madison to go out of the city to staff his FL roster. Madison's boldest move was to sign George Stovall away from the St. Louis Browns even after the AL team had rejected the first baseman's request for a release from his reserve clause option year. In becoming the first player to jump to the Feds, Stovall defied existing NL-AL threats that anyone ignoring reserve clause rights would be suspended from Organized Baseball for three years. He justified his defection to the Packers in the language of the day by declaring that "no white man ought to be bartered like a broken-down horse." As Kansas City's playing manager, Stovall hit .284 for the sixth-place 1914 team, then slumped off to .231 the following year, when the club moved up to fourth.

The Packers started their inaugural year at home to a crowd of 9,000—the smallest opening day attendance in the league, but double what the AA Blues drew. Several days later, the team did visiting honors for the home opener of the Chicago Whales. No sooner had the game against Chicago begun than Kansas City pitcher Chief Johnson was served with an injunction requested by the Cincinnati Reds, from whom he had jumped, and had to leave the ballpark. Unlike Stovall, Johnson had not merely ignored the reserve clause claims of his former organization, but had broken a contract to join the Packers—an offense that the established leagues had warned that they would penalize with a five-year suspension. A Chicago judge ruled in favor of the Cincinnati petition, but that verdict was overturned on appeal and Johnson returned to Kansas City.

The 1914 stars of the team were second baseman Duke Kenworthy, who hit .317 and tied for the league lead in homers with 15; catcher Ted Easterly, who led the club with a .335 average; and pitcher Gene Packard, who won 21 and lost 13. Their efforts notwithstanding, the team lost so much money that,

in February 1915, the FL planned to turn it over to Patrick Powers, former president of the International League, and oilman Harry Sinclair, who had every intention of uprooting the club and bringing it to Newark. Determined resistance, including a lawsuit by the organization's board of directors, halted the move. For their second season, the Packers' directors reorganized the front office, installing Charles Baird (and later Conrad Mann) as president. The team rose to fourth place, winding up only 5½ games out of first. The improvement in the standings was largely due to pitching—Packard going 20–11 and Nick Cullop coming in at 22–11.

The improvement on the field did nothing to help the franchise financially, and FL president James Gilmore went to Kansas City in a last-ditch attempt to recruit fresh money. Eventually, Sinclair had to step in to keep the club afloat. On November 10th, the FL declared the franchise forfeit and assumed responsibility for it. Sinclair and Gilmore talked about plans to relocate the team in New York, but it was little more than a ruse to get a better deal for an eventual buyout. The scam was an elaborate one. Announcing that he would abandon his holdings in Newark and transfer the best of the Peppers and the Packers to a new $800,000 stadium in upper Manhattan, Sinclair even went so far as to lease offices in New York, to apply to the city for permission to close off streets at the proposed construction site, and to produce designs by architect C. B. Comstock for a two-tier, 55,000-seat grandstand with no obstructing posts. The playing field would have been huge—388 feet down each line and 450 feet to dead center.

With groundbreaking scheduled for January 15, 1916, Sinclair, then one of the wealthiest men in the United States, issued a figurative challenge to the owners of the New York clubs in the NL and AL: "I'll stand at the Battery, and I'll match any of them in pitching dollars into New York Harbor. We'll see who quits first." Several years later, Gilmore admitted that the whole thing had been "one big bluff," since he, Sinclair, and a couple of other owners had known by the beginning of July that the FL lacked the resources to begin another season. But the bluff helped Sinclair pad his pockets with his share of the buyout and the proceeds from player sales.

KANSAS CITY PACKERS

Annual Standings and Managers

Year	Position	W	L	Pct.	GB	Managers
1914	Sixth	67	84	.444	20	George Stovall
1915	Fourth	81	72	.529	5½	George Stovall

Kansas City Athletics

American League, 1955–1967	**BALLPARK:** MUNICIPAL STADIUM
	OTHER NAMES: A'S
RECORD: 829–1224 (.404)	

The worst team in baseball history for the length of its survival and failure to reach .500 even once, the Athletics owed most of their importance to executive suite innovations and manipulations that influenced the major leagues out of all proportion to what they accomplished on the field. Kansas City also served as the stepping stone for Charlie Finley to enter big league councils.

The Athletics became a glimmer in the eye of the American League in 1954, when Kansas City voters approved a $2-million bond issue to purchase and enlarge Blues Stadium, then the home of the New York Yankees' farm club in the American Association; the vote followed local dismay that Milwaukee, a Kansas City rival in the minor loop for years, had been awarded the NL Braves in 1953. The municipal takeover met no resistance from stadium landlord Arnold Johnson, an executive of the Chicago-based Automatic Canteen Company of America who had purchased both the Missouri facility and Yankee Stadium a couple of years earlier; on the contrary, Johnson declared his readiness to promote efforts for

What owner Charlie Finley couldn't provide on the field, he sought to offer with such publicity gimmicks as a mule mascot. *UPI/Bettmann Newsphotos*

a big league club, provided others bought it and ran it. The most obvious target for a buyout was the Philadelphia Athletics, then sagging under the debts accumulated by Connie Mack and his two sons, Roy and Earle. Facing the prospect of seeing the debt-ridden Athletics go into receivership on the eve of the 1955 season, the league increased pressures on Johnson to step in and coordinate the disorganized interest of several Missouri business groups. With the financial help of Nathaniel Leverone, chairman of the board of Automatic Canteen, Johnson changed his mind about getting involved in a franchise and, on November 8, 1954, announced a $3.375-million deal with the Macks.

The only clubs opposed to the sale were Cleveland, whose president, Hank Greenberg, insisted that the AL had to give priority to getting to Los Angeles before the NL did, and Washington, whose owner Clark Griffith didn't like the idea of Baltimore being pushed into the Eastern Division of the league to make room for Kansas City in the west, with the result that the Senators and Orioles were usually playing at home at the same time. Another source of misgivings for both Greenberg and Griffith was Johnson's close association with Yankees' co-owners Dan Topping and Del Webb, established when the Chicago businessman had bought Yankee Stadium and Blues Stadium and immediately confirmed when New York announced that it was waiving the indemnity payments due it for pushing its farm affiliate out of Kansas City to make room for the Athletics.

Collusion between the franchises outlasted even Johnson's ownership, with the A's little more than a New York farm club on a major league level; between 1955 and 1960 alone, the teams completed sixteen trades involving some sixty players. In almost every instance, the deals brought the Yankees prize prospects like Roger Maris, Ryne Duren, and Clete Boyer, while leaving the Athletics with over-the-hill stars like Ewell Blackwell, Johnny Sain, and Don Larsen. Two of the more blatant cases centered around third baseman Boyer and righthander Ralph Terry. Wanting the infielder but not wanting to have him clog their roster for two years as an under-used bonus baby, the Yankees financed Kansas City's purchase of Boyer, watched him develop major league experience, and then went through with a prearranged deal that made him their regular third baseman. Similarly, Terry was too raw for Yankee tastes when he came up to the AL in 1956, so he was shipped off to the Athletics for major league experience before being reacquired.

Footnote Player: All four of Tommy LaSorda's major league decisions came with Kansas City in 1956. The southpaw lost all four games, and had an ERA of 6.15.

But the collusion charges were a distant thought amid the celebrations that marked the Athletics' first major league game on April 12, 1955 in rebaptized Municipal Stadium. After former president Harry Truman threw out the first ball, 32,147 watched manager Lou Boudreau's home team defeat Detroit, 5–2; the crowd was the largest in the history of Kansas City for a public event, sporting or otherwise. Fans continued to turn out for the rest of the season, with attendance totaling 1,393,054. What they got for showing up was a sixth-place club whose main assets were the fancy fielding and solid hitting of first baseman Vic Power (.319, 19 homers) and the slugging of left fielder Gus Zernial (30 homers, 84 RBIs). For owner Johnson, the big turnout for his decidedly second-division club was sugar in his coffee, because the terms of his lease on Municipal Stadium obligated the city to cover any losses accruing from fall-offs in attendance below a million; the sweetheart deal also gave him the right to break the lease after three years if similar attendance minimums were not met. But over and beyond his financial leverage with the city, Johnson had a far more lasting effect on baseball coffers in general when he had his attorneys contact the Internal Revenue Service for a definitive ruling on the status of players as organization property; thanks to the IRS response to Kansas City, major league franchises honed their accounting skills to project depreciation tables and similar beneficial barometers around a player's abilities.

Boudreau lasted until the middle of the team's third year, by which time the Yankee Shuttle had begun to drive away with players like Boyer, Duren, and pitchers Art Ditmar and Bobby Shantz. The second-rate arrivals from the Bronx not being the answer to the team's poor performance, Johnson and general manager Parke Carroll replaced Boudreau with Harry Craft.

Under Craft, the club improved slightly in 1958, in good part because of Bob Cerv's career year (.305, 38 homers, and 104 RBIs) and a mid-season deal with the Indians that brought over Maris in exchange for Power and shortstop Woodie Held. When some AL owners protested that the trade was just a setup for another swap that would send Maris on to the Yankees, the league office warned Kansas City and New York to keep the lefty-hitting outfielder out of their postseason discussions. The warning worked insofar as it wasn't until after the 1959 campaign that Maris finally landed in the Bronx. Despite a starting rotation that began and ended with southpaw Bud Daley, Craft kept the team in the first division over the first part of 1959, but then collapsed from exhaustion at the end of July, triggering a ruinous two months that once again left the Athletics barely out of the basement. In November, Bob Elliott was named to replace the frazzled Craft.

Elliott's managerial task in 1960 was something of an afterthought following a spring training heart attack that proved fatal to Johnson. While the club floundered around in last place, a parade of prospective buyers descended on the owner's remarried wife, Mrs. Warren Humes, to pry away the 52 percent share of the franchise that Johnson had left to her and their son. At first, Humes rejected the suitors, declaring that she wanted to keep the team for her son, but then she was forced to change her mind by the need to use sale money to pay off the taxes on Johnson's $5-million estate. In November 1960, a court approved the sale of 32 percent of the stock to St. Louis investment banker Elliott Stein for $1.8 million, but then Stein had second thoughts about the franchise's drain on his resources and pulled out. A couple of weeks later, a group of Kansas City businessmen bought up the 48 percent not held by Humes, but announced their inability to meet her demands. At this juncture, Indiana insurance executive Finley appeared on the scene, purchasing the Humes stock for $1.975 million and then, a few weeks later, also buying out the Kansas City group to assume total control.

Blowhard, innovator, petty tyrant, and miser, Finley wasted little time in putting his imprint on the club by ousting Carroll and Elliott and replacing them with Frank Lane and Joe Gordon, respectively. In his first of endless media events, he staged the burning of an old bus, declaring that the era of the Yankee Shuttle was over; in his first of equally end-less contradictions, he then promptly turned around and traded Daley, the Athletic's best pitcher, to New York. With deals of the kind keeping the club in the nether regions of the standings, Finley sought to attract fans through one dog-and-pony show after another. He dressed up players in flamboyant kelly green and gold uniforms, introduced livestock to Municipal Stadium in promotions aimed at farmers, had his team enter the ballpark on a mule train (and adopted one of the animals as a mascot), set aside an area behind the outfield fences for grazing sheep, had a mechanical rabbit pop up to resupply home plate umpires with baseballs, had players autograph the balls used in play so that fans could catch what he described as "personalized" foul balls and home runs, and engaged in a war of attrition with the league office over his right to shorten the right field line with a Yankee Stadium-like grandstand porch. Even when the team was on the road, Finley found ways to keep the team the most talked about subject in Kansas City. Responding to an off-the-cuff challenge, he hired Betty Caywood to do color on the club's radio broadcasts; the first woman to be part of a team's regular broadcasts, Caywood concentrated most of her remarks on events in the grandstand or in the dugouts. When the indignant owners of the White Sox refused to let Finley lead his mascot Charlie O around the field at Comiskey Park before a twi-night doubleheader with the A's, the Kansas City owner rented a parking lot across the street and, with a ten-piece band and six beautiful models to help draw a crowd, denounced the White Sox for being "unfair to Charlie O the man, Charlie O the mule, baseball, and muledom."

But when Finley wasn't making Kansas City laugh, he was making it cringe. In one of his first acts as owner, he ordered the business staff to cut out personal deliveries of season tickets, then banned ticket orders by telephone. Ignoring protests that conveniences of the kind had given Kansas City one of the largest season ticket sales volumes in the league, he alienated so many customers that by the summer of 1961 the atmosphere was ripe for a campaign to buy tickets to "save the A's." In what initially appeared to be a goodwill gesture toward the city, he called a news conference in the office of Mayor H. Roe Bartle, where he proceeded to burn the lease that had given Johnson such advantageous terms for using Municipal Stadium and that had become a sore point for numerous local politicians; it was only a few weeks later that he admitted he had burned a blank piece of paper and was still holding the city to the original terms of the lease. Both the

In one of his first moves after buying the team, Charlie Finley announced that he was changing its name from the Athletics to simply the A's. According to Finley, the name Athletics was too closely associated with the losing clubs of former Philadelphia owner Connie Mack.

ticket and lease episodes assumed new significance when Finley acknowledged that he had sounded out the league about the possibility of shifting the franchise to Dallas. Although the other owners were sufficiently discouraging to prevent the request coming up for a formal vote, it turned out to be only the first of several threats, demands, and petitions to go elsewhere. In 1963, Finley set his sights on Atlanta, then on Oakland. Although he denied it at the time, league president Joe Cronin encouraged a transfer to the Bay Area so that the circuit could have two California clubs, making traveling to the west coast far more feasible for everybody. But the notion was rebuffed by San Francisco President Horace Stoneham, whose territorial rights were involved.

Whether or not he had Cronin's backing for a shift to Oakland, Finley certainly didn't have it for another threatened transfer to Louisville in 1964. In what was variously interpreted as a try at presenting the league with a fait accompli and as a bluff aimed at getting the A's to Oakland ultimately, the Kansas City owner signed a conditional two-year lease on Fairgrounds Stadium and formally petitioned the league for a move to Kentucky. Aggravated by the annual campaigns to go elsewhere and anywhere, the other owners rejected the request by a 9–1 margin, and then ordered Finley to conclude a new pact for Municipal Stadium or face expulsion. Never at a loss for putting a few extra spins on situations, Finley first signed a new four-year lease on the stadium with the city, then sued to reclaim rights to the original seven-year pact with Johnson (which had the critical escape clause that the newer agreement did not have), and then announced that he was putting up the A's for sale for $8 million. Suitors from San Diego and Denver made unsuccessful bids for the franchise, though not without scads of publicity in Kansas City. Then, suddenly, Finley withdrew his lawsuit and took the team off the market; it emerged later that he did so after receiving private assurances that he would be allowed to move to Oakland within three years.

Finley's relations with his general managers and field managers were of a piece with his dealings with the city and the league. Lane didn't survive one year of his two-year agreement; after being fired, the veteran general manager filed a breach of contract suit. Lane was replaced by Pat Friday, an executive at Finley's insurance company in Chicago; Ed Lopat and Hank Peters also had stints as general managers. Finley's first pilot, Gordon, lasted about a half season before his talents were found to be wanting. Gordon's successor was Hank Bauer, then winding down his career as an outfielder; Bauer walked out at the end of the 1962 season, after being told that his contract was not about to be renewed. Next up was Lopat, who held down a number of jobs in the organization despite a reputation for not being the most insightful of talent evaluators (among other things, he loudly proclaimed that Minnesota farmhand Tony Oliva would never hit in the major leagues). Mel McGaha and Haywood Sullivan also had tenures for parts of seasons.

Although Kansas City would not benefit from it, Finley started giving the Athletics their future look in the mid-1960s, when he insisted that Bert Campaneris and Dick Green be installed as the regular shortstop and second baseman, respectively. Equally important was the arrival of Jim Hunter, who with the Finley-invented name of Catfish ("People like players with nicknames") would convert his 224 victories into Hall of Fame membership in 1987. By 1967, the team's last year in Kansas City, such other future stars as Reggie Jackson, Sal Bando, Joe Rudi, and Blue Moon Odom had appeared on the twenty-five-man roster.

If Finley's A's had been a center of turmoil previously, they became synonymous with chaos in 1967. Through the first few months of the season, the club waddled along in its customary cellar position amid cost-cutting measures that pointed to an imminent move of the franchise and began to get on the players' nerves. The explosion came in mid-August, when Finley fined pitcher Lew Krausse $500 for what he called "rowdyism" on a flight from Kansas City to Boston. Deciding that the fine was merely a tactic for saving some money on Krausse, the players drafted a petition protesting Finley's high-handedness, as well as his cutbacks in everything from food to clubhouse supplies. Alerted to the revolt, Finley summoned manager Alvin Dark and told him that his inability to handle the club meant that he wouldn't be coming back in 1968; when Dark protested that the players were only responding to Finley's actions, the owner had a change of heart and announced his readiness to give the pilot a new two-year contract. Dark was still taking in this shift of gears when an assistant brought the player's petition to Finley, whereupon the owner fired the manager outright. Dark promptly went out to newsmen and termed the players' petition "one of the most courageous things I've ever seen in baseball."

Ken Harrelson of the 1964 Athletics was the first major leaguer to wear batting gloves.

Outfielder Rick Monday was the very first selection in major league baseball's inaugural draft of college and high school players in 1965. Monday was called up from the minors by Kansas City in 1966.

A day after Dark was fired and replaced by Luke Appling, A's first baseman Ken Harrelson, one of the drafters of the petition, called Finley "a menace to baseball." The owner's response was to order the player's immediate release, even disdaining waivers because, he said, he didn't want "blood money." Harrelson was about to issue a public apology for his remark when he realized that he was a free agent and entitled to sign with any club that approached him; he ended up going to the Red Sox.

Following the Krausse and Dark events, the Players Association also swung into action against Finley, requesting a hearing with Commissioner William Eckert. When Finley sought to obstruct that meeting, the National Labor Relations Board (NLRB) was called in to hear harassment charges against the owner. In the end, both the association and Finley backed off in an agreement centered around his commitment not to obstruct any baseball investigation of franchise matters if so warranted. For a while, Krausse maintained a separate appeal to Eckert about the fine, but then he too withdrew after an enigmatic shooting incident in Kansas City in which two bullets were fired at an office building from a hotel across the street; although several players living in the hotel were said to have been questioned by the police, the only one specifically named as having been "cleared" was Krausse.

Following the season, the AL dropped the other shoe with the announcement that it approved the transfer of the franchise from Kansas City to Oakland. A simultaneous announcement after a league meeting that efforts would be made to give Kansas City an expansion team by 1971 satisfied neither Mayor Ilus Davis, who threatened court injunctions to keep the Athletics, nor Missouri Senator Stuart Symington, who declared that he was ready to open another investigation of the antitrust exemption enjoyed by major league baseball. AL President Cronin, who had expected the 1971 deadline to be enough for the politicians, scrambled to reconvene the league meeting before the legal threats became fact, declaring that the session had been only recessed, not adjourned; when he discovered that many of the AL owners had already gone off, he collected the five franchises still represented, declared them a quorum, and railroaded through a new motion promising Kansas City a new team by 1969. Davis and Symington accepted the compromise, though the senator spent a few days describing Finley as "one of the most disreputable characters ever to enter the American sports scene" and comparing his impact on Kansas City to that of the atomic bomb on Nagasaki. The final result of the decision to accelerate AL expansion was a protest from NL President Warren Giles that Cronin had betrayed an accord between the leagues to proceed more slowly; the NL's anger would eventually lead to the inclusion of Montreal and San Diego in the senior circuit in tandem with the creation of the Kansas City Royals and Seattle Pilots in the AL.

KANSAS CITY ATHLETICS

Annual Standings and Managers

Year	Position	W	L	Pct.	GB	Managers
1955	Sixth	63	91	.409	33	Lou Boudreau
1956	Eighth	52	102	.338	45	Lou Boudreau
1957	Seventh	59	94	.386	38½	Lou Boudreau, Harry Craft
1958	Seventh	73	81	.474	19	Harry Craft
1959	Seventh	66	88	.429	28	Harry Craft
1960	Eighth	58	96	.377	39	Bob Elliott
1961	Ninth*	61	100	.379	47½	Joe Gordon, Hank Bauer
1962	Ninth	72	90	.444	24	Hank Bauer
1963	Eighth	73	89	.451	31½	Ed Lopat
1964	Tenth	57	105	.352	42	Ed Lopat, Mel McGaha
1965	Tenth	59	103	.364	43	Mel McGaha, Haywood Sullivan
1966	Seventh	74	86	.463	23	Alvin Dark
1967	Tenth	62	99	.385	29½	Alvin Dark, Luke Appling

* Tie

Kansas City Royals

American League, 1969–Present	**BALLPARKS:** MUNICIPAL STADIUM (1969–1972) ROYALS STADIUM (1973–Present)
RECORD: 1977–1843 (.518)	

The Royals have almost given expansion teams a good name. Since entering the American League, their six division titles, eligibility for the special 1981 postseason divisional series, and eight second-place finishes have put them in a class with Oakland and Baltimore as the most successful franchises of the era. The club's usual status as a contender has been all the more striking for a city that had previously hosted only losing major league teams.

The franchise owes its existence to the turmoil created by the AL's decision in 1967 to allow the Athletics of Charlie Finley to go from Kansas City to Oakland. League president Joe Cronin was stunned when his pledge to find another franchise for the city within a few years was rejected as too little too late and powerful Missouri politicians like Senator Stuart Symington threatened to stir up Congress against baseball's exemption from antitrust statutes. Cronin hastily hammered out a compromise between the city and the league that bound the latter to place a new team in Kansas City in time for the 1969 season. The franchise was awarded to Ewing Kauffman on January 11, 1968; the head of Marion Laboratories, Kauffman paid $5.5 million for the club.

Kauffman's first move was to appoint Cedric Tallis general manager. His second was to organize a contest to find a nickname for the team, with Royals emerging as the choice over such other proposals as Hearts, Zoomers, and Eagles because of the popularity of the city's annual American Royal livestock show. In September 1968, Tallis named Joe Gordon as the team's first manager. Kansas City's first pick in the expansion draft was Baltimore righthander Roger Nelson; among the others selected was future Hall of Famer Hoyt Wilhelm. In December, the team completed its first big league trade, by sending Wilhelm to the Angels for catcher-outfielder Ed Kirkpatrick and catcher Dennis Paepke. On the eve of the 1969 season, Tallis made another deal in acquiring outfielder Lou Piniella from the Pilots; it turned out to be the first of many transactions that earned Tallis his reputation as major league baseball's best trader of the period.

An enraged George Brett has to be restrained from attacking umpire Tim McClelland for voiding the infamous Pine Tar Home Run against the Yankees in 1983. *UPI/Bettmann Newsphotos*

Kansas City made its AL debut on April 8, 1969 with a 4–3, 12-inning win over Minnesota before a Municipal Stadium crowd of 17,688. The rest of the season was not quite as positive, although even the team's sub-.500 performance was better than those of Chicago and Seattle. Individual honors for the year went to Piniella, whose .282 average got him named AL Rookie of the Year. As soon as the season ended, Gordon announced his resignation, saying that he was not up to coping with the new, independent breed of player; he was replaced by scouting chief

Charlie Metro. Metro had even more of a problem with losing than Gordon had with independence, and the Royals' slow start in 1970 had him climbing walls; by early June, he was gone in favor of the more patient Bob Lemon. The club once again finished fourth, with only Piniella batting .300 and only southpaw Jim Rooker breaking into double figures in wins.

In the offseason between 1969 and 1970, Tallis pulled off one of the franchise's all-time steals by sending infielder Joey Foy to the Mets for outfielder Amos Otis and pitcher Bob Johnson. In June 1970, he obtained slick-fielding second baseman Cookie Rojas from the Cardinals, then after the season repackaged hurler Johnson with shortstop Jackie Hernandez and catcher Jim Campanis for the Pirates in return for shortstop Freddie Patek, pitcher Bruce Dal Canton, and catcher Jerry May. The result in 1971 was a club that moved into second place in the Western Division in late May and remained there for the rest of the year. Offensively, the leaders were Otis (league-leading 52 steals and a .301 average) and Patek (49 steals and the league leader in triples), while Drago topped the pitchers with 17 wins.

Tallis made another big swap during the 1971 winter meetings in obtaining slugging first baseman John Mayberry from the Astros. Although Mayberry clouted 25 homers and became the first Royal to drive in 100 runs, the team sagged under bad pitching, slipping back to fourth place again. Kauffman, who only a year before had seconded Lemon's honor as AL Manager of the Year, decided that his pilot was too easygoing and fired him for Jack McKeon. Tallis, who eluded full responsibility for the axing of Lemon, went back into the trade market again, this time sending original draft pick Nelson and outfielder Richie Scheinblum to the Reds for pitcher Wayne Simpson and outfielder Hal McRae; in the development of the team through the 1970s, McRae proved to be not only one of its offensive stars, but also a clubhouse leader of tremendous importance.

For the 1973 season, the club moved into the Royals Stadium part of the $43-million Truman Sports Complex. With its multicolored water fountains and twelve-story scoreboard, the facility became one of the league's primary showcases, drawing 1,345,341 fans; equally important, its artificial surface was the basis for the contact philosophy of hitting imparted by coach Charlie Lau. The team's most productive hitters were Otis and Mayberry, who clouted 52 homers between them. On the mound, the big stories were southpaw Paul Splittorff, who won 20, and righthander Steve Busby, who posted the franchise's first no-hitter with an April 27 blanking of the Tigers. What it all added up to was a return to second place, but also with some intimations of the franchise's first serious internal problems.

The tensions began shortly before the end of the 1973 season, when Kauffman announced that Joe Burke, most recently general manager of the Rangers, was being brought in to oversee the club's financial affairs; Kauffman denied that Burke's arrival meant any curtailing of Tallis's power. Playing the good soldier, Tallis went to the winter meetings, where he promptly completed a bad trade in shipping Piniella to the Yankees for aged reliever Lindy McDaniel. When McDaniel got off to a bad start in 1974 (and Piniella started hitting his way toward a .305 season), the second-guessers went into action. Finally, on June 11th, Kauffman announced that he had too many general managers and that because Burke had more ability in financial matters, Tallis was the superfluous one.

Also in 1974, McKeon started another brouhaha when, only days before the team closed out a bad season in fifth place, he announced the firing of Lau. The coach charged that his ouster had followed the habit of some of the players to come to him instead of to McKeon or to pitching tutor Galen Cisco when they had problems in the batting box or on the mound. Lau was backed by several players, including Patek, who called the firing "the dumbest thing yet," and Busby, who suggested that the former catcher had been as helpful to the pitchers as Cisco. The hardest hit of all was rookie third baseman George Brett, who broke down in tears after being informed of the firing. In the years that followed, Brett would stand as Lau's most conspicuous pupil, and with enough long-ball power to refute claims that the batting instructor's methods precluded home runs as a regular offensive weapon.

The atmosphere did not get much better in 1975. Busby, Kansas City's ace, got into several disputes with McKeon and Cisco in spring training and in the early-season, culminating in threats in May to jump the team. There were other run-ins between the manager and Patek and McRae. Finally, on July 24, with the team 11 games behind Oakland, Burke announced that McKeon was being replaced by Whitey Herzog. One of Herzog's first moves was to bring back Lau, immediately improving the atmosphere and starting the club on a solid second-half that once again left it as the division's chief runnerup. The best performance of the year was turned in by Mayberry, who finished second to Boston's Fred Lynn in AL

MVP honors for slugging 34 homers, driving in 106 runs, and batting .291.

Kauffman spent a good part of the offseason in 1975 serving as the point man for major league owners in their attempt to avoid going to arbitration over the free agent claims of pitchers Andy Messersmith and Dave McNally. In a motion filed with a Missouri court, Kauffman claimed that the attack on the reserve clause integral to the Messersmith-McNally case fell beyond the purview of baseball's arbitration panel. He also insisted that part of the basis of his investment in the Royals was the assumption that there would be a continuation of the reserve clause; failure to maintain it, the Royals' owner contended, jeopardized his investment unfairly. Both the arbitration panel and the Missouri court came down on the side of the players and against Kauffman and his fellow owners.

The Royals won their first division title in 1976, despite losing Busby to shoulder surgery for all but thirteen games. Herzog's biggest gamble was replacing the slowing Rojas at second base with rookie Frank White; a graduate of the organization's special baseball academy in Florida, White wasted little time in flashing the defensive form that would gain him eight Gold Gloves. In a second key move, the manager pulled McRae out of the outfield and made him a full-time designated hitter; although not the worst of fielders, McRae's barreling style of play had proved costly to walls, other players, and himself in pursuit of balls. In his DH role, the righthanded hitter battled Brett all year for the batting crown. Without Busby, the staff was led by righthanders Dennis Leonard, who won 17, and Al Fitzmorris, who notched 15 victories. The single most important pitching performance of the campaign, however, came from southpaw Larry Gura on September 29th. With the team looking like it was on the edge of collapsing before the surging A's, the seldom-used Gura tossed a shutout against Oakland, yielding only four hits. The victory proved decisive when Kansas City blew its last three games to Minnesota and had to back in to the division title on an Oakland loss to California.

The final weekend series against the Twins was also the setting for a bitterly contested batting race among Brett, McRae, and Minnesota stars Rod Carew and Lyman Bostock. By the final game of the year, Royals' pitchers had knocked Carew and Bostock out of the running, but the outcome remained in doubt right down to the last at bats by Brett and McRae in the ninth inning. Brett led off the inning with what appeared to be a routine fly to left, but Minnesota outfielder Steve Brye misjudged the ball, and it fell for what turned out to be an inside-the-park homer. After McRae then bounced out to short, effectively giving the title to Brett, the designated hitter screamed over at Twins' manager Gene Mauch, accusing him of having ordered Brye, one of the best defensive outfielders in the league, to foul up the fly ball. After the game, a still-seething McRae escalated the charges, saying Mauch wanted the white man Brett to win the crown instead of a black like himself. Both Mauch and Brye denied the allegations.

The LCS against the Yankees got off to the worst start possible for the Royals when Otis sprained his ankle in the first inning of the first game and was lost for the rest of the series. But Kansas City hung in for four games and then came back in the eighth inning of the finale on a three-run blast by Brett to tie that contest. All went for nought when New York first baseman Chris Chambliss tagged reliever Mark Littell for a pennant-winning homer to lead off the home ninth.

If the 1976 Royals had danced through the raindrops to their first title, the 1977 club created most of its own thunder with a quartet of regulars (Mayberry, Brett, McRae, right fielder Al Cowens) each of whom hit at least 20 homers. With Leonard topping the AL with 20 wins, Jim Colborn winning 18, and the lefty Splittorff 16, the team won 24 out of 25 at one stretch in September and ended up with a franchise-high 102 victories. But once again the Yankees were waiting in the LCS, and once again New York advanced to the World Series after a fifth-game triumph. Instead of a homer by Chambliss, the crusher this time was a sloppy ninth inning in which Leonard, Gura, and Littell were accomplices in surrendering a one-run lead. Herzog did not take the loss lightly, and he ended up turning most of his wrath on Mayberry, strongly hinting that the first baseman's 4-for-18 effort in the series was the result of drugs. When he insisted that "Mayberry goes or I go," Burke immediately dealt the slugger to Toronto.

In more than one way, the 1978 season played out like a familiar tune. Once more, the club won the division title behind the pitching of Leonard (21 wins), Splittorff (19), and Gura (16), and the hitting of regulars like Otis (22 homers, 96 RBIs) and Brett (.294). Also again, the Yankees took the LCS, though accomplishing it this time in four games (and despite three homers by Brett in the third game). Then, in an even older echo, Herzog announced that he would be coming back in 1979, but without Lau; the main bone of contention was the manager's charge that Lau had tried to get every player on the team to hit in the same way. Lau's departure caused another ruckus among the players, with McRae and Brett wondering aloud why Herzog couldn't have settled his problems privately "without penalizing the team." Herzog preferred to joke instead about his own precarious position after losing three straight postseason series. Even after signing a new two-year contract in November, he predicted to reporters that "the first time we lose, I'm gone."

Herzog was right. When bad pitching prevented the club from converting solid offensive years from Brett, catcher Darrell Porter, and outfielder Willie Wilson into a fourth straight division title, he was replaced by Jim Frey.

Although he had already established himself as one of the AL's best hitters, Brett gained superstar status in 1980 for his year-long attempt to become the first player since Ted Williams in 1941 to hit .400. In the end, he had to settle for .390 and an MVP award, as the club pulverized the rest of the division, finishing 14 games up on second-place Oakland. In addition to compiling the highest average since Williams, Brett collected 24 homers, 33 doubles, and 118 RBIs. Leonard was again the anchor of the rotation with 20 wins, while Gura won 18 and Dan Quisenberry won 12 and saved a league-leading 33. In their fourth shot against the Yankees, the Royals finally prevailed, grabbing their first flag in a three-game sweep of the Eastern Division titlists. On the other hand, the World Series against the Phillies was torture. Although he got nine hits against Philadelphia pitching, Brett was slowed considerably by a well-publicized case of hemorrhoids. Principally because of Wilson's inability to make contact (12 strikeouts) and rocky relief performances from Quisenberry, the team went down in six games. The big men in defeat were Otis, who had 11 hits and drove in 7 runs, and first baseman Willie Mays Aikens, who belted 4 homers and drove across 8.

During the World Series, Brett had tried to make light of his pain, but his humor was in short supply the following season, despite offseason surgery. In one episode, he swung a crutch at a photographer who thought he was being cute about the player's

ailment; in another, he broke up a dugout toilet after making out in a crucial situation; in a third incident, he shoved a woman reporter. Brett's outbursts reflected tensions on the club made only more acute by atrocious play at the beginning of the season and the June walkout by players that kept big league parks closed until August. When the team showed little improvement after the strike, Frey was kicked out in favor of Dick Howser. With Aikens (17 homers, 53 RBIs) and Otis (57 RBIs) leading the offense, and Leonard (13 wins) and Quisenberry (18 saves) the pitching, the team rebounded to win the second-half piece of the Western Division title. The comeback ended ignominiously in the special postseason divisional series against Oakland, when the A's yielded only one earned run in their three-game sweep.

Prior to the 1982 season, the franchise promoted Burke to the presidency and brought in John Schuerholz as general manager. Going against the club tradition of dealing age for youth, Schuerholz completed two separate trades with the Giants that would haunt the club for years: In the first swap he acquired veteran outfielder Jerry Martin, in the second former Cy Young winner Vida Blue. Both Martin and Blue played largely supporting roles during the campaign, which concluded with the team blowing 10 of 11 games in the final two weeks to hand California the Western Division title. The two bright notes on the year were McRae's AL-leading 46 doubles and 133 RBIs and Wilson's league-leading 15 triples and .332 average.

Consolations were far fewer in 1983. The first major happening was a May announcement that an ailing Kauffman had surrendered 49 percent of his interest in the franchise to Memphis real estate developer Avron Fogelman for $10 million; Fogelman also threw in another $1 million to gain the first option on buying out Kauffman altogether before 1991. Then, in midseason, Wilson, Aikens, Blue, and Martin were named in a state drug investigation for sell-

In 1982, John Wathan established the record for steals by a catcher in a season when he swiped 36 bases.

ing and possessing cocaine. Blue was released, Martin advised that his contract would not be renewed for the following season, and Aikens later traded to the Blue Jays. The four players ended up serving three-month terms in jail after a plea-bargaining arrangement had reduced the charges from felonies to misdemeanors. Commissioner Bowie Kuhn then tried to suspend the indicted players for a year, but an arbitration panel upheld the penalty only against Blue, named as having been the original source of the drugs. For the 1984 season, Wilson was back with the Royals, Aikens with the Blue Jays, and Martin with the Mets.

The drug investigation hung over the team for the last half of the 1983 season, but it wasn't the only cloud. Early on in the year, Leonard, who had been sidelined by a broken hand in 1982, snapped a knee tendon, effectively ending his career. Then, on July 24th, Brett, who had been having a solid season up to that point, precipitated a three-week farce when he slammed a two-run home run with two out in the ninth inning off Goose Gossage at Yankee Stadium, only to have the blast (which gave the Royals a one-run lead) annulled on umpire Joe Brinkman's ruling that there had been too much pine tar on the third baseman's bat. An enraged Brett had to be pulled away from Brinkman, and the Yankees went off the field in the belief that the ruling had amounted to a last out and given them a win. After taking four days to review all the evidence, AL President Lee MacPhail upheld a Kansas City protest on the grounds that the pine tar rule was too vague, and ordered the game resumed from the point of Brett's home run. New York owner George Steinbrenner suggested that MacPhail go "house hunting in Kansas City" and declared that he would rather forfeit the game than continue it. When warned that a forfeit would indeed be the alternative to the Yankees' taking the field again on August 18, however, Steinbrenner went to court in an attempt to overturn the decision. Other actions were filed by New York fans in protest against the New York owner's declared intention of charging $2.50 as an admission fee for watching what might only amount to four outs. Hearings of the various petitions lasted until late afternoon on August 18, when the way was finally cleared for resuming the contest.

When the teams took the field again at 6:05 before an estimated 1,245 fans, the roster-short Yankees had pitcher Ron Guidry in center field and lefthand-throwing Don Mattingly at second base. New York manager Billy Martin attempted a final ploy by appealing that Brett and the other Kansas City runner, U. L. Washington, had missed first and second bases, respectively, while scoring on the homer, but umpire Dave Phillips met the challenge by whipping out a notarized statement from the Brinkman crew that both runners had touched every bag. After McRae made the last out in the top of the frame, Quisenberry came in to retire the Yankees in order and make the 5–4 score stand up. Later on, Kuhn fined Steinbrenner $250,000 both for his remarks against MacPhail and his suspicious support of the separate suits filed by the New York fans.

Thanks largely to a bullpen moored by Quisenberry's 44 saves, the Royals came back as the Western Division's only team to play better than .500 in 1984. The offense was minimal, and despite the promise shown by a young rotation that featured Bret Saberhagen and Mark Gubicza, and a career year (17 wins) from southpaw Bud Black, the club was little match for the Tigers in the LCS, going down in three straight games. The following year was much better, with Brett returning to form (.335, 30 homers, 38 doubles, and 112 RBIs), first baseman Steve Balboni hitting another 36 homers, Wilson and Lonnie Smith combining for 83 steals, and Quisenberry racking up 37 more saves. All of them, however, took a back seat to the righthander Saberhagen, who came into his own to capture Cy Young honors for his 20 wins and 2.87 ERA. The big years proved imperative in a season-long duel with the Angels that saw the teams still separated by only one game with seven to go. Then, in a reversal of their fold in 1982, the Royals took three games out of four in a showdown series with California to secure the division.

In the LCS against Toronto, Kansas City established a pattern for the postseason by losing the first two games and then three of the first four, but still ending up on top. The turning point proved to be a Game Five shutout by lefty Danny Jackson just as the Jays appeared on the verge of taking their first pennant. In the World Series against the Cardinals, the Royals once again put themselves in a hole by losing the first two games and three of the first four—and then once again got a big win from Jackson in the fifth game to stay alive. But the real turning point came in the ninth inning of the sixth game when, with the club trailing 1–0, Jorge Orta was called safe at first base by umpire Don Denkinger on a throw from first baseman Jack Clark to pitcher Todd Worrell. The call enraged Clark, Worrell, and St. Louis manager Herzog—all the more so when Clark then dropped an easy foul ball off the bat of Balboni, Balboni singled, and pinch-hitter Dane Iorg ended up singling in the tying and winning runs. Kansas City won its first world championship the following night in an 11–0 massacre that was made even more embarrassing by attempts by St. Louis pitcher Joaquin Andujar to start a couple of brawls. Saberhagen, who won two games and posted an 0.50 ERA in his 18 frames of work, capped his big year by being named Series MVP.

Although never slipping below third place, the Royals labored through the rest of the 1980s. The franchise was sent reeling after the 1986 All Star Game, when it was revealed that Howser was suffering from a brain tumor. With first Mike Ferraro and then Billy Gardner appointed as interim pilots, the organization kept up the front that Howser would be back until spring training in 1987; only then did the fatally ill manager officially step down, a few months before his death in June at the age of 51. Gardner lasted until August 27, 1987, by which time the club had not only been cast down by the death of Howser, but also by the announcement that Bo Jackson, the Heisman trophy winner who had made his major league debut the previous September, intended pursuing professional football as "a hobby" after the baseball season. Club reaction was negative, with veterans like Brett questioning whether Jackson wanted to develop his baseball talents or become some kind of professional sports freak. The righthand-hitting outfielder, who had started the 1987 campaign by showing signs of the tremendous power that had attracted club scouts, responded badly to the criticism of his teammates and the booing of Royals Stadium fans, hitting only .188 after he had made known his football playing intentions. With the team in disarray, Gardner was fired in favor of former catcher John Wathan.

Even Wathan's appointment created a clubhouse problem. With Gardner poised for the axe, Schuerholz had first gone to McRae to ask him to take over, but the veteran designated hitter had refused unless he were signed for more than the remainder of the 1987 season. The question of why the front office had not acceded to McRae's condition hung over the clubhouse well into 1988, when McRae, who had been a bridge between the club's various factions for most of his stay, was no longer on the premises. Brawls and finger-pointing suddenly became a regular occurrence, with Jackson and

third baseman Kevin Seitzer, Brett and Wilson, and Saberhagen and outfielder Danny Tartabull squaring off against one another at one point or another. Even more symptomatically, the campaign saw big individual efforts by Gubicza (20 wins), Brett (24 homers, 103 RBIs), Tartabull (26 homers, 102 RBIs), and a couple of others, but little sign of field cohesion, making another third-place finish inevitable. There was only relative improvement the following year. Although Saberhagen took another Cy Young honor for his record of 23–6 (2.16 ERA) and Jackson boomed 32 homers and drove in 105 runs, the club had to settle for second place behind Oakland.

The advent of the 1990s brought a change at the top, but even worse playing on the field. Following their initial agreement in 1983, Fogelman had purchased another one percent of team stock to become a 50-50 partner with Kauffman. By 1990, however, Fogelman had seen his real estate holdings dry up to the point that he needed to borrow $34 million from his baseball partner. Kauffman secured the loan with Fogelman's stock, in effect returning to sole ownership of the club. Another element of the deal absolved the pharmaceuticals industrialist of responsibility for much ballyhooed lifetime contracts that had been given to Brett, Wilson, and Quisenberry on Fogelman's initiative following the 1985 World Series; the Memphis developer subsequently bought out or worked out the accords with the three players.

The 1990 season was no kinder to Schuerholz than it was to Fogelman. Although he had made a couple of key trades for the team over the years, especially the acquisition of Tartabull in 1987, Schuerholz had seldom been allowed to forget his bloopers—particularly the dealing away of such fine arms as Danny Jackson, David Cone, and Melido Perez. In 1990, the general manager's foray into the free agent market was even more of a disaster, with 1989 Cy Young winner Mark Davis, Storm Davis, and Rich Dotson all playing large roles in dooming the team to its first sixth-place finish. At the end of the year, Schuerholz and the Royals parted company, with Herk Robinson taking over as general manager.

The sixth-place finish in 1990 was abetted by a shoulder separation suffered by Jackson in a dive for a liner at Yankee Stadium on July 17. Jackson sustained the injury after walloping three homers in his three at bats; on August 26, in his first return to the batter's box, he saw one pitch from Seattle's Randy Johnson and drove it 450 feet for a record-tying fourth consecutive home run. The year also saw Brett become the first major leaguer to win batting titles in three different decades.

The 1991 season got off to a startling start when Robinson announced that the Royals were releasing Jackson, who had suffered a serious hip injury while playing with the football Los Angeles Raiders. By the end of the season, Jackson was back as the designated hitter for the White Sox, but would eventually undergo a career-threatening hip replacement operation. Without Bo around, much of the attention was focussed on Brian McRae, Hal's son, who was put in center field to stay by Wathan at the beginning of the year. The fleet switch hitter became even more of a talking point when the front office finally pulled the trigger on Wathan in the middle of the season and replaced him with Brian's father. This time with a guarantee that he would be managing the club beyond the season, the elder McRae immediately announced his dissatisfaction with veteran infielders Kurt Stillwell and Seitzer and sat them down for rookies; he also spurred Tartabull into an MVP-type year with a .316 average, 31 homers, 100 RBIs, and the league's slugging crown (.593). Although the team again finished sixth, it wound up above the .500 mark.

After the season, Robinson stunned Kansas City fans a couple of more times—first, by agreeing to sign free agent first baseman Wally Joyner to a mere one-year contract, then, by pulling off a blockbuster trade with the Mets that sent Saberhagen and utility man Bill Pecota to New York in exchange for infielder Gregg Jefferies, outfielder Kevin McReynolds, and utility man Keith Miller. The general manager justified the swap of the popular Saberhagen by noting the team's corps of young starters (Gubicza, Tom Gordon, and Kevin Appier) and the need to replace Tartabull, a free agent who had signed with the Yankees.

What neither Robinson nor McRae was able to justify was an abysmal 1992 season, when a combination of injuries, subpar performances, and a general sense of disorder doomed the club to its worst showing since 1970. The only positive notes of the year were sounded by Appier's emergence as the staff ace and Brett's 3,000th hit off California's Tim Fortugno on October 1st. After the season, the club went marketing in a big way, retrieving Cone and satisfying McRae's two-year-old desire for a strong middle of the infield by acquiring second baseman Jose Lind and shortstop Greg Gagne.

KANSAS CITY ROYALS

Annual Standings and Managers

Year	Position	W	L	Pct.	GB	Managers
1969	Fourth	69	93	.426	28	Joe Gordon
1970	Fourth*	65	97	.401	33	Charlie Metro, Bob Lemon
1971	Second	85	76	.528	16	Bob Lemon
1972	Fourth	76	78	.494	16½	Bob Lemon
1973	Second	88	74	.543	6	Jack McKeon
1974	Fifth	77	85	.475	13	Jack McKeon
1975	Second	91	71	.562	7	Jack McKeon, Whitey Herzog
1976	First	90	72	.556	+2½	Whitey Herzog
1977	First	102	60	.630	+8	Whitey Herzog
1978	First	92	70	.568	+5	Whitey Herzog
1979	Second	85	77	.525	3	Whitey Herzog
1980	First	97	65	.599	+14	Jim Frey
1981	Fifth	20	30	.400	12	Jim Frey
	First	30	23	.566	+1	Jim Frey, Dick Howser
1982	Second	90	72	.556	3	Dick Howser
1983	Second	79	83	.488	20	Dick Howser
1984	First	84	78	.519	+3	Dick Howser
1985	First	91	71	.562	+1	Dick Howser
1986	Third*	76	86	.469	16	Dick Howser, Mike Ferraro
1987	Second	83	79	.512	2	Billy Gardner, John Wathan
1988	Third	84	77	.522	19½	John Wathan
1989	Second	92	70	.568	7	John Wathan
1990	Sixth	75	86	.466	27½	John Wathan
1991	Sixth	82	80	.506	13	John Wathan, Hal McRae
1992	Fifth*	72	90	.444	24	Hal McRae

* Tie

Postseason Play

LCS				WS		
	2–3 versus New York	1976		WS	2–4 versus Philadelphia	1980
	2–3 versus New York	1977			4–3 versus St. Louis	1985
	1–3 versus New York	1978				
	3–0 versus New York	1980				
	0–3 versus Detroit	1984				
	4–3 versus Toronto	1985				

Los Angeles Dodgers

National League,
1958–Present

RECORD: 3014–2566 (.540)

BALLPARKS: LOS ANGELES MEMORIAL COLISEUM
(1958–1961)
DODGER STADIUM (1962–Present)

In the circumstances surrounding their birth, in their organization, and in their development, the Los Angeles Dodgers have been a symbol of the business of major league baseball. While the argument could be made that one or the other of the New York teams represented the game's most profitable franchise entering the 1990's, it is Los Angeles that has been most conspicuous in identifying athletic and economic

Walter O'Malley looks over the plans for the Chavez Ravine facility that became the cornerstone of the Dodgers' fortunes in Los Angeles. *AP/Wide World Photos*

success with meticulous management and long-range investment. At the same time, in the usual corollary with corporations priding themselves on their providence, the team has assiduously promoted an image of a Dodger Family that embraces every one of its employees, from a superstar on the diamond to a night watchman at its training complex in Vero Beach, Florida. The management approach has been vindicated by a stability reflected in a mere two managers in more than three decades; it has been put into question repeatedly by acrimonious clubhouse scenes and bitter player departures.

When Walter O'Malley announced on October 8, 1957 that he was moving the Dodgers from Brooklyn to California, he did so after less than a year of practical preparation. In fact, it was not until the winter of 1956 that the Dodger owner got a look at the section of Los Angeles known as Chavez Ravine that was to be the linchpin of his gamble in transferring one of baseball's most legendary teams. Once he had convinced himself of the lucrative future of the site, the ongoing talks in New York to keep the Dodgers in Brooklyn became academic. Faced with a National League stipulation that a second club would also have to shift to California to make the transfer feasible for travel schedules, he persuaded New York Giants' owner Horace Stoneham to pull up stakes for San Francisco. In need of political and economic collateral to get rights to the 315-acre Chavez Ravine property, he set his sights on Los Angeles's Wrigley Field (then operated by Phil Wrigley as a Pacific Coast League facility), arranged a trade of minor league franchises with the owner of the Chicago Cubs, and then turned around and made a grand public gesture of deeding his newly obtained stadium to the city. In return, the city gave him the title to Chavez Ravine, plus $4.7 million to help get construction work underway on a new stadium. Asked why he wanted to build the first privately financed major league park since Yankee Stadium in 1923, O'Malley could reply with perfect seriousness: "Because I like the free enterprise system."

Although O'Malley's sweetheart deal caused an uproar among political opponents of city hall, it was sanctioned in a city referendum held in June 1958, though by a surprisingly narrow margin of 345,435 to 321,142. O'Malley, a veteran of Brooklyn's Democratic machine, was later to admit that he relished the brawl and spent as much time working the telephones during the referendum campaign as he did paying attention to the baseball club that he had brought west from Brooklyn. What he would have noticed if he had taken a closer look was the end of the Boys of Summer team that had reigned in Brooklyn for a decade.

Even before the Dodgers took the field for their first California game (an 8–0 loss to the Giants in San Francisco on April 15, 1958), Hall of Fame catcher Roy Campanella had been paralyzed from the shoulders down in an offseason automobile accident. The season went downhill from there. After losing his only six decisions, one-time pitching ace Don Newcombe was sent off to Cincinnati. Carl Erskine won the first game played in Los Angeles (on April 18, 1958 against San Francisco), but went on to a total of only four wins for the year. Other Ebbets Field luminaries such as Duke Snider, Gil Hodges, Carl Furillo, and Jim Gilliam found themselves battling mediocrity all year. The team's moral center, shortstop Pee Wee Reese, batted a mere .224 in a reserve role and announced his retirement after sixteen years. What it all added up to was the worst club record since the World War II year of 1944—and an attendance of 1,845,556 (a gain of more than 800,000 over 1957 in Brooklyn)!

There was a connection between the big crowds and the bad years suffered by, in particular, Snider and Hodges. While waiting for Dodger Stadium to be built, O'Malley moved the team into the Memorial Coliseum. No stadium was less suited for baseball. While right field dropped away to an alley distance of more than 440 feet, left field down the line extended no more than 250 feet from home plate and even left-center field started at a laughable 320 feet before dropping off into a normal alley distance. The dimensions prompted numerous preseason conferences between O'Malley and Commissioner Ford Frick. But when Frick ordered O'Malley to erect a second screen eighty feet behind an existing one in left field and to have that serve as a home run boundary (balls hit between the nets would have been doubles), he found himself up against California earthquake laws that prohibited such an additional structure. The commissioner had to accept the Coliseum for what it was—including some center field seats that were 700 feet from the batter's box.

If O'Malley had perceived any home team advantage in the dimensions aside from that accruing from filling up the nose-bleed sections, it was not a vision shared by his players. The left-swinging outfielder Snider, who had hit more than 40 homers for five consecutive years, saw his long ball production plunge to 15 when shot after shot was run down in deep right field. Predictions that the righthand-hitting Hodges would make a run at Babe Ruth's record because of the proximity of the left field fence overlooked the fact that the first baseman was a line-drive hitter whose rising blasts kept smacking the screen and dropping down to become relatively harmless singles; Hodges managed only 22 home runs. It didn't take long for NL players to dub the Coliseum O'Malley's Chinese Theater, or in the words of one newsman, "the only ballpark that can hold 94,000 spectators but only two outfielders."

In his move westward, O'Malley brought along his three most important front office aides—general manager Buzzy Bavasi, farm system chief Fresco Thompson, and scouting supervisor Al Campanis. Along with manager Walt Alston, Bavasi, Thompson, and Campanis had been used to fielding teams that had been culled almost exclusively from the Dodgers' elaborate minor league system. After the disastrous 1958 season, however, Bavasi went into the trade market to come up with seasoned outfielders Wally Moon and Rip Repulski.

While Repulski contributed little, Moon proved to be the team's best clutch hitter, smacking 19 homers and 74 RBIs to go along with his .302 average. More pointedly, the lefthand-hitting slugger made the Coliseum his private batting tee by repeatedly stroking drives to the opposite field over the screen. Together with some restored power from Snider and Hodges, the agile play of Maury Wills at shortstop and on the bases, and Don Drysdale's 17 victories, the "Moon shots" got Los Angeles into a best-of-three playoff against Milwaukee.

Thanks to a decisive 11th-inning error by Braves shortstop Felix Mantilla in the second game, the Dodgers then went on to the World Series, where they defeated the White Sox four games to two. The highlights of the series were the two wins and two saves by Dodger reliever Larry Sherry and the 92,000-plus fans who showed up for each of the three games played in the Coliseum.

Next to the O'Malley bloodline, the most important continuum for the franchise from Brooklyn to Los Angeles has been radio-TV announcer Vin Scully. A protégé of Red Barber when he joined the Dodgers in 1950, Scully's mellifluous play-by-play on the radio has been credited with blunting much of the criticism fired at the franchise for severely restricting its television coverage. Among the more noted Scullyisms over the years was his report that the prognosis for an injured player was that he would be "day to day"; after a beat, he added: "Aren't we all!"

As large as they were, the crowds that descended on the Coliseum for the World Series did not even establish the year's attendance record for a single game. That distinction belonged to a May 7 exhibition game against the Yankees organized to honor the immobilized Campanella, when 93,103 fans were on hand. The sentimental tribute to Campanella (who never played a single game for Los Angeles) contrasted sharply with the treatment meted out to other Ebbets Field stars. After fifteen years in a Dodger uniform, an injured Furillo was asked by Bavasi in 1960 to accept a demotion to the minor leagues so the team could bring up another player. When Furillo refused, he was immediately released. The embittered outfielder had to sue for the remainder of his 1960 salary and eventually got it, but suddenly found himself unwanted by fifteen other clubs as well. In another case, reliever Clem Labine, who had been the mainstay of the team's bullpen for most of the 1950s, discovered from a press box announcement that he had been dealt to the Tigers.

The team's last two years in the Coliseum were mainly significant for the development of the players who would become the franchise's cornerstones for a good part of the 1960s. Instead of Furillo and the rapidly declining Snider and Hodges, there were Frank Howard, Ron Fairly, Willie Davis, and Tommy Davis. Johnny Roseboro had settled in as Campanella's successor, and Wills was for Los Angeles what Reese had been for Brooklyn. Among the position players, only Gilliam, switched back and forth between second and third base, had played for any length of time in Brooklyn. Aside from Drysdale, the pitching staff had a southpaw look, with 1955 World Series hero Johnny Podres, reliever Ron Perranoski, and, especially, Sandy Koufax. Originally signed as a bonus baby in 1955, Koufax confirmed the baseball wisdom that lefthanders took longer to mature than righthanders; in fact, it wasn't until 1961, his seventh major league season, that he provided consistent evidence of the form that was to lead him to the Hall of Fame.

Dodger Stadium was unveiled on April 11, 1962, with Los Angeles defeating Cincinnati 6–2. O'Malley had prepared for the opening in every way possible, including leaving it up to the city to oust the 1,800 Chicanos who had been living on the land. Although he had once toyed with the idea of building seating for as many as 200,000, the owner allowed at the opening as how he expected fans to be interested enough in the team and so pleased by the better sight lines (in comparison to the Coliseum) that the park's

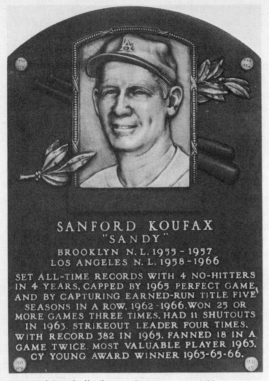

SANFORD KOUFAX
"SANDY"
BROOKLYN N.L. 1955 - 1957
LOS ANGELES N.L. 1958 - 1966
SET ALL-TIME RECORDS WITH 4 NO-HITTERS
IN 4 YEARS, CAPPED BY 1965 PERFECT GAME,
AND BY CAPTURING EARNED-RUN TITLE FIVE
SEASONS IN A ROW, 1962-1966. WON 25 OR
MORE GAMES THREE TIMES. HAD 11 SHUTOUTS
IN 1963. STRIKEOUT LEADER FOUR TIMES,
WITH RECORD 382 IN 1965. FANNED 18 IN A
GAME TWICE. MOST VALUABLE PLAYER 1963.
CY YOUNG AWARD WINNER 1963-65-66.

National Baseball Library, Cooperstown, NY

56,000 capacity would suffice to fulfill his prediction of an annual attendance of 3 million. This actually did not happen until 1978, but it wasn't for lack of effort in the meantime. To encourage more people at the ticket windows, the club even went back on its pioneering policy in Brooklyn of televising most home games, restricting telecasts to a minimum and usually only in the interests of pumping up the team's deflated rivalry with the Giants.

But 1962 was not without its problems, even for O'Malley. Irritated that the American League had expanded into southern California in 1961, he had to swallow a little more pride when, as part of the negotiating ploys around getting New York back into the NL, his fellow owners prevailed on him to host the California Angels at Dodger Stadium until the new club's own park was ready in Anaheim. The arrangement was uncomfortable for both teams until the Angels moved out after the 1965 season.

Down on the field, the Dodgers won as many games (102) as they would win in their first thirty-three seasons on the West Coast. Drysdale was given the Cy Young Award for his 25–9 record. Wills received the Most Valuable Player trophy for batting .299 and setting a new record of 104 stolen bases in

one season. Tommy Davis not only won the first of two straight batting titles with his .346 mark, but also led both leagues with 153 RBIs. The only trouble was that the team did not win the pennant—collapsing in the ninth inning of the decisive third game in a best-of-three playoff against the Giants. The players marked the loss by trooping back to the clubhouse, finding some champagne that had been laid out for them prematurely, and smashing all the bottles against the walls.

As if the playoff defeat hadn't been bad enough, manager Alston had to spend the offseason reading charges from his coach Leo Durocher that he had blown the pennant with faulty strategy and a lack of nerve in key situations. As in the cases of Charlie Dressen and Bobby Bragan before and after, Durocher had been O'Malley's idea of "creative tension"—flanking the stoical Alston with experienced big league managers who would never be accused of hiding their own self-esteem. With Durocher, however, even Alston cracked, leading to scenes on the bench and periodic reports that The Lip was about to take over the reins of the team. The rumors reached a crescendo after the 1964 season, when the team did a bellyflop into sixth place after having won the World Series from the Yankees the year before. But partly because the local media had increased attacks on O'Malley and Bavasi for putting Alston in an intolerable position, the club announced another solution—Alston was being retained for still another year, Durocher was being fired, but so was Alston's chief confidant Joe Becker (so that nobody got an impression that the front office had been completely wrong in silently seconding Durocher's criticisms).

Durocher aside, the mid-1960s were Alston's most successful period as Dodger manager. With Koufax coming into his own as the Player of the Decade, Drysdale putting together the numbers that would also earn him a Cooperstown berth, the farm system continuing to turn out promising hitters, and veterans like Claude Osteen and Phil Regan arriving via trades, the man who had once been Walter Who? in Brooklyn won pennants in 1963, 1965, and 1966. The team also went all the way to a world championship in a four-game sweep of the Yankees in 1963 and in a seven-game struggle with the Twins in 1965, before going down meekly in a sweep to the Orioles in 1966. The collapse before Baltimore (which featured three blankings by the AL team) served as a fitting prelude to two years in the wilderness, when the club dropped back down to eighth in 1967 and seventh in 1968.

The team didn't have to look too far for the reasons for its tumble in 1967. Though nobody knew it at the time, Koufax's pennant-clinching game against the Phillies in the final days of the 1966 season was also his last win. After receiving his third Cy Young Award during the offseason, he announced that fears for his long-tormented left arm were forcing his premature retirement. More trouble arose when Wills declined to accompany the team on a postseason tour of Japan. An infuriated O'Malley, disregarding the counsel of Bavasi, ordered him traded off, and the shortstop found himself in a Pittsburgh uniform in exchange for Gene Michael and Bob Bailey.

The changes on the field were more than matched by those in the front office. In 1968, Bavasi went off to head up operations for the expansion San Diego Padres. A few months later, Thompson died, leaving only Campanis representing the old guard from Brooklyn. Although Campanis took over much of the general manager duties, Bavasi's departure and Thompson's death also accelerated the rise of O'Malley's son Peter in the organization. After a year as executive vice-president, O'Malley *fils* was elevated further to the club presidency, with his father taking over the newly created post of chairman of the board. It would, however, be almost another decade before Peter would be credited with calling his own shots.

In 1969, Alston got 20-victory seasons from Osteen and righthander Bill Singer and solid years from Willie Davis and reliever Jim Brewer to bounce back over the .500 mark. The same players, along with Sutton, figured prominently in two second-place finishes in 1970 and 1971. The main change in the pitching staff with the onset of the new decade was the retirement of Drysdale, the last of the Dodgers to have played in Brooklyn.

The early 1970s saw two significant developments among the position players. The first was the club's rent-a-slugger approach in acquiring Dick Allen in 1971, Frank Robinson for 1972, and Jimmy Wynn for 1974. In immediate terms, only Wynn paid off, belting 32 homers and driving in 104 runs in a pennant-winning year. But from a long-term point of view, all three veterans proved valuable when the Dodgers were able to get Tommy John for Allen, Andy Messersmith for Robinson, and Dusty Baker for Wynn. By the end of 1973, the club had also established an infield of Steve Garvey (first base), Davey Lopes (second base), Bill Russell (shortstop), and Ron Cey (third base) that would go on to establish major league records for longevity as a playing unit.

The pennant-winning season of 1974 matched the franchise high (102 games) set in 1962. For all that, it took some big wins in the final days of the year to avoid surrendering the Western Division title to the surging Reds. The team prevailed in the LCS over Pittsburgh, three games to one. The club's main strengths during the season were Wynn, Garvey (21 homers, 111 RBIs, .312), and Cey (97 RBIs) among the hitters, and Messersmith (20 wins) and Sutton (19) among the pitchers. But towering above them all was relief specialist Mike Marshall, obtained in a trade with Montreal, who won 15 games, saved 21 others, and appeared in a staggering 106 contests.

Even for an organization that saw its share of conspicuous characters come and go in the 1970s, Marshall stood out. For one thing, his diamond achievements notwithstanding, he regarded himself primarily as an educator in the physiological field of kinesiology, not as a baseball player. Second, he had little use for the tried-and-true routines for developing pitchers that the Dodgers had been practicing since the days of Branch Rickey in Brooklyn. Third, he had even less use for the constant questions of newsmen, considering them useless at best. Finally, he objected to signing autographs, and more than once queried an autograph-seeker about the relevance of his quest to anything meaningful. Given the Los Angeles attitude toward cultivating one and all for the greater good of the Dodger Family, it was a minor miracle that Marshall lasted on the team until the middle of 1976 when, according to one front office official, he was traded to Atlanta because he was "too difficult."

Marshall wasn't the only pitcher who gave the Dodgers worries in the mid-1970s. Southpaw John appeared well on his way to some extraordinary numbers when, with a record of 13–3, he snapped the ligament in his pitching elbow. The injury would lead to reconstructive surgery and a long recuperation that would cause him to miss all of 1975, but that would then permit his comeback as the Bionic Arm who would go on to pitch for more years than any other hurler in baseball history except for Nolan Ryan.

If the Dodgers missed John in 1975, they were even more concerned at the prospect of missing Messersmith after the season. In what proved to be the most effective challenge by a player against baseball's venerable reserve clause, Messersmith (and Montreal's Dave McNally) refused to sign a contract for the year, forcing the team to renew the existing pact automatically. Once the season was over, the pitcher declared himself a free agent, and won backing for his stand from the Players Association. With the Dodgers (and other teams) claiming that management had the right to renew contracts perpetually through option clauses, the controversy ultimately ended up in the lap of arbitrator Peter Seitz. Seitz's ruling—that renewals of contracts were good for only one year and that players who played out that year were free to negotiate with any team for their services—marked the real beginning of free agency. Although O'Malley insisted in public that he would still be interested in signing Messersmith, he in fact went to a meeting of league owners ten days after the Seitz decision with detailed proposals for blackballing free agent players. The strategy came to nothing when Ted Turner of Atlanta signed Messersmith.

Despite losing the 1974 World Series to Oakland in five games, the Dodgers were emboldened enough by their season to predict another pennant the following year. But in both 1975 and 1976 they had to accept second-place finishes behind Cincinnati's Big Red Machine. The 1976 season also marked the end for Alston, who had managed the club through twenty-three one-year contracts since the 1954 season in Brooklyn. To take over, the O'Malleys chose Tommy LaSorda, the club's third base coach and as much of a cheerleader as Alston had been a quiet observer.

LaSorda, who liked to tell people that he bled "Dodger blue," represented a fusion of the organization's assumptions of total loyalty and Hollywood's assumptions of relentless self-promotion. If Casey Stengel had been the darling of sportswriters, LaSorda was the paramour of television, showing up not just on sports shows, but on talk programs and even variety hours to spout a well-rehearsed line of anecdotes, cracks, and homilies to the spiritual strengths to be gained by working for the O'Malleys. Frequently lost amid all the huckstering were his abilities as a manager—which were considerable in many areas, but which were also circumscribed by the use of starting pitchers to excess and by mood swings that ended up alienating many of the players he was fond of embracing before the cameras. At least one of the players, pitcher Rick Sutcliffe, tore up LaSorda's office and had to be restrained from throttling the manager after being informed that he was being left off the club's 1981 postseason roster. Another, Garvey, called the pilot's frequent outbursts after losing efforts "irrational." A third, Sutton, was

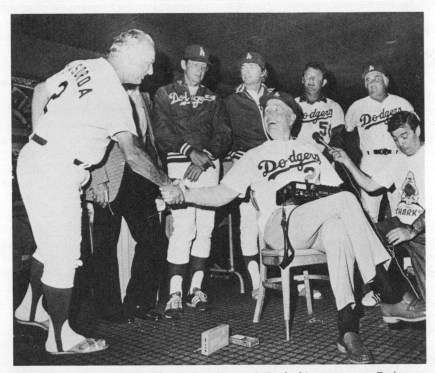

Walter Alston accepts congratulations from Tommy LaSorda, his successor as Dodgers manager, upon his election to the Hall of Fame in 1983. *National Baseball Library, Cooperstown, NY*

given to rebutting LaSorda's semi-serious but completely sanctimonious references to the Big Dodger in the Sky by observing that "God might not even like baseball."

In 1977, with third baseman Cey leading the way with a record 29 RBIs in April, the club won 17 of 20 games at the start and created the momentum that would produce a division title. Cey, Garvey, Baker, and Reggie Smith each hit at least 30 homers—another record. Another decisive factor in the race was the return of John, whose reconstructed arm churned out 20 wins to lead the staff. Although the team went on to topple the Phillies in the LCS, it fell to the Yankees four games to two in the World Series.

Broadly speaking, 1978 mirrored 1977—a division win over the Reds, a pasting of the Phillies in the LCS, and a loss in six games to the Yankees in the World Series. But there were also some differences. On the positive side, the franchise realized O'Malley's prophecy of three million fans, and knuckle-curve specialist Burt Hooton led the starters with 19 wins. On the other side of the fence, the team was shaken by the death of former player and popular coach Gilliam and by a series of clubhouse incidents that suggested deep fissures between players who accepted the Dodger Family propaganda and those who didn't. The most notorious fracas exploded when Sutton told a newsman that the team's most valuable player was Smith, not Garvey, whose straight arrow looks and smooth manner before a camera had made him as much of an organization emblem as LaSorda. When Garvey confronted Sutton, particularly over the pitcher's charges that the first baseman went out of his way to attract media attention, punches were exchanged.

The atmosphere was even worse the following year. Despite the arrival of Sutcliffe and the first of four straight NL Rookie of the Year awards to the team (the others would be given to lefty reliever Steve Howe, southpaw starter Fernando Valenzuela, and second baseman Steve Sax), few weeks passed without LaSorda finding a reason for going into a rage. Even before the season had started, John had gone off to the Yankees as a free agent. Messersmith came back as a now-faded righthander, won two games, and then spent the rest of the year on the disabled list. After a promising start in 1978 and a couple of dramatic duels with the Yankees' Reggie Jackson in the World Series, righthander Bob Welch revealed that he had an alcohol problem.

Shortly before the beginning of the season, the Dodgers renegotiated shortstop Russell's contract, but turned a deaf ear to a similar request from sec-

ond baseman Lopes. Although he denied it publicly, Lopes, according to teammates, retaliated by refusing to steal bases. Writers covering the club also had a field day with LaSorda, who responded to all his troubles by stepping up his already ample intake of pasta. By the time the Dodgers had closed the season with their worst record in eleven years, the manager was waddling more than walking and reading about himself described as Bozo in the Los Angeles press.

Less than a year after he had fulfilled his dream of attracting three million fans to what some called the Taj O'Malley, Walter O'Malley died of cancer. Twenty-two years after mortgaging everything he could and after talking Los Angeles into giving him Chavez Ravine, he left a personal estate to his son Peter and daughter Terry valued at $20 million, a family trust estimated as equal to that, plus a controlling interest in the Dodgers that was then valued at about $60 million and four times that by the 1990s. He also left an organization that, under his vigilance as chairman of the board, had gradually adopted the corporate management techniques picked up by Peter at the Wharton School of Business. It was an organization that kept computerized track of everything from junior college prospects to a receptionist's salary, that hired as many marketing strategists and public relations experts as scouts and ushers, and that called its attention to potential customers community relations. Whereas Walter O'Malley had once crassly promoted the team's transition from the east coast to the west coast by putting a pair of sunglasses on the Brooklyn Dodger symbol of a bum designed by New York *World Telegram* cartoonist Willard Mullin, the franchise presided over by Peter O'Malley had no room for bums, either real or symbolic.

The younger O'Malley also had his circle of confidants—men (and they were all that), who, if they hadn't been drawn to the Elysian Park Avenue of Dodger Stadium, would have probably ended up on Madison Avenue in New York. The most important of these was Fred Claire, who was to rise from an assistant in the publicity department in 1969, to vice-president for public relations and promotions in 1975, to general manager in 1987. Second only to O'Malley in the team hierarchy, it was Claire who created the Dodger Blue promotion that quickly became the franchise slogan.

By his own standards, Walter O'Malley had reason to roll over in his grave only a couple of months after his death when the organization reversed its five-year policy of not signing high-priced free agents. Ironically, it was Campanis, the last of the old Brooklyn hands, who instigated the move, persuading the younger O'Malley to shell out $3 million for righty starter Dave Goltz and another $2.1 million for reliever Don Stanhouse. Both pitchers proved to be double disasters—for Campanis, when it was revealed that he had been bidding against himself in the negotiations with agents more practiced in the game than he was; for the club, when Goltz won a mere seven games and Stanhouse managed only seven saves before going on the disabled list.

Despite the free agent failures, the Dodgers staged a dramatic comeback in the division race by going head to head with the Astros in the final three games of the year, making up a three-game deficit, and forcing a sudden death playoff. That was it, however, with the team going down rather meekly in the winner-take-all contest. By way of consolation, LaSorda was able to point to the vital contributions made over the last two weeks of the season by the Mexican lefty Valenzuela, who worked 17 innings in relief, yielded only 8 hits, fanned 16, and emerged without giving up a single earned run.

For the next several years, the Dodgers' fortunes were intimately tied to Valenzuela, whose portly figure and skyward look in the act of delivering a pitch made him as colorful as he was effective. In his first full season, the southpaw walked to Cy Young and Rookie of the Year awards; his 13 wins in the strike-shortened year included five shutouts in his first seven games and eight blankings overall. Even more happily from the point of view of the franchise, the pitcher's every appearance on the mound became something of an international event, with millions of Mexican radio listeners and television viewers on the team's Spanish-language networks joining coast-to-coast viewers on United States network coverage in living room attendance. The Dodger Stadium turnout wasn't bad, either, with Valenzuela drawing capacity crowds eleven times. Thanks in good part to his outings, the team drew 2.3 million fans despite the cancellation of twenty-five home dates because of the strike.

Aside from Valenzuela and steady offensive

Fernando Valenzuela's habit of peering skyward before the delivery of the pitch only increased his popularity with the fans throughout the North American continent. *Los Angeles Dodgers Inc.*

years from Garvey, Cey, and Pedro Guerrero, the Dodgers had few tangibles to point to in accounting for a season that reached its climax with a comeback 3-games-to-2 victory over Houston in the pre-LCS playoffs and a ninth-inning home run by Rick Monday in the fifth and deciding game of the LCS against Montreal. In fact, if not for the contorted half-and-half playoff formula devised by the commissioner's office for dealing with the strike, the better overall record of the Reds would have entitled them rather than Los Angeles to go into the LCS. Hardly about to question their fortune, the Dodgers marched into the World Series and avenged their 1977 and 1978 defeats by overcoming two initial losses to take the Yankees in six games.

In 1982, the Big Dodger had to share its sky with dollar signs. Shortly before the start of the season, the team broke up its veteran infield by dealing Lopes to Oakland. On the other hand, it found itself

It was because of Goose Gossage's beaning of Ron Cey in the 1981 World Series that helmets with double ear-flaps soon after became mandatory in the major leagues.

in a no-win situation when Valenzuela, only too aware of what he had meant for the gate, held out for three weeks. Although the impasse was resolved in time for opening day, it served as a prelude to another contract battle the following season, when the lefthander went to arbitration, where he became the first player to earn $1 million a year through some avenue other than free agency or threatened free agency. Still another 1982 contract problem was Garvey, considered the equal to LaSorda in blue haemophilia since his days as a bat boy in the spring training complex at Vero Beach. But when the first baseman rejected a three-year offer from the team, he took his first step toward eventual free agency.

On the field, the plusses for the year were rookie Steve Sax's performance at second in place of Lopes, an MVP-type season from Guerrero (32 homers, 100 RBIs, .304), and a combined 37 wins from Valenzuela and southpaw Jerry Reuss. Despite staging a mid-season surge to wipe out a 10½ game lead by the Braves, the team had to settle for second place when, on the final day of the season, it lost to the Giants by the margin of a Joe Morgan home run, allowing Atlanta to back into the LCS. The following season made up that one game when Guerrero produced an almost identical year (32, 103, .298) to lead the team into the championship series against the Phillies. But then Steve Carlton's two victories sparked a Philadelphia pennant win.

The franchise had to swallow some heavy doses of reality in 1983. The first was administered indirectly by Yankees owner George Steinbrenner who, liking what he had seen in the World Series in 1981, offered LaSorda a multiyear pact to double as manager and general manager for New York. Stunned by the possibility of losing their most valuable ambassador, the Dodgers tossed out the one-year-at-a-time contract policy that had been in effect for managers since the days of Charlie Dressen in Brooklyn and gave LaSorda a three-year deal for $1 million. The franchise also had to come to grips with the fact that Dodger Blue was not as addictive as cocaine when Howe, following two unexplained absences and three team suspensions, was barred from baseball for a year for drug abuse. On the diamond, there was the

belated awareness that Garvey would not be easily replaced when highly touted rookie Greg Brock flopped. Over the next few years, first base would be something of a revolving door for Brock, Guerrero, the perennially injured Mike Marshall, and the perennially struck-out Franklin Stubbs.

With Howe missing from the bullpen and Valenzuela becoming increasingly hittable, 1984 was a bad memory from start to finish. But the following year, Guerrero found his form again to lead the league in both slugging and on-base average, catcher Mike Scioscia finished second in on-base average, and Orel Hershiser went 19–3 (with five shutouts) to boost the club into the LCS against the Cardinals. Their efforts were squeezed between two lesser performances— two more absences from Howe that prompted his outright release and two gopher balls served up by reliever Tom Niedenfuer to Ozzie Smith and Jack Clark that provided the margin of victory for St. Louis in the championship series.

The Cardinal victory was the start of something bad, with the Dodgers winning only 73 games in each of the next two years and finishing closer to the cellar than to first place. In 1986, a mere half-game prevented the team from becoming the first one in the NL ever to drop from first to last from one season to the next. The main problems were injuries to key players, an inconsistent bullpen, and a porous defense. Then, too, there were the usual clubhouse flareups, more than one of them centering around the power-hitting but apparently fragile Marshall. In 1987, Marshall exchanged blows with both Guerrero and veteran Phil Garner, who had accused him of exaggerating complaints about his back and taking too may days off. For his part, veteran third baseman Bill Madlock decided that Marshall wasn't the only one who had gotten used to calling it in. Given such an atmosphere both on and off the field, it did not come as too much of a surprise that Dodger Stadium attendance dipped below 3 million in 1987 for the first time in a full season since 1979.

The heaviest blow of all to the franchise's image was delivered by the oldest guardian of the seal, Campanis. On April 7, 1987, the ABC-TV public affairs program "Nightline" devoted a segment to the fortieth anniversary of Jackie Robinson's debut with the Brooklyn Dodgers. Campanis, a last-minute substitute for one-time Robinson teammate Don Newcombe, turned the commemoration into an unconscious admission of how strongly racism persisted in major league hierarchies and of how personally sotted he was with racist stereotypes. Among Campanis's observations was the assertion that blacks "may not have some of the necessities" to be managers or general managers, and that this was why so few of them had ever made it as pitchers in baseball or quarterbacks in football—positions requiring a lot of mental ability. Against a storm of nationwide criticism, O'Malley and his general manager issued apologies for the remarks the following day. But when that did nothing to abate the protests, O'Malley fired Campanis and turned his responsibilities over to Claire. Over the ensuing months, Los Angeles and every other team in the majors came under intense scrutiny for hiring policies regarding blacks and other minorities. One of the Dodgers' responses was to appoint Tommy Hawkins, a former basketball star and veteran Los Angeles sports announcer, to the newly-created position of vice-president for communications. Hawkins immediately became the highest ranking black in the franchise's history.

For all the team's travails in 1987, LaSorda went into 1988 confident about what he called his Awesome Foursome—a middle of the lineup that consisted of Kirk Gibson (obtained as a free-look free agent after a collusion ruling against the owners), Guerrero, Mike Davis (another free agent), and John Shelby. As it turned out, Davis and Shelby were next to invisible for the season, and Guerrero ended up being exchanged to the Cardinals for southpaw John Tudor. On the other hand, the gung-ho Gibson proved to be enough of an awesome force unto himself to lead the team to a division win. When he wasn't driving home runs on the field, the lefty-swinging outfielder was driving his teammates to intensity levels that managed to camouflage their relatively modest abilities. His counterpart on the pitching staff was Hershiser, whose 23 wins included a season-closing (and record) 59 consecutive scoreless innings. Gibson easily won MVP honors, Hershiser took the Cy Young trophy, and LaSorda was named NL Manager of the Year. In postseason play, the team stumped baseball experts by using Hershiser's apparently tireless arm and dramatic homers from Gibson and Scioscia to defeat the heavily favored Mets in the LCS and the even more touted Athletics in the World Series.

The team closed the decade with a thud back into fourth place. The leg-sore Gibson, who had been heroic in hobbling up to the plate in 1988 postseason play, became simply leg sore and of limited offensive use. Without his bat clinching most of his arguments, his intensity became indistinguishable from tension, and the same players who had admired his leadership qualities the year before began criticizing his

temper. Hershiser also declined to a 15–15 record, but through little fault of his own; in his losses, the Dodgers scored a grand total of 17 runs.

Worse awaited Hershiser in 1990, when, after only four starts, he came down with an arm ailment that was ultimately diagnosed as a torn rotator cuff requiring reconstructive surgery. The injury, together with other ailments that had just about put an end to the effectiveness of Valenzuela, refocused attention on LaSorda's use (or overuse) of pitchers. In fact, however, it was a criticism that had been heard even before LaSorda had replaced Alston, back in 1959 in the almost frenzied use of reliever Art Fowler over the first half of the season. It would be heard again in 1991 when arm problems began to assail righthander Ramon Martinez.

In the culminating reversal of his father's thumbs-down policy on free agents, O'Malley announced the signing of slugger Darryl Strawberry after the 1990 season for a then-league-high $5 million a year for four years. A couple of months later, the team gave another big contract to free agent centerfielder Brett Butler. Some said the signings were the final proof that the franchise's long-vaunted farm system had run dry; others said that it was evidence that the Dodgers were beginning to accept the fact that they had to spend as much as collect in the vast market they had been so instrumental in creating.

The positive side of 1991 was that Butler showed himself to be the best leadoff man in the game next to Rickey Henderson, that Mike Morgan finally fulfilled 10 years of expectations by emerging as a mound winner, and that the team finished a mere game behind the division-winning Braves. The down side was that, outside of Butler, receiver Scioscia, and veteran first baseman Eddie Murray, the club barely had a player it could call a regular, especially after Strawberry missed significant time with various injuries. With so little lineup consistency, terrible defense, and an erratic bullpen, LaSorda depended for much of the season on Morgan and fellow righthander Ramon Martinez to stay close—a managerial effort that was considered his best since taking over from Alston.

The one-game difference with the Braves led the organization into a lot of what-if thinking in the off-season. It was a distraction that proved fatal. On the assumption that he had enough starting pitching, Claire peddled Tim Belcher to the Reds for outfielder Eric Davis, a childhood friend of Strawberry's whose regular visits to the disabled list had undercut his potential as a superstar. On the same assumption, Morgan was allowed to go off to the Cubs as a free agent. When the team would offer him only a one-year contract, slugger Murray also packed his bags, ending up with the Mets. The only significant addition came with the signing of knuckleballer Tom Candiotti.

What it all added up to was not only the worst team in Los Angeles history, but the first cellar finish by any Dodger club since Brooklyn had occupied the basement in 1905. Once again, Strawberry missed a good part of the season, this time with back problems that forced him to undergo an operation in the fall. Davis also lived up to his reputation by spending more time ailing than playing. Among the starting pitchers, Martinez was sidelined with elbow problems, and Hershiser showed that, while he was valiant in rebounding so quickly from his surgery, he was hardly the same dominating hurler he had been. The defense went from dreadful to catastrophic, with the team making as many as seven errors in games and shortstop Jose Offerman becoming the first NLer

in 14 years to commit at least 40 miscues. About the only bright light in the season was first baseman Eric Karros, who took Rookie of the Year honors for his 20 homers and 88 RBIs. This was not enough, however, to prevent attendance from plunging and critics and fans from insisting on a total organization overhaul, beginning with those responsible for the bankruptcy of the farm system.

In the 1992–93 off-season, the Dodgers' luck with free agents didn't seem to be getting any better. Only a couple of weeks after signing Todd Worrell to a three-year pact for $9 million, the veteran reliever admitted that he still felt pain in his arm from the miseries that had plagued him in St. Louis. Otherwise, the club's major moves were to acquire two infielders well past their prime—second baseman Jody Reed (obtained in a trade with Colorado after the Rockies had drafted him from the Red Sox) and third baseman Tim Wallach (from the Expos).

LOS ANGELES DODGERS

Annual Standings and Managers

Year	Position	W	L	Pct.	GB	Managers
1958	Seventh	71	83	.461	21	Walter Alston
1959	First	88	68	.564	+2	Walter Alston
1960	Fourth	82	72	.532	13	Walter Alston
1961	Second	89	65	.578	4	Walter Alston
1962	Second	102	63	.618	1	Walter Alston
1963	First	99	63	.611	+6	Walter Alston
1964	Sixth	80	82	.494	13	Walter Alston
1965	First	97	65	.599	+2	Walter Alston
1966	First	95	67	.586	+1½	Walter Alston
1967	Eighth	73	89	.451	28½	Walter Alston
1968	Seventh	76	86	.469	21	Walter Alston
1969	Fourth	85	77	.525	8	Walter Alston
1970	Second	87	74	.540	14½	Walter Alston
1971	Second	89	73	.549	1	Walter Alston
1972	Third	85	70	.548	10½	Walter Alston
1973	Second	95	66	.590	3½	Walter Alston
1974	First	102	60	.630	+4	Walter Alston
1975	Second	88	74	.543	20	Walter Alston
1976	Second	92	70	.568	10	Walter Alston, Tommy Lasorda
1977	First	98	64	.605	+10	Tommy Lasorda
1978	First	95	67	.586	+2½	Tommy Lasorda
1979	Third	79	83	.488	11½	Tommy Lasorda
1980	Second	92	71	.564	1	Tommy Lasorda
1981	First	36	21	.632	+½	Tommy Lasorda
	Fourth	27	26	.509	6	Tommy Lasorda
1982	Second	88	74	.543	1	Tommy Lasorda
1983	First	91	71	.562	+3	Tommy Lasorda
1984	Fourth	79	83	.488	13	Tommy Lasorda
1985	First	95	67	.586	+5½	Tommy Lasorda
1986	Fifth	73	89	.451	23	Tommy Lasorda

1987	Fourth	73	89	.451	17	Tommy Lasorda
1988	First	94	67	.584	+7	Tommy Lasorda
1989	Fourth	77	83	.481	14	Tommy Lasorda
1990	Second	86	76	.531	5	Tommy Lasorda
1991	Second	93	69	.574	1	Tommy Lasorda
1992	Sixth	63	99	.389	35	Tommy Lasorda

Postseason Play

LCS				WS		
	3–1 versus Pittsburgh	1974			4–2 versus Chicago	1959
	3–1 versus Philadelphia	1977			4–0 versus New York	1963
	3–1 versus Philadelphia	1978			4–3 versus Minnesota	1965
	3–2 versus Montreal	1981			0–4 versus Baltimore	1966
	1–3 versus Philadelphia	1983			1–4 versus Oakland	1974
	2–4 versus St Louis	1985			2–4 versus New York	1977
	4–3 versus New York	1988			2–4 versus New York	1978
					4–2 versus New York	1981
					4–1 versus Oakland	1988

Louisville Grays

National League, 1876–1877   **BALLPARK:** LOUISVILLE BASEBALL PARK

RECORD: 65–61 (.516)

Charter members of the National League, the Grays are remembered almost exclusively as the source of major league baseball's first great scandal. The response to that scandal, lifetime banishment for all four of the so-called Louisville Crooks, became a threat held over the head of every player, not only for the crime of deliberately losing games, but also for a host of other infractions. The NL also took the opportunity presented by the scandal to tighten its reins on all elements of the game, imposing new restrictions on independent clubs and the reserve rule on players.

In one sense, the NL was born in Louisville. It was in the Kentucky city in 1875 that William Hulbert of Chicago met with representatives from St. Louis, Cincinnati, and Louisville to explore the idea of subverting the player-dominated National Association and replacing it with the investor-dominated NL. In Louisville, the investors included a cross-section of local businessmen. Walter N. Haldeman, publisher of the Louisville *Courier-Journal,* was chosen president; the most active officer was Charles E. Chase, a liquor company executive. Haldeman's son,

John, also owned one share of stock—a gift from his father; more important, the younger Haldeman was a *Courier-Journal* sportswriter who kept after his father to devote more space in the paper to baseball.

Almost from the beginning, the Grays were starcrossed. On April 13, 1876, less than two weeks before the opening of the NL's first year, a tornado ripped through Louisville Baseball Park, severely damaging the grandstand. The team itself finished an unexciting fifth in its first year. Jim Devlin pitched more games (68) than anyone else in the league, compiling a 30–35 record; he also led the Grays in hitting with a .315 average. The pitcher played a central role in a minor scandal that was a prelude to more noto-

Footnote Player: Johnny Ryan's major league career consisted of one game for the Grays, a no-decision on July 22, 1876. In 8 innings of relief work, he gave up 22 hits and established a never-broken record of 10 wild pitches.

The Grays were the victims of the first shutout in major league history, a 4–0 blanking at the hands of Al Spalding of Chicago in their first game in 1876.

rious events in 1877. It started when the Grays lost a game to the New York Mutuals on May 30th; Louisville right fielder George Bechtel provided the margin of difference in a 7–2 score when he allowed three hits to get past him. Several weeks later, the club directors announced that they were investigating allegations that Bechtel had wired Devlin suggesting that they could make $500 if they were to lose the game to be played on June 10th. Bechtel insisted that he had not sent the telegram, and the outfielder's denial was supported by an anonymous letter from Philadelphia that claimed the name on the wire was a forgery. Unconvinced, the directors offered Bechtel a choice between resigning and being expelled; he chose the latter.

A completely revamped Louisville squad emerged as the favorite to win the 1877 pennant. Rookies Juice Latham (first base), Bill Crowley (center field), and Orator Shaffer (right field) were signed, along with shortstop Bill Craver (from New York) and left fielder George Hall (from Philadelphia). In fact, the club was comfortably in first place on August 16th, 5½ games ahead of Boston with only 20 games left to play. Then the bottom fell out. Between August 17th and September 6th, the Grays lost eight in a row on the road, dropping them four games off the lead. When they could do no better than split the next 8 games with the Reds, Boston, on the way to winning 20 of its last 21 games, had a clear path toward the pennant.

One view of the collapse was that the Grays' bats simply went dead and that Devlin, suffering from a case of boils, lost the effectiveness of his deadly sinker ball at the same time that Boston began one of the most torrid pennant drives in baseball history. Chase, Louisville's vice-president, was the first to smell the bad odor surrounding his team. During an August series against Brooklyn, he received an anonymous telegram from Hoboken, where gamblers had set up shop, warning him to "watch your men." A second telegram informed the executive that the next day's game was fixed and that Louisville would lose (which it did). At first, suspicion settled on utility player Al Nichols, who had been picked up from the independent Pittsburgh

Alleghenys in mid-season on Hall's recommendation. But with concrete evidence lacking, Chase had to bide his time.

More than a month later, on September 24th and 25th with the pennant already decided, the Grays split a pair of exhibition games against an Indianapolis squad; John Haldeman accused Devlin and Hall of losing deliberately. After Louisville's next league game, a meaningless 9–6 loss to fifth-place Chicago in which the Grays made 16 errors, Haldeman made his first veiled suggestion that something was amiss: Commenting on the fact that the oddsmakers in New York and Philadelphia favored Chicago in the next day's game, the sportswriter asserted: "This looks somewhat strange."

Next it was Chase's turn, charging Devlin with having thrown two games with the Hartfords during the losing streak in August. Although he denied the accusation, Devlin did admit that he had pitched "carelessly" against independent teams. The pitcher did little to persuade Chase and Haldeman of his honesty when, the season over, he suddenly recovered his form and pitched well in postseason exhibitions. It was, in the end, Hall who confessed, prompting the club's board of directors to hold closed-door hearings. Second baseman Joe Gerhardt, who had made costly errors in the August slump, and third baseman Bill Hague, who had been unable to buy a hit during the streak, were exonerated; Devlin, Hall, and Nichols, on the other hand, confessed to transgressions.

The announcement that Devlin, Hall, Nichols, and Craver had been suspended came in a brief notice in the *Courier-Journal* on October 30th. Aside from the interrogations of the players, the investigation consisted of an examination of telegrams received by the players to corroborate the confessions. All of them except Craver signed a release allowing the team to examine the wires, which involved a simplistic code involving the use of the word "sash" to indicate a game would be thrown. But who actually did what remained somewhat vague. Nichols, Hall, and Devlin were suspended specifically for "selling games," Craver for the decidedly more amorphous "disobedience of positive orders, of general misconduct, and of suspicious play in violation of his contract and the rules of the League."

Nichols, who had been known to associate with gamblers when he had played for the Mutuals in 1876, was the easiest to eliminate, if only because he was a lowly sub who batted .211. He was blackballed not for what he did or didn't do on the field, but as the link between the players and the gamblers. The evidence against him included his own admission that he had bet on games, Shaffer's testimony that Nichols had admitted a willingness to throw games, and several incriminating telegrams.

Hall, about whom there had been unsavory rumors since his days in the pre-NL National Association, confessed to conspiring with Nichols to throw an August 30th exhibition game in Lowell, Massachusetts and another against the Pittsburgh Alleghenys four days later. Claiming that the whole affair had been Nichols's idea, Hall testified that he had told his co-conspirator that he would have nothing to do with throwing official league games. Despite his transgressions, Hall had a remarkable season, a fact recognized even by the *Courier-Journal*. His .323 batting average was seventh in the NL and his 11 errors in 61 games was the lowest among regular outfielders.

The collusion between Hall and Devlin began on September 5th in Columbus, where the Grays had traveled for yet another exhibition. At first, Hall claimed that Devlin had sounded him out; later he admitted that he had instigated the conspiracy, but insisted that he had done so at Nichols's urging. Hall and Devlin cut Nichols out of the deal and wired a New York gambler, who paid the pitcher $100 to throw one game to Cincinnati and another $100 for a loss to Indianapolis. Devlin denied being involved with Nichols, but offered the gratuitous observation that he suspected Craver's play and had actually spoken to manager Jack Chapman about it.

Craver's was a different story altogether. He admitted no wrongdoing, but simply refused to allow the team to read his telegrams and suffered from damaging testimony given not only by Devlin but also by Gerhardt, Shaffer, and Latham, who claimed the shortstop had "rattled" them repeatedly and caused them to make errors. His admission that he played cards and drank late into the night, so much so that he wasn't able to play up to his abilities on occasion, didn't help his case. Haldeman's description of Craver's fate was that "misconduct compelled his expulsion."

The scandal did not erupt in a vacuum. While Louisville had a reputation for paying high salaries, the directors had taken a punitive approach to players who had signed with other clubs before the season ended. Devlin, Hall, and catcher Pop Snyder had signed with St. Louis; Craver and Hague with the Hartfords. Even Snyder, who was guilty of nothing, had to wait until a special NL resolution in December forced Louisville to pay him what he was owed. The organization's vindictiveness was well known in

baseball circles, and the St. Louis *Globe-Democrat* pointed out that "money matters have a good deal to do with the expulsions" and issued an admonishment that, "Contracts, unlike pie crusts, were not made to be broken."

The NL as a whole also invited the scandal by its attitude toward its players. Not only did the clubs conspire to hold down salaries, but in 1877 they also instituted a policy of charging players $30 for their uniforms and 50 cents a day for meal money on the road. Haldeman, writing in the *Courier-Journal* on January 4, 1877, had sided with the players in their battles with the owners. "Ball players do not like the idea of being charged for their uniforms and a certain rate per diem while away from home." " 'Tis very sad," he wrote. "They are a much-imposed-upon and cruelly down-trodden set. How they manage to live on the mere pittance received for hard work rendered is a conundrum."

The games involved were, as Devlin and Hall always insisted, meaningless exhibitions. There is no evidence to support Haldeman's assessment of the crucial eight-game losing streak: "There is not a man in Louisville who is not thoroughly satisfied that the last games with the Bostons and the Hartfords were purposely lost. The directors believed that men who would sell games with Alliance clubs for one hundred dollars would not hesitate to sell league games for a consideration." Even the Cincinnati game involved was with a team that at the time was threatened with suspension from the league and the elimination of its games from the standings.

At a December 4, 1877 meeting, the league made the Louisville club's decision permanent, banning all four players, as well as outfielder Bechtel, for life. It was a bit kinder to the organization, with both sides keeping up the pretense that there would be a Louisville entry in 1878. As late as January, Chapman was publicly seeking players who were "above suspicion." But several weeks later, on March 7th, the Louisville directors voted not to field a team for the coming season, and the NL, playing out the charade, accepted the club's resignation on April 2nd. The game had been exposed earlier, however, when the NL announced an 1878 schedule that did not include Louisville.

As for the Louisville Crooks, Hall returned to Brooklyn and became a successful engraver, while Craver became a policeman in Troy, N.Y. Nichols defied the ban by playing for a minor league club called the Brooklyn Franklins in 1884; he may also have played, using Williams as an alias, for Jersey City in the Eastern League in 1886 before disappearing into an obscurity so deep that his date and place of death are unknown. Devlin persistently sought reinstatement. He wrote to Boston manager Harry Wright three times describing his impoverished state, admitting his guilt, citing the circumstances of his acts, and finally requesting any job in baseball, even as a groundskeeper. The NL's ultimate response to Devlin's pleas was to adopt a resolution at its December 1880 annual meeting promising never to undo the penalty imposed on the Louisville Four nor to entertain any future request for reinstatement. The pitcher eventually found work as a Philadelphia policeman.

LOUISVILLE GRAYS

Annual Standings and Managers

Year	Position	W	L	Pct.	GB	Managers
1876	Fifth	30	36	.455	22	Jack Chapman
1877	Second	35	25	.583	7	Jack Chapman

Louisville Colonels

American Association, 1882–1891	**BALLPARK:** ECLIPSE PARK
	OTHER NAMES: ECLIPSE, CYCLONES
RECORD: 575–638 (.474)	

While never a success financially or on the field, the Colonels were at the center of the turbulence that wracked the American Association in its final years. It was more than appropriate that, at least for the 1890 season, the club was nicknamed the Cyclones. The team also produced the AA's most extraordinary player, Pete Browning.

Led by the rookie Browning, who won the first of two batting crowns, and by Tony Mullane, who went 30–24 in his first full season, Louisville finished third in 1882 under manager-shortstop Denny Mack. In 1883, with second baseman Joe Gerhardt taking over as manager, the Eclipse (as the team was called in its first few years) slipped back to fifth, but had a hand in deciding the race when a Guy Hecker wild pitch with two out in the tenth inning of the next to last game of the season brought home the pennant-winning tally for the Philadelphia Athletics. The er-

rant toss proved very costly to Hecker, because the Louisville players had gone into the game with a promise from St. Louis owner Chris Von der Ahe that they would earn a new suit if they could beat the Athletics, who held a one-game lead over the entrepreneur's Browns. Deprived of their reward, Eclipse players vented their resentment on Hecker for years, and their animosity eventually ended up costing him a shot at the manager's job.

If anyone might have deserved more respect from his teammates, it was Hecker, the only player ever to win a batting title (.341 in 1886) and also lead a league in victories (52 in 1884). Although he put together a busy mound record of 175–146 in nine seasons, he appeared even more often as a first baseman or outfielder, compiling a career average of .283. Hecker's twin prowess enabled him to set more than

The first twins to play in the major leagues were third baseman Phil and outfielder John Riccius, who were with Louisville together in 1882 and 1883.

Mike Walsh, the Colonels manager in 1884, had been an American Association umpire the year before—the first umpire to work for a salary. Previous arbiters had worked either for a per-game fee or just for the fun of it.

one offensive record for pitchers, including being one of only two hurlers to hit three homers in a game (August 15, 1886). In the same game, he set the all-time mark—for pitchers and non-pitchers alike—for runs scored in one game (7).

Even more important to the AA than Hecker was Browning. Easily the best hitter in the association, he averaged .345 in eight seasons, climbing as high as .402 in 1887. The outfielder became almost equally known for his conversation—always loud because of a hearing problem and always centered around his batting average, his eyes, or his bats. Browning lavished great care on his bats, constantly rubbing oil on them and speculating on the number of hits each one contained. During an 1884 slump, he had a local woodworker named J. F. Hillerich make him a stick to his own specifications. Hillerich's shop eventually grew into Hillerich and Bradsby, the sporting goods manufacturer, and the bat model made for Browning was soon enough known as the Louisville Slugger.

Even in 1883, the AA's most successful season, the Colonels could do no better than break even. This prompted the franchise's majority stockholder, J. H. Park of the Kentucky Malt Company, to give way to a group of owners headed by brothers Zach and John Phelps. A succession of mediocre seasons led to another ownership transfer to Mordecai Davidson after the 1887 campaign. It was Davidson who sought to make Hecker the manager and who came up against the resentful players who made it clear that they wanted somebody else as their field boss. The owner first appointed John Kelly, found him wanting, then took over himself for three games. Next came John Kerins, but by then Davidson was so taken with his own skills on the bench that he dumped him equally fast so he himself could get back on the job. The owner ran up a record of 35–54.

Having proven to the world (or at least to himself) that he could manage, Davidson decided to take over the team presidency in 1889, supplanting W. L. Lyons and ushering in a reign of terror that fell short of destroying the franchise only because the AA stepped in to end the abuses. On the way to baseball's first 100–loss season, including a record 26 in a row, Davidson ran managers in and out of the clubhouse frantically: Dude Esterbrook (10 games), Chicken Wolf (65), Dan Shannon (56), and Jack Chapman (7). As if that were not enough to demoralize the club, the owner kept up constant public criticism of his players, while imposing fines on them for making errors or failing in the clutch. By June, the team was in open revolt, and six players walked out in what amounted to baseball's first strike. When a league inquiry established that Davidson had collected $1,425 in fines, sometimes withholding huge chunks of paychecks and leaving players on the road without money, he was finally removed from control of the franchise.

New president Lawrence Parsons kept Chapman as manager, approved a proposal to rename the club after a tornado that had ripped through Louisville on March 27, 1890 (killing seventy-five people), and then watched his Cyclones breeze from the cellar to first place—the first "worst to first" team and the last for 102 years. Much of the miracle climb stemmed from the fact that many of the AA's best players had defected to the Players League. The biggest contributions on the club came from former manager Wolf, who went from a .291 average in 1889 to a league-leading .363; Red Ehret, who improved his record from 10–29 to 25–14; and, most amazing of all, Scott Stratton, who zoomed from 3–13 to 34–14.

Having made a small profit while the rest of the AA was being devastated, the Cyclones went back to their old name and their old ways in 1891, slipping to sixth despite the addition of future stars Hughie Jennings and Patsy Donovan. By midseason, however, it was also evident that the club's problems were secondary to those of the association, which endured an administrative turmoil involving three changes in

Colonel's right fielder Chicken Wolf was the only player to last in the American Association for all ten seasons of its existence.

the president's office. The solution to the circuit's crisis turned out to be an agreement by the NL to absorb four AA franchises and buy out the others. Despite its shaky finances and even shakier roster, Louisville was one of the clubs absorbed by the senior loop with the dissolution of the AA after the 1891 season.

LOUISVILLE COLONELS

Annual Standings and Managers

Year	Position	W	L	Pct.	GB	Managers
1882	Third	42	38	.525	13	Denny Mack
1883	Fifth	52	45	.536	13½	Joe Gerhardt
1884	Third	68	40	.630	7½	Mike Walsh
1885	Fifth*	53	59	.473	26	Jim Hart
1886	Fourth	66	70	.485	25½	Jim Hart
1887	Fourth	76	60	.559	19½	John Kelly
1888	Seventh	48	87	.356	44	John Kelly, Mordecai Davidson
						John Kerins, Mordecai Davidson
1889	Eighth	27	111	.196	66½	Dude Esterbrook, Chicken Wolf
						Dan Shannon, Jack Chapman
1890	First	88	44	.667	+12	Jack Chapman
1891	Sixth	55	84	.396	40	Jack Chapman

*Tie

Louisville Colonels

National League, 1892–1899   **BALLPARK:** ECLIPSE PARK

RECORD: 419–683 (.380)   **OTHER NAMES:** WANDERERS

No more successful in their National League incarnation than they had been in the American Association, the Colonels began their second career under a financial cloud, suffered through nine losing seasons, and then disappeared when the NL reverted to eight teams after the 1899 season.

Before their admission to the NL in December 1891, the Colonels changed owners: Lawrence Parsons, the owner of the AA franchise, was forced to sell the club at auction on November 16th to satisfy a $6,459.40 mortgage. The new owner, Dr. T. Hunt Stuckey, retained Jack Chapman as manager and kept seven players. The rest of the squad came from a variety of defunct AA teams, and it was a sorry crew, finishing next to last and ninth in the two halves of the twelve-team NL's split season, and

dead last (.226) in hitting. Second baseman Fred Pfeffer succeeded Chapman as manager before the end of the first half of the split season.

Stuckey's major act before selling out to Fred Dresler in 1892 was to follow the lead of his fellow owners and slash the salaries of about half of his players. Pfeffer surrendered the managerial reins to Billy Barnie in 1893, but stayed around another year to lead the club in batting with a .308 mark. In late 1894, after Barnie had been fired and Pfeffer had pleaded injuries to secure his release, the pair became involved in an abortive effort to form a New American Association. Reacting quickly to this latest threat to its monopoly, the NL suspended both players, but gave them until the end of the year to recant and sign a loyalty oath. Barnie agreed to appear at a hearing before NL president Nick Young and, though he refused to sign the loyalty oath, was reinstated. Pfeffer refused even to appear, claiming that, as a released player, he was free to pursue whatever business interests he chose.

Pfeffer signed to coach baseball at Princeton University, but made it clear that he wanted to resume his playing career; he was backed by letters from some ten thousand fans threatening a boycott if the NL didn't agree to a reinstatement. Defying the NL, Dresler offered Pfeffer a contract. The league proposed a compromise by agreeing to accept the second baseman back into the fold if he paid a $500 fine and signed the oath; Pfeffer's friends raised the money within an hour.

The Colonels didn't fare half as well on the field as Pfeffer did off it. Barnie had brought the team home eleventh and twelfth with the NL's highest ERA (5.90) in 1893 and the lowest batting average (.269) in 1894. On August 17th of the latter year, righthander Jack Wadsworth surrendered all 36 hits as the Phillies established a record for most safeties in a game. John McCloskey led the Colonels to last place again in 1895, when the club was last in both ERA (5.90) and hitting (.279), and shared the reins with Bill McGunnigle for a third consecutive cellar finish in 1896. The only bright spot in three years was the arrival of future Hall of Fame left fielder Fred Clarke, who hit .347 in 1895 (his first full year). Clarke never dropped below .300 in his five seasons in Louisville, reaching a high of .390 in 1897. In 1897, Clarke became manager, succeeding Jim Rogers a third of the way into the season. The year also brought new owners—Barney Dreyfuss and Henry C. Pulliman—and Honus Wagner, who hit .338 in 61 games, mostly as an outfielder.

Clarke was able to lift the club to ninth place in the final two seasons, but the twelve-team league was doomed, with the prognosis particularly grim

Colonels third baseman Jerry Denny was the last player to take the field without a glove. He did not adopt the new style until 1894.

for Louisville. If the team's fate had ever been in question, a fire that destroyed Eclipse Park in August 1899 sealed it. Temporary bleachers were hurriedly put up, but delays in the insurance settlement set back the construction of a covered grandstand. When most of its late-season home games were moved to the road, the team became known as the Wanderers.

On December 6, 1899, Dreyfuss revealed that he and Pulliam had purchased a half-interest in the Pittsburgh Pirates. At the same time, he announced what was probably the most one-sided trade in the history of baseball, with Pittsburgh sending pitcher Jack Chesbro (6–9 in 1899), catcher Paddy Fox (.244), second baseman John O'Brien (.226), utility infielder Art Madison (.271), and $25,000 to Louisville, in exchange for Wagner (.336), Clarke (.342), third baseman Tommy Leach (.288), second baseman Claude Ritchey (.300), catcher Chief Zimmer (.298), first baseman Mike Kelley (.241), and pitchers Deacon Phillippe (21–17), Rube Waddell (7–3), and Walt Woods (9–13), along with backup players Tacks Latimer and Patsy Flaherty. With the demise of the Colonels, Chesbro ended up back in Pittsburgh, and Fox, O'Brien, and Madison never played in another major league game. Wagner, Clarke, and Waddell had Hall of Fame careers, while Phillippe, Leach, Ritchey, and Zimmer were genuine stars. The Louisville press somehow concluded that the Colonels had gotten the better of the deal.

Louisville's remaining directors set out for the annual December meeting of the league with a buyout price of $20,000 in mind. For its part, the NL wanted both to keep the price down and to drag out the process to prevent Ban Johnson's American League or the newest version of the American Association from taking over the four territories the NL was about to abandon. The ploy decided on was the establishment of a Circuit Reduction Committee that dragged its feet until March 9, 1900, adroitly sidestepping efforts by a group of Louisville businessmen to set up a new franchise by offering a berth in yet another rebirth of the AA, this time as an NL subsidiary. In the end, the worn down Louisville directors accepted a $10,000 buyout as part of the final reduction of the NL to eight teams.

LOUISVILLE COLONELS

Annual Standings and Managers

Year	Position	W	L	Pct.	GB	Managers
1892	Eleventh	30	47	.390	25½	Jack Chapman, Fred Pfeffer
	Ninth	33	42	.440	19½	Fred Pfeffer
1893	Eleventh	50	75	.400	34	Billy Barnie

1894	Twelfth	36	94	.277	54	Billy Barnie
1895	Twelfth	35	96	.267	52½	John McCloskey
1896	Twelfth	38	93	.290	53	John McCloskey, Bill McGunnigle
1897	Eleventh	52	78	.400	40	Jim Rogers, Fred Clarke
1898	Ninth	70	81	.464	33	Fred Clarke
1899	Ninth	75	77	.493	28	Fred Clarke

Milwaukee Grays

National League, 1878   **BALLPARK:** MILWAUKEE BASEBALL GROUNDS

RECORD: 15–45 (.250)

The Milwaukee Grays, unimaginatively named for the color of their uniforms, spent the 1877 season in a loose federation organized by the National League to prevent unallied teams from forming a rival circuit. Milwaukee won 19 and lost 13 in its intrafederation games, good for fourth place, and filled out its schedule against all manner of opponents, from college teams to NL clubs. The following season, Milwaukee joined the parent loop itself.

John L. Kaine, editor-in-chief of the Milwaukee *Sentinel* and president of the major league Grays, hired Jack Chapman to manage a mixture of NL veterans and newcomers that looked decent enough on paper but whose league-leading total of errors cost far too many games. Injuries only made matters worse. Starting catcher Charlie Bennett came down with a sore arm the first week of the season, and a foul ball split one of backup Bill Holbert's fingers. Attendance reflected the team's poor performance, and by June revenue had dropped so low that the Grays were in danger of folding. On July 2nd, William P. Rogers bought the team, but the purchase did little to alleviate the club's financial problems.

Bennett's return to the lineup did nothing to stop what eventually became a fifteen-game losing streak. So poor was the team's performance that the *Sentinel,* with Kaine unburdened of any responsibility for the franchise, stopped publishing accounts of its games, confining coverage to the final score.

Fiscally, matters became so dire that on August 31st the players staged a mini-strike because they had not received their paychecks. Persuaded to play the day's scheduled game against Indianapolis, the players had to wait several days more to be paid. At the annual NL meeting in December, infielder Johnny Peters, outfielder Mike Golden, and utility-man Joe Ellick brought formal charges of nonpayment against the organization. Rogers claimed that the amount owed to Peters was in dispute and that he had paid Golden and had a receipt to prove it. Nevertheless, Milwaukee was given twenty days to pay its debts, including those to its players, and withdraw honorably from the league. Rogers left the meeting and went to the opera. A few weeks later he dissolved the Grays.

MILWAUKEE GRAYS

Annual Standings and Manager

Year	Position	W	L	Pct.	GB	Manager
1878	Sixth	15	45	.250	26	Jack Chapman

Milwaukee Grays

Union Association, 1884   **BALLPARK:** WRIGHT STREET GROUNDS

RECORD: 8–4 (.667)

Possessors of the best won-lost percentage in major league history, the Grays began the 1884 season in the minor Northwestern League before moving into the Union Association in September as a replacement for the Wilmington Quicksteps.

The Northwestern League, a vital element in the National League's battle plan against the UA, began the 1884 season with representation in twelve cities ranging geographically from Minnesota to Indiana. Initially, Milwaukee team president John C. Iverson and his associates had a commitment from Albert Spalding not only to have the Chicago White Stockings play exhibition games in the Wisconsin city, but also to allow a twenty-five-cent admission charge instead of the established circuit's mandated fifty cents. In the event, the number of teams, the vast distances between cities, and predatory raids by the UA all took a toll on the Northwestern League. Throughout the season, franchise after franchise collapsed, finally forcing the creation of a reduced four-team schedule in August. Although the Grays were the best team in the league, they were even more impressive at the gate: Crowds of up to 2,000 showed

up on weekends , and a fifteen-game road trip late in May and early in June showed a profit of $1,800.

UA founder Henry V. Lucas took note of the team's box office success and opened negotiations for the Grays to join his circuit. Gray's manager Tom Loftus met with Lucas in St. Louis where they agreed that the Milwaukee Club would join the Unions as soon as Wilmington exited. That condition met, the Grays opened their brief major league tenure with flair. On September 27th, they shut out the visiting Washington Nationals 3–0 on one hit. The next day they shut out the Nationals again, this time by a score of 5–0 on Ed Cushman's no-hitter. About 4,000 fans showed up for what proved to be the club's final game, a 5–2 victory over Baltimore on October 12th.

The Grays' management, optimistic about 1885, made an appearance at the last two UA meetings, but when Lucas deserted to the NL and the Unions folded, the Milwaukee team returned to the minor leagues in the Western Association. No other major league team has topped Milwaukee's .667 won-lost percentage.

MILWAUKEE GRAYS

Annual Standings and Manager

Year	Position	W	L	Pct.	GB	Manager
1884	Partial Season	8	4	.667	—	Tom Loftus

Milwaukee Brewers

American Association, 1891   **BALLPARK:** MILWAUKEE ATHLETIC PARK

RECORD: 21–15 (.538)

As the second war between the National League and the American Association unfolded during the 1891 season, it became increasingly clear that the weaker

association was unable to compete and that some AA clubs would pay a stiff price. The Brewers replaced one of those victims late in the season, then joined the ranks of the victims themselves at the end of the season.

On August 10th, the Brewers were leading the minor Western League with a record of 59–35, when the team hierarchy was approached by the AA about replacing the Cincinnati Porkers. Five days later, manager Charlie Cushman was called off the field by club president H. E. Gillette; with his team leading the Sioux City Indians by a score of 4–1, Cushman returned to the game in the bottom of the seventh inning to announce that, because Milwaukee had just accepted membership in the AA, he was taking his players off the field and forfeiting the contest. Two days later, the Milwaukee management paid $12,000 to take over the Cincinnati franchise. Five Porkers joined the core of the Western League team when it opened its abbreviated AA season the next day by beating second-place St. Louis, 7–2.

The Brewers played their first 15 games on the road, winning only 5 of them. The club returned home on September 7th to beat Washington 30–3, the beginning of a stretch in which they won 17 of their last 22 games. Catcher Farmer Vaughn led the hitters with a .333 average after joining the team from Cin-

cinnati, but the fan favorite was left fielder Abner Dalrymple, who had been a rookie with the NL Grays in 1878 and who closed his major league career by batting in a different league but in the same city where it had begun.

Fans and management looked forward to a full season in 1892; Gillette even lured budding star Bill Dahlen from Chicago with a $3,500 contract. Plans had been underway since August, about the same time Milwaukee entered the AA, to have the NL absorb four of the league's franchises and buy out the rest. Chris Von der Ahe, the St. Louis owner, was charged with securing the buyout of the western clubs in the AA. Having first settled with Columbus, which became the sixth vote for consolidation, Von der Ahe ignored Milwaukee as irrelevant. Miffed, Gillette came to the joint NL-AA meeting in Indianapolis demanding $20,000. Soon realizing that he had little bargaining leverage and that the deal was done with or without him, Gillette quickly reduced his asking price to $13,000 finally settling for $6,000, and took his team into a reconstituted Western League for the 1892 season.

MILWAUKEE BREWERS

Annual Standings and Manager

Year	Position	W	L	Pct.	GB	Manager
1891	Partial Season	21	15	.583	—	Charlie Cushman

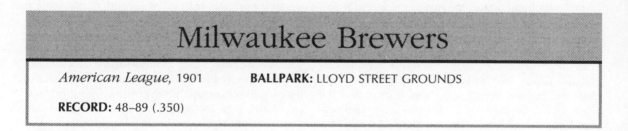

Milwaukee Brewers

American League, 1901   **BALLPARK:** LLOYD STREET GROUNDS

RECORD: 48–89 (.350)

In 1900, when the American League was still a minor circuit, the Brewers finished second in the standings, third in attendance (88,000), and second in profits ($6,700). A year later, as a major league franchise, the club could do nothing right, and became the first of two AL teams (the other being the 1969 Seattle Pilots) to last only one season.

Things got off to a bad start when 1900 manager Connie Mack departed for Philadelphia in preparation for the league's rise to major status; Mack was replaced by center fielder Hugh Duffy, who wasted

little time in criticizing owner Henry Killilea for not spending more to attract National League stars. Killilea's only response was the admission that he didn't have any money. In their very first game, the Brewers led the Tigers 13–4 going into the ninth inning, when Detroit erupted for ten runs.

Duffy's .308 average in the twilight of his Hall of Fame career was second on the team to first baseman John Anderson's .330. The ace of the pitching staff was supposed to have been nine-year NL veteran Pink Hawley, but he fell ill in midseason and Bill

Reidy emerged as the head of the staff with a 16–20 record.

By August, it was clear that Milwaukee's AL future was limited. Killilea was allowed to buy into the Boston franchise, and soon afterward league president Ban Johnson made clear his intention to invade the St. Louis market. After a last-place finish, the Brewers were indeed transferred to St. Louis, where they became the Browns.

MILWAUKEE BREWERS

Annual Standings and Manager

Year	Position	W	L	Pct.	GB	Manager
1901	Eighth	48	89	.350	35½	Hugh Duffy

Milwaukee Braves

National League, 1953–1965   **BALLPARK:** MILWAUKEE COUNTY STADIUM

RECORD: 1146–890 (.563)

The most successful National League franchise in this century, the Braves never played below .500 in their thirteen-year Milwaukee sojourn between Boston and Atlanta. From the perspective of baseball history, the team was even more noteworthy as the first franchise created in either league in fifty years and as the spur to the other organizational transfers that were to follow in the 1950s.

For better or worse, much of the fate of the Braves was tied up with the number thirteen. It was on November 13, 1952, for example, that Boston Braves majority stockholder Lou Perini announced that he and his brothers were ready to buy out the club's minority shareholders in order to assume total control. It was on March 13, 1953 that Perini made clear his buyout objective by announcing that the team would be moving to Milwaukee for that season. Exactly one month later, on April 13, 1953, Max Surkont pitched a three-hit shutout against the Reds in Cincinnati to inaugurate twentieth-century NL ball in Milwaukee. And the following year, on March 13, 1954, outfielder Bobby Thomson broke his ankle in a spring training slide—an injury that cleared the way for the insertion into the lineup of Hank Aaron, the star who was to dominate the team's thirteen years in Wisconsin.

The speed with which Perini managed to move the team from Boston to Milwaukee (and with which the league endorsed the shift only five days after receiving a formal request) was the result of several miscalculations, the organized fervor of Wisconsin public opinion, and major league baseball's disdain for Bill Veeck.

The first miscalculation was Perini's, when he publicly assured Milwaukee in 1952 that he would never use his territorial right to the area (through Boston's Milwaukee Brewers farm club affiliate in the American Association) to block the entry of a major league franchise. The second miscalculation was also Perini's, when he decided that the $6.6-million County Stadium built by Milwaukee for the 1953 season would—through attendance at Brewers games—provide a test ground for the city's readiness to support a major league team, and specifically his own Braves within a year or two. The third miscalculation was the league's, when it assumed that Perini's vague timetable for deciding about a shift by the Braves was the best way of dealing with the increasing impatience of Milwaukee for big league ball.

In fact, no sooner had Milwaukee digested the importance of its new playing facility and heard Perini's promise not to impede the entry of a major league team than a statewide campaign was launched for buying out his territorial prerogatives and covering his expenses for moving the Brewers out of the way to Toledo. Whipped on daily by the Milwaukee *Journal* and other newspapers, city politicians demanded that Perini's lease on County Sta-

Milwaukee fans, baseball's most conspicuous twenty-sixth player for many years, turn out to welcome the Braves to Wisconsin on April 8, 1953. *AP/Wide World Photos*

dium be rescinded, state legislators called for boycotts of Brewer games, and Wisconsin congressmen in Washington suggested that the time had come for another look at baseball's curious exemption from antitrust regulations.

Milwaukee also played its Veeck card. The St. Louis Browns' owner had approached Perini more than once with the idea of shifting his downtrodden franchise north, but the Braves' boss had dragged his feet on selling his territorial rights. Convinced that Perini's real intention was to move to Milwaukee himself, Veeck then switched his priorities to Baltimore. Knowing that Veeck would almost certainly be turned down by American League owners hostile to his rambunctious style, but that St. Louis was unable to keep supporting two teams, Milwaukee representatives made an end run by offering $4 million to the financially troubled Fred Saigh of the Cardinals. Alarmed by the maneuver, NL owners quickly decided that they would rather lose Boston than St. Louis. They encouraged Perini to move fast, while also making it clear to Saigh that he should accept another, lower offer for the Cardinals made by the Anheuser-Busch brewery.

The swift turn of events caught Boston by surprise, but not Milwaukee. While Braves Field was shuttered overnight and simply left to go to seed, County Stadium became the symbol of Milwaukee civic pride. With the season opener less than a month away, the park was besieged by tens of thousands of ticket requests, while politicians fell over each other to claim credit for having sponsored the county's financing of the facility. What remained a question amid all the euphoria was whether Milwaukee, having secured a franchise, had also gotten a major league team, since the Bostonians of 1952 had finished a miserable 33 games out of first place with a record of 64–89.

Those who wanted to see them found hopeful signs. Lefty Warren Spahn, a 20-game winner four times in Boston, anchored the pitching staff. Rookie Eddie Mathews's 25 home runs had set off predictions that he would be guarding third base for years to come. Moreover, during the winter of their metamorphosis from the Boston Braves to the Milwaukee Braves, the club had gotten potential slugger Joe Adcock from Cincinnati and frequent all-star Andy Pafko from the Dodgers. The rookies and untested players included shortstop Johnny Logan, catcher Del Crandall, and pitchers Lew Burdette, Johnny Antonelli, Bob Buhl, and Ernie Johnson.

If such a roster hardly promised a pennant winner, it was enough to get the team from spring training in Florida to Milwaukee, where it immediately picked up what was arguably the most important 26th player ever to support a major league club. With more than 12,000 people on hand to welcome the team at the train station and another 60,000 attending an official parade the next day, the die was cast for the love affair between the field and the grandstand that was to inspire the Braves for most of their years in Milwaukee. By May 20, in its thirteenth home game, the team would match the attendance (281,278) that it drew for its entire 77 games in Boston the previous year. The overall 1953 attendance of 1,826,397 would be topped in 1954 when the Braves became the first NL team to attract two million customers. On the road, hundreds, sometimes thousands, of boosters traveled with the team, ringing their cow bells and tooting their horns with a particular delight in enemy camps.

Between 1953 and 1957, the Braves' chief rival was the Brooklyn Dodgers' Boys of Summer team. To the expectations of no one but Milwaukee's own faithful, the Braves climbed from their seventh-place finish in 1952 to second in 1953, coming in 13 games behind Brooklyn but serving notice that they were on the rise. In 1954, both the Braves and Dodgers took a temporary back seat to the pennant-winning Giants, but the arrival of Aaron proved to be more than a consolation prize for a third-place finish. In 1955, the club found itself up against what was probably Brooklyn's strongest postwar team and again fell shy despite almost 100 home runs from Mathews, Aaron, and a first base combination of the injured Adcock and George Crowe.

Having established themselves as the league's chief pretender, the Braves began to show their impatience for greater rewards when, 46 games into the 1956 season, Fred Haney was named as manager in place of Charlie Grimm, who had piloted the team from Boston. Down to the final weekend, the Braves led the faltering and aging Dodgers by one game. They had gotten that far thanks to the usual charac-

ters—38 homers and 103 runs batted in from the recovered Adcock, 37 homers from Mathews, 26 from Aaron, 20 from Bobby Thomson, and a combined 57 wins from Spahn, Burdette, and Buhl. But with only three games separating them from the World Series, they lost two to St. Louis while the Dodgers were sweeping the Pirates in Brooklyn.

Two key additions were made to the Milwaukee lineup in 1957. Before Haney's insistence that the infield needed a take-charge second baseman with some offensive consistency, the front office acquired veteran Red Schoendienst from the Giants; Schoendienst went on to bat .310 and lead the league in hits. The second addition was outfielder Bob Hazle, a half-year wonder dubbed Hurricane for the sudden wind that blew in him and his astonishing .403 average after a midseason call-up. Together with Aaron's only officially acknowledged MVP season (.322, 44 homers, 132 RBIs), 32 homers from Mathews, 21 from Wes Covington, and 56 wins from the Spahn-Burdette-Buhl trio, Schoendienst and Hazle provided the fire to outdistance the Cardinals by 8 games and present Milwaukee with its first NL championship. With Burdette's three wins tying or breaking various records and Aaron's three homers and eleven hits spearheading the offense, the Braves then went on to defeat the Yankees four games to three in the World Series.

Except for the World Series finale, the same script was followed in 1958. No longer the youngest franchise in the league because of New York's departure for San Francisco and Brooklyn's for Los Angeles, the mellower, more experienced Braves won their second pennant with more of a show of solidity than flair, barely paying heed to the fact that just about every one of their key players except Spahn, Burdette, and Covington fell off statistically from the previous year. In the World Series, however, the team squandered a three-games-to-one edge over the Yankees, allowing New York to claim the championship.

Another page fell out of the script in 1959 when, despite strong comeback years from Aaron (39 homers, 123 RBIs) and Mathews (46 homers, 114 RBIs), the Braves found themselves in a dogfight with the two new California teams down to the final weekend of September. Playing without Schoendienst, who had been sidelined with tuberculosis for all but three at bats for the year, the team finally eked out a dead heat with the Dodgers, precipitating a best-of-three playoff. After losing the first game, Milwaukee went into the 9th inning of the second contest with a three-run lead, but then blew it and had to straggle into

Warren Spahn. *National Baseball Library, Cooperstown, NY*

overtime, until a 12th-inning throwing error by handyman infielder Felix Mantilla gave the Dodgers their first West Coast flag.

Having come so close to a third straight NL pennant, the Braves spent the winter of 1959–1960 generally ignoring widespread warnings about the team's widening holes up the middle and on the pitching staff behind the Spahn-Burdette-Buhl triumvirate. For the front office headed by general manager John McHale, the only conspicuous problem to be resolved was the mild managerial style of Haney. Haney was jettisoned for pepperpot Charlie Dressen. And in fact, with the only other significant change being the installation of rookie Chuck Cottier at second base for the physically questionable Schoen-

dienst, the team did wind up playing two games better in 1960 than it had in 1959. But once again the effort was good only for second place—this time behind the Pittsburgh Pirates.

For the last five years of their stay in Milwaukee, the Braves never won fewer than 83 games and generally finished with the kind of winning percentage that had previously guaranteed them at least a second-place finish. But the numbers were deceptive because of the 107 losses sustained by the Phillies in 1961 and the ineptitude of the expansion Mets and Astros which enabled almost all of the league's other teams to roll up a lot of victories. In spite of winning between 83 and 88 games every year between 1961 and 1965, therefore, the Braves never managed to finish higher than fourth.

The honeymoon between the team and the Milwaukee community started to end around the same time that the Braves began to realize that not every October would be spent playing the Yankees in the World Series. In particular, two latent issues that had been smoothed over during the halcyon years came to the fore with increasingly bitter stress, especially in the writings of influential Milwaukee *Journal*

Footnote Player: Hitting guru Charlie Lau was evidently only at the beginning of his offensive education when he played for the Braves in 1960 and part of 1961. In only occasional duty, he batted .189 in 1960 and .204 in 1961, before being traded to the Orioles.

sportswriter Russ Lynch. The first had to do with the fact that Perini, for all his local honors for having brought the franchise to Milwaukee, had remained very much an absentee owner, continuing to reside near his other business interests in Massachusetts. For critics like Lynch, this made it impossible to completely trust the team owner and in fact perpetuated a threat that, for the sake of the bottom line, he might one day shift the club out of Milwaukee as abruptly as he had moved it in. In this context, Lynch and others noted the growing role played by television in the ledgers of a baseball franchise and Milwaukee's scant potential in this area. Another sore point, made more and more important in the push to get Perini either to sell the team to local interests or move his base of operations to Wisconsin, was the team's policy of forbidding fans to bring beer into County Stadium, forcing them to purchase it from ballpark concessionaires. The issue was aired to full censorious effect and, together with the team's relatively more humdrum play on the field, lessened enthusiasm for the Braves at the turnstiles.

Worn down by all the criticism and aware that no other member of his family was as enthusiastic as he was about the franchise, Perini finally satisfied his critics in 1962 by selling the Braves to a joint Milwaukee-Chicago syndicate headed by Illinois insurance broker Bill Bartholomay. But not even the comparatively local ownership could reverse the declining fortunes of the team on the field or at the gate. Although Aaron continued to amass the numbers that would one day get him to the Hall of Fame and put him ahead of Babe Ruth on the all-time home run list, Mathews, Spahn, Adcock, and Burdette, were clearly on the downside of their major league careers. The main bright spots during the rest of the team's tenure in Milwaukee were catcher Joe Torre and pitcher Tony Cloninger. Otherwise, the team was overladen with journeymen who could hit but couldn't field, could field but couldn't hit, or could throw a lot of innings but not especially brilliant ones.

With the attendance falling as rapidly as the batting averages of some of the veterans, it did not come

Although overshadowed throughout his career by Hank Aaron and Eddie Mathews, there were few more prodigious home run hitters in the '50s and '60s than Joe Adcock. Among his 336 career blasts were four in one game against the Dodgers, the first ball ever hit completely over the left field grandstand of Ebbets Field, and the first ball ever hit to the left-center field bleachers in the Polo Grounds (an estimated distance of 465 feet). In the July 31, 1954 game in which he belted his four homers, he also clouted a double to set the record for the most total bases (18) in a major league game. Adcock will also always be remembered for hitting the "non-homer" that ended Harvey Haddix's 12-inning perfect game on May 26, 1959; when he passed Aaron on the bases, the hit was ruled a double.

as a complete shock in 1964 when the Bartholomay group announced that it had accepted an offer to move to Atlanta for the 1965 season. Aside from providing an extremely low-cost playing facility, Atlanta had the sort of attractive television market potential that journalist Lynch and others had been warning about for years. But, for one last time, a Braves owner underestimated Milwaukee public opinion. Led by a group headed by future AL Milwaukee Brewers president Bud Selig, city interests sued Bartholomay and the NL for violating stadium lease agreements and for ignoring alternative local buyers for the franchise. Although the league would eventually prevail in the suits (through attorney and future commissioner Bowie Kuhn), the Braves were forced to play a lame duck season in Milwaukee in 1965. With disillusion and resentment running high in the city, many of the games drew fewer than a thousand people. The attendance for the final NL game in County Stadium on September 22, 1965—an 11-inning 7–6 loss to the Dodgers—was 12,577, about the same number that had welcomed the first Braves team at the Milwaukee train station in 1953.

MILWAUKEE BRAVES

Annual Standings and Managers

Year	Position	W	L	Pct.	GB	Managers
1953	Second	92	62	.597	13	Charlie Grimm
1954	Third	89	65	.578	8	Charlie Grimm
1955	Second	85	69	.552	13½	Charlie Grimm
1956	Second	92	62	.597	1	Charlie Grimm, Fred Haney

1957	First	95	59	.617	+8	Fred Haney
1958	First	92	62	.597	+8	Fred Haney
1959	Second	86	70	.551	2	Fred Haney
1960	Second	88	66	.571	7	Charlie Grimm
1961	Fourth	83	71	.539	10	Charlie Grimm, Birdie Tebbetts
1962	Fifth	86	76	.531	15½	Birdie Tebbetts
1963	Sixth	84	78	.519	15	Bobby Bragan
1964	Fifth	88	74	.543	5	Bobby Bragan
1965	Fifth	86	76	.531	11	Bobby Bragan

Postseason Play

| WS | 4–3 versus New York | 1957 |
| | 3–4 versus New York | 1958 |

Milwaukee Brewers

American League,
1970–Present

BALLPARK: MILWAUKEE COUNTY STADIUM

RECORD: 1791–1870 (.489)

Officially the successors to the bankrupt Seattle Pilots, the Brewers entered the American League as the spiritual heirs of the National League Braves, who had deserted Milwaukee after the 1965 season. A product of local boosterism, the franchise has been a model of stability from the start—having boasted only one chief executive (Bud Selig) and keeping together key elements of its 1982 flag winner (Robin Yount, Paul Molitor, Jim Gantner) for more than a decade and a half. On the other hand, the organization never found its footing in developing pitchers—or in keeping healthy the few hurlers that it has nurtured through its minor league system.

Even before the Braves had left, Selig, an automobile dealer, had put together a civic association committed to restoring Milwaukee to the big leagues. The group was instrumental in getting the White Sox to play twenty-one home games at County Stadium in 1968 and 1969, and big turnouts encouraged speculation that Chicago would move its team to Wisconsin. But AL disapproval and a new White Sox ownership killed that idea, and the city lost out again in the 1969 expansion of both leagues. It was only when one of the expansion teams, the Pilots, flopped that Selig and his associates (among them, Robert Uihlein of the Schlitz Breweries, Ralph Evinrude of

the outboard motor company, and meatpacker Oscar Mayer) gained another opening to offer $10.8 million for a franchise. While the league accepted the tender during the 1969 World Series, legal delays kept the deal up in the air until March 31st of the following year.

On April 7, 1970, the new Brewers took the field with their Milwaukee lettering barely covering the hastily removed Seattle logo; their performance was as ragged as their appearance, going down to California's Andy Messersmith, 12–0. The entire offense for the first year was provided by third baseman Tommy Harper, who became the second 30-30 player in history with 31 homers and 38 steals. The club's struggle to a fourth-place tie was as high as it would get until 1978.

Selig tried to change things by replacing general manager Marvin Milkes (a holdover from Seattle) with Frank Lane; if nothing else, Lane's effort to overhaul the team was thorough. By opening day of 1972, only pitchers Skip Lockwood and Ken Sanders had survived from the first-year club. The general manager's biggest deal was a ten-player swap with the Red Sox in October 1971 that packaged Harper and pitchers Matty Pattin and Lew Krausse among others, for first baseman George Scott and righthander

Robin Yount's 3,000th hit. *Courtesy of the Milwaukee Brewers*

Hank Aaron and catcher Phil Roof were the only ex-Milwaukee Braves who also played for the Brewers.

In 1973, the Brewers staged what might have been the most insensitive promotion in baseball history. Called the Chinese Aviator Look-Alike Contest, it was spurred by Detroit manager Billy Martin's equally crass crack that "if the Brewers can win with what they've got, I'm a Chinese aviator."

Jim Lonborg. A couple of months later, he picked up starter Jim Colborn from the Cubs for outfielder Jose Cardenal. Although both trades paid dividends a season later, they could not help Bristol hang on to his job beyond the opening month of the 1972 campaign when he was replaced by Del Crandall. Lane himself only lasted through the year before being succeeded by Jim Wilson. In addition to their mediocrity, the Brewers played the season under the additional handicap off having been moved from the Western to the superior Eastern division of the league because of the transfer of the Washington franchise to Texas.

Aided by an offseason Wilson trade that had brought Don Money in as the regular third baseman, the Brewers improved slightly in 1973, boasting several franchise firsts: Scott became the club's first 100-

RBI man, outfielder Dave May its first .300 hitter, and Colborn its first 20-game winner. The first of the 1982 champions to arrive on the scene was the 18-year-old Yount, who broke in at shortstop in 1974. The righthand-hitting Yount, who would win MVP awards in both 1982 and 1989, eventually became the franchise player, first as an infielder and then as a center fielder. In 1978, however, he had become so discouraged by the futility of the team that he retired, at age 22, to play professional golf. He returned only when Molitor seemed on the verge of taking over his position.

Molitor was to spend his years in Milwaukee

Milwaukee is the only AL club to produce back-to-back MVPs and Cy Young winners in the same years. Reliever Rollie Fingers took both honors in 1981, and Robin Yount (MVP) and Pete Vuckovich (Cy Young) followed in 1982.

being shifted from position to position to accommodate the Brewers' various needs and his own injuries. The team's shortstop while Yount decided between baseball and golf, he became the second baseman until Gantner was ready for full-time duty in 1980. At other points, he was the team's regular center fielder, right fielder, third baseman, first baseman, and designated hitter. With almost equal regularity, however, he ended up on the disabled list for lengthy stays.

Milwaukee's losing ways in 1975 (the team won only 25 of its last 84 games) erupted into a major confrontation between manager Crandall and several players. Second baseman Pedro Garcia and Crandall clashed all season long, most significantly when the infielder stood on second base during batting practice and refused to pick up ground balls. In a follow-up incident with racial overtones, a fellow Puerto Rican, outfielder Sixto Lezcano, rebelled after Garcia was directed to apologize both to the team and to the manager. In late July, a team meeting was called to let players vent their grievances, but, when word leaked to the manager that first baseman Scott had told his teammates that the Brewers were "the laughingstock of baseball," a bad situation only grew worse. Selig and new GM Jim Baumer fired Crandall at the end of the season, recruiting Cincinnati coach Alex Grammas as his successor.

Grammas's disciplinary solution of clean-shaven, short-haired players, failed to ease the team's problems. On the field, the 1976 season got off on a sour note when, in the second game, Money hit a bottom-of-the-ninth grand slam to beat the Yankees 10–9 only to have it invalidated because Yankee first baseman Chris Chambliss had requested time from umpire Jim McKeon. Money returned to the plate and made out; the Brewers lost. The season ended equally sourly in an incident involving home run king Hank Aaron, who had been acquired in 1975 to provide additional punch to the lineup and additional fans in the stadium. While wearing a Brewer uniform, Aaron had already moved past Babe Ruth on the all-time RBI list, and wanted to pass The Bambino in runs scored, as well. Grammas added insen-

sitivity to the list of charges against him when he removed the slugger for a pinch-runner after a single in his last major league at bat. The pilot's intention had been to facilitate an ovation for Aaron as he left the field; the result was that the home run king was miffed at losing the chance to break a tie with Ruth for second place in career runs scored as pinch-runner Gantner crossed the plate a few minutes later.

During the season, Baumer had promised wholesale changes, and he delivered. On one day, December 6th, he made what was possibly the franchise's worst trade, sending Colborn and catcher Darrell Porter to the Royals for outfielder Jim Wohlford and DH Jamie Quirk, and one of its best, getting first baseman Cecil Cooper from Boston for Scott and outfielder Bernie Carbo. In addition, Selig signed free agent third baseman Sal Bando.

Early in the season, the club sent promising outfielder Danny Thomas, a first-round draft pick in 1972, back to the minors in a move that would end tragically three years later. Thomas was a member of The World Wide Church of God and a devout observer of the sect's prohibition against any kind of labor between sundown Friday and sundown Saturday. Unwilling to keep a six-day-a-week outfielder, the Brewers demoted him, even though he had hit .276 in 32 games in 1976 and was batting .271 in the new campaign. Thomas eventually left baseball and, in 1980, died a suicide in an Alabama jail cell while awaiting trial on a rape charge.

By the end of the season, in which only the presence of the expansion Blue Jays spared the Brewers a second consecutive cellar finish, Grammas was talking to neither the players nor Baumer. On November 19th, in one dramatic sweep, Selig got rid of the manager, the general manager, and several coaches and front-office staffers. The wholesale firing led to a Baltimore connection, when new GM Harry Dalton recruited several former associates with the Orioles; Dalton's staff included ex-Oriole pitching coach George Bamberger as manager and scouting director Ray Pointevint. Before Dalton and Pointevint had arrived, the Brewers had relied heavily on the Major League Scouting Bureau, but the Dalton Gang, as it came to be known, developed an internal scouting network that grew to thirty in number. With the exception of Bamberger, whose health forced him to leave twice, the front office team of former Oriole employees would remain largely intact through 1991.

Dalton developed close ties with baseball reporters across the country; one of these relationships, with Tom Boswell of the Washington *Post*, caused the general manager considerable grief when, on

March 6, 1981, the newsman printed what Dalton had considered an off-the-record dissident opinion of management's position in the impending players' strike. (The nationally syndicated Boswell quoted the Milwaukee official: "I hope management is really looking for a compromise and not a victory, but I'm not certain that's the case. The Players Association is genuinely looking for a compromise if we'll just give them something they can accept without losing too much face.") While Dalton's opinion was an informed one because he had served on a joint player-management committee to explore solutions to the impasse over how to compensate teams for lost free agents, it also violated a gag rule imposed on baseball executives. The violation almost cost him $50,000, which would have been the largest fine ever imposed on a non-owner; it was canceled when the strike ended.

Dalton's most significant contribution to the Brewers was a December 1980 trade that brought relief specialist Rollie Fingers, starter Pete Vuckovich, and catcher Ted Simmons from the Cardinals. Fingers and Vuckovich won back-to-back Cy Young Awards in 1981 and 1982.

With Gorman Thomas leading the AL with 45 homers, Bamberger took a power-packed Brewer team to second place in 1979. Unfortunately, the manger's heart attack in spring training the following year kept him out of action until June and forced his retirement before the season was over. Coach Buck Rodgers filled in while Bamberger recuperated, then took over on his own in September. In 1980, outfielder Ben Oglivie led the league with 41 homers, Thomas hit 38, Cooper 25 and an AL-leading 122 RBIs, and Yount 23 in an attack that produced 203 round trippers. The Fingers-Simmons trade made it possible for Milwaukee to win the second-half championship in the split season of 1981, only to lose the AL East playoff to New York, three games to two. Rodgers, however, never exerted the authority Bamberger had shown. A slow start in 1981 had produced a clubhouse meeting, called by Dalton so that he could lecture his players on their nocturnal habits and their inattention to matters such as running out ground balls. A second meeting called by team captain Bando, whom many saw as the manager-in-waiting, allowed Rodgers's detractors to accuse the pilot of every sin that had been laid on Crandall and Grammas—childish dress codes, remoteness from the players, and overmanaging, among others. Rodgers confronted his accusers (chief among them were Simmons, Vuckovich, Thomas, and pitcher Mike Caldwell) at yet a third meeting, only to have every-

one deny responsibility for the daily newspaper stories detailing his supposed inadequacies. The manager's Milwaukee career ended in 1982 after he brought Caldwell in to protect a one-run lead in the ninth inning of a game against the Seattle Mariners; the starter gave up a game-tying hit, the Brewers lost the game, and Fingers, who had been warming up and who had expected to get the call from the bullpen, exploded. Dalton offered the job first to Bando, who was serving as a front-office assistant after his retirement as a player; when Bando declined, the post went to Harvey Kuenn.

The Brewers' batting coach since 1971, Kuenn had survived the wholesale firings of 1977; more significant, he had also survived quadruple bypass surgery in 1976, kidney failure that caused him to lose fifty pounds in 1977, and, in 1980, a leg amputation necessitated by blood clots. He accepted Dalton's offer of the job on an interim basis and proceeded to indulge his fondness for elaborate charts detailing the location of every fair ball hit by every opposing batter against every Brewers pitcher. These he posted on the dugout wall where they were largely ignored by the players, who, instead of studying the charts, took Kuenn's advice to have fun. Harvey's Wall-bangers, the successors to Bambi's Bombers of 1980, banged 216 home runs. Thomas tied for the AL lead with 39, while Ogilvie (34), Cooper (32), Yount (29), and Simmons (23) all reached 20 and Molitor, with 19, just missed. The late-season acquisition of Don Sutton helped make up for the September loss of Fingers to a torn muscle and fend off a last-minute rush by the Orioles.

AL East champions by only one game, the Brewers defeated the California Angels in the LCS, three games to two. Both the pitching (a team ERA of 4.19) and the hitting (a .219 average) were ragged, and the absence of Fingers hurt not only in the playoffs but also in the World Series, which Milwaukee dropped to St. Louis in seven games. Molitor had 5 hits in the first game, a Series record, and Yount had two 4-hit games, but only Caldwell pitched effectively.

In 1983, the Brewers reached two million in paid attendance for the only time in team history, but the club the fans came to see was not the same one that had knocked down fences the year before. Fingers developed bone chips in his elbow and sat out the entire season, Vuckovich tore his rotator cuff and appeared in only three games, the power shut down, and Kuenn's interim job ended with a fifth-place finish. An interlude under Rene Lachemann led to a last-place standing in 1984. Vuckovich missed the entire season after an operation to remove a bone spur; Molitor missed all but thirteen games with a torn muscle, and back problems cost the team Fingers for the final two months.

The most that could be said for the managerial tenure of Tom Trebelhorn was that the Brewers kept their heads above water, and even vaguely began to resemble a contender with third-place finishes in 1987 and 1988. An advocate of computer storage of information about players and pitcher-batter matchups, Trebelhorn got an opportunity to manage only because of a near-tragic accident at the 1986 spring training camp in Chandler, Arizona, when a gas heater exploded, severely burning coaches Tony Muser, Herm Starrette, and Larry Haney. Trebelhorn, slated to manage in the minors that year, was promoted to third base coach because of Muser's injuries and was in the right place when Bamberger, called out of retirement for a second stint, quit for good in September.

Injuries continued to haunt the team. Gantner, who had become one of the best second basemen in the AL, missed parts of 1987, 1989, and 1990; slugging outfielder Rob Deer went down in 1988 and 1989; southpaw Teddy Higuera, who had won 20 games in 1986, spent time on the DL in 1989, 1990, 1991, and 1992; and ace reliever Dan Plesac added his name to the list in 1991. For his part, Dalton was able to retain the nucleus of the team by re-signing free agents Molitor and Gantner in 1988 and Yount in 1989. But what had been intended as a surge based on farm club prospects, fizzled into a collection of underachieving and injury-prone infielders and pitchers.

Over the years, Selig bought up chunks of stock from the partners who had become disillusioned by the club's play and pessimistic that the franchise would ever have the financial resources to become an AL power. One particular sore point was the league's refusal to table serious talks about sharing revenues from superstation TV coverage, such as that provided by the nearby WGN in Chicago. Although revenue sharing was also one of his battle horses, Selig did not allow the issue to divert him from acquiring a majority interest in the franchise. In late 1991, the owner engineered his second mass overhaul, putting Dalton in charge of vaguely defined special projects and removing Trebelhorn altogether. Bando was promoted to general manager, with Phil

Garner coming in as manager. Bando's choice of Garner raised hackles in more than one quarter because of earlier indications that Trebelhorn's successor would be hitting coach Don Baylor. Because Garner had no more experience than Baylor for the post, the selection stirred charges that blacks such as the hitting coach were still being ignored routinely for managerial positions. Bando didn't help matters with some ambiguous remarks that suggested that he did indeed have a double standard on minor league experience where black and white candidates were concerned.

If nothing else, Garner improved Bando's public relations posture by leading the team to its most wins in ten years. Even more than Trebelhorn, he stressed a running game, with shortstop Pat Listach swiping 54 bases, outfielder Darryl Hamilton 41, and the veteran Molitor 31. Listach's .290 average and nimble defense were other ingredients that enabled him to take Rookie of the Year honors. The biggest what-if of the season centered around righthander Cal Eldred, who was called up in midseason and dominated AL batters for an 11–2, 1.79 ERA record. Garner was the first to admit that if he had been less hasty in farming out Eldred in spring training, the club might have overtaken Toronto for the division title. The mound staff also got 17 victories from Jaime Navarro and 16 from Chris Bosio. Aside from the running, the club's biggest offensive headline came on September 9, when Yount cracked out his 3,000th hit.

Selig also had plenty to keep him busy off the field in 1992. After several years of on-and-off discussions, he announced agreement on construction of a new stadium for the 1995 season. Even those negotiations with the county, however, were a picnic compared to his maneuvers in baseball's back rooms, first over the feasibility of working for a lockout of the players in 1993 as the prelude to new contract talks, then as the co-leader with Chicago's Jerry Reinsdorf of the hard-line ownership bloc that forced the resignation of Commissioner Fay Vincent. Shortly after Vincent stepped down, the Milwaukee owner himself was named pro tem commissioner. In that role, he was given a lot of the blame for the

On April 15, 1987, southpaw Juan Nieves hurled the franchise's only no-hitter, a 7–0 blanking of Baltimore.

Bob Uecker has kept his job as a Milwaukee TV broadcaster despite success as an author and sitcom actor. Among the ex-catcher's most often quoted lines is his solution to catching the knuckleball: "You wait until it stops rolling, then you pick it up."

inability of the owners to come to authoritative decisions on such matters as the racist remarks attributed to Cincinnati's Marge Schott.

While Selig was busy telling everyone that the future of the game would depend on boardroom events in 1993, the immediate future of the Brewers became clouded when Molitor took a free agency offer from the Blue Jays and Bosio chose to go to the Mariners. Gantner's service with the club also ended in 1992. The organization's biggest off-season pickups were outfielders Kevin Reimer and Tom Brunansky.

MILWAUKEE BREWERS

Annual Standings and Managers

Year	Position	W	L	Pct.	GB	Managers
1970	Fourth*	65	97	.401	33	Dave Bristol
1971	Sixth	69	92	.429	32	Dave Bristol
1972	Sixth	65	91	.417	21	Dave Bristol, Del Crandall
1973	Fifth	74	88	.457	23	Del Crandall
1974	Fifth	76	86	.469	15	Del Crandall
1975	Fifth	68	94	.420	28	Del Crandall
1976	Sixth	66	95	.410	32	Alex Grammas
1977	Sixth	67	95	.414	33	Alex Grammas
1978	Third	93	69	.574	6½	George Bamberger
1979	Second	95	66	.590	8	George Bamberger
1980	Third	86	76	.531	17	George Bamberger, Buck Rodgers
1981	Third	31	25	.554	3	Buck Rodgers
	First	31	22	.585	+1½	Buck Rodgers
1982	First	95	67	.586	+1	Buck Rodgers, Harvey Kuenn
1983	Fifth	87	75	.537	11	Harvey Kuenn
1984	Seventh	67	94	.416	36½	Rene Lachemann
1985	Sixth	71	90	.441	28	George Bamberger
1986	Sixth	77	84	.478	18	George Bamberger, Tom Trebelhorn
1987	Third	91	71	.562	7	Tom Trebelhorn
1988	Third*	87	75	.537	2	Tom Trebelhorn
1989	Fourth	81	81	.500	8	Tom Trebelhorn
1990	Sixth	74	88	.457	14	Tom Trebelhorn
1991	Fourth	83	79	.512	8	Tom Trebelhorn
1992	Second	92	70	.568	4	Phil Garner

*Tie

Postseason Play

LCS	3–2 versus California	1982	WS	3–4 versus St. Louis	1982

Minnesota Twins

American League,
1961–Present

RECORD: 2593–2520 (.507)

BALLPARKS: METROPOLITAN STADIUM (1961–1981)
HUBERT H. HUMPHREY METRODOME
(1982–Present)

Like their original owner, the erratic and often neanderthal Calvin Griffith, the Twins have seldom been a model of big league orthodoxy, and their successes have usually been as surprising as their failures.

Rod Carew slides safely across the plate with his record-tying seventh steal of home during the 1969 season. He actually had an eighth theft that year that was missed by an umpire. *UPI/Bettmann Newsphotos*

Only in the 1970s did the club seem anchored to a role—that of a respectable but uninspired also-ran; otherwise, it has shot back and forth from the top to the bottom of the Western Division of the American League practically from one year to the next. The franchise's one constant has been the ability to produce hitters from its farm system as regularly as the St. Louis Cardinals did between the 1930s and 1960s. Between 1964 and 1978 alone, thanks to Tony Oliva and Rod Carew, the team claimed ten batting titles.

The luring of Griffith's Washington Senators to Minneapolis-St. Paul after the 1960 season climaxed years of lobbying by Minnesota officials to gain a major league team. The final negotiations were especially delicate because of fears that any leaks about moving out of the nation's capital would incite Congress to lift baseball's exemption from antitrust laws; for the same reason, the majority of other AL owners were known to be opposed to the abandonment of the Washington market. What ultimately rescued

At the league meeting that approved Washington's move to Minnesota, Baltimore reversed its initially positive vote with the argument that it hadn't fully understood the significance of the ballot. The change of mind, which would have kept the franchise in Washington, was ruled inadmissible by AL President Joe Cronin, who was Calvin Griffith's brother-in-law.

both Griffith and Minnesota was the league's desire to expand from eight to ten teams. With the crucial help of Chicago White Sox owner Bill Veeck, Griffith persuaded the league that relocating his franchise to Minnesota would not only save his family ownership financially after several losing years in Washington, but also open the way for an expansion team in the capital that would satisfy would-be congressional investigators and give fans a new start. The AL owners bought the idea, accepting the California

Angels and the second version of the Senators for the 1961 season.

Griffith was welcomed as a hero when he moved his organization into Metropolitan Stadium in the Minneapolis suburb of Bloomington. Advance ticket sales for the 1961 season ran ahead of total attendance figures for his final years in Washington, and local builders made good on guarantees to have the ballpark's capacity raised from 25,000 to 30,000 by opening day. Aside from sluggers Harmon Killebrew and Bob Allison, who had combined for 46 homers in their final year in Washington, the team's biggest jewels were shortstop Zoilo Versalles, catcher Earl Battey, and pitchers Camilo Pascual, Jim Kaat, and Pedro Ramos.

Ramos took the mound for the club's first game at Yankee Stadium on April 12th and proceeded to shut out New York by a 6–0 margin. The inaugural game was deceptive in more ways than one: the club ended up a disappointing seventh, 38 games behind the pennant-winning Yankees, and Ramos himself recorded 20 losses to lead the league. On the other hand, first baseman Killebrew produced the second of the eight 40-plus-homer years that would get him elected to the Hall of Fame in 1984 and Allison hit 29 homers and drove in 105 runs.

In moving to Bloomington, the Twins took along Cookie Lavagetto, who had been managing the Senators since 1957. But Lavagetto had been ailing from ulcers for some time, and his inability to get the team off on a winning track before the new, enthusiastic throngs in Minnesota only aggravated his condition. On June 6th, following a fight in the dugout between Allison and Pascual, Griffith announced that the manager was going to take a few days of "rest" and be replaced on an interim basis by coach Sam Mele. A week later, Lavagetto came back, but only long enough to get fired on the grounds that he had lost control of the club. Mele assumed command on a permanent basis.

It only took until 1962 for the Twins to show their penchant for careening up and down in the AL standings. With Pascual (20 wins) and Kaat (18) leading the pitchers and Killebrew leading the league in both homers and RBIs, Minnesota kept pace with the Yankees most of the year, closing five games off the pace. The season also saw southpaw Jack Kralick

In 8,147 official at bats over twenty-two years, Harmon Killebrew never bunted for a sacrifice.

fashion the franchise's first no-hitter against Kansas City. Curveballing Pascual's 20-win record prompted a postseason contract squabble with Griffith that was to become an annual winter event and that familiarized the Minnesota public with the owner's well-earned reputation as a penny-pincher. Following a disastrous 1964 season, with attendance down some 200,000 for the sixth-place club, Griffith went so far as to cut Mele's salary as a condition for his return as manager. Mele agreed to the terms and was at the helm when the team popped right back up in the standings to win its first AL pennant.

The 1965 triumph, which effectively put an end to the Yankees' postwar dominance of the league, was cobbled together from several things: Oliva's second straight batting title; Versalles's MVP season (among other things, he led the league in both total bases and runs scored); more than 20 homers each from Killebrew, Allison, Don Mincher, and Jimmy Hall; the only 20-win season put together by Mudcat Grant; and the tireless relief work of NL veterans Al Worthington and Johnny Klippstein. When Griffith wasn't counting his victories, he was counting the profits from a gate that totalled 1,463,258.

In the World Series against the heavily favored Dodgers, the Twins almost did the unthinkable when they beat Los Angeles aces Don Drysdale and Sandy Koufax in the first two games, but then had to settle for a valiant defeat in seven games, mainly because Koufax came back to shut them out twice.

The mid-1960s saw frictions involving coach Billy Martin, particularly with traveling secretary Howard Fox and pitching instructor Johnny Sain. The Fox episode, which ended with punches exchanged in a hotel lobby, was a harbinger of several things to come, affecting both Martin's entire coaching and managerial career and decisions later taken by the Minnesota franchise. Although nominally only a traveling secretary, Fox was known to "report" messages to managers, coaches, and players from Griffith that were frequently of his own interpretation, if not outright invention; in the same way, he had the owner's ear for what went on—or what he said had gone on—in the clubhouse or during team flights. As the years went on, Griffith leaned more heavily on Fox for baseball and business advice (even when he wasn't altogether aware that he was doing so).

By the end of the 1967 season, the focus of Fox's reports to Griffith was not Mele, but Cal Ermer, who had been called in as manager after the team had split its first 50 games of the year. With rookie Rod Carew and NL acquisition Cesar Tovar setting the table for power hitters Killebrew and Allison, and with Dean Chance bearing down on a 20-win season, the Twins climbed from sixth place to first under Ermer, and went into the final weekend of the season needing a single victory to secure their second pennant in three years. They didn't get it; led by the fierce clutch hitting of Carl Yastrzemski, the Red Sox thumped Chance, Kaat, and knuckleball reliever Ron Kline to sneak away with the flag. The main consolation for the bitter defeat was the arrival of Carew, who over nineteen years would win seven batting titles and compile a lifetime .328 average. The lefty slap hitter became the byword for hitting proficiency in the 1970s and early 1980s, with his crouched, open stance serving as an influence on hitting coaches as much as players. In his early years, he was also a gifted runner, as evidenced by his record-tying seven steals of home in 1969 (he lost an eighth, successful steal of the plate when a bowled over umpire failed to see that he had not been tagged by the catcher). Carew was elected to the Hall of fame in 1991.

Calvin and Clark Griffith. *National Baseball Library, Cooperstown, NY*

Griffith had several reasons for wanting to forget 1968, about the least of which was another typical club tumble down to seventh. In the season of the dead ball in which even vaunted hitters like Oliva and Carew could bat no higher than .289 and .273,

respectively, Griffith's biggest problem was with his son Clark, who declared little enthusiasm for entering the family business with Minnesota's Charlotte farm club and made it clear that he thought that the organization required some of his Dartmouth-instilled marketing techniques if it was going to flourish. The rift made Calvin dig in even deeper in his traditional approach to the game, to the point that he took delight in voting against recommendations put forth by his son at family-controlled board sessions. The conflict also exacerbated tensions between the team owner and his wife Natalie, who had always resented the move from Washington because it deprived her of the capital's social and cultural life. About the only one who didn't mourn the clash was Griffith's sister Thelma Haynes, who had feared that Clark's ascendancy would deny her own son Bruce an effective voice in the organization. (Under the terms of the legacy left by the late Clark Griffith, Calvin and his son controlled 26 percent of the franchise, with Haynes and her family another 26 percent. The biggest minority shareholder was H. Gabriel Murphy, who owned 43 percent).

Deciding after the club's seventh-place finish that Ermer was too low-key in his handling of players, Griffith turned to Martin for the 1969 season. The appointment was, in fact, something of a referendum result, with fans bombarding the front office during the 1968 season with letters and phone calls demanding the promotion of the volatile coach; most of the sportswriters in Minneapolis and St. Paul pressed for the same end.

Between the lines, Martin didn't disappoint, steering the club through its first year of divisional play to a relatively easy title over runner-up Oakland. Rebounding from the year of the dead ball, Carew hit .322 for a batting crown, Killebrew took MVP honors with his AL-leading 49 homers and 140 RBIs, Oliva batted .309 with 24 homers and 101 RBIs, and Rich Reese took over first base with a .322 mark.

Asked about his wife's laments that she missed the social and cultural life of Washington in Minnesota, Calvin Griffith told *Sports Illustrated* in 1974: "I like to look at magazines, read a few stories, read the captions. I don't like to socialize too much. You run into people who are not athletic-minded. They're bookworms or symphony patrons, and that's all they want to talk about." The Griffiths eventually separated.

The pitching staff was led by Jim Perry and Dave Boswell, both of whom won 20, and relief ace Ron Perranoski, who won 9 and saved another 31. Off the field, however, Griffith didn't have to wait until the Twins were swept in three games by Baltimore in the League Championship Series to declare that the season was one of his worst since leaving Washington.

The owner's first complaint was with former staff aces Chance and Kaat, who both held out during spring training, maintaining that "Calvin throws quarters around like manhole covers"; when the contracts were finally settled, Chance went down with a sore pitching arm that left him sidelined for a good part of the season and Kaat registered barely .500 numbers. Already irritated that he had been steamrollered into hiring Martin (although admitting that he would have done so anyway), Griffith seethed whenever the manager staged one of his noted scenes with umpires, convinced that their aim was as much to win personal headlines as some argument related to the game. Then, on August 7th, Martin got all the headlines that he would need when he punched out pitcher Boswell during a brawl in a Detroit bar. The most accepted version of the episode was that Martin had intervened in a fight between Boswell and Allison, had been struck unintentionally, then lost his head and worked over the pitcher while the latter was being held by two other bar patrons. For public consumption, Griffith backed Martin's demand that Boswell be fined for starting the trouble; privately, he told Fox and others that Martin had broken one of his most basic club rules—that managers should never drink in the same bars with players. Following the saloon fight, Griffith and Fox began sounding out Kaat, Killebrew, and other veterans for further compromising information that would make it easier for him to get rid of Martin after the season.

Still, even after the LCS loss, Griffith showed reluctance to pull the trigger, mainly because of Martin's enormous popularity with fans and the press. As it turned out, it was these same media allies of the manager who provided the *coup de grâce:* first by asking Griffith for a reaction to rumors that Martin had already approached the Seattle Pilots for a managerial job, then by relaying Martin's own belief that he was about to be fired. It was in this sense that Griffith insisted in the years to come that "Billy fired himself." However that might be, few people in Minnesota believed it, and a bombardment of mail and telephone calls similar to the one that had demanded his hiring erupted to protest his firing.

The uproar over Martin was followed in December 1969 by one of Griffith's worst trades, when he sent pitchers Chance and Bob Miller, outfielder Ted Uhlaender, and third baseman Graig Nettles to the Indians in return for righthanders Luis Tiant and Stan Williams. Cleveland had been ready to accept Nettles's younger brother Jim, but Griffith's advisors thought he was a better prospect than the future All Star third baseman because of his speed. Even though he had contributed little to the 1969 division title, the departure of Chance was also viewed as a mean-spirited retaliation by Griffith for the contract dispute during spring training.

It was within this baleful atmosphere that Bill Rigney replaced Martin and promptly directed the club to another division title, even winning a game more than in 1969. Once again, Perry (a Cy Young Award for his 24 wins) and Perranoski (34 saves along with 7 wins) were the big stories on the mound. Offensively, the team had to overcome an injury to Carew that limited him to 191 plate appearances, and did so with Killebrew (41 homers, 113 RBIs) and Oliva (23 homers, 107 RBIs, .325) delivering characteristic seasons and role players like outfielder Brant Alyea (16 homers, 61 RBIs, and .291 in 258 at bats) coming through in the clutch.

Unfortunately for the Twins, the Orioles were again waiting in ambush in the LCS, and again the Twins went down in three straight games, losing by a combined score of 27–10. Griffith later estimated that the quick elimination of the club in the two postseason series cost the organization about $4 million.

In 1970 and 1971, the winds of change that began to blow over all of baseball found in Griffith a reed particularly unwilling to bend. The initial sign of trouble came in the fall of 1970, when the owner denounced that year's strike by umpires as "a disgrace to humanity" and went on to analyze the role of unions in general in similar terms. The following year, when the Supreme Court ruled against Curt Flood's challenge to the reserve clause, the Minnesota owner released management's loudest sigh of relief and announced his hard line against a threatened players' walkout over health and pension benefits in 1972. When the strike took place, disrupting the start of the 1972 season, he declared himself ready to remain shut down for the entire year, then denounced other owners as "appeasers" when they reached an agreement with the Players Association in less than two weeks.

Griffith railed against his boardroom colleagues even more in 1973, when they consented to changes in the Basic Agreement that opened the way to salary arbitration. In a fitting turn of events, the very first player to benefit from a binding arbitration hearing was Twins' lefthander Dick Woodson in 1974. After losing to Woodson by some $20,000, Griffith told newsmen that he would make up for the loss by dealing the pitcher for cash, then denied that he had ever made such a statement to avoid a fine. Shortly afterward, he peddled the southpaw to the Yankees. By then, however, he should have been used to being a co-star in baseball's new contract dramas because, the year before, pitchers Perry and Kaat had been the first two ALers to take advantage of their 10-and-5 status (10 years in the big leagues, 5 years with the same club), requiring their approval for sales to the Tigers and White Sox, respectively. It was a fourth Minnesota pitcher, reliever Bill Campbell, who would become the first regular free agent signee, going to the Red Sox after the 1976 season.

After winning the division in 1970 and plummeting back down to fifth the following year, the Twins settled into a nine-year rut in which they finished either third or fourth; most of the suspense of the period came from wondering whether the team would play .500 and whether Carew would win another batting title.

On July 6, 1972, Rigney was dispatched in favor of former Minnesota infielder Frank Quilici. Explaining his reasons for selecting Quilici, Griffith said that one factor had been his Italian roots, since previous Italian-American managers Lavagetto, Mele, and Martin had all been popular in the Minneapolis area. By then, the franchise could have used help from any ethnic quarter, with the club attracting fewer than a million fans a year and season tickets barely reaching the 2,000 mark. The main reasons for fan disenchantment were the lingering effects of the Martin firing, the general deterioration of Metropolitan Stadium, and a growing sense that Griffith was going to avoid going after big names on the trade market because of the salaries attached to them.

On another question, Griffith had more than a philosophic interest in being one of the most outspoken advocates of Oakland owner Charlie Finley's proposal for introducing a designated hitter into AL lineups; as the Minnesota farm system had been demonstrating for years, nobody believed in offense as a gate magnet more than the Twins' owner. Moreover, the DH turned out to be the solution for Oliva, one of the team's most popular players and effective hitters but whose legs had started to go on him at an early age.

Following the 1973 season, with still more red numbers to contemplate, Griffith held exploratory talks with Bob Short, owner until only weeks before of the Texas Rangers, about a possible sale of the franchise. The discussions didn't go very far, but they proved to be only the first of similar contacts held over the years with representatives of Seattle, Indianapolis, New Orleans, Tampa, Toronto, and Vancouver. Lacking big money from a sale—or even the conviction that selling was what he wanted to do—Griffith sought economy by attacking his own payroll. The first big move was the release of Killebrew in January 1974, after the slugger had rejected lower paying positions as either a minor league manager or a coach on the varsity. Then, over the next three years, the Twins' owner effectively dismantled the team by trading away or simply ignoring players in the walk year of their contracts. In June 1976, it was the turn of righthander Bert Blyleven, who had put together six straight years of double-figure wins for the team; months away from his free agency, he was swapped to the Rangers along with infielder Danny Thompson for pitchers Bill Singer and Jim Gideon, infielders Roy Smalley and Mike Cubbage, and the not inconsiderable sum of $250,000. At the end of the 1976 season, the club declined to enter into a serious bidding war for reliever Campbell, who went to Boston, or third baseman Eric Soderholm, who took his services to the White Sox. The following year was even worse, with seven members of the Twins walking away as free agents at the end of the 1977 season.

Griffith's aversion to free agents, and the money they were demanding, became so notorious that his own managers began bemoaning the frustration of piloting clubs that had no future even when they might have a passable present. Gene Mauch, who took over for Quilici in 1976, had to be talked out of quitting after Griffith allowed outfielders Lyman Bostock and Larry Hisle to leave, declaring that he wanted to "manage a team with a chance to win." Although Mauch stayed, he did so with enough leverage gained from his outburst to pressure Griffith into signing reliever Mike Marshall as a free agent in 1978; as Mauch, who had managed the righthander

In the midst of his attendance crisis in 1975, Calvin Griffith went along with an idea to stage a special day for Harmon Killebrew, the longtime Twins' slugger who spent his final year with the Kansas City Royals. Although he had been a fan favorite for many years, the promotion for retiring Killebrew's number during a visit by the Royals drew only 2,946 fans.

in Montreal had predicted, Marshall made it a sound investment by winning 20 games and saving 53 others over his first two years with the club. Not even that was enough to convince Griffith, however, and right up to the closing hours of the decade, he was waving goodbye to free agents such as 20-game winner Dave Goltz and southpaw Geoff Zahn. But the most traumatic of all departures was that of Carew.

Trouble between the star first baseman and Griffith had been building since 1977, when Carew had accused the owner of being offensive and rude to his agent Jerry Simon during contract renewal negotiations. Although Griffith claimed that he had only been aggravated in having to deal with agents in general, the insinuation was that the owner had vented some anti-Semitic crudities during the talks. Then, on September 28, 1978, in a public relations fiasco second only to Al Campanis's appearance on *Nightline* in 1987, an inebriated Griffith let loose with a flood of racial and sexual invective before a Lions Club group in Waseca, Minnesota; among his passing remarks was the smirking observation that Carew had been "a damn fool" for agreeing to the 1977 pact that was paying him the relatively low salary of $170,000 a year. Two years later, in his walk season and with both the Simon episode and the Waseca speech firmly in mind, Carew was much less of a fool when he asked for $3.5 million over five years. When Griffith said no, the Twins announced that Carew, who had 10-and-5 trade approval rights, was available to the highest bidder.

The first team to step forward was San Francisco, which satisfied Griffith with a player package, but happened to be in the wrong league as far as Carew was concerned. Next up was the Angels, who satisfied Carew with an offer of $4 million over five years, but who left Griffith uninterested when they refused to include third baseman Carney Lansford in the trade. At this point, Commissioner Bowie Kuhn ruled that prospective suitors had to complete accords with Griffith before approaching Carew; failure to do so, he warned, would leave clubs liable to tampering charges. The Yankees immediately concluded a deal with Griffith that would have dispatched first baseman Chris Chambliss, outfielder Juan Beniquez, and minor leaguers Rex Hudler and Chris Welsh, along with $250,000, to Minnesota, but Kuhn came right back to veto the idea of money being part of the deal. It turned out to be an academic objection when the New York-reared Carew said that he had no desire to play for Yankees' owner George Steinbrenner. Finally, with no other offer on the table, Griffith went back to the Angels, dropped his demand for Lansford, and agreed on a package of pitcher Paul Hartzell, outfielder Ken Landreaux, and two minor league prospects—southpaw Brad Havens and catcher Dave Engle. Carew signed for the originally offered $4 million over five years.

Even the fallout from Carew's departure was secondary to the civic embarrassment and alienation generated by Griffith's appearance before the Waseca Lions Club. Among the owner's other cracks on the occasion were that he had welcomed the opportunity to move out of Washington for Bloomington because of the large black population in the capital, that blacks were more disposed to attending wrestling matches than baseball games, and that catcher Butch Wynegar had batted only .229 during the 1978 season because he had spent more time during spring training chasing his new wife around the bedroom than baseballs around the field; according to Griffith, Wynegar would have been better off staying single and picking up women for one-night stands because "love comes pretty cheap for ballplayers these days and they should take advantage of it." No sooner had the remarks been published by Nick Coleman in the Minneapolis *Star & Tribune* than the Urban League suggested that the Griffiths make their next transfer to South Africa and state legislators demanded that Kuhn open an investigation with an eye to forcing new ownership for the Twins. In response, Griffith denied the racial slurs attributed to him by Coleman, but in the same breath insisted that anything he might have said had been off the record anyway; even ten years later, he would voice regret only for his references to Wynegar, allowing as how they might have been in bad taste.

Carew's exit also spurred Mauch into again declaring his dissatisfaction with the franchise, to the point that he asked Griffith for permission to explore the possibility of taking a job with the Angels. Griffith reserved his decision until he talked to California about obtaining a couple of prospects in exchange, finally concluding that the players he might get wouldn't be worth another wave of criticism over allowing the popular manager to go. Mauch had built up most of his capital with the fans in 1977, when his "little ball" tactics of the hit-and-run, the stolen base, and the sacrifice had been primarily responsible for the club's fifty-one-day occupation of first place before a late-season swoon produced still another fourth-place finish. The manager had also gained more public relations points with his insistence on the signing of free agent Marshall. But it was also at least partly because of Marshall that he finally called it quits in 1980. The season had begun with threats of a player strike for sometime in late May and with Marshall as one of the most visible union activists. When the reliever got off to a slow start, Griffith released him, insisting that the move had nothing to do with the union. Although Marshall later lost a grievance claiming that he had been jettisoned for his off-the-field activities, the incident was another indication to Mauch, who was otherwise as anti-union as the owner, that Griffith was more interested in personal vindication and saving money than winning; he submitted his resignation on August 24th and was replaced by coach John Goryl. Ironically, it was only a couple of months later that Griffith sprang for the heftiest free agent contracts of his tenure, holding onto shortstop Smalley (Mauch's nephew) and catcher Wynegar.

Goryl had little to show for his resume, not even lasting until the players' strike in 1981 interrupted play in mid-June; on May 22nd he was replaced by coach Billy Gardner, who would hold on to the job until 1985. Griffith was the first to admit that the strike turned out to be a boon for the Twins, because the club's $2-million share of insurance indemnities was more than it probably would have made if the season had gone on normally (and also provided another reason for him to denounce any compromise with the Players Association). Otherwise, the club had little to crow about, descending to the AL West's basement for the first half of the split season and finishing near the bottom in the second half. At the gate, the franchise finished last in the major leagues for the second straight year. Injuries were also prominent, with both free agents, Smalley and Wynegar, giving Griffith more ammunition for his views by missing substantial portions of the schedule. Another blow came when John Castino, who shared the Rookie of the Year award in 1979 with Toronto's Alfredo Griffin, had to undergo a spinal fusion operation; back troubles would eventually abort the promising infielder's career. The happiest footnote to the season was written in September, when three of the organization's best prospects—first baseman Kent Hrbek, third baseman Gary Gaetti, and catcher Tim Laudner—all hit home runs in their first major

league games. All three moved into the starting lineup in 1982, when the team carried so many rookies (fifteen) that the entire twenty-five-man payroll amounted to less than what Montreal was paying catcher Gary Carter that year.

The 1982 season also marked the transfer of the Twins from rotting Metropolitan Stadium in Bloomington to the Metrodome in downtown Minneapolis. Negotiations to get the club into the new facility with the football Vikings had been protracted, and often acrimonious. Since the project had first been contemplated in the late 1970s, Griffith's reservations about the dome had assumed different forms: his traditionalist opposition to indoor stadiums with artificial turf, his apprehension that the keenly competitive residents of St. Paul would resent the Minneapolis property, alleged favoritism being shown the Vikings, and concession and novelty stand percentages that did not compare to what he had gotten in Washington and Bloomington. On the other hand, he had not needed to be convinced that the Met had deteriorated to the point of peril in some areas of the grandstand or that Twins' fans living in the Dakotas and other far-flung regions would be much quicker to drive to Minneapolis if they knew for sure that bad weather wasn't going to affect a scheduled game. While balancing these two sets of factors at the beginning of 1980, Griffith also took a closer look at the alternative of moving the team out of Minnesota altogether. What finally swayed him to stay was an escape clause concession in a thirty-year lease on the dome that allowed the Twins to pull out if attendance was shown to be suffering from the structure's lack of air conditioning or if the franchise failed to be profitable over a three-year period (the barometer being an annual average attendance of 1.3 million).

The good news was that some 52,000 showed up for the team's first home indoor game; the bad news was that they got a look at the worst club in the history of the franchise, destined to lose 102 games and finish 33 games behind the Angels. Even with the new stadium as a novelty, Minnesota was the only franchise in the majors not to draw one million. Once again, the main problem was the owner Griffith, who unloaded relief pitcher Doug Corbett and

In 1979, reliever Mike Marshall established the AL record for appearances when he strode to the mound 90 times. In 1974, Marshall had set the NL record in the same category with 106 appearances.

In 1982, righthander Terry Felton went 0–13 for the Twins. Together with an 0–3 mark in 1980, this gave him the big league record for the most losses without a win.

After the Twins pulled out at the end of the 1981 season, Metropolitan Stadium became the first modern baseball facility to be razed to the ground.

free agents Smalley and Wynegar within the first month of the season. Few were ready to believe that the Twins had actually benefited from the Corbett deal by acquiring slugger Tom Brunansky from California or from the Smalley exchange by obtaining reliever Ron Davis and shortstop Greg Gagne from New York; his credibility long gone, Griffith's swaps only increased sales for the TRADE CALVIN buttons in evidence everywhere around the state. They also prompted confrontation with Clark Griffith, who had been left out of the negotiations for the exchanges and who, a year later, would walk away from the organization to return to law school.

The failure of the Metrodome to supply instant adrenaline to the franchise concerned not only Griffith, but the Minneapolis interests that had agreed to the escape clause for the facility. It also became increasingly obvious that Griffith's sister Haynes was no longer rubberstamping her brother's decisions, but, in the long-range interests of her son Bruce, urging closer examination of offers from cities such as Tampa. The city's first response was a Chamber of Commerce initiative called the Major League Task Force, which set as its task the purchase of thousands of tickets to close down the escape hatch in the team's lease agreement for the dome. While a great deal of publicity was given to this effort, and it helped spawn an image of Minneapolis as the most civic-minded metropolis in the country, it actually had little impact on the developments immediately preceding the sale of the team. Of far more importance—psychological as much as financial—was the announcement in April 1984 that minority stockholder Murphy had sold his 43 percent interest in the franchise to the same Tampa businessmen who had been approaching Griffith and Haynes. Although Griffith insisted that the Murphy transaction meant simply that he had a new minority partner, Minneapolis banker Carl Pohlad quickly put together a group of buyers who had previously been reluctant to match the figures Griffith and Bruce Haynes had said they had heard from the Florida interests. On June 22, 1984, Pohlad and Griffith appeared together at the dome and formally signed the papers that took the Washington-Minnesota organization out of the

hands of the Griffiths for the first time in sixty-five years. The sale price was $32 million. A few weeks later, Pohlad, considered one of the 100 wealthiest people in the United States, also picked up the Murphy shares from the Tampa buyers, for an estimated $12.5 million. In his first administrative appointments, the new owner made Griffith chairman of the board and the persistent Fox president. On the other hand, the revamped organization made it clear immediately that there would be no room for Clark Griffith.

As though eager to send one last message to Griffith, Minnesota fans flocked to the dome and set a franchise total attendance record of 1,598,422. It helped no little that Gardner kept the club tied for the lead in a generally weak division right down to the final week of the season; even the game that officially eliminated the team was memorable in its own way, with the Twins blowing a 10–0 lead over the Indians to go down 11–10. The principal ingredients of the comeback to a second-place tie were southpaw Frank Viola's 18–12 record, Hrbek's 27 homers and 107 RBIs, and Brunansky's 32 homers; the campaign also marked the debut of center fielder Kirby Puckett, who demonstrated his batting eye with a .296 average, but had no homers in 559 plate appearances.

With expectations once again high, the team fell down quickly in 1985, running up separate nine- and ten-game losing streaks over the first two months. The chief problem was pitching, so the organization brought in long-time Baltimore pitching coach Ray Miller to take over from Gardner, but he had little success either that year or the next with a staff that by and large consisted of Viola, the reacquired Blyleven, and hopes that righthander Mike Smithson would show an ability to be better than a .500 performer. Thanks in part to his inclination for throwing gophers anywhere and in part to the stadium that was becoming known as a Homer Dome, Blyleven surrendered a record-breaking 50 homers in 1986. Miller wasn't altogether surprised when he was ousted for coach Tom Kelly in early September.

The Twins went into 1987 with more new faces than Kelly. During the offseason, Pohlad replaced Fox as president with Jerry Bell, a long-time official with the commission that operated the Metrodome. Executive vice-president (and, later, general manager) Andy MacPhail moved to patch up at least part of the club's pitching woes by obtaining relief ace Jeff Reardon from the Expos and then picking up the veteran Juan Berenguer as a setup man. Both deals proved crucial in a bizarre season that saw the Twins go ricocheting back up to the division title despite only two starters (Viola and Blyleven) with wins in double figures. The two-game margin of victory over Kansas City was one part Reardon (31 saves), one part slugging offense (Hrbek, Gaetti, and Brunansky all with more than 30 homers), one part Puckett (an MVP-type year with 28 homers, 99 RBIs, and an average of .332), and one part strong defensive middle of the infield (second baseman Steve Lombardozzi and shortstop Gagne). But more significant than any of the parts was the whole of the club's domination at home, going 56–25 for the season. The same syndrome was at work in the postseason, first against the Tigers in the LCS, then against the Cardinals in the World Series. In the matchup against Detroit, the Twins beat Doyle Alexander and Jack Morris in the opening contests at the dome, giving them enough of a cushion to go into Tiger Stadium, where they won two out of the next three for a fairly easy pennant in five games. Brunansky was the hitting star, with 2 homers and 9 RBIs.

In the World Series, the home field advantage was even more on display. With 50,000 handkerchief-waving fans screaming them on at ear-splitting decibel levels in the enclosed arena, the Twins shattered the Cardinals in the first two games by the scores of 10–1 and 8–4. Without the thunderous backing of the grandstands, the club went down to defeat three straight times in St. Louis. But then, back at home for the last two games, Minnesota belted around John Tudor in the sixth game and rode strong pitching by Viola and Reardon in the final contest to win the franchise's first world championship. The heroes were Viola, who won twice, Puckett, who had ten safeties, and left fielder Dan Gladden, who knocked in seven runs with nine hits. As elated as people in Minnesota were by the triumph, baseball purists in other parts of the country lamented the handkerchief waving and the TV-hyped screaming of the fans as another blow to the integrity of the game.

On paper, the 1988 season was even more successful in several respects. For one thing, Kelly fulfilled a spring training promise that he wouldn't be resting on his laurels by guiding the team to six more wins than the year before. Second, Viola moved to the head of the pitching class in the AL by capturing the Cy Young Award for his 24 victories and 2.64 ERA. Third, lefty Allan Anderson won the ERA title with 2.45. Fourth, Reardon picked up more saves (from 31 to 42). Fifth, Puckett had an even better year (24 homers, 121 RBIs, .356). And most important of all to the organization, the Twins became the first franchise in the AL to break the three-million mark

in attendance. But with all those positives, the club failed to overcome a disastrous trade of Brunansky to St. Louis for second baseman Tommy Herr and pitching shorts so severe that over-the-hill 43-year-olds Steve Carlton and Joe Niekro were eyed briefly as saviors; it ended up 13 games behind Oakland.

The turn of the decade saw the Twins collapsing even further, with the added problem of some bad will in the clubhouse. Like Herr before him, ex-Mets second baseman Wally Backman arrived in 1989, took one look around, and decided that the AL was not a major league. Gaetti, who had been a clubhouse leader for years, withdrew into his newly found fundamentalist faith. Viola entered the 1989 season so dissatisfied with a MacPhail contract offer that he let it be known that he would be a lame duck ace. Although a three-year deal was worked out before mid-season, the Twins jumped at a Mets' trade offer for the southpaw on July 31 that brought them five hurlers—righties Rick Aguilera, Kevin Tapani, Jack Savage, and Tim Drummond, and lefty David West. Most of the rest of 1989 and all of 1990 were spent sorting out these acquisitions, with Aguilera becoming the bullpen stopper (32 saves in 1990) and Tapani a key to the rotation (a team-leading 12 wins in 1990). The 1989 season also saw Puckett add to the club's collection of batting titles.

Having landed in the basement of the division in 1990, Minnesota entered the 1991 season with the clock ticking for Kelly and a lot of questions about such offseason free agent pickups as the aging right-hander Jack Morris, third baseman Mike Pagliarulo, and designated hitter Chili Davis. As it developed, the three acquisitions were pivotal to an extraordinary comeback that made the team the first in the AL to rebound from last to first in one year. The Minnesota native Morris contributed 18 wins, Pagliarulo and righty hitting Scott Leius platooned effectively at third in place of the departed free agent Gaetti, and Davis clouted 29 home runs. Other big years came from 20-game winner Scott Erickson, Aguilera with another 42 saves, Tapani with 16 wins and a 2.99 ERA, and Puckett with a .319 average.

Postseason play once again highlighted the Metrodome, with the Twins scoring two more home victories and then going on to Toronto to make relatively quick work of the Blue Jays in the LCS. Not too many people remembered the five-game series a week later when the Twins and Braves found themselves in one of the noisiest, most dramatic World Series ever played. With the handkerchief wavers again out in force, the Twins took the first two games. In Atlanta, however, they came up against the equally zealous tomahawk choppers, who roared the Braves onto three straight victories, including two extra-inning thrillers. Back in Minneapolis, it was the turn again of the handkerchief wavers, who shrieked their way through still another overtime contest, finally decided by an 11th-inning Puckett homer off Charlie Leibrandt. But even these games turned out to be a mere prelude to the finale that matched Morris against Atlanta's John Smoltz for seven scoreless innings. In the eighth, a critical base-running failure by Braves outfielder Lonnie Smith cost the visitors a chance to score and set up a double play that got Morris out of a jam; in the bottom of the frame, Hrbek hit into another double play to squelch a rally and keep the game scoreless. The teams went into the 10th inning, when, finally, pinch-hitter Gene Larkin touched reliever Alejandro Peña for the bases-loaded single that gave the Twins their second World Series championship in five years and gave the valliant Morris an extra-inning shutout.

Less than forty-eight hours after being toasted

as the Series MVP, Morris declared himself a free agent, eventually signing with Toronto. To replace him, MacPhail sent two prospects to the Pirates to obtain southpaw John Smiley. It was the only significant move made by the 1992 club, and wasn't nearly enough. With only Puckett and outfielder Shane Mack delivering with any consistency, the Twins made a midseason run at the Athletics, but crumbled over the last two months and were lucky to finish second. The pitching was as spotty as the hitting, with an overused Aguilera saving 41 games but also blowing some decisive contests.

After months of foot dragging, the club resigned Puckett in the off-season amid indications that he was on the verge of going to Boston. Davis and Gagne were allowed to walk, as was Smiley after he received a big offer from the Reds. The most important free agent signing for 1993 was that of Minnesota native Dave Winfield, penciled in as Davis's successor as the designated hitter.

MINNESOTA TWINS

Annual Standings and Managers

Year	Position	W	L	Pct.	GB	Managers
1961	Seventh	70	90	.438	38	Cookie Lavagetto, Sam Mele
1962	Second	91	71	.562	5	Sam Mele
1963	Third	91	70	.565	13	Sam Mele
1964	Sixth*	79	83	.488	20	Sam Mele
1965	First	102	60	.630	+7	Sam Mele
1966	Second	89	73	.549	9	Sam Mele
1967	Second*	91	71	.562	1	Sam Mele, Cal Ermer
1968	Seventh	79	83	.488	24	Cal Ermer
1969	First	97	65	.599	+9	Billy Martin
1970	First	98	64	.605	+9	Bill Rigney
1971	Fifth	74	86	.463	26½	Bill Rigney
1972	Third	77	77	.500	15½	Bill Rigney, Frank Quilici
1973	Third	81	81	.500	13	Frank Quilici
1974	Third	82	80	.506	8	Frank Quilici
1975	Fourth	76	83	.478	20½	Frank Quilici
1976	Third	85	77	.525	5	Gene Mauch
1977	Fourth	84	77	.522	17½	Gene Mauch
1978	Fourth	73	89	.451	19	Gene Mauch
1979	Fourth	82	80	.506	6	Gene Mauch
1980	Third	77	84	.478	19½	Gene Mauch, John Goryl
1981	Seventh	17	39	.304	18	John Goryl, Billy Gardner
	Fourth	24	29	.453	6	Billy Gardner
1982	Seventh	60	102	.370	33	Billy Gardner
1983	Fifth*	70	92	.432	29	Billy Gardner
1984	Second*	81	81	.500	3	Billy Gardner
1985	Fourth*	77	85	.475	14	Billy Gardner, Ray Miller
1986	Sixth	71	91	.438	21	Ray Miller, Tom Kelly
1987	First	85	77	.525	+2	Tom Kelly
1988	Second	91	71	.562	13	Tom Kelly

1989	Fifth	80	82	.494	19	Tom Kelly
1990	Seventh	74	88	.457	29	Tom Kelly
1991	First	95	67	.586	+8	Tom Kelly
1992	Second	90	72	.556	6	Tom Kelly

* Tie

Postseason Play

LCS	0–3 versus Baltimore	1969	WS	3–4 versus Los Angeles	1965
	0–3 versus Baltimore	1970		4–3 versus St. Louis	1987
	4–1 versus Detroit	1987		4–3 versus Atlanta	1991
	4–1 versus Toronto	1991			

Montreal Expos

National League,
1969–Present

BALLPARKS: JARRY PARK (1969–1976)
OLYMPIC STADIUM (1977–Present)

RECORD: 1854–1966 (.485)

Like the San Diego Padres, the Expos were born prematurely in 1969 as the result of some hasty maneuvering between National and American league owners. From both competitive and financial points of view, the franchise has been generally hard put to carry its weight ever since.

A mainstay of the International League in the Dodger farm system for decades, Montreal had long been viewed as an attractive candidate for eventual expansion by the NL. But with Dodger owner Walter O'Malley acting as the most equal of equals in the inner circles of the league, the move had been put on

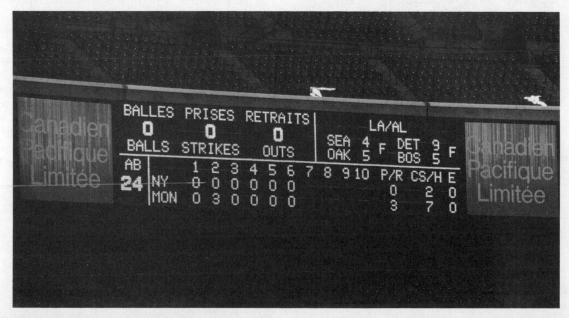

Baseball goes bilingual. *Gilles Corbeil/Expos de Montréal*

hold until sometime in the 1970s. That timetable was scratched when the AL announced unilaterally that it intended moving into Kansas City and Seattle for the 1969 season and adopting a twelve-team, two-division structure. While some NL owners threatened lawsuits against their junior circuit cousins and others warned that the Kansas City-Seattle move was merely a prelude to further incursions aimed at establishing an "American League within an American League," O'Malley came forward with a proposal to bring in Montreal and San Diego immediately. The other NL owners weren't very hard to convince: In addition to splitting the $10 million each new franchise had to cough up for league membership, they were able to deal off their second-rate players to the Expos and Padres at $175,000 a man.

With Charles Bronfman of the Seagram distilleries paying the bills, the Expos took the field in 1969 as the first major league team to play outside the United States. Having adopted an expansion draft strategy midway between that of the Mets (veterans) and Astros (rookies) in 1962, the team had a little bit of everything. The most conspicuous player proved to be Rusty Staub, until then primarily a contact hitter who had been obtained not through the draft but through a preseason trade with Houston. With his flaming red hair and conversion to power hitting in the small confines of Jarry Park (29 homers, 79 RBIs, .302), Staub became an instant favorite, known to both Anglo- and French-speaking fans as Le Grand Orange. Another grandstand pet was third baseman Coco Laboy, whose melodious name ended up overshadowing his solid offensive contribution of 18 homers and 83 RBIs. As for the pitching staff, it more or less began and ended with Bill Stoneman (11–19), who raised a few eyebrows when he no-hit the Phillies only ten days into the season. Much less of a surprise was the team's final record of 52–110 (exactly the same as the Padres).

For their first seven years, the Expos were in the hands of Gene Mauch, the manager synonymous with both hard luck and one-run-at-a-time baseball. Although familiar with Montreal from his days in the Brooklyn Dodger farm system and regarded by many as something of a walking encyclopedia of the game's subtleties, Mauch seemed a curious choice to many because of a roster laden with mid-career wild swingers and pitchers who called for more patience than their skipper had displayed in his previous posts. Nevertheless, after digesting their woeful 1969 play, the Expos went out the following year to win twenty-one games more than they had in their maiden season, in no small part because of Mauch's rabbit-out-of-the-hat tactics. Another vital contribution came from Carl Morton, a righthander who won Rookie of the Year honors for his 18–11 record.

Over the next couple of seasons, the team played at the 1970 level, although they managed to get out of the Eastern Division cellar past the Phillies. Journeymen came and went, plugging pitching, fielding, and hitting holes more out of expediency than according to some long-range development plan. In 1971, righthander Balor Moore posted a record of 9–9—a noteworthy occurrence only insofar as he was the first player to have been selected by the Expos in the amateur draft and not an arrival from some other team's bench or farm system. Prior to the 1972 season, the Expos risked the wrath of their fans by deal-

English-speaking fans in Montreal have had to learn more than Le Grand Orange to be able to follow the Expos in their full local flavor. Among the other basic baseball terms in French are:

Pitcher—lanceur
Infielder—interieur
First Base—premier but
Third Base—troisième but
Shortstop—arrêt-court
Strike—prise
Strikeout—retrait au baton
Inning—manche
Error—erreur
Double—deux-buts
Home Run—circuit
Stolen Base—but vole
Foul Ball—balle fausse
Relief Pitcher—lanceur de relève

Catcher—reçeveur
Outfielder—voltigeur
Second base—deuxième but
Home Plate—marbre
Mound—monticule
Ball—balle
Out—retrait
Hit—coup sur
Bunt—coup retenu
Triple—trois-buts
Grandslam—grande quatre
Sacrifice Fly—ballon sacrifice
Grounder—roulant
Pinch-Hitter—frappeur de relève
Umpire—Arbitre

Few teams have had as many colorfully named players as the Expos. While Coco Laboy remains the favorite of most fans, it has gotten competition in some quarters from Razor Shines and Boots Day. Another favorite of the public address announcer in Montreal (and elsewhere around the league) was John Boccabella—with the accent on every single syllable.

ing the popular Staub to the Mets in exchange for three regular position players—outfielder Ken Singleton, first baseman Mike Jorgenson, and shortstop Tim Foli. Predictably denounced at the time, that deal—plus earlier acquisitions of second baseman Ron Hunt and relief ace Mike Marshall—put the team in its first genuine division race the following year.

Although still falling short of the .500 mark with a record of 79–83, the Expos remained in contention until the final week of 1973, ending up in fourth place only three-and-a-half games behind the winning Mets and earning Mauch honors as the league's Manager of the Year.

While realists might have noted that none of the Eastern Division clubs in 1973 brought the 1927 Yankees to mind, that in fact only the first-place Mets played better than .500 ball, Expo fans went into 1974 expecting at least as much as the previous year's effort from the team. What they got was slightly less than the same. Although the team managed 79 victories for the second consecutive year (and, because of a rainout, even one less loss), stronger teams in Pittsburgh and St. Louis cost them an additional five games in the standings. Moreover, for the first time since the establishment of the franchise, the media began to persistently criticize Mauch's conservative managing and the front office's often inexplicable player moves. Particularly glaring was a trade with Los Angeles prior to the season that had sent bullpen specialist Marshall to the Dodgers in exchange for outfielder Willie Davis. Montreal president John McHale and general manager Jim Fanning justified the swap by saying that Marshall, who had his own theories on physical conditioning and who didn't pay a lot of attention to people who didn't share them, had become impossible to manage. However true that might have been, the righthander went on to establish the major league record for pitching game appearances in one season (106) and win a Cy Young Award for the Dodgers. On the other hand, Davis, while turning in a respectable enough year, overwhelmed the Expo front office with his constant demands for salary advances and loans to pay off his creditors.

There was worse coming. As with Marshall, Staub, and some others, Singleton and righthander Mike Torrez (16 wins in 1972, 15 in 1974) were players whom Montreal had obtained in deals that did the team credit—and players whom McHale and Fanning then couldn't seem to get rid of fast enough again. In the worst fiasco of the kind, Singleton and Torrez were dealt to Baltimore in December 1974 in return for outfielder Rich Coggins and pitchers Bill Kirkpatrick and Dave McNally. Singleton became one of the American League's most feared sluggers and Torrez gave the Orioles a 20-win season. Meanwhile, Coggins managed a total of 37 at bats before going on the disabled list and then being peddled off to the Yankees, Kirkpatrick never got out of the high minors, and McNally went into voluntary retirement while he and Andy Messersmith successfully challenged the reserve clause and opened the door all the way to free agency.

During the transition years of 1975 and 1976, it was evident that the club was determined to put more stress on the products of its own farm system and that it was in need of a manager committed to what was, in effect, starting from scratch again. What this translated to in reality was a fifth-place finish in 1975, Mauch's ouster in favor of Karl Kuehl, and a disastrous tumble back into the cellar of the division in 1976, 46 games behind Philadelphia. It also meant ugly scenes during the 1976 season when shortstop Tim Foli decided that Kuehl wasn't up to managing a big league club, showed him up in front of the other Expos, and by and large got away with it.

In return for suffering through the team's worst year since its inaugural season, Expo fans got a look at the first important pieces of the club that was to take the field for a good part of the next decade. What they also saw were players—among them, Gary Carter, Steve Rogers, Warren Cromartie, Ellis Valentine, and Larry Parrish—who had gotten to Canada almost in spite of the front office inasmuch as none of them had been a first-round draft pick. Instead, between 1969 and 1973, the club had wasted its favorable drafting position on college players like Frank Hale, Tom Ford, Wayne Piper, and Bobbie Goodman. The most notable first-round selection in the period was Jack Scalia, who soon quit baseball for modeling and acting.

On July 13, 1973, Hal Breeden hit pinch-homers for Montreal in both ends of a double-header. The only other player to accomplish this feat was Red Sox shortstop Joe Cronin on June 17, 1943.

Footnote Player: Jose Morales set the all-time record for pinch hits in a season when he hit safely 25 times coming off the bench in 1976.

Significant changes came in 1977—some that would provide immediate payoffs, others that would prove more beneficial in the short run than over the long haul. The most marked difference was the transfer of the team from Jarry Park to Olympic Stadium, the facility that had been built for the 1976 Olympics and that—foul lines, scoreboards, and a couple of dugouts notwithstanding—would always look like a facility that had been built for the 1976 Olympics. From a financial standpoint, the Big O (or Big Oh, as its critics were wont to call it) was a white elephant costing hundreds of millions of dollars that bred a few extra white elephants of its own over the next fifteen years with start-and-stop projects to cap the stadium with a dome. From a baseball point of view, it was more arena than ballpark, with the stands so far from the field and the roof absorbing so much of the grandstand noise that it became commonplace for players to compare its atmosphere to that of a funeral parlor. Conditions on the artificial turf diamond were not much better, especially for day games when the sun would glare down through the hole in the roof and practically blind batters. When the facility was finally domed in the mid-1980s, it became an erratic exercise to open it again for the summer months. Still another fiasco occurred in September 1991, when the toppling of a fifty-ton beam (the stadium was empty at the time) forced the Expos to play the last three weeks of the season on the road.

In 1977, however, the Big O was mainly a symbol of the new start by the club. There were other signs, as well. Dick Williams, who had won AL pennants with the Red Sox and Athletics, let it be understood that he had signed on as manager to get into the World Series again. The veteran Tony Perez, the first baseman for Cincinnati's Big Red Machine teams, was acquired to further instill a winning attitude. Last but not least, the franchise's most highly touted prospect, center fielder Andre Dawson, was slipped between Cromartie and Valentine in the outfield.

The lesson for the year was that people (1.4 million of them) would come to see a promising team in a new ballpark, even if the club had some way to go in learning how to play as a unit. On the plus side, Dawson was selected Rookie of the Year for his 19 homers, 65 RBIs, .282 average, and nimble defense; after having been stashed in the outfield for a good part of his first two seasons, Carter took giant strides toward becoming the league's premier catcher; Perez and Valentine hit with power; and Rogers began to fulfill expectations with 17 wins and 206 strikeouts. But the team couldn't hide the generally mediocre pitching behind Rogers, the ninety-plus stikeouts by Dawson, Carter, and Perez, or the shaky defense in the middle infield.

The gain from 1976 to 1977 was 20 victories and 20 games in the standings. Putting exactly the same players out on the field and adding free agent pitcher Ross Grimsley (20–11) in 1978, the team won only one more game but shaved a further 12 games off its standing behind the division winner. Deciding that it had a solid, if not the best, nucleus in the Eastern Division, the Expos prepared for 1979 by going out for another starter (Bill Lee from Boston), another reliever (Elias Sosa, signed as a free agent), and a second baseman (Rodney Scott from the Cubs) who could give them more range in the infield and more speed at the top of the lineup. With Parrish, Dawson, Carter, and Valentine each contributing at least 20 homers, the Expos ended up compiling the best record in the history of their franchise—but still finished second to the Pirates by two games.

The 1980 season saw more of the same frustration. As in 1979, the division race wasn't settled until the final weekend of the season. But whereas one year before Philadelphia had waited until the eleventh hour to knock off Montreal so Pittsburgh could get into the League Championship Series, this time the Phillies delivered the knockout blow on their own behalf, with a Mike Schmidt homer in the eleventh inning on the next to last day. The only consolation for Expo fans was the fact that the team had been beaten as much by its own disabled list as by the NL opposition: Because of injuries, the eight regulars had taken the field together only twenty-three times during the season.

The first and only time that the Expos were to make the division playoffs—the strike year of 1981— was also the season that the team's frustrations reached a boiling point in the clubhouse. Already, there had been incidents indicating that the players were bristling under Williams's martinet rule (in one episode, elderly administrative assistant Charlie Fox belted Rogers) and that the front office was worried that the manager had inherited Mauch's mantle as an ingenious but hard-luck also-ran. Finally, in September of 1981, general manager Fanning went down to the dugout to replace Williams and lead the team into the playoffs.

The keys to the 1981 win were the running of Tim Raines, the slugging of Dawson and Carter, and the pitching of Rogers, journeymen Woodie Fryman and Ray Burris, and novice bullpen ace Jeff Reardon. Despite playing only 88 games, Raines swiped 71 bases and had seemed safely on his way to the all-time record when the strike intervened in June. Daw-son produced 24 homers and 64 RBIs, and Carter came through for 16 homers and 68 RBIs. After being obtained in May in a trade with the Mets for Valen-tine, Reardon fashioned the first eight of the saves that were to make him Montreal's most dependable pitcher for much of the 1980s. In addition to his twelve regular season wins, Rogers beat Steve Carl-ton twice in the best-of-five first round of the play-offs, including a fifth-game 3–0 shutout. Excitement ran so high in Canada for the games that one Quebec independence spokesman was widely reported as la-menting the fact that the Expos had become the Ot-tawa government's best propaganda argument for national unity.

The LCS against Western Division winner Los Angeles was a more painful story. Despite a shutout from Burris and another tightly pitched win from Rogers, the Expos went down to defeat three games to two on the strength of a ninth-inning home run off Rogers in the final game by Dodger outfielder Rick Monday.

With Fanning returning to the helm in 1982, the club slipped to third place. The few bright spots in-cluded a batting championship for first baseman Al Oliver and another pace-setting year for Raines as a base thief (78 steals). They did not include persisting stresses in the clubhouse, particularly in the resent-ment of Rogers and Dawson toward Carter's alleged me-first attitude.

In 1983 and 1984, the team continued to decline, under Fanning, Bill Virdon, and then Fanning again. By the time Buck Rodgers took over the managerial reins in 1985, Cromartie was long gone, Rogers was eking out his final hours as a big league pitcher, and Carter had been shipped to the Mets in a blockbuster deal that had brought Hubie Brooks and Mike Fitz-gerald to Canada. After a fifteen-year reign with Fan-ning and Fox, McHale had also ceded some of his authority, bringing in Murray Cook as general man-ager. Against all expectations, Rodgers piloted the team to its first season over .500 in three years and appeared on the verge of repeating the trick in 1986 when a series of injuries to Brooks, Fitzgerald, first baseman Andres Galarraga, and pitcher Bryn Smith dropped the team back to a fourth-place finish.

Unlike Mauch and Williams, Rodgers did not come to Canada with press clippings attesting to his genius. But considering that Dawson went to Chicago as a free agent at the end of the 1986 sea-son, Reardon was dealt to Minnesota during the same winter (before he too became a free agent), and his pitching staff consisted of two rehabilitat-ing righthanders, Dennis Martinez and Pascual Perez (recovering from alcohol and drug depen-dencies, respectively) along with a lot of guys named Joe, Rodgers's ability to steer the club to within four games of division-winning St. Louis in 1987 was probably the best effort ever turned in by a Montreal strategist.

For the rest of the 1980s, Montreal played under the shadow of owner Bronfman's expressed desire to sell the club, even if that meant a transfer to another city. Aside from its other problems, the franchise be-came weighed down by the realization that free agents wanted no part of Montreal and that the Expo players themselves couldn't get away fast enough. The main reasons for this attitude were the financial disadvantages accruing from the exchange rate of the dollar and higher Canadian taxes, and the feeling of expatriation that was felt far more keenly by many players in the French-speaking province of Quebec than by those playing for the Blue Jays in Ontario. In 1990, Bronfman finally found his buyer in a consor-tium of Canadian business interests assembled un-der Claude Brochu, an executive in the outgoing-owner's distillery company. The NL formally approved the sale in June 1991.

After years of stability (some said stolidity) un-der McHale, the Montreal front office underwent a series of changes between 1985 and 1991. Although credited with righting the team, Cook found himself out of a job following romantic entanglements with the wife of another club official. He was followed as general manager by one-time Montreal pitcher Stoneman, then by David Dombrowski. For a couple of years, Dombrowski and Rodgers fought behind the scenes about player moves or non-moves, with the general manager finally prevailing in 1991 by bringing in Tom Runnells as the new skipper. The decision to bounce Rodgers enthused few of the Expo

On July 26, 1991, Montreal righthander Mark Gardner hurled hitless ball against Los Angeles for nine innings, only to lose the no-hitter, shut-out, and game in the tenth inning. Two days later, righty Dennis Martinez fashioned a perfect game against the same Dodgers. Martinez's catcher was Ron Hassey, the only receiver in major league history to call two perfect games; as a member of the Cleveland Indians, Hassey was also behind the plate for Len Barker's May 15, 1981 masterpiece against the Blue Jays.

players, all the more so when Runnells showed more of a bent for maintaining military discipline than for out-thinking the opposing manager. Dombrowski didn't have to listen to all the grumbling because, in September 1991, he abruptly resigned to take over baseball operations for the expansion Florida Marlins. In the weeks that followed in the 1991–92 off-season, he made such a raid on Montreal's front office personnel that NL President Bill White finally had to step in and order an end to the defection of Expos' officials to Florida.

With Dan Duquette in place as the new general manager for 1992, the players had a more sympa-

A**s** of the early 1990s, five native Canadians had worn the Expo uniform: pitcher Claude Raymond (1969–71), pitcher Larry Landreth (1976–77), pitcher Bill Atkinson (1976–79), outfielder Doug Frobel (1985), and outfielder-first baseman Larry Walker (1989-present).

thetic ear for their complaints against Runnells. One move that was particularly criticized was the manager's insistence that the veteran Tim Wallach, a Gold Glove winner and one of the most popular players in the history of the franchise, switch from third base to first base. Only a few weeks into the season, Runnells was given his walking papers and replaced by Felipe Alou. Under Alou, the team blossomed into a strong second-place entry. Leading the effort were center fielder Marquis Grissom (14 home runs and 78 steals), second baseman Delino DeShields (.292 with 46 steals), and especially, right fielder Larry Walker (.301 with 23 homers and 93 RBIs). The key man on the mound was reliever John Wetteland, who racked up 37 saves.

With so many of their younger players coming through, Duquette and Alou spent the 1992–93 off-season clearing positions for still more of them, especially shortstop Will Cordero, first baseman Greg Colbrunn, and catcher Tim Laker. Among the veterans traded away or allowed to depart as free agents were shortstop Spike Owen, slugger Ivan Calderon, and Wallach.

MONTREAL EXPOS

Annual Standings and Managers

Year	Position	W	L	Pct.	GB	Managers
1969	Sixth	52	110	.321	48	Gene Mauch
1970	Sixth	73	89	.451	16	Gene Mauch
1971	Fifth	71	90	.441	25½	Gene Mauch
1972	Fifth	70	86	.449	26½	Gene Mauch
1973	Fourth	79	83	.488	3½	Gene Mauch
1974	Fourth	79	82	.491	8½	Gene Mauch
1975	Fifth*	75	87	.463	17½	Gene Mauch
1976	Sixth	55	107	.340	46	Karl Kuehl, Charlie Fox
1977	Fifth	75	87	.463	26	Dick Williams
1978	Fourth	76	86	.469	14	Dick Williams
1979	Second	95	65	.594	2	Dick Williams
1980	Second	90	72	.556	1	Dick Williams
1981	Third	30	25	.545	4	Dick Williams
	First	30	23	.566	+½	Dick Williams, Jim Fanning
1982	Third	86	76	.531	6	Jim Fanning
1983	Third	82	80	.506	8	Bill Virdon
1984	Fifth	78	83	.484	18	Bill Virdon, Jim Fanning
1985	Third	84	77	.522	16½	Buck Rodgers
1986	Fourth	78	83	.484	29½	Buck Rodgers
1987	Third	91	71	.562	4	Buck Rodgers
1988	Third	81	81	.500	20	Buck Rodgers
1989	Fourth	81	81	.500	12	Buck Rodgers
1990	Third	85	77	.525	10	Buck Rodgers
1991	Sixth	71	90	.441	26½	Buck Rodgers, Tom Runnells
1992	Second	87	75	.537	9	Tom Runnells, Felipe Alou

* Tie

Postseason Play

LCS	2–3 versus Los Angeles	1981

Newark Peppers

Federal League, 1915   **BALLPARK:** HARRISON FIELD

RECORD: 80–72 (.526)

New Jersey's only venture into the major leagues, the Federal League Newark Peppers were oil tycoon Harry F. Sinclair's proposed gateway to the New York baseball market. The assumption was that, inheriting the bulk of the roster of the 1914 pennant-winning Indianapolis Hoosiers, the Peppers would take the 1915 pennant and sufficiently threaten the Brooklyn Dodgers, New York Yankees, and New York Giants that the American and National leagues would sue for peace. The reality was that the Peppers finished fifth, drew poorly, and finally served only as a vehicle for Sinclair to negotiate a settlement with the two older circuits.

Before there even was a Newark club, there were Sinclair, an Oklahoma oil millionaire, and Patrick T. Powers, who had served as president of both the minor Eastern League and the National Association, the governing body of the minor leagues. Sinclair's money made the Feds giddy. When FL President James Gilmore sought more information about Sinclair, Philip Ball, president of the St. Louis Terriers, wired him: "Rockefeller has half the money in the world, Sinclair the other half."

To use Sinclair's money and exploit Powers's baseball knowhow in the New York metropolitan area, the FL had to move a franchise. The first choice had been the sixth-place, poorly attended Kansas City Packers, but a restraining order secured by the Kansas City directors shifted attention to the pennant-winning but debt-ridden Indianapolis Hoosiers. For a time, the Newark *Evening News*, not knowing which of the two clubs New Jersey would inherit, actually covered the spring training sites of both. At the same time, Powers used all his resources to complete construction on a $100,000, 20,000-seat stadium in Harrison, just across the Passaic River from and within walking distance of downtown Newark.

Sinclair wanted John McGraw of the Giants as his manager, but McGraw rejected a $100,000 offer and became a bitter foe of the Federals. Instead, Bill with the exception of 1914 batting titlist Benny Kauff, looked very much like the squad that the Hoosiers had fielded the year before. The Packers opened on April 16th to a crowd of more than 26,000, with several thousand more turned away. The club enjoyed a few days in first place, spent the better part of the summer bouncing between second and sixth, and finally settled into fifth place, six games out of first. In June, Phillips was replaced by third baseman Bill McKechnie, who would go on to a Hall of Fame managerial career.

Without Kauff, the Peppers' best hitter was right fielder Vin Campbell (.310), followed by future Hall of Fame center fielder Edd Roush (.298). The most interesting, if not the best, player on the team was 38-year-old utility player Germany Schaefer, who was picked up from the Washington Senators more for the entertainment value of his antics than for his performance.

What kept Newark over .500 for the season was a pitching staff that led the FL with a 2.60 ERA. The anchor was aging Ed Reulbach, who had been cut by the NL Brooklyn team because of his activities on behalf of the Players Fraternity, an early attempt to-

Harry Sinclair built one of the great oil fortunes of the nineteenth century after he left baseball. He also became one of the central figures of the Teapot Dome Scandal. Allegedly, Sinclair bribed Secretary of State Albert B. Fall and others in 1922 in order to secure government oil leases. While acquitted of conspiracy charges, he was found guilty of contempt of Congress and sentenced to three months in jail.

organize players in a protective association. Reulbach went 20–10, with a 2.23 ERA.

Initially at least, the Peppers' major competition was not the AL and NL clubs across the Hudson River, but the International League Newark Indians, who were owned by Charlie Ebbets of Brooklyn. The Feds eventually forced the minor league team to move to Harrisburg, Pennsylvania. Even with that victory, however, the Peppers set no attendance records. Sinclair first tried to boost the gate with bicycle races. In July, he threatened to move the club unless the local trolley line was extended across the Passaic River to his ballpark. In August, he experimented with reduced prices—ten cents in the bleachers, twenty-five cents in the pavilion, and fifty cents in the grandstand. When 18,000 fans poured into Harrison Park, six other FL clubs announced price cuts.

Sinclair went on to play a central role in the negotiations to settle the FL war. His assumption of control over the Kansas City Packers and subsequent threat to move them into New York gave him unparalleled leverage. As a result, he came out of the settlement unique among FL backers: He made a

Footnote Player: First baseman Rupert Mills was the last FL holdout. Long after the owners had abandoned the cause, Mills insisted on honoring his two-year contract with Newark. Refusing a $600 buyout of the $3,000 owed him for the 1916 season, Mills accepted Patrick Powers' demand that he work out every day for seven hours. For sixty-five days, until he agreed in July to play for Harrisburg in the New York State League, Mills showed up at Harrison Field for "practice," making him the only FL player in 1916.

profit. Not only did he receive a direct $100,000 buyout over ten years, but he assumed control over FL player contracts and sold them off to AL and NL teams. Some reports had Sinclair and James Gaffney, a former owner of the Boston Braves, on the verge of purchasing the Giants, but with the demise of the FL, the oilman returned to Texas and Oklahoma, where profits were more readily available.

NEWARK PEPPERS

Annual Standings and Managers

Year	Position	W	L	Pct.	GB	Managers
1915	Fifth	80	72	.526	6	Bill Phillips, Bill McKechnie

New York Mutuals

National League, 1876   **BALLPARK:** UNION GROUNDS

RECORD: 21–35 (.375)

William Hulbert was certainly aware of the Mutuals' longstanding reputation for throwing games when he invited them to join his plot to sabotage the National Association and create the National League in 1876. But faced with a choice between upholding the new league's stated intention of driving gamblers out of professional baseball or having representation in the gigantic New York market, Hulbert went for expediency.

The Mutuals had been formed as an amateur club in 1857 by members of New York City's Mutual Hook and Ladder Company Number One. By 1864, they were charging a ten-cent admission fee for their games at the Union Grounds in Brooklyn and splitting the proceeds among themselves. Soon afterward, the club fell under the influence of the notorious Boss Tweed, who maintained the facade of the players' amateur standing by providing them with patronage jobs, frequently in the New York City Coroner's Office. In 1871, the team entered the National Association, drawing crowds of up to 6,000 at the Union Grounds at fifty cents a head. With the fall of Tweed's empire in 1871, management of the club fell to William Cammeyer, the owner of the Union Grounds, who endured long enough to suffer the losses of the club's only year in the NL.

The Mutes, as they were called colloquially, were involved in the first publicized baseball scandal: On September 28, 1865, they lost 28–11 to the Eckfords of Brooklyn in a game that they had been heavily favored to win. It came out subsequently that two Mutuals players, Ed Duffy and William Wansley, had bribed shortstop Thomas Devyr to help throw the contest. The National Association of Base Ball Players, which regulated the amateur clubs of the day, suspended Duffy and Wansley for several years, but shelved charges against Devyr.

The Union Grounds was the center of baseball gambling (and of "hippodroming," as fixing a game was called) throughout the NA years and in the first NL season. Newspapers discussed the situation openly, with catcher Nat Hicks and shortstop Jimmy Hallinan mentioned several times. The Mutuals were eventually expelled for failure to complete their schedule rather than for crooked play, but the gamblers and fixers were indirectly responsible for their demise insofar as constant reports about their activities at the ballpark were hardly an inducement to fans. As the crowds grew smaller, the team lost money and the players sought employment elsewhere; by September, nine members of the roster had signed to play somewhere else in 1877.

To plug the financial drain, Cammeyer canceled the Mutuals' last trip West, the sort of ploy NA teams had gotten away with time after time. But Hulbert insisted the games be played; joining with the St. Louis management, he offered Cammeyer a $400 guarantee if the Mutuals would play two games in St. Louis and three games in Chicago. Cammeyer refused; he didn't even bother to show up at the league's annual meeting in December, when the NL made good on an expulsion threat.

NEW YORK MUTUALS

Annual Standings and Manager

Year	Position	W	L	Pct.	GB	Manager
1876	Sixth	21	35	.375	26	William Cammeyer

New York Metropolitans

American Association, 1883–1887

RECORD: 270–309 (.466)

BALLPARKS: POLO GROUNDS (1883–1885)
METROPOLITAN PARK (1884)
ST. GEORGE CRICKET GROUNDS (1886–1887)
WEST NEW YORK FIELD CLUB GROUNDS (1887)
WILD WEST GROUNDS (1887)

The most controversial club in the ten-year history of the American Association, the Metropolitans were haunted in their first three years by John B. Day's joint ownership of both the Mets and the National League New York Giants, by suspicions that manager Jim Mutrie was a fifth column for the NL within the AA's ranks, and by their status as New York's "other" team. In their last two years, the Mets were simply a doormat performing in out-of-the way Staten Island, a dropout waiting to happen.

Before Day pulled off his coup of placing teams in both the AA and the NL in 1883, there had been no major league baseball in either New York or Brooklyn since 1877. Day, a Manhattan tobacconist, and Mutrie, a former pitcher, had started the club in 1880, playing minor league games both in New Jersey and in Brooklyn until they leased the Polo Grounds at Fifth Avenue and 110th Street from James Gordon Bennett, Jr., the son of the owner of the New York *Herald*. On September 29, 1880, the Mets played the first professional game ever in New York City. (New York clubs in the old National Association, as well as the NL New York Mutuals of 1876, had played in Brooklyn, a separate city until 1899.)

Day's club joined the Eastern Championship Association in 1881, and promptly won the pennant; the team averaged a handsome 3,000 patrons a game. At the end of the following season, the Mets were invited to the organizational meetings of the AA, a budding rival to the NL. Mutrie went to Cincinnati, the site of the meeting, but attended none of the sessions; instead, he hung around the periphery, keeping the club's major league option open, but unwilling to sacrifice the lucrative NL exhibitions that had become the basis of the club's profits. Mutrie agreed to attend the next AA meeting on March 13, 1882, but, working both sides of the street, went directly from Cincinnati to Chicago for a private session with NL president William Hulbert, after which he announced that the Mets would stay out of the AA.

A year later, the ground rules had changed, and Day was offered berths in both the NL and the AA. To replace Troy in the NL, he created an entirely new club with himself as president; the Mets, with W. S. Appleton as president and Mutrie as manager, entered the AA, making their major league debut on May 12, 1883, at the West Diamond of the Polo Grounds. The New Yorkers lost to the Philadelphia Athletics by a score of 11–4.

The Giants and Mets played their home games side-by-side at the Polo Grounds, the former occupying the Mets' old field with the Fifth Avenue entrance, while the latter were relegated to a makeshift area that fronted on Sixth Avenue. A canvas fence—and a clear attitude about which club was more important—separated the two. Led by Tim Keefe's 41–27 record, the Mets came in a respectable fourth.

When the AA objected to the condominium Polo Grounds, the Mets moved their home games to newly leveled grounds on the East River and 108th Street; by June of 1884, however, it was apparent that Metropolitan Park, built atop a city dump, was unsuitable. Pitcher Jack Lynch described the facility as a place where "A player may go down for a grounder and come up with six months of malaria." By July, most games were back in the poor man's half of the Polo Grounds, all complaints about the proximity to the Giants silenced. The shifting home field did not prevent the Mets from getting off to a torrid start, and by mid-June the club was in first place to stay. The offensive stars were Dave Orr (.354, 9 homers) and Dude Esterbrook (.314); Lynch (37–15) and Keefe (37–17) pitched every game except the last one, combining to give the opposition fewer than 2.5 earned runs a contest.

Mutrie proposed a postseason matchup between the NL and the AA champions. Negotiations on the duration and terms of the series began during the season, when it was clear that the Mets and the Prov-

TIMOTHY J. KEEFE
1880 – 1893
RIGHTHANDER WHO WON 346 GAMES
FOR TROY, METS, GIANTS AND PHILS
IN ONLY 14 SEASONS.
HIS RECORD STREAK OF 19 STRAIGHT TRIUMPHS
PACED GIANTS TO FLAG IN 1888.
ONE OF FIRST PITCHERS
TO USE A CHANGE OF PACE DELIVERY.

National Baseball Library, Cooperstown, NY

idence Grays would win their leagues' titles. The Grays swept three games from the New Yorkers in what was the first officially sanctioned interleague championship.

Day, distressed that he had lost $8,000 despite winning the pennant, boldly transferred Esterbrook and Keefe to his fifth-place Giants, where he could charge patrons fifty cents, instead of the AA's mandated twenty-five cents, to see them play. To get around a rule requiring a 10-day wait between a player's release and signing with another club, he sent Esterbrook and Keefe on a cruise to Bermuda so they couldn't be approached by another team.

Irate over Day's maneuver, the AA, at an April meeting, proposed ejecting the Mets, but could not muster enough votes. Instead, the association settled for a $500 fine and a bit of vengeance in the form of a personal fine and suspension for Mutrie, whom many in the Association had long considered a spy for the NL. There was some truth to the accusation. In addition to his open contract with the Mets, the manager also had a secret contract with the Giants.

To earn his money from Day's other purse, Mutrie had leaked the AA club's schedule sufficiently in advance of publication to give Day time to persuade the NL to alter the Giants' schedule. Undismayed by the penalties levied against him, Mutrie followed Esterbrook and Keefe and took over as manager of the Giants. He also scoffed at the AA's declaration that it would no longer honor the reserve clause, thereby precipitating a mini-war with the NL. "Baseball is a business as much as anything else," he said, writing off any suggestion of a conflict as the invention of a "rattle-brained idiot."

Mutrie was right. After all its initial bluster, the association came down to voting to convene the joint conference committee that had been established to resolve difficulties between the leagues. At a secret Atlantic City meeting (from which the Mets were deliberately excluded on the grounds that the AA did not want "its private business known prematurely to the League"), the association rescinded its abandonment of the reserve clause. This concession paved the way to another committee meeting in Saratoga on August 24th at which the rules governing the transfer of players from one club to another were revised. The ten-day rule was modified to allow the other clubs in a released player's league to negotiate with him and to preclude teams in the other league from doing so during the ten days; in effect, the Saratoga agreement created an embryonic waiver rule. The conference failed to provide a mechanism for the sale of player contracts, but that too came, in 1889, as a direct outgrowth of the Saratoga talks.

The Mets, under a new president (Frank Rhover) and a new manager (Jim Gifford), slipped to seventh place in 1885. In December, Day sold the club for $25,000 to Erastus Winman, whose Staten Island Amusement Company promoted circuses, concerts, fountain displays, and Buffalo Bill's Wild West Show. Winman also owned something called the Staten Island Rapid Transit Railway, which was actually a ferry that had a contract with the Baltimore and Ohio Railroad to provide transportation to Manhattan from its Staten Island terminus. Winman's fee from the railroad was based on the volume his ferry carried, and the Mets appeared to him as a volume booster.

But the AA, suspecting that Winman was nothing more than a shill for Day, who was trying to keep Manhattan as a preserve for the Giants, expelled the Mets prior to its annual meeting and doled out the club's players to other teams. Realizing that he suddenly had no franchise, Winman sought an injunction against the expulsion in the Philadelphia Court of Common Pleas. The association contended that it was an organization that had to reconstitute itself every year and that Winman had forfeited his franchise by scheduling games at the St. George Cricket Grounds in Staten Island. But Judge M. Russell Thayer ruled that not only was the AA a permanent body, but also that a league franchise was "as sacred as any property" and that changing the location of home games was insufficient grounds for expulsion. The AA had no alternative but to reel back all the players it had strewn about.

Winman's schemes and machinations, while they may have increased his revenue from the B & O, did little to improve the Mets; they finished seventh in each of their last two seasons. Bob Ferguson succeeded Gifford as manager after seventeen games of the 1886 season and was himself replaced for eight games in 1887 by Orr, who yielded to O. P. Caylor for the franchise's final ninety-five games. In both seasons, Orr continued to be the main thrust of the Mets offense with a .338 average and an AA-leading 7 homers in 1886 and a .368 average in 1887.

Winman lost $30,000 in 1886 and 1887 before giving up. At the close of the 1887 season, the entrepreneur sold out to Charles Byrne of the Brooklyn Trolley Dodgers. Byrne kept Orr, O'Brien, Mays, catcher Bill Holbert, and outfielder Paul Radford, released the rest of the players, and then returned the franchise to the AA, which awarded it to Kansas City.

NEW YORK METROPOLITANS

Annual Standings and Managers

Year	Position	W	L	Pct.	GB	Managers
1883	Fourth	54	42	.563	11	Jim Mutrie
1884	First	75	32	.701	+6½	Jim Mutrie
1885	Seventh	44	64	.407	33	Jim Gifford
1886	Seventh	53	82	.393	38	Jim Gifford, Bob Ferguson
1887	Seventh	44	89	.331	50	Bob Ferguson, Dave Orr, O. P. Caylor

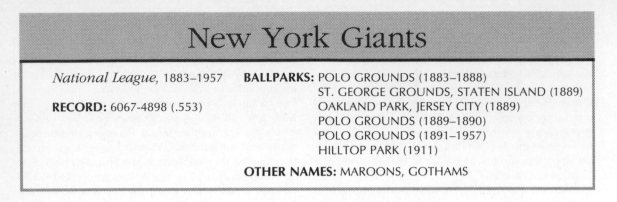

New York Giants

National League, 1883–1957

RECORD: 6067-4898 (.553)

BALLPARKS: POLO GROUNDS (1883–1888)
ST. GEORGE GROUNDS, STATEN ISLAND (1889)
OAKLAND PARK, JERSEY CITY (1889)
POLO GROUNDS (1889–1890)
POLO GROUNDS (1891–1957)
HILLTOP PARK (1911)

OTHER NAMES: MAROONS, GOTHAMS

For much of their existence, the Giants were a very Manhattan concoction of swaggerers and staggerers whose owners, managers, and players were as inspired by Boss Tweed and Damon Runyon as by baseball's Basic Agreement. In the first three decades of the twentieth century under John McGraw, the team lived up to its name by dominating the National League in a way never achieved by any other club, and even its bleakest periods in the 1800s, 1940s, and 1950s were peppered by record power feats and remarkable pennant wins. From Mickey Welch to Willie Mays, no franchise sent more players to the Hall of Fame; from Fred Merkle to Bobby Thomson, none produced more players identified with a single dramatic diamond moment.

The Giants were the creation of tobacco merchant John Day and sports promoter Jim Mutrie, who were invited into the NL at an 1882 owners' meeting that decided to dissolve small-market Worcester and Troy franchises in favor of moving into Philadelphia and New York. The original intention of the owners had been to bring in Day and Mutrie's minor league New York Metropolitans, but the two entrepreneurs trumped that idea by entering the Metropolitans in the American Association, creating an entirely new franchise for the NL, and then shifting their best players from the existing club to the one that was called either the Maroons and Gothams at first and later became known as the Giants. For a playing field, Day and Mutrie used the rectangle of land bordered by 110th and 112th streets and Fifth and Sixth Avenues that they had leased from the son of New York *Herald* publisher James Gordon Bennett in 1880; they divided the area (once very much a polo grounds) with a shabby canvas fence, put the new NL entry in the old Mets' diamond, and built a new field for the AA team. The fence was more than a physical divider; it was also a social separator of the generally unruly fans who paid a quarter to drink beer and see

the Mets and the tonier crowds who paid a half-dollar to watch NL action.

The NL team played its first game on May 1, 1883, struggling through to a 7–5 win over Boston before an estimated crowd of 15,000; among those on hand was former President Ulysses Grant. With Mutrie deciding to keep an eye on his Mets' investment, the club was managed by John Clapp. In what was to become a trademark for the franchise, the very first three batters in the lineup (catcher Buck Ewing, first baseman Roger Connor, and center fielder John Montgomery Ward), as well as starting pitcher Welch, all ended up in Cooperstown. Welch, one of several players picked up from the disbanded Troy franchise, wasted little time in familiarizing New Yorkers not only with the skill that would earn him 311 victories with a career 2.71 ERA, but with the jingles that he sang to celebrate his capacity for beer drinking; one of them ("Pure elixir of malt and hops/ Beats all the drugs and all the drops") caused something of a scandal when it began being heard with too much regularity in the city's schools.

In spite of the presence of so many names in the lineup, New York stumbled through its inaugural season, not even up to playing .500. Over the next four years, it cleared the break-even mark—and then some—but found itself denied first-place honors by even stronger Chicago and Detroit squads. At the end of the 1884 season, Day and Mutrie decided that the more successful but less profitable Mets were the answer to their NL problem, so they brewed up a scheme to switch the AA club's best pitcher Tim Keefe and star third baseman Dude Esterbrook to the Gothams. Making sure that the players couldn't be approached by other bidders during a ten-day grace period after the expiration of their contracts, the owners sent Keefe and Esterbrook on a cruise to Bermuda, ostensibly as a reward for their vital contributions to the Mets' 1884 pennant win. When

The single greatest moment in franchise history occurred on October 4, 1951, when Bobby Thomson clouted a three-run home run off Brooklyn's Ralph Branca to give New York a playoff victory. As Thomson is mobbed by teammates, Branca starts the long walk toward the Polo Grounds clubhouse and Jackie Robinson tries to absorb the momentous defeat. *UPI/Bettmann Newsphotos*

the players returned, they were put under contract by the Gothams. A short while later, Mutrie also came over to the NL club, leaving the Mets to plunge to the bottom of the AA.

Although Esterbrook was gone by then, Keefe proved to be an invaluable contributor to New York's first two NL pennants in 1888 and 1889. In 1888, the righthander led the league with 35 victories and an ERA of 1.74, combining with Welch for 61 wins; the following season, he contributed 28 wins to go with Welch's 27. Keefe was elected to the Hall of Fame in 1964 for a career mark of 344 wins and a 2.62 ERA. The biggest offensive stick on the two pennant winners was the first baseman Connor, who clouted 14

homers and drove home 71 runs with a .291 mark in 1888, then came back to lead the league with 130 RBIs and bat .317 the next year. It was while watching the 1888 team drive toward the pennant that Mutrie popularized the name Giants, usually running around in the stands (while Ewing, Ward, or somebody else made the tactical decisions on the field) and urging the crowd on to cheer "my giants."

The most influential of all the early Giants was Ward, the inspiration for generations of management sneers at rebellious players as "clubhouse lawyers." Originally a successful pitcher (he won 161 games and threw the second perfect game in NL history), Ward was forced by an arm injury to convert first to the outfield and then to shortstop, where he became one of the league's most dominant infielders. Despite the fact that he spent the better part of six seasons on the mound, he still managed to accumulate 2,123 hits in his seventeen-year career, topping the .300-mark three times; he was also one of baseball's first deers, twice leading the NL in stolen bases and running up more than 50 thefts five times.

For all his diamond accomplishments, however, it was off the field that Ward left a deeper imprint—as a union organizer, attorney, and even advocate of racial integration. As a unionist, he was the brains of the Brotherhood of Professional Base Ball Players that, failing to obtain satisfaction from NL owners for its objections to the reserve clause, formed the rival Players League in 1890. As an attorney, he went to court for numerous players and ex-players in contract suits against clubs and leagues, usually emerging victorious. It was also Ward who pushed the Giants to sign black lefthander George Stovey for the 1887 season; the signing was aborted when, around the same time, Chicago manager Cap Anson refused to allow his team to face the southpaw even in an International League exhibition contest, thereby frightening league owners and sealing baseball's doors to blacks until the arrival of Jackie Robinson in 1947. With an assiduousness not always evident in some of its other selections, the Veterans Committee of the Hall of Fame did not vote him into Cooperstown until 1964.

A second straight pennant notwithstanding, 1889 was not Day's best year. Not too long before the season got underway, he was abruptly informed by the city that the Polo Grounds was going to be demolished to enlarge an area known as Douglass Circle. Day quickly arranged for the team to take title to another site at Eighth Avenue and 155th Street, but when construction still wasn't completed on the new Polo Grounds by Opening Day, he had to move two games to Jersey City and another twenty-five to Staten Island; it was not until July 8th that the Giants were able to play their first game in their new home.

The losses incurred by the franchise in having to construct a new park and having to play tag with its fans at the outset of the 1889 season were nothing compared to those registered the next year. Day stumbled first (for the whole league as much as for

On September 10, 1889, pitcher Mickey Welch became the first pinch-hitter in major league history. He struck out.

On May 12, 1890, outfielder Mike Tiernan ended a thirteen-inning scoreless duel between Amos Rusie and Boston's Kid Nichols with a long home run that cleared the center field fence of the Polo Grounds and then banged against the fence of adjoining Brotherhood Park. As Tiernan trotted around the bases, he was cheered by fans in both ballparks.

himself) in losing petitions before the New York State Supreme Court and the U.S. Circuit Court aimed at preventing Ward and Ewing, respectively, from jumping the club to the Players League. As it developed, the Brotherhood circuit lasted only one season, but that was long enough to decimate the Giants' roster and drive Day to the brink of financial ruin. While Ward went off to manage and play shortstop for Brooklyn's entry in the rebel league, Ewing (manager-catcher), Connor, Keefe, Orator Jim O'Rourke, Hank O'Day, Cannonball Crane, George Gore, Danny Richardson, Mike Slattery, and Art Whitney all defected to a New York Brotherhood franchise that set up for business at Eighth Avenue and 157th Street, right next to the NLers; moreover, the insurgents also called themselves the Giants, and with a lot more plausibility than the team they had abandoned. In no mood to lose its New York franchise, least of all to the upstart Brotherhood, NL owners persuaded the Indianapolis owner John T. Brush to sell some of its best players to Day and Mutrie as part of its own shutdown. When not even that was enough to draw the fans whose paid admissions would assist Day out of his money problems, the other owners held a July meeting at which they agreed to invest in New York, with Chicago's Albert Spalding and Boston's Arthur Soden investing $25,000 apiece, Brooklyn's Ferdinand Abel and Philadelphia's Al Reach each tossing in $6,500, and Brush cancelling the $25,000 still due him from the earlier sale of his players. When all the dust had settled, the Giants were in sixth place playing to small crowds, and Day found himself with a bloc of partners who could outvote him at board meetings.

In 1891, following the collapse of the Players League, things got a little better for the Giants, but not for Day. With the majority of the Brotherhood Giants back in the fold, and now seconded by the players obtained from Indianapolis, New York was a preseason favorite to win its third pennant in four years. In fact, it finished a distant third behind Boston and Chicago, largely because stars like Keefe, Welch, and Buck Ewing were beginning to show their years. On the other hand, Ewing's brother John led the league in both ERA and winning percentage, and right fielder Mike Tiernan (with Welch, the only star not to have jumped to the Players League) was the NL home run champion. New Yorkers also had every reason to believe that they had a replacement for Welch in the fireballing Amos Rusie, one of the players obtained from Indianapolis. After winning 29 games in the troubled season of 1890, Rusie came back to notch 33 more, including the team's first no-hitter. In his eight years with the club, he would never win fewer than 20, and ended up with 243 career victories. But although Rusie's numbers were good enough to get him elected to the Hall of Fame in 1977, he would become equally noted for two developments in which he had only an indirect role. The first occurred in 1893, when, in good part because of the righthander's velocity, the NL decided to move the pitching mound to the 60'6" from home plate that it has remained ever since. The second event was the December 1900 trade that sent Rusie to the Reds in exchange for Christy Mathewson; probably the single worst trade in the history of baseball, the sore-armed Rusie didn't win even one game for Cincinnati, while Mathewson went on to establish the NL record of 373 victories (all but one for the Giants).

As for Day, he went from the frying pan of having the other NL owners as partners to the fire of attorney Eddie Talcott. The chief backer of the Brotherhood Giants, Talcott had little trouble buying his way into the NL club and reducing Day to a minority stockholder before the 1891 season. One of the attractions of Talcott's money to Day and the other NL owners was that it also eased negotiations for the Giants to move to the better-equipped Brotherhood version of the Polo Grounds for the 1891 campaign. No sooner had the new general partner taken over than he demanded that Day fire Mutrie and replace him with Buck Ewing. With the backing of other NL owners who did not want to appear too capitulative to Players League forces, Day held firm for Mutrie throughout the season. But then, only a couple of weeks after the final game, Talcott found an ally in minority stockholder Brush, who had moved his major holdings to Cincinnati, and left Day little option but to oust his long-time associate. The lawyer and the owner of the Cincinnati franchise waited a few more months, then they teamed up again to get rid of Day, as well.

The principal developments under the Talcott ownership were the return of Ward as a manager-second baseman and the naming of minority shareholder C.C. Van Cott as president in place of Day; Van Cott's appointment proved far more significant. On the credit side, Ward got the club back up to second place in 1894. But then came a postseason Temple Cup series between the Giants and the pennant-winning Orioles that saw Baltimore sleepwalk through games after members of both teams had allegedly agreed to split the proceeds fifty-fifty no matter who emerged the winner. As for Van Cott, without his appearance on the scene and subsequent money problems, Andrew Freedman might never have found enough disposable stock to buy up and assume majority control over the organization on January 17, 1895.

Even in a business noted for breeding crooks, incompetents, misers, and paranoids, real estate lawyer Freedman stood out as a superlative species. As a long-time bagman for Tammany Hall's Boss Croker, he was in characteristic form in slowly putting together stock in the Giants not in his own name, but in that of future circus entrepreneur James Bailey—and without bothering to inform Bailey. His first move in taking over was to fire Ward in favor of third baseman George Davis; this would be only the first of seventeen managerial changes under Freedman's aegis. His second move was to cancel all the complimentary passes traditionally given to former players and friends of the club. He followed that up by demanding that the Brooklyn franchise pull out of the league and transfer to some minor circuit so that New York would be the only game in town; when Brooklyn owner Charles Byrne ridiculed the notion, Freedman went to his cronies on the City Council to make sure that none of the new subway lines then being projected would go near the Bridegrooms' facility at Washington Park. As much as anything, the uproar over this maneuver consolidated the tempestuous New York-Brooklyn rivalry that would mark the NL for the next half-century.

The first conspicuous critic of Freedman's methods was Sam Crane, a former infielder who had become one of the city's leading sportswriters through commentaries in the New York *Commercial Advertiser*. When Crane accused the owner of trying to destroy the Giants' franchise, Freedman responded by voiding his press credentials to the Polo Grounds, and then by alerting his ticket sellers not to allow him in the park even with a paid admission. When other New York writers came to Crane's defense, they were also put on the blacklist. Particular targets included the New York *Sun*, against whom Freedman filed twenty-five (unsuccessful) lawsuits in five years, and *The New York Times*, whose beat writer the owner slugged one day for suggesting that he was the source of the franchise's problems. When baseball rules pioneer Henry Chadwick joined the chorus of protests in a Brooklyn *Eagle* column, Freedman wrote a letter reminding him that he was drawing a $500-a-year pension from the league and warning him against "biting the hand that fed" him; Chadwick's response was to boycott the Polo Grounds and urge his readers to do the same.

If possible, Freedman's relations with his managers and players were even worse. Davis lasted two months as pilot, after which he was replaced by first baseman Jack Doyle. Considering the fact that he lashed out at Freedman at every opportunity, it was a wonder that Doyle lasted the five weeks that he did. Next came Harvey Watkins, a ham actor whose greatest qualification for managing a big league club was that he had been working until then as an errand boy in Bailey's circus offices. When the Giants ended the 1895 season buried in ninth place, the owner decided that part of the blame for the bad showing rested with the ace Rusie, who had led the staff with 22 wins. Announcing that he had detected an "indifference" in the pitcher's final performances, Freedman deducted $200 from his final paycheck. The irate Rusie not only demanded the $200 back, but served notice that he would sit out the 1896 season if he did not receive a contract for $5,000. When Freedman sent him a pact for less than half that amount, the dispute evolved into a war of attrition that saw even Manhattan stockbrokers demonstrating for the popular pitcher and calling for Freedman's ouster. To make matters worse for the other NL owners, Rusie retained Ward as his attorney in challenging the $200 fine before a league committee. Although the committee quickly ruled that the fine was unjustified, Freedman refused to bend, this in turn prompting Ward to announce that he was filing a suit against the Giants in civil court.

The conflict dragged on for months, with Rusie demanding both the fine money and the $5,000 for 1896, Freedman refusing even to negotiate until Rusie dropped his civil suit, and the other owners not liking their odds in a civil court with Freedman's reputation, Rusie's popularity, and Ward's agility. It was not, however, until Rusie made good on his threat to sit out the 1896 season that the NL realized that it was going to have to break ranks with one of its own by reimbursing the pitcher his $200 and making up the difference between Freedman's salary offer and his own demand. Feeling vindicated, Rusie

returned to action in 1897, compiling a record of 29–8 and leading the league in ERA.

One of the nastiest incidents centering around Freedman developed on July 25, 1898 in a game against Baltimore. The trouble began when Orioles' outfielder and former Giant Ducky Holmes responded to a Polo Grounds heckler by shouting, "I'm glad I don't have to work for no Sheeny anymore!" If anybody could have made something worse out of the remark, which was indicative of the casual anti-Semitism of the day, it was Freedman, and he did so by promptly charging down from the stands with several security guards behind him, intent on removing Holmes from the ballpark. When the other Orioles saw Freedman coming, they got up from the bench and formed a bat-wielding circle around Holmes, defying the security guards to make a move. With the increasingly hostile crowd beginning to urge on the guards to use their truncheons on the Orioles, Freedman demanded that umpire Thomas Lynch eject Holmes from the game. Instead, Lynch warned that the game would be forfeited to Baltimore if Freedman and his guards didn't get off the field. When Freedman refused, Lynch declared the game a Baltimore victory and then ran to the clubhouse with the visiting team to get away from the infuriated crowd. Even when the league censured Freedman for his actions, the Giants' owner wasn't through. After Baltimore declined his demands to give back its share of the gate receipts for the game, he stopped payment on the check. Baltimore then went to NL President Nick Young, asking not only for the money due from the turnstiles but for a $1,000 fine to be imposed on the Giants for deliberately forfeiting the contest. Advised to get out of town for a few weeks, Freedman sailed off to Europe, where he was informed a couple of weeks later that the league had voted to uphold both the fine and forfeit against New York; the consolation for Freedman was that the NL had also decided to suspend Holmes for the remainder of the year.

The NL's plague-on-both-your-houses verdict set off storms of protest from both the nation's press and players around the league, all of whom saw the suspension of Holmes as a concession to Freedman's powerful Tammany Hall connections in New York. In quick order, newspapers demanded a closer investigation of Freedman's ties to Boss Croker, players threatened to strike future games against the Giants, and a Baltimore judge granted an injunction against the suspension of Holmes. With so much opposition, Young reconvened the league committee and reinstated Holmes. For the rest of the season,

Freedman formally protested every game in which Holmes appeared, but to no avail. One of the outcomes of the whole episode was that it strengthened the self-righteousness and obliviousness of baseball writers where ethnic questions were concerned; typical was the reaction of *The Sporting Life*, which declared itself aghast that Holmes should have been disciplined for "the trifling offense . . . of insulting the Hebrew race."

In the dugout, meanwhile, managers continued to come and go. In 1898, Bill Joyce lasted for 44 games, after which came Cap Anson, brought in at NL insistence in an attempt to bring order to the team. Anson needed a mere three weeks to clash with Freedman and walk off, forcing a return by Joyce to play out the schedule. In a move that impressed many as pure sadism, Freedman then hired the broke and broken former owner Day, who scraped listlessly through the first half of the 1899 schedule before he was replaced by Fred Hoey, a Tammany Hall hanger-on who had absolutely no credentials for managing. The only positive thing to be said about Day's tenure was that it represented one of his last moments in the sun: The founder of the Giants would end up in a Bowery tenement, too ill and paralyzed to care for his wife, dying of cancer in the same room. Day died at the age of 77 as a ward of the state.

As for Freedman, he wasn't beyond claiming some method to all his madness—specifically, to devalue the franchise to such an extent that the other owners would realize how badly they needed a New York team (with political connections) and would cave in to his various demands. However this might have been (and there was little evidence of his patience for such long-term strategies in his other investment fields), he achieved his goal in 1900 by watching the team play before sparse crowds as it plopped into the cellar of the standings. It was then that he and Brush lifted the drape off their scheme for syndicate baseball.

The Freedman-Brush concept of the league as a whole controlling players in a common trust and assigning them to teams each season, was triggered most immediately by the rise of the American League, but it had a longer pedigree than that, especially around the Polo Grounds. The most obvious example of the league's pooled interests was the 1890 bailout of Day, with the owners of Chicago, Brooklyn, Boston, and Philadelphia, plus Brush, buying into the club. In 1893, as well, Ward's return from Brooklyn to manage the team was a direct result of NL pressures, and for which the Brooklyn franchise

received a share of the Giants' gate; even Ward himself owned stock in the two clubs. By March of 1900, the crossfunding had grown so common that a rundown of some major boardroom players showed the following:

John Brush—owner of Cincinnati; stockholder in New York.

Arthur Soden—one-third owner of Boston; principal minority stockholder in New York.

Ferdinand Abel—owner of 40 percent of Brooklyn; owner of 40 percent of Baltimore; stockholder in New York.

Frank Robison—owner of Cleveland and St. Louis.

Harry Von Der Horst—owner of 40 percent of Brooklyn; owner of 40 percent of Baltimore.

Ned Hanlon—owner of 10 percent of Brooklyn; owner of 10 percent of Baltimore.

Charlie Ebbets—owner of 10 percent of Brooklyn; owner of 10 percent of Baltimore.

Albert Spalding—owner of a large portion of Chicago; significant stockholder in New York.

In short, the trust scheme was merely a logical extension of tested custom, and Freedman and Brush found quick understanding for their idea from Soden and Robison. But when the New York *Sun* published an outline of the plan before a December 1901 owners' meeting, it caused enough of a sensation for the other four owners—Charlie Ebbets of Brooklyn, John Rogers of Philadelphia, Barney Dreyfuss of Pittsburgh, and John Hart of Chicago—to mend their fences on other issues and set up an opposing four-man bloc. The opposition was primarily based on a projected breakdown of common league stock that would have given the Giants 30 percent, the other three pro-trust clubs 12 percent each, and, carrying up the rear, Philadelphia and Chicago 10 percent, Pittsburgh 8 percent, and Brooklyn 6 percent. The Dodgers and Pirates had additional reasons for battling the plan: the former a suspicion that any Freedman scheme had the dissolution of the Brooklyn franchise as an ultimate target, the latter a championship club that had nothing to gain from having players reassigned around the league.

At the owners' meeting, the clash came down to the choice of a new NL president, with the Freedman-Brush faction backing incumbent Young for another term and the other four advancing the candidacy of Spalding. The submission of Spalding's name was not only an eleventh-hour surprise, but a test of hypocrisy insofar as the new standard bearer for the antitrust faction had himself sought to float a syndication scheme a couple of years before. After twenty-five ballots showing a 4–4 deadlock, Freedman and his cohorts left the conference room to plot strategy, but made the mistake of leaving behind a representative of the Giants; the trust opponents immediately claimed they had a quorum and voted in Spalding. Although Freedman wasted little time in getting to a judge who enjoined Spalding from taking over, the months that followed gave the major league pioneer and the four antitrust owners plenty of opportunities for denouncing the Freedman-Brush group, to the point that they were viewed as defenders against monopolies. None of this did anything for the image of the NL as a whole, and a compromise was finally worked out on the eve of the 1902 campaign, with Spalding withdrawing as president in favor of long-time Dreyfuss associate Henry Pulliam.

The agreement that made Pulliam president also signalled an end to the NL's patience with Freedman. Despite his outrages in running the Giants, he had been tolerated for his connections to Tammany Hall, especially when Ban Johnson began announcing plans to set up an AL franchise in New York; it was usually because of Freedman's political clout that city surveyors were prone to arriving on the scene where Johnson wanted to build an AL stadium and voicing their regret that a new street would have to be paved there instead. In the 1901 municipal elections, however, Tammany was dealt a heavy enough blow by a reform ticket that even Boss Croker decided to take an extended vacation in Europe. With his syndication plan thwarted and this usefulness to the other NL owners becoming frayed at the edges, Freedman surrendered to suggestions that he sell out to Brush and put some distance between baseball and any criminal investigation problems he might have with the new administration of Mayor Seth Low.

There were, however, two footnotes to the deal. The first was that Freedman still had enough power to see to it that the AL's new Highlanders franchise in New York fell into the hands of Tammany disciples like gambler and saloon keeper Frank Farrell. The second was that his unloading of the Giants turned out to be a protracted arrangement, with Brush not taking over completely until the 1903 season. This turned out to be time enough for Freedman to make both his most potentially disastrous and most inspired choices for manager.

When the 1902 season got underway, the New York manager was Horace Fogel. A Philadelphia sportswriter most of the time, Fogel had as his pet project the conversion of Christy Mathewson from a pitcher to a first baseman—and this after the future Hall of Famer had won 20 games and thrown a no-hitter in his rookie year. Fogel's experiment got sidetracked—sort of—when he was fired after forty-one games. His replacement, second baseman Heinie Smith, thought it was crazy to turn a player with Mathewson's arm into a first baseman, so *he* began working out the pitcher at shortstop and in the outfield. To complicate matters a little more, Fogel was kept around as a full-time advisor, meaning that he kept a wary eye on the ruination of his first baseman during pregame drills, sometimes becoming so exasperated with Smith's way of doing things that he returned to the dugout to manage the ensuing game. In the thirty-two games in which Smith either called the shots or served as Fogel's front man, the Giants won five times. The manager for the thirty-third game was John McGraw.

Both Freedman and Brush claimed credit for bringing McGraw to New York, with most evidence suggesting that Brush did all the negotiating on Freedman's initial inspiration. The scene was set for the dramatic hiring when Ban Johnson's increasingly sharp rebukes to McGraw for his umpire baiting and other on-field antics made it clear that the then-Baltimore manager was not going to be permitted to pilot the AL's new franchise in New York in 1903. McGraw was enthusiastic about the opportunity to manage in New York in competition with Johnson's Highlanders, and he signed a four-year contract with the Giants at $11,000 a year.

What followed over the next few days was a McGraw-inspired rondo of stock trades leaving Brush with a majority share in the Orioles and McGraw free to import to New York the Orioles he deemed essential to reanimating the Giants. The players he chose were hurlers Joe McGinnity and Jack Cronin, catcher-outfielder Roger Bresnahan, first baseman Dan McGann, and second baseman Billy Gilbert. Brush was also still formally running Cincinnati, so he added to the ransacking by transferring Cy Seymour and Joe Kelley to the Reds.

Within 10 minutes of his first meeting with Freedman and the Giants on the field of the Polo Grounds, McGraw had released nine players; he also warned the owner that he didn't want to see Fogel around anymore. In his first half-season, all this added up to more bark than bite, with not even the man known as Muggsy able to lift the Giants out of their cellar dwelling.

From 1903 to the beginning of the 1930s, however, McGraw and his New York teams held sway over baseball with a dynastic consistency that only the Yankees would ever match on an organizational level and that nobody ever matched on an individual basis. In twenty-nine full seasons and parts of two others at the helm, McGraw guided the Giants to ten pennants, eleven second-place finishes, and six other first-division showings.

McGraw's success was the result of several ingredients whipped into an original whole: an eye for baseball talent and a freedom from front office constraints to go after it; his nerve-wracking "old Oriole" style of play that kept adversaries as defensive against the stolen base and the Baltimore chop as the opposite-field drive or the home run; a deliberately provoked image of the Giants as couldn't-lose swaggerers, which only made the opposition press more against them; constant umpire baiting aimed at getting the next call; and the thriving of Mathewson. He was also a master psychologist, both in seeming to play up to the superstitions of his players while tactfully turning them to the team's advantage and in channeling most of his confidence-building to players who were being pilloried by the fans or the press for a perceived shortcoming. In agreement with Connie Mack, who once declared that "there has been only one manager and his name is John McGraw," the Hall of Fame elected him as a member in 1937.

Once he got Fogel and Smith off his back, Mathewson turned in the numbers that made him one of the first five players elected to Cooperstown in 1936. Between 1903 and 1914, the lowest number of games won by the righthander in any season was 22. Four times he topped the 30-mark, five times he led the NL in ERA (and posted a career average of 2.13), and five times he struck out more opposition hitters than any other pitcher in the league. With all his diamond grit, Mathewson, a one-time member of the Bucknell Glee Club, also offered a contrast in style to the tobacco-chewing fireballers of his era—relying on a fadeaway screwball as his decisive out pitch, reading avidly, refusing to pitch on Sundays for religious reasons, and possessing the handsome, clean-cut features that were to inspire fictional baseball heroes for children. He became so close to McGraw that the manager didn't shy away from descriptions of the pitcher as his adopted son.

One testament to the effectiveness of McGraw's "total team" slap-and-run tactics was the fact that until outfielder Ross Youngs came into the league in 1917, the well-traveled Bresnahan was the only New York position player who eventually got into Cooperstown; by then, the Giants had finished first or second ten times. On the other hand, the New York pitching staff during that period boasted not only

Mathewson, but fellow Hall of Famers McGinnity and Rube Marquard and solid starters like Red Ames and Jeff Tesreau. McGraw further strengthened his pitching corps by being one of the pioneers in the use of relievers; among the bullpen specialists for the club in the first decade of the century were Claude Elliott, George Ferguson, and Doc Crandall.

McGraw won his first pennant in 1904, with a franchise-high 106 victories. The principal contributors were McGinnity and Mathewson, who won a staggering 68 games between them, and shortstop Bill Dahlen, who led a weak offensive league with 80 RBIs. The pennant was almost overshadowed, however, by the refusal of Brush and McGraw to meet Boston in the World Series; still vindictive toward Johnson, neither was ready to lend credibility to the AL by agreeing to the postseason games. A year later, however, after another pennant romp, McGraw agreed to go up against Mack's Athletics in what turned out to be the greatest pitching series in the history of postseason play. In the opening game, Mathewson shut out Philadelphia; in game two, it was the turn of Chief Bender to blank the Giants; in the third game, Mathewson came back to throw nine more blanks; game four saw McGinnity twirl a five-hit whitewash; and then, finally, it was Mathewson again for his third shutout in five games.

As though the Giants needed another weapon to bruise the feelings of opposition players and their fans, the win over the Athletics inspired McGraw to have special uniforms made for the players that said WORLD CHAMPIONS. It was in these togs that the team traveled by horse and carriage from their hotel to visiting ballparks, infuriating the local population (and prodding them to buy tickets) along the way. In the odd circumstance that crowds figured to be kept down by bad weather or a host team out of the pennant race, Brush and McGraw would send telegrams ahead to their next stop requesting police

On September 22, 1904, the Giants clinched the pennant with 52-year-old Orator Jim O'Rourke behind the plate. O'Rourke, a former Giants' star, had been out of the game for eleven years, but was invited back to play in the clincher by John McGraw. He had one single in four at bats. O'Rourke's appearance made him the only player from the National League's inaugural season in 1876 to appear in a twentieth-century game.

protection against some anonymous threat to the club; the sight of policemen waiting at a train station for the team train was generally enough to resuscitate interest in the game to be played. Given the arrogance of McGraw and his players, on-field brawls became commonplace, frequently going on long enough to encourage rowdier fans to clamber down from the grandstand to join in. The club's reputation became such that even in the rare instance when the Giants were on the side of the angels, they ended up taking the blame for trouble. In one 1908 episode in Boston, McGraw and McGinnity attempted to go to the aid of a Braves' fan who was being roughed up by security men in the stands and, despite having most of the spectators on their side during an ensuing melee, the two men were arrested for fomenting a riot.

When McGraw wasn't baiting umpires or opposition players and managers, he was going after NL owners. In one instance, he began shouting at Ebbets, who was sitting next to the Dodger dugout; when the Brooklyn owner stood up and demanded to know whether McGraw had called him "a bastard," the manager replied, "No, I called you a son of a bitch!" Of much more consequence was his baiting of Dreyfuss during an early-season game at the Polo Grounds in 1905 between the Giants and Pirates. With a taunting cry of "Hey, Barney!", McGraw launched into accusations that the Pittsburgh owner controlled certain umpires and that he had become known as a deadbeat around the league for his failure to pay off gambling debts. Dreyfuss, who prided himself as a model of rectitude, filed a protest with NL president Pulliam, who opened an investigation. That was enough for McGraw to remind everybody that Pulliam had been a long-time Dreyfuss employee and to call the president himself to warn him against acting like a puppet for Pittsburgh. When Pulliam responded by fining the manager $150 and suspending him for fifteen days for the presumptuousness of his admonition, the New York *Evening Journal* collected more than 12,000 signatures on a petition demanding that the league directors put an end to the investigation and overturn the fine and the suspension. In an atmosphere permeated by the harangues of McGraw and Brush against Dreyfuss and Pulliam, the league directors decided that the Polo Grounds episode had really been Dreyfuss's fault, and they censured him for engaging in a public brawl; they also congratulated the hapless Pulliam for having handled the situation so wisely.

In upholding both the fine and suspension against McGraw, the board really resolved nothing, because the New York manager promptly announced that he still had no intention of abiding by them. When the team traveled to Boston for a series, it was accompanied by an attorney who obtained an order from Boston Superior Court restraining Pulliam from seeking to execute the penalties. McGraw put on his uniform and returned to the dugout without ever missing a game. Pulliam, who ultimately saw the whole matter peter out and who would often refer back to the incident as a major reason for losing enthusiasm for his job, became a frequent target of cartoonists, especially in New York. As for Dreyfuss, he would be haunted for the rest of his life by wiseacre cries of "Hey, Barney!"

Mathewson's stint in the Bucknell Glee Club notwithstanding, few of McGraw's players could be confused with choir boys. Shortstop Dahlen was known as Bad Bill for his readiness to start a fight at the slightest provocation and for his constant attacks on other teams as minor league franchises. Pitcher Bugs Raymond, who was to die as an alcoholic at the age of 30, accepted assignments to the bullpen only because it left him closer to a saloon across the street from the Polo Grounds. The strutting Turkey Mike Donlin was charged with drunkenly assaulting a conductor and menacing a porter with a gun during an offseason train trip in 1906; Donlin also took off the entire 1907 season to pursue a career in vaudeville with his wife Mabel Hite. McGinnity, known as the Iron Man for having worked in an iron foundry as a youth, was fined on a number of occasions for precipitating mass brawls. In one instance McGinnity was accused by Pulliam of "attempting to make the ballpark a slaughterhouse"; the righthander also had the frightening major league record of hitting one out of every nineteen batters that he faced.

The Polo Grounds fans were of a piece with their team. On opening day in 1907, they pelted umpire Bill Klem so relentlessly with snowballs that he declared a forfeit victory for the Phillies. A month later, some 10,000 spectators rushed onto the field after a loss to the Cubs to protest the umpiring; umpires Hank O'Day and Bob Emslie had to be escorted to their dressing room by policemen with drawn revolvers. In September 1908, part of a crowd of 35,000 began mocking Donlin about his vaudeville career, prompting the outfielder to charge into the stands and punch the nearest jaw; police had to drag him

In 1907, Arlie Latham was put under contract by the Giants as baseball's first full-time coach.

out of a pile of bodies feet first and then had to ring the outfield for the rest of the game in case the hostilities broke out again.

Not all Giants' fans were unruly, of course. Practically from birth, the club was a magnet for Broadway performers, sports stars, and other luminaries. Part of the reason was simple proximity; another was the franchise's ties to Tammany Hall politicians who attracted entertainers and other celebrities to their coteries. There was also McGraw's own attraction to such people and their fascination with somebody who could growl like a mongrel during a game, then show off his university-honed intelligence during dinner at a fancy restaurant.

Inevitably, some of the Giants themselves undertook show business ventures. After his 1907 taste of the stage, Donlin became less and less interested in baseball, and eventually drifted to Hollywood, where he became a bit player in the movies. McGraw not only went on vaudeville tours with baseball anecdotes, but was talked into playing the title role in a silent film entitled *The Detective*. Marquard toured the country with the reigning queen of vaudeville, Blossom Seely, then later married her after being chased through several states by her estranged husband and various process servers; he also appeared in the Hollywood film *Nineteen Straight* with Maurice Costello.

In the first decade of the century, the nightmare season for the Giants was 1908, as symbolized by the Polo Grounds game on September 23rd against the Cubs when Fred Merkle committed his notorious "boner." At the start of the game, the clubs were tied for first place; in the ninth inning, they were still tied, with Merkle leading off first, Moose McCormick leading off third with the potential winning run, and Al Bridwell at the plate. When Bridwell singled to center off Jack Pfeister, McCormick crossed home with what appeared to be the winning run. With the crowd jumping down from the grandstand to celebrate the ostensible victory, Merkle didn't bother to touch second, but jogged straight to the clubhouse. Chicago second baseman Johnny Evers called frantically for the ball so he could register a forceout.

It was while passing the Polo Grounds in 1908 that composer Jack Norworth got the inspiration for the song "Take Me Out to the Ball Game." Norworth himself never saw a major league game until many years after the song had become the sport's unofficial anthem.

Outfielder Solly Hofman fired the ball over Evers's head. McGinnity, coaching third base that day, sensed what Evers was up to and fought his way through jubilant fans to get to the ball. No sooner had he seized it than Chicago shortstop Joe Tinker jumped on his back to prevent him from losing the ball. McGinnity shook Tinker off him and fired the ball toward the left field stands. Just then a second ball landed somewhere near the shortstop position, and was spotted simultaneously by Cubs' pitcher Rube Kroh and a New York fan. Kroh punched the fan, retrieved the ball, and handed it to Evers, who immediately stepped on second and demanded an out verdict from umpire Emslie. Emslie said he hadn't seen the play and appealed to fellow-arbiter O'Day, who agreed with Evers that Merkle had not touched second and called the runner out, disallowing the run.

Although that decision necessitated an immediate resumption of the game, O'Day and Emslie looked around at the unleashed fans, recalled their past troubles in the Polo Grounds, and retreated. It was not until 10 o'clock that evening that O'Day, after making a game report to Pulliam, officially called Merkle out.

Then the real trouble started. McGraw noted instantly that a third out call on Merkle had obligated the umpires to clear fans off the field and continue the game into the tenth inning; failure to do so, he said, amounted to an umpiring forfeit for the home team. Most sportswriters—around the country as well as in New York—observed that, though in the rulebook, the touching-second regulation had always been ignored by umpires.

What proved to be the worst reaction of all was Pulliam's: After upholding umpire O'Day's belated call, he allowed the Giants and Cubs to play another game in the Polo Grounds series without insisting on continuing the tied game first, then even let Chicago leave town and several more days pass before finally declaring that the squads would have to meet again after the season if the contest were necessary for deciding the NL pennant. The game did indeed turn

On April 11, 1907, Roger Bresnahan became the first catcher in the big leagues to wear shin guards openly. Soon afterward, as a result of a beaning, Bresnahan also became the first player to add a protective lining to his cap.

out to be extremely necessary, and despite being pelted by cushions and other objects thrown at them by Polo Grounds fans during the game, the Cubs prevailed by a count of 4–2. For McGraw, the game was merely a confirmation of how the Giants were "robbed" of a pennant, not by Merkle (whom the manager always defended stoutly) but by Pulliam.

On top of the 1905 incident involving Dreyfuss, Pulliam's untimely silences and belated pronouncements in 1908 cemented the hostility of McGraw and Brush. A year later, a disturbed NL president shot himself to death in the New York Athletic Club; the only franchise not represented at the funeral by an owner and manager was the Giants.

Because of the 1908 makeup game, the Giants not only lost another pennant, but also their team physician. Shortly before going out on the field to officiate the contest, umpire Klem was accosted by Dr. Joseph Creamer, who offered $2,500 if the home team were the beneficiary of some calls. By Klem's subsequent account, Creamer said that he had been put up to his approach by three players whom he did not name. Although the physician denied any such bribery attempt, he was banned from baseball for life.

After a couple of more runnerup seasons, New York got back to the World Series in 1911—a campaign that started off in the most inauspicious way possible when an April 14th fire destroyed the Polo Grounds. While a concrete-and-steel structure was being erected in place of the old wooden stands, the team took up quarters in Hilltop Park, where it proceeded to run the league ragged with an attack centered around a never-equalled 347 stolen bases. The principal thieves were outfielders Josh Devore and Fred Snodgrass, who combined for 112 steals. Overall, the best offensive player was second baseman Larry Doyle, who led the league in triples with 25, and also had 25 doubles, 13 homers, and 77 RBIs to go with his .310 average. A sparkplug for the team since coming up in 1907, Doyle had become something of a franchise emblem ever since Damon Runyon had recorded his effusive declaration after a club victory that "Goddam! It's great to be young and a New York Giant!" The pitchers were led by Mathewson and Marquard, who put together 50 wins between them; one or the other led the league in ERA, winning, percentage, and strikeouts.

The 1911 season also marked the arrival on the scene of Charlie Faust. With a name that tantalized McGraw from the start, Faust presented himself to the manager before an early-season game in St.

Louis, declaring that a fortune teller had predicted that if he pitched for the team, the Giants would win the pennant. Although he was no good as a pitcher, fielder, or hitter, McGraw kept him around for a few days as a good luck charm. When the Giants suddenly embarked on a lengthy winning streak, the players began referring to their teammate as Victory Faust and welcomed his company.

On the last weekend of the season, with the pennant already decided, Faust was permitted to appear against the Dodgers twice, yielding a run in two innings in what was clearly a burlesque performance by everyone except the pitcher. After the season, Faust took to the vaudeville circuit to explain how he had helped the Giants win the flag. During losing streaks in both 1912 and 1913, he was called back to the team, which immediately began winning again on both occasions. By 1913, however, McGraw was beginning to have doubts about what he had wrought, all the more so when he tried to explain without success to some of the players that it hadn't been Faust, but their own looseness around him, that had accounted for their improved performance on the diamond. But before the manager had to tell the team that it was going to go through 1914 without its good luck charm, Faust himself disappeared, not showing up again until many months later in an Oregon mental institution. He died in a Washington State asylum in 1915.

The good news between 1911 and 1913 was that the Giants won three straight pennants; the bad news was that the club lost all three appearances in the World Series, twice to Mack's Athletics and in between to the Red Sox.

Brawls continued to be a trademark of the team, even in exhibition contests and during hours of supposed respite. In the middle of a November 1911 barnstorming tour of Cuba, McGraw and NL umpire Cy Rigler got into a drunken fight with Cuban fans in a Havana bar and were arrested for disturbing the

Footnote Player: Jim Thorpe, who in 1912 became the first man to win the decathlon at the Olympic Games, joined the Giants as an outfielder in 1913. His less than sparkling major league career was spread out over six seasons, during which he compiled a .252 average for the Giants, Reds, and Braves. The famed runner had only 29 steals.

peace. In a May 1912 exhibition against a black team in New Jersey, the Giants walked off the field to protest some umpiring calls, causing incensed fans to come after them with sticks and rocks. In June 1913, a fight between McGraw and Phillies' pitcher Ad Brennan ended with dozens of Philadelphia fans pummeling the manager to the ground. In October of that year, the long relationship between McGraw and Wilbert Robinson came to a snarling end when the pilot blamed his righthand man for missing the sign that supposedly cost the Giants a rally against the Athletics in the World Series; Robinson soon moved over to the Dodgers and became a thorn in the side of his former friend. McGraw was thrown for another loss in November 1912, when the long-ailing Brush died and was replaced as president by his son-in-law Harry N. Hempstead. Hempstead knew next to nothing about baseball, so he leaned heavily on the advice of club secretary John Foster, who never disguised his antipathy toward McGraw or his own ambition to wrest effective control of the team away from the manager. Tensions between Foster and McGraw finally exploded in December 1913, after the club secretary and Hempstead had taken it upon themselves to trade infielder Buck Herzog and catcher Grover Hartley to the Reds for outfielder Bob Bescher; declaring that he had always made the team's deals and would continue to do so, McGraw forced the executives to usurp his authority once and for all or back down. They backed down.

Of all the individual performances at the beginning of the second decade of the century, the most remarkable was Marquard's nineteen consecutive victories in 1912. Scoring rules of the day robbed him of a twentieth straight for a game in which the team regained a decisive lead while he was on the mound as a reliever. In 1915, Doyle won the club's only batting title over a forty-year-period stretched between Jack Glasscock in 1890 and Bill Terry in 1930. Two of McGraw's special projects—Merkle and outfielder Fred Snodgrass, whose error in the decisive game of the 1912 Series against Boston had been as vilified as Merkle's celebrated running boner—vindicated the pilot's defense of them with a number of solid reasons.

Raids by the insurgent Federal League in 1914 cost many organizations key players. With the Giants, however, the big question was McGraw himself, who received two bonafide offers—a one-year contract for $100,000 that would allow him to pick any team he wanted to manage and a five-year pact at $50,000 a year that would be predicated on establishing a New York team. When the Giants' boss turned down both offers, his players also remained at the Polo Grounds, especially after Hempstead was persuaded to hand around hefty raises.

The Federals came back into Giants' history a number of ways following the league's dissolution after the 1915 season. To begin with, McGraw spent a lot of the organization's money picking up suddenly available players like outfielders Benny Kauff and Edd Roush, third baseman Bill McKechnie, pitcher Fred Anderson, and catcher Bill Rariden. Then, in July 1916, having to admit that Mathewson had won all that he was going to win and seeking a managerial spot for his friend, McGraw packaged the righthander, Roush, and McKechnie to the Reds to reacquire Herzog. The exchange not only provided Mathewson with a managerial opportunity and wiped out Foster's foray into wheeling and dealing, but became a curious footnote to baseball lore insofar as all three players bundled off to Cincinnati ended up in the Hall of Fame.

Even though he had a couple of solid years for the Giants, the lefty swinger Kauff never became the superstar McGraw had envisioned. Near the end of the 1920 campaign, he was released to Toronto; a short time later, he was named in connection with an auto theft ring. Although eventually cleared of any crime, Kauff was regarded as compromised enough to be banned from baseball for life.

The 1916 Giants set new standards for inconsistency. After an eight-game losing streak in April, the club went on a seventeen-game winning binge in May, all the victories coming on the road. In September, even the seventeen wins became a memory when the team ripped off a record twenty-six straight triumphs. For all that, New York not only finished a mere fourth, but clouded the outcome of the entire pennant race when McGraw hinted that his team might have thrown a season-ending contest to the Dodgers that allowed Brooklyn to sneak past Philadelphia into the World Series. When the Phillies demanded a league investigation into why a visibly disgusted McGraw had left in the fifth inning of the crucial game against the Dodgers, the manager claimed that it was only because he couldn't stand watching inept baseball. Though no formal charges were ever pressed against the Giants, suspicions lingered that some members of the already-eliminated team had wanted Brooklyn to beat out Philadelphia because of their attachment to former coach Robinson and Merkle (traded across the river earlier in the year).

If McGraw harbored resentment over the game with the Dodgers, he hid it well, because practically the entire team was back in 1917, when the Giants once again went all the way. The campaign got underway in classic Giants' style during an exhibition series against the Tigers, when Herzog and others got into brutal mixups with Ty Cobb both on and off the field and McGraw himself tried to slug the Detroit star in a hotel lobby. In June, an even nastier story began to unfold after McGraw slugged umpire Bill Byron under the stands in Cincinnati for allegedly declaring that Muggsy had been "run out of Baltimore." League president John Tener, a former governor of Pennsylvania, fined McGraw $500 and suspended him for two weeks. McGraw's reaction, delivered to New York *Globe* writer Sid Mercer and then to other reporters, was to accuse Tener of being a puppet for the Phillies and to write off all NL arbiters as incompetents. Although he subsequently repeated the charges to other journalists in Boston, he then backtracked completely after a meeting with Hempstead, denying that he had ever attacked Tener or the umpires. The Baseball Writers Association demanded a hearing before Tener, where various witnesses confirmed that the New York manager had indeed made the incriminating allegations to Mercer. Despite the fact that he had the nimble Ward as his attorney, McGraw lost at the hearing, and had to pay an additional fine of $1,000 for slander.

Back on the field, the team had little trouble with the runnerup Phillies. The stars of the pennant drive were southpaw Ferdie Schupp, who had a career year with 21 wins and the second best ERA in the league, right fielder Dave Robertson, who led the league in homers, and third baseman Heine Zimmerman, who threw in a NL-leading 102 RBIs to go with his .297 average. In the World Series against the White Sox, however, it was the same old story, with an AL team defeating McGraw for the fourth time in a row. The main reasons for the loss were Chicago ace Red Faber's three wins, woeful New York defense, and another Giant Moment when Zimmerman chased Eddie Collins across home plate in a botched rundown play in the decisive game.

Like other teams during World War I, the Giants lost some of their most important players to military service or defense plant work. But as McGraw was the first to admit, their main problem in three straight second-place finishes was the advanced age of some pivotal position players and pitchers and the need to find young blood. This was accomplished, and then some; among those who made their debut on the eve of the 1920s were future Hall of Famers Youngs,

The only major leaguer killed in either world war was backup Giants' third baseman Eddie Grant, a World War I casualty. Grant's body was never found, but a monument was erected in his honor at the center field wall of the Polo Grounds.

George (High Pockets) Kelly, and Frankie Frisch. The club's most reliable pitcher at the turn of the decade was righthander Jesse Barnes, a 25-game winner in 1919 and a 20-game winner the following season.

The team continued to generate stories of smears, brawls, and arrests, but the biggest development of the period was the January 14, 1919 announcement that Hempstead and the Brush estate had concluded an agreement to sell the franchise for $1 million. Although the sale had been anticipated for some months, every indication had been that the buyer would be George Loft of the candy-making company or George M. Cohan of the flag-waving companies; instead, the buyer turned out to be Charles Stoneham, who was identified at first as a Wall Street broker. In fact, Stoneham ran a bucket shop that allowed bettors to buy and sell stock hypothetically and that, though legal as an enterprise up to the Crash of 1929, resembled nothing so much as a casino. One of his partners in the speculation venture was gambler Arnold Rothstein, who would become implicated in the 1919 Black Sox scandal; more to the point for any New York Giants' owner, one of Stoneham's closest associates was Governor Alfred E. Smith, who carried with him the endorsement of Tammany's politicos. At several junctures in the 1920s, Stoneham would need every one of his political allies to slip out from under various grand jury indictments handed down in connection with his bucket shops.

McGraw's reaction to the sale was totally positive because it meant an end to interference, effective or not, from Hempstead and Foster. The manager was all the more enthusiastic when Stoneham invited him into the ownership for a $50,000 purchase of seventy shares in the franchise; with the investment, McGraw also became an organization vice-president. But if he wasn't bothered by the new owner's connections to Rothstein, McGraw was considerably irritated by gambling's pull on two of his players—Zimmerman and first baseman Hal Chase. By September, the manager began benching both players without explanation; then, some days before the end of the season, he sent them both home. Testifying during the hearings into the Black Sox scandal, the New York pilot revealed that he had washed his hands of the players both for throwing games themselves and for trying to get outfielder Kauff and pitchers Fred Toney and Chauncey Dubuc to go along with them. Chase, Zimmerman, and Dubuc were banned from baseball for life.

McGraw's position at the center of the action in New York enabled him to have a say in more than Giants' matters. Between 1912 and 1923, for example, he had a crucial role in resolving the various ownership crises of the Boston Braves, mainly by promoting the candidacies of various Tammany associates who had some money to burn in Massachusetts; the matchmaking role usually paid off in trades between the clubs that benefited the Giants much more than the Braves.

In New York itself, McGraw was instrumental in Colonel Jacob Ruppert's purchase of the Yankees, and also had the decisive say in allowing the AL club to use the Polo Grounds during Giants' road trips. By 1920, however, he was having lots of second thoughts about the Yankees as a tenant, most of them named Babe Ruth. Whenever he got the chance, he exploded into diatribes against the new emphasis on power-hitting precipitated by Ruth. Pique turned to vindictiveness when he pressured Stoneham to serve an eviction notice on the Yankees in December 1920. The move brought sharp criticism of McGraw, and only gave more emphasis to the differences between his brand of baseball (now viewed as old-fashioned) and that being marketed by the Yankees.

To an increasing extent, there was less of Muggsy and more of Little Napoleon in the public perception of the manager. Even his relations with some long-time cronies from show business and Tammany hit rocky ground after a drunken brawl at the Lambs' Club with actor William (Hopalong Cas-

sidy) Boyd and a subsequent beating of a second actor that left the latter in a coma for three days. Although felony charges were never filed against McGraw, Prohibition agents used the incident as an excuse for cracking down on the Lambs' Club. The club retaliated by suspending McGraw's membership, who countered by cancelling passes for members at the Polo Grounds. The upshot of all these entanglements was that, almost as much as Ruth himself, McGraw solidified the standing of the Yankees with the New York public.

But McGraw was far from finished; to the contrary, he established the NL record for most consecutive pennants by leading the Giants into the World Series every year from 1921 to 1924. With some of the teams having as many as seven future Hall of Famers on the roster, the Giants made the most of generally shaky pitching while slashing and running their way over the rest of the league. In 1921, the stalwarts were Kelly (league-leading 23 homers, 122 RBIs, .308), Youngs (102 RBIs, .327), Frisch (100 RBIs, .341), and lefthander Art Nehf (20 wins); in 1922, it was Irish Meusel (16 homers, 132 RBIs, .331), Kelly (17 homers, 107 RBIs, .328), and five other regulars who topped .320; in 1923, outfielder Meusel led the league

No National League team has ever been as synonymous with one man as were the Giants with John McGraw.
UPI/Bettmann Newsphotos

Although John McGraw blamed Babe Ruth for inspiring what he considered bad baseball, he invited the Yankee slugger to join his team for a game on October 3, 1923. The occasion was an exhibition contest against the minor league Orioles, with the proceeds ticketed for the impoverished and ailing founder of the Giants, John Day. Wearing an ill-fitting Giants' uniform, Ruth clouted a 400-foot home run in his only plate appearance.

with 125 RBIs, while Frisch and Kelly also reached the 100-plateau; and in 1924, it was Kelly leading the circuit with 136 RBIs, while he, Frisch, Youngs, Meusel, shortstop Travis Jackson, and catcher Frank Snyder all cleared .300. The offense of the early 1920s' clubs was such that, though he batted .295 in his only season as a regular, another future Hall of Famer, Hack Wilson, was sent to the minor leagues and later traded away.

For McGraw, however, the four pennants were merely a warmup to his ultimate goal—thrashing the Yankees in a World Series faceoff. In 1921, in the last of the best-of-nine formulas, he had a conniption when the ALers took the first two games and was not much happier when, because the Yankees were still tenants in the Polo Grounds, the Giants had to wear gray road uniforms in their own park. He brightened considerably, however, when Meusel provided the offensive spark in leading the club to five victories in the next six games. In 1922, Meusel had his second straight Series with seven runs batted in, and the Yankees failed to win a single game.

Over the first two World Series, McGraw's pitchers held Ruth to 7 hits in 33 at bats with one meaningless home run. The eruption came in 1923 when the Bambino clouted three round-trippers in the Yankees' championship win in six games. What slugging did to the Giants in 1923, pebbles accomplished in the 1924 World Series against Washington. With the team leading by a score of 3–1 in the eighth inning of the seventh game, Bucky Harris slapped a bad hop single over the head of New York third baseman Fred Lindstrom to send two runners home for a tie. Then, in the bottom of the twelfth frame, after catcher Hank Gowdy had missed a foul ball by tripping over his mask and the Senators had put on the winning run, Earl McNeely scooted another shot toward Lindstrom that hit a second pebble and caromed over his head to bring the championship to the nation's capital.

Even by Giants' standards, the early 1920s were rambunctious. In April 1921, first baseman Kelly and coach Cozy Dolan were ordered by an Alabama court to pay $600 each to a minor league umpire for assaulting him during an exhibition contest. In April 1922, McGraw and outfield prospect Ralph Shinners jumped on Philadelphia pitcher George Smith months after the hurler had beaned the rookie; Shinners, once thought by McGraw to have the potential of Kelly, never fully recovered from the beaning. In August 1922, hurler Phil Douglas, one of the heroes of the previous year's World Series with the Yan-

kees, reacted to a tongue lashing from McGraw by first drinking himself into a near-stupor and then writing a letter to St. Louis outfielder Les Mann offering to "go fishing" for the rest of the season if the Cardinals, then in a tight pennant race with the Giants, paid him enough money; by the time Douglas had sobered up, the letter was making its way from Mann to St. Louis manager Branch Rickey to Commissioner Kenesaw Landis, and the pitcher was eventually kicked out of the league. An even uglier bribery scandal exploded in October 1924, when outfielder Jimmy O'Connell approached Philadelphia shortstop Heinie Sand and offered him $500 not to bear down against the Giants. Within 24 hours, the naive O'Connell was telling Commissioner Landis that he had merely done what coach Dolan and stars Frisch, Kelly, and Youngs had told him to do. Although the three veteran players denied any involvement, Dolan's only defense was that he "couldn't remember" having sent O'Connell to Sand. Landis exonerated Frisch, Kelly, and Youngs, and put O'Connell and Dolan on the permanently ineligible list.

As it turned out, McNeely's pebble-aided hit in the last game of the 1924 Series marked McGraw's farewell to postseason competition. Although the club remained a contender just about every season except 1926, the second half of the 1920s was a period of extended melancholy interspersed with growls for him. In 1925, he lost two of his closest friends, Mathewson and the veteran sportswriter Sam Crane; in 1927, he went into a long funk over the death of Youngs, who succumbed to Bright's Disease at the age of 30. Over the winter of 1925–26, McGraw also found himself exploited by two hustlers who used his image in newspaper ads to sell Florida land. When the victims discovered that they had been conned out of their down payments, they demanded justice from the Polo Grounds; although McGraw himself had no role in the swindle, he made it a private crusade to reimburse more than $100,000 to the victims because his likeness had made them such prey.

McGraw's biggest problem on the team was Frisch, whose McGraw-like bearing and manner of play made him both the manager's alter ego and his favorite whipping boy. In August 1926, Frisch suffered one verbal beating too many and jumped the team in St. Louis. Although he rejoined the Giants a few days later, it was clear that his days in New York were numbered. What came as a shock was the manner of his departure—a December 20th trade with St.

Louis that brought nothing less than Rogers Hornsby to New York. In his increasingly vindictive style, Mc-Graw also sent to St. Louis journeyman pitcher Jimmy Ring and some money, telling friends that he didn't want Frisch to get the idea that he was worth Hornsby even-up. Not too long afterward, the manger and just about everyone else connected with the Giants would have preferred Frisch's occasional absences to Hornsby's presence. The first major problem came in January 1927, when the second baseman was sued by the Kentucky Gambling Commission for some $70,000 in gambling debts. Hornsby fought the suit and won it, but not before the Giants suffered through some anxious moments that Landis might open an investigation and leave them without a batting champion in the middle of the infield. No sooner had that threat evaporated than NL President John Heydler reminded Hornsby that he was still the second biggest stockholder in the Cardinals and that he could not play for New York until he unloaded his shares in the Missouri team. When Hornsby demanded some 300 percent profit on the price he paid for the stock, Cardinals' president Sam Breadon balked. The standoff galvanized McGraw into public warnings that he was contemplating a suit against the league for placing obstacles in the way of playing his second baseman. This was enough for the owners of the six teams not directly involved to throw some money into the pot to accommodate Hornsby.

With his .361, Hornsby was one of six New York regulars to go over .300 in 1927. Everything else about his stay was negative. A former manager himself, he was not the least impressed with either Mc-Graw's reputation or some of his strategical moves, and was firm about telling his teammates so. Whenever McGraw was away from the team for health or business reasons, Hornsby took every opportunity in his role as temporary skipper to contradict standing instructions. It did not come as too much of a surprise when the Giants retraded the Rajah after the 1927 season; what was news was that their only return from the Braves was catcher Shanty Hogan and outfielder Jimmy Welch.

Three of the franchise's greatest players stepped into the limelight in the second half of the 1920s. The first was first baseman Bill Terry, whose abilities with a bat and glove were equalled only by his blunt manner with sportswriters, other players, and fans. A lifetime .341 hitter, the lefty-swinging Terry eschewed the short (257 feet) right field line of the Polo Grounds in favor of the gaps, ending up with 1078 RBIs on only 154 home runs. For six consecutive sea-sons between 1927 and 1932, he topped the 100-mark in both RBIs and runs scored. His 1930 average of .401 represented the last time that a NL player reached .400.

The opposite of Terry in almost every way was outfielder Mel Ott, who remained the people's choice as a player and manager from 1926 to 1948. A six-time home run champion, the lefty-swinging Ott thrived on the comfortable measurements of the Polo Grounds, clouting almost two-thirds of his 511 homers at home. A lifetime .304 hitter, Ott appeared in a New York lineup for the first time in 1926 at the age of 16, attracting immediate attention for a batting stance that saw him elevate his front foot almost to the knee of the other leg when stepping into a pitch.

The third future Hall of Famer to break in with the club in the 1920s was southpaw screwballer Carl Hubbell, who registered the first 10 of his 253 career victories in 1928. Over five straight seasons between 1933 and 1937, Hubbell won a minimum of 21 games, leading the league in ERA three times during the stretch. Among the lefty's many accomplishments were 24 straight wins in a period between 1936 and 1937 and the fanning of Ruth, Lou Gehrig, Jimmie Foxx, Al Simmons, and Joe Cronin in succession in the 1934 All Star Game.

Between 1928 and 1933, the franchise was in and out of courtrooms in a bitter dispute with Francis X. McQuade, a significant minority stockholder who was bounced from his position as organization treasurer behind Stoneham charges that he had sought to "destroy the club." In a succession of suits and countersuits, it emerged that Stoneham had been using Giants' money for years to finance other ventures, that McQuade had tried to draw McGraw into a plot to overthrow the owner, and that the one-time treasurer himself had not been above borrowing franchise money for private purposes. In the end, however, the case turned on an appeals court reminder that, whatever agreements McQuade had or had not entered into with Stoneham and McGraw and however shabbily he might have been treated by the club president and vice-president, his position as a New York magistrate precluded activities like being an officer of a baseball team. McQuade had troubles besides Stoneham and McGraw; his name also figured prominently in the Seabury Commission's probe of corruption in the Tammany administration of Mayor Jimmy Walker.

In September 1930, Stoneham announced a new five-year accord with McGraw that would keep him as manager through the 1935 season. But the agreement could not disguise the growing alienation between the pilot and his players or McGraw's failing health. Terry, for one, acknowledged that he had not exchanged a word with the manager off the field in almost two years; even the mild-mannered Hubbell protested the pilot's insistence on calling every pitch from the bench.

Adding to McGraw's grief was the consolidation of the Yankees as the biggest draw in baseball with their Murderers' Row teams of Ruth and Gehrig; rather than try to adapt to the new style of play, McGraw became more critical of anything that smacked of innovation, even rejecting the idea of uniform numbers because, he said, real baseball fans should know the players from their appearance. He also lobbied for the pitching mound to be placed two feet closer to home plate so that pitchers might have greater leverage against free-swinging hitters.

The end came on June 3, 1932, when McGraw called Terry into his office and asked him whether he would be interested in managing the club; when Terry said that he would, McGraw made known his intentions to Stoneham to retire. As something of a consolation prize in his losing publicity fight against the Yankees, the news of McGraw's retirement the next day deprived Gehrig of the main sports headlines for having hit four homers in a game against the Athletics. Less than two years later, on February 23, 1934, McGraw died of uremia in a New Rochelle hospital.

The Giants were always on the lookout for a Jewish star who would help attract New York's large Jewish population. Among those to arrive at the Polo Grounds amid a great deal of club ballyhoo were outfielders Benny Kauff, Moses Solomon, and Sid Gordon, first baseman Phil Weintraub, and second baseman Andy Cohen. In an effort to offset the box-office power of Babe Ruth, John McGraw encouraged Solomon's tag as the Rabbi of Swat; the minor league power hitter ended up with only eight big league at bats. Cohen came in for even more pressure, when he succeeded Rogers Hornsby at second base, had a couple of game-winning hits, then found his stats compared with those of the departed Rajah for the rest of the season in daily update boxes in the New York press. Even the usually surly Hornsby asked the dailies to stop increasing pressure on the infielder. Cohen held down the keystone position for only two years.

Terry didn't have an easy start to his 9½-year tenure as manager, not least because of the club's sixth-place finish in 1932. As soon as his appointment was announced, coach and former All Star shortstop Dave Bancroft handed in his walking papers because he hadn't been given the job. Third baseman Lindstrom was even more incensed, saying that he had been led to expect that he would be McGraw's eventual successor; Lindstrom was traded to the Pirates as soon as the season was over. Terry's own first appointment of Billy Southworth as a coach ended badly when the two got into a fist fight during spring training in 1933.

All of the resentments quickly lost their importance when Terry defied all preseason expectations and steered the Giants to the pennant. With the hop taken out of the ball that had made pitching a high-risk profession at the beginning of the 1930s, New York rode the hurling talents of Hubbell, Hal Schumacher, and Freddie Fitzsimmons to the full, clipping the runner-up Pirates by five games. Ott led the offense with 23 homers and 103 RBIs, with Terry himself turning in a .322 average. In a rematch against the Senators in the World Series, the team encountered no pebbles in its path and prevailed in five games, with Hubbell winning twice.

The 1933 world championship was the start of another franchise roll, with the club finishing second in 1934, third in 1935, and again at the top of the pack in both 1936 and 1937. More than for the two pennants, however, the period became memorable for an off-the-cuff remark made by Terry to Roscoe McGowen of *The New York Times* during the February 1934 winter meetings. After discussing the deals made by other clubs during the gathering, Terry wondered aloud about the failure of the Dodgers to complete some kind of trade, asking "Is Brooklyn still in the league?" As soon as the remark appeared in print, Dodgers' officials used it as a rallying cry for their then-miserable team, in the process making it sound as though Terry had been referring to Brooklyn's playing abilities. The upshot was that, on the final weekend of the season, Brooklyn defeated New York twice to allow St. Louis to win the pennant. In the two World Series in which they did appear, in 1936 and 1937, the Giants proved little match for the Yankees of Gehrig and Joe DiMaggio; with Lefty Gomez winning twice in each Series, the ALers took the first confrontation in six games and the second in five games.

By the end of the 1930s, the team was treading water more seriously than at any time since the arrival of McGraw at the start of the century; aside from Ott, who was himself beginning to slip, there was nobody exceptional in the everyday lineup. There was also some uncertainty about the organizational abilities of owner Horace Stoneham, who took over upon the death of his father Charles in January 1936. Although the elder Stoneham had always claimed that he had bought into the club in the first place to leave it someday to his son, the most popular perception of Horace was that of a hard but convivial drinker who talked baseball into the wee hours with some of his favorite players and others whom he regarded as a part of the "Giants' family." In the forty years that he ended up operating the Giants in both New York and San Francisco, Stoneham succeeded in changing that image only to the extent that he became a knowledgeable owner who drank into the wee hours with his favorite players and others whom he considered part of the team's family.

Terry lasted through the 1941 season. A couple of years earlier, amid reports that he was mulling an offer to manage the Indians, he had been given a new five-year contract that also made him the general manager in title as well as fact, and the combination of extra administrative duties and the club's poor performance on the field convinced everyone concerned that a change would be for the better. But, contradicting expectations that his successor would be either shortstop Billy Jurges or third baseman Dick Bartell, the job was given to Ott.

With Terry taking over the farm system and himself assuming the decisive say in trades, Ott made his first move a big one—acquiring first baseman Johnny Mize from St. Louis in exchange for first baseman Johnny McCarthy, catcher Ken O'Dea, pitcher Bill Lohrman, and $50,000. In implicit opposition to the philosophies of McGraw and Terry, Ott described the home run hitting Mize as the "kind of player New York wants," noting that nobody had ever booed him, either, for all his round-trippers in the Polo Grounds. In fact, the Ott-Mize tandem proved to be one of the most potent in the NL in 1942, with the first baseman walloping 26 home runs and a league-leading 110 RBIs, while the manager led the circuit with 30 homers and drove in 93 runs.

But the spark provided by Mize was dowsed quickly when he was among the first league stars to be drafted into military service for World War II. Attempts to land another power hitter, Dolf Camilli, in a July 1943 trade with the Dodgers were rewarded with the first baseman's announcement, after the deal had been completed, that he preferred retirement to wearing a New York uniform.

The end of the war brought a lot of hope and a lot of disillusion. In addition to getting back Mize and outfield power prospects Sid Gordon and Willard Marshall from the army, the Giants opened their purse for $175,000 to pick up Cardinals' catcher Walker Cooper, considered the premium receiver in the league before he had been drafted. The season had hardly gotten underway when Cooper broke his finger, the first of several injuries that would limit him to 280 at bats. Overall, the team's hitting was so poor that only Mize drove in more than 50 runs, and he batted across a mere 70.

The team was also one of the hardest hit by the 1946 raids of Mexican millionaire Jorge Pasquel on the major leagues. With backing from the Mexico City government to upgrade the caliber of play in the Latin country, Pasquel offered inflated salaries to outfielder Danny Gardella, bullpen stopper Ace Adams, second baseman George Hausmann, first basemen Nap Reyes and Roy Zimmerman, and pitchers Sal Maglie, Harry Feldman, and Adrian Zabala. The defectors were banned for five years, but Gardella, changing his mind about playing south of the border, instituted a $300,000 suit challenging the blacklist in terms guaranteed to question baseball's exemption from antitrust laws. Although he lost his case in a first go-round in July 1948, an appeals tribunal not only upheld his claim, but issued a blistering indictment of baseball that effectively reversed the 1922 Supreme Court decision that declared that the sport did not engage in interstate commerce; one of the key points of the ruling was that radio and television coverage of games alone constituted an adequate definition of interstate commerce.

The appeals court verdict sent baseball owners into near hysteria, and they immediately lodged their own appeal. Given the Cold War climate of the period, it was practically inevitable that Branch Rickey, for one, would denounce the pro-Gardella finding as the work of "people with avowed Communist tendencies." With the owners' appeal to the Supreme Court still pending, Commissioner Happy Chandler suddenly announced an amnesty for the Mexico League jumpers in June 1949. The ploy worked: A few months later, Gardella settled out of court for $60,000, saving the owners another legal hearing that they were hardly confident of winning. Gardella's own hopes of resuming his major league career were quickly scotched, with the outfielder getting only one further at bat—for the 1950 Cardinals. Of all the players reinstated, the most significant by far was New York righthander Maglie.

The Giants' last-place finish in 1946 did nothing

for manager Ott's job security, and there were constant reports that he was on the verge of being replaced by Lefty O'Doul. Contributing to his shaky position was a widely quoted comment attributed to Brooklyn's Durocher that maybe Ott didn't have the right attitude to lead a winning ballclub. As originally stated to Brooklyn announcer Red Barber and recorded by New York *Journal-American* sportswriter Frank Graham, the exact Durocher quote was: "Look over there. Do you know a nicer guy than Mel Ott? Or any of the other Giants? Why, they're the nicest guys in the world. And where are they? In last place!" Durocher's observation was later telescoped into the maxim that "nice guys finish last," earning him a line in Bartlett's *Famous Quotations*.

Although Stoneham was viewed as sharing some of Durocher's reservations about the manager, Ott came back in 1947, and presided over the biggest power splurge in NL history when the team clouted 221 home runs. Leading the onslaught was Mize, who hit 51 balls out of the park to tie Pittsburgh's Ralph Kiner for the league lead; in chief supporting roles were right fielder Marshall (36), Cooper (35), and center fielder Bobby Thomson (29). But despite the record slugging (Cincinnati would tie the mark in 1956) and a 21–5 effort from rookie righthander Larry Jansen, the club rose no higher than fourth. There was no mystery about the reasons for the team's mediocrity: It could hit home runs and do little else. For example, the entire club stole 29 bases, which was exactly how many Jackie Robinson stole for the Dodgers that year.

Change finally came on July 16, 1948, and it came as a shock. Eager to hire Burt Shotton as Ott's successor, Stoneham contacted Brooklyn president Branch Rickey to obtain permission to negotiate with the veteran manager, coach, and scout. Rickey's reply was to disclose that Shotton, who had led the

---

Although there had been busts before him, outfielder-pitcher Clint Hartung came to embody the skeptical definition of a baseball pheenom when he joined the Giants in 1947. Hailed as a new Babe Ruth and new Christy Mathewson rolled into one, the Hondo Hurricane, as the press liked to call him, spent six seasons at the Polo Grounds moving back and forth from the outfield to the mound; as a hitter he ended up with 14 homers and a .238 average, and as a pitcher he had a 29–29 record with a 5.02 ERA.

Dodgers in 1947 while Durocher had been serving a season-long suspension, was about to be named again as the Ebbets Field diamond boss; did Stoneham want to talk to the incumbent Durocher, instead? The stunning announcement took a while to set in on both sides of the East River, with even Durocher admitting to feeling queasy about suddenly managing "the enemy." He got over it quickly enough, however, to see that the team he guided to a 41–38 second half in 1948 wasn't one he wanted to manage again in 1949.

Durocher's relations with Stoneham were not unlike those he had with Brooklyn general manager Larry MacPhail in the early 1940s, with allowances made for MacPhail's habitual bluster. As with his one-time Dodger boss, Durocher sat into the night with Stoneham for increasingly inebriated dissections of the team and major league baseball in general, there being plenty of opportunity for the manager to suggest that his employer didn't know what he was talking about. Also as with MacPhail, Durocher departed from the sessions aware of which players his employer doted on and determined to play them into the ground if he didn't happen to like them.

In the case of the Giants, Stoneham was enamored of the so-called "window breakers," especially because their power hitting had proven as popular at the gate as Ott had predicted; sure that only a pennant-winning club could assure spectators in the long run, Durocher set about showing up the deficiencies of the home run hitters, then winning Stoneham's approval to deal them away. In December 1949, he completed what proved to be the Giants' best trade since the acquisition of Mathewson by shipping Marshall, Gordon, and shortstop Buddy Kerr to the Braves in return for shortstop Alvin Dark and second baseman Eddie Stanky. Dark and Stanky, the best double-play combination in the league at the time, had led Boston to a pennant in 1948; Durocher called both of them "my kind of player."

By the end of the 1940s, the New York farm system had produced a number of hitters who seemed born to play within the erratic confines of the Polo Grounds; among them were banjo-hitting outfielders Whitey Lockman and Don Mueller. Also on hand were infielder Hank Thompson and outfielder-first baseman Monte Irvin, who in July 1949 became the first blacks on the team. The usual disaster zone of the pitching staff was relieved somewhat by the July 1950 acquisition of righthander Jim Hearn from the Cardinals and even more by the sudden flourishing of Maglie. Known as The Barber for his ability to shave corners with his curve and chins with his fastball, the righthander was the dominant mound force for the Giants in the early 1950s, not least because of his success against the Dodgers. His scowling image and reputation for winning the big game (meaning against the Dodgers) were such that he overshadowed Jansen, who put up much better numbers before being injured.

After a couple of seasons of tantalizing fans with glimpses of what *his* kind of club could accomplish, Durocher entered the 1951 campaign under some put-up-or-shut-up pressures; the 35-year-old Stanky, for one, had had to deny reports that he had been sounded out as an eventual manager. The atmosphere around the Polo Grounds didn't get any better when the team got off to a lethargic start and was already behind Brooklyn by an appreciable distance by the end of April. But then, in mid-May, Durocher made a series of moves that were to make possible the Miracle at Coogan's Bluff. With his defense even wobblier than his offense, he moved Lockman from left field to first base, Irvin from first base to left field, Thomson from center field to third base, and Thompson to the bench. What made all these changes possible was the calling up of center fielder Willie Mays from the minors. In what became a fabled instance of

managerial patience, Durocher held Mays's hand through a disastrous offensive start of only one hit (a home run off Warren Spahn) in 25 at bats; amidst growing concern that the outfielder was nothing more than a case of overblown front office promotion and Mays's own depressed requests to be sent back down, Durocher declared flat out that the righthand-hitting rookie would stay in the lineup no matter what. By the beginning of June, Mays had found the stride that made him one of the greatest players, offensively and defensively, in the history of baseball. In twenty-two big league seasons, he amassed 660 homers with 1,903 RBIs and a lifetime average of .302. Among his statistical marks were a batting championship, leading the NL in homers and steals four times, and becoming the first big leaguer to clout at least 300 round-trippers and swipe a minimum of 300 bases. But not even Mays's eleven straight Gold Gloves conveyed fully the dash and excitement of his outfield play, as he covered about three-quarters of the outer perimeters to chase down mammoth drives, grab them at the belt in his patented basket catch, then uncork howitzer throws back to the infield. On August 15, 1951, his catch of a long smash off the bat of Brooklyn's Carl Furillo and his estimated 325-foot line drive to double up Billy Cox at home had most spectators calling it the

Although he will always be identified with his catch of Vic Wertz's drive in the 1954 World Series, Willie Mays always singled out this snare of Carl Furillo's line drive on September 22, 1954, as his best defensive play. No sooner had he caught the ball than Mays fired a strike to the plate to double up Billy Cox. *UPI/Bettmann Newsphotos*

greatest catch-and-throw play ever made. Although he had a vested interest in saying so, Durocher's contention that Mays was the best all-around player of the twentieth century was shared by many people. He was elected to the Hall of Fame in 1979.

Despite the energy that Mays brought to the lineup, the Giants remained buried behind the Dodgers well into August; by August 11, Brooklyn's lead had grown to a seemingly insurmountable 13½ games. But then the Giants ripped off sixteen consecutive wins, closing the gap to five games by early September. For the rest of the month, both teams slapped around the NL, but the Giants a little harder than the Dodgers, so that when the season ended, they were in a tie and facing a best-of-three postseason playoff. The first game went to New York behind homers by Thomson and Irvin off righthander Ralph Branca. The second contest was a Dodger slaughter, with four homers supporting rookie Clem Labine's 10–0 whitewashing. With everything on the line in the third game on October 3rd, both teams went to their aces—the Dodgers to fireballing righthander Don Newcombe and the Giants to Maglie. Over the first seven innings, the teams remained deadlocked at 1–1, but then Brooklyn took advantage of some sloppy infield play and singles from Gil Hodges and Cox to score three runs in the top of the eighth and take a 4–1 lead. After Brooklyn failed to add to its lead against Jansen in the top of the ninth, the stage was set for the most memorable half-inning since Harry Wright had paid his first player.

Dark started the ninth by blooping a single. For reasons never explained, Hodges held Dark on first, allowing a potential double play grounder by Mueller to scoot through the infield for another single. With Robinson screaming for the weary Newcombe to get it together, the righthander came back to get Irvin to foul out to Hodges. But then Lockman sent the Polo Grounds into pandemonium by flicking an opposite-field double over third base, scoring Dark and sending Mueller to third. In getting to third, however, Mueller suffered a broken ankle and had to be carried off the field on a stretcher.

In the meantime, Brooklyn manager Charlie Dressen finally saw that Newcombe was indeed exhausted and motioned to the bullpen. At the time, the Dodgers had three pitchers warming up—Labine mainly for show, Branca, and Carl Erskine. Just before leaving the dugout, Dressen was informed by bullpen coach Clyde Sukeforth that Erskine had bounced a curve in the dirt. That left Branca as the choice. In his first pitch to Thomson, Branca got a

called strike. In his second, he got a three-run home run—The Shot Heard 'Round the World. The drama of the moment was underscored by New York announcer Russ Hodges's hysterical mantra of THE GIANTS WIN THE PENNANT.

No World Series could top the playoff finale, and the Giants proved that by losing to the Yankees in six games. The final game of the Series was clouded by disclosures that Durocher had received a combination bribe-threat by mail offering him $15,000 if the Giants lost to the Yankees and threatening his wife, Hollywood actress Laraine Day, if he didn't play along.

What Durocher had not counted on was that the next two seasons would be as anticlimactic as the 1951 World Series. The club suffered its biggest blow when Mays was drafted into the army after only a handful of games in 1952; he did not get back into the lineup until 1954. Another big setback in 1952 was a broken ankle by Irvin, limiting him to fewer than 50 games. Despite these critical losses, the team made another charge at the Dodgers, only to be turned back in very unmiraculous fashion. Among the standout performers of the year were knuckleball reliever Hoyt Wilhelm (who began his trek to the Hall of Fame with 15 wins, 11 saves, and a NL-leading 2.43 ERA), Maglie (18 wins), and Thomson (24 homers and 108 RBIs). In 1953, Thomson was again the big hitter with 26 homers and 106 RBIs, while Thompson, the forgotten man since Durocher's position switches in May 1951, came on with a solid 24 homers and .302 average.

The 1952 season marked an escalation in the bitterness between the Giants and Dodgers; although the clubs had never been sweethearts, beanball exchanges became commonplace, with Durocher and Dressen openly egging on their players. One of the worst incidents took place at the Polo Grounds on September 6, 1953, when Brooklyn outfielder Furillo responded to a fastball on the wrist from Ruben Gomez and a subsequent taunting from Durocher by charging the New York dugout and swinging at whatever Giant got in his way. The brawl ended with Furillo breaking some fingers—but also winning a batting title by being able to sit on a .344 average for the final month of play. In another episode a couple of years later at Ebbets Field, Robinson pushed a bunt down the first base line to get at a New York pitcher, but instead trampled over second baseman Davey Williams. The next inning, an infuriated Dark deliberately went through second base on a double to get at Robinson spikes first at third and precipitate a fist fight. The leg and back injuries suffered by the slight Williams in the collision with Robinson just about ended his career.

Durocher himself was thrown out of games and suspended regularly. More often than not, he withdrew to a press box seat behind Barney Kremenko of the *Journal-American* and flashed signs down to his players and coaches through the sportswriter. On more than one occasion, an innocent gesture by Kremenko had Giants stealing or bunting when they should not have been.

With Mays back in 1954, the Giants had New York to themselves for the first time in more than twenty years. While the Yankees and Dodgers had to settle for runnerup status, the Giants feasted from the return of their star outfielder to win the NL flag. Mays took MVP honors by leading the league in hitting with .345, bashing 41 homers, 33 doubles, and 13 triples, driving in 110 runs, and scoring 119. Other big contributions came from Mueller, who finished right behind Mays in hitting at .342, Thompson, who had another big offensive year with 26 homers and 86 RBIs, and Dusty Rhodes, who hit .333 as a pinch-hitter and .341 overall, with 15 homers and 50 RBIs as a part-time performer. The pitching staff was anchored by southpaw Johnny Antonelli, obtained prior to the season in a deal with the Braves for 1951 hero Thomson; Antonelli had a 21–7 record, with a league-leading 2.30 ERA. The World Series against the Indians—a sweep by the Giants—was most memorable for The Catch, Mays's incredible over-the-shoulder grab against Vic Wertz in the first game that aborted a big Cleveland rally and allowed Rhodes to settle matters with a three-run pinch-hit homer off Bob Lemon in the tenth inning. The lefty-swinging Rhodes, who became almost as known in New York for his bourbon hangovers as for his ability to come off the bench, also had decisive pinch-hits in the second and third games, and ended up driving home seven runs in only six at bats.

The Giants' last three years in New York were mainly a matter of running out the ground ball. With only Mays and (to a lesser extent) Antonelli offering distractions on the field, most attention was focused on Stoneham's warnings that the team required a new park or would be forced to consider leaving town. Unlike the situation in Brooklyn, where Walter O'Malley was making identical threats a daily news item, the Giants had some real financial problems because of a sharp drop in attendance and Stoneham's profligate ways with a dollar. The fact that the Polo Grounds was located in Harlem did not help attract the carriage trade, particularly after a spectator was killed in 1956 by a sniper firing across the street from the stadium. Throughout 1955 and 1956, various proposals were aired for moving the Giants into Yankee Stadium, building a brand new facility on the Upper West Side of Manhattan or near the present location of Madison Square Garden, or moving both the Giants and Yankees into a dome. What became clear through all the rumors, especially after reports that former manager Terry was ready to buy the club, was that Stoneham had no intention of selling, whether the franchise was in New York or elsewhere.

Durocher quit the club a few days before the end of the 1955 season; indications were that he had hit enough of a low in his up-and-down relations with Stoneham that he would have been fired anyway. Taking the helm for the team's last two years in New York was former infielder Bill Rigney, who filled out most of his lineup cards with Mays and one-time stars who would never play again in an All Star Game; among them were Hank Sauer, Red Schoendienst, and Thomson (reacquired in a trade with the Braves). An even bigger name in his twilight hours, the Dodgers' Robinson, was obtained in a December 1956 trade for southpaw Dick Littlefield and $35,000, but he opted for retirement rather than go to New York.

Through the first part of 1957, the question wasn't so much if the Giants would move, but where they would go. For some weeks, the likely destination seemed to be Minneapolis, where the club had its chief farm club. But then in May, the NL gave its formal approval for the Dodgers to move to Los Angeles and the Giants to San Francisco if they were unable to conclude local deals. With O'Malley turning on the pressure (the league had made it a condition that both clubs had to move west if one did), Stoneham went before his board of directors on August 19th to get an 8–1 sanction for shifting the franchise to the Bay Area; the only negative vote was cast by M. Donald Grant, who would become a major voice in the New York Mets in 1962. The New York Giants played their last game in the Polo Grounds on September 29, 1957, getting mauled by the Pirates, 9–1. McGraw's widow, who was on hand for the event, commented that the team's departure "would have broken John's heart."

NEW YORK GIANTS

Annual Standings and Managers

Year	Position	W	L	Pct.	GB	Managers
1883	Sixth	46	50	.479	16	John Clapp
1884	Fourth*	62	50	.554	22	James Pierce, John Montgomery Ward
1885	Second	85	27	.759	2	Jim Mutrie
1886	Third	75	44	.630	12½	Jim Mutrie
1887	Fourth	68	55	.553	10½	Jim Mutrie
1888	First	84	47	.641	+9	Jim Mutrie
1889	First	83	43	.659	+1	Jim Mutrie
1890	Sixth	63	68	.481	24	Jim Mutrie
1891	Third	71	61	.538	13	Jim Mutrie
1892	Tenth	31	43	.419	23	Pat Powers
	Sixth	40	37	.519	13½	Pat Powers
1893	Fifth	68	64	.515	19½	John Montgomery Ward
1894	Second	88	44	.667	3	John Montgomery Ward
1895	Ninth	66	65	.504	21½	George Davis, Jack Doyle, Harvey Watkins
1896	Seventh	64	67	.489	27	Art Irwin, Bill Joyce
1897	Third	83	48	.634	9½	Bill Joyce
1898	Seventh	77	73	.513	25½	Bill Joyce, Cap Anson, Bill Joyce
1899	Tenth	60	90	.400	42	John Day, Fred Hoey
1900	Eighth	60	78	.435	23	Buck Ewing, George Davis
1901	Seventh	52	85	.380	37	George Davis
1902	Eighth	48	88	.353	53½	Horace Fogel, Heinie Smith, John McGraw
1903	Second	84	55	.604	6½	John McGraw
1904	First	106	47	.693	+13	John McGraw
1905	First	105	48	.686	+ 9	John McGraw
1906	Second	96	56	.632	20	John McGraw
1907	Fourth	82	71	.536	25½	John McGraw
1908	Second*	98	56	.636	+ 1	John McGraw
1909	Third	92	61	.601	18½	John McGraw
1910	Second	91	63	.591	13	John McGraw
1911	First	99	54	.647	+ 7½	John McGraw
1912	First	103	48	.682	+10	John McGraw
1913	First	101	51	.664	+12½	John McGraw
1914	Second	84	70	.545	10½	John McGraw
1915	Eighth	69	83	.454	21	John McGraw
1916	Fourth	86	66	.566	7	John McGraw
1917	First	98	56	.636	+10	John McGraw
1918	Second	71	53	.573	10½	John McGraw
1919	Second	87	53	.621	9	John McGraw
1920	Second	86	68	.558	7	John McGraw
1921	First	94	59	.614	+ 4	John McGraw
1922	First	93	61	.604	+ 7	John McGraw
1923	First	95	58	.621	+4½	John McGraw
1924	First	93	60	.608	+1½	John McGraw
1925	Second	86	66	.566	8½	John McGraw
1926	Fifth	74	77	.490	13½	John McGraw
1927	Third	92	62	.597	2	John McGraw
1928	Second	93	61	.604	2	John McGraw
1929	Third	84	67	.556	13½	John McGraw
1930	Third	87	67	.565	5	John McGraw

1931	Second	87	65	.572	13	John McGraw
1932	Sixth*	72	82	.468	18	John McGraw, Bill Terry
1933	First	91	61	.599	+ 5	Bill Terry
1934	Second	93	60	.608	2	Bill Terry
1935	Third	91	62	.595	8½	Bill Terry
1936	First	92	62	.597	+ 5	Bill Terry
1937	First	95	57	.625	+ 3	Bill Terry
1938	Third	83	67	.553	5	Bill Terry
1939	Fifth	77	74	.510	18½	Bill Terry
1940	Sixth	72	80	.474	27½	Bill Terry
1941	Fifth	74	79	.484	25½	Bill Terry
1942	Third	85	67	.559	20	Mel Ott
1943	Eighth	55	98	.359	49½	Mel Ott
1944	Fifth	67	87	.435	38	Mel Ott
1945	Fifth	78	74	.513	19	Mel Ott
1946	Eighth	61	93	.396	36	Mel Ott
1947	Fourth	81	73	.526	13	Mel Ott
1948	Fifth	78	76	.506	13½	Mel Ott, Leo Durocher
1949	Fifth	73	81	.474	24	Leo Durocher
1950	Third	86	68	.558	5	Leo Durocher
1951	First	98	59	.624	+1	Leo Durocher
1952	Second	92	62	.597	4½	Leo Durocher
1953	Fifth	70	84	.455	35	Leo Durocher
1954	First	97	57	.630	+5	Leo Durocher
1955	Third	80	74	.519	18½	Leo Durocher
1956	Sixth	67	87	.435	26	Bill Rigney
1957	Sixth	69	85	.448	26	Bill Rigney

* Tie

Postseason Play

WS	refused to play Boston	1904
	4–1 versus Philadelphia	1905
	2–4 versus Philadelphia	1911
	3–4 versus Boston	1912
	1–4 versus Philadelphia	1913
	2–4 versus Chicago	1917
	5–3 versus New York	1921
	4–0 versus New York	1922
	2–4 versus New York	1923
	3–4 versus Washington	1924
	4–1 versus Washington	1933
	2–4 versus New York	1936
	1–4 versus New York	1937
	2–4 versus New York	1951
	4–0 versus Cleveland	1954

New York Giants

Players League, 1890	**BALLPARK:** BROTHERHOOD PARK
RECORD: 74–57 (.565)	

To a great extent, the Players League war was a battle for the New York market between two teams with the same name, the Giants. The National League edition, which had used the name almost since the beginning of its existence in 1883, finished sixth and drew slightly more than 60,000 fans; the upstart PL version, having pirated almost all of its rival's players, finished third and drew more than 140,000 fans. But although the Brotherhood won the battle on the field, at the turnstiles, and in the courts, it still ended up losing the war.

The Brotherhood arose in 1885 when nine members of the NL Giants formed its first chapter. When the players announced in 1889 their plans to form

WM. B. "BUCK" EWING

GREATEST 19TH CENTURY CATCHER. GIANT IN STATURE AND GIANT CAPTAIN OF NEW YORK'S FIRST NATIONAL LEAGUE CHAMPIONS 1888 AND 1889. WAS GENIUS AS FIELD LEADER, UNSURPASSED IN THROWING TO BASES, GREAT LONG-RANGE HITTER. NATIONAL LEAGUE CAREER 1881 TO 1899 TROY, N.Y. GIANTS AND CLEVELAND; CINCINNATI MANAGER.

National Baseball Library, Cooperstown, NY

their own league, virtually the entire roster followed captain Buck Ewing to the new Brotherhood Giants. The highest paid player in the NL at $5,000 a year and, according to many fans and sportswriters, the best player in baseball, Ewing became an immediate focus of the NL's legal battle with the PL. Giants' owner John B. Day, with the backing of the rest of the NL, sought an injunction in federal court to prevent Ewing from playing for the New York PL team. But Judge William P. Wallace refused to restrain Ewing on the grounds that the reserve clause was nothing more than "a contract to make a contract" for the next season provided the player and the club could reach an agreement. According to Wallace, the reserve clause in Ewing's contract gave the Giants only a "prior and exclusive" right to negotiate with him; as a binding document, it was "wholly nugatory" because no salary was specified and the terms were decidedly one-sided.

Defeated in the courts in the Ewing case and in another against Brotherhood founder John Montgomery Ward, the NL tried to subvert the PL more obliquely. During the season, NL president A. G. Mills stayed in contact with Ewing, perceived as a weak link in the Brotherhood because of his personal liking for Day. With Chicago manager Cap Anson as the go-between, Ewing held clandestine meetings with Mills in the back room of a suburban cigar store and during a late night carriage ride. The objective was to get the catcher to sign a recantation prepared by Mills and expressing Ewing's promise to return to the NL Giants in 1891 after the inevitable demise of the PL. But when Ewing solicited other players to sign as well and was rebuffed, he backed away from Day, claiming that he had been spying for the PL all along and had reported all his meetings to Al Johnson, the backer of the PL Cleveland Infants.

Whatever the truth, the players' suspicion of Ewing failed to compromise their performance for him as the PL Giants' manager. First baseman Roger Connor led the PL with 13 homers, while batting .372 and driving in 103 runs. Right fielder Jim O'Rourke drove in 115 on the strength of a .360 average and 9 home runs. Ewing himself hit .338 and led the club to a third-place finish. The club led the PL in homers with 64 and scored 1,018 runs in 131 games. Hank O'Day (23–15) led the pitching staff.

Ewing's crew played at a new version of the Polo Grounds near where their NL rivals played. The park, located under Coogan's Bluff (named for an upholsterer who had once been elected Borough President of Manhattan), was newer, larger, and better appointed than the NL facility; it even contained a fancy bar, the Seeley and Rappleyea Cafe, under the grandstand.

Despite the new ballpark and the edge in attendance, the financial backers of the club—Edwin A. McAlpin (a New York real estate speculator who was also PL president) and Edward Talcott—lost about $8,000. Right after the season's close, Talcott joined with fellow PL backers Wendell Goodwin of Brooklyn and Johnson of Cleveland in a meeting with three NL owners—Day, Albert Spalding of Chi-

cago, and Charles Byrne of Brooklyn. Talcott and his associates held nothing back, confessing to their rivals the full details of the sorry state of the PL's finances. The NL contingent, whose league was in even worse shape, held their counsel. In less than a month, the PL ranks had broken, with Talcott the first to collapse. Claiming that he and McAlpin had been spending $3,000 a month for nothing but "high-priced ballplaying," he cut a deal that gave him and his partner NL Giants' stock as compensation for allowing the Brotherhood Giants to be absorbed by their NL competitors. The players, as well as the backers of several other clubs, howled in protest, but there was little they could do to alter the outcome.

With the Giants gone, other PL backers scurried to get the best deal they could. The final outcome included several convoluted solutions, but the one undisputed fact was that the Brotherhood was dead.

NEW YORK GIANTS

Annual Standings and Manager

Year	Position	W	L	Pct.	GB	Manager
1890	Third	74	57	.565	8	Buck Ewing

New York Yankees

American League, 1903–Present

RECORD: 7855–6060 (.564)

BALLPARKS: HILLTOP PARK (1903–1912)
POLO GROUNDS (1913–1922)
HARRISON FIELD (1918)
YANKEE STADIUM (1923–1973)
SHEA STADIUM (1974–1975)
YANKEE STADIUM (1976–Present)

OTHER NAMES: HIGHLANDERS

By far the most successful franchise of the twentieth century, the Yankees won twenty-nine pennants between 1921 and 1964, then added four more and an American League East championship in the era of divisional play. Reaping the benefits of its diamond superiority, the club was the first (in 1920) to draw one million fans at home, notched five more million-plus seasons before any other team reached that level even once, and broke the two-million mark for five straight years after World War II. In the age of television, the Yankees have maintained their financial

dominance of the rest of the league with a monster cable contract valued at almost $500 million. Such a steady revenue flow has enabled the organization to reign over the player market for long periods by offering the highest salaries and, later, the biggest free agent contracts. In various eras, the club also exerted financial muscle with other teams (the Boston Red Sox and Kansas City Athletics) in order to keep talent streaming to the Bronx. Many quality players gave rise to a vaunted Yankee tradition of quiet heroes such as Lou Gehrig and Joe DiMaggio; but the

Babe Ruth's power hitting revolutionized the sport, consolidating it as the national pastime. *National Baseball Library, Cooperstown, NY*

team's heritage has also included the less dignified off-field behavior of other superstars such as Babe Ruth and Mickey Mantle. For the better part of the franchise's existence, the front office mirrored the self-assurance of the players and dominated to the point of arrogance the inner councils of baseball; more recently, however, in the second decade of the George Steinbrenner ownership, the persisting arrogance has mainly served to mask the absence of any cause for self-assurance.

From the AL's first claim to major league status in 1901, league president Ban Johnson was acutely aware that a successful New York franchise was essential to the prosperity, if not the survival, of the infant circuit. The major obstacle was the Tammany Hall connections of Andrew Freedman, who retained a large voice in the operation of the Giants even after he sold the club to John T. Brush in 1901. Through his influence with Tammany chieftain Boss Croker, Freedman threatened to have a streetcar line run over second base at any prospective AL ballpark site, while Brush, with his money, was always ready to purchase the sites. The breakthrough came when the

NL, noting that Johnson's circuit had drawn 2.2 million customers to its own 1.6 million, sued for peace in December 1902. The tradeoff for the AL's unimpeded entrance into New York was its promise to stay out of Pittsburgh; only Brush, among NL owners, objected.

Sportswriter Joe Vila of the New York *Sun* introduced Johnson to prospective backers of a New York franchise who could counterbalance Brush's money and Freedman's political influence. The key men were Frank Farrell, a former saloon keeper who had made a fortune running a gambling operation with more than two hundred outlets, and former New York City Police Chief William Dever, who had spent his law enforcement career turning a blind eye to illegal activities of every variety and his time since retirement building a real estate fortune with his payoffs from gambling and prostitution interests. The pair was hardly the sort that the sanctimonious Johnson wanted in his league, but Farrell had offered $25,000 as a binder to demonstrate their good intentions, and Dever had connections with Tim Sullivan, the Tammany boss after the fall of Croker in 1901. The new owners paid the AL $18,000 for the defunct Baltimore franchise, built Hilltop Park in upper Manhattan for $300,000, and hired as club president coal dealer Joseph W. Gordon, whose only previous connection to baseball had been as president of the American Association New York Mets.

The Highlanders, so named partly because Hilltop Park was on one of the highest elevations in Manhattan and partly because of the romantic connotations of Gordon's Highlanders, a prominent British military unit, lost their first game, played in Washington on April 22, 1903, by a 3–1 score. Manager-pitcher Clark Griffith, imported from the Chicago White Sox, got the franchise off to an inauspicious fourth-place beginning. Griffith's major assets were two future Hall of Famers who had jumped from the NL before the truce: Outfielder Willie Keeler (.318), who came from Brooklyn for a $10,000 contract, the largest in the AL up to that time, and spitballer Jack Chesbro (21–15), from Pittsburgh.

In its very first game in the American League in 1903, New York was the home team even though it played in Washington. Figuring to intimidate the new franchise right from the start, the Senators elected to bat first in their own park. The rule obligating home teams to bat last was not passed until after World War II.

In 1904, Chesbro set a twentieth-century record with 41 wins but surrendered the pennant-losing run to Boston with a wild pitch in the bottom of the ninth inning on the last day of the season. A disappointing sixth-place finish in 1905 was followed in 1906 by another runner-up season on the strength of Al Orth's AL-leading 27 wins, Chesbro's 24 wins, and .300-plus seasons by first baseman Hal Chase (.323), shortstop Kid Elberfeld (.306), and Keeler (.304). The team slipped to fifth in 1907, and collapsed altogether in 1908, losing a franchise record 103 games. During the season, Gordon was fired, Farrell became club president, and Dever, despite earlier contentions that he had no stock in the franchise, began to play a more visible role. Griffith quit as manager and Chase, who had counted on succeeding him, defected to the outlaw California State League when Elberfeld got the job.

In 1909, Chase was permitted to return after paying a token fine, but soon was endeavoring to undercut new manager George Stallings, the first pilot to suspect the notorious first baseman of throwing games. Stallings's accusations received no support from Johnson, who could not bear having one of the AL's biggest stars tarnished; Farrell, whose self-interest was involved, concurred. Chase finally took over the reins at the tail end of the 1910 season. Trouble began almost at once, when he insisted on wiping the slate clean and recruiting replacements for almost everyone on the roster. Chase lasted only long enough to escort the team into fifth place; he was succeeded by Harry Wolverton, whose flamboyant sombreros and long cigars had brought him attention at Williamsport in the Tri-State League but were objects of ridicule in New York. Another basement finish, the franchise's last until 1990, didn't help Wolverton's credibility, either.

The 1913 season brought several changes, including the shift of home games to the Polo Grounds, where the club became tenants of the Giants. (Relations between the two clubs had improved after Farrell had offered the Giants the use of Hilltop Park following a 1911 fire at the Polo Grounds.) With Gordon long gone and Hilltop Park abandoned, the team became known as the Yankees, a name in use at least since 1904 by headline writers who could not accommodate the lengthier Highlanders. Finally, former Cubs manager Frank Chance was persuaded by a $40,000 contract to abandon his plans to retire and to become manager. Chosen as much for the sake of a name to rival McGraw's as for his exceptional managerial skills, Chance was an overbearing authoritarian, making strife with Chase inevitable.

Chance barely tolerated his first baseman's ongoing mockery; the breaking point came when the manager became convinced that Chase was once again deliberately losing games and voiced his conviction to columnist Heywood Broun. Farrell and Dever defended the first baseman, and Chance and Dever almost came to blows after the manager traded Chase to the White Sox on June 23rd for two mediocre players. That Chase lasted long enough to see a seventh-place end to the 1913 season and to get within several weeks of the end of the 1914 season was testimony only to a distracting feud that had erupted between the co-owners. Shortstop Roger Peckinpaugh, who took over for Chance, became, at 23, the youngest manager in major league history, although he lasted only seventeen games.

The Farrell-Dever regime came to an end on January 11, 1915, when, with Farrell's gambling debts catching up to him and Dever unwilling to go it alone, the franchise was sold for $460,000 to Jacob Ruppert, who had inherited his father's brewery and fortune, and Tillinghast L'Hommedieu Huston, a self-made millionaire engineer. The new owners—one an elegant socialite and honorary colonel in the New York governor's staff and the other a rumpled Army Corps of Engineers captain—made an odd pair. Introduced by McGraw, Ruppert and Huston had both wanted to buy the Giants, but, when the NL manager suggested the Yankees instead, they shifted their ambitions accordingly. Ruppert, who became club president, planned to rechristen the team the Knickerbockers after his biggest selling beer, but was foiled by an uncooperative press corps.

With a new field manager, Bill Donovan, and business manager, McGraw's friend Harry Sparrow, the rebuilding began immediately. The purchases of Wally Pipp from Detroit for $7,500 and Bob Shawkey from Philadelphia for $18,000 not only brought the team a better-than-average first baseman and a pitcher who would win more than 20 games in four different seasons, but also signaled the new ownership's willingness to spend money to build a winner. After a stop at fifth place in their first season, the two millionaires confirmed their intentions by paying the Athletics $37,500 for the right to talk third baseman Frank Baker out of retirement. With Pipp leading the AL with 12 homers, Baker contributing another 10, and Shawkey turning in a 24–10 performance, the club climbed a notch to fourth in 1916, before falling again to sixth in 1917. The partners recouped some of the money they had spent from a handful of illegal Sunday games, the first of which was a 2–1 loss to the St. Louis Browns on June 17, 1917. In 1918, the team repaired to Harrison Park in New Jersey, the former home of the Federal League Newark Peppers, for Sunday contests. New York legalized Sunday ball the following year.

With Huston in France with the army in 1918, Ruppert decided to fire Donovan and, on the recommendation of Johnson, hire St. Louis Cardinals manager Miller Huggins. Huston concurred with the first decision, but preferred a different successor—50-year-old Dodgers' pilot Wilbert Robinson, whom Ruppert considered too old. Huston, now also a colonel, fumed by cable and letter during the war-shortened 1918 season, in which the Yankees finished fourth, and in person after he returned. He never forgave his partner for the Huggins signing and spent the rest of his time with the organization trying to undermine the manager. Huggins, a diminutive lawyer with a string of physical ailments that often made him disagreeable, was not received well by the New York players, press, or fans; in 1920, he was even punched by Sammy Vick, one of his outfielders.

On December 18, 1918, the two colonels dispatched four players and $15,000 to the Red Sox for outfielder Duffy Lewis and pitchers Ernie Shore and Dutch Leonard. The significance of the deal, a product of the friendship between Huston and Boston owner Harry Frazee, was less the players involved than that it marked the beginning of a relationship in which Ruppert and Huston would repeatedly send cash to the financially strapped Red Sox president for players who would help build the first Yankee dynasty. When the colonels next reached into the Boston grab bag, they came up with temperamental submarine pitcher Carl Mays, precipitating a battle that would divert them from their differences, destroy their relationship with AL president Johnson, and reshape the governance of baseball.

Mays, who had earlier demanded a trade to New York, had been suspended by Johnson for throwing a tantrum after being taken out of a game. The pitcher's sale to the Yankees, announced while he was still under suspension, aroused Johnson's suspicion that the incident had been staged, and the president ordered the deal be put on hold. Accustomed to getting his way with AL owners, Johnson was totally unprepared for the defiance of Ruppert and Huston, who obtained an injunction barring the league from interfering in the club's affairs. Backing the colonels were Frazee, the beneficiary of the Mays sale, and Charles Comiskey, who had broken with Johnson over another contract dispute. The other five clubs threatened to boycott games with the Yankees for their temerity in taking the league's affairs into a

courtroom. Ruppert and Huston came back with charges that Johnson had been planning to ship Mays to cronies in Cleveland, then called a meeting of AL owners, pointedly slighting the league president by inviting him merely to sit in on the session. That tactic failing, the colonels summoned a session of the AL board of directors; when only Ruppert, Frazee, and Comiskey showed up, they declared themselves a quorum, reinstated Mays, and ratified the pitcher's sale. For his part, Johnson had the ruling National Commission withhold the Yankees' third-place World Series money, but in the end he gave in, largely because the dispute had made big inroads into his authority. A year later, the same three AL clubs ganged up with the NL against him in forcing through the election of Kenesaw Mountain Landis as the first commissioner.

The controversy over Mays was soon eclipsed in the history of New York-Boston relations by the even more dramatic purchase of Babe Ruth from Frazee. Ruth played for twenty-two seasons in which he led or tied for the lead in home runs twelve times, batting average once, slugging thirteen times, RBIs six times, runs scored eight times, and walks eleven times. His career marks in slugging (.690) and walks (2056) are still tops on the all-time lists, and he ranks second among all players in homers (714) and RBIs (2211), and is tied for second in runs scored (2174). The lefty slugger's election to the Hall of Fame among the first entrants in 1936 was automatic. Beyond the numbers, however, Ruth dominated baseball as no one else ever has. The outfielder's budding power, which drew large crowds wherever he played, persuaded the AL to adopt a livelier ball, which added to his home run totals and to the figures at the turnstiles. He made undreamed-of amounts of money, not only in salary but also in endorsements, barnstorming appearances, movies, and vaudeville shows. And around him grew the legend of The Babe, whose voracious appetite for fast cars, willing women, and huge quantities of food and alcohol was as prodigious as his hitting. Also important to the myth was Ruth's affection for children. He actually did call on sick children in hospitals, the most noted episode being the speedy recovery of a suburban New Jersey boy named Jimmy Sylvester following such a visit. It was equally true (and equally typical) that, a year later, Ruth had no recollection of the event.

Ruth's purchase (for $125,000 and a $350,000 loan secured by a mortgage on Fenway Park) paid immediate dividends. In his first two seasons in New York, he posted batting averages of .376 and .378, homer totals of 54 and 59, 137 and 171 RBIs, 158 and 177 runs, and slugging averages of .847 and .846. In 1920, when Ruth hit more home runs than any other AL team (a feat he duplicated in 1927), the Yankees drew 1,289,422 fans, a major league record that would hold until 1946.

The Yankees finished third in 1920, a season marred by Mays's fatal beaning of Cleveland shortstop Ray Chapman. Ruppert and Huston went back to the Boston well in October, this time to draft Red Sox manager Ed Barrow to succeed business manager Sparrow, who had died in May. Barrow, who would be elected to the Hall of Fame in 1953, was a hot-tempered baseball man of the old school. Never fully accepting the changes that Ruth's long-ball hitting had wrought, he always thought his most famous player should have hit .400 instead of playing the power game. During his front office tenure, the Yankees would win fourteen pennants and ten world championships, but he was at least as famous for his humorlessness and tight-fistedness as for his success in building winning teams; his philosophy was that overpaid players lacked the motivation that the prospect of a World Series check offered.

Barrow's first move was to hire Paul Krichell as chief scout; in his more than three decades in the job, Krichell would sign Lou Gehrig, Tony Lazzeri, Phil Rizzuto, and Whitey Ford. Barrow's first trade, on December 15, 1920, with, of course, the Red Sox, brought the Yankees pitcher Waite Hoyt, catcher Wally Schang, and infielder Mick McNally for catcher Muddy Ruel, infielder Del Pratt, Vick, and a pitcher. Schang turned in two .300-plus seasons in his five years in New York, but the real object of the deal was Hoyt, who spent ten of his twenty-one seasons in New York. The righthander was elected to the Hall of Fame in 1969 on the basis of a lifetime 237–182 record.

While Barrow could control the club, no one could control Ruth, whose lack of self-discipline infuriated Huggins more for the influence the outfielder had on other members of the team than for its effect on Ruth's own output. Capable of epicurean feats that would have felled lesser men, Ruth could carouse mightily all night, then swing a bat equally mightily the next day. (In 1920, outfielder Ping Bodie, nominally Ruth's roommate on the road, noted that he mainly roomed with the star's suitcase.) One major reason Huggins had little effect on Ruth's off-field exploits was that the outfielder and co-owner Huston shared a friendship based on carousing and a shared enmity toward the manager.

The Yankees rollicked their way to their first pennant in 1921. In his second year with the club, Bob Meusel, who switched between left and right field with Ruth, was the second most potent source of power (a .318 average, 24 homers, 135 RBIs). Overall, the team clouted 134 homers to break the major league-record of 115 it had established the year before. Mays, 27–9, led the AL in both victories and won-lost percentage (.750). The World Series with the Giants, the first Subway Series, ended with a record attendance of 269,977, but with the AL on the short end of a 5-games-to-3 margin. McNally stole home in the first game, Meusel in the second—after loudly announcing his intention to do so. The games were clouded by charges that Mays, who followed up a five-hit shutout in the opening game with a fourth-game loss, had been paid for the defeat. Although a detective they had hired found nothing amiss, Huston and Huggins remained convinced that Mays was guilty of throwing the fourth game and possibly the seventh as well, which the Giants won, 2–1, by making the most of only six hits. Huggins used Mays only sparingly in 1922 and, after another suspicious loss in the fourth game of the 1922 Series, virtually not at all in 1923 except to refuse to relieve him in a humiliating 20-hit, 13-run thrashing on July 17. Mays was finally waived to Cincinnati in December 1923.

No sooner had the 1921 World Series ended than Ruth found himself in trouble with Landis for flouting an old baseball rule prohibiting World Series participants from offseason barnstorming. Huston talked Ruth into canceling the trip after just a few stops; attendance had been far less than expected, and Ruth had a $3,000-per-week offer to hit the vaudeville circuit. The mistake was in not going to see Landis, who did not suffer defiance with equanimity and who suspended Ruth and Meusel (also involved in the venture) for the first thirty-one days of the 1922 season. The suspension did not deter Ruppert and Huston from acceding to Ruth's request for a $52,000-per-year, five-year, contract, "because I always wanted to make a grand a week."

With the highest paid player in baseball history scheduled to sit out the first six weeks of the season, the Yankees sought reinforcements in Boston again, this time obtaining pitchers Joe Bush and Sam Jones and shortstop Everett Scott, for Peckinpaugh, Jack Quinn, and two other pitchers. The distractions of training in New Orleans proved so compelling that even the usually compliant sportswriters of the day filed stories about the team's partying, led by Ruth. One dispatch, under a headline announcing "Yankees Training on Scotch," inspired Ruppert and Huston to hire another detective, who ingratiated himself with the players and finally persuaded Ruth, Meusel, and several others to attend a party at a Joliet brewery to pose for a group picture. The incriminating evidence found its way into the hands of Landis, who invaded the Yankee clubhouse to issue admonitions about cavorting with bootleggers.

The 1922 season also added brawling to the Yankees' list of riotous activities. Ruth, fighting a slump on his return to the lineup, climbed into the stands on May 25th to go after a heckling fan and was fined $200, suspended for one game, and forced to give up his nominal title of Yankee captain. The club engaged in a series of intramural bouts in the dugout and clubhouse, with Ruth taking a punch from Pipp, Hoyt tussling with Huggins, Mays and catcher Al DeVormer going at it, and DeVormer switching sparring partners to fellow catcher Fred Hofman. Although it was clear that Huggins was losing control, Barrow persuaded Ruppert and Huston to stay out of the clubhouse, at least after losses, because their habitual grilling of the manager only undercut his authority further. On June 19th, with the team languishing, Ruth was suspended for the fourth time (for three days) when he protested a call by umpire Bill Dinneen a little too strenuously, and a fifth time (for two more days) when he went after the umpire the next day. To shake up the team, Barrow turned again to the Red Sox for help, coming up, on July 23rd, with third baseman Joe Dugan and outfielder Elmer Smith for four players and $40,000. The outcry from pennant contenders St. Louis and Chicago about the Yankees buying a pennant was enough to force a new rule prohibiting the sale or trade of any players after June 15th without first obtaining waivers.

The pennant race came down to a decisive three-game September series with the Browns. Center fielder Whitey Witt had to be carried off the field after being knocked out by a bottle thrown at him in the middle of a 2–1 Yankee victory in the first game. Rewards offered by the Browns for the identity of the culprit produced only fanciful tales (one said that the bottle had been thrown by a small boy and that it had landed on the outfield grass where Witt stepped on it, sending it spinning upwards to his head). Witt exacted his revenge when he returned to stroke a game-winning single in the third game, sending the Yankees on their way to an eventual one-game margin in the pennant race.

After a few years of a best-of-nine formula, the 1922 World Series (again against the Giants) reverted to a best-of-seven format at the insistence of Landis.

But when the second game ended in a 3–3 tie, allegations that both teams had conspired to create the draw in order to get back some of the money lost by reducing the number of games compelled the commissioner to give the proceeds from the contest to charity. The other four games ended in Giant victories, with McGraw's pitchers holding the Yankees to a .203 average.

More big changes came after the World Series. Blaming the manager for the loss of a second consecutive Series, Huston told friends that Huggins had skippered his last game for the Yankees. But in a showdown with Ruppert, he backed down and sold out his half of the franchise to his partner for $1.5 million; at the same time, Barrow purchased about 10 percent of the operation for $300,000. Construction was already underway on Yankee Stadium, following a subtle eviction notice from Giants' owner Charles Stoneham pointing out that separate homes would enable both clubs to schedule more Sunday dates. Relations between the two organizations had become strained by the Yankees' success and by Ruth's attractiveness to New York fans; Yankee Stadium thus became The House that Ruth Built. But there was more to the building of Yankee Stadium than the Giants' ire over Ruth's popularity. As early as 1919, Ruppert and Huston had approached Stoneham with a plan to build a new 100,000-seat home for both clubs. Rebuffed, the Yankee owners, fearful that Stoneham would extract a burdensome rent increase on what amounted to a year-to-year lease, had bought the Bronx site where the new stadium would be built for $600,000. Following Stoneham's letter, AL president Johnson, with little to do since the appointment of Landis as commissioner but to plot against his enemies, tried to buy the Yankees' Polo Grounds lease with the intention of evicting the tenants. Ruppert hurriedly constructed a new triple-decked facility at a cost of $2.3 million. Yankee Stadium opened on April 18, 1923 with a 4–1 Shawkey victory over Boston, the margin provided by a third-inning, three-run shot by Ruth. The announced crowd for the park's first game was 74,217, but that was probably a Barrow exaggeration by about 10,000.

In 1923, Barrow turned twice more to the Red Sox to add to an already formidable pitching staff. On January 3rd he obtained young righthander George Pipgras in a straight cash deal; then, on January 30th he got southpaw Herb Pennock for three players and $50,000. Pipgras would take a few years to mature, but Pennock (19–5) moved directly to the forefront of the staff and toward a Hall of Fame career (he was elected in 1948) with a 240–162 record over twenty-two years.

With Ruth winning the Most Valuable Player Award for a career high .393 batting average, the club swept to the 1923 pennant by a 16-game margin over the Tigers. In the World Series, which produced the first one million dollar Series gate, the Yankees avenged themselves on the Giants for their two earlier losses. Second baseman Aaron Ward hit .417 and Pennock won 2 games, but Ruth stole the show with a .368 average, 3 homers, and 8 RBIs in the 4-games-to-2 victory. The following year, despite the midseason arrival of center fielder Earle Combs, the team slipped to second. Combs played for New York for all twelve of his major league seasons—a career cut short by a head-on collision with the outfield wall in St. Louis. His lifetime average of .325 (with a career high of .356 in 1927) and three AL-leading totals in triples won him a spot in Cooperstown in 1970.

On April 7, 1925, on the way home from spring training, Ruth, feeling ill, got off the train in Asheville, North Carolina, and collapsed. Hustled back onto the train, he passed out again and cracked his head open. Reports of his death appeared as far away as London. Despite the stress of marital problems and the 270 pounds he was carrying around, the slugger had been batting .447 in spring training games, and was only approaching the peak of his powers when his excessive eating and drinking had created intestinal problems that dictated immediate abdominal surgery. (Reporters and others around the team suspected, but never wrote, that Ruth's problems were the result, not of food and liquor, but of his third excess, women; the speculation about which combination of venereal diseases he had contracted reached Ruthian proportions, but the postoperation scar Ruth carried was clearly abdominal.)

Ruth's illness, which kept him out of the lineup until June 1st, won him no sympathy from Huggins.

In 1923, Babe Ruth batted righthanded on three occasions in an attempt to thwart the numerous walks he had been receiving. The first time, against Cleveland, he took one pitch, then jumped back over to his normal lefthand-hitting position, and cracked a home run; on the other two occasions, against St. Louis, he was walked anyway.

Babe Ruth was undefeated as a Yankee pitcher, going 5–0 in five starting appearances, two of them complete games, stretching from 1920 to 1933.

On the contrary, his unaltered habits both during his recuperation and after he returned only increased the pilot's deep-seated hostility toward the outfielder. The manager continued to seethe when Ruth stayed out all night during a trip to Cleveland and even when he twice ignored signs—first bunting when he had been told to swing away and then swinging away when he had been told to bunt. The climax came on August 29th when Ruth showed up late for a game in St. Louis, and Huggins, with prior approval from Ruppert and Barrow, slapped him with a $5,000 fine, the largest in history up to that time, and an indefinite suspension. In a fury, Ruth laid the blame for the team's languishing in seventh place on the manager and laid down an ultimatum: "Either he quits or I quit." Returning to New York for a closed-door session with Ruppert, the slugger was confident of victory; but emerging from Ruppert's office, he was forced to listen as the owner repeated for the press his unequivocal position that "Huggins is in absolute command," then had to apologize in front of the team. Ruth never again publicly challenged Huggins' authority.

The 1925 season also marked the beginning of Gehrig's Iron Man streak of 2,130 consecutive games. The lefty first baseman was sent in to pinch hit for shortstop Pee Wee Wanninger June 1, 1925, and put in the lineup the next day to give Pipp a rest. Taking over at first base permanently, he hit .295 with 21 homers for the season, after which Pipp was sold to Cincinnati. In his seventeen-season Yankee career, he led the AL in batting once, tied for the lead or led in homers three times, and topped the list in RBIs five times, including an AL record 184 in 1931; he also led in runs four times, slugging and doubles twice each, and hits and triples once apiece. Gehrig's lifetime statistics—a .340 average, 493 home runs, 1990 RBIs (third on the all-time list), and a .632 slugging average (also third among all players)—got him into Cooperstown in 1939, when the five-year waiting period was waived because of a well-publicized fatal illness.

With a subdued but hardly reformed Ruth batting .372 with 47 homers and 145 RBIs, and Pennock leading the pitching staff with a 23–11 record, the

Lou Gehrig's 2,130 consecutive games were not all played at first base. The streak at first ended at 885 games in 1930, when he appeared in the outfield. He played another game in the outfield in 1933, and, in 1934 he was in the lineup as the shortstop and leadoff hitter long enough to single in the top of the first and be removed for a pinch-runner.

Yankees charged back into first place in 1926. The newest Hall of Fame addition was second baseman Lazzeri, who in fourteen major league seasons would hit .292 (with a high of .354 in 1929) and would reach double numbers in homers ten times. In that year's World Series against the Cardinals, Ruth became the first player to hit three homers in the postseason competition, but he also ended the seven-game duel by being thrown out trying to steal second base with two out in the ninth inning of the finale. Barrow called it "the only dumb play I ever saw Ruth make."

Many people consider the 1927 Murderers Row Yankees the greatest team of all time. Not only did the New Yorkers coast to a 19-game margin of victory over Philadelphia on the strength of 110 victories, but they did so without making a single roster change. Ruth added a .356 batting average and 164 RBIs to his 60 home runs; Gehrig (.373, 47, 175), kept pace with the outfielder's home run total until mid-August and took the MVP Award because Ruth, who had won in 1923, was barred by AL rules from taking it more than once. Meusel and Lazzeri also contributed more than 100 RBIs, and Combs hit a career high .356 leading off. Hoyt led the AL in wins (22) and ERA (.2.63). To no great surprise, the club swept the Pirates in the World Series.

Less dominant in 1928 because of injuries to half a dozen key players, the team, nevertheless, was 17 ahead of Philadelphia in mid-summer, only to slip to second place on September 8th before a late-season surge to finish 2½ games up on Connie Mack's rebuilt Athletics. The World Series, another four-game rout, this time against the Cardinals, marked the first time any team had won eight consecutive World Series games. Ruth blasted three consecutive homers in the fourth game, while hitting .625 overall, but Gehrig, with 3 homers, 9 RBIs, and a .545 average, set a Series slugging record of 1.727.

The 1928 victory gave rise to the first demands to "Break Up the Yankees," a cry that would be heard periodically for the next three and a half decades.

The Yankees had drawn 3.26 million fans in the three pennant-winning seasons, breaking every record for World Series gate receipts and adding substantially to Ruppert's already healthy coffers. Most of the players, however, did not share in the prosperity. Ruth, of course, was handsomely rewarded. He had a three-year, $70,000-per-year contract through the 1929 season, after which he received a raise to $80,000; given the Depression economy and the minimal taxes at the time, this may have amounted to the most money ever paid to a ballplayer. Others made considerably less; Pennock was the next-best-paid member of the 1927 team, at $17,500. Gene Robertson, who batted .291 filling in for the injured Dugan at third base in 1928, was denied a raise on the grounds that the organization would go broke if it gave raises to every utility infielder.

As it turned out, there was no need to break up the Yankees. They fell to second place, the victims of instability on the left side of the infield, where Mark Koenig, Robertson, Lyn Lary, and Leo Durocher each took turns at short, third, or both. The bright spot in 1929 was backstop Bill Dickey, who, in a seventeen-year all-Yankee career hit .313 (with a high of .362 in 1936), reached double numbers in home runs nine times (peaking at 29 in 1937), and posted four consecutive seasons with more than 100 RBIs. He was elected to the Hall of Fame in 1954. Huggins, suffering all year from a variety of ailments, was aware of the team's lack of fire but unable to overcome it. On September 25th, the manager died of erysipelas, brought on by a carbuncle on his eye. He, too, was elected to the Hall of Fame, in 1964.

The search for a new manager ran into several dead ends. Ruppert's and Barrow's first choice, Donie Bush, had signed to pilot the White Sox hours before they reached him; the second and third choices, Athletics' Hall of Fame second baseman Eddie Collins and Yankee coach Art Fletcher, turned them down. The fourth choice, pitcher Shawkey, who had retired in 1927, no sooner accepted the post than he ran into the usual problems faced by managers who had been one of the boys. Ruth, for one, sulked at being passed over for the job; others didn't appreciate the new distance in their ex-teammate. Tensions reached critical mass when the manager clashed with Hoyt over how to pitch to certain batters. The newest addition to the pitching staff was Red Ruffing, who arrived from the Red Sox in May in exchange for outfielder Cedric Durst and $50,000. The righthander became one of the mainstays of the rotation for fifteen years, compiling a twenty-two-year career record of 273–225, including four consecutive 20-win seasons. His career year came in 1938, when he led the AL in victories (21) and won-lost percentage (.750), and tied for the lead in shutouts with 4. He was elected to Cooperstown in 1967.

The end for Shawkey came when the Cubs fired Joe McCarthy; the unsuspecting Shawkey learned his fate when he walked in on a press conference called to announce McCarthy as his successor. Ruth once again thought the manager's job should have been his, only to be told by Ruppert that a player-manager wasn't part of the club's plans. McCarthy, whose severe manner would add to the Yankee image of cold efficiency, managed the team for more than fifteen seasons, winning eight pennants and seven World Series and never finishing out of the first division. His .614 lifetime won-lost percentage (.627 with the Yankees) is the highest of any manager with any longevity and earned him a Cooperstown plaque in 1957. McCarthy, whom Jimmy Dykes called a "push button manager," preferred personnel as colorless as he was. He had the card table in the clubhouse smashed. There was a dress code. Shaving was prohibited in the clubhouse because he expected players to be clean shaven when they arrived at work. Nevertheless, he won over the Yankee players—except Ruth. Growing more vocal about his desire to manage the Yankees, Ruth had to swallow the bitter pill of having been passed over for an NL manager who had never even played in the major leagues. McCarthy's approach to the slugger's frustration and resentment was to bide his time. For all practical purposes, the team rules applied to everyone but Ruth; everyone knew it and accepted it.

In his first New York season, McCarthy finished second with a team that set a twentieth-century record by scoring 1067 runs and began a streak of 308 games, between August 3, 1931 and August 2, 1933, without being shut out. Gehrig tied Ruth for the AL lead in homers with 46. (He was deprived of a 47th homer and exclusive right to the homer crown when shortstop Lary thought a Gehrig blast had been caught and left the basepath; the first baseman was called out for passing Lary and credited with a triple.) Newcomers included third baseman Joe Sewell, for the final three years of his Hall of Fame career, and Lefty Gomez, who in his first full season, led the staff with a 21–9 record. The southpaw would go on to complement righthander Ruffing on the teams of the 1930s; his best year came in 1934 when he had 26 victories, an .839 won-lost percentage, a 2.33 ERA, 159 strikeouts, and 6 shutouts, all AL-leading figures. His 189–102 record over fourteen seasons and perfect 6–0 World Series record, along with AL-

leading totals in just about every pitching category in one season or another, earned him admission to the Hall of Fame in 1972.

With the Red Sox connection dried up because of new ownership in Boston, Ruppert and Barrow decided belatedly in 1932 to establish a farm system. Hired to build and then run the system was George Weiss, who had first come to Barrow's attention when he refused to pay the Yankees their share of the gate receipts for an exhibition with his Eastern League New Haven club because Ruth, the central attraction, had not made the trip to Connecticut. Until his forced retirement in 1960, Weiss was to play an increasingly important role in the Yankee organization, and dour personality that he was, in the developing public image of the Yankees as a brutally effective corporate machine.

New York won the pennant in 1932, making McCarthy the first manager to capture flags in both leagues. Gomez (24–7) led the pitchers, while Gehrig (.349, 34, 151) sparked the offense and became, on June 2nd, the first ALer to sock four homers in a game. The World Series against the Cubs was a rout; the New Yorkers scored 37 runs in the four games. Ex-Yankee Mark Koenig, who hit .353 in thirty-three games for the Cubs, had been awarded only half of a World Series share, prompting the New Yorkers to get all over Chicago for being cheap. The legend of Ruth's response to the counter-jockeying, his famous called home run in the third game, has been attributed by some to sportswriter Joe Williams of the New York *World-Telegram*, the only writer present to suggest that the slugger had pointed to the center field bleachers before hitting the ball into the area. Ruth did little to discourage the spread of the myth, and became evasive when asked if his hand motions had actually been only macho reminders to the Chicago bench of how many strikes he had left before teeing off.

Over the next two seasons, however, Ruth became a burden. He had slowed down considerably, and feuded with teammates, including Gehrig, once his close friend and admirer. Ruth also loathed McCarthy, but the manager, unwilling to precipitate a showdown, let the aging star pick his spots to play. Ruppert and Barrow had no such compunction, cut-

---

Babe Ruth hit the first All Star Game home run, when he connected for a two-run shot in the third inning of the inaugural exhibition in 1933.

ting the slugger's salary to $52,000 in 1933 and $35,000 in 1934. Ruth himself forced the issue of his future when, after the 1934 season, he virtually demanded that the owner and general manager fire McCarthy and give him the manager's job. For their part, Ruppert and Barrow had hoped all along that Ruth would land a managerial job with one of he clubs that had sent out feelers to him. (Boston, Detroit, and Philadelphia had all expressed interest at some point.) A painless solution precluded, the brass rejected the demand, even after McCarthy had offered to step down; instead, Ruppert suggested that Ruth take the manager's job at Newark. When Ruth refused, the owner felt free to orchestrate the deal that sent Ruth to the Boston Braves in a position that the outfielder was led to believe would carry front office responsibilities and eventually the manager's job, but that Ruppert knew was mere window dressing.

Not even Gehrig's Triple Crown season in 1934 saved McCarthy from the tag Second Place Joe for three successive runner-up finishes. That changed with the arrival of center fielder Joe DiMaggio in 1936. A sensation with the San Francisco Seals of the Pacific Coast League, DiMaggio had injured his knee in 1934, decreasing major league interest in his services and causing Barrow to sour on him; Weiss, on

the other hand, insisted on the deal, and Ruppert landed his biggest catch for the bargain basement price of $25,000. In his thirteen seasons with the Yankees, DiMaggio led the AL twice each in batting, homers, RBIs, and slugging, and once in runs scored. More important, he became the franchise player—not only for his performance but also for his quiet self-assurance, that, in contrast to Ruth's boisterousness, was precisely the image the Yankee front office wished to project. His election to the Hall of Fame came in 1955.

With DiMaggio complementing Gehrig (who won a second MVP in 1936), Dickey, and Lazzeri, the Bronx Bombers ran roughshod over the AL to win four consecutive pennants, none by fewer than 9½ games, and faced as little difficulty with NL rivals in the World Series, losing only three games in the four series between 1936 and 1939. The 1936 team boasted a record five players with more than 100 RBIs.

On January 13, 1939, Ruppert succumbed to phlebitis. The 71-year-old bachelor left most of his $100 million estate to a variety of relatives, with his baseball holdings going jointly to two nieces, Mrs. Joseph Holleran and Mrs. J. Basil Maguire, and to Helen Winthrope Weyant, a chorus girl whose name had never before surfaced publicly. The three women

Joe DiMaggio ties the major league record batting streak of 44 consecutive games. *National Baseball Library, Cooperstown, NY*

owners rarely interfered in club operations, leaving all business and player affairs to Barrow, who became club president.

Gehrig's streak of 2,130 consecutive games ended on May 2nd, when the first baseman removed his name from the starting lineup. McCarthy and everyone else had watched with concern the first baseman's slow start (.143), and Gehrig himself knew something was wrong, when, after the final out of his last game, on April 30, relief pitcher Johnny Murphy and Dickey congratulated him for what had been a routine play; he learned soon afterward that he was suffering from amyotrophic lateral sclerosis. On July 4, 1939, between games of a doubleheader, Gehrig delivered his "luckiest man on the face of the earth" farewell speech. Ruth, who joined other members of the 1927 club at the ceremonies, patched up his differences with the first baseman, who would be dead within two years.

By the end of the four consecutive pennants, the expensive farm system directed by Weiss had begun to pay dividends. Second baseman Joe Gordon came up from Newark in 1938 and left fielder Charlie Keller in 1939. Also in 1939, in a move that would

Lou Gehrig's tearful goodbye to baseball. *UPI/Bettmann Newsphotos*

eventually become a multimillion-dollar media operation, the Yankees became the first team to offer regularly scheduled radio broadcasts of games; Arch McDonald was joined on the air by Alabaman Mel Allen, who would remain The Voice of the Yankees on radio and television for twenty-five years. The streak of pennants ended in 1940, partially because of a miscalculation by Barrow and Weiss who, deciding that righthander Ernie Bonham needed another year in the minors, did not bring him up until August 12th, after which he went 9–3 with a league-leading 1.90 ERA.

The return to the top of the AL in 1941 was highlighted by DiMaggio's 56-game hitting streak, which ended on July 17th only because Cleveland third baseman Ken Keltner made two spectacular plays to take doubles away from the outfielder, who won his second MVP. (The first had been in 1939.) The World Series turned on a fourth-game, ninth-inning passed ball by Brooklyn catcher Mickey Owen that allowed Tommy Henrich to reach first on a strikeout and Keller to double home two runs in a four-run rally that won the game. Repeat pennants in 1942 and 1943 were accompanied by MVP awards for Gordon (.322, 18 homers, 103 RBIs) and righty Spud Chandler (20–4, 1.64). In the 1942 World Series, Cardinal pitching stopped everyone except third baseman Red Rolfe (.353), with the New Yorkers dropping their first World Series since 1926. The club avenged the loss in a return match against St. Louis in 1943, as Chandler won two games. A third-place finish in 1944 was an achievement given the loss of almost the entire starting lineup to the military. The biggest beneficiary of the depleted league was first baseman Nick Etten, who led the AL with 22 homers.

Like the Giants across the river, the Yankees of the 1930s and 1940s were always on the look-out for a Jewish player who would draw the city's numerous Jews. To this end, they ballyhooed the arrival of first baseman Ed Levy in 1942. The only trouble was, Levy was actually only the name of the step-father of Edward Clarence Whitner, who had been raised as an Irish Catholic. "You may be Whitner to the rest of the world," team president Ed Barrow told the player, "but if you're going to play with the Yankees, you'll be Ed Levy." Levy-Whitner batted .215 in less than 200 appearances during his two-year stay with the team.

The Yankees' gray corporate image underwent a change on January 26, 1945, when the club was sold for the comparatively low figure of $2.8 million to Larry MacPhail, a boisterous gadfly with a history of innovative promotions in Cincinnati and Brooklyn, and silent partners Dan Topping and Del Webb. Barrow was given the title of chairman of the board, but was stripped of all duties or authority. With Barrow, who scorned night games and promotions, out of the way, MacPhail launched a razzle-dazzle program that made more money for the franchise in three years than any other team made in the decade. But bizarre player moves such as the midseason sale for $100,000 of pitcher Hank Borowy to the Cubs, dropped the club to fourth in 1945, McCarthy's lowest finish with the club. The main compensations for the year were second baseman Snuffy Stirnweiss' league-leading batting average (.309), slugging average (.476), and totals in stolen bases, runs, hits, and triples, and Etten's topping the RBI list with 111. Troubled by the team's performance and MacPhail's interference, McCarthy quit in July, but MacPhail was able to talk him into returning.

The reconciliation lasted only until May 1946, when the manager retired to nurse stomach ailments brought on in equal parts by MacPhail's antics and the continued foundering of the team. On May 28, 1946, the Yankees beat the Washington Senators 2–1 in the first game at Yankee Stadium under the lights. MacPhail's other initiatives included selling the first major league television contract to Dumont, for $75,000, when there were only about 500 television sets in New York City; courting season ticket holders and building the Stadium Club for their convenience; introducing fashion shows and nylon stocking giveaways to attract women fans; and moving the club's front office to lavish accommodations on Fifth Avenue that so discomforted Barrow that he wouldn't go there.

MacPhail's innovations weren't always popular with players. On May 13, 1946, he upset a lot of stomachs by arranging for the first air swing through the league's western cities. By August, when he unveiled a plan to expand the schedule to 168 games to compensate owners for concessions made to the players on pension fund contributions (an idea ultimately squashed by Boston's Tom Yawkey), he had every player in the AL gunning for him. On September 9th, he hired Bucky Harris to fill an undefined front office job, so angering Dickey, McCarthey's successor, that he too quit three days later. Coach Johnny Neun finished out the season, then gave way to Harris. Despite a third-place finish, the club drew

2,265,512 fans, the first two-million gate in history.

In April 1947, MacPhail took on Commissioner Happy Chandler by violating a gag rule Chandler imposed on all the principals in a sequence of events that had led to the one-year suspension of Dodgers' manager Leo Durocher. The proceedings had included MacPhail's successful tampering with Brooklyn coach Charlie Dressen, his unsuccessful tampering with Durocher, and his public flaunting of the rules barring public association with gamblers. After paying a $2,000 fine and agreeing to remain silent about Chandler's March hearings on the various accusations and counter-charges, the New York owner blasted the commissioner for suspending Durocher on insufficient evidence; let Dressen suit up for games even though the coach had been suspended; alleged that Durocher had approached him about the Yankee manager's job; and claimed that his sitting with gamblers at a Yankee-Dodger spring training game had been the result of his willingness to switch boxes with Dodger President Branch Rickey.

Relations with the players deteriorated further early in the 1947 season, when MacPhail levied fines on Keller and DiMaggio, among others, for their failure to participate in some of his promotional stunts. DiMaggio, who had had two operations for calcium deposits on his heel during the offseason and who had returned to action with a home run in his first game, overcame his personal problems with the owner to team up with manager Harris to head off a player insurrection. Through all the turmoil, which included several near-accidents in the old C-54 transport plane that flew the club around the league, the Yankees put together a 19-game winning streak and ended up winning the pennant by 12 games. DiMaggio won a third MVP Award, while the pitchers were led by Allie Reynolds, who won 19, and reliever Joe Page, who won 14 and saved another 17. The pennant triumph was soured by the resignation of team physician Mal Stevens, who declared his disgust with MacPhail's interference and who suggested that the owner was close to a nervous breakdown.

The season-long fireworks were followed by a seven-game victory over Brooklyn in a World Series notable for Bill Bevens' fourth-game near-no-hitter,

The Yankees were the first team to retire a uniform number, when they hung up Babe Ruth's #3 at ceremonies in 1947.

broken up in the bottom of the ninth by pinch-hitter Cookie Lavagetto's two-run double, and Al Gionfriddo's game-saving catch of a DiMaggio drive in the sixth game. What followed the Yankee victory was even more dramatic than the season itself. First, Harris threw MacPhail out of the festive Yankee clubhouse because the owner had upbraided outfielder Johnny Lindell for leaving the sixth game of the series with a cracked rib. Next, the owner announced tearfully that he was selling out and leaving baseball for good. Finally, MacPhail moved to a front office victory party, where he tried to punch both Topping and Weiss and eventually did land one on old friend John McDonald. The next day, Topping and Webb bought out MacPhail's one-third share for $2 million.

Topping, who became club president, restored the old order immediately, appointing Barrow protégé Weiss general manager. While as cold-blooded and tight-fisted as Barrow, Weiss also added a mean-spiritedness and even a viciousness. His salary battles with Reynolds were monumental, and he was always ready to trade away a valuable player who gave him trouble over money, as he did with pitcher Vic Raschi in 1953. His distaste for players who enjoyed the nightlife bordered on the obsessive, and detectives hired to catch the culprits were ubiquitous. Lindell, especially, took great pride in how much he cost Weiss in detective fees. Unable either to curb Mickey Mantle's free spirit or to get rid of the star slugger, Weiss focused his attack on the outfielder's sidekick, second baseman Billy Martin. The GM's most insensitive move was releasing veteran shortstop Rizzuto on Old Timers' Day in 1956. Overriding all else was Weiss's open racism, pointed out by the Dodgers' Jackie Robinson at every opportunity.

Weiss fired Harris after a third-place finish in 1948, despite the fact that the club was not eliminated until the next-to-last day of the season. The open hostility to the move from the players and the media turned to bewilderment at the announcement of Harris's successor: Casey Stengel, a prankster as a player and a loser as a manager with Brooklyn and Boston in the NL. As it turned out, Stengel was also, at the beginning at least, a tireless tutor of young players. In addition, the press appeal of his jabber, endless stories, and barroom conviviality took some of the heat off Weiss. The dour general manager and the zany manager formed an unlikely working tandem that endured for twelve Yankee years, during which Stengel won the ten pennants and seven World Series that earned him a Cooperstown plaque in 1966.

Stengel inherited a pitching staff of Raschi, who

Casey Stengel. *Courtesy of the New York Yankees*

would post 21 victories in each of Stengel's first three seasons; Reynolds, who would excel as a starter and in relief; lefty Ed Lopat (obtained from the White Sox for catcher Aaron Robinson on February 24, 1948 in Weiss' first deal); and lefty reliever Page, who recorded 13 wins and 27 saves in 1949. Among the problems the new manager inherited were DiMaggio's health and a host of young players with potent bats but no set positions. DiMaggio had just signed baseball's first $100,000 contract, but he had also had another operation on his heel that would keep him out of the lineup until late June. Moreover, Weiss began causing trouble as early as spring training by ordering Stengel to restrict players' attendance at Florida's dog tracks and to apply the same 11 o'clock curfew imposed on players living in the team barracks on those staying with their families.

Throughout the 1949 season, Stengel juggled lineups to compensate for injuries and platooned at almost every position, eventually using seven first basemen, including Henrich and future Cooperstown honoree Johnny Mize, purchased from the Giants in August. No one except Rizzuto had as many as 500 at bats; no one hit over .300 or had 100 RBIs. The return of DiMaggio—4 homers and 9 RBIs in three games against the Red Sox in a key midseason series—provided a boost. The emergence of Yogi

Berra as the regular catcher, after several tries in the outfield, was also a key element in the pennant. Elected to Cooperstown in 1972, Berra played eighteen seasons with the Yankees, batting .285 with 358 home runs, hitting more than 20 round-trippers in ten consecutive years, and winning Most Valuable Player awards in 1951, 1954, and 1955. Stengel's first pennant was not decided until the last two games of the season. To beat the Red Sox 5–4 in the first game, the New Yorkers had to overcome a 4–0 deficit, with the key hit a homer by Lindell; a Henrich homer and a three-run double by rookie second baseman Jerry Coleman gave Raschi a 5–3 victory in the second. The World Series, a 4–1 affair over the Dodgers, featured a .500 performance by third baseman Bobby Brown, later the AL president.

Stengel had treaded softly in 1949, but with his position more firmly established in 1950, he became more acerbic and dictatorial. The new assertiveness led to difficulties with DiMaggio. In 1949, the manager had insisted to anyone who would listen that his center fielder was the best player he had ever managed; the following year, he seemed to go out of his way to humble DiMaggio, whose lack of respect for the manager was acute. Stengel had Topping persuade the star to move to first base, an experiment that lasted one game; he dropped DiMaggio from cleanup to fifth and later sat him down a few games for "a rest" without discussing the moves beforehand; and he sent Cliff Mapes to replace DiMaggio in the field mid-inning, whereupon the star waved his substitute off the field, then took himself out of the game at the end of the inning. DiMaggio, who had wanted to retire before the season to avoid embarrassing himself, nevertheless let himself be talked into another $100,000 contract by Topping, and had his last great year (.301, 32, 122). Rizzuto won the MVP award with a .324 average and 125 runs scored; lefty Whitey Ford went 9–1 after being brought up in late June; and the Yankees swept the Phillies in the World Series. After a hitch in the military, Ford was to become the ace of the staff from 1953 to 1965, winning 236 while losing only 106 and compiling a 2.75 ERA in sixteen seasons. He paced AL pitchers in wins three times and in won-lost percentage and ERA twice each; he also won more World Series games (10) than any other pitcher. He was elected to the Hall of Fame in 1974.

A bottom-of-the-ninth Rizzuto suicide squeeze to beat Cleveland, 2–1, put the Yankees into first place to stay on September 17, 1951. Rookie of the Year Gil McDougald, who could play all over the infield, would give Stengel ten years of the flexibility

he desired. Reynolds pitched two no-hitters, the second a tie-clinching victory against the Red Sox in which Berra dropped a two-out, ninth-inning foul pop by Ted Williams, only to have the Boston slugger hit another pop up in the same area. The Giants were disposed of in the World Series in five games, after which DiMaggio announced his retirement. His successor in center field was Mantle, who had stepped in an open drain in the outfield grass during the 1951 World Series and severely damaged his knee. That injury and the many that followed may have limited his output in his eighteen years with the team, but the switch hitter's .298 average, 536 homers, MVP Awards in 1956, 1957, and 1962, and Triple Crown in 1956 (.353 average, 52 homers, 130 RBIs), were sufficient for a ticket to Cooperstown in 1974. Nonetheless, the apparent disparity between Mantle's potential and his productivity caused constant tension with Stengel, with the manager trying to prod the outfielder into being the greatest player of all time. Mantle's taste for nightlife and his home run swing irritated the pilot because they produced too many strikeouts, although the latter also generated towering tape-measure homers. The most famous Mantle shots were the first ball ever hit over the left field roof in Washington's Griffith Stadium (April 17,

Mickey Mantle. *Courtesy of the New York Yankees*

1953 off Chuck Stobbs), and two almost identical drives off the right field upper deck facade (May 30, 1956 off Pedro Ramos of Washington and May 22, 1963 off Bill Fischer of Kansas City) that came as close as any fair balls to leaving Yankee Stadium.

In November 1953, the Yankees were party to a U.S. Supreme Court decision that reiterated the 1922 ruling that had exempted baseball from federal anti-trust statutes. The case, coupled with two similar suits, involved minor league pitcher George Earl Toolson's refusal to accept a demotion from Newark to Binghamton and his contention that the reserve clause was a monopolistic practice that prevented the pitcher from advancing himself. The high court found in favor of organized baseball by a 7-to-2 majority not because it agreed that baseball was not "commerce" and therefore exempt from anti-trust laws, but on the grounds that the remedy for the problem had to be legislative and that the U.S. Congress had chosen not to act in the 31 years since the original decision.

The Stengel-Weiss pennants became almost as automatic as Stengel's maneuvering and platooning were obsessive. When new pitchers were needed, as they were in 1954, the organization dipped into the farm system for Rookie of the Year Bob Grim (20–6), and pulled off an eighteen-player trade (the largest in history) with Baltimore that brought to New York righthanders Bob Turley, the 1958 Cy Young Award winner, and Don Larsen, best remembered for his perfect game against the Dodgers in the fifth game of the 1956 World Series. After 1955, when the Philadelphia Athletics moved to Kansas City, Weiss used the new franchise as a Yankee farm club, reaching out to make seventeen separate deals between April 1955 and May 1960 that netted the New Yorkers frontline pitchers Art Ditmar, Bobby Shantz, Ralph Terry, and reliever Ryne Duren; third baseman Clete Boyer; and outfielders Roger Maris, Enos Slaughter, Hector Lopez, and Bob Cerv. The Kansas City connection centered around Arnold Johnson, who had owned Yankee Stadium before taking over the Athletics, and Kansas City GM Parke Carroll, who had worked for Weiss in the Yankee front office.

The Yankees finally broke the franchise color ban in 1955 with catcher Elston Howard, who was deemed sufficiently in the Yankee mold. (Weiss had traded Vic Power, a flashy black Puerto Rican, to Philadelphia in December 1953 because the first baseman had been considered not docile enough.) Howard took considerable abuse of the Uncle Tom variety, especially after he defended Stengel's treatment of him in the face of the manager's remark that

"When I finally get a nigger, I get the only one who can't run." Neither a speedster nor a crusader, Howard lasted twelve productive seasons in New York, winning an MVP award in 1963.

Despite the end of the five-pennant streak in 1954 (the Yankees won 103 games, the most under Stengel, but fell to Cleveland's superior pitching) and a World Series loss (to Brooklyn) the following year, the Yankee machine churned on. But while the manager looked the other way when his players kicked up their heels off the field, Weiss looked only for an opportunity to break up the clique that inspired most of the fun without breaking up the team. The general manager's chance came with an altercation at the Copacabana nightclub in New York on May 15, 1957. With Mantle, Ford, Berra, outfielder Hank Bauer, pitcher Johnny Kucks and their wives gathered to celebrate Martin's birthday, an argument erupted between Bauer and a drunk who had been abusing both the Yankee players and performer Sammy Davis, Jr.; Bauer and his antagonist stepped to the men's room to settle the affair, and the police arrived to find the drunk unconscious and the outfielder swearing that he had never laid a finger on him. A grand jury investigation and a $1 million lawsuit followed. Outraged over the tarnishing of the Yankee image, Weiss fined the players involved and convinced himself that Martin, whom he considered a bad influence on Mantle, had thrown the offending punch. A month later, the second baseman, who had shone in both the 1952 and 1953 World Series, was peddled to Kansas City. The fact that Martin had also been Stengel's pet amounted to very little, especially because Bobby Richardson was considered ready to take over at second base.

Richardson and his double play partner Tony Kubek, the 1957 Rookie of the Year, were principal players in the club's 1957 and 1958 pennants. Both flags led to World Series meetings with Milwaukee, with the Braves winning the first encounter and the Yankees the second. Southpaw Shantz led the league in ERA in 1957, and Turley compiled the most victories and won the Cy Young Award the following season.

After only its second pennant loss of the decade in 1959, the club rebounded for what turned out to be Stengel's last flag in 1960. The World Series was another matter. The Yankees outhit the Pirates .338 to .256, outscored them 55 to 27, out-homered them 10 to 4, and outpitched them with a 3.54 ERA to 7.11, but still lost in seven games because they squandered runs in lopsided 16–3, 10–0, and 12–0 victories. Even so, it took a bad hop into Kubek's throat, a three-run homer by pinch hitter Hal Smith, and, after the Yankees had come back for a tie, a conclusive homer in the ninth inning of the finale by Bill Mazeroski to put down New York. The Yankee offense was led by Richardson's 12 RBIs and Mantle's .400 average and 3 homers.

After the Series, Stengel was criticized for giving Ford only two starts and warming up seventh-game losing pitcher Terry four times before bringing him into the game. Moreover, while he had once been a great instructor of young talent, he had become a grumpy old man intolerant of mistakes when he wasn't dozing on the bench. Deciding that former bullpen catcher and Denver manager Ralph Houk might be lost to another organization if they did not move immediately, Topping and Webb instructed Weiss to announce Stengel's retirement on October 15th. The ousted manager put up no pretense that the move had been his idea; "I'll never make the mistake of being 70 again," Stengel complained. Weiss, only four years Stengel's junior, failed to see the handwriting on the wall; on November 2nd he too was gone, replaced by Roy Hamey.

Houk's first year at the helm produced a record 240 home runs by a team some consider the equal of the 1927 squad. Assisted by two expansion teams that put twenty or so additional pitchers in the AL, a record six Yankees hit more than 20 homers. Maris led the pack, breaking Ruth's 1927 record with 61 to win his second consecutive MVP. Mantle kept pace most of the summer, but, hobbled and then sidelined by injuries in the stretch, fell behind and finished with 54. Maris's pursuit of Ruth's record produced a press circus that tormented the reticent outfielder with repetitive questions and that set up a rivalry with Mantle, who had grown to be the fans' darling and their favorite to surpass the 60-mark. The stress on Maris was so intense that his hair fell out; he grew surly with fans. To make matters worse, Commissioner Ford Frick, a former ghostwriter for Ruth, announced his intention of attaching an asterisk to Maris's home run total if the outfielder did not reach number 61 before the Yankees' 154th game; in fact, the record-breaking homer came off Tracy Stallard of the Red Sox in the last game of the season, number 162 in the expansion schedule, before a Yankee Sta-

dium crowd of only 23,154. The final five games of the season, during which Maris tied and broke the record, averaged only about 18,000, the number held down by the public awareness that the record would only be a half-record. Cy Young Award recipient Ford racked up a 25–4 record, helped by reliever Luis Arroyo (15–5, 29 saves). The World Series was a replay of the season: Six players combined for seven homers, Ford won twice, and the Reds went down in five games.

Although not apparent at first, the decline of the franchise began almost immediately afterwards, when Topping and Webb agreed privately early in 1962 to sell the club at the earliest opportunity and to spend as little as possible in the interim. Given that approach, it was just a matter of time before the organization broke down. Still, the Topping-Webb Yankees won three more pennants, two of them under Houk, and a final one in 1964 under Berra, whom Topping pushed into the manager's seat to combat the popularity of Stengel, then managing the expansion Mets, with Houk getting kicked upstairs to replace the retiring Hamey. In 1962, the Yankees beat the Giants in their final World Series victory until 1978; in 1963, they lost to the Los Angeles Dodgers in four games, and in 1964, to the Cardinals in seven, despite Richardson's record 13 hits.

By 1964, the signs of decay were inescapable. Injuries nagged at aging stars, such as Mantle and Ford. The four top farm teams in the system had finished last in 1963. Finally, the Houk-Berra switch failed on both counts. Houk as a front office figure could make little use of his ability to motivate players; unable to adjust to his new role, he resorted to indulging the players' gripes about Berra. For his part, Berra turned out to be sour rather than lovable, and not only failed to win over Stengel's public following, but barely steered the club to the flag through his own ridiculed tactical mistakes. The poisoned atmosphere exploded on August 20th on a bus ride following a fourth straight loss to Chicago. Infielder Phil Linz insisted, over Berra's objections, on playing a harmonica. The manager suggested that whoever was playing the instrument shove it, Linz tossed it at Berra and suggested that the manager try. Webb and Houk, concluding that Berra had lost control of the situation, decided that, win or lose, the pilot would have to go.

Meanwhile, Topping and Webb were negotiating a deal to sell 80 percent of the organization to CBS for $11.2 million. This set off league fears that the media conglomerate would interfere with baseball's lucrative television contract and that the wrath

Roger Maris actually hit 62 home runs in 1961, but one of them was wiped out of the record book when the game was rained out.

of the U.S. Congress or the Justice Department would descend on baseball for a possible antitrust violation. Only with assurances that Topping and Webb would continue to run the club for five years did the other owners relax and approve the move in a nonchalant telephone vote. The main repercussion for the other AL owners was that five of them had to sell their CBS stock. As for the promise of transitional management by the sellers, Webb sold his remaining 10 percent to CBS in February 1965 and Topping held out only until September 1966; the two took away another $3.2 million between them for their final 20 percent.

The players felt betrayed by the switch in the club's identity to a line item in the budget of a giant corporation, and the press had a field day. Rooting for the Yankees had often been likened to rooting for General Motors or U.S. Steel; now the derogatory joke had come true. The humor very quickly turned to farce with the next act, the signing of a new manager. Midway through the 1964 season, Houk had decided on Johnny Keane, who was about to be fired from his job managing the languishing Cardinals. All at once, however, the Cardinals caught fire as the frontrunner Phillies collapsed, and, with the Yankees also pulling themselves together in the final month of the season, Keane found himself managing in the World Series against the team he had agreed to take over the following year. After the St. Louis victory, Berra was dumped immediately. Houk, compelled to engage in a charade, denied even knowing that Keane had quit the Cardinals; within weeks, however, the switch was announced. Having already lost the respect of some players for his tolerance of the backstabbing of Berra, Houk sank to a new public relations low when he dumped popular broadcaster Allen in December.

The circumstances of Keane's hiring got him off on the wrong foot, and his sanctimonious airs during clubhouse lectures on proper behavior made matters worse. For his part, Keane knew he was being judged by his charges, as he once indicated with his hotel lobby greeting to a group of them, "Good afternoon, gentlemen of the jury." Keane's inflexibility and his secrecy (with Houk's complicity) about the extent of injuries to Howard and Maris hastened an otherwise inevitable collapse. For the first time in thirty-nine years, the Yankees fell below .500. The bitterest pill was that Berra resurfaced as a coach with Stengel's Mets, whose fans at least had fun while their team was losing.

Keane lasted until May 6, 1966, when Houk stepped down from the front office for a second tour as manager. Dan Topping, Jr. took over the general manager's desk. Also gone was Red Barber, fired from the broadcasting booth in retaliation for suggesting that a camera pan empty Yankee Stadium seats to underscore his point about the doldrums into which the team had fallen. Houk, once a dugout hero, returned with considerably less credibility not only because of his role in Berra's removal but also because he had become the one to tell the players that their salary demands were out of line. In 1966, when modish CBS executive Mike Burke took over as club president, he inherited a team that had fallen into last place for the first time since 1908 and that had no farm system to speak of (shortstop Bobby Murcer was the only prospect at the time). What's more, the old route of rebuilding with young players enamored of signing a Yankee contract was no longer open because of the amateur free agent draft.

The CBS regime, with Lee MacPhail, Larry's son and later AL president, as general manager, was a shambles. For six seasons, the team stumbled along with adequate pitching, primarily from Mel Stottlemyre, Fritz Peterson, Stan Bahnsen (1968 Rookie of the Year), and reliever Lindy McDaniel; but the offense was abysmal. Mantle was reduced to playing first base for two seasons before following Richardson, Kubek, Ford, and others into retirement. His successor in center, Joe Pepitone, suffered a breakdown brought on by hot pursuit by various bookies, and went AWOL three times in 1969. The low point of the era came on December 2, 1971, when the club bellowed that it had traded Bahnsen to the White Sox for Rich McKinney; touted as the third baseman of the future, McKinney couldn't throw, and lasted only thirty-seven games.

In 1971, the first rumblings arose about moving the club to the New Jersey Meadowlands sport complex—a theme that would recur several times in the next two decades. Burke, more interested in increasing the parking facilities around Yankee Stadium and renovating the deteriorating stadium itself, appealed to New York City Mayor John Lindsay, who agreed to finance what he thought would be a $24 million facelift. The beginning of work was held up by the Mets, whose permission the Yankees needed to become tenants in Shea Stadium during the two-year reconstruction; the Mets, who were already outdrawing the Yankees, would just as soon have seen their AL rivals in New Jersey, a move that would have left them with a monopoly on New York City baseball and precluded an NL rival from inhabiting the Meadowlands. With negotiations underway to offer the Mets financial concessions for agreeing to become the Yankees' landlord, a new study projected the cost of the Yankee Stadium overhaul at $36 million, causing the Lindsay administration considerable political discomfort. When the project was finally completed in 1976, the price tag had risen to $125 million, all of it public money.

By then, however, Steinbrenner had arrived. Unwilling to spend the money required to rebuild the franchise, CBS board chairman William Paley told Burke in 1972 either to buy the club himself or to find an outside buyer. Thinking he had done both, Burke became part of a partnership headed by Steinbrenner, the owner of the Cleveland-based American Ship Building Co., that put up $10 million (a $4 million loss for CBS) and assumed control on April 30, 1973. Burke was quickly disabused of any assumption that he would continue to direct the operation, and he resigned the club presidency in favor of Cleveland general manager Gabe Paul. MacPhail followed him out the door in October to assume the AL presidency. Left behind were Roy White, the left fielder since 1965; Murcer, no longer an infielder who threatened the safety of fans behind first base with every throw, but now the center fielder; catcher Thurman Munson, AL Rookie of the Year in 1970; and southpaw reliever Sparky Lyle, who arrived from Boston in MacPhail's best trade.

Paul began wheeling and dealing immediately. In November 1972, he made his first trade, getting third baseman Graig Nettles from Cleveland for four spare parts. The following December, he added outfielder Lou Piniella by giving up McDaniel to Kansas City. In April 1974, the club president shipped four pitchers—Peterson, Steve Kline, Fred Beene, and Tom Buskey—to Cleveland for first baseman Chris Chambliss and pitchers Dick Tidrow and Cecil Upshaw.

Houk, uncomfortable with the new front office, had resigned at the end of the 1972 season, giving Paul the opportunity to exert his power in the managerial realm, as well. His first choice to replace Houk was Dick Williams, who, at the height of his success, had quit as manager of the Oakland A's because of the meddling of owner Charlie Finley. Told by the A's owner that the price for permission

In 1972, Yankee pitchers Fritz Peterson and Mike Kekich traded lives by moving in with each other's families. Peterson eventually married Suzanne Kekich, while the relationship between Kekich and Marilyn Peterson did not last.

to negotiate with Williams, still under contract to Oakland, was Murcer, Munson, Lyle, or young lefthander Scott McGregor, Paul went ahead and signed his man without Finley's approval. When Finley lodged a protest with AL president Joe Cronin, Paul retaliated with a similar complaint against Detroit for signing Houk in the hope that the Tigers would send the A's a player and make everyone happy. Cronin foiled the plan by ruling against the Yankees on both counts, so Paul settled on Bill Virdon, who, in 1974, led the Yankees to a second-place finish.

In buying the franchise, Steinbrenner had promised an "absentee ownership," with himself "sticking to building ships." Into 1974, he had kept his word, if only because he had been busy defending himself against an indictment for illegally contributing $100,000 to President Richard Nixon's 1972 election campaign. Pleading guilty on August 23, 1974, he was fined $15,000; the Watergate-related felony would haunt Steinbrenner, who attributed to himself every traditional American value, until, after intense lobbying, he was finally pardoned by President Ronald Reagan in 1989. More immediately, he was suspended from all club operations for two years by Commissioner Bowie Kuhn. While the Yankee managing partner never publicly violated the ban, he did send taped pep talks to the clubhouse. It was also considered unlikely that Paul would have made the moves that he did—trading Murcer to San Francisco for outfielder Bobby Bonds on October 22, 1974 and signing free agent pitcher Catfish Hunter to a five-year, $3 million contract on the following Christmas Eve—without approval. Kuhn ignored the probable violations of his ban and even reinstated Steinbrenner, in March 2, 1976, five months prematurely—some months after the Yankees had switched sides at a joint AL-NL meeting to cast the deciding vote in awarding the commissioner a second term. Steinbrenner's return, and the August 2, 1975 replacement of Virdon with former second baseman Martin, set the stage for the Yankees' return to pennant winning ways and for the most tumultuous period in the club's history since the Huggins-Ruth battle of 1925.

Martin, whose earlier managerial stops at Minnesota, Detroit, and Texas had been tempestuous affairs, was uncharacteristically quiet while completing the third-place finish of 1975. Then, on December 11th, Paul converted a probable 1976 contender into a favorite by sending Bonds to California for center fielder Mickey Rivers and righthander Ed Figueroa, and by then shipping pitcher Doc Medich to Pittsburgh for second baseman Willie Randolph and pitchers Dock Ellis and Ken Brett. The Yankees played their first game in the new Yankee Stadium on April 15, 1976, beating Minnesota 11–4 behind Tidrow. Death Valley in left center field had been reduced from 457 feet to 430 feet (and would be further reduced to 399 by 1988), and seating capacity had been cut to about 56,000, but the renovation removed the iron columns that had blocked the view from many seats and generally made the stadium more comfortable. In midseason, Paul had one of his most publicized deals voided when Kuhn invalidated the $1.5 million purchase of pitcher Vida Blue from Oakland on the grounds that it was detrimental to the best interests of baseball. Paul also made what turned out to be his worst Yankee trade that spring, giving up pitchers McGregor, Tippy Martinez, Rudy May, and Dave Pagan and catcher Rick Dempsey for Baltimore pitchers Ken Holtzman, Doyle Alexander, and Grant Jackson and catcher Ellie Hendricks.

With the ill effects of the Baltimore swap still in the future, the Yankees coasted to a 10½-game AL East margin over the Orioles in 1976. Nettles led the league with 32 homers, Munson won the MVP, Rivers hit .312 and stole 43 bases, and Lyle won the Cy Young Award with 26 saves. The League Championship Series against Kansas City was settled on a sudden-death home run by Chambliss. A four-game World Series sweep by Cincinnati's Big Red Machine ended the year on a sour note.

The advent of free agency in 1976 altered the approach of the newly reactivated Steinbrenner, who threw his money around to win headlines not only for the signing of some of the game's biggest names, but also to gain attention for himself. His first free agent acquisition, of Cincinnati lefty Don Gullett, also set a pattern of recruiting high-priced pitchers who would develop physical or psychological disabilities that restricted their usefulness. Following Gullet would be Andy Messersmith (1978), Luis Tiant (1979), Rudy May (1980), Rick Reuschel (1981), Doyle Alexander (1982), Bob Shirley and John Montefusco (1983), Ed Whitson (1985), Britt Burns (1986), Steve Trout (1987), Andy Hawkins (1988), and Tim Leary (1990).

The signing of Gullett was eclipsed by Steinbrenner's pursuit of future Hall of Famer Reggie Jackson. The Yankee owner escorted the slugging

In 1976, Mickey Rivers walked only thirteen times, the lowest total ever for a player who appeared in 150 or more games.

outfielder to cocktail parties and posh restaurants all over New York, making the official signing in November 1976 a foregone conclusion. Unfortunately for organization chemistry, he never bothered to consult the ever-sensitive Martin about the deal. Before the 1977 season was a month old, Steinbrenner and Paul completed two other transactions that also annoyed the manager. The first sent outfielder Oscar Gamble (a Martin favorite), pitcher LaMarr Hoyt, and $200,000 to Chicago for Bucky Dent, a shortstop who displaced Fred Stanley, another of the manager's pets. The second deal added pitcher Mike Torrez from Oakland for Ellis, a third Martin favorite whose earring had irritated Paul. The manager, already saddled with Holtzman, a pitcher he would ignore throughout the 1977 season, let it be known that he wasn't happy.

The inevitable explosion took a few months, during which players conspired against Martin, Steinbrenner fired the manager on at least five occasions and threatened to do so on dozens of others, and everyone resented Jackson's talk about "the magnitude of me." The eruption came with the publication of a magazine article in which the outfielder called himself "the straw that stirs the drink," and ridiculed the idea of Munson taking on such a role. Jackson only exacerbated the situation by pointedly ignoring the extended hands of his teammates after hitting a home run the night the article appeared. Sulking over the coolness of teammates and Martin's day-to-day decisions to drop him from the cleanup spot or take him off the field altogether as a designated hitter, Jackson played a bloop single into a double in a nationally televised game on June 18th and found himself replaced in right field mid-inning by Paul Blair. The ensuing dugout scene showed the outfielder screaming at his manager, while the latter tried to break out of a cordon of coaches to get at the player.

Despite all the frictions, the Yankees won the AL East by 2½ games, beat Kansas City in a five-game LCS for the second consecutive year, and defeated the Dodgers in a six-game World Series. In the Series with Los Angeles, Jackson hit .450 and set Series records with 5 home runs, 25 total bases, and 10 runs, earning the sobriquet of Mr. October. Three of the homers came on consecutive pitches off three different Dodger hurlers in the final game.

The 1978 season was different, primarily because, with the departure of Paul, Steinbrenner's constant references to his "baseball people" took on a hollow ring. The owner and new president Al Rosen simply collected players, often opting for the biggest

> The attitude of Yankee players toward George Steinbrenner was summed up by third baseman Graig Nettles: "The more we lose, the more he'll fly in. And the more he flies in, the better chance that there'll be a plane crash."

name available, sometimes acting only on whim. For half of the 1978 season, the Yankees carried Jim Spencer, Jay Johnstone, and Gary Thomasson, all lefthanded outfielder-first basemen-designated hitters. (Spencer's contract included an unenforceable provision, inserted at Steinbrenner's insistence, that the player start every game in which the Yankees faced a right-handed pitcher.) Before the season, Steinbrenner had signed free agent reliever Goose Gossage, sending Lyle, in Nettles's phrase, "from Cy Young to Sayonara." The owner meddled constantly in Martin's handling of the team, dictating lineups, calling the dugout with advice, even bugging the phone in the manager's office. Jackson was even more trouble, defying orders to bunt in a game against Kansas City and complaining to the front office about one thing or another. For his part, Martin further alienated his slumping star by batting him near the bottom of the lineup against southpaws and by making him a permanent DH, even if that meant sending an ailing Munson to right field. Finally, when Jackson decided on July 17th to bunt with a two-strike count in a game against the Royals and fouled off the pitch for a strikeout, Martin suspended him for five days. Jackson showed no contrition, and even baldly defended his bunt ploy. The team fell to 14 games behind Boston, a season low. Then Martin found out from Chicago owner Bill Veeck that Steinbrenner had discussed trading him for his White Sox counterpart Bob Lemon. Feeling defied by Jackson and betrayed by Steinbrenner, an overwrought manager told reporters that "the two of them deserve each other—one's a born liar, the other's convicted."

Martin was fired on July 25th. His successor was Lemon, who had in the meantime been bounced by Veeck and whose low-key style set the team on a 48–20 pace that brought it to a season-ending tie. The one-game playoff victory was keyed by Dent's three-run home run into the left field screen at Fenway Park. On the season, the mound star was Cy Young winner Ron Guidry, whose 25 wins (against only 3 losses), 1.74 ERA, and 9 shutouts all topped the league. The campaign was also marked by a surprise announcement before an Old Timers Day crowd that Martin, booted only a couple of weeks before, would be back to manage in 1980, with Lemon moving up to the general manager's chair. The Yankees swept the Royals in three straight games in the LCS, then came back from an 0–2 deficit to beat the Dodgers in the World Series. The stars against Los Angeles were Dent, who batted .417, and second baseman Brian Doyle, who filled in for the injured Randolph by swatting .438.

The death of Lemon's 26-year-old son in an auto accident ten days after the World Series took a great deal out of the manager, and, on June 18, 1979, Martin was back, earlier than expected. The addition of free agent pitchers Tiant and Tommy John and of lefthander Dave Righetti from Texas (for Lyle) raised expectations of another pennant. But the Yankee hopes effectively ended with an early-season shower room tussle between Gossage and catcher Cliff Johnson that put the reliever on the sidelines for several months with a torn ligament in his thumb. Then, on August 2nd, Munson was killed when his private jet crashed. Finally, in October, after months of Steinbrenner's taunting Martin with the necessity for good behavior, the manager got into a fist fight in a Minnesota hotel with a marshmallow salesman named Joseph Cooper and was fired for the second time. Martin would return for three more terms as Yankee manager—in 1983 and parts of 1985 and 1988—in what became an obsessive quest to please Steinbrenner sufficiently to be named to the post permanently. By that time, however, the various hirings and firings of managers had become a travesty that bored as many fans as it angered. Rumors of Martin's return for a sixth tour continued right up to his death in an automobile accident in December 1989.

Former Yankee coach Dick Howser followed Martin in 1980 and won the AL East title, but was fired after a month of public hand wringing by Steinbrenner over how to deal with a manager who had won 103 games but lost the LCS in three games. The issue came down to a replacement for third base coach Mike Ferraro, who had fallen victim to the owner's wrath for sending Randolph home to a bang-bang out in the second game of the LCS. When Steinbrenner publicly asked Don Zimmer to take Ferraro's place, Howser sealed his fate by asserting that he should have final say on the make-up of the coaching staff; on November 2nd, Steinbrenner announced Howser's decision to go into real estate in Florida rather than return to manage the team. (Actually, he turned up as pilot of the Kansas City Royals in 1981.) In 1981, former shortstop Gene Michael was moved

Billy Martin. *Courtesy of the New York Yankees*

into the dugout because of his loyalty (an attribute Steinbrenner often invoked), then was fired in September for disloyalty after refusing to apologize for a public plea for an end to the unrelenting badgering.

Winners of the first half of the strike-induced split season, the Yankees beat second-half winner Milwaukee in a five-game playoff for the AL East championship, then swept Oakland (managed by Martin) in the LCS, before losing the World Series to the Dodgers in six games. Righthanded reliever George Frazier lost a Series-record three games. Following the defeat, Steinbrenner apologized "for the performance of the Yankees in the World Series." On the other hand, he did not apologize for an alleged run-in with two Dodger fans in an elevator; rather, he displayed his bruised knuckles as a badge of honor, although there was much speculation that the victim of the fisticuffs had been the elevator itself. The front office confusion was such that, in three separate announcements, Lemon was rehired, Michael was said to be returning in 1983, and Michael's contract was extended through 1985.

By 1985, the Yankees had endured six more managerial changes, with Lemon giving way to Michael and then Clyde King in 1982; Martin return-ing for all of 1983; and Berra serving for all of 1984, but getting the axe in favor of Martin seventeen games into the 1985 season. The front office picture was no clearer than who was in charge on the field. In rapid succession, Cedric Tallis, Michael, Bill Bergesch, Murray Cook, King, Woody Woodward, Lou Piniella (between two managerial stints), Syd Thrift, and Michael again either held the title or theoretically exercised the authority of general manager. The confusion reached its height in 1991, when vice president-general manager George Bradley kept busy offering second baseman Steve Sax a contract extension that would make him untradeable for a couple of years, while vice president Pete Peterson was trying to peddle the infielder to make room for prospect Pat Kelly.

As the treatment of Ferraro suggested, coaches were interchangeable parts in the Steinbrenner cosmos. In 1982 alone, there were three batting coaches and five pitching coaches. Players never knew where to turn, and sometimes didn't even know who their teammates were. When outfielder Dave Collins asked in 1982 which of the new faces was even-more-recent arrival Juan Espino, he was told that the catcher had already been shipped to Columbus.

Nineteen players rode the infamous Columbus shuttle that year, with pitcher Dave LaRoche alone making four round trips. The reason for all the movement back and forth was that Steinbrenner had decided on a speed-oriented offense, signed free agent Collins and got outfielder Ken Griffey from Cincinnati toward that end, then decided that the departure of Jackson had left the team with too little power, and made hurried deals to correct the power shortage. The April acquisition of shortstop Roy Smalley from Minnesota was supposed to add even more punch to the lineup, but it left everyone, especially Smalley and incumbent shortstop Dent, wondering what was going on until the latter was shipped to Texas in August. Similar indecisiveness kept lefty Righetti baffled for years about whether he would continue as bullpen stopper, a role he assumed in 1984 with the departure of Gossage, or go back to the starting rotation.

Young players suffered the most in the turmoil. The fortunate prospects were those (like McGregor, Martinez, Hoyt, Greg Gagne, Doug Drabek, Tim Burke, and Fred McGriff) who were traded away to stardom elsewhere before they could get a taste of Steinbrenner's version of the Yankee tradition. The less fortunate took merciless abuse for their mistakes. In June 1978, righthander Jim Beattie had his courage as well as his ability questioned in Steinbrenner-seeded headlines for giving up four runs in three innings in a key game; he was soon packed off to the minor leagues. Shortstop Bobby Meacham was summarily dispatched to Columbus when his error cost the Yankees the fourth game of the 1984 season. Other prospects abused in public included pitchers Ken Clay and Scott Nielsen. Some of the biggest heat was turned on Jose Rijo, when he was rushed to the major leagues in 1984 in an attempt to counter the publicity being garnered by the Mets with the arrival of Dwight Gooden; Rijo was traded off before his failures at Yankee Stadium prompted additional psychological burdens laid on him by Steinbrenner. In another incident, during an August 1982 doubleheader, the owner had Yankee Stadium public address announcer Bob Sheppard, the embarrassment obvious in his voice, offer everyone present a free ticket to any home game for having had to endure a 1–0 loss in the first game and a 14–2 drubbing in the second. Frazier, who had escaped a tongue whipping after his three losses in the 1981 World Series, sat on the mound, his head hung in humiliation.

The veterans who showed up in the Bronx in the 1980s were a mixed bag. DH Don Baylor and knuckleballer Phil Niekro (who won his 300th game for the Yankees in the last game of the 1985 season) tried to be calming clubhouse influences after signing on as free agents. Signed to a five-year, $4.5 million contract in 1984, pitcher Whitson suffered attacks from both Steinbrenner and the fans because of his 10–8 record and 4.88 ERA; the pitcher's disparaging remarks about New York, threatening letters to his family, and a fistfight with Martin in 1985 hastened his departure back to San Diego. The New York hex ruined the career of outfielder-designated hitter Steve Kemp, a 1984 free agent acquisition, without an assist from the Yankees' principal owner; he was struck on the cheek by a batting practice line drive. Even Yankee old timers had to put up with Steinbrenner's accusations; outfielder White, who had signed to play in Japan after retiring in 1978, was charged with being a mole for Japanese leagues and attempting to recruit pitchers Righetti and Bill Gullickson for the Far East.

Steinbrenner did not confine his outbursts to employees. In 1983 alone, he took on White Sox owner Jerry Reinsdorf, the Umpires Association, Commissioner Kuhn, and AL President MacPhail. In January, he called Reinsdorf and partner Eddie Einhorn "The Abbott and Costello of Baseball" in response to charges of irresponsibility for signing ex-White Soxer Kemp to a $5.5-million, five-year contract; Kuhn fined him $5,000 for the crack. In spring training, the Yankee owner accused umpire Lee Weyer of being under instructions from NL President Chub Feeney to call all close plays in interleague games for the NL team; the fine for this was $50,000. What became known as the Pine Tar Incident involved a ninth-inning home run by the Royals' George Brett on July 24, 1983 that put Kansas City ahead 5–4 but that was disallowed when Martin pointed out that the bat used by the third baseman had pine tar more than the allowed eighteen inches up the handle. MacPhail reallowed the homer four days later, precipitating a series of court cases and a Steinbrenner outburst against the league president; for this, Kuhn imposed a $250,000 fine and required reimbursement of $50,000 in legal fees. In 1987, the Yankees owner won a court case brought by the Umpires Association over an accusation that arbiter Dallas Parks was incompetent. Two years after that, Steinbrenner took on his own fans when he had Yankee Stadium security guards confiscate signs saying "George Must Go"; only an action brought by the American Civil Liberties Union prevented a recurrence.

Although they were almost always overshadowed by the front office shenanigans, there were bright moments on the field. Second-place finishes in

In 1986, Don Mattingly set a record when he went to bat 677 times without a single attempt to steal a base.

1985 and 1986 were largely the result of left fielder Rickey Henderson's AL-leading totals both seasons in runs scored (146 and 130) and stolen bases (80 and 87); Henderson also had sufficient power to hit 24 homers in 1985 and 28 the next year. First baseman Don Mattingly led the AL in batting in 1984 with a .343 average, drove in a league-high 145 runs to win the MVP Award in 1985, and gave evidence of becoming the next franchise player until a back problem slowed him later in the 1980s. Outfielder Dave Winfield battled Mattingly for the 1984 batting crown down to the last game of the season and averaged more than 100 RBIs in his eight years with the team.

Piniella, first named manager in 1986, was subjected to the favorite Steinbrenner ploy of being promoted to general manager (in 1988, so Martin could take over for the fifth time), then being demoted back to the dugout later that season. The former Yankee outfielder was also the victim of another Steinbrenner gambit, insisting that employees be available for phone calls at all hours and firing them when they didn't answer the phone. Piniella's successor, Dallas Green ("one of the biggest mistakes I ever made," according to the owner), failed to finish as the 1989 manager. Firing Bucky Dent in 1990 and replacing him with Stump Merrill in 1990 were sideshows to Steinbrenner's problems with the commissioner's office.

The difficulty indirectly involved Winfield. Signed as a free agent in 1981, the ex-Padre insisted that part of his ten-year $23-million salary be put into the Winfield Foundation, a charitable trust intended to fund youth programs. It wasn't long, however, before the Yankee owner was calling his new slugger Mr. May—an unfavorable comparison with the departed Mr. October, Jackson. The battle between player and owner focused on the Winfield Foundation, which Steinbrenner refused to fund until what he considered financial irregularities had been straightened out. The depths to which the feud had

In 1987, catcher Rick Cerone became the only player to pitch and catch in the same game twice.

degenerated did not become public knowledge until July 30, 1990, when an investigation by Commissioner Fay Vincent's office revealed that Steinbrenner had, two years earlier, paid Howard Spira, a professional gambler and a one-time employee of the foundation, $40,000 to provide information damaging to Winfield. Vincent was about to suspend the Yankee owner for two years when Steinbrenner offered to remove himself from club affairs permanently, provided the word suspension was not used. The Yankee Stadium announcement of the arrangement was greeted by a standing ovation.

With the advent of the 1990s, the team on the field threatened to be as bad as the clubs that had labored under the CBS ownership in the 1960s. Mattingly's back problems practically eliminated his extra-base power, while Winfield was already gone in spirit before finally being dealt to the Angels. Emblematic of the club's state was righthander Hawkins, who had come over as another free agent from San Diego in 1989. Although his 15–15 record in that season was the staff's best, he won only 5 games in 1990, and his losses included a July 1st embarrassment, when he dropped a no-hitter to the White Sox because of errors, 4–0. Like Whitson and so many others, Hawkins was soon gone.

Steinbrenner in exile proved to be as ubiquitous as Steinbrenner in power. When his successor as general partner, Robert Nederlander, was ousted late in 1991, Vincent turned down the selection of Daniel McCarthy, the owner's personal attorney, who admitted that, while serving as acting managing partner, he had discussed the free agent signing of outfielder Danny Tartabull with Steinbrenner. All sides finally agreed on Steinbrenner's son-in-law Joseph Molloy as the new head of the team in April.

Molloy's appointment did little to end the farce. For one thing, former Steinbrenner associate Leonard Kleinman, who had been denied the organization's top job in 1990 because of his involvement in the Spira affair, brought a $22-million lawsuit against Vincent. General Manager Michael exhibited less of an inclination to be a good soldier, not least when he asserted during the 1992 season that the Yankees didn't have enough money to go after the free agents

In 1991 and 1992, the Yankees set a major league record by going 93 straight games without a complete effort from one of their pitchers. The string was broken by Greg Cadaret on April 19, 1992, in a 14–0 blanking of Cleveland.

that he wanted. The reason that they didn't, as it turned out, was that they had been borrowing heavily against an unprecedented $486-million contract with the cable Madison Square Garden (MSG) network and WABC radio to distribute profits to team partners and to help Steinbrenner bail out his ailing shipbuilding company. Although Kleinman eventually went away and Michael subsequently played down his criticisms with the usual I-was-misquoted excuse, the public disarray of the organization prompted other owners to pressure Vincent for a specific date for Steinbrenner's return. In one of his final pronouncements as commissioner, Vincent announced that the owner would be permitted to resume full control of the club in March 1993.

Things did not go too much better on the field in 1992. While new manager Buck Showalter gave the club a veneer of hustling play, he was quickly undermined by renewed drug charges against starter Pascual Perez and reliever Steve Howe, both of whom had been suspended previously by other teams for substance abuse. But while Perez was summarily suspended, the ouster of Howe (the eighth of his career) led to another circus that pitched its big tent in Vincent's office. Without waiting for a Montana court to hand down a verdict on the possession and dealing charges against the southpaw, the commissioner kicked him out of the game as an incurable recidivist. When the Players Association responded to a formal complaint by the pitcher by summoning officials of the Yankees to give testimony on the case, Vincent decided that his authority was being usurped and, in turn, issued threats to Michael and another team official to adhere to his line or think about other employment. The upshot was that Howe pleaded *nolo contendere* in Montana, the Yankees had another reason to support moves for Vincent's ouster in September, and the pitcher was reinstated with a big contract after the season. The legal implications of Vincent's move against Howe aside, the different fates of the bullpen ace and Perez reawakened charges in some quarters that it was one thing to be a repeat drug offender and another thing to be a repeat Latin drug offender.

Without Perez and Howe, the 1992 pitching staff was as much of a sometime thing as ever, with only Melido Perez showing any consistency, and even he finished three games under .500. The most significant offense came from Tartabull, who, despite nagging injuries, hit 25 home runs. The fourth straight losing season matched the franchise's worst slide, first recorded between 1912 and 1915.

With Michael operating in New York and Molloy in Florida, the 1992–93 offseason saw the team's two top officials continually talking at cross-purposes about whom they were seeking on the free agent market. If anything emerged clearly, however, it was that Michael was only marking time until Steinbrenner's return, when the general manager was likely to be replaced. In the meantime, the organization took a couple of more black eyes when such highly desired free agents as Greg Maddux, David Cone, and Barry Bonds indicated that they had no wish to don Yankee pinstripes. The club made another miscalculation when it left third baseman Charlie Hayes available to the Colorado Rockies in the expansion draft for no better stated reason than Michael's excuse that "we thought they'd miss him." On the credit side, the team plunged into both the free agent and trade market to come up with pitchers Jim Abbott and Jimmy Key, third baseman Wade Boggs, shortstop Spike Owen, and outfielder Paul O'Neill. The main costs were outfielder Roberto Kelly and highly touted prospect J. T. Snow.

In 1992, New York outfielder Roberto Kelly reached first base on catcher's interference a record eight times.

NEW YORK YANKEES

Annual Standings and Managers

Year	Position	W	L	Pct.	GB	Managers
1903	Fourth	72	62	.537	17	Clark Griffith
1904	Second	92	59	.609	1½	Clark Griffith
1905	Sixth	71	78	.477	21½	Clark Griffith
1906	Second	90	61	.596	3	Clark Griffith
1907	Fifth	70	78	.473	21	Clark Griffith
1908	Eighth	51	103	.331	39½	Clark Griffith, Kid Elberfeld
1909	Fifth	74	77	.490	23½	George Stallings
1910	Second	88	63	.583	14½	George Stallings, Hal Chase

1911	Sixth	76	76	.500	25½	Hal Chase
1912	Eighth	50	102	.329	55	Harry Wolverton
1913	Seventh	57	94	.377	38	Frank Chance
1914	Sixth*	70	84	.455	30	Frank Chance, Roger Peckinpaugh
1915	Fifth	69	83	.454	32½	Bill Donovan
1916	Fourth	80	74	.519	11	Bill Donovan
1917	Sixth	71	82	.464	28½	Bill Donovan
1918	Fourth	60	63	.488	13½	Miller Huggins
1919	Third	80	59	.576	7½	Miller Huggins
1920	Third	95	59	.617	3	Miller Huggins
1921	First	98	55	.641	+4½	Miller Huggins
1922	First	94	60	.610	+1	Miller Huggins
1923	First	98	54	.645	+16	Miller Huggins
1924	Second	89	63	.586	2	Miller Huggins
1925	Seventh	69	85	.448	30	Miller Huggins
1926	First	91	63	.591	+3	Miller Huggins
1927	First	110	44	.714	+19	Miller Huggins
1928	First	101	53	.656	+2½	Miller Huggins
1929	Second	88	66	.571	18	Miller Huggins, Art Fletcher
1930	Third	86	68	.558	16	Bob Shawkey
1931	Second	94	59	.614	13½	Joe McCarthy
1932	First	107	47	.695	+13	Joe McCarthy
1933	Second	91	59	.607	7	Joe McCarthy
1934	Second	94	60	.610	7	Joe McCarthy
1935	Second	89	60	.597	3	Joe McCarthy
1936	First	102	51	.667	+19½	Joe McCarthy
1937	First	102	52	.662	+13	Joe McCarthy
1938	First	99	53	.651	+9½	Joe McCarthy
1939	First	106	45	.702	+17	Joe McCarthy
1940	Third	88	66	.571	2	Joe McCarthy
1941	First	101	53	.656	+17	Joe McCarthy
1942	First	103	51	.669	+9	Joe McCarthy
1943	First	98	56	.636	+13½	Joe McCarthy
1944	Third	83	71	.539	6	Joe McCarthy
1945	Fourth	81	71	.533	6½	Joe McCarthy
1946	Third	87	67	.565	17	Joe McCarthy, Bill Dickey, Johnny Neun
1947	First	97	57	.630	+12	Bucky Harris
1948	Third	94	60	.610	2½	Bucky Harris
1949	First	97	57	.630	+1	Casey Stengel
1950	First	98	56	.636	+3	Casey Stengel
1951	First	98	56	.636	+5	Casey Stengel
1952	First	95	59	.617	+2	Casey Stengel
1953	First	99	52	.656	+8½	Casey Stengel
1954	Second	103	51	.669	8	Casey Stengel
1955	First	96	58	.623	+3	Casey Stengel
1956	First	97	57	.630	+9	Casey Stengel
1957	First	98	56	.636	+8	Casey Stengel
1958	First	92	62	.597	+10	Casey Stengel
1959	Third	79	75	.513	15	Casey Stengel
1960	First	97	57	.630	+8	Casey Stengel
1961	First	109	53	.673	+8	Ralph Houk
1962	First	96	66	.593	+5	Ralph Houk
1963	First	104	57	.646	+10½	Ralph Houk
1964	First	99	63	.611	+1	Yogi Berra
1965	Sixth	77	85	.475	25	Johnny Keane
1966	Tenth	70	89	.440	26½	Johnny Keane, Ralph Houk
1967	Ninth	72	90	.444	20	Ralph Houk

1968	Fifth	83	79	.512	20	Ralph Houk
1969	Fifth	80	81	.497	28½	Ralph Houk
1970	Second	93	69	.574	15	Ralph Houk
1971	Fourth	82	80	.506	21	Ralph Houk
1972	Fourth	79	76	.510	6½	Ralph Houk
1973	Fourth	80	82	.494	17	Ralph Houk
1974	Second	89	73	.549	2	Bill Virdon
1975	Third	83	77	.519	12	Bill Virdon, Billy Martin
1976	First	97	62	.610	+10½	Billy Martin
1977	First	100	62	.617	+2½	Billy Martin
1978	First	100	63	.613	+1	Billy Martin, Bob Lemon
1979	Fourth	89	71	.556	13½	Bob Lemon, Billy Martin
1980	First	103	59	.636	+3	Dick Howser
1981	First	34	22	.607	+2	Gene Michael
	Sixth	25	26	.490	5	Gene Michael, Bob Lemon
1982	Fifth	79	83	.480	16	Bob Lemon, Gene Michael, Clyde King
1983	Third	91	71	.562	7	Billy Martin
1984	Third	87	75	.537	17	Yogi Berra
1985	Second	97	64	.602	2	Yogi Berra, Billy Martin
1986	Second	90	72	.556	5½	Lou Piniella
1987	Fourth	89	73	.549	9	Lou Piniella
1988	Fifth	85	76	.528	3½	Billy Martin, Lou Piniella
1989	Fifth	74	87	.460	14½	Dallas Green, Bucky Dent
1990	Seventh	67	95	.414	21	Bucky Dent, Stump Merrill
1991	Fifth	71	91	.438	20	Stump Merrill
1992	Fourth	76	86	.469	20	Buck Showalter

*Tie

Postseason Play

LCS	3–2 versus Kansas City	1976	WS	3–5 versus New York	1921
	3–2 versus Kansas City	1977		0–4–1 versus New York	1922
	3–2 versus Kansas City	1978		4–2 versus New York	1923
	0–3 versus Kansas City	1980		3–4 versus St. Louis	1926
	3–0 versus Oakland	1981		4–0 versus Pittsburgh	1927
				4–0 versus St. Louis	1928
				4–0 versus Chicago	1932
				4–2 versus New York	1936
				4–1 versus New York	1937
				4–0 versus Chicago	1938
				4–0 versus Cincinnati	1939
				4–1 versus Brooklyn	1941
				1–4 versus St. Louis	1942
				4–1 versus St. Louis	1943
				4–3 versus Brooklyn	1947
				4–1 versus Brooklyn	1949
				4–0 versus Philadelphia	1950
				4–2 versus New York	1951
				4–3 versus Brooklyn	1952
				4–2 versus Brooklyn	1953
				3–4 versus Brooklyn	1955
				4–3 versus Brooklyn	1956
				3–4 versus Milwaukee	1957
				4–3 versus Milwaukee	1958
				3–4 versus Pittsburgh	1960
				4–1 versus Cincinnati	1961
				4–3 versus San Francisco	1962
				0–4 versus Los Angeles	1963

3–4 versus St. Louis	1964
0–4 versus Cincinnati	1976
4–2 versus Los Angeles	1977
4–2 versus Los Angeles	1978
2–4 versus Los Angeles	1981

New York Mets

National League,
1962–Present

RECORD: 2313–2637 (.467)

BALLPARKS: POLO GROUNDS (1962–1963)
SHEA STADIUM (1964–Present)

Like the Houston Astros, the Mets were created as a compromise solution to the Continental League's threatened incursion into major league baseball. Unlike Houston, New York was able to avail itself of a rich legacy of National League baseball, left in escrow in 1957 with the departures of the Brooklyn Dodgers and New York Giants for California. The franchise's first moves included adopting the blue (Dodgers) and orange (Giants) colors of its local predecessors.

For a team aimed primarily at New York's starved NL fans, the Mets had a decidedly Yankee look in their first years. The major reason was the reluctance of principal owner Joan Payson and club

Nobody was more of a franchise player than Tom Seaver for the Mets in the late 1960s and for most of the 1970s. Here, on September 4, 1976, Seaver delivers the pitch that gave him a record 200 strikeouts for 9 consecutive seasons. *AP/Wide World Photos*

No sooner had the club been organized with the official name of the Metropolitan Baseball Club than Dan Daniel and other sportswriters started referring to it as the Mets. In a subsequent contest, more than 1,000 newspaper readers cast ballots in favor of one of the ten names selected by the owners: Mets, Jets, Continentals, Burros, Avengers, NYBs, Rebels, Skyliners, Skyscrapers, and Meadowlarks. Skyliners finished a close second to Mets. Payson herself was said to have preferred Meadowlarks.

It was in the team's inaugural year that Casey Stengel started to refer to his motley collection of has-beens and never-would-be's as the Amazin' Mets—a description that would stick to the team, in sarcasm and earnestness, for the next thirty years. Other Stengelisms from his Mets days:
—"We was going to get you a birthday cake, but we figured you'd drop it" (at a birthday party for Marv Throneberry).
—"We traded him while he was hot" (after trading Don Zimmer, who had just doubled to break up an 0–34 slide, to Cincinnati).
—"I got a kid, he's 19 years old and in 10 years he's got a chance to be 29" (on the limited prospects of Mets outfielder Greg Goossen).
—"You gotta have a catcher. If you don't have a catcher, you'd have all passed balls" (on why the Mets made receiver Hobie Landrith their first choice in the expansion draft).

chairman M. Donald Grant to give in to the financial and power demands of their first choice for general manager, Continental League point man Branch Rickey. As their second choice, Payson and Grant turned to George Weiss, the 66-year-old architect of the great Yankee teams of the late 1940s and 1950s who had been forced into retirement in the Bronx. Although given a five-year contract as a part-time "advisor," Weiss made little secret of his resentment at the way he had been treated by the Yankees, and jumped at the Mets offer. To put the cherry on his decision, he got the Mets to give him the title of president rather than general manager, thereby remaining technically within a stipulation of his retirement contract with the Yankees and obligating them to continue paying him for his advice even as he moved into the executive offices of the Mets. The Yankees had more reason to see red when Weiss then went out to recruit such former Bronx names as Johnny Murphy, Gil McDougald, Whitey Herzog—and, in particular, Casey Stengel. Nobody was surprised when the Yankees turned a cold shoulder to the notion of hosting the Mets at Yankee Stadium while a new ballpark was being built for the fledgling franchise.

Stengel, who had also been forcibly retired by the Yankees, signed on with the team as a manager, but that turned out to be only one of his roles. Confronted with expansion players who were to constitute one of the worst teams in baseball history, Stengel, who was over 70 years old, worked the press and television (and, through them, the fans) tirelessly to represent his charges as New York's biggest entertainment attraction. From February to October for almost four years, hardly a day went by without the sports pages reporting some new bizarre (or bizarrely stated) observation from the Old Professor on the sorry state of his team. The public relations

performance worked to endear the incompetent Mets to many of the same fans who, only a few years before, would have gone into a deep depression if their Dodgers or Giants had failed to win the pennant. Along with a $6-million radio-television contract signed with the Rheingold breweries, this New Breed of fan was to more than cover the $50,000 induction fee and $1.8 million in expansion player purchases required to enter the NL in 1962.

Going for familiar names in the expansion draft and subsequent trades, the Mets filled their roster with aged stars like Gil Hodges, Richie Ashburn, Gus Bell, and Gene Woodling. Also found appealing were players with an Ebbets Field pedigree—Hodges, Charlie Neal, Don Zimmer, Roger Craig, and Clem Labine. What it all added up to was a record-shattering season of 40 wins and 120 losses that included nine straight losses to open the season, an eleven-game losing run between July 15th and July 26th, a thirteen-game losing streak between August 9th and August 21st and a seventeen-game losing skein between May 21st and June 6th. The team was officially eliminated from the pennant race on August 7.

Despite the concentration of ex-Dodgers like Hodges and declining stars like Ashburn, the New Breed ended up devoting most of its attention to other players—perceived as more appropriate symbols for whatever flaws in the human condition the Mets brought constantly to mind. Among these were

Rod Kanehl, who could play all the infield and out-field positions, but none of them well; Choo Choo Coleman, a catcher whose main skill was chasing down passed balls; Elio Chacon, a shortstop whose lack of English extended to "I've got it" and led him into almost daily collisions with oncharging outfield-ers; and Al Jackson, a pitcher of genuine talent who seemed particularly burdened with the task of get-ting six outs an inning and who, in the words of Stengel, had to be relieved on occasion before "he committed suicide on the mound." Most of all, there was Marv Throneberry, a first baseman whose feats of missing popups, ground balls, and bases became the most enduring emblem of the early Mets.

The groaning laughter from the grandstands and the media failed to impress Weiss, accustomed to collecting pennants and World Series trophies from his days with the Yankees. Already irritated that the team had to play its first two years in the deteriorating cavern that was the Polo Grounds, he imported and exported dozens of players in the vain attempt to match the play of at least fellow-expansion Houston. But the only reminders of his past glories came when rival general managers evened the score for his past Yankee trade pillagings by fobbing off on the Mets their bench and farm system mediocrities. A dour man, Weiss was also slow to realize the pro-motional value of the sheets and placards carried to the Polo Grounds by fans bent on proclaiming their sentiments about the team; only after his confiscation policy was blasted in the press did he rescind the order and give impetus to the banners that were to become a cardinal feature of the ballpark.

In their first four seasons, the Mets never lost fewer than 109 games and never ended a season closer to first place than 40 games. The "instant rec-ognition" philosophy of players continued with the purchase of all-but-done stars (and future Hall of Famers) like Duke Snider, Yogi Berra, and Warren Spahn. Another 1963 import was Jimmy Piersall, the *Fear Strikes Out* center fielder who marked his 100th home run by trotting around the bases backward and who was then quickly traded because, according to Stengel, there wasn't room for two clowns on the team. For those seeking signs of an eventual im-provement in the play of the club, the main sources of hope were second baseman Ron Hunt and first baseman Ed Kranepool. Hunt, whose specialty was getting hit by pitched balls, finished second only to Pete Rose in the voting for the 1963 Rookie of the Year; a year later, he became the first Met elected to a starting berth in the All Star game. Kranepool, who was a member of the team even in its maiden year

after being signed out of a local high school, so im-pressed owner Payson that she made it clear to the front office that she never wanted him traded. De-spite several tries in that direction over the years, the order was obeyed: Although he reached 60 RBIs only once and closed with a lifetime batting average of .261, Kranepool spent his entire eighteen-year career with the Mets.

The most immediate result of the team's move from the glum Polo Grounds to Shea Stadium in 1964 was a dramatic hike in attendance. After two seasons of barely missing and barely topping the 1 million mark, the team reeled off annual attendance totals of 1.7, 1.7, 1.9, 1.5, and 1.7 million in its first five years in the new Queens facility.

What the fans mainly got for their money were memorable games that the Mets, for all their David-versus-Goliath valor, still ended up losing. In 1964, for instance, the team observed Memorial Day by battling the Giants in a record-breaking ten-hour doubleheader that featured a twenty-three-inning nightcap during which the Mets pulled off a triple play, San Francisco's Willie Mays was forced to play shortstop, and Gaylord Perry pitched ten shutout in-nings thanks to his first big league use of a spitball. Three weeks later, on Father's Day, twenty-seven Mets trooped to the plate and then back to the bench again as Philadelphia's Jim Bunning tossed a perfect game against them.

The out-with-the-old-in-with-the-new attitude spurred on by the team's shift to Shea Stadium came close to costing Stengel his position as manager for the 1965 season. After still another cellar finish, the press stepped up its quotes from the usual anony-mous players accusing him of falling asleep on the bench during games and no longer even being able to identify his personnel. Weiss rejected the sallies and, although he brought in former managers Yogi Berra and Eddie Stanky as coaches, insisted that Ca-sey would stay on. In a move seen as reflecting in-creased edginess on the part of Payson and Grant about the accomplishments of Weiss himself, Bing Devine, mastermind of the Cardinals' successful 1964 pennant drive, was added as the team president's own special assistant.

Stengel's ties to the team were unraveled, then severed altogether, by two accidents during the 1965 season. In the first one, on May 10, the 74-year-old manager fractured his wrist in a fall at West Point, where the Mets had gone to play an exhibition game. The injury forced him to turn over the club, at least temporarily, to coach Wes Westrum. Then, in late July, during a banquet held to honor the former stars who would appear the following day at an old-timers' game, another fall fractured his hip. Although there was never any definitive word on how or even where the accident occurred, the popular impression was that Stengel had taken his tumble in the midst of a little too much celebrating. In any case, with explicit blessings from Stengel and despite previous indications that Berra would be tapped as a successor, coach Wes Westrum was given a contract as the new manager. It was under Westrum in 1966 that the team avoided 100 losses for the first time and even got out of the cellar past the Cubs.

Because of the improved showing, 1967 was the first season in which the hopes of the New Breed did not appear completely unrealistic. They did, however, prove groundless when the team slipped back to last place with 101 losses. The responsibility for the reversal was equally shared among the players, the manager, the front office, and the ownership—and with important ramifications for the team that was to excite the nation only a couple of years later.

On the field, the 1967 team's only effective offense came from the leg-sore Tommy Davis, who batted .302 with 16 homers and 73 RBIs after being obtained in a trade with the Dodgers for Hunt. On the bench, Westrum managed with a defensiveness that observers attributed to his fears that he would be replaced any day by the far more popular Berra. Up in the general manager's office, Devine, who had fulfilled expectations by replacing Weiss before the start of the season, behaved as though his only priority was to put a personal imprint on the team; at one time or another during the season, twenty-seven different pitchers and twenty-seven different position players wore the Mets uniform. On the other hand, some attributed Devine's frantic dealing to a

Casey Stengel was not the only Mets manager with a talent for idiosyncratic phrasemaking. Stengel's successor Wes Westrum, for example, once described a close game as being "a real cliff-dweller." On another occasion, he allowed as how "when they made Stengel, they threw away the molding."

One of the most worn of all baseball bromides was coined in the final weeks of the 1973 season when, aiming to reassure sportswriters that he thought the Mets still had a chance to win the division, manager Yogi Berra asserted that "it ain't over till it's over."

desire to confuse Grant, who had taken Weiss's departure as a signal for having more of a say of his own in the day-to-day business of the club.

The first to crack was Westrum who, with less than two weeks to go in the season, asked for a contract renewal, got turned down, and resigned on the spot. Grant immediately stepped into this breach with orders to Devine to get the one and only man he wanted as the next manager—the then-skipper of the Washington Senators, original Met Hodges. Devine had two reasons for not protesting Grant's usurpation of his prerogatives as general manager: Hodges was tailored for the job and he himself was about to quit the Mets and return to the Cardinals. It fell to Devine's assistant, Johnny Murphy, to work out a deal with the Senators under which Hodges was released from his managerial contract in Washington in exchange for minor league pitcher Bill Denehy and $150,000. At least partly in acknowledgement of his deft handling of the negotiations, Murphy was tapped as Devine's successor as general manager.

Even before the start of the 1968 season, the tandem of Hodges and Murphy signalled a new Mets era. For one thing, Hodges politely but firmly insisted that he would select his own coaches—an ordinary option for the mangers of most teams, but a privilege denied to both Stengel and Westrum. The new skipper also dealt quickly with the habitual speculation about Berra's status by announcing that he wanted the former Yankee pilot around as his NL expert (Hodges's coaches—Rube Walker, Eddie Yost, and Joe Pignatano—had been with him in Washington). For his part, Murphy was no Devine where Grant was concerned: The new general manager not only put up roadblocks against the chairman's attempted intrusions, but seemed to enjoy player development chief Herzog's even more outspoken criticism of Grant. As for his relations with Hodges, Murphy underwrote the new manager's philosophy of maintaining as much personnel stability for the season as possible; in 1968, twenty fewer players wore the Mets uniform than had under Devine the previous year.

In raw numbers, the 1968 accomplishments of the Mets were modest. At the end of the season, they found themselves out of the cellar and 12 games better off than in 1967, but they were still 16 games below a break-even mark. On the plus side, however, was the near-emergence of a nucleus of young players who were to make the team competitive for years to come. These included catcher Jerry Grote, shortstop Bud Harrelson, outfielder Cleon Jones, and pitchers Jerry Koosman (19 wins in 1968), Nolan

Ryan, and Jim McAndrew. Most of all, there was the righthander who was to become known as The Franchise, Tom Seaver.

Seaver came to the Mets through the sheerest luck—via a special lottery drawing held by the commissioner's office after his earlier signing by the Braves had been ruled as being in violation of the amateur drafting rules. As soon as the Mets were awarded first negotiation rights (the Indians and Phillies were the other contenders), the team signed the Fresno native to a $50,000 bonus contract and installed him in the rotation as the number two starter behind Jack Fisher in May of 1967. Seaver responded with the most wins (16) ever by a Mets pitcher and surprised nobody by being voted the NL Rookie of the Year. In 1968, he won another 16 games and struck out more than 200 batters for the first of nine consecutive seasons. It would not be until 1974 that his earned run average for a season would touch 3. Seaver became the franchise's first Hall of Famer when he was elected to Cooperstown in 1992.

With so much promise on the mound, the main problems confronting the Mets at the end of 1968 were the team's hitting and the health of Hodges. On September 24, the manager complained of chest pains during a road game in Atlanta and was soon diagnosed as having suffered a heart attack. Although the Mets were quick to issue reassurances about his condition, conjecture was rife in most New York dailies that the search for another manager was already underway and that, once again, it was likely to be Berra. The major exception to the rumor mongering was *Daily News* sports columnist Dick Young, a friend of the Hodges family from the days of the Brooklyn Dodgers and an intimate of more than one Mets executive. Some years later, Young's privileged access to Mets officials would create problems for both his paper and the team, but in the winter of 1968 it mainly led to exclusive photographs in the *News* showing a Hodges who was relaxed, off his three-pack-a-day habit, and ready to go to spring training.

On the eve of the 1969 season, the team's hitting problems appeared to have been resolved with a trade for Joe Torre, the Brooklyn-born catcher for the Braves who had been feuding with his own front office. But just when the deal appeared done, Atlanta suddenly upped its asking price, and talks broke off. Ironically, the eleventh-hour Braves demand—considered too costly by the Mets—was for fastball specialist Ryan and outfielder Amos Otis, who would eventually go in separate trades that were about the two worst in Mets history. Finally, in May, the Mets got their man when they obtained power-hitting first baseman Donn Clendenon from Montreal in exchange for four minor league prospects.

Even with Clendenon's bat and Hodges's clear determination to make the clownish Mets of Stengel a thing of the remote past, there was little reason to think that the club would mark the first year of divisional play by marching on to a World Series championship. Particularly debatable to many was Hodges's declared intention of maintaining a season-long platoon in right field and at all the infield positions except shortstop. As it turned out, almost all the platoon players had career or near-career years, the shortstop Harrelson emerged as one of the league's deftest fielders, catcher Grote shone as a defensive backstop at least the equal of Cincinnati's Johnny Bench, left fielder Jones batted .340, and center fielder Tommie Agee overcame a horrendous season in 1968 to lead the club offensively with 26 homers and 76 RBIs. But both on and off the mound, it was the pitchers—and primarily, Seaver—who proved to be the key.

As early as February, Seaver moved into a team leadership role when, during a player-management dispute that delayed the opening of spring training camps, he organized informal drills for Mets hurlers. While hardly as taxing as the regular camp practices would have been, Hodges and pitching coach Rube Walker would later point to the exercises as one of the main reasons why New York's pitchers got off to a fast start for the season. It was also Seaver who responded furiously when fellow players decided that reaching the .500 mark called for some kind of celebration; as Hodges's number one pupil, he made it clear that, whatever the odds, he wouldn't be satisfied until the Mets had won the division. On the mound, the righthander backed up his words with the first of his three Cy Young Award seasons, posting a 25–7 record and an ERA of 2.21.

The Mets' drive to the Eastern Division title remained highly improbable as late as the second week of August, when the team was still behind the first-place Cubs by 9½ games. By winning 38 of its next 49 games, however, the club ended up with its own eight-game lead over Chicago and built the legend of the Miracle Mets. Down the stretch, omen seekers were more than satisfied by one game against the Cubs in which a black cat strolled out of the stands at Shea Stadium and scampered over to vex Chicago manager Leo Durocher, and by another game in which Philadelphia ace Steve Carlton struck out a record 19 batters—but still lost to the Mets on two home runs by right fielder Ron Swoboda. Another turning point, according to many of the Mets themselves, was a midseason game in which Hodges called time to take a long stroll out to left field and order Jones to accompany him back to the dugout for being less than energetic in his defensive play.

In their first taste of postseason competition, the Mets resorted to hitting rather than pitching to sweep the Braves in the League Championship Series. In the World Series against heavily favored Baltimore, they fell back on pitching, the timely slugging of Clendenon and second baseman Al Weis, and the spectacular outfield defense of Agee and Swoboda to win four out of five against the Orioles. New York was the first expansion team to take a world championship, and would continue to stand alone in that category until the Kansas City Royals defeated the Cardinals sixteen years later.

The miracle ended even before the calendar year was over. During the Christmas holidays, general manager Murphy suffered a heart attack that proved fatal two weeks later. To replace him, Grant returned to throwing his weight around by ignoring the obvious candidacy of his tormentor Herzog and tapping special assignment scout Bob Scheffing. It was clear from the start that Scheffing was less than enthusiastic about the job and more than ready to lend an ear to Grant's various suggestions. Sensing greater interference from the front office, Hodges effectively cut it off by tightening his control over the clubhouse. In view of Hodges's enormous popularity with both players and fans, there was little that Grant or Scheffing could do. The executives were also galled by the manger's benign attitude toward a player walkout, led by Seaver and Tug McGraw, at a Florida banquet presided over by Governor Claude Kirk; using the forum of a Mets' victory celebration, Kirk went into a lengthy defense of the White House's pursuit of the Vietnam war. When the players excused themselves from the dais, Hodges limited himself to questioning the appropriateness of the governor's speech.

On the field, the Mets finished third in both 1970 and 1971. A big reason for the dropoff was Koosman, who suffered serious injuries in both seasons. Equally important were declines by most of the platoon players in 1969 and the failures of Joey Foy (in 1970) and Bob Aspromonte (in 1971) to resolve the team's perennial third base problem. It was because of these latter flops that, in preparation for the 1972 season, the club felt compelled to go after Jim Fregosi of the California Angels, no matter that the price was the fireballer Ryan, outfielder Leroy Stanton, and a couple of other minor league prospects.

Beginning with the dealing away of Ryan, 1972 was as vexatious a season as 1969 had been miraculous. On April 2nd, while golfing with some of his coaches, Hodges suffered a second and fatal heart attack. Finally, after all the years of rumors, Berra was given the managerial reins, but in circumstances that cast a pall over all of New York. Thanks mainly to the acquisition of outfielder Rusty Staub, the Mets gave early indications of being able to play through the tragedy, getting off to the fastest start in their history and entering June with a five-game lead over the rest of the Eastern Division. But then injuries to Staub, Harrelson, and Grote dropped the team back to still another third-place finish. The consolations for the year were another 21 wins by Seaver, the naming of southpaw Jon Matlack (15–10, 2.32 ERA) as Rookie of the Year, and the sentimental return to New York of Willie Mays, acquired from the Giants in a May deal.

Off the field, things were not much better. The trouble began when the *Daily News* rushed into print with the story of Hodges's attack before it was certain that the manager's family had learned of his death. Although the Mets mumbled about such questionable ethics, it did not prevent them from delivering "exclusive last photos" of Hodges, his wife, and children to the *News* a few days later. This in turn caused considerable grumbling among New York's other papers and prompted more stories criticizing the Mets front office and accenting the efforts of the Yankees to improve themselves. Back at the *News*, meanwhile, columnist Young, no longer deterred by whatever feelings he had for Hodges, began taking off the gloves where Seaver was concerned. Always irritated politically by the pitcher's union activism and by his visible stance against the war in Vietnam, Young began to suggest that Seaver (along with Koosman and Grote) did not respect Berra as a manager and would have preferred Herzog as the new pilot. Although the stories had a grain of truth to them, their main effect was to pit publicly the city's most popular player against one of major league baseball's most folkloristic figures.

Sour odors continued to circulate around the club the following season. Smarting under criticism from the Ryan trade, Grant had Scheffing unload Fregosi on the Rangers and then blamed sportswriter Jack Lang for having "forced" him to deal for the over-the-hill infielder. The 1972 disabled list looked almost unfilled by comparison when Harrelson (twice), Grote, Jones, Mays, and first baseman John Milner were all sidelined for weeks at a time. In what initially appeared to be the most serious injury of all, Matlack took a line drive squarely in the forehead and was diagnosed as having a fractured skull; less than two weeks later, however, he was back on the mound. On August 1st, with the team dead last in the Eastern Division, a New York daily (not the *News*) conducted a poll among its readers asking who should be fired first—Berra, Scheffing, or Grant. Scheffing attracted the most thumbs down, with Grant in second place.

Through all their early-season travails, the Mets did manage to keep their starting rotation in pretty good shape, so that Seaver, Koosman, Matlack, and southpaw George Stone were primed in August and September when the position players trooped back from the disabled list and McGraw overcame a disastrous first half in the bullpen to register 12 saves and 5 wins in his final 25 relief appearances. It was also McGraw who symbolized (if inadvertently in the beginning) the team's dizzying climb from the basement to the top of the standings over the final weeks of the season. After sitting through a locker room pep talk by Grant in late August, the southpaw punctuated the speech with a cry of "You gotta believe!" Although even Grant suspected that the shout had been sarcastic, McGraw talked himself out of his ticklish situation and then allowed the media to interpret his outburst as an expression of the team's determination not to quit on the season.

By the end of the year, with the Mets settled over the Cardinals by a game-and-a-half, nobody seemed to remember the sardonic origins of the slogan. What came more readily to mind after another unexpected division win was a September 20th game at Shea Stadium with Pittsburgh, when Dave Augustine hit what appeared to be a decisive ninth inning-home run against the Mets, only to have the ball carom directly off the top of the fence into Jones's glove. The left fielder whirled and fired to third baseman Wayne Garrett, who relayed to Grote at home to cut off Pittsburgh's Richie Zisk at the plate. When the Mets finally won the game in the thirteenth inning, the Augustine drive became 1973's equivalent of the black cat omen in 1969.

The Mets' division win was greatly abetted by the fact that the Eastern clubs were all pretty mediocre (only New York and St. Louis even reached the .500 mark). But in taking three games out of five from the powerhouse Reds in the LCS, the team astonished experts almost as much as the 1969 Mets had caused dismay by running over Baltimore in the World Series. Almost equally stunning, a team on which Staub's .279 average and 76 RBIs represented hitting highs battled the dynastic Oakland Athletics down to the seventh game of the Series before finally succumbing. The most glaring disappointment in the postseason contests was Mays, who had announced that he would retire at the end of the season and whose markedly reduced abilities cost the club a key game against Oakland.

The 1973 comeback proved to be the Mets' last moment of glory for more than a decade. In the mid-1970s, the team alternated between errors of standing pat and of installing a revolving door outside the clubhouse. While the erratic decision-making was producing middle-of-the-pack finishes on the field, it was also casting a sorry light on the state of the team's front office and ownership. Following the 1974 season, Scheffing retired and was succeeded as general manager by Joe McDonald, till then the farm director. McDonald was viewed as even more obeisant to Grant than his predecessor had been, and it was considered only a matter of time before the chairman carried out his simmering intention of axing Berra. Before he got around to that, however, Grant conducted an embarrassing press conference in May of 1975 when he dragged outfielder Jones before the media to apologize for having been seized by police in a Florida trailer on charges of having sexual relations with a woman in public. The "indecent exposure" charges were eventually dropped for lack of evidence, but that didn't prevent Grant from staging his press show and levying a $2,000 fine against Jones for "betraying the image of the New York Mets."

As it turned out, it was also Jones who provided Grant with a reason for getting rid of Berra. On July 18th, the manager got into a shouting match with the outfielder in the dugout during a game with Atlanta; Jones then refused to play defense for the last few innings of the contest. Insisting that the player be suspended for insubordination, Berra was left twisting in the wind for four days while Grant and McDonald kept silent. Finally, after some half-hearted attempts at mediating the crisis, the executives announced that they were acceding to Berra's wishes and releasing Jones. Berra had about a week to savor his triumph—and to read daily stories about how he had lost control of the team, didn't even know basic baseball rules, and was costing the club game after game because of his deficiencies as a strategist; then he too was bounced and replaced by coach Roy McMillan. When McMillan proved to be less than a scintillating leader over the last two months of the campaign, the club announced that Joe Frazier, the manager of the Mets' top farm team at Tidewater, would be taking over in 1976.

For a few critical years, Grant's influence was also felt more sharply in the ownership suite. Following the death of Payson in 1975, control of the franchise was passed to her widower Charles, who in turn delegated his authority to his daughter Lorinda de Roulet and her daughters Whitney and Bebe. In her turn, de Roulet leaned heavily on Grant for major decisions. One of the chairman's first counsels—one that would help bury the team in last place for years—was for the Mets not to panic before the prospect of re-entry draft free agency and to keep a tight grip on the purse strings. De Roulet, not nearly as well off as her late mother had been, had little trouble heeding the advice and eventually went further in introducing a series of austerity measures affecting every aspect of the franchise.

The first victim of the ownership's attitude toward free agency was Staub, who was peddled off to Detroit when he insisted on a long-term contract that would recompense him for staying out of the re-entry draft. The second victim was almost Seaver; rather than meet the pitcher's demands for a long-term pact, Grant authorized McDonald to pursue a trade with the Dodgers in which The Franchise would be sent to California in exchange for Don Sutton. The deal was scotched only after press reports of the Mets' intentions caused an uproar among fans in New York, and Seaver was given the biggest contract in the team's history. The embarrassment over the proposed Seaver swap had very little impact on the team's anti-free agency stance, however; in fact, for the rest of the decade, while the crosstown Yankees were signing stars like Catfish Hunter and Reggie Jackson, the only free agents to put their names to a Mets contract were journeyman pitcher Tom Hausman and handyman infielder-outfielder Elliott Maddox.

The fallout from the club policy on free agents occurred during spring training in 1977, when Seaver and several other veterans lamented that the front office was doing nothing to find necessary offensive support for the team's still lustrous pitching. In particular, there was bitterness that the Mets, still one of the richest franchises in the major leagues, had not pursued Gary Matthews, a slugging outfielder picked up by the Braves. Grant's retort was that the club did not need Matthews and that the controversy was being stirred up by Seaver (supposedly resentful that he had settled for less than Matthews the previous year) and Dave Kingman (a crowd-pleasing home run hitter in the final year of his contract). With Young of the News once again stating the front office case day in and day out, Seaver was portrayed as an "ingrate" and Kingman was a pawn in the pitcher's campaign to pressure the team into open-

ing its coffers. With the bitterness rising on both sides, de Roulet finally stepped in and personally ordered a three-year extension on Seaver's contract.

The free agency dispute was put on the back burner for a few days when, on May 31st, the club announced that Frazier was being fired in favor of Torre. Through his year-plus tenure, Frazier had been the squarest of pegs in the roundest of holes—compounding his decidedly unNew York-like personality with on-field incidents that suggested that he did not think as highly of black players and umpires as he did of their white counterparts.

On June 15th, Young wrote another column in the News in which he charged that the real culprit in all the contract controversy was Seaver's wife Nancy, who was jealous that Ryan had received a bigger contract from the Angels than her husband had from the Mets. Entertaining few doubts that Young's sally had been inspired by the Mets front office (aside from his personal ties with team executives, the sportswriter also had a son-in-law employed by the club), Seaver instantly demanded a trade. Having already been ordered to do the groundwork for such a deal, McDonald quickly tied up the final details with Cincinnati for a package that included pitcher Pat Zachry, infielder Doug Flynn, and minor league outfielders Steve Henderson and Dan Norman. (McDonald was later to claim that his own teenage son insisted on the inclusion of Norman and that he wouldn't have recommended the swap without the prospect who ended up batting .227 in 338 plate appearances for New York and Montreal.) Before the clock struck twelve on the midnight trading deadline, McDonald and Grant also shipped Kingman to San Diego.

New York reaction to what became known as The Midnight Massacre ran the gamut from rage to fury. While Seaver broke down in tears on television, Grant and Young were blamed equally for the hasty deals by both fans and rival dailies of the News. Some fans picketed Shea Stadium, others canceled season tickets, and cranks began bombarding Grant with threats by phone and mail. (Not taking any chances, he hired a bodyguard for the rest of the season.) Attendance, which had risen as high as 2.6 million in 1970 and which had still reached 1.4 million in the dreariness of 1976, dropped precariously to the 1-million mark in 1977 and 1978, then plunged to 788,000 in 1979.

Presiding over the Era of Bad Feeling, Torre could do little to prevent cellar finishes in 1977, 1978, and 1979, with bare improvement to fifth in 1980 and for the overall standings of the split season of 1981.

The few bright spots on the field came from pitcher Craig Swan (when healthy) and outfielders Henderson and Lee Mazzilli. Lacking any other drawing card, the team's publicity office put particular emphasis on the darkly handsome Mazzilli, and never let anyone forget that he drove in the tying and winning runs in the 1979 All Star Game. More typical of the players in the period were Joel Youngblood, who declined to play in the infield because he didn't want to be knocked down by baserunners, and Richie Hebner, who spent most of his single season with the club telling everybody how he hated New York, Shea Stadium, and Mets fans.

At the end of the 1978 season, de Roulet surprised everyone by announcing that she was going to replace Grant as chairman. While Grant fumed that he had never been appreciated by the players, fans, or media, it gradually emerged that his exit was at the behest of Charles Payson, who might not have known much about baseball but who knew that he had never liked Grant's influence over his late wife and other members of the family. In what was meant as a dramatic declaration of the team's resolve to turn things around, de Roulet also announced that the Mets would pursue free agent Pete Rose. Rose said no thanks, he didn't play for losers, and it would be another thirteen years before the club went after—and landed—a front-line free agent (Vince Coleman in 1991).

De Roulet's hands-on management was brief, and cheap. With rumors dogging the club throughout 1979 that a sale was imminent, she increased her cost-cutting pressures, opposing Torre's recommendations to sign veterans when minimum-salary rookies would do and, at one widely reported meeting, even suggesting that used baseballs be washed after games so they could be employed again. While fans continued to stay at home, she concentrated an inordinate amount of energy on a mule mascot dubbed Mettle that was kept in a stall behind home plate and that was hitched to a buggy so that daughter Bebe could drive it around the field before every home game. Among the other casualties of de Roulet's economics was popular announcer Lindsay Nelson, who broke up the longest-running baseball broadcast team (with Ralph Kiner and Bob Murphy) in 1979 by indicating that he couldn't stand the atmosphere around the club any longer. More idiosyncratically, she turned thumbs down to a deal that Torre and McDonald had worked out with the California Angels that would have sent Swan and backup catcher Ron Hodges to the American League in exchange for four-star prospects Dickie Thon and Willie Mays

Aikens. Her reason for saying no was that Swan was a Connecticut neighbor.

The other shoe finally fell on January 24, 1980, when it was announced that the team had been sold for $21.3 million to a group headed by publisher Nelson Doubleday and realtor Fred Wilpon. One month later, the new owners signed former Orioles general manager Frank Cashen to a five-year contract to head up baseball operations. Although Cashen in turn brought in knowledgeable baseball aides like Lou Gorman, Joe McIlvaine, and Al Harazin, he also kept McDonald around in a reduced administrative capacity and declined to buy out a new contract that Torre had signed with de Roulet only one month before the team's sale.

Cashen warned New York fans from the start that it would require five years to make the Mets competitive again. For the first two of those years, he engineered some good deals (obtaining Claudell Washington for a pitcher who never made it to the majors) and some bad ones (swapping Jeff Reardon to Montreal for Ellis Valentine), while focusing most of his energies on scouting and signing high school prospects. Although Torre won kudos for keeping the team out of the cellar in both 1980 and 1981 with a pitching staff that boasted only a single double-figures winner in either year (Mark Bomback with 10 victories in 1980), it was never forgotten on either side that the manager had been foisted on the new management with the eleventh-hour contract signed with the de Roulets. What turned out to be the breaking point between the dugout and front office was Torre's insistence on carrying righthander Tim Leary on the major league roster for the 1981 season. Considered a "second Seaver" by everyone in the organization, Leary went to the mound in the second game of the season on a foul and bitter day in Chicago, hurt his arm, and never fulfilled his promise. Only the strike and the split season delayed the inevitable announcement, made on the final day of the year, that Torre would not be back for 1982. Named as the new manager was George Bamberger, the pitching coach of the champion Orioles when Cashen had been Baltimore's general manager.

The 1982–83 teams, both of which finished in the cellar, were a conglomerate of young players who would play significant roles in the team's revival and

In 1982, Dave Kingman set the record for the lowest batting average (.204) by a league leader in home runs (37).

familiar faces who tried to keep the fans interested. Among the first group were speedster Mookie Wilson, scrappy infielder Wally Backman, line-drive hitter Hubie Brooks, southpaw relief specialist Jesse Orosco, and, most of all, slugger Darryl Strawberry, who was to be named Rookie of the Year in 1983 for his 26 home runs and 76 RBIs. The older group included returning veterans Staub and Kingman, as well as Big Red Machine cog George Foster, obtained in a trade with Cincinnati and signed to one of the biggest contracts ever given to a prospective free agent. More dramatically, Cashen engineered another deal with the Reds that brought Seaver back to New York for 1983 and that precipitated a New York Love-In when the righthander went to the mound to oppose the Phillies on opening day (he pitched seven shutout innings, but didn't get the win).

The most important transaction of all, however, took place on June 15, 1983, when the Mets dealt pitchers Neil Allen and Rick Ownbey to the Cardinals in exchange for first baseman Keith Hernandez. Why Hernandez, a former batting champion and MVP, should have been available remained a mystery for some time, with even St. Louis officials passing on the ludicrous story that manager Herzog didn't like the way he spent time on crossword puzzles in the clubhouse. As it turned out, Hernandez would eventually be named in a major trial involving cocaine use among big league players. But with the acquisition of the first baseman and his subsequent acceptance (after great wooing by Cashen and teammate Staub) of a multiyear contract, the team had in place its offensive, defensive, and spiritual keystone for the rest of the decade.

Shortly into the 1983 season, Bamberger, who had suffered in the past from heart problems, begged out of the manager's job and was succeeded by batting coach Frank Howard. It was clear from the start that Howard was only a stopgap solution, and on October 13th, Cashen announced that Davey Johnson would be taking over for the following year. Never one to hide his light under a bushel, Johnson immediately ruffled a few front office feathers when he indicated that he would like to bring along some of the pitchers who had helped him win the Triple-A World Series for the Tidewater farm club for the Mets; these included Dwight Gooden, Ron Darling, and Walt Terrell. Cashen, only too mindful of the Leary incident with Torre, said that such questions would have to be settled in spring training and noted that the team was stocked with a lot of veteran hurlers, including Seaver, Mike Torrez, Swan, and Dick Tidrow. It was in light of this mini-controversy that some sportswriters later interpreted an avowed "mistake" by the Mets in leaving Seaver's name off the protected forty-man roster and exposing him to a draft by the Chicago White Sox. While the pitcher once again appeared in public to question the ways and motives of the Mets front office, Cashen criticized the White Sox for being insensitive to the feelings of New York fans and Johnson didn't say much of anything. Within a few weeks of the 1984 season, however, Gooden, Darling, and Terrell had deposed Torrez, Swan, and Tidrow on the staff.

The 1984 season fulfilled Cashen's promise to turn the Mets into a contender within five years. With Hernandez, Strawberry, and Foster keying the offense, the club battled the Cubs down to the final weeks of September before settling into second place. The home attendance of 1.8 million was the highest since 1973—many of the fans attracted in particular by the dazzling feats of righthander Gooden. Dubbed Doctor K for his strikeout prowess, Gooden compiled a mark of 17–9 with an ERA of 2.60, established a major league rookie record for whiffs (276), and easily won Rookie of the Year honors. The following

Darryl Strawberry. *Marc Levine/NY Mets*

year, he was even better, becoming the youngest pitcher in NL history to win the Cy Young Award for his record of 24–4, 2.53 ERA, and 268 strikeouts. So dominating was the Florida native during the season that Las Vegas bookmakers refused to accept bets on the Mets when he was scheduled to pitch.

Despite Gooden's astonishing performance and the preseason acquisition of All Star catcher Gary Carter, the Mets fell short once again in 1985, this time to the Cardinals. The three-game margin between the teams at the end of the season was largely due to injuries to Strawberry and Wilson. Certain that the fallen outfielders were the one and only reason that the team hadn't qualified for postseason play, Johnson got his 1986 spring training camp off to a bang by telling newsmen that "we don't want to just win, we want to dominate." The remark went a long way toward portraying the club as arrogant— all the more so when it then proceeded to make a travesty of the division race by winning 108 games and finishing 21½ lengths ahead of second-place Philadelphia. Among the pitchers, every member of the starting rotation (Gooden, Darling, Bob Ojeda, Sid Fernandez, Rick Aguilera) won in double figures, Orosco and Roger McDowell combined for 43 saves, and both Gooden and Fernandez fanned 200 batters. The offense came from practically everyone in the lineup, with Ray Knight, Len Dykstra, and Kevin Mitchell providing especially valuable support for the heart of the order. The only sour note came from Foster, who complained that he had lost playing time to Mitchell and Wilson because he was black. Although he quickly retracted the charge (particularly when it was noted that Mitchell and Wilson were also black), the outfielder was given the gate by Cashen and an infuriated Johnson; he was replaced on the roster by Mazzilli, the one-time gate attraction who returned as a valuable pinch-hitter.

Both the LCS against Houston and the World Series against Boston revolved around incredible sixth-game comebacks by the Mets that rank with the most exciting in baseball history. In the playoffs, the club went into the ninth inning of the sixth game trailing 3–0 and facing the dim prospect of having to take on Astros' ace Mike Scott in a seventh and decisive contest the following day. The Mets rallied to tie, went ahead in the 14th inning, were tied by a Billy Hatcher home run, went ahead again by three runs in the top of the 16th inning, and barely escaped in the bottom half of the frame when Houston scored twice and had the tying and winning runs on base. Against the Red Sox, the situation appeared even more hopeless when, one out away from a Boston

championship in the bottom of the 10th inning and two runs down, Carter, pinch-hitter Mitchell, and Knight singled, Red Sox reliever Bob Stanley uncorked a wild pitch to tie the game, and first baseman Bill Buckner let Wilson's grounder go through his legs for the error that gave New York the win. The Mets capped their championship in the seventh game when, again trailing by three runs as late as the sixth inning, they rallied to tie and then got decisive homers from Knight and Strawberry. The irony behind both triumphs was that, in rolling up 108 regular season wins, the team had seldom been called upon to stage late-inning dramatics—usually jumping off to an early lead and then leaving the game in the hands of the exceptional starting staff and bullpen.

Most betting was that the 1986 World Series victory over Boston would serve as the cornerstone of a Mets dynasty, especially when outfielder Kevin McReynolds and pitcher David Cone were added in postseason trades. But on the eve of the 1987 season, Gooden was admitted to a clinic for drug abusers, causing shockwaves in New York second only to those provoked by the Midnight Massacre in 1977. Although the righthander returned in June and ended up leading the staff with 15 victories, his absence for the first couple of months forced pressures on Darling and Fernandez that they could not handle. Together with injuries to Ojeda, Cone, Aguilera, and McDowell, the result was chaos on a staff that, only one year before, had been thought of as among the best in decades. One of the few bright spots was the emergence of third baseman Howard Johnson (36 homers, 99 RBIs, 32 steals) as a power complement to Strawberry.

With everyone but Aguilera healthy again in 1988, the team rebounded to win the Eastern Division. Cone turned in a dominating mark of 20–3, with Gooden and Darling winning 18 and 17, respectively. In place of the traded Orosco, Randy Myers earned 26 saves. The offense featured three players (Strawberry, Johnson, McReynolds) with 24 homers or more. In the Year of Hershiser, however, the club lost the LCS to Los Angeles four games to three.

For the final weeks of the 1988 season, the Mets offense was galvanized by Gregg Jefferies, a switch-hitter who had been even more switched from one infield position to another during his minor league career. While admitting that he lacked consistent defensive skills, the Mets ballyhooed Jefferies's arrival in much the same terms that they had Strawberry's earlier in the 1980s, and did nothing to deter media predictions that he would be 1989 Rookie of the Year.

When the infielder got off to a miserable start, and compounded his woes by slamming helmets and bats in frustration, the snickers began coming out of the Mets clubhouse. Within a couple of months, Johnson had a full-scale morale problem on his hands—to go along with others that had bubbled up in the wake of a scuffle between Strawberry and Hernandez and amid a growing feeling that the manager himself had lost enthusiasm for his job.

Although Jefferies came back for a strong second half, the clubhouse atmosphere remained grim throughout the season. Co-captains Hernandez and Carter, both suffering from career-threatening injuries, took their leadership off the field in favor of snipings from the bench. Strawberry, Myers, and McDowell (among others) continued their snickering at Jefferies. Strawberry and McReynolds, already under criticism for lackadaisical play on the field, did not hesitate to leave the bench to go home while a game was still underway. A major deal for Juan Samuel imploded when the Phillies import didn't hit or field, told everybody he hated New York, and constantly reminded fans that he had cost the popular Dykstra and McDowell. Another major deal for Minnesota lefty and former Cy Young Award winner Frank Viola produced little in the way of clutch pitching. The whole year was encapsulated in the final play of the Mets' last game when Jefferies and McDowell got into a Shea Stadium punchup, both benches emptied, and a Philadelphia player suggested the rookie had to take on "25 Phillies and 24 Mets."

Through all the turmoil, Cashen kept his own counsel, to such a degree that Johnson declared that he expected to be fired. He was wrong—and right. At the end of the season, the team announced a new contract for the manager, but not for his closest aide, coach Sam Perlozzo. Also shown the door were Hernandez and Carter (neither of them offered free agent contracts), Samuel (traded to the Dodgers), and Myers (traded to the Reds). Acknowledging that the release of Perlozzo had not been his idea, Johnson entered the 1990 season with the image of somebody who had lost the "battle of the egos" with Cashen. The *coup de grace* was administered at the end of May when, with the Mets stumbling and continued grumbling coming from the clubhouse, the manager who had never finished below second was replaced by former shortstop Harrelson.

It did not take long for Harrelson's by-the-book managing to precipitate charges that he was too timid for the job and had only gotten it in the first place because he was a yes-man for Cashen. The once-popular shortstop only made matters worse in 1991 when he shrank from media criticism and made it clear that he would do anything to avoid hearing boos (including sending out a coach to change pitchers). In the wake of some televised incidents, Harrelson was also hard put to persuade people that he had won the respect of his players.

But the Mets of the early 1990s lacked more than Johnson as manager. On the final week of the 1990 season, assistant general manager McIlvaine, long thought to be Cashen's eventual successor, lost patience with his boss's conflicting retirement signals and took over the Padres' front office. Even more dramatically, Strawberry announced a couple of weeks later that the Mets had not met his free agent demands and that he had decided to sign with the Dodgers. Whether or not he had ever seriously considered resigning with New York, Strawberry asserted that one of the main reasons for his decision was a midseason statement by Cashen that he wasn't worth the money he was asking. Cashen reassured Mets fans that the team would survive without Strawberry, spent a good part of the offseason pursuing free agent batting champion Willie McGee, and ended up with NL stolen bases king Coleman as the first bonafide free agent star in the history of the franchise.

With Strawberry in Los Angeles and only Johnson a reliable power source, the Mets' offense came close to disappearing. Making matters worse, the continual moving of Johnson and Jefferies around the infield created enough defensive uncertainties to undermine the efforts of the team's vaunted pitching staff; during the 1991 season, there were games in which as many as six of the eight starters were out of position. Other blows on the year included a rotator cuff injury to Gooden and a knee ailment suffered by Fernandez that was aggravated by the southpaw's overweight condition. A few days before the end of the campaign, Harrelson was let go, while Harazin was named to succeed Cashen as head of baseball operations. The final word on the dreary fifth-place season was written before the concluding game against Philadelphia, when the team was informed that Cone was under investigation for alleged rape. The righthander took his scheduled turn against the Phillies anyway, struck out 19 batters to tie the NL record, and then found out that there would be no charges pressed against him because of the ambiguous statement of the woman involved.

Harazin's first announcement in his new role was the selection of Jeff Torborg as the new manager. Through the fall months of 1991, he then disclosed one startling agreement after another: the signing of sluggers Bobby Bonilla and Eddie Murray as free agents for a combined $34 million; a blockbuster trade with Kansas City that brought Cy Young winner Bret Saberhagen and infielder Bill Pecota in exchange for McReynolds, Jefferies, and second baseman Keith Miller; and the signing of local favorite Willie Randolph as another free agent. All the goodwill recouped by the franchise through the deals proved necessary when the 1992 spring training camp was beset by lurid charges that Gooden, Coleman, and outfielder Daryl Boston had raped a woman the previous year, that Cone had exposed himself to other women who had somehow found their way into a bullpen bathroom, and that gossip-hungry tabloid writers had taken to wiretapping the phones of some of the players. Although no formal charges were brought in the rape case, the affair offered some flickering lights on the sexual escapades of ballplayers and team groupies, the vulnerability of athletes to lawsuits and criminal prosecution, and the arrogance of players in their relations with women.

If spring training was a nightmare, the regular season wasn't much better. With the exception of Murray, the offense had already broken down before midseason injuries put just about every one of the team's regulars on the disabled list for extended periods. Bonilla made his arduous season worse by getting into a public squabble with an official scorer about an error charged to him, then by lying about the incident. On another occasion, the switch-hitting

In 1992, Eddie Murray eclipsed Mickey Mantle's mark of 1510 for the most career RBIs by a switch-hitter. By going 10–15 with 27 RBIs, the first baseman also added to his astonishing numbers of batting with the bases loaded. Entering the 1993 season, Murray had a lifetime average of .429 (81–189), with 17 homers and 247 RBIs, whenever he found three teammates on base.

outfielder wore earplugs so as not to have to hear the booing from the grandstands at Shea Stadium. Even more of a disaster was Coleman, who for the second straight year spent more time on the disabled list than in the field and who, even when he did play, shunned the base stealing he had been signed to provide. Among the pitchers, Saberhagen missed most of the year with a finger injury and relief ace John Franco was shelved for two months with elbow problems. Still another problem was Torborg's relentlessly cautious managing style.

With the team in a shambles by early August after so much offseason spending, it became clear that the ownership was going to begin tightening its belt. The first victim was potential free agent Cone, who was dealt to Toronto for two prospects. On the other hand, the club was able to profit from a similar austerity campaign by the Padres to pick up all-star shortstop Tony Fernandez at little sacrifice shortly after the end of the season.

NEW YORK METS

Annual Standings and Managers

Year	Position	W	L	Pct.	GB	Managers
1962	Tenth	40	120	.250	60½	Casey Stengel
1963	Tenth	51	111	.315	48	Casey Stengel
1964	Tenth	53	109	.327	40	Casey Stengel
1965	Tenth	50	112	.309	47	Casey Stengel, Wes Westrum
1966	Ninth	66	95	.410	28½	Wes Westrum
1967	Tenth	61	101	.377	40½	Wes Westrum, Salty Parker
1968	Ninth	73	89	.451	24	Gil Hodges
1969	First	100	62	.617	+8	Gil Hodges
1970	Third	83	79	.512	6	Gil Hodges
1971	Third*	83	79	.512	14	Gil Hodges
1972	Third	83	73	.532	13½	Yogi Berra
1973	First	82	79	.509	+1½	Yogi Berra
1974	Fifth	71	91	.438	17	Yogi Berra
1975	Third*	82	80	.506	10½	Yogi Berra, Roy McMillan
1976	Third	86	76	.531	15	Joe Frazier
1977	Sixth	64	98	.395	37	Joe Frazier, Joe Torre
1978	Sixth	66	96	.407	24	Joe Torre

1979	Sixth	63	99	.389	35	Joe Torre
1980	Fifth	67	95	.414	24	Joe Torre
1981	Fifth	17	34	.333	15	Joe Torre
	Fourth	24	28	.462	5½	Joe Torre
1982	Sixth	65	97	.401	27	George Bamberger
1983	Sixth	68	94	.420	22	George Bamberger, Frank Howard
1984	Second	90	72	.556	6½	Davey Johnson
1985	Second	98	64	.605	3	Davey Johnson
1986	First	108	54	.667	+21½	Davey Johnson
1987	Second	92	70	.568	3	Davey Johnson
1988	First	100	60	.625	+15	Davey Johnson
1989	Second	87	75	.537	6	Davey Johnson
1990	Second	91	71	.562	4	Davey Johnson, Bud Harrelson
1991	Fifth	77	84	.478	20½	Bud Harrelson
1992	Fifth	72	90	.444	24	Jeff Torborg

*Tie

Postseason Play

LCS	3–0 versus Atlanta	1969	WS	4–1 versus Baltimore	1969
	3–2 versus Cincinnati	1973		3–4 versus Oakland	1973
	4–2 versus Houston	1986		4–3 versus Boston	1986
	3–4 versus Los Angeles	1988			

Oakland Athletics

American League, 1968–Present	**BALLPARK:** OAKLAND-ALAMEDA COUNTY COLISEUM
	OTHER NAMES: A'S
RECORD: 2094–1893 (.525)	

In shifting from Kansas City to Oakland after the 1967 season, the Athletics went from being the major league team with the longest history of failure to the big league franchise with the most immediate record of success. It would not be the last 180-degree turn by an organization that has always been assailed by doubts that the Bay Area could support two clubs and that, on occasion, has acted ready to cede the territory back to the San Francisco Giants.

The Oakland version of the Athletics was a Caesarian delivery forced on the American League by owner Charlie Finley after several years of skirmishes over transferring the club out of Missouri. Although most of the other owners couldn't stand Finley, either for his endless rush of innovative ideas or his crass personality, they were too wary of his litigious nature to go back on a string of promises they had made about relieving his financial situation

Sporting the team's trademark mustaches, Mike Epstein, Dave Duncan, Joe Rudi, and Sal Bando celebrate Oakland's 1972 World Series victory. *Ron Riesterer/Oakland Tribune*

in Kansas City. The league itself had also been looking for another California outlet since the creation of the Angels to make travel schedules more economical. Thus, once agreement was reached with Missouri politicians to create a new expansion franchise for Kansas City, Finley was allowed to go west.

He didn't go alone. Over their last two years in the Midwest, the A's had introduced more young talent to the league than any other team; the first Oakland roster featured the likes of Catfish Hunter, Rollie Fingers, Blue Moon Odom, Sal Bando, Reggie Jackson, Bert Campaneris, Dick Green, Joe Rudi, and Rick Monday. With these still somewhat unblended makings, and with veteran manager Bob Kennedy calling the shots, the team debuted on April 10 with a 3–1 loss to the Orioles in Baltimore. It turned out to be a somewhat misleading opening because the club ended up two games over .500 for the season—the first time any Athletics franchise had achieved that since the Philadelphia version sixteen years before. Moreover, it marked the first of nine straight seasons with records of .500 or better—the A.L. record for a franchise setting up quarters in a city.

The inaugural year was filled with harbingers of the accomplishments and problems that would mark the AL for the next decade. On the plus side, the righthander (and future Hall of Famer) Hunter took to the mound on May 8th against the Twins and produced the league's first perfect game since Charlie Robertson of the White Sox had stifled the Tigers in 1922. The other side of the coin was that the franchise established its erratic attendance pattern at once by attracting more than 50,000 to its home opener against Baltimore on April 17th and by then drawing a mere 5,000 the next day. Despite a team that had some flair on the mound, at the plate, and on the bases, attendance for the year was only 837,466, and was helped considerably even to that modest level by a late September crowd of some 44,000 eager to see the Tigers' Denny McLain win his thirtieth game. The club would not reach the one million-mark until 1973.

During his first few years in the Coliseum, Finley worked tirelessly at promotions aimed at drawing more fans. As he had done in Kansas City, he had players milking cows or chasing greased pigs before games. Charlie O, the mascot mule that had made the traditional white elephant of Connie Mack's Athletics superfluous (not to say competitive) in Kansas City, continued generating almost as many front office press releases as the players. Bats, caps, helmets, and even hot pants were exchanged for tickets at the turnstiles. To go along with their gaudy gold and green uniforms, Finley promised a bonus to the players if they would grow mustaches; so many of them did, in every conceivable variation, that facial hair and shoulder-length locks became the trademark of the club, much to the consternation of other owners and their belief in clean-shaven players.

Finley also brought some of his other habits from Missouri. The first was his impatience with managers who weren't available to confer with him on the phone when he called from his Chicago office or home, no matter that they might have been in the dugout in the middle of a game. After one season, Kennedy was out in favor of Hank Bauer, who had managed briefly and uncomfortably for Finley in Kansas City. Despite guiding the team to second place in the first year of divisional play in 1969, Bauer was again dropped two weeks short of the end of the season with the club 11 games above .500; in his place came John McNamara. The drive to second place was led on the field by future Hall of Famer (1993) Jackson, who blossomed into one of the league's power stars with 47 homers and 118 RBIs. Other big efforts came from Bando (31 homers and 113 RBIs) and Odom (15–6, 2.92 ERA), while Fingers (6 wins and 12 saves) gave an inkling of the form that made him one of the few relief pitchers to be elected to the Hall of Fame (in 1992). But as good a season as Jackson had on the field, his postseason was equally disastrous when he came up against a Finley determined to nickel-and-dime him on a new contract. The wrangling between the owner and the outfielder's representatives—the first of many such tussles with Oakland players—continued through the winter, the following spring training, and right into the 1970 campaign. At one point, Finley was so infuriated by the slugger's bargaining stance that he ordered McNamara to bench him. The result of all the tension was a contract that satisfied neither side, a bad year by Jackson, and another second-place finish. For all his pains, McNamara was replaced by Dick Williams.

With the heavy-handed Williams at the helm, the emotional level of the A's for the first part of the 1970s was at a fever pitch: When the players weren't busy hating Finley, they were hating the pilot. The difference was that Williams couldn't have cared less; moreover, he turned his instinctive distance from players into an asset by ignoring their relentless goadings of one another over inferior performances. When the clubhouse critiques exploded into fisticuffs, as they did quite often, Williams was usually content to let the players resolve matters by themselves. Williams's additional strength was that he knew how to run a pitching staff in a way that Bauer and McNamara did not.

The result in 1971 was a division title with a very big accent on pitching. While Jackson's 32 homers and 80 RBIs led the offense (his .277 was also the highest batting average among the regulars), Vida Blue took both MVP and Cy Young honors for going 24–8 with a league-leading 1.82 ERA. The club was so impressive with its 101 victories and runaway 16-game margin over second-place Kansas City that even Finley professed not to be bothered by Baltimore's three-game sweep in the League Championship Series.

As after Jackson's stellar year in 1969, the southpaw Blue's big numbers in 1971 made for a tumultuous offseason. Even more than Jackson, Blue had a media appeal—comprising one part performance (he also had a no-hitter in his rookie year of 1970) and one part esoteric name. This was translated into a *Time* cover and several television commercials, with these in turn bringing out even more fans to AL ballparks when he was scheduled to pitch. Ever ready to gild a lily, Finley kept after Blue to change his first name to True, but the pitcher refused. What he didn't reject, on the other hand, was a suggestion from President Richard Nixon during a visit to the White House after the 1971 season that he was the most underpaid player in the major leagues. Blue promptly got himself an agent and, with every detail being reported by the press, waged another contract battle with Finley, eventually entering spring training as an official holdout. An agreement was finally reached, but the lefthander went through a nightmare year, managing a record of only 6–10 and drawing a lot of heat from local fans.

Even without Blue, Oakland played its second straight season of .600 ball, leaving western division runner-up Chicago behind by five-and-a-half games. The key to the race turned out to be an offseason trade that brought the A's southpaw starter Ken Holtzman; although Holtzman had originally been slotted as the team's second lefty behind Blue, he ended up as Hunter's major backup with 19 wins and a 2.51 ERA. As for Hunter himself, he regained his status as the staff ace by going 21–7 with a 2.04 ERA. Not one of the staff's eight most used hurlers yielded an average of three runs a game. The offensive leaders were Jackson and first baseman Mike Epstein, who combined for 51 homers.

In the LCS against Detroit, Oakland prevailed for its first pennant in a tough five-game showdown that featured three one-run games and two overtime affairs. The series was lit up by a second-game brawl

Although Charlie Finley was most directly responsible for the introduction of the designated hitter in the American League in 1973, the Oakland owner was not the first official to propose such an offensive innovation. As far back as the 1920s, National League President John Heydler also advocated a DH in the lineup, but received support for the idea only from the Dodgers and Giants.

sparked when Tigers' reliever Lerrin LeGrow beaned Campaneris and the shortstop responded by firing his bat at the mound and then following up with a charge at the pitcher; Campaneris was suspended for the rest of the LCS and for several games at the beginning of the 1973 season. Williams accounted for the crucial decision of the Series when he started Odom in the final game and then with a 2–1 lead, yanked the righthander and brought in lefty Blue to shut down the Tigers over the last four innings. The winning run in the fifth game came home on catcher Gene Tenace's single—his only hit in seventeen at bats. But then, in the World Series against Cincinnati's Big Red Machine, Tenace clouted homers in his first two at bats of the first game, then went on to hit two more and drive in nine runs in subsequent games to lead the team to a world championship.

The 1972 season marked the first of three straight world championships for Oakland, but Finley wasn't happy. Noting that the season attendance had been little more than 921,000 and that advance sales indicated little improvement for 1973 (the final figure turned out to be 1,000,673), he began making noises about having overestimated the Bay Area's enthusiasm for baseball and started looking into such other markets as Seattle and Toronto. If this was familiar music for the AL owners who had heard it for years when the A's had been in Kansas City, it was new to Oakland, and created more sympathy in the press and in letters-to-editor columns for the players who were constantly blasting their employer.

Soon, though, even the transfer threats got buried in the ongoing melodramatics of a team that, almost coincidentally, was also pushing toward a third straight division title. One problem was Jackson, who told everybody that he wasn't appreciated enough and who charged Williams and his coaches with being dictatorial; Finley promptly extended the contracts of the manager and his aides. Another problem was outfielder Billy North, who came into the league to hit .285 and steal 52 bases—and to lead the clubhouse in major brawls, with three. A third problem was Hunter, who fractured a thumb early in the season. But none of this was enough for runner-up Kansas City. When Jackson wasn't moaning, he was leading the AL in homers and RBIs, on his way to an MVP cup. When North wasn't rolling around on the floor, he was teaming with Campaneris as the best table-setting tandem in the division. And when Hunter got over his injury, he won 21 games. Playing a special role in the win was Deron Johnson, who clouted 19 homers and drove in 81 runs as the team's first designated hitter; the DH was a Finley proposal that had been accepted by the league the previous winter.

Hunter starred in the LCS against Baltimore by winning Game Two and then twirling a shutout in the fifth and decisive contest. Again though, Finley had more to cheer on the field than in the grandstands; less than 30,000 showed up for the fourth game in the Coliseum and less than 25,000 for the finale. Attendance was better in the World Series against the Mets, but by then the owner had other sources of irritation. The Mets found their way to his doghouse when they rejected a request to add infielder Manny Trillo to the Oakland roster, which injuries had reduced to 24 players. When Finley told Commissioner Bowie Kuhn that he would tell the Coliseum fans of the Mets' attitude during the opening game, Kuhn warned him against any public address announcement of the kind. Finley went through with the announcement anyway, and Kuhn responded by fining the owner. In the second game, the A's owner ignored the major league rule about turning on lights in a twilight situation only at the start of an inning, waiting for Oakland to come to bat before ordering his technicians to pull their levers. Kuhn, in attendance, immediately countered the order and fined Finley a second time. In the twelfth inning of the same game, Mike Andrews was sent out to play second base, committed errors on back-to-back plays, and handed the Mets a 10–7 victory; the miscues also gave several people something to sue, countersue, and threaten to sue about for the next year.

Infuriated by the errors, Finley ordered Oakland's team doctor to pronounce Andrews unfit to play further in the Series because of an old shoulder injury, then had the infielder sign a consent form and told him to go home. But when the owner petitioned Kuhn to have Andrews declared disabled and to have Trillo put on the roster as a replacement, the commissioner declined and instantly reinstated Andrews. This emboldened several Oakland players, who told the media that they were considering a solidarity strike for their maligned teammate; in the event, they settled for affixing a number 17 (the infielder's number) to their uniforms.

For Williams the Andrews fiasco was the last straw, and he told the team before the third game at Shea Stadium that, win or lose, he intended quitting Finley after the Series. He made good on the threat, and attracted immediate attention from the Yankees, looking for a manager since allowing Ralph Houk to leave their employ and go to Detroit. Holding the ace of another year on Williams's contract, Finley demanded various New York regulars in exchange for the services of his erstwhile manager, turning down an offer of two minor leaguers and $150,000. Undaunted by the Oakland contract, the Yankees signed Williams to a new pact, this prompting a lawsuit from Finley. New York then sought to buttress its case by alerting the Tigers that, if forced to compensate Finley for Williams, it would also demand compensation from Detroit for Houk. After several more skirmishes in the courtrooms and the league's offices, AL president Joe Cronin came down against the Yankees twice: that Williams still owed his services to Finley and that New York had no right to compensation in the Houk case because it had played a voluntary role in his leaving. Williams ended up sitting out the final year of his Oakland contract before returning to manage the Angels.

With their lame duck pilot, the A's outlasted the Mets in seven games in the 1973 Series. Clubhouse celebrations were relatively muted, however, with Jackson summing up the team mood by telling reporters that "Finley takes all the fun out of winning." The fun was even scarcer in 1974. Over the winter, Finley stepped up threats to move the franchise out of Oakland or sell it to interests in Toronto or Denver; whenever an outside buyer expressed optimism that a deal was imminent, however, he increased his money demands. At the same time, he resorted to his Kansas City tactics of slashing costs, firing employees, and cutting back on ticket plans and promotions. It wasn't even until the eve of spring training that he signed a new manager—Alvin Dark, who had been at the center of a stormy firing in Kansas City in 1967. For the first couple of months of the new season, Dark and his fundamentalist Christian views on life alienated the players even more than Williams had. Bando, for one, became a team hero when he declared after a game, and within earshot of the manager, that "Dark couldn't manage a meat market." Relations with the manager only began to improve when Dark blasted Finley for firing coaches Irv Noren and Vern Hoscheit. Like Williams, the new pilot also learned to stay out of the clubhouse fights that continued to erupt with regularity. The worst explosion came on June 5th, when catcher Ray Fosse sought to break up a fight between Jackson and North, and got a crushed disc in his neck for his trouble; Fosse was forced to undergo surgery to have the disc removed and missed the remainder of the season except for the very last game.

As in previous years, the club seemed to thrive on its internal chaos, winding up five games ahead of the Rangers for another division title. Hunter took the Cy Young Award fairly easily by notching 25 victories, leading the league in ERA, and allowing fewer combined hits and walks than innings pitched. The 1974 season was also the year of the Washingtons: Claudell came up from A ball in July to hit .285 and solidify the top of the lineup, and Herb, a sprinter with no previous experience in baseball, became Finley's experiment in designated running when he went through the year without a bat or glove, merely going in as a pinch-runner. The experiment became another source of ridicule of Finley among the players; even Dark objected that Washington's ratio of success in stolen bases (29–45, 64 percent) was far below respectable levels, all the more so for somebody who was useless as either a hitter or fielder. The manager did not win his point until Washington got off to an even worse start in 1975.

In the 1974 LCS, the A's made pretty quick work of the Orioles, taking the pennant in four games; both Holtzman and Blue racked up shutouts. The World Series against the Dodgers got off to a raucous start when Fingers and Odom got into a vicious fight before the opening game; Fingers then went out to pitch 4⅓ innings of relief and gain the first-game victory. Oakland ended up taking the Series in five games, but once again the championship lacked

something in the fun department. Finley availed himself of national media attention to take his complaints about Oakland fans to the country, observing that the club had attracted only 845,000 to the Coliseum during the season while playing before almost double that number on the road. Second baseman Green announced that he was tired of all the hassle and, contrary to the previous two years, was not going to be talked out of retirement. Most of all, there was the cloud around the status of pitching ace Hunter.

At the beginning of 1974, Hunter agreed to a two-year contract calling for him to receive $100,000 a year, with half the amount to be paid directly by Finley into an annuity. On the eve of the World Series against Los Angeles, the press reported that Finley had reneged on the annuity payment, Hunter said he didn't want to talk about it until after the season was over, and league president Lee MacPhail ridiculed reports that Finley's omission amounted to violating a contract and left the pitcher a free agent. When Finley attempted to hand Hunter a check for the missing $50,000, the player's representatives cautioned him against accepting it. As soon as the Series was over, the Players Association formally filed for a hearing aimed at making Hunter a free agent, and eventually secured a positive decision from arbitrator Peter Seitz. Finley immediately went to court to seek an injunction against the ruling, but had his petition rejected. Hunter's liberation prompted a twofold reaction from other owners: shock that he had been able to win his case and eagerness to be first in line for his services. After considering competitive offers from the Angels, Twins, and Padres, the pitcher agreed to a $3-million contract with the Yankees. Although free agency did not really come until the decisions in the Andy Messersmith and Dave McNally cases were handed down a year later, the Hunter affair made it clear to everybody how much the players had to gain from liquidating the reserve clause once and for all.

Even without Hunter, the A's took a fifth straight divisional title in 1975. Blue led the pitchers with 22 wins, while Holtzman won 18 and Fingers added 24 saves to his 10 victories. Jackson again led

After the A's cut Herb Washington in 1975, they tried a modified version of the designated runner with outfielder Don Hopkins. In 82 game appearances, Hopkins got to play the outfield five times and to swing the bat six times (with one single). As a designated runner, he stole 21 bases and scored 25 runs. Outfielder Matt Alexander was used in a similar role, but he played the field far more often.

In the final game of the 1975 season, Vida Blue, Glenn Abbott, Paul Lindblad, and Rollie Fingers combined for the only four-pitcher no-hitter against the Angels.

the offense (and the league) with 36 homers. But in contrast to previous years, the atmosphere around the club was more expectant than volatile; there were no major clubhouse brawls, and most speculation was that Finley had been sufficiently traumatized by the Hunter case to sell out for real before the improving legal situation of players made his plantation-master's attitudes as costly as they were oppressive. Throughout the season, however, he was uncharacteristically quiet, saving most of his energies for an aborted attempt to overthrow Kuhn as the commissioner. But then, shortly before the LCS against Boston in which the A's went down meekly in three straight games, Dark got Finley's attention in a big way by telling a congregation of fundamentalists that "to God, Charlie Finley is just a very little, bitty thing. If he doesn't accept Jesus Christ as his personal savior, he's going to hell." Finley waited until the end of the season, then bounced Dark for being distracted by "too many church activities"; Chuck Tanner was named as the new manager.

The 1976 season more than made up for the relative quiet of the previous year. On the eve of the season opener, Finley sent rumbles of protest through the Bay Area by shipping Jackson, Holtzman, and a minor league prospect to Baltimore for designated hitter Don Baylor and pitchers Mike Torrez and Paul Mitchell. The exchange was only the first step in ridding the Oakland roster of players whose high salaries or expectation of higher wages made the franchise less attractive to prospective buyers. Within a twenty-four-hour period in June, the owner sold Blue to the Yankees for $1.5 million and both Fingers and Rudi to the Red Sox for $1 million each. Or so he thought, anyway. No sooner had he been informed of the sales than old foe Kuhn announced that he was putting them on hold; then, a couple of days later, he canceled them altogether as "not being in the best interests of baseball." An enraged Finley called Kuhn "the village idiot," and proceeded to file a $10-million lawsuit against him. Lost in the shuffle were the three players who had been announced as sold; in fact, Fingers and Rudi had even donned their Boston uniforms for a couple of games. When they came back to the A's pending the outcome of the lawsuit, they (and Blue) were told by Finley that they couldn't play since this might

In 1976, the A's established the team record for stolen bases in the American League with 341.

prejudice the suit against Kuhn. The rest of the team took this for two weeks, then began more strike talk in protest against having to go up against the other league teams with only twenty-two players. Finley finally granted permission for Tanner to use the trio, but the two weeks without the three stars proved significant when Oakland ended up losing the division title to Kansas City by only two-and-a-half games. Finley also ended up losing his suit against Kuhn.

As soon as the season ended, the mass exodus began. Fingers, Rudi, Bando, Tenace, Baylor, and Campaneris all signed with other clubs as free agents; only Blue, who had been signed to a new contract hours before being peddled to the Yankees, remained. When he was asked if it was difficult leaving after so many years, Bando replied that "it's about as hard as leaving the Titanic." Tanner also announced that one year with Finley was enough, and he went to Pittsburgh as the manager in a deal for catcher Manny Sanguillen and $100,000; named as the new pilot was Jack McKeon. For the next two years, McKeon and Bobby Winkles went back and forth as managers of a club that went from being the class of the league to a shambles. Hardly a week passed without some player blasting Finley or the owner retaliating. In 1977, North demanded that the league take over the franchise. When Blue walked away from the club during spring training, he was suspended for two weeks. Dick Allen had his attempt at a comeback ended abruptly when Finley found him taking a shower in the middle of a game. Bay Area fans stayed away from the Coliseum to such an extent that the ballpark became known around the league as the Mausoleum; even when Finley resorted to a half-price scheme for games played between Monday and Thursday, annual attendance dipped below the half-million mark. The rights to broadcast coverage of A's games were given to a college radio station. The Coliseum scoreboard went untended, and ballpark amenities, from concession stands to rest rooms, were the worst in the major leagues since the dark ages of Ebbets Field in the early 1930s.

Finley persisted. On the player front, he again tried to deal Blue in 1977, this time sending him to the Reds for first baseman Dave Revering and $1.75 million. Once again, Kuhn intervened to kill the transaction, this time with the justification that Cincinnati's Big Red Machine was already too superior to the rest of the NL's West Division for the best interests of baseball to be served by the acquisition of Blue. In 1978, Finley finally succeeded in unloading

The seven players received by Oakland from the Giants for Vida Blue on March 15, 1978 are the most ever received by a club for one player. The Giants who went in the deal were pitchers Dave Heaverlo, Alan Wirth, John Henry Johnson, and Phil Huffman, catcher Gary Alexander, shortstop Mario Guerrero, and outfielder Gary Thomasson. The A's also received $300,000.

Blue in an unprecedented seven-for-one trade with the Giants. Finley gloated that not even Kuhn could object to a transaction that emphasized such a welter of players (whatever their abilities) rather than cash.

Right through to the end of the decade, however, there were very few deals that didn't bring Finley at least a little cash. In October 1978, he sent designated hitter Rico Carty to the Blue Jays for $200,000. The following season, he picked up $500,000 from New York for catcher Bruce Robinson and pitcher Greg Corcoran, and $400,000 in a deal with Texas for reliever John Henry Johnson. Together with the organization's practically nonexistent overhead, the transactions solidified the impression that the team might have been atrocious and the Coliseum a crypt, but that Finley wasn't doing all that terribly. The impression was borne out a couple of years later when the Internal Revenue went after him for back taxes.

The turmoil on the boardroom front never stopped. Near the end of 1977, Finley voiced optimism that he would be able to unload the franchise on Denver-based oilman Marvin Davis for $10 million; AL president MacPhail went beyond even optimism in publicly welcoming Davis to the league. But then Oakland Mayor Lionel Wilson and the operators of the Coliseum sued the league and the A's for $35 million over the ten years still remaining on the ballpark lease and got an order blocking the team's transfer to Colorado. This prompted a long round of negotiations, and then what appeared to be a compromise solution by which the A's would be allowed to go to Denver if the Giants were to play half their home games at the Coliseum. Despite initially reassuring signs from across the bay, the San Francisco Board of Supervisors came down against any such arrangement, declaring itself disposed to moving a maximum of twenty games to Oakland. Even then the deal didn't seem dead because of a proposal that the AL and NL would pass the hat to make up the difference between the reduced number of San Francisco games and any revised indemnity against Finley by the Coliseum; subsequently, however, several teams in both leagues revealed that they were not prepared to cough up hundreds of thousands of dollars merely to soothe those determined to get rid of Finley at any cost.

In 1978, more buyers came forward. The first was Broadway producer James Nederlander, whose reported bid of $12 million gained a lot of local headlines because of the rumored involvement of actors Walter Matthau and Angie Dickinson as minority investors. The second offer came from two Oakland furniture dealers who were widely viewed as front men for Oakland Raiders' owner Al Davis; their $13-million proposal satisfied Finley, but came a cropper before demands that the Coliseum agree to a three-year lease with a highly favorable escape clause. The Coliseum lease also stymied the efforts of Edward DeBartolo, Sr., the shopping mall and race track owner who sought to shift the team to New Orleans. The following year, Marvin Davis came back with a new offer: $12 million to buy the team and transfer it to Colorado, and $1 million each from him, Finley, the American League, and San Francisco owner Bob Lurie to buy out the Coliseum lease. For once, the Coliseum acted enthusiastic, but then money problems on other fronts cooled Davis's ardor for the deal.

With the dawning of the 1980s, Finley was still in Oakland—and as hated as he had been over his last couple of years in Kansas City. The chief distinction of the 1979 team, which had sunk below even the expansion Mariners in the standings, was that manager Jim Marshall had often been forced to play three catchers (Jeff Newman, Mike Heath, and Jim Essian) simultaneously for lack of backup infielders and outfielders.

But then, in a surprise move, Finley appointed Billy Martin as Marshall's successor, promising that there would be a radical improvement on the diamond. For once, the record was on the owner's side because Martin had scored his greatest successes in his first years as pilot of the Twins, Tigers, Rangers, and Yankees. Oblivious to the surrounding problems of the franchise, the new manager concentrated his efforts on the five-man rotation of Mike Norris, Marty Keough, Steve McCatty, Rick Langford, and Brian Kingman, and, practically ignoring the bullpen, got more than 200 innings out of each of them. Among the position players, the infield was barely above Triple A caliber, but the outfield trio of Rickey Henderson, Dwayne Murphy, and Tony Armas suddenly surged forward as one of the best in the league, defensively as much as offensively. The payoff was an unexpected second-place finish, with the new manager's impact most obvious in the team's running game. Aside from Henderson's AL-leading 100 stolen bases, the club as a unit pulled off one triple steal, fourteen double steals, and seven thefts of home. Billy Ball, as it was quickly called, also intrigued the fans; although the final attendance total of 842,259 hardly amounted to much in itself, it represented a rise of more than a half-million over the wretched 1979 total of 306,763.

There was also other good news for the locals: On August 23rd, in failing health and worn out by his battles with the league, the Coliseum, and the city of Oakland, Finley finally agreed to sell the A's for $12.7 million. The buyers, who took over officially in November, were the very Bay Area-minded heads of Levi Strauss—Walter Haas, his son Wally, and his son-in-law Roy Eisenhardt. In bidding goodbye to Finley, MacPhail kept a straight face in hailing him for the "new ideas" he had brought to the game.

Eisenhardt's first move as president was to give Martin a second job as vice-president for player personnel decisions. Thanks to Finley's savage cutbacks, the team's main office had been reduced to six employees, including a receptionist, by whose count only 19 percent of the incoming calls over 1979 and 1980 had been answered. The organization's farm system was in even worse condition than the major league club, and there wasn't a single independent scout on the payroll. While addressing all these problems, Eisenhardt also reemphasized the traditions of the A's with such gestures as putting Finley's mule out to pasture and restoring Connie Mack's white elephant as a franchise symbol. He also covered the walls of the team office with pictures of the Philadelphia Athletics stars that Finley had never wanted to acknowledge. Later on in the decade, Oakland would also return to its nickname of the Athletics rather than merely A's.

After all the publicity that had been given to Billy Ball the year before, Oakland ended up pinning its success in the strike season of 1981 on the power of outfielders Armas and Murphy and designated hitter Cliff Johnson. What carried over, on the other hand, was the speed of Henderson (AL-leading 56 steals) and near-exclusive reliance on the starting corps. Whereas Norris had been the most equal of equals in 1980 with 22 victories, the strike-shortened campaign saw McCatty emerge to lead the league in both wins (14) and earned run average (2.32). McCatty, Norris, and Langford also made quick work of the Royals with a three-game sweep in the postseason divisional series, but then Oakland went down just as fast in the LCS against the Yankees.

The end of Martin's enchanted period with the Athletics came in 1981, and he was soon into the irrational scenes that had always arisen during his second or third year with a club. The trouble began in the middle of the 1982 season when the manager's attorney demanded that the team extend Martin's contract to ten years. The demand was made amid rising criticism that Martin's overuse of his starters was the reason behind the arm woes of Langford, Norris, and McCatty (among others). While Eisenhardt procrastinated, Martin went into a rage after an early August loss to Milwaukee, ripping up his office and then getting on the phone to scream at a couple of team officials for the delay on his pact extension demand. With the team bumbling along in fifth place, the incident was enough for Eisenhardt to fire Martin in October and replace him with Steve Boros. The main consolations on the season were a record attendance high of 1,735,489 and Henderson's unprecedented 130 steals (the previous mark had been Lou Brock's 118).

Under Boros and then Jackie Moore, Oakland limped along closer to the bottom than the top of the Western Division. There were good trades (obtaining third baseman Carney Lansford from the Red Sox for Armas), not-so-good trades (sending Henderson to the Yankees for pitchers Jose Rijo, Jay Howell, and others), and free agent signings of more flash than substance (Joe Morgan). Among the others joining the club in the middle of the decade was Dave Kingman, the righthand-hitting slugger as noted for his strikeouts and surliness as his gargantuan home runs. Kingman's notions of humor were caught in a June 1986 episode, when he had a live rat delivered to a woman sportswriter for the Sacramento Bee; he was fined $3,500 by the team and, though Oakland's leading power hitter, was not offered another contract.

Steve McCatty won the ERA title in 1981 although he had a higher runs-per-innings percentage than Sammy Stewart of Baltimore. Under rules then in force, however, Stewart's ERA was rounded off to the nearest whole inning, giving him a more inflated number. The rounding off rule was abandoned after protests over awarding the title to McCatty.

Dave Kingman's 442 home runs are the most by a player not elected to the Hall of Fame.

By 1985, the club's moping play had once again chilled the enthusiasm of fans and once again raised the specter of a move to Denver; on several occasions, Eisenhardt questioned whether two clubs could ever thrive in the Bay Area. The organization also started to smart under its modest television contract ($1.5 million), and was one of the louder voices at league councils in pressing for some kind of revenue-sharing plan on TV money. But just before the situation deteriorated to Finley levels, the team announced a new lease on the Coliseum that extended to the end of the century.

The 1986 season marked the fifth consecutive year that the team played less than .500 ball. But it was also a turning-point year with the arrival of Tony LaRussa in June as Moore's successor as manager. No sooner had LaRussa and his pitching coach Dave Duncan set foot in the Coliseum than they pulled journeyman righthander Dave Stewart out of the bullpen where he had been an undistinguished middle reliever and made him a starter. Stewart, who had drifted around earlier from the Dodgers to the Rangers to the Phillies, won nine of his first ten assignments and was launched on a rejuvenation that would see him win 20 games four years in a row. The new dugout team also inherited Jose Canseco, a brash righthand-hitting slugger who became the first of three consecutive Oakland rookies of the year by belting 33 home runs and driving home 117 runs. While Stewart used his success to become a highly visible spokesman for community problems, the free-swinging Canseco set up a cottage industry in ego, jauntily lending his name to personal 900 numbers and other enterprises for fans who couldn't get enough of the right fielder's boasts, views, and hiccoughs; he also became synonymous with speeding violations in a couple of states.

In 1987, LaRussa and new general manager Sandy Alderson added more pieces. The biggest moves saw veteran righthander Dennis Eckersley obtained from the Cubs and converted into a bullpen closer, and power-hitting Mark McGwire installed at first base. Eckersley became the league's dominant reliever by the end of the decade, while McGwire became the first player in major league history to hit at least 30 homers in his first four seasons. The third Rookie of the Year, after Canseco and McGwire, was

the deft-fielding Walt Weiss, who took over at shortstop in 1988.

The club's first of three consecutive pennants in 1988 established a franchise record of 104 wins. In addition to Stewart (21 wins) and Eckersley (45 saves), the mound contributors included veteran righties Bob Welch (17 wins) and Storm Davis (16). The offense was galvanized by Canseco, a unanimous choice for MVP honors for his 42 homers, 124 RBIs, and .307 average. Canseco clouted three more home runs in the four-game sweep of the Red Sox in the LCS; Eckersley earned a save in every one of the contests. In the World Series against the Dodgers, however, it was the bullpen ace who yielded a dramatic two-out ninth-inning pinch-hit home run to the gimping Kirk Gibson that would send Los Angeles off to a world championship in five games.

The following year was more of the same, though the team had to battle through serious injuries to Canseco, McGwire, Eckersley, and Weiss. Despite missing the first 89 games of the year with a fractured wrist, Canseco still came back to wallop 17 homers and drive in 57 runs; Eckersley's elbow problems for a month did not prevent him from racking up another 33 saves, either. Much of the club's success, however, was due to righthander Mike Moore (19 wins), signed as a free agent, and Rickey Henderson, reacquired from the Yankees. Henderson turned the LCS against Toronto into a personal showcase by reaching base fourteen out of twenty-three times; his statistics included six hits, seven walks, one hit-by-pitch, five runs batted in, eight runs scored, and eight stolen bases. Toronto went down in five games. Stewart and Moore both won two games in a sweep of the Giants in the World Series, but the games were of secondary importance to an October 17th earthquake in the Bay Area that took sixty-seven lives and caused hundreds of millions of dollars in damages. The quake hit only moments before the start of the third game at Candlestick Park, and there was lengthy debate about whether or not to resume the postseason competition. Commissioner Fay Vincent finally gave the go-ahead to continue ten days later.

Oakland's third straight pennant in 1990 spotlighted the efforts of Welch, who stormed to a Cy

In 1988, Jose Canseco became the first major leaguer to hit 40 home runs and steal 40 bases in the same season.

On May 1, 1991, Rickey Henderson steals his unprecedented 939th base. *Ron Riesterer/Oakland Tribune*

May and eclipsed Brock's mark of 938 the following season. The LCS against Boston was another 4–0 rout, but then, contradicting all expectations, the Athletics themselves were swept by the Reds in the World Series. The two losses in three World Series reflected badly on the dynastic claims of LaRussa's team—doubts that were sharpened further by the club's fall to fourth place in 1991.

But then, just when the club seemed on the verge of going back to the shop for a total overhaul, it emerged as a surprise division winner again in 1992. Of the familiar faces, the standouts were McGwire, who slugged 42 homers and drove in 104 runs to rally from a pitiful 1991 season, and Eckersley, who captured both the Cy Young and MVP trophies for his league-leading 51 saves, 7 victories, and 1.91 ERA. Otherwise, it was LaRussa's astute use of role players such as Mike Bordick and Jerry Browne and an eight-man bullpen that proved to be the difference over Minnesota and that earned the manager plaudits for his best tactical effort since taking over the team. Even LaRussa ran out of ploys in the LCS against Toronto, however, and the Athletics went down in five games.

Next to the division win, the biggest news of the year was a startling August trade that sent Canseco to Texas for switch-hitting outfielder Ruben Sierra and pitchers Bobby Witt and Jeff Russell. The swap followed numerous Canseco rifts with his manager and teammates, and for a couple of months exposed Oakland to ending up with nothing for one of the league's premier RBI men since Sierra was on the walk year of his contract. Agreement was finally reached on a new pact in November.

Faced with another dozen players on the roster eligible for free agency, Alderson picked and chose, resigning Eckersley, McGwire, catcher Terry Steinbach, and starter Ron Darling; permitting Stewart (to Toronto) and Moore (to Detroit) to depart; and re-signing Baines, only to trade him then to Baltimore. The club also unloaded Weiss on Florida in a deal after the expansion draft and, after Lansford announced his retirement, signed third baseman Kevin Seitzer.

Young Award with a record of 27–6 and a 2.95 ERA. The righthander's performance overshadowed another 22 wins from Stewart and an additional 48 saves from Eckersley. Rickey Henderson took MVP honors for his 28 homers, 65 steals, and .325 average, and had big support from the Bash Brothers Canseco, McGwire, and Dave Henderson, who combined for 96 homers. Alderson sealed the division title in late August with two stunning trades on the same day that brought in slugger Harold Baines and NL batting titlist Willie McGee. A franchise-high 2.9 million fans were also drawn to the Coliseum by Rickey Henderson's pursuit of Ty Cobb's AL record and Lou Brock's major league record in steals; the outfielder swiped base number 893 to pass Cobb in late

OAKLAND ATHLETICS

Annual Standings and Managers

Year	Position	W	L	Pct.	GB	Managers
1968	Sixth	82	80	.506	21	Bob Kennedy
1969	Second	88	74	.543	9	Hand Bauer, John McNamara
1970	Second	89	73	.549	9	John McNamara
1971	First	101	60	.627	+16	Dick Williams

1972	First	93	62	.600	+5½	Dick Williams
1973	First	95	68	.580	+6	Dick Williams
1974	First	90	72	.556	+5	Alvin Dark
1975	First	98	64	.605	+7	Alvin Dark
1976	Second	87	74	.540	2½	Chuck Tanner
1977	Seventh	63	98	.391	38½	Jack McKeon, Bobby Winkles
1978	Sixth	69	93	.426	23	Bobby Winkles, Jack McKeon
1979	Seventh	54	108	.333	34	Jim Marshall
1980	Second	83	79	.512	14	Billy Martin
1981	First	37	23	.617	+1½	Billy Martin
	Second	27	22	.551	1	Billy Martin
1982	Fifth	68	94	.420	25	Billy Martin
1983	Fourth	74	88	.457	25	Steve Boros
1984	Fourth	77	85	.475	7	Steve Boros, Jackie Moore
1985	Fourth*	77	85	.475	14	Jackie Moore
1986	Third*	76	86	.469	16	Jackie Moore, Tony LaRussa
1987	Third	81	81	.500	4	Tony LaRussa
1988	First	104	58	.642	+13	Tony LaRussa
1989	First	99	63	.611	+7	Tony LaRussa
1990	First	103	59	.636	+9	Tony LaRussa
1991	Fourth	84	78	.519	11	Tony LaRussa
1992	First	96	66	.593	+4	Tony LaRussa

*Tie

Postseason Play

LCS	0–3 versus Baltimore	1971	WS	4–3 versus Cincinnati	1972
	3–2 versus Detroit	1972		4–3 versus New York	1973
	3–2 versus Baltimore	1973		4–1 versus Los Angeles	1974
	3–1 versus Baltimore	1974		1–4 versus Los Angeles	1988
	0–3 versus Boston	1975		4–0 versus San Francisco	1989
	0–3 versus New York	1981		0–4 versus Cincinnati	1990
	4–0 versus Boston	1988			
	4–1 versus Toronto	1989			
	4–0 versus Boston	1990			
	1–4 versus Toronto	1992			

Philadelphia Athletics

National League, 1876   **BALLPARK:** JEFFERSON STREET GROUNDS

RECORD: 14-45 (.237)

One of only three clubs to participate in all five of the National Association's seasons between 1871 and 1875, the Athletics were an obvious choice for charter membership in the National League. But the team paid a price: In exchange for gaining exclusive right to the Philadelphia territory, it had to surrender first baseman Cap Anson to the Chicago franchise headed by NL founder William Hulbert.

Footnote Player: On June 14, 1876, Philadelphia outfielder George Hall became the first major leaguer to hit for the cycle when he collected a single, a double, two triples, and a home run in a game.

On April 22, 1876, Philadelphia hosted the NL's first game—a 6–5 loss to Boston that featured 20 errors. Needless to say, the club contributed a slew of major league firsts—including the first error, by third baseman Ezra Sutton on a wild throw past first. During the contest, center fielder Dave Eggler caught a fly ball and threw a Boston runner out at home for the first double play, while outfielder-third baseman Levi Meyerle was credited with the first double and first walk. A couple of days later, Meyerle, whose .492 average for the National Association Athletics in 1871 is still the highest ever recorded in a professional league, contributed the league's first triple.

The first day loss was a sign of things to come for the club, which stumbled through the season to a seventh-place finish, failing to draw crowds because of rival free public events, such as the Centennial Exposition, the Regatta, and the Fireman's Parade. In addition, the franchise was weighed down by its assumption of the NA Athletics' debts. Things got so bad that the team couldn't find train fare for its final western trip, prompting organization president G. W. Thompson to offer Chicago and St. Louis 80 percent of the gate receipts if they would come to Philadelphia for their final series with his club. When both refused, Thompson canceled the eight-game road trip, as well as the last three games of the season against the Mutuals of New York. The league's response was to expel the Athletics (along with the Mutuals, who were guilty of the same offense) at its annual meeting in December. Philadelphia would not have another NL franchise for six years.

PHILADELPHIA ATHLETICS

Annual Standings and Manager

Year	Position	W	L	Pct.	GB	Manager
1876	Seventh	14	45	.237	34½	Al Wright

Philadelphia Athletics

American Association, 1882–1891	**BALLPARKS:** OAKDALE PARK (1882) JEFFERSON STREET GROUNDS (1883–91)	

RECORD: 633–564 (.529)

The original riches-to-rags franchise, the Athletics set new standards of profitability in their early years, only to fall so hard during the 1890 Players League war that they had to be taken over by the league before the end of the season.

In late 1881, there were two applicants to the American Association from Philadelphia. One, called the Philadelphias, was headed by sporting goods manufacturer Al Reach; the other, the Athletics, was the property of theatrical producer Bill Sharsig, who borrowed his mother's life savings to start the club. The Athletics were awarded the franchise, mainly because Sharsig had secured a permanent lease on Oakdale Park, which had been abandoned for six years.

Sharsig and two co-owners, Charlie Mason and Lew Simmons, alternated in the various club offices. Sharsig, the senior partner, was president from 1882 to 1886, secretary from 1887 to 1890, and manager for parts of 1884 and 1886 and from 1888 to 1890. Simmons managed the club in 1883 and part of 1886, and served as president in 1887. Mason managed in the beginning of 1884 and all of 1887. It was Simmons who managed the club to its lone pennant, a thriller won by one game over St. Louis on a wild pitch in the bottom of the tenth inning in the next to last game of 1883.

The slugging and running Athletics won over Philadelphia fans, who ignored the new National League Phillies and gave the AA club a profit for their first two years (estimated at between $200,000 and $300,000, an unheard of amount at the time). A scheduled championship series with NL-pennant winning Boston was canceled when the team fared badly in some postseason exhibitions.

The team's best players were pitcher Bobby Mathews, who chalked up 30 wins a year for three seasons (1883–1885), and first baseman-outfielder Harry Stovey, who led the AA in homers five times and won the 1884 AA batting crown with a .326 average. Stovey was also one of only two Athletics' managers who were not part of the ownership trio holding the reins in 1885. (The other was his predecessor at first base, Juice Latham, in 1882.)

Following the 1883 pennant, four successive uninspired seasons caused profits to plummet. In 1888, the owners chose as president an outsider, H. C. Pennypacker, who presided over a club decision defying a new association rule that increased admission prices to fifty cents. Philadelphia fans, accustomed to the AA's traditional twenty-five-cent baseball, rebelled against the association-imposed admission fee. In early July, the Athletics, in a move to restore some of their lost patronage, reverted unilaterally to twenty-five-cent tickets; by the end of the month, the entire AA had followed their lead.

Through thick and thin, the Athletics retained their reputation for producing sluggers. Outfielder-first baseman Harry Larkin (four .300-plus seasons) and third baseman Denny Lyons (three .300-plus seasons) complemented Stovey. When Mathews faded after 1885, he was succeeded as the mound ace first by Al Atkinson (25–17 in 1886), then by Guy Weyhing (84 wins between 1887 and 1889), Ed Seward (35 victories in 1888 and 21 in 1889), and, finally, by Sadie McMahon (29–18 in 1890).

The entire AA was fading, however, and despite placing third in both 1888 and 1889, Philadelphia shared the league's fate. The turning point came during the Brotherhood war of 1890. Weyhing, Larkin, Stovey, and second baseman Lou Bierbauer all absconded to the Players League. Furthermore, with the Athletics, Phillies, and PL Quakers all sharing the Philadelphia market, everyone suffered. Having shown a $30,000 profit in 1889, the Athletics should have been able to survive the war; instead, the club was $17,000 in the red by September 17th when Pennypacker released the players and disbanded the club. The president blamed the PL for the team's financial woes, but the root of the problem lay in the large salaries paid to Pennypacker and treasurer William Whittaker.

With the AA assuming responsibility for the franchise for the remaining twenty-two games, Sharsig fielded a team of amateurs, semi-pros, and cast-offs. The result was a twenty-two-game losing streak. On November 22nd, the franchise was awarded to J. Earl Wagner and his brother George, the backers of the PL Quakers.

The Wagners retained Sharsig, but he lasted only seventeen games before being replaced by left fielder George Wood. Wood was one of several players the Wagners brought to the Athletics from the Quakers; others were second baseman Bill Hallman, third baseman Joe Mulvey, and catcher Jocko Mulligan. Two players they were not permitted to keep, on the other hand, were first baseman Stovey and second baseman Bierbauer, who had played for the Athletics in 1889 and who, by the terms of the agreement dissolving the PL after one season in 1890, should have reverted to the Athletics. But when the Wagners neglected to include the two players on their reserve list, Stovey signed with Boston and Bierbauer with Pittsburgh in the NL. The consequences of the omissions were dramatic and far reaching: A decision by the three-man National Board, which governed organized baseball, in favor of the NL; a new NL-AA war; and, at the end of the season, the folding of the overmatched AA.

The Wagners, as they were to do several times in their baseball careers, came out ahead. With the NL planning to admit four AA franchises and buy out as many others as necessary, the Wagners were the first to succumb. At a joint NL-AA meeting in Indianapolis, the brothers accepted a two-part deal—$56,000 for their Philadelphia interests and the right to apply that money to the purchase of the Washington franchise that had just been transferred to the NL from the AA. Their capitulation effectively guaranteed the demise of the association.

The youngest player ever to appear in a major league game was Fred Chapman, who was four months shy of his fifteenth birthday when he pitched 5 innings for the Athletics in July of 1887. Chapman gave up 8 hits, 2 walks, and 4 earned runs in a game that ended in a tie after 5 innings.

PHILADELPHIA ATHLETICS

Annual Standings and Managers

Year	Position	W	L	Pct.	GB	Managers
1882	Second	41	34	.547	11½	Juice Latham
1883	First	66	32	.673	+1	Lew Simmons
1884	Seventh	61	46	.570	14	Charlie Mason, Bill Sharsig
1885	Fourth	55	57	.491	24	Harry Stovey
1886	Sixth	63	72	.467	28	Lew Simmons, Bill Sharsig
1887	Fifth	64	69	.481	30	Charlie Mason
1888	Third	81	52	.609	10	Bill Sharsig
1889	Third	75	58	.564	16	Bill Sharsig
1890	Seventh	54	78	.409	34	Bill Sharsig
1891	Fourth	73	66	.525	22	Bill Sharsig, George Wood

Philadelphia Phillies

National League,
1883–Present

RECORD: 7681–8837 (.465)

BALLPARKS: RECREATION PARK (1883–1886)
HUNTINGTON GROUNDS (1887–1894)
UNIVERSITY OF PENNSYLVANIA ATHLETIC FIELD
(1894)
BAKER BOWL (1895–1938)
COLUMBIA PARK (1903)
SHIBE PARK or CONNIE MACK STADIUM (1927;
1938–1970)
VETERANS STADIUM (1971–Present)

OTHER NAMES: QUAKERS, LIVE WIRES, BLUE JAYS

Anything that has ever been wrong with a major league franchise has been wrong with the Phillies at one time or another. Miserly and larcenous owners, miserable teams, mean-spirited and drunken players, inept managers, intolerable ballparks, and rowdy fans—all have been part of the Philadelphia history. In their eleven decades of existence, the Phillies have won only one world championship in four World Series appearances. Even worse, the club's NL records include those for most seasons (fourteen) with at least 100 losses, for most consecutive defeats (twenty-three) in one season, and for the most owners (two) thrown out of baseball.

The franchise got its start following the 1882 season, when NL president A. G. Mills approached sporting goods manufacturer Al Reach with information that the league intended moving out of

Worcester into the larger market offered by Philadelphia. Reach seized on the news as an opportunity for expanding his business, and he and partner Ben Shibe put up capital for 50 percent of the new team, with the other half in the hands of Pennsylvania attorney John Rogers. As was to be evident from the outset, Rogers contemplated nothing but direct profits from his investment, while Reach and Shibe had a subsidiary interest in using the team to promote bats and balls. The team was known as the Phillies from the beginning, although city dailies persisted in referring to the players as Quakers, a throwback to the Philadelphia club in the National Association. For his first manager, Reach selected Bob Ferguson.

The franchise had acquired nothing but the right to take over from Worcester, so its opening day lineup in Recreation Park on May 1, 1883 was com-

Dick Sisler ends the Phillies' 35–year pennant drought with a tenth-inning, three-run homer on the last day of the 1950 season. *UPI/Bettmann Newsphotos*

John Coleman, the ace of the Philadelphia staff in the team's inaugural 1883 season, holds the record for most losses in a season with his 12–48 record. But Coleman still towered above the rest of the 1883 staff, which went 5–33.

posed largely of pickup players that Ferguson and Reach had found in various minor and semi-pro leagues around the nation. It therefore came as something of a surprise that the Phillies prevailed over the Providence Grays and ace Charlie Radbourne by a slim 4–3 margin. But before fans could become too optimistic, the club revealed its flimsy foundations, and began compiling the worst record ever for a franchise that was to suffer through many more nightmarish seasons. Even before the end of the first season, Ferguson had tired of the losing and been replaced by outfielder Blondie Purcell, and speculation was rife that the franchise would fold as quickly as it had arisen. But Reach and Shibe, with their additional interest in staying in the public eye, went out after as storied a figure as baseball could have in the 1880s—Harry Wright, the English-born organizer of the 1869 Cincinnati Reds. Wright would remain at the club's helm for ten years, the longest tenure of any Philadelphia manager.

After an initial season of working the team toward respectability, Wright steered the Phillies through a series of second, third, and fourth-place finishes that compare favorably with the record of any of baseball's expansion clubs in their fledgling years. Between 1885 and 1893, the team slipped below .500 only twice, and each time by only a single game; its 1886 mark of 71–43 remained the franchise's best for ninety years and misses being the best ever by fractions of a decimal point. The biggest contributor to the 1886 season was pitcher-outfielder Charlie Ferguson, who compiled a 30–9 record and led the league with a 1.98 ERA. Unfortunately, after amassing 99 victories in four years and averaging .288 with signs of increasing power, Ferguson died of typhoid fever in April 1888. Another important player in the Phillies' first years was Art Irwin, a

While managing the Phillies, Harry Wright initiated the idea of pregame batting practice and hitting fungos to outfielders for defensive preparation.

shortstop (and eventual successor to Wright) who endeared himself to Reach and Shibe by offering his employers a license on an infielder's glove he had designed.

After the 1886 season, the Phillies moved into Huntington Grounds (named for adjoining Huntington Street). To supplement income from the facility during team road trips, Reach built a fifteen-foot track around the outfield for bicycle races, then a national craze; this made it necessary for outfielders to negotiate a series of banked turns when pursuing long drives. The first game in the new park took place on April 30, 1887, when an overflow crowd of 20,000 saw the Phillies outslug the Giants 19–10. The ace of the club's staff that year was Dan Casey, a 28-game winner who would insist in his later years that he directly inspired Ernest Thayer's "Casey at the Bat" by striking out with the bases loaded in a game against the Giants.

Before the decade was over, the team had two future Hall of Famers in uniform—outfielders Ed Delahanty (elected in 1945) and Sam Thompson (1974). Coming up as a second baseman, Delahanty showed little that was exceptional during two years with the Phillies, a third with the Cleveland franchise in the Players League, and a fourth back with Philadelphia. But between 1892 and his swan song years for Washington in 1902 and 1903, he never batted below .300, reached .400 three times, won two batting titles, and led the league in slugging average five times, doubles five times, RBIs three times, and triples and homers once each; he would close out his sixteen-year career with an average of .345. Thompson, who came to the Phillies after Detroit liquidated its NL franchise following the 1888 season, was a lifetime .331 hitter who drove in more than 160 runs twice and who stood out as a longball threat in the nineteenth century with seasons of 18 and 20 home runs.

Like other NL clubs, the Phillies suffered a body blow from the organization of the Players League in 1890. Among the most important defectors were pitcher Charlie Buffinton, who had won 76 games for the club over the previous three seasons, and regulars Bill Hallman and Sid Farrar. Delahanty went the one-time jumpers better by first signing a PL contract, then jumping back to Philadelphia when Reach and Rogers waved more money at him, then reversing himself another time when the Brotherhood's Cleveland franchise beckoned with a still better contract. The year of the PL defections also saw the arrival in Philadelphia of outfielder Billy Hamilton, baseball's first great base stealer. With allowances made for the scoring of the day that credited runners with stolen bases for merely advancing an extra base on hits, Hamilton still ended up leading the league in thefts seven times, in walks four times, and in runs scored four times. Together with his career batting average of .344, these numbers were sufficient to get him elected to Cooperstown in 1961.

After the collapse of the PL after the 1890 season, Reach indicated his willingness to accept most of the defectors back to the Phillies, but Rogers became strident about slamming the door on all of them. In a sign of Rogers's growing power within the partnership, only outfielders Delahanty and Jim Fogarty were ultimately allowed to return—Delahanty because the owners were agreed that his best days were still ahead of him, Fogarty because he was dying of tuberculosis (and would in fact be dead before Opening Day 1891).

At first, Rogers's stubbornness won him little sympathy in Philadelphia, especially after pitcher Buffinton, spurned by the Phillies, signed with the American Association's Boston team and led the league with 28 wins. But after another couple of fourth-place finishes, Rogers sounded a more popular note when he inquired why the team, which arguably had the best hitting in the league, seemed unable to get out of its middle-of-the-pack rut. Finally, in the waning days of the 1893 season, Rogers persuaded Reach that one of the main problems was Wright, that the 59-year-old baseball pioneer had become that in a negative sense and that the game had passed him by. Wright's successor was former shortstop Irwin.

In his two years as pilot, Irwin accomplished just about what Wright had—a fourth- and third-place finish. This prompted more of the same rhetorical questions from Rogers, especially after outfielders Delahanty, Thompson, and Hamilton all hit around .400 for 1894 and around .390 the following year. (In 1894, the team batted .349, the highest average in big league history.) Less diplomatic than Wright, Irwin gave as good as he got in his public exchanges with Rogers, but he was also happy to accept a managerial offer from the Giants for the 1896 season.

In 1890, catcher Harry Decker designed the forerunner of modern catching mitts. The first player to use the Decker Safety Catching Mitt in a game was Buck Ewing.

Irwin's ostensible successor was Bill Shettsline, a one-time organizer of the Union Association's Philadelphia club who had subsequently worked his way up through the ranks of the Phillies from ticket-taker to secretary to business manager. Shettsline was responsible only for overall strategic policy, with the grittier game details left to third baseman Billy Nash, named as captain and assistant manager.

To get Nash from Boston, Rogers traded Hamilton—the first of many disastrous deals that would haunt the franchise. Bad became worse when Nash had to give up the ghost as a player after only sixty-four games and had to share logistic responsibility for the last half of the year with backup catcher Jack Boyle.

The one positive development during Nash's brief reign was the arrival in Philadelphia of Nap Lajoie—still another Hall of Famer to wear a Phillies uniform in the nineteenth century (and also another to do some of his best playing elsewhere). Lajoie came to the Phillies as an afterthought in a minor league signing of outfielder Phil Geier, but wasted little time in breaking into the lineup near the end of 1896 and batting .328. The following year, he led the league in slugging, the year after that in RBIs and doubles, and never in his five years with the club did he slip below the .328 of his first season. Lajoie's hitting and graceful defense (initially at first base, more impressively at second base) immediately won over Philadelphia fans, who took to calling him La-Joy.

With the Shettsline-Nash experiment a failure, Rogers brought in George Stallings to lead the team in 1897. Only 28, Stallings was a walking profanity who spent as much time establishing team regulations and lashing into his players as he did trying to outwit opposing clubs. The results were predictable: a tenth-place finish in 1897 and the contempt of his players. The following season, the rancor turned to open revolt when a delegation of Phillies led by outfielder Dick Cooley warned Rogers and Reach that the team would strike if Stallings were not replaced immediately. The owners got the message and once again installed Shettsline, this time with no intermediary captains or assistant managers.

On April 21, 1898, pitcher Bill Duggleby hit a pinch-hit grand slam in his first major league at bat. He is the only one to have accomplished this feat.

The formation of the American League in 1901 posed particular problems for the Phillies. Although Reach and Shibe had been drawn to the franchise originally for the opportunity it appeared to offer for peddling their sports goods, they had in fact been unable to break rival dealer (and Chicago club president) Albert Spalding's monopoly on the baseballs used in the NL. When Ban Johnson approached Shibe with a commitment to give him exclusive rights to the supply of baseballs for the AL if the manufacturer would take over the presidency of the new circuit's Philadelphia entry, the Athletics, Shibe agreed. This latest twist on turn-of-the-century syndicate baseball left Shibe as the president of the Athletics, his partner Reach as the president of the Phillies, and their mutual partner Rogers fuming. Rogers had even more to rail against as soon as Connie Mack was named manager of the Athletics and started going after such Phillies stars as Delahanty and Lajoie. Like other players in the NL, Delahanty and Lajoie were especially vulnerable to rival offers because of the arbitrary $2,400 salary ceiling that the league had imposed on its players. Like other owners, Rogers took the rise of the AL as a justification for trying to skirt the agreed upon maximum with various under-the-table "incentives." But then he got caught in a series of lies and equivocations between Delahanty and Lajoie about who was making more than whom, and watched the second baseman jump to the Athletics anyway. Among those who went with Lajoie were pitchers Bill Bernhard, Chick Fraser, and Wiley Piatt, who had combined for more than half the team's wins in 1900. The situation was no better the following season when Mack snatched outfielder Elmer Flick, shortstop Monte Cross, and Pitcher Bill Duggleby. Even Delahanty accepted Rogers's "incentives" for only a single year before jumping to the Senators for the 1902 season.

But the issue didn't end there. Shortly after the 1902 season got underway, the Pennsylvania Supreme Court ruled that the option clause held by the Phillies on their departed players remained valid and that the defectors could not play for the Athletics. AL president Johnson immediately arranged for LaJoie, Flick, and Bernhard to switch to his Cleveland franchise and ordered them to stay out of the Pennsylvania court's jurisdiction. Fraser and Duggleby returned to the Phillies, but Cross, who had never gotten along with Rogers and who had not impressed the owner as a great loss, was permitted to play out the year for the Athletics. As for Delahanty, his jump to Washington (unaffected by the Pennsylvania ruling) brought him an AL batting title in 1902.

The AL raids not only took their toll on the team (plunges to the bottom of the standings for three straight years), but were also the breaking point for the Reach-Shibe-Rogers ownership. A couple of months before the start of the 1903 season, Pittsburgh owner Barney Dreyfuss mediated the sale of the franchise to a group headed by Philadelphia broker and socialite Jimmy Potter for $200,000. Dreyfuss threw in one of his own Pirate catchers, Chief Zimmer, as a managerial successor to Shettsline. The changing of the guard led to little that was positive. In early August, a section of the left field stands collapsed, killing twelve people, injuring more than 200 more, and opening the franchise to numerous lawsuits. After another seventh-place finish, Potter and his syndicate bounced Zimmer for a marquee name, Hugh Duffy, but that only produced an even more humiliating eighth-place standing. Weary of the fallout from the collapse of the stands and the team's bad play, Potter resigned from the presidency after only two seasons; his successor was Mister Phillie, Shettsline.

The Potter syndicate retained ownership of the club for another five dim years. Although some good players (outfielder Sherry Magee, catcher Red Dooin, outfielder Roy Thomas) put in appearances in the period, none of them could compare to the Delahantys, Hamiltons, and Thompsons. Moreover, the Philadelphia personnel in the opening decade of the century had a decided snarl to it. Magee, for example, became notorious throughout the league for his bullying of Phillies rookies. For Kid Gleason, there was no levity intended when he displayed a leather strap and a knuckle-duster in his locker to underline his standing as field captain. Few weeks went by without some Phillies player taking out a strikeout or an error on the opposing team by instigating a brawl.

One of the ugliest scenes in baseball history exploded in April 1906, when New York manager John McGraw heckled Phillies third baseman Paul Sentell and Sentell responded by throwing punches at the New York skipper. After both combatants had been thrown out of the game, they met again under the stands and went another couple of rounds. Meanwhile, back in the stands, Philadelphia fans sat in growing irritation as the Giants pasted the locals. When the Giants headed for the barouches they fancied to take them back and forth from road ballparks, some of the fans pulled blankets off the horses and others started pelting the New York players with lemon rinds and pieces of ice obtained from street-corner vendors. Mainly by swinging their whips, most of the drivers got their barouches away from the mob. Less fortunate was Giants catcher Roger Bresnahan, who was quickly surrounded in the last coach by an estimated thousand screaming fans. Shooting his fists and spiked shoes at anybody who came near, Bresnahan somehow managed to get to a grocery store and shut himself up inside. It took the police more than a half-hour to arrive and when they did, they served the catcher with a summons for disturbing the peace.

After three years of the tough-talking Duffy, who proved that as a manager he was a good outfielder, Shettsline took the opposite tack by bringing in the soft-spoken Bill Murray as pilot. The change in style brought no dramatic change in the standing of the club, although righthander George McQuillan generated special interest at the gate in 1908 by winning 23 games and challenging New York's Christy Mathewson for the ERA title. Where Murray was significant was in bringing together representatives of the club's ownership with Israel Durham and James McNichol, then the city's most powerful Republican Party bosses. Together with banker Clarence Wolf, the two politicos purchased the club shortly before the start of the 1909 season, with Murray tagging along for a minority share. In the boardroom shakeup that followed, Durham took over the presidency and the ever mobile Shettsline went back to being business manager. But cartoonists on Philadelphia's leading dailies were just getting used to two politicians as the owners of the team when, on June 28, Durham died at the age of 52. From there the season went downhill. While the team floundered around in fifth place, Murray spent a good part of his time exercising his trade-approval rights as a stockholder by turning down ill-conceived deals cooked up by McNichol and Wolf.

There was little surprise when, on November 26, 1909, McNichol and Wolf announced that their dabbling in baseball was over and that they had sold the team for $350,000. What was astonishing was the identity of the buyer—Horace Fogel, long-time

Turn-of-the-century outfielder Roy Thomas became so proficient at fouling off pitches (in one recorded instance, twenty-two in a row) that the National League introduced the rule of making the first two fouls strikes in the interests of both speeding up the game and saving franchises money.

sportswriter for the *Evening Star* and other local dailies. Between his stints as a reporter, the blustering Fogel had served as manager of the NL Indianapolis team in 1887 and as a McGraw predecessor with the 1902 Giants. The $350,000 came from the millionaire Tafts of Cincinnati, the same family that had earlier financed Charles Murphy's purchase of the Chicago Cubs. While they were both in the league, there were not too many issues that found Fogel and Murphy on opposite sides.

Having also bought out Murray's minority interest in the club, Fogel wasted little time in replacing him as manager with Red Dooin, then still Philadelphia's starting catcher. According to the owner, Dooin had a "live wire" personality that was in keeping with an energetic image that he intended bringing to the team. It was not an idle phrase: For the next couple of years, Fogel labored zealously for the press and fans to refer to the club as the Live Wires, dismissing Phillies as meaning nothing and Quakers as having too many passive connotations. To abet his cause, he sold or gave away thousands of watch fobs adorned with an eagle carrying sparking wires. To open the 1910 season, he negotiated with the Philadelphia Zoo to borrow an eagle, got turned down, then settled for one hundred pigeons that he festooned with free admission tickets and set loose. In the end, however, few people outside of Fogel's immediate circle learned to accept the team as the Live Wires.

With Dooin, as with several managers before him, the Phillies were respectable but not much more. To go along with Magee (batting champion in 1910), the team picked up steady players like outfielder Dode Paskert, third baseman Hans Lobert, and first baseman Fred Luderus; but there were just as many rookie busts and so-so journeymen. The most conspicuous exception was righthander Grover Cleveland Alexander, who narrowly missed out wearing another uniform after Fogel brushed off a tip to sign him before the 1910 winter draft. Even after the club did draft him in open competition, Dooin had to have his arm twisted to bring the pitcher north from spring training. In his first season, Alexander led the league with 28 wins; before the end in 1930, he would rack up 373 victories, leaving him tied with Mathewson for the most in NL history and earning a Cooperstown induction in 1938. Along the way there would be three straight seasons of 30 or more wins, another six 20-game seasons, five ERA titles, six strikeout titles, and ninety career shutouts, including a record-breaking sixteen in 1916. The grim side to Alexander's career was that he was plagued

Grover Cleveland Alexander. *National Baseball Library, Cooperstown, NY*

by both epilepsy and alcoholism. After his baseball days were over, he ended up working for a Times Square flea circus. None of these details emerged in the Hollywood movie made of his life in the 1950s, with Ronald Reagan portraying the hurler.

Despite the arrival of Alexander, Tom Seaton, and Eppa Rixey (another future Hall of Famer) for the nucleus of a strong pitching staff, the Phillies veered from injury to mediocre season to injury in trying to put together a potent lineup. It didn't help, either, when Magee slugged umpire Bill Finneran midway through the 1911 season and lost more than a month to a suspension. It especially didn't help when the suspension led Fogel to issue periodic bulletins on what he considered the sad state of umpiring. A year later, he was still at it, by now charging that the umpires favored the Giants over the Cubs in the pennant race and were making their calls accordingly. Although the majority of Fogel's accusations came during drinking bouts with his writer cronies,

In 1911, the Phillies and Giants were the first teams to use different home and away uniforms.

he became quoted so frequently (especially in Chicago) that the umpires demanded that the league vindicate their name. With the Giants backing the call, the league set up a hearing in New York after the 1912 season for Fogel to prove his charges. The Philadelphia owner emerged from the session banned from baseball for life for having undermined the integrity of the game.

Fogel's removal prompted more scrambling in the Phillies' organization. Albert Wiler took over the presidency in the name of the Tafts, but only to negotiate the sale of the franchise. Once again, it was Pittsburgh owner Dreyfuss who came to the rescue. Aware that the secretary of his club, William Locke, was interested in buying the Phillies, Dreyfuss energetically endorsed the bid among the other NL owners, noting in particular that Locke's group included former New York City police commissioner William Baker, precisely the image the league needed after the Fogel scandal.

After the Potters, Durhams, and Fogels, Locke was hailed as a genuine baseball man by comparison. It was a short-lived celebration. On July 15, 1913, with the reanimated Phillies in first place, Locke dropped dead, leaving the club in the hands of the New York-based Baker. The Phillies still made a fight of it for another month or so, before finally succumbing to the Giants. Even with its disappointing 12½-game deficit to New York, it amounted to the best season for the franchise since Shettsline's 1899 team. The stars on the field included outfielder Gavvy Cravath, who topped the league in both homers (19) and RBIs (128). Cravath helped make the Phillies the most potent long-ball team of the pre-Babe Ruth era, thanks in no small part to the friendly right field wall (officially, 280 feet down the line) of what would become known as Baker Bowl. But just as the franchise had had little time to congratulate itself for the arrival of Locke, it had barely gotten through patting itself on the back about challenging the Giants when the newly formed Federal League began going after its regulars. The club plunged again to sixth in 1914.

Federal League or no Federal League, Baker decided that the team's collapse was in good part Dooin's doing, so at the end of the season, he announced a switch to backup catcher Pat Moran. With his new manager's backing, Baker then defied popular opinion by dealing Magee to the Braves for outfielder Possum Whitted. He also completed several other transactions that seemed relatively minor at the time but that brought the team vital ingredients for its 1915 pennant—shortstop Dave Bancroft, third baseman Milt Stock, second baseman Bert Niehoff, and

pitcher Al Demaree. With Cravath once again leading the NL with 24 homers and 115 RBIs, Alexander winning 31, Erskine Mayer notching 21, and even Whitted hitting a point higher than Magee did for Boston, the club took its first flag by a 7-game margin over the Braves. Several superior Phillies teams had failed to get into the World Series, so much of the credit for the triumph went to Moran. The ex-catcher was not only adamant about hitting and fielding fundamentals, but he devised sophisticated signs (for example, adding elaborate indicators to the signs proper) that stymied other clubs.

In their first World Series, the Phillies went down to Boston in five games. The series was a string of pitching masterpieces and cliff-hanging dramatics: the scores were 3–1, 2–1, 2–1, 2–1, and 5–4, and four of the five games were decided in the victor's last at bat.

Although the 1916 team won a game more than the 1915 NL champions, it finished 2½ games behind the Dodgers of Wilbert Robinson. Moran thought he knew why, too: because New York Giants' players so resented their manager McGraw and so liked their former coach Robinson that they threw crucial games to Brooklyn near the end of the season. To back up his charges, Moran (and later Baker) noted that McGraw had stalked away from one Giant-Dodger game muttering insinuations about the integrity of the contest. NL President John Tener looked into the accusations, but then declared himself satisfied that nothing illegal had occurred. The next season, the Phillies again finished second on the strength of Alexander's third straight 30-victory season, but were effectively out of the race from June. It was to be the club's last decent showing for some three decades; between 1917 and 1949, only the 1932 team would even top the .500 mark. The same period showed sixteen cellar finishes, eight more in seventh place, and twelve years with at least 100 setbacks.

If there was one theme to the dark ages of the Phillies, it was Baker's quest for money. The owner had already provided a taste of things to come in 1914, when he declined to give a small raise to 27-game winner Seaton and watched the righthander defect to the Brooklyn team in the FL. When, following the 1917 season, he heard that Alexander was likely to be drafted into the army over the winter, he didn't hesitate to unload his ace and catcher Bill Killefer on the Cubs for $60,000 and a couple of negligible players. Flag-winning manager or not, Moran had to get along without a coach because of the franchise's reputed lack of funds. In 1918, Baker turned down an opportunity to buy up Philadelphia's entire spring training complex in St. Petersburg, Florida because (as he told Mayor Al Lang) he had "better things to do with (his) money"; rebuffed in his asking price of a mere $25,000, Lang sold the property a few years later for $500,000. When outfielder Chuck Klein became the talk of the league in the 1930s for his homer-hitting prowess, Baker had an extension placed atop the wall in right field so the slugger wouldn't outdo Babe Ruth and improve his contract bargaining position. More generally, the Phillies owner made sure to save every negative reference to his players that appeared in print for use in contract negotiations.

Among those who were most heated about the trading of Alexander was Moran. The manager's criticisms, along with a sixth-place finish in 1918, made it easy for Baker to replace him after the season with one-time Athletics pitching ace Jack Coombs. Coombs lasted only until July 1919, when he got into a screaming match with Baker about the organization's inability to pick up talented players; his successor for the next season-and-a-half was Cravath, then on his last legs as a player. The most significant event during Cravath's reign was the blacklisting of first baseman Gene Paulette for suspected game fixing during a previous stay with the Cardinals.

While managers like Cravath, Bill Donovan, and Kaiser Wilhelm went through the motions of playing out the schedule, Baker pursued his philosophy of netting money from player sales rather than from giving Philadelphia a decent team. Among those sold out from under the managers in the early 1920s were Bancroft, pitchers Rixey, Lee Meadows, and Red Causey, second baseman Johnny Rawlings, and outfielders Irish Meusel and Casey Stengel. The owner also wasn't above trying to use the baseball scandals of the day as an excuse for his actions. Following the trade of Meusel in 1921, for instance, he dropped some heavy hints that the outfielder had been dogging it for some time and very suspiciously. After firing Donovan as manager, he made the same insinuations. Alerted to the veiled charges, Commissioner Kenesaw Landis sent an investigator to question everybody involved, decided that Baker had only been trying to fend off criticism and lay the groundwork for not honoring Donovan's contract, and blasted the Philadelphia owner.

In the final week of the 1924 season, the Phillies were in the bribery news more substantially, when Giants outfielder Jimmy O'Connell accosted Philadelphia second baseman Heinie Sand with an offer of $500 if he would be a little lax about chasing groundballs. Sand reported the bribery attempt to

his manager Art Fletcher, who in turn contacted NL President John Heydler and Landis. When the commissioner completed his investigation, he banned O'Connell and New York coach Cozy Dolan for life. The scandal created bad blood between Fletcher and his mentor McGraw, who rebuked the Phillies' pilot for not having gone to him instead of to Heydler.

Until the arrival of Klein in 1928, the Phillies' fan of the 1920s came awake only when center fielder Cy Williams strode to the plate. In his nineteen-year career, the lefty-swinging Williams topped the NL in homers four times (three times with Philadelphia, once with Chicago), including 41 round-trippers in 1923. A lifetime .292 hitter, his season averages included marks of .345, .331, and .328 during his Baker Bowl days. Williams was so quick in the outfield that his flankers in left and right saw little reason to move for anything not hit directly at them; in mock recognition of this, local sportswriters once decided that the club's slogan for the 1920s was GET IT, CY, GET IT.

By the time the 1928 season rolled around, Baker had so dismembered the franchise that it was referred to around the league as the Phoolish Phillies. Baker Bowl had become so dilapidated that when a foul ball hit the roof or grazed a beam, fans sitting immediately below would be showered with rust. Baker's only consolation was that there were few fans sitting anywhere in the Bowl who might have sued him. Even before Connie Mack had rebuilt his Athletics into a powerhouse across town, the Phillies were mainly drawing pensioners who had nothing better to do in the afternoon. Local gamblers refused to accept bets on the team unless they were wagers on how much it would lose by. Players left as soon as they were assigned a price tag, managers were fired as soon as they began to complain about their lack of players.

Even within the general malaise, the 1928 club under Burt Shotton stood out as especially bad. An associate of St. Louis general manager Branch Rickey, Shotton's arrival in Philadelphia sparked speculation

Although the Williams Shift has become associated with Cleveland manager Lou Boudreau's stationing of three infielders between first and second to defend against Ted Williams, the strategy was actually employed by NL managers in the 1920s against Cy Williams of the Phillies and later borrowed by the Indians' pilot.

that Baker's latest deal was to use his franchise as something of an additional farm club for the Cardinals and their overabundant minor leaguers; the rumors resurfaced whenever the teams announced another of their regular deals during Shotton's tenure. Among the players who began the season on the roster were outfielder Russ Wrightstone, who once explained an error by saying that the ball had been batted "too goddam high"; wisecracking Fresco Thompson, who once disdained to enter a game as a pinch-runner because he had just had his shoes polished; and Russ Miller, who had been counted on as a mainstay of the staff (and another attractive commodity in the window) until he went 0–12. Not even Ferguson's 1883 team had finished further away from first place than Shotton's Phillies.

Surprisingly, amid all the wreckage, the club came up with not one, but two, potent bats. The first belonged to first baseman Don Hurst, who got his major league career going with a season that included 19 homers. In the years to follow, the lefty swinger batted over .300 four straight times, clubbed as many as 31 homers in a season, and led the NL in RBIs. In 1932, Hurst combined with outfielder Klein to rack up even more total bases (737) than the fabled Yankee duo of Babe Ruth and Lou Gehrig (672).

Until the arrival of Mike Schmidt more than four decades later, the lefty-hitting Klein was the franchise's most powerful twentieth-century offensive player. Before he was shipped off to the Cubs in another Baker fire sale, he batted .360, .356, .386, .337, .348, and .368 in six seasons. These years included a Triple Crown in 1933 (when he also led the NL in doubles and slugging average); other home run titles in 1929, 1931, and 1932; another RBI crown in 1931; three consecutive years (1930–32) of leading the league in runs scored; and even a base-stealing title in 1932. Many of Klein's numbers were reduced significantly following his trade to Chicago after the 1933 season, prompting his career-long reputation as "a Baker Bowl hitter." The impression seemed only confirmed when he was dealt back to the Phillies in 1936, going on to hit more round-trippers than he had in either year in Wrigley Field. He ended up with a career average of .320, and was elected to the Hall of Fame in 1980.

Although 1930 has usually been cited as the year for the extra-lively ball, it wasn't too dead around Baker Bowl in 1929, either, as the team led the league in hitting (.309) and slugging (.467) despite finishing in fifth place. On the other hand, of the fifteen pitchers who took the mound during the season, only righthander Lou Koupal managed an ERA under

First baseman Monk Sherlock batted .324 in 299 plate appearances for the 1930 Phillies, and his brother Vince went 12-for-26 for the 1935 Dodgers. Their combined batting average of .335 is the highest for brothers in the big leagues.

5.00, and that was 4.76. The team's 1930 staff became legendary: it had a composite ERA of 6.71, allowed an opposition batting average of .346, and set major league records in the number of hits and runs yielded. But the pitching staff had nothing on Baker Bowl, where the league's eight teams batted .352, as opposed to .296 in the other seven parks. What this added up to for the Phillies was a club batting mark (.315) that was even higher than the previous season—but they still were short of New York's average of .319 and once again found themselves back in the basement. Even Klein's torrid 170 RBIs finished behind the all-time record of 190 amassed by Hack Wilson of Chicago.

On the surface, the offensive gore (the league as a whole hit .303) delighted NL owners for the half-a-million more customers who trooped through the circuit's turnstiles during the season. But the numbers racked up at Baker Bowl were also something of an embarrassment, prompting more behind-the-scenes agitation about the state of the Philadelphia facility and the franchise in general. Suddenly, however, amid reports that the owners had enough votes to impose a change in the Phillies' hierarchy, Baker died of a heart attack while attending a December meeting in Montreal. Minority stockholder Charlie Ruch took over temporarily as president. A short while later, Baker's will revealed that he had left the largest chunk of his stock not to his widow, but to club secretary (and former personal secretary) May Mallon Nugent. When Baker's widow died a few years later, she too left her stock to Nugent. Nugent's husband Gerald, a former shoe salesman from Philadelphia, benefited from one of Baker's last moves when he was named as Shettsline's successor as business manager; by 1933, he had climbed the ladder higher to take over from Ruch as organization president.

The big difference between Baker and Nugent was that, whereas the aloof former police commissioner was severely criticized for selling off Philadelphia's best players, the cordial ex-salesman received widespread sympathy for doing the same thing more frequently. Nugent helped assure this reaction by

Baker Bowl with its infamous right field wall. *National Baseball Library, Cooperstown, NY*

persuading Philadelphia beat writers and many fans that the alternative to his sales was the loss of the franchise to the city. It was an argument that sustained him through the departures of Klein, Hurst, Pinky Whitney, Dolf Camilli, Bucky Walters, Claude Passeau, Spud Davis, Dick Bartell, Kirby Higbe, and Morrie Arnovich, among others. When the reaction wasn't a regrettable sigh, it was a bizarre attempt to believe that the players carrying the cash back to the Phillies were better than those leaving Philadelphia. But even in the few instances where this might have been true (for example, the 1934 trade of Hurst to the Cubs for Camilli), it was so only temporarily, until the received player had established credentials of his own for being resold.

Of the players who did stick around long enough to be recognized, many were the stuff of pressbox lore rather than diamond ability. One of these was pitcher Flint Rhem, most noted for missing a start because, he said, he had been kidnapped, brought blindfolded to some place in New Jersey, and then forced at the point of a gun to drink a bottle of whiskey. Another was Hugh Mulcahy, known to everyone as Losing Pitcher Mulcahy even before his lifetime 45–89 record gave him the worst percentage (.336) ever compiled by a pitcher with at least 100 decisions.

Nugent's managers were also known for something other than a strategic genius. Jimmie Wilson, otherwise considered close to the owner, became known for his "O'Rourke checks" during games—ascertaining whether Patsy O'Rourke, the organiza-

tion's one and only scout, was in his regular seat (as he always was) instead of being on the road doing some actual scouting. Doc Prothro was a managerial equivalent to Mulcahy for pilots with at least 400 games—a final record of 138–320 (.301) for three last-place clubs. Hans Lobert's chief contribution to the team in the war year of 1942 was the patriotic gesture of marching all the players out on the field before games with their bats on their shoulders.

Nugent's most important innovations were the introduction of Sunday baseball on April 29, 1934 and a move out of Baker Bowl to Shibe Park on July 4, 1938. The latter change had been discussed in NL boardrooms for years, but finally came to pass only after Nugent was persuaded by fire experts that Baker Bowl was a tragedy waiting to happen. The switch to Shibe Park as tenants of the Athletics was hardly a dream come true for the franchise: No sooner had the club moved its quarters than even its previously small attendance was undermined further by the faithful who resented having to sit in the park of the municipal enemy and by the less than faithful who, once into the habit of invading Connie Mack's territory, saw that Philadelphia's AL entry was offering better baseball entertainment for their money.

As if he needed it, Nugent found another problem with Landis in 1940 when he drafted 6'5" right-hander Rube Melton from the Cardinals for $7,500. Although Melton had been touted for a couple of years as one of the best prospects in the minor leagues, there was only more shrugging in Philadelphia when Nugent turned right around and dealt the pitcher to Larry MacPhail of the Dodgers for $15,000. But even as Nugent's press cronies were pointing out that, if nothing else, the Phillies owner had made a 100 percent profit on the dealing, St. Louis general manager Rickey called on the commissioner's office to investigate.

What was established as fact was that MacPhail had sought Melton from Rickey prior to the draft, been told that the price would be $30,000, and replied that he would wait and acquire the hurler for half that price; what was rumored but never proven was that the Dodger boss had not only asked Nugent to draft Melton for Brooklyn with the guarantee of the $15,000, but that he had even advanced the $7,500 to the Phillies owner for the original purchase. Declaring that he sensed "something smelly," Landis canceled the deal with the Dodgers, ordered the Phillies to keep Melton for at least two years, and censured both Nugent and MacPhail.

In baseball terms, Nugent came out the loser when Melton put together records of 1–5 and 9–20 for Philadelphia; in terms much more significant to the Philadelphia president, he came out ahead when, after the 1942 season, he finally sold the pitcher to the Dodgers, and for double the originally planned $15,000.

It was around the time that he was counting his money from the Melton sale that Nugent also blew his last chance for baseball glory. Indications had been strong for months that the other NL owners were fed up with their meager earnings from trips to Philadelphia and had decided to impose the same changes on Nugent that they had been about to force on Baker before the latter's death. This made Nugent particularly receptive to an offer from outsider Bill Veeck, then owner of the AAA Milwaukee Brewers, to buy the Phillies. The only trouble was, Veeck had already intimated his intentions of stocking his new Phillies with Negro League stars, making the franchise immediately competitive, not to say revolutionary. Whether or not the scheme would have ever overcome the prejudices of the other owners if it had simply been presented as a fait accompli, will never be known; instead, Veeck informed Landis of his intentions, and the project died right then and there. Within days, the league had taken over the Philadelphia franchise and the Nugent regime was over.

It was NL President Ford Frick who found the next Phillies owner—lumber magnate William Cox. The good news about Cox was that, unlike his immediate predecessors, he had the kind of wealth that indicated an ability to buy players rather than sell

them and that his very first move as president was to give the manager's job to Bucky Harris, the first Phillies' pilot since Harry Wright who came to the organization as a pennant-winning strategist. The bad news was just about everything else, not least the fact that Cox was the essence of the hands-on owner.

In his first spring training in 1943, Cox insisted on filling in the roster holes left by Nugent's eleventh-hour housecleaning by pitching and playing shortstop himself. To get his charges into better shape, he brought in a former coach for the Hungarian Olympic team who scheduled hours of calisthenics every day and who tried to get chewing tobacco banned from the bench in favor of orange slices. With the same fervor that had once led Fogel to call the club the Live Wires, Cox changed the team's name to the Blue Jays. It was all to no avail, or worse. His spring training exploits on the diamond merely provoked ridicule from the players. The exercise coach had his tenure terminated after nodding off on the bench during a game. Not only did sportswriters and fans continue referring to the team as the Phillies, but a group of Johns Hopkins University students called on the team not to use their nickname of Blue Jays because it "brought disgrace and dishonor to the good name" of the school.

But the biggest backfire of all turned out to be the hiring of Harris. The first strain in the relationship between the manager and the owner appeared in spring training, when Harris began to complain to writers that Cox was calling him at all hours of the day or night with this or that idea. The strain escalated into tension when Cox brought in the exercise coach over Harris's objections and when the manager was only too happy to report the coach's sleeping problem and insist that he be bounced for the morale of the team.

Some ninety games into the season, Harris was replaced by Freddie Fitzsimmons. As soon as the players heard of the change, they erupted against Cox. With pitcher Schoolboy Rowe acting as their chief spokesman, they threatened to sit out a game against the Cardinals unless the owner rescinded his decision. It finally took a personal appeal by Harris to get the team to call off its action. Unfortunately for Cox, however, Harris didn't leave the scene completely until he had a farewell drink with a few Philadelphia writers during which he charged that the owner bet frequently on the team's games. The accusation eventually got back to Landis, who summoned Cox following the season and heard him admit that he had indeed made some "small sentimental bets" on the Phillies; his defense was that he had not been aware that baseball's regulations against gambling also covered owners betting on their own clubs. Landis ordered the executive to attend another hearing in December with his attorney, but, knowing how that session would go, Cox submitted his resignation. Like Fogel, he was then blacklisted for life.

In view of the pressures that they themselves had brought to bear on Nugent to sell the team to Cox, both Landis and Frick were acutely embarrassed by the incident. But that didn't prevent them from again demanding a new ownership in Philadelphia as quickly as possible. The point man this time turned out to be minority shareholder Babe Alexander, who brought together the ousted owner and Robert Carpenter, Sr., a multimillionaire member of the DuPont family. Before the end of the year, Cox completed the sale of the franchise to Carpenter for $400,000.

Initial reaction in Philadelphia to the latest sale was skeptical, in good part because Carpenter had made it clear that his main interest in buying the team was to find something to do for his son Robert, Jr., who was seated as organization president. But as the jokes started coming hot and heavy about the Phillies as a rich man's tinker toy, the younger Carpenter hired Herb Pennock, then the farm director of the Red Sox, as general manager. Pennock moved into his office with the decided philosophy that the only way to rebuild the franchise was to develop young players, not go for quick-fix veterans. If this sounded like another call for Philadelphia fans not to expect much for awhile, they could at least say they had been advised ahead of time. Even with every club in the league reduced to the aged, the inexperienced, and the simply bad because of the war, the Phillies remained in the cellar in both 1944 and 1945. The 1945 pitching staff in particular had a beer league look to it; the situation got so bad that even slugger Jimmie Foxx, then making his last stop before retirement and the Hall of Fame, was pressed into service as a pitcher nine times (and even won once).

Given his illustrious career as a pitcher with the Yankees, it figured that Pennock would bring some former New York cronies to the Phillies with him. The first two were scout Johnny Neun and pennant-winning minor league manager Eddie Sawyer. The third, obtained in a June 1945 trade with the Dodgers, was Ben Chapman. Chapman, an outfielder throughout his career who had been fancying himself in his later years as a pitcher, underwent another vocational change when Pennock appointed him manager in place of Fitzsimmons. The two of them

then brought in Bennie Bengough, Cy Perkins, and Dusty Cooke (all with a Yankees connection of some kind) as coaches.

Chapman's two full seasons as manager, in 1946 and 1947, showed only minimal improvement for the team in the standings. But the period also saw the gradual arrival of the farm system players that Pennock had argued represented the future of the organization. Making a particularly big impression in 1946 was outfielder Del Ennis, who batted .313 with 17 homers and 73 RBIs to lead the club in all three categories. The same two years saw southpaw Curt Simmons, third baseman Willie Jones, and shortstop Granny Hamner get a taste of big league competition.

The Phillies also got in on the postwar attendance boom that benefited just about all the NL clubs: The 1946 total of 1,045,247 not only marked the franchise's first million-plus season and not only more than doubled the previous high attracted by Pat Moran's 1916 incumbent league champions, but also represented 423,454 more fans than were drawn to the Athletics.

One of the club's main problems in 1947 was Chapman's virulent opposition to racial integration and his hateful baiting of Jackie Robinson throughout games against the Dodgers. Years later, some of Robinson's teammates would say that Chapman's nonstop slurs from the Philadelphia dugout accelerated unity on the Brooklyn club; in the year that they were being spewed, they caused a great deal of embarrassment within the Phillies organization, and for more than one reason. Never to be confused with a social innovator, Carpenter would keep the Phillies lily-white longer than any other NL club (until the arrival of John Kennedy in 1957); at the same time, however, he didn't need Chapman's performance keeping the issue hot in Philadelphia and focusing attention on the franchise's racial policies. This would turn out to be strike one against the manager.

Strike two came during the offseason, after Pennock was felled by a fatal stroke at the age of 48. Hardly had the general manager been buried and Carpenter announced his intention of taking over the club's baseball operations directly, than Chapman began egging on some of the beat writers to suggest to the president that he wasn't qualified to succeed Pennock and that the organization needed somebody like George Weiss of the Yankees. The advice infuriated Carpenter, who was bent on demonstrating to his father that he didn't need somebody like Pennock holding his hand to make a go of the franchise.

Strike three came around the 1948 All Star game,

when Carpenter decided that Chapman had not been getting enough out of his players (then five games under .500) and fired him. After a week or so under Cooke, the team was turned over to Sawyer, then managing a Philadelphia affiliate in Toronto.

Among the players Sawyer found waiting for him when he replaced Cooke were two who became synonymous with the 1950 Whiz Kids—center fielder Richie Ashburn and pitcher Robin Roberts. In his rookie season, the speedy, lefthand-hitting Ashburn finished second only to Stan Musial with his .333 average and led the league in steals with 32. Over a fifteen-year career that was mainly spent with the Phillies, he hit .308, won two batting titles, led the league in hits three times, in walks four times, and in triples twice. Roberts, who got off to a slow start in the majors with a 7–9 record in 1948, eventually compiled a 286–245 mark in nineteen years, most of them with the Phillies. His distinctions include six 20-game seasons, five consecutive years of leading the league in complete games, and two years of totaling the most strikeouts. The righthander, who was elected to the Hall of Fame in 1976, also gained a footnote in baseball history in the 1970s, when he introduced labor lawyer Marvin Miller to player association representatives.

In his first full year at the helm in 1949, Sawyer guided the club from sixth to third. In addition to farm products like Ashburn, Roberts, Ennis, Hamner, and Jones, the team had slugger Dick Sisler (obtained in a deal with the Cardinals), reliever Jim Konstanty (a former pitcher for the Reds and Braves who had worked for Sawyer in Toronto), and first baseman Eddie Waitkus (acquired in a trade with the Cubs). It was Waitkus who raised the most eyebrows—first by leading the club with a .306 average over the first fifty-four games, then by almost getting himself killed. During a mid-June road trip to Chicago, the first baseman received a note at the team hotel from one Ruth Ann Steinhagen asking him to come to her room because it was "important." Waitkus went, knocked on the door, and was met with a .22 caliber bullet in the chest. The bullet penetrated a lung, narrowly missing the spine, and Waitkus remained in critical condition for almost a week. It turned out that the player had never met Steinhagen, that she had developed a long-distance crush on him at Wrigley Field, and had then decided to kill him so nobody else would have him. The woman was placed in an Illinois mental institution.

A number of Philadelphia sportswriters picked the Phillies to win the pennant in 1950, and they were not disappointed. The team's 91 wins represented the most for the franchise since 1916. The greatest contributions came from Ennis (31 homers, a league-leading 126 RBIs), Ashburn (.303), catcher Andy Seminick (24 homers), Roberts (20 wins), and Simmons (17 wins before being drafted in September). But towering over everyone was bullpen ace Konstanty, who was named NL MVP for his 16 victories, 22 saves, and 74 game appearances.

Although the final 1950 standings showed the Phillies finishing ahead of the Dodgers by two games, it was more like two feet. After leading the league comfortably for most of the year, the team went into a swoon in mid-September after losing Simmons to the military and starters Bubba Church and Bob Miller to injuries. By the final day of the regular season at Ebbets Field, Brooklyn was only a single game behind. With the score tied at 1–1 in the bottom of the ninth inning and Dodger runners on second and first with none out, Duke Snider singled to center off Roberts. Charging the hit, Ashburn fired a perfect strike to Seminick to nab what would have been the winning run. The play seemed to calm down Roberts, who then proceeded to get the next two batters on easy popups and sent the contest into the tenth inning. Sisler then hit one of the most dramatic homers in NL history—an opposite-field, three-run shot into the left field seats off Dodger ace Don Newcombe that clinched the pennant.

With Roberts worn out by the season finale, Simmons in military service, and Church and Miller ailing, Sawyer opened the World Series against the Yankees by giving Konstanty his first start of the year. The righthander pitched valiantly, but went down 1–0 to Vic Raschi. Roberts had the same luck the next day, bowing 2–1 to Allie Reynolds in ten innings. With no alternatives, Sawyer called on backup southpaw Ken Heintzelman and then the sore-armed Miller for the next two games, but the results were the same. The sweep by the Yankees marked Philadelphia's last appearance in postseason play for more than a quarter-century.

There were several reasons for the club's slip back to mediocrity (and worse), not least the fact that the 1950 team wasn't of dynastic strength to begin with. Another significant factor was the organization's aversion to signing black players; it was not until 1960 that the club had its first black regular, second baseman Tony Taylor. Also important, Carpenter and aides like Roy Hamey were timid, and not always bright, traders. The only blue-chip players in or approaching their prime to be acquired by the Phillies in the 1950s were catcher Smokey Burgess in 1951 and outfielder Johnny Callison in 1959.

As with all so-so teams, there wasn't much stability at the managerial helm, either. Despite the praise for his efforts in 1950, Sawyer, a college biology instructor in the off-season, had never earned high marks for team chemistry, and the two seasons after the pennant triumph featured one episode after another of stated player dissatisfaction with the manager, Sawyer countercharges that the players were swell-headed or lazy, the imposition of petty rules intended to get the players back into line, and, finally, squabbles among the players themselves. When Carpenter at last decided that the club needed somebody new as field leader, he went to the relatively uninspired choice of AL veteran Steve O'Neill. Next was Mayo Smith, who managed to keep three largely humdrum teams in the middle of the pack before the roof caved in halfway through the 1958 season. His successor for the rest of the decade was the same man who had launched the Phillies into the 1950s so successfully—Sawyer.

Fortunately for the Phillies, there was one development in the decade that kept the franchise out of even murkier waters—the departure of the Athletics for Kansas City after the 1954 season. This not only made the Phillies the only game in town, but also enabled Carpenter to purchase outright Connie Mack Stadium (rebaptized Shibe Park) and get out from under onerous lease conditions. With their ranks swollen by abandoned AL rooters, the always vociferous Philadelphia fans stepped up their virulent booing and hectoring of hometown sluggers they regarded as busts in the clutch. Two of the most prominent victims in the 1950s were Ennis and catcher Stan Lopata; later on, Dick Allen and Mike Schmidt would receive the same treatment.

At first, the 1960s brought little that was new except in the names of the personnel. After watching the team being trashed on opening day in 1960, Sawyer stepped down for the second time, telling reporters that he wasn't up for the job anymore. A couple of days later, Carpenter and general manager John Quinn named Gene Mauch as the new manager. Al-

On April 16, 1959, Dave Philley cracked a record ninth consecutive pinch hit. The first eight had come at the end of the previous season.

though Mauch would become noted in later years for "little ball" tactics that emphasized moving runners along even if that meant sacrificing in the first inning, his patchwork roster in Philadelphia made such refinements a luxury. In 1961, he presided over a twenty-three-game losing streak that set the modern record for futility. When the 1962 club rose to a game above .500, it was in good part because of four 20-plus home run hitters—Callison, Don Demeter, Tony Gonzales, and Roy Sievers. With second baseman Taylor and shortstop Bobby Wine tightening up the middle of the infield, the team improved another six games in 1963, rising to fourth place after five straight years of finishing seventh or eighth. The most consistent pitcher of the period was reliever Jack Baldschun, who was also the staff workhorse.

The 1964 squad had two significant additions—third baseman Allen and pitcher Jim Bunning. Allen, a product of the Phillies' farm system, was the first genuine slugger to arrive on the scene in almost twenty years, demonstrating that in Ennis-like fashion by clouting 29 homers, driving in 91 runs, and leading the league in runs scored with 125 in his first full season. Bunning, acquired in an offseason deal with Detroit, was brought in to anchor the staff, and did just that by winning 19 games. On June 21st, the righthander also pitched the league's first perfect game (against the Mets) since John Montgomery Ward had accomplished the feat for Providence in 1880.

With Allen, Bunning, and Callison (31 homers, 104 RBIs) leading the way, the Phillies broke out to a surprisingly comfortable lead over the rest of the league in August, continuing hot for weeks. But disaster struck in mid-September when the club dropped ten in a row while the Reds reeled off nine straight wins, the Cardinals took eight in a row, and the Giants played almost .800 ball. When St. Louis finally emerged from the heap with the pennant, the Phillies had joined the short list of memorable stretch-drive flops. Mauch was especially criticized for his almost exclusive reliance on Bunning and southpaw Chris Short over the final weeks.

In 1965, the club was once again a distant also-ran despite another 19 wins from Bunning, 18 from Short, and banner production from Allen, Callison,

Footnote Player: Except in one area, Glen Gorbous was an outfielder of modest talents for the Phillies in the 1950s. The exception was his throwing arm, and in 1957 Gorbous responded to a challenge by firing a ball 445' 10" on the fly. There is no recorded instance of anyone throwing a baseball farther.

and first baseman Dick Stuart. But the most publicized slugging of the year took place before a July 3rd game, when Allen and backup outfielder Frank Thomas swapped blows during batting practice over some alleged racial insults. During the game Thomas came off the bench to pinch-hit a home run that evened the score, then returned to the clubhouse to be told that he was being released. The episode was the loudest of many involving Allen with teammates and the front office over reputed racial cracks and attitudes. Matters would deteriorate further when the slugger began taking on owners and front offices with observations such as: "Baseball is a form of slavery. Once you step out of bounds, that's it, they'll do everything possible to destroy your soul." Allen himself, however, showed decreasing concern about the bounds, skipping exhibition games and missing team planes with feeble excuses.

There was a showdown of sorts in June 1969, when manager Bob Skinner, who had taken over from Mauch the previous year, fined the slugger for not showing up for a game against the Mets. When Carpenter first hesitated to collect the money, then rescinded the fine altogether on the grounds that there had been only some kind of "misunderstanding," Skinner submitted his resignation. This only turned Philadelphia's already hostile fans against Allen even more, and prompted the player himself to request a trade.

The deal that did come—in October 1969—was one of the most influential in baseball history. In sending Allen, pitcher Jerry Johnson, and infielder Cookie Rojas to the Cardinals, the Phillies expected to receive in return catcher Tim McCarver, pitcher Joe Hoerner, and outfielders Curt Flood and Byron Browne. But then Flood refused to report, setting in motion the years of legal and union challenges to the reserve clause that would ultimately end with free agency.

The club entered the 1970s under Frank Lucchesi, who managed no better than a fifth-place finish under the new divisional system in his two full years. The brightest moments in the Lucchesi period were April 10, 1971, when the Phillies inaugurated Veterans Stadium with a 4–1 victory over Montreal before a franchise-record crowd of 55,352, and February 5, 1972, when the club obtained Steve Carlton in a straight swap with the Cardinals for Rick Wise.

Over the next fourteen years, Carlton would take four Cy Young awards to go along with five 20-win seasons, an ERA title, and five seasons of leading NL pitchers in strikeouts. His career total of 329 victories left him behind only Warren Spahn for most wins by a lefthander, and his 4,131 strikeouts have been topped only by Nolan Ryan. Carlton's most dominating performance came in 1972, his first year with the Phillies, when he won the pitching Triple Crown of most wins, most strikeouts, and lowest ERA; his 27 victories that season for a last place club represented 45 percent of all the games won by Philadelphia—a proportion unmatched in modern baseball.

After a couple of years of getting only desultory performances from the team on the field and doing little to ease clubhouse tensions (in one incident, outfielder Larry Hisle was criticized for reading books on black history), Lucchesi was replaced by general manager Paul Owens; Owens, in turn, handed the reins over to Danny Ozark for the start of the 1973 season. Aside from Carlton, Ozark inherited shortstop Larry Bowa and power-hitting left fielder Greg Luzinski. In his first year as manager, he added as regulars third baseman Schmidt and catcher Bob Boone.

What Carlton was to the pitchers, Schmidt was to the position players. Arguably the greatest third baseman in major league history, the righthand-hitting slugger compiled 548 homers and set a long list of fielding records during his sixteen-year career, all spent in the Phillies uniform. His feats included leading the league in home runs eight times and in RBIs four times. At Wrigley Field on April 17, 1976, he hit four homers in a single game. He is also one of only three NL players (the others being Stan Musial and Roy Campanella) to win the MVP award three times (in 1980, 1981, and 1986). But for all his accomplishments and durability (a torn rotator cuff in 1988 was his first serious injury), Schmidt could not escape the Veterans Stadium boobirds, and his slumps and strikeouts precipitated relentless torment from the grandstands. Unlike some predecessors like Allen, however, he insisted on being philosophical about the treatment he received from the fans.

Philadelphia's climb to its first Eastern Division win in 1976 was not without incident. Ozark's first three years at the helm produced incessant criticism that he was anything but a strategic genius, that he was content to leave the outcome of most games to the power hitting of Schmidt and Luzinski and the pitching of Carlton and Jim Lonborg. In 1974, the outcries were particularly loud, with some of the players quoted as saying that the team needed either another manager or another power hitter who would make Ozark's job even more mechanical. When even team broadcaster and former star Ashburn began to press Owens and Carpenter, the front office opted for the extra hitter—the redoubtable Allen, reobtained from the Braves. In part because of injuries and in part because of his declining abilities, the slugger was not the Dick Allen of the 1960s, but he did contribute several clutch performances from first base while showing his old flair for what sympathizers called "creative turmoil." For Ozark and the front office, however, there was little of the creative in the player's decision to boycott the division win celebrations in 1976 because the club had failed to include veteran second baseman Tony Taylor on the postseason roster. Although Schmidt and others also protested Taylor's exclusion, it was Allen who paid for the rebellion by being released at the end of the season.

For three straight years, in 1976, 1977, and 1978, the Phillies got to the LCS, and no further. In 1976, the nemesis was the Big Red Machine of Cincinnati, which romped to a three-game sweep. In 1977, the turning point came in the third game against the Dodgers, when aged pinch-hitters Vic Davalillo and Manny Mota struck with two out in the ninth inning of an apparent Philadelphia victory to give Los Angeles the win and grease the way to another Dodger pennant. In 1978, it was the Dodgers again, with the unlikely culprit being Gold Glove center fielder Garry Maddox, whose error sealed a three-out-of-four games win for the California team.

The good news for the franchise despite its three losses in the playoffs was attendance. In 1976, the team drew 2.48 million fans, half a million more than its previous high. Two years later, the total was up to 2.58 million. The bad news was that most of the fans entering the ballpark had joined the press in scoring not just Ozark, but also Owens, for not making the moves geared to getting the club into the World Series.

Then the general manager jumped into the free agent market after the 1978 season and snared the biggest prize of all—Pete Rose. To get the long-time Cincinnati star, the Phillies not only had to compete with several other teams in the NL (primarily the Braves and Pirates), but also had to satisfy Rose's own demand that the final contract make him the highest paid player for any team sport; specifically, that he earn more than David Thompson of the National Basketball Association Denver Nuggets, then

Mike Schmidt's four home runs against the Cubs on April 17, 1976 came in a game in which the Phillies were trailing by the score of 13–2 after four innings. Powered by the Schmidt drives, Philadelphia eventually won the game, 18–16.

It was Mets broadcaster Ralph Kiner who, referring to Garry Maddox's wide range in the outfield, originated the quip that "two-thirds of the world is covered by water and the other one-third by Garry Maddox."

the title holder. Owens and Carpenter fulfilled that condition by offering $3.225 million over four years, but only after local television station WPHL came forward to guarantee $600,000 of the payment per year.

If Philadelphia fans were expecting great things from Rose in 1979, they got them; if they were expecting great things from the team, they were disappointed. While the free agent acquisition batted .331 and had his name on the lineup card for every one of Philadelphia's 163 games (including one tie), the club dropped to fourth place under a wave of injuries. With the team beginning to sleepwalk through the dog days of August, Owens finally pulled the plug on Ozark, replacing him with minor-league operations director Dallas Green. The blisteringly aggressive Green steered the team to 19 wins in its last 30 games and was handed the job for 1980.

Philadelphia's one and only world championship came with only two notable additions—pitchers Bob Walk and Marty Bystrom—made to the 1979 roster. Other pivotal mound performances came from Carlton (24 wins for another Cy Young award), Dick Ruthven (17 wins), and reliever Tug McGraw, who came off the disabled list on July 19th and then turned in a record of 5–1 with 13 saves and an ERA of 0.52. Offensively, Rose provided the spark that had been expected by again appearing in every single game, leading the league in doubles, and aver-

Asked his opinion of playing on the artificial surface at Veterans Stadium, Dick Allen, a horse trainer and breeder at the time, replied: "If horses can't eat it, I don't want to play on it."

It was as a Phillie that Pete Rose passed Stan Musial (on August 10, 1981) for most hits by a NL player and Hank Aaron (on August 14, 1982) for most major league at bats.

aging .282; Schmidt led the league in homers, RBIs, and slugging percentage; and outfielder Bake Mc-Bride batted .309 with a surprising 87 RBIs near the top of the lineup. But while Green went through the year preaching his We-Not-I philosophy, the atmosphere around the club still reeked of a lot of I until early September, when Owens took it upon himself to hold a clubhouse meeting at which he lashed into several players for spending too much time worrying about their own statistics and baring their frustrations to any sportswriter who happened to be handy.

For once, the Phillies were up to the postseason competition. In a dramatic LCS against Houston, the team battled through three extra-inning contests to win in five games, even though only Rose and Manny Trillo among the regulars hit with any consistency. A six-game World Series against the Royals saw Carlton win twice, McGraw save two games, and Schmidt clout a pair of homers and account for seven runs. All but the final game of the Series was a one- or two-run affair.

In 1981, turmoil returned to the team in a big way. To begin with, there was the players strike that forced the split season. In going 34–21 over the first half of the year, the Phillies assured themselves a spot in the pre-playoff playoffs at the end of the season as they doddered along under .500 in August and September.

Mike Schmidt. *Courtesy of the Philadelphia Phillies*

Scheduled postseason appearance or not, Carpenter interpreted the strike as "the final nail in the coffin" of a game he professed no longer able to recognize because of the advent of free agency, and declared his intention of selling the franchise. After delays caused by the player walkout, general partner Bill Giles and the Taft Broadcasting Company of Cincinnati (heirs of the family that had once financed Horace Fogel) bought the organization for an estimated $30 million. What they got for their money immediately was a team that lost the Eastern Division Series to the Expos in five games, with Carlton bowing twice to Montreal ace Steve Rogers. What they also got was a commitment by Owens to stay on as general manager for another five years. What they didn't get was Green, who quit after the season to become general manager of the Cubs. Pat Corrales was named manager for 1982.

Under Corrales, the team made a season-long run at the Cardinals, but ended up three games short. The marquee players were again Rose, Schmidt, and Carlton (whose 23 victories represented the first time in major league history that only one pitcher in baseball won at least 20 games).

With opinion divided in the front office about the real value of the club's chief minor league prospects, Owens and Giles decided to go for broke in 1983 with some Last Hurrah personnel that might get the team into another World Series through sheer diamond experience. Thus, to go along with the 42-year-old Rose, the 38-year-old Carlton, the 38-year-old McGraw, and the 40-year-old reliever Ron Reed, they imported 39-year-old Joe Morgan, 41-year-old Tony Perez, and 40-year-old Bill Robinson. With even Schmidt, Maddox, and outfielder Gary Matthews well into their thirties, it didn't take too long for the club to gain the nickname of the Wheeze Kids. In another gamble, Owens packaged minor league standout Julio Franco along with second baseman Trillo, outfielder George Vukovich, pitcher Jay Baller, and catcher Jerry Willard to Cleveland for outfielder Von Hayes; in the years to come, Hayes would become known to Phillies fans as 5-for-1, especially when he was going bad and came in for the kind of booing that Ennis, Lopata, Allen, and Schmidt had suffered through before him.

In general terms, Owens's gambles paid off. The veteran players did indeed put it together for one more year, with Philadelphia ending up atop the division by six games over Pittsburgh. Some of the details of the win, however, had not been anticipated. For one thing, it was Owens himself who had to win the title when, in July, he heard one criticism too many about Corrales's inability to get along with the veterans and decided to take over in the dugout. On the day he was removed, Corrales actually had the team in first place, and this small particular was not forgotten by players who *had* gotten along with the ousted manager when the Phillies went into a slump shortly afterward. At one point, Owens and Schmidt exchanged barbs in public, with the third baseman complaining that no one knew who the actual manager was because Owens depended completely on his coaches.

As the season wore on, however, the feuding died out, especially when Morgan awoke from a first-half slumber and righthander John Denny stepped up a 19-win pace that would earn him the Cy Young nod. In September, the club marched through the NL with a 22–7 record, fully vindicating Owens's contention that the veterans would get better in the stretch. Aside from Denny and Carlton (15 wins), the strongest pitching came from southpaw Al Holland, who took over from McGraw and Reed as the ace of the bullpen and posted 25 saves.

The veterans remained dominant in the LCS against the Dodgers, with Carlton winning twice and Matthews clouting three homers and driving in eight runs in a four-game series. In the World Series against Baltimore, however, the club went down in five games.

In view of the one-year plan with which he had entered 1983, Owens surprised nobody by clearing the decks shortly after the end of the World Series. Whether through outright releases, trades, or decisions not to renew contracts, he got rid of Rose, Morgan, Perez, Matthews, Bob Dernier, and Reed. Much more difficult was finding suitable replacements, and for the most part he didn't. The Phillies slumped to fourth place with an even .500 record. The main reasons were an atrocious defense, listless hitting from the first base and outfield positions, and an injury to Denny. Although Holland had 29 saves again, only four of them came in August and September. One of the worst fielders was rookie second baseman Juan Samuel, who atoned for some of his glove work with the first of four straight years in which he attained double figures in steals, doubles, triples, and homers; on the other hand, Samuel also launched a four-year string of leading the NL in strikeouts. At the end of the season, Owens announced his resignation as manager and went back upstairs to concentrate on being general manager; John Felske took over as pilot for 1985.

For the rest of the decade, the Phillies had only one season (1986) of winning more than losing, and even that second-place finish left them 21½ games behind the steamrolling Mets. It was for the most part a period of swan songs, with Carlton being released in 1986, Maddox retiring the same year, and Schmidt coming to the end in May 1989. Felske, who often seemed embarrassingly outmanaged by his counterpart in the opposition dugout, lasted about sixty games into 1987, when he was replaced by Lee Elia. Elia hung on through one 1988 change of general managers from Owens to Woody Woodward, but was then fired in September after Woodward was derricked for Lee Thomas and the latter brought in a former Cardinal associate, Nick Leyva, to take over. Another executive suite change came in 1986, when Giles bought out the Taft interests.

The organization entered the 1990s with very few arrows in its quiver. Its best position player was center fielder Lenny Dykstra, obtained in a 1989 trade with the Mets for Samuel. But after almost becoming the first Philadelphia player since Ashburn in 1958 to win a batting title in 1990, Dykstra went through a horrendous 1991—first being put on probation for a year for associating with gamblers, then almost losing his life in a May car crash caused by drunk driving, then, after months on the disabled list, coming back only to break his collarbone and sit out what remained of the season.

In 1991, Thomas replaced Leyva with Jim Fregosi, regarded as more adept at handling the team's young pitching staff. Although the team did not break .500, it did manage to finish ahead of the Cubs and Mets, both of which had been cited as superior clubs. The general manager was the first one to attribute the surprise showing to Fregosi's patience with starters Terry Mulholland, Jose DeJesus, and Tommy Greene. Both Mulholland and Greene threw no-hitters.

Nineteen ninety-two was another step back, with Dykstra and Greene spending great chunks of time on the disabled list and DeJesus missing the season altogether with a rotator cuff injury. Well into August, first baseman John Kruk appeared to have the batting title in his sights, but then shoulder injuries did him in. The positive notes of the year were sounded by catcher Darren Daulton, who clouted 27 homers and drove in a league-leading 109 runs, third baseman Dave Hollins, who belted another 27 roundtrippers, and righthander Curt Schilling, who came over in a trade with the Astros to pace the starters with 14 wins and an ERA of 2.35.

In the 1992–93 off-season, Thomas's biggest move was to obtain southpaw Danny Jackson from the Marlins in a deal worked out following the expansion draft.

PHILADELPHIA PHILLIES

Annual Standings and Managers

Year	Position	W	L	Pct.	GB	Managers
1883	Eighth	17	81	.173	46	Bob Ferguson, Blondie Purcell
1884	Sixth	39	73	.348	45	Harry Wright
1885	Third	56	54	.509	30	Harry Wright
1886	Fourth	71	43	.623	14	Harry Wright
1887	Second	75	48	.610	3½	Harry Wright
1888	Third	69	61	.531	14½	Harry Wright
1889	Fourth	63	64	.496	20½	Harry Wright
1890	Third	78	54	.591	9½	Harry Wright
1891	Fourth	68	69	.496	18½	Harry Wright
1892	Third	46	30	.605	7	Harry Wright
	Fifth	41	36	.532	12½	Harry Wright
1893	Fourth	72	57	.558	14	Harry Wright
1894	Fourth	71	57	.555	18	Art Irwin
1895	Third	78	53	.595	9½	Art Irwin
1896	Eighth	62	68	.477	28½	Billy Nash
1897	Tenth	55	77	.417	38	George Stallings
1898	Sixth	78	71	.523	24	George Stallings, Bill Shettsline
1899	Third	94	58	.618	9	Bill Shettsline
1900	Third	75	63	.543	8	Bill Shettsline
1901	Second	83	57	.593	7½	Bill Shettsline
1902	Seventh	56	81	.409	46	Bill Shettsline
1903	Seventh	49	86	.363	39½	Chief Zimmer
1904	Eighth	52	100	.342	53½	Hugh Duffy
1905	Fourth	83	69	.546	21½	Hugh Duffy
1906	Fourth	71	82	.464	45½	Hugh Duffy
1907	Third	83	64	.565	21½	Billy Murray
1908	Fourth	83	71	.539	16	Billy Murray
1909	Fifth	74	79	.484	36½	Billy Murray
1910	Fourth	78	75	.510	25½	Red Dooin
1911	Fourth	79	73	.520	19½	Red Dooin
1912	Fifth	73	79	.480	30½	Red Dooin
1913	Second	88	63	.583	12½	Red Dooin
1914	Sixth	74	80	.481	20½	Red Dooin
1915	First	90	62	.592	+7	Pat Moran
1916	Second	91	62	.595	2½	Pat Moran
1917	Second	87	65	.572	10	Pat Moran
1918	Sixth	55	68	.447	26	Pat Moran
1919	Eighth	47	90	.343	47½	Jack Coombs, Gavvy Cravath
1920	Eighth	62	91	.405	30½	Gavvy Cravath
1921	Eighth	51	103	.331	43½	Bill Donovan, Kaiser Wilhelm
1922	Seventh	57	96	.373	35½	Kaiser Wilhelm
1923	Eighth	50	104	.325	45½	Art Fletcher
1924	Seventh	55	96	.364	37	Art Fletcher
1925	Sixth*	68	85	.444	27	Art Fletcher
1926	Eighth	58	93	.384	29½	Art Fletcher
1927	Eighth	51	103	.331	43	Stuffy McInnis
1928	Eighth	43	109	.283	51	Burt Shotton
1929	Fifth	71	82	.464	27½	Burt Shotton
1930	Eighth	52	102	.338	40	Burt Shotton

1931	Sixth	66	88	.429	35	Burt Shotton
1932	Fourth	78	76	.506	12	Burt Shotton
1933	Seventh	60	92	.395	31	Burt Shotton
1934	Seventh	56	93	.376	37	Jimmie Wilson
1935	Seventh	64	89	.418	35½	Jimmie Wilson
1936	Eighth	54	100	.351	38	Jimmie Wilson
1937	Seventh	61	92	.399	34½	Jimmie Wilson
1938	Eighth	45	105	.300	43	Jimmie Wilson, Hans Lobert
1939	Eighth	45	106	.298	50½	Doc Prothro
1940	Eighth	50	103	.327	50	Doc Prothro
1941	Eighth	43	111	.279	57	Doc Prothro
1942	Eighth	42	109	.278	62½	Hans Lobert
1943	Seventh	64	90	.416	41	Bucky Harris, Freddie Fitzsimmons
1944	Eighth	61	92	.399	43½	Freddie Fitzsimmons
1945	Eighth	46	108	.299	52	Freddie Fitzsimmons, Ben Chapman
1946	Fifth	69	85	.448	28	Ben Chapman
1947	Seventh*	62	92	.403	32	Ben Chapman
1948	Sixth	66	88	.429	25½	Ben Chapman, Dusty Cooke, Eddie Sawyer
1949	Third	81	73	.526	16	Eddie Sawyer
1950	First	91	63	.591	+2	Eddie Sawyer
1951	Fifth	73	81	.474	23½	Eddie Sawyer
1952	Fourth	87	67	.565	9½	Eddie Sawyer, Steve O'Neill
1953	Third*	83	71	.539	22	Steve O'Neill
1954	Fourth	75	79	.487	22	Steve O'Neill, Terry Moore
1955	Fourth	77	77	.500	21½	Mayo Smith
1956	Fifth	71	83	.461	22	Mayo Smith
1957	Fifth	77	77	.500	19	Mayo Smith
1958	Eighth	69	85	.448	23	Mayo Smith, Eddie Sawyer
1959	Eighth	64	90	.416	23	Eddie Sawyer
1960	Eighth	59	95	.383	36	Eddie Sawyer, Andy Cohen, Gene Mauch
1961	Eighth	47	107	.305	46	Gene Mauch
1962	Seventh	81	80	.503	20	Gene Mauch
1963	Fourth	87	75	.537	12	Gene Mauch
1964	Second*	92	70	.568	1	Gene Mauch
1965	Sixth	85	76	.528	11½	Gene Mauch
1966	Fourth	87	75	.537	8	Gene Mauch
1967	Fifth	82	80	.506	19½	Gene Mauch
1968	Seventh*	76	86	.469	21	Gene Mauch, George Myatt, Bob Skinner
1969	Fifth	63	99	.389	37	Bob Skinner, George Myatt
1970	Fifth	73	88	.453	15½	Frank Lucchesi
1971	Sixth	67	95	.414	30	Frank Lucchesi
1972	Sixth	59	97	.378	37½	Frank Lucchesi, Paul Owens
1973	Sixth	71	91	.438	11½	Danny Ozark
1974	Third	80	82	.494	8	Danny Ozark
1975	Second	86	76	.531	6½	Danny Ozark
1976	First	101	61	.623	+9	Danny Ozark
1977	First	101	61	.623	+5	Danny Ozark
1978	First	90	72	.556	+1½	Danny Ozark
1979	Fourth	84	78	.519	14	Danny Ozark, Dallas Green
1980	First	91	71	.562	+1	Dallas Green
1981	First	34	21	.618	+1½	Dallas Green
	Third	25	27	.487	4½	Dallas Green
1982	Second	89	73	.549	3	Pat Corrales
1983	First	90	72	.556	+6	Pat Corrales, Paul Owens

1984	Fourth	81	81	.500	15½	Paul Owens
1985	Fifth	75	87	.463	26	John Felske
1986	Second	86	75	.534	21½	John Felske
1987	Fourth*	80	82	.494	15	John Felske, Lee Elia
1988	Sixth	65	96	.404	35½	Lee Elia, John Vukovich
1989	Sixth	67	95	.414	26	Nick Leyva
1990	Fourth*	77	85	.475	18	Nick Leyva
1991	Third	78	84	.481	20	Nick Leyva, Jim Fregosi
1992	Sixth	70	92	.432	26	Jim Fregosi

*Tie

Postseason Play

LCS	0–3 versus Cincinnati	1976	WS	1–4 versus Boston	1915
	1–3 versus Los Angeles	1977		0–4 versus New York	1950
	1–3 versus Los Angeles	1978		4–2 versus Kansas City	1980
	3–2 versus Houston	1980		1–4 versus Baltimore	1983
	3–1 versus Los Angeles	1983			

Philadelphia Keystones

Union Association, 1884   **BALLPARK:** KEYSTONE PARK

RECORD: 21–46 (.313)

Backed by Thomas Pratt and William Shettsline, the Union Association Keystones were simply outclassed in the crowded Philadelphia market that already included teams in both the National League and the American Association. Although the NL Phillies and the AA Athletics finished sixth and seventh in their respective leagues, the Keystones, a feckless collection of rookies and castoffs, attracted almost no interest from the public.

Left fielder Buster Hoover led the team with a .364 batting average. Jersey Bakely, the regular pitcher, led the UA with 30 losses. Only rookie southpaw catcher Jack Clements went on to a solid career, mostly with the Phillies.

The Keystones lasted until early August, when, having failed to win even a third of their games and $10,000 in the red, they folded. Several players were signed by the Phillies, and the Wilmington Quicksteps were recruited from the Eastern League to complete the Keystones' schedule.

PHILADELPHIA KEYSTONES

Annual Standings and Managers

Year	Position	W	L	Pct.	GB	Managers
1884	Partial	21	46	.313	—	Fergy Malone, Tom Pratt

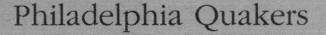

Philadelphia Quakers

Players League, 1890   **BALLPARK:** FOREPAUGH PARK

RECORD: 68–63 (.519)

With both National League and American Association clubs already operating in Philadelphia, the creation of the Quakers was a strategic error on the part of the Players League: There just wasn't room for three teams in the city.

Chief investor J. M. Vanderslice and player representative George Wood, who jumped from the AA Athletics and played left field, recruited a squad with a decidedly Philadelphia flavor. Third baseman Joe Mulvey came from the Athletics with Wood. First baseman Sid Farrar, right fielder Jim Fogarty, and pitchers Ben Sanders and Charlie Buffinton came from the NL Phillies. Fogarty and Buffinton also managed the team, with the outfielder giving way to the pitcher after only sixteen games.

In March, Phillies' President John Rogers sued to prevent utilityman Bill Hallman from joining the team. He was rebuffed by Judge M. Russell Thayer, who took exception to the lack of mutuality in a contract that essentially tied a player to a club for as long as the club desired but that, once a player's

services were no longer desired, allowed his employer to dismiss him on ten days' notice. Thayer released Hallman from any obligation to the Phillies in a major setback for the champions of the reserve clause.

Despite both their legal triumphs and the .322 average and 10 home runs of shortstop Bill Shindle, the Quakers were on the verge of collapse when they were rescued in July by minority shareholders J. Earl and George Wagner, local meat wholesalers. The Wagners blew hot and cold about a compromise with the NL: At first they opposed any deal, but, when it became clear that the PL was finished, they settled for an opportunity to run a new Philadelphia franchise in the AA.

> **S**hortstop Bill Shindle's 115 errors for the Quakers in 1890 is the most ever made by any player at any position in one major league season.

PHILADELPHIA QUAKERS

Annual Standings and Managers

Year	Position	W	L	Pct.	GB	Managers
1890	Fifth	68	63	.519	14	Jim Fogarty, Charlie Buffinton

Philadelphia Athletics

American League,   **BALLPARKS:** COLUMBIA PARK (1901–1908)
1901–1954   SHIBE PARK (1909–1954)

RECORD: 3886–4248 (.478)

No other twentieth-century major league franchise has been as nearly the work of one man as the Athletics were of Cornelius McGilicuddy. Through fifty years as manager and fifty-four as at least part-owner, Connie Mack, as he came to be known, won nine pennants, more than any other American

Connie Mack flicks the scorecard that was his main strategic weapon in running a ball game. *National Baseball Library, Cooperstown, NY*

League club except the Yankees during the period; he also finished last seventeen times as manager and eighteen overall, one of every three years of the club's existence. A major organizer of the AL, Mack outlived almost all of his contemporaries to become Mr. Mack to his players and The Grand Old Man of Baseball to columnists.

> **C**onnie Mack was never ejected from a game in his fifty years as Athletics manager.

Mack threw his lot in with what would become the American League in 1897, when he took over the Milwaukee franchise of Ban Johnson's minor Western League. In 1901, when Johnson decided to challenge the National League, Mack was given $50,000 and a mandate to establish an AL club in Philadelphia. He spent $35,000 of the amount on a parcel of land surrounded by breweries and built Columbia Park, a 12,000-seat, single-deck, wooden grandstand. (His difficulties in finding a suitable location had prompted John McGraw to predict that "The Athletics will be the white elephants of the league," sug-

gesting the team emblem that would endure for its entire history.) Mack himself owned 25 percent of the franchise, with the largest share (50 percent) belonging to Ben Shibe, a partner of A.J. Reach, the sporting goods manufacturer and a major stockholder in the NL Phillies. The final 25 percent was divided between Frank Hough, sports editor of the Philadelphia *Inquirer*, and Sam Jones of the Associated Press Philadelphia bureau.

Mack's biggest surprise for the inaugural 1901 season was the signing of Phillies' star second baseman Nap Lajoie, who jumped leagues for more money. Lajoie collected three hits in the Athletics' first game on April 26, 1901, a 5–1 defeat at the hands of the Washington Senators. The game attracted 10,524 fans, while the Phillies were drawing a mere 779 for their home opener. It was a portent of things to come, with the fourth-place A's outdrawing their second-place city rivals for the season by a count of 206,329 to 112,066. Lajoie fulfilled the promise of the first game by establishing the AL batting record (.422) and completing the Triple Crown by leading in homers (14) and RBIs (125); he also set the pace in hits (219), doubles (48), and runs scored (145). The pitching was handled by Chick Fraser (22–16) and Bill Bernhard (17–10), both of whom had accompanied Lajoie in bolting the Phillies, and rookie Eddie Plank (17–11). Plank, who was elected to the Hall of Fame in 1946, was the first lefthander to win 300 games; he pitched for seventeen years, fourteen of them for Mack, winning 20 or more seven times, and finished his career with a 327–193 record.

The franchise's first major crisis occurred when Phillies' owner John Rogers sought an injunction to prevent Lajoie from playing for the Athletics. After losing in a lower court, Rogers appealed to the Pennsylvania State Supreme Court, which, two days before the opening of the 1902 season, handed down a decision that barred the second baseman from playing in the state of Pennsylvania for anyone but the Phillies. Mack, who had already gone back to the

> **W**hen third baseman Lave Cross jumped to the Athletics in 1901, he became the only player in history to wear the uniforms of teams in four different leagues in the same city: Cross had earlier played for Philadelphia clubs in the American Association (1889 and 1891), the Players League (1890), and the National League (1892–97).

Phillies to lure away outfielder Elmer Flick and pitcher Bill Duggleby, ultimately had to agree to a Johnson proposal to send Bernhard, Lajoie, and Flick to Cleveland, where the two hitters went on to Hall of Fame careers. Duggleby and Fraser scurried back to the Phillies. Franchise losses on the year also included rookie righthander Christy Mathewson, who, six weeks after signing with the Athletics, thought better of switching leagues and returned to the Giants.

To fill the new holes, Mack dipped into the minor leagues for second baseman Danny Murphy, who, in his first game for the A's on July 8th went 6-for-6; with his .313, Murphy was one of six regulars to bat over .300 for the season. Right fielder Socks Seybold also led the AL with 16 homers, a league high until Babe Ruth hit 29 in 1919. But what gave Mack his first pennant was the arrival on July 26 of Rube Waddell to back up Plank (20–15). A professional alligator wrestler in the offseason, the southpaw was childlike and frustrating to managers, but he possessed a blazing fastball and superior curve. Mack, who hired him from a Los Angeles minor league team called the Looloos for $400 a month, handled the pitcher gently, assigning someone to prevent him from chasing after fire engines, doling out money a bit at a time to undercut a penchant for wild spending, and indulging Waddell's predilection for disappearing for days at a time to go fishing. The result was a 24–7 record and a league-leading 210 strikeouts that lifted the Athletics from fourth to first. A favorite of the fans, Waddell went on to three more 20-plus seasons and six consecutive league-leading totals in strikeouts. He entered the Hall of Fame along with Plank in 1946.

In 1903, the staff gained a third Hall of Fame pitcher, Chief Bender, a graduate of Carlisle Indian School who compiled a 210–127 lifetime record and a 2.46 ERA in fifteen seasons. He was installed in Cooperstown in 1953. Still, despite 20-win seasons from all three hurlers, the A's slipped to second, 14½ games behind Boston. The 1904 season, in which the A's fell further, to fifth, was memorable for two reasons: Waddell struck out 349 batters, a twentieth-century mark that endured until 1965, and first baseman Harry Davis led the AL in homers for the first of four consecutive seasons with a total of 10.

The 1905 season brought Mack his second pennant and the first of three World Series matchups with McGraw's Giants. The flag came largely on the strength of Waddell's league-leading 26 victories and 1.48 ERA, Plank's 25–12 record, a 20–7 contribution by rookie Andy Coakley, and Bender's 16 wins. The World Series promised a matchup of baseball's best, Waddell and Mathewson, but it never happened because the lefthander injured his shoulder in a playful train-station tussle with Coakley over the latter's straw hat. Mathewson went on to hurl three shutouts against the A's, Joe McGinnity threw a fourth, and the Athletics' only win came in a 3–0 effort by Bender in the second game.

Mack spent the next few years patching and then rebuilding his aging team. In 1906, Eddie Collins appeared in six games, using the alias Eddie Sullivan, because he was still a student at Columbia University and in violation of intercollegiate rules. Collins eventually played in the major leagues for twenty-five years en route to the Hall of Fame (in 1939) on the strength of a .333 lifetime average, 3,311 hits, and 743 stolen bases.

Toward the end of the 1907 season, Waddell, whose antics had become more violent and more alcohol-affected, blew a 7–1 lead in a crucial late-September game with the Tigers. When the A's lost the pennant to Detroit by a game and a half, Mack had had enough. Despite his often-repeated claim that a close, second-place finish was more profitable than a pennant because the runner-up's crowds would be just as large as the winner's while its players' salary demands would be lower, the manager packed Waddell off to the Browns. He was far more reluctant to part with Shoeless Joe Jackson, the best hitter outside the Hall of Fame, but had little choice when the slugging outfielder, who loathed Philadelphia and who had been taunted by teammates for his rural manners, returned to his native South Carolina after only a few games in 1909. Jackson was traded to Cleveland for outfielder Bris Lord, a lifetime .256 hitter, in one of the most one-sided deals in history.

The opening of Shibe Park on April 26, 1909 was marred by the collapse of catcher Mike Powers, following his crash into a wall in pursuit of a pop-up. The catcher, who died following surgery, was baseball's first onfield fatality.

In 1909, Mack unveiled Shibe Park and the beginnings of his One Hundred Thousand Dollar Infield. The new stadium, built to seat 20,000, at a cost of $500,000, was the first steel and concrete baseball facility. After a few false starts, The One Hundred Thousand Dollar Infield began to take shape after Collins was moved permanently to second base and Murphy shifted to right field. Jack Barry took over at shortstop early in the season and formed, with Collins, the most impressive middle infield in the AL. Frank Baker was installed at third, where he would remain for six years, leading the AL in homers in his final four Philadelphia seasons, adding league-leading totals in RBIs twice; his .313 average and timely power hitting over fourteen seasons won him a Cooperstown plaque in 1955.

John Kull was baseball perfection. Debuting in relief for the 1909 Athletics, the righthander not only gained a victory, but singled in his only turn at bat. Kull never appeared in another big league game, so he retired with pitching and batting marks of 1.000.

The young A's, who finished second in 1909, were hardly brawlers by the standards of the day, but they were involved in their fair share of onfield incidents. On August 24th in a game with first-place Detroit, Ty Cobb spiked Baker on the arm as the third baseman reached across his body for a bare-handed tag. Baker stayed in the game with a bandaged arm, but Mack, in one of his few public outbursts, accused Cobb of being "the dirtiest player in history."

In 1910, the A's matured from a good team into a great one, winning 102 games and finishing 14½ games ahead of second-place New York. Collins (.322) led the hitters, but Plank (16–10) and Bender (23–5) gave way to a new ace, Jack Coombs, whose 31–9 mark led the AL and whose 13 shutouts are still an AL record. Continuing the roll in the World Series, the A's wiped out the Chicago Cubs in five games: Collins hit .429, Baker .409, and Coombs won three games.

Footnote Player: Earle Mack was the first major leaguer to have his father for a manager. The younger Mack appeared in five games over three seasons (1910, 1911, and 1914) as a catcher, first baseman, and third baseman, collecting 2 hits in 16 at bats for a .125 average.

The 1911 season was a replay of 1910. The One Hundred Thousand Dollar Infield was completed when Stuffy McInnis, one of the best fielding first basemen of all time, took over in June for the aging Davis and hit .321. Collins, at .365, again led the team

and Baker (.334) led the AL in homers with 11 and drove in 115 runs. The front line mound trio— Coombs (28–12), repeating as the AL leader in wins; Plank (23–8); and Bender (17–5)—once more dominated the league, enabling the A's to finish 13½ games ahead of the Tigers. In the World Series, the A's took their revenge on the Giants in a six-game victory. The Big Three, who did all the pitching, posted a joint 1.29 ERA, and Bender and Coombs each beat old nemesis Mathewson. Baker hit .375 to lead the club and earned his nickname, Home Run, with two timely clouts—the first a two-run shot to break a 1–1 tie in Game Two, the second a ninth-inning solo shot to tie Game Three (eventually won by the Athletics). The Series was prolonged when catcher Jack Lapp didn't notice that the Giants' Larry Doyle had missed the plate while sliding past the catcher with the winning run in the bottom of the tenth of Game Five, but the A's clinched matters the next day anyway.

The 1912 team, which Mack considered the best of the decade, won 90 games, but it finished third, well behind Boston and Washington. Plank was the big winner at 26–6, while the club led the league in hitting for the third consecutive year. The return to pennant-winning form in 1913 was the result of an outfield revitalized by rookies Jimmy Walsh and Eddie Murphy, both purchased from the International League Baltimore Orioles, which became a major supplier of talent for Philadelphia over the years. A corps of young hurlers, including Joe Bush and Bob Shawkey, allowed Mack to use Plank and Bender increasingly in relief. Collins (.345), Baker (.336), and McInnis (.326) again provided the offense; Baker added a second league-leading total in RBIs (126) to his third homer title (12). The team then rolled to a five-game World Series victory over the Giants. Baker hit a game-winning homer in the final contest, batting .450 with 7 RBIs for the Series.

After Mack's third pennant in four years, owner Frank Farrell offered him the managerial reins of the Yankees. As a counter-offer, Shibe provided his manager with the 25 percent of the A's stock that had been held by sportswriters Hough and Jones, raising him to a full partner.

The tedium of winning set in the following year. The statistics were still there: Collins batted .344 and won the Chalmers award as the AL's most valuable player; Baker and McInnis both hit over .300; Baker's 9 homers led the league once again; the team topped the AL in batting for the fifth consecutive season and scored 749 runs, 134 more than the next best total; and seven pitchers won in double figures. Mack, however, claimed that the team had lost its drive; finishing 8½ games in front of the pack was no feat, as he saw it, because the A's were so much better than the rest of the AL. The fans recognized, and returned, the indifference; the turnstiles at Shibe Park clicked only 346,641 times, the lowest total since 1901 and almost 330,000 fewer than in the second-place 1909 season. Mack ended what he later called "my unhappiest season" by being swept by the Miracle Braves in the World Series.

The root of the manager's unhappiness was money. The malaise of winning had increased salaries and decreased attendance. With the outbreak of the Federal League war, it was necessary to pay out even more to keep players from defecting. Mack was also deeply embittered by the fact that the chief FL recruiter hovering over the team was former second baseman Murphy. Unable even to approach FL offers for some players, he dispatched them elsewhere, asking waivers on Plank and Bender and selling Collins to the White Sox for $50,000. For a long time, Baker was indecisive about returning to Philadelphia, going to the Feds, or retiring to his Maryland farm; he finally chose the farm. Mack later asserted that he was "disgusted and discouraged with the lot of them."

Despite all the departures, Mack insisted that he was not breaking up the team. Half of the infield was still intact, and there was a pack of young pitchers. While he had to turn down an opportunity to buy southpaw Babe Ruth from the International League Orioles because of a cash shortage, the manager did sign the 39-year-old Lajoie to replace Collins. But it was all an illusion. Lajoie had lost his grace afield, tying an AL record of five errors in one game, and batted only .280. By May, the Athletics were in seventh place, and Mack the salesman went to work. Barry went to the Red Sox for only $8,000, Shawkey to the Yankees for $18,000, Eddie Murphy to the White Sox for $13,500, and Herb Pennock and his Hall of Fame arm to the Red Sox for the waiver price. The result for the Athletics was the first of seven consecutive last-place seasons, 58½ games behind Boston, the deepest the team would ever sink into the cellar. Attendance dropped to a franchise low of 146,223. Fifty-six players, a major league record, contributed to the effort.

If the 1915 A's were bad, the 1916 club was one of the worst ever. The club should have expected as much in spring training, when hunchbacked batboy Louis Van Zelt, hired as a good luck charm, died. Despairing of Baker's ever returning, Mack sold the third baseman to the Yankees for $37,500 in February. Shortstop Whitey Witt made 78 errors. Third base-man Charlie Pick had an .899 fielding average, the last below-.900 performance by a regular for sixty-three years. Despite a 3.47 ERA, Jack Nabors posted a 1–20 record for the worst one–season won-lost percentage (.048) in history; right behind was roommate Tom Sheehan at 1–16 (3.69). To plug the holes left by injuries, Mack paraded collegians, semi-pros, amateurs, even high school boys onto and off the roster. The net result: a 36–117 record for a .235 won-lost percentage, the lowest of the twentieth century.

More of the same followed—55–98 (.359) in 1917 and 52–76 (.406) in the war-shortened 1918 season. In December 1917, Wally Schang, Amos Strunk, and Bush went to the Red Sox for three unknowns and $60,000. The following month, McInnis followed, only this time Mack collected three serviceable players—third baseman Larry Gardner, catcher Forrest Cady, and outfielder Tilly Walker, who tied Ruth for the league lead in homers with 11. The other bright spots were first baseman George Burns's .352 average and Scott Perry's 21–19 record. But Perry's presence also created a dispute with the Boston Braves that changed press perception of Mack from The Tall Tactician to The Slim Schemer.

The Braves owned the rights to Perry's contract even though he had never played a game for them, preferring to play in an independent league until Mack purchased him from Atlanta, the same club that had earlier sold the pitcher to Boston. After Perry started winning, the Braves claimed their rights. While the National Commission sided with the Braves, Mack secured an injunction barring Perry from playing for anyone but him. The NL was incensed at Mack, both for refusing to accept a compromise in which the Browns would have accepted another player and for resorting to legal action. The issue was resolved only when NL president John Tener threatened to boycott the 1918 World Series, NL owners refused to back him for fear of creating a new war between the leagues, Tener resigned, and John Heydler took over as head of the league. It was Heydler who persuaded Mack to pay the Braves $2,500 and withdraw the lawsuit.

Mack underlined his scheming image at the end of the 1918 season when he joined the owners in releasing every player on his roster, giving only the required ten days' notice. All the owners had agreed not to sign anyone else's players, so the collusion saved an overall $200,000 in salaries. Mack, who at the beginning of the season had asked his players to accept a profit-sharing plan in exchange for lower salaries, came off looking even more niggardly than most, especially after he publicly defended the mass release by announcing that "It was only natural that we should enter into an agreement to protect our interests."

On March 1, 1919, Mack made one of his infrequent forays into the trade market, sending outfielder Charlie Jamieson and two other players to Cleveland for outfielder Braggo Roth; Jamieson went on to an eighteen-year, .303 career, while Roth failed to finish the season in Philadelphia.

After two more basement finishes, some of the elements of the next great Athletics team began to appear. Jimmy Dykes, who had been around since 1918, displayed the versatility that enabled him to play every infield position and the outfield in his twenty-two years, fifteen of them with the Athletics. Rookie first baseman Joe Hauser broke in with a .323 average and, two years later, would hit 27 homers; Hauser would not be a part of the powerhouse A's at the end of the decade only because one of his knees cracked in spring training in 1925 and the other during the 1927 season. The team showed a modest improvement to seventh place, largely on the strength of kunckleballer Ed Rommel's league-leading 27 wins, and the team total of 111 homers, also an AL high.

Sharing in the general prosperity of the 1920s, Mack began to buy the players who would push the A's beyond respectability to dominance. The biggest purchase resulted in the biggest flop, however; in 1924 Mack laid out $40,000 for outfielder Paul Strand, who had hit .394 with 43 homers and 187 RBIs for Salt Lake City. When Strand brought his bat down from the mountain air of Utah, his statistics descended to earth as well. Outfielder Bill Lamar's .330 average in 1924 and .356 in 1925 were more what Mack was looking for, but he could have done without Lamar's Broadway Bill image and behavior that caused him to be unloaded in 1928. More permanent was the presence of second baseman Max Bishop, a .271 lifetime hitter acquired from the IL Orioles, who walked almost as often as he got a hit. Also arriving in 1924 was outfielder Al Simmons, who was purchased from Milwaukee and who made an immediate impression with his .308 average despite a foot-in-the-bucket swing that prompted Mark to proclaim that anyone who hit like Simmons "could stand on his head if he wants." The outfielder played twenty big league seasons and hit for a .334 average, including batting crowns in 1930 (.381) and 1931 (.390); he also clouted 307 home runs en route to the Hall of Fame in 1953.

In 1925, Mack's program for improvement went into high gear. First, he doubledecked Shibe Park and added left field bleachers. Then, to fill the seats, he acquired three future Hall of Famers from the minor leagues. Perhaps the greatest catcher of all time, Mickey Cochrane proved worth the $50,000 paid to Portland when he hit .320 over a thirteen-year career. Though he never led the league in a major category, Cochrane reached highs of .357 in 1930 and 23 homers and 118 RBIs in 1932. Twice the winner of the AL award for Most Valuable Player, he entered Cooperstown in 1942.

Jimmie Foxx, a 17-year-old catcher-third baseman recommended by former third baseman Baker, took a few seasons to find his way to first base, but once he did, he became the most prodigious right-handed slugger of his time, swatting 534 homers with a .325 average in twenty seasons. His 58 round-trippers in 1932 (later tied by Hank Greenberg) set the record for righties; he also led the AL five times in slugging, three times in RBIs, and twice in batting, as well as on three other occasions in homers. The winner of three MVP awards, Foxx entered Cooperstown in 1951.

On June 15th, the lineup Mack had been assembling showed the sort of damage it could do when the A's overcame a 15–4 deficit, scoring 13 runs in the bottom of the eighth off a shell-shocked Cleveland pitching staff, to tie the major league record for the greatest comeback. But even with an offense that could generate this kind of firepower, the Athletics of the late 1920s were a club built primarily on pitching. The backbone of the staff was Lefty Grove, purchased for $100,000, the highest amount paid for a minor league player to that time, in what was the culmination of Mack's use of Jack Dunn's International League Baltimore Orioles as a substitute for a farm system. As irascible as he was overpowering, Grove went into the Hall of Fame in 1947, after seventeen seasons in which he compiled a 300–141 lifetime record and a 3.06 ERA. Among his other feats were leading the AL in strikeouts in his first seven seasons, in ERA nine times, in won-lost percentage five times, in wins four times, and even in saves once.

In 1926, Mack took a big bite out of the Pennsylvania blue laws prohibiting Sunday baseball. Noting that a municipal fair to mark the 150th anniversary of the Declaration of Independence was allowed to remain open on Sundays and seeing little difference between a fair and a baseball game, he got an injunction prohibiting the police department from foiling his plans and played a game with the White Sox on Sunday, August 22nd. The following year, after the Pennsylvania State Supreme Court had upheld the ban, Mack and the Shibe family bought land in Camden, New Jersey and made tentative plans to pull up stakes and move across the Delaware River. The Pennsylvania legislature quickly stepped in and made Sunday ball a local option; municipal officials vacillated for eight years before finally making Philadelphia the last AL city to permit Sunday contests. The A's played their first legal Sunday game on April 22, 1934, losing to Washington 4–3.

The 1927 team boasted seven future Hall of Famers on the roster. In addition to those already on the club, Collins returned as a backup infielder and outfielder Zach Wheat came over from Brooklyn for his last season. Most prominently, Cobb, having survived accusations of fixing games, was signed for $40,000 after his release by the Tigers. But despite winning 91 games, the club finished 19 games behind the Murderers Row Yankees.

In 1928, Mack still had seven Cooperstown-bound players (Tris Speaker came aboard, replacing Wheat), but this time he tried a different approach. Collins barely played at all; Cobb and Speaker played limited roles. The more youthful Mule Haas, acquired from Atlanta, moved to center field, and Bing Miller went to right. With the acquisition of George Earnshaw from cooperative Baltimore to provide righthanded balance for Grove, the A's endured a second consecutive second-place finish, this time with 98 wins, only 2½ games behind the Yankees.

For the next three years, Philadelphia rolled over the rest of the AL, winning 313 games and finishing first by margins of 18, 8, and 13½ games. Mack, 67 years old when the A's clinched the first of the three pennants, was not the same manager he had been with his last winner in the 1910s. Less the teacher now than the leader, he began to develop the image that was to endure through the hard years ahead: the gaunt figure sitting on the bench in a dark suit and hat waving his signature scorecard to move a player into position. The 1929 World Series, an Athletics' victory over the Cubs in five games, began with surprise starter Howard Ehmke beating the Cubs, 3–1, and striking out 13 to set a series record that stood until 1953; Ehmke, a journeyman who ended his career with a 166–166 record and who had appeared in

Ty Cobb's 4,000th hit came in 1927 while he was with the Athletics; the milestone was reached against the outfielder's alma mater, the Tigers.

only eleven games during the season, got the nod over Grove (20–6), Earnshaw (24–8), and Rube Walberg (18–11), because Mack had a hunch his sidearm delivery would baffle the Cubs' predominantly right-handed lineup. In Game Four, the Cubs, leading 8–0, were about to tie the Series and Mack was about to send in his benchwarmers, when the A's exploded for ten runs in the seventh inning. The turning point came when Chicago center fielder Hack Wilson lost Haas's fly ball in the sun, allowing it to become a three-run inside-the-park home run. Dykes expressed his excitement by slapping the man next to him on the back, sending his manager to his knees. "It's all right, Jimmy. Anything's all right now," Mack told Dykes, whose .421 average lead the A's in the Series.

It was all right the following year, as well, when the Athletics, batting only .197, made the most of 35 hits by knocking 18 of them for extra bases, 6 for home runs, to defeat the Cardinals 4 games to 2. Mack's final World Series, in 1931, ended less satisfactorily as the Cardinals, bolstered by third baseman Pepper Martin's .500 average and daring baserunning, won in seven games. One reason offered for the World Series loss—Cochrane's inability to concentrate because of heavy stock market losses—was symptomatic of the team's situation. Mack had built the best team in baseball, but he had also created the highest payroll up to that time.

Two events of 1932 doomed the latest Philadelphia dynasty: The Yankees won the last of their Ruth-era pennants, and the bank that had provided most of the franchise's financing called in a $400,000 note. Foxx chased Ruth's home run record all year, ending with 58, but the A's, who won 90 games, finished 13 behind New York. As soon as the season ended, Mack sold Simmons, Haas, and Dykes to the White Sox for $150,000 to pay part of the club's debt.

The White Sox deal was minor compared to what followed the third-place finish of 1933. On one day, December 12th, Mack completed three deals that would cause the franchise to crash and burn: Cochrane went to Detroit for $100,000; Grove, Bishop, and Walberg brought $150,000 from the Red Sox; and Earnshaw's sale to the White Sox added another $20,000. What little remained didn't last long: Foxx, irate over a $6,000 pay cut, was sold to Boston for $150,000 in December, 1935; a month later, center fielder Doc Cramer and shortstop Eric McNair followed for $75,000.

Attendance in 1935 was a paltry 233,173, which prompted Mack to sue to prevent residents of buildings behind the twelve-foot wall in right field from watching games for free. Losing his suit, he constructed a twenty-two-foot corrugated iron fence on top of the existing wall.

The 1935 team led the AL in homers while winding up in the cellar, establishing a pattern of unproductive power that would prevail for more than a decade. Outfielder Wally Moses hit over .300 every year between 1935 and 1941 with a high of .345 in 1936; outfielder Bob Johnson had nine consecutive years with 21 or more homers and seven consecutive seasons of collecting better than 100 RBIs. The late 1930s were otherwise brightened only by Mack's 1937 selection to the Hall of Fame and Philadelphia's hosting of the first AL night game, a ten-inning 8–3 loss to Cleveland on May 16, 1939.

Mack celebrated his fiftieth anniversary as a manager in 1944 with a great deal of hoopla throughout the league. The achievement was tarnished somewhat by the fact that Mack had always been a part-owner and, since the death of Ben Shibe's heir John in 1937, the majority stockholder. Several members of the Shibe family had held onto their stock, but Mack assumed the presidency and absolute control of the franchise. He further solidified his hold by bringing his sons into what was now a family business. Earle sat in the dugout as a coach and later as assistant manager (and often managed, most visibly in 1937 and 1939, when his father wasn't up to the chore); Roy moved into the front office as a vice-president; and Connie, Jr. became assistant treasurer.

In 1946, when Robert Murphy tried to organize a Philadelphia local of the American Baseball Guild, Mack used security men to bar his entry to the Athletics' clubhouse. Also in 1946, Mack refused to compensate players returning from the military but unable to make the roster, as he was obliged to do under the Veterans Act. When pitcher Bob Harris sued for restitution, Mack used the U. S. Attorney, who should have been representing the player, to con Harris into settling for $3,000 (two-thirds of what he was owed) and posing for the cameras shaking hands with a beaming, generous, and patriotic Philadelphia owner.

The youngest player to appear in an American League game was pitcher Carl Scheib, 16 years old when he pitched in six games for the 1943 Athletics; Scheib was 0–1 with a 4.34 ERA that year.

What generosity Mack expressed went toward his family, and even that caused trouble. In 1946, he divided some of his shares in the club among his three sons. The second Mrs. Mack, mother of Connie, Jr., took exception to an arrangement that gave the first Mrs. Mack's sons double the number of shares held by her son. The Macks even separated over the issue for a time, and the franchise's life was thereafter plagued by intermittent warfare between Earle and Roy on one side and Connie, Jr., his mother, and the Macfarland brothers, Ben and Frank, who had inherited the Shibe interests, on the other.

The team's relative success in 1947—fifth place and the first record on the plus side of .500 since 1933—surprised Mack as much as it did everyone else. At first, the team appeared to be more of the same journeymen infielders, less-than-mediocre pitchers, and a few slugging outfielders. But something inexplicably jelled as Ferris Fain, Pete Suder, Eddie Joost, and Hank Majeski became, if not the equivalent of the One Hundred Thousand Dollar Infield, at least a cohesive defensive unit. Fain hit .291, and outfielders Barney McCosky and Elmer Valo hit .328 and .300, respectively. Phil Marchildon's 19–9 record topped a staff of unusually promising young pitchers.

Mack aged rapidly in the late 1940s. Practically deaf, he relied heavily on coaches Simmons and, especially, Earle Brucker, who handled the pitchers. The manager often fell asleep on the bench; his mind would wander and he would call for sluggers long retired to get up to pinch hit. As often as not, players would refer to him as The Old Man, no longer with the respect that had once been attached to the name. The team he had collected on the cheap was good enough to stay in the 1948 race until August, but 84 victories and fourth place was the best it could manage. Mack vented his frustration over the not-quite-good-enough status of his team by publicly berating 37-year-old Nelson Potter; when the reliever blew a game in the ninth inning, Mack delivered a tirade in the dugout and released the pitcher then and there.

In 1949, the A's dropped to fifth, even though they won 81 games. The defense was exceptional, as the club turned a major league record 217 double plays. Alex Kellner emerged as the ace with a 20–12 record, for the Athletics' first 20-win season since the departure of Grove, but the staff (4.23 ERA) put too many men on base, which helped the infielders set the double-play record but didn't help in the victory column.

After the season, trouble erupted in the board

room, which, in the A's case, meant the family room. In October, longtime coaches Brucker and Simmons were let go and replaced by former players Cochrane and Miller. Mack let it be known that the dismissals were not his doing, but that Connie, Jr. and the Macfarlands had engineered the ouster. Exerting his authority, he made two deals, both of which were disasters. On October 19th, he traded second baseman Nellie Fox to the White Sox for catcher Joe Tipton. On December 13th, he laid out $100,000 and gave up two players to get third baseman Bob Dillinger from the Browns. The manager expected Dillinger, who had led the AL in stolen bases in the three previous seasons, to be the final ingredient that would push the A's to the top; as it turned out, Dillinger's moodiness caused more trouble than his .309 average (in 84 games) could compensate for and he was sold to Pittsburgh in July for $35,000. The team lost 102 games and finished in the cellar.

Exacerbating the collapse on the field was the completion of the coup in the front office. On May 26th, Connie, Jr. and the Macfarlands relieved Earle, whom everyone assumed would succeed his father in the dugout, of his duties as assistant manager, and reduced his status to that of chief scout. Dykes was moved in as assistant manager, with Cochrane moving upstairs to become the club's first general manager. The victory of Connie, Jr. and the Macfarlands was only temporary, however. On August 28th, Roy and Earle bought out their half-brother, the Macfarlands, and several other Shibe heirs, and with their father's support—and a $1.75 million loan, secured by a mortgage on Shibe Park, from Connecticut General Life Insurance Co.—assumed control of almost 80 percent of the club's stock.

Two months shy of his 89th birthday, Mack retired without fanfare on October 18th. Publicly, the elder sons, who now held the real power in the franchise, had maintained that their father could stay on as manager as long as he chose; privately, they had applied pressure on him to step down.

The new manager was Dykes. Art Ehlers, the farm director, was promoted to replace Cochrane as GM. Mack, who retained the title of president, kept a promise not to second-guess his successor. In 1951, Dykes pulled the club up to sixth on the strength of the first of Fain's back-to-back batting championships (.344), lefty Bobby Shantz's 18–10 record, and league-leading totals in homers (33) and RBIs (129) by left fielder Gus Zernial. Fain (.307), Zernial (29 homers, 100 RBIs), and an MVP year by Shantz (24–7 to lead the AL in victories, along with a 2.48 ERA)

sparked a fourth-place finish in 1952 and renewed optimism. But although Zernial blasted 42 homers in 1953, the team fell again to seventh place. In 1954, when Ehlers and Dykes departed for the new Baltimore Orioles, the franchise suffered a major blow. Even the rechristening of Shibe park to Connie Mack Stadium was a hollow gesture; only 326,113 fans showed up to watch the A's.

Left to themselves, the Mack brothers appointed shortstop Joost manager; it was the last decision on which they agreed. By July, they were feuding and offering to buy each other out for improbable amounts neither of them possessed. The usual rumors circulated that the franchise would be moved to Los Angeles or Dallas; names of buyers, including insurance executive Charlie Finley, were bandied about. Philadelphia construction magnate John McShain, who had fronted the money for the Macks in 1950 while they waited for Connecticut Life to come through with its loan, entered the bidding. But the only concrete offer, $3.375 million, came from Chicago vending machine and real estate millionaire Arnold Johnson, who made no pretense about his intention to move the club to Kansas City.

Meanwhile, Joost's club had landed in eighth place, 60 games behind the Yankees. The eighteenth last-place finish was a team effort: The pitching staff compiled a joint 5.18 ERA, 1.30 higher than the next-worst team's, while the hitters compiled a composite .236, 15 points behind the next-worst figure in the AL. Only 304,666 fans paid to see the A's in their final year; this was 115,000 fewer than had paid to see them in Columbia Park in 1902.

In the six weeks after the close of the 1954 season, ownership of the franchise became as convoluted as it had been stable for the club's first half-century. On September 28th, the AL held a special meeting to consider Johnson's offer. Connie and Earle Mack had reconciled themselves to the move to Kansas City, but the AL owners were hesitant. Some of them anticipated the unnatural relationship between the Yankees and Johnson, who included Yankee Stadium in his real estate empire; others, out of deference to Mack, preferred salvaging Philadelphia's place in the league; still others were eyeing a more lucrative West Coast location for the club. The solution was to do nothing other than to give holdout Roy Mack two weeks to come up with $1.364 million to buy out his father and brother and cover overdue bills amounting to $310,000. On October 12th, at a second special league meeting, the AL approved the sale to Johnson. Roy Mack, however, had one more card up his sleeve—an offer by a Philadelphia syndicate headed by former Phillies' employee Jack Rensel to match Johnson's offer, include Roy Mack in the purchasing group, and keep the team in Philadelphia. Roy and a reconverted Earle Mack signed a contract with the Philadelphia group on October 18th.

Johnson immediately threatened a breach of contract suit and, at a third AL meeting, on October 28th, the AL rejected the Rensel offer despite sentimental pleas by the Old Man, who went to New York to argue for the Philadelphian's offer against Johnson (to which he had already agreed and the rejection of which would have landed him in a major legal wrangle). At the meeting, Earle changed sides yet again, agreeing to Johnson's offer, provided his father agreed. On November 1st, at yet a fourth gathering, the league reaffirmed its approval of the Johnson offer: $604,000 to Connie Mack; $450,000 to each of his sons; assumption of the $1.2 million mortgage on Connie Mack Stadium and other debts amounting to $800,000; and jobs for Earle, Roy, and Roy's two sons. The final act of the Athletics' history took place three days later, in Connie Mack's home in Germantown, where Johnson presented the ailing Mack with a check for $604,000 in exchange for his 302 shares in the club. The exchange was consummated with a handshake.

PHILADELPHIA ATHLETICS

Annual Standings and Managers

Year	Position	W	L	Pct.	GB	Managers
1901	Fourth	74	62	.544	9	Connie Mack
1902	First	83	53	.610	+5	Connie Mack
1903	Second	75	60	.556	14½	Connie Mack
1904	Fifth	81	70	.536	12½	Connie Mack
1905	First	92	56	.622	+2	Connie Mack
1906	Fourth	78	67	.538	12	Connie Mack
1907	Second	88	57	.607	1½	Connie Mack
1908	Sixth	68	85	.444	22	Connie Mack
1909	Second	95	58	.621	3½	Connie Mack
1910	First	102	48	.680	+14½	Connie Mack
1911	First	101	50	.669	+13½	Connie Mack
1912	Third	90	62	.592	15	Connie Mack
1913	First	96	57	.627	+6½	Connie Mack
1914	First	99	53	.651	+8½	Connie Mack
1915	Eighth	43	109	.283	58½	Connie Mack
1916	Eighth	36	117	.235	54½	Connie Mack
1917	Eighth	55	98	.359	44½	Connie Mack
1918	Eighth	52	76	.406	24	Connie Mack
1919	Eighth	36	104	.257	52	Connie Mack
1920	Eighth	48	106	.312	50	Connie Mack
1921	Eighth	53	100	.346	45	Connie Mack
1922	Seventh	65	89	.422	29	Connie Mack
1923	Sixth	69	83	.454	29	Connie Mack
1924	Fifth	71	81	.467	20	Connie Mack
1925	Second	88	64	.579	8½	Connie Mack
1926	Third	83	67	.553	6	Connie Mack
1927	Second	91	63	.591	19	Connie Mack
1928	Second	98	55	.641	2½	Connie Mack
1929	First	104	46	.693	+18	Connie Mack
1930	First	102	52	.662	+8	Connie Mack
1931	First	107	45	.704	+13½	Connie Mack
1932	Second	94	60	.610	13	Connie Mack
1933	Third	79	72	.523	19½	Connie Mack
1934	Fifth	68	82	.453	31	Connie Mack
1935	Eighth	58	91	.389	34	Connie Mack

1936	Eighth	53	100	.346	49	Connie Mack
1937	Seventh	54	97	.358	46½	Connie Mack
1938	Eighth	53	99	.349	46	Connie Mack
1939	Seventh	55	97	.362	51½	Connie Mack
1940	Eighth	54	100	.351	36	Connie Mack
1941	Eighth	64	90	.416	37	Connie Mack
1942	Eighth	55	99	.357	48	Connie Mack
1943	Eighth	49	105	.318	49	Connie Mack
1944	Fifth*	72	82	.468	17	Connie Mack
1945	Eighth	52	98	.347	34½	Connie Mack
1946	Eighth	49	105	.318	55	Connie Mack
1947	Fifth	78	76	.506	19	Connie Mack
1948	Fourth	84	70	.545	12½	Connie Mack
1949	Fifth	81	73	.526	16	Connie Mack
1950	Eighth	52	102	.338	46	Connie Mack
1951	Sixth	70	84	.455	28	Jimmy Dykes
1952	Fourth	79	75	.513	16	Jimmy Dykes
1953	Seventh	59	95	.383	41½	Jimmy Dykes
1954	Eighth	51	103	.331	60	Eddie Joost

* Tie

Postseason Play

WS	1–4 versus New York	1905
	4–1 versus Chicago	1910
	4–2 versus New York	1911
	4–1 versus New York	1913
	0–4 versus Boston	1914
	4–1 versus Chicago	1929
	4–2 versus St. Louis	1930
	3–4 versus St. Louis	1931

Pittsburgh Alleghenys

American Association,
1882–1886

BALLPARKS: EXPOSITION PARK (1882–1884)
RECREATION PARK (1885–1886)

RECORD: 236–296 (.444)

A charter member of the American Association, the Alleghenys were at the center of every one of its major controversies, largely because principal owner H. Denny McKnight was also president of the circuit. Finding itself in the minority on too many important issues, Pittsburgh eventually became the first club to pull out of the AA and join the National League.

The club took its name from the location of Exposition Park, on the current site of Three Rivers Stadium, in what was then the town of Allegheny. It came into the AA thanks to a bartender. Justus Thorner and O. P. Caylor had gone to Pittsburgh for what they had expected to be a meeting of teams willing to take on the NL. Realizing that they were the only ones who were going to show up, the disappointed Thorner and Caylor repaired to a saloon to drown their sorrows; there they met bartender Al Pratt, who directed them to McKnight, president of two former independent teams in the area. Assisted by McKnight and a successful ruse in getting other teams to attend a second organizational meeting, Thorner and Caylor were able to get the AA off the ground.

Managed by Pratt, who gave up his bartender's apron, the first major league team to represent Pittsburgh boasted few stars. Its leading hitter the first three seasons (and the AA leader in 1883 with a .356 average) was first baseman-right fielder Ed Swartwood. Harry Salisbury compiled a 20–18 record the first season, and Denny Driscoll (13–9) had the AA's lowest ERA (1.21).

As the competition for player talent intensified, the AA began signing NL players to pledges to sign contracts the following season. Detroit Wolverines catcher Charlie Bennett accepted $100 in August as a binder to sign a Pittsburgh contract for 1883, but then got cold feet and resigned with Detroit. In response, McKnight sought a restraining order to compel Bennett to honor his agreement or to force Detroit to pay $1,000 in damages for depriving the Alleghenys of the catcher's services. A court ruled for Bennett because the parties had not reached mutually agreeable terms.

When Northwestern League President Elias Matter sought an alliance between his minor league and the Nationals, NL president A.G. Mills diplomatically suggested that Matter invite McKnight to a three-way meeting because, without the AA in their combine, it would be impossible to enforce contracts. The resultant Harmony Conference, held in New York, produced a Tripartite Agreement (later renamed the National Agreement) that was the real beginning of organized baseball. Among other things, it spelled out the responsibilities and privileges of participating leagues, including the right to territorial exclusivity and the sanctity of player contracts.

Peace failed to bring prosperity to the Alleghenys, who, despite Swartwood's batting crown, dropped from fourth to seventh in the now eight-club circuit. Pratt gave way after thirty-two games to Ormond Butler, who in turn left the manager's chair to shortstop Joe Battin for the final thirteen games. The club lost $3,000 in a year when almost every other AA franchise turned a profit.

The slide continued in 1884, as Swartwood's average dropped to .288 and the pitching staff yielded 4.35 runs a game. Five managers wandered in and out of the dugout during a tenth-place finish. One of them was George Creamer, who entered the record books as the manager with the most career losses (eight, all in 1884) without a victory. The last of them, was Horace Phillips, who produced a winning record

(9–4) and some promise of stability. Promises weren't all Phillips brought, however. When the AA cut back from twelve to eight teams for the 1885 season, Columbus failed to make the final cut, making available numerous players whom Phillips had managed previously on the Ohio club. Among those coming to Pittsburgh were new ace pitcher Ed Morris (39 24) and right fielder Tom Brown, who led the team in hitting with a .307 average. The infusion of talent, under new President William A. Nimick, enabled Pittsburgh to climb to third in 1885 and second in 1886. Morris led the league in 1886 with 41 wins.

The Alleghenys also sought to improve themselves by acquiring St. Louis Browns second baseman Sam Barkley, but ended up embroiled in an intramural battle that cost McKnight his job and eventually led to the transfer of the franchise to the NL. Barkley had agreed to terms with Pittsburgh, but subsequently signed a contract with the Baltimore Orioles, who sent St. Louis owner Chris Von der Ahe $1,000 as compensation. Von der Ahe felt committed to Pittsburgh, and persuaded Barkley to honor the agreement with the Alleghenys. Baltimore appealed to the AA board of directors, which fined Barkley $100, suspended him for the 1886 season, and awarded Pittsburgh the rights to his services for 1887. McKnight refused to accept the decision, but a vote of the full league upheld the penalties. The AA president then neglected to forward the formal indictment to Barkley or to attend the AA meeting that was to have imposed the penalty.

On March 20, 1886, the AA fired McKnight and promoted Secretary-Treasurer Wheeler Wikoff to the presidency. Barkley went to the Pittsburgh Court of Common Pleas to get an injunction to prevent any AA club from playing the Alleghenys unless he were on the team; he later settled out of court, agreeing to a $500 fine (which was probably paid by Nimick) in return for a lifting of the suspension. The Orioles were assuaged when they received first baseman Milt Scott from Pittsburgh.

Barkley hit .266, but he had never been the issue; McKnight's weak leadership was. That there was no improvement with his successors, and that the AA club owners wouldn't have stood for a strong president, hardly mattered. They would eventually founder on a reef of petty interfranchise squabbles. The first big crack in the hull came in November 1886, when an embittered Nimick, who had spent the season protesting the shabby treatment directed at his club by the other owners, withdrew from the AA and joined the NL.

PITTSBURGH ALLEGHENYS

Annual Standings and Managers

Year	Position	W	L	Pct.	GB	Managers
1882	Fourth	39	39	.500	15	Al Pratt
1883	Seventh	31	67	.316	35	Al Pratt, Ormond Butler, Joe Battin
1884	Tenth	30	78	.278	45½	Denny McKnight, Bob Ferguson Joe Battin, George Creamer Horace Phillips
1885	Third	56	55	.505	22½	Horace Phillips
1886	Second	80	57	.584	12	Horace Phillips

Pittsburgh Stogies

Union Association, 1884   **BALLPARK:** RECREATION PARK

RECORD: 7–11 (.389)

When the situation of the Chicago Browns became untenable in August 1884, Henry V. Lucas, president of the Union Association, and A.H. Henderson, a Baltimore mattress manufacturer who had been president of the Browns, moved the franchise to Pittsburgh. Lucas had sought to place a club there from the beginning of the season, because, as a major railhead, it was an ideal stopover for teams traveling between eastern and western cities. The ideal franchise lasted a mere eighteen games.

Footnote Player: Kid Baldwin caught one game for the Stogies, although he was under contract to the UA Kansas City Unions at the time. When the Stogies' two regular catchers Tony Suck and Bill Krieg were unable to play one day, Kansas City loaned Baldwin to Pittsburgh. The receiver got a hit in his only official at bat for the Stogies, then returned to Kansas City.

Most of the Pittsburgh players were Chicago retreads. First baseman Jumbo Schoeneck led the Stogies' regulars in hitting, with a .286 average. Joe Battin, recruited from the American Association Pittsburgh Alleghenys to play third, hit a mere .188 and managed the team for its first six games before being replaced by shortstop Joe Ellick. In trying to give the lie to National League President A.G. Mills's contention that the UA was little more than a refuge for drunkards who couldn't find employment elsewhere, the team left behind in Chicago outfielder Jack Leary and outfielder-catcher Emil Gross, two of the Browns' more prodigious drinkers, even though Gross was batting .318 at the time of the move. The club did, however, take outfielder Gid Gardner, who had been expelled from the AA Baltimore Orioles for his drinking.

Few fans bothered to show up to see if the players were drunk or sober. With the dissolution of the Stogies, many of the players went to the UA Baltimore Monumentals. Lucas, in an act of desperation, invited the St. Paul Saints of the Northwestern League to complete the schedule.

PITTSBURGH STOGIES

Annual Standings and Managers

Year	Position	W	L	Pct.	GB	Managers
1884	Partial season	7	11	.389	—	Joe Battin, Joe Ellick

Pittsburgh Pirates

National League,
1887–Present

RECORD: 8351–7765 (.518)

BALLPARKS: RECREATION PARK (1887–90)
EXPOSITION PARK (1891–1909)
FORBES FIELD (1909–1970)
THREE RIVERS STADIUM (1970–Present)

OTHER NAMES: ALLEGHENYS, INNOCENTS

On and off the field, the Pirates have rarely been subtle. In their century-plus of existence, their good years have almost always been the result of some Lumber Company propping up adequate pitching and their dismal years have almost always stemmed from some Toothpick Company collapsing under the same pitching. From Honus Wagner in 1900 to Bill Madlock in 1983, their emphasis on offense produced an unrivaled twenty-four batting titles; from Jimmy Williams in 1899 to Andy Van Slyke in 1988, the same stress yielded twenty-five league leaders in tri-ples. Suggestive of a team at the mercy of the streaks and slumps of its hitters, the Pirates have also had few equals in the drastic rises and falls of their fortunes—whole decades, and even generations, passing with the club remaining at the top or near the bottom of the league.

Pittsburgh entered the National League after the 1886 season, when the circuit decided that its mostly eastern seaboard teams were spending too much money traveling to Kansas City and needed a franchise closer to the main action in New York, Boston,

Bill Mazeroski tries to cross the plate after his home run on October 13, 1960, that gave Pittsburgh a World Series victory over the Yankees. *UPI/Bettmann Newsphotos*

and Philadelphia. William A. Nimick, president of the Pittsburgh Alleghenys of the American Association, seized the opportunity for personal as well as financial reasons. Aside from his optimism that the Alleghenys would draw better in the older league, Nimick was furious at the AA for dumping its organizer-president and fellow Pittsburgher Denny McKnight that year in a fallout over various legal squabbles.

Pittsburgh opened the 1887 season on April 30th with a 6–2 victory over Chicago before an estimated 10,000 fans jammed into Recreation Park. For at least that day, there was some reason to believe manager Horace Phillips's prediction that the club that he had steered to a second-place finish in the AA the year before would win the NL pennant. But thereafter there were few things to crow about in western Pennsylvania; for the rest of the nineteenth century, in fact, the team would manage only one finish as high as second, spending most years in sixth place or lower. What NL baseball in Pittsburgh mainly came down to before 1900 was figuring out the reasons for the franchise's mediocrity—and there were a lot of those.

To begin with, there were the tragedies. In the team's maiden season, for instance, the chief offensive threat for the first few months was first baseman Alex McKinnon, who carried a .340 average into a July 4th game against Philadelphia. Complaining of stomach cramps to Phillips, McKinnon asked to sit out the contest, was still ill the following day, and finally had to be sent home; three weeks later, he was dead of typhoid fever. Manager Phillips himself came under fire the next season for "losing concentration" during games—a criticism that carried over into 1889, when Nimick finally recognized that his field leader was suffering a nervous breakdown. Shortly after being given a leave of absence, Phillips was admitted to a mental institution, from which he never emerged.

Phillips's incapacity led to, first, Fred Dunlap and, then, Ned Hanlon taking over the club in 1889. Then Hanlon led a massive defection of Alleghenys to the rebellious Players League in 1890, leaving behind one of the worst teams in major league history. With a mere four players coming back for new manager Guy Hecker, the club had to scramble through most of the season just to find enough teenagers and old men to fill out the roster. The final record of 23–113 included a twenty-three game losing streak and the loss of all three games in a Labor Day tripleheader against Brooklyn. Attendance was so bad (one game was seen by only seventeen fans) that

Ned Hanlon in an early ad for a cigarette company.
National Baseball Library, Cooperstown, NY

Nimick and his righthand man J. Palmer O'Neil scrapped a number of home games at Recreation Park in favor of taking them to various towns in western Pennsylvania, Ohio, and West Virginia that might show more curiosity about the team. Given the club's ineptitude and the inexperience of many of its players, it did not take long for the wits of the day to redub the Alleghenys the Innocents, and the name was taken up by the franchise itself.

With the collapse of the PL after the 1890 season, Pittsburgh retrieved many of its players, and even welcomed back Hanlon as manager. The most noteworthy acquisition for 1891, however, was second baseman Lou Bierbauer, a member of the AA's Philadelphia club prior to the widespread jumpings to the PL. When Bierbauer and outfielder Harry Stovey discovered that their names had been inadvertently left off the printed reserve lists that would have forced them to return to their original teams for the 1891 season, they negotiated free agent contracts—Bierbauer with Pittsburgh and Stovey with Boston. The AA protested and submitted a document to an arbitration panel that described the complicity of Pittsburgh in the signing as "piratical." When the arbitration panel ruled in favor of the players, the franchise not only had a new second baseman, but Pirates as a new nickname.

In 1891, the club took up quarters at Exposition Park—a relatively more spacious facility, but one that was also subject to overflows from the adjoining Allegheny River. On some days, the problem was so bad that, rather than cancel what might have been only the first of many annulled games, the Pirates and their opponents agreed to special groundrules, such as declaring any hit to the swampy outfield an automatic single. It was also because of the high water on the Allegheny in April that the club took to requesting that it open the season on the road—a practical move insofar as this reduced the chances of playing on a flooded field, but also counterproductive in exposing Pittsburgh's mediocre teams to defeat away from home before local fans could generate enthusiasm for them.

The franchise's other glaring problem before the dawning of a new century was the ownership. Almost as soon as he finalized the details for Pittsburgh's move to the NL, Nimick began displaying less interest in the team and gradually shifted most of the day-to-day responsibilities over to O'Neil. The latter's major contribution to the team turned out to be his well-publicized insouciance during the disastrous 1890 season, when he never cut back on his lavish life style even as he was scraping around for the dollars that would pay the players or guarantee them something to eat on the road. With a Barnumesque flair, O'Neil also had little problem justifying Pittsburgh's "road-home" games in Ohio and West Virginia as attempts to bring major league ball to other communities rather than admitting that they were a desperate attempt to have some kind of a gate for the dreary Innocents.

Principally because he managed to arrive at the end of the season with the organization still relatively intact, O'Neil was given Nimick's presidency the following year. But it was a short-lived promotion. Only weeks into the 1891 season, O'Neil and Hanlon were differing publicly over the quality of their players and over who should not be playing. Hanlon lasted until August 1st, only because O'Neil hadn't found as suitable a replacement as Bill McGunnigle before then. But even with McGunnigle at the helm for the final weeks, the club ended up in the same eighth place that it had occupied in the fiasco year of 1890. With public criticism of Nimick and O'Neil rife, there was little surprise when, a few weeks after the end of the season, coffee magnate William Kerr and long-time associate Phil Auten announced that they had purchased the club. In their

first move, Kerr and Auten bounced O'Neil as president in favor of William Temple, the Pittsburgh sportsman who would become most identified with the postseason Temple Cup games played between the NL's first- and second-place teams from 1894 to 1897.

In naming Al Buckenberger as McGunnigle's successor, Kerr initially had nothing but praise for his new manager as the latter spent the offseason using his connections to import such noted players of the period as Joe Kelley, Elmer Smith, Red Ehret, Adonis Terry, Jake Stenzel, and Tom Burns. But on the eve of what was to be the league's one-year experiment in a split-season, the owner had a change of heart, deciding that Burns would be a better motivator on the field and kicking Buckenberger upstairs to what was the equivalent of the general manager's post. This arrangement lasted only until the Pirates finished the first half of the season buried in sixth place. For the second half, Kerr sent Burns back to third base and brought Buckenberger back down to the dugout. It was a pattern that would be repeated several times during the decade, with Kerr jerking Buckenberger, Patsy Donovan, and Bill Watkins back and forth between the diamond and the front office, usually after some public harangue against the ineptitude of the man he was replacing. Only Connie Mack, who took over as manager at Kerr's original insistence in 1894, refused to tolerate the owner's tantrums and quit before he could be fired.

As bleak as the 1890s as a whole were for the team, there were some bright spots. One of these was catcher-manager Mack, who developed receiving into a sophisticated craft (which for Mack also included a talent for tipping the bats of hitters). Another was Hall of Fame first baseman Jake Beckley, whose offensive contributions to the team included five .300-plus years and whose trade to the Giants in 1897 precipitated the first serious calls for Kerr to sell the team. In 1893, the team's unexpectedly strong second-place finish was due in large part to southpaw Frank Killen's 34 wins.

The 1899 club counted in its ranks six-time 20-game winner Jesse Tannehill, future batting cham-

It was while managing the Pirates that Connie Mack devised his "iceball" gimmick. When the team was up against a particularly strong offensive club, Mack saw to it that the balls to be used in the game were put on ice to deaden them.

pion Ginger Beaumont, and future Hall of Famer Jack Chesbro. Two others who were to make an impact on the game were business manager Ed Barrow and caterer Harry M. Stevens, who worked out a deal early in the decade for control of the concessions at Exposition Park.

Kerr's sovereign rule ended up lasting only the eight years (1892–99) in which the league consisted of twelve teams. In the winter of 1899, amid growing indications that the circuit would be cut back to eight teams, Kerr and Auten made a conditional agreement to sell the franchise to former manager Bill Watkins and his backers, who included Cincinnati owner John T. Brush. But when Brush pulled out and was replaced by Barney Dreyfuss, owner of the Louisville franchise that was earmarked to be one of the four teams eradicated, Kerr had second thoughts and sought to get out of the agreement with Watkins. Some tough bargaining followed, resulting in Dreyfuss's taking over 50 percent of the Pirates, Kerr's retaining control of the other 50 percent, and the mass importing of Louisville players to Pittsburgh.

The Kentucky franchise had not yet been officially liquidated by the league, so the player transaction had to take the form of a trade between the Pirates and the Colonels; specifically, Pittsburgh giving Louisville $25,000 and players Chesbro, George Fox, John O'Brien and Art Madison for manager-outfielder Fred Clarke, Honus Wagner, Claude Ritchey, Tommy Leach, Chief Zimmer, Tacks Latimer, Deacon Phillippe, Patsy Flaherty, Rube Waddell, Walt Woods, Bert Cunningham, and Mike Kelley. When the Louisville franchise was formally terminated some weeks later, Chesbro came right back to Pittsburgh, along with Fred Ketcham and Louis Deal. By the time the dust had settled on what was arguably the greatest trade in baseball history, the Pirates had secured the services of four future Hall of Famers, not to mention a number of 20-game winners, batting champions, and even one home run leader (Leach). In the accompanying reorganization of the club, Dreyfuss took over as president, with Auten vice-president, Kerr treasurer, Dreyfuss confidant Harry Pulliam secretary, and Clarke the manager.

Primarily because of the Louisville deal, the Pirates were as good in the first decade of the twentieth century as they had been bad in the last decade of the nineteenth century. Between 1900 and 1909, they finished first four times, second four times, and third and fourth once each. Twice, in the pennant-winning years of 1902 and 1909, they won more than 100 games—the only times the franchise would accomplish this feat. Their finish 27½ games ahead of Brooklyn in 1902 set a league mark for runaway victories.

At the center of the team's success was Wagner, considered by some the greatest player ever to put on an NL uniform. A first-year entrant into the Hall of Fame in 1936 (he was voted in before Babe Ruth), Wagner moved back and forth between first base, third base, and the outfield, before finally settling in as a shortstop in his seventh big league season. At bat, he hit .300 or better seventeen years in a row, falling shy of the mark for the first time in 1914, when he was already 40 years old. His career average of .329 included an NL record eight batting titles, 3,430 hits, 651 doubles, 252 triples, 101 homers, 1,740 runs, and 1,732 RBIs. He also led the NL in stolen bases five times.

Wagner had plenty of help. The 1901 pennant-winning team boasted an entire outfield of .300 hitters and two 20-game winners in Chesbro and Phillippe. The 1902 winners featured batting champion Beaumont, homer leader Leach (if only with 6 round-trippers, the lowest number to lead a league in the twentieth century), and three 20-game winners in Chesbro, Phillippe, and Tannehill. In 1903, the main contributors to the flag included Phillippe with another 24 wins, Sam Leever with 25 victories and a

Honus Wagner. *National Baseball Library, Cooperstown, NY*

league-leading ERA of 2.06, and .340-plus years from both Beaumont and Clarke. Before the end of the decade, 20-win seasons would come again from Phillippe and Leever, Howie Camnitz, Lefty Leifield, Nick Maddox, and, most conspicuously, Vic Willis (four consecutive years).

The team's turnaround with the arrival of Dreyfuss and Louisville's top stars once again saw Kerr fuming—this time because of the general perception that he had little, if anything, to do with the revival. Matters came to a head after the 1900 season, when he called a board meeting to force out Pulliam as the club secretary. After a series of boardroom maneuvers, however, Dreyfuss, knowing that his partner's ultimate aim was to dislodge him as president, rounded up enough votes to reconfirm himself as head of the club and Pulliam as secretary. Kerr went to court to challenge the vote, lost his case, and then dared Dreyfuss to buy him out or sell. Dreyfuss chose the former option and, at the age of 35, became the full owner. He would remain so for thirty-two years; in that time, Pittsburgh would fall to the second division only six times.

For all his club's success on the field, Dreyfuss had more to worry about than Kerr in his first years as president. To begin with, the one-time distillery bookkeeper was something of a prude who gave his charges failing marks for smoking, drinking, or acting in a rowdy fashion. While this made the family-oriented Wagner his personal favorite, the same attitude led him to dismiss recommendations to sign Tris Speaker, who smoked, and Walter Johnson, who had been touted by a cigar salesman. It also led to some friction with manager Clarke, who was second to nobody in defending himself on the field with his fists and who expected similar aggressiveness from his players.

Honus Wagner has no peers among baseball card collectors. In 1990, a group headed by hockey star Wayne Gretzky paid $451,000 for a 1910 depiction of the shortstop produced by Sweet Caporal cigarettes. The following year, another (but more worn) card from the series was auctioned off for $220,000. The rarity of the cards is due to the fact that Wagner, a non-smoker, objected to the Sweet Caporal printing and demanded that his likeness be withdrawn from the market. Experts say that about forty cards printed by the tobacco company still exist.

Dreyfuss's *bête noire* in baseball's executive councils was New York Giants owner Andrew Freedman. The animosity between the men went back to Louisville, when Freedman had led an attempt to deprive the Colonels of essential Sunday home games and thereby force them into withdrawing from the league. Although Dreyfuss had survived that attack, he found himself up against Freedman again after the 1901 season, when the New York official spearheaded a move to have all teams share players and then pool their profits for the season, redividing them according to a fixed scale of percentages.

Dreyfuss had three reasons to laugh off the proposal: the pennant-winning Pirates had made the most money on the year, the Giants would have received the largest share of the redistributed monies, and Freedman still hadn't reimbursed his share of the league indemnity for the folding of Louisville. But then he discovered that Boston, Cincinnati, and St. Louis were also in favor of it. After initial skirmishes on the pool scheme itself, the issue came down to the owners' vote on a new NL president, because he would provide any tiebreaking ballot. With Brooklyn, Chicago, and Philadelphia supporting him, Dreyfuss nominated Albert Spalding for the post against the incumbent (and pro-Freedman) Nick Young. Twenty-five ballots later, no one had budged from a 4–4 deadlock.

The issue was resolved after a fashion when, with the Young forces out of the room and the Giants secretary Fred Knowles just killing time until his boss Freedman returned, Philadelphia owner John Rogers ordered another ballot, insisted that Knowles's presence made for a quorum, and quickly elicited a 4–0 poll in favor of Spalding. Freedman and his allies immediately went to court to obtain an injunction against Spalding and, though it took some months, eventually prevailed in their demand that the vote be overturned.

However, with the league threatening to come apart at the seams, a compromise was worked out under which a three-man executive council would replace a single president and Young would function as a secretary-treasurer. Freedman's ultimate triumph was that two members of the three-man committee were his allies from Boston and Cincinnati; Dreyfuss's consolation prize was that there was no more talk about taking away Pittsburgh's gate receipts and redistributing them.

Compared to other NL teams, the Pirates emerged relatively unscathed from the initial player raids launched on the circuit by Ban Johnson's new

Pittsburgh catcher Chief Zimmer was the president of the Protective Association of Professional Baseball Players, a 1900 group that represented the first attempt to form a players union since the collapse of the Players League in 1890. Using the emerging American League for leverage, Zimmer and other association leaders sought to pressure the National League into limiting the reserve clause, giving players a voice in where they could be traded, and eliminating excessive fines. When union attorney Harry Taylor raised the demands to include a board of arbitration, a player's right to release in the case of contract violations, and a limit on suspensions, NL owners went from stalling to halting negotiations with the players altogether. Only then did the association encourage players to take advantage of the impending war with the AL and jump over to Ban Johnson's circuit.

American League at the beginning of the century. The only noteworthy defection over the first couple of years was catcher Harry Smith, and he jumped right back to Pittsburgh after a single year in the AL.

For awhile, in fact, it appeared that the biggest result of the AL recruitment drive in Pittsburgh would be Dreyfuss's discovery that shortstop Bones Ely had been serving as something of a fifth columnist for Johnson in the Pirates clubhouse; in dumping Ely immediately, Dreyfuss opened up shortstop to Wagner. But then, toward the middle of the 1902 season, the president learned that five of his players—pitchers Tannehill and Chesbro, catcher Jack O'Connor, infielder Wid Conroy, and outfielder Lefty Davis—had already signed contracts to play for the AL's new franchise in New York in 1903. O'Connor, identified as Ely's successor as the team recruiter, and Davis were released before the close of the season, and Tannehill was informed before taking the mound for his final start of the year (which he won) that his services would no longer be required. All five players played for New York in 1903.

Where the AL was concerned, Dreyfuss had more to worry about than the defection of his players. During his frequent trips to Pittsburgh in the pursuit of Pirate players, AL boss Johnson also sounded out local businessmen on the possibility of shifting the new league's Detroit franchise to the Pennsylvania city. Hardly needing any such competition, Dreyfuss insisted—successfully—that the Jan-

uary 1903 peace agreement between the NL and AL include a commitment by the latter to stay out of Pittsburgh; his *quid pro quo* was to accept the defection of Chesbro and Tannehill to the Highlanders.

Despite his problems with the AL, Dreyfuss did as much as anybody to legitimize the new circuit when, in 1903, he endorsed public calls for his pennant-winning Pirates to meet the AL's Boston franchise in what become the first World Series. Although the Pirates lost the best-of-nine series five games to three, Dreyfuss declared himself proud enough of his players to add his own profits to their pool, so that members of the losing club ended up with more money than the victorious ALers. Dreyfuss also rejected the protests of other NL owners that his participation in the World Series had given undue publicity to the junior league. In fact, so adamant was he about the pledge that he had made to meet "an American League team of corresponding standing" following regular season play that, when the Giants of John McGraw refused to play Boston in a 1904 World Series, Dreyfuss set up a series of postseason games between his fourth-place club and the fourth-place AL Indians.

One of the keys to Boston's victory over Pittsburgh in the inaugural World Series of 1903 was the ineffectiveness of Pirates pitcher Ed Doheny. On the last day of the Series, Doheny attacked medical aide Oberlin Howarth with a castiron stove footrest, knocking him unconscious. The pitcher was pronounced insane and committed to a Massachusetts asylum.

Although Freedman sold out his interests in the Giants following the 1902 season, Dreyfuss was able to maintain his animosity toward the New Yorkers because of the arrival of McGraw as manager. However successful Pittsburgh was in the first decade of the century, it galled Dreyfuss no end that the Giants won two pennants over the same period.

Between June 2nd and June 8th in 1903, the Pirates pitched six consecutive shutouts. The blankings came from Deacon Phillippe, Sam Leever, Kaiser Wilhelm, Ed Doheny, and then Phillippe and Leever again.

The worst explosion between the teams occurred in 1905, when the New York manager publicly taunted Dreyfuss to bet $10,000 on the outcome of a particular Giants-Pirates game and then, in equally sarcastic tones, withdrew the challenge with the insinuation that the owner was infamous for not paying off his gambling debts. Dreyfuss was so furious that he immediately wrote a letter to Pulliam, his former protégé who had since become NL president, demanding that McGraw be suspended for vilifying his character. Instead of writing off the incident as typical McGraw needling, a compliant Pulliam made everything worse by suspending the manager for fifteen days and fining him $150—this inevitably bringing forth charges from New York that the president was indeed in Dreyfuss's pocket. With the integrity of the league office once again at issue, NL owners held an emergency meeting at which they upheld McGraw's suspension and fine and reaffirmed their confidence in Pulliam, but also slapped Dreyfuss for "undignified" behavior. The Pittsburgh owner went to his grave in embarrassment and resentment that he, the paradigm of clean living, should ever be tainted with accusations of consorting with gamblers and behaving badly in public.

> Forbes Field was named for General John Forbes, a British officer in the French and Indian War who captured Fort Duquesne in 1758 and renamed it Fort Pitt.

In more ways than one, 1909 represented the close of Act I of the Dreyfuss ownership. It was in that year that the club won more games than it ever would in franchise history and moved from Exposition Park to Forbes Field. On the one hand, the 25,000-capacity steel and concrete stadium was very much like the facility that the Athletics opened in Philadelphia in the same year to prevent the sort of fires that had devoured several wooden ballparks since the 1890s. But Forbes Field also differed from Philadelphia's Shibe Park insofar as it contained far more reserved grandstand seats for more affluent customers—this reflecting Dreyfuss's view that the franchise's long-term prosperity did not rest with bleacher fans. An overflow crowd of 30,338 showed up for the park's first game on June 30th and saw the Cubs beat the Pirates, 3–2. When Chicago's very first batter, Johnny Evers, singled, he launched Forbes Field's sixty-one-year history of never hosting a no-hit game.

There were also some dark moments in 1909 for Dreyfuss. He was sent reeling when, not quite a month after he had presided over the opening of Forbes Field, long-time friend and NL president Pulliam blew his brains out in the midst of a nervous breakdown. The suicide and the stresses that had contributed to it were thought to be the main reason why Dreyfuss thereafter showed more of a hardened attitude toward just about everything connected to baseball. One early victim of the new outlook was Pittsburgh first baseman Bill Abstein, who had barely finished celebrating Pittsburgh's World Series triumph over Detroit when he was informed that he had been sold to a minor league team. The move followed some very public fuming by Dreyfuss for Abstein's errors and inability to hit in the clutch against the Tigers.

Over the next fifteen years, the hapless Abstein would have plenty of company in not hitting in the clutch. Through a combination of aging stars (Wagner would win his last batting title in 1911, Clarke's playing career would effectively end in 1912), bad trades, and overrated prospects, the club would not return to the World Series until 1925. Its best showings along the way were a couple of second-place finishes in 1912 and 1921. The initial phase of the slide took place under Clarke, who displayed much less intensity as a manager once he had quit as a player. Finally, after twenty-two years as a player, manager, or both for Dreyfuss, Clarke bowed out altogether after the end of the 1915 season and was replaced by Nixey Callahan.

After so many years with Clarke at the helm, Callahan's arrival took some getting used to—and not too many people succeeded at the task. On the one hand, the former 20-game winner for the Cubs prided himself as a McGraw-type slavedriver and soon had most of his team hating him as much as the opposition; on the other hand, he became so vulnerable to the team's bad play that, during a late-season trip, he simply took off with a couple of drinking pals, leaving Wagner to handle games in Philadelphia and New York. Fearful that the manager was on the verge of the kind of nervous collapse that had once claimed Phillips, road secretary Pete Kelly covered for Callahan while enlisting newsmen to help him find the pilot. In the end, everything came to light anyway and Dreyfuss fired Kelly for showing more loyalty to Callahan than to him. Conversely (or, perversely), the owner also decided that if Callahan could get people to risk their jobs for him, he merited another chance in 1917. It was a mistake: By June 30th, the Pirates were well embarked on their worst year since the 1890 Innocents and Callahan had been replaced by Wagner, this time officially.

But Wagner's tenure lasted only five games (which included four losses). He in turn was succeeded by Hugo Bezdek, one of the strangest managerial choices in baseball history. The team's business manager in the front office, Bezdek had absolutely no experience as a field skipper, having made his name first as a college football player and wrestler and then as a successful football coach at the University of Oregon. As it turned out, he ended up handling the club better than anyone had a right to expect. After a few bruising moments in his debut season (calling for runners on both third *and* second to try to score on a suicide squeeze, a violent fight with Pittsburgh pitcher Burleigh Grimes that left both men bloodied), Bezdek led the team back up to .500-plus finishes in both 1918 and 1919, good enough each time for a first-division, fourth-place finish. But then, just when originally skeptical sportswriters and fans had warmed to the unlikely manager, Bezdek announced that he had accepted a job as a coach of the Penn State football team. George Gibson, a fourteen-year catcher for the Pirates and Giants, took over.

When he convened the club in spring training in 1920, Gibson had one asset that the Pirates had been missing since Kerr had traded Jake Beckley in 1896—a first baseman who showed that he could both hit and field. With the arrival of Charlie Grimm the previous season, in fact, Dreyfuss had gone out of his way to promise Pittsburgh fans the end of the nightmare that had, by his own admission, led him into any number of misconceived deals over the years. (To make matters worse, Pittsburgh had ostensibly solved the first base problem in 1915 with the signing of Ohio high school phenom George Sisler, but had then lost the future Hall of Famer to the St. Louis Browns in an arbitration hearing over conflicting contracts.)

Aside from Grimm, the team's main strengths entering the new decade were league-leading base stealer Max Carey, four-time 20-game winner Wilbur Cooper, and spray-hitting outfielder Carson Bigbee. Of much greater importance for the future, the 1920 season also marked the major league debut of Pie Traynor, the third baseman who would become second only to Wagner in franchise legend.

The 1921 season offered a taste of things to come. With the high-living shortstop Rabbit Maranville imported from Boston in a preseason trade, the Pirates solidified their defense and a "little ball" offense sufficiently to streak out of the gate and remain in first

Pittsburgh station KDKA provided the first radio broadcast of a baseball game on August 5, 1921. The Pirates' opponent was the Philadelphia Phillies. The broadcaster was Harold Arlin.

place until the end of August. But then, largely because of a disastrous series in the Polo Grounds in which Pittsburgh lost five straight games, the Giants came with a rush, ending up with the pennant by four games. Although the club had surpassed most predictions that it would have ended up in the middle of the pack again, Dreyfuss was not amused by the September collapse, especially because it brought another pennant to his old foe McGraw. When the owner wasn't wondering aloud if Gibson hadn't failed to motivate the team enough down the stretch, he was growling about the well-publicized antics of Maranville, Grimm, and a couple of other Pirates. On one occasion, Dreyfuss himself became the object of a mocking (and somewhat drunken) tribute from Maranville and a Pawnee pitcher named Chief Moses Yellowhorse, leading him to order Gibson to crack down on the players. Instead, Gibson attempted a middle course, pleasing nobody. In July of 1922, tired of attacks on all sides, he announced his resignation, and was succeeded by Bill McKechnie.

McKechnie had two directives: to develop young prospects Traynor and outfielder Kiki Cuyler into vital centers of a pennant winner and to cut down on the clowning that, according to Dreyfuss, was destroying the team's image. In his first task, McKechnie had little to do but watch. In seventeen major league seasons, Traynor (elected to Cooperstown in 1948) compiled a batting average of .320, while Cuyler's (elected in 1968) eighteen years ended with a .321 mark. Where imposing discipline was concerned, however, McKechnie didn't do much better than Gibson. Deciding that the best way of handling Maranville and Yellowhorse was to room with them on the road, the manager returned to his hotel after an early movie one evening to discover the two players sleeping off another drinking bout. When he opened the bottom drawer of his bureau, a dozen pigeons flew up into his face. With such pranks as the background, it was only a question of time before Maranville and the Chief were dispatched elsewhere.

McGraw's Giants remained the dominant team in the NL for the first half of the 1920s, so Dreyfuss had a lot to be irritated by. His irritation rose again to fury in September of 1924 following disclosures that

Giants coach Cozy Dolan had been involved in an attempt to bribe Philadelphia shortstop Heinie Sand to throw some crucial games New York's way. With the Giants, Dodgers, and Pirates all within a hair of each other at the top of the standings, Dreyfuss awaited the response of Commissioner Kenesaw Landis to the revelations, and particularly to unconfirmed reports that Dolan had not been the only New Yorker to approach the Phillies. When Landis finally came forward with a verdict blacklisting only Dolan and intermediary Jimmy O'Connell, Dreyfuss exploded, telling the commissioner to investigate further and, in the meantime, annul the scheduled World Series between the Giants and Senators. But even with AL President Ban Johnson also urging Landis to censure New York by authorizing the runner-up Dodgers to play in the Series, the Judge turned a deaf ear except to make it clear that he didn't appreciate Dreyfuss's insinuations that he had not conducted a thorough inquiry.

If nothing else, the episode galvanized Dreyfuss into action. Announcing that he was tired of the competent "little ball" that the team had been playing for years and that he wanted a pennant sooner than later, he shocked most of the league by trading pitcher Cooper, Maranville, and Grimm to the Cubs for George Grantham, a hitter who played first base and second base with equal mediocrity, and pitchers Vic Aldridge and Al Niehaus. Then, in a move that was seen as aimed at both lighting a fire under McKechnie and blunting the bad press over the departure of the popular Maranville and Grimm, he brought back Fred Clarke from his retirement ranch in Kansas. Depending on the day, Dreyfuss variously described Clarke's function as coach, assistant manager, and vice-president; but the main point was that he was in uniform on the field.

The pennant success of the 1925 Pirates was no mystery: Of the eight regular position players and the two most used backups, only second baseman Eddie Moore and substitute catcher Johnny Gooch failed to bat .300—and they both hit .298! The overall club average was .307, with the principal contributions coming from Cuyler (.357), Carey (.343), Grantham (.326), outfielder Clyde Barnhart (.325), and a midseason pickup from the American League, long-time Red Sox star Stuffy McInnis (.368). Four players—Cuyler, Traynor, Barnhart, and shortstop Glenn Wright—both scored and batted in more than 100 runs. With Traynor and Wright providing the strongest defense in the league on the left side of the infield, the unexceptional pitching staff struggled through, despite the fact that Aldridge led the staff

with an ERA of 3.63. In the World Series against Washington, the team spotted Walter Johnson and the Senators a 3–1 lead in games, then became the first club ever to overcome such a steep deficit to take the championship. The victory was locked up with a 15-hit pounding of Johnson in the seventh game. While Dreyfuss was not ready to admit it, the turning point of the Series came after the fourth game when McGraw, reduced to a spectator, advised manager McKechnie to bench the slumping and defensively erratic Grantham in favor of McInnis. McKechnie took up the suggestion, and McInnis steadied the infield over the final three games.

Throughout the team's pennant-winning year, Dreyfuss had singled out Clarke as one of the fundamental reasons for what he viewed as a positive change in the spirit of the club. When it came to sharing out the World Series pool, however, a majority of players argued that Clarke, as a vice-president and minority shareholder in the Pirates, was not entitled to the same money as the other coaches. When he was given a $1,000 consolation prize, the former manager returned the check, setting the mood for the following season. The first blowup came in May, when Grantham spurned some batting tips from Clarke and sportswriters began speculating that the coach had lost the confidence of the players. Then, in August, Clarke urged McKechnie to bench Carey for his slumping offense and when asked by the manager to suggest a replacement, shot back: "Anybody, even the batboy." Outfielder Carson Bigbee heard the crack and reported it to Carey, who immediately called a players-only meeting to discuss the tensions between Clarke and most of the team. In the course of the meeting, Carey asked pitcher Babe Adams his opinion of the situation, and Adams said that "managers should manage, and no one else should interfere." Emboldened by such apparent antagonism toward Clarke, Carey and Bigbee organized a vote among the players on the question of whether Clarke ought to be allowed to remain on the bench. To their surprise, the team voted by an 18–6 margin to keep the coach around; among those endorsing his stay was Adams, who had debuted in the major leagues under the old outfielder-manager.

But Clarke could not leave well enough alone. Buoyed by the favorable vote, he demanded that Dreyfuss get rid of what were then being referred to as the A(Adams)B(Bigbee)C(Carey) Mutineers. Dreyfuss acquiesced, releasing Adams and Bigbee unconditionally and selling Carey to the Dodgers. When Adams protested that his only involvement had been to answer Carey's apparently innocuous question, the owner insisted that this still amounted to insubordination. The three players took their case to NL President John Heydler, but Heydler, while absolving them of the insubordination charge, upheld the right of the Pirates to get rid of any player the team wanted to.

The fallout didn't end there. In late September, Dreyfuss decided that McInnis had been talking out of both sides of his mouth during the controversy and also released the first baseman. Then, a couple of days after the close of the season, McKechnie was handed his walking papers for not showing enough authority during the crisis. No sooner did the press begin to speculate that Clarke was going to crown his victory by being reappointed manager than he also departed the scene, resigning from all his posts and even liquidating his very small interest in the franchise. With every one of the scandal's principals gone, Dreyfuss tapped former Detroit shortstop Donie Bush as the new manager.

Although the Clarke fracas overshadowed much of the 1926 season, Pittsburgh remained in contention right down to the wire, ending up in third place, 4½ games behind St. Louis. The campaign marked the arrival of outfielder Paul Waner, who batted .336, clouted 35 doubles, and led the league with 22 triples. Over the next twenty years, Waner (elected as a Hall of Famer in 1952) would win three batting crowns as part of a lifetime .333 mark, lead the league in hits twice, in doubles twice, in triples twice, in runs scored twice, and in RBIs once. Like Wagner, he would not dip below a .300 average until well into his career (in his thirteenth season), then come back the following year to hit .328 again.

With four future Cooperstown residents in the 1927 lineup, the Pirates once again clouted their way to the top of the league with a team average of .305. To get there, though, they had to post a record of 22–9 in September to eke by the Cardinals and Giants, each of which also could boast of numerous all-stars.

Indicative of the Pirates punch was the fact that Traynor batted .342—and was only the third highest hitter in the everyday lineup. Leading the attack was Waner, whose .380 average, 131 RBIs, and 17 triples led the NL in those categories. The next most consistent hitter was Waner's brother Lloyd, who debuted by batting .355 and leading the league in runs scored (133). Known as Little Poison in tandem with Paul's Big Poison, Lloyd Waner was a classic leadoff hitter whose speed converted numerous ground balls into infield singles. In an eighteen-year career,

he would average .316 and establish himself as a premier defensive outfielder. He was elected to Cooperstown in 1967.

With the two Waners and Cuyler starting the season in the outfield, there was a great deal of expectation that the team would be settled in those three positions for years to come. But that optimism was deflated in June when Bush, trying to shake the club out of a minor slide, bumped Cuyler from third to second in the lineup. The outfielder protested, saying that he wasn't a good hit-and-run man and was better suited to driving in runs from the third spot, then went hitless in a few games to back up his case. But the more Cuyler remonstrated, the more adamant Bush became that the player was merely questioning his authority. Finally, after almost a week of tensions, Bush snapped when Cuyler failed to slide into second base to break up a double play and fined him $25. The two got into a shouting exchange that ended with Cuyler's being benched indefinitely. When a group of Cuyler loyalists in the grandstands and the press began to blast Bush for his attitude, Dreyfuss came to the defense of his manager. The stubbornness of both the manager and the owner were enough to keep Cuyler on the bench for the rest of the season and even the World Series. After the season, he was traded to the Cubs in exchange for two unknowns and picked up his brilliant career where he had left off.

The other sour note of 1927 was the World Series, where the Murderers Row lineup of the Yankees ran over Pittsburgh in four games. Although three of the four games were closer than the sweep might have indicated, the Pirates were no match for Babe Ruth, Lou Gehrig, and the rest of the New York lineup.

If the Pirates had always been a team more gifted with hitters than pitchers, the emphasis became even more marked during the next stage of the team's evolution. Following Carmen Hill's 22 victories for the 1927 pennant winners, Pittsburgh's only 20-game winners until the middle of World War II were the veteran spitballer Burleigh Grimes in 1928 and Ray Kremer in 1930. Year after year, the club seemed to have to turn over its staff, not merely to find support for one or two reliables as in the days of Cooper and Willis, but to come up with an annual ace. The only Pirate hurler of the period who earned consistent respect from the rest of the league was reliever Mace Brown, and even he ended up yielding the most notorious home run in the history of the franchise.

On the other hand, the Pirates continued to hit—

and to find players who would eventually walk into Cooperstown as honored guests. In the 1930s, the chief find was Arky Vaughan, a shortstop who went both Wagner and Waner one better by *never* batting below .300 in a Pittsburgh uniform. In his ten-year stay with the team, Vaughan won batting and slugging championships, led NL batters in triples three times, in runs scored twice, and in bases on balls three times; his career average came out to .318, entitling him to the Hall of Fame in 1985.

Dreyfuss swept away both Bush (in 1929) and his successor Jewel Ens (in 1931) in his impatience for another flag. The Bush exit was notable insofar as it popularized the kiss-of-death interpretation of public votes of confidence in a manager (Dreyfuss having insisted only a short time before that there wasn't a better field leader in baseball) and also carried on the Pittsburgh tradition of managers "resigning" rather than being fired.

Managerial changes were the least of the shocks to hit the franchise with the dawning of the 1930s. In 1931, Dreyfuss's son Samuel, vice-president-treasurer-business manager and heir apparent to the team, died of pneumonia at the age of 36. The grief-stricken father went around in a daze for months. Finally, under subtle pressures from NL President Heydler, he agreed to bring in somebody to run the team, found nobody to his liking, and turned to his son-in-law Bill Benswanger. Benswanger, an insurance company executive by profession, consented only to a temporary post. In January 1932, however, Dreyfuss himself was operated on for a glandular condition, contracted pneumonia, and, after a one-month battle, also died. Immediately after being named as the club's new chairwoman of the board, Dreyfuss's widow pleaded with Benswanger to stay on. With less than a year's experience, the son-in-law withdrew from his insurance business and took over the team on a full-time basis.

Aside from the passing of Dreyfuss and the arrival of Vaughan, Pittsburgh baseball in the 1930s came down to three things: the reappearance of Wagner, Sunday games, and a Mace Brown pitch to Cubs catcher Gabby Hartnett. Shortly before the start of the 1933 season, the team announced that its greatest player, Wagner, was returning as a coach. Wagner himself had requested the position after years of menial jobs and the onset of the Depression had driven him to the edge of poverty. Although there were to be periodic rumors of Wagner taking over the club, he in fact remained only as a coach for some twenty years, willy-nilly becoming an enduring reminder of the Dreyfuss regime. On the other hand, Benswanger

made one decisive break with his late father-in-law when he brought Pittsburgh its first Sunday home game on April 29, 1934. Dreyfuss had always opposed playing on the sabbath, not because of religious principles but because of a fear that Sunday games would cut into attendance on Saturdays, traditionally a gold mine at both the gate and at concession stands.

On September 28, 1938, the Pirates experienced something like the anguish felt in New York after Fred Merkle's boner and felt in Brooklyn after Bobby Thomson's home run. In what amounted to an eleventh-hour contest for the pennant, Pittsburgh took on Chicago in Wrigley Field with a half-game lead. With darkness descending over a 5–5 tie in the ninth inning, the umpires made it clear that there would be no extra innings. With two out and two strikes on Hartnett, Brown shook off a fastball sign, threw a curve, and watched what became known as The Homer in the Gloamin'. The Pirates never recovered from the evening blow, and Chicago went on to win the pennant.

Not counting the questionable standards of World War II ball, the Pirates would not rise again as high as second for twenty years. Before that achievement in 1958, there would be years of edging back and forth over the .500 mark and then a plunge to the basement that only the 1890 Innocents would have truly appreciated. The 1930s also marked the peaking of the Waners and Traynor, with the latter becoming Gibson's successor as manager in 1934. For a couple of years, Traynor tried to do double duty as a third baseman and pilot, but then hung up his spikes for good at the age of 35. Over five-and-a-half seasons as manager, he compiled a winning percentage of .530, but this also included being at the helm for Hartnett's homer and for the team's 1939 flop into sixth place. In keeping with franchise tradition, Traynor "resigned" after the 1939 season; his replacement was the Fordham Flash, Frankie Frisch.

Like his mentor, McGraw, Frisch did nothing by halves. His abrasive style and tart tongue cut umpires, opposing players, and his own players alike; he whooped with every victory; he went into heavy brooding after every defeat. During his seven-year tenure, he got into one or more personality clashes with all of the team's offensive stars of the period, including Vaughan, Vince Dimaggio, and Bob Elliott.

The rift with Vaughan became so deep that Frisch lobbied for the deal that eventually sent the shortstop to Brooklyn in exchange for Pete Coscarat, Luke Hamlin, Babe Phelps, and Jimmy Wasdell. As bad as all these players turned out for Pittsburgh, they were about as good as it got when Frisch and Benswanger went into the trade market in the early 1940s. The chief exception was a December 1943 deal with the Phillies that brought Pittsburgh first baseman Babe Dahlgren in exchange for Phelps and cash; Dahlgren went on to hit .289 and drive in 101 runs in 1944.

Like other managers, Frisch received the benefit of the doubt from the front office and fans alike during the war years because of the decimation of rosters through the military draft. He was even regarded as something of a mastermind for piloting the team's overripe and unripe squad into second place in 1944. His main assets were 21-game winner Rip Sewell, famous for his floating "Eephus ball"; third baseman Elliott, who batted .297 with 108 RBIs; outfielder Johnny Barrett, who led the league in triples and stolen bases; and Dahlgren.

In the years immediately after World War II, the club didn't get any better (it actually got worse), but it got more interesting. Among those returning from military service for 1946 were the organization's two most highly touted prospects—shortstop Billy Cox and outfielder Ralph Kiner. Scouted by Traynor and coached by Wagner, the spidery Cox was hailed as the team's best defensive infielder since Maranville, and he didn't disappoint; in addition, he ended up leading the club with a .290 average. It was Kiner, though, who turned out to be the true sensation, in his rookie year becoming the first Pirate to lead the NL in home runs since Tommy Leach back at the beginning of the century.

For all the Wagners, Waners, and Traynors who had played for Pittsburgh, Kiner was the franchise's first genuine long-ball slugger. Although he remained in the majors for only ten seasons, the future Hall of Famer (1975) bashed 369 homers in that time, including five straight years of 40 or more, and ended up second only to Babe Ruth in home run frequency. Kiner's slugging was all the more remarkable in that he spent years of his Pittsburgh career in lineups that not only seldom boasted a second power threat, but that arguably didn't even have other major league talents. This situation became so marked in the early 1950s that many fans didn't bother showing up at Forbes Field until the second inning, on the assumption that the first three Pirates would be retired in the first inning and Kiner would only be coming up to hit as the cleanup batter in the second; by the same token, his final at bat in the eighth inning usually signaled a mass exit for the street. Given his lack of protection, it was not too surprising that the out-

fielder received at least 100 walks for seven years in a row; despite that, he still managed to drive in more than 100 runs in five consecutive years. As he was to realize to his regret in later years, Kiner came as close to being a "one-man team" as any player in the modern era.

But Kiner wasn't the only new wind blowing through the Pirate clubhouse in 1946. Early in spring training, a Harvard-educated attorney named Robert Murphy sounded out the players about representing them in a union. Although Murphy had also been in contact with other teams, he zeroed in on Pittsburgh because of the city's strong union tradition and the well-publicized chafing of players under Frisch. By early June, to the consternation of Benswanger and other owners, Murphy was claiming that he had enrolled a majority of the Pirates and that he would soon be pressing such demands as resolving salary disputes through collective bargaining and giving players a percentage of the money exchanged for their sale; another aim of the so-called American Baseball Guild was to arrive at a limited form of free agency. On June 8th, Murphy called a meeting of the players prior to a night game at Forbes Field and asked them to go out on strike. Despite indications that only Sewell and infielder Jimmy Brown opposed the union idea, the players came up just short of the three-fourths majority that would have sanctioned the walkout. Lee Handley, a second baseman who had been one of the more outspoken unionists, admitted later that he had cast one of the negative votes because "we're not radicals." Arguing that the ballot result had been preordained by an air of intimidation around the club, Murphy appealed to Pennsylvania's Labor Relations Board. The board conducted its own poll of the players to see whether they wanted the Guild as their bargaining agent, and Murphy lost by a count of 15–3, with ten players abstaining. The lawyer withdrew his charges against Benswanger and faded from the scene. Later that year, Commissioner Happy Chandler presented Sewell with a wristwatch for taking his pro-management stand. This in turn prompted a series of clubhouse clashes between the pitcher and his teammates. For his part, infielder Brown was beaten up one evening by unidentified assailants as he was leaving Forbes Field.

Rumors that Dreyfuss's widow Florence and Benswanger were interested in unloading the team had been circulating in Pittsburgh throughout the first half of 1946. Finally in July, Benswanger acknowledged that he had been reviewing offers from several sources and that the controversy over the unionization attempt had only strengthened Florence

Dreyfuss's resolve to get out. As announced officially on August 8th, the purchasers were a group headed by Indianapolis banker Frank McKinney, Columbus realtor John Galbreath, Pittsburgh attorney Tom Johnson, and entertainer Bing Crosby. The sale price was $2.5 million. To run the day-to-day baseball operations, the new owners brought in Roy Hamey, most recently president of the American Association.

For better or worse, the first Pirate club without a Dreyfuss since 1899 wasted little time in making an imprint. The first to go—regarded as a positive—was Frisch. The first to come—also considered a positive—was Detroit slugger Hank Greenberg, talked out of retirement for a one-year contract of $80,000 not only to furnish some power, but also to take Kiner under his wing and smooth out the outfielder's rougher edges.

Then there was a simultaneous coming and going that turned out to be only the first in a series of bad trades engineered by McKinney and Hamey. Resolved to get Boston second baseman Billy Herman as a player-manager successor to Frisch, the Pirates allowed themselves to get into a bidding war with Cincinnati for the future Hall of Famer's services. With Braves owner Lou Perini using one suitor against the other, Pittsburgh finally agreed to surrender Elliott in exchange for Herman, infielder Whitey Wietelman, outfielder Stan Wentzel, and pitcher Elmer Singleton. The trade was so weighted in Boston's favor that even Herman, the object of the transaction, told McKinney upon joining the club that Pittsburgh had given away too much. Herman was right. After an arm injury just about ended his value as a player, he proved to be an even more glaringly unable manager, and had to be replaced before the end of the year by Bill Burwell. On the other hand, Elliott went on to become the league's most valuable player for Boston's pennant-winning team of 1948.

Surprisingly, the club's second straight seventh-place finish was not reflected at the gate, where the franchise went over the one-million mark for the first time. The sole reason for the enthusiasm was the swatting duo of Kiner and Greenberg. To get even more bang for their buck, the Pirates installed a bullpen in left field that shortened the distance from home plate by some thirty feet. At first called Greenberg Gardens, then Kiner's Korner, the structural addition became the most noted feature of Forbes Field as it contributed significantly to Greenberg's 25 homers and Kiner's league-leading 51.

With Billy Meyer taking over the managerial reins in 1948, the club rode Kiner's bat and some solid hitting from second baseman Danny Murtaugh

and outfielder Wally Westlake to an unexpected fourth in the standings. But as was to be the case for years to come, Meyer had to juggle an army of journeymen pitchers who seemed to arrive in the morning, get battered in the afternoon, and then leave again in the evening. In 1947 and 1948 alone, McKinney earned his sobriquet of The Old Clothes Man by plucking off the waiver wire Hi Bithorn, Hugh Mulcahy, Jim Bagby, Lou Tost, Bob Malloy, Roger Wolff, Mel Queen, Al Lyons, Elmer Riddle, Paul Erickson, and Bob Muncrief; in two deals with the Dodgers alone, the team acquired pitchers Kirby Higbe, Hank Behrman, Cal McLish, Hal Gregg, and Vic Lombardi. The last two not only didn't bring much to the Pittsburgh table, but cost the club Cox and southpaw Preacher Roe, integral pieces of the Boys of Summer championship teams in Brooklyn.

The fourth-place finish in 1948 was as high as Meyer or his immediate successors Fred Haney and Bobby Bragan would ever get the club. In the 1950s, the franchise plunged to an all-time low with five cellar finishes in six years and three consecutive 100-game losing seasons. In 1950, the club broke spring training with an outfield phenom named Dino Restelli. In the third batting slot ahead of Kiner and Westlake, Restelli became a Pittsburgh hero when he belted two homers off Warren Spahn in his second big league game and clouted nine within the first two weeks of the season. But he hit only three more for the year and ended up back in the minors in 1951.

Around the same time that the league discovered that Restelli couldn't hit a curve, McKinney came to the conclusion that he wasn't cut out for the rough treatment he was receiving in the press and sold his interest in the franchise to Galbreath. Galbreath had an even more startling announcement of his own after the 1950 season, when he hired Branch Rickey to take over the team's baseball operations.

Rickey arrived in Pittsburgh with a reputation for having put together some of the greatest teams ever to take the field in St. Louis and Brooklyn; by the time he left, he had added to his resume the singular feat of having made bad Pittsburgh clubs even worse. Part of the problem was that, Kiner and a couple of other players aside, the Pirates had nowhere near the talent that the Cardinals and Dodgers had possessed prior to Rickey's entrance on the scene. Another difficulty was that the aging Mahatma executed one bad trade after another, following his long-tested principle of giving away players at the peak of their careers in exchange for quantities of prospects that he hoped would produce at least one star. Without too many Pirates in a position to boast about peaks, however, Rickey ended up having to accept as many over-the-hill players as promising minor leaguers. Typical was his first big deal in June 1951, when he peddled Westlake and southpaw pitcher Cliff Chambers to the Cardinals for catcher Joe Garagiola, outfielder Bill Howerton, infielder Dick Cole, and graying hurlers Howie Pollett and Ted Wilks. An even bigger disaster was the shipping of all-star outfielder Gus Bell to the Reds in October 1952 for outfielder Cal Abrams, catcher Joe Rossi, and infielder-outfielder Gail Henley. A third debacle was the December 1953 trade of second baseman Danny O'Connell to the Braves in exchange for outfielders Sid Gordon and Sam Jethroe and pitchers Max Surkont, Larry Lasalle, Curt Raydon, and Fred Walters. But it was the June 4, 1953 trade of Kiner that truly alienated Rickey from Pittsburgh fans.

The slugging outfielder and the team general manager had been at odds almost from the moment of Rickey's arrival. Among other things that Rickey didn't like about Kiner were the outfielder's visibility in player association causes and the frequency of his name in gossip columns for being linked with this or that Hollywood actress. On another level, Kiner also irritated Rickey for winning over Pittsburgh fans with the generally one-dimensional skills (power) that the executive had always preached against in dispensing his views about ideal players. For his part, Kiner didn't hesitate to describe Rickey as a liar and hypocrite for his devious negotiation tactics with players. The end came on June 4, 1953, when Rickey packaged Kiner, Garagiola, Pollett, and first baseman George Metkovich to Chicago in return for six undistinguished players and $150,000. Rickey's only defense against the general uproar in Pittsburgh was to assert that the team could finish last without Kiner as easily as with him.

What Rickey had no answer to, on the other hand, were repeated Kiner charges about his cheapness. The executive was in fact so tight that he was reluctant to replace injured players with others who would require salaries and travel expenses; during the 1952 season alone, the team had to make two road trips with only eighteen players, seven under the limit. In another example of dollar-stretching, Rickey signed so many players to serf-scale minor league contracts that the franchise ended up with more than 400 athletes in the fold in the early 1950s. Ninety percent of these players were in their teens.

For the most part, the prospects who arrived in Pittsburgh during Rickey's reign displayed little but their willingness to work for baseball's minimum salary. These included infielders Curt Roberts (the

Branch Rickey's animosity toward Ralph Kiner reached such a peak that he wrote a piece of free verse mocking the slugging outfielder. The ditty, mainly intended for the ears of owner John Galbreath, declared in part:
Babe Ruth could run. Our man cannot.
Ruth could throw. Our man cannot.
Ruth could steal a base. Our man cannot.
Ruth was a good fielder. Our man is not.
Ruth could hit with power to all fields. Our man cannot.
Ruth never requested a diminutive field to fit him. Our man does.

team's first black), Clem Koshorek (a mere 5'5"), Tony Bartirome (later a club trainer), and the O'Brien twins Johnny and Eddie. Minor league pitching phenoms like Paul Pettit, Ron Necciai, Joe Trimble, and Bill Bell came and went every year, with few of them toting up any major league victories. Finally, after still another cellar finish in 1955, Galbreath had enough and asked Rickey to vacate the premises. His successor was Joe L. Brown, the general manager of the franchise's minor league team in New Orleans and until then mostly known for being the son of actor-comedian Joe E. Brown, the Alibi Ike of the movies.

By any significant standard, Brown was the official most responsible for reviving the organization in the late 1950s. But it was also true that he arrived on the scene in time to oversee the final development of several players gathered up by the net that Rickey had thrown over the country's high schools with little discrimination. Among the potential talents already on hand were outfielders Frank Thomas and Bob Skinner, infielders Dick Groat and Bill Mazeroski, and pitchers Bob Friend, Ron Kline, Vern Law, and Bob Purkey. There was also future Hall of Famer Roberto Clemente, obtained by Rickey from the Dodger farm system because the right fielder's access to Ebbets Field was blocked by Carl Furillo. One of Brown's first moves was to bolster this core with Bill Virdon, a speedy center fielder acquired fairly cheaply from the Cardinals.

While waiting for this Pirate team to mature into the pennant winners of 1960, Pittsburgh fans had Dale Long, Bragan, Dick Stuart, and Harvey Haddix to entertain them. In 1956, first baseman Long hit home runs in eight consecutive games to set a new major league mark (and, for his eighth game, to draw the biggest crowd to Forbes Field since Kiner's hey-day in 1951). The lefthand-hitting slugger seemed well on his way to other feats when, a couple of weeks later, he injured his ankle, changed his stance to compensate for a persisting ache, and never re-gained his form. Bragan, whom Brown had named manager on Rickey's recommendation, was only mildly impressed with the heroics of Long and not impressed at all with the rest of the club. In one interview after another, the Rickey protege sug-gested that he was piloting a team not much better than the Bad News Bears. He also irked Brown by batting former outfielder-turned -pitcher Johnny Lin-dell ahead of Mazeroski and the catcher and pushing slugger Thomas to the top of the order so he could have an extra plate appearance. The breaking point came in 1957, when he declared that pitcher Friend and shortstop Groat were the only major leaguers on the roster. Furious that Bragan hadn't at least kept his two preferences anonymous, Brown tapped first base coach Murtaugh to take over.

Under Murtaugh, the team surged from seventh to second in 1958, in the process drawing more than a million fans again. The keys to the rise were Friend's league-leading 22 wins, Thomas's 35 hom-ers and 109 RBIs, and the double play combination of Groat (who also batted .300) and Mazeroski (.275 with 19 homers). After an aging Ted Kluszewski demonstrated that he was not the slugger he had once been for Cincinnati, the Pirates gave more play-ing time at first base to Stuart—a Kinerlike slugger who kept tape measures useful but who was so inept defensively that he later came to be called Doctor Strangeglove. On one occasion, Stuart was so embar-rassed by an error that he dug a hole for the ball near first base, earning immediate public relations points from the fans.

Although the club dropped back to fourth again in 1959, two pitching performances stood out. The first was by reliever Roy Face, who compiled 17 straight wins in relief and closed the season with an astonishing record of 18–1. Even more amazing was the southpaw Haddix's May 26th performance against Milwaukee, when he pitched a perfect game through twelve innings, only to lose everything in the thirteenth frame on an error, an intentional walk, and a blast by Braves first baseman Joe Adcock that went out of the park but that was ruled only a double after the stunned hitter passed Hank Aaron on the basepaths. Many baseball historians cite the Haddix effort as the single greatest pitching performance in major league history.

The 1960 pennant winners were the most suc-cessful Pirate club since the NL champions of 1925. But despite Law's 20 wins (good for the Cy Young trophy) and Groat's .325 average (good for the bat-ting title and the MVP award), there was very little that was dominating about the team: None of the hitters clouted as many as 25 homers or drove in 100 runs, none of the starters had an ERA under 3.00. As often as not, it was the bench (Dick Schofield, Hal Smith, Gino Cimoli) that supplied the late-inning he-roics that added up to a seven-game edge over the runner-up Braves. Especially important was Scho-field, who batted .403 in September after Groat, the team leader and most consistent offensive threat, was sidelined with a broken wrist.

The World Series turned out to be one of the most unusual in postseason history. When all the statistics were in, the Pirates ended up being out-scored by the Yankees 55–27, outhit by them 91–60, and outhomered by them 10–4; their pitching was no better, combining for an ERA of 7.11 against New York's 3.54. But the seventh and decisive game still went to the Pirates because of first, a late-inning clutch homer by backup catcher Smith and then, a leadoff ninth-inning blast by Mazeroski. Mazeroski's shot, which made the final tally 10–9, represented the only time that a World Series has been decided by a game-ending home run.

Even those who had expected 1961 to be some-what anticlimatic were not prepared for the club's collapse back to sixth place. For the rest of the de-cade, in fact, the Pirates never rose higher than third, and within three years of celebrating the world championship, such stalwarts of the 1960 team as Groat, Stuart, Skinner, and third baseman Don Hoak were wearing other uniforms. Except for catcher Jim Pagliaroni, acquired from the Red Sox in the trade for Stuart, none of the players received in exchange had appreciable tenures as regulars. On the other hand, the decade saw the gradual arrival of the play-ers who would make the Pirates the Eastern Divi-sion's foremost power in the 1970s (Willie Stargell, Gene Alley, Richie Zisk, Richie Hebner, Manny San-guillen, Al Oliver, Steve Blass, Bob Moose, Dock El-lis) and the establishment of Clemente as a Hall of Famer. To go along with one of the strongest arms in the game, the right fielder won four batting titles and, in 1966, was named the league's MVP. Also in 1966, banjo-hitting outfielder Matty Alou added his name to the franchise players who led the league in hitting.

Alou's emergence as an offensive force was at-tributed directly to Harry Walker, who took over from Murtaugh as manager in 1965. Walker himself lasted little more than two years and restored the reins to Murtaugh in July 1967. Despite Brown's urgings to remain on the job, Murtaugh claimed the same health reasons that had led to his original departure in 1965 as reason for quitting again after the season. He was replaced by Larry Shepard, a minor league manager for eighteen years who demonstrated in short order that he was not up to the promotion. After some conspicuous strategic mistakes in the course of games, Shepherd became a target of critical sportswriters and hectoring fans; on one occasion, he explained away a tactical error by saying simply, "I forgot."

Brown had at first defended his manager, but five games before the end of the 1969 season, he fired Shepard and turned the team over to coach Alex Grammas for the last week. The search for Shepard's successor prompted a tragic coincidence, if not a direct tragedy. As in 1967, the man most often mentioned in the press as the next likely pilot was former Pirate third baseman Hoak, an intense competitor as known for his short temper as his bat and glove during his playing days. But Brown kept his own counsel until he flew down to Florida to confer with old friend Murtaugh, from whom he was seeking a short list of recommendations. When Murtaugh announced instead that his doctor had given him a clean bill of health and that he was eager to get back to the dugout for another term, Brown looked no further. The general manager, sensing a news coup, flew Murtaugh secretly back to Pittsburgh, then sprang his big surprise on sportswriters October 8th. The following day, October 9th, the 42-year-old Hoak was felled by a fatal heart attack.

From 1970 to 1979, the Pirates ripped through the Eastern Division by finishing first six times, second three times, and as low as third only once. If the decade became more closely associated with Cincinnati's Big Red Machine, it was because the Pirates stumbled over the Reds three times in the League Championship Series (1970, 1972, and 1975), defeated them in only one playoff (1979), and arrived in only two World Series (1971 and 1979).

In general, Murtaugh held very loose reins on the club. In contrast to Charlie Dressen's noted remark that he would "think of something" if his team contained the opposition to a nine-run lead, the Pittsburgh manager made a ritual of telling players at preseason meetings that "if you keep me close in the eighth inning, I'll lose it every time." What his humor belied was a winning percentage of .540 spread out over fifteen different years and at the helm of teams that varied widely in talent.

Murtaugh's relaxed approach also disguised his ability to deal with characters like righthander Ellis, who made as many headlines during his nine-year career with the Pirates for his off-the-field problems as for his diamond accomplishments. On one occasion, the pitcher was maced by a security guard at Cincinnati's Riverfront Stadium to end a dispute that had started when Ellis refused to show his identification; on another road trip, he moved out of a San Francisco hotel to protest what he called the Pirates' cheap accommodations; and, as he was to reveal many years later in an autobiography, he pitched a June 12, 1970 no-hitter against San Diego while under the influence of LSD.

Neither Murtaugh nor his teammates ever questioned Ellis's determination to win games. In particular, before one game against the Reds in 1971, he announced that he intended hitting every Cincinnati batter who came to the plate, proceeded to do exactly that to the first five hitters, and had to be lifted. Even Murtaugh, who was furious at the time, conceded at the end of the season that it had been Ellis's abbreviated performance—and the edginess of Cincinnati's feared hitters against him—that made the Pirates less intimidated in subsequent games against the Big Red Machine.

Midway through their division-winning 1970 season, the Pirates moved out of Forbes Field to Three Rivers Stadium, a typical oval-and-artificial surface facility of the period. The official opening came on July 16, 1970 (a 3–2 loss to the Reds) after a decade of planning, building, and overly optimistic inauguration dates. The lefty swinger Stargell was particularly quick to baptize the park with the mammoth clouts that had become his trademark and that would lead him into the Hall of Fame in 1988. By the time he ended his twenty-one-year career in a Pittsburgh uniform in 1982, the first baseman-outfielder had amassed 475 homers and 1,540 RBIs to go with his .282 batting average (and 1,936 strikeouts).

As typified by players like Stargell, Clemente, Oliver, righty-swinging first baseman Bob Robertson, and others, the teams that won the East in 1970, 1971, and 1972 (and, for that matter, in 1974, 1975, and 1979) were very much like the Pittsburgh pennant winners in the early part of the century—long on hitting and adequate in pitching. Especially in the first part of the decade, Brown's main problem was making room on the roster for the offensive-minded outfielders (Zisk, Gene Clines, Dave Parker, Mike Easler) and second basemen (Dave Cash, Rennie Stennett, Willie Randolph) who seemed to arrive in bunches every spring; in the best of cases, he thinned out the numbers by trading for pitchers. The team's only 20-game winner in the decade was John Candelaria in 1977; in fact, the southpaw was the sole Pittsburgh pitcher to reach that mark in a thirty-year span between Cy Young winner Law in 1960 and Cy Young winner Doug Drabek in 1990.

The offense was especially in evidence in the club's championship 1971 season. In the LCS against the Giants, Robertson led a home run barrage by clouting three in one game. In the seven-game World Series against the Orioles, Clemente went on a .414 tear (and made a series of brilliant defensive plays). It was following the win over Baltimore that Murtaugh once again cited health reasons for stepping down and turning the club over to Virdon. The change came as no surprise, because Murtaugh had missed almost a month of regular season games because of illness.

In 1972, Virdon managed the club into the LCS with relative ease, but then watched Moose wild-pitch home the run that gave the Reds the pennant. Then, on New Year's Eve, the nation was stunned by the news that Clemente had been killed in the crash of a plane that was carrying relief supplies to earthquake victims in Nicaragua. As a tribute to the outfielder, the Hall of Fame waived its usual five-year rule and inducted him into Cooperstown in 1973.

The tragedy seemed to unhinge the entire organization, including Brown. In September, with the entire division still in the race, the general manager rejected Murtaugh's advice to announce a new contract for Virdon, and instead, fired the pilot. Called on still again to lead the club, Murtaugh made little attempt to disguise his uneasiness about his fourth term, hinting to one and all that he thought Virdon had gotten a raw deal and that only his friendship with Brown had convinced him to return. Insofar as this was also the general feeling among the players, Murtaugh at least had a common bafflement to work off as he steered the Pirates back into the playoffs in both 1974 and 1975.

Division wins or not, the team's inability to get past Los Angeles in 1974 and Cincinnati in 1975 increased tensions in the front office. Even before the 1975 season had begun, Galbreath had shrugged off predictions that the Pirates would go all the way by commenting, "I've heard that before." Not even the emergence of Parker and reliever Kent Tekulve during the season proved to be enough of a solace after the loss to the Reds. As frazzled by pressures from Galbreath as he was determined to right the team's pitching, Brown made a disastrous deal with the Yankees in which he surrendered Randolph, Ellis, and lefty Ken Brett in exchange for Doc Medich. Even

Roberto Clemente connects for his 3,000th hit. *National Baseball Library, Cooperstown, NY*

more unpopular was the organization's announcement that it was cutting loose announcer Bob Prince, who had been the voice of the Pirates for almost thirty years. Behind management's generic explanation that it wanted to "go in new directions" was Galbreath's irritation that Prince had become less than a 100 percent loyalist in discussing the moves of the organization.

With a few games to go in the 1976 season, Brown announced that he was resigning in favor of his assistant Harding Peterson. Over and above the team's inability to collect more World Series checks for the premier talent that it fielded, Brown was held responsible for a steady decline in attendance. With Brown gone, Murtaugh did the inevitable by also quitting. And then tragedy struck the club twice. On October 9th, pitcher Moose was killed in an auto accident at the age of 29. A few weeks later, less than two months after his resignation, Murtaugh succumbed to the illnesses that had dogged him for so long.

Through the gloom Peterson set about remaking the team. His first significant move was to send catcher Sanguillen and $100,000 to Oakland in exchange for manager Chuck Tanner and install the A's skipper as Murtaugh's successor. Before the 1977 season had gotten underway, he had also sent infielders Craig Reynolds and Jim Sexton to Seattle for southpaw reliever Grant Jackson; packaged Zisk and pitcher Silvio Martinez to the White Sox for blaze-ballers Goose Gossage and Terry Forster; unloaded the caravan of pitchers Dave Giusti, Doug Bair, Rick Langford, and Medich, along with outfielders Tony Armas and Mitchell Page, to Oakland in return for infielders Phil Garner and Tommy Helms; and acquired slugger Easler from California in exchange for a minor league pitcher. The four interleague trades suggested to many that Peterson was relying heavily on the advice of Tanner.

For a couple of years, the changes brought only two more second-place finishes. The chief attraction

was Parker, who won batting titles in both 1977 and 1978 and who was rewarded with a million-dollar contract (covering five years). Together with the runner-up status of the club, a growing economic crisis in Pittsburgh as a whole depressed attendance figures even further, with the total going below one million in 1978.

In 1979, however, the club came back. To the theme song of "We Are Family" and with a swaggering style reminiscent of the franchise's most gloried Lumber Companies, the aging Stargell and Parker led the Pirates to a division win on the last day of the regular season, a three-game sweep of the Reds in the LCS playoffs, and a tensely fought World Series victory over the Orioles in seven games. The keys to the championship were two deals that Peterson pulled off after the start of the season, obtaining sparkplug shortstop Tim Foli from the Mets and line drive-hitting Bill Madlock from the Giants. With Tekulve and Jackson doing workhorse duty from the bullpen, six pitchers won in double figures, but none more than Candelaria's 14 victories. Stargell was named co-winner of the MVP award with St. Louis's Keith Hernandez; he was the oldest player (38) ever to receive the trophy.

The 1979 World Series turned out to be the last hurrah before another black period. In the 1980s, the Pirates were the only Eastern Division team not to reach the playoffs—and that was the least of it. In obtaining players such as Garner and Madlock for quick returns, Peterson discovered that he had practically bankrupted the organization's farm system, with players like Reynolds, Armas, Whitson, and Langford going on to star elsewhere. His ability to sign or just hold on to free agents was even worse—with only over-the-hill players like Gene Tenace and Amos Otis proving available for Pittsburgh prices. About the only trade made by Peterson that wasn't a catastrophe or a non-event was an August 1981 swap that brought the Pirates second baseman Johnny Ray from Houston in exchange for Garner. Not only weren't fans patient, they became markedly abusive toward Parker for making the kind of money that the city's unemployed could only dream about. When the outfielder's bad knees cost him appreciable playing time and his idleness added to his waistline, the same fans who were amused by Stargell's balloon proportions began pelting Parker with batteries and other objects. He left the team after the 1983 season to sign with Cincinnati as a free agent; it was while he was with the Reds that he was named as having been a heavy drug user in his last years with the Pirates.

Galbreath's solution to the thinning talents on

Pittsburgh's turn-of-the-century caps were one of baseball's hottest promotional items in the late 1970s and early 1980s, but it wasn't the first time that the team's attire caused a stir. In the late 1880s, the club had such gaudy blue-and-black-striped uniforms that they acquired such monikers as the Smoked Italians, the Zulus, and the Potato Bugs.

the field and thinning customers in the stands was to demand in 1981 that the city negotiate new terms for the club's rental of Three Rivers Stadium. Among other things, the owner wanted the city to foot the bill for repairs, maintenance, and new access roads, claiming that this was the only way for the franchise to reverse some $6 million in losses and prevent it from having to be sold or transferred to another city. As soon as the latter threat was aired, New Orleans Superdome general manager Cliff Wallace flew to Pittsburgh to see what it would take to move the Pirates to Louisiana. The city of Pittsburgh immediately filed suit to keep New Orleans out of the picture, and Wallace went back home. Over the next couple of years, the battle between the city and the team blew hot and cold, with nominal concessions on both sides and persistent rumors of a franchise move. In 1983, Galbreath tried another path by taking on Warner Communications as a 48 percent partner. But after several months of rumors that the Warner involvement was a prelude to the pay-for-view coverage of Pirate games, both the media giant and Galbreath announced that they wanted out altogether.

While he was waiting for buyers to come forward with a feasible offer, Galbreath asked Brown to return in place of Peterson. Brown agreed, on the condition that his second tenure last only through the 1985 season, by which time he expected Galbreath to have sold the franchise. With the Pittsburgh drug trials underway and former Pirate players like Parker, Milner, Lee Lacy, Dale Berra, and Rod Scurry being mentioned prominently, Brown didn't need to be told that he was inheriting a mess even worse than the one he had cleaned up after Rickey. His first move was to unload Candelaria and outfielder George Hendrick—both of whom had become laughing-stocks of effort—on the California Angels. Next to go was Madlock, whom Brown decided was a bad influence on the younger players for his constant criticisms of the organization; the four-time batting champion was traded to the Dodgers for first baseman Sid Bream and outfielders Cecil Espy and R.J. Reynolds. Finally, Brown got rid of Tanner, whose constantly upbeat assurances to the media could not cover the disorder that had overtaken the team. As for Tanner's assertions that he knew nothing about the heavy drug taking that was going on in the locker room and even on the team bus during the early 1980s, they were interpreted most benignly as the admissions of a pilot totally removed from his players.

Around the same time that Brown was winding up his sweep of the clubhouse, Galbreath announced that he had completed the sale of the franchise to a local coalition from both public and private sectors headed by Mayor Richard Caliguiri. Among the most prominent investors were Malcolm Prine and Carl Barger. Under the terms of an unusual arrangement, thirteen companies or individuals put up $2 million each, with the city expected to match that $26 million with another $25 million raised through a bond issue. From the projected $51 million, $22 million was to go to Galbreath and his partners, $9 million for team debts, and some $20 million for operating expenses. (It would be some years before the city would come up with its share of the investment.)

With Prine replacing Galbreath as club president, the first move by the new ownership was to hire Syd Thrift as general manager. In turn, Thrift named Jim Leyland, a long-time manager in the Tiger organization and a coach for the White Sox, as the successor to Tanner. The results in 1986 were negligible, with the club finishing in the basement of the Eastern Division for the third consecutive year. But between July of that season and the following April, Pittsburgh pulled off three trades that were to provide the underpinning for a triumphant start to the 1990s. The first transaction allowed the club to reacquire outfielder-third baseman Bobby Bonilla (he had been lost in the draft) from the White Sox, the second imported 1990 Cy Young winner Drabek from the Yankees, and the third brought the club outfielder Andy Van Slyke, catcher Mike Lavalliere, and pitcher Mike Dunne from the Cardinals. With these players and farm products Barry Bonds and Jose Lind winning regular jobs, the Pirates moved up to fourth in 1987 and to second in 1988.

Never one to hide his light under a bushel, Thrift let everyone know that he was the one mainly responsible for what he called "resurrecting the dead." When he demanded that he be given greater control over the organization as a whole, Prine declined, necessitating various peacemaking sessions before the board in 1987. Finally, with Barger and the other directors having to choose between Prine and the general manager who was making good on his vow to reanimate the franchise, they threw their weight behind Thrift. Prine resigned, Barger took over the presidency, and Douglas Danforth was elected chairman of the board. The pro-Thrift vote seemed vindicated the following year, when the club's second-place finish drew 1,866,713 fans—a franchise record. But there was a big fly in the ointment. Determined to overtake the Mets in the latter part of the season, Thrift began to spend liberally for veterans like Gary Redus, Glenn Wilson, Ken Oberkfell, and Dave LaPoint as backup players. When the team still came in a full 15 games behind New York, Barger and Danforth had their excuse for firing Thrift. To accusations that he had gone over his budget, the general manager countercharged that Barger and Danforth were mainly interested in running the team themselves. Organization man Larry Doughty was appointed the new general manager.

With Thrift cackling from the sidelines, the Pirates sagged to fifth in 1989, but mainly because of a plague of injuries. The essential solidity of the club became apparent in 1990, when Leyland beat off a late rise by the Mets to win the division by four games. In classic Pittsburgh fashion, Drabek's 22 wins were ten more than runner-up Neal Heaton's, with only the two of them in double figures. On the other hand, Bonds snagged the MVP for his 33 homers, 114 RBIs, 52 stolen bases, and .301 average; Bonilla cracked 32 homers and drove in 120 runs; and Van Slyke belted 17 homers while consolidating himself as the best defensive center fielder in the NL. But in the reprise of a familiar story, the so-called Killer Bees (Bonds, Bonilla, Bream, regular shortstop Jay Bell, platoon third baseman Wally Backman) dropped the LCS to Cincinnati.

The 1991 season brought still another division title, with Bonds and Bonilla again keying the offense and southpaw John Smiley leading the staff with a record of 20–8. In the playoffs against Atlanta, however, the two outfielders and the lefthander were particularly ineffective, and the Pirates went down in seven games. The drive to the division title was clouded all year by the impression that the club was not going to be able to meet Bonilla's free agent demands at the conclusion of the season; in fact, the switch-hitting slugger moved to the Mets in the fall.

In the middle of the 1991 season, Barger got permission from Commissioner Fay Vincent to remain as president despite the announcement that he intended taking over the Florida Marlins' expansion organization at the end of the year. It was only after a barrage of media criticism that Vincent had second

thoughts and asked the Pirates' official to step down immediately. Barger was replaced by Mark Sauer, who shortly afterward fired Doughty for "too many mistakes." Among Doughty's most criticized lapses were prematurely identifying "players to be named later" in 1990 deals with the Expos and Phillies, allowing Leyland favorite Bream to get away to Atlanta as a free agent, alienating Bonilla with some ill-timed remarks, and spending more money than had been budgeted for free agent righthander Bob Walk. In taking over as general manager, former catcher Ted Simmons acknowledged that the club was probably not going to be able to resign its big name free agents, and signaled the start of an organization overhaul by trading Smiley to Minnesota for a couple of prospects.

Just when the team seemed on the verge of getting the best possible deals for Bonds and Drabek as well, however, Leyland had the Pirates back in its familiar place atop the Eastern Division. Two moves in the middle of the season were to prove particularly vital to the club's third straight division win. The first was the swap of third baseman Steve Buechele to the Cubs, which not only added useful lefty Danny Jackson to the starting rotating, but also opened up a position for a revived Jeff King in the infield. The second move was the promotion from the minors of knuckleballer Tim Wakefield, who went 8–1 with an ERA of 2.15 over the last part of the season. When he wasn't making it clear that he was headed to another team after the season, Bonds was amassing the numbers (34 homers, 103 RBIs, .311, 39 steals) that would give him another MVP trophy. Other key contributors were Van Slyke (.324) and Drabek (15 wins with a 2.77 ERA).

The LCS against the Braves was the same old story—in spades. With only one out to get in the ninth inning of the seventh game to get into the World Series for the first time since 1979, the team saw Atlanta pinch hitter Francisco Cabrera single in two runs off reliever Stan Belinda to send Pittsburgh home once again without a pennant.

As anticipated, both Bonds (to San Francisco) and Drabek (to Houston) took off after the season. More unexpected was a Simmons deal that sent Lind to the Royals to open up second base for prospect Carlos Garcia. Throughout the fall and winter, the club adhered to its money-saving philosophy by signing only second-line free agents such as the aging outfielder Lonnie Smith and the equally weathered reliever Alejandro Peña. The off-season also saw Sauer consolidating his control of the front office.

In 1989, the Pirates had to use outfielder-first baseman Benny DiStefano as a catcher. DiStefano thus became the third lefthand-throwing receiver in the postwar era. The others were Dale Long for the Cubs in 1958 and Mike Squires for the White Sox in 1980.

PITTSBURGH PIRATES

Annual Standings and Managers

Year	Position	W	L	Pct.	GB	Managers
1887	Sixth	55	69	.444	24	Horace Phillips
1888	Sixth	66	68	.493	19½	Horace Phillips
1889	Fifth	61	71	.462	25	Horace Phillips, Fred Dunlap, Ned Hanlon
1890	Eighth	23	113	.169	66½	Guy Hecker
1891	Eighth	55	80	.407	30½	Ned Hanlon, Bill McGunnigle
1892	Sixth	37	39	.487	16	Tom Burns, Al Buckenberger
	Fourth	43	34	.558	10½	Al Buckenberger
1893	Second	81	48	.628	5	Al Buckenberger
1894	Seventh	65	65	.500	25	Al Buckenberger, Connie Mack
1895	Seventh	71	61	.538	17	Connie Mack
1896	Sixth	66	63	.512	24	Connie Mack
1897	Eighth	60	71	.458	32½	Patsy Donovan
1898	Eighth	72	76	.486	29½	Bill Watkins
1899	Seventh	76	73	.510	25½	Bill Watkins, Patsy Donovan
1900	Second	79	60	.568	4½	Fred Clarke
1901	First	90	49	.647	+7½	Fred Clarke
1902	First	103	36	.741	+27½	Fred Clarke
1903	First	91	49	.650	+6½	Fred Clarke
1904	Fourth	87	66	.569	19	Fred Clarke
1905	Second	96	57	.627	9	Fred Clarke
1906	Third	93	60	.608	23½	Fred Clarke
1907	Second	91	63	.591	17	Fred Clarke
1908	Second*	98	56	.636	1	Fred Clarke
1909	First	110	42	.724	+6½	Fred Clarke
1910	Third	86	67	.562	17½	Fred Clarke
1911	Third	85	69	.552	14½	Fred Clarke
1912	Second	93	58	.616	10	Fred Clarke
1913	Fourth	78	71	.523	21½	Fred Clarke
1914	Seventh	69	85	.448	25½	Fred Clarke
1915	Fifth	73	81	.474	18	Fred Clarke
1916	Sixth	65	89	.422	29	Nixey Callahan
1917	Eighth	51	103	.331	47	Nixey Callahan, Honus Wagner, Hugo Bezdek
1918	Fourth	65	60	.520	17	Hugo Bezdek
1919	Fourth	71	68	.511	24½	Hugo Bezdek
1920	Fourth	79	75	.513	14	George Gibson
1921	Second	90	63	.588	4	George Gibson
1922	Third*	85	69	.552	8	George Gibson, Bill McKechnie
1923	Third	87	67	.565	8½	Bill McKechnie
1924	Third	90	63	.588	3	Bill McKechnie
1925	First	95	58	.621	+8½	Bill McKechnie
1926	Third	84	69	.549	4½	Bill McKechnie
1927	First	94	60	.610	+1½	Donie Bush
1928	Fourth	85	67	.559	9	Donie Bush
1929	Second	88	65	.575	10½	Donie Bush, Jewel Ens
1930	Fifth	80	74	.519	12	Jewel Ens
1931	Fifth	75	79	.487	26	Jewel Ens
1932	Second	86	68	.558	4	George Gibson
1933	Second	87	67	.565	5	George Gibson

1934	Fifth	74	76	.493	19½	George Gibson, Pie Traynor
1935	Fourth	86	67	.562	13½	Pie Traynor
1936	Fourth	84	70	.545	8	Pie Traynor
1937	Third	86	68	.558	10	Pie Traynor
1938	Second	86	64	.573	2	Pie Traynor
1939	Sixth	68	85	.444	28½	Pie Traynor
1940	Fourth	78	76	.506	22½	Frankie Frisch
1941	Fourth	81	73	.526	19	Frankie Frisch
1942	Fifth	66	81	.449	36½	Frankie Frisch
1943	Fourth	80	74	.519	25	Frankie Frisch
1944	Second	90	63	.588	14½	Frankie Frisch
1945	Fourth	82	72	.532	16	Frankie Frisch
1946	Seventh	63	91	.409	34	Frankie Frisch
1947	Seventh*	62	92	.403	32	Billy Herman, Bill Burwell
1948	Fourth	83	71	.539	8½	Billy Meyer
1949	Sixth	71	83	.461	26	Billy Meyer
1950	Eighth	57	96	.373	33½	Billy Meyer
1951	Seventh	64	90	.416	32½	Billy Meyer
1952	Eighth	42	112	.273	54½	Billy Meyer
1953	Eighth	50	104	.325	55	Fred Haney
1954	Eighth	53	101	.344	44	Fred Haney
1955	Eighth	60	94	.390	38½	Fred Haney
1956	Seventh	66	88	.429	27	Bobby Bragan
1957	Seventh*	62	92	.403	33	Bobby Bragan, Danny Murtaugh
1958	Second	84	70	.545	8	Danny Murtaugh
1959	Fourth	78	76	.506	9	Danny Murtaugh
1960	First	95	59	.617	+7	Danny Murtaugh
1961	Sixth	75	79	.487	18	Danny Murtaugh
1962	Fourth	93	68	.578	8	Danny Murtaugh
1963	Eighth	74	88	.457	25	Danny Murtaugh
1964	Sixth*	80	82	.494	13	Danny Murtaugh
1965	Third	90	72	.556	7	Harry Walker
1966	Third	92	70	.568	3	Harry Walker
1967	Sixth	81	81	.500	20½	Harry Walker, Danny Murtaugh
1968	Sixth	80	82	.494	17	Larry Shepard
1969	Third	88	74	.543	12	Larry Shepard, Alex Grammas
1970	First	89	73	.549	+5	Danny Murtaugh
1971	First	97	65	.599	+7	Danny Murtaugh
1972	First	96	59	.619	+11	Bill Virdon
1973	Third	80	82	.494	2½	Bill Virdon, Danny Murtaugh
1974	First	88	74	.543	+1½	Danny Murtaugh
1975	First	92	69	.571	+6½	Danny Murtaugh
1976	Second	92	70	.568	9	Danny Murtaugh
1977	Second	96	66	.593	5	Chuck Tanner
1978	Second	88	73	.547	1½	Chuck Tanner
1979	First	98	64	.605	+2	Chuck Tanner
1980	Third	83	79	.512	8	Chuck Tanner
1981	Fourth	25	23	.521	5½	Chuck Tanner
	Sixth	21	33	.389	9½	Chuck Tanner
1982	Fourth	84	78	.519	8	Chuck Tanner
1983	Second	84	78	.519	6	Chuck Tanner
1984	Sixth	75	87	.463	21½	Chuck Tanner
1985	Sixth	57	104	.354	43½	Chuck Tanner
1986	Sixth	64	98	.395	44	Jim Leyland
1987	Fourth*	80	82	.494	15	Jim Leyland
1988	Second	85	75	.531	15	Jim Leyland
1989	Fifth	74	88	.457	19	Jim Leyland

1990	First	95	67	.586	+4	Jim Leyland
1991	First	98	64	.605	+14	Jim Leyland
1992	First	96	66	.593	+9	Jim Leyland
*Tie						

Postseason Play

LCS	0–3 versus Cincinnati	1970	WS	3–5 versus Boston	1903
	3–1 versus San Francisco	1971		4–3 versus Detroit	1909
	2–3 versus Cincinnati	1972		4–3 versus Washington	1925
	1–3 versus Los Angeles	1974		0–4 versus New York	1927
	0–3 versus Cincinnati	1975		4–3 versus New York	1960
	3–0 versus Cincinnati	1979		4–3 versus Baltimore	1971
	2–4 versus Cincinnati	1990		4–3 versus Baltimore	1979
	3–4 versus Atlanta	1991			
	3–4 versus Atlanta	1992			

Pittsburgh Burghers

Players League, 1890   **BALLPARK:** EXPOSITION PARK

RECORD: 60–68 (.469)

In 1889, Ned Hanlon, one of the most active members of the Brotherhood of Professional Baseball Players, was both the manager of the National League Pittsburgh franchise and the principal organizer of the Players League Pittsburgh team. With backing from John M. Beemer and M. B. Lennon, Hanlon rebuilt the old American Association Exposition Park and recruited virtually all of his 1889 teammates to join him on the Burghers.

First baseman Jake Beckley (.334 with 10 homers, 120 RBIs, and a league-leading 22 triples) provided almost all of the offensive punch on a team that tied for the worst batting average in the PL (.260). The pitching wasn't much better, despite the efforts of workhorse Harry Staley (21–25).

With an uninspired sixth-place finish and a disappointing 117,000 patrons, the Burghers were easy prey when the NL began to dismember the PL, and it was the second Brotherhood franchise to collapse. The financial backers of the club joined their rivals in a new corporate structure, the Pittsburgh Athletic Company, which assumed ownership of the NL Alleghenys.

PITTSBURGH BURGHERS

Annual Standings and Manager

Year	Position	W	L	Pct.	GB	Manager
1890	Sixth	60	68	.469	20½	Ned Hanlon

Pittsburgh Rebels

Federal League, 1914–1915   **BALLPARK:** EXPOSITION PARK

RECORD: 150–153 (.495)   **OTHER NAMES:** STOGIES, PITTSFEDS

The Rebels were a prime example of what aggressive player procurement could do to improve a team. After waving money at National and American league players to get them to jump aboard, the club was able to climb from a drab seventh-place finish in 1914 to only ½ game out of first in 1915, in one of the closest pennant races in history. For all its improvement, however, the team couldn't break the lock that the NL Pirates held on Pittsburgh fans.

Originally called the Stogies, the Pittsburgh FL franchise was the property of William Kerr, whose financing going into the 1914 season was woefully inadequate. Then railroad contractor Edward W. Gwinner agreed to take over the ailing franchise in partnership with Brooklyn architect C. B. Comstock. The new ownership took over Exposition Park, where the NL Pirates had played from 1891 to 1909, and hired as manager Doc Gessler, who was replaced after only eighteen games by center fielder Rebel Oakes. The new manager not only tied third baseman Ed Lennon for the team lead in batting (.312), but also gave his nickname to the team.

Following a grim seventh-place finish, Gwinner sent Oakes out with a bankroll to raid other teams for players for 1915. New arrivals over the winter included first baseman Ed Konetchy (.314, 10 home runs) from the St. Louis Cardinals and third base-

man Mike Mowry (.280) from the Pittsburgh Pirates. The recruiting didn't stop once the season began: Left fielder Al Wickland was picked up from the Chicago Whales, and he batted .301 for the final three quarters of the season.

Pitching was the difference for the Rebels in 1915. Frank Allen (23–12), Elmer Knetzer (18–15), and rookie Clint Rogge (17–12) led the staff to a 2.75 ERA, down from 3.56 the year before. But even the close third-place finish couldn't save the franchise, which lost the all-important war of the turnstiles to the Pirates. Gwinner ended up losing about $150,000 in his venture, but even so, he sought to buy the Cleveland Indians as part of the settlement. Failing at that, he had to settle for a $50,000 buyout paid out in five equal installments, ostensibly for his ballpark, and even this came over the loud protestations of AL President Ban Johnson. The contractor picked up another $3,500 by selling a few players and the team equipment.

While all Federal League players were officially reinstated to organized baseball for the 1916 season, about 100 former American and National leaguers failed to find roster spots. Among the unemployed was manager-outfielder Oakes, who was ignored because of his aggressive recruitment of AL and NL players for the FL.

PITTSBURGH REBELS

Annual Standings and Managers

Year	Position	W	L	Pct.	GB	Managers
1914	Seventh	64	86	.427	22½	Doc Gessler, Rebel Oakes
1915	Third	86	67	.562	½	Rebel Oakes

Providence Grays

National League, 1878–1885   **BALLPARK:** MESSER STREET GROUNDS

RECORD: 438–278 (.612)

Among the first eighteen cities that entered and left the National League in its first decade (some of them more than once), only the Providence Grays were consistent winners. The Grays had only one losing season, their last, and their overall won-lost percentage was second only to that of Chicago (.648), the NL's showcase franchise. Unlike Chicago, however, the Grays suffered from bickering among shareholders, and were also undone by fans who rarely turned out in numbers larger than 1,000.

Rhode Island had a rich history of local amateur and minor league baseball that attracted large, fiercely partisan crowds. Early in 1878, Benjamin Douglas, Jr., a member of a wealthy Hartford family, arrived in Providence and began assembling the backing for a new NL franchise. Among others, he recruited Col. Henry B. Winship, Marsh B. Meade, Col. J. Lippett Snow, Newton Earl, and Henry T. Root, all of whom would play major roles in the front office squabbling to follow. Root became the club's first president, and Douglas, appointed manager, put together a team and oversaw the siting and construction of Messer Park. The facility was completed only five minutes before the start of the Grays' first game on May 1, but by then Douglas had been fired for an unspecified "incompetency" and replaced by George Ware.

The Grays were responsible for several innovations. They were the first team to abandon white uniforms, sporting a gray trimmed with blue that accounted for their nickname. They were the first to install turnstiles, apparently as early as 1878. They were the first to put up a wire mesh screen behind home plate and in front of the grandstand to protect the spectators from foul balls and to facilitate the recovery of the balls. They also built what they called a "bullpen" along the left field foul line for young fans; although the function of the bullpen has changed, the term dates from this structure.

Sparked by the slugging and defense of center fielder Paul Hines, the team recruited by Douglas finished third in the six-team NL. The biggest surprise of the year was pitcher John Montgomery Ward, who had been added to the roster when it became apparent that the original pitcher, Tricky Nichols, was washed up. The 18-year-old Ward pitched shutouts in his first two starts and went on to win 22 while losing 13.

In 1879, Root raided Boston for legendary shortstop George Wright as a player-manager and outfielder Orator Jim O'Rourke, who batted .348. Hines led the NL with a .357 average, Ward (47–19) was the best pitcher in the league, and the result was Providence's first pennant. Boston, managed by George's brother Harry Wright, finished second, and Providence fans found the fraternal conflict between the Wrights sufficiently interesting to file through the turnstiles in encouraging numbers—but only for contests with Boston. Despite newspaper ads, leaflets, and posters exhorting the fans to come to the ballpark, the Grays' average paid attendance for forty-two home games was just slightly over 1,000, sufficient for a modest profit of $2,000, most of which was spent on ballpark alterations and improvements.

Providence barely had time to savor its pennant when George Wright resigned as manager to form Wright and Ditson, a sporting goods business. His retirement made him the only major leaguer ever to win a pennant in his only season as a manager.

Over the next four seasons, the Grays, built around pitching and defense, played at a .580 clip, but had to be content with three second-place finishes and one third-place showing. Among the members of the team was shortstop Art Irwin, who may or may not have invented the hit-and-run, but who

In the third game of the 1878 season, center fielder Paul Hines made the first unassisted triple play, still the only one ever completed by an outfielder.

was certainly one of its most proficient early practitioners. In 1883, Irwin invented the fielder's mitt (the common practice at the time was to use an ordinary glove) by padding a buckskin driving glove to protect two broken fingers. Another key player was Charlie Radbourne, who was first hired in 1881 as Ward's change pitcher. Radbourne had appeared in six games (none of them as a pitcher) for Buffalo the year before, but had gone home to Illinois, so disgusted with his .143 batting average that he was prepared to resume his earlier career as a butcher's apprentice. The Grays, who were looking for a utility player, wired him, but got no reply. A friend answered in his name, asked for $750 (to which Providence agreed), and persuaded Radbourne to report. When Ward came down with a sore arm, Radbourne stepped in and won 25 and lost 11, following that up with a 31–19 record in 1882.

The first two consecutive second-place finishes did little to increase crowds or placate stockholders. On August 1st and 12th, 1881, shareholders' meetings turned the club completely upside down over a projected shortfall of $1,500. A hardline faction at-

CHARLIE RADBOURNE
"OLD HOSS"

PROVIDENCE, BOSTON AND CINCINNATI
NATIONAL LEAGUE 1881 TO 1891. GREATEST
OF ALL 19TH CENTURY PITCHERS. WINNING
1884 PENNANT FOR PROVIDENCE, RADBOURNE
PITCHED LAST 27 GAMES OF SEASON, WON
26. WON 3 STRAIGHT IN WORLD SERIES.

National Baseball Library, Cooperstown, NY

tacked the management of the club for leniency toward players (including the policy of paying the salaries of the injured) and failure to win the support of fans. The conflict led to the ouster of president Root, two other directors, manager Jim Bulloch, and captain Jack Farrell. The new business-oriented board of directors, which elected John D. Thurston president for the 1882 season and Colonel Winship for 1883, brought in Harry Wright from Boston as manager in 1882.

All the record books show Chicago finishing three games ahead of Providence in 1882. What they fail to show are the controversy over whether to count games played by Worcester (which withdrew from the NL toward the end of the season, then withdrew its withdrawal), and the switch of three late-season games from Buffalo to Chicago that helped the financially ailing Bisons, but that also shifted the home-team advantage. After the season, Providence challenged Chicago to a nine-game series to decide the championship. Chicago president Albert Spalding originally wanted to play the games as mere exhibitions, then relented when faced with Providence's insistence that they be championship games. At first, Chicago toyed with the Grays; manager Cap Anson kept both left fielder Abner Dalrymple and second baseman Joe Quest out of the lineup. But after Providence had won the first three games, the White Stockings showed their superiority by winning five of the next six contests. It was clear that neither the Chicago management nor the players did their utmost to win every game and that the sole attraction for the pennant winners was the gate. Although no formal charges were ever brought, the fiasco brought little credit to the pennant winners and was promptly eradicated from the official record.

The new regime also had other problems that were beyond its control. It could only protest ineffectively the NL's blacklisting of catcher Lew Brown and Ernie Gross for "dissipation and insubordination" after the 1881 season. Nor could it do much about the fact that as of 1883, with Troy and Worcester out of the league, Providence (with a population of 180,000) was the NL's smallest city. At the same time, the club's salaries soared from about $13,000 in 1881 to $18,000 (the highest in the league) in 1882, to

Paul Hines was the first outfielder to wear sunglasses in the field, a practice he started in 1882.

more than $20,000 in 1883 because of the American Association war.

By the fall of 1883, with the Grays slipping out of the pennant race, new rumors spread that the directors were planning to take the team out of the NL and concentrate their sporting interest on harness racing at nearby Narragansett Park. The directors did nothing to vitiate the speculation when they voted a 100 percent dividend, almost universally interpreted as an effort to deplete the club's treasury and in effect disband the club. The board set out to answer the charges at a shareholders' meeting on September 25th. Before resigning, Winship in particular had to defend himself against charges that he had intended to abandon baseball for the trotters and that he had bet on Grays games. The rest of the directors also resigned; Colonel Snow was elected interim president and Root rejoined the board, pending the completion of an investigation. When the meeting resumed on October 5th, the only provable—and easily curable—transgression was an over-subscription of stock—by $25. To head the latest administration the board chose George Flint.

Harry Wright left Providence to manage the Philadelphia Phillies in 1884. In his place came Frank Bancroft, a 38-year-old veteran of three previous managing jobs. Bancroft looked at the new 112-game schedule and, like most other NL managers, decided that his team needed more than a change pitcher to spell the regular starter. Bancroft's plan was to alternate not just pitchers but entire batteries, with veteran Billy Gilligan catching Radbourne (who continued to throw underhand despite a new league rule allowing overhand deliveries) and Cuban rookie Sandy Nava behind the plate for Charlie Sweeney. Unfortunately, both his pitchers were more than a little high-strung. The bad-tempered, arrogant, hard-drinking Radbourne was unhappy sharing the limelight; 21-year-old Sweeney was equally hot-headed and an even heavier drinker. Despite the bad chemistry, the Grays broke fast from the gate, winning 17 of their first 19 games.

By Memorial Day, Radbourne had a 12–1 record, Sweeney was 8–3, and the Grays were in first place by percentage points over Boston. The two top teams met June 6th when they began a six-game series split

On August 21, 1883, the Grays beat the Phillies, 28–0, for the most one-sided shutout in baseball history.

between the two cities. The first game in Providence attracted just under 4,500 fans, a spectacular crowd made possible by the thousand or more Bostonians who had come down for the contest. They saw Radbourne and Jim Whitney of Boston duel for 16 innings in a 1–1 tie in which both runs were unearned. The next day, in Boston, 7,400 fans saw Sweeney strike out 19 to win 2–1. After four Boston victories, Radbourne notched a 4–3 win in 15 innings, and, when the series ended, Providence was only four games out.

The two New England teams met for their second six-game series on July 11th with Boston two games in front. Sweeney had strained his forearm in July, putting Radbourne where he wanted to be—alone at the center of the diamond—every day. He won two of the first three games to pull the Grays to within a game of first place before they slipped back a game the next day. Despite the unshared limelight and his success in the box, Radbourne had been behaving erratically for about three weeks. Henry Lucas, president of the Union Association, was in Boston for a series between his St. Louis Maroons and the Boston Unions, leading to reports that he had offered Radbourne a $2,000 bonus to jump to his league; others said the pitcher had been drinking.

What had been a distraction erupted into a crisis in the eighth inning of the game against Boston on July 16th. The Grays had been complaining that Charlie Buffinton, the Boston pitcher, had been balking regularly. Umpire Stewart Decker ignored the protest, but when he called a balk on Radbourne in the eighth, the righthander exploded. He began throwing erratically, seemingly more determined to punish his catcher Gilligan than to retire Boston batters. Several walks, a wild pitch, a passed ball, and a throwing error by Gilligan, another error by the third baseman, and a single resulted in three runs and a victory for Boston.

The next day, the Providence board of directors suspended Radbourne for "insubordination." For the next two games, manager Bancroft had to rely on Cyclone Miller, who needed help from the recovering Sweeney both times. Then, during an exhibition game on July 21st in Woonsocket, Sweeney started drinking in the dressing room, stayed behind with Nava to continue the spree after the rest of the team had returned to Providence, and missed a morning workout the next day. Bancroft, somewhat desperate for pitching, put the bleary Sweeney in the box against Philadelphia that afternoon for his first start in two weeks. After four innings, the manager decided to switch his pitcher and Miller, who was playing right field, but Sweeney refused. In the seventh, with the Grays ahead 6–2, Bancroft again told Sweeney to go to right field; Sweeney again refused and left the field. The Grays survived the eighth inning with only two outfielders; but in the ninth, several hits fell between the pair, the rattled infielders made a few errors, and Philadelphia scored eight times to win the game.

The Providence directors expelled Sweeney, who immediately signed a lucrative contract with the UA St. Louis Maroons. Rumors circulated that the Grays, without a star pitcher, would have to disband. Reenter Radbourne, who offered to pitch every day if the club would tear up his contract at the end of the season. The directors reinstated him with a raise and, while Radbourne did not pitch every game after July 22nd, he did turn in thirty-five complete efforts plus four innings of relief, in the process winning 30, losing 4, and tying 1. Between August 21st and September 25th, Radbourne pitched every inning of all twenty-two games the Grays played, a streak that overlapped a personal eighteen-game winning streak and a club streak of twenty in a row and twenty-eight out of twenty-nine. What had looked like a close pennant race between Providence and Boston turned into a rout, with the Grays finishing 10½ games in front.

Radbourne, whose cricket-like running delivery was outlawed after the 1886 season, won 60 (including one in relief), lost 12, and tied 2. His seventy-three complete games so wearied his arm that he could barely raise it over his head each morning. He capped his stunning season by winning all three games against the AA New York Metropolitans in the first officially sanctioned postseason championship between the two leagues. At the end of the season, the directors, keeping their word, offered the hurler a blank contract, on which he gave himself only a modest raise to $4,000.

The Grays' final season began with the election of Root to the club presidency. Also elected, as secretary-treasurer, however, was Marsh B. Mead, who by the end of the season would control a majority of the stock to the undoing of the franchise. Large, enthusiastic crowds greeted the early season

games, but as the team's play fell off, so did the crowds. Injuries accelerated the slide.

Reports began circulating in July that Radbourne and Gilligan would be sold to Boston and the franchise abandoned. There was also a widespread impression that the players were keeping late hours and deliberately performing laxly so they would be released. The Providence *Journal*, once the club's strongest supporter, began running its stories on the Grays below those on New York and Chicago games, a far cry from the days when the daily would attract large crowds by posting scores in its front window every half-inning.

On August 1st, Root resigned and was replaced by J. Edward Allen, Mead's ally. The day after Root's resignation, Allen and fellow director George J. West went to an NL meeting to fight the planned expulsion of Providence. New York abandoned the majority to create a 4–4 tie on the expulsion vote, presumably in the interests of stopping Providence's reported deal with Boston. Allen and West, who had been authorized to unload players if the opportunity arose, returned home with the roster intact. On September 9th, the club's directors voted to field a team in 1886; on October 17th, at another NL meeting, the club declared its intention to continue; and as late as November 18th, Allen accepted a place on the NL board of directors, Meanwhile, the demoralized team lost thirteen consecutive games before beating Philadelphia in an errorless, flawlessly played 3–1 game on the last day of the season.

The deal with Boston was finally announced on November 30th. The purchase price for the entire franchise was $6,000. Boston kept Radbourne and catcher Con Daily, rather than Gilligan; the rest of the players scattered about the league. The directors' final unashamed word was that the NL's larger cities were responsible for the Grays' demise because the league wanted the franchise "transferred to a larger city where the game would be more profitable." That was the last the NL heard from Providence. As late as March 3, 1886, the NL stated its willingness to accept the franchise's formal resignation as soon as it was offered. It never was.

PROVIDENCE GRAYS

Annual Standings and Managers

Year	Position	W	L	Pct.	GB	Managers
1878	Third	33	27	.550	8	George Ware
1879	First	59	25	.702	+5	George Wright
1880	Second	52	32	.619	15	Jim Bullock
1881	Second	47	37	.560	9	Jim Bullock, Bob Morrow

1882	Second	52	32	.619	3	Harry Wright
1883	Third	58	40	.592	5	Harry Wright
1884	First	84	28	.750	+10½	Frank Bancroft
1885	Fourth	53	57	.482	33	Frank Bancroft

Richmond Virginias

American Association, 1884   **BALLPARK:** ALLEN PASTURE

RECORD: 12–30 (.286)

When Washington deserted its ranks in August of 1884, the American Association reached out to the Virginia Club of Richmond in the Eastern League as a replacement. When the Virginias played their first AA game on August 5th, Richmond became the first major league franchise from the Old Confederacy— and the last one for seventy-eight years.

The capital of the Confederate States, Richmond was a stronghold of Jim Crow sentiment in the years after Reconstruction. Predictably, a scheduled three-game series with Toledo in October aroused local racist sentiment against that team's black catcher, Fleet Walker; a letter warned of violence by "75 determined men" if Walker played in the city. As it turned out, Walker was released be-

cause of injuries in September, before the series took place.

Financed by William Siddon and Felix Moses, the Virginias, mostly carryovers from the Eastern League franchise, performed abysmally. Only right fielder Mike Mansell (.301), at the end of his career, and center fielder Dick Johnston (.281), at the beginning of his, had creditable years. Furthermore, Richmond was too small to support a major league franchise; only Toledo and Columbus in the AA had fewer people.

When the AA cut back to eight teams after the defeat of the Union Association, the franchise, never more than a stopgap entry, was cut from the circuit and rejoined the Eastern League.

RICHMOND VIRGINIAS

Annual Standings and Manager

Year	Position	W	L	Pct.	GB	Manager
1884	Partial Season	12	30	.286	—	Felix Moses

Rochester Hop Bitters

American Association, 1890   **BALLPARK:** CULVER FIELD
JONES SQUARE
RECORD: 63–63 (.500)   WINDSOR BEACH

With four vacancies for the 1890 season, the American Association cast a wide net in search of new franchises; part of the catch was the Rochester Hop

Bitters of the International Association. The president of the club was General Henry Brinker, a railroad and brewery owner.

With the same squad that had finished third in the IA in 1889, manager Pat Powers was able to produce a .500, fifth-place finish in the debilitated AA. Center fielder Sandy Griffin (.307) was the leading batsman; Bob Barr won 28 (and also tied for the league lead with 24 losses), while Cannonball Titcomb contributed a no-hitter among his 10 wins. The Hop Bitters might have done even better had it not been for a brouhaha surrounding pitcher Will Calihan (18–15), who talked shortstop Marr Phillips into a drinking spree and was suspended. After thirty days, Powers reinstated the pitcher without consulting Brinker; when the general found out, he released

Calihan altogether and never completely forgave Powers.

The AA, struggling for its life, could not survive another season with its Little Three of Rochester, Syracuse, and Toledo. Although Rochester, with 133,000 people, was the biggest of the trio and also larger than AA member Columbus, it was no major league city. Sunday games at Windsor Beach in nearby Irondequoit helped, but not enough. Brinker, eager to get out of baseball completely, settled for a share of a $24,000 buyout to remove his club from the AA, and the Hop Bitters went back to the minor league they had left.

ROCHESTER HOP BITTERS

Annual Standings and Manager

Year	Position	W	L	Pct.	GB	Manager
1890	Fifth	63	63	.500	22	Pat Powers

St. Louis Brown Stockings

National League, 1876–1877   **OTHER NAMES:** BROWNS

RECORD: 73–51 (.589)   **BALLPARK:** SPORTSMAN'S PARK

The first step in William Hulbert's subversion of the National Association and the formation of the National League was to recruit St. Louis as an ally. Toward that end, he secured the cooperation of Charles Fowle, president of the association's St. Louis club, and Campbell Orrich Bishop, a St. Louis attorney who served as vice-president of the circuit. Fowle and Bishop proved crucial to spelling out the provisions of the NL's constitution.

In the new league's first season, the Browns finished second, percentage points ahead of Hartford; they used only ten players, seven of whom had been part of the St. Louis NA club the year before. The outstanding performances were by center fielder Lip Pike (.323), catcher John Clapp (.305), third baseman Joe Battin (.300), and pitcher George Washington Bradley (45–19, including a no-hitter).

President John R. Lucas, a member of a wealthy St. Louis family, turned the reins of the club over to his nephew, John C.B. Lucas, for 1877, and George McManus succeeded Herman Dehlman as manager. A series of injuries dashed the team's pennant hopes

Footnote Player: Dickey Pearce played in the National League only two years, 1876 and 1877, and batted a mere .198 in thirty-three games. Forty years old at the time of the NL's founding, Pearce, with the Brooklyn Atlantics in 1856, had been one of the first two players to be paid for his services. He is credited with being the first shortstop to confine his positioning to the infield. On June 29, 1876, Pearce also started the first major league triple play.

early, but prospects for the future seemed brighter after McManus went to Louisville and persuaded several members of the Grays to join the team in 1878. But then umpire Dan Devinney accused McManus of offering him a $250 bribe to fix a game with Louisville, and the younger Lucas fired McManus and took over as manager himself. At the same time, two of the Louisville players McManus had signed— Jim Devlin and George Hall—were suspended by

Louisville for throwing games. When the NL made Louisville's suspension of the four players permanent, St. Louis was left in the lurch.

Lucas, angry over suggestions that he had known about the Louisville Crooks' activities and

had chosen to ignore them, resigned from the league in a huff. When he walked out, club stockholders were also under fire for non-payment of the third installment of the purchase price and had $8,000 in losses, the most by any franchise in the league.

ST. LOUIS BROWN STOCKINGS

Annual Standings and Managers

Year	Position	W	L	Pct.	GB	Managers
1876	Second	45	19	.703	6	Herman Dehlman
1877	Fourth	28	32	.467	14	George McManus, John C.B. Lucas

St. Louis Browns

American Association,
1882–1891

RECORD: 782–433 (.644)

BALLPARK: SPORTSMAN'S PARK

OTHER NAMES: BROWN STOCKINGS

The most successful franchise in the American Association, the Browns won four pennants and finished second four times in the Association's ten-year existence. Their left fielder Tip O'Neill had the single greatest offensive season of the nineteenth century and their pitching dominated the AA for the better part of the decade. As for their owner, the flamboyant Chris Von der Ahe, he was the colossus of the AA.

At first, the independent Brown Stockings (as they were known originally) played only other local clubs, but, in 1881, Alfred H. Spink, who was later to found *The Sporting News*, invited Cincinnati sportswriter O. P. Caylor to bring a club to St. Louis for an exhibition. The Browns won 15–8 before a substantial crowd. Later that year, the Brooklyn Atlantics and the Philadelphia Athletics were also invited for match games. So successful were the exhibitions that Spink and Caylor set out to form a league to rival the NL. After a series of false starts, they established a six-team circuit with the help of H. Denny McKnight of Pittsburgh. The AA was modeled along the lines of the NL with four major exceptions: a twenty-five-cent admission fee (half that of the NL), Sunday games, a guarantee of $65 for visiting clubs (instead of the NL's percentage split), and the sale of beer and liquor in ballparks.

Enter Von der Ahe. A German immigrant with a

Chris Von der Ahe, impressed by the enthusiasm of the patrons pouring into his ballpark in 1882, referred to them as fanatics. St. Louis manager Ted Sullivan abbreviated that to "fans." The term quickly replaced the then-current "kranks."

comic strip accent, a comic opera physiognomy, and a comic wardrobe of diamond stickpins, checkered pants, and spats, he had operated a saloon and grocery store near Sportsman's Park where the independent Brown Stockings had played. Although he knew almost nothing about baseball, he knew the financial rewards of quenching the thirst of large crowds before and after the games. He had also made enough money from his enterprise to invest in local real estate and to become a political power, so that when Spink approached him in 1882, the saloon keeper bought $1,800 worth of stock in the new Brown Stockings and, significantly, received the beer and alcohol concession in the ballpark. Within a few years, Von der Ahe had bought out Spink and the other major stockholders.

The Brown Stockings got off to a rocky start in 1882, suffering their only losing AA season and finishing fifth under Ned Cuthbert, an itinerant outfielder who had worked for Von der Ahe as a bartender. In 1883, as the abbreviated name Browns came into common currency, the club jumped to second, losing the pennant to Philadelphia in the second to last game of the season. Tony Mullane won 35, while center fielder Fred Lewis batted a team-high .301. Also on hand were Ted Sullivan and Charlie Comiskey. Sullivan, one of the great early baseball promoters, handled business affairs, and also managed the club for a while in the season; Comiskey took over as manager from Sullivan, and, except for a brief stint by Jimmy Williams early in 1884, the first baseman stayed at the helm until the Players League war of 1890, leading the Browns to four consecutive pennants between 1885 and 1888.

> In 1884, dismayed by the loss of lucrative home games to bad weather, Von der Ahe was the first owner to use a tarpaulin to protect the playing field from the rain.

In 1884, the Union Association Maroons cut deeply into Von der Ahe's profits and compelled him to make some nominal concessions to the new league. To retain the services of catcher Pat Deasley in 1884, for instance, the owner agreed to a contract without a reserve clause. But when Deasely tried to sell his services elsewhere in 1885, the AA refused permission on the grounds that his contract had been nothing more than a subterfuge. The impasse was resolved only when Von der Ahe let Deasley go to the NL New York Giants. The AA had still made its point—that even a contract without an explicit reserve clause would be interpreted as binding a player to his team for the next season.

Von der Ahe ended up playing a major role in the UA peace settlement. First, he agreed to share his territory with the Maroons, who had been admitted to the NL, although he exacted a payment estimated at $2,500 for the privilege. In addition, he used his

> The rule awarding a batter first base when hit by a pitched ball was introduced by the American Association in 1884. The motivation for the new rule was the tendency of Jack Schappert, who had pitched for St. Louis in 1882, to throw at batters.

prestige to have the AA join the NL in reinstating the players blacklisted for jumping to the UA.

The Browns ran away with their first three flags, from 1885 to 1887, and took the fourth straight by a comfortable margin of 6½ games; they compiled a .689 (357–162) won-lost percentage over the four years. Comiskey's crew was built on superior hitting and extraordinary pitching. O'Neill, the major offensive threat, racked up batting averages of .350, .328, .435, and .335 in the pennant-winning years. In 1887, he led the AA not only in hitting, but also in hits (225), home runs (14), doubles (52), triples (19), runs scored (167), and slugging (.691). With solid support from pitcher-right fielder Bob Caruthers (.357), Comiskey (.335), third baseman Arlie Latham (.316), and second baseman Yank Robinson (.305), O'Neill was the biggest gun in an overpowering attack that generated 1,131 runs scored in 1887, the first time a team cracked the 1,000 mark in a season. At the same time, the mound staff led the AA in earned run average in three of the four seasons. Caruthers and Dave Foutz carried the burden in 1885 and 1886,

National Baseball Library, Cooperstown, New York

with records of 40–13 and 30–14 for the former and 33–14 and 41–16 for the latter.

Ever the enterprising entrepreneur, Von der Ahe saw the potential profit in a postseason series between the AA and NL pennant winners. Scheduling a twelve-game series, Von der Ahe and Chicago owner Albert Spalding each put up $1,000 as a purse, and their clubs embarked on a championship tour that was to include games in five neutral cities (all in the AA), as well as in Chicago and St. Louis.

The series never got that far. The first game ended in an eight-inning tie, and the second concluded in a fiasco caused by an objectionable sixth-inning call that sent irate St. Louis fans pouring onto the field and umpire David Sullivan scurrying for his hotel room, from the safety of which he declared a forfeit for Chicago. The bad feeling between the teams reached such a level of intensity that the series was canceled after only five more games, three of which were victories by the Browns, who claimed the championship. Spalding maintained the series stood at a 3–3 tie, including the forfeited game, and denied that he had ever agreed that the championship of the world was at stake in the first place.

In 1886, Von der Ahe, who could never accept anything less than being the best, sent Comiskey to negotiate another series with Spalding after St. Louis and Chicago had once again won their respective pennants. Spalding refused to accept any terms but a seven-game winner-take-all match with all games played in Chicago and St. Louis. Chicago took two of the first three at home, but the Browns swept three in a row at home to claim the championship.

The final game of the series was an early candidate for "the greatest contest ever known to the history of baseball," as the St. Louis *Republic* put it. Chicago, behind John Clarkson, was leading 3–0 in the eighth when the Browns, sparked by Latham's

two-run triple, tied the score. St. Louis won it in the tenth when center fielder Curt Welch stole home on a high pitch that glanced off catcher King Kelly's glove. Welch's fabled but superfluous "$15,000 slide" was actually worth just under $13,000, the total gate for the six games. Von der Ahe pocketed $6,900 and gave each player a $580 bonus.

In 1887, Caruthers and Foutz were joined by Silver King, whose 34–11 record convinced Von der Ahe that he could do without the other two. The three pitchers' combined salary was $9,000; the total payroll, $40,000. Not that Von der Ahe couldn't afford it; a Decoration Day crowd of 25,000 fans alone brought in $10,000. But Von der Ahe blamed the players for the loss of the 1887 postseason championship (ten games to five to the Detroit Wolverines), and, as ungracious a loser as he was generous as a winner, refused to share the $12,500 losers' share with the team. In November, Gleason and Welch were sold to the Philadelphia Athletics for $5,000. A month later, Caruthers, Foutz, and Catcher Doc Bushong went to Brooklyn for $18,500.

Comiskey, who until now had been able to curb Von der Ahe's inclination to cash in on the team's success, plugged the holes with catcher Big Milligan, shortstop Shorty Fuller, and center fielder Tommy McCarthy, and relying on King, who led the AA with 45 victories (against 21 losses) and a 1.64 ERA, and Nat Hudson (25–10), took his fourth consecutive pennant in 1888. But the team lost a second consecutive postseason match, this time to the New York Giants, six games to four. Von der Ahe walked away with another $12,000 from the 1888 series. The nucleus of a strong team still existed in 1889. O'Neill hit .335. The pitchers—King (33–17), Icebox Chamberlain (32–15), and Jack Stivetts (13–7 and an AA-leading ERA of 2.25)—led all Association staffs with a 3.00 ERA. But Brooklyn, strengthened by its purchases from the Browns, took the pennant by two games.

The Browns survived a major attack on their flow of revenue in 1887, when a state law banning baseball on Sunday was struck down by a state supreme court justice's ruling that baseball was "a reasonable sport" and not work. But then, even the club's success began working at curtailing profits. As

Chris Von der Ahe's ignorance of baseball is legendary. Told by Charlie Comiskey that all baseball diamonds are the same size after the owner had boasted that his Browns had the largest one in the world, Von der Ahe shot right back, "Well, I haff de biggest infield anyway." On another occasion he demanded that his players stop hitting the ball to the other team. And he never quite overcame his inclination to blame every opposition hit on one of his players for being out of position.

In 1887, first baseman-manager Charlie Comiskey became the first ballplayer to endorse a product, Merrell's Penetrating Oil.

long as the crowds kept pouring into Sportsman's Park, Von der Ahe had been quite content with the AA's standard guarantee to visiting teams. But as St. Louis fans became more and more accustomed to winning, the crowds dwindled at home, while continuing to turn out for the Browns on the road. Accordingly, Von der Ahe sought to bully the rest of the AA into altering the rules to provide visiting teams with a percentage of the gate, even threatening to take his Browns into the NL if he did not get his way. In 1888, he clashed with Charles Byrne of Brooklyn over the issue, finally compromising on a visitors' share of 30 percent with a $130 guarantee (later adjusted to 20 percent and a $100 guarantee). By 1891, Von der Ahe had gotten his way, as the AA adopted a straight 40 percent for visitors (50 percent on certain holidays).

By then, however, the St. Louis owner had just about wrecked the AA—with a little help from the Players League. His antics during a September 1889 series against Brooklyn led to a riot and a double forfeit. At the end of the season, Byrne bolted to the NL over the selection of a new AA president. Cincinnati joined him, and their allies, Baltimore and Kansas City, quit the AA to join minor leagues.

The Boss President, as he liked to call himself, was as extravagant in his personal life as he was difficult in his business relations. A real estate millionaire, he had a lifesize statue of himself made (it was later placed on his grave). A bibulous womanizer, he reveled in marching at the head of a column of uniformed players on the way to the park while sporting a top hat and leading his two greyhounds, Snoozer and Schnauzer. He encouraged umpire-baiting and paid player fines for such run-ins. Otherwise, his attitude toward his players was even more obnoxious than it was toward his fellow owners. He berated them for errors. He accused them of not appreciating all he had done for them. On one occasion, he ripped into them for refusing to play an exhibition against the Cuban Giants, a black team, because, he was convinced, they were acting out of spite rather than "honest prejudice." He insisted that the players drink in his saloon and no other and often raided rival establishments looking for the disobedient; the players often got away with patronizing his competition by scampering away when they saw his signature spats and greyhounds under the saloon doors.

As his empire began to dissipate, Von der Ahe's excesses became more outrageous. He fined Robinson $25 for showing up at the park in dirty uniform

pants and then cursing out a gatekeeper who wouldn't readmit the young man to the park after he had been sent back to the hotel for a clean pair. The team almost struck over Von der Ahe's refusal to rescind the fine and his threats to blacklist Robinson. As so often happened, the fracas was settled only by Comiskey's intervention. But the 1890 PL war removed Comiskey, who jumped to the Chicago Pirates, as a buffer between the owner and the players. That season, the team again finished second in a much depleted league, as Von der Ahe moved star players in and out as manager: Right fielder Tommy McCarthy, left fielder Count Campau, and part-time center fielder Chief Roseman each took a turn. The idiosyncratic owner interfered at every turn. His worst scrap was not with one of his own players, but with Mark Baldwin, a former AA Columbus pitcher who was recruiting players for the new league. Von der Ahe had Baldwin arrested twice on charges of conspiracy to destroy the Browns. When the charges were thrown out of court, the pitcher slapped Von der Ahe with a $20,000 lawsuit for false arrest. Four years later, a jury awarded Baldwin $2,500 in damages.

After the PL settlement, Comiskey returned to manage the Browns again in 1891. He led them to a third consecutive second-place finish on the strength of Stivetts' 33–22 record and the hitting of O'Neill (.321), McCarthy (.310), and shortstop Denny Lyons (.315), but his relationship with Von der Ahe was never the same.

Neither was the AA. No sooner had the PL war ended than the NL and AA began feuding over the relocation of players. To bolster the AA, Von der Ahe financed the ill-conceived Cincinnati Porkers, who folded in August. At about the same time, negotiations started for combining the two rival leagues. Spalding had been advocating "one great league" since the mid-1880s, but Von der Ahe and other AA owners had been reluctant to give up their cheaper admission charge and the money they made both from selling alcohol and playing on Sunday. But realizing that he would have to sink a fortune into what promised to be a losing battle anyway, Von der Ahe yielded to the inevitable.

The St. Louis president became the NL's whip charged with rounding up AA votes for the amalgamation. He succeeded, but in his usual heavy-handed way. Assured of the votes of Louisville, Washington, and Baltimore, the three other clubs slated to be transplanted into the NL, as well as his own, Von der Ahe convinced Columbus to accept a buyout. The sixth, and decisive, vote came from Philadelphia. As a result, Von der Ahe neglected to talk to the owners in Milwaukee and Chicago, which had been admitted to the AA after the 1891 season. That oversight—plus a holdout by the Boston owners—almost ruined the NL's scheme. At a joint NL-AA meeting in Indianapolis on December 15th, it took

considerable effort—and considerably more money than originally budgeted—to buy out the reluctant owners in Milwaukee, Chicago, and Boston and avoid a lawsuit. Von der Ahe brought his Browns into the NL, but no one was waiting for him with open arms.

ST. LOUIS BROWNS

Annual Standings and Managers

Year	Position	W	L	Pct.	GB	Managers
1882	Fifth	37	43	.463	18	Ned Cuthbert
1883	Second	65	33	.663	1	Ted Sullivan, Charlie Comiskey
1884	Fourth	67	40	.626	8	Jimmy Williams, Charlie Comiskey
1885	First	79	33	.705	+16	Charlie Comiskey
1886	First	93	46	.669	+12	Charlie Comiskey
1887	First	95	40	.704	+14	Charlie Comiskey
1888	First	92	43	.681	+6½	Charlie Comiskey
1889	Second	90	45	.667	2	Charlie Comiskey
1890	Second	78	58	.574	12	Tommy McCarthy, Chief Roseman, Count Campau
1891	Second	86	52	.623	8½	Charlie Comiskey

St. Louis Maroons

Union Association, 1884   **BALLPARK:** PALACE PARK OF AMERICA

RECORD: 94–19 (.832)

The Maroons, the Union Association's showcase franchise, were managed by 26-year-old UA president Henry V. Lucas, heir to a million-dollar streetcar, shipping, and real estate fortune. To many, including himself, Lucas *was* the UA. Questioned once about making a decision without consulting other association owners, he claimed unabashedly, "Whatever I do is all right."

The UA was the first organized protest against the combined imperiousness of the National League and the American Association. While Lucas's moral ire was aroused by the unfairness of the reserve rule, his business instinct was equally aroused by the success of the two-year-old AA. The revolt against the reserve rule, blacklisting, and related NL-AA practices had actually begun with plans by an entrepreneur named James Jackson to form an "American

League." By the time the UA held its organizational meeting on September 12, 1883, however, Jackson had lost so much influence that even his bid for a New York franchise was denied and the members elected H.B. Bennett of Washington their first president. At its next meeting, on December 18, 1883, the association replaced Bennett with Lucas.

The Unions faced a united opposition. A peace settlement between the NL and the AA on February 17, 1883 had established the Tripartite Agreement among the two circuits and the Northwestern League, which became a recognized minor league and a party to all provisions of the accord.

When the UA directly challenged the monopolistic limitations that the National Agreement had imposed on both players and entrepreneurs, the established leagues declared war. On December 12th, the AA placed itself in the reluctant position of re-instating previously blacklisted players to keep them out of the clutches of the "Onions," while simultaneously keeping faith with the National Agreement obligations to blacklist those who deserted to the UA. The association also expanded to twelve teams (and an 111-game schedule) to reserve as many players as possible.

Three months later, the NL increased its schedule to 112 games, and, more significantly, adopted a resolution proposed by John B. Day of the Giants that called for the expulsion of any player who signed a UA contract. Day intended not only to keep the rosters intact, but also to preclude rewarding "revolvers" with higher salaries to return to the fold. The AA adopted a modified version of the Day Resolution that applied the blacklist only to players who actually appeared in a Union Association game. Several franchises in both circuits formed reserve teams, prototypes of farm clubs, to assert control over even more players, as well as to provide a pool of talent for the future.

At first, Lucas and his associates, while refusing to recognize "any agreement whereby . . . ball-players may be reserved for any time beyond the terms of their contracts," refused to challenge the validity of agreements for the 1884 season; as a result, the eight Union teams began the season with fewer than fifty players (more than thirty of them out of the weaker AA) from the rosters of 1883. Only during a July 1st meeting in Baltimore did the Union managers acknowledge that they were in a full-scale war and agree to raid other leagues. The NL and AA retaliated with an effort to get back as many jumpers as possible, even though such tactics violated their stated policies. The inevitable results were more money for the players and instability for the clubs.

Fear of blacklisting kept many players from accepting relatively lucrative UA offers. Lucas lavished much of his spending on the Maroons—too much, in fact, for the overall good of the association because too many of the league's best players starred in St. Louis. Third baseman Jack Gleason, lured from Louisville (AA), finished fourth in batting. The sterling outfield included Orator Shaffer, second in batting,

from Buffalo (NL); Dave Rowe from Baltimore (AA); and Lew Dickerson from Pittsburgh (AA). The Maroons began the season with Billy Taylor, formerly with Pittsburgh (AA), as their ace pitcher, but when he jumped to the AA Philadelphia Athletics after a 24–7 record, Lucas reached into his deep pockets and signed Providence's Charlie Sweeney, who won 25 and lost only 4 in the second half. The central jewel in the Maroons' crown was second baseman-captain Fred Dunlap, who came to St. Louis from Cleveland (NL) and who led the Unions in both batting (.412) and home runs (13). Led by Dunlap, the Maroons overpowered the competition, winning their first twenty-one games, compiling the best-ever won-lost percentage (.832), and taking the association title by twenty-one games over Cincinnati.

However satisfied Lucas may have been with his team's performance, its overwhelming success spelled disaster for the fledgling league. There was little interest in a pennant race so one-sided, and several teams went bankrupt during the season and had to be replaced. Leaving the day-to-day operation of the club to Ted Sullivan, Lucas scurried about moving franchises and cheering the ever dwindling number of the faithful. Even though a five-team meeting reelected Lucas president on December 18th in an atmosphere of cautious optimism over the 1885 season, the end came less than a month later. On January 15, 1885, only two teams—midseason replacements Kansas City and Milwaukee—showed up at the final league meeting, where they voted to disband. Among the absent was Lucas himself, who was already negotiating to move his Maroons to the NL. The price he paid was $6,000, variously interpreted as a fine for raiding other teams and a fee for the privilege of keeping his own players. For Lucas, the price also included the humiliation of publicly endorsing the necessity of the reserve clause and even accepting an 1886 increase to twelve reserved players for each team.

Lucas estimated his losses at $17,000. NL propaganda put the losses at his entire fortune, but that seems to have been an exaggeration. The probable figure was about $100,000.

ST. LOUIS MAROONS

Annual Standings and Manager

Year	Position	W	L	Pct.	GB	Manager
1884	First	94	19	.832	+21	Henry V. Lucas

St. Louis Maroons

National League, 1885–1886   **BALLPARKS:** PALACE PARK OF AMERICA (1885)
VANDEVENTER LOT (1885–1886)

RECORD: 79–151 (.343)

When Henry Lucas transferred the Maroons from the Union Association to the National League, effectively terminating the Union Association, he paid a high price for the privilege. Accepting the reserve rule, which he had battled so fiercely, and paying out $6,000 were only the beginning; not only did his former associates regard him as a turncoat, but his new colleagues treated him with disdain.

Obliged to buy out the Cleveland franchise for $2,500, Lucas handed over a cash deposit of $500. Assuming that he was purchasing player contracts as well as a franchise, he had reason to believe that, with the best of the Forest Citys added to the core of his UA team, the NL edition of the Maroons would be competitive. But when Cleveland released its players, as it was obliged to do under the rules of the day, the American Association Brooklyn Bridegrooms violated the rule requiring teams to wait ten days before entering into contracts with new free agents and immediately signed five of the newly available players. When the rest of the Forest Citys signed with other teams, Lucas was left with little more than a $2,000 debt that he refused to pay until Cleveland sued him for it.

At Lucas's insistence, the NL lifted the blacklist on players who had jumped to the Unions, a concession that hardly damaged the victors, because mid-season contract jumpers were all fined $1,000 and reserve clause violators were each assessed $500. The NL's extra profit from the players did not sit well with league president A.G. Mills, the hardest of the hardliners. Mills was so convinced that commuting the sentence of expulsion from organized baseball would cause the players to lose respect for management that he turned to other business interests and at the NL's November 19, 1884 meeting refused to run for reelection.

The NL's unilateral decision on reinstatement was looked upon as treachery by the AA and almost wrecked the coalition between the two victors. Nick Young, elevated to the NL presidency after Mills's retirement, responded to the AA's objections with a bit of Jesuitical reasoning—that the joint policy on reinstatement was merely a wartime policy and not part of the National Agreement. AA owners and officials fulminated, but in the end they had no choice but to come around and reinstate the defectors.

Lucas was the primary beneficiary of the leniency policy. Second baseman Fred Dunlap and outfielder Orator Shaffer had ignored the reserve clause and signed with the Maroons for the 1884 season. Pitcher Charlie Sweeney had jumped his contract with Providence and joined the Maroons in mid-season. Shortstop Jack Glasscock and catcher Fatty Briody had also switched leagues in mid-season, going from Cleveland (NL) to Cincinnati (UA). Lucas got to keep all five, the last two by virtue of the reversion of their contracts to Cleveland.

The Maroons were formally admitted to the NL on January 10, 1885—conditional upon the willingness of Chris Von der Ahe, the successful but eccentric owner of the AA St. Louis Browns, to accept the new club's violation of his territorial rights. Von der Ahe was initially sympathetic to the idea because he had seen the potential profit in an intracity exhibition series the previous year when the Maroons had been in the outlaw UA. But when Lucas took his time about contacting him, Von der Ahe became irked and demanded compensation both for the damage done to him during the UA war and for the future "valuable business privilege" he would be surrendering. Lucas declined to pay any such fee.

At this point, the NL intervened by trying to exclude St. Louis from the National Agreement provision that extended territorial rights to each club. In a power play, the league confronted AA President H. Denny McKnight and offered not to pursue Brooklyn's violation of the ten-day rule regarding the Cleveland players in return for the association's cooperation in stripping Von der Ahe of his territorial rights. But McKnight and the Association were spared anguish when John J. O'Neill, vice-president of the Browns and a U.S. Congressman, met Lucas on a train and offered to serve as an intermediary for him with Von der Ahe. The two St. Louis magnates resolved their differences over a private dinner at the fashionable Tony Faust's Restaurant.

Despite the surface amity, there was an inevitable battle for patronage in which the two teams were unevenly matched from the beginning. Lucas had an exemption from the established NL admission price of fifty cents and permission to match the AA's twenty-five cent tickets, but that and his holdover players were all that he had. For his part, Von der Ahe could schedule Sunday games and sell liquor at his park, both of which the NL prohibited. He also

had a team that would win the first of four consecutive pennants in 1885, while the Maroons stumbled home last in 1885 and sixth in 1886.

At the end of the 1886 season, with the Maroons unable to compete with the Browns at the gate, Lucas applied to the NL for permission to play Sunday games. That permission denied, he gave up and sold the franchise to Indianapolis interests that immediately moved the team to Indiana for the 1887 season.

Lucas left baseball for good. Years later, his fortune dissipated, he had to take a job as a railroad ticket manager.

ST. LOUIS MAROONS

Annual Standings and Managers

Year	Position	W	L	Pct.	GB	Managers
1885	Eighth	36	72	.333	49	Henry V. Lucas
1886	Sixth	43	79	.352	46	Gus Schmelz

St. Louis Cardinals

National League,
1892–Present

RECORD: 7805–7659 (.505)

BALLPARKS: SPORTSMAN'S PARK (1892; 1901; 1920–1966)
LEAGUE PARK (1893–1920)
BUSCH STADIUM (1966–Present)

OTHER NAMES: BROWNS, PERFECTOES

The Cardinals needed a considerable amount of time to achieve respectability after their move into the National League from the American Association. It was not until their twenty-third season that they rose even as high as third, and not until their thirty-fifth year that they won a pennant. From that 1926 triumph, however, and through the introduction of divisional playoffs, the advent of free agency, and various episodes of front office turbulence, the club has been a serious contender more often than not. In general, it has also enjoyed a fan following far more reliable and enthusiastic than its relatively small market might have promised.

St. Louis (then known as the Browns) was admitted to an enlarged NL of twelve teams at the December 1891 conclave in Indianapolis that liquidated the AA. As an Association franchise the season before, the Browns of owner Chris Von der Ahe had finished second; in the six seasons before that, they had won four straight pennants and never finished

Enos Slaughter completes his sprint from first base with the tally that gave St. Louis the world championship over Boston in the seventh game of the 1946 World Series. *UPI/Bettmann Newsphotos*

below third. But that record of success was turned upside-down in the NL, when the club dove toward the cellar in the split season of 1892 and stayed around there for most of the rest of the nineteenth century. An important reason for the plunge was the defection of player-manager Charlie Comiskey to the Reds after the final AA season in 1891. Von der Ahe took it upon himself to succeed Comiskey and demonstrated that, as a manager, he was an energetic beer garden proprietor and brewer; over the rest of the decade, he would ignore criticism of his strategic talents and move in and out as manager with a frenzy unmatched in the history of the game. At that, Von der Ahe was at least a familiar signpost for St. Louis fans endeavoring to keep up with his Rent-A-Manager tactics; in the years 1895, 1896, and 1897 alone, the franchise made twelve managerial changes. At the end of the 1897 season, there was nobody at all as manager in a cost-cutting move. It fell to a fourteenth pilot in 1898, former umpire Tim Hurst, to stagger home as the head of the St. Louis club with the most losses (111) in one season.

The teams of the 1890s had a decidedly German air to them, beginning with Von der Ahe's own depiction on the sports pages as a real-life version of "The Captain" from the Katzenjammer Kids comic strip ("You will drive me crazy vit your chokes," he was quoted as raging at one of his players on one occasion). The owner's righthand man as team treasurer and then president was Stewart Muckenfuss. When he ran out of other candidates for manager in 1896, Von der Ahe turned to his closest friend and drinking companion, sports writer Harry Diddlebock. The German influence was also visible among the players, especially in the so-called Pretzel Battery of pitcher Theodore Breitenstein and receiver Heinie Peitz. The Breitenstein, as he was known, was the ace of the staff for most of the decade. Offensively, first baseman Roger Connor had a couple of solid seasons at the end of his eighteen-year Hall of Fame career, and shortstop Bones Ely turned in a stellar perfor-

Joe Quinn, the Cardinals' regular second baseman between 1893 and 1895, was the first Australian to play major league baseball. The Sydney native had two other tours of duty with the club, in 1898 and 1900. There was not another Australian in the majors until infielder Craig Shipley was called up by the Dodgers in 1986.

mance in 1894 with a .306 average that included 12 homers and 89 RBIs. For the most part, however, the players from the earliest St. Louis teams were perceived as showing up for work mainly because Sportsman's Park was directly across the street from a race track that was of far more interest to them.

Because he didn't have much to offer fans in the way of baseball talent, Von der Ahe sought their patronage by making games little more than a sideshow attraction in what he called his Coney Island of the West. The amusements ran the gamut from carousels and Magic Carpet rides in the outfield to band playing contests, boxing matches, and horse racing. Von der Ahe also did not hesitate after a while to sell the few talented players he had for the cash needed to install a new carnival ride. By 1898, such tactics had so alienated NL owners and the segment of the St. Louis populace that preferred baseball to cotton candy, that Von der Ahe passed his presidency of the organization over to Muckenfuss and tried to assume a lower profile. The gesture proved to be in vain. Barely had the season begun than a nearly catastrophic fire devoured the entire grandstand, the left field bleachers, the club's offices, and most of the personal effects that Von der Ahe had kept on the premises. Miraculously, the casualties came to only a couple of hundred injuries. Maddened by the blaze, Von der Ahe ordered manager Hurst and the players to assist firemen in cleaning up the debris so that a scheduled contest against Chicago could be played the very next day. With the aid of 4,000 hastily erected seats, the game was indeed played (the weary St. Louis squad lost 14–1), but after that, the Browns were on the road for a good part of the season.

The lawsuits stemming from the fire were a godsend for the NL owners. Not only were they determined to get rid of Von der Ahe because of his debt-ridden franchise, but they considered his private life, in the words of *The Sporting News*, "an affront to the community." What was particularly shocking to the other owners was a Von der Ahe mistress who became such a public fact that his wife ended up suing him for divorce on the grounds of adultery; his son lodged another suit for property. As though that weren't enough, Pittsburgh owner William A. Nimick, exasperated by a years-old debt that he had been unable to collect, had private detectives kidnap Von der Ahe, whisk him out of Missouri, and throw him into a Pennsylvania jail, where he stayed for several days before his attorneys could bail him out. When Der Boss President (as he had come to call himself) sought to end his miseries by putting the Browns up for sale, court receivers arrived on the scene to thwart even that move.

Finally, after the 1898 season, a judge ordered the sale of the franchise to St. Louis business speculator G.A. Gruner for some $33,000. Gruner turned right around and sold the team to St. Louis attorney Edward Becker for an estimated $40,000. Nobody bothered to deny that Becker was a front man for both the NL and the owners of the Cleveland Spiders. Only a few days after the papers were signed giving Becker nominal control, the league announced that it was approving the trade of practically every key player on the Spiders to the Browns, with St. Louis in turn sending a contingent of players to Lake Erie. The mass move benefited both the NL and Spiders' owners Frank and Stan Robison: the former because it could finally boast a respectable club in the St. Louis market, the latter because they could finally anticipate the kind of enthusiastic following that not even hotly contested pennant races had attracted in Cleveland.

If St. Louis fans were ready to celebrate the abrupt transformation of their team into a contender, Von der Ahe was not. Charging that the league had stolen the team away from him, he first filed a $50,000 damage suit against Becker and Frank Robison. Then he waited for the first home series of the 1899 season, at which point he served notice on the visiting Pittsburgh Pirates that he was suing them for $25,000 for having been in on the plot against him and intended doing the same thing against the other teams coming in to play. The league dispensed with both threats through the simple expedient of formally expelling the old St. Louis club that had been owned by Von der Ahe and rechartering the team under another corporate name, with Frank Robison as organization president. Von der Ahe didn't even get the satisfaction of being banned from his old haunt: Although Becker had first declared him *persona non grata* at the ballpark, he changed his mind with the sarcastic observation that Von der Ahe's presence would amount to "a good advertisement for the St. Louis club— what it was before and after."

One source of minor confusion during the 1899 season was the name of the club that the Robisons had taken over. Still known as the Browns at the beginning of the year, that nickname became inappropriate when the new owners decided some weeks into the campaign that the club had to get away from its dingy look as much as its dingy record, and switched to the cardinal red socks and piping that has helped to distinguish the team ever since. Still, it took some time for people to accept the proposal of St. Louis *Republic* sportswriter William McHale that the club be called the Cardinals; many of those who didn't persist in referring to them as the Browns went along with a *Sporting News* practice of calling them the Perfectoes.

The players who moved to St. Louis from Cleveland for the 1899 season counted some of the biggest names of the day, including eventual Hall of Famers Cy Young, Bobby Wallace, and Jesse Burkett. But despite this, the club, managed by first baseman Patsy Tebeau, could finish no higher than fifth, a full 18½ games behind Brooklyn. Although even this standing represented a 45-game improvement over 1898, St. Louis fans who had been led to expect a flag grew progressively unruly as the season unfolded, particularly toward umpires. On one occasion, the veteran arbiter Hank O'Day had to be rescued by a squadron of gun-wielding police from a mob shouting for the umpire to be lynched for reputedly bad calls against the Cardinals.

With the NL's decision to cut back from twelve to eight teams for 1900, the Robisons trained their sights on third baseman John McGraw, catcher Wilbert Robinson, and second baseman Billy Keister—the last three important Orioles who had not been committed to Brooklyn with the dismantling of the Baltimore franchise. The brothers got their wish for the 1900 season, but it was an empty achievement. In agreeing to a pact without a reserve clause option, McGraw not only brushed off Robison notions that he think about managing St. Louis down the road, but made it clear that he intended jumping to the new American League the very next year. Robinson and Keister were also on a one-year lease before returning to the new AL Baltimore team.

The presence of the three Orioles seemed to demoralize the entire club, not least when McGraw deliberately provoked umpires so he could be thrown out of games and be free to go to the track across the street. Tebeau, already aggrieved that the Robisons had tried to flank him with a manager-in-waiting, took out his insecurities on the team and was gone by mid-August. The Robisons then turned what had been a crisis into a travesty by hiring concessions supervisor Louis Heilbronner as the new pilot. The five-foot-tall Heilbronner commanded no respect at all, and spent the rest of the season trying to get away from the practical jokes of his ostensible charges. The brightest spot of the season was outfielder Burkett's .402 average; while he lost the hitting title to Ed Delahanty's .408, Burkett became the first of only four major leaguers (the others were Delahanty, Ty Cobb, and Rogers Hornsby) to bat .400 three times.

The return of the three Orioles to Baltimore was far from the stiffest price paid by St. Louis for the dawning of the AL. Among the other players who skipped to the junior circuit for the 1901 season were pitchers Young and George Cuppy, catcher Lou Criger, outfielder Mike Donlin, and third baseman Lave Cross. The Cardinals had barely absorbed these defections when, a year later, Ban Johnson shifted his Milwaukee franchise to St. Louis in direct competition with the Robisons. Adopting the old name of the Browns and moving into the old Sportsman's Park that had been occupied by Von der Ahe's AA club, the new franchise proceeded to lure away outfielders Burkett and Emmett Heidrick, infielders Wallace and Dick Padden, and pitchers Jack Powell, Charlie Harper, and Willie Sudhoff.

The raids proved lethal to the Cardinals at the gate and on the field. While the Browns were able to deflect attention from their own mediocre play with the novelty of their existence, the Cardinals fell into a second-division subsistence that did not end until 1914. Managers came with optimistic forecasts and left again with disillusioning records fairly regularly; among them were two future Hall of Famers— pitcher Kid Nichols and catcher Roger Bresnahan. Another was co-owner Stanley Robison, who decided to save his brother and himself some money by taking over the team for the last fifty-seven games of the 1905 season (his 22–35 record was not radically different from the efforts of more experienced managers). The organization compounded its problems by cutting back on its scouting and giving short shrift to prospects in the name of getting quick cash or some reasonably familiar name that might draw a few more customers; among those jettisoned in this fashion was future Hall of Fame pitcher Mordecai Brown.

At the end of the 1906 season, Frank Robison, physically ailing and still brooding about the Cleveland Spiders players who had deserted him during the AL raids, announced that he was through with baseball as an active owner and was turning the club over to Stanley. Frank returned to his home in Cleveland, where he died of a stroke within two years.

Less self-assured than his older brother, Stanley did not hesitate to go to other NL owners when he sought a new manager for the 1909 season. The good news was that he succeeded in obtaining the highly respected Bresnahan as pilot; the bad news was that,

to obtain the catcher, St. Louis had to tear apart its relatively respectable pitching staff by first dealing Ed Karger and Art Fromme to the Reds for receiver Admiral Schlei, then package Schlei, pitcher Bugs Raymond, and RBI-man Red Murray to New York. In addition, Robison agreed to pay Bresnahan a rather high $10,000 and give him carte blanche in the running of the team.

As a Cardinal, Bresnahan managed one .500 year in four seasons, and that year, 1911, was a checkerboard of loss, tragedy, hope, and success. Before the season even got underway, Stanley Robison was felled by a fatal heart attack. This left the club in the hands of his niece Helen Hathaway Robison Britton, the first woman to assume an active role in the running of a major league team. When the season got underway, the Cardinals surprised everyone by winning, and doing so regularly; at the beginning of July, the club was still in a five-corner race, a mere three games out of first place. Then, on July 11th, in what many were to claim was a trauma from which the team never totally recovered, the train carrying the Cardinals to a series in Boston plunged down an embankment near Bridgeport, Connecticut, killing fourteen people and injuring forty-seven more. Most of the casualties occurred in a coach that had been switched with the team's Pullman to the front of the train after Bresnahan had complained that his players were unable to sleep because of the noise of the engine. Even when the club faded from the pennant race, St. Louis fans continued to flock to the ballpark and cheer for Bresnahan and the players who had distinguished themselves during rescue operations at the train wreck site. The franchise ended up having the best financial year since its inception and paid off most of the debts that had been pressing down on the Robisons. Britton was so elated by the team's showing that she rewarded Bresnahan with a new five-year contract and a separate agreement giving him 10 percent of the profits.

The good feelings didn't last long. In 1912, the

On August 9, 1906, Jack Taylor was knocked out of the box, thus breaking an incredible record of 188 consecutive complete games. During the streak, which began when the right-hander started for the Cubs on June 20, 1901, Taylor also made fifteen relief appearances for a grand total of 1,727 innings without respite.

Cardinals won three of their first four games, then collapsed. Although injuries to Bresnahan and a couple of other players had something to do with the fall, the more fundamental reason was that the club simply didn't have the personnel to compete with either New York or Pittsburgh.

Britton had her own problems: No sooner had she liquidated many of the organization's old debts than she had to start paying attorneys astronomical fees to settle the issue of who was the legal executor of the Robison estate. This outflow gave her some second thoughts about her largesse with Bresnahan, especially with the team floundering around in pre-1911 form. In September, the owner and the manager found another bone of contention in accusations by Phillies' owner Horace Fogel that Bresnahan had rested his front-line players in games against the Giants because he wanted his former boss McGraw to beat out the Cubs and Pirates. Although Fogel was unable to prove the charges, Britton was not amused when Bresnahan protested his innocence in her home with language she considered more suitable for a locker room. A couple of weeks later, she told organization president James Jones to get rid of him and replace him with second baseman Miller Huggins. Bresnahan didn't go so easily, and it wasn't until the following June that the long wrangling over his contract ended with the Cubs stepping in to pick up the final four years of the pact and the Cardinals kicking in $20,000 to pay off the agreement.

Huggins was anything but the People's Choice when he assumed the managership. Although his gritty infield play had won him some local following, he had also been repeatedly singled out by Bresnahan as a back-stabber who had been Britton's conduit to the team in 1912. Others were skeptical that Huggins could command the respect of the St. Louis veterans, a constant test even for the hard-bitten Bresnahan. All the criticism seemed merited when St. Louis flopped back into the cellar in 1913. But a year later, the same Huggins was celebrated throughout the city for keeping the Cardinals in contention until September with a squad that was almost as much of a surprise as the Miracle Braves that won the pennant.

As with Tebeau in 1899, Patsy Donovan in 1901, and Bresnahan in 1911, Huggins's affair with .500 lasted only a single season, and the Cardinals sagged back to sixth the following year. The Federal League's hovering presence didn't help, with outfielder Lee Magee defecting to the Brooklyn club in the new circuit and both pitcher Pol Perritt and catcher Ivy Wingo having to be traded well below their value before they also jumped.

Although few people realized it at the time, the club's most significant moment came on September 10th, when Rogers Hornsby made his major league debut. Considered by many to be the greatest righthand-hitter in the history of baseball, Hornsby batted only .246 in 57 plate appearances after being called up from a Class D league, but thereafter set off in serious pursuit of the .358 average he would compile over twenty-three seasons. Originally a shortstop and then a third baseman before going over to his dominant position at second, Hornsby batted .400 in three seasons, won an NL record six consecutive batting crowns (1920–25) and seven overall, led the league in hits four times, in doubles four times, in triples twice, in homers twice, in runs scored five times, in RBIs four times, and in slugging average no less than nine times. His .424 in 1924 is the highest single-season average in this century. Originally signed by St. Louis scout Bob Connery for $500, Hornsby was elected to the Hall of Fame in 1942.

Rogers Hornsby. *National Baseball Library, Cooperstown, NY*

More interested in the present than in the future represented by Hornsby, Britton let it be known that she was tiring of her financial struggles with the team. In 1916 she took even tighter rein on franchise operations by assuming the presidency and instigating the club's only deal of the year (the sale of pitcher Slim Sallee to the Giants for $10,000). At the end of the season, she called in Huggins and team counsel (and ex-president) Jones to confirm her selling intentions and give them first crack at the purchase. Never the closest of associates, the manager and the attorney left the meeting determined to beat one another to the finish line. Jones won. While Huggins was in Cincinnati to get the financial backing of the millionaire Fleischmann brothers, the lawyer put together a coalition of scores of St. Louis businessmen to buy out Britton for $375,000. Investors put up anywhere from $50 to $10,000, with each $50 share also the guarantee of a Knot Hole Gang seat for an underprivileged child. With the sale depicted as something of a civic duty, as opposed to Huggins's mercenary trip to Cincinnati, Jones became something of a local hero.

The lawyer also gained public relations points by gathering a group of St. Louis writers together and asking for recommendations for somebody to take over the club's day-to-day baseball operations. All those present chose Branch Rickey, then business manager of the Browns. Although the new Browns ownership of Phil Ball had been trying to get rid of Rickey after inheriting him from the previous administration, it changed its mind quickly when the rival Cardinals asked him to be president. Eventually, Ball went to court to block Rickey's attempts to get out of his contract. Many weeks and thousands of dollars later, the Browns' owner withdrew his legal obstacles, allowing his employee to go over to the NL, but also consolidating the enmity between the two franchises.

With the Cardinals, Rickey set down his foundations as one of the two or three most influential executives in big league history. In a career that encompassed every conceivable job with a baseball franchise (player, coach, manager, scout, instructor, business manager, general manager, president, owner), it was during his twenty-six-year tenure with St. Louis that the teetotaling Sunday school teacher varnished the sport's monopolistic grain by devising the farm system and committing hundreds of players to one organization. In the mid-1930s, at the height of his power, Rickey had an estimated 800 major and minor leaguers under Cardinal contract

In the 1930s, the St. Louis farm system put together by Branch Rickey showed:

Class	Team	League
Major	St. Louis	National
AA	Rochester	International
AA	Columbus	American Association
AA	Sacramento	Pacific Coast
A-1	Houston	Texas
B	Asheville, N.C.	Piedmont
B	Columbus, Ga.	South Atlantic
B	Decatur, Ill.	Three-I
B	Mobile, Ala.	South Eastern
C	Jacksonville, Tex.	East Texas
C	Pine Bluff, Ark.	Cotton States
C	Portsmouth, O.	Middle Atlantic
C	Springfield, Mo.	Western Association
D	Albany, Ga.	Georgia-Florida
D	Albuquerque, N. M.	Arizona-Texas
D	Cambridge, Md.	Eastern Shore
D	Caruthersville, Mo.	Northeast Arkansas
D	Daytona Beach, Fla.	Florida State
D	Duluth, Minn.	Northern
D	Fostoria, O.	Ohio State
D	Gastonia, N. C.	North Carolina State
D	Grand Island, Neb.	Nebraska State
D	Greensburg, Pa.	Penna. State Association
D	Johnson City, Tenn.	Appalachian
D	Kinston, N. C.	Coastal Plain
D	Martinsville, Va.	Bi-State
D	Midland, Tex.	West Texas-New Mexico
D	Monett, Mo.	Arkansas-Missouri
D	New Iberia, La.	Evangeline
D	Paducah, Ky.	Kitty
D	Taft, Tex.	Texas Valley
D	Union Springs, Ala.	Alabama-Florida
D	Williamson, W. Va.	Mountain States

on more than thirty teams that St. Louis owned wholly or partially. Mainly because of his ability to draw on such numbers, he traded freely and often at the big league level, frequently keeping a significant detail or two (the seriousness of a player's injury, the military draft notice sent to the player he was unloading) away from his trading counterpart. In St. Louis, this industry translated into five pennants in nine years (1926–34), and a sixth in 1942, after which Rickey went to the Dodgers, where he rocked baseball even more by signing Jackie Robinson and breaking the color line. Still later, he was a pivotal figure in the Continental League origins of the New York Mets and Houston Astros. Rickey was elected to Cooperstown in 1967.

The settlement of the dispute with Ball did not end the controversy over Rickey's move to the Cardinals. Although Huggins was again the manager in 1917, he simmered through most of the season at what he considered a fast shuffle by Britton in allowing him to go off to Cincinnati while Jones was putting together the deal locally. Even the team's surge back to third place proved to be a mixed blessing, with many sportswriters giving Rickey equal credit for the comeback. Also irritated was AL President Ban Johnson, who had planned to keep Rickey in his own tent by proposing him as a manager-general manager for the New York Yankees. With so much resentment in the air, it did not come as too much of a shock when Huggins moved to the Yankees as pilot for 1918 at twice the salary he had pocketed in St. Louis. Jack Hendricks was named as the new Cardinal field boss.

Although every NL team suffered from the loss of key players in the war year of 1918, the Cardinals ached the most, dropping to the cellar. That did it for Hendricks, with Rickey announcing after the season that he would double as president and manager. For the next six years, he continued to wear both hats, steering the club to a couple of third-place finishes and three .500-plus records. It was also during this period that he stepped up his reputation for trading, completing eleven deals in 1919 alone. Among the imports was outfielder Burt Shotton, a slap hitter who was Rickey's righthand man for more than four decades; it was Shotton, for instance, who managed the Cardinals on Sundays, when Rickey's religious beliefs compelled him to observe the Sabbath.

The sheen of the "civic duty" sale to the group put together by Jones wore off rather quickly, especially after public concern with World War I drastically reduced attendance. By 1918, Britton was demanding to know what had happened to the second half of the $375,000 she had been promised for the franchise, and shareholders were grousing about the debts that the organization was piling up for what remained an essentially mediocre club.

Among the irritated stockholders was Sam Breadon, an automobile salesman who had invested the maximum $10,000 originally and who had been solicited subsequently for another $6,000 to help shore up the treasury. When Jones called an investor's meeting before the 1918 season, Breadon initially indicated that he wouldn't even show up to be dunned for more money, but then did go and ended up lending the team another $5,000. It was because of this performance that Jones approached him after the 1919 season with an offer to take over the team presidency; it was because he was already in too deep to say no that Breadon said yes. In taking over formally as president from Rickey in January 1920, Breadon effectively ended the organization's "civic ownership" period. For his part, Rickey claimed no hurt feelings as long as he remained in charge of the franchise's baseball operations.

But there were other hurt feelings. In one of his first presidential moves, Breadon announced that the Cardinals had to get out of ramshackle League Park (Robison Field, previously) before rotting grandstands caused a disaster. Stressing the dangerousness of the facility rather than its limited seating capacity, he got city officials to back him in pressures on Ball to lease Sportsman's Park to the Cardinals when the Browns were on the road. At first, Ball turned a deaf ear to the idea, even blasting Breadon for not having the ability to run a respectable franchise. By way of reply, the Cardinals' president rented an abandoned quarry in South St. Louis and then took out newspaper ads urging readers to bring their dirt to the location so the franchise could build a stadium with genuinely popular support. The prospect of thousands of people descending on the area with tons of dirt prompted City Hall into increasing pressures on Ball, who himself admitted to friends that he had been outflanked.

On June 1, 1920, the Cardinals moved into Sportsman's Park. Aside from attaining his objective of playing in a modern facility, Breadon sold the League Park site to the St. Louis Board of Education for $200,000 and some adjoining lots to the city's public transportation agency for an additional $75,000. The money from the sales—which raised some eyebrows, but no definite evidence of City Hall hanky-panky—ended up seeding Rickey's farm system.

Breadon's rise to the presidency did not slake his ambition. Modestly at first, he began buying out the other members of the Jones purchasing group. With those shares safely in his pocket, he took on Fuzzy Anderson, an associate from the automobile business who had originally talked him into investing in the team. Breadon didn't have enough money

In 1920, St. Louis pitcher Bill Doak used the first glove with a preformed pocket and reinforced webbing.

to buy out Anderson himself, so he accepted Rickey as a full partner, underwriting his manager's note for a bank loan. By the time all the paper had been put into vaults, Breadon had almost 80 percent of the organization, and Rickey had a hold over the owner that went far beyond his job title.

Breadon's business acumen could also benefit the fans. It was he, for instance, who started the practice of scheduling doubleheaders on Sunday from the conviction that people sought more than two hours of entertainment on their day off. As early as 1930, he was also active in NL councils trying to win acceptance for night baseball. After two years of dogged arguments, the league finally gave him permission to try it, but Ball wouldn't hear of installing any lights in Sportsman's Park, even after Breadon volunteered to pay all wiring costs.

Rickey always claimed that his farm system scheme grew out of necessity. Certainly, with the Giants and Cubs in particular showing a willingness to spend generously both for young prospects and for the scouts to seek them out, money-tight franchises such as St. Louis were at a disadvantage. Even when a St. Louis scout was the first to discover a raw talent, a minor league operator, college coach, or parent would waste little time in contacting more affluent teams to reveal Rickey's interest in the player and dicker for more money than that being offered by the Cardinals. To hear the St. Louis manager, the situation grew so bad that he couldn't even rely on his own underhanded practice of "hiding" former college players in the boondocks until they were ready for the majors; after awhile, minor league franchise owners forgot about such "gentlemen's agreements" and sold the stashed player to the highest bidder.

It was thus to reverse all these tendencies that, in 1919, Rickey persuaded Breadon to purchase an 18 percent interest in the Houston club of the Texas League. A short time after that, the Cardinals bought into an Arkansas team in the Western Association and the Syracuse club of the International League. What started as a trickle took less than a decade to become a flood, and at one point, before the intervention of Commissioner Kenesaw Landis, Rickey and Breadon even controlled two entire leagues (the Nebraska State League and the Arkansas-Missouri League).

Although the extent of St. Louis's involvement in minor league operations varied from minority investment to half-ownership to total control, only the last-named circumstance was a guarantee against surprise maneuvers by the management of a minor league organization. The first player to arrive in St. Louis via the farm system vindicated both this suspiciousness and the value of nurturing players in one corporate cradle.

Following the 1921 season, the Cardinals "called up" Jim Bottomley, a lefthand-hitting first baseman, from the Syracuse team in which they held 50 percent of the stock. Forgetting about his commitment to develop Bottomley for St. Louis, Syracuse President Ernest Landgraf replied that so many major league clubs had shown interest in the first baseman that he was going to hold an auction for his services.

With the validity of the whole farm system approach at stake, Rickey got to Syracuse as fast as he could and, after several hours of intense negotiating, hammered out an agreement with Landgraf that allowed Bottomley to join the Cardinals for the 1922 season. After several weeks of dodging questions about the exact nature of the concessions made to Landgraf, Breadon let it slip that he had purchased the other 50 percent of Syracuse and had become the sole owner of the International League team. As for Bottomley, he batted .310 over sixteen big league seasons—good enough to get him elected to the Hall of Fame in 1974. In 1924, he set a single-game record by driving in twelve runs.

When Bottomley joined Hornsby in the infield in 1922, he became the third member of the club destined for the Hall of Fame. The other was pitching ace Jesse Haines (elected in 1970), who turned in three 20-win seasons in the 1920s and who ended up with 210 career victories in eighteen years with the Cardinals. (A fourth future Cooperstown resident, outfielder Chick Hafey, who was elected in 1971, arrived on the scene in 1924.)

Despite such cogwheels, Rickey could not get the team higher than third in the early part of the decade. One reason was that after Haines, the club didn't have a consistent starter. Another reason was that, for all his greatness as a hitter, Hornsby kept the clubhouse unsettled with his manic self-absorption, real or imagined ailments, and ongoing feud with Rickey over whether or not he was contributing as much to the team as he was able. There was also

On May 30, 1922, between games of a Memorial Day doubleheader, the Cardinals acquired outfielder Max Flack from the visiting Cubs in exchange for outfielder Cliff Heathcote. The players switched uniforms and dugouts and then played against their former teams.

some thought in both the press box and the front office that Rickey was too much of a theorist for a managerial job and that his dedication to the long view frequently cost the Cardinals in the here and now of a ballgame. On top of all these factors, St. Louis suffered a couple of tragedies in 1922, when both catcher Pickles Dillhoefer (pneumonia) and outfielder Austin McHenry (brain tumor) died before they reached their prime; McHenry, in particular, had been tagged as a future all-star.

By the beginning of the 1925 season, Breadon was stating his impatience with the club's inability to charge toward the top. Adding a little fuel to his anxiety were regular approaches from the Giants and Cubs for Hornsby's services, with the offers going as high as $250,000. The final straw came on the eve of Memorial Day, when, with the Cardinals in last place, Breadon was informed that there had been next to no advance sale for a home game against Cincinnati. Before the holiday game could be played, Rickey was out as manager in favor of Hornsby. Although maintaining his titles as vice-president and business manager, Rickey insisted on selling all his stock in the team; Hornsby bought it with the help of another Breadon note to the bank.

After getting the team over .500 in 1925, Hornsby brought home the Cardinals' first pennant in 1926. The keys to the flag were catcher Bob O'Farrell's MVP season, 20 victories by Flint Rhem, the acrobatic defense of shortstop Tommy Thevenow, and a midseason trade with Boston that brought in outfielder Billy Southworth. The season went so well that even the franchise's oldest antagonist, Ball of the AL Browns, contributed to it by increasing the capacity of Sportsman's Park to more than 33,000. Although Ball was confident when he approved the project that it would be his team to benefit from a flag-winning campaign, it was the Cardinals who ended up swimming in the extra gate receipts.

Hornsby himself had a rather mediocre season,

In 1924, Sam Breadon persuaded the National League of the promotional value of an annual Most Valuable Player award. In view of the fact that Rogers Hornsby had batted .424 during the season, the St. Louis owner counted on the trophy being presented to his second baseman, with attendant positive publicity for the Cardinal franchise. Instead, the award went to Dodger righthander Dazzy Vance.

batting a relatively low .317 after six straight batting titles. But anybody who had any doubt that he was still his old self was brought up short on the eve of the World Series against the Yankees, when the pilot announced that he would remain with the club rather than attend his mother's funeral in Texas. The announcement left a sour taste even in the mouth of Breadon, but the owner seemed to get over it when Hornsby led the Cardinals to the championship over the Murderers' Row Yankees. The most dramatic moment of the Series came in the seventh inning of the seventh game when the hungover Grover Cleveland Alexander appeared in relief to strike out Tony Lazzeri with the bases loaded, effectively preserving a 3–2 victory. The finale ended when O'Farrell got Babe Ruth at second on an attempted steal.

While St. Louis fans celebrated their first world championship, Breadon counted his profits and added up his grievances against manager Hornsby. One of the deepest sores was Hornsby's refusal to play an exhibition game during the September stretch drive on the grounds that the team had to concentrate on the pennant race rather than add a few more dollars to the owner's pocket. Another was Hornsby's rejection of a one-year, $50,000 contract to return as player-manager in 1927; the Rajah demanded a multiyear pact instead.

The upshot was a December announcement that St. Louis had traded Hornsby to the Giants for second baseman Frankie Frisch and catcher Jimmy Ring. The fallout was immediate and thunderous. Fan groups threatened to boycott the team in 1927. Cranks made so many menacing calls to Breadon's home that he had to disconnect the telephone. Editorialists demanded that he sell the team to Rickey or somebody else. Even when the first wave of protests subsided, the issue was kept alive by Hornsby's refusal to sell the stock he had purchased from Rickey unless he came out of the deal with a substantial profit. With league rules prohibiting a player on one team from owning stock in a second, NL President John Heydler was dragged into the controversy. In the end, Hornsby traded his St. Louis holdings for $116,000, a profit of $66,000 in less than two years. The money came from Breadon ($80,000), the NL ($18,000), and the Giants ($18,000).

Breadon deflected some of the criticism over Hornsby's departure by appointing the popular O'Farrell to succeed him. As the 1927 season wore on, he got even more help from the brilliant defensive and offensive play of Frisch, who was not only a better fielder than Hornsby, but who batted .337 and led the league in steals; it was to be the first of seven seasons in which the Hall of Famer would average .300 for the team. Another box-office performance came from the 40-year-old Alexander, who notched 21 wins and finished second only to Pittsburgh's Ray Kremer in the ERA category. But despite these efforts, and other good years from Bottomley, Hafey, and Haines, St. Louis never quite managed to get over a bad season from Rhem and a broken leg suffered by Thevenow in June, and ended up a game-and-a-half behind the Pirates. Breadon immediately dumped O'Farrell for Bill McKechnie.

Under McKechnie, St. Louis returned to the pennant circle—indirectly because of O'Farrell. When the catcher got off to a slow start in 1928, he was traded to the Giants for outfielder George Harper, who joined Hafey and Taylor Douthit in giving the club a solid-hitting picket line. Moreover, with the backstop position open, Rickey obtained Jimmie Wilson from Philadelphia. Considered the best defensive catcher of his time, Wilson also hit enough to be singled out as the club's most important acquisition of the season. Also having big years were Bottomley (MVP for a .325 average, 31 homers, and 136 RBIs) and pitchers Bill Sherdel (21 wins) and Haines (20 wins). The World Series was another story, with the Yankees gaining retribution for 1926 by trampling St. Louis in a four-game sweep.

Developing a taste for ousting managers who had compiled good records, Breadon decided that McKechnie hadn't prepared the Cardinals sufficiently for the World Series and demoted him back to Rochester, bringing up Southworth to replace him for 1929. One of the most popular and easy-going of Cardinals when he had been a player, Southworth seemed to have taken courses in sourness in the meantime—a change that first stunned, then simply alienated his ex-teammates.

At the beginning of July, with St. Louis in fourth place and showing no sign it could rise any higher, Breadon once again switched McKechnie and Southworth. For a couple of months, McKechnie kept the team at the .500 mark and earned general praise for getting as much out of it as possible. But then, in the closing weeks of September, he began skipping games to campaign for public office back in his hometown in Pennsylvania. When the Braves came calling at the end of the season for permission to talk with McKechnie about their managerial opening, Breadon quickly consented, and shed few tears when the future alderman departed for Boston. Gabby Street was named as the pilot for 1930.

Street got off to the best possible start, by winning the NL flag in his first two years at the helm.

The story of his first season was a dazzling comeback that saw the club go 39–10 after trailing the Cubs by 10 games as late as August 17th. In the Year of the Hitter, only backup third baseman Andy High failed to bat .300, and the team's three main replacements were Showboat Fisher at .374, Ray Blades at .396, and Gus Mancuso at .366. Among the regulars, the biggest sticks were Hafey (.336 with 26 homers and 107 RBIs), outfielder George Watkins (a rookie record .373 average with 17 homers and 87 RBIs), and, again Frisch (.346 with 114 RBIs). The surprise pitching performance came from the veteran Burleigh Grimes, who brought his spitball to St. Louis from Boston in June; Grimes not only won thirteen games, but was that rare 1930 pitcher in the NL who had a reasonable ERA (3.01). A footnote to franchise history was also written by a pitcher on the last day of the season, when Dizzy Dean made his big league debut with a 3–1 victory over Pittsburgh.

Despite losing the 1930 World Series to the Athletics in six games, Street was back the following season, and at the head of a club that took no prisoners. For the first time in their existence, the Cardinals won a race in a romp, then went on to edge the same A's of Connie Mack in a seven-game World Series. Another standout year from Frisch defensively as well as offensively (.311 with 82 RBIs) netted him MVP honors. In addition to 18-game winner Paul Derringer, the Rickey farm system made its presence felt through the additions of Pepper Martin and Rip Collins, mainstays of the Gas House Gang that was waiting in the wings. Martin, who began as an outfielder before moving to his more familiar third base position, was the difference in the World Series against Philadelphia, with 12 hits in 24 at bats, 5 RBIs, 5 runs scored, and 5 stolen bases.

It was, however, the same Martin who became the emblem of the club's unexpected flop back into a sixth-place tie in 1932: not only did he bat a mere .238, but his nine stolen bases for the year were only four more than he had swiped in the World Series. Also attracting criticism for the turnaround was Rickey because he dealt away Hafey and Grimes before the season, even though both players ended up confirming his intuition that their best years were behind them. On the other hand, the season marked the rise of righthander Dean to ace of the pitching staff. The original Yogi Berra in his predilection for ungrammatical observations that often contained common sense, Dean so dominated the league for five years in a Cardinal uniform that not even a career-abbreviating injury and a relatively meager 150 wins could prevent his election to the Hall of

The most quoted Dizzy Deanism was probably that said about him rather than by him, when a St. Louis newspaper headlined the results of a hospital examination of a possible concussion by declaring: DEAN'S HEAD EXAMINED, X-RAYS REVEAL NOTHING. But the player and subsequent broadcaster, who often had runners "sludding" into third, had a few gems of his own, including:

"The series is already won, but I don't know by which team" (on the eve of the 1934 World Series between St. Louis and Detroit);

"Don't fail to miss tomorrow's game" (a broadcasting promo);

"The runners have returned to their respectable bases";

"He's standing confidentially at the plate"; and

"The Good Lord was good to me. He gave me a strong body, a good right arm, and a weak mind."

Fame in 1953. His numbers included 30 wins in 1934 and 28 in 1935, four consecutive years of leading the league in strikeouts, and an average of 25 wins over the four-year period from 1933 to 1936. In 1934 and 1935, he was paired on the St. Louis staff by his brother Paul, who won 19 games in each of the two seasons.

As might have been expected, the team's flop in 1932 persuaded Rickey to make some offseason moves, and he didn't wait long to dispatch Bottomley and turn first base over to Collins. A second transaction was forced on him when, in November, regular shortstop Charlie Gelbert almost shot his leg off in a hunting accident; to replace Gelbert, Rickey had to part with Derringer in a deal with Cincinnati for Leo Durocher. Another important change came with the installation of Joe Medwick in left field. The righthand-hitting Medwick would end up playing in the league for seventeen years, during which he would compile a .324 average, win a batting championship, and drive in 100 runs for six straight seasons. The last National League player to win the triple crown (in 1937), Medwick was elected to the Hall of Fame in 1968.

Though all three new regulars performed up to expectations, the 1933 campaign picked up where 1932 had left off, with the team slipping out of the race fairly early. In fact, the main source of interest

for many by June was picking the day Street would be fired and speculating on the identity of his successor. During the winter of 1932–33, there hadn't appeared to be much doubt about the latter, especially after Breadon rejected a Giants' offer to reacquire Frisch and name him as McGraw's successor as New York manager. But then Breadon and Rickey clouded the issue by signing Hornsby as a pinch-hitter. Well past his prime and broke from backing too many losing horses, the one-time batting king had nevertheless fought the image of a charity case, dropping leaden hints that he had returned for more than a regular paycheck. Finally, in July, Breadon and Rickey made their choice: They released Hornsby so he could take over the reins of the Browns, then a few days later fired Street and replaced him with Frisch.

The 1934 Cardinals were a prime illustration of Rickey's promotional skills. From the beginning of the season, he started feeding sportswriters around the country with exaggerated tales of the daffy or bruising doings of the team's most conspicuous players, inventing out of whole cloth nicknames like The Wild Hoss of the Osage (Martin) and Ducky (Medwick). Abstemious as he was personally, he did not hesitate to depict his personnel as inveterate drunks who were better at their jobs than their sober contemporaries around the rest of the NL. It didn't take long for some of the players to believe their own publicity, and by midseason they were taking up much of the slack for Rickey with raucous performances on and off the field. It was in this context that Durocher, as cited by New York *Sun* sportswriter Frank Graham, referred to himself and his scruffy, hard-nosed teammates as "gas house ball players" who wouldn't be allowed to play in the snobbier precincts of the AL.

As legendary as it was to become, the Gas House Gang snared its one and only pennant in 1934. Even that success remained in doubt until the final hours of the season, when the Cardinals finally passed the Giants to eke out a two-game supremacy. The St. Louis drive was spearheaded by the Dean brothers, who combined for 49 wins; Collins, who led the league with 35 homers while batting .333 with 128 RBIs; Medwick, who contributed a .319 mark and 106 RBIs; and catcher Bill DeLancey, who batted .316 with 13 homers in part-time duty.

Against the Tigers in the World Series, Martin, Collins, and Medwick proved to be the difference in a seven-game struggle. The seventh game degenerated into the ugliest in World Series history when, with St. Louis clearly on its way to the championship

THE WORLD CHAMPIONS, 1934
Dizzy Dean · Durocher · Orsatti · Delancey · Collins
Medwick · Frisch · Rothrock · Martin

The Gas House Gang. *National Baseball Library, Cooperstown, NY*

in a lopsided contest, Tiger fans began pelting Medwick with any object that came to hand—in part out of general principles, in part because of a scuffle earlier in the game between the left fielder and Detroit third baseman Marv Owen. Peace was reimposed only when Commissioner Landis, in attendance, requested that Frisch take Medwick off the field.

Notwithstanding the team's second World Series win in four years, Breadon was not a happy owner when he counted up the season's attendance as a mere 327,000. Convinced that the Depression was going to linger for some time and that the Cardinals and Browns were going to be sharing an increasingly besieged market, he entered into negotiations with Oklahoma oil millionaire Lew Wentz for sale of the club. The talks appeared headed for a successful conclusion when they became unstuck at the last minute over the value of St. Louis's farm system properties. Breadon then sought to move the Cardinals to Detroit, but that idea died when the Tigers and the AL warned Landis that he could expect a revival of tensions between the leagues if he approved the move. Ultimately, Breadon found the solution to his money problems in the tried-and-true big league practice of selling off his players for big wads of cash; unlike his counterparts in Philadelphia and Boston around the same time,

however, the St. Louis owner was able to count on the steady stream of arrivals from the minor leagues to fill in the gaps caused by the sales, so that the Cardinals remained a contending club throughout the 1930s and 1940s. Rickey also embraced the sale ploy eagerly once Breadon assured him of a 10 percent return on every cash exchange he worked out.

Footnote Player: Branch Rickey was second to nobody in building up untalented prospects as a prelude to trading them for more than they were worth. One of his most successful deceptions was a promotion of outfielder Tom Winsett, whom he constantly described as "a coming Babe Ruth" and whom he managed to palm off on Brooklyn in December 1936 in exchange for Frenchy Bordagaray, Dutch Leonard, and Jimmy Jordan. After Winsett had hung up his spikes with a grand total of eight homers over parts of seven seasons, Rickey offered a more honest evaluation of the outfielder: "Woe unto the pitcher who throws the ball where the Winsett bat is functioning. But throwing it almost anywhere else in the general area of home plate is safe."

Though they generally remained in the hunt, often to the final days of the season, the Cardinals did not win another flag until 1942. Sometimes the reason was a rival's extraordinary year (Chicago's 21 consecutive wins in September 1935), other times injuries to key players (Paul Dean in 1936, Dizzy Dean in 1937), most frequently ineffective pitching behind the first and second starters. On the other hand, the team continued to churn out impressive position players, including Terry Moore, Marty Marion, and eventual Hall of Famers Johnny Mize (1981) and Enos Slaughter (1985). Mize, in particular, was in the club's tradition of slugging first basemen who didn't let their power affect their consistency. Over a fifteen-year career that also included stellar moments with the Giants and Yankees, Mize hit .312 with one batting title, led the league in homers four times, and drove in at least 100 runs eight times. For his part, Slaughter got to Cooperstown with a nineteen-year career average of .300 and an image as baseball's ultimate hustler.

Given Breadon's track record with even winning managers, not too many were surprised when he began playing Musical Pilots again with the teasing performances of the Cardinal clubs of the late 1930s; Frisch led to Mike Gonzalez, who led to Ray Blades, who led to Gonzalez again.

In 1938, however, the Cardinal owner had a much bigger problem on his plate when Landis, who had been trying for years to dismantle the St. Louis farm system on the grounds that it was a monopolistic practice against the long-range interests of baseball, announced that he was summarily granting free agent status to seventy-four of the organization's farm hands. In what became known as the Cedar Rapids Case, the commissioner ruled that the Cardinals, and Rickey in particular, had entered into a number of "secret understandings" with minor league officials that violated rules covering competitive opportunity. Initially, Breadon rushed to Rickey's defense, charging that Landis had never gotten over a court ruling earlier in the decade that substantially upheld the validity of the farm system. But with additional disclosures that some of Rickey's cro-

nies in the minors had sought to disguise their relationship with St. Louis by altering checks and ledgers, the owner adopted a cooler stance toward his vice-president, even charging him with having betrayed his trust. For his part, Rickey, only too aware that Landis had banned others from the game for relatively more minor offenses, urged Breadon to file a lawsuit so that the entire issue might be aired in a courtroom. In one sense the counterattack was successful, insofar as Landis never quite got around to informing the Cardinals of formal charges, obliquely confirming Rickey's suspicion that the Judge was mainly interested in vaunting his own sense of self-righteousness over that of the St. Louis vice-president. On the other hand, the Landis initiative succeeded in tearing a hole in Breadon's relationship with Rickey, to the point that the embarrassed owner refused even to insist on the franchise's right to the seventy-four farm hands. Among those lost to the organization were outfielder Pete Reiser, who went on to star for the Dodges, and infielder Skeeter Webb, a cog in Detroit's pennant-winning club of 1945.

The tensions between the organization's two highest officials became clear to all in 1940, when Rickey dismissed rumors that manager Blades was on his way out. Little more than a week later, following an embarrassing loss to Durocher's Dodgers at the first home night game at Sportsman's Park, Breadon held a press conference of his own to announce that Blades was indeed out, and was being replaced by Southworth.

In his second tour of duty with the club, Southworth strove to erase the dictatorial image that he had created in 1929. That he succeeded—and in the process became the most victorious manager in Cardinal history—was due not only to his more patient handling of the team, but also to the growingly negative perceptions of Breadon and Rickey by comparison.

Even for an organization confident of finding replacements in its farm system, the cash-for-player spree undertaken by Breadon and Rickey in the early 1940s had few parallels. From June 1940 to July 1942, St. Louis completed fourteen transactions primarily aimed at bringing in money (10 percent of which still went into Rickey's bank account); among the players sent off were Medwick, Mize, catcher Mickey Owen, and pitcher Lon Warneke. Southworth also won points for himself by keeping the 1941 club in contention down to the final weekend of the season despite serious injuries to such key players as Slaughter, catcher Walker Cooper, and his brother and batterymate, Mort Cooper.

One-time St. Louis manager Mike Gonzalez is credited with coining the baseball expression "good field, no hit." The original object of Gonzalez's appraisal was catcher Moe Berg, being scouted by the Cardinals for a possible deal.

The 1942 season was another watershed year for the franchise: not only did it return to the winner's circle, but it also said goodbye to Rickey. In addition, the season saw the insertion into the regular lineup of Stan Musial, who had provided a glimpse of the future at the end of 1941 by going 20-for-47. In a twenty-two-year career spent solely with the Cardinals, the lefthand-hitting Musial established himself as one of the league's all-time greats, winding up in the top ten of practically every offensive category upon his retirement in 1963. Adding to the first baseman-outfielder's charisma was a batting stance that was all crouch and coil, giving him the appearance of a clamp gripping an invisible shelf. Musial's numbers included a lifetime average of .331, seven batting titles, eight years of leading the league in doubles, five seasons with the most triples, ten years with 100 RBIs, and eleven with 100 runs scored. Although he never led the NL in home runs, he topped the 30-mark six times and ended up with 475. Often applauded as much on the road as at home for his offensive prowess, Musial achieved the odd feat of closing out his career with exactly 1,815 hits in away games and 1,815 in St. Louis. Stan the Man, as Brooklyn Dodger fans were the first to call him for his

relentless tattooing of the Ebbets Field rightfield wall, was elected to Cooperstown in 1969.

With Musial and Slaughter providing much of the punch, Southworth's 1942 Cardinals had to struggle with still another epidemic of injuries to overcome the favored Dodgers and, on the very last day of the season, clinch the flag. The single most valuable player on the team (and so recognized by the NL with an MVP award) was righthander Mort Cooper, who came back from his arm miseries the previous year to lead the league in both victories (22) and ERA (1.78); ten of Cooper's wins were shutouts. The pennant race also brought out the best in Johnny Beazley, who had a career year at 21–6 (he never again won more than seven games). Beazley remained in the spotlight in the World Series, where he won two games in St. Louis's triumph over the Yankees.

The showdown between Breadon and Rickey came in the summer of 1942, when the owner confided his intention of assigning sponsorship rights for the radio coverage of St. Louis games to Hyde Park Beer. When the anti-alcohol Rickey objected that a brewery was an inappropriate choice for games that would be heard by tens of thousands of chil-

Stan Musial. *Fred Roe*

dren, Breadon exploded, declaring that he was going to begin operating the team as he saw fit. Rickey got the message and, in October, tendered his resignation. After a few days of reports that he was about to enter the insurance world or become a political candidate for the Republican Party, he signed with the Brooklyn Dodgers.

With Musial and Mort Cooper again leading the way, the Cardinals romped through both the 1943 and 1944 seasons, capturing the NL title by 18 and 14½ games, respectively. The franchise broke even in postseason face-offs, losing to the Yankees in five games in 1943 and beating the Browns in six the following year. The latter duel, referred to locally as The Streetcar Series, practically closed down St. Louis while it was going on. Strong favorites going in, Cardinal players won few public relations points with their barely disguised wonder that they should end up playing for the championship against a team that had been giving drudgery a bad name for decades. When the Browns won two of the first three games, national sympathies became all the more pronounced in favor of the underdog club. But then reality set in, and the ALers had to content themselves with the knowledge that they had given a clearly superior club a scare.

With Musial joining other front-line St Louis players in the service for the 1945 season, not even big pitching efforts from Red Barrett (21–9) and Ken Burkhart (19–8) could get the club past Chicago for a fourth straight pennant. At the end of the season, Breadon made some observations about Southworth's managing that, as in the case of McKechnie in 1929, prompted a Cardinal pilot to accept a better offer in Boston. When organization man Eddie Dyer was named to succeed Southworth, the change was viewed as still one more cost-cutting measure.

Breadon didn't stop there: Between the conclusion of the 1945 season and the opening of the 1947 campaign, he borrowed a page from Rickey's book to pull off sixteen deals, only one of which (a May 1946 trade for catcher Clyde Kluttz) brought him a player instead of cash. No fewer than eight of the cash purchases were with Boston, where Southworth was using his knowledge of the St. Louis organization to put together a pennant winner for New England.

In 1946, in the tightest NL race in history to that point, the Cardinals and Dodgers closed their regular seasons in a tie, necessitating a best-of-three playoff. When the Cardinals won the first two games for the pennant, they could again point to Musial (batting title) and Slaughter (most RBIs in the league) as the difference between the first and second spots in the standings. Other standouts were second baseman Red Schoendienst (elected to Cooperstown in 1991), third baseman Whitey Kurowski, and southpaw Howie Pollett, whose 21 wins and 2.10 ERA topped the NL in both categories. An intense seven-game World Series against the Red Sox ended up being decided in the Cardinals' final at bat in the last game when Slaughter scored from first on a Harry Walker double after Boston shortstop Johnny Pesky hesitated on a relay throw to the plate. The pitcher of the Series was St. Louis lefty Harry Brecheen, who won twice as a starter and picked up his third win in relief as a result of the Slaughter dash around the bases.

With attendance zooming in St. Louis as in other major league cities, Breadon had little to complain about in 1946—with one exception. That was the early-season defection of pitchers Max Lanier and Fred Martin, infielder Lou Klein, and several lesser Redbirds to the Mexican League organized by multimillionaire Jorge Pascual. When Lanier skipped off to accept the big dollars being waved at him by Pascual, he had been 6–0 and generally regarded as the ace of the staff. It was mainly because of him and Giants' pitcher Sal Maglie that Commissioner Happy Chandler viewed Pascual's ambitions to set up a third major league as a serious threat and that he had little trouble in getting backing from the owners in blacklisting the defecting players for a minimum of

The 1943 World Series became a propaganda issue for the Nazis after armed forces radio broadcast the games to Europe. Commenting on the results, a Nazi broadcast declared: "There are fresh atrocities in the United States. The Yankees, not content with their pious interference all over the world, now are beating up their own cardinals in St. Louis."

First baseman-outfielder Stan Musial was the first of five players to appear in at least 1,000 games at two different positions. The others have been shortstop-first baseman Ernie Banks, first baseman-outfielder Ron Fairly, second baseman-first baseman Rod Carew, and shortstop-outfielder Robin Yount.

five years. When the Mexican initiative collapsed, Lanier organized his fellow jumpers in a barnstorming tour of the United States. His money ran out just when Chandler rescinded his ban and allowed the players to rejoin their teams for the 1949 season.

Musial aside, the Cardinals spent the rest of the 1940s and a good part of the 1950s making charges at the Dodgers, but then falling back to second place or lower. The shift in league power from St. Louis to Brooklyn was the result of three main developments: (1) the blossoming of a Dodger farm system under Rickey; (2) the refusal of the Cardinals to accept black players, as the Dodgers had done; and (3) the predominantly righthand-hitting lineup of Brooklyn's Boys of Summer teams, which allowed them to beat up regularly on a St. Louis staff that was dominated by lefties (such as Pollett, Brecheen, Lanier, and Al Brazle). Breadon himself did not stick around to watch the eclipse of the franchise; at the end of the 1947 season, he sold the team to lawyer Fred Saigh and Postmaster General Robert Hannegan. The following year, Saigh bought out Hannegan, setting himself up as something of a one-man band as owner, president, and general manager.

With first the Dodgers and then the Braves setting the pace in the 1950s, the Cardinals settled into the role of also-ran, always in need of a couple of pitchers. Saigh and his successors kept up the wheeling-and-dealing tradition of Rickey, but with distinctly more modest names; in the entire decade of the 1950s, for example, the biggest star to come St. Louis's way was knuckleball specialist Hoyt Wilhelm, who went 1–4 in 1957 before moving on again to resume a Hall of Fame career.

On the other hand, the ownership kept itself in the headlines, and not only on the sports pages. Following the 1950 season, Saigh emerged as the most prominent spokesman among NL and AL owners for dumping Chandler as commissioner and replacing him with Ford Frick. Saigh's pet peeve was that Chandler had turned down a request that the Cardinals be allowed to play at home on Sunday nights during the hot summer months. Few as they were, the Chandler loyalists didn't forget Saigh's role in the change of commissioners a couple of years later when the St. Louis owner was found guilty of tax evasion and sentenced to fifteen months in prison. When he sought to resolve some of his financial problems by selling the franchise for over $4 million to a Wisconsin group that intended moving it to Milwaukee, the NL stepped in to veto the deal and pressure him to sell out to Anheuser-Busch in St. Louis for a substantially lower figure.

The Anheuser-Busch purchase allowed the makers of Budweiser to get a foot firmly into the door of big league baseball, from where they would sign exclusive contracts with a majority of stadium concessionaires around both leagues, become a dominant force in network and local radio-television coverage of games, and consolidate themselves as a sponsorship power in all professional sports. Especially as of the late 1980s, the beer company's relationship to the Cardinals and to baseball in general became troubling to many, not least because of the enormous logos that festooned most stadiums with encouragements to drink; a few teams eventually eliminated the signs, while others dealt with the bat-and-beer issue by reserving small grandstand sections for fans who didn't want to be seated in the vicinity of drinkers. For its part, Anheuser-Busch took to publicity campaigns emphasizing the historic roots of beer and the need to be "responsible" in its use, but otherwise insisted on the right to reach potential customers. Particularly during the regime of August A. Busch, Jr. (1953–1989), the company not only didn't apologize for its links to sports, but celebrated them in such stunts as having the owner drive an old beer wagon around the ballpark. In the face of earlier assertions that his purchase of the Cardinals would never lead him to use the team as a vehicle for his brewery interests, Busch even had to be talked out of renaming the club's home Budweiser Park.

Busch's first move in assuming command of the franchise was to give then-manager Eddie Stanky the broader mandate of also being responsible for player moves. Then, taking advantage of the cash-short Browns' franchise of Bill Veeck, he purchased Sportsman's Park for $800,000 and renamed it Busch Stadium. The latter move proved to be a much longer investment than the former. Increasingly irritated by the club's inability to rise above the middle of the NL, Stanky became the bane of umpires with his constant arguments, and was booted from games regularly. He was all the more displeased when, during the 1953–1954 offseason, Busch decided to entrust personnel decisions to company man Dick Meyer.

A breaking point of sorts was reached July 18, 1954, when Stanky's stalling tactics during a game that St. Louis was losing by seven runs precipitated a free-for-all with the Phillies and umpire Babe Pinelli's decision to forfeit the contest to Philadelphia. Although the manager got off with the relatively light penalty of $100 and a five-game suspension, the episode sent Busch and Meyer off in pursuit of a replacement. While they were looking, the Cardinals finished the season under .500 for the first time since 1938. Mainly because Busch was not altogether convinced of Rochester manager Harry Walker's credentials for taking over the big league team, Stanky was still at the helm for the start of the 1955 season. But little more than a month into the campaign, with no sign of any changes on the field, the owner pulled the trigger—firing Stanky, promoting Walker, and hiring the latter's brother Dixie as pilot for Rochester.

Walker presided over the team's worst showing since 1919. Although the club had offensive assets in Musial, third baseman Ken Boyer, and the slash-hitting outfield of Wally Moon, Rip Repulski, and Bill Virdon, it was Walker himself who provided the season's most memorable punch when, during a melee with the Reds over another stalling gambit by the Cardinals, he ended up exchanging blows with Cincinnati manager Birdie Tebbetts. To no great surprise, the end of the year produced another shakeup, with Frank Lane replacing Meyer as general manager and Fred Hutchinson succeeding Walker. Lane, known as The Trader for his fast and furious deals in the AL, lived up to his reputation in St. Louis by completing twenty-six transactions with other big league clubs in less than two years. The most significant, which helped boost the team temporarily back to second place in 1957, were a June 1956 blockbuster with the Giants that involved Schoendienst going to New York for Alvin Dark and a November 1956 swap of Repulski and infielder Bobby Morgan to the Phillies for slugger Del Ennis.

Lane's tenure came to an abrupt end at the end of 1957, when Busch declared himself unhappy with a second-place finish. Saying that he had no desire to work for an "irrational organization," Lane jumped back to the AL to the Indians, leaving his post to Bing Devine. Devine went into 1958 with Lane's man Hutchinson still calling the shots from the dugout, but the club's return to humdrum form made it a foregone conclusion that there would be another manager in 1959. The successor turned out to be Solly Hemus, obtained in an end-of-the-year swap with the Phillies. Hemus was to Stanky what Stanky had been to Durocher: a younger, sharp-tongued provocateur who sought to make up in theatrics and spikes-first play what he could not attain through natural talent. In 1959 alone, he was tossed out of games eight times, and watched approvingly as his players and coaches also made regular walks down the dugout runway after exchanges with umpires. With nothing better than Boyer's slugging to watch on a seventh-place team, St. Louis fans initially found Hemus entertaining. But the next year he risked be-

ing driven out of town on a rail when he announced that he was instituting a youth movement in the lineup and that Musial was going to be benched. Although there was little doubt that The Man's best years were behind him, he was still the most popular player in the history of the franchise, and his benching prompted boycott warnings and innumerable protest calls. In the event, Hemus kept Musial out of the lineup only for a short time, and mostly for road games.

In entering the 1960s, the organization could look back on two major accomplishments over the previous decade. The first was the departure of the Browns for Baltimore after the 1953 season, which left the Cardinals in a one-team market for the first time in a half-century. The second positive development (not yet clear even to the front office) was the filtering in of some of the players who would play critical roles in the club's renaissance in the 1960s. In the first move completed after he replaced Lane, Devine obtained outfielder Curt Flood from the Reds. In March 1959, he swapped veteran right-hander Sam Jones and minor league hurler Don Choate to the Giants for first baseman Bill White and third baseman Ray Jablonski. A third deal one month into the 1960 season sent pitcher Vinegar Bend Mizell and third baseman Dick Gray to the Pirates for second baseman Julian Javier.

The Flood and White trades brought the franchise more than the center fielder and first baseman for the pennant-winning team of 1964. In acquiring Flood, the Cardinals finally had an everyday black player—eleven years after Jackie Robinson's debut for Brooklyn and four years after reserve first baseman Tom Alston and pitcher Brooks Lawrence had broken the club's color line. Future NL President White helped bring about an even bigger change when, during spring training in 1960, he protested the exclusion of black players from a public function in Florida to which the Cardinals and Yankees had been invited. When a black newspaper in St. Louis got wind of the incident, it called for a nationwide boycott of Anheuser-Busch, which in turn prompted blacks in other training camps to denounce Florida's segregationist policies in hotels and other public enterprises. Faced with the threat of the boycott, Busch warned officials in St. Petersburg that the team would pull out of its traditional spring camp unless integrated accommodations were provided. The ultimatum persuaded a local businessman to buy two of the best motels in the city and make them available to the team. In what was later viewed as a crucial step in the solidarity of the 1960s St. Louis clubs,

Musial and Boyer gave up their private beachfront homes to move their families into the motels with the other members of the team.

With the club eight games under .500 midway through 1961, Hemus was jettisoned for Johnny Keane. Keane kept the team a surprising 14 games above the break-even mark for the rest of the year, and never went under .500 over his subsequent three years of calling the shots. For the most part, however, the Cardinals remained very much a hit-or-miss proposition in the early 1960s, with only Boyer, White, and Flood hitting with any consistency and pitchers Ray Sadecki, Ernie Broglio, and Larry Jackson taking turns at having off-years. Another member of the staff was Bob Gibson, who, after a slow start in 1959 and 1960, improved to 18 wins in 1963. Before hanging up his glove after seventeen seasons with St. Louis, Gibson would turn in 251 victories, including five 20-win seasons. In his most astonishing performance, in 1968, he overwhelmed NL hitters with 22 wins, 13 shutouts, a league-leading 268 strikeouts, and an incredible 1.12 ERA. A nimble athlete who could also hit and field his position, Gibson became a byword for on-field competitiveness. The imposing righthander was elected to the Hall of Fame in 1981.

In a move that caused nothing but trouble, Busch announced after the 1962 season that he was bringing Rickey back into the organization as a special advisor. The decision infuriated both Devine and Meyer (still around as vice-president), who knew that not even Rickey's 81 years were going to deter him from having a lot to say about front office decisions. Rickey wasted little time in fulfilling their fears, declaring only days after his appointment that Musial's return to a .330 average in 1962 was his last hurrah as a productive player and that he should announce his retirement. Both the player and Devine blasted what they termed "embarrassing" and "unpleasant" advice and confirmed that Stan the Man would return for another season; as it turned out, however, 1963 was indeed Musial's swan song. Devine and Meyer also remonstrated with Busch over Rickey's public prognosis that the 1963 team was too weak to be considered a genuine contender; the Cardinals did in fact stay in the race against the Dodgers until well into September, but fell apart because of the lack of deep pitching that the veteran baseball executive had detected before the start of the season.

By the start of the 1964 season, the situation in the executive suite had become so snarled that Devine realized that only Busch would ultimately emerge as the winner, so he changed tactics by trying to enlist Rickey's help against the owner's reported intention of changing general managers. By his own testimony, Rickey claimed that he sought to intercede with Busch when the latter started pushing Devine toward the door in July 1964; however that might have been, Devine officially "resigned" in July and Rickey protégé Bob Howsam was put in charge of baseball operations, both developments inflaming Meyer.

Shortly after Howsam took over, the Cardinals began playing steadier ball, so that they remained in a four-team race with Philadelphia, Cincinnati, and San Francisco down to the final weekend of the season and, overcoming a scare from the lowly Mets in the year's very last series, wound up snatching the flag. The key players in the pennant drive were MVP Boyer (.295 with 24 homers and 119 RBIs), White (.303 with 21 homers and 102 RBIs), and the strong defensive middle of center fielder Flood, second baseman Javier, the veteran shortstop Dick Groat, and catcher Tim McCarver. The pitching was led by the threesome of Gibson, Sadecki, and Curt Simmons, who combined for 57 wins, and reliever Barney Schultz, who gained most of his 14 saves in the final weeks. But no single player was more responsible for the team's first World Series appearance in eighteen years than left fielder Lou Brock, obtained in June from the Cubs for pitchers Broglio and Bobby Shantz. Displaying the form that ran him into Cooperstown in 1985, the lefty-swinging Brock batted .348 for St. Louis, scored 111 runs, and ended the season with 43 stolen bases. In the succeeding years of his nineteen-season career, he would establish the all-time record for steals at 938 (surpassed by Rickey Henderson in 1991) and bang out 3,023 hits.

In a topsy-turvy World Series against the Yankees, the Cardinals rode the hitting of McCarver and Boyer and the gutsy hurling of Gibson to a championship in seven games. As had happened in 1926 and 1942, however, the celebrations were dampened considerably by palace intrigues, this time emanating from an August memo that bore Rickey's signature that had been given to St. Louis sportswriter Bob Broeg by a Devine-Meyer loyalist in the front office. The gist of the memo was a series of Rickey recommendations on player moves that, if followed, would have denied the Cardinals their flag. Rickey was snubbed at the team's victory dinner and, soon afterward, informed that his services were no longer required. Howsam considered quitting in protest, but stayed on the scene when Busch asked his help in resolving another mess created by Keane's decision to resign as manager and go over to the Yankees. Keane had been under fire from Busch from the beginning of the year, with Leo Durocher waiting in the wings to take over the team in 1965.

The new manager actually turned out to be Schoendienst, and he ended up staying at the post for a franchise-record twelve years. Few would have bet on such longevity when the former second baseman's 1965 team became the first in baseball history to topple all the way from world champions to seventh place. This led to a housecleaning at the end of the year, with Boyer, White, and Groat all sent elsewhere. The 1966 season was dominated by the club's move from old Busch Stadium (Sportsman's Park) to a new artificial-surface facility called the same thing. A month into the campaign, Howsam pulled off the most significant deal of his tenure when he shipped Sadecki to the Giants for first baseman Orlando Cepeda. But not even Cepeda's Comeback Player of the Year season and 21 wins from Gibson could boost the club higher than sixth.

Howsam made another critical deal in December by acquiring right fielder Roger Maris from the Yankees. St. Louis fans were still absorbing the arrival of the record-holder for home runs in one season when the general manager announced his resignation to take over baseball operations for the Reds. If there had been any thought that Schoendienst was going to join the exiles, it was immediately quashed with the news that Howsam's successor was Musial, the manager's long-time roommate during their playing days and one of his closest friends.

Already the owner of a drawerful of hitting records, Musial established a first as a front office executive by becoming the only general manager to preside over a pennant in his sole year of heading baseball operations. The team's comeback from 12 games behind to 10½ in front, with relatively little competition from the Giants and Cubs, stemmed from a number of factors. Cepeda, for one, took MVP

honors for his .325 average with 25 homers and 111 RBIs. Playing its first full season on the artificial turf of the new Busch Stadium, the outfield of Brock, Flood, and Maris mastered the alleyways with a defensive prowess that was to be a prerequisite for all successful Cardinal teams in the years that followed. When Gibson was sidelined with a broken leg in July after racking up 13 wins, 29-year-old rookie Dick Hughes, Nelson Briles, and Steve Carlton took up the slack by posting a combined 44 victories. The World Series against Boston showcased the returning Gibson, who won three times and had an overall ERA of 1.00, Brock with 12 hits and 7 steals, and the veteran Maris with 10 hits and 7 RBIs.

In line with franchise tradition, the 1967 world championship produced another front office change, with Musial stepping down to return to his private business interests and Devine coming back after a few years with the Mets. In the Year of the Pitcher, St. Louis absorbed diminished production from just about every one of its position players except Flood and third baseman Mike Shannon to take its second straight flag. In addition to Gibson's daunting ten-shutout, 1.12-ERA performance, the club received 19 wins from Briles, 14 from Ray Washburn, and 13 from Carlton, with all four starters averaging less than three runs a game. Another contributor was lefty reliever Joe Hoerner, who won 8, saved 17, and had an ERA of 1.47. Gibson won two more games in the seven-game World Series against the Tigers, but was overshadowed by Detroit southpaw Mickey Lolich's three victories. Brock picked up 13 more hits and 7 more steals in the losing effort.

The advent of divisional play in 1969 marked the beginning of another stretch of mediocrity for the franchise, with St. Louis not returning to postseason play until 1982. The era got off to a bad start when Busch, in defiance of all geographic reality, had to accept the inclusion of the Cardinals in the Eastern Division, while the more eastern teams of Cincinnati and Atlanta were put in the West. The arrangement was largely the result of the insistence of the Mets, who, foreseeing fewer lucrative home dates with the Dodgers and Giants, threatened to torpedo the divisional system altogether if they couldn't at least count on three additional games a year against the then-reigning power of the league, St. Louis. Busch agreed, but only after making sure that his team's regional rival, the Cubs, would also be included in the East.

The Mets could have saved themselves the trouble. Rather than embarking on a dynastic rule over the NL, the Cardinals started alternating between

In 1966, southpaw Larry Jaster faced the pennant-winning Dodgers five times and shut them out each time, yielding only 24 singles in 45 innings. The only other pitchers who blanked a team as often in one season were Tom Hughes of the 1905 Senators, who mastered the Indians, and Grover Cleveland Alexander of the 1916 Phillies, who whitewashed the Reds.

being the league's biggest pretenders and biggest disappointments. The only category that the organization led the league in was trades: Between 1969 and 1979, Devine and his successor John Claiborne completed no fewer than 193 deals (an average of sixteen a year) with other major league clubs. Among the most prominent names to come and go were Joe Torre, Vada Pinson, Matty Alou, Rick Wise, Tommie Agee, Claude Osteen, Reggie Smith, Willie Davis, Joe Ferguson, Larry Dierker, Ted Sizemore, Rawley Eastwick, George Hendrick, and Bobby Bonds—for the most part, players who even in their prime were a half-notch below all-time all-star status and who put on Cardinal uniforms when they were approaching the end of the road.

On October 7, 1969, however, the team announced a deal that ultimately helped to revolutionize baseball. In the swap, the Cardinals sent McCarver, Flood, Hoerner, and outfielder Byron Browne to the Phillies in return for slugger Dick Allen, second baseman Cookie Rojas, and pitcher Jerry Johnson. But, in a challenge to the legality of the reserve clause and its hold over players, Flood refused to report to Philadelphia and went to court to pursue his demand for free agency. Although the outfielder himself lost, his defiance proved to be the opening salvo in the player-management war that, in the middle of the 1970s, did indeed usher in free agency and arbitration.

In the early 1970s, the club had other trade troubles, especially with a February 1972 deal that sent Carlton to Philadelphia in exchange for Wise. Busch and Devine decided to unload the southpaw after a contract wrangle involving less than $10,000. Standout performances of the period included Torre in 1971, who was named NL MVP for clouting 24 homers and leading the league in both batting (.363) and RBIs (137); switch-hitting catcher Ted Simmons, who drove in 100 runs in both 1974 and 1975; Brock, who established a new single-season steal record with 118 in 1974; and southpaw reliever Al Hrabosky, who won 13 and saved 22 other games in 1975 while gaining national attention for his Mad Hungarian act of glaring at the baseball and then pivoting back up the hill with a manic stomp.

The 1976 season turned out to be another one of

> **A**lvin Dark, a Baptist fundamentalist, turned down an offer to manage the Cardinals in the 1970s because the team was owned by a brewer.

> **I**n 1972, Ted Simmons waited until August 9th to sign a contract for the season. Emboldened by the Curt Flood challenge to baseball's reserve clause, the catcher had announced his own intention of playing out a single option year. Even though he then signed a pact for 1972–73, he was the first player to go through most of a season without a formal contract.

transition. On the negative side, the Cardinals finished fifth with their worst won-lost percentage since 1955, had no left side of the infield to speak of, and next to no power. On the other hand, righthander John Denny led the league in ERA, Keith Hernandez took over the first base position that he would practically redefine defensively, and shortstop Garry Templeton and outfielder Jerry Mumphrey became the prototypical switch-hitting speedsters who would account for so much of the team's success in the 1980s. But Denny's ERA and the potential of Hernandez, Templeton, and Mumphrey were not enough to bring back Schoendienst for a thirteenth year; at the end of the season, he was fired for Vern Rapp.

Rapp took over with a reputation for being a strict disciplinarian, but that was the least of it. When he wasn't laying down military academy-like rules, he was publicly blasting his players as "minor leaguers," "losers," or worse. In a little more than a year with the team, he had highly publicized clashes with, among others, Hrabosky (who charged that Rapp's edict to shave his Fu Manchu mustache was the reason for his overnight ineffectiveness), Simmons, and Templeton, and opposing players around the league began to savor horror tales relayed to them by Cardinal players. Busch and Devine finally got the message fifteen games into the 1978 season, when they named Boyer the new pilot. Despite (or because of) being more popular than his predecessor, Boyer could get little out of the club, and it ended up with its worst record since 1924.

Busch got rid of Devine again at the end of the 1978 season, replacing him with Claiborne. Even more dramatically, the owner and his new general manager made it clear that Brock, who had suffered through a miserable 1978, had thirty days from the start of the season to prove that he still had something or he would be sold or released. In fact, it turned out to be an exceptional year for the outfielder, who placed himself among the NL's top hitters as early as April and later on both banged out his 3,000th career hit and passed Billy Hamilton for most career steals in the NL. It was also a banner season for Hernandez, who won the batting title with .344 and shared MVP honors with Willie Stargell of Pittsburgh, and Templeton, who became the first switch-hitter to get 100 hits from each side of the plate. Nevertheless, because of faulty pitching, the club came in a distant third, and when Boyer got off to a woeful start (18–33) the following season, he was fired. Whitey Herzog was then named the new manager.

Herzog impressed Busch immediately by keeping a club essentially without front-line pitching three games over .500 well into August. The owner rewarded this effort by yanking him out of the dugout and naming him general manager in place of Claiborne, with Schoendienst returning to the pilot's job. When he had finished his shakedown season, Herzog took back his managerial title to go with his general managership, appointed Joe McDonald to handle front office details, then set off for the winter meetings where he conducted a blitz of deals within four days. A first swap with the Padres netted him pitchers Rollie Fingers and Bob Shirley and catcher Gene Tenace; next he sent first baseman Leon Durham and infielders Ken Reitz and Ty Waller to Chicago for relief ace Bruce Sutter; next he sent Fingers, Simmons, and pitcher Pete Vukovich to the Brewers for pitchers Lary Sorensen and Dave LaPoint and outfielders Sixto Lexcano and David Green; finally, he signed Darrell Porter, the catcher from his previous Kansas City teams, as a free agent. The deals involving Reitz and Simmons also set a contractual precedent when the two players were paid significant sums to waive their no-trade privileges.

The first result of Herzog's dealing binge was the best record in the NL East—and nothing to show for it. Because of the split season in 1981, the Cardinals (like the Reds in the West) were shut out of postseason play, finishing a game-and-a-half behind Philadelphia before the players' strike and a half-game behind Montreal after the settlement.

There were also unpleasant moments during the

season involving Templeton and Busch. Exasperated by the heckling he had been receiving for alleged lackadaisical play, Templeton gave St. Louis fans the finger while returning to the dugout after making an out in a late August game, prompting Herzog to pull him down the steps and shove him on the bench. The shortstop was subsequently admitted to a hospital for depression, then came back to hit a blazing .367 in September, but there was little doubt that he had exhausted Herzog's not-always-infinite patience.

Busch alienated even more natives in April, when he declared his intention of buying Busch Stadium outright from the Civic Center Redevelopment Corporation that had spearheaded the construction project back in the 1960s and that had employed a bond issue to build up surrounding land as well. Under the terms of the original agreement, Anheuser-Busch had a 25 percent interest in the corporation and had ceded parking and concession stand money to the group. Claiming that the franchise now needed the parking and concession profits to pay rocketing player salaries, Busch made two offers for the stadium, was rebuffed each time, and then threatened to sell the team. When he appeared to be making good on his threat by entering into negotiations for the club with a Missouri-based oil company, Civic Center caved in, eventually selling the stadium for an estimated $53 million.

Herzog had another busy offseason in 1981–82. After obtaining switch-hitting minor league outfielder Willie McGee from the Yankees for pitcher Bob Sykes, he acquired Lonnie Smith for hurlers Sorensen and Silvio Martinez in a three-way deal with Cleveland and Philadelphia, and then fulfilled expectations by unloading Templeton in an exchange with the Padres that brought acrobatic shortstop Ozzie Smith to St. Louis. The transactions achieved everything they were supposed to when the Cardinals captured their first division title, then went on to sweep the Braves in the League Championship Series and edge the Brewers in a seven-game World Series. There were many keys to the team's success, starting with an infield of Hernandez, Tommie Herr, Smith, and Ken Oberkfell that committed a mere 44 errors and an outfield of McGee, Lonnie Smith, and George Hendrick that batted .280 or better. The pitching staff was headed by 15-game winners Joaquin Andujar and Bob Forsch, but was mainly dependent on Sutter, who came out of the bullpen to record 9 victories and 36 saves.

Just when it appeared that the Cardinals had indeed established the dynasty that the Mets had foreseen back in 1969, the team was sent reeling by a

In 1979, Garry Templeton upset baseball traditionalists by declaring that he would not join NL reserves for the annual All Star game. Said Templeton: "If I ain't startin', I ain't departin'."

Ozzie Smith's acrobatics added a startling new dimension to playing shortstop. *UPI/Bettmann Newsphotos*

series of injuries and drug problems that consigned it back to the middle of the pack for a couple of years. On June 15, 1983, Herzog startled everyone by announcing the trade of Hernandez to the Mets for pitchers Neil Allen and Rick Ownbey. Although the manager issued several fatuous reasons for dealing Hernandez, such as the player's preoccupation with crossword puzzles before a game, it emerged eventually that the first baseman had been a heavy user of cocaine for some time. Also in 1983, Lonnie Smith was admitted to a clinic for drug and alcohol rehabilitation. The following season, David Green, obtained in the big trade with the Brewers for Fingers, went into a rehabilitation program for alcohol abuse. On the bright side of the ledger, 1983–1984 saw Ozzie Smith consolidate his reputation as possibly the best fielding shortstop in baseball history, Forsch pitch his second no-hitter (1983), the team establish an all-time attendance record of 2,343,716 (1983), and Sutter leave other relievers in the dust with a 1984 performance of 45 saves and an ERA of 1.54.

Sutter had another kind of impact when he signed with Atlanta as a free agent following his big 1984 season. Lacking any premier reliever to replace him, Herzog went to a bullpen by committee (Ken

Dayley, Jeff Lahti, Rickey Horton, Todd Worrell) that was to be an increasingly important part of his strategy in the decade. In 1985, the combination of relievers, 21-win seasons from Andujar and lefty John Tudor, and big offensive years from McGee (batting title and MVP), Herr (.302 with 110 RBIs), and first baseman Jack Clark (22 homers, 87 RBIs) gave the team another division title after a tight race with the Mets. The season also saw the debut of Vince Coleman, who shattered previous rookie records by stealing 110 bases and jump-starting the run-and-hit offense. In the LCS against the Dodgers, Clark hit a dramatic three-run homer off reliever Tom Niedenfuer in the ninth inning of the sixth game to give the team another pennant. The seven-game I-70 Series (named for the highway connecting the two cities) against Kansas City ended less happily, especially after a controversial call at first base in the ninth inning of the sixth game that went against St. Louis and set up a Royals' victory. Smarting over the call by AL umpire Don Denkinger and their own inability to win the championship after being up three-games-to-one, the Cardinals embarrassed themselves in the finale by being clubbed 11–0, having Tudor punch out a window and slice up his hand after being knocked out of the box, and being forced to relieve Andujar after he sought to instigate fights against both the umpires and the Royals. Herzog wasted little time in trading away Andujar over the winter.

Aside from reliever Worrell gaining Rookie of the Year honors, 1986 was a bust, with the team finishing 28½ games behind pitching-strong New York. A similar scenario seemed on the verge of being played out in 1987 until September 11th, when third baseman Terry Pendleton spiked a Mets' surge to the top by belting a ninth-inning homer off Roger McDowell in a tense game at Shea Stadium. The following day, the Cardinals walloped Dwight Gooden, and were not headed again. Although Pendleton and Clark boasted the biggest hitting numbers, and Coleman stole 109 bases, the club's unofficial MVP was utility player Jose Oquendo, who played all the infield and outfield positions and was even called on to pitch in a game. In the LCS with San Francisco, steady relief pitching and a seventh-game shutout by righthander Danny Cox allowed the Cardinals to prevail over Jeffrey Leonard's MVP series for the Giants. The World Series was again a disappointment, however, with the Cardinals unable to overcome a Minnesota team spurred on by deafening, hankie-waving crowds at the Minneapolis Metrodome.

The Cardinals ended the decade on a series of bleak notes, including a devastating wave of injuries to pitchers; among those put out of action for entire years or substantial portions of them were Cox, Worrell, Lahti, Dayley, and southpaw Greg Mathews. Suspicions arose that the epidemic had something to do with the minor league training or big league use of the hurlers, but the organization insisted that the ailments were coincidental; it held to this line in 1991, when ace southpaw Joe Magrane also missed the entire season. On September 29, 1989, another organization era came to an end when Busch died at the age of 90; he was replaced in the boardroom by his son August Busch III.

Herzog showed increasing impatience with the club in 1988 and 1989, and his nickname, The White Rat, became less endearing to a lot of his players. One of his regular targets—in the clubhouse and in interviews—was Coleman, whom he accused of stealing bases for the sake of amassing numbers and without regard for the specific game situation. It did not come as a complete surprise when the manager announced his resignation on July 6, 1990 with the despondent admission that "I can't get these guys to play." Schoendienst returned on an interim basis for a month before the job was officially given to Joe Torre. Torre and general manager Dal Maxvill spent what remained of the season evaluating the many Cardinals who would be eligible for free agency at the end of the year. In the end, McGee was traded to Oakland for switch-hitting outfielder Felix Jose, and Dayley, Coleman, and Pendleton were allowed to walk. McGee's departure for the AL in late August froze his batting average at .355—ultimately enough to win the hitting title.

With the veteran Lee Smith providing invaluable relief, Torre surprised the league in 1991 by melding a substantially new lineup of rookies (outfielders Ray Lankford and Bernard Gilkey) and near-rookies (Jose and third baseman Todd Zeile) with the veterans Ozzie Smith and Pedro Guerrero to get the Cardinals into second place. Emboldened by the power potential of Jose and Zeile in particular, the team moved in the fences for the 1992 season, thereby putting an end to the priority on line-drive-hitting speedsters that had worked so well for Herzog. To the same long-ball ends, promising righthander Ken Hill was traded to the Expos for slugging first baseman Andres Galarraga.

The results were decidedly mixed. While the team did establish a new record for Busch Stadium home runs, the number still came out to a mere 55, and even that mark wasn't set until the last day of the season. More surprising, the lineup's main slugger was not Jose, Zeile, or Galarraga, but center fielder Lankford who blossomed with 20 home runs, 86 RBIs, 42 steals, and a .293 mark. While Jose had a decent season, both Zeile and Galarraga were disasters—with the third baseman even farmed out for a month to get back his stroke and the first baseman missing half the season with a broken wrist and coming back to contribute minimally. The pitching was a two-man story—Lee Smith coming in for another league-leading 43 saves and junkball starter Bob Tewksbury going 16–5 with a 2.16 ERA and yielding only 20 walks in 233 innings. It all added up to a third-place finish.

The club's biggest public relations problem during 1992 was a clear hesitation about resigning the popular Ozzie Smith. Only when the issue had been turned into something of a local plebiscite by St. Louis fans did Maxvill agree to a new contract for the aging but still nimble shortstop. Otherwise, the off-season was more notable for the free agents (Galarraga, Guerrero, Worrell) that the club let go elsewhere than for those it signed to back up what had become one of the youngest teams in the league.

ST. LOUIS CARDINALS

Annual Standings and Managers

Year	Position	W	L	Pct.	GB	Managers
1892	Ninth	31	42	.425	22½	Chris Von der Ahe
	Eleventh	25	52	.325	28½	Chris Von der Ahe
1893	Tenth	57	75	.432	30½	Bill Watkins
1894	Ninth	56	76	.424	35	George Miller
1895	Eleventh	39	92	.298	48½	Al Buckenberger, Joe Quinn, Lew Phelan, Chris Von der Ahe
1896	Eleventh	40	90	.308	50½	Harry Diddlebock, Arlie Latham, Chris Von der Ahe, Roger Connor, Tommy Dowd

1897	Twelfth	29	102	.221	63½	Tommy Dowd, Hugh Nicol, Bill Hallman, Chris Von der Ahe
1898	Twelfth	39	111	.260	63½	Tim Hurst
1899	Fifth	84	67	.556	18½	Patsy Tebeau
1900	Sixth*	65	75	.464	19	Patsy Tebeau, Louie Heilbroner
1901	Fourth	76	64	.543	14½	Patsy Donovan
1902	Sixth	56	78	.418	44½	Patsy Donovan
1903	Eighth	43	94	.314	46½	Patsy Donovan
1904	Fifth	75	79	.487	31½	Kid Nichols
1905	Sixth	58	96	.377	47½	Kid Nichols, Jimmy Burke, Stanley Robison
1906	Seventh	52	98	.347	63	John McCloskey
1907	Eighth	52	101	.340	55½	John McCloskey
1908	Eighth	49	105	.318	50	John McCloskey
1909	Seventh	54	98	.355	56	Roger Bresnahan
1910	Seventh	63	90	.412	40½	Roger Bresnahan
1911	Fifth	75	74	.503	22	Roger Bresnahan
1912	Sixth	63	90	.412	41	Roger Bresnahan
1913	Eighth	51	99	.340	49	Miller Huggins
1914	Third	81	72	.529	13	Miller Huggins
1915	Sixth	72	81	.471	18½	Miller Huggins
1916	Seventh*	60	93	.392	33½	Miller Huggins
1917	Third	82	70	.539	15	Miller Huggins
1918	Eighth	51	78	.395	33	Jack Hendricks
1919	Seventh	54	83	.394	40½	Branch Rickey
1920	Fifth*	75	79	.487	18	Branch Rickey
1921	Third	87	66	.569	7	Branch Rickey
1922	Third*	85	69	.552	8	Branch Rickey
1923	Fifth	79	74	.516	16	Branch Rickey
1924	Sixth	65	89	.422	28½	Branch Rickey
1925	Fourth	77	76	.503	18	Branch Rickey, Rogers Hornsby
1926	First	89	65	.578	+2	Rogers Hornsby
1927	Second	92	61	.601	1½	Bob O'Farrell
1928	First	95	59	.617	+2	Bill McKechnie
1929	Fourth	78	74	.513	20	Bill McKechnie, Billy Southworth
1930	First	92	62	.513	+2	Gabby Street
1931	First	101	53	.656	+13	Gabby Street
1932	Sixth*	72	82	.468	18	Gabby Street
1933	Fifth	82	71	.536	9½	Gabby Street, Frankie Frisch
1934	First	95	58	.621	+2	Frankie Frisch
1935	Second	96	58	.623	4	Frankie Frisch
1936	Second*	87	67	.565	5	Frankie Frisch
1937	Fourth	81	73	.526	15	Frankie Frisch
1938	Sixth	71	80	.470	17½	Frankie Frisch, Mike Gonzalez
1939	Second	92	61	.601	4½	Ray Blades
1940	Third	84	69	.549	16	Ray Blades, Mike Gonzalez, Billy Southworth
1941	Second	97	56	.634	2½	Billy Southworth
1942	First	106	48	.688	+2	Billy Southworth
1943	First	105	49	.682	+18	Billy Southworth
1944	First	105	49	.682	+14½	Billy Southworth
1945	Second	95	59	.617	3	Billy Southworth
1946	First	98	58	.628	+2	Eddie Dyer
1947	Second	89	65	.578	5	Eddie Dyer
1948	Second	85	69	.552	6½	Eddie Dyer
1949	Second	96	58	.623	1	Eddie Dyer
1950	Fifth	78	75	.510	12½	Eddie Dyer

1951	Third	81	73	.526	15½	Marty Marion
1952	Third	88	66	.571	8½	Eddie Stanky
1953	Third*	83	71	.539	22	Eddie Stanky
1954	Sixth	72	82	.468	25	Eddie Stanky
1955	Seventh	68	86	.442	30½	Eddie Stanky, Harry Walker
1956	Fourth	76	78	.494	17	Fred Hutchinson
1957	Second	87	67	.565	8	Fred Hutchinson
1958	Fifth*	72	82	.468	20	Fred Hutchinson, Stan Hack
1959	Seventh	71	83	.461	16	Solly Hemus
1960	Third	86	68	.558	9	Solly Hemus
1961	Fifth	80	74	.519	13	Solly Hemus, Johnny Keane
1962	Sixth	84	78	.519	17½	Johnny Keane
1963	Second	93	69	.574	6	Johnny Keane
1964	First	93	69	.574	+1	Johnny Keane
1965	Seventh	80	81	.497	16½	Red Schoendienst
1966	Sixth	83	79	.512	12	Red Schoendienst
1967	First	101	60	.627	+10½	Red Schoendienst
1968	First	97	65	.599	+9	Red Schoendienst
1969	Fourth	87	75	.537	13	Red Schoendienst
1970	Fourth	76	86	.469	13	Red Schoendienst
1971	Second	90	72	.556	7	Red Schoendienst
1972	Fourth	75	81	.481	21½	Red Schoendienst
1973	Second	81	81	.500	11½	Red Schoendienst
1974	Second	86	75	.534	1½	Red Schoendienst
1975	Third*	82	80	.506	10½	Red Schoendienst
1976	Fifth	72	90	.444	29	Red Schoendienst
1977	Third	83	79	.512	18	Vern Rapp
1978	Fifth	69	93	.426	21	Vern Rapp, Ken Boyer
1979	Third	86	76	.531	12	Ken Boyer
1980	Fourth	74	88	.457	17	Ken Boyer, Whitey Herzog, Red Schoendienst
1981	Second	30	20	.600	2½	Whitey Herzog
	Second	29	23	.558	½	Whitey Herzog
1982	First	92	70	.568	+3	Whitey Herzog
1983	Fourth	79	83	.488	11	Whitey Herzog
1984	Third	84	78	.519	12½	Whitey Herzog
1985	First	101	61	.623	+3	Whitey Herzog
1986	Third	79	82	.491	28½	Whitey Herzog
1987	First	95	67	.586	+3	Whitey Herzog
1988	Fifth	76	86	.469	25	Whitey Herzog
1989	Third	86	76	.531	7	Whitey Herzog
1990	Sixth	70	92	.432	25	Whitey Herzog, Red Schoendienst, Joe Torre
1991	Second	84	78	.519	14	Joe Torre
1992	Third	83	79	.512	13	Joe Torre

* Tie

Postseason Play

LCS	3–0 versus Atlanta	1982	WS	4–3 versus New York	1926
	4–2 versus Los Angeles	1985		0–4 versus New York	1928
	4–3 versus San Francisco	1987		2–4 versus Philadelphia	1930
				4–3 versus Philadelphia	1931
				4–3 versus Detroit	1934
				4–1 versus New York	1942
				1–4 versus New York	1943
				4–2 versus St. Louis	1944

4–3 versus Boston	1946
4–3 versus New York	1964
4–3 versus Boston	1967
3–4 versus Detroit	1968
4–3 versus Milwaukee	1982
3–4 versus Kansas City	1985
3–4 versus Minnesota	1987

St. Louis Browns

American League,
1902–1953

BALLPARK: SPORTSMAN'S PARK

RECORD: 3414–4465 (.433)

Lawsuits and losses dominate the fifty-two year history of the American League Browns. With the worst overall record of the eight AL franchises that lasted from the 1900s to the 1950s, the team is remembered mainly as the instigator of bizarre promotions and as the inspiration for the parodic rhyme, "First in shoes, first in booze, and last in the American League." What is less well remembered is that, for the first half of their existence, the Browns were also first in the affections of St. Louis fans.

For a team that finished last ten times, seventh twelve times, and sixth eleven times, the Browns' beginnings were quite promising. After the 1901 season, AL President Ban Johnson summarily removed the last-place Milwaukee Brewers to St. Louis, then the fourth largest city in the United States, to challenge the National League Cardinals. Ralph Orthwein, the Browns president, did more than challenge the Cardinals, he raided them for their best players: future Hall of Famers Jesse Burkett and Bobby Wallace; outfielders Emmett Hendrick and Billy Maloney; and pitchers Jack Powell, Jack Harper, and Willie Sudhoff.

Hoping to benefit from an association with the past as well as looking to the future, Johnson and Orthwein resurrected the name of the nineteenth-century Browns and refitted their old home, Sportsman's Park. On April 23, 1902, pitcher Jiggs Donohue beat Cleveland, 5–3, in the club's first outing. Manager Jimmy McAleer then took the Browns to second place, their best finish for the next twenty years. The franchise also survived the first of numerous court actions—a request by the Cardinals for an injunction preventing the pirated players from appearing for the new AL team.

Unhappy with Orthwein and his sportsman friends who owned the club, Johnson persuaded Robert L. Hedges, a Cincinnati carriage maker, to purchase the Browns for $30,000. Hedges's thirteen-year reign produced little glory. Left fielder George Stone, acquired in January 1905 from the Red Sox, won a batting crown in 1906 with a .358 average, but the team finished in the first division only once. Nevertheless, Hedges showed an overall profit of $765,000 even after pumping considerable amounts back into both the park and the team. He completely overhauled Sportsman's Park in 1908, in the process shifting the playing field around by 180 degrees; the following year he increased the capacity to 18,000 by adding a second deck around the infield. The club finished second in league attendance, with 618,947. Hedges was also relatively generous with his players, granting them salary advances to tide them over the winter. His liberality threatened the sale of the club to Philip De Catesby Ball in 1915, when buyer and seller reached a temporary impasse over who should be owed thousands of dollars of what had been, in effect, loans to employees.

When the Browns slumped to seventh place in 1909, Hedges fired the affable McAleer and replaced him with catcher Jack O'Connor, a crustier type who undid himself on the last day of the 1910 season. With his club mired in the cellar, O'Connor took it upon himself to determine the outcome of the AL batting championship. Ty Cobb, with what he thought was a comfortable lead over Nap Lajoie, sat out the final day, failing to reckon with the depth of his unpopularity with fellow players. Lajoie, whose Cleveland club played a doubleheader with St. Louis on the final day of the season, collected eight hits, six of them bunt singles toward third base that Browns rookie Red Corriden failed to handle because he was playing too deep on orders from O'Connor. An investigation by Johnson led to the expulsion of the manager and pitching coach Harry Howell, who had offered the official scorer a new suit if he changed his ruling on one of Lajoie's at bats; Corriden was banished to the minors. Lajoie lost the batting crown anyway. O'Connor, who had a two-year contract, sued the Browns for his $5,000 1911 salary and won.

Wallace succeeded O'Connor, but his closeness to the players, not to mention a second consecutive 107-loss, eighth-place finish in 1911 and a rocky start in 1912, led to his departure in favor of George Stovall. The feisty first baseman lasted only parts of two seasons (seventh and eighth again) and suffered the same fate as O'Connor, dismissed not by his employer, but by Johnson, for spraying an umpire with tobacco juice over a called third strike.

After a brief tenure by third baseman Jimmy Austin, Hedges settled on puritanical Branch Rickey to take over the club; following a brief career as a catcher, Rickey had been coaching baseball at the University of Michigan. Assisted by Austin and outfielder Burt Shotton (who ran the team on Sundays because Rickey would not violate the Sabbath),

Rickey brought only marginal improvement in the standings over the first couple of years, but began the turnaround that made the Browns financially successful contenders in the early 1920s.

Rickey's most enduring contribution to the Browns was securing the services of first baseman George Sisler. The foremost college player of the early 1910s, Sisler, while still a minor, had signed a contract with Akron that had eventually been purchased by the Pittsburgh Pirates. As the teenager approached graduation, Pittsburgh president Barney Dreyfuss pressed his claim with the National Commission. Advised by Rickey, who had coached him at Michigan, Sisler argued successfully against the Pittsburgh claim, was declared a free agent, and then signed with the Browns for $7,400. He went on to a fifteen-year Hall of Fame (in 1939) career over which he hit .340, leading the AL twice in that category (.407 in 1920 and .420 in 1922) as well as once in triples and runs scored, twice in hits, and four times in stolen bases. Sisler's 257 hits in 1920 set a major league mark that still stands.

On December 18, 1915, with the Federal League war drawing to a close, Hedges, his health failing, sold the Browns for $525,000 to the curmudgeonly Ball, a millionaire cold-storage-unit manufacturer and president of the FL St. Louis Terrapins. The new owner's first act was to kick Rickey upstairs to the front office where his true genius could flourish. Never popular with the players as a field manager,

The stunt of stunts: On August 19, 1951, Bill Veeck sent Eddie Gaedel up to bat against the Tigers. *UPI/Bettmann Newsphotos*

George Sisler. *National Baseball Library, Cooperstown, NY*

Rickey made them dislike him even more as a general manager: Taking advantage of the death of the FL, he advised the players that salary offers for the 1916 season were good only for ten days; heeding the implied threat, twenty players mailed their contracts back in time.

At spring training a year later, Ball discovered that Rickey had signed on as president of the rival Cardinals. Although he had no desire to hold on to a general manager who wanted to be elsewhere, the Browns' owner was a stickler for the sanctity of contracts, and Rickey's had five years remaining. To make a point, Ball won a court injunction preventing Rickey from assuming his new position—but only for twenty-four hours.

Ball's legendary irascibility found objects everywhere, from his own players to Commissioner Kenesaw Landis. On one occasion, he released a player for having breakfast in bed, because "I don't have time to eat breakfast in bed. He shouldn't have that much time either." In another incident, he flew to Detroit to see a game only to find none of the players in the hotel dining room. When he learned that the players ate at inexpensive local restaurants to keep the difference from their $5-a-day meal money, Ball issued instructions for them to sign for food at the hotel, a practice other clubs soon adopted.

The bad blood between Ball and Landis went back to the FL war, when the commissioner, then a federal judge, had sat for almost a year on a suit filed by the Feds against the NL and AL. Opposing Landis's selection as commissioner in 1921, Ball refused even to sign the final papers of appointment, leaving that task to general manager Bob Quinn. Nevertheless, the commissioner's first case, a dispute between the Browns and the Cardinals over rights to first baseman Phil Todt, went in Ball's favor, and the Browns' owner later offered the resolution to re-elect Landis at the end of his first term. The reconciliation ended in 1930, when the commissioner declared outfielder Fred Bennett a free agent on the grounds that St. Louis had been hiding him in the minor leagues, and Ball sued. On the only occasion that Landis's authority was challenged in court, Federal Judge Walter Lindley upheld the broad powers the owners had bestowed on the commissioner. Wary that his suit could open the thorny question of baseball's antitrust exemption, Ball did not pursue the matter further.

Surprisingly, Ball interfered very little in personnel decisions. These he left to Quinn, who sat in the general manager's chair from 1917 to 1923, when he left to become part-owner of the Boston Red Sox. Fielder Jones, who had succeeded Rickey as field manager, lasted only until June 15, 1918, when he walked out after the team had blown a six-run lead in the ninth inning. Jones had actually started out on the right foot, finishing fifth with a winning record in 1916 before slipping back to seventh in 1917. One high point of the latter season occurred when no-hitters were thrown on consecutive days by southpaw Ernie Koob on May 5th and righthander Bob Groom in the second game of a May 6th doubleheader. The low point came in 1917, when Ball found himself in court yet again, this time in a $50,000 slander suit brought by Browns' shortstop Doc Lavan and second baseman Del Pratt. Ball had accused the pair of "laying down" in a game against the White Sox; the issue was settled out of court only through the intervention of Johnson and Washington manager Clark Griffith. No sooner was the case settled than Quinn sold Lavan to the Senators and traded Pratt to the Yankees for, among others, pitcher Urban Shocker, second baseman Joe Gedeon, and $15,000. Shocker became the mainstay of the staff, winning at least 20 games every year from 1920 to 1923, including an AL-leading total of 27 in 1921. Gedeon, on the other hand, proved more trouble than Pratt when he testified before the grand jury hearing the Black Sox case that he had bet on the

Cincinnati Reds to win the 1919 World Series. Although Gedeon denied knowledge of the fix, he did admit discussing the series with gamblers and was expelled from baseball by Landis.

To replace Jones as manager, Quinn again installed Austin temporarily, then hired Jimmy Burke, who brought the team home fifth in both 1918 and 1919 and fourth in 1920. Too placid for Quinn, Burke gave way to Lee Fohl in 1921. By then, Quinn had assembled the team that, between 1920 and 1925, would notch five first-division finishes. In 1922, the Browns had their most successful year, 93 wins and 61 losses. Sisler hit .420 despite a shoulder injury late in the season; Shocker won 24; and catcher Hank Severeid hit .321 and second baseman Marty McManus .312. The outfield of Jack Tobin (.331), Baby Doll Jacobson (.317), and Ken Williams (.332 and an AL leading 39 homers and 155 RBIs) was the best in baseball. The Browns fell short of a pennant by one game.

The Sportsman's Park turnstiles clicked about 713,000 times, a franchise record in 1922, and Ball made a $350,000 profit, $125,000 of which he doled out to the players in the form of bonuses. A wealthy man long before he came to baseball, the owner treated the Browns as a hobby, pouring whatever profits he realized back into the club and taking whatever losses he suffered philosophically. In May 1922, after a particularly grueling win that followed the reversal of an umpire's decision and the summoning of the players back to the field from the locker room, Ball chastised road secretary Willis Johnson for bothering him with "such unimportant details" as the $12,000 gate share owed to the visiting Browns.

Ball's generosity led to the departure of Quinn, who used his bonus to purchase a part-interest in the Red Sox in 1923. Worse, Sisler was lost for the season with an eye problem. Then Fohl was fired for refusing to sign a petition defending pitcher Dave Davenport against accusations of doctoring the ball. Despite permanently impaired vision, Sisler returned in 1924 not only to play first base, but also to take over as manager. Fourth place in 1924 and a notch higher in 1925 raised Ball's hopes: He extended the

In 1922, Browns' rookie lefthander Hub Pruett struck out Babe Ruth ten of the first fourteen times that he faced the slugger. Ruth homered in his fifteenth at bat.

second deck of Sportsman's Park to the foul lines in 1925, then, anticipating a pennant in 1926, added bleachers to bring the park's capacity to almost 34,000. But the Browns had crested, and plummeted to seventh place in 1926. The World Series was played in Sportsman's Park that year, but the home team was the Cardinals, tenants since 1920. This reversal of fortune, largely the work of Rickey, shifted the balance of St. Louis baseball power to the NL team.

Ball's last years were frustrating. Dan Howley succeeded Sisler as manager in 1927 with Bill Killefer supplanting him in 1930. Hall of Famers Heine Manush and Goose Goslin moved on and off the roster, as did pitcher Alvin Crowder and outfielders Sam West, Smead Jolley, and Carl Reynolds, but the team remained unrelentingly mediocre, climbing as high as third place only once (in 1928). Ball showed flashes of his old free spending, shelling out $25,000 for catching prospect Rick Ferrell in 1929, but, hit hard by the Depression, later sold Ferrell, who went on to a Hall of Fame career with the Red Sox and Indians.

Ball died in October 1933. His last official act, dismissing interim manager Alan Sothoron and hiring Hall of Fame second baseman Rogers Hornsby, was also his worst. The executors of Ball's estate—business associate Louis B. Von Weise, personal friend Walter Fritsch, and general manager Carle McEvoy—had no particular baseball expertise and easily fell victim to Hornsby's bullying. A sixth-place finish in 1934 and two seventh-place seasons in 1935 and 1936 failed to convince the trustees that Hornsby was not the man to lead the team.

The former Cardinal slugger alienated the players with his bluntness and incorrigible abusiveness. In 1935, he got rid of outfielder Debs Garms and pitcher George Blaeholder for laughing after a de-

In 1922, Ken Williams hit 39 home runs and stole 37 bases to make him the first player to reach 30 or more in both categories in a single season. The feat was not duplicated until 1970.

On September 26, 1926, the Browns and the Yankees played the quickest doubleheader in history; the two games at Sportsman's Park were over in 2 hours and 7 minutes.

feat. He fined Rollie Hensley repeatedly for the catcher's carousing. Worse still, patronage became almost non-existent, slipping to a twentieth–century record low of 80,922 in 1935.

Von Weise, desperate to extricate both himself and the Ball heirs from the franchise, offered a $25,000 finder's fee to anyone who could come up with a buyer. The reward went to none other than Rickey, the master peddler of damaged goods, who landed Donald Barnes, the president of American Investment Company of Illinois. In early 1936, Barnes and Bill De Witt headed a syndicate that took over the club for $325,000, almost a third of which came from the sale of stock to the public. The team showed no improvement through the end of the decade despite the removal of Hornsby in mid-1937. After swearing repeatedly to Barnes that he had mended his gambling ways, a Pinkerton wiretap established that Hornsby had been wagering heavily on horse races, even stooping to the subterfuge of using the clubhouse boy as his runner during games.

Succeeding the Rajah for the remainder of the 1937 season was Jim Bottomley, another former Cardinals slugger, who, in turn, gave way to Gabby Street, a one-time pennant-winning manager for the local NLers. The result was an eighth-place finish in 1937 and a slight improvement to seventh in 1938. In the latter season, Bobo Newsom, in his second of three tours with the Browns, won 20 games despite a 5.08 ERA. Looking for yet another new manager for 1939, Barnes and De Witt resisted an unsolicited offer by Babe Ruth to take over because, while they recognized that the Bambino would be a terrific drawing card, they also viewed him as a less than positive influence on young players. Instead, they settled on Fred Haney. Ruth could not have done worse: The team suffered its worst season, 111 losses against only 43 wins and a major league record margin of 64½ games out of first place.

The 1930s ended with few positive memories for the Browns. Right fielder Beau Bell had had a pair of seasons batting better than .340 and led the AL in hits and doubles in 1937, and third baseman Harlond Clift had back-to-back seasons with 29 and 34 home runs (and identical 118 RBIs) in 1937 and 1938. In 1938, the club acquired George McQuinn from the Yankees' farm system in a blatantly illegal waiver deal. The two organizations prearranged both the first baseman's transfer and the subsequent sale of a player to Newark in exchange. McQuinn immediately showed he was worth the trouble by batting .324 and .318 in his first two seasons with the Browns.

Attendance dropped below 100,000 three times during the decade (including the record year of 1935), and never rose as high as 180,000. Losses averaged about $100,000 a year. Budgets were so tight that keeping the outfield grass trim became the responsibility of a goat.

In 1940, the other clubs voiced concern that they couldn't recoup their travel and hotel expenses for trips to St. Louis, AL President Will Harridge suggested that the owners "go a little socialistic for their own good" and each sell the Browns a player for $7,500. Only two players of any value were proffered: aging submariner Eldon Auker, whose 16 wins kept the mound staff from collapsing altogether, and outfielder Walt Judnich, whose .303 average and 24 homers made him the team's biggest offensive threat. Not only did the organization go on the dole, but individual players, strapped by paltry salaries, received offseason unemployment compensation of $15 a week.

The 1940 season was brightened by the addition of lights at Sportsman's Park, the $150,000 cost shared equally by the Browns and the Cardinals. The lights were installed eight years after Ball had scorned a Cardinals suggestion that St. Louis inaugurate night ball in the major leagues.

The Browns played their first night game on May 24, 1940, with Auker losing to Cleveland 3–2. The game drew 24,827, the biggest crowd in a dozen years; in fact, half of the 240,000 home fans who came out to see the Browns that season showed up for the club's fourteen night games (double the number permitted other clubs).

By late 1941, reduced to only seven night games, the franchise had reached its nadir, despite modest on-field improvement to two successive sixth-place finishes. The cumulative effect of too many years of insufficient income had taken its toll. Bills remained unpaid. Particularly irritating were contractual obligations that required the Browns to pay for half of all costs for ushers and maintenance staff at Sportsman's Park, even though the Cardinals, with their far larger crowds, used considerably more of both. The dearth of operating capital dictated the abandonment of five farm teams and the release of the entire scouting staff; this in turn dropped the value of club stock to 40 percent of the original purchase price. The AL had to intervene with a $25,000 loan to meet expenses.

Then, in early December, Barnes orchestrated a shift of the franchise to Los Angeles for the 1942 season. Cubs' president Phil Wrigley agreed to surrender not only his territorial rights to the California city, but also his minor league park there. The other AL owners gleefully agreed to the move in the hope of improving road attendance; Barnes had a schedule drawn up to include Los Angeles and had priced the cost of air transportation to the West Coast for all teams; even Cardinals owner Sam Breadon indicated a willingness to cough up cash and speed the Browns on their way, so that he could have St. Louis all to himself. All that was required was official ratification of the move at the AL annual meeting on December 8th. But then the bombing of Pearl Harbor exploded all of the transfer plans.

The next best thing was to find an angel; the rescuer turned out to be Richard Muckerman, head of the St. Louis Ice and Fuel Co., who laid out $300,000 for a new issue of Browns' stock and assumed the title of vice-president; Barnes and De Witt remained as president and vice-president–general manager, respectively.

The boost provided by Muckerman's money was mirrored by improved play on the field under manager Luke Sewell. Sewell pushed an old pitching staff headed by Auker and Denny Galehouse and a youthful offense led by Chet Laabs (.275 average, 27 homers and 99 RBIs) and rookie shortstop Vern Stephens (.294, average, 14 homers, and 92 RBIs) to a third-place finish, the club's best since 1928.

With Judnich and Jack Kramer off in war plant work and everyone else except Stephens slumping badly, the Browns fell back to sixth in 1943, but by then the 4F Club that would end forty-two years of pennantless futility was in place. There were, in fact, eighteen 4F's on the 1944 opening day roster; among them was catcher Frank Mancuso, discharged from the military for a back injury suffered in a parachute jump that made him incapable of looking straight up for pop flies.

While not the prettiest pennant winning team, the 1944 Browns got out of the gate quickly, winning their first nine games. (A mere 894 people saw the ninth win at Sportsman's Park; the Browns at the time had 1,132 stockholders.) Led by Nelson Potter (19–7) and Kramer (17–13), the staff produced a 3.17 ERA, second in the AL. Stephens led the AL in RBIs with 109, to go with his .293 average and 20 homers. St. Louis's pennant hopes came down to a four-game series with the third-place Yankees on the last weekend of the season. The team slipped into first place,

ahead of Detroit, in the season finale on fourth- and fifth-inning home runs by Laabs, who had otherwise been having a disappointing season. Stephens added a homer for a 5–2 victory and a one-game margin over the Tigers. The game attracted the largest crowd ever to see the Browns at home—34,625.

The Streetcar Series with the Cardinals was a letdown: The Browns could only manage a .183 batting average to support the pitching staff's 1.49 ERA. Just as bad, ten errors led to seven unearned Cardinal runs (out of a total of sixteen). After two victories in the first three games came three straight losses and a Cardinals' world championship.

Having succeeded with draft rejects, the club went one step further in 1945 and brought up one-armed Pete Gray from Memphis. Although Gray batted only .218 in 77 games, he attracted the admiring and the merely curious. Teammates never warmed to the outfielder, partly because of his surliness and partly because of their resentment over the attention paid to him. A third-place finish, the Browns' last in the first division, did not deter Muckerman from buying out Barnes on August 10th.

Stephens began 1946 by bolting to the Mexican League for promised riches, but after only two games in Jorge Pascual's private domain, he thought better of his decision. Stephens fared better than other Mexican League jumpers, however, because Commissioner Happy Chandler declared that, since he had not signed a contract with St. Louis before going south, he was eligible for immediate reinstatement. Otherwise, the season had few happy endings. On the way to a seventh-place finish, Sewell was fired, largely because he refused to play third baseman Bob Dillinger. Under Sewell's successors, starting with coach Zach Taylor, Dillinger became a productive hitter (.321 and .324 in 1948 and 1949, respectively) and led the AL in stolen bases three times.

Muckerman spent another $750,000 to buy Sportsman's Park from the Ball estate in 1947; $500,000 more went on refurbishing the park and an additional $750,000 for a new facility for the organization's San Antonio farm club. The 1947 campaign saw the organization's first black players, second baseman Hank Thompson and outfielder Willard

On July 20, 1944, Nelson Potter became the first pitcher ejected, fined, and suspended for throwing a spitball.

On September 28, 1947, the Browns activated radio announcer Dizzy Dean; only 36 years old at the time, Dean pitched four scoreless innings against the White Sox, giving up only three hits.

Brown, but the infielder only managed to hit .256 in twenty-seven games and the outfielder .179 in twenty-one games; to Muckerman's chagrin, St. Louis fans preferred descending on the rebuilt park to see Brooklyn's Jackie Robinson thrash the Cardinals. In a year when almost every other major league team made money, the Browns drew only 320,000 fans in response to a cellar finish under Muddy Ruel. With Taylor back in 1948, the team rose to sixth, but Muckerman had had enough.

When the expected rewards had not materialized, players were sold off to recover losses. From January 1947 to January 1949, the club worked twenty deals, sixteen of which brought cash. The biggest swaps were with the Red Sox in November 1947. In the first, Stephens and Kramer got tickets to Boston for six journeymen and $310,000; in the second, pitcher Ellis Kinder and infielder Billy Hitchcock made the trip east in return for shortstop Sam Dente and $65,000. In another deal, infielder Johnny Berardino, later to become noted as the star of the *General Hospital* television soap opera, was swapped to Washington for second baseman Gerry Priddy. When Berardino retired to pursue his acting career, the Browns substituted $25,000 and came away with Priddy anyway. Berardino promptly unretired, then was unloaded on the Indians for first baseman-outfielder George Metkovich and $50,000, later increased to $65,000 when Metkovich, discovered to have a broken finger, was sent back to Cleveland. Between the two Berardino trades, promising slugger Jeff Heath was shipped off to the Braves for $25,000.

The fire sale continued throughout 1948. Then, on February 2, 1949, Muckerman sold his almost 57 percent of the franchise to Witt and his brother Charley, both of whom had begun their Sportsman's Park careers as vendors. Muckerman claimed that he had rejected better offers from interests in Baltimore, Los Angeles, Milwaukee, and Dallas in order to keep the team in St. Louis, but the choice of the buyer seemed mainly a response to the deals that Bill De Witt had engineered to recoup Muckerman's losses. On the surface, the transfer of ownership carried a $1 million price tag, but the structure of the transaction was identical to that of a corporate raid: A three-step process of borrowing the money to make the deal, selling off the most valuable assets one at a time, then selling the shell of the structure. To assume control of the club, the De Witts put up $75,000 of their own money and borrowed the rest—$300,000 from the AL (on the condition that they stay in St. Louis) and $650,000 from Muckerman.

> Browns' owner Bill De Witt hired Dr. David F. Tracy in 1950 to instill self-confidence in the players through hypnosis. The experiment was short-lived when the Browns lost two games to the Red Sox soon after Dr. Tracy's arrival—a 20–4 drubbing on June 6 and, the next day, a 29–4 fiasco.

To retire the debts, Bill De Witt continued selling players. Between March 1949 and June 15, 1951, he engaged in eleven major transactions, ten of which brought in money; the only difference was that now it was his own head, rather than Muckerman's, that had to be kept above water. Together with the sale of the Browns' Toledo farm club to Detroit, the player transactions netted more than $500,000.

When the De Witts weren't selling off the future for quick cash, they were trying to evict the Cardinals from Sportsman's Park on the grounds that Fred Saigh's purchase of the NL club had violated the terms of the lease. A court ruling held that the Cardinals' tenancy remained valid until the end of 1961. On the field, Taylor presided over two seventh-place finishes and was in the process of bringing the team home last in 1951 when Bill Veeck entered the scene to take over the franchise.

Veeck arrived in St. Louis with a large reputation and even larger plans. The former was as baseball's premier promoter and Peck's Bad Boy whose antics had done as much to alienate his fellow owners as to revive the minor-league Milwaukee and major-league Cleveland franchises; the latter was nothing less than to drive the Cardinals out of St. Louis. It was a tall order, for not only had the Cardinals been the top team in St. Louis for twenty-five years, but Veeck's syndicate was woefully underfinanced. The fragile coalition had Veeck owning a third of the shares, minority investors such as Arthur Allyn and Newton Frye providing a piece of the financing, and Bill De Witt surrendering most of his 56 percent but retaining enough to stay on as vice-president.

So precarious was the group's economic footing that it was in default of the heavy mortgage on Sportsman's Park from the first day, because the sale had dissolved the corporate entity that had officially owned the stadium. In another move that would later add to his fiscal problems, Veeck signed a contract with Falstaff Brewery, the teams' radio sponsor, that called for a $250,000 payment to the club if it won the pennant, but also for a sliding scale down to $1 for a seventh- or eighth-place finish.

The new regime got off to an explosive start on the Fourth of July with a sign that read "Open for Business Under New Management," a fireworks display between games of a holiday doubleheader, and a free beer or soda for each of the 10,392 patrons. Baseball clowns Max Patkin and Jackie Price were brought in to entertain the crowd. Millie the Queen of the Air slid down a tightrope that stretched from right field to third base. On August 19, 1951, Veeck pulled the stunt that he would later say would inspire his inescapable epitaph: "He sent a midget up to bat." To celebrate the birthdays of both the AL and Falstaff Brewery, the St. Louis owner wheeled out an oversized birthday cake between games of a doubleheader; out of the cake popped 3'7" Eddie Gaedel wearing a Browns uniform with the number 1/8. Veeck then sent Gaedel up to pinch-hit for leadoff hitter Frank Saucier in the first inning of the second game. Assured by manager Taylor that the midget had signed a valid contract, umpire Ed Hurley let Gaedel keep his appointment with baseball immortality—a base on balls issued by Detroit's Bob Cain, whose laughter as much as Gaedel's minuscule strike zone contributed to his wildness. The unamused AL President Harridge banned midgets from the league the next day and ruled that Gaedel's name and record should not appear in the official 1951 averages.

Five days after Gaedel's lone plate appearance, Veeck held Grandstand Managers Day. Originally, the promotion was to have been the selection of the Browns starting lineup from mail-in ballots printed in the St. Louis *Globe-Democrat;* each voter received a free ticket to the game and the right to contribute to the strategy against the Philadelphia Athletics. When the editors of the paper killed the ballot after only one edition and Philadelphia General Manager Art Ehlers threatened to protest the "travesty," Veeck went all out. Each of the 4,000 special ticket holders, joined by Veeck and former Athletics manager Connie Mack, received a placard with a green "yes" on one side and a red "no" on the other. Browns PR director Bob Fishel held up cards with proposed moves—steal, warm up pitcher, and the like—to which the grandstand managers flashed their opinions. A circuit court judge tabulated the results and relayed the consensus to the players. All the while, Taylor, in street clothes and slippers, puffed on a pipe as he sat in a rocking chair first atop the dugout and, after umpire Bill Summers objected, in a box

seat. The fans called an excellent game: The Browns triumphed 5–3 to end a four-game losing streak.

The antics drew twice as many fans in the second half of the season, after Veeck had taken over, as the team had in the first half, but there was no improvement on the field: The Browns lost 102 games and finished last. The high points of the season were Ned Garver's 21–12 record, the first time a pitcher had won 20 for a tailender, and outfielder Bob Nieman's pair of home runs on September 14th, the only time a player has hit two round-trippers in his first two big league at bats.

For 1952, Veeck tweaked Saigh's nose by hiring such familiar Cardinals as Hornsby (as manager for a second time), Harry Brecheen (as a pitcher-coach), Marty Marion (as a player-coach), and Dizzy Dean (as radio announcer). Hornsby did a reprise of his Captain Bligh act in the clubhouse and went about his field duties lackadaisically. When Veeck fired him in June for protesting a blatantly incorrect fan interference call too late, the St. Louis press sided with Hornsby; the dailies intensified their criticism when the players presented Veeck with a two-foot loving cup for liberating them from Hornsby's tyranny. Veeck always swore that the cup was Garver's idea; Garver concurred, but almost everyone else concluded it was just another of Veeck's publicity stunts.

Marion, the new manager, could do no better than seventh place despite the contributions of Satchel Paige (a 12–10 record, 10 saves, and a 3.07 ERA), who had joined the Browns the previous year at the official, but probably underestimated, age of 46. Attendance was 518,796, higher than in the pennant-winning season of 1944, while the Cardinals drew fewer than a million customers for the first time since the end of World War II.

Veeck's undoing—and that of the franchise—came immediately after the 1952 season. The trouble began when he proposed two radical changes for the AL—an unrestricted draft that would make all minor leaguers free agents after one season and the sharing of television revenue with the visiting clubs. Voted down 7–1 on the second issue, Veeck refused to sign releases to allow the televising of games in which the Browns were the visitors. The rest of the league retaliated by changing the schedule to eliminate the lucrative night games in St. Louis. While contemplating whether to sue over this collusion, Veeck learned that Saigh, who had been indicted for tax evasion, had sold the Cardinals to Anheuser-Busch Breweries. Realizing that the resources of the new Cardinals' owner were overwhelming, he resorted to attempts to move the franchise. He was blocked out of his first choice, Milwaukee, by Lou Perini, who was about to move his Boston Braves there. Settling on Baltimore, where Jerry Hoffberger of the National Brewing Company offered $300,000 to sponsor the games of the relocated franchise, Veeck took his case to the AL. Although assured by his fellow AL owners of a swift approval, he found himself on the short end of a 6–2 vote at the winter meetings in Tampa.

Left as a lame duck in St. Louis, the man who in 1951 had finished second to Cardinals' star Stan Musial in a sportswriters' poll for the city's outstanding sports figure, was exorciated by both press and fans. Veeck shot back at the fans for wanting to keep the Browns without wanting to support them. Having laid out $400,000 for prospects he had expected to showcase in Baltimore, he sold Sportsman's Park to the Cardinals for $800,000. (There was little alternative because the city was about to condemn the structure for multiple violations that ended up costing $1 million to correct.) Selling his Arizona ranch to purchase some unissued stock helped; so did the sale of pitcher Virgil Trucks and outfielder Bob Elliot to the White Sox for $90,000.

The old magic was gone, however. Even a 6–0 no-hitter by Bobo Holloman over the Athletics in his first major league start on May 6th ended up costing money, when the unexpected performance forced Veeck to exercise a $25,000 option on a pitcher who could do no better than a 3–7 record and a 5.23 ERA. Exercising the option on Holloman also prevented Veeck from scraping together the $31,500 asking price for slugging shortstop Ernie Banks, who was about to emerge from the Negro Leagues. The icing on the cake was that Holloman's only complete game came on a rainy night with only 2,473 fans in the stands, each of whom had been given a rain check for their hardiness before the first pitch had been thrown. Aside from Holloman's performance, what few Browns' fans remained had little to distract them except a colossal April 28th brawl provoked by

catcher Clint Courtney's nasty slide into Yankee shortstop Phil Rizzuto; six players were fined for their roles in the melee.

On the last day of the season, September 27th, two days after a sparse crowd had hung the owner in effigy during the final night game, Veeck found himself thwarted again in his efforts to move the club to Baltimore when the AL voted 4–4. Told by Yankees co-owner Dan Topping that the rest of the league would bankrupt him and then dispose of the franchise, Veeck became effectively powerless before an offer by a syndicate headed by attorney Clarence Miles and Baltimore mayor Thomas D'Alesandro to buy the club for $2.475 million. With Veeck abstaining, his partners accepted what amounted to a 48 percent profit only to find the AL also willing to consider an alternative $2.5 million offer from a Los Angeles group sponsored by Topping's partner Del Webb that included aircraft manufacturer-movie mogul Howard Hughes. For a full day, until Veeck convinced the other owners that Miles would sue, the AL had committed the Browns to Los Angeles. When the madness subsided, the Miles offer and the shift to Baltimore were approved unanimously.

Meanwhile, back in St. Louis, the Browns had played their last game, a 2–1 twelve-inning loss (their 100th of the season) to the White Sox in which the home team had ignominiously run out of fresh baseballs; the last out was recorded with a recycled ball with a gash in it. As fitting as this ending was, it almost wasn't because a holder of eight shares was so averse to losing the young hurlers (Bob Turley and Don Larsen) and sluggers (first baseman-outfielder Vic Wertz and outfielders Johnny Groth and Roy Sievers) that Veeck had assembled for transport to Baltimore that he got an injunction to prevent the franchise shift. Veeck, who probably could have defeated the suit, knew that no St. Louis judge could easily have dismissed the case and kept his position; fearing that a year or more might be lost before the move could be consummated, he settled the case for one final indignity—and $50,000.

ST. LOUIS BROWNS

Annual Standings and Managers

Year	Position	W	L	Pct.	GB	Managers
1902	Second	78	58	.574	5	Jimmy McAleer
1903	Sixth	65	74	.468	26½	Jimmy McAleer
1904	Sixth	65	87	.428	29	Jimmy McAleer
1905	Eighth	54	99	.354	40½	Jimmy McAleer
1906	Fifth	76	73	.510	16	Jimmy McAleer

1907	Sixth	69	83	.454	24	Jimmy McAleer
1908	Fourth	83	69	.546	6½	Jimmy McAleer
1909	Seventh	61	89	.407	36	Jimmy McAleer
1910	Eighth	47	107	.305	57	Jack O'Connor
1911	Eighth	45	107	.296	56½	Bobby Wallace
1912	Seventh	53	101	.344	53	Bobby Wallace, George Stovall
1913	Eighth	57	96	.373	39	George Stovall, Jimmy Austin, Branch Rickey
1914	Fifth	71	82	.464	28½	Branch Rickey
1915	Sixth	63	91	.409	39½	Branch Rickey
1916	Fifth	79	75	.513	12	Fielder Jones
1917	Seventh	57	97	.370	43	Fielder Jones
1918	Fifth	58	64	.475	15	Fielder Jones, Jimmy Austin, Jimmy Burke
1919	Fifth	67	72	.482	20½	Jimmy Burke
1920	Fourth	76	77	.497	21½	Jimmy Burke
1921	Third	81	73	.526	17½	Lee Fohl
1922	Second	93	61	.604	1	Lee Fohl
1923	Fifth	74	78	.487	24	Lee Fohl, Jimmy Austin
1924	Fourth	74	78	.487	17	George Sisler
1925	Third	82	71	.536	15	George Sisler
1926	Seventh	62	92	.403	29	George Sisler
1927	Seventh	59	94	.336	50½	Dan Howley
1928	Third	82	72	.532	19	Dan Howley
1929	Fourth	79	73	.520	26	Dan Howley
1930	Sixth	64	90	.416	38	Bill Killefer
1931	Fifth	63	91	.409	45	Bill Killefer
1932	Sixth	63	91	.409	44	Bill Killefer
1933	Eighth	55	96	.364	43½	Bill Killefer, Allen Sothoron, Rogers Hornsby
1934	Sixth	67	85	.441	33	Rogers Hornsby
1935	Seventh	65	87	.428	28½	Rogers Hornsby
1936	Seventh	57	95	.375	44½	Rogers Hornsby
1937	Eighth	46	108	.299	56	Rogers Hornsby, Jim Bottomley
1938	Seventh	55	97	.362	44	Gabby Street
1939	Eighth	43	111	.279	64½	Fred Haney
1940	Sixth	67	87	.435	23	Fred Haney
1941	Sixth*	70	84	.455	31	Fred Haney
1942	Third	82	69	.543	19½	Luke Sewell
1943	Sixth	72	80	.474	25	Luke Sewell
1944	First	89	65	.578	+1	Luke Sewell
1945	Third	81	70	.536	6	Luke Sewell
1946	Seventh	66	88	.429	38	Luke Sewell, Zack Taylor
1947	Eighth	59	95	.383	38	Muddy Ruel
1948	Sixth	59	94	.386	37	Zack Taylor
1949	Seventh	53	101	.344	44	Zack Taylor
1950	Seventh	58	96	.377	40	Zack Taylor
1951	Eighth	52	102	.338	46	Zack Taylor
1952	Seventh	64	90	.416	31	Rogers Hornsby, Marty Marion
1953	Eighth	54	100	.351	46½	Marty Marion

* Tie

Postseason Play

WS	2–4 versus St. Louis	1944

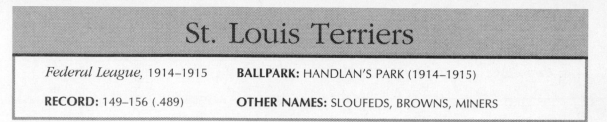

St. Louis Terriers

Federal League, 1914–1915	**BALLPARK:** HANDLAN'S PARK (1914–1915)
RECORD: 149–156 (.489)	**OTHER NAMES:** SLOUFEDS, BROWNS, MINERS

A Federal League franchise that had to compete against both an American and a National League rival, the Terriers rarely had a home game when another contest between more established teams wasn't also being held. The daily confrontation was a conscious decision on the part of the FL organizers, who knew they had to succeed in St. Louis, one of only two major league cities to permit Sunday baseball at the time, if their enterprise was to flourish.

At first, Otto F. Stifel, a wealthy brewer, provided the financial backing for the club, but despite an opening day crowd that approached 20,000, losses were soon so great that new money was soon required. It came from Philip De Catesby Ball, a wealthy ice-machine manufacturer and cold-storage plant operator who had played minor league ball in Louisiana until he lost the use of his left hand in a knife fight.

The Terriers' biggest catch was pitcher-manager Mordecai (Three Finger) Brown, a future Hall of Famer who bolted the Cubs. Late in the summer, having proven that as a manager (a 50–63 record) he was still a pretty good pitcher (a 12–6 record), Brown moved to the Brooklyn Tip Tops. His removal eliminated the informal club nicknames (Browns for the manager's last name and Miners for his middle name) that had gained currency among fans.

Fielder Jones was Brown's replacement. Doc Crandall, 13–9 on the mound and a .309 average in an additional sixty-three games at second base, was the biggest attraction on the last-place club. On the other hand, the club had to get through all but nine games of the 1914 season without Armando Marsans, the Cincinnati outfielder whose jump to the Terriers provided the NL with a test case against the Federals; a federal judge ruled that Marsans had to

go back to the Reds because of a previous contract with Cincinnati. The injunction was lifted at the end of the season, but the outfielder was a bust for the Terriers.

Not content with a tailender, Ball went on a shopping spree, signing future Hall of Famer Eddie Plank (21–11 in 1915) from the Philadelphia Athletics, third baseman Charlie Deal (.323 in 65 games) from the NL Boston club, and first baseman Bob Barton (.286) from the New York Yankees. The one that got away was Walter Johnson, probably the greatest righthanded pitcher of all time. Johnson, in the middle of a contract dispute with the Washington Senators, was offered $20,000 by Jones to join the Terriers, but ultimately went back to Clark Griffith.

The new Terriers helped boost the club all the way to second place, only one percentage point behind the Chicago Whales, in the closest pennant race in major league history. The Terriers actually won one more game than the Whales, but they also lost one more to finish with a .566 won-lost percentage to Chicago's .567. (Pittsburgh finished third, four percentage points out of first.)

As early as April, 1915, Ball, at the instigation of *Sporting News* editor J. G. Taylor Spink, had met twice with AL President Ban Johnson for ice-breaking talks aimed at easing the Terriers' owner out of the Federal League and into one of the older circuits. In his second season with the Sloufeds, Ball lost $182,000, but made it clear that he thought there was more to baseball than the Federal League. The upshot was that the final settlement of the FL war included Ball's purchase of the Browns for $525,000. It also contained a curious $2,500 payment by Cincinnati owner Garry Herrmann as compensation for having deprived the Terriers of the services of Marsans.

ST. LOUIS TERRIERS

Annual Standings and Managers

Year	Position	W	L	Pct.	GB	Managers
1914	Eighth	62	89	.411	25	Mordecai Brown, Fielder Jones
1915	Second	87	67	.565	(.001)	Fielder Jones

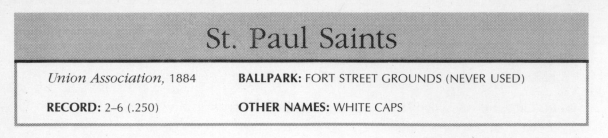

St. Paul Saints

Union Association, 1884	**BALLPARK:** FORT STREET GROUNDS (NEVER USED)
RECORD: 2–6 (.250)	**OTHER NAMES:** WHITE CAPS

The Saints hold two distinctions among major league franchises: They were the shortest-lived team, playing only nine games (one of them a tie), and they are the only club never to have played a home game.

A charter member of the Northwestern League, the first minor league recognized by the National League and the American Association, St. Paul was one of only three survivors of that circuit's rocky inaugural season of 1884. Following the end of the Northwestern League campaign, Saints' backer H. W. Cory and manager Andrew Thompson planned to spend September touring the midwest playing games against local teams. But fate intervened when the Omaha club declined an invitation to replace the ailing Pittsburgh franchise in the Union Association, and UA President Henry V. Lucas turned instead to St. Paul to complete the season, with all remaining games scheduled on the road.

The lineup brought to the UA was hardly of major league caliber. Rightfielder Scrappy Carroll hit .097; shortshop Joe Werrick, .074. The highest batting average (.313) belonged to pitcher Jim Brown, who also went 1–4 on the mound. Of the team's eleven players, only two achieved any distinction: Catcher Charlie Ganzel played for thirteen more seasons, all of them in the NL, and Billy O'Brien, who pitched a 1–0 shutout over St. Louis for the Saints' first victory, led the NL with 19 homers for Washington in 1887.

The final series of the year was scheduled in Milwaukee, but, at St. Paul's request, it was called off after what proved to be the Saints' last game, a 14–1 loss to St. Louis on October 14th.

ST. PAUL SAINTS

Annual Standings and Manager

Year	Position	W	L	Pct.	GB	Manager
1884	Partial Season	2	6	.250	—	Andrew Thompson

San Diego Padres

National League, 1969–Present	**BALLPARK:** SAN DIEGO JACK MURPHY STADIUM
RECORD: 1722–2152 (.450)	

Of all the excuses offered for losing ball clubs, few have been as inventive as that traditionally put forward for explaining the negative records usually compiled by the Padres: that the team is playing in an atmosphere too pleasant for winning. While this undoubtedly comforts the San Diego chamber of commerce in a perverse sort of way, it does little for illuminating the reasons for the franchise's history of disappointing prospects, erratic deals and free agent signings, and front office chaos. Nor does it explain how the team managed to win a pennant in 1984.

Anybody looking for omens about the future course of the franchise might have found a few in 1969, the first year for a team that had been created hastily amid fears by National League owners that the American League was on the verge of expanding

WASHINGTON   **1st BASE**

NATE COLBERT   **"NAT'L LEA."**

Rumors were so rife concerning an imminent move by the Padres to Washington in 1974 that even baseball card companies were caught in the middle. *Copyright The Topps Company, Inc.*

into one of the country's richest markets. One omen might have been C. Arnholt Smith, a California banker and close acquaintance of then-President Richard Nixon who had gotten into the habit of investing in ambitious projects (like the Padres) with everybody's money but his own. Another omen might have been the distinctly Dodger look to much of the franchise after Los Angeles owner Walter O'Malley had personally steered San Diego's candidacy through meetings with other NL executives. The most conspicuous of the Dodger alumni was former general manager Buzzy Bavasi, who took over as Padres president under Smith and brought along his son Peter. The Bavasi family would in turn start a San Diego tradition of hiring field managers with connections to the Dodgers: Preston Gomez, Don Zimmer, Roger Craig, Frank Howard, and Dick Williams. On the other hand, apprehensive about the smallest public hint of the kind of collusion that had transpired between the New York Yankees and Kansas City Athletics, the two teams went out of their

way to avoid player deals with each other: In the first ten years of the Padres' existence, over which they completed more than 100 transactions, the only swap with the Dodgers was a 1969 exchange in which pitcher Al McBean went to Los Angeles for shortstop Tommy Dean and minor league hurler Leon Everitt.

Most ominous of all for the team's beginnings was the roster of has-beens and might-someday-be's that the franchise had put together from the expansion draft and subsequent trades. With only 23,000 people on hand to see the Padres' first game on April 8, 1969, the lineup included three players (Rafael Robles, Bill Davis, and Larry Stahl) who wouldn't hit .200 for the season. And though the team won its opening game against Houston 2–1, it was not lost on local pundits that the victorious battery, pitcher Dick Selma and catcher Chris Cannizzaro, had until then been associated with the woeful expansion teams of the New York Mets. It was, therefore, something less than a shock when Gomez could produce nothing better than a 52–110 record, 41 games to the rear of the division-winning Braves.

The next four years of the Smith-Bavasi regime produced almost identical results—last-place Western Division finishes, losses in the neighborhood of 100, and yearly attendance totals around 550,000. The few cheers that came out of the grandstands were for the power hitting of first baseman Nate Colbert (149 homers between 1969 and 1973, including five in a doubleheader against Atlanta on August 1, 1972) and the tuba playing of a Marine drill instructor who had assumed the role of unofficial mascot.

Even when there appeared to be something to get excited about, grayer minds prevailed. In one particularly notorious incident, on July 22, 1970, righthander Clay Kirby came off the mound in the eighth inning only three outs shy of a no-hitter. But because Kirby was trailing in the game 1–0, manager Gomez sent Cito Gaston up to bat for him with two out in the bottom of the inning (Gaston struck out). While Gomez defended his decision by saying that his job was to win games, Bavasi went berserk up in the press room, raging about the lost opportunity for having a no-hit pitcher as a drawing card.

When he took over the Padres in 1969, Cuban Preston Gomez became the first native of Latin America to be given a regular managerial contract. Another Cuban, Mike Gonzalez, served as interim manager for the Cardinals for a handful of games in both 1938 and 1940.

Through all the losing of games and money, periodic rumors had Smith on the verge of selling the club to various San Diego and non-San Diego interests. Finally, in May 1973, the rumors became something like a fact when Smith announced that he was ready to unload the team on a Washington grocery chain owner named Joseph Danzansky, who had already indicated his intention of moving the franchise to the District of Columbia in time for the 1974 season. What followed was a boardroom circus that lasted eight months and that, at least for those not directly involved, was more entertaining than anything the Padres were doing on the field.

Although the club's red ink alone would have been enough reason for many owners to try to sell, Smith had a few extra incentives in the crumbling of his banking empire, the growing impatience of his creditors for repayments on the loans made to purchase the team, and a possible indictment for having failed to pay almost $23 million in taxes. So desperate was he for the $12 million promised for the Padres by Danzansky that, pending the league's approval of the transaction, he agreed to accept a $100,000 "deposit" from the Washington entrepreneur in exchange for a pledge that he would not permit Bavasi to make any player deals without the prospective buyer's approval. What Smith hadn't counted on was the league's lack of enthusiasm for abandoning San Diego for a market that had already lost two AL teams in the century because of lack of support. In line with this attitude, the NL owners repeatedly put off meetings at which they would have to vote on the sale, in the meantime searching high and low for another San Diego-based buyer.

At first, Smith kept up a brave front, insisting that the deal would go through and confiding to intimates that he had an ace in the hole in Commissioner Bowie Kuhn, who had been lobbying both leagues for another Washington franchise for some time. But his declared optimism notwithstanding, he also kept seeing red ink in the team's ledgers and, with Danzansky's approval, authorized Bavasi to peddle pitcher Fred Norman to the Reds and second baseman Dave Campbell to the Cardinals in exchange for some quick cash. (Conversely, Bavasi was blocked by Danzansky from dealing the almost-no-hit pitcher Kirby to St. Louis because the righthander was from the Washington area and was viewed as a potential gate attraction for the transplanted franchise in 1974.) As the season wore on and the NL owners continued their delaying tactics, Smith's confidence seeped away to the point of near-paranoia, charging at one point that there was a "plot" afoot

against him because of his ties to Nixon, then on the threshold of the Watergate affair.

For their part, the NL owners had their own problems. After receiving several warnings, they were hit by a $85-million suit from the city of San Diego for allegedly conniving with Smith in helping the Padres jump their Jack Murphy Stadium lease (which had another fifteen years on it). The search for a San Diego alternative to Danzansky had also proved fruitless. Then, just when it appeared that the situation could not be more complicated, it became just that. In an attempt to break the stalemate, Bavasi introduced Smith to Marjorie Everett, main stockholder in the Hollywood Park race track and the daughter of the one-time owner of the Arlington and Washington tracks in Chicago. Everett and a group of associates offered Smith the same $12 million that Danzansky had tendered and added a commitment to keep the Padres in San Diego "for at least a couple of years." Vague as the latter commitment was, it was better than anything else on the table and appeared to have resolved the impasse.

Until, that was, the league owners decided that Everett and her group were unacceptable.

Opposition to Everett came mainly from John Galbreath of Pittsburgh and Joan Payson of New York, fellow horse investors who had had run-ins with her within the racing industry. Other owners were chilled by a recent scandal involving Everett's father and his Chicago tracks that had reached right into the governor's mansion in Illinois. So opposed to the Everett group was the league that it let Smith know that it was ready to review the Danzansky offer in a definitive way, even if that meant transferring the franchise to Washington. But Smith, never chary of making a bad situation worse, suddenly decided to accept Everett's offer and told the league so. This resulted in Danzansky suing Smith for breach of contract and the NL taking a formal (9–3) vote rejecting the Everett sale.

Back in no-man's land, both Smith and the league seemed to have no alternative but to return to Danzansky. But after all the months of turmoil, the Washington chain owner had second thoughts of his own—specifically about business people who found it second nature to jerk him around and about rocketing interest rates that had made his proposed purchase less attractive with every passing month. Tired of the whole business, Danzansky got his deposit back and pulled out. The most lasting trace of his near-ownership would appear in January 1974, when that season's baseball cards would start to show up in stores: So convinced had the companies been that the Padres would be shifted to the nation's capital that the team's players were described as playing for Washington.

It was also in January 1974 that the sale farce finally ended, with McDonald's hamburger king Ray Kroc stepping forward and handing Smith $12 million in cash for the franchise. Kroc, already well into his 70s, said that he had waited "all [his] life to go into the locker room to kick one player in the fanny and pat another on the back." He also promised to keep the team in San Diego.

The team that Kroc inherited in 1974 was as inept as the five that had preceded it—a fact noted by the owner himself on opening day when, in the midst of a pasting by the Astros, he used the public address system to bemoan "some of the most stupid ballplaying I've ever seen." Remonstrances of the kind were embraced by the long-suffering Padres fans who, though treated to a team that ended up with precisely the same record as the 1973 club (60–102), showed up during the season 1,075,399 strong, marking the first time that the franchise had reached one million customers and representing an increase of 431,000 over the previous year. Though largely lost among all the aging veterans on the roster, the 1974 team also sported two players—pitcher Randy Jones and outfielder Dave Winfield—who suggested some hope for the future.

Some of the promise was cashed in the following year when, for the first time, San Diego escaped the cellar to finish fourth in the Western division, ahead of Atlanta and Houston. With John McNamara at the helm, the team's eleven-game improvement was largely the result of a 20–12 record by Jones, 23 homers and 68 RBIs from the veteran Willie McCovey, and 15 homers and 76 RBIs from Winfield (who had in fact been tied for the league lead in homers up to the All-Star break, before being sidelined by wrist injuries).

Footnote Player: Pitcher Steve Arlin was probably the first player on the Padres to encourage the notion that San Diego would never have a consistently winning team because of the ease of southern California living. Arlin, in fact, threatened to quit baseball in the early 1970s amid the initial rumors that the franchise was considering a move from San Diego to Washington. He came out with his threat around the same time that he was posting consecutive seasons of 19 and 21 losses.

When all else failed to divert fans in the 1970s, the Padres fell back on the San Diego Chicken, the first of many grandstand mascots that cavorted atop dugouts, along outfield fences, and (between innings) on the field. The Chicken (Ray Geriulatis) eventually got into a dispute with the Padres over the ownership of his costumed character and had to take it elsewhere in the majors and minors without the San Diego tag.

In 1976, the good news was in the pitching: Jones taking the Cy Young award for his second consecutive 20-win season (22–14) and reliever Butch Metzger sharing the award (with Pat Zachry of Cincinnati) for Rookie of the Year for his 11 wins and 16 saves. The bad news was another injury to Winfield (this time to his leg) that curtailed his fast start, and total collapses in the latter part of the season by such graying regulars as McCovey, Tito Fuentes, Willie Davis, and Doug Rader. The team dropped back to fifth.

On both the field and in the team's executive suites, the years that followed marked a return to some of the worst moments of the Smith regime. Entering the free agent market to sign relief ace Rollie Fingers and catcher Gene Tenace for 1977 and clearing the decks of most of the veterans who had collapsed in the second half of the previous season, the Padres still ended up fifth again. The campaign also saw the resignation of Bavasi after months of feuding with Kroc's wife Joan over the direction of the club, and the firing of McNamara 48 games into the season in favor of Alvin Dark.

Dark, a Baptist fundamentalist with precise ideas about race, sins of the flesh, and delegation of power, turned out to be the biggest disaster of all. From the moment he announced that there would be no beer drinking within his purview, the team was in constant revolt against his authority. Some of his coaches even joined the players in the criticism that Dark insisted on being his own pitching, hitting, and infield coach and on being so determined to outsmart opposing managers during a game that he frequently ended up only outsmarting himself and his own players.

Dark was fired during spring training in 1978 in favor of pitching coach Roger Craig, and the team's relief was translated into a season record over .500 (84–78)—the first in the history of the franchise. Spearheaded by Winfield, Cy Young winner Gaylord Perry's 21 victories, bullpen specialist Fingers's 37 saves, and the nifty defense of Ozzie Smith at shortstop, the club found itself in contention all the way to August before its generally weak offense and bad second-line pitching took their toll.

It turned out to be a short moment in the sun. One year later, despite a big season from Winfield (34 homers, 118 RBIs, .308), the same players who had raised expectations in 1978 were back to 25 games under .500. The casualties for the poor showing included not only Craig (who was replaced by Padres' radio-television announcer Gerry Coleman) and general manager Bob Fontaine, who had to give up the reins to his assistant Jack McKeon early the following season, but even Kroc himself. Weary of the team's play and furious that he had been forced to pay the league $100,000 for allegedly tampering with free agents Graig Nettles and Joe Morgan, the hamburger king turned the club over to his son-in-law, Ballard Smith.

Kroc didn't miss much. With manager Coleman concluding that the pundits had it wrong that pitching was 75 percent of the game, that "it was 90 percent," his moundless staff led the team to its first cellar finish in six years, which caused attendance to plummet. Criticized anonymously by his players all year in the press for not knowing how to manage and for being nothing more than a company man,

Coleman couldn't wait for the season to end so he could get back up to the broadcast booth.

Coleman didn't suffer much more than Winfield. Playing out the last year of his contract before becoming a free agent, Winfield and his agent submitted a list of contract demands to Smith on the eve of the season that were his conditions for remaining with San Diego. When Smith made a point of releasing some of the details of the demands (which included a ten-year contract at $1.3 million per season), the outfielder went from local hero to local ingrate and was heavily booed whenever he came to bat. Everybody pretended to be happy when he signed with the Yankees the following season.

Under Frank Howard in the split season of 1981, the Padres managed to finish last in both halves of the year. Then, with McKeon coming into his own as Trader Jack and Dick Williams taking over as manager, the team posted two identical 81–81 records and fourth-place finishes. The key moves over the period—all of them instrumental in the franchise's only pennant in 1984—included a six-player exchange with the Cardinals that brought Garry Templeton for shortstop Smith, a three-player deal with the Indians that landed righthander Ed Whitson, the acquisition of Nettles from the Yankees, and the free agent signings of first baseman Steve Garvey and veteran reliever Goose Gossage.

While there was little doubt that the Padres' win was abetted by a generally lackluster Western Division, the 1984 team boasted not only veterans like Nettles, Garvey, and Gossage from other organizations, but also home-grown products like league batting titlist Tony Gwynn (.351), long-ball threat Kevin McReynolds (20 homers, 75 RBIs), and pitchers Eric Show (15 wins) and Mark Thurmond (14). The combination proved to be enough for Chicago in the League Championship Series, with San Diego staking the Cubs to a two-game lead and then, thanks particularly to the hitting of Garvey and Gwynn, storming back to take the next three games. Despite the heroics of utility man Kurt Bevacqua (7–17, 2 home runs), the World Series was another story, with the team going down rather lamely to the Tigers in five games.

Until July 4th of the following year, the club seemed about to repeat its success, leading the division at that point by five games. But then the roof fell in, and the Padres ended up no better than in a third-place tie with the Astros, 12 games behind the Dodgers. The flop came amid more turmoil in the clubhouse, with players accusing Williams of returning to the martinet ways that had gotten him fired

Although he was forgettable as a single-season manager in 1981, Padres broadcaster Gerry Coleman has become part of baseball lore for his on-the-air trips of the tongue. Among the Colemanisms:

—"Rich Folkers is throwing up in the bullpen."

—"We're all sad to see Glenn Beckert leave. Before he goes, though, I hope he stops by so we can kiss him goodbye. He's that kind of guy."

—"George Hendrick simply lost that sun-blown popup."

—"Grubb goes back, back, he's under the warning track, and he makes the play."

—"There's a fly ball to deep center field. Winfield is going back, back. . . . He hits his head against the wall. It's rolling toward second base."

—"He slides into second with a standup double."

—"Those amateur umpires are certainly flexing their fangs today."

from other big league jobs and themselves becoming divided along several political and racial lines. Usually at the center of the troubles were pitchers Show, Thurmond, and Dave Dravecky, self-proclaimed members of the John Birch Society. None of this improved Williams's bargaining position when he demanded a contract extension after the season, but then McKeon made the mistake of firing the manager's close associate, coach Ozzie Virgil, bringing Joan Kroc into the picture. Kroc, who had taken over the ownership with her husband's death, overruled McKeon on Virgil, ordering him to settle the contract issue with her son-in-law Smith. That goal seemed within reach until shortly before spring training, when Williams insisted that coach Harry Dunlop, whom he considered a spy for McKeon, be ousted. On the very day that pitchers and catchers reported to camp, the club announced that Williams had been bought out on what remained of his contract, that Virgil had resigned, and that Steve Boros would be the pilot for 1986.

Boros, who prided himself on his computer printouts on players' performances in every situation, had very little to encourage him when he looked up from his stat sheets. With only Gwynn's league-leading 211 hits and McReynolds's 26 homers and 96 RBIs to cheer about, the Padres dropped to fourth, 22 games behind Houston. It was also a very unhappy fourth-place team after Smith announced that the club would no longer serve beer in the clubhouse after games because of new insurance costs affecting the practice. Reliever Gossage blasted the decision, noting that Jack Murphy Stadium was plastered with Budweiser signs and calling the new policy "hypocritical." Before he was through, he also ripped Smith as "gutless" and accused Kroc of "poisoning the world with her hamburgers." Smith retaliated by suspending Gossage indefinitely; the pitcher eventually issued a humiliating public apology, asserting that he and his family were regular customers at McDonald's.

During the 1986 season, Smith also tried to play hard ball on the drug issue, announcing that the club would agree only to one-year contracts with players who refused to agree to drug testing. The Players Association immediately challenged the decision, which cost the team the services of free agent Tim Raines. Raines, who had a history of drug abuse, had been about to sign with the team before Smith's pronouncement. After the season, McKeon swung into action again, first by firing the "too passive" Boros for Larry Bowa and then by sending McReynolds to the Mets in exchange for Kevin Mitchell and several

prized New York farmhands. The deal backfired almost completely when the farmhands (outfielders Shawn Abner and Stanley Jefferson, among them) all turned out to be examples of New York's public relations hoopla and Mitchell spent more time hanging out with toughs from his old neighborhood than delivering on the field. The following July, the team packaged the third baseman-outfielder with Dravecky and reliever Craig Lefferts to the Giants, receiving back third baseman Chris Brown and hurlers Mark Davis, Keith Comstock, and Mark Grant. Although Mitchell turned into one of the league's premier sluggers in Candlestick Park and Brown brought even more attitude problems to San Diego, the club gained some satisfaction from the deal when Davis won the Cy Young award in 1989.

In March 1987, Kroc announced that she had reached an accord with Seattle Mariners' owner George Argyros to sell the team for $60 million. The announcement came after long months of media criticism of Kroc and Smith for doing nothing to improve the franchise; it also came amid indications that Smith's marriage to Linda Kroc was falling apart and that he would soon be out as organization president. Disclosure of the deal turned out to be extremely premature when Argyros couldn't find a buyer willing to put up the $45 million that he needed to get out from under the Mariners and when NL owners made it clear that they would not endorse the sale.

First baseman Garvey, near the end of his career, also came forward as the head of a syndicate with an offer for the club, but Kroc rejected his offer as insufficient. After all the dust had settled, Smith was out, his marriage to Kroc's daughter was over, and former NL President Chub Feeney was named president. For the next couple of years, Feeney was more embarrassment than president, alienating the players, the press, the team's broadcasters, and the San Diego fans with one wrong step after another. He became so notorious for his refusal to sign free agents or even attempt to hold on to Padres in their walk year that SCRUB CHUB banners became commonplace at Jack Murphy Stadium. Spotting one of them on Fan Appreciation Night in 1988, Feeney gave the bearers the finger, leading to his dismissal and replacement by executive vice-president Dick Freeman.

As Boros's successor, Bowa lasted little more than a year, contributing little but constant explosions against umpires, opposition players, and his own charges. Having tried Boros's mild approach and Bowa's volatility, McKeon himself entered the dugout 46 games into the 1988 season, instantly effecting a change in atmosphere reminiscent of that when Craig had succeeded Dark in 1978. The 16–30 effort that the team had made under Bowa gave way to a 67–48 record for the rest of the campaign, good enough for a third-place finish. The following year, with perennial batting leader Gwynn smoothing the way, the team put together the second best season in the history of the franchise, finishing as a runner-up by three games to division-winning San Francisco.

Until midway through the 1990 season, McKeon was in effect the Padres franchise—sometimes bowing to the arrival of other executives, but generally functioning as both manager and general manager. The multiplicity of his titles was not to be confused with job security, however, because Kroc continued to send signals that she wanted to sell out. Unlike C. Arnholt Smith, she was equally adamant that any prospective buyer commit himself to keeping the team in San Diego—a condition that discouraged groups in New Orleans, Denver, and Florida. Indicative of her seriousness on the point, she offered to sell the franchise to the city at the beginning of 1990, but was immediately talked out of the idea by NL owners who had no desire to see any municipal ownership. Finally, on April 2, 1990, Kroc announced that she had found a buyer in a syndicate headed by television producer Tom Werner; the sale price was given as $75 million.

McKeon hung on as manager until the middle of 1990, when he turned the reins over to protege Greg Riddoch. Riddoch inherited a club that was bogged down in fourth place and riven by clubhouse jealousies. At the center of the tensions were Gwynn and slugger Jack Clark. Backed by a handful of teammates, Clark spent most of the year grumbling that Gwynn was interested only in his personal statistics; Gwynn's usual retort was to note how much time Clark spent on the bench or on the disabled list with cuts, bruises, and pulls of one kind or another. As the franchise player, Gwynn prevailed; after the season, Clark went off to the Red Sox as a free agent.

Shortly after stepping down as manager, McKeon also had to clean out his general manager's desk when Werner brought in Joe McIlvaine from the Mets to oversee still another overhaul. McIlvaines's most noteworthy move in the first year was a major swap with the Blue Jays that landed slugging first baseman Fred McGriff and shortstop Tony Fernandez in exchange for two equally talented players—outfielder Joe Carter and second baseman Roberto Alomar. In large part because of McGriff's power and the maturing of righthander Andy Benes, San Diego inched up to third place in 1991.

The club finished third again in 1992, with McGriff leading the league with 35 homers. But an even bigger story was third baseman Gary Sheffield, obtained in a preseason deal with the Brewers after years of being written off as an "attitude problem" by the Milwaukee front office. Well into September, Sheffield was within sight of the NL's first Triple Crown since 1937; he ended up winning only the batting title (.330), though also amassing 33 homers and 100 RBIs. Until injuries to Gwynn and a slump by Fernandez in the closing weeks of the season curtailed their production, the first four batters in the Padres' lineup gained a reputation around the league as the Fab Four.

In the closing days of the season, McIlvaine pulled the plug on Riddoch, replacing him with Jim Riggleman. The move hardly came as a surprise after season-long reports of tension between the manager and ace southpaw Bruce Hurst and other indications that both Werner and McIlvaine wanted their own man in the dugout. Riddoch's firing was also the opening salvo in the club's announced intention of sharply cutting back on costs, beginning with salaries. The next to go was Fernandez, who was asked to take his contract to the Mets in return for middle reliever Wally Whitehurst and two prospects. After hearing grandstand catcalls all year for his reported free agent demands, catcher Benito Santiago was also allowed to seek his fortune elsewhere and ended up with the Marlins. Another departure (to the Cubs) was that of reliever Randy Myers, whose 38 saves during the season had been notched in between numerous blown leads. The austerity program gave rise to rumors that McIlvaine felt hamstringed in his general manager's role and would also soon be leaving.

SAN DIEGO PADRES

Annual Standings and Managers

Year	Position	W	L	Pct.	GB	Managers
1969	Sixth	52	110	.321	41	Preston Gomez
1970	Sixth	63	99	.389	39	Preston Gomez
1971	Sixth	61	100	.379	28½	Preston Gomez

1972	Sixth	58	95	.379	36½	Preston Gomez, Don Zimmer
1973	Sixth	60	102	.370	39	Don Zimmer
1974	Sixth	60	102	.370	42	John McNamara
1975	Fourth	71	91	.438	37	John McNamara
1976	Fifth	73	89	.451	29	John McNamara
1977	Fifth	69	93	.426	29	John McNamara, Alvin Dark
1978	Fourth	84	78	.519	11	Roger Craig
1979	Fifth	68	93	.422	22	Roger Craig
1980	Sixth	73	89	.451	19½	Gerry Coleman
1981	Sixth	23	33	.411	12½	Frank Howard
	Sixth	18	36	.333	15½	Frank Howard
1982	Fourth	81	81	.500	8	Dick Williams
1983	Fourth	81	81	.500	10	Dick Williams
1984	First	92	70	.568	+12	Dick Williams
1985	Third	83	79	.512	12	Dick Williams
1986	Fourth	74	88	.457	22	Steve Boros
1987	Sixth	65	97	.401	25	Larry Bowa
1988	Third	83	78	.516	11	Larry Bowa, Jack McKeon
1989	Second	89	73	.549	3	Jack McKeon
1990	Fourth	75	87	.463	16	Jack McKeon, Greg Riddoch
1991	Third	84	78	.519	10	Greg Riddoch
1992	Third	82	80	.506	16	Greg Riddoch, Jim Riggleman

Postseason Play

LCS	3–2 versus Chicago	1984	WS	1–4 versus Detroit	1984

San Francisco Giants

National League,
1958–Present

BALLPARKS: SEALS STADIUM (1958–59)
CANDLESTICK PARK (1960–Present)

RECORD: 2864–2716 (.513)

When owner Horace C. Stoneham announced on August 19, 1957, that the New York Giants would be moving to San Francisco for the following season, he made them California's first major league team. It was very much a technical first, however, because the shift had been coordinated with a parallel decision by the Dodgers to go from Brooklyn to Los Angeles—a move that was not acknowledged publicly for another couple of months. Prior to the agreement with Brooklyn owner Walter O'Malley, Stoneham had given every indication of being about to uproot his cash-strapped, attendance-poor franchise to Minneapolis, which at the time had an American Association team in the New York farm system. But with the Dodgers also transplanting their operations, Stoneham was persuaded that worries about the extra travel expenses incurred from playing on the Pacific coast would be more than outweighed by the nascent California market, not to mention by the opportunity to continue the extremely profitable rivalry with the Dodgers.

In moving to San Francisco's Seals Stadium for the 1958 season, the Giants had to resist a local campaign to rename themselves the Seals after the Pacific Coast League team that had played in the city from 1922 to 1957. But for Stoneham, it was "one thing to move a team, another to erase a glorious past." The only other attempt to get the Giants to change their name came in 1978 when, confronted by the rumored defection of the Oakland Athletics to Denver, some local groups proposed redubbing the team the Bay Area Giants or San Francisco-Oakland Giants and

The first major league pitch on the West Coast is delivered by Giants' righthander Ruben Gomez to the Dodgers' Gino Cimoli at Seals Stadium in San Francisco. *AP/Wide World Photos*

having it play half its home games at the Oakland Coliseum. This campaign became academic when the Athletics stayed put in California.

The Giants' first year on the West Coast confirmed the business wisdom of their move from the east. After having drawn only 650,000 in New York's spacious Polo Grounds (which had a capacity of 56,000) in 1957, the team attracted more than 1,272,000 customers in 1958—and this in a relatively ramshackle facility that had a seating capacity of less than 23,000. The 1959 turnout was almost identical, after which the team moved into newly constructed Candlestick Park.

On the field, the Giants moved west with only one proven asset—future Hall of Famer Willie Mays. But, to the surprise of the National League and even some of the organization's own executives, a band of rookies headed by Orlando Cepeda, Jim Davenport, Leon Wagner, Willie Kirkland, Felipe Alou, and Bob Schmidt made the team instantly respectable, to the point that it went from a 1957 record of 69–85 (26 games out of first place) to 80–74 (12 behind) in 1958 and 83–71 (4 behind) in 1959. As it turned out, the

two winning years at Seals Stadium initiated a fourteen-year streak by the Giants of playing at least .500—a feat never accomplished by the New York version of the franchise.

In their makeup, the earliest San Francisco Giants set what was to be an organization pattern in featuring outfield sluggers with more than a little speed, powerhouse first baseman, average infielders, less than average catchers, and pitching staffs heavy on the journeymen starters and relievers. Ingredients of the kind made for a somewhat passive strategic philosophy, with the majority of San Francisco managers up to Roger Craig's arrival in 1985 relying on the long ball as a cure-all. (The 1967 team, for instance, holds an NL record for having stolen only 22 bases.)

Although welcomed to San Francisco as the exciting star that he was, Mays soon discovered that he was still too much of a New Yorker for a lot of fans, especially after numerous interviews in which he made it clear that he would never forget his beginnings in the Polo Grounds. Until he had reestablished himself through longevity in the late 1960s, the outfielder usually finished second in grandstand acceptance—first behind Baby Bull Cepeda and then, for most of the 1960s, behind Willie McCovey, both of whom were adopted as immaculately local heroes.

Despite records over .500 their first four years in California, the Giants were developing a reputation as a single-dimension (power) also-ran until 1962, when key Dodger injuries and career years by a couple of veteran San Francisco pitchers set up a West Coast rerun of the 1951 postseason playoff that had ended with Bobby Thomson's dramatic home run. As had been the case eleven years earlier in New York, the Giants won the first game, lost the second one, and were only an inning away from going home for the winter when their fortunes suddenly turned. Instead of coming up with an epic home run this time, they mainly kept their bats on their shoulders as Dodger pitchers Ed Roebuck and Stan Williams walked and wild pitched them around the bases and into the World Series. Given the other similarities to 1951, it was only appropriate that their World Series opponents were once again the Yankees and that, also as in 1951, they were defeated by the New Yorkers—despite going all the way down to their 27th out in a 1–0 seventh game before McCovey lined out with the tying and winning runs on base.

Including their playoff victories, the Giants finished 1962 with 103 wins and 62 losses—the best record of any San Francisco squad. But another twenty-seven years would pass before the club could again hang World Series bunting around Candlestick Park. The main reasons for the drought were inconsistent pitching, horrendous trades, and a ballpark that seemed to deprive the team of a home-field advantage.

As was to be the case with the 1989 pennant-winning team, the 1962 NL champions got as far as they did because, in addition to the usual power hitting, they received banner years from veteran pitchers—specifically from ex-Phillie Jack Sanford (24 wins), one-time Oriole Billy O'Dell (19 wins), former White Sox ace Billy Pierce (16 wins), and even Yankee perfect game maestro Don Larsen (5 wins and 11 saves). Within two years, however, all these major league nomads were either in retirement or mop-up men for other clubs. The one exception to the turnover was 18-game winner Juan Marichal, who went on to become the dominant righthander in the league for the next decade and whose mark of 154–65 (.703) between 1963 and 1969 was the highest in the majors. The Dominican's lifetime 243–142 record and 2.89 ERA earned him a Hall of Fame plaque in 1983. But neither alone nor with the support of Gaylord Perry from the mid-1960s could Marichal constitute a mound staff.

It was also in the mid-1960s that the team completed the first of many terrible trades that it was to make over the next couple of decades, in dealing fan favorite Cepeda to the Cardinals for southpaw pitcher Ray Sadecki. While Cepeda went on to lead St. Louis to two World Series, Sadecki put together a record of 32–39. Before the end of the decade, the team would also unload all three Alou brothers (Felipe, Matty, and Jesus) in exchange for mediocre pitchers and over-the-hill catchers. In the 1970s, front

Willie McCovey crosses the plate after one of his 521 homers as Willie Mays greets him. *National Baseball Library, Cooperstown, NY*

Although the Giants have played only eleven World Series games since moving to California, they have been spread out over almost a month of time. In 1962, the seven-game series against the Yankees opened on October 4th, but because of rain postponements was not concluded until October 16th. In their 1989 confrontation with the Athletics, the Giants went down in four straight games—but only after the October 17th earthquake in the Bay Area caused a ten-day interruption between the second and third games.

Few diamond fights have been as violent as the August 22, 1965 brawl between the teams that saw Juan Marichal attack Los Angeles catcher John Roseboro with his bat. The incident was sparked by Marichal's belief that Roseboro was returning the ball to Dodger pitcher Sandy Koufax by way of his ear in retaliation for some alleged knockdown pitches by the San Francisco ace. When Marichal turned around in the batter's box and whacked the catcher with his bat, a free-for-all ensued. The pitcher was eventually fined $1,750 and suspended for nine days.

office moves stirred even more dread among fans, with the likes of George Foster, Bobby Bonds, Garry Maddox, Dave Kingman, Ken Henderson, Gaylord Perry, and Bill Madlock moving on elsewhere for little, questionable, or no return.

In 1964, manager Alvin Dark came close to causing baseball's only twentieth-century racial strike when he attacked the team's black and Latin players. In the midst of that season's hot pennant race, Dark was quoted as telling a New York sportswriter: "We have trouble because we have so many Negro and Spanish-speaking players on the team. They are just not able to perform up to the white players when it comes to mental alertness. One of the biggest things is that you can't make them subordinate themselves to the best interest of the team. You don't find pride in them that you get in the white player."

Dark's assertions prompted a majority of the team's blacks and Latins to call for a boycott of games until the manager was replaced. But Mays, while stressing that he found Dark's comments repugnant, cooled tempers by pointing out that the pilot's racial views had never prevented him from fielding a majority of blacks and Latins. Because of Mays's intervention, Dark was able to hold on to his job, but only for the rest of the season.

Footnote Player: In 1964 and 1965, the San Francisco pitching staff included Masanori Murakami, the only Japanese ever to play in the majors. He compiled a record of 5–1 in 53 relief appearances and one start, then returned home when his father insisted that the honor of his family dictated that he pitch in his homeland.

For all its deficiencies, the club remained competitive until 1972. In 1964, 1965, and 1966, for example, it was not eliminated from contention until the final days of the season. But not even tense pennant races were always able to overcome the franchise albatross of Candlestick Park—a damp, wind-blown stadium that not only proved increasingly unattractive to fans, but also played so much havoc with the game that visiting players moaned about having to go to San Francisco and home team players moaned about not being able to depart with the visitors. The facility's defects became only too clear to the entire country during the 1961 All-Star game, when relief pitcher Stu Miller was blown off the mound in the course of his windup. In the first years of free agency, the stadium was also an obstacle to signing or holding onto stars.

The last hurrah for the Stoneham regime turned out to be the 1971 team, which eked out a Western Division win over the Dodgers before going down three games to one in the League Championship Series against Pittsburgh. The keys to the division win were Bobby Bonds's 33 home runs and 102 runs batted in, Marichal's 18 wins, and reliever Jerry Johnson's 12 wins and 18 saves. One season later, however, the Giants could finish ahead of only the expansion Padres. Even worse from the point of view of club accountants, the first losing San Francisco season was the final straw for fans already put off by bone-chilling Candlestick: In spite of some modest enclosures against the wind that had been added in the winter of 1971–72, attendance dipped below even the nadir that had been reached in the Giants' last year in New York.

It took Stoneham another four years to sell the club that had been in his family since 1919, but not for lack of trying. Prospective buyers came and went amid demands by Mayor George Moscone's office that any deal include a commitment to keep the team in San Francisco, the threatened alternative being lawsuits against the franchise and the league. Stoneham paid lip service to the commitment, but then in 1975 announced that he had concluded an agreement with a Canadian beer company that made little secret of its intention of moving the club to Toronto. For its part, the NL seemed willing to sanction the move just to get rid of Stoneham; in fact, the team's finances had become so chaotic that the league ordered Spec Richardson into the Giants' front office to make sure that checks were issued on time. But once again, Mayor Moscone tightened the screws and, with various bureaucratic tactics, succeeded in delaying the transaction until real estate developer Bob

Lurie and Arizona meatpacker Arthur Herseth stepped forward with $8 million and a vow to remain in the city.

Stoneham's sale of the Giants in time for the 1976 season reflected more than a change in the ownership of a single club. As a representative member of baseball's old guard, he had been intransigent before the free agency that preempted his paternalistic concern that Giants players always be paid a few dollars more than their counterparts on other teams. Moreover, as he told more than one intimate in his later years, the advent of agents, obsessively conditioned athletes, and boardroom-operated franchises had begun to dull his sense of a personal contact with players and other owners, not least that to be established over a bottle in the wee hours of the morning. Stoneham had also been disillusioned by the fact that the traditional rivalry between the Giants and Dodgers, a touchstone of NL baseball for generations, had been eroded by the new competition between Los Angeles and San Diego.

Between 1972 and 1977, the Giants had only one winning season, with the attendance to prove it. The scarcity of customers was abetted by the lack of any individual drawing card on the field: After so many years of seeing Mays galloping in the outfield and on the bases, McCovey hitting torrid line drives over the right-field wall, and Marichal going into acrobatic kicks on the mound, fans reacted gingerly even to the multi-talented (but somewhat aloof) Bonds, then had nobody at all to watch when Bonds was traded to the Yankees after the 1974 season for the unspectacular Bobby Murcer. So pressing did the need for a gate attraction become that, after dealing him away three years earlier, the club repurchased the aged McCovey for the 1977 season. He promptly hit 28 home runs, far and away the most any Giant had hit in four years.

The Giants' traditional rivalry with the Dodgers lost a good part of its edge with the shift of both teams to California, but there have been some reminders of the old New York-Brooklyn competition. The only conspicuous trades between the teams in all their years on the Pacific Coast, for example, have been a 1968 deal in which San Francisco acquired infielders Ron Hunt and Nate Oliver for catcher Tom Haller and a 1985 exchange in which the Giants gave the Dodgers catcher Alex Trevino for outfielder Candy Maldonado.

While it lasted, the 1978 season seemed to mark a positive turn in the team's fortunes. With the old formula of a veteran as the anchor of the pitching staff (Vida Blue, who won 18) and home runs in the middle of the lineup (Jack Clark with 25 and Darrell Evans with 20), the Giants streaked through most of the summer atop the West before falling back to third place. Particularly encouraging were an additional million fans over 1977 and the apparent blossoming of right fielder Clark as the Lurie ownership's first superstar. But it took only a few weeks into the 1979 season for hopes for further improvement to be dashed. While Clark and another one-season wonder, first baseman Mike Ivie, supplied some power, the team fell apart in just about every phase of its game, with only two pitchers managing even to get into double figures in victories. Manager Joe Altobelli, who had been hailed as the league's tactical genius in 1978, fell out with the front office over player moves and non-moves and was gone before the end of the season. The team's 71–91 effort restored rust to the turnstiles, where it was to remain for a succeeding losing season in 1980.

Both Altobelli and his replacement Dave Bristol had an additional problem to go along with on-the-field ineptitude and front office conflicts: a divided clubhouse. Led by Clark, pitchers Bob Knepper and Gary Lavelle, and infielder Rob Andrews, the Giants had a particularly militant clutch of born-again Christians who tended to correlate every team fortune and misfortune with the desires of a higher power. This outlook in turn sowed a suspicion among other players that the born-agains did not play aggressively enough, and it wasn't too long before the clubhouse was split between what one player called "a prayer meeting on one side and the street corner wiseguys on the other." It was the worst behind-the-scenes tension on the club since the early 1960s, when Dark had vented his racist remarks, and it foreshadowed the locker room controversies over religion and desire that were to continue well into the 1990s in all college and professional sports. If there was any San Francisco player immune to the stresses, it was probably third baseman Evans, who ascribed his turnaround as a major leaguer to the sighting of a UFO in his backyard after the 1976 season.

The Giants returned to a winning record for the strike-shortened 1981 season. Taking over from Bristol, the no-nonsense Frank Robinson became the league's first black manager, and brought in veteran sparkplug Joe Morgan to play second base. With Andrews released, Knepper dispatched to Houston, and

Lavelle on the disabled list most of the season, Robinson restored order in the clubhouse. He was even more successful in 1982 when, despite an especially lackluster starting rotation, he steered the team from 10 games below .500 prior to the All-Star break to within 2 games of division-winning Atlanta by the time the curtain finally fell.

The 1982 season was the high point of Robinson's tenure as manager. Over the following winter, long-simmering problems with general manager Tom Haller (appointed to his post by Lurie after Robinson had been signed as manager) erupted when the front office refused to give in to a relatively modest contract demand by Morgan and traded him off to the Phillies. Robinson also accused Haller of being shy about pulling the trigger on deals deemed necessary by the manager. Lacking reliable starters, the team became dangerously dependent on relievers Greg Minton and the rehabilitated Lavelle over the next couple of seasons. At the same time, Clark began to get acquainted with the disabled lists that were to become an increasingly important part of his career, and would eventually be sent to St. Louis in another bad deal prior to the 1985 season. With the team mired in last place after 106 games in 1984, Robinson was replaced by Danny Ozark, who in turn was dropped for Jim Davenport for the start of 1985, who in turn was succeeded by Roger Craig for the final weeks of that season. Combined, the four managers presided over two last-place division finishes, with the 1985 record of 62–100 representing the lowest point of the franchise in either New York or California.

With little to lose for 1986 and only outfielders Jeffrey Leonard and Chili Davis certain regulars, Craig installed rookies Will Clark at first base and Robby Thompson at second, withstood criticism of second-year players Jose Uribe and Chris Brown at the other infield positions, and generally promoted a spirit on the team that had been absent since 1982. Although finishing third behind Houston, the 1986 Giants turned around a franchise that then went on to a division title in 1987, continued to play winning ball in 1988, and captured its first pennant in twenty-seven years in 1989. In true San Francisco fashion, the winning recipe concocted by Craig and team president Al Rosen was composed in good part of sluggers (Clark, Leonard, Davis, Candy Maldonado, Kevin Mitchell) and hurlers who had been around the block several times in other uniforms (Rick Reuschel, Don Robinson, Mike Krukow, Dave Dravecky, Steve Bedrosian). Added to this were Craig's own special skills as an unorthodox strategist and as the pitching guru who spread the gospel of the split-finger fastball among his charges.

For all its revival on the field, the San Francisco version of the Giants entered the 1990s with one particularly dark cloud over its future. After several years of agitating about a new stadium to replace the ever-unfriendly Candlestick Park, the Giants finally succeeded in getting the question put on a referendum ballot in 1990. Unfortunately for the Lurie ownership, the vote was held in the immediate aftermath of the earthquake that rocked the Bay Area during the 1989 World Series and that, in the view of a majority of residents, made public appropriations for a new ballpark less than a priority. Stymied at the polls, Lurie made it clear that he would not keep the team in Candlestick past the 1993 season and opened serious negotiations to shift the franchise down the peninsula to rapidly growing San Jose. He was backed in the initiative by Commissioner Fay Vincent, especially after San Jose announced its intention of building a new stadium. But then two referendums on the San Jose facility were also vetoed by voters, leaving the team where it had started.

Aside from the earthquake, the Giants were rattled in the 1989 World Series by the Oakland pitching staff, and went down in four games. With the onset of the 1990s, the club's chief cachet was a slugging trio in the middle of the lineup (Clark, Mitchell, and third baseman Matt Williams) that was second to none; on the other hand, the team continued to be bedeviled by injuries to its most promising pitchers, and such hopes as Kelly Downs, Scott Garrelts, and Trevor Wilson spent long periods on the disabled list. Partly to redress this problem and partly to end its exasperation with his numerous off-field run-ins with the police for one reason or another, the club traded Mitchell to the Mariners in the 1991–92 offseason, getting in return young hurlers Bill Swift, Mike Jackson, and Mike Burba.

The good news in 1992 was that Swift won the ERA title with a 2.08 mark. But even he missed six weeks of the season to two injuries, depleting further an already mediocre staff. Making matters worse, Clark's power numbers declined sharply and Williams spent most of the year hovering around the .200 mark. The club's patchy effort on the field, however, soon gave way to another circus involving the future of the franchise.

The opening act came in August, when Lurie announced agreement with a Tampa Bay group headed by businessman Vincent Naimoli to sell the

Players and fans wander about in the first moments following the terrifying earthquake that occurred just before the third game of the 1989 World Series between San Francisco and Oakland. *Courtesy of San Francisco Giants*

team for $111 million, with the understanding that the team would play in Florida in 1993. According to the owner, the deal was backed by Vincent. Even as some civic groups were organizing to protest the sale, George Shinn, owner of the Charlotte Hornets basketball team, flew into San Francisco behind claims that he was ready to improve on the Tampa offer and keep the club in California. What this mainly produced was some literal grandstanding by Shinn as he toured Candlestick during a game to hear the cheers of fans for his ostensible championing of their cause. A couple of days later, he was back in Charlotte, never to be heard from again.

In the meantime, however, the same owners who were working to get rid of Vincent decided that Lurie had overstepped his bounds in making commitments to Naimoli before a formal league vote and that the commissioner had once again demonstrated that his view of the "best interests of baseball" wasn't theirs. NL President Bill White then took the eyebrow-raising step of allowing Bay Area groups more time to come up with a counter-offer, specifically asserting that even a lower bid than the $111 million might be acceptable. Behind the scenes, NL owners were not only bent on putting Vincent in his place, but also on promoting other interests viewed as endangered by a Giants' move. Marlins' owner Wayne Huizenga, for example, had no desire to share

his newly gained Florida territory with a more familiar team. For their part, the Dodgers weren't too enthusiastic about surrendering what remained of their traditional rivalry with the Giants. Others protested the added expense of travel.

In November, the league formally rejected the sale by a margin of 9–4. This left Lurie with little alternative but to accept another offer of $100 million put together by a Bay Area group headed by Peter Magowan, chairman of the Safeway supermarket chain. The sale did not contain any specifics about the future of Candlestick.

In the middle of all the turmoil, Rosen resigned, making it clear that he had no desire either to go to Florida or to work under a new ownership in San Francisco. He was replaced by Bob Quinn, fired from a similar post with the Reds at the end of the 1992 season. After the Magowan sale had been finalized, Craig also departed from the scene, and was replaced by his hitting coach Dusty Baker.

The Magowan ownership's first player move was the biggest one of all—signing free agent outfielder Barry Bonds to an unprecedented $43.75 million for six years. The club also announced that the two-time MVP's father, former Giant Bobby Bonds, would be back as the hitting coach and that his godfather, Mays, would play a more prominent front office role.

SAN FRANCISCO GIANTS

Annual Standings and Managers

Year	Position	W	L	Pct.	GB	Managers
1958	Third	80	74	.519	12	Bill Rigney
1959	Third	83	71	.539	4	Bill Rigney
1960	Fifth	79	75	.513	16	Bill Rigney
1961	Third	85	69	.552	8	Alvin Dark
1962	First	103	62	.624	+1	Alvin Dark
1963	Third	88	74	.543	11	Alvin Dark
1964	Fourth	90	72	.556	3	Alvin Dark
1965	Second	95	67	.586	2	Herman Franks
1966	Second	93	68	.578	1½	Herman Franks
1967	Second	91	71	.562	10½	Herman Franks
1968	Second	88	74	.543	9	Herman Franks
1969	Second	90	72	.556	3	Clyde King
1970	Third	86	76	.531	16	Clyde King, Charlie Fox
1971	First	90	72	.556	+1	Charlie Fox
1972	Fifth	69	86	.445	26½	Charlie Fox
1973	Third	88	74	.543	11	Charlie Fox
1974	Fifth	72	90	.444	30	Charlie Fox, Wes Westrum
1975	Third	80	81	.497	27½	Wes Westrum
1976	Fourth	74	88	.457	28	Bill Rigney
1977	Fourth	75	87	.463	23	Joe Altobelli
1978	Third	89	73	.549	6	Joe Altobelli
1979	Fourth	71	91	.438	19½	Joe Altobelli, Dave Bristol
1980	Fifth	75	86	.466	17	Dave Bristol
1981	Fifth	27	32	.458	10	Frank Robinson
	Third	29	23	.558	3½	Frank Robinson
1982	Third	87	75	.537	2	Frank Robinson
1983	Fifth	79	83	.488	12	Frank Robinson
1984	Sixth	66	96	.407	26	Frank Robinson, Danny Ozark
1985	Sixth	62	100	.383	33	Jim Davenport, Roger Craig
1986	Third	83	79	.512	13	Roger Craig
1987	First	90	72	.556	+6	Roger Craig
1988	Fourth	83	79	.512	11½	Roger Craig
1989	First	92	70	.568	+3	Roger Craig
1990	Third	85	77	.525	6	Roger Craig
1991	Fourth	75	87	.463	19	Roger Craig
1992	Fifth	72	90	.444	26	Roger Craig

Postseason Play

LCS	1–3 versus Pittsburgh	1971	WS	3–4 versus New York	1962
	3–4 versus St. Louis	1987		0–4 versus Oakland	1989
	4–1 versus Chicago	1989			

Seattle Pilots

American League, 1969   **BALLPARK:** SICKS STADIUM

RECORD: 64–98 (.395)

The Pilots were a bad idea whose time had come. Underfinanced in the boardroom, undertalented on the field, and under siege even long after it had ceased to exist, the franchise proved profitable to few people outside of attorneys in several states and *Ball Four* author Jim Bouton.

The expansion Pilots were created in December 1967 as part of the agreement between the American League and Missouri politicians that also sired the Kansas City Royals in return for allowing Charlie Finley's Athletics to migrate from Kansas City to Oakland. The $6-million admission tab (including expansion draft purchases and contributions to the players' pension fund) was picked up by William Daley, the chairman of the Reading Railroad who controlled 60 percent of the stock, and Pacific Coast League President Dewey Soriano, who with his brothers Max and Milton represented another 34 percent. Among the league conditions for awarding the franchise to Daley and the Sorianos were that minor league Sicks Stadium would be enlarged to provide a temporary playing site, that Seattle voters would get behind a $40-million bond issue for building a domed facility, and that the owners would pay the Pacific Coast League $300,000 in indemnities for invading its territory. None of these conditions was met in the way the AL intended. Before and throughout the 1969 season, Soriano and Seattle Mayor Floyd Miller swapped charges about who was responsible for the delays in refurbishing Sicks Stadium, to the point that the mayor threatened to evict the team altogether. Although voters eventually endorsed the bond issue for what became the Kingdome, the project turned into an $80-million political football that was not pulled down in the end zone until after the Pilots had expired. As for the indemnities to the PCL, they were not paid off fully until Class A teams were back as the only baseball action in town.

With Daley anchored to Cleveland as an absentee owner, Soriano assumed the club presidency and appointed Marvin Milkes as general manager; Milkes recomended Joe Shultz as manager. The first player under contract was first baseman-outfielder Mike

On the eve of the season, the Pilots made the worst trade of their brief history by acquiring outfielder Steve Whitaker and pitcher John Gelnar from Kansas City in exchange for outfielder Lou Piniella. Piniella went on to become Rookie of the Year for the Royals.

Hegan, acquired from the Yankees a couple of months before the October 1968 expansion draft. The club's first selections at the draft were slugging first baseman Don Mincher and speedster third baseman Tommy Harper. Other familiar names on the roster were Bouton, Tommy Davis, Diego Segui, Mike Marshall, and Gary Bell. It was Bell who, before 15,014, began the team's brief existence with a ten-hit shutout over Chicago on April 11, 1969.

For a couple of months, the Pilots remained respectable, but then hit a summer skid that dropped them down to the cellar finish that had been predicted for them. The bright spots were Harper (a league-leading 73 steals), Mincher (25 homers and 78 RBIs), and Segui (12 wins and 12 saves). Although the 15,000 seats in Sicks Stadium made high attendance impossible, the final total of 677,944 was bigger than that registered by the White Sox, Indians, Padres, and Phillies.

Like so much else connected to the Daley-Soriano organization, even the mildly admirable attendance total was achieved in spite of the ownership, because the Pilots had sought to compensate for a lack of television revenues by charging more for tickets than any other team in the league. In the same vein of the counterproductive, Soriano spent a good part of the season ducking bills for the Pilots' spring training facility in Tempe, Arizona; the bills evolved into subpoenas and a lawsuit a few months later. In the category of the ingenuous went such other items as the President's five-year rental of Sicks Stadium at $175,000 annually, even though the Kingdome should have required only three years to be completed. As unlikely a spokesman for the league as he was, Oakland owner Finley summed up the mood of the boardroom fraternity when he declared during the season that "we made a mistake in awarding the franchise to the Sorianos."

And they continued to make mistakes. Although Daley had gotten involved in the franchise in the first place because the Sorianos had been unable to find sufficient backing in Seattle, the AL continued to insist that it wanted to stay in the northwestern city. In the fall of 1969, even as Daley and the Sorianos were fielding offers from Lamar Hunt to buy the club and move it to Dallas and from a Milwaukee syndicate bent on purchasing the franchise for Wisconsin, league representatives met with Fred Danz, operator of a Washington theater chain, to see if he could keep the club where it was. They were so impressed with Danz that they voted conditional approval of his purchase—only to discover that he didn't have the $10.5 million he claimed to have and that due notes from the Bank of California on Soriano's loans would have wiped out the money even if it had existed.

Not even the Danz experience was enough for the AL. When still another Seattle group headed by Edward Carlson came along to tender a new approach based on a non-profit charter, league owners laughed a quick no, but also pressed the Washington businessman to find an orthodox way of resolving their problem. Carlson was in the process of putting together a Seattle syndicate when word leaked of a $13.5-million deal between Daley-Soriano and Milwaukee interests. In rapid succession, this produced local injunctions against letting the team leave Seattle, a countermove by the Sorianos in applying for bankruptcy protection, and another suit by Seattle citizen Alfred Schweppe demanding to know how bankruptcy could be granted to people who admitted that they would make more than one million dollars off the sale to Milwaukee. While all these legal duels went on, the other AL clubs had to put up $50,000 each to finance 1970 spring training for the Pilots and to pay off some of the franchise's most pressing debts. Finally in late March, after a cross-examination of Schweppe had revealed that his own desire to buy the franchise would have foundered on his inability to finance even a single day of a major league club's expenses, a bankruptcy referee ruled that the sale of the club to Milwaukee was in order. The league had approved the transaction 24 hours before, so the referee's decision was the green light for the Milwaukee Brewers to succeed the Pilots.

The sale to Milwaukee created new problems for the league. As might have been expected, Washington's U.S. senators, Warren Magnusson and Henry Jackson, called for a congressional investigation of baseball's exemption from antitrust laws; equally predictably, they fell quiet as soon as the AL committed itself to putting a new franchise in Seattle sometime in the early 1970s. By the time the Mariners were actually created in 1977, both the city of Seattle and the state of Washington had filed lawsuits totaling some $32.5 million against the league.

Aside from the Mariners, the most notable result of the Daley-Soriano franchise was Bouton's book, which scandalized both players and the baseball establishment by naming names in a diaristic narrative of the three-quarters of a season that the righthander spent with the club. Commissioner Bowie Kuhn helped make the book a best-seller by summoning Bouton to his office and demanding that he make a public apology for it. When he refused to accommodate the commissioner, according to Bouton, Kuhn spent the rest of the meeting attempting to win reassurances that he would not be accused of trying to censor the book. Much of the uproar over *Ball Four* was over its casual depiction of the sex-obsessed lives of big leaguers, especially while on the road; but it also unnerved front office executives with its specific instances of settling rosters through racial quotas and of management hypocrisy during contract negotiations. It also made manager Schultz one of the characters of the game with his refrains that the team "get in there and pound those Budweisers."

Gene Brabender's 13 wins for the Pilots is the most recorded by a pitcher on a first-year expansion team. Dave Lemanczyk also won 13 for the 1977 Blue Jays.

SEATTLE PILOTS

Annual Standings and Manager

Year	Position	W	L	Pct	GB	Manager
1969	Sixth	64	98	.395	33	Joe Schultz

Seattle Mariners

American League, 1977–Present	**BALLPARK:** KINGDOME

RECORD: 1084–1452 (.427)

Although the impeccable 0–13 Kansas City Athletics might have given them a run for their money if they had lasted longer, no big league team waited as long (fifteen years) as the Mariners to reach the .500 mark for a season. Even when the franchise finally attained the plateau in 1991, it fired its manager for not doing enough and threatened to pull out of Seattle behind a similar grievance against the city. Most of the rest of the club's history has been equally shoddy.

Along with the Toronto Blue Jays, the Mariners entered the American League in November 1976 with the league's expansion from twelve to fourteen squads. The franchise represented the fulfillment of a pledge that the AL had made the city of Seattle following the defection of the Pilots to Milwaukee after only one season in 1969; its establishment also staved off some $32.5 million in lawsuits that the jilted city and the state of Washington had pending against the league for the unhappy experience with the Pilots. Organization backers, who anted up $7 million as an admission fee and millions more to buy players in the expansion draft, were led by West Coast businessman Lester Smith and entertainer Danny Kaye. Lou Gorman was the chief baseball man in the front office, with Darrell Johnson as manager.

The nearest thing to a name that the Mariners plucked out of the draft was 40-year-old righthander Diego Segui, familiar to locals because he had been the best pitcher on the 1969 Pilots. Two significant trades with the Pirates landed shortstop Craig Reynolds and southpaw Rick Honeycutt. The club played its first game before 57,762 in the Kingdome on April 6, 1977—a 7–0 whipping at the hands of the Angels. The loser was Segui, who was driven to shelter quickly in his 600th major league mound appearance; after going 0–7, he was released, thereby cutting the team's last link to the 1969 Pilots. Mainly because of the long-ball hitting of Leroy Stanton (27 homers, 90 RBIs), Ruppert Jones (24 homers, 76 RBIs), and Dan Meyer (22 homers, 90 RBIs), the Mariners finished a half-game out of the cellar. The combination of novelty and slugging heroics within the Kingdome's narrow confines promoted an attendance of 1,388,511—far more than even front office optimists had predicted.

Reality set in the following season in more ways than one. In the kind of public relations blunder that would typify three successive ownerships, the team announced a substantial increase in the price of tickets for 1978, and then compounded that crassness by moving general admission fans from the second to the third deck. Although the latter decision was eventually revoked after loud protests, the moves rekindled regional suspicions toward the money-grubbing priorities of the league and its owners. It

Ken Griffey, Sr. (left) with Ken Griffey, Jr. on August 30, 1990, after the elder Griffey's signing made him the only major leaguer ever to play on the same team with his son. *AP/Wide World Photos*

The very first player under a Mariners' contract was pitcher Jim Minshall, obtained from the Pirates a month before the November 1976 expansion draft. Minshall never saw any AL action for the team.

didn't help, either, that by the time sports fans had finished watching the special television coverage of the Supersonics in the NBA finals, the Mariners had settled into the cellar position from which they would never again rise. With little more to watch than second baseman Julio Cruz's 59 stolen bases and left fielder Leon Roberts's 22 homers and 92 RBIs, almost a half-million fewer fans than the previous season walked through the turnstiles.

Still another 30,000 fewer showed up in 1979, when first baseman Bruce Bochte (16 homers, 100 RBIs, a .316 average), designated hitter Willie Horton (29 homers, 106 RBIs), and ace Mike Parrott (14 wins) led the club back up to sixth place again. The year also marked the debut of switch-hitting outfielder Rodney Craig, the first product of the organization's farm system to reach the majors.

After only two years of flagging fortune at the gate, the ownership let it be known in early 1980 that it would consider offers for the franchise. This sparked considerable criticism that the Smith-Kaye group had been undercapitalized from the start and should have never been approved by the league; those with longer memories of the Pilots and of a more conspiratorial turn of mind, suggested that the franchise had been meant to fail so that it could be transferred to Washington D.C. without valid objection. The first potential buyer to approach the club was shopping mall magnate and sports entrepreneur Edward J. DeBartolo, Sr., but he lost interest when he saw a greater opportunity (ultimately thwarted) to buy the Chicago White Sox. Next up was Nelson Skalbania, half-owner of the NHL Calgary Flames, who offered Smith, Kay, and their partners a reported $12.25 million for the team. The apparently completed deal became unstruck at the last moment when the Canadian sportsman could not come up with a required 60 percent down payment in cash. More successful was California and Idaho real estate tycoon George Argyros, who talked the increasingly fidgety Smith-Kaye group down to $11 million before taking over the club officially at the beginning of 1981. Argyros's attorney, Warren Finley, bought in for a minority share, as did Kaye and a couple of the other original owners.

The big news on the field in 1980 was the August 4th ouster of Johnson as manager and his replacement by Maury Wills. The former National League speed king did little to lift the Mariners out of the cellar; what he did do was to provide numerous reasons why he should have never been given the job. Already deeply dependent on drugs for a number of years, he acted erratically on the bench, occasionally

sending out conflicting signs to his third base coach, other times not sending out any at all. As he later admitted, he was also obsessed by an affair with a woman who was simultaneously seeing California designated hitter Don Baylor, making his stragetic decisions in games against the Angels all the more unpredictable. Whether because they knew about his drug problem or simply didn't like him, most local sportswriters were unrelenting in their criticism of Wills, becoming eager ears for the complaints of players; Wills only aggravated the problem by maintaining a disdainful silence before some of the writers and supplying more grist for the mill with gratuitous attacks on some of the players. Another battlefront opened when the manager flew to Japan in February 1981 to honor a long-standing coaching commitment, knowing this would make him late for his first spring training with the Mariners. When he finally did arrive in Arizona, he got into a series of wrangles with general manager Dan O'Brien about removing regulars too early from exhibition games; the front office executive was also appalled by the manager's hostility toward outfielder Dave Henderson, one of the organization's prize prospects. There was little astonishment at the May 6th announcement that Wills was being replaced by Rene Lachemann.

After limping through the strike season, Lachemann approached 1982 with the modestly stated goal of "not losing 100 games." He succeeded, and then some, when the club registered the best winning percentage it would have over its first decade and climbed to fourth place. The rise was largely the result of two deals swung by O'Brien on the eve of opening day: the purchase of outfielder Al Cowens (20 homers, team-leading 78 RBIs) from the Tigers and the acquisition of relief ace Bill Caudill (12 wins, 26 saves) from the Yankees. The season was also enlivened by Future Hall of Famer Gaylord Perry's 300th victory—and by the suspension of the right-hander for ten days for being caught doctoring the baseball. For the first time since 1977, the team drew more than a million fans.

That was the end of the good news. By the following June, both Lachemann and Perry were gone and Del Crandall was filling the managerial slot for a club once again scraping the floor of the Western Division. In addition to all its other problems, the team went through the season without its most consistent hitter, Bochte, who announced that he was tired of baseball and was retiring.

Much less retiring was Argyros, who tightened his control over the organization by buying out Kaye and most of the other minority partners and then brought in Chuck Armstrong, an executive from his real estate company, to serve as franchise president. In another change, the owner bounced O'Brien for not producing more major league prospects from the farm system, replacing him with Hal Keller. Crandall survived the rest of 1983 and most of 1984, but then he got into a dispute with pitching coach Frank Funk over the staff's work routines and was backed up far too loudly by catcher Bob Kearney, who got into a newsmaking punchup with the pitching tutor. Although Crandall drew first blood by getting Keller's backing in firing Funk, the pitchers soon made known their resentment toward the manager for forcing out the coach; a month before the end of the season, Crandall was removed as a divisive force and replaced by third base coach Chuck Cottier. The bright side of the 1984 season was that it produced the first two major league stars in Seattle uniforms to come through the organization's farm system—Rookie of the Year first baseman Alvin Davis (.284, 27 homers, 116 RBIs) and AL strikeout leader Mark Langston.

If the only thing worse than watching the Mariners lose was not being able to watch them play at all, Argyros forced the city to entertain such a prospect for a good part of 1985, with alternate threats of declaring bankruptcy and moving the franchise elsewhere. What he ultimately settled for was an agreement that gave him an additional $1.3 million out of the Kingdome and, far more important, an escape clause from the facility that permitted him to pull out of Seattle after 1987 if season ticket sales fell below 10,000 or attendance fell below 1.4 million over any two-year period between 1985 and then. The most benign interpretation of the pact was that it was a rallying cry for Seattle to demonstrate that it could support a big league franchise; the more prevalent view was that King County had buckled under blackmail. The escape clause hung over the franchise for the rest of the decade, with Argyros trying again and again to sell or move, or threatening as much. The closest call came in March 1987, when Argyros and Joan Kroc held a joint press conference to announce that she intended selling the San Diego Padres to the developer for some $60 million as soon as he found a buyer for the Mariners for a requested $45 million. In the event, Argyros couldn't find his buyer, and had also been informed unofficially that the National League would not approve his purchase of the Padres.

On the field, the Mariners continued changing managers and losing. Cottier lasted until May 1986, when he was succeeded by Dick Williams. Under Cottier in 1985, the club had flexed some muscle, with six regulars reaching double figures in homers.

When Dick Williams took over from Chuck Cottier on May 8, 1986, he tied Jimmy Dykes for the most clubs managed (six) this century. Before the Mariners, Williams had called the shots for the Red Sox, Athletics, Angels, Expos, and Padres.

But the season had also been plagued by injuries to the entire starting rotation and by a decision by general manager Keller to farm out second baseman Jack Perconte after he got off to a lethargic start. Regarded as the team's sparkplug, Perconte's demotion ignited protests from both fans and other members of the organization, finally leading to Keller's dismissal for Dick Balderson.

When he took over the following year, Williams declared that the club had nothing to lose by concentrating on youth and backed up his intentions immediately by releasing veterans like Barry Bonnell, Gorman Thomas, and Cowens, recalling second baseman Harold Reynolds and outfielder John Moses, and installing slugger Danny Tartabull as the full-time right fielder. In a deal that paid pennant dividends to the Red Sox, he also promoted the trading of Henderson and shortstop Spike Owen to Boston in exchange for another shortstop, Rey Quinones. Despite good years from Tartabull (25 homers, 96 RBIs) and third baseman Jim Presley (27 homers, 107 RBIs), however, the team was again doomed to the cellar by a starting staff that had a combined ERA close to five runs per game.

The 1987 team won more games (78) than any of its predecessors, rising back to fourth place. But in the long run, it became a season more notable for the absence of Tartabull, who was lost to Kansas City in the franchise's worst trade—for sore-armed right-hander Scott Bankhead and backup outfielder Mike Kingery. As Tartabull drove toward another big year with the Royals, and Argyros continued playing tag with the city of Seattle, outfielder Phil Bradley and others voiced trade demands. Balderson made the mistake of accommodating Bradley after the season,

In 1987, Seattle batting coach Bobby Tolan was fired for alleged lack of communication with the team's hitters. The following year, batting coach Frank Howard was let go because of complaints that he talked to the players too much.

sending him to the Phillies for relief pitcher Mike Jackson and outfielder Glenn Wilson. Jackson chipped in for only 6 wins and 4 saves in 1988, while Wilson produced an almost invisible 3 homers and 17 RBIs. Along with the Tartabull fiasco, the Bradley trade cost Balderson his job; Woody Woodward took over as general manager in July. A few weeks before he got the axe, Balderson dismissed Wiliams after the manager's vow to retire at the end of the season had created a lame duck atmosphere in the clubhouse. Williams left blasting ace southpaw Langston for being ''gutless''; Langston's mistake had been to question whether the lame duck pilot had been sufficiently motivated to lead the team through the season.

The 1989 season began with Jim Lefebvre at the helm and with Argyros and Woodward making it very clear that they would not be able to meet Langston's expected free agent demands after the campaign. After shopping around the three-time AL strikeout leader, they completed a deal with the Expos on May 25th in which they received lefty Randy Johnson and righthanders Brian Holman and Gene Harris. Johnson went on to win 28 games over the next two years and, on June 2, 1990, threw the club's first no-hitter, against the Tigers. The club also danced through the raindrops to ultimate praise by force-feeding 19-year-old center fielder Ken Griffey, Jr. on major league pitching in 1989. Before he broke his hand in a midseason accident, Griffey appeared to be a lock for Rookie of the Year.

The promotion of the lefty swinger while his father Ken Griffey, Sr. was still active with the Reds, marked the first time that a father and son played in the majors simultaneously. A year later, the Mariners fulfilled a promotion man's dream by signing the father as his son's teammate. The Griffeys appeared together in a lineup for the first time on August 30, 1990; both of them singled and scored a run in the first inning. The enthusiasm for the younger Griffey in Seattle as The Franchise was such that a local confectioner named a candy bar after him. Recovered from his hand problem, the outfielder delivered on his promise in 1990 by batting .300 with 22 homers and 80 RBIs, and in 1991 by hitting .327 and driving in 100 runs. After an injury-filled season, the older Griffey retired at the end of the 1991 campaign.

The Argyros saga finally came to an end on August 22, 1989, with the announcement that he had sold the franchise to the Indianapolis-based Emmis Broadcasting Company for $77 million. Two key provisos of the deal were that the team would not be relocated and that one of the new owners would settle in the Seattle area. A mere year later, however, Emmis chief

Jeff Smulyan was already lamenting cash shorts and the scarce television-contract possibilities in the Northwest. In the fall of 1991, Smulyan unloaded several of the media company's radio stations in what he insisted was a necessary step to keep the franchise going. Then, without missing a beat, he acknowledged that he had had contacts with officials from St. Petersburg interested in moving the club to Florida.

Matters quickly became even muddier. When the Seattle-based Japanese owners of the Nintendo company came forward with an offer to buy the club from Smulyan and keep it in Washington, Commissioner Fay Vincent abruptly jumped onto a Japan-bashing bandwagon to insist that baseball was opposed to foreign ownership. The racist response by Vincent and some AL owners aroused Seattle, which began to smell some rats disinterred from the days of the Pilots and set off a public relations drive to spike plans for the relocation of the franchise; it didn't hurt that the Washington State congressional delegation also raised the familiar specter of a new look at the game's exemption from antitrust statutes. In June 1992, a compromise was reached under which Nintendo president Hiroshi Yamauchi contributed $75 million for a 49 percent interest in the franchise, with a substantial part of the rest of the money coming from Chris Larson, a Microsoft executive. Although he ended up with less than one percent of the team, local businessman John Ellis was named as chief executive officer, therby keeping the club in white hands.

> First baseman Pete O'Brien signed with the team as a free agent for the 1990 season after turning down a couple of other offers because of his stated fear that the clubs tendering them would be contenders.

Mainly because of the excitement generated by Griffey and a series of fan promotions, the Kingdome registered a record attendance of 1.5 million in 1990. A year later, the fans had even more to see when the team, led by Griffey, Reynolds, and third baseman Edgar Martinez, finally broke .500. The achievement had its price, however, with Lefebvre criticizing Woodward for being satisfied with the break-even plateau instead of going after the extra player or two that would make the club a genuine contender. For his part, Woodward noted the financial restraints put on him by Smulyan, then, as soon as the season was over, fired Lefebvre. Bill Plummer, the ninth manager in the team's sixteen-year history, was named to take over in 1992.

Prior to the season, Woodward pulled off one of the biggest trades in franchise history, when he obtained slugger Kevin Mitchell from the Giants in exchange for pitchers Jackson, Bill Swift, and Mike Burba. The deal was a double disaster: a foot fracture reduced Mitchell's power numbers to a minimum and the loss of the three pitchers doomed a staff that was overworked, injured, and ineffective. The only bright note on the mound was rookie Dave Fleming, who won 17 games. Offensively, third baseman Martinez led the league with a .343 mark and Griffey again came through with a banner 27 homers, 103 RBIs, and .308 average, but the rest of the lineup was inconsistent at best.

No sooner had the season ended than Woodward dispatched Plummer for Lou Piniella. Piniella,

> On September 25, 1992, the Mariners set the major league record for the most pitchers (11) used in a game. The sixteen-inning affair with the Rangers also established a mark for the most players used by two teams—54.

who had managed the Reds for three years, immediately engineered a deal with his old club by sending Mitchell to Cincinnati in exchange for lefty reliever Norm Charlton. The team also allowed free agent Reynolds to accept an offer from the Orioles, confident that Bret Boone would be a fixture at second base for years to come. When he made his debut during the 1992 season, Boone, grandson of Ray Boone and son of Bob Boone, became the first third-generation player in baseball history.

SEATTLE MARINERS

Annual Standings and Managers

Year	Position	W	L	Pct.	GB	Managers
1977	Sixth	64	98	.395	38	Darrell Johnson
1978	Seventh	56	104	.350	35	Darrell Johnson
1979	Sixth	67	95	.414	21	Darrell Johnson
1980	Seventh	59	103	.364	38	Darrell Johnson, Maury Wills
1981	Sixth	21	36	.368	14½	Maury Wills, Rene Lachemann
	Fifth	23	29	.442	6½	Rene Lachemann
1982	Fourth	76	86	.469	17	Rene Lachemann
1983	Seventh	60	102	.370	39	Rene Lachemann, Del Crandall
1984	Fifth*	74	88	.457	10	Del Crandall, Chuck Cottier
1985	Sixth	74	88	.457	17	Chuck Cottier
1986	Seventh	67	95	.414	25	Chuck Cottier, Dick Williams
1987	Fourth	78	84	.481	7	Dick Williams
1988	Seventh	68	93	.422	35½	Dick Williams, Jimmy Snyder
1989	Sixth	73	89	.451	26	Jim Lefebvre
1990	Fifth	77	85	.475	26	Jim Lefebvre
1991	Fifth	83	79	.512	12	Jim Lefebvre
1992	Seventh	68	94	.395	32	Bill Plummer

* Tie

Syracuse Stars

National League, 1879   **BALLPARKS:** NEWELL PARK
                                 LAKE SIDE PARK

RECORD: 22–48 (.314)

The brief, unhappy major league career of the Syracuse Stars is the sharpest example of how the National League's insistence on a fifty-cent admission fee damaged the opportunity for smaller cities to participate in major league baseball. Before their entry into the league, the Stars had been among the most successful independent professional teams.

In 1877 and 1878, the Stars were members of the International Association, a confederation that vainly attempted to unite as many clubs as possible against the NL's efforts to subordinate all baseball to its interests. But from the start, the International's teams were also highly ambivalent toward the NL. Syracuse, for instance, expressed its willingness to "act promptly, and with firmness, against any attempt at monopoly" by the major circuit, but also considered two offers to join that monopoly. On the third try, they ceded to temptation, consenting not only to the fifty-cent charge required at all NL parks, but even to an additional twenty-five-cent charge for cushioned reserve seats. (One Syracuse paper suggested a sliding scale of prices to keep the social classes separate.)

The NL wanted the Stars among its ranks because they were one of the strongest teams outside the league. Their pitcher, curveballer Harry McCormick, won 142 games against association, independent, and NL opponents between 1876 and 1878,

including 59 wins in 1877 and 50 in 1878. Other members of the club were catcher Bill Holbert and manager-utilityman Mike Dorgan, the only two with previous major league experience. Never an offensive powerhouse, Syracuse struggled against NL pitching and, though McCormick pitched well, he only won 18 games while losing 33. The players spent considerable energy fighting among themselves and with management over late paychecks.

The club's initial hesitation over increasing prices turned out to be well placed; the fans would not pay fifty cents to see a bad team. President Hamilton S. White pleaded with the NL for an exemption, but the league refused to acknowledge its miscalculation. To attract fans, White scheduled Sunday games, but to avoid a city ordinance against Sunday ball, they had to be played at Lake Front Park in neighboring Geddes, where a soggy, weed-infested marsh covered the outfield and diminished even further the quality of the team's play. On September 11th, with two weeks to go in the season and the team $2,500 in debt, White disbanded the club and forfeited the rest of its games.

SYRACUSE STARS

Annual Standings and Manager

Year	Position	W	L	Pct.	GB	Manager
1879	Seventh	22	48	.314	30	Mike Dorgan

Syracuse Stars

American Association, 1890   **BALLPARK:** STAR PARK
THREE RIVERS PARK

RECORD: 55–72 (.433)

Ravaged by franchise defections after the 1889 season and facing the loss of still more players to the Players League in 1890, the American Association prepared for battle as best it could by filling its empty slots with teams in smaller cities. Syracuse, run by George Kasson Frazer with the backing of a local streetcar company and a brewer, was drafted out of the International League on January 7, 1890.

Frazer acted as both president and manager. His best player was second baseman Cupid Childs, who hit .345. Other contributions came from first baseman Max McQuery (.308) and center fielder Rasty

Wright (.305). Dan Casey won 19 and lost 22, while John Keefe tied for the AA lead in losses with a 17–24 mark. On April 22, catcher Grant Briggs allowed a record 19 Philadelphia runners to steal bases. The bottom line was a sixth-place finish.

No great draw, the Stars, in a market of only 88,000 people, were high on the list of clubs to be cut when the PL war ended and the AA tried to recoup its strength. The cost of eliminating the Little Three franchises in Rochester, Syracuse, and Toledo was $24,000.

Annual Standings and Manager

Year	Position	W	L	Pct.	GB	Manager
1890	Sixth	55	72	.433	33½	George Frazer

Texas Rangers

American League,
1972–Present

BALLPARK: ARLINGTON STADIUM

RECORD: 1579–1752 (.474)

Asked once how he viewed his club, Rangers' general manager Tom Grieve replied: "Over the course of time, the emphasis subtly shifts from development to winning. We're somewhere in the middle." Indeed, the Rangers have usually been somewhere in that middle since leaving Washington for Dallas after the 1971 season. Over the club's two decades of existence, only the Indians and Mariners have had comparably perfect records as postseason spectators. Only once has the team won as many as 90 games, and that season (1977) saw four managers taking turns at the reins. Entering the 1990s, the organization's most notable contribution to baseball was the intolerable Texas summer heat that made it easier to advance the cause of Sunday night games.

The prime movers behind establishing American League baseball in Texas were Arlington Mayor Tom Vandergriff and Minneapolis hotel owner and freight-line executive Bob Short. Vandergriff had the demographics of the metropolitan Dallas–Fort Worth region as his most powerful argument; what Short had were an estimated $2.6 million in losses over three years of operating the expansion Senators in Washington. With his club showing little sign of attracting more fans through improved play and with Baltimore dominating the television market around the nation's capital, Short successfully pleaded imminent bankruptcy to other AL owners to win their approval for the transfer. The move took place in the face of President Richard Nixon's declared "grief" over the decision and amid threats by various congressmen that they would reopen investigations into major league baseball's exemption from antitrust statutes. The congressmen fell quiet before vague

(and unfulfilled) promises that Washington would eventually get another team.

In setting up operations at Arlington Stadium, Short's principal assets were the legendary reputation of manager Ted Williams and the relatively more recent power feats of 35-year-old slugger Frank Howard. Neither could prevent a season in the cellar of the AL West—or even get the year off to its scheduled home start. Because of a players' strike called to pressure higher ownership contributions to the pension pool, the Rangers were forced to cancel their first homestand, and made their debut against the Angels in Anaheim on April 15th. The game was an excruciating 1–0 loss decided on a ninth-inning wild pitch by Texas reliever Paul Lindblad. Over the next 153 games, the club's closest thing to a power hitter was outfielder Ted Ford, who hit 14 homers and drove in 50 runs, and its pitching ace was Rich Hand, who went 10–14. Short, who had targeted 800,000 fans as the break-even point, fell some 130,000 short; even before the end of the season, he tried to make up for some of the loss by selling Howard to Detroit for $100,000. He didn't protest, either, when Williams (and his ample salary) resigned at the end of the year. Mainly on the advice of general manager Joe Burke, the owner tapped Whitey Herzog as manager.

Herzog got his reign off to a start by comparing the Rangers to the 1962 expansion Mets, calling them "one of the worst" teams he had ever seen. They proceeded to get worse in 1973, setting a franchise record of 105 losses and offering only outfielder Jeff Burroughs (30 homers, 85 RBIs) as an offensive threat. But the most notorious story of the year was

Nolan Ryan completing his sixth no-hitter, against the Athletics in the Oakland Coliseum on June 11, 1990. On May 1, 1991, he chalked up number seven against the Blue Jays.
AP/Wide World Photos

the one that began unfolding on the evening of June 27th when Short ran 18-year-old southpaw David Clyde out to the mound at Arlington Stadium to take on the Minnesota Twins. The first pick in that year's amateur draft, Clyde was billed as the future of the franchise so relentlessly by Short and his publicists that Mayor Vandergriff led the first sellout crowd (slightly under 36,000) to watch his debut. Although

When Bob Short moved the Senators to Texas, he also moved the team from the Eastern to the Western Division of the American League. To replace Washington, the Milwaukee Brewers were moved from the West to the East.

he walked seven and threw 112 pitches in five innings, the lefty had a 4–2 lead when he retired in favor of reliever Bill Gogolewski, and four innings later had his first victory. With only Herzog counseling care, the Rangers banged the drums even more loudly before every Clyde game, to the point that his twelve starts at home accounted for almost one-third of the year's total attendance of 686,085. Unfortunately for Clyde, the short-term benefits to the franchise from all the ballyhoo did absolutely nothing for his career. In his rookie year, he went an uninspiring 4–8 with a 5.03 ERA, and never won more than 8 games in a season (and even that for the Indians). His final career record was 18–33 with a 4.63 ERA.

Herzog's cautious stand on Clyde did not help his relations with Short; nor did his assumption that his two-year contract allowed him at least that much time to bring along some of the youngest players in the Texas chain. But what hurt him most of all was a late August decision by the Tigers to fire Billy Martin as manager and make him available to Short. Or, as the owner declared during a September 2nd press conference in announcing Herzog's ouster: "If my mother were managing the Rangers, and I had the opportunity to hire Billy Martin, I'd fire my mother." Martin barely had time to act flattered; a few months later, Short decided that he had only added to his losses by moving from Washington to Texas, and announced the sale of the franchise to a group headed by industrial parts manufacturer Brad Corbett. The Corbett syndicate, which included Fort Worth publisher Amon Carter and future AL President Bobby Brown, agreed to pay Short $9.5 million, plus cover another $1 in carryover debts.

If Short always seemed to be counting his pennies, Corbett's actions over the next five years had many baseball people wondering if he had any sense. A typical comment was that of long-time general manager Frank Lane, who asserted that "having Corbett run a baseball team is like giving a 3-year-old a handful of razors." Though again and again denying that he had any interest in being a hands-on owner, Corbett constantly intruded in the daily operations of his front office, often pulling off trades behind the

backs of his general managers and overriding their warnings. When deals came back to haunt him, he retreated behind the classic baseball tactic of blaming it on the manager; the Rangers averaged a new pilot a year during his tenure. At other times, he stacked his front office with executives who either operated in competition with one another or ultimately had to defer back to him for resolving disputes.

In 1974, however, both Corbett and Martin were heroes for Texas fans when their Turn-Around Gang bolted from last place to second in a dramatic 27-game gain from the previous season. As late as mid-September, the club was only four games behind the powerhouse Athletics before finally settling into the runner-up spot for good. Spearheading the surge were Burroughs (AL MVP for his 25 homers, 33 doubles, 118 RBIs, and .301 average), first baseman Mike Hargrove (AL Rookie of the Year for batting .323), and Ferguson Jenkins (a league-leading 25 victories).

The surprise showing turned out to be something of a mixed blessing when Corbett, deciding that the pickup of veterans like Jenkins paid off more handsomely than waiting for the farm system to develop, pressed general manager Dan O'Brien to go after more seasoned players in order to go all the way to a title in 1975. The results were the acquisition of 35-year-old outfielder Willie Davis, who batted only .249 in 42 games and who infuriated Martin with his work habits, and 34-year-old southpaw Clyde Wright, who won only four games. In the same vein, Corbett sent three present or future starters—Jim Bibby, Jackie Brown, and Rick Waits—to the Indians, along with $100,000, to obtain the services of 36-year-old Gaylord Perry. Although Perry still had a few decent seasons left in his Hall of Fame career, his arrival only added to the win-now pressures that soon had the otherwise untried club buckling. Martin, never too smooth with his players or the press when somebody was turning on the heat, was gone before the end of July, replaced by third base coach Frank Lucchesi. It was Lucchesi who steered the team to a third-place finish in 1975 and a further drop to fourth the following year.

In the middle years of the decade, Corbett had a little bad luck to go with his general lack of astuteness. On paper, for instance, he appeared to have made a good trade with the Twins in June 1976 by acquiring righthander Bert Blyleven and shortstop Danny Thompson in return for the over-the-hill Bill Singer, shortstop Roy Smalley, and third baseman Mike Cubbage. As it turned out, the Rangers were about the only team in Blyleven's long journey around the major leagues where he was merely a

.500 pitcher; more tragically, Thompson was dead of leukemia a few months later. The middling to bad results of some of the club's other deals in 1975 and 1976 were more predictable. Among the worn-down veterans who made brief stopoffs in Arlington were Ed Brinkman, Nelson Briles, Juan Beniquez, Gene Clines, George Stone, and Fritz Peterson. Then, in December 1976, Corbett had his first serious run-in with Rangers' fans when he traded the apple of the franchise, Burroughs, to the Braves for outfielders Ken Henderson and Dave May and pitchers Rogelio Moret, Carl Morton, and Adrian Devine. Underscoring the relative worth of the players it was parting with, Atlanta also threw in $250,000.

But the Burroughs trade, and the negative fan reaction to it, was the least of the troubles for the franchise in 1977. General manager O'Brien, squeezed out of some of his responsibilities by the naming of Eddie Robinson to a special vice-presidency, regained some attention by musing aloud that he would like to sign free agent Larry Hisle; this cost the team $25,000 for tampering. When Corbett gave up a whopping $400,000 to Oakland's Charlie Finley to reobtain the lefty Lindblad, who had lost the team's very first game to the Angels in 1972, Commissioner Bowie Kuhn first threatened to squash the deal as he had other Finley fire sales of the period, then reluctantly gave his okay after pointing out that the hurler was 36 years old and had nowhere near the value placed on him by the Rangers. Corbett was still swallowing this criticism when, before a spring training game in Orlando, infielder Lenny Randle attacked Lucchesi with a left-right combination, then continued to pound on him until restrained by teammates. The nearest thing to an explanation for the assault was Randle's contention that Lucchesi had called him a "punk"—a detail denied by the manager from his hospital bed, where he was treated for a concussion, a broken cheekbone, and a lacerated lip. Randle was fined $10,000 and suspended for thirty days by the team and subsequently arrested on felonious assault charges. The criminal count was eventually reduced to a misdemeanor carrying a $1,000 fine, by which time the infielder had been sent off to the Mets.

Any sympathy that Lucchesi might have gained from Corbett over the clash with Randle was spent by June, when the owner began telling reporters that the club needed a manager who wasn't a symbol of divisiveness. A whispering campaign that he was on the way out just about broke down Lucchesi, and he was more than ready for an announcement on June 21st that he was being replaced by Eddie Stanky,

then serving as coach for the University of Alabama baseball team. The person who turned out not to be at all ready for the announcement was Stanky, who managed the Rangers to a 10–8 victory over the Twins, then decided that he preferred being back in Mobile with his family and university job. While Corbett sought to talk Stanky back to Texas and third base coach Connie Ryan ran the team, Robinson and O'Brien went after recently retired slugger Harmon Killebrew to see if he might be interested in the post. A week later, Lucchesi, Stanky, Ryan, and Killebrew were all out of the picture, and the team's fourth manager of the year was former Baltimore shortstop Billy Hunter.

When Hunter took over, the team had a record of 34–35 and appeared set for another drowsy third- or fourth-place finish. When he won only three of his first eight games, the new manager only abetted a July 4th scene at Arlington Stadium that saw a drunken Corbett staggering around after another loss, declaring that he was going to sell the team because it was filled with "dogs." From that point on, however, the Rangers caught fire and, notwithstanding all the chaos around them, went on to compile their best record in franchise history. The keys to the effort on the mound were the veterans Perry (15 wins) and free agent acquisition Doyle Alexander (17), while the offense was led by third baseman Toby Harrah (27 homers and 87 RBIs), Hargrove (18 homers and .305), and designated hitter Willie Horton (15 homers, 75 RBIs, and .289). Catcher Jim Sundberg added to his reputation as one of baseball's best defensive receivers by also showing some hitting ability (65 RBIs and a .291 average).

As had been the case after the 1974 season, Corbett followed up the club's second-place finish in 1977 with another whirlwind round of deals aimed at bringing in still more veterans. Among those added either through trades or free agent signings were Doc Medich, Jon Matlack, Richie Zisk, Al Oliver, and Bobby Bonds. But though Matlack and Bonds, in particular, delivered, the club was ultimately undone by the shallowness of its starting rotation, no bullpen, and no shortstop. It didn't help, either, that Hunter overcame the relative shyness of his first half-season to assert the authoritarian personality that had earned him the nickname of Little Hitler. Despite the fact that the club had only two regular position players and two starters under 28, the manager became infamous around the league for treating the players as children. This prompted several clashes in the clubhouse and during road trips, including one scene on a plane when pitcher Doc

Ellis openly urged his teammates to ignore Hunter's ban on drinking during flights. Corbett generally affected indifference to the clashes, and near the close of the season even offered to extend his pilot's contract by five years. But when Hunter decided that such an extension was longer than he wanted to commit himself, Corbett ousted him, cracking to reporters that "we didn't fit into his long-range plans." The announcement that Pat Corrales was taking over was treated with relief in the clubhouse.

Many of those who welcomed Corrales's arrival were not around too long to play under him. Once again promising that it would take "only one or two pieces" for the Rangers to win the division title, Corbett threw himself into another winter of frantic trading, completing nine deals before spring training. The best of them brought third baseman Buddy Bell from the Indians for Harrah; the worst of them were all of the others. To get help for the bullpen, the team sent Bonds and starter Len Barker to Cleveland for Jim Kern. To replace Bonds, Oscar Gamble was imported from San Diego for Hargrove, the team's most consistent hitter. Then, in a deal that would haunt the franchise for years, Corbett insisted on negotiating directly with George Steinbrenner to obtain aging lefty Sparky Lyle, shortstop Domingo Ramos, and catcher Mike Heath in exchange for Beniquez, prize prospect Dave Righetti, and several others. Aside from getting the washed-up Lyle for Righetti, Corbett also confused the Latin infielders in the New York chain, bringing home Ramos instead of Damaso Garcia, as he had been instructed by Robinson and other front office aides.

Corrales kept the team fairly competitive in 1979, largely on the strength of hitting from Bell and Oliver and Kern's one effective year out of the bullpen for the team. But the season was clouded by Corbett's increasingly public money shorts; at one point, he stepped back from bankruptcy only thanks to an infusion of new capital (some $900,000) from Texas oilman Eddie Chiles, who took the occasion to complain that the franchise was being run "like a toy." By January 1980, Corbett had broken his last

Despite an eighteen-year career spanning 2,405 games, Buddy Bell never appeared in postseason competition. That is the major league record for unfulfilled expectations in the era of divisional play. In addition to the Rangers, Bell played for the Indians, Reds, and Astros.

yo-yo string, and was forced to sell out to Chiles and two other stockholders, publisher Carter and attorney Dee Kelly, for $4 million. The last straw for the investors had been a commitment by Corbett to give Sundberg a $5.1-million contract covering six years as an active player and a subsequent career as a Rangers's broadcaster. Although Sundberg had agreed to a more limited pact after the organization's board of directors vetoed the original accord, Corbett had taken the rejection as a personal humiliation and announced his readiness to sell. Chiles promoted Robinson to the post of president, though the title was to last for only one year and Robinson's presence at all only for two.

Overall, the 70-year-old Chiles proved to be something of a surprise. Long known as much for his right wing America-First bluster as for his oil fortune, he stayed relatively in the background for a couple of years, content to second Robinson's recommendation to replace Corrales with Don Zimmer after a fourth-place finish in 1980. On the other hand, the new owner made it clear from the start that he was not about to use his greater financial resources to emulate Corbett's often wild spending; by 1984, in fact, he had the club's payroll all the way down to twenty-third place in the major leagues. The only significant free agent signing that he authorized over the first half of the 1980s was that of southpaw Frank Tanana, who had still not completed his transition from fireballer to finesse pitcher and who would promptly lead the league in losses in 1982.

The lack of free agents wasn't the only cause of the club's gradual sinking back to the bottom of the division in the first part of the decade; more fatal were the trades executed by Robinson and his successor Joe Klein. The worst swap of all—again in the name of acquiring "one last piece"—was an April 1982 transaction that sent prize pitching prospects Ron Darling and Walt Terrell to the Mets in exchange for outfielder Lee Mazzilli. Mazzilli not only hit a mere .241 and had a poor outfield arm, but never disguised his gloom at having been traded away from the lights of New York; before he had completed a single season with the Rangers, he was peddled to the Yankees. Klein also acquiesced to Chiles's money priorities by dealing ERA leader Rick Honeycutt to the Dodgers for $200,000 and Dave Stewart (still many years away from becoming a big winner), and sent Sundberg to the Brewers for hapless Ned Yost.

The Sundberg deal, which precipitated a years-long search by the franchise for a first-string catcher, also pointed up another club problem in the early

When the Rangers traded Rick Honeycutt to the Dodgers during the 1983 season, they also froze the southpaw's AL ERA at a level low enough to help him end up as the league leader in that category.

The Rangers ended the 1984 season by being the victims of a perfect game thrown by California's Mike Witt. The very last Texas batter of the game—and of the season—was pinch-hitter Marv Foley, who never hit again in the major leagues.

1980s—manager Doug Rader. Rader was hired to take over the club for the 1983 season, after Zimmer and Darrell Johnson had divided the responsibility for a sixth-place finish the year before. Never one to walk when he could swagger, Rader began publicly questioning Sundberg's hustle even before he had met the team in spring training. The catcher had become a target for two reasons: He himself had been mentioned as a possible managerial candidate before the appointment of Rader, and he had exercised his contract veto power over a December 1982 swap that would have sent him to the Dodgers for pitchers Stewart, Orel Hershiser, and Burt Hooton. The feud between the manager and the catcher continued throughout the 1983 season, especially after Sundberg tried to explain away some stolen bases against him by saying that he had a sore shoulder and Rader rejoindered that he was either a whiner or a liar. By the time that the deal for Yost (who would hit .182 and throw as though he, too, had a sore arm) was announced the following winter, Sundberg was happy to leave the team, other players were accusing Rader of trying to manage through intimidation, and fans were beginning to protest the treatment of one of their few stable players. In retrospect (but only then), Texas officials would also concede that Rader's caustic manner and tendency to lash out at players on the field or in the dugout had seriously hampered, if not curtailed altogether, the development of prospects like Jeff Kunkel, George Wright, and Tom Henke.

Of the players Rader did approve of, the most productive during his tenure were Bell, designated hitter Larry Parrish, and the knuckleballer Charlie Hough, who led the staff in victories for seven consecutive years in the 1980s. As a whole, however, the team was going nowhere fast, and there was little astonishment when Chiles bounced Klein as general manager in September 1984, replacing him with former Texas outfielder Tom Grieve. Somewhat more surprising, given the mounting accusations against him in the media, Rader was not simply retained, but was put in charge of the Texas delegation to the winter meetings in Houston. But when the club got off to

a horrendous start in 1985, winning only 9 of its first 32 games, Grieve had gained enough power behind his title to press successfully for the appointment of Bobby Valentine as Rader's replacement.

Valentine was the dominant figure of the franchise for the remainder of the decade. Those who liked him noted that his high-octane energy involved him in every aspect of the team's preparations for a game, and also made him the organization's best salesman. Those who didn't like him accused him of being a tireless, glib self-promoter who sought to gloss over the fact that, for all his public relations panache, he was no more successful than any of his predecessors.

Just as with Martin's first full season in 1977, Valentine's 1986 team engendered nothing but superlatives for his managing efforts, with the Rangers going from 37 games under .500 in the cellar to 12 games above the break-even mark to finish second. The principal contributors to the turn-around were outfielder Pete Incaviglia (30 homers, 88 RBIs), first baseman Pete O'Brien (23 homers, 90 RBIs), and DH Parrish (28 homers, 94 homers). For the first time since the franchise had been created, the pitching staff was composed largely of rookie and second-year hurlers; of the six most used pitchers, four of them (Ed Correa, Bobby Witt, Mitch Williams, and Jose Guzman) were 23 or younger. Pitching coach Tom House attracted a lot of media attention for such unorthodox drills as having his charges loosen up by throwing footballs instead of baseballs.

The team's revival provided little solace for Chiles, who had been watching his fortune dwindle with crude oil prices for several years. As early as

In 1986, the Rangers acquired Pete Incaviglia from the Expos after the just-drafted slugger refused to sign with Montreal. The deal prompted passage of the so-called Incaviglia Rule that barred teams from trading amateur draft selections until at least one year after signing them.

1984, he had needed money from Oklahoma publisher and television magnate Edward Gaylord to keep going, and had required the eleventh-hour help of Commissioner Peter Ueberroth to allay the fears of other AL owners that Gaylord would use his 33 percent interest in the team as leverage to launch superstation coverage of the Rangers around the country in the way that the Mets, Cubs, and Braves were already swamping small markets. Now, once again, Chiles turned to Gaylord, offering his 58 percent share of the franchise for $50 million. This time, however, Milwaukee and Kansas City lobbied successfully against ratifying the agreement, getting enormous assistance from statements by a Gaylord Broadcasting official that the company did indeed intend competing against the other superstations once it had control of the Rangers.

Chiles continued to look for a buyer. In the spring of 1987, he appeared near a deal with a New York syndicate headed by Warren Crane, but that fell through when the prospective buyers wouldn't offer ironclad guarantees that the team would stay in Texas. Less than a year later, however, with his flagship Western Company of North America forced to file for Chapter 11 bankruptcy, it was Chiles himself who was telling people that the general economic situation in Texas had made it impractical to restrict his search for buyers to the state. In August 1988, acknowledging that he had not insisted on a clause committing the franchise to Texas, Chiles announced that he was going to sell his majority interest in the team for $46.4 million to Florida auto dealer Frank Morsani and New Jersey developer Bill Mack, two of the point men in the well-organized campaign to bring major league baseball to Tampa. The obstacle this time was Gaylord, who had first refusal rights on Chiles's stock and who announced that he was going to use the entire month he was allowed to decide his position. The thirty days were long enough for Chiles to lament publicly that he hadn't insisted on a condition binding Morsani and Mack to Arlington and for a storm of protest to blow up around the pact. When Gaylord finally came out against the agreement, asserting that it was his "duty to keep the team out of the hands of New Yorkers and other foreigners," he was hailed as a local hero.

AL owners remained unmoved. Even before Chiles's plea that his minority partner was the only plausible buyer on the horizon, the league again rejected Gaylord's application. Suspicious that Chiles might not have been as energetic as he claimed in looking for alternatives to Gaylord, Ueberroth flew to Texas twice in February 1989 to sound out a group headed by George W. Bush, the son of the President of the United States, and Rusty Rose, a Dallas banker. While Chiles took the public posture that he appreciated Ueberroth's assistance, he complained mightily to friends that the commissioner was trying to run his business for him. It was mainly because of this resentment that he dragged out signing sale papers, threatening second thoughts on everything, even after a late winter announcement that the Bush-Rose group had bought the franchise for the same $46.4 million that had been discussed with Morsani and Mack. With a commitment by the new owners to stay put in Texas, Gaylord gave his approval to the sale, declaring his intention of retaining his minority interest.

The Rangers' second-place finish in 1986 turned out to be just another tease, with the club staying closer to the tail of the division than the top for the rest of the 1980s. After every campaign, Valentine and Grieve bemoaned the hitting and praised the pitching, or vice versa, then spent the offseason creating the reverse problem for the following year. Before he sold the team, Chiles accepted the blame for the team's inconsistent performance, saying that Valentine and Grieve were working within his restrictive financial parameters and couldn't be expected to effect miracles; he rewarded both of them with contracts extending into the 1990s.

The manager and general manager had more off-the-field troubles than their budget. In July 1987, Grieve announced that the club had signed Steve Howe to a minor league contract; the lefty had lost roster spots on both the Dodgers and Twins for repeated drug offenses, and at the time was under suspension from organized ball for another drug episode with the minor league San Jose Bees. Under the terms of an agreement with Ueberroth, the Rangers were allowed to sign Howe for Oklahoma City but would have to await the commissioner's explicit approval before promoting him back to the majors. Less than a month later, Texas recalled Howe without Ueberroth's permission. The bad news was that he turned out to be only another mediocre pitcher on a mediocre pitching staff; the worse news was that the defiance of Ueberroth cost the franchise $250,000 in fines; and the worst news was that Howe had a relapse into drug use over the winter and was once again suspended from baseball.

In 1989, the club had another substance abuse episode when outfielder Rick Leach disappeared during a trip to New York. After a twenty-four-hour search by police, Leach resurfaced to admit that he had been holed up with drugs.

In 1989, Valentine began being eclipsed as the biggest story of the franchise with the signing of Nolan Ryan as a $2-million-a-year free agent. Although other teams had bid even higher for the righthander's services after he had declined to resign with the Astros, the Rangers prevailed largely because of the proximity of Arlington to the 42-year-old's home. If there was any doubt that Ryan still had something left besides gate appeal, it disappeared quickly when he led the staff with 16 wins, struck out 301 batters, and held the league to a .187 average. On August 22nd, he also recorded his 5,000th strikeout by fanning Oakland's Rickey Henderson.

Even that performance turned out to be mere prelude to the sensation Ryan caused nationally in the early 1990s. On June 6, 1990, he fashioned career no-hitter number six against Oakland. On July 31, before more than 51,000 screaming fans in Milwaukee, he got his 300th career victory. Then, in 1991 at the age of 44, he struck out sixteen Blue Jays on his way to his seventh no-hitter. Despite protracted periods on the disabled list both years, he struck out more than 200 batters in both 1990 and 1991. Entering the 1993 season, the righthander had a significant number of baseball's compilation and longevity records, including most seasons played (27).

Ryan aside, the Rangers of the early 1990s had a decidedly offensive look, mainly because of their two-three-four-five batters in the lineup (Julio Franco, Rafael Palmiero, Ruben Sierra, Juan Gonza-

lez), dubbed by some as the Latin Quarter. While not as much of a power hitter as the others, Franco became one of the few righthanded batters in the postwar AL to win a Silver Bat when he averaged .341 in 1991.

Hopes that such a solid lineup (bolstered further by designated hitter Kevin Reimer and third baseman Dean Palmer) would produce the team's first division title in 1992, lasted little more than a few weeks into the season. This time, however, Valentine couldn't dodge the bullet, and he was replaced by coach Toby Harrah. To the surprise of many, Grieve held on to his post, and spent most of the year moving legions of relief pitchers back and forth between Texas and the minor leagues in a vain attempt to put together a bullpen. The only bright spots on the mound were Kevin Brown's 21 wins and a long-awaited emergence by the often-injured Guzman, who won 16.

The offense was all or nothing. The all included an AL-leading 43 home runs from Gonzalez, the nothing a murderous strikeout rate from the middle of the lineup and a hand injury that confined Franco to the sidelines all year. Then in August, amid reports that the club was not going to be able to sign potential free agent Sierra in the offseason, Grieve pulled off the trade of the year by dispatching the switch-hitting outfielder along with pitchers Witt and Jeff Russell to Oakland in exchange for slugger Jose Canseco.

The team's humdrum play over the final months of the campaign doomed Harrah's hopes of returning as manager; in November, Montreal coach Kevin Kennedy was named as his successor. In an effort to correct its feeble bullpen and shoddy middle infield defense, the club went into the free agent market for relievers Tom Henke and Craig Lefferts, shortstop Manny Lee, and second baseman Billy Ripken. Lefty starter Charlie Leibrandt also came over in a trade with Atlanta. The biggest offseason losses were those of Guzman, who went to the Cubs as a free agent, and Reimer, who was picked up by Colorado in the expansion draft.

> On August 12, 1990, the Rangers were part of the longest rain delay in baseball history, when an afternoon game in Chicago was not called off until 7½ hours after its scheduled start. The official reason given for the procrastination was that it was the final appearance by Texas at old Comiskey Park. The game was later made up in Arlington. Fewer than 200 fans were on hand when the contest was finally called.

TEXAS RANGERS

Annual Standings and Managers

Year	Position	W	L	Pct.	GB	Managers
1972	Sixth	54	100	.351	38½	Ted Williams
1973	Sixth	57	105	.352	37	Whitey Herzog, Billy Martin
1974	Second	84	76	.525	5	Billy Martin
1975	Third	79	83	.488	19	Billy Martin, Frank Lucchesi
1976	Fourth*	76	86	.469	14	Frank Lucchesi

1977	Second	94	68	.580	8	Frank Lucchesi, Eddie Stanky, Connie Ryan, Billy Hunter
1978	Second*	87	75	.537	5	Billy Hunter, Pat Corrales
1979	Third	83	79	.512	5	Pat Corrales
1980	Fourth	76	85	.472	20½	Pat Corrales
1981	Second	33	22	.600	1½	Don Zimmer
	Third	24	26	.480	4½	Don Zimmer
1982	Sixth	64	98	.395	29	Don Zimmer, Darrell Johnson
1983	Third	77	85	.475	22	Doug Rader
1984	Seventh	69	92	.429	14½	Doug Rader
1985	Seventh	62	99	.385	28½	Doug Rader, Bobby Valentine
1986	Second	87	75	.537	5	Bobby Valentine
1987	Sixth*	75	87	.463	10	Bobby Valentine
1988	Sixth	70	91	.435	33½	Bobby Valentine
1989	Fourth	83	79	.512	16	Bobby Valentine
1990	Third	83	79	.512	20	Bobby Valentine
1991	Third	85	77	.525	10	Bobby Valentine
1992	Fourth	77	85	.475	19	Bobby Valentine, Toby Harrah

* Tie

Toledo Blue Stockings

American Association, 1884   **BALLPARKS:** LEAGUE PARK
                                                  TRI-STATE FAIR GROUNDS

RECORD: 46–58 (.442)

The admission of Toledo into the American Association, the club's subsequent expulsion after only one season, and the acquisition and disposal of its star player, pitcher Tony Mullane, are a case study in the convoluted dealings of nineteenth century baseball club owners. The Blue Stockings are also noteworthy as the team that broke the color line (however, briefly) by employing black catcher Fleet Walker.

Toledo gained entry to the AA as part of the attempt to expand the association to twelve teams and lock up as many players as possible against anticipated Union Association talent raids. Blue Stockings' president William J. Colburn and manager Charlie Morton were willing to go through the season with the same personnel that had won the Northwestern League pennant in 1883, but then they were suddenly handed Mullane, who had won 30 games with Louisville (AA) in 1882 and 35 with St. Louis (AA) the following year. With a salary increase from $1,900 to $2,500 as an incentive, Mullane had bolted the Browns and signed with the UA St. Louis Maroons for 1884. But when the AA adopted the Day

Resolution that called for the blacklisting of players who jumped their contracts, Mullane had second thoughts about his move and approached Browns' president Chris Von der Ahe about returning to the fold. Knowing that Mullane was unlikely to come back for $1,900, Von der Ahe concluded that the next best option was to hustle him out of St. Louis altogether. NL president A.G. Mills then suggested a gentleman's agreement whereby both NL and AA clubs would ignore Mullane's release, allowing him to land with remote and harmless Toledo so that he could help keep the franchise afloat.

Mullane's 35–25 record was a decisive factor in Toledo's finishing as high as eighth. But not everyone was happy with the NL-AA solution. Henry V. Lucas, the Maroons' president and the UA's chief

---

The Blue Stockings were the first team to offer rain checks, allowing free admission to another game in the event of rain.

angel, obtained a court order restraining Mullane from appearing in games in St. Louis (thereby playing into Von der Ahe's hands by keeping the pitcher out of five home games between the Browns and the Blue Stockings). Seeking further redress, Lucas sent attorney Newton Crane to Cincinnati to obtain another injunction, but this one was thrown out on appeal on the grounds that baseball's intramural battles were too insignificant to be of concern to the courts because they related to a sport and not a business. Nevertheless, the St. Louis injunction remained in force until 1887.

Mullane's contributions, while sufficient to keep the Blue Stockings on their feet, did little to save the franchise when, the war with the UA over, it was time to pare the AA back to eight teams; as the smallest city in the league, Toledo failed to make the cut. Assuming responsibility for liquidating the club's assets, Colburn offered Cincinnati (AA) its pick of players. When he received no response, he offered the same deal to Von der Ahe, who anted up $2,500, half in advance, for negotiating rights. Von der Ahe secured notarized commitments from Mullane (to whom he paid $500 as an advance on a $3,500 salary), center fielder Curt Welch, and two other players. Released by Toledo, the four were sequestered in a hotel room to ride out the required ten-day free agency period, but on the ninth day, Mullane, enterprising as ever, pretended he was sick and escaped to sign a $5,000 agreement with the AA Reds.

In a rage, Von der Ahe brought charges against Mullane, whose punishment was a one-year suspension for "conduct tending to bring discredit on the baseball profession." Mullane also had to return the advances he had received from both clubs—$500 from St. Louis and $2,000 from Cincinnati. Mills, who had suggested the chicanery that had sent Mullane to Toledo in the first place, refused to criticize the pitcher; almost always when a player breaks the rules governing contract signings, he said, "the fault is directly traceable to the club managers." The defunct Toledo franchise, however, was forced to sue Von der Ahe for the rest of its money, ending up with the unprincely sum of $659.30.

Amid the Mullane controversy, Toledo also de-fied the unofficial ban that had kept black players out of the major leagues. One of about fifty blacks who played in the minors in the nineteenth century, Fleet Walker, a good defensive catcher but mediocre hitter, had already gained some attention in 1883 when Cap Anson had refused to allow Chicago to play a scheduled exhibition if the receiver were in the lineup. Blue Stockings' manager Charlie Morton had had every intention of keeping Walker, who had a sore hand, on the bench that day, but Anson's ultimatum forced him to deliver a counter-ultimatum: Either Walker would play or there would be no game. Anson, with his eye on the gate receipts, capitulated. When Toledo joined the AA the following year, Colburn included the backstop.

The reaction by the rest of the association, with its strong minority of teams in southern cities, was mixed. There was no hostility in Baltimore, Washington, or Cincinnati. Fans in Louisville, however, were abusive and threatening, and the Louisville team refused to take the field against Walker. In Richmond, there were threats of mob action. Walker's batterymate Mullane was not much friendlier. Thirty-five years later, Mullane acknowledged his aversion to blacks, but also said that Walker was "the best catcher I ever worked with." The compromise they worked out was that as long as Mullane insisted on disregarding Walker's signs, they would work without signs, a situation that did not prevent Walker from catching "everything I pitched without knowing what was coming."

In the end, it was neither the racism of opponents or teammates nor threats of mob violence that ended Walker's career; a foul tip that broke one of his ribs in July took care of that. In September, when the catcher's injuries prevented him from playing, he was released.

Footnote Player: The second black player to appear in the major leagues was Welday Walker, Fleet's younger brother, an outfielder who batted .222 in five games for Toledo.

TOLEDO BLUE STOCKINGS

Annual Standings and Manager

Year	Position	W	L	Pct	GB	Manager
1884	Eighth	46	58	.442	27½	Charlie Morton

Toledo Maumees

American Association, 1890	**BALLPARK:** SPERANZA PARK
RECORD: 68–64 (.515)	**OTHER NAME:** BLACK PIRATES

One of four new clubs admitted to the American Association in the wake of the AA's near-dissolution at the end of 1889, Toledo was neither an adequate substitute for the losses nor a bulwark against the forthcoming attack by the Players League. The Maumees represented the smallest city (with a population of 81,000) in the major leagues in 1890.

President Valentino H. Ketcham, Jr. and manager Charlie Morton fielded a team that featured veteran right fielder Ed Swartwood (.327), first baseman Perry Werden (.295), and a running attack that led the AA in both stolen bases and triples. Egyptian

Healy (22–21) led the mound staff.

Even a fourth-place finish couldn't save the Maumees. With the prospect of placing clubs in established major league cities like Boston, Cincinnati, and Washington in the wake of the PL war, the AA wasted little time in getting rid of its Little Three franchises in Syracuse, Rochester, and Toledo. Ketcham didn't go without a fight, securing an injunction against his club's expulsion. Eventually, however, he accepted part of the $24,000 package set aside by the AA for buying out the Little Three.

TOLEDO MAUMEES

Annual Standings and Manager

Year	Position	W	L	Pct.	GB	Manager
1890	Fourth	68	64	.515	20	Charlie Morton

Toronto Blue Jays

American League, 1977–Present	**BALLPARKS:** EXHIBITION STADIUM (1977–1989) SKYDOME (1989–Present)
RECORD: 1256–1277 (.496)	

The Blue Jays gained respectability faster than any modern expansion team except the Mets, but, until 1992 also struggled with a reputation for not winning the big games that would make them the class of the American League East. On the other hand, the club's general competitiveness on the field and success at the gate in the latter part of the 1980s and early 1990s did a great deal to offset prejudices that baseball would always have something of a diluted taste in Canada.

The Blue Jays officially entered the AL at a meeting at New York's Plaza Hotel on November 5, 1976.

Some of the owners present would not have foreseen a gathering of the kind only a few months earlier; some certainly were sorry that it had been called. As far back as the nineteenth century, Albert Spalding had pointed to Toronto as the site for a future big league club. More often than not, however, such predictions over the years had been merely rhetorical, political, or both—when a franchise sought to hold a league to ransom, when a league tried to make a franchise understand that it wasn't indispensable, or when some budding league tried to create an impression that it had far-flung resources. It was not

Skydome, home of baseball's first four-million-plus season attendance. *Courtesy of Stadium Corporation of Toronto Limited*

until 1971 that Montreal financier Robert Webster made a serious bid to buy the San Diego Padres and relocate the franchise to Ontario. Although Webster's try failed, it provided incentive for the city fathers to expand the existing Canadian National Exhibition Stadium for baseball use.

In January 1976, a group that included Webster but that was dominated by Donald McDougall of the Labatt's Breweries, announced an agreement to purchase the San Francisco Giants for $13.5 million. The deal foundered when San Francisco Mayor George Moscone obtained a court injunction that delayed matters long enough for Bob Lurie to step forward with the money that kept the Giants in California. Less than a month later, however, AL owners voted by a margin of 11–1 to expand into Toronto and Seattle. To some extent, the vote was only a tactical ploy aimed at persuading the National League to accept the idea of regular-season interleague play, in exchange for which AL owners declared their readiness to set up two thirteen-team leagues, with Toronto being given to the senior circuit in order to

stimulate a rivalry with Montreal. But when NL owners reiterated their opposition to interleague play, the Blue Jays remained within the AL. The city also got a scare from Commissioner Bowie Kuhn, who was so intent on setting up a franchise for cronies in Washington that there were brief indications that Toronto might be sacrificed for the nation's capital.

The new club, which paid an entry fee of $7 million, named Webster chairman of the board and Labatt's executive Peter Hardy vice-chairman. To run baseball operations, the team picked 34-year-old Peter Bavasi. Bavasi's choice for manager was Roy Hartsfield, a veteran of the Dodger organization. More important, he hired away Yankees' farm director Pat Gillick as chief of player personnel decisions; Gillick's first-hand knowledge of the New York farm system would benefit the Blue Jays repeatedly over the years. Another significant hire was scout Espy Guerrero, who made Toronto especially aggressive in pursuing Latin American players; it was Guerrero's intimacy with the sandlots of San Pedro de Macoris that brought the club, either directly or through deals with other teams, such Dominican stars as George Bell, Tony Fernandez, and Manny Lee.

Even before the team had played its first game, Toronto ranked among baseball's biggest marketing successes through T-shirts, caps, and other paraphernalia that attracted buyers throughout the United States and Canada. The main element of the team logo—a blue jay in profile—was conceived after some 30,000 fans had submitted entries in a Name the Team contest in the summer of 1976; among the rejected names were Dingbats, Blue Bats, and Maple Leafs. Although some members of the franchise objected to the tag of Blue Jays because of its past (if brief) association with wretched Philadelphia Phillies' teams, it carried the day fairly easily. More difficult to accept in some quarters was the introduction of the "balanced schedule." With the arrival of the Blue Jays and Mariners on the scene, each division had an odd number of clubs, meaning there would always be a swing team playing outside its own regional group; moreover, the need to accommodate thirteen adversaries for two home and two road series each created bizarre schedule situations in which rival contenders within a division might finish playing one another as soon as early August, lessening the impact of stretch drives in September.

In approaching the expansion draft, Bavasi and Gillick harbored few illusions about being able to stock the team with all-stars. Even the advent of free agency meant next to nothing where Toronto was concerned because many players were reluctant to play across the border and none of them were interested in paying Canada's higher taxes. Within these limitations, the Blue Jays ended up obtaining promising minor league performers like Bob Bailor (the very first pick), Jim Clancy, Pete Vukovich, and Ernie Whitt, along with wizened veterans like Rico Carty and Bill Singer.

Before he even left the Plaza Hotel site of the draft, Gillick completed his first significant deal by obtaining catcher Alan Ashby from Cleveland in exchange for pitcher Al Fitzmorris. A month later, he also sent Carty to the Indians, in return for outfielder John Lowenstein and catcher Rick Cerone. But Gil-

lick's most significant swap of all was one that he could not pull off because of Bavasi. Having agreed to trade Singer to the Yankees for a New York farmhand, Gillick was told that the veteran pitcher had to remain on the Blue Jays because he was on the cover of the team's media guide and it would have not looked good for the fledgling franchise if it got rid of its cover boy at the first opportunity. The minor leaguer whom the Blue Jays would have received from the Yankees was southpaw Ron Guidry.

Toronto hosted its first major league game at Exhibition Stadium on April 7, 1977, with 44,649 fans braving freezing temperatures and snow flurries to see the Blue Jays hammer the White Sox, 9–5. The hero of the day was first baseman Doug Ault, who hit two homers; outfielder Alvis Woods also entered the record book by becoming the eleventh major leaguer to hit a pinch-hit home run in his first at bat. When the fans weren't jumping up and down to keep warm, they were letting loose with the "We Want Beer!" chant that would be heard at Exhibition Stadium until city blue laws against drinking in public were rewritten in 1982; the beer ban prompted some residents to refer to the Blue Jays' ballpark as Prohibition Stadium.

Most of the season after opening day was downhill, with the club fulfilling expectations of finishing at the bottom of the division. The main respites from 107 losses were Bailor's .310 average (the highest by a regular on a first-year expansion team) and Roy Howell's club-record nine runs batted in against the Yankees in an early September game. Setting a pattern for some years to come, the pitching was ragged, with Jerry Garvin's 22 pickoffs the only impressive statistic.

The next two seasons were just as bad—and worse. While veterans like John Mayberry and Carty (who came and went three times in three years) were brought in to offer some immediate power lift, the organization generally preached patience while prospects matured in the farm system. But especially during the ebb season of 1979, there were increasing calls in the local press for some of the minor leaguers to do their developing in Toronto. That same year also brought out the resentment of many players toward Hartsfield, viewed as a petulant yes-man whose main task was to keep the team together until somebody else took over the next stage of development. According to reliever Tom Buskey, Hartsfield was totally ignorant about handling a pitching staff. Outfielder Rick Bosetti, the team's resident clown, got serious enough to complain that Hartsfield op-

The first player signed by Toronto was catcher Phil Roof, obtained from the White Sox before the expansion draft. Roof went to bat five times without a hit before being released.

erated under strict orders to spend his time with rookies and ignore everyone else. Catcher Ernie Whitt, who clashed with the manager during spring training in 1979, blamed Hartsfield for keeping him in the minor leagues just out of pique.

Bavasi was no more popular than Hartsfield in the clubhouse. The club president offended many when, following a disclosure that a woman ticket-taker at Exhibition Stadium had been fired for being seen getting into the car of a Toronto player, he cracked that "I certainly wouldn't want my daughter dating a Blue Jay." He didn't rise any higher in the esteem of the players with his periodic talks expounding on his "artichoke theory" of the team; i.e., that some of the players were hearts that would last on the club for some time, but that some others were just leaves that would be thrown out sooner rather than later.

In spite of its pitiful on-field performance in 1979, the club kept its fans interested with moves that epitomized the dice-tossed fortunes of an expansion team. On the positive side, a winter trade with the Indians brought over shortstop Alfredo Griffin, who wound up sharing Rookie of the Year honors with Minnesota's John Castino. On the other hand, ceding to pressures to accelerate the promotion of prospects, the Blue Jays called up righthander Phil Huffman after only a handful of games in the minors, and he went on to lead the league in losses (18) with an ERA of 5.77. Although the move paid off initially in publicity, the franchise made another mistake in its eager pursuit of infielder Danny Ainge. Ainge, then about to graduate from high school, had made it clear that he preferred going on to college basketball rather than professional baseball, but the Blue Jays made him a series of financial and schedule concessions that allowed him to do both. After three partial seasons adding up to 211 games and a .220 average, Ainge quit baseball to concentrate on professional basketball.

A source of more bizarre interest in 1979 was pitcher Mark Lemongello, obtained in a trade with the Astros. Arguably the hardest loser in the history of baseball, Lemongello had had a well-publicized record of crazed behavior (biting his own shoulder until it bled, pounding on his pitching hand) after losses in Houston. The Blue Jays got their first taste of it when the righthander dropped out of sight for almost a month after the trade, refusing to talk to Toronto officials and only issuing periodic bulletins through third parties that he would rather drive a truck than pitch in a foreign country. He eventually reported to the team in time for spring training, after

which the Blue Jays began to wonder why they had so avidly pursued his services. Lemongello went 1–9 with an ERA of 6.29, fired a ball at Hartsfield when he was removed from his last starting assignment, dropped down to the minors, and never returned to Toronto or any other big league team.

With Bobby Mattick taking over from Hartsfield and easing tensions in the clubhouse, the club showed relative improvement in 1980 by winning 14 more games than it had the previous year. Over and above the statistical improvement, Bavasi was able to point to the emerging roles played during the year by such prospects as pitchers Dave Stieb and Clancy, catcher Whitt, outfielder Lloyd Moseby, and second baseman Damaso Garcia, acquired in a Gillick raid on the Yankee farm system. On the other hand, the club suffered the loss of more home dates than most teams during the strike-shortened year of 1981, and the season produced little that was positive except for Stieb's record of 11–10. Almost as soon as the campaign was over, Bobby Cox came in to replace Mattick as manager and Bavasi resigned as general manager to make room for Gillick.

With another former Yankee farmhand Willie Upshaw installed at first base and slugger Jesse Barfield taking over in right field, the 1982 Blue Jays took on a much more competitive look. The offensive star of the year was Garcia, who batted .310, stole 54 bases, and only once went two straight games without a hit. Stieb was the workhorse of the league with 288 innings and 17 victories, while Clancy won 16. Cox's nimble use of platoon players and pinch hitters was attested to by the club's record-tying 71 pinch-hits.

In 1983, the Blue Jays made their first serious run for the division title, with Upshaw, Barfield, Moseby, Whitt, and designated hitter Cliff Johnson all hitting at least 17 homers and making Exhibition Stadium the launching pad of the league. Stieb again won 17, but a blister on his pitching hand cost him and the club several other important starts. The turning point of the season came on August 24th when, trailing the division-leading Orioles by only 1½ games, the Blue Jays blew a 3–1 edge in the ninth inning, but still had the consolation of entering extra innings with backup infielder Lenn Sakata pressed into service as the Baltimore catcher. After Johnson had hit a home run in the tenth inning to regain the lead for Toronto, three consecutive Blue Jays tagged Orioles' reliever Tippy Martinez for singles, all three took big leads off first base against the inexperienced Sakata, and all three were promptly picked off by Martinez. Sakata later hit a home run to win the game for Baltimore and crush Toronto's title hopes. In another game that month, the front office suffered a different kind of embarrassment when New York outfielder Dave Winfield was arrested for having killed a seagull with a warmup toss between innings. The charge of willful destruction of wildlife was eventually dropped.

Although the club finished with the same won-lost percentage in 1984 as it had the previous year, and even climbed a couple of notches up to second place, it was never really in the fight against the steamrolling Tigers. On the other hand, the season marked the blossoming of left fielder George Bell as the club's most reliable offensive force and vindicated still another Gillick deal with the Yankees when veteran Doyle Alexander won 17 games. Moreover, the franchise topped two million fans in a facility notorious for having large sections of the grandstand barely within television distance. It was also in 1984 that the fans started to overcome their earlier reputation as polite spectators as likely to applaud an opposition player's home run as one tagged by a Blue Jay. One of the first victims of the new ardor was reliever Dennis Lamp, a costly free agent who disillusioned expectations of a settled bullpen by picking up only one save after May, thereby earning choruses of catcalls whenever he entered a late-season contest.

No longer counting on Lamp as the stopper, Gillick spent the offseason acquiring Bill Caudill from the Mariners and Gary Lavelle from the Giants to shore up the relief corps. But it was a relatively more minor transaction with the Rangers for Tom Henke that proved decisive. The fireballing righthander, working up to his reputation as The Terminator of the AL, saved 13 games and won 3 others down the stretch to make the late-inning difference in Toronto's first division title. Altogether, Henke, Caudill, Lavelle, Lamp, and Jack Acker notched 30 wins and 47 saves; more comfortable with a setup role, Lamp bounced back with a record of 11 wins and no defeats. Among the starters, Alexander again had 17 wins, lefty Jimmy Key pitched in for 14, and Stieb backed his 14 victories with a league-leading 2.48 ERA. The offense was led by Bell and Barfield, who

combined for 45 homers; along with Moseby, the two righthand-hitting sluggers were hailed as baseball's best all-around outfield.

The team also showed some grit, as evidenced in a July game when backup catcher Buck Martinez broke his leg making an out at home, fired wildly to third in an attempt to nail a second runner, but then held his ground at the plate to take a throw from left field to make the second out anyway. The League Championship Series against Kansas City had a different ending, when the Blue Jays blew a 3–1 lead in games to go down to the Royals in seven games. The playoff loss marked the beginning of Toronto's reputation for being unable to win the big game.

The season was barely over when Cox tendered his resignation to take over as general manager of the Braves. Named to replace him was third base coach Jimy Williams, a central figure in what turned out to be more than three years of clubhouse turmoil. There were three main sources of trouble: Williams's growing impatience with Bell's defensive play, the manager's equal concerns with the born-again Christian movement on the club, and the gradually mutual isolation of black, white, and Latin players. Although Bell quickly established himself as one of the league's most potent offensive threats, Williams never accepted the left fielder's defensive shortcomings and indicated from the beginning of his tenure that he preferred using him as the designated hitter. This did not sit well with Bell, all the more so when fielding lapses prompted boos from the grandstand; according to the outfielder, the reaction had been caused primarily by the manager's public questioning of his abilities. The feud simmered for a couple of seasons with Bell remaining in the outfield, until Williams announced that he was going with rookies Sil Campusano and Rob Ducey defensively in 1988. That experiment ended rather quickly when neither Campusano nor Ducey got beyond spring training, but Bell carried the insult into the season with him, to the point that only an explosion in August and September brought him back up to creditable offensive numbers. When he challenged the front office at the end of the year to choose between him and Williams, the organization signed the manager to an extension.

Williams set off another round of clubhouse dissension when, in 1988, he ordered an end to chapel sessions on the road, charging that they were disrupting workout routines and creating resentment from players who preferred to leave religion outside the game; among those denouncing the decision were Barfield and shortstop Tony Fernandez. Once

> **A**s a member of the Blue Jays in 1984, Cliff Johnson collected his nineteenth career pinch-hit homer to establish a new major league record.

again, the front office backed the manager, this time to the extent of prohibiting Fernandez and Kelly Gruber from wearing team jackets while promoting a religious organization's fund-raising drive for hungry children. The controversy over religion overlapped even longer tensions among some of the team's black, white, and Latin members, with the combinations of Whitt-Clancy, Barfield-Moseby, and Bell-Fernandez often accusing one another of thinking more about clanning together than making a joint effort on the field. Still another source of discontent were charges from Stieb and Henke that the front office had ordered Williams to use them sparingly so they would not be able to meet incentive clauses for game appearances.

Under Williams, the club consolidated its reputation as a group of underachievers. Even though there were strong individual performances through the middle of the decade (Barfield leading the league in homers in 1986, Key winning the ERA title in 1987, and Bell emerging as MVP in 1987), the club as a whole continued to lack cohesion. The most devastating of all failures occurred in 1987, when the Blue Jays entered the final seven games of the season with an apparently comfortable lead over Detroit and then proceeded to lose all seven games, including a season-concluding series with the division-winning Tigers. Playing for all the marbles the final Sunday of the season, Key yielded only a home run to Larry Herndon, but that proved to be enough for Detroit southpaw Frank Tanana and a 1–0 loss.

Stieb added a footnote to the frustration of the period by entering the ninth inning of back-to-back turns in September 1988 with a no-hitter, getting the first two outs, and then surrendering hits. On August 4, 1989, the righthander went himself one better (or worse) by throwing a perfect game until the twenty-seventh batter, Roberto Kelly of the Yankees, lashed a double. In that same season, he added two more one-hitters in his exasperating quest. (He would eventually get his no-hitter, against Cleveland on September 2, 1990.)

On September 14, 1987, the Blue Jays set a single-game record by clouting ten homers in an 18–3 crushing of the Orioles. Leading the long-ball onslaught were Ernie Whitt with three and Rance Mulliniks and George Bell with two each. The other homers were hit by Fred McGriff, Rob Ducey, and Lloyd Moseby.

The 1989 season wasn't all frustration. On June 5th, the club moved to Skydome, a $572-million indoor facility that featured a nine-story-high scoreboard and a retractable roof. It also boasted a seating capacity of more than 50,000, enabling the franchise to reach three million fans even after losing some dates to Exhibition Stadium in April and May of 1989. By the early 1990s, the dome complex (including attached hotels, restaurants, and malls) had become one of Toronto's biggest tourist attractions, and getting a ticket to a game became as arduous as Stieb's getting the last out in a no-hitter. In 1990, the club set an all-time attendance record in baseball with 3.8 million fans, and in the next two years it topped the four-million mark.

There was success on the field in 1989, too, especially after Gillick changed his mind about the contract extension he had given to Williams and derricked the manager only thirty-six games into the schedule. With batting coach Cito Gaston named to the post on an interim basis, the general manager approached Yankees' owner George Steinbrenner for permission to talk to Lou Piniella, then an advisor to New York. By the time Steinbrenner decided that keeping Piniella was more important than exploring a possible trade for a Toronto prospect or two, Gaston had the Blue Jays on a winning streak, and he was given the job on a full-time basis. After going 12–24 under Williams, the team responded with a torrid 77–49 pace the rest of the year, finally edging Baltimore by two games.

Although most of the main players in the effort (Bell, Fernandez, Stieb, Key, Henke) were from the usual cast, there were some significant additions. The first was first baseman Fred McGriff, who followed up a 34-homer season in 1988 by banging out a league-leading 36 more and giving Gillick still another notch on his gun in cleaning out the Yankees' farm system. In August, responding to a Gaston request for a leadership figure with pennant-winning experience, the front office acquired outfielder Mookie Wilson from the Mets and, a day later, purchased pinch hitter Lee Mazzilli on waivers from the same team. Both New York veterans proved invaluable in the dugout and in the clubhouse as much as on the field, and were often referred to by the joint nickname of Mazzookie. Wilson, especially, was regarded as so crucial to the club's success that he made the cover of the Canadian weekly *MacLean's* before the season was over. But once again the LCS turned into a fiasco, with Rickey Henderson running, hitting, and hitting with power to lead Oakland over the Jays in five games.

The 1990s began with the club reeling off at least 85 victories for the eighth year in a row, but otherwise playing too inconsistently to overtake the Red Sox, even though the race wasn't decided until the last day of the season. Key was lost to the team for a lengthy period with a leg injury, and neither John Cerutti nor Todd Stottlemyre could compensate for his absence. The plusses were again McGriff (35 homers), Stieb (18 wins, 2.93 ERA), Henke (32 saves, 2.17 ERA), and third baseman Gruber, who contributed a career year of 31 homers and 118 RBIs.

Although the Blue Jays had earned praise in the 1980s for a corps of stable regulars, the club's failure to get into a World Series had turned the same plaudits to criticism by the new decade, with the general manager branded as Stand Pat Gillick for his disinclination to complete any major transactions. Gillick changed that before the 1991 season, first by letting Bell go to the Cubs as a free agent, then by acquiring center fielder Devon White from the Angels, and, especially, by working a blockbuster trade with the Padres that sent McGriff and Fernandez to San Diego in return for second baseman Roberto Alomar and outfielder Joe Carter. The benefits were twofold: an improved clubhouse with the departure of Bell and Fernandez and the arrival of Carter, and another division title in good part because of the offensive trio of White, Alomar, and Carter at the top of the lineup.

Except for Henke (who once again saved 32 games) and the tireless short and long relief of Duane Ward, the pitching remained questionable through most of the season, with Stottlemyre, rookie Juan Guzman, and Tom Candiotti trying to take up the slack for the briefly injured Key and the seriously ailing Stieb. Even Gaston missed several weeks with back maladies, and had to turn the reins of the club over to coach Gene Tenace. Tenace's fill-in tenure revived some of the clubhouse problems from Williams's days, but Gaston returned in time to soothe tempers and lead the club through still another miserable LCS, this time against Minnesota.

After the 1991 season, Gillick went in search of free agents who might lift the club into its first postseason competition with the NL. He found them in 1991 Twins' World Series hero Jack Morris and veteran outfielder Dave Winfield. Although the Brewers and Orioles took shots at the division lead during the 1992 season, it was really a question of whether the Blue Jays would lose it—and they didn't. Morris more than lived up to his billing with 21 wins, while Guzman overcame some arm problems to win 16 and post an ERA of 2.64. For the stretch run, Gillick picked up NL strikeout king David Cone from the Mets in exchange for two prospects, and the right-hander filled the gap left by the still ailing Key and Stieb. Equally important was the bullpen, where Henke saved another 34 and Ward did double duty as a setup man and occasional closer.

Offensively, the biggest numbers in 1992 came from Carter's 34 homers and 119 RBIs, but Winfield wasn't too far behind with 26 round-trippers and 106 RBIs. It was the first time that a big leaguer over 40 knocked in 100 runs. In addition to his power hitting, Winfield proved indispensable in stirring up Toronto fans to show more enthusiasm for the team and in keeping order in the clubhouse.

For once, the LCS had a happy ending for the Blue Jays, with Alomar's clutch hitting leading the way in a five-game victory over the Athletics. In the World Series against Atlanta, the club ignored some artificially pumped up hoopla about a nationlistic struggle between the U.S. and Canada, gaining its first world championship in six games. Although the Toronto effort was spread around fairly evenly among starters, relievers, and hitters, catcher Pat Borders took MVP honors for his offensive and defensive brilliance.

Borders's performance in the World Series defused expectations that he would be exposed in the November expansion draft for stocking Colorado and Florida; at that, he was one of the few Blue Jays' regulars not to depart during the offseason. In a turnover normally associated with losing teams, the club bade farewell to free agents Stieb (White Sox), Key (Yankees), Cone (Royals), Henke (Rangers), regular left fielder Candy Maldonado (Cubs), regular shortstop Lee (Rangers), and even Winfield (Twins), and came perilously close to losing Carter to Kansas City, as well. Another transaction sent Gruber to the Angels for infielder Luis Sojo. To fill some of the holes, Gillick signed free agents Paul Molitor, Dave Stewart, and Dick Schofield. In the expansion draft, the organization's main loss was minor league outfielder Nigel Wilson, Florida's very first pick.

TORONTO BLUE JAYS
Annual Standings and Managers

Year	Position	W	L	Pct.	GB	Managers
1977	Seventh	54	107	.335	45½	Roy Hartsfield

1978	Seventh	59	102	.366	40	Roy Hartsfield
1979	Seventh	53	109	.327	50½	Roy Hartsfield
1980	Seventh	67	95	.414	36	Bobby Mattick
1981	Seventh	16	42	.276	19	Bobby Mattick
	Seventh	21	27	.438	7½	Bobby Mattick
1982	Sixth*	78	84	.481	17	Bobby Cox
1983	Fourth	89	73	.549	9	Bobby Cox
1984	Second	89	73	.549	15	Bobby Cox
1985	First	99	62	.615	+2	Bobby Cox
1986	Fourth	86	76	.531	9½	Jimy Williams
1987	Second	96	66	.593	2	Jimy Williams
1988	Third*	87	75	.537	2	Jimy Williams
1989	First	89	73	.549	+2	Jimy Williams, Cito Gaston
1990	Second	86	76	.531	2	Cito Gaston
1991	First	91	71	.562	+7	Cito Gaston
1992	First	96	66	.593	+4	Cito Gaston

* Tie

Postseason Play

LCS	3–4 versus Kansas City	1985	WS	4–2 versus Atlanta	1992
	1–4 versus Oakland	1989			
	1–4 versus Minnesota	1991			
	4–1 versus Oakland	1992			

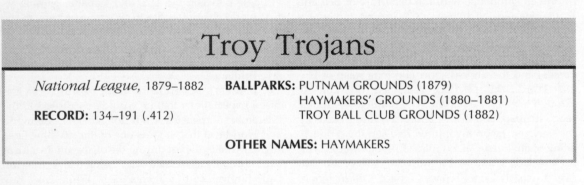

Troy Trojans

National League, 1879–1882   **BALLPARKS:** PUTNAM GROUNDS (1879)
                                 HAYMAKERS' GROUNDS (1880–1881)
RECORD: 134–191 (.412)   TROY BALL CLUB GROUNDS (1882)

OTHER NAMES: HAYMAKERS

Both the surprising entry of Troy into the National League and its abrupt departure four years later were components of larger schemes by the NL to fend off potential rival organizations.

In 1878, the Haymakers of Lansingburg (a suburb of Troy) were one of the ten members of the New York State Association, a peculiar organization that offered no championship and that existed mainly to provide the solace of unity against NL bullying. Since the New York State Association lacked a competitive purpose, five of its members were also part of the parallel International Association. To break the backs of both organizations, the NL admitted three clubs that belonged to both—Buffalo, Syracuse, and Troy—for its 1879 season. Troy (57,000) and Syracuse (50,000) had to be voted into the NL unani-

mously, a requirement for cities with populations under 75,000.

The club was rechristened the Trojans (although it never shook its pre-NL name) and began its first season with a lineup drawn entirely from International Association teams. Toward the end of the season, Bob Ferguson joined the club from Chicago, first to play third base and then to take over from Horace Phillips as manager, a position he held for the rest of the franchise's life.

The 1879 Trojans were horrible. Rookie Dan Brouthers, a future Hall of Famer, led them in batting with a .274 average. George Washington Bradley led the league with 40 losses. Crowds of 400 were the average. The club lost money steadily.

One reason Troy lost so much money was that

under the terms of its admission to the NL, it had been forced to forsake lucrative exhibition games with Albany, its trans-Hudson River rival. Albany had made a perfunctory application to join the NL as well, but the NL would not countenance a nine-team league, insisting that the New York capital would have to be content with twenty-five-cent exhibitions against NL teams on their way to and from Troy. This offered the advantage of exposing Albany fans to NL teams without exposing the club to the league's onerous travel expenses and fifty-cent admissions. Troy objected to the arrangement on the grounds that, even though the two clubs' parks were separated by eight miles, the cities themselves were only 4.75 miles apart, making any exhibition game in Albany a violation of the Trojans' five-mile territorial rights. The rule also banned exhibitions between Troy and Albany.

The Troy directors, facing a somewhat desperate situation, reorganized in late July. President Gardner Earl, secretary C. R. DeForest, and the new board assumed a more aggressive posture toward the league and its rules. In October, the directors voted not to be a part of any circuit that required a fifty-cent admission, but the vote was little more than a gesture. Overmatched, Troy had to settle for a change in the territorial limit so it could resume its rivalry with Albany.

So important were the exhibitions that, early in 1880, the Trojans risked expulsion from the NL to play one of them. On Saturday, May 15th, the rained-out final game of a three-game series with Providence was rescheduled for Monday the 17th, but the Trojans had already scheduled an exhibition with Albany that day and chose to meet the latter commitment rather than stay in Rhode Island. The Grays claimed a forfeit and their president, Henry Root, wanted Troy expelled from the league for its infraction, but the NL board of directors found a mere "technical violation" because, as Troy vice-president E. L. Fursman observed, there had been no scheduled game on May 17th. The Board also ruled that any similar transgressions in the future would result in expulsion.

Boston and Providence had been so sure that the vote would go against Troy that both clubs had begun negotiations with some of the Trojan players. Boston wanted shortstop Ed Laskin, first baseman Ed Cogswell, catcher Bill Holbert, and pitcher Mickey Welch. Boston's scouting reports were off the mark: Roger Connor, Buck Ewing, and Tim Keefe, all of whom went on to Hall of Fame careers with Welch on the New York Giants, were also on the 1880 Trojans.

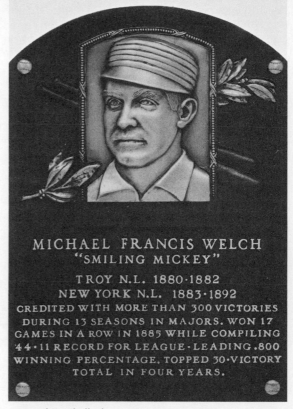

National Baseball Library, Cooperstown, NY

Despite the presence of such future luminaries, the Trojans never rose above fourth place. In 1881, new club president A. L. Hotchkin moved Troy's home games to Haymakers' Grounds on Center Island, where the Mohawk River joins the Hudson. It was there that, on September 27, 1881, the Trojans set an all-time-low major league attendance record of twelve (tied in 1885 by Buffalo) in a rain-soaked game against Chicago.

Earlier in 1881, the directors had discussed disposing of the franchise to Pittsburgh. They also tried playing some home games at Riverside Park in Albany as early as 1880. (In one of those games in Albany, on September 10, 1881, first baseman Roger Connor hit the first major league grand slam against Worcester.)

In 1882, under another new president, Francis N. Mann, the Trojans moved again, this time to the inappropriately named Troy Ball Club Grounds, which was actually in the Albany County community of Watervliet on the west bank of the Hudson. By this time, the club's finances were so poor that the rest of the league had to subsidize the operation.

With the successful advent of the AA, the NL realized that it could no longer afford to prop up its small-city teams. The six-city AA had a combined population of more than 2.3 million (more than twice as much as the eight NL cities) and was about to expand into New York. On December 6, 1881, at its annual meeting, the NL shoved Troy and Worcester out of the league. Connor, Ewing, Welch, Keefe, and outfielder Pete Gillespie were gobbled up by the New York franchise. Troy's consolation was honorary NL membership.

TROY TROJANS

Annual Standings and Managers

Year	Position	W	L	Pct.	GB	Managers
1879	Eighth	19	56	.253	35½	Horace Phillips, Bob Ferguson
1880	Fourth	41	42	.494	25½	Bob Ferguson
1881	Fifth	39	45	.464	17	Bob Ferguson
1882	Seventh	35	48	.422	19½	Bob Ferguson

Washington Nationals

American Association, 1884   **BALLPARK:** ATHLETIC PARK

RECORD: 12–51 (.190)

The Nationals were the product of the American Association's expansion to fight the Union Association. The theory was that a twelve-team league would deprive the Unions of 50 percent more players than an eight-team league.

However valid the theory, its application had unintended consequences, not least the inadequate funding of the new teams. Washington was one of the franchises with shaky backing. The other association members, suspecting as much as early as the December, 1883 meeting when the club was admitted, sought assurances of financial security. Club president L. Moxley, the city billposter, enthusiastically provided the assurances, but little else.

A second unintended consequence was that a twelve-team league dramatically increased expenses. The 1884 schedule called for 110 games, twelve more than in 1883; that meant six more dates on the road with attendant travel costs. Thus, while NL teams traveled between 5,500 and 7,500 miles to complete their 112-game, eight-team schedule in 1884, AA clubs had to cover between 6,200 and 8,500 miles, with four teams topping 8,000 miles.

The third consequence of expansion—deterioration of the quality of play in 1884—prevented the team from offering prospective fans attractive entertainment. Aside from the need to stock four new clubs, playing ranks were thinned out further by UA raids. In the case of Washington, this meant that shortstop Frank Fennelly led the offense with a soft .292 and four regulars hit under .200. The defense was the worst in the association; on May 10th, in his only major league game, catcher Alex Gardner showed how bad it could get, allowing 12 passed balls in a seven-inning game.

In their sporty red, white, and blue uniforms, the Washingtons (as they were popularly known) were managed by Holly Hollingshead, who needed all his local popularity after the team lost 23 of its first 28 games. On August 1st, with only 12 wins in 63 games, Hollingshead was fired; on the same day, Moxley was reported seriously ill. Two days later, the Washingtons were disbanded. Fennelly was sold to Cincinnati for $600. The UA Washington Nationals picked up three of the players, and three more found a home with the Richmond Virginias, which took Washington's place in the AA. In an act of magnanimity, the Nationals played an intra-squad benefit game and distributed the proceeds among their vanquished rivals.

WASHINGTON NATIONALS

Annual Standings and Manager

Year	Position	W	L	Pct.	GB	Manager
1884	Partial Season	12	51	.190	—	Holly Hollingshead

Washington Nationals

Union Association, 1884   **BALLPARK:** CAPITOL GROUNDS

RECORD: 47–65 (.420)

The Nationals were one of only two Union Association teams to turn a profit. The surplus, perhaps as much as $7,000, was mainly the result of the fact that the Nationals, unlike the other seven clubs that started the season in Henry Lucas' league, were the established team in their city.

Begun in 1883 as an independent squad, the team name dated to the 1873 Nationals of the National Association. Their owner, grain and feed merchant Robert C. Hewett, had an even longer association with Washington baseball, going back to the NA Washington Olympics in 1871. Hewett's original intention in 1884 had been to join the more established American Association, but, while he was trying to raise additional capital, the upstart club of L. Moxley grabbed that franchise and Hewett had to settle for the UA.

Manager Mike Scanlon, owner of a prominent D.C. pool hall and an intimate of presidents Andrew Johnson and Ulysses Grant, had built the first enclosed baseball park in Washington in 1870; he was also an expert on the rules of baseball. But none of this was much help in juggling fifty-three players, most of whom were local amateurs. Seventeen appeared in only one game; twenty-two of them never played major league ball before or after their tenure with the Nationals. The team lost 18 more games than it won and finished sixth in the convoluted, franchise-shuffling UA.

Although the Unions did not survive beyond one season, the Nationals did, surfacing in the Eastern League in 1885 and going on to play four years in the NL after that.

WASHINGTON NATIONALS

Annual Standings and Manager

Year	Position	W	L	Pct.	GB	Manager
1884	Sixth	47	65	.420	46½	Mike Scanlon

Washington Senators

National League, 1886–1889	**BALLPARK:** SWAMPOODLE GROUNDS
RECORD: 163–337 (.326)	**OTHER NAMES:** STATESMEN

The Washington club that entered the National League just in time for the 1886 season was the same organization that had acquitted itself so well, at least financially, in the Union Association in 1884. After the collapse of the Unions, club president Robert Hewett had taken the club into the Eastern League where it won a pennant in 1885 with a record of 72 wins and 24 losses. The franchise's return to the majors was aided no little by Hewett's long association with NL President Nick Young, who plumped for Washington to fill one of the vacancies in the league left by the departure of Buffalo and Providence in 1885.

The nucleus of the Washington team came from the 1885 Eastern League franchise and from Providence. Paul Hines, one of five ex-Grays, batted .312, but four regulars hit below .200 and no one besides Hines was over .240. Mike Scanlon, who had been managing Washington teams since the 1870s, was replaced by John Gaffney in late August, and the squad finished last, an astounding 60 games out of first place. The only bright spot in the season was the acquisition of catcher Connie Mack, one of five players purchased from Hartford of the Eastern League by team secretary Walter Hewett, the owner's son. Mack batted .361 in nineteen games and went on to become one of the NL's best defensive receivers.

At first, Hewett was no harsher than most nineteenth-century owners. In 1886, he fined Hines, Cannonball Crane, and Jimmy Knowles $100 each for nonchalance on the field. It cost pitcher Frank Gilmore an equal amount for taking an unauthorized day off for what he lyingly called his wedding day. The following year, Hewett released pitcher Dupee Shaw for drinking himself out of shape. But none of this was adequate preparation for the draconian rules announced publicly in 1887. Total abstinence was the order of the day. Offenses met with incremental fines: $25 for first offenders; $50 for recidivists; and $100 for three-time losers. Players found out of condition for any reason would be suspended without pay.

The rules accomplished nothing. Under managers Walter Hewett and then Ted Sullivan, the Senators, the club's new name in 1888, won two more games than the year before, but with the schedule expanded from 126 games to 140, they also lost ten more and fell back into the cellar, largely because of a miniscule .208 team batting average.

When president Hewett died on September 1st, Walter assumed ownership of the club and went after players more aggressively. In November, at a time when sales still required player consent, he "bought" the contract of John Montgomery Ward from the Giants for $12,000. Then in Honolulu on Albert Spalding's round-the-world tour, the shortstop, who also served as president of the Players Brotherhood, was unwilling to accept the concept of being sold like property. Ward was also opposed to leaving New York because his wife, Helen Dauvray, was a Broadway star. Not even Hewett's offer of a $6,000 salary could get him to change his mind.

The new owner chose first baseman John Morrill as the new manager in 1889, replaced him with shortstop Art Irwin before the season was half over, and rode out the Senators' second consecutive last-place finish. At season's end, eleven Washington players—including Mack, Dummy Hoy, Sam Wise, Ed Beecher, Art Irwin (the manager), and pitchers Alex Ferson (17–7) and George Haddock (11–9)—jumped to the Buffalo club in the Players League. The NL, preparing for the impending battle with the PL, ousted Washington from the league and assigned its place to the Cincinnati Reds.

WASHINGTON SENATORS

Annual Standings and Managers

Year	Position	W	L	Pct.	GB	Managers
1886	Eighth	28	92	.233	60	Mike Scanlon, John Gaffney
1887	Seventh	46	76	.377	32	John Gaffney

1888	Eighth	48	86	.358	37½	Walter Hewett, Ted Sullivan
1889	Eighth	41	83	.331	41	John Morrill, Art Irwin

Washington Statesmen

American Association, 1891   **BALLPARK:** BOUNDARY FIELD
                                GENTLEMEN'S DRIVING PARK
RECORD: 43–92 (.319)

As part of the settlement of the Players League war, Washington, which had been dropped by the NL in 1889, was readmitted to the American Association after a seven-year hiatus. With more than 230,000 people, the capital was then the fourteenth largest city in the country and, despite its dismal major league track record, a predictable market choice.

Not as predictable was the assignment of the franchise to Harrison Bennett, one of the organizers of the successful Union Association Nationals. Bennett, finding himself a part of the league that he had run out of town in 1884, capitalized his venture with the help of prominent businessmen. (One of them was Walter Hewett, whose franchise had been appropriated by the NL in 1889.) Deciding that the Nationals needed a brand new home, Bennett had 125 oak trees felled at Seventh Avenue and Florida Avenue and the stump holes filled to make an infield. The resulting Boundary Field, which held 4,000, was in the same location as Griffith Stadium, home of the American League Senators.

The team itself was a reprise of Washington seasons past. The first manager was Sam Trott, who had played with the Washington entry in the minor league National Base-Ball Association in 1880, while outfielders Paul Hines and Ed Beecher had played for the city's earlier NL entry. Equally familiar was the National's last-place finish, which came despite more than three dozen players being shuttled in and out of the lineup and four managers taking turns at calling the shots.

In December, the NL announced that it would expand to twelve teams by absorbing four AA clubs, including Washington, but without Bennett. The franchise went to George and J. Earl Wagner, who allowed the association to buy their Philadelphia club for $56,000, then paid Bennett and his shareholders $16,000 for the District of Columbia franchise.

WASHINGTON STATESMEN

Annual Standings and Managers

Year	Position	W	L	Pct.	GB	Managers
1891	Eighth	43	92	.319	50	Sam Trott, Pop Snyder, Dan Shannon, Sandy Griffin

Washington Senators

National League, 1892–99   **BALLPARK:** BOUNDARY FIELD
                              GENTLEMEN'S DRIVING PARK
RECORD: 410–697 (.370)

If there were ever a contest for the most rapacious owners in baseball history, the Wagner brothers, who controlled the last National League version of the Senators for all eight years of their existence, would certainly be finalists. J. Earl and George Wagner were fast-talking, money-hungry, hit-and-run entrepreneurs who had built up their bankroll on a meat-packing business in Philadelphia. The difference between them and later-day abusive self-promoters like Charlie Finley and George Steinbrenner is that Finley and Steinbrenner showed an interest in winning games.

The Senators were not the Wagners' first baseball venture: They had also operated Players League (1890) and American Association (1891) franchises in their home city and had walked away from each with substantial buyouts. The second buyout (for $56,000) came from the NL when its owners decided to form a twelve-team monopoly by paying off several AA franchises and absorbing four others. The Wagners reinvested a piece of their Philadelphia profits in the Senators, one of the four clubs absorbed into the NL; they paid $16,000, about half of what the franchise was worth. With George maintaining a base in Philadelphia and coming to Washington at irregular intervals (for the most part to provoke trouble) and Earl running the club (first as vice-president and secretary, then as president), the brothers sought every available method to turn a profit while doing nothing to prevent the Senators from languishing in the lower regions of the expanded league.

Early in their first season in Washington, Earl fired manager Billy Barnie for "talking back" to brother George; Barnie's transgression had been refusing to resign. In August, they fired Barnie's successor, Art Irwin, claiming that he was unpopular with the fans. Later that year, George ordered Danny Richardson, Irwin's successor, to pull the team off the field in the middle of a game in St. Louis because Chris Von der Ahe, the St. Louis owner, had neglected to include $300 he owed George in the Washington share of the gate; Wagner relented only when Richardson reminded him that such a move would result in a forfeit and that forfeits carried an automatic $1,000 fine.

In February 1893, the brothers traded second baseman-manager Richardson to Brooklyn for third baseman Bill Joyce and $2,000; Joyce, who had earned $2,800 with Brooklyn, refused to sign for $1,800 and sat out the 1893 season. Frank Killen, the Senators' best pitcher (29–26), also refused to sign for $1,800 and was traded to Pittsburgh for catcher Duke Farrell; after Killen beat the Senators for the third time in 1893, George Wagner's only response to criticism of the deal was an announcement that he was getting married. In June, Willie Wagner, a third brother who was serving as team secretary, an-

nounced the release of pitcher Cy Duryea, but Earl overruled him saying he had no authority to release players. In late July, after the Senators had drawn a crowd of 15,000 in Philadelphia, the Wagners, figuring that the visitors' share of a huge crowd was more than the home share of a modest one, moved three home games against the Phillies to Philadelphia and three against the Spiders to Cleveland; the NL let them get away with it but created a rule calling for a $1,000 fine for any future violation. At the end of the season, the brothers shipped Farrell and pitcher Jouett Meekin to the Giants for $7,500; Farrell hit .284 for the Giants in 1894 and Meekin led the league with 36 wins.

Manager-outfielder Jim O'Rourke survived a last-place finish in 1893 and retired. His successor, Gus Schmelz, brought the Senators home eleventh in 1894. Nominally still the Washington pilot, Schmelz spent the early part of the 1895 season running The Texas Show, a Wagner-backed wild west traveling extravaganza. In Schmelz's absence, captain-third baseman Joyce directed the team. Later that summer, after Joyce had been criticized in the press for his inability to handle the players, the Wagners traded him to the Giants for none other than Farrell. When Joyce went on to bat .333 and lead the NL in home runs with 14, the press lambasted the Wagners; Earl responded with a lengthy statement detailing alleged Joyce shortcomings (his lack of leadership, his unwillingness to bunt, his unpopularity with the fans, his suspicious nature) that had made him expendable. Earl also claimed to have offered $5,000 to Baltimore for John McGraw as a replacement for Joyce at third and, for good measure, $2,500 to the Giants for Amos Rusie; both offers were shams. What Earl did do, on the other hand, was deal shortstop Gene DeMontreville to Baltimore. Later, he admitted convincing the official scorer to add base hits to DeMontreville's record to increase his worth.

Schmelz was fired early in June 1897 and, when his successor Tom Brown brought the Senators into a tie for sixth place, their best finish, the Wagners gave him a bonus and a new contract; Brown was fired on June 6, sixteen games into the 1898 season. The Wagners chose first baseman Jack Doyle as Brown's suc-

> **D**uke Farrell still holds the major league record for throwing out the most runners in a game. On May 11, 1897, he gunned down 8 Orioles; nonetheless, the Orioles won the game.

cessor, then, a week later, announced that the pilot was taking two weeks off because of illness. Less than two weeks after that, Doyle was fired and then sold to the Giants for $2,000. The next victim was Deacon McGuire; ten days after his appointment, Earl announced that he himself would be the co-manager and McGuire was soon gone. The next manager, Irwin, was said to have bought into the club, but all subsequent player deals were made by the Wagners, so there was little evidence that the transaction ever took place.

Such a history of contradiction, hyperbole, double-dealing, profiteering, and downright lying did little to endear the Wagners to Washington fans. The brothers couldn't have cared less. By 1899, they had pocketed a considerable sum from their player sales, and were known to be exploring further deals. But the NL finally had enough: At their December meeting, league owners declined to reelect Earl Wagner to their board of directors. A month later, they voted to revert to an eight-team league by eliminating Baltimore, Cleveland, Louisville, and Washington. True to form, Earl denied the inevitable, first claiming that the Senators would be around for a long time, then asserting that Washington would be a part of a new ten-team league, a possibility never even considered in the NL's deliberation.

Wagner's actions belied his bravado, however,

When Buck Freeman hit 25 home runs to establish a new major league record, his celebrity permitted him to become the first ballplayer to endorse non-sports merchandise. Freeman's picture appeared in newspaper ads for Squinksquillet's suspenders.

because he was already discussing terms for the inevitable buyout. Offered $25,000, he demanded double that figure, pointing out that he could get $45,000 for his five best players—Bill Dinneen, Buck Freeman, Dan McGann, and pitchers Win Mercer and Gus Weyhing. He set about doing just that, selling Freeman and Dinneen to Boston for $7,500. Then when Boston owner Arthur Soden insisted that Wagner deliver players with signed contracts for the 1900 season, Wagner abandoned his charade about remaining in the league and signed Freeman to a $2,000 contract not with Washington but with Boston.

On March 9th, the Wagners gave up their franchise for $46,500, less the $7,500 Boston had paid for Dinneen and Freeman. The NL assumed responsibility for the disposition of all players still under obligation to Washington. The upshot was that the Wagners left town $230,000 richer than they had arrived eight years earlier.

WASHINGTON SENATORS

Annual Standings and Managers

Year	Position	W	L	Pct.	GB	Managers
1892	Seventh	35	41	.461	18	Billy Barnie, Art Irwin
	Twelfth	23	52	.307	29½	Art Irwin, Danny Richardson
1893	Twelfth	40	89	.310	46	Jim O'Rourke
1894	Eleventh	45	87	.341	46	Gus Schmelz
1895	Tenth	43	85	.336	43	Gus Schmelz
1896	Ninth	58	73	.443	33	Gus Schmelz
1897	Seventh	61	71	.462	32	Gus Schmelz, Tom Brown
1898	Eleventh	51	101	.336	52½	Tom Brown, Jack Doyle, Deacon McGuire, Art Irwin
1899	Eleventh	54	98	.355	49	Art Irwin

Washington Senators

American League, 1901–1960	**BALLPARKS:** AMERICAN LEAGUE PARK (1901–1910) GRIFFITH STADIUM (1911–1960)
RECORD: 4223–4864 (.465)	**OTHER NAMES:** NATIONALS

It was vaudevillians in the early part of the century who popularized the taunt that Washington was first in war, first in peace, and last in the American League. They had a point, but it didn't always hold true. In fact, the team's three pennants were two more than the St. Louis Browns ever won and are just as many as the Cleveland Indians have won despite on additional thirty-two years in the league. The Senators also had in Walter Johnson the greatest pitcher in AL history and in Clark Griffith one of the major reasons the league ever had a last place to call its own.

Long before he owned Washington, Griffith had a seminal influence on the franchise insofar as it was he, Ban Johnson, and Charlie Comiskey who turned the then-minor American League into a major league circuit. It was also Griffith who, as a representative of the Ball Players Protective Association, got first word of the National League's refusal to incorporate AL franchises into the senior circuit and who was decisive in luring slews of fellow NLers over to the fledgling enterprise. While Griffith himself took over the White Sox as a playing manager, Johnson assigned the franchise in the nation's capital to Jimmy Manning, owner and manager of the Kansas City team in the minor American League. Although Detroit hotel owner Fred Postal was announced as the club's first owner-president, it emerged subsequently that Johnson himself held a majority 51 percent of the organization's stock.

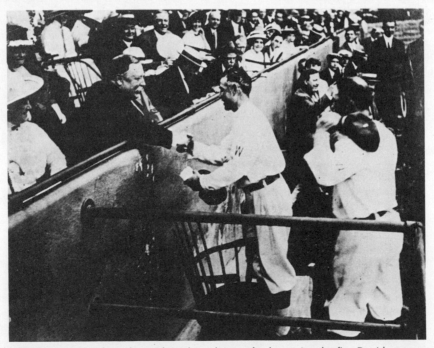

William Howard Taft confers with Walter Johnson after becoming the first President to throw out the ball on Opening Day, on April 14, 1910. Johnson shut out Philadelphia, 3–0. *National Baseball Library, Cooperstown, NY*

With its roster heavy with Manning's Kansas City players, the Senators got off to a flying start by beating Connie Mack's Athletics twice in Philadelphia, then opening at home on April 16, 1901 and, before an overflow crowd of 9,772, defeating John McGraw's Orioles, 5–2. Thereafter, however, the inaugural season was an exercise in mediocrity, with the Senators winding up in sixth place, more than 20 games behind Griffith's flag-winning White Sox. It was not until Griffith donned a Washington uniform in 1912 that the club rose any higher in the standings.

The first episode of organizational grief occurred after the 1901 season, when Manning announced that he couldn't continue with Johnson's tight-fisted money policies where procuring new players was concerned, and quit; he was replaced by Tom Loftus. In one of his first moves, Loftus, suddenly finding funds that had not been available to Manning, waved big contracts at several members of the NL Phillies and came away with four players, most conspicuously Ed Delahanty. Delahanty more than justified his high salary for the period ($4,000 a year) by capturing the AL batting title. Otherwise, there was not much good news, with the club once again finishing sixth and the year's attendance of 188,158 about half of that totaled in 1901.

Against a background of rumors that he was about to shift the franchise to Pittsburgh, Johnson reached a peace agreement with the NL that, among other things, provided for a New York franchise to displace the one in Baltimore, in exchange for which the AL would not go near the Steel City. The evaporation of the Baltimore organization immediately eased Washington's market problems.

Even with his agreement with the NL, Johnson had problems in Washington. The first was the tragic death of Delahanty in July of 1903 in circumstances never fully explained. All that was officially established was that the apparently drunk outfielder got into a fight with a train conductor near the Ontario border and was left to fend for himself near the International Bridge; whether he fell, jumped, or was

The first public address announcer at a baseball stadium was E. Lawrence Phillips, who used a megaphone to relay lineups at American League Park in 1902.

pushed into the Niagara River, his lifeless body was washed ashore a few days later. A few weeks after that, Loftus took up Manning's refrain about not having enough money to pursue decent players, blaming it all on Postal. When Postal denounced his untenable position between the manager and Johnson, it amounted to the first public confirmation that the league president was also the behind-the-scenes owner of the franchise. Johnson sought to patch over the rift by buying out Postal, but then he too got into a spat with Loftus and ended up firing the manager with the justification that "he failed to please the Washington people." Subsequent editorial criticism persuaded Johnson that he wasn't too pleasing, either, and in March 1904 he sold his controlling interest in the team to a group of Washington businessmen put together by sportswriter-turned-promoter William Dwyer. The syndicate's chief financial backer was Thomas Noyes, a member of the publishing family that operated Washington's *Evening Star*. Wilton Lambert, the team's attorney from its first year, took over as president, while Dwyer himself assumed decision-making powers as vice-president and business manager.

Dwyer's first act was to get rid of Loftus. The move was aimed at clearing the manager's post for Patsy Donovan, but when Donovan got bogged down in a dispute over his existing contract with the St. Louis Cardinals, veteran catcher Malachi Kittredge was handed the reins to open the season. It turned out to be a starcrossed choice, with Kittredge racking up one of the all-time records for managerial failure by guiding the club to only one win in seventeen tries. Not that Donovan fared much better with what turned out to be the worst team in franchise history: From the day that the outfielder settled his dispute with the Cardinals and entered the Washington dugout, the club won 37 and lost 97. Dwyer wasn't around for most of the 113 losses. Once Donovan's arrival had convinced him that the problem was the team rather than Kittredge, he abandoned his brief career as a big league administrator.

The following winter, Noyes also ousted Lambert as president, holding onto the post for the next eight years. With the *Evening Star*'s publisher as their

When he took over the Senators in 1902, Tom Loftus became the only man to manage in four different major leagues. Before Washington, Loftus had piloted Milwaukee in the Union Association, Cleveland in the American Association, and Cleveland, Cincinnati, and Chicago in the National League.

chief executive and Scott Bone, managing editor of the Washington *Post*, buying in as a substantial stock-holder, the Senators didn't get much better on the field, but they suddenly weren't quite so bad in the local newspapers.

With first baseman Jake Stahl taking over as manager and Noyes ordering a name change from Senators to Nationals, the club teetered along to a couple of seventh-place finishes in 1905 and 1906. Further tragedy struck before the 1906 season when Joe Cassidy, heralded as one of the best defensive shortstops in the league after taking over the position at the age of 21, died of typhoid fever.

The next manager was Joe Cantillon, a former umpire who had been more skilled in starting fights than resolving them. As a manager, Cantillon's three-year tenure came down to a single order that he gave backup catcher Cliff Blankenship in the early part of the 1907 season: Out of action with a broken finger, Blankenship was told to go to Kansas and Idaho to scout a couple of players Cantillon had heard were worth signing. In Wichita the receiver signed out-fielder Clyde Milan, in Weiser he inked Walter Johnson.

The lefthand-hitting Milan played his entire six-teen years in the majors with the Senators, becoming one of the best slap hitters and base stealers of his era. A lifetime .285 batter, he led the league in steals twice and swiped a minimum of 34 bases seven years in a row between 1910 and 1916. Another career-long Senator (for twenty-one seasons), the righthander Johnson probably has more claims than anyone to being considered the single greatest pitcher in base-ball history. Although Cy Young won more games, Johnson's 416 victories (the most in the AL) all came for a team that called the second division home and that didn't win a pennant until he was 37 years old. Despite that kind of support, he won more than 30 games twice, had ten straight seasons of 20 wins or more, and led the AL in wins six times, in ERA five times, and in strikeouts twelve times. Until Nolan Ryan and Steve Carlton passed him in the 1980s, he led the major leagues with 3,508 strikeouts, accom-plishing them almost exclusively with a side-armed fastball; he didn't develop a curve until he was well

One of Walter Johnson's greatest pitching feats was throwing three shutouts in four days against the Yankees in September 1908.

over 30 years old. His single greatest year was 1913, when he went 36–7 with an ERA of 1.09, yielding less than six hits per nine innings and fanning 243 batters while walking a mere 38. In 1936, Johnson (known as the Big Train) was one of the first five players elected to the Hall of Fame.

Even with Johnson in the rotation as of 1908, Washington moped through the league under Can-tillon. The pilot lasted through the 1909 campaign, when he was shown the door behind a widely quoted crack (sometimes attributed to Noyes) that "he might have been fired, but he didn't leave any va-cancy." On Ban Johnson's recommendation, the team went next to Jimmy McAleer, who hung around for another couple of seventh-place finishes. The most notable moment of McAleer's managerial stay came on April 14, 1910, when Johnson started the first of fourteen opening day assignments and recorded the first of his seven shutouts on the occasion. Before the 3–0 whitewash of the Athletics, William Howard Taft initiated the custom of having presidents of the United States throw out the first ball at Washington openers. The game almost put an end to the career of Secretary of State Charles Bennett, who, sitting in the presidential box, took a foul ball off the bat of Frank Baker directly in the head; Bennett recovered with-out serious consequences.

Before the 1911 season, both Johnson and Milan demanded more money for their conspicuous efforts on such a bad team. While Noyes settled quickly for the smaller raise demanded by Milan, he refused Johnson's demands for a salary equal to that of Ty Cobb ($9,000 per year), whereupon the pitcher calmly walked out of the team's spring training camp in Atlanta. In response to fan protests against the club's stand, Noyes initially seeded both his family's paper and the *Post* with "reports" that the balking Johnson might be headed to the Tigers; he dropped that tactic when the protests grew even louder. The two sides eventually agreed on a three-year pact at $7,000 a year.

Shortly before the end of the 1911 season, Mc-Aleer made a mark as the first Washington manager not to be fired by submitting his resignation and moving over to the Red Sox as a part-owner. On October 27th, Noyes announced that Griffith was coming in not only as the manager, but as a 10-percent stockholder that made him the single biggest investor in the organization. Griffith's enthusiasm for the new venture was not shared by his league co-founders; in fact, both Comiskey and Ban Johnson were so pessimistic about the future of the Washington franchise that they refused to lend Griffith the money to buy the stock—a rejection that did not help relations among the men for some years.

As manager, Griffith made short work of the team's aged roster, dropping ten veterans within weeks of taking over. Building the team around the starting rotation of Johnson, Bob Groom, and Long Tom Hughes, he fielded a club that by the end of the season had only two players—Hughes and shortstop George McBride—who were over 30 years old. In another critical move, he brought in Chick Gandil as the regular first baseman. The result was a totally unexpected drive to second place, with the team not only reaching the .500 level for the first time, but coming to within a percentage point of playing .600. Johnson was the club's anchor, with 32 wins and a league-leading ERA of 1.39, while Groom won 24 and both Milan and Gandil batted over .300. The underside of the season was in the sudden death of Noyes in August at the age of 44; he was replaced as organization president by Ben Minor, the club attorney and a long-time associate of Griffith.

The Senators picked up where they had left off in 1913, moving into second place early in the season and making periodic surges toward the top spot. Convinced that he needed only one more slugging outfielder to pass Philadelphia, Griffith cornered Detroit owner Frank Navin during a game and handed him a $100,000 personal check for the services of Cobb. When Navin expressed surprise that Griffith had so much money, the Washington boss confessed that he didn't, but promised that he would within two weeks. While Navin agreed to think about the offer for that much time, Griffith went to work on hostile shareholders, outlining a plan by which he would place exactly 100,000 tickets on sale for $1 each to raise the money to buy Cobb. Although some of the club's directors agreed that Washington fans might go for a scheme that brought Cobb to the capital and would almost assure a pennant, the whole question became academic when Navin returned the check, saying he wasn't interested in dealing his star player. Washington had to settle for another second-place standing.

The team weathered the first year of the Federal League fairly well, but then Minor wrote a letter to Johnson in which he told the pitcher that his "mere 28 wins" did not entitle him to the same $12,000 contract that he had been given after his 36-win performance in 1913. Johnson was so furious with the letter that he promptly signed with the FL's Chicago club for an annual salary of $16,000 plus an inking

bonus of $10,000. Without consulting Minor, Griffith went to the Johnson home and talked his ace into signing an identical pact with the Senators. Then, aware that he would never get his team's board of directors to approve the signing bonus, Griffith called on Ban Johnson to come up with the $10,000 out of a special fund the AL maintained for emergencies. But as he had when Griffith had asked for the stock purchase money, Johnson said no. Griffith had more success with Comiskey: While also initially reluctant to bail out the Senators, the White Sox owner changed his tune when he was reminded of how much his club would suffer from having a Walter Johnson pitching in competition in the Windy City.

The 1915 season saw the debuts of two players who became fixtures on the Washington scene. One was first baseman Joe Judge, who would end up playing eighteen of his twenty major league seasons in the capital, compiling a lifetime average of .298 that included ten years of .300 or better. The other was future Hall of Famer Sam Rice, who came to the club as a pitcher, attracted more attention for his pinch-hitting, and then converted to a .322-lifetime-hitting outfielder. The lefthand-swinging Rice was a paradigm of consistency, never once in his twenty-year career (nineteen with the Senators) batting below .293, and dipping that low only in his final campaign with Cleveland, when he was already 44 years old. A classic contact hitter with little power (his home run high was six), he struck out only 275 times in more than 10,000 plate appearances. Rice was elected to Cooperstown in 1963.

During World War I (and again during World War II), Griffith proved invaluable to both leagues in persuading the U.S. Government not to eliminate baseball as a nonessential activity. In 1918, after Ban Johnson had failed to gain deferments from military service for players and had only sharpened the antagonism of Federal bureaucrats toward the big leagues, Griffith worked out a deal with Secretary of War Newton Baker by which the players would perform pregame drills (with bats instead of rifles) in exchange for remaining exempt from the draft until Labor Day. The Washington manager also spear-

---

On July 19, 1915, the Senators stole a record eight bases in one inning against the Indians. The Cleveland catcher was Steve O'Neill.

headed a fund-raising drive for $100,000 to buy bats and balls for servicemen in Europe. Although the first supply of baseball gear ended up at the bottom of the Atlantic thanks to a U-boat attack, Griffith's public relations adroitness kept major league baseball going for all but a few weeks in September. For the future, it didn't hurt, either, that one of the participants in the drills before the Washington games was Assistant Navy Secretary Franklin Delano Roosevelt.

For all his importance to the league as a whole, Griffith used up a lot of his clout at home with his failure to get the Senators out of .500 territory and into a World Series; with the collapse of the club back to seventh place in 1919, dissatisfaction turned to open demands for his firing by some members of the board of directors. Griffith's response was to round up enough capital from the Metropolitan National Bank and from Philadelphia grain exporter William Richardson to take over as majority owner and president; a key part of the deal allowed him to speak for Richardson's minority holdings as well as his own. The boardroom transactions accented an Horatio Alger complex in Griffith, who never got tired of asking visitors to his office "how many people in this game of baseball can start out as a player and end up as an owner?"

With the dawning of the 1920s, Griffith found himself increasingly bogged down by administrative matters, forcing him to turn the daily managing over to shortstop McBride. It turned out to be a short-lived solution, however, when McBride was struck in the face by a line drive in batting practice in August 1921 and had to be replaced by Milan. Milan remained at the helm through a dismal 1922 season,

a good part of which Griffith attributed to the outfielder's inability to take charge of his long-time teammates. Declaring that the club needed "more energy" from the bench, Griffith released Milan at the end of the season and brought in Donie Bush.

Although the team did little more than tread water at the beginning of the 1920s, the period saw the gradual insertion into the lineup of players who would have pivotal roles in the franchise's first two pennants in 1924 and 1925. The first was Bucky Harris, who would settle down the keystone position for most of the 1920s. The second was outfielder Goose Goslin, who brought his lifetime .316 mark to the capital in 1921. Unlike Milan and Rice, the lefty-hitting Goslin also had considerable power, and would reach double figures in home runs in ten of his eighteen big league seasons. (He entered the Hall of Fame in 1968.) A third addition was third baseman Ossie Bluege, who debuted in 1922 and became the club rock at his position for most of the next eighteen years.

The good news about Bush's 1923 Senators was that, for a team that had been synonymous for so long with Johnson, it had five .300 hitters in the regular lineup. The bad news was that, in the era of the lively ball, the club's overall .274 still left it sixth in offense and fourth in the standings. To make matters worse, Johnson had clearly seen his best days, failing to win 20 games four years in a row. Not quite ready yet to deal away his franchise hurler for a couple of mound prospects and not able to swap a spray hitter or two for a slugger, Griffith fell back on the classic choice of firing Bush. What was not so expected was his naming of the 27-year-old Harris as the new manager; the second baseman was younger than every other key player on the team except for Goslin and Bluege.

Harris made it work (and helped himself along to Cooperstown—in 1975—in the process). After a bad April in which the young manager was ridiculed as Griffith's Folly by local sportswriters, the club picked up steam and found itself in a dogfight with the Tigers, Athletics, and Yankees. The turning point came in a late August series at Yankee Stadium, when the team took three games out of four from New York. Rallying to the possibility of playing in the postseason for the first time in his career, Johnson rediscovered his old form, reeling off thirteen consecutive victories down the stretch and winding up with AL-leading numbers in both wins (23) and ERA (2.72). The other big pitching contribution came from reliever Firpo Marberry, who won 11 and saved 15. Offensively, the most potent bat belonged to Goslin,

Athough a relatively staid franchise for most of its history, Washington had its antic side. At the beginning of the century, catcher Gabby Street grabbed a ball thrown down to him from the top of the Washington Monument. Both Nick Altrock and Al Schacht, the clown princes of baseball, also got their start with the Senators. Altrock, a southpaw, wore a big league uniform over five decades from 1898 to 1933 (the last two as a publicity stunt), winning 82 and losing 75. The righthander Schacht had a 14–10 record for Washington between 1919 and 1921, and also managed the club for a few games at the end of the 1934 season.

who led the league with 129 RBIs, scored 100 runs, and batted .344. Another significant ingredient was defense, with Harris and the veteran Roger Peckinpaugh excelling in the middle of the infield.

President Calvin Coolidge joined the hysterical capacity crowds that jammed Griffith Stadium for the first two games of the World Series against the Giants, and saw the Senators split two 4–3 decisions. In the Polo Grounds they weren't so lucky, losing two out of three. Back in Washington, however, southpaw Tom Zachary got things even again with a 2–1 squeaker over Art Nehf, leaving everything up to a seventh game.

In a ploy aimed against New York's lefty-swinging first baseman Bill Terry, Harris sent right-hander Curly Ogden to face the first two batters, then, daring Giants' manager John McGraw to use up his platooning righthanded hitters, immediately brought in lefty George Mogridge. The tactic seemed in vain when the Giants took a 3–1 lead in the sixth inning. But then came the pebbles. In the bottom of the eighth inning, with the tying runs on base, Harris slapped a shot down the third base line that took an erratic skip over Freddie Lindstrom's glove and bounded down into the corner to knot the contest. Behind grandstand roars for the Big Train, Johnson then came out of the bullpen to hurl scoreless ball into the twelfth inning, along the way escaping a couple of serious New York threats. Finally, in the bottom of the twelfth, catcher Muddy Ruel got a second life when Giants' catcher Hank Gowdy tripped over his mask in going after an easy foul pop and promptly doubled the winning run to second base. Johnson then reached first safely on shortstop Travis Jackson's error, while Ruel held at second. With the stadium howling for one more hit, Earl McNeely sent a grounder to Lindstrom that looked like a double-play ball; at the last second, however, another pebble intervened, sending the ball over the third baseman's head and Ruel home with the franchise's only world championship.

As it developed, it wasn't Johnson's last victory in a World Series. Defying every logical argument that he should have rejuvenated the pitching staff over the winter, Griffith took the opposite tack of bringing in 36-year-old Stan Coveleski, 31-year-old Dutch Reuther, and 40-year-old Vern Gregg.

While Gregg turned out to be a bust, Coveleski ended up winning 20 and leading AL hurlers with an ERA of 2.84, and the southpaw Reuther chipped in 18 victories, as Washington prevailed over Mack's Athletics. Among the other pitchers, both Johnson (20 wins) and Marberry (8 wins and 15 saves) came back strong. The hitters were again led by Goslin, who hit .334, with 34 doubles, 20 triples, 18 homers, 113 RBIs, and 116 runs scored. Other prime performers were Rice (.350, 87 RBIs) and part-timer Joe Harris (.323 and 59 RBIs in only 300 at bats).

Despite two wins (one of them a shutout) from Johnson, the World Series had a less happy ending, with Pittsburgh taking advantage of a record eight errors by Peckinpaugh and coming out on top after seven games. What made the loss even harder to take was a bitter telegram from Ban Johnson after the finale criticizing Harris for using the Big Train three times (he was the loser in Game 7) "for sentimental reasons."

With the exception of one positive development, nothing very good happened to the franchise for the rest of the decade. In both 1927 and 1928, Johnson had hellish springs (the first because of a broken leg, the second because of a serious bout with influenza), and finally took the hint to retire at the age of 40. Goslin, gifted with one of the strongest throwing arms in the league, sharply reduced his value to the team in the spring of 1928 when he got into a shotput contest with some high school athletes for more than a half-hour and woke up the following morning to realize that he couldn't even comb his hair; his arm never completely recovered. Little more than a year after he had been the toast of Washington, Harris became a regular target for Griffith Stadium boobirds. His first sin was that he had slowed down perceptibly in the field; his second, relayed through anonymous quotes from the clubhouse, was that his marriage to the daughter of a U.S. senator had made him stuck up and increasingly distant from his players.

After three straight finishes in the middle of the league, Griffith decided on a change, bringing in Johnson as manager. Griffith came in for his own share of criticism for a May 1927 trade that sent promising second baseman Buddy Myer to the Red Sox in exchange for shortstop Topper Rigney. The swap was one of the worst in the history of the franchise, but was effectively nullified before the 1929 season when the Senators reacquired Myer, a life-

---

Asked once whom he most admired in America, Clark Griffith replied: "The Lone Ranger has been my guiding star, the sort of man I wanted to be." Griffith kept a picture of the fictional radio and comics character in his office.

time .303 hitter, and kept him in Griffith Stadium for the rest of his seventeen-year career.

The brightest note of the period was the July 1928 pickup of shortstop Joe Cronin, who had failed to impress the Pirates in two brief trials. With Washington, the righthand-batting Cronin emerged as one of the power hitters of the league, driving in more than 100 runs for five straight seasons with averages that went as high as .346. Before his career was over, he would be a manager, general manager, and president of the league. Cronin was voted into the Hall of Fame in 1956 for his .301 average, his exceptional RBI punch as a shortstop, and his lengthy managing career (from 1933 to 1947, with a winning percentage of .540).

Johnson's career as a manager got off to a laborious start in 1929 with a fifth-place finish and reliever Marberry having to anchor the rotation as well as come out of the bullpen. Although Goslin had another decent year offensively with 18 homers and 91 RBIs, his batting average slipped below .300 for the first time since his debut as a backup player in 1921. When reports began circulating that one of the outfielder's problems was Johnson's impatience with Goslin's working habits, Griffith denied them vociferously. But then, in June of 1930, the team announced one of its most significant deals in shipping Goslin to the Browns in return for pitcher Alvin (General) Crowder and outfielder Heinie Manush. In his first three-and-a-half seasons for Washington, the righthanded Crowder won 83 games, while Manush solidified his Hall of Fame career with four-and-a-half years of batting averages above .300. The deal became even more of a steal for Griffith when Goslin was reacquired after the 1932 season.

In his four years as manager, Johnson brought the team back up to .600 ball, but somewhat deceptively. Typical was 1932, when Washington blazed through September with a 24–4 record but still finished 14 games off the pace because it had been so far behind to start with. As in the case of Milan a decade earlier, Griffith decided that Johnson didn't create enough pressure in the dugout, so he fired him after the 1932 campaign. Initial indications were that Griffith himself might return to the helm, but then, falling back on his Harris formula, the president selected the 26-year-old Cronin. Cronin's first response was to present Griffith with a wish list of three pitchers he declared necessary for a Washington pennant. Within two days at the winter meetings in New York that December, Griffith had secured all three of them—Earl Whitehill from the Tigers, Jack Russell from the Indians, and Lefty Stewart from the

Browns. It was through the Stewart trade that Goslin also returned to the capital.

Cronin had been right. With Whitehill, Russell, and Stewart providing 49 wins and 14 saves, the 1933 Senators rolled up a franchise-high 99 victories, finishing 7 games ahead of the Yankees. In addition to the three hurlers acquired in the December trades, Crowder led the league with 24 wins, both Cronin himself and first baseman Joe Kuhel knocked in more than 100 runs, and six regulars batted over .295.

The season was punctuated by a series of nasty brawls between the Senators and Yankees. The ugliest one took place in Griffith Stadium on April 25, when a spikes-first slide by New York's Ben Chapman into Myer at second base precipitated a near-riot. After police finally cleared the field, several players were on their way to fines and suspensions and five spectators were headed for disorderly conduct and assault charges. The Giants were once again the foe in the World Series, and this time they avoided pebble incidents to run over the Senators in five games.

Washington never appeared in another World Series, and even its two lone second-place finishes over the next twenty-seven seasons occurred during the war years, when most of the league's prime talent was in khaki. There was nothing subtle about the fall, either, with the team collapsing under a series of spring training and early season injuries in 1934 and plunging all the way to seventh place. Among those sidelined for significant parts of the season were Cronin himself, Bluege, Kuhel, Myer, and catcher Luke Sewell. The slide to the nether regions was hastened further by Cronin's clashes with Goslin and Crowder. After Goslin objected to being platooned against southpaw pitching, he was shipped off to the Tigers; Crowder also ended up with Detroit after he made a scene over Cronin's decision to play rookie Cecil Travis at third base instead of the sure-handed Bluege.

As though he needed any more aggravation, Cronin finished off the 1934 season listening to grandstand catcalls over the announcement that he intended marrying Griffith's niece in the fall. Griffith heard them, too, and, unlike the nepotist who would later staff the organization with relations and inlaws, wondered aloud if Cronin would ever be at his best under so much extra pressure. Helping the doubts along was a $250,000 offer from Boston for Cronin's services. On October 26, 1934, only a few days after returning from his honeymoon, Cronin agreed to go to the Red Sox as a player-manager in exchange for shortstop Lyn Lary and $225,000. Griffith stemmed some of the uproar in Washington over the deal by bringing back Harris as the team pilot.

Harris's second tenure lasted eight years, but yielded none of the miracles of his first go-round; in fact, the club managed merely one first-division finish between 1935 and 1942, never coming closer than twenty games from the top. Aside from a batting title for the pesky Myer in 1935 and the stolen bases of outfielder George Case in the late 1930s and early 1940s, there were few Washington diamond heroics to be celebrated in the period. Most of the diversion offered by the team came from its often bizarre mix of personalities. At the top of the list was the bombastic righthander Bobo Newsom, who never met a fact he couldn't exaggerate or a lie he couldn't defend indignantly as a fact. In his twenty-year career, Newsom changed uniforms a record seventeen times, including five separate stints with the Senators. For lack of any other logical reason for his recurrent pursuit of a hurler who seemed to save his most mediocre years for Washington and who ended up with a record of 211–222 (3.98 ERA), Griffith once admitted that he had always looked forward to playing pinochle with Newsom.

A second character of the era was Zeke ("Boy, what a physique!") Bonura, a lumbering first baseman from the Dick Stuart School of Defense. In his only full season with the club, in 1938, Bonura bashed 22 homers and drove in 114 runs; he also led the league in waving at ground balls through the infield, in watching foul balls drop between the foul line and the seats, and in waving off pitchers on grounders and losing foot races to the first base bag. Bonura's biggest fan was Vice-President James Nance Garner, who spent his every free moment at Griffith Stadium cheering on the slugger and embracing him whenever he crossed home plate after hitting a ball in the seats.

Footnote Player: At the end of the 1934 season, Clark Griffith went for a quickie gate attraction by signing righthander Allen Benson, a bearded pitcher from the House of David team. After getting pounded in his debut against the Tigers, Benson asked for another start and for the right to shave off his beard. Griffith granted the start but not the shave, declaring that it was Benson's facial hair that made him "special." The pitcher was banged around again by the Browns, retiring from the major leagues with a record of 0-1 and an ERA of 12.10.

For many years, Griffith's scouting department was made up of Joe Engel, a one-time pitcher of modest accomplishments who spent a lot of his time worrying about the owner's responses to his recommendations. To his credit, Engel wore down minor league executives to sign such future Washington stars as Bluege and Cronin; on the other hand, he was not above approaching the team's best pitchers during spring training to urge them to get into mid-season form against some hitter Griffith wanted to observe so that his own thumbs-down view wasn't contradicted. By the mid-1930s, Griffith was also opening his ears to the recommendations of Joe Cambria, a long-time operator of minor league franchises who got into more than one scrape with Commissioner Kenesaw Landis over his hit-and-miss understanding of contract obligations. Among Cambria's first significant tips to Griffith was the speedster Case, who ended up leading the league in stolen bases five years in a row and six times overall. Another big recommendation was first baseman Mickey Vernon, who won two batting titles as a Senator, in 1946 and 1953. But, in the long run, Cambria proved even more valuable to Washington (and, eventually, other major league organizations) as an assiduous tracker of baseball talent in Cuba and other parts of Latin America.

Griffith didn't need to have his arm twisted about the potential of the Cuban market: As manager of the Reds in 1911, he had tutored outfielder Armando Marsans and third baseman Rafael Almeida. In 1935, he told Harris to play Cambria protégé Bobby Estalella at third base. An instant fan favorite for his .314 bat and a glove that gathered up only what his chest had knocked down, Estalella hung around for a couple of years mainly because he was box office; in the end, however, his lack of defense made him a hazardous proposition for a number of teams, and he drifted back to the minor leagues. Estalella turned out to be the first of a long parade of Cubans who found their way—through Cambria—to Griffith Stadium. The majority were run-of-the-mill players or worse, and were often included on the roster for no better reason than they came cheaply to the increasingly miserly Griffith. But their presence in the majors, however brief in individual cases, spurred the development of the Latin American stars who began arriving in the 1950s. Ironically, the best of the Latins to wear a Washington uniform was righty Camilo Pascual, who did not begin to blossom until after Griffith's death and when the franchise was on the verge of moving to Minneapolis.

The most promising aspect of the team at the

turn of the 1940s was its pitching. In 1939, knuckle-baller Dutch Leonard won an unexpected 20 games. The following season, the team weathered seven consecutive brutal outings by prospect Sid Hudson, then thrived behind his charge to 17 wins. It was also in this period that future Hall of Famer Early Wynn started his march to 300 career wins. But despite the talents of all three righthanders, their lack of hitting support would give them only one category in common during their stays with the Senators—leading the AL in losses for a season.

The mediocrity of his teams in the late 1930s did not do too much for Griffith's already thin sense of humor, and he was especially irritated to see the Yankees topping the league season after season. In a move that found immediate favor from other franchises resentful of the New York success, he sponsored a resolution at the 1940 winter meetings that prohibited a previous year's pennant winner from making trades with other AL clubs. The ploy turned out to affect very little, because it had been years since the Yankees had picked up a player via a swap who had proved critical to their pursuit of a flag. Moreover, in the season in which the regulation was in effect, Detroit won the flag; the owners quickly scrapped the no-trade provision after the World Series. Griffith had considerably more satisfaction where the Yankees were concerned in a 1942 transaction involving Mike Chartak. Hearing that New York was about to sell the first baseman-outfielder to the Browns for $14,000, the Washington owner sounded the patriotic note that the wartime capital would benefit more from showcasing such a prospect, got him from the Bronx for $12,000, then promptly turned around and peddled him to St. Louis for the originally discussed $14,000.

Griffith's last big moments followed the outbreak of World War II, when he was once again baseball's chief lobbyist in persuading the Government that the game should not be curbed as an inessential activity. His connections with Roosevelt proved particularly important, and he made numerous visits to the White House in January and February 1942 to argue his case that night games were a perfect relaxant for people who had to put in long hours at military plants or other war-related jobs. (The sudden stress on the appeal of night games amused a number of league officials who had been exposed to Griffith's tirades against installing lights in AL stadiums only a short time before.) Not only did he convince Roosevelt of his cause, but Griffith also dined regularly with draft officials who, while not about to declare blanket exemptions from military service, saw

little problem in granting some Washington players months-long deferrals. Together with the numerous Cubans and other Latin players who did not have to register for the draft until 1944 (there were twelve of them at Washington's spring training camp that season), the deferrals kept the club well-stocked while other teams scurried just to find enough bodies for a lineup.

The first war year, 1942, also saw Calvin Griffith assuming a more active role in the franchise as vice-president. The elder Griffith's nephew, Calvin and his sister Thelma went to live with their uncle at young ages because their own parents—the Robertsons—were bending under the weight of trying to support a house full of children. Although he eventually changed his name from Calvin Griffith Robertson to Calvin Robertson Griffith, the boy was never adopted legally by the Senators' president because he was too old when he applied. It was Calvin's sister Mildred who married Cronin, his sister Thelma who would marry Senators' pitcher Joe Haynes, and his brothers Sherry (an AL outfielder for ten years), Billy, and Jimmy who would gradually move into key positions in the organization and make it almost as much of a family operation as the Macks had with the Athletics.

When Harris's 1942 club finished with the franchise's weakest winning percentage since 1919, the manager did not have to be asked twice to resign. To replace Harris, the owner brought in Bluege—the ninth straight appointment of a pilot who had played for the organization. Bluege inherited a radically revamped team, with the lefty-hitting Vernon installed at first, Gerry Priddy at second, and solid-hitting Stan Spence moving into the outfield. To the astonishment of the league, the Senators were the Yankees' chief pursuers all year, and might have even made it closer if third baseman Harlond Clift, an important midseason acquisition, had not been disabled with mumps only a week after joining the team. But no sooner did the Senators begin envisioning overtaking the Yankees altogether in 1944 than the draft deferrals expired, decimating the roster and plunging the club to the cellar. For all the cracks of the early vaudevillians, it was actually the first time that Washington had occupied the basement since 1909 and the first time ever with Griffith running the organization. Spence, one of the few regulars to escape the draft for the season, pointed up the team's wretched offense by hitting 18 home runs—three more than the rest of the club as a whole hit. At one point, the Senators got so desperate for position players that they signed up Eddie Boland, an outfielder who had failed in brief trials with the Phillies in the early 1930s and who was playing with a New York City Sanitation Department squad when he asked for a tryout. (He didn't do that badly, either, batting .271 in nineteen games.) The only significant game of the year for the club was the very last one, when the knuckleballer Leonard ignored a $10,000 bribe to lose to the Tigers and went out to beat them; Detroit lost the pennant to the Browns by a single game.

If World War II had given Griffith one reason to think differently about night baseball, his 1945 pitching staff gave him another one. With a starting rotation that included knuckleballers Leonard, Roger Wolff, Mickey Haefner, and Johnny Niggeling, the club suddenly found itself boomeranged back up to second place, in good part because the flawed night lighting of the period made it even harder for AL batters to catch up to butterfly deliveries. With the solid-hitting outfield of Case, Buddy Lewis, and Bingo Binks backing up the unusual rotation, the Senators tussled with the Tigers all the way to the end of September, with only one game separating the two clubs. Then two culprits emerged. The first was Binks, who handed a crucial game to the Athletics because he forgot to put on his sunglasses and lost an easy out in the glare of the sky; teammates were so infuriated with the outfielder that a number of them voted to deprive him of his second-place money. The other goat was Griffith, who had been so pessimistic about the Senators' chances of being a contender that he agreed to schedule a slew of doubleheaders at Griffith Stadium in September in order to clear a couple of Sundays for the football Redskins; the consensus was that the twinbills had proved too much for a staff that, in addition to the knuckleballers, depended almost entirely on Marino Pieretti and Alex Carrasquel. Detroit ended up winning the pennant by 1½ games, with Wolff's 20 wins the main consolation prize.

With the return of major league stars at the end of the war, the franchise went into eclipse for good, never again rising higher than fourth and reaching the .500 level only twice in fifteen years. Like many other franchises, Washington benefited from the immediate postwar atmosphere to register one million in attendance for the first time in 1946, but thereafter

Joe Kuhel hit the only Washington home run in Griffith Stadium in 1945—and even that was an inside-the-park shot.

Under rules then in effect, outfielder Taft Wright should have won the 1945 AL batting title by virtue of his 100 game appearances. Because many of his appearances were as a pinch-hitter, however, the commissioner's office stepped in to deny Wright the title and give it to New York infielder George Stirnweiss.

fans became scarcer and scarcer until even a target of a half-million in the late 1950s seemed to be asking for too much. Bluege lasted through the 1947 season, but barely. For most of the 1947 campaign, Washington pitchers complained loudly that the manager was using them out of turn. Pitchers and non-pitchers alike also ganged up on him for not protesting to Griffith over haphazard travel arrangements that sometimes saw the club arriving in a city to find no hotel rooms waiting. Amid press reports of his imminent firing, Bluege finally called the team together and demanded that everyone sign a statement saying that the newspaper stories were wrong and that there was no revolt against him. When Priddy refused to sign, he was put down as a troublemaker and, as soon as the season was over, dealt to the Browns. The swap turned into a fiasco when Johnny Berardino, the infielder who should have come to the Senators in the exchange, told Griffith to talk to his agent to work out a new contract for 1948. When Griffith railed at the notion of talking to anyone's agent, Berardino announced his retirement rather than go to Washington. Griffith was incensed enough by Priddy's arrogance to accept cash instead of Berardino; Berardino, an aspiring actor who would later make his career on the soap opera *General Hospital*, was smart enough to unretire immediately afterward and accept a second trade to the Indians, where owner Bill Veeck had not only promised him playing time, but also an introduction to a Hollywood producer who would give him a screen test.

In the Griffith tradition of hiring only former Senators for the managerial post, the owner replaced Bluege with one-time first baseman Kuhel for the 1948 and 1949 seasons. Kuhel was at the helm when Griffith made one of the franchise's worst trades in December 1948—Vernon and Wynn to Cleveland for first baseman Ed Robinson and pitchers Joe Haynes and Eddie Kliemann. As with the Buddy Myer swap in the 1930s, the exchange might have been still worse if the Senators had not reacquired Vernon a year later; nevertheless, the trading of the future Hall of Famer Wynn for Haynes, the husband of Griffith's niece, became ridiculed around the league as Thelma's Deal. It was in this same period that Griffith Stadium fans were becoming more vocal in their skepticism about the playing abilities of Sherry Robertson. Griffith's nephew (and Calvin's brother) had been billed in his minor league days as a steady hitter, but he ended up with a career average of .230; he had also been ballyhooed in some quarters as another Case on the bases, but he never had more than ten steals in a season.

But on the eve of the 1950s, Griffith had more to worry about than charges of nepotism. After thirty years of operating the organization on the strength of his stock plus that of Philadelphia grain exporter Richardson, he learned belatedly that the latter's heirs had sold their 40 percent stake in the club to young wheeler-dealer John Jachym. Furious that the Richardson family had ignored an agreement to give him first shot at its stock, but also aware that his own mere 44 percent holding made him vulnerable to a takeover, Griffith raced Jachym to minority shareholders for a majority edge. To his chagrin, even long-time associates refused to sell him the shares that would give him control, consoling him only with a board of directors voting bloc big enough to deny Jachym an executive position with the club. With the message clear that the next board vote might go to Jachym if the team didn't improve, the 80-year-old president brought back Harris as manager for the third time. When the Senators got off to an unspectacular start, Griffith seemed finished. But then, partly because the club began improving on the field and partly because of indications that the old man intended using every ounce of clout he had in Washington to remain as head of the franchise, Jachym suddenly backed down from a showdown by taking a six-month capital gain on his investment and selling out to local insurance broker H. Gabriel Murphy. Murphy immediately sold Griffith enough of his stock to give the latter 52 percent of the club; in return, Murphy obtained an option to buy the Griffith stock when and if the family decided to sell.

In his third tour of duty, Harris lasted five years,

Despite his financial problems, Calvin Griffith turned down a Cincinnati offer of a half-million dollars each for Harmon Killebrew and Camilo Pascual, saying they were the future of the franchise. They were—of the Minnesota franchise.

squeezing out the last two .500 seasons enjoyed by the franchise. If nothing else, he had the decisive say in a couple of deals that were among the best ever completed by the organization. Using his familiarity with the farm system of the Yankees (by whom he had been employed for a number of years), Harris obtained pitchers Bob Porterfield, Fred Sanford, and Tom Ferrick in 1951, and slugger Jackie Jensen and pitcher Spec Shea in 1952. Porterfield led the league in wins (22) and shutouts (9) in 1953, while Jensen found his footing as one of the AL's top power hitters of the 1950s. Unfortunately for the Senators, however, they were talked into another deal with Boston in 1954 in which the right fielder was sent off again to the Red Sox in exchange for southpaw Mickey McDermott. Another deal with the Browns brought over 1948 Rookie of the Year Roy Sievers.

With the team nowhere near contention, fans had to be satisfied with the efforts of individual players. One particular grandstand favorite was third baseman Eddie Yost, who in 1950 began redefining the ideal leadoff man by drawing at least 100 walks for the first of eight times in his career. In 1953, most attention was centered on Vernon, who went down to the last day of the season in a dead heat with Cleveland's Al Rosen for the batting championship. In his first four at bats in the season finale, the first baseman got two hits, but then word came from Cleveland that Rosen had already collected three. In full awareness that another out by Vernon would have cost him the title, his teammates conspired over the last two innings of the contest to make sure that he would not have another plate appearance—merely going through the motions with their own turns in the batting box and, in the case of catcher Mickey Grasso, getting picked off deliberately. Vernon won the title by a single point.

Because of the vastness of Griffith Stadium, the Senators were almost always at the bottom of the league in home runs. In the mid-1950s, however, Calvin Griffith brought the stadium fences in by as much as 30 feet, changing front office priorities in trades and minor league signings. The first beneficiary of the smaller park was outfielder-first baseman Sievers, who belted 21 or more homers in a Washington uniform every season between 1954 and 1959; in 1957, the righthand-hitting slugger topped the league with 42 round-trippers. Before the end of the decade, Sievers would be joined in the lineup by other bashers like Jim Lemon and Bob Allison.

The most exceptional player to join the Senators in the 1950s was another righthand-hitting longballer—Harmon Killebrew. Recommended to the or-

Clark Griffith, who ran the Washington Senators as a family
business, celebrates his 83rd birthday surrounded by his official and
actual family. Among those on hand were Mrs. Griffith (seated), Joe
Judge (far left), Sherry Robertson, Joe Cronin, Jack Bentley
(obscured), Ossie Bluege, Commissioner Ford Frick, Bucky Harris,
Nick Altrock, and Joe Haynes. *AP/Wide World Photos*

ganization by Idaho Senator Herman Welker,
Killebrew was a near-caricature of the one-
dimensional player, shifting from third base to first
base to the outfield and back again during his
twenty-two-year career to hide his glove. With a bat
in his hand, however, he clouted 573 home runs, the
most by a righthanded hitter in AL history. His ratio
of one homer every 14.22 at bats ranked him third
behind only Babe Ruth (11.76) and Ralph Kiner
(14.11). For the Senators in 1959, he led the league
with 42 homers—the first of six times that he topped
that category and the first of eight times that he went
over the 40-mark; his 105 RBIs that year also represented the first of nine times that he drove across at
least 100 runs. The Hall of Fame elected Killebrew as
a member in 1984.

Calvin Griffith pressed another kind of change
on his uncle after the 1954 season, when he announced the firing of Harris for the veteran pilot
Charlie Dressen. Dressen was the first Washington
skipper since McAleer in 1911 who had not played
for the club. Where the standings were concerned,
the outsider's arrival coincided with the nadir of the
franchise, with the Senators ending up in the cellar
four out of the next five years.

Although it hardly needed another factor to discourage fans from coming to Griffith Stadium, the
team found one when, over the strenuous objections
and filibustering tactics of Calvin Griffith, the AL

approved the transfer of the St. Louis Browns to
nearby Baltimore for the 1954 season. The vote on the
move occasioned a rift between the Griffiths when
Clark, who had pledged his support for the shift
because of personal commitments, discovered belatedly that his nephew had been going against his instructions at league meetings; the 84-year-old owner
himself attended the session that finalized the transfer. It turned out to be one of Clark Griffith's last
major decisions for the club; on October 27, 1955, the
owner who had become known as The Old Fox died
at the age of 85.

Under the terms of Griffith's will, Calvin and
Thelma each acquired 26 percent of the franchise,
with the binding condition that neither could sell out
without the other's permission. Calvin assumed
practical control of the franchise, with Thelma content to rubber-stamp his decisions for many years.
The true worth of what they had inherited was another matter. By Calvin's account, the franchise had
little more than $25,000 in the treasury when Clark
Griffith passed away. In an era when most organizations had farm clubs scattered around the country,
the Senators had only three—in Charlotte, Chatta-
nooga, and Orlando. The chief sources of profit were
the concession stands and the rental fees paid by the
Redskins. The tattered state of the franchise both on
and off the field repopularized the old vaudeville
taunts and made the Senators the perfect team for

the setting of a Broadway musical fantasy like *Damn Yankees*, in which a losing club overcomes the Bronx Bombers thanks to the devil's intervention. The greater mockery implied in headline references to Washington as the Nats also had team officials insisting with new ardor that the club was called the Senators.

Griffith had another problem in minority stockholder Murphy, who had held out hopes that Clark Griffith's death would have made the rest of the family ready to offer him the first option on the team that he had gained in 1950. When that didn't transpire, Murphy began attacking Calvin's ability to run the franchise. One of his favorite targets was the all-family front office, with Thelma's husband Haynes as vice-president, brother Sherry as farm director, brother Jimmy as head of concessions, and brother Billy as chief of stadium operations; other key posts were in the hands of family retainers like Howie Fox (traveling secretary) and Bluege (comptroller). Throughout the late 1950s and into the 1960s, when the team had already moved to Minnesota, Murphy filed various lawsuits aimed at wresting away control from Griffith. None of them succeeded.

The frail financial condition of the franchise inevitably attracted suitors interested in moving the club to another city. The first big pitch came from former baseball commissioner Happy Chandler, who attended a team board meeting in October 1956 to promise that Louisville was ready to build a 50,000-seat stadium and underwrite guarantees for at least a million fans a year for three years. Representatives of San Francisco and Minneapolis offered similar deals. Shortly after Happy Chandler had tried to lure the Senators to Kentucky, namesake Norman Chandler, publisher of the Los Angeles *Times*, undertook a middleman role between Griffith and Mayor Norris Poulson to see if the franchise could be shifted to Los Angeles as quickly as the 1957 season. Griffith later claimed that the transfer was aborted only because his radio advertisers wouldn't let him out of his contract, but the fact was that Poulson had already opened talks with the Brooklyn Dodgers of Walter O'Malley and, as a former congressman in Washington, had never been captivated by the Griffiths or their ballclub. Earl Warren, Chief Justice of the Supreme Court and a former governor of California, was also active behind the scenes trying to put Griffith together with some San Jose businessmen, but his efforts came to nothing when the Giants agreed to go to San Francisco.

Reports of the various moves being contemplated increased pressures on both Griffith and the city of Washington to do something to keep the team where it was. Griffith's most appreciable response was a declaration published by the Washington *Post* on January 15, 1957 that said in part: "This is my home. I intend that it shall remain my home for the rest of my life. As long as I have any say in the matter, and I expect that I shall for a long, long time, the Washington Senators will stay here, too. Next year. The year after. Forever." Under municipal urging, Congress agreed to look at a proposal for a new $6-million stadium to replace Griffith Stadium, but that went nowhere after Griffith objected that the facility would be placed in the predominantly black northeast section of the capital rather than in the more affluent southern or western suburbs. Griffith also made it clear that he did not regard a new stadium, wherever it was located, as the solution to his economic problems; on the contrary, as he noted often, a new park that would be run by some government body and enlist the Senators and Redskins as co-tenants, would deprive him of the concession and rent profits he had been counting on from the football team.

The final act began in May 1958, when Commissioner Ford Frick gave authoritative voice to the possibility that the Senators would not be in Washington too much longer. "From the standpoint of baseball," Frick told reporters, "it is not good to be leaving the nation's capital. But you have to think of the poor devil who is holding the franchise." For a couple of more years, other AL owners did their best not to think about the poor devil and to think instead about the fallout that might result from leaving the capital; the major fear was that congressmen already fired up by the defection of the Dodgers and Giants to California after the 1957 season would react to the loss of Washington by pushing for legislation that would deprive baseball of its exemption from antitrust statutes. But as Houston, Dallas, and Toronto joined Minneapolis and Louisville in courting the Senators, Griffith's pledges of staying put sounded decreasingly convincing; the owner admitted to being particularly impressed by the persistence of the Minnesota delegation and its head, lobbyist Gerald Moore.

By the end of the decade, only the Yankees, Red Sox, and Indians seemed to have special reasons over and above apprehension about Congress for opposing a shift: New York because the championship team was drawing what few fans still went to Griffith Stadium and was not losing money there, and because the ownership of Dan Topping and Del Webb did not want any investigators, in or out of

Congress, snooping into their tangled business affairs; Boston because the tandem of Tom Yawkey and Cronin wasn't ready for a league without Washington, and because the Red Sox had just moved their American Association affiliate to Minneapolis; and Cleveland because it had its eye on some of the same cities that Griffith did.

What ultimately settled the issue was the league's desire to expand from eight to ten teams. With the help of Chicago White Sox owner Bill Veeck, Griffith persuaded the rest of the circuit that relocating to Minnesota would not only save him

financially, but also open the way for an expansion club in the capital that would defuse worries about congressional investigations. The 1961 season saw the Griffith franchise playing in Bloomington as the Minnesota Twins, the first AL team on the West Coast with the California Angels, and a new Senators franchise in the capital. The roster of Griffith's last Washington team, managed in 1960 by Cookie Lavagetto, included Killebrew, Allison, shortstop Zoilo Versalles, catcher Earl Battey, pitchers Pascual and Jim Kaat, and several others who would not be such easy marks for vaudeville cracks.

WASHINGTON SENATORS

Annual Standings and Managers

Year	Position	W	L	Pct.	GB	Managers
1901	Sixth	61	72	.459	20½	Jimmy Manning
1902	Sixth	61	75	.449	22	Tom Loftus
1903	Eighth	43	94	.314	47½	Tom Loftus
1904	Eighth	38	113	.251	55½	Malachai Kittredge, Patsy Donovan
1905	Seventh	64	87	.421	29½	Jake Stahl
1906	Seventh	55	95	.367	37½	Jake Stahl
1907	Eighth	49	102	.325	43½	Joe Cantillon
1908	Seventh	67	85	.441	22½	Joe Cantillon
1909	Eighth	42	110	.276	56	Joe Cantillon
1910	Seventh	66	85	.437	36½	Jimmy McAleer
1911	Seventh	64	90	.416	38½	Jimmy McAleer
1912	Second	91	61	.599	14	Clark Griffith
1913	Second	90	64	.584	6½	Clark Griffith
1914	Third	81	73	.526	19	Clark Griffith
1915	Fourth	85	68	.556	17	Clark Griffith
1916	Seventh	76	77	.497	14½	Clark Griffith
1917	Fifth	74	79	.484	25½	Clark Griffith
1918	Third	72	56	.563	4	Clark Griffith
1919	Seventh	56	84	.400	32	Clark Griffith
1920	Sixth	68	84	.447	29	Clark Griffith
1921	Fourth	80	73	.523	18	George McBride, Clyde Milan
1922	Sixth	69	85	.448	25	Clyde Milan
1923	Fourth	75	78	.490	23½	Donie Bush
1924	First	92	62	.597	+2	Bucky Harris
1925	First	96	55	.636	+8½	Bucky Harris
1926	Fourth	81	69	.540	8	Bucky Harris
1927	Third	85	69	.552	25	Bucky Harris
1928	Fourth	75	79	.487	26	Bucky Harris
1929	Fifth	71	81	.467	34	Walter Johnson
1930	Second	94	60	.610	8	Walter Johnson
1931	Third	92	62	.597	16	Walter Johnson
1932	Third	93	61	.604	14	Walter Johnson
1933	First	99	53	.651	+7	Joe Cronin
1934	Seventh	66	86	.434	34	Joe Cronin, Al Schacht
1935	Sixth	67	86	.438	27	Bucky Harris
1936	Fourth	82	71	.536	20	Bucky Harris
1937	Sixth	73	80	.477	28½	Bucky Harris
1938	Fifth	75	76	.497	23½	Bucky Harris
1939	Sixth	65	87	.428	41½	Bucky Harris

1940	Seventh	64	90	.416	26	Bucky Harris
1941	Sixth*	70	84	.455	31	Bucky Harris
1942	Seventh	62	89	.411	39½	Bucky Harris
1943	Second	84	69	.549	13½	Ossie Bluege
1944	Eighth	64	90	.416	25	Ossie Bluege
1945	Second	87	67	.565	1½	Ossie Bluege
1946	Fourth	76	78	.494	28	Ossie Bluege
1947	Seventh	64	90	.416	33	Ossie Bluege
1948	Seventh	56	97	.366	40	Joe Kuhel
1949	Eighth	50	104	.325	47	Joe Kuhel
1950	Fifth	67	87	.435	31	Bucky Harris
1951	Seventh	62	92	.403	36	Bucky Harris
1952	Fifth	78	76	.506	17	Bucky Harris
1953	Fifth	76	76	.500	23½	Bucky Harris
1954	Sixth	66	88	.429	45	Bucky Harris
1955	Eighth	53	101	.344	43	Charlie Dressen
1956	Seventh	59	95	.383	38	Charlie Dressen
1957	Eighth	55	99	.357	43	Charlie Dressen, Cookie Lavagetto
1958	Eighth	61	93	.396	31	Cookie Lavagetto
1959	Eighth	63	91	.409	31	Cookie Lavagetto
1960	Fifth	73	81	.474	24	Cookie Lavagetto

* Tie

Postseason Play

WS	4–3 versus New York	1924
	3–4 versus Pittsburgh	1925
	1–4 versus New York	1933

Washington Senators

| *American League,*
1961–1971 | **BALLPARKS:** GRIFFITH STADIUM (1961)
ROBERT F. KENNEDY STADIUM (1962–1971) |
| **RECORD:** 740–1032 (.418) | **OTHER NAMES:** NATS |

Like the Kansas City Royals, the expansion Senators were created as an expedient to ease the way out of town of a previous franchise. Unlike the Royals, the club never developed winning ways, getting to the .500 mark only once in eleven years. The team's main distinctions were the slugging of outfielder Frank Howard and the celebrity of managers Mickey Vernon, Gil Hodges, and Ted Williams.

The Senators came into being during the frantic American League meetings in the fall of 1960 that sanctioned the transfer of Calvin Griffith's Senators from Washington to Minnesota. Fearing new political sallies against baseball's exemption from antitrust statutes if the capital were left without a club, AL

Hector Maestri was one of six players to appear for both twentieth-century Washington teams. Maestri's feat was particularly noteworthy insofar as he pitched in only two big league games— one for each Washington franchise.

owners accelerated plans for expansion by rushing both the California Angels and a new Senators franchise into the league for the 1961 season. The team was awarded to a group headed by Elwood (Pete) Quesada, then head of the Federal Aviation Authority. Quesada's group paid $2.2 million to cover admission fees and the right to select players at an expansion draft. Ed Doherty was named general manager, while Vernon, who had been a batting star for Griffith's Senators, was named manager.

With selections made by position, Doherty and Vernon went for outfielder Willie Tasby, pitcher Bobby Shantz, catcher Pete Daley, and infielder Coot Veal as their first category choices. In their first player transaction, they sent Shantz to the Pirates for pitchers Bennie Daniels, third baseman Harry Bright, and first baseman R. C. Stevens. Among the more familiar names on the first-year roster were Dale Long, Gene Woodling, Claude Osteen, Mike Garcia, and Dick Donovan. With 26,725 in attendance, Donovan lost the opening day game to the White Sox, 4–3, on April 10, 1961; because the Angels didn't start play until the next day, the game was the first to feature a modern expansion club. To the surprise of just about everybody, Vernon kept the Senators near .500 until August, when they went into a tailspin that included a stretch of 24 losses in 25 games. Their consolation prizes for the year were a ninth-place tie with the Athletics and Donovan's league-leading 2.40 ERA.

The team got off to a better start in 1962 by inaugurating $24-million D.C. Stadium (later renamed Robert F. Kennedy Stadium) with a 4–1 win over Detroit before a near-capacity 42,143. The omens were deceptive, however, and the club ended up in the cellar for the first of two straight years. Aside from mediocre play, the team was bedeviled most of the year by frictions between Doherty and Vernon, forcing Quesada to get rid of his general manager at the end of the campaign. One of the owner's charges against Doherty was that his development policy effectively excluded black players (there were only two in the entire Washington farm system at the time). A couple of months later, Quesada himself took to the door with the announcement that he had sold the franchise to a group headed by investment bankers James Johnston and James Lemon. George Selkirk took over baseball operations.

With Quesada no longer behind him, Vernon realized how short a leash he had when, a mere 40

On September 12, 1962, Tom Cheney of the Senators set the record for the most strikeouts in a game of any length when he fanned 21 Orioles in 16 innings. Cheney won the game, 2–1.

Footnote Player: First baseman-outfielder Tom Brown, who hit .147 in 61 games for the 1963 Senators, is the only major leaguer ever to play in a Super Bowl. Brown, a safety for the Green Bay Packers, appeared in Super Bowl I and Super Bowl II.

games into the 1963 season, he was replaced by Gil Hodges. As his baptism of fire, Hodges led the team to an organization low, 106 defeats and 48½ games out of first place. The club's leading performers were outfielders Don Lock and Jim King, who hit 51 homers between them; on the other hand, nobody batted higher than outfielder Chuck Hinton's .269, and southpaw Osteen's nine wins topped the pitching staff. The attendance of 535,604 was the lowest in the major leagues.

Over the next four years, Hodges built his managerial credentials by improving the team's play each season, minimal as the advance was. Until 1967, when Washington rose to a sixth-place tie with Baltimore, the progress made little public impression, with attendance declining from year to year and sparking periodic rumors of another imminent sale. The main source of entertainment for fans was wondering whether the 6'7" Howard would ever break out the huge numbers that had been expected from him (and glimpsed) since coming up to the Dodgers to stay in 1960. In what was easily the organization's best trade, the Senators had obtained the righthand-hitting slugger in a December 1964 swap that also landed pitchers Pete Richert and Phil Ortega and first baseman Dick Nen from Los Angeles in return for Osteen, infielder John Kennedy, and $100,000. It was in the relatively banner year of 1967 that Howard finally made good on all the expectations by belting 36 homers and knocking in 89 runs. Even that performance was mere prelude to the next three seasons, when he topped the 40-mark in round-trippers and the 100-mark in RBIs each season. Between May 12th and May 18th of 1968, he inscribed his name forever among the game's great sluggers by belting ten homers in twenty at bats.

Following the 1967 season, the Brooklyn-born Hodges was dealt back to the Mets, from whom he had come, to manage the New Yorkers; Washington named one-time local slugger Jim Lemon (no relation to the investment banker in the front office) as the new pilot. Lemon spent the 1968 season like everybody else in Washington—watching Howard's power feats and wondering where the rest of the team was. Aside from the outfielder, not a single regular hit even .250.

The aftermath of the 1968 season brought big changes when the Johnston-Lemon ownership announced that the franchise was for sale. Initially, the club appeared headed to comedian Bob Hope, who went so far as to indicate Bill DeWitt as his general manager; but then, facing a serious eye operation, Hope withdrew his bid, leaving the field open to Bob Short, a Minnesota-based hotel entrepreneur and treasurer of the Democratic National Committee.

Short took control of the organization on January 28, 1969 for $9 million. Although he immediately offered back a minority share to James Lemon, he wasted little time in jettisoning the Lemon in uniform with a startling announcement—the appointment of Hall of Famer Ted Williams as the new manager. Williams, who until then had stayed away from baseball except for some spring training tutoring of Boston hitters, signed a five-year agreement at $100,000 annually; the pact also gave him a vice-presidency.

In the first year of divisional play, hopes that the new manager would improve the club's puny offense were realized, and then some. In a showing that would bring Williams Manager of the Year honors, the club improved its overall batting average by 25 points while landing in a franchise-high fourth, 10 games over .500. In addition to Howard, the lineup featured career years from first baseman Mike Epstein and third baseman Ken McMullen, who combined for 49 homers and 172 RBIs. The pitching proved to be equally surprising, with righthander Dick Bosman leading the way with 14 victories and an AL-leading 2.19 ERA. But then, just when Washington fans were acknowledging the hope that they might have a team truly on the rise, it skidded back to less than mediocrity in the cellar of the AL East Division.

Most of the interest generated by the franchise in its final two years in the capital was the result of Short's transactions. On October 9, 1970, in a bizarre press conference presided over by Commissioner Bowie Kuhn, the owner announced that he had acquired righthander Denny McLain, outfielder Elliott Maddox, third baseman Don Wert, and minor league hurler Norm McRae from Detroit in return for pitchers Joe Coleman and Jim Hannan, third baseman Aurelio Rodriguez, and shortstop Ed Brinkman. Kuhn's presence was motivated by the fact that McLain, a one-time 30-game winner for the Tigers, was then officially under suspension for associating with gam-

blers; in handling all questions related to the disciplinary action, the commissioner declared that he was lifting the suspension and approving the trade because psychiatrists had concluded that there was nothing "mentally wrong" with the pitcher. Although Kuhn did not go into what had raised the question in the first place, Williams raised a more immediate issue when he decried the trade as a giveaway of the Washington infield and of a prize arm in Coleman. As it turned out, McLain won only 10 games for the Senators, while Coleman racked up 88 for the Tigers, including two 20-win seasons. With Rodriguez and Brinkman settling down the left side of Detroit's infield defense for years, the trade was indeed what Williams had feared—the worst in franchise history.

Four days after getting McLain, Short grabbed more headlines by signing outfielder Curt Flood. Then in the midst of his challenge to baseball's reserve clause, Flood agreed to the one-year $110,000 pact only after a complicated series of negotiations involving Kuhn and the Philadelphia Phillies, which still had formal rights to the outfielder's services after the deal with the Cardinals that had precipitated the lawsuit. Most of the discussions turned on demands that the contract declare explicitly that playing for Washington would not prejudice Flood's court case. Kuhn ruled out such a proviso (originally agreed to by Short) on the grounds that it would amount to an attack on the automatic option clause, thereby undercutting baseball's position in the courtroom. He also vetoed Philadelphia's consent to accepting a minor league Washington player in exchange for allowing the Senators to negotiate with Flood, asserting that this was tantamount to paid tampering and still another inroad into a franchise's exclusivity privileges. The deal that finally emerged was, except for the Phillies, written on the wind. Although he was prohibited from spelling out the non-prejudicial significance of the contract, Short offered verbal assurances in the same vein—suggesting to some people that he *might* have undermined baseball's case. Although he had verbal assurances, Flood left himself open to subsequent denials by Short— suggesting to others that he *might* have jeopardized his challenge. As for the Phillies, they picked up three minor leaguers in return for giving up their rights to the outfielder. Then, with everything apparently settled, Flood reported to Washington for the 1971 season, got 7 hits in 35 at bats, and then bolted to Europe, never to play in another major league game.

Practically since buying the Senators in 1969, Short had pleaded poverty—and won over some ad-

The Senators ended their unsuccessful existence on an appropriate note on September 30, 1971. With two out in the ninth inning and holding a 7–5 lead over the Yankees in the final game of the season, the club was denied victory when fans jumped from the grandstand and swarmed over the field in search of souvenirs. After an unsuccessful attempt to get the fans back to their seats, umpires awarded the game to the Yankees by a 9–0 forfeit.

herents to his claim by ignoring rent payments on RFK Stadium. In 1971, he issued an ultimatum to the league: either he found somebody in Washington in a position to pay him $12 million for the franchise or he would accept an offer to move the franchise to Dallas–Fort Worth. The either-or sent Kuhn and other owners scrambling for months in search of a local buyer, their energies galvanized by the prospect of finding themselves back in the same awkward position they had been in when Calvin Griffith had wanted to jump to Minnesota. But instead of an expansion team, all they could come up with this time was a would-be buyer in Joseph Danzansky, the owner of a chain of supermarkets and the president of the Washington Board of Trade. Despite the fact that Short turned down Danzansky's offer of $8.4 million as insufficient immediately, Kuhn and AL

owners continued to court the retailer in the hope that he could sweeten the pot. In this, they were led along by Danzansky, who made periodic claims of having discovered new financial backers. Finally asked to put up or shut up, Danzansky shut up. When another eleventh-hour attempt to talk World Airways chairman Ed Daly into buying out Short also failed, the AL had little choice but to approve the transfer to Dallas–Fort Worth and give birth to the Texas Rangers. The only teams voting against the shift were Chicago, whose owner John Allyn was close to Danzansky, and Baltimore, which feared that the AL's departure from Washington would leave it vulnerable to an NL invasion and make the Roses, Seavers, Clementes, and McCoveys unwanted regional competition for the Orioles.

One of the biggest losers in Short's departure for Texas was Kuhn, who had put his prestige on the line in trying to keep the Senators in the city. In the years that followed, he floated various unsuccessful plans for restoring baseball to the capital, including a shift by the San Diego Padres and a scheme to have every team play two games at RFK Stadium in 1975. In 1976, still fearful that some congressmen might dust off another threat to examine baseball's exemption from antitrust statutes, he tried to have Washington replace Toronto in the 1977 expansion. Aside from the Padres, the Athletics, Giants, and Astros were mentioned at one time or another as being on the verge of moving to the capital. The city's most recent defeat was the 1991 decision to award the NL's newest franchises to Denver and Miami.

WASHINGTON SENATORS

Annual Standings and Managers

Year	Position	W	L	Pct.	GB	Managers
1961	Ninth*	61	100	.379	47½	Mickey Vernon
1962	Tenth	60	101	.373	35½	Mickey Vernon
1963	Tenth	56	106	.346	48½	Mickey Vernon, Gil Hodges
1964	Ninth	62	100	.383	37	Gil Hodges
1965	Eighth	70	92	.432	32	Gil Hodges
1966	Eighth	71	88	.447	25½	Gil Hodges
1967	Sixth*	76	85	.472	15½	Gil Hodges
1968	Tenth	65	96	.404	37½	Jim Lemon
1969	Fourth	86	76	.531	23	Ted Williams
1970	Sixth	70	92	.432	38	Ted Williams
1971	Fifth	63	96	.396	38½	Ted Williams

* Tie

Wilmington Quicksteps

Union Association, 1884   **BALLPARK:** WILMINGTON GROUNDS

RECORD: 2–16 (.111)

The Quicksteps, who compiled the worst won-lost percentage of any major league team, actually began their dismal 1884 season by winning a championship, if only a minor league one.

By clinching the Eastern League pennant on August 15th with a 51–12 record, Wilmington almost destroyed a circuit that was to become (after several name changes) the present Triple A International League, the oldest continuous minor league. The club was so dominant that attendance suffered, several teams disbanded, and even the Quicksteps found themselves $1,000 in the red. The seemingly rosier alternative was to join the Union Association as a replacement for the ailing Philadelphia Keystones. This Wilmington did on August 18th, after having received assurances from president Henry V. Lucas that the association would subsidize the team's salaries and travel expenses in addition to its usual $75 share of road game receipts. The team had more reason for optimism when it won its first game, beating Washington 4–3.

Then everything fell apart. Unlike most UA replacement teams, Wilmington had entered with its minor league roster intact. But after only two games, Oyster Burns, the shortstop, captain, and star slugger, accepted an offer from the American Association Baltimore Orioles of $900 a month—six times what he had been making. Outfielder Dennis Casey joined Burns in Baltimore for $700 a month, a more modest increase of $565.

Next, the National League Phillies claimed rights to Ed (The Only) Nolan and Tony Cusick, the Wilmington starting battery, when the two players took advantage of an off-day to play an exhibition game with Philadelphia. Nolan refused to jump and later was the winning pitcher in Wilmington's second and last victory, also against Washington. Cusick, whose salary with Wilmington was $150 a month, accepted Philadelphia's offer of $375. The Quicksteps never recovered from the loss of Burns, Casey, and Cusick, and compiled a sorry .175 team batting average in their eighteen games.

Neither as winners in the Eastern League nor as losers in the UA did the Quicksteps draw enough fans to survive. After the season ended, the Wilmington *Morning News* estimated that an average attendance of 800 (double the number that actually showed up) would have kept the team afloat. Lucas, skeptical from the start about Wilmington's long-term prospects as a major league city, went to Plan B very quickly by opening negotiations with Milwaukee of the Northwestern League. By repeatedly postponing an association meeting to vote the money to cover Wilmington's special incentives, the official sought to force the Quicksteps to step aside for Milwaukee. On September 15th, after not a single fan showed up for a home game against Kansas City, manager Joe Simmons conceded a forfeit, and the Quicksteps ceased to exist.

WILMINGTON QUICKSTEPS

Annual Standings and Manager

Year	Position	W	L	Pct.	GB	Manager
1884	Partial Season	2	16	.111	—	Joe Simmons

Worcester Brown Stockings

National League, 1880–82   **BALLPARK:** AGRICULTURAL COUNTY FAIR GROUNDS

RECORD: 90–159 (.361)   **OTHER NAMES:** RUBY LEGS

Of the various maneuvers by which the National League dropped and admitted teams in its first decade, none was as cynical as the fast and loose interpretation of the rules that brought Worcester into the NL on February 3, 1880.

In the 1880s, the NL required an applicant's home city to have a population of at least 75,000; exemptions required the unanimous consent of the rest of the league. With only about 58,000 people, Worcester could not get unanimous consent because Troy wanted Albany, its natural trans-Hudson River rival, to fill the vacancy created by the departure of Syracuse. An impasse was avoided when the league's board of directors coupled the population requirement with a four-mile territorial exclusivity rule, in effect obviating the need for unanimity by creating something similar to a modern media market or metropolitan area with a population above the required minimum.

The NL's enthusiasm for Worcester was largely an enthusiasm for its ace pitcher, Lee Richmond. In 1879, the team, then a member of the shaky National Base-Ball Association, offered Richmond, the first lefty curveball pitcher, $10 to pitch an exhibition against the NL Chicago club. Richmond accepted only because his catcher with the Brown University team had received the same offer and needed a new pair of pants. In his first professional game, the southpaw startled both his temporary employers and their opponents by pitching a seven-inning no-hitter. He won five other exhibitions (and lost two) against NL competition, and won one late season league contest pitching for Boston.

While Richmond spent the winter studying and practicing with catcher Doc Bushong in Providence, the club's directors were busy accumulating the capital to support their major league venture. They sold shares in the team for $35, a price that included a season ticket; sponsored a walking race that attracted 3,000 people; sold for-women-only season tickets for $9, less than half the full fifty-cent price for forty-two home games; arranged for discount train fare–baseball ticket packages for fans from outlying areas; and held benefit concerts and dramatic performances. Each player's uniform had a colored band with the colors cross-referenced in the team's scorecards for easy identification. All of Worcester was baseball mad. A downtown clothing store placed a scoreboard in its window, and the local telephone company offered what was probably the first sportsphone service, charging subscribers twenty-five cents a call for updated scores.

The results did not measure up to expectations. The Brown Stockings started fast, actually occupying first place for a few days in May, but sank quickly, dropping below .500 in July and ending in fifth place with a record of 40 wins and 43 losses. The high point of the season was the major league's first perfect game by Richmond against Cleveland on June 12th.

Toward the end of the season, provincial Worcester became the ramrod in the NL's war against cosmopolitan Cincinnati. The *Spy*, a Worcester newspaper with an appetite for guarding public morals, published an editorial attacking Sunday games and the sale of beer in Cincinnati. Eventually, Cincinnati was expelled and replaced by a Detroit entry that lured manager Frank Bancroft away. Free-

The first perfect game in the major leagues was pitched by Lee Richmond against Cleveland on June 12, 1880. Richmond worked under rules and conditions somewhat different from modern ones. Some of these gave him advantages present-day pitchers would envy: The pitcher's box was only fifty feet away from home plate, and it took eight balls (lowered from nine just that year) to walk a batter. Others put him at a disadvantage: He was required to throw the ball from below the waist, and his fielders wore gloves designed more to offer protection from the cold than to be of much help in picking up ground balls—if they wore gloves at all.

man Brown, who had been secretary-treasurer, took over as the new pilot.

Worcester, with a $3,000 profit in hand, added third baseman Hick Carpenter and outfielders Mike Dorgan and Pete Hotaling to its lineup, and began preparations for the 1881 season by offering season tickets to shareholders for $12.50 and to the general public for $15. The franchise also held a series of walking races to raise additional money. Within a month of opening day, however, the rowdiness, umpire baiting ("kicking" in the contemporary jargon), and internal strife that had erupted occasionally in 1880, overwhelmed the team.

Richmond, accused of arrogance, had trouble with the fans, his fellow players, and management. In July, he was released at his own request, then was recalled in August after Dorgan was suspended. He closed out the season by getting into a nasty beanball war with Boston's Grasshopper Jim Whitney. Dorgan, who as captain directed the team on the field, also fell out with manager Brown. In June, the outfielder was benched because of a sore arm; in August, he was suspended and replaced as captain by first baseman Harry Stovey for accusing the directors of arbitrary behavior toward the players. After the season, Dorgan and outfielder Buttercup Dickerson were blacklisted for insubordination. The culmination of the clubhouse strife was the accusation, by several players, that 36-year-old veteran Lip Pike, a late-season addition, threw a game against Boston in which he made three outfield errors.

Brown took charge at season's end—at least temporarily. Armed with the new title of executive director and a recently awarded seat on the NL board of directors, he held a third annual walking contest to raise money and sold new stock. In an effort to get rid of the dissensions and rowdiness, he broke up the team and carried into 1882 only six players from the 1881 club. The shakeup failed. Early in the season, Richmond came down with a sore arm. His successors on the mound were dismal, and Richmond himself was erratic on his return. A fourteen-game losing streak sealed Brown's fate, and Tommy Bond moved in to manage—with similar results. At a special shareholders' meeting on September 20th, President C. B. Pratt tried to resign, but the directors refused to accept his resignation; instead, three of the directors were replaced. The new board raised $1,000 to complete the season, fired Bond, and hired Jack Chapman away from the Holyoke club in the National Association. It was too little too late.

Worcester's performance, both on the field and at the turnstiles, did not go unnoticed by the rest of the league, which, as the first year of the war with the American Association drew to a close, realized it could no longer afford the luxury of small cities within the fold. In September, at a secret meeting in Philadelphia, Worcester and Troy were voted out of the league and plans laid to replace them with Philadelphia and New York. Worcester retaliated by threatening to resign on the spot, cancel the rest of its games, and force the league to apply its rule disallowing the results of the entire season of clubs that drop out in mid-season. This would have made the result of the tight Providence-Chicago pennant race questionable, so the league voted to hold a nine-game postseason championship between the first- and second-place teams. Arthur Soden, head of the Boston franchise and acting president of the NL, persuaded Worcester to complete the season; a cash advance from the league made Worcester's about-face more palatable.

Meanwhile, the Brown Stockings' performance deteriorated even further. Richmond gave up twenty-eight runs in two late September games against Cleveland; in another game, the team made twenty-one errors. The last game of the season drew only eighteen fans, an embarrassing decline from the rowdy crowds that had turned out in numbers as large as 3,652. On December 12th, Worcester succumbed to the inevitable, officially resigning from the NL and selling its franchise rights, although not its players, to interests in Philadelphia.

WORCESTER BROWN STOCKINGS

Annual Standings and Managers

Year	Position	W	L	Pct.	GB	Managers
1880	Fifth	40	43	.482	26½	Frank Bancroft
1881	Eighth	32	50	.390	23	Freeman Brown
1882	Eighth	18	66	.214	37	Freeman Brown, Tommy Bond, Jack Chapman

Bibliography

Nick Acocella & Donald Dewey, *The All-Stars All-Star Baseball Book* (Avon Books, New York, 1986).

Charles C. Alexander, *John McGraw* (Viking Penguin, New York, 1988).

Charles C. Alexander, *Ty Cobb* (Oxford University Press, New York, 1984).

Lee Allen, *The American League Story* (Hill and Wang, New York, 1961).

Lee Allen, *The Cincinnati Reds* (Putnam's, New York, 1948).

Lee Allen, *100 Years of Baseball* (Bartholomew House, New York, 1950).

Maury Allen, *You Could Look It Up* (Times Books, New York, 1979).

Harry H. Anderson, "The Ancient Origins of Baseball in Milwaukee," *Milwaukee History*, Summer 1983.

Bob Bailey, "Four Teams Out: The NL Reduction of 1900," *Baseball Research Journal*, 1990.

Frank Bancroft, " 'Old Hoss' Radbourn," *Baseball Magazine*, July 1908.

Red Barber, *1947—When All Hell Broke Loose in Baseball* (Doubleday, New York, 1982).

The Baseball Encyclopedia, 8th ed. (Macmillan, New York, 1990).

Morris Beale, *The Washington Senators* (Columbia Publishing Co., Washington, 1947).

Michael Benson, *Ballparks of North America* (McFarland & Company, Jefferson, NC, 1989).

Art Berke and Paul Schmitt, *This Date in Chicago White Sox History* (Stein and Day, New York, 1982).

Richard E. Beverage, *The Angels* (The Deacon Press, Placentia, CA, 1981).

Peter Bjarkman, *The Toronto Blue Jays* (Gallery Books, New York, 1990).

Thomas Boswell, *Why Time Begins on Opening Day* (Doubleday, New York, 1984).

Jim Bouton, *Ball Four Plus Five* (Stein and Day, New York, 1984).

Jim Bouton, *"I Managed Good, But Boy Did They Play Bad"* (Dell, 1973).

Larry Bowman, "Moses Fleetwood Walker: The First Black Major League Baseball Player," *Baseball History*, ed. Peter Levine (Stadium Books, Westport, CT, 1988).

Jimmy Breslin, *Can't Anybody Here Play this Game?* (Ballantine Books, New York, 1970).

Jim Brosnan, *The Long Season* (Grosset & Dunlap, New York, 1960).

Jim Brosnan, *Pennant Race* (Penguin, New York, 1962).

Jim Brosnan, *The Ted Simmons Story* (Putnam's, New York, 1977).

Warren Brown, *The Chicago Cubs* (Putnam's, New York, 1946).

Warren Brown, *The Chicago White Sox* (Putnam's, New York, 1952).

Michael Bryson, *The Twenty-Four Inch Home Run* (Contemporary Books, Chicago, 1990).

Harry Caray, with Bob Verdi, *Holy Cow!* (Villard Books, New York, 1989).

Tom Carson, "Major League Baseball's First Post-Season Champions: The Providence Grays", typescript, The Rhode Island Historical Society, 1983.

Craig Carter, ed., *The Series* (The Sporting News, St. Louis, 1991).

Happy Chandler, *Heroes, Plain Folks, and Skunks* (Bonus Books, Chicago, 1989.

Bob Chieger, *Voices of Baseball* (Atheneum, New York, 1983).

Tom Clark, *One Last Round for the Shuffler* (Truck Books, New York, 1979).

Ed Coen, "Early Big Time Teams Left Milwaukee Bitter," *Baseball Research Journal*, 1985.

Richard M. Cohen and David S. Neft, *The World Series* (Collier Books, New York, 1986).

Anthony J. Connor, *Baseball for the Love of It* (Macmillan, New York, 1982).

Anthony J. Connor, *Voices From Cooperstown* (Collier Books, New York, 1982).

Robert Creamer, *Babe: The Legend Comes to Life* (Simon and Schuster, New York, 1974).

Robert Creamer, *Stengel: His Life and Times* (Simon and Schuster, New York, 1984).

William Curran, *Mitts* (Morrow, New York, 1985).

Dennis D'Agostino, *This Date in New York Mets History* (Stein and Day, New York, 1981).

Donald Davidson, with Jesse Outler, *Caught Short* (Bantam Books, New York, 1973).

H. L. Dellinger, *The Kansas City Unions* (Two Rivers Press, Kansas City, 1977).

H. L. Dellinger, *One Year in the National League: An Account of the Kansas City Cowboys* (Two Rivers Press, Kansas City, 1977).

Donald Dewey and Nick Acocella, *The All-Time All-Star Baseball Book* (The Elysian Fields Press, Dubuque, IA, 1992).

Paul Dickson, ed., *Baseball's Greatest Quotations* (HarperCollins, New York, 1991).

James M. DiClerico and Barry J. Pavelec, *The Jersey Game* (Rutgers University Press, New Brunswick, NJ, 1991).

Joe Dittmar, *Baseball's Benchmark Boxscores* (McFarland & Company, Jefferson, NC, 1990).

Frank Dolson, *Beating the Bushes* (Icarus Press, South Bend, IN, 1982).

James DuPlacey and Joseph Romain, *The Athletics* (Gallery Books, New York, 1991).

Leo Durocher, with Ed Linn, *Nice Guys Finish Last* (Simon and Schuster, New York, 1975).

Joseph Durso, *Baseball and the American Dream* (The Sporting News, St. Louis, 1986).

James Dworkin, *Owners Versus Players* (Auburn House, Boston, 1981).

Lenny Dykstra, with Marty Noble, *Nails* (Doubleday, New York, 1987).

Morris Eckhouse and Carl Mastrocola, *This Date in Pittsburgh Pirates History* (Stein and Day, New York, 1980).

Richard Egenriether, "Chris Von der Ahe: Baseball's Pioneering Huckster," *Baseball Research Journal*, 1989.

Charles Einstein (ed.), *The Baseball Reader* (McGraw-Hill, New York, 1983).

James Elfers, "Pro-Diamonds in the Diamond State," Typescript, The Delaware Historical Society, 1986.

Ed Fitzgerald, ed., *Sport Magazine's Book of Major League Baseball Clubs: The American League* (Grosset & Dunlap, New York, 1955).

Ed Fitzgerald, ed., *Sport Magazine's Book of Major League Baseball Clubs: The National League* (Grosset & Dunlap, New York, 1955).

Mark S. Foster, "Foul Ball: The Cleveland Spiders' Farcical Season of 1899," *Baseball History*, Summer 1986.

Harvey Frommer, *New York City Baseball* (Macmillan, New York, 1980).

Harvey Frommer, *Primitive Baseball* (Atheneum, New York, 1988).

Harvey Frommer, *Rickey & Robinson* (Macmillan, New York, 1982).

Mark Gallagher, *The Yankee Encyclopedia* (Leisure Press, New York, 1982).

Peter Gammons, *Beyond the Sixth Game* (Houghton Mifflin, Boston, 1985).

Peter Golenbock, *Bums* (Putnam's, New York, 1984).

Peter Golenbock, *Dynasty* (Prentice-Hall, Englewood Cliffs, NJ, 1975).

Charles Brian Goslow, "There Was A Ballpark in Worcester," Typescript, Worcester Historical Society, 1988.

Frank Graham, *The Brooklyn Dodgers* (Putnam's, New York, 1945).

Frank Graham, *The New York Giants* (Putnam's, New York, 1952).

Frank Graham, *The New York Yankees* (Putnam's, New York, 1958).

Lee Green, *Sportswit* (Harper & Row, New York, 1984).

Donald Gropman, *Say It Ain't So, Joe!* (Lynx Books, New York, 1979).

J. Scott Gross, "Wilmington Quick Steps—Glory to Oblivion," *Baseball Research Journal*, 1986.

Mike Gunther, *Basepaths* (Scribner's, New York, 1984).

Allen Guttman, *Sports Spectators* (Harper & Row, New York, 1984).

Gary Hailey, "Anatomy of a Murder: The Federal League and the Courts," *The National Pastime*, 1985.

David Halberstam, *Summer of '49* (Morrow, New York, 1989).

Jack E. Harshman, "The Radbourn and Sweeney Saga," *Baseball Research Journal*, 1990.

Tommy Holmes, *The Dodgers* (Collier Books, New York, 1975).

Donald Honig, *The American League* (Crown, New York, 1983).

Donald Honig, *Baseball America* (Macmillan, New York, 1985).

Donald Honig, *Baseball When the Grass Was Real* (Berkeley Publishing Corp., New York, 1975).

Donald Honig, *The National League* (Crown, New York, 1983).

John Richmond Husman, "J. Lee Richmond's Remarkable 1879 Season," *The National Pastime*, Winter 1985.

Noel Hynd, *The Giants of the Polo Grounds* (Doubleday, New York, 1988).

Frederick Ivor-Campbell, "1884: Old Hoss Radbourne and the Providence Grays," *The National Pastime,* 1985.

Jerry Izenberg, *Great Latin Sports Figures* (Doubleday, New York, 1976).

Reggie Jackson, with Mike Lupica, *Reggie* (Villard Books, New York, 1984).

W. Lloyd Johnson, "The Short, Spectacular Career of Harry McCormick," *Baseball Research Journal,* 1987.

Harold Kaese and R. G. Lynch, *The Milwaukee Braves* (Putnam's, New York, 1954).

Roger Kahn, *The Boys of Summer* (Harper & Row, New York, 1971).

Roger Kahn, *Good Enough to Dream* (Signet, New York, 1985).

Roger Kahn and Al Helfer, eds., *The Mutual Baseball Almanac* (Doubleday, New York, 1954).

Jon Kerr, *Calvin: Baseball's Last Dinosaur* (William C. Brown, Madison, WI, 1990).

Kevin Kerrane and Richard Grossinger, eds., *Baseball Diamonds* (Anchor Books, New York, 1980).

Edward Kiersh, *Where Have You Gone, Vince DiMaggio?* (Bantam Books, New York, 1983).

Leonard Koppett, *Sports Illusion, Sports Reality* (Houghton Mifflin, Boston, 1981).

John Krich, *El Beisbol* (The Atlantic Monthly Press, New York, 1989).

Tony Kubek and Terry Plato, *Sixty-One* (Macmillan, New York, 1987).

Richard S. Kubik, *Baseball Trades and Acquisitions* (Exposition Press, Smithtown, NY, 1981).

Bowie Kuhn, *Hardball* (McGraw-Hill, New York, 1988).

Dick Lally, *Pinstriped Summers* (Arbor House, New York, 1985).

Jack Lang and Peter Simon, *The New York Mets* (Henry Holt and Co., New York, 1986).

Jim Langford, *The Game Is Never Over* (Icarus Press, South Bend, IN, 1980).

Ernest Lanigan, *Baseball Cyclopedia* (Baseball Magazine Co., New York, 1922).

Jerry Lansche, *The Forgotten Championships* (McFarland & Co., Jefferson, NC, 1989).

Richard Lapchick, *Broken Promises* (St. Martin's, New York, 1984).

Tommy Lasorda and David Fisher, *The Artful Dodger* (Arbor House, New York, 1985).

Bill "Spaceman" Lee, with Dick Lally, *The Wrong Stuff* (Penguin, New York, 1984).

John Leptich and Dave Baranowski, *This Date in St. Louis Cardinals History* (Stein and Day, New York, 1983).

Peter Levine, *A. G. Spalding and the Rise of Baseball* (Oxford University Press, New York, 1985).

Allen Lewis and Larry Schenk, *This Date in Philadelphia Phillies History* (Stein and Day, New York, 1979).

Franklin Lewis, *The Cleveland Indians* (Putnam's, New York, 1949).

Fred Lieb, *Baseball As I Have Known It* (Tempo Books, New York, 1977).

Frederick Lieb, *The Baltimore Orioles* (Putnam's, New York, 1955).

Frederick Lieb, *The Baseball Story* (Putnam's, New York, 1950).

Frederick Lieb, *The Boston Red Sox* (Putnam's, New York, 1947).

Frederick Lieb, *Connie Mack: Grand Old Man of Baseball* (Putnam's, New York, 1948).

Frederick Lieb, *The Detroit Tigers* (Putnam's, New York, 1950).

Frederick Lieb, *The Pittsburgh Pirates* (Putnam's, New York, 1948).

Frederick Lieb, *The St. Louis Cardinals* (Putnam's, New York, 1944).

Frederick Lieb, *The Story of the World Series* (Putnam's, New York, 1950).

Frederick Lieb and Stan Baumgartner, *The Philadelphia Phillies* (Putnam's, New York, 1953).

Ed Linn, *Steinbrenner's Yankees* (Holt, Rinehart, and Winston, New York, 1982).

Ralph E. LinWeber, *The Toledo Baseball Guide of the Mud Hens 1883–1943* (Publisher unknown, Toledo, 1944).

Lee Lowenfish and Tony Lupien, *The Imperfect Diamond* (Stein and Day, New York, 1980).

Philip J. Lowry, *Green Cathedrals* (SABR, Cooperstown, NY, 1986).

Ron Luciano & David Fisher, *Remembrance of Swings Past* (Bantam Books, New York, 1988).

Ron Luciano & David Fisher, *Strike Two* (Bantam Books, New York, 1984).

Ron Luciano & David Fisher, *The Umpire Strikes Back* (Bantam Books, New York, 1983).

Sparky Lyle and Peter Golenbock, *The Bronx Zoo* (Crown, New York, 1979).

Connie Mack, *My 66 Years in Baseball* (Philadelphia, Winston, 1950).

Rich Marazzi, *The Rules and Lore of Baseball* (Stein and Day, New York, 1980).

Rich Marazzi and Len Fiorito, *Aaron to Zipfel* (Avon Books, New York, 1985).

Rich Marazzi and Len Fiorito, *Aaron to Zuverink* (Avon Books, New York, 1984).

Billy Martin, *Billyball* (Doubleday, New York, 1987).

Billy Martin and Peter Golenbock, *Number 1* (Dell, New York, 1980).

Tim McCarver, with Ray Robinson, *Oh Baby, I Love It!* (Villard Books, New York, 1987).

Denny McLain, *Strikeout* (The Sporting News, New York, 1988).

William B. Mead, *Even The Browns* (Contemporary Books, New York, 1978).

William B. Mead, *The Official New York Yankees Hater's Handbook* (Putnam's, New York, 1983).

Ernest Mehl, *The Kansas City Athletics* (Henry Holt and Company, New York, 1956).

John Mercurio, *Chronology of Major League Baseball Records* (Harper's, New York, 1989).

James Edward Miller, *The Baseball Business* (University of North Carolina Press, Chapel Hill, NC, 1990).

Jim Miller, "The Old Orioles' First Pennant," *The National Pastime*, 1990.

Minor League Baseball Stars (SABR, Kansas City, 1985).

George L. Moreland, *Balldom* (Horton Publishing Co., St. Louis, 1989—originally published 1914).

John Mosedale, *The Greatest of All* (Dial, New York, 1974).

Eugene Murdock, *Mighty Casey: All American* (Greenwood Press, Westport, CT, 1984).

Bruce Nash and Allan Zullo, *Baseball Confidential* (Pocket Books, New York, 1988).

Bruce Nash and Allan Zullo. *The Baseball Hall of Shame* (Pocket Books, New York, 1985).

David S. Neft and Richard M. Cohen, *The Sports Encyclopedia: Baseball* (St. Martin's Press, New York, 1985).

Kevin Nelson, *The Greatest Stories Ever Told About Baseball* (Perigee Books, New York, 1986).

David Nemec, *Great Baseball Feats, Facts & Firsts* (Plume, New York, 1987).

Graig Nettles and Peter Golenbock, *Balls* (Putnam's, New York, 1984).

Sadaharu Oh and David Faulkner, *A Zen Way of Baseball* (Times Books, New York, 1984).

Marc Okkonen, *The Federal League of 1914–15* (SABR, Garrett Park, MD, 1989).

Daniel Okrent, *Baseball Anecdotes* (Oxford University Press, New York, 1989).

Daniel Okrent, *Nine Innings* (Ticknor & Fields, New York, 1985).

Marc Onigman, *This Date in Braves History* (Stein and Day, New York, 1982).

Preston D. Orem, *Baseball from the Newspaper Accounts*, vol. 2 (privately published, Altadena, CA, 1961).

Joshua B. Orenstein, "The Union Association of 1884: A Glorious Failure," *Baseball Resarch Journal*, 1990.

Joseph M. Overfield, *The 100 Seasons of Buffalo Baseball* (Partners Press, Kenmore, NY, 1985).

Phil Pepe and Zander Hollander, *The Book of Sports Lists #2* (Pinnacle Books, Los Angeles, 1980).

William D. Perrin, *Days of Greatness: Providence Baseball* (SABR, Cooperstown, NY, 1984).

Robert Peterson, *Only the Ball was White* (Prentice-Hall, Englewood Cliffs, NJ, 1970).

David Pietruza, *Major Leagues* (McFarland & Co., Jefferson, NC, 1991).

Players' National League, *The Players' National League Official Guide for 1890* (F. H. Brunnell, Chicago, 1889).

Terry Pluto and Jeffrey Newman, eds., *Baseball Winter* (Macmillan, New York, 1986).

Murray Polner, *Branch Rickey* (Signet, New York, 1983).

Shirley Povich, *The Washington Senators* (Putnam's, New York, 1954).

Martin Quigley, *The Crooked Pitch* (Algonquin Books, Chapel Hill, NC, 1988).

Benjamin G. Rader, *American Sports* (Prentice-Hall, Englewood Cliffs, NJ, 1983).

Reach Baseball Guides, 1883–1939.

Zach Rebackoff, *Tough Calls* (Avon Books, New York, 1983).

David Reddick and Kim Rogers, *The Magic of Indians Baseball 1887–1987* (Indianapolis Indians, Indianapolis, 1988).

Joseph Reichler, *The Baseball Trade Register* (Collier Books, New York, 1984).

Lowell Reidenbaugh, *First Hundred Years* (The Sporting News, St. Louis, 1985).

Lawrence S. Ritter, *The Glory of Their Times* (Random House, New York, 1985).

George Robinson and Charles Salzberg, *On A Clear Day they Could See Second Place* (Dell, New York, 1991).

Ray Robinson, *The Homerun Heard 'Round The World* (HarperCollins, New York, 1991).

Phil Rogers, *The Impossible Takes a Little Longer* (Taylor Publishing Company, Dallas, 1990).

Donn Rogosin, *Invisible Men* (Atheneum, New York, 1983).

John M. Rosenberg, *They Gave Us Baseball* (Stackpole Books, Harrisburg, PA, 1989).

Harold Rosenthal, *The 10 Best Years of Baseball* (Van Nostrand-Reinhold Co., New York, 1981).

Edna and Art Rust, Jr., *Art Rust's Illustrated History of the Black Athlete* (Doubleday, New York, 1985).

Nathan Salant, *This Date in New York Yankees History* (Stein and Day, New York, 1979).

Dick Schaap, *Sport* (Arbor House, New York, 1975).

Dick Schaap, *Steinbrenner* (Putnam's, New York, 1982).

Dan Schlossberg, *The Baseball Catalog* (Jonathan David Publishers, New York, 1983).

Gene Schoor, *The Complete Dodgers Record Book* (Facts on File, New York, 1984).

Gerald W. Scully, *The Business of Major League Baseball* (University of Chicago Press, Chicago, 1989).

Charles Segar, ed., *Official History National League 75th Anniversary* (Jay Publishing Co., New York, 1951).

Jack Selzer, "Baseball in the Nineteenth Century: An Overview" (SABR, Cooperstown, NY, 1986).

Harold Seymour, *Baseball: The Early Years* (Oxford University Press, New York, 1960).

Harold Seymour, *Baseball: The Golden Age* (Oxford University Press, New York, 1971).

Harold Seymour, "St. Louis and the Union Baseball War," *Missouri Historical Review,* April, 1957.

Bill Shannon and George Kalinsky, *The Ballparks* (Hawthorn Books, New York, 1975).

Mike Shatzkin and Jim Charlton, *The Baseball Fan's Guide to Spring Training* (Addison-Wesley Publishing Co., Reading, MA, 1989).

Myron J. Smith, *Baseball: A Comprehensive Bibliography* (McFarland & Co., Jefferson, NC, 1986).

Red Smith, *Out of the Red* (Alfred A. Knopf, New York, 1950).

Red Smith, ed., *Press Box* (Avon Books, New York, 1974).

Red Smith, *The Red Smith Reader* (Vintage Books, New York, 1983).

Robert Smith, *Illustrated History of Baseball* (Madison Square Press, New York, 1973).

Robert Smith, *Pioneers of Baseball* (Little, Brown, Boston, 1978).

Bob Smizik, *The Pittsburgh Pirates* (Walker & Company, New York, 1990).

A. G. Spalding, *Baseball: America's National Game 1839–1915* (Halo Books, San Francisco, 1991).

Spalding Official Baseball Guides, 1878–1939.

Sporting Life, 1883–1903.

The Sporting News, 1886-to date.

The Sporting News Official Baseball Dope Book, 1955–85.

The Sporting News Official Baseball Guides, 1940-to date (*Spink Official Baseball Guides* through 1979).

Fred Stein and Nick Peters, *Giants Diary* (North Atlantic Books, Berkeley, CA, 1987).

Fred Stinson and Richard Waldbauer, "The Providence Grays as a Franchise" (Paper delivered at the 1984 SABR Annual Meeting).

Bert R. Sugar, *Rain Delays* (St. Martin's Press, New York, 1990).

Dean Alan Sullivan, *The Growth of Sport in a Southern City* (Thesis, George Mason University, Fairfax VA, 1989).

Ted Sullivan, *Humorous Stories of the Ball Field* (Donohue, Chicago, 1903).

James Tackach, "Hazards and Tips for Researchers," *Baseball Research Journal,* 1986.

A. H. Tarvin, *Seventy-Five Years on Louisville Diamonds* (Schumann, Louisville, 1940).

S. C. Thomson, *All-Time Rosters of Major League Baseball Clubs* (A. S. Barnes and Co., New York, 1973).

John Thorn, *The Relief Pitcher* (E. P. Dutton, New York, 1979).

John Thorn & Pete Palmer, *The Hidden Game of Baseball* (Doubleday, New York, 1984).

John Thorn and Pete Palmer (eds.), *Total Baseball* (Warner Books, New York, 1989).

Stew Thornley, "The St. Paul Unions," Typescript, Minnesota Historical Society, 1983.

Campbell B. Titchener, *The George Kirksey Story* (Eakin Press, Austin, TX, 1989).

Gerald Tomlinson, *The Baseball Research Handbook* (SABR, Cooperstown NY, 1987).

John Tullius, *I'd Rather Be A Yankee* (Macmillan, New York, 1986).

George Tuohey, *A History of the Baseball Club* (M. F. Quinn & Co., Boston, 1897).

Hy Turkin and S. C. Thompson, *The Official Encyclopedia of Baseball* (A. S. Barnes & Co., New York, 1951).

Jules Tygiel, *Jackie Robinson and His Legacy* (Random House, New York, 1984).

Bill Veeck, with Ed Linn, *Veeck As In Wreck* (Signet, New York, 1962).

David Quentin Volight, *American Baseball,* 3 vols. (The Pennsylvania State University Press, University Park, PA, 1983).

Glen Waggoner, *Baseball By The Rules* (Taylor Publishing Co., Dallas, 1987).

Richard Waldbauer, "A Social History of the Providence Grays" (Paper delivered at the 1984 SABR annual meeting).

Ed Walton, *Red Sox Triumphs and Tragedies* (Stein and Day, New York, 1980).

Charles W. Westlake, *Columbus Baseball History* (Pfeifer Printing Co., Columbus, 1981).

Mike Whiteford, *How To Talk Baseball* (Dembner Books, New York, 1983).

Ted Williams, with John Underwood, *My Turn at Bat* (Simon & Schuster, New York, 1988).

Jerry Jay Wright, "Major League Baseball Comes to Altoona, Pennsylvania—Or Did It?" (Paper delivered at the 1990 annual meeting of the North American Society for Sport History).

Andrew Zimbalist, *Baseball Billions* (Basic Books, New York, 1992).

Joel Zoss & John Bowman, *Diamonds in the Rough* (Macmillan, New York, 1989).

About the Authors

NICHOLAS ACOCELLA lives in Hoboken, New Jersey, the birthplace of baseball. He is the author of several books about baseball, including *The Official Baseball Record Book* and *The All-Time All-Star Baseball Book*, the latter in collaboration with Donald Dewey, and has published numerous magazine articles.

DONALD DEWEY has been a writer, editor, and screenwriter for more than twenty-five years. He is the author of several works of fiction and non-fiction, and was a founding editor of the award-winning monthly magazine *Attenzione*. Dewey was the recipient of the 1990 Nelson Algren Award for fiction, and recently published a biography of actor Marcello Mastroianni. He lives in Jamaica, New York.